MW01671155

FREE COPY NOT TO BE SOLD FREE COPY NOT TO BE SOLD FREE COPY NOT TO BE SOLD

Exploring Human Sexuality

MAKING HEALTHY DECISIONS

Second Edition

Richard D. McAnulty
University of North Carolina at Charlotte

M. Michele Burnette

PEARSON

Boston New York San Francisco
Mexico City Montreal Toronto London Madrid Munich Paris
Hong Kong Singapore Tokyo Cape Town Sydney

FREE COPY NOT TO BE SOLD FREE COPY NOT TO BE SOLD FREE COPY NOT TO BE SOLD

FREE COPY NOT TO BE SOLD FREE COPY NOT TO BE SOLD FREE COPY NOT TO BE SOLD

FREE COPY NOT TO BE SOLD FREE COPY NOT TO BE SOLD FREE COPY NOT TO BE SOLD

FREE COPY NOT TO BE SOLD FREE COPY NOT TO BE SOLD FREE COPY NOT TO BE SOLD

Editor: Kelly May
Editorial Assistant: Marlana Voerster
Senior Developmental Editor: Lisa McLellan
Senior Marketing Manager: Wendy Gordon
Production Administrator: Susan Brown
Editorial/Production Services: Lifland et al., Bookmakers
Text Designer: Pearson Education Design Group
Formatting/Page Layout: Omegatype Typography, Inc.
Cover Administrator: Linda Knowles
Composition Buyer: Linda Cox
Manufacturing Buyer: Megan Cochran
Photo Researcher: Katharine Cook

Copyright © 2004, 2001 Pearson Education, Inc.

All rights reserved. No part of the material protected by this copyright notice may be reproduced or utilized in any form or by any means, electronic or mechanical, including photocopying, recording, or by any information storage and retrieval system, without written permission from the copyright owner.

To obtain permission(s) to use material from this work, please submit a written request to Allyn and Bacon, Permissions Department, 75 Arlington Street, Boston, MA 02116 or fax your request to 617-848-7320.

LIBRARY OF CONGRESS CATALOGING-IN-PUBLICATION DATA

McAnulty, Richard D.
Exploring human sexuality : making healthy decisions / Richard D. McAnulty, M. Michele Burnette.—2nd ed.
p. cm.
Includes bibliographical references and index.
ISBN 0-205-38059-X
1. Sex. 2. Hygiene, Sexual. I. Burnette, M. Michele. II. Title.

HQ21.M4624 2003
306.7—dc21

2003041843

Printed in the United States of America
10 9 8 7 6 5 4 3 2 1 07 06 05 04 03

Credits appear on page 563, which constitutes a continuation of the copyright page.

FREE COPY NOT TO BE SOLD FREE COPY NOT TO BE SOLD FREE COPY NOT TO BE SOLD

FREE COPY NOT TO BE SOLD FREE COPY NOT TO BE SOLD FREE COPY NOT TO BE SOLD

Exploring Human Sexuality

FREE COPY NOT TO BE SOLD FREE COPY NOT TO BE SOLD FREE COPY NOT TO BE SOLD

FREE COPY NOT TO BE SOLD FREE COPY NOT TO BE SOLD FREE COPY NOT TO BE SOLD

FREE COPY NOT TO BE SOLD FREE COPY NOT TO BE SOLD FREE COPY NOT TO BE SOLD

Exploring Human Sexuality

MAKING HEALTHY DECISIONS

Second Edition

Richard D. McAnulty
University of North Carolina at Charlotte

M. Michele Burnette

PEARSON

Boston New York San Francisco
Mexico City Montreal Toronto London Madrid Munich Paris
Hong Kong Singapore Tokyo Cape Town Sydney

FREE COPY NOT TO BE SOLD FREE COPY NOT TO BE SOLD FREE COPY NOT TO BE SOLD

FREE COPY NOT TO BE SOLD FREE COPY NOT TO BE SOLD FREE COPY NOT TO BE SOLD

FREE COPY NOT TO BE SOLD FREE COPY NOT TO BE SOLD FREE COPY NOT TO BE SOLD FREE COPY NOT TO BE SOLD FREE COPY

Editor: Kelly May
Editorial Assistant: Marlana Voerster
Senior Developmental Editor: Lisa McLellan
Senior Marketing Manager: Wendy Gordon
Production Administrator: Susan Brown
Editorial/Production Services: Lifland et al., Bookmakers
Text Designer: Pearson Education Design Group
Formatting/Page Layout: Omegatype Typography, Inc.
Cover Administrator: Linda Knowles
Composition Buyer: Linda Cox
Manufacturing Buyer: Megan Cochran
Photo Researcher: Katharine Cook

FREE COPY NOT TO BE SOLD FREE COPY NOT TO BE SOLD FREE COPY NOT TO BE SOLD FREE COPY NOT TO BE SOLD

Copyright © 2004, 2001 Pearson Education, Inc.

All rights reserved. No part of the material protected by this copyright notice may be reproduced or utilized in any form or by any means, electronic or mechanical, including photocopying, recording, or by any information storage and retrieval system, without written permission from the copyright owner.

To obtain permission(s) to use material from this work, please submit a written request to Allyn and Bacon, Permissions Department, 75 Arlington Street, Boston, MA 02116 or fax your request to 617-848-7320.

LIBRARY OF CONGRESS CATALOGING-IN-PUBLICATION DATA

McAnulty, Richard D.
Exploring human sexuality : making healthy decisions / Richard D. McAnulty, M. Michele Burnette.—2nd ed.
p. cm.
Includes bibliographical references and index.
ISBN 0-205-38059-X
1. Sex. 2. Hygiene, Sexual. I. Burnette, M. Michele. II. Title.

HQ21.M4624 2003
306.7—dc21

2003041843

Printed in the United States of America
10 9 8 7 6 5 4 3 2 1 07 06 05 04 03

Credits appear on page 563, which constitutes a continuation of the copyright page.

FREE COPY NOT TO BE SOLD FREE COPY NOT TO BE SOLD FREE COPY NOT TO BE SOLD

FREE COPY NOT TO BE SOLD FREE COPY NOT TO BE SOLD FREE COPY NOT TO BE SOLD

brief contents

FREE COPY NOT TO BE SOLD FREE COPY NOT TO BE SOLD FREE COPY NOT TO BE SOLD

FREE COPY NOT TO BE SOLD FREE COPY NOT TO BE SOLD FREE COPY NOT TO BE SOLD

FREE COPY NOT TO BE SOLD FREE COPY NOT TO BE SOLD FREE COPY NOT TO BE SOLD

contents

FREE COPY NOT TO BE SOLD FREE COPY NOT TO BE SOLD FREE COPY NOT TO BE SOLD

FREE COPY NOT TO BE SOLD FREE COPY NOT TO BE SOLD FREE COPY NOT TO BE SOLD

FREE COPY NOT TO BE SOLD FREE COPY NOT TO BE SOLD FREE COPY NOT TO BE SOLD
FREE COPY NOT TO BE SOLD FREE COPY NOT TO BE SOLD FREE COPY NOT TO BE SOLD

FREE COPY NOT TO BE SOLD FREE COPY NOT TO BE SOLD FREE COPY NOT TO BE SOLD

FREE COPY NOT TO BE SOLD FREE COPY NOT TO BE SOLD FREE COPY NOT TO BE SOLD

Part Three The Social Context of Sexuality

FREE COPY NOT TO BE SOLD FREE COPY NOT TO BE SOLD FREE COPY NOT TO BE SOLD

FREE COPY NOT TO BE SOLD FREE COPY NOT TO BE SOLD FREE COPY NOT TO BE SOLD

FREE COPY NOT TO BE SOLD FREE COPY NOT TO BE SOLD FREE COPY NOT TO BE SOLD

FREE COPY NOT TO BE SOLD FREE COPY NOT TO BE SOLD FREE COPY NOT TO BE SOLD

FREE COPY NOT TO BE SOLD FREE COPY NOT TO BE SOLD FREE COPY NOT TO BE SOLD

FREE COPY NOT TO BE SOLD FREE COPY NOT TO BE SOLD FREE COPY NOT TO BE SOLD

FREE COPY NOT TO BE SOLD FREE COPY NOT TO BE SOLD FREE COPY NOT TO BE SOLD

FREE COPY NOT TO BE SOLD FREE COPY NOT TO BE SOLD
FREE COPY NOT TO BE SOLD FREE COPY NOT TO BE SOLD

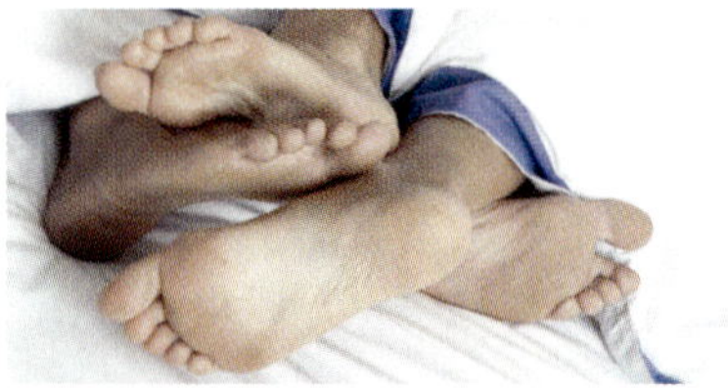

FREE COPY NOT TO BE SOLD FREE COPY NOT TO BE SOLD FREE COPY NOT TO BE SOLD

FREE COPY NOT TO BE SOLD FREE COPY NOT TO BE SOLD FREE COPY NOT TO BE SOLD

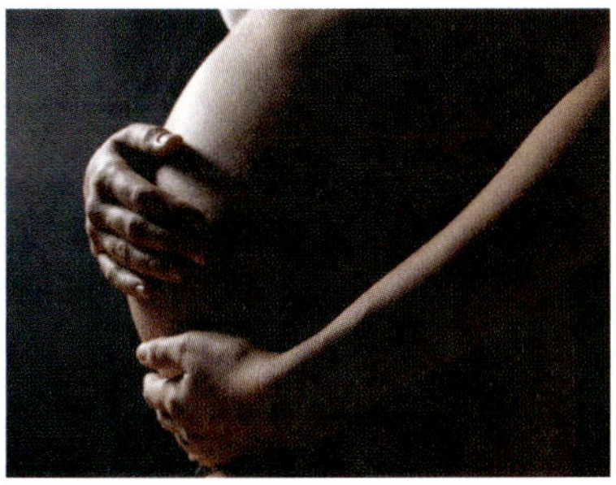

FREE COPY NOT TO BE SOLD FREE COPY NOT TO BE SOLD FREE COPY NOT TO BE SOLD

FREE COPY NOT TO BE SOLD FREE COPY NOT TO BE SOLD FREE COPY NOT TO BE SOLD

FREE COPY NOT TO BE SOLD FREE COPY NOT TO BE SOLD FREE COPY NOT TO BE SOLD
FREE COPY NOT TO BE SOLD FREE COPY NOT TO BE SOLD FREE COPY NOT TO BE SOLD

FREE COPY NOT TO BE SOLD FREE COPY NOT TO BE SOLD FREE COPY NOT TO BE SOLD

FREE COPY NOT TO BE SOLD FREE COPY NOT TO BE SOLD FREE COPY NOT TO BE SOLD

FREE COPY NOT TO BE SOLD FREE COPY NOT TO BE SOLD FREE COPY NOT TO BE SOLD

FREE COPY NOT TO BE SOLD FREE COPY NOT TO BE SOLD FREE COPY NOT TO BE SOLD

FREE COPY NOT TO BE SOLD FREE COPY NOT TO BE SOLD FREE COPY NOT TO BE SOLD

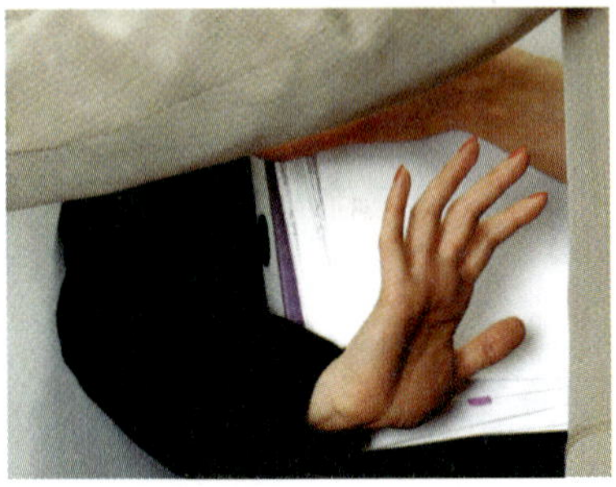

BOOKS
VIDEOS
MAGS
FULLY
LICENSED
BAR
BOOKS
MAGS
VIDEOS

preface

Sex permeates our society. The Internet, television, film, music lyrics and videos, newspapers and magazines—all reflect our culture's almost obsessive fascination with sex. It is easy to feel inundated. Scientific surveys and reports on sexual attitudes and practices; sexual health and safer sex messages; marketing campaigns for birth control methods, pregnancy tests, ovulation kits, and HIV tests; reports of sex crimes in the news; and pornography in all media—these are only a few of countless "resources" on sexuality. All are readily available to us in the privacy of our homes just by clicking a computer mouse, opening a newspaper or magazine, or switching on the television. It is frequently difficult to make sense of it all. Our goal in writing this text is to arm students with information that will help them to make healthy decisions about their sexuality. In our second edition, we continue to promote sexual health within a framework that integrates the social, psychological, and physiological aspects of sexuality.

OUR GOALS

This book has three main objectives:

1. To present information in a "friendly advisor" style to enhance students' interest and learning. The focus of our book is proactive; we promote sexual health at all levels: physical, emotional, and interpersonal.
2. To offer an integrated view of physiological, psychological, social, and cultural factors that affect human sexuality. Because sexuality is as influenced by psychosocial and cultural factors as it is by biological makeup, these factors are given equal treatment throughout the book where appropriate.
3. To provide information on the most recent developments and findings. Our clinical, research, and teaching experiences, as well as our determination to stay abreast of the literature in human sexuality, enable us to provide the most current information that is available on each topic we cover.

SEXUAL HEALTH

One of the themes of this text is an emphasis on sexual health and healthy decision making. Sexual health is a major concern in cultures around the world today, and sexual health involves so much more than simply prevention of disease: It extends to emotional and interpersonal fulfillment. In this edition, total sexual health is a major theme throughout. We include special *Health Matters* features throughout the text, and we conclude each chapter with a section called Healthy Decision Making. We cover the full spectrum of sexual health issues, both physical and psychological, because we believe that an understanding of both is critical for achieving and maintaining sexual health.

GENDER ISSUES, CULTURAL DIVERSITY, AND ALTERNATIVE LIFESTYLES

In addition to our focus on sexual health, we strive to include appropriate coverage of gender issues, cultural diversity, and alternative lifestyles. We devote an entire chapter specifically to gender, and we interweave important cultural comparisons and gender issues into the text whenever they are relevant. *Close Up on Gender* and *Close Up on Culture,* features that appear in most chapters, discuss gender and culture in greater detail. Furthermore, we made a special effort to discuss how research on sex differences is often misinterpreted and to clarify the interpretation of such research and the limitations of the methods it employs. Drawing on our personal and professional experiences, we have sought to provide complete and balanced coverage of sexuality from the perspective of both genders. (See the Index of Gender and Cross-Cultural Issues on page xxxvi.)

The book also includes a chapter on sexual orientation in which we take a broad "sexualities" approach. In other words, we do not hold homosexuality up as an unusual or aberrant condition. Rather, we discuss it as one of several possible sexualities, while making sure to thoroughly educate readers about homosexuality and related cultural and personal concerns. Perhaps more importantly, we emphasize, in our choice of words and coverage throughout the text, that not all relationships are between men and women. For example, we recognize in the childbirth section of Chapter 9 that a woman's birthing partner might not be a man, and we include sexual positions for same-sex partners in Chapter 8.

ORGANIZATION

The book is divided into five major parts. Each part focuses on either physical or psychological factors related to sexuality. Because we know that students are eager to get into love and communication issues early on, we have reorganized the text for the second edition so that the chapters addressing the social context of sexuality come before those devoted to reproduction and development.

PART ONE **Introduction to Sexuality and Sexual Health** comprises the first two chapters, which provide social, cultural, historical, and scientific backdrops for the study of human sexuality and sexual health.

PART TWO **The Biological Basis of Sexuality** includes Chapters 3 and 4, which establish the biological backdrop for human sexuality and health. However, this part title merely suggests the primary focus of the chapters. We do not limit the discussion to "biological" topics. The myriad psychological and social factors that affect the adequacy of physiological responses are well integrated into the discussion of this topic.

PART THREE **The Social Context of Sexuality** includes Chapters 5 though 8, which look at interactions between the social and sexual realms and factors that influence those interactions. Both gender roles and sexual orientation have a tremendous impact on interpersonal sexual interactions, as do sexual and communication skills, which are discussed in Chapter 8. The emphasis in this part is on psychological, rather than physical, health.

PART FOUR **Reproduction and Sexual Development** includes Chapters 9 through 12, which cover those life processes that are invariably governed by sexuality and sexual health. Although we see reproduction and sexual development as heavily controlled by biological givens, we also emphasize the social, attitudinal, and behavioral factors that are important.

PART FIVE **Issues and Challenges in Sexuality** includes Chapters 13 through 17, which cover issues in sexuality that are both highly personal and socially controversial. This part focuses on factors that impair sexual health—both physical factors and psychological ones. We place special emphasis on prevention and treatment of sexual problems and resolution of sexual controversies.

FEATURES

Each chapter includes several basic learning aids that make the text more user-friendly and engaging. These include an introductory outline, boldfaced key terms, a marginal glossary, and a bulleted chapter summary of major findings and issues. In the second edition we have incorporated several exciting new features designed to enhance student interest and learning.

New to the Second Edition

- **Looking At . . . Thinking About** features appear several times in each chapter and include a provocative photo followed by a question aimed at getting students to think critically about the subject matter. For example, in Chapter 6 we ask students to look at a photo of a same-sex couple in a social setting and encourage them to think about the importance of community in the development of a healthy sexual identity.

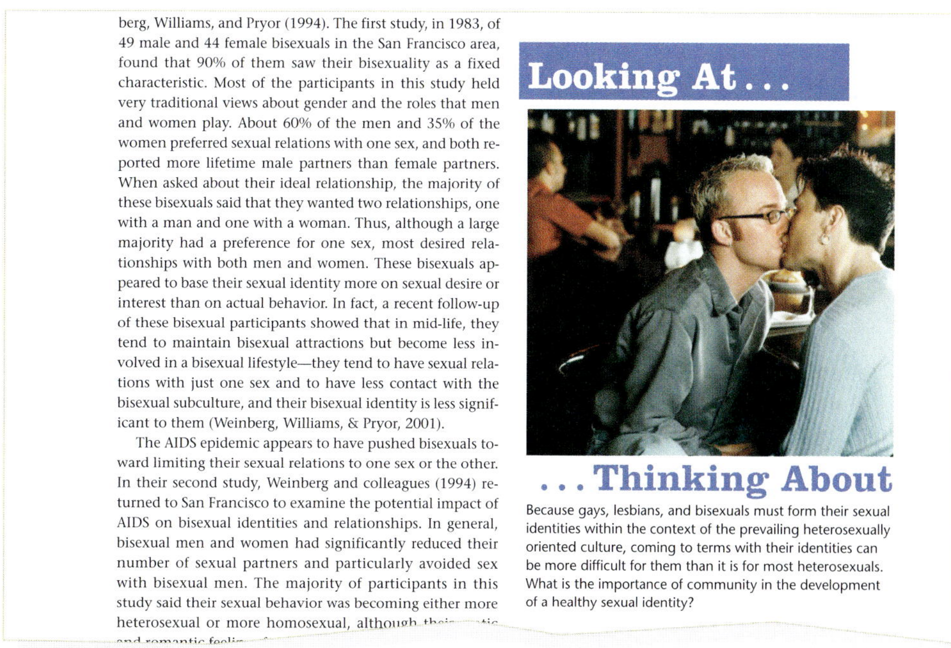

berg, Williams, and Pryor (1994). The first study, in 1983, of 49 male and 44 female bisexuals in the San Francisco area, found that 90% of them saw their bisexuality as a fixed characteristic. Most of the participants in this study held very traditional views about gender and the roles that men and women play. About 60% of the men and 35% of the women preferred sexual relations with one sex, and both reported more lifetime male partners than female partners. When asked about their ideal relationship, the majority of these bisexuals said that they wanted two relationships, one with a man and one with a woman. Thus, although a large majority had a preference for one sex, most desired relationships with both men and women. These bisexuals appeared to base their sexual identity more on sexual desire or interest than on actual behavior. In fact, a recent follow-up of these bisexual participants showed that in mid-life, they tend to maintain bisexual attractions but become less involved in a bisexual lifestyle—they tend to have sexual relations with just one sex and to have less contact with the bisexual subculture, and their bisexual identity is less significant to them (Weinberg, Williams, & Pryor, 2001).

The AIDS epidemic appears to have pushed bisexuals toward limiting their sexual relations to one sex or the other. In their second study, Weinberg and colleagues (1994) returned to San Francisco to examine the potential impact of AIDS on bisexual identities and relationships. In general, bisexual men and women had significantly reduced their number of sexual partners and particularly avoided sex with bisexual men. The majority of participants in this study said their sexual behavior was becoming either more heterosexual or more homosexual, although

Looking At . . .

. . . Thinking About

Because gays, lesbians, and bisexuals must form their sexual identities within the context of the prevailing heterosexually oriented culture, coming to terms with their identities can be more difficult for them than it is for most heterosexuals. What is the importance of community in the development of a healthy sexual identity?

LOOKING AT . . . THINKING ABOUT

- **Did You Know?** marginal features throughout every chapter offer interesting statistics and comments on hot topics and cross-cultural differences, such as "Did you know that the Internet porn industry reportedly generates over $366 million in revenues each year?"

The Internet

The newest medium to offer sexual materials is the Internet. Although the use of technology to disseminate sexual materials is not new, the Internet does so on an unprecedented scale (Stern & Handel, 2001). Studies show that sexual pursuits, which may range from visiting pornography sites to participating in online sexual exchanges, are the most common use of the Internet (Cooper, Scherer, Boies, & Gordon, 1999). There are over 8,000 chat rooms devoted to cybersex, or interactive discussions of sex (McKenna, Green, & Smith, 2001). Users can access picture libraries, video clips, live strip shows, live sex shows, and Web-cam sites that offer public access to the most private lives of volunteers (Griffiths, 2001). Available materials range from sexually explicit educational materials, online virtual sex shops, and sexual fantasy aids. Internet users can even meet prospective sexual partners online through chat rooms, personal advertisements, or escort services (Griffiths, 2000). People can form intimate relationships online, and

did YOU know?

The Internet porn industry reportedly generates over $366 million in revenues each year (Spenger, 1999).

DID YOU KNOW?

- **In Your Own Words** is an engaging new marginal feature, in which current college students discuss some aspect of sexuality in their own lives. These student quotes represent a variety of viewpoints on a number of different topics—some of them controversial—and are meant to serve as springboards for discussion.

IN YOUR **own words**

Tina Rae Sparks
Trinity College

I think that abstinence should be encouraged much more highly than contraception and condom usage. We have gotten so far

Abstinence Education

Abstinence-based sexuality education programs were originally developed in reaction to so-called value-free programs. Essentially, the label "value-free" was used as a criticism of sexuality education programs that did not exclusively promote sexual abstinence prior to heterosexual marriage. There are several abstinence-based curricula. Among the best known is a curriculum named *Sex Respect*. This program is widely used and has received some government funding through the United States Office of Adolescent Pregnancy Programs.

The *Sex Respect* curriculum consists of eleven lessons designed to help students "realize that true sexual freedom includes the freedom to say 'no' to sex outside of marriage" (Mast, 1990). Most notable about *Sex Respect* are its imbalanced coverage, exclusions, and gender stereotypes (Goodson & Edmundson, 1994). For instance, although there are drawings of male genitals, there are no illustrations of female genitals. The labia and the clitoris are not even mentioned. Contraception is conspicuously omitted. The curriculum manual claims that teaching contraception increases sexual promiscuity and does not reduce pregnancy or abortion rates. Several gender stereotypes are perpetuated by *Sex Respect*. Males are described as "more readily excitable" and as often feeling "pressured to go further than they want to sexually (by girls who want to have sex)." Females are stereotyped as less impulsive, more level-headed

IN YOUR OWN WORDS

Retained Features

Exploring Human Sexuality contains the following pedagogical features designed to engage the reader and stimulate interest:

- **Health Matters** features highlight important issues in sexual health—issues that may be personally relevant to readers. For example, in Chapter 11 on sexual development in adolescence, Health Matters discusses the negative health effects of unplanned teen pregnancy. Because the negative health consequences are a result of inadequate prenatal care and not a result of the youthfulness of the mother, this topic provides a wonderful example of how social factors can have a tremendous impact on health.

HEALTH Matters

Health Risks of Unplanned Teenage Pregnancy

From a purely biological perspective, middle to late adolescence represents an optimal age for child-bearing. However, a healthy pregnancy and delivery require high-quality prenatal care and services. Quality prenatal care includes regular medical checkups, proper diet and nutrition, and a healthy lifestyle. Unfortunately, one-third of pregnant adolescents do not receive proper prenatal care, thereby increasing the risks of problematic pregnancies and deliveries (Alan Guttmacher Institute, 1994). Furthermore, many pregnant teenagers smoke cigarettes (Ventura, Martin, Curtin, & Mathews, 1999), which is a known risk factor for problems during pregnancy.

Younger teens need more intensive prenatal care but are less likely to receive such care than older adolescents. Younger teenaged mothers may be unaware of the resources that are available for prenatal care. An additional obstacle to obtaining prenatal care is the stigma associated with being an unmarried adolescent parent. Because of inadequate prenatal care, teenagers are likely to have problematic pregnancies and deliveries. Low birth weight and premature birth are more common among infants of teenagers than among those born to women in their 20s. Infants born to women younger than 15 are twice as likely to have low birth weight and nearly three times as likely to die within the first month of life (American Academy of Pediatrics, 1999; Stevens-Simon & White, 1991). Low birth weight is an important risk factor for infant mortality and later health problems. Newborns who weigh less than 2 pounds at birth have a low survival rate, and those who do survive almost always have permanent neurological problems. Overall, babies born to young mothers have more health problems and spend more time in the hospital than babies of adult mothers. Various respiratory, digestive, and neurological problems are common in premature infants, because many of their organs are not fully developed at birth. Fortunately, some of these problems can be resolved with proper medical care. In the long term, children of teenaged mothers have more problems with school performance.

In order to improve conditions for teenaged mothers and their children, a number of family planning centers and school-based programs have been developed. By providing day care and special courses, some programs offer teenaged mothers the opportunity to complete school or receive job training. The most comprehensive programs offer classes on prenatal care, infant care, and parenting skills (Solomon & Liefeld, 1998). These programs enhance prenatal care among pregnant teenagers, reduce risks of low-birth-weight infants, and increase the mother's economic prospects (Alan Guttmacher Institute, 1994). Such programs have also been shown to reduce risks of future unplanned pregnancies and to decrease school dropout rates (Solomon & Liefeld, 1998).

- A **Healthy Decision Making** section closes each chapter and highlights some aspect of healthy decision making about sexual health. For example, the Healthy Decision Making section in Chapter 8, Sexual Communication and Techniques, provides tips for improving sensual communication.

HEALTHY DECISION MAKING

If there is one key concept to be derived from this chapter, it is that communication is essential to a successful relationship. As Byers and Demmons (1999) discovered in their study of nearly 100 college students in dating relationships, people who feel that they communicate effectively with their partners are also better at sharing their sexual likes and dislikes. The following tips should help you improve sensual communication with your partner.

1. *Identify the barriers to effective communication.* Don't be hard on yourself for not having all of the answers. (Even "sexperts" who write textbooks don't know it all!) If you find it embarrassing to talk about your sexual preferences, practice giving your partner feedback while engaged in nonsexual touching, such as a backrub. Then gradually work up the courage to talk about your sexual relationship with your partner.
2. *Remember that communication, like all skills, requires practice.* Find opportunities to practice sensual communication with your partner. Begin by talking about things you like that you find easiest to talk about. Many people, for example, find it easier to start by describing how they like being kissed or held. As you become more comfortable, progress to sharing preferences that are more awkward for you to discuss.
3. *Remember that effective communication is a two-way street.* Find opportunities to share *and* opportunities to listen. Because people have busy schedules, they often

- **Reflect on This** features appear in most chapters and challenge students to apply what they have read to their own lives or to assess their thinking on particular topics. In addition to enhancing students' interest in the topic, this approach will facilitate learning of the material. For example, in Chapter 10 we ask students to reflect on their views on abortion. This approach encourages students not only to memorize facts and understand issues surrounding abortion, but also to analyze how this information meshes with the beliefs they brought to the classroom. By personalizing the information, students are more likely to remember it and make use of it.

reflect ON THIS

Where Do You Stand on Abortion?

Read the following questions and jot down your responses to each. After doing that, ask yourself, "Am I pro-choice, pro-life, or a mixture of the two?" Explain why you selected the position you did.

1. At what point does human life begin: at conception, at quickening, at viability, at birth?
2. When does the fetus become a person?
3. How should the definitions of "human life" and "personhood" enter into decisions regarding the legality of abortion?
4. Should abortion remain legal? Why or why not?
5. If it remains legal, should any restrictions be placed on it?
   - Should abortions be only therapeutic, or should they be available on demand? (If therapeutic only, how does one determine when abortion is essential for a woman's physical or emotional health?)
6. How should the following circumstances affect the right to and/or the decision to abort, if at all?
   - The pregnancy results from a rape.
   - The woman is an unwed teenager.
   - The woman is on Medicaid and has several children.
   - The fetus is severely deformed at 5 or 6 months gestation.
   - The woman is a high school senior with aspirations to go to college and have a career.
   - The fetus is determined to have Tay-Sachs disease, which will cause death by the time the child is 4 or 5.
   - The parents are a separated or divorced couple, and the man wants the woman to have the child.
   - A 17-year-old woman was molested by her own father, and she must gain consent for an abortion from a judge who is anti-abortion.

REFLECT ON THIS

■ **Close Up on Gender** features spotlight important gender issues. For example, the Close Up on Gender feature in Chapter 10 examines the question: Who is responsible for contraception?

CLOSE UP ON

gender

Who Is Responsible for Contraception?

A continuing question concerns which person, male or female, should be responsible for providing contraception and protection against STIs and ensuring that contraception is used properly. In general, this responsibility has traditionally been placed in the hands of women, which is why the majority of contraceptives have been developed for them. The justification for this may be that it is an effort to empower women to protect themselves from unwanted pregnancy, since they ultimately have the higher price to pay if they get pregnant.

Society's tendency to place responsibility for contraception on women is probably also influenced by gender stereotypes, such as the belief that women are sexual "gatekeepers" and can better control their sexual impulses—a stereotype that has clearly been challenged by gender ...

... aim to arm women with an understanding of the risks of unprotected sex and the benefits of protection, with the expectation that this knowledge will lead them to practice safer sex. However, this approach ignores the sociocultural context—specifically, the expectations and roles of men and women. For example, if a woman purchases or carries a condom with her, she may develop a reputation of being "loose." In many cultural settings, "good" women are expected to at least feign ignorance of and take a passive role in sexual interactions. Men, on the other hand, have greater sexual freedom, and they are usually expected to take control in sexual encounters (Gage, 1998).

In addition, men wield greater sexual power in most cultures (Wingood & DiClemente, 1998) and may resist women's attempts to control sexual decision-making. Particularly in more "macho" cultures, if a woman attempts to enforce her will with respect to contraceptive use, she may threaten her male partner's manhood, give him the impression that she does not trust him, or inadvertently incite a violent reac-

... you're gonna get something, you might as well do it. I have it on me, and I have it just for that use, but it kind of pisses me off. It's like, "Do you think I'm dirty, or what?"

Nathan: I'd be very uncomfortable, 'cause girls aren't supposed to do that.

Other gender-specific factors that may play a role in determining whether a woman takes precautions against pregnancy are the high value that some cultures place on childbearing and motherhood and the bond that parenting a child together is expected to create in a relationship. These factors may have a particularly strong influence among African Americans as well as in rural settings, where there is greater social acceptance of childbearing at a young age (Cochran & Mays, 1993; Wingood & DiClemente, 1992).

Researchers, medical professionals, and sex educators need to take these and other gender-related issues into account when trying to influence contraceptive use. It is important not to strip women of a sense of power and personal self-efficacy ...

CLOSE UP ON GENDER

■ **Close Up on Culture** features provide special consideration of cross-cultural factors and emphasize how cultural norms and practices influence sexual behavior and beliefs. For example, the Close Up on Culture feature in Chapter 9 considers the experience of childbirth across cultures.

CLOSE UP ON culture

The Experience of Childbirth across Cultures

The physiological processes of pregnancy and childbirth are very similar for all women, but varying social standards produce birth experiences that differ tremendously across cultures. Anthropologists have observed that the differences appear on several dimensions and are largely determined by the extent to which the medical establishment is involved in pregnancy and childbirth. Cultures differ with regard to the amount and type of birth preparation women receive, who is present to assist and support women during labor and delivery, where delivide most of the prenatal care in the United States.

In the Mayan culture of the Yucatan region of southeastern Mexico and northern Central America, preparation does not occur until the woman is actually in labor and is provided by any of a number of individuals who are there to support and assist during the birth. However, because most women give birth at home, it is unlikely that a woman and her partner will not have observed many births throughout their lives. Thus, they are likely to be fairly well informed before the birth of their first child.

The individuals present at a birth may be either specialists or nonspecialists. The United States is unusual compared to other cultures in that, up until the 1970s, only medical specialists assisted women giving birth. Today, it is increasingly common for one or more family members or friends to be pre-

tal; in Holland, most births used to take place at home, but most now occur in hospitals. Birthing rooms within hospitals or birthing centers, which have cropped up in the United States over the years, are intended to create the feel of a home birth while offering ready access to high-tech interventions in an emergency. Although these are still unfamiliar environments with unfamiliar attendants, for the most part, women seem to feel more comfortable in them than in standard hospital rooms. Nonetheless, the medical personnel maintain ultimate authority over the birth process in these settings.

As noted, cross-cultural differences in birth processes are heavily influenced by who is assigned the role of decision maker. In the Yucatan, everyone present participates in the decision-making process via "negotiated consensus." In Holland, even hospital deliveries are attended by midwives,

CLOSE UP ON CULTURE

- **On the Web** activities appear in the margins of each chapter. These activities encourage students to take advantage of the endless resources on the Web and to think critically about the information that they retrieve from "cyberspace." Students are directed to the companion Web site located at www.ablongman.com/mcanulty2e, where they can link directly to the Web sites mentioned in the On the Web activity.

The Effects of Aging

Better health resulting from improved quality of life, advances in medicine, and better education has tremendously increased the average life expectancy of humans. Thus, an increasing proportion of the population can be classified as elderly, and accurate information about the effects of aging on sexuality is clearly of value to many people. Common cultural views of the elderly depict them as asexual. The stereotype might cause many aging individuals to view changes in their sexual responses as signs of failing sexuality. As a result, they might forgo sexual experiences prematurely. While it is true that several physiological changes occur as a result of the aging process, it is not clear that these changes consistently interfere with sexual behavior. Poor health or lack of a sexual partner may affect sexual expression; however, there is no reason to assume that the elderly cannot have very healthy sexual desires or satisfying sexual relationships. In fact, the lifestyle that many older adults enjoy may enhance sexual expression. Many older couples are no longer distracted by children or the stresses of work. Nor do they have to concern themselves with birth control. Slowed orgasm in an elderly male allows more time for an elderly female partner to enjoy extended stimulation and a greater opportunity to have an orgasm herself. Older couples who have shared many years together have typically worked out the "kinks" in their relationship, which means they are free to enjoy each other more fully.

4.2 on the web

When we are young, many of us have a difficult time imagining that people enjoy sex in old age. Read the article entitled "Older Women Talk about Sex" at **www.ablongman.com/mcanulty2e.**

Describe the overall findings regarding older women and sexuality discussed in this article and your reactions to them.

ON THE WEB

WHAT'S NEW IN THE SECOND EDITION?

Every chapter is brimming with new research and cutting-edge coverage. Some of the key changes in the second edition are listed below.

Chapter 1 Sexuality: Yesterday and Today

- Chapter has been largely rewritten
- Extensive new section on sexuality around the world
- Updated coverage of sociocultural influences, including new material on the Internet and popular music and videos
- Section on religion expanded to include Islam and Buddhism
- New section on the family's influence on sexuality
- New section on the learning perspective
- 70 new references, over half of which are from the period 2000–2002

Chapter 2 Research Methods in Sexuality

- Expanded coverage of correlational designs
- Expanded coverage of computer-assisted interviewing
- New discussion of Internet-based sex research
- New discussion of the National Longitudinal Survey of Adolescent Health and the Youth Risk Behavior Surveillance System
- 9 new references added, 7 from 2000–2002

Chapter 3 Sexuality and Reproductive Anatomy

- Greater focus on normal, healthy anatomy; coverage of insignificant diseases of reproductive anatomy deleted
- Updated discussion of female genital mutilation
- Updated coverage of ovarian and cervical cancer
- Extensive new discussion of menstrual problems
- Coverage of advances in pap smear technology
- Updated coverage of circumcision
- Updated coverage of testicular and prostate cancer
- 57 new references added, the majority from 2000–2002

Chapter 4 Physiology of Sexual Arousal and Response

- Chapter reorganized so that interpersonal aspects of sexual responses are discussed first
- Updated discussion of the G-spot, with new figure added
- Significantly expanded and updated discussion of pheromones (including discussion of menstrual synchrony)
- Updated coverage on hormonal influences on female and male sexual behavior
- Update on Viagra
- New material on use of Ecstasy as a "love drug"
- 30 new references added, 16 from 2000–2002

Chapter 5 Gender Roles and Sexuality

- Now includes coverage of sex differentiation
- Updated coverage of intersexuality
- New material on transgenderism
- Updated coverage on gender typing in the classroom
- Updated coverage of media influences
- New Healthy Decision Making section that invites readers to evaluate how androgynous they are
- 22 new references added, 12 from 2000–2002

Chapter 6 Sexual Orientation

- New research on sexual identity formation
- New material on bisexual identity formation
- Updated coverage of same-sex marriage
- New table highlighting common characteristics of people who are homophobic

- New section on internalized homophobia
- 7 new references added, all from 2000–2002

Chapter 7 Intimacy and Love

- New expanded chapter on intimacy and love
- Expanded coverage of intimacy
- New section on the attachment theory of love
- Expanded coverage of evolutionary perspective on attraction
- New table highlighting the fundamentals of effective communication
- New section on relationship problem-solving strategies
- New table providing guidelines for "soft startups"
- Updated coverage of jealousy
- New Healthy Decision Making section that includes an interactive "Love Map Questionnaire"
- 15 new references added, 9 from 2000–2002

Chapter 8 Sensual Communication and Techniques

- New expanded chapter on sensual communication and techniques
- New student quotes on sexual pleasure
- Significantly expanded discussion of sexual communication—including topics such as talking about sex, communicating sexual needs, and sexual self-disclosure
- New Close Up on Gender feature dealing with gender differences in sensual communication
- New table highlighting reasons for masturbation, by gender
- Expanded coverage of foreplay
- New Close Up on Culture feature on sexual differences around the globe
- New Healthy Decision Making section providing tips for improving sensual communication
- 22 new references added, 9 from 2000–2002

Chapter 9 Conception, Pregnancy, and Childbirth

- Expanded coverage on the role of the placenta
- New table summarizing possible, probable, and positive signs of pregnancy
- New Close Up on Gender box addressing the issue of pregnancy among women over 35
- Updated information on male infertility factors
- Expanded discussion of birthing options, including coverage of midwives
- 23 new references added, all from 2000–2002

Chapter 10 Contraception and Abortion

- Completely updated coverage of new contraceptive options for women—including Implanon (new implant), Lunelle (new hormone injection), Nuva-Ring (new vaginal ring), Mirena (modern IUD), and Ortho Evra (new contraceptive patch).
- Completely updated coverage of new contraceptive options under investigation for men—including the bi-directional polyurethane condom, hormonal

methods, "plugs" to block sperm passage, chemical injections into the vas deferens, and heating of the scrotum

- Updated coverage of RU 486
- New section on historical perspectives on abortion
- New Healthy Decision Making section including an interactive table that lists questions to consider when selecting a birth control method, and possible responses
- 27 new references added, almost all from 2000–2002

Chapter 11 Sexual Development from Birth through Adolescence

- Updated information on self-stimulation and orgasm in childhood
- Updated information and statistics on masturbation and sexual interactions in preadolescence
- Expanded and updated section on psychosocial development in adolescence
- Updated information and statistics (including several new figures) on sexual interactions in adolescence
- New section that examines factors contributing to early first intercourse
- New section on same-sex sexual behavior in adolescence
- Updated information and statistics on sexually transmissible infections
- Updated information and statistics on teenage pregnancy
- Updated discussion of sexuality education
- New Healthy Decision Making section providing tips on talking with children about sex
- 48 new references added, 33 from 2000–2002

Chapter 12 Sexual Development in Adulthood

- Updated statistics on prevalence of marriage
- New material on the advantages of single life
- New material on modern dating rituals (including online dating and speed dating)
- New Health Matters feature including advice on safe cyberdating
- Updated statistics on marital status and median age of first marriages
- New material on "covenant marriages"
- 8 new references, all from 2000–2002

Chapter 13 Sexual Dysfunctions

- New Close Up on Culture feature on *koro* (genital retraction syndrome)
- Expanded section on drugs and sexual functioning
- Expanded section on psychological factors and sexual dysfunction
- Expanded section on relationship problems and sexual dysfunction
- New section on medical treatment of female sexual dysfunction
- New Healthy Decision Making section encouraging self-assessment of sexual functioning
- 27 new references added, 25 from 2000–2002

Chapter 14 Sexually Transmissible Infections

- More streamlined coverage (two STI chapters combined into one)

- Updated statistics and data on vaginal and parasitic infections
- Updated prevalence data and coverage of chlamydia, gonorrhea, syphilis, herpes, and genital warts
- New Health Matters feature on HPV and cancer
- Updated coverage of HIV/AIDS
- New research on STI risk reduction
- New Healthy Decision Making section on discussing condom use with a resistant partner
- 52 new references added, 43 from 2000–2002

Chapter 15 Atypical Sexual Behavior

- Updated data on transvestic fetishists
- New material on high-tech voyeurism—including webcams
- New material on Internet pedophilia
- New figure illustrating a multifactor theory of coercive pedophilia
- 10 new references added, all from 2000–2002

Chapter 16 Sexual Coercion

- Completely revised and reorganized section on sexual assault
- New data on prevalence of rape
- Expanded coverage of date rape drugs
- New coverage of evolutionary explanations for rape
- New data on sexual harassment in the workplace and academia
- New information on sexual harassment of men
- Revised Healthy Decision Making section including guidelines for what to do if you or someone you know has been raped
- 19 new references added, 15 from 2000–2002

Chapter 17 Commercial Sex

- Expanded coverage of sexuality in the media
- New section on online pornography
- New section on child pornography
- New section on "cybersex"
- Updated coverage of HIV and prostitutes
- 14 new references added, 12 from 2000–2002

ANCILLARY PACKAGE

Exploring Human Sexuality can be supplemented by any of the following teaching and learning aids.

For the Instructor

- **Instructor's Manual.** Written by Janet Elizabeth Snoyer of Cornell University, this is a wonderful tool for classroom preparation and management. Each chapter includes an At-a-Glance grid, with detailed pedagogical information about links to other available supplements; a detailed chapter outline; teaching objectives covering major concepts within the chapter; a list of key terms with page references; lecture material, including outlines and suggested discussion questions; demonstrations and activities; an updated list of video, media, and Web resources; and an updated list of suggested readings. In addition, this manual includes a preface, a sample syllabus, and an appendix containing a comprehensive list of student handouts.

- **Test Bank.** Written by David Libhart of University of Phoenix, Hawaii Campus, the Test Bank helps students prepare for exams with challenging questions that target key concepts. Each chapter includes over 100 questions, including multiple choice, true/false, short answer, and essay questions, each with an answer justification. Page references, a difficulty rating, and type designation are included for each question. In addition, the appendix includes a sample open-book quiz. This product is also available in TestGen computerized version, for use in creating tests in the classroom.
- **Computerized Test Bank.** This computerized version of the Test Bank is available with easy-to-use TestGenEQ software, which lets you prepare printed, network, and online tests. It includes full edition capability for Windows and Macintosh.
- **PowerPoint Presentation.** Prepared by Michael Heimlich of Stanford University, this is an exciting interactive tool for use in the classroom. Each chapter includes key points covered in the textbook; images from the textbook, with demonstrations; a link to the companion Web site for corresponding activities; and electronic files of the Instructor's Manual.
- **Transparencies.** A collection of over 100 full-color acetates is available to adopters, to enhance classroom lecture and discussion. The collection includes images from Allyn and Bacon's major human sexuality texts.
- **Interactive Video for Human Sexuality.** Michael Bailey of Northwestern University prepared the video after interviewing a sex researcher, a gynecologist, transsexuals, a sex therapist, an exotic dancer, and more. In addition, the video guide provides further critical thinking questions and Internet resources for more information.
- **CourseCompass.** Powered by Blackboard, this course management system uses a powerful suite of tools that allow instructors to create an online presence for any course.

For the Student

- **Companion Web Site.** This unique resource for connecting the text to the Internet can be accessed at www.ablongman.com/mcanulty2e. Each chapter includes text-specific learning objectives; chapter summaries; updated and annotated Web links for additional sources of information; flash card glossary terms; and online practice tests.
- **Grade Aid Study Guide.** Developed by Janet Elizabeth Snoyer of Cornell University, this is a comprehensive and interactive study guide. Each chapter includes "Before You Read," with a brief chapter summary and chapter learning objectives; "As You Read," a collection of demonstrations, activities, and exercises; "After You Read," containing three short practice quizzes and one comprehensive practice test; "When You Have Finished," with Web links for

further information; and crossword puzzles using key terms from the text. An appendix includes answers to all practice tests and crossword puzzles.

- **Research Navigator™ for *Human Sexuality*.** Research Navigator™ is designed to help students select and evaluate research from the Web to find the best and most credible information available. The booklet contains a practical and to-the-point discussion of search engines; detailed information on evaluating online sources; citation guidelines for Web resources; Web activities for *Human Sexuality;* Web links for *Human Sexuality;* and the access code to explore Research Navigator™.

  Research Navigator™ is the easiest way for students to start a research assignment or research paper. Complete with extensive help on the research process and three exclusive databases of credible and reliable source material (including EBSCO's ContentSelect Academic Journal Database, *New York Times* Search by Subject Archive, and "Best of the Web" Link Library), Research Navigator™ helps students use their research time most efficiently.

ACKNOWLEDGMENTS

A project of this magnitude can only be brought to fruition with the assistance of numerous individuals. We are indebted to many colleagues who provided substantive contributions. Our research assistants provided tireless support, even through the tedious details of tracing missing information. Finally, much credit goes to the devoted team at Allyn & Bacon that spearheaded this project and brought it to completion, providing the necessary prodding and encouragement throughout.

We wish to acknowledge a number of colleagues who shared their expertise in the following areas through the development of first drafts:

Betty Fisher (Cook County Hospital), physiology
Paul Rasmussen (Furman University), love and sensual communication
Michael Kauth (VA Medical Center, New Orleans), sexual orientation
Patricia Long (Oklahoma State University), sexual coercion
Seth Kalichman (Center for AIDS Research), HIV and AIDS
Kent Koehn (Marquette General Hospital), STIs

Our research assistants helped with much of the detail work. They and many of our students generously agreed to read portions of the manuscript and offered useful feedback. We are also thankful to our professional colleagues, who contributed significantly to the refinement of this work through their reviews of the manuscript at various stages of its development. We thank each of the following colleagues for their help in shaping this second edition:

Veanne Anderson, Indiana State University
Elaine Baker, Marshall University
Sharon Ballard, University of Tennessee–Knoxville
M. Betsy Bergen, Kansas State University
Robert Castleberry, University of South Carolina–Sumter
Lorry Cology, Owens Community College
Craig Cowden, Northern Virginia Community College

Keith Davis, University of South Carolina
W. Michael Fleming, University of Northern Iowa
Francine Gentile, Rogue Community College
Kathleen Greaves, Oregon State University
Kevin Gross, East Carolina University
Gary Gute, University of Northern Iowa
Robert Hensley, Iowa State University
Greg Janson, Ohio University
Shelli Kane, Nassau Community College
Elena Mikalsen, University of Houston
Amy Miron, Community College of Baltimore County–Catonsville Campus
Cynthia Pury, Clemson University
Peggy Skinner, South Plains College
Paul Twelker, Trinity International University
Nancy Walbek, Gustavus Adophus College

We also gratefully acknowledge the following reviewers, who provided insightful feedback during the development of our first edition:

Leslie Barnes-Young, Francis Marion University
Sheri A. Berenbaum, Southern Illinois University School of Medicine
Robert B. Castleberry, University of South Carolina
Shelly Cavin, Tarrant County College, Northwest Campus
Charles Chase, West Texas A&M University
Lorry Cology, Owens Community College
Judy C. Drolet, Southern Illinois University
Vera Dunwoody, Chaffey College
Philip Duryea, University of New Mexico
Richard N. Feil, Mansfield University
Randy Fisher, University of Central Florida
David Gallagher, Pima County Community College
C. Globiana, Fitchburg State College
Michael Goslin, Tallahassee Community College
Kevin H. Gross, University of Tennessee, Knoxville
Sally Guttmacher, New York University
Morton G. Harmatz, University of Massachusetts, Amherst
Karen Hicks, Moravian College
Barbara Hunter, Belleville Area College
Kathleen J. Hunter, SUNY Brockport
James Johnson, Sam Houston State University
Molly Laflin, Bowling Green University
Bruce LeBlanc, Black Hawk College
R. Martin Lobdell, Pierce College
Jim W. Lochner, Weber State University
Ronald McLaughlin, Juniata College
David W. Moore, Wake County Human Services School of Health
Calvin D. Payne, University of Arizona
Lauren Perdue, Central Connecticut State University
Cynthia Pury, Clemson University
Daphne Long Rankin, Virginia Commonwealth University

Peggy Skinner, South Plains College
Sherman K. Sowby, California State University–Fresno
Susan Sprecher, Illinois State University
Katherine Stewart, University of Alabama
Sergei Tystsarey, University of Central Florida
Nancy H. Walbek, Gustavus Adolphus College
Carl Westerfield, University of Alabama
Susan L. Woods, Eastern Illinois University
Andrea Zabel, Midland College

Finally, there is no way to accurately describe the contributions of our editors. We are particularly grateful for the commitment and untiring support we received from the entire editorial team, including Lisa McLellan, who has been with us since the first edition. We remain most impressed with the openness and enthusiasm that the entire Allyn & Bacon team offered at every phase. We could not have hoped for a better team, and we remain convinced that they are the best. We have come to count them as friends.

Richard D. McAnulty
M. Michele Burnette

FEATURE LIST

CLOSE UP ON culture

Global Sex in Perspective (Chapter 1)
Female Genital Mutilation (Chapter 3)
The Influence of Gender Roles on Safe Sex Practices (Chapter 5)
Religion and Sexual Orientation (Chapter 6)
Love and Attraction around the World (Chapter 7)
Sex around the Globe . . . A World of Differences (Chapter 8)
The Experience of Childbirth across Cultures (Chapter 9)
Adolescent Sexuality across Cultures (Chapter 11)
Sexual Attitudes around the World (Chapter 12)
Ethnicity, Race, and Transmission of STIs (Chapter 14)
Worldwide and U.S. Trends in HIV/AIDS (Chapter 14)
The History of Cross-Dressing (Chapter 15)

CLOSE UP ON gender

Do Men Lie More about Their Sex Lives? (Chapter 2)
Types of Orgasms in Women and Men (Chapter 4)
Gender Identity Disorder (Chapter 6)
Gender Differences in Love Attitudes (Chapter 7)
"Not Tonight Dear": Gender Differences in Sensual Communication (Chapter 8)
Pregnancy after Age 35 (Chapter 9)
Who Is Responsible for Contraception? (Chapter 10)
"Was it Good For You?" Reactions to First Intercourse (Chapter 11)
Myths about Sex in the United States (Chapter 13)
Women's Risks of HIV Infection (Chapter 14)
Female Perversions? (Chapter 15)
Coercive Sexuality in Same-Sex Relationships (Chapter 16)

HEALTH Matters

Does Masturbation Cause Blindness? (Chapter 1)
Epidemiology (Chapter 2)
Circumcision—The Medical Controversy (Chapter 3)
Cowper's Gland Emission and Pregnancy Risk (Chapter 4)
(Mis)Communication in the Bedroom (Chapter 5)
Gays and Lesbians—Easing the Burden (Chapter 6)
Are Relationships Good for Your Health? (Chapter 7)
How to Have Great Sex with Your Partner (Chapter 8)
Is Breast Milk Best? (Chapter 9)
A Note on Toxic Shock Syndrome (Chapter 10)
Do Oral Contraceptives Cause Cancer? (Chapter 10)
Health Risks of Unplanned Teenage Pregnancy (Chapter 11)
Cyberdating Safety Advice (Chapter 12)
Too Much of a Good Thing? (Chapter 13)

Myths about HIV Transmission (Chapter 14)
Taking Precautions against Being Raped (Chapter 16)
What You Can Do if You Experience Sexual Harassment (Chapter 16)
HIV and Prostitutes (Chapter 17)

reflect ON THIS

Would You Volunteer for Sex Research? (Chapter 2)
For Women—Increasing Comfort with Your Sexual Anatomy (Chapter 3)
Penis Envy for Men? (Chapter 3)
Concerns about Sexual Performance (Chapter 4)
Are You Open Minded about Sex Differences? (Chapter 5)
Analyzing Your Own Feelings and Attitudes (Chapter 6)
Who Do You Love, and How Much? (Chapter 7)
To Be or Not to Be a Parent? (Chapter 9)
Where Do You Stand on Abortion? (Chapter 10)
Memories of Early Sexual Thoughts and Feelings (Chapter 11)
The Lonely Hearts Club (Chapter 12)
Are You at Risk for Acquiring an STI? (Chapter 14)
Rape Myths about Women (Chapter 16)
Assessing Your Attitudes toward Sexually Explicit Materials (Chapter 17)

INDEX OF GENDER AND CROSS-CULTURAL ISSUES

Integrated Coverage of Gender Issues

Gender stereotyping in the media (Chapter 1, pp. 12–16, Chapter 5, pp. 148–149)
Double standards regarding male and female sexuality (Chapter 2, p. 51)
Gender differences in orgasm (Chapter 4, p. 120)
Intersexuality (Chapter 5, p. 134)
Gender roles and stereotypes (Chapter 5, pp. 135–138)
Transgenderism (Chapter 5, pp. 137–138)
Gender identity disorder (Chapter 5, pp. 140–141)
Gender-role conflict (Chapter 5, pp. 149–154)
Androgyny (Chapter 5, pp. 152–154)
Similarities and differences in male and female sexuality (Chapter 5, pp. 155–159)
Gender differences in love attitudes (Chapter 7, pp. 208–209)
Gender differences in sensual communication (Chapter 8, p. 234)
Pregnancy after age 35 (Chapter 9, p. 266)
Gender issues in contraception decision making (Chapter 10, p. 294)
Preadolescent girls' and boys' views on self-stimulation (Chapter 11, p. 335)
Gender differences in reactions to first intercourse (Chapter 11, p. 343)
Sexual scripts for men and women (Chapter 12, pp. 370–372)
Gender differences in extramarital infidelity (Chapter 12, p. 379)
Myths about sex in the United States (Chapter 13, pp. 398–399)
Women's risk of HIV infection (Chapter 14, p. 447)
Atypical sexual behavior in women (Chapter 15, p. 465)
Gender socialization and rape myths (Chapter 16, p. 499)
Gender differences in sexual harassment (Chapter 16, p. 514)

Integrated Coverage of Cross-Cultural Issues

Sexuality around the world (Chapter 1, p. 7)
Influence of media and religion on cultural norms and beliefs (Chapter 1, pp. 16–18)
Genital mutilation (Chapter 3, p. 70)
Menstruation across cultures (Chapter 3, pp. 77–78)
Influence of gender roles on safe sex practices around the world (Chapter 5, p. 154)
Cross-cultural trends in sexual identity formation (Chapter 6, pp. 169–171)
Religion and sexual orientation (Chapter 6, p. 178)
Gay and lesbian ethnic minorities (Chapter 6, pp. 180–181)
Love and attraction around the world (Chapter 7, pp. 206–207)
Cultural standards of attractiveness (Chapter 7, pp. 207, 208)
Cultural variations in sexual techniques and practices (Chapter 8, p. 232)
Experience of childbirth across cultures (Chapter 9, p. 256)
Cultural differences related to contraceptive use (Chapter 10, p. 294)
Adolescent sexuality across cultures (Chapter 11, p. 338)
Attitudes toward premarital sex, homosexual sex, and extramarital sex across cultures (Chapter 12, p. 360)
Koro (genital retraction syndrome) (Chapter 13, p. 402)
Cultural factors and sexual dysfunction (Chapter 13, pp. 411–412)
Ethnicity, race, and STI transmission (Chapter 14, p. 427)
Worldwide and U.S. trends in HIV/AIDS (Chapter 14, p. 443)
Coercive sexuality in same-sex relationships (Chapter 16, p. 493)
Cultural factors involved in rape (Chapter 16, p. 498)
Prostitution in various cultures throughout history (Chapter 17, pp. 539–541)

about the authors

The authors are both clinical psychologists who received specific training in sexual dysfunctions and disorders while studying at the University of Georgia. Diverging areas of professional emphasis and different employment settings provide the authors with a broad perspective in the area of human sexuality; this perspective encompasses sexuality and health, including the host of physical, psychological, and interpersonal nuances and factors in sexual adjustment.

Dr. Richard D. McAnulty is a professor in the Department of Psychology at the University of North Carolina–Charlotte. He currently teaches human sexuality and an advanced topics course in sexuality. He has written about and conducted research on such topics as measurement of sexual arousal, patterns of sexual arousal in accused child molesters, child sexual abuse, expert testimony in child sexual abuse cases, sexual coercion and dating relationships, religiosity and pedophilia, and topless dancers. He co-edited *The Psychology of Sexual Orientation, Behavior, and Identity* and has served on the editorial boards of several journals including *The Journal of Sex Research.* He currently specializes in the assessment and treatment of sexual disorders.

Dr. M. Michele Burnette is a former tenured associate professor in the Department of Psychology at Western Michigan University. She taught human sexuality at the undergraduate level for several years as well as courses on sexual dysfunction and therapy at the graduate level. Her research activities included outcome research on the behavioral management of genital herpes recurrences, AIDS attitudes and behaviors, acquaintance rape, and the impact of exercise on sexual function. Her years of clinical work included conducting relationship therapy and counseling clients on sexual dysfunctions and disorders, posttraumatic stress disorder (including post-rape trauma), recovery from childhood sexual abuse, infertility, and perinatal complications and bereavement. Dr. Burnette also completed a Research Fellowship in the Department of Epidemiology at the University of Pittsburgh's Graduate School of Public Health. While conducting research on the impact of health behaviors on cardiovascular health in women, Dr. Burnette obtained a Master of Public Health degree. Currently, she is a full-time writer and part-time teacher at area colleges, including the University of Pittsburgh.

Exploring Human Sexuality

CHAPTER 1

Sexuality: Yesterday and Today

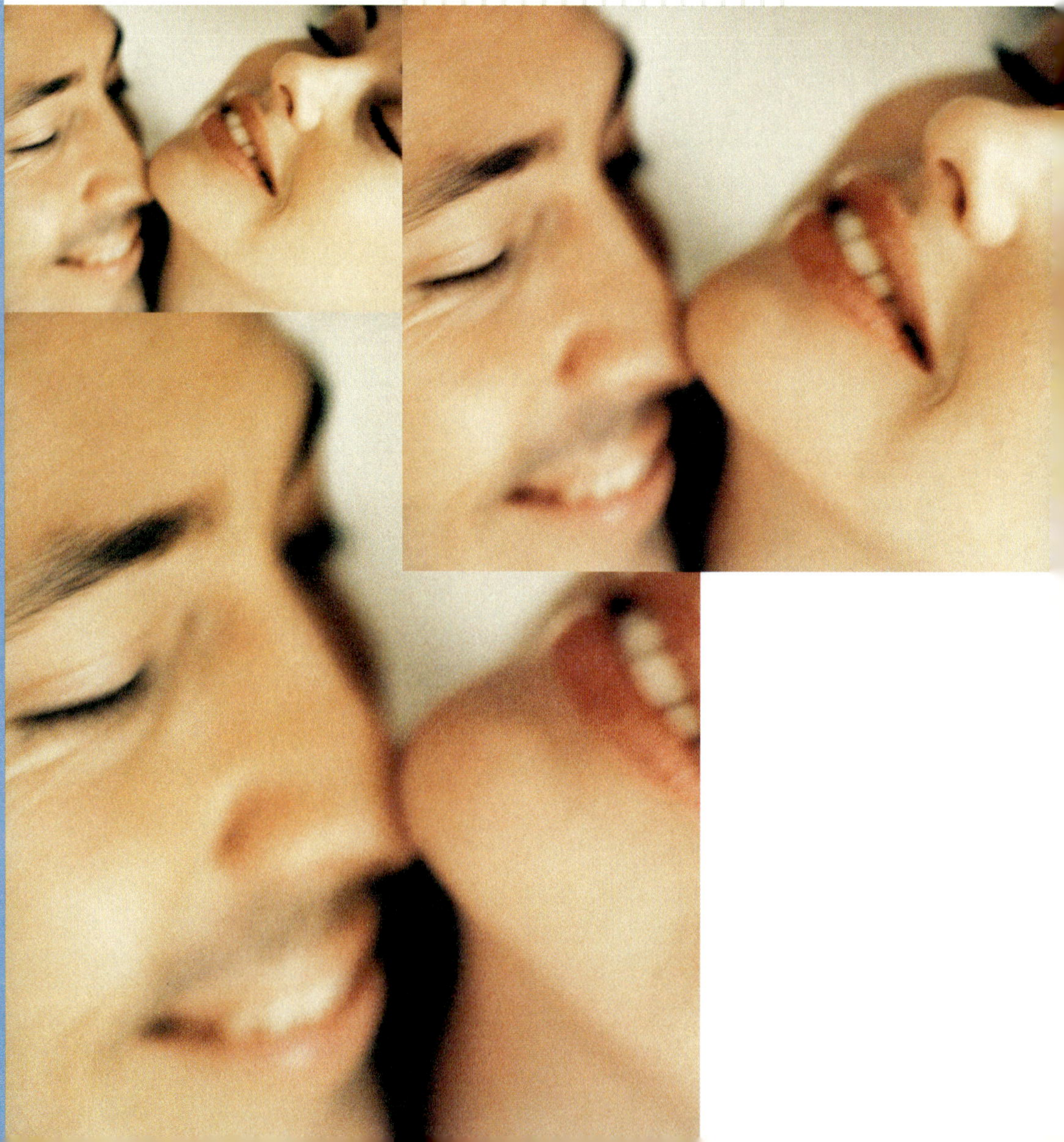

Growing up, I was taught that you weren't supposed to have sex until you were married. I was planning on living up to that belief until I reached high school and realized that everyone, even the "good girls," was having sex. It made me sit back and figure out what I really believed.

(A 20-year-old female college student)

I'm so sick of America complaining about teenage pregnancy and sexually transmitted diseases. What else can society expect from a generation that is being raised on ignorance rather than knowledge about sex? Our schools are not allowed to teach about sex, and our parents seem to think that it is best not to talk about it in the home.

(A 19-year-old male college student)

I consider myself to be a very respectable young lady, yet I'm having sex with two guys. I'm searching for that ultimate high. I think everyone's attitude toward sex today is that it is recreational, a great way to burn some calories, to release tension, and make time go by.

(A 21-year-old female college student)

Sex is a natural way of showing affection.

Sex today is public, live porno out in the open. Marriage is not important. We meet people today with the thought of sex, and only sex, on our minds. . . . Sex is seen as a natural way of showing affection to someone, so it should not be embarrassing to talk about or see on television.

(A 24-year-old male college student)

Few topics are more fascinating than sex. Sex is exciting and mysterious. Sex means pleasure, fun, and intimacy. But sex may also seem taboo, forbidden, and risky. It may be associated with negative feelings—shame, fear, and embarrassment. These contradictory reactions to sex occur in all of us to some extent as we are bombarded with mixed messages about it.

Sexuality pervades contemporary U.S. society, and contradictory messages about it come from many sources. Cultural ambivalence about sexuality is evident in the media—from television and films to novels, magazines, newspapers, and even computer networks. Mixed messages also come from various societal institutions, such as religious groups, governments (as reflected in existing laws), schools, and health professionals (DeLamater, 1987). We often experience this sexual ambivalence on a more personal level, in interactions with our families or peers and in our sexual relationships. Our mixed feelings about sexuality are evident even in our language. Consider, for example, some of the colloquial and even crude references to genitals that are used as insults. When someone is called a "dick," it is perfectly obvious that the word is not a compliment. Curiously, we don't use references to other body parts as insults.

Sexuality encompasses a wide range of topics, from sexual behavior and attitudes to anatomy and gender.

(Calling someone a "toe" or an "eyeball" clearly does not have the same negative connotation.)

Many popular TV programs and movies seem to promote sexual openness and experimentation. Peers may reinforce this message, and you may experience pressure to conform to peer norms. On the other hand, other influential sources emphasize sexual restraint. Many families and most religious groups in the United States teach that people should abstain from sex until marriage. With respect to sex, U.S. culture is viewed as quite conservative in comparison to most European cultures (Widmer, Treas, & Newcomb, 1998). It is not surprising, then, that many Americans experience some ambivalence in their views about sexuality.

So what is it about sex that is so mysterious and exciting but also uncomfortable and "dirty"? What is "sexuality"? We all share some curiosity about the mysteries of sex, yet finding a universally accepted definition of sexuality is no easy matter. The difficulty stems not only from cultural and individual ambivalence about the topic but also from the extraordinary variability in human sexuality. There are vast cultural differences in sexual attitudes and practices (Hatfield & Rapson, 1996). And sexual attitudes and behaviors have changed over the course of history. Furthermore, sexuality encompasses a wide range of topics. The words *sexuality* and *sex* can refer to anatomy—especially the genitals, or external sexual organs. They can refer to sexual behavior, thoughts, and feelings—including masturbation, sexual intercourse (or *coitus,* as it is more technically called), kissing, and sexual fantasies. Sex also refers to *gender,* the psychosocial condition of being feminine or masculine.

Although everyone has ideas about what sexuality means, coming up with a good definition is no simple feat (Reiss, 1986). This book will borrow the definition offered by Aron and Aron (1991), who define sexuality as consisting of all the sensations, emotions, and cognitions that an individual associates with physical sexual arousal and that usually give rise to sexual desire and/or behavior. More than any other species, humans are sexual creatures. We are the only species that engages in sexual activity for pleasure only, in private settings (as a rule), and according to certain rules or guidelines (that may not be rigidly adhered to). In summary, human sexuality is characterized by extraordinary diversity, and this will be a recurring theme throughout this book.

CONTEMPORARY TRENDS

Several interesting trends influenced sexual attitudes and behaviors in the United States during the latter half of the 20th century. The first, which emerged during the sexual revolution of the 1960s, was a trend toward increased openness about sex (Thornton & Young-DeMarco, 2001). U.S. culture at large is more open to sexual images and discussion of sexual issues now than it was prior to the 1960s. Sexual freedom has become an ideal, and many old taboos have been abandoned. The ideal of sexual freedom includes the right to choose one's personal sexual standards and values (Mosher, 1991; Sands, 2000). Accordingly, sexual experimentation has become more common and acceptable.

A second and related trend concerns the range of sexual relationships. Although most Americans still view sex as properly belonging in a committed relationship, the frequency of sexual relationships outside of traditional marriage has increased in the past several decades. An ever increasing number of young adults are postponing marriage or choosing to live together without being married. Yet, young adults in the United States are more sexually active than ever before (Seidman & Rieder, 1994). Along with increasingly tolerant views of sex outside of marriage, there is growing acceptance of sexual diversity and alternatives. People are more likely than ever before to view masturbation as a healthy sexual outlet, to recognize that aging does not bring the end of one's sex life, and to understand that many differences between men and women are culturally determined rather than biologically imposed. More than ever before, Americans are able to discuss homosexuality and alternative sexual practices in objective language. But although U.S. society seems to have made some progress toward a consistent and healthy perspective on human sexuality, considerable ambivalence remains (Donovan, 1998). There is still tremendous controversy and prejudice surrounding such topics as homosexuality, sexuality education, and abortion. Many stereotypes about men and women endure, and sex is still equated with youth and beauty.

The third trend that has been apparent in the United States over the past few decades is a growing awareness that sex can be risky. A number of diseases can be sexually transmitted, and partners who do not take precautions may infect one another. The threat of sexually transmissible infections is not new, although the seriousness of the threat escalated in the 1980s with the spread of the human immunodeficiency virus (HIV). The realization that sex can be associated with untreatable and life-threatening illnesses led to a renewed emphasis on open discussions about sex. It also led many experts to advocate safer sex, which refers to sexual practices that reduce the risks of contracting sexually transmissible infections. Although *safer sex* is a household word today, it was not introduced until the mid-1980s. The trend toward openness emphasizes the importance of being explicit about the potential dangers of sex, a message that has paradoxically reinforced the cultural ambivalence about sex. For a number of people, the potential health risks of sexual interactions have contributed to the decision to abstain from sex. Others, such as some college students, for example, choose to remain virgins because they feel they have not met the "right person" (Sprecher & Regan, 1996).

did YOU know?

People who are not in a committed relationship report having more sexual partners over time, but they also report an overall lower rate of sexual activity.

Sexual Behavior in the United States

One of the oldest sexual norms in the United States is the idea that sexual activity should be postponed until marriage. For centuries, sexual purity, or virginity, was the moral, religious, and social ideal. Today, postponing sexual activity may still be an ideal, but it is an ideal that is frequently not lived up to. Several surveys have revealed that the majority of teenagers and young adults view sex before marriage as acceptable, at least under certain circumstances (Ku et al., 1998; Robinson, Zeiss, Ganja, Katz, & Robinson, 1991; Smith, 1994).

Today, the vast majority of unmarried adults are sexually experienced. From their review of surveys of sexual behavior among young adults, Seidman and Rieder (1994) concluded that approximately 90% of young adults are sexually experienced, and most of these individuals have sex regularly. Surveys of college students have found that 74–88% of men and 69–88% of women report being sexually experienced, and most of these young adults have had several sexual partners (Anderson & Dahlberg, 1992; MacDonald et al., 1990; Weinberg, Lottes, & Gordon, 1997). According to one large national survey, the National Health and Social Life Survey (NHSLS; discussed in detail in Chapter 2), approximately one-third of women and men aged 18 to 24 reported having had two or more sexual partners in the 12 months prior to being interviewed (Laumann, Gagnon, Michael, & Michaels, 1994).

Other noteworthy trends include a tendency to be older when marrying for the first time and a tendency to have a first sexual experience at a younger age (Seidman & Rieder, 1994; Weinberg et al., 1997). In other words, people are marrying at a later age yet beginning sexual activity at an earlier age, showing that the norm of waiting until one finds the "right person" is changing. For most people, however, initiation into sex still occurs in the context of a relationship. Sex and love are perceived as belonging together, the so-called love effect. For the majority of teenage boys and girls, first sexual

1.1 on the web

People today are more likely than ever to view masturbation as a healthy sexual outlet. Yet, for many it still remains a taboo and the topic of jokes rather than serious discussion. Visit "Sex with Ourselves" at **www.ablongman.com/mcanulty2e.**

Can you relate to any of the attitudes toward self-pleasuring expressed in the excerpts? Are your attitudes toward masturbation mostly positive or negative? What experiences shaped your attitudes?

did YOU know?

Although young adults in the United States are more likely than ever before to use contraceptive devices, the major reason is still for birth control rather than prevention of disease.

intercourse occurs with someone they are dating steadily (Sprecher, Barbee, & Schwartz, 1995).

Gender is also an important factor in determining contemporary sexual behavior. Overall, men report higher levels of sexual activity than women do, and younger unmarried men are the most sexually active group in the U.S. population, as measured by the self-reported number of sexual partners. Approximately 15% of never-married young men have had five or more sexual partners over the past year, compared to 6% of never-married young women (Laumann et al., 1994). This trend reflects a cultural double standard. Being sexually active is tolerated or even expected for males, yet females are still expected to be more sexually restrained. This double standard for sexual behavior has been changing over the past several decades, but ever so slowly. Society still frowns on women having sex in a casual or uncommitted relationship, although men are generally not judged negatively for the same behavior (Baumeister & Tice, 2001; Cohen & Shotland, 1996). This trend is not limited to the United States. As you'll read in Close Up on Culture: Global Sex in Perspective, sex surveys from France, Great Britain, and Finland reveal that men in those cultures also report higher numbers of sexual partners over their lifetimes than do women (Johnson et al., 2001).

Sexual behavior in the United States varies across ethnic and racial backgrounds, which reveals that not only cultural norms but also subcultural norms influence sexual practices. Overall, Caucasian Americans (whites) and African Americans (blacks) report more sexual partners in their lifetimes than do Hispanic Americans, Asian Americans, and Native Americans (Laumann et al., 1994). About 70% of whites and 80% of African Americans reported having had more than one sexual partner since age 18, compared to fewer than 50% of Asian Americans. Historically, African Americans have reported higher levels of sexual activity than other racial or ethnic groups. The differences between whites and African Americans, however, have been declining, and few differences are found with respect to lifetime sexual behavior patterns (Laumann et al., 1994). Many of the reported differences in sexual behavior may be attributable to socioeconomic status rather than to racial or ethnic background (Staples & Johnson, 1993). In fact, middle-class African Americans appear to subscribe to mainstream sexual norms. Among other racial or ethnic groups, sexual practices are heavily influenced by the extent of acculturation, or the degree to which the group has adopted the norms of the dominant culture. Members of an ethnic or racial minority group who reject the norms of their subculture in favor of those of the dominant U.S. culture typically share the mainstream sexual values. Differences in the reported sexual practices of Hispanic Americans and Asian Americans may therefore reflect a lower degree of acculturation for these two groups compared to African Americans.

Although most people today are marrying at a later age, for the majority, sexual activity in adolescence is initiated in the context of a steady dating relationship.

Sex around the World

Examining sexual beliefs and practices across diverse cultures serves two purposes. First, such a comparison can help reveal the role that cultural norms and traditions play in shaping people's sexual behavior. Second, finding nearly universal sexual practices can reveal influences that are *not* culture-dependent, such as biological factors. Either way, cross-cultural comparisons can contribute to an understanding of sexuality from a different perspective.

Sexual practices and customs across the world are extraordinarily diverse. Yet, we're all familiar with the growing

CLOSE UP ON culture

Global Sex in Perspective

Americans' attitudes toward sex can be characterized as ambivalent. Some other cultures are more definite in their views. On the permissive end of the spectrum are the Polynesian cultures of the Pacific islands, which have a very liberal and tolerant view of sex. Sex is considered a great pleasure that is to be shared freely, beginning early in life. Parents encourage and expect sexual experimentation. Unmarried young adults in Mangaia (Central Polynesia) are expected to be unrestricted sexual athletes. Once they marry and start family life, however, their sex drive is expected to decline drastically. Among the Canela tribe of South America, sexual intercourse may start at age 11 or younger for girls. Extramarital sex is permissible, even expected, for a married woman, but only before her first pregnancy. Once she becomes pregnant, she is expected to settle down and remain monogamous with few exceptions (Crocker & Crocker, 1994). At the other extreme, people of the rural Irish village of Inis Beag associate any type of sex with sin, guilt, and shame (Messenger, 1971). Breast-feeding of infants is avoided because of its "erotic connotation," and married couples have sex only in the dark after removing the least amount of clothing possible. Because of the taboo associated with the human body, inhabitants of Inis Beag do not learn how to swim, since it is impossible to do so fully dressed. Between these two extremes are such cultures as the Muria from the Bastar State of India, who tolerate sexual experimentation as long as it does not involve complete penetration for unmarried teenage couples. The intent is not to preserve the girl's virginity but to prevent pregnancy (Elwin, 1968). Most American college students are surprised to learn that kissing is not a universal practice. Popular in Western cultures (including France, of course), kissing is practiced less commonly than stimulation of a partner's genitals in some cultures (Frayser, 1985).

In examining sexual attitudes in 24 countries, Widmer, Treas, and Newcomb (1998) concluded that it is overly simplistic to categorize countries as either conservative or permissive. Sexual attitudes in a given culture may vary widely depending on the type of sexual behavior in question. Premarital sex is accepted in most cultures, but only for persons aged 16 or older. Extramarital sex is strongly condemned in the majority of cultures. Homosexual behavior is rejected in most countries, although there are exceptions. In the Netherlands, for example, nearly two-thirds of people are tolerant of sexual relations between same-sex adults. The Philippines, on the other hand, stands apart from virtually every other country: Its people disapprove of all forms of sex outside of marriage (Widmer et al., 1998). Indeed, if there is one truly universal sexual norm, it is the belief that marriage provides the preferred context for a sexual relationship (Davenport, 1987).

trend toward *globalization,* a worldwide blending of views and practices. And sex has not been immune to this trend. The convergence of sexual practices across cultures has been attributed to the spreading influence of Western values, modernization, economic factors, and an ideology that promotes love, sex, and pleasure (Altman, 2001; Dowsett & Aggleton, 1999). Of all Western cultures, the United States in particular has a strong influence in many parts of the world. Ching (1997), for example, noted that Japan was "plugged into every trend of Western, especially American, pop culture" (p. 171). Similarly, Chinese critics have deplored the materialism of U.S. culture that is increasingly evident in their media (Keane, 1998). As Middleton (2002) observed, "globalization alters local institutional structures, breaks down taboos, and engenders cultural clashes and misunderstandings" (p. 87).

Most cultures, however, do retain distinct sexual values that are reinforced by various belief systems and institutions. In many countries, tradition is a powerful force that shapes sexual values. Similarly, religious precepts and social norms play important roles in all cultures as they guide individual beliefs and practices. Some sexual values, such as the importance of fidelity to one's partner, are explicitly articulated and promoted on many levels. Other values, however, are subtle and unwritten, yet they can be just as influential. All cultures, for example, have certain rules and norms based on gender. Some cultures prize female virginity, although they rarely place the same value on male virginity (Altman, 2001). In parts of Africa and Asia, virginity is still used as a measure of a woman's value as a mate and as a marker of her character in the eyes of her partner, family, and community or tribe (Dowsett & Aggleton, 1999).

The coverage of cross-cultural perspectives on sexuality that follows is limited for several reasons. We have attempted to sample from all major regions of the world to illustrate the breadth of sexual views and practices. We are forced, however, to report only on the cultures that have been studied. There is no central repository for global sex statistics, and this type of research is prohibited in some countries, particularly those with repressive sexual norms (Mackay, 2001). In many cases, the existing data pertain to fertility and diseases, such as birth rates and number of cases of HIV infection, rather than to sexual practices and attitudes.

Europe

The continent of Europe is marked by significant regional variations in sexual norms and practices. The different sexual perspectives that are evident in European countries can be traced in part to their religious traditions (Eder, Hall, & Hekma, 1999). Countries with Protestant traditions generally disapprove of nonmarital sex. Yet, prostitution is tolerated in many countries as an unfortunate necessity for men. Countries with a Catholic legacy have advocated a more restrictive lifestyle but practiced tolerance and lenience. The resulting gap between doctrine and actual sexual practices allows a broad range of expressions. Owing to their Orthodox Christian religious backgrounds, the countries of eastern Europe, including Russia, were historically viewed as very conservative in their sexual values (Amirkhanian, Tiunov, & Kelly, 2001; Eder et al., 1999). The fall of the Soviet Union marked the beginning of dramatic social, cultural, and economic changes in eastern Europe, along with changes in sexual behavior. Current practices in Russia reflect those in many countries in the region, which are experiencing a new openness hampered by lingering taboos and gross misinformation (Kon, 1999), all of which contribute to the region's growing pains. During the Soviet era, governmental policies in many countries prevented open discussions of sexuality, and variations from the norm, such as homosexuality, were considered illegal. The Soviet Union was officially dissolved in 1991, marking the beginning of widespread changes at all levels of society. On the positive side, Russians experienced more freedom and openness, including the freedom to explore their sexuality. Homosexuality was decriminalized. On the negative side, however, stigma remain evident in most areas, and severe economic problems, including unemployment and shrinking resources, prevent most people from pursuing their sexual needs in a healthy fashion. The social and political upheaval in these countries, following decades of sexual repression and misinformation, have resulted in rampant sexually transmitted infections (Amirkhanian et al., 2001; Zhuravleva, 2001). The longstanding inhibitions against sexual expression prevent many people from seeking information on sexually transmissible infections, disease prevention, and contraception. Although young adults in Russia and other eastern European cultures now enjoy freedom for sexual experimentation, they lack the requisite knowledge and information for healthy sexual expression. Consequently, "the HIV epidemic now unfolding in Eastern European and former Soviet countries is new, rapidly moving, and still understudied" (Kelly et al., 2002, p. 74).

On the other end of the sexual spectrum, the Netherlands is often touted as sexually permissive, progressive, and tolerant (Kraaykamp, 2001). It was the first European country to officially recognize gay and lesbian marriages (Russell, 2001). Sexuality education is widespread and readily accepted by adults and children alike. The average age for the first experience of intercourse is 18, and 84% of those who are sexually active use contraception. Over 90% of young people report that they always use contraception. The pregnancy rate is only 4.2 per 1,000, as is the abortion rate; both are among the lowest in the world. In Holland, adolescents claim that the main motivation for initiating sexual intercourse is affection for a partner rather than social pressure (Roberts, 2000).

During the past decade, the amount of sexually explicit programs on Dutch television has increased significantly. Viewers are offered a variety of sexual formats ranging from pornography to explicit documentaries about people's sex lives (Vanwesenbeeck, 2001). The city of Amsterdam is notorious for offering a wide range of sexual services and opportunities, including "kinky parties" that are reportedly well attended (Oosterhuis, 1999). The government and public alike are tolerant of sexual diversity and alternative lifestyles. Despite this openness to sexuality, surveys reveal that Dutch college students subscribe to sexual scripts that are fairly traditional. Men are viewed as the active initiators of sexual encounters, with women playing the part of cautious and sometimes reluctant participants (Vanwesenbeeck, Bekker, & van Lenning, 1998).

The Netherlands is an example of a country with a sexually liberated and tolerant culture. It was the first country to officially recognize gay and lesbian marriages.

France enjoys a reputation of being a land of love and passion, both of which are prevalent themes in its rich traditions and cultural history (Nye, 1999). Indeed, the French pride themselves on their alleged prowess and expertise in the bedroom. Public displays of affection are socially acceptable in France. Laws regarding sexual conduct, under the Napoleonic Code, are fairly liberal, regulating only harmful acts such as rape and child molestation. Public sentiment is that consenting adults should be allowed to engage in any sexual activity as long as it is in private. In reality, though, France is less tolerant of homosexuality than some other European countries (Nye, 1999).

Rates of divorce in France are lower than in most other Western cultures, in part because of higher rates of cohabitation. Although young French women are slower to enter sexual relationships than young women in the United States, older French women enjoy richer sex lives, regardless of their relationship status. Children born to unmarried couples have the same legal benefits and cultural acceptance as children whose parents are married (Nye, 1999). Despite its status as the "most sexually celebrated of Western cultures" (Gagnon, Giami, Michaels, & de Colomby, 2001), monogamy is valued in France, and most couples enter exclusive relationships earlier and for longer than their counterparts in the United States. In general, the French place more value on commitment in their sexual relationships than do people in the United States (Gagnon et al., 2001).

did YOU know?

In the United States, the French are credited with the invention of deep kissing, the **French kiss*****, and even a condom, the*** **French tickler.**

Africa

No other continent shows the diversity that characterizes sexual practices in Africa. Traditional African beliefs promote the idea that sex can lead to immortality through procreation (Van Dyk, 2001). For many traditional Africans, especially women, the failure to have children is stigmatizing and leads to profound disadvantages. In many African societies, a woman's worth is measured by her fertility. In parts of Nigeria, "a childless woman is considered a monstrosity" (Ogundipe-Leslie, 1984, p. 501). To the Shona of rural Zimbabwe, those who die childless are doomed to wander the earth aimlessly because they cannot be accepted into the spirit world of their ancestors (Scott & Mercer, 1994). Not only does childbearing impart social privileges, children also provide additions to the labor force for poor rural families and an investment for the future.

Polygamy is still practiced in some parts of Africa. Some tribes have traditional rules to ensure that co-wives are treated equally, sometimes even going so far as to establish a quota for the sexual relations between the husband and his wives. In many African societies, unmarried women are placed in the same stigmatized group as childless women (Altman, 2001). To the Gabra of east Africa, choosing not to marry is unthinkable or absurd (Wood, 1999). One tribal custom requires a widowed woman to become

Looking At . . .

. . . Thinking About

In many African tribes, childbearing imparts social privileges. Are there social privileges associated with having children in the United States?

the second wife of her husband's brother. Traditional beliefs about sexual behaviors are also varied. In Rwanda, the exchange of fluids during sexual intercourse represents a "gift" that is essential to both partners' health—hence, the opposition of Rwandans to using condoms (Taylor, 1990). Another belief, common in east Africa and Zaire and among the Zulus of South Africa, is that a growing fetus requires regular injections of semen to ensure its "ripening" (Van Dyk, 2001). Some youths practice "thigh sex" (rubbing the penis between a partner's closed thighs) as a way of preserving virginity; thigh sex is also practiced by some married men when their wives are menstruating (Green, Zokwee, & Dupree, 1995). The Kikuyu people of Kenya encourage sexual play among adolescents of both sexes, but actual penetration and mutual masturbation are off limits (Kenyatta, 1953). However, in sharp contrast, women in parts of Nigeria are socialized to deny any sexual interest or enjoyment (Blanc, 2001; Jung, Hunt, & Balakrishnan, 2001). Similarly, the Fulbe of north Cameroun in West Africa view romance and passion as threats to social order. Those who are accused of public displays of affection are subject to reprimand or even exorcism (Middleton, 2002). In parts of Africa, the practice of kissing is unknown or is viewed as disgusting.

Unfortunately, the diverse belief systems of Africa have also contributed to a number of problems, some of which can be traced to people's adherence to age-old customs in a changing world. Sub-Saharan Africa is suffering from epidemic rates of sexually transmissible infections, including HIV (Lawson, 1999; UNAIDS [Joint United Nations Programme on HIV/AIDS], 2002). The soaring rates of infection can be tied to social, economic, and cultural factors that interact in complex ways. Women in Africa are often disadvantaged on many levels, and male domination is evident in intimate relationships as well as in social and political contexts (Lugalla & Emmelin, 1999). In rural Zimbabwe, young women are often initiated into sexual activity by older men who make promises of marriage and material resources (Gregson et al., 2002). Insisting on fidelity or safer sex could have disastrous consequences for poor women with children: Abandonment or rejection by their husbands would threaten their very survival. As one woman from Tanzania put it, "In our tradition the husband is the boss of the household. He decides and plans everything. Women are not allowed to question. . . . If you disobey, you risk divorce. Getting divorced means losing husband's wealth and children" (Lugalla & Emmelin, 1999, p. 385). Economic problems and political instability have compromised the traditional values and lifestyles in many African communities. The decline in traditional practices has led to greater sexual experimentation along with increased sexual risk-taking (Gregson et al., 2002). Migrant workers often acquire sexually transmissible infections in encounters with commercial sex workers (Susser & Stein, 2000). These men then infect their partners when they return to their local communities.

Current sexual practices in Africa remain varied, although traditional beliefs and lifestyles continue to change. These changes stem not only from globalization, but also from the economic and political upheaval that is prevalent in many African regions.

Asia

An ancient culture, China has a rich history that is replete with traditions. Many contemporary Chinese attitudes toward sex can be traced to religious traditions but are colored by contemporary political ideologies. Overall, the Chinese perspective is quite restrictive. There is significant misinformation about sex and corresponding prudishness (Hatfield & Rapson, 1996). Recent research confirms that Chinese college students are more sexually restricted than their U.S. counterparts. One survey revealed that only 24% of students from Hong Kong admitted to being sexually active during the preceding year (Wong & Tang, 2001). Another survey found that less than 10% of Chinese students had experienced vaginal intercourse; as in the United States, males were more likely than females to report the experience (Liu, Ng, Zhou, & Haeberle, 1997). These relatively low rates of sexual activity, by Western standards, are due to a higher emphasis on academics, greater parental influence, and a lack of opportunities to engage in sexual activity. Cultural norms deter many Chinese from sexual experimentation, as premarital sex is still officially condemned. In one case, a male student was expelled from a public university after authorities learned that he had engaged in premarital sex (Southerland, 1990).

As in most Western cultures, a double standard is evident in China. Males were more likely than females to report engaging in casual sex. One survey found that Chinese college students share many of the same body-image concerns as their Western counterparts: Males were most concerned with penis size, and women worried about having small breasts (Liu et al., 1997). A majority of Chinese students deny any masturbatory experience (Liu et al., 1997), most likely because of the traditional Chinese belief that the practice is harmful to a person's health.

The historical heritage of Japan is vastly different from that of Western cultures. One key difference is that the religious tradition is not Judeo-Christian; rather, Shintoism and Buddhism have been the dominant religious influences. Followers of Buddha are instructed to copy his example of morality, kindness, and wisdom to achieve spiritual enlightenment (Bullough, 1995). Self-control and moderation are valued. Another difference relates to broader cultural norms and values. In Japan, beginning in elementary school, productivity and achievement are emphasized more than they are in most other cultures. Officially, the Japanese culture promotes sexual abstinence until marriage, especially for girls (Caron, 1998). In actuality, Japanese sexual norms are unique. Like people from most other countries, the Japanese frown on extramarital affairs and sexual relationships for adolescents. Their views of premarital sexuality are more ambivalent than those of people in most other cultures, though (Widmer et al., 1998). The Japanese are apparently tolerant of premarital sexual behavior as long as it is discreet and does not interfere with social duties (White, 1993). Hatano (1991) reported that although the Japanese started experimenting with intimacy later than adolescents in Western cultures, they tended to proceed rapidly once they started. Although most Japanese men and women did not experience their first kiss until age 20, within a year or two they had experienced sexual intercourse.

Historically, Japan was a male-dominated society where women had few rights. Even today, Japanese women have a lower social status. Traditional norms teach that women should be submissive to their husbands. Although there has been a movement toward promoting equal rights in recent years (Learner, 1999), Japan's Equal Employment Opportunity law of 1986 apparently did little to rectify the situation. One obstacle to gender equality in Japan is the culture's emphasis on motherhood as the ultimate goal for all women (Kodera, 1996); everything else is secondary in a Japanese woman's life.

Although prostitution is not legal, there is a thriving sex trade in Japan. Female college students commonly work for "date clubs," which are essentially escort services (Greenlees, 1997). Such work offers a relatively quick way to earn a lucrative income. Comic magazines, often with sexually explicit content, are immensely popular in Japan. Mass-circulation comics commonly feature a variety of sexual situations and graphic portrayals of sexual acts, including rape. In contrast, Japanese culture is quite intolerant of homosexuality.

Thailand is unique among Asian countries in allowing men the freedom of exercising their autonomy, including in their sex lives (Beyrer, 1998). Wealthy Thai men maintain mistresses, a practice that is tolerated as long as it is discreet. Visits to prostitutes are also permissible. As Beyrer (1998) observed, "the use of commercial sex services, highly stigmatized in many Asian cultures, is an acknowledged outlet for northern Thai men, the great majority of whom have bought sex at some time in their lives. Like nearly all societies, however, this sexual freedom applies much less to women" (p. 27). Social norms historically prohibited sex before and outside of marriage for women in Thailand. The values are beginning to change, however, as evidenced by an increase in premarital sex among teenage girls and a corresponding decrease in visits to prostitutes by male adolescents. However, commercial sex continues to thrive in Thailand (Beyrer, 2001).

MAJOR SOCIOCULTURAL INFLUENCES

As the anthropologist F. A. Beach (1977) noted, "Every society shapes, structures, and constrains the development and expression of sexuality in all of its members" (p. 116). Three societal institutions are particularly powerful agents in shaping cultural norms regarding sexuality: the mass media, religions, and the family.

The Mass Media

The media disseminate information and a variety of messages about sexuality, and their presentations of sex reflect many contemporary trends and issues. The changes in U.S. attitudes seen in the latter half of the 20th century (as well as advances in technology) have allowed the various media in the United States to become increasingly open in addressing sexuality and to increase the quantity (and quality) of sexual materials they make available. Although media critics often deplore the apparent increase in sexual materials, the trend is not new, only more obvious today than it was 50 years ago (Stern & Handel, 2001).

Television and Films

As a consequence of the increased incidence of sexually transmissible infections, public health messages on national television have begun to warn of the potential risks of unprotected sex. Advertisements for condoms first appeared in the mass media during the 1990s. Topics that were previously taboo are now regularly presented on television. Banned from mass media in the past, words such as *oral sex, masturbation, homosexuality,* and *semen* are used in national broadcasts.

NBC's Will and Grace *was the first successful television series to revolve around the life of a gay man. Both Eric McCormack and Sean Hayes have won Emmy Awards for their groundbreaking roles as gay pals Will Truman and Jack McFarland.*

The popular HBO series Sex and the City *depicts relationship issues and sexual issues from the perspective of four professional women. The show is considered groundbreaking in addressing sexual topics that are usually avoided on television, such as whether women should fake orgasms and how to coach an inept male partner in the bedroom.*

In 1992, for the first time ever, an entire episode of a prime-time TV show was devoted to masturbation. An award-winning episode of the immensely popular comedy *Seinfeld* featured a contest between the characters to determine who could resist the urge to masturbate for the longest time. Challenging popular gender stereotypes, the lead female character lost the competition. A few years later, actress Ellen DeGeneres made headlines when she became the first to portray an openly gay lead character on a prime-time network show. In a 1997 episode, her character in the series *Ellen* revealed her sexual orientation, earning the actress an Emmy for writing the episode and turning her into a popular-culture pioneer. The show paved the way for *Will and Grace,* which premiered in 1998 and was the first prime-time U.S. comedy in which the lead male character is openly gay. Perhaps in anticipation of controversy, the gay character has a heterosexual female roommate, although the relationship is only platonic.

The popular HBO series *Sex and the City* features the romantic and sexual adventures of four over-30 professional women. The Emmy award–winning show portrays the characters' candid discussions of their quests for love and pleasure. The "lusty Samantha" is depicted as sexually adventuresome and uninhibited, making her one of the more controversial characters on the show (Poniewozik, 1999).

The media in other countries also reflect and reinforce cultural norms in their presentations of sex and gender roles. In France, for example, seminude models are commonly shown on TV ads, and sexually suggestive language is permissible, but commercials for contraceptives are prohibited. In fact, advertising for contraceptives is viewed as unacceptable in most cultures. In Middle Eastern cultures with an Islamic belief system, displaying any part of a woman's body is strictly forbidden. In Malaysia, when a man and woman (both clothed) are shown alone in a room for more than 3 seconds, the implication is that they had sexual intercourse. Such scenes are prohibited unless the actors are identified as a married couple. In the United States, men and women are displayed in sexually suggestive poses, but frontal nudity is generally avoided. Scandinavians, on the other hand, are very tolerant of nudity but object to advertising that perpetuates gender-role stereotypes.

The media in the United States also convey messages about gender roles, which may powerfully influence viewers' attitudes and expectations. From the late 1920s to the mid-1980s, men and women on television and in Hollywood films behaved according to rigid gender-role stereotypes. Historically, women on television were portrayed as housewives, nurses, and airline stewardesses. Men were shown as physicians, police officers, and politicians. Only recently have the media in the United States started challenging gender-role stereotypes.

Sex is commonly featured in regular media programming in the United States. Many TV programs depict couples kissing, often with the implicit message that the kissing will lead to sexual intercourse. Daytime soap operas regularly show couples in erotic encounters, although full nudity is excluded. According to one analysis, the typical one-hour "soap" features four implied sexual encounters (Greenberg, 1994). The encounters typically involve passionate kissing, but the majority of the couples shown are not married to one another, and contraception is practically never mentioned (Greenberg & Woods, 1999). Although extramarital encounters are common in soaps, homosexuality is virtually never mentioned (Greenberg & Busselle, 1996). Finally, contrary to popular belief, soap opera viewers are not just middle-aged housewives—soaps are very popular among college students as well (Perse & Rubin, 1990).

Daytime talk shows are another popular genre on American television. These shows differ widely in their formats, but most share one common feature: controversial topics, with sexuality high on the list (Greenberg, Sherry, Busselle, Hnilo, & Smith, 1997). At one time, more than twenty syndicated talk shows competed for daytime TV audiences. Shows that focused on sensationalism, scandal, and confrontation thrived (Gamson, 1996). Many talk shows made it a point to feature guests whose behavior would be considered unusual or deviant by the majority of the audience, in what has been described as a "parade of pathology" (Heaton & Wilson, 1995) and a "psychological freak show"

IN YOUR own words

Vinita Acklin
Virginia Commonwealth University

Sex is everywhere: it is on TV, it is on the radio, and there is unlimited access to it on the Internet.

One popular genre, so-called reality TV, combines elements of talk shows, soap operas, and game shows, all allegedly set in real-life situations (Grimm, 2001). Relationship problems and sexual innuendos are common features in several reality TV shows, including Temptation Island, *which features four couples who are sent to an exotic island where their commitment to their relationships is tested by "sexy singles."*

(Oliver, 1995). Consider the promotional lines for some of these shows: "Bizarre stories of transvestites and their lovers," "My mom is a slut," "My husband slept with the baby-sitter," "Women who marry their rapists," "I have sex with my sister," and so on. One analysis of the most popular daytime talk shows revealed that relationship issues, including parenting, marriage, and dating, formed the single most common topic (48% of shows)—and sex was a major theme. Popular sexual topics included frequency of sexual activity (36%), sexual infidelity (21%), and sexual orientation (12%). The authors of the study concluded that the "viewer, then, is cascaded with interpersonal family and dating problems and often with sex as a component of these problems" (Greenberg et al., 1997, p. 431). Note, however, that not all talk shows thrive on sensationalism. *The Oprah Winfrey Show,* for example, has consistently tried to address important topics in a sensitive and objective fashion.

Sexual topics are regularly the focus of news programs and prime-time talk shows as well. Although this could be seen as healthy and a positive endorsement of human sexuality, that is not really the aim of such coverage. Media coverage is almost invariably biased. News and talk shows often focus on the sensational and negative aspects of sex. Lies, deception, and drama are often the mainstays of other forms of programming, especially soaps and films. This is because the mass media primarily intend to entertain, not to educate. Their business is to make a profit, which is achieved by drawing audiences. Ultimately, the media offer what they perceive to be popular and interesting—and sex sells.

Magazines

The prevailing norms of the culture determine what is considered acceptable to media audiences (Boddewyn & Kunz, 1991). The teen magazine *Seventeen,* for example, did not even mention the topic of oral sex until 1994, and that year was also the first time it referred to masturbation as "a normal part of life" (Carpenter, 1998). *Cosmopolitan* magazine is reportedly one of the leading sources of information about sex for many female U.S. college students. Its most popular features are articles dealing with sexual skills and how to please one's partner (Bielay & Herold, 1995). A number of messages are promulgated in *Cosmopolitan,* including the acceptability of sex outside of marriage and the importance of sexual enjoyment. Articles about power and conflict in relationships are also common, while contraception receives minimal coverage (Kunkel, Cope, & Biely, 1999). *Maxim* is *Cosmopolitan*'s counterpart for men. The leading men's magazine in the United States, *Maxim* usually features a scantily clad celebrity on its cover (Gray, 2000). Its feature articles typically offer tips for sexual conquests.

1.2 on the web

Magazines provide much information about sex and sexuality for women of all ages. *Cosmopolitan,* a magazine for female U.S. college students, offers frank advice and tips on sex, and even *Seventeen,* a magazine for preteen and teenage girls, presents articles on sexual behavior. Visit the Web sites for these magazines at **www.ablongman.com/mcanulty2e.**

Do you think that the material you find on these sites is appropriate for the audiences? Do these magazines contribute to the increasing acceptance of frank discussions of sex in modern Western society?

Advertising

Sex does indeed sell, and this is most evident in advertising (Telford, 1997). Eroticism is evident in all forms of advertising, where it is used to build associations between sex and almost any imaginable product. The sexual content of ads in print has become increasingly explicit since the early 1980s (Reichert, Lambiase, Morgan, Carstarphen, & Zavoina, 1999). Attractive young women in suggestive poses or clothing are commonly used as attention-getters in ads aimed at men. Attractive men and women may be displayed together in ads for perfume or clothing. Eroticism is seen as being as legitimate in advertising as it is in art, as long as it is appropriate to the context. For example, few people object to sexually suggestive ads for perfume and clothing, but most would object to such content in ads for real estate or office supplies. The line between acceptable and unacceptable use of sexuality in advertising is not always obvious, however. Designer Calvin Klein generated intense controversy in 1998 when he used unusually young models in sexually suggestive ads. The ensuing controversy, coupled with threats of legal reprisals, forced the company to withdraw the ads.

Sexist stereotyping is common in advertising and is often used as a shortcut technique for reaching particular audiences (Brentl & Cantor, 1988; Lovdal, 1989). Automobile advertising aimed at women tends to emphasize the car's appearance, ease of parking, and convenience for shopping. Car ads aimed at men accentuate performance and economy (Courtney & Whipple, 1983). The message conveyed is that men care about substantive matters, whereas women's interests are more superficial and vain. Gender-role stereotyping is most evident in advertising for household products and laundry detergents (Boddewyn & Kunz, 1991). How often do you see ads for household products that show a man putting dirty clothes in a washing machine or doing the dishes?

Music

Recent studies reveal that children and adolescents in the United States are exposed to as many as 38 hours of media per week (American Academy of Pediatrics, 2001; Roberts, Foehr, Rideout, & Brodie, 1999), and the average teenager may be exposed to 14,000 sexual references per year, often in the content of music videos. Music networks such as MTV, VH1, and BET are very popular with adolescents and young adults. Nearly 60% of homes that subscribe to cable services receive MTV, and one-third of its viewers are younger than 18 (Seidman, 1999). Teens report watching MTV for anywhere from 25 minutes to 2 hours daily. Approximately 75% of music videos contain sexual imagery (Sherman & Dominick, 1986).

Both males and females are typecast in traditional sex roles in music videos. Males are depicted as more adventuresome and aggressive than females, who in turn are portrayed as nurturing, affectionate sex objects (Seidman, 1999). Women are often shown wearing skimpy and provocative clothing and being pursued by eager males. These themes are certainly not unique to music videos; they are also evident in commercials aired on MTV (Signorielli, McLeod, & Healy, 1994), in prime-time TV shows (Davis, 1990), and in the lyrics of music popular among teens (Christenson & Roberts, 1998).

The sexual content of music-related media is not only potentially inaccurate and misleading, it may also distort viewers' perceptions of normative sexual behavior. Extensive exposure to sex in the media may cause adolescents to overestimate their peers' sexual activity. This exposure may normalize sexual activity and create pressure to conform to the perceived norm.

The Internet

The newest medium to offer sexual materials is the Internet. Although the use of technology to disseminate sexual materials is not new, the Internet does so on an unprecedented scale (Stern & Handel, 2001). Studies show that sexual pursuits, which may range from visiting pornography sites to participating in online sexual exchanges, are the most common use of the Internet (Cooper, Scherer, Boies, & Gordon, 1999). There are over 8,000 chat rooms devoted to cybersex, or interactive discussions of sex (McKenna, Green, & Smith, 2001). Users can access picture libraries, video clips, live strip shows, live sex shows, and Web-cam sites that offer public access to the most private lives of volunteers (Griffiths, 2001). Available materials range from sexually explicit educational materials, online virtual sex shops, and sexual fantasy aids. Internet users can even meet prospective sexual partners online through chat rooms, personal advertisements, or escort services (Griffiths, 2000). People can form intimate relationships online, and some develop online romances outside of their marriages, so-called *cyberaffairs* (Young, Griffin-Shelley, Cooper, O'Mara, & Buchanan, 2000).

did YOU know?

The Internet porn industry reportedly generates over $366 million in revenues each year (Spenger, 1999).

The newest technology to offer sexual materials, the Internet offers countless porn sites and thousands of chat rooms devoted to cybersex.

The popularity of Internet sex may be due to easy access, safety, affordability, and the enormous range of materials and services (McKenna et al., 2001). Users can access materials and make numerous contacts almost instantaneously, day or night. The anonymity of the Internet affords safety: Users face little risk of being embarrassed, rejected, or exposed. The anonymity, combined with reduced risks, may lower inhibitions and encourage more risk-taking. Some people have been described as suffering from *Internet sex addiction.* According to Griffiths (2001), a small but significant proportion of Internet users experience serious problems, which may include compulsive usage, sexual risk-taking with partners whom they have met online, and a pattern of Internet usage that persists despite harmful consequences in the person's life. The ever-growing popularity of the Internet and the expanding role of computer technology in people's lives suggest that use and misuse of this medium will continue to grow.

Religions

Every culture in the world includes some form of religion, and some cultures have several. Religions, however, vary widely in their doctrines: Some are very conservative, others are liberal, and most probably fall somewhere between these extremes. Some religions devote much effort to the control of sexual behavior, attempting to maintain morality and sexual purity through various prohibitions. Other religions, especially in Eastern cultures such as India, view sex as a source of pleasure and even as a means of spiritual enlightenment (Bullough, 1995). All religions teach moral precepts, or rules, addressing sexual behavior (Parrinder, 1987; Runzo & Martin, 2000). One way or another, religions have always sought to define, control, and direct sexuality (Haffner, 1997; Sands, 2000).

1.3 on the web

Worldwide, the number of different religions is countless. Different religions have diverse, often even opposite, views of sex. As an example, consider Tantra, which is a tradition within Buddhism and Taoism. Visit **www.ablongman.com/mcanulty2e.** Note that one Eastern religion, Shaktiism, had ceremonies devoted to the worship of female genitalia.

How do religions that promote "sex worship" differ from the predominant religions in the United States? What are your reactions to reading about Tantric and other Eastern religious viewpoints?

Judaism and Christianity

The dominant religious influence in the United States is Christianity, which is a derivative of Judaism. Both of these religions have shaped beliefs and values of Western cultures, including sexual attitudes and practices, for centuries. The Judeo-Christian tradition teaches that men and women are created by God, and they are to marry and form lifetime partnerships. They are instructed by the Bible to "be fruitful and multiply and replenish the earth." Procreation and childbearing are the justification for sexuality in the Judeo-Christian tradition. By implication, nonprocreative activities are discouraged (Parrinder, 1987). The Bible, however, is silent on such sexual practices as masturbation, oral sex, and contraception (Haffner, 1997). These topics were addressed by later Christian writers, such as Augustine (354–430 C.E.) and Aquinas (1225–1274), and their views became part of certain church traditions. It is important to remember, then, that much of the Judeo-Christian tradition is based on the views and interpretations of such later religious writers, many of whom had negative views of sex (Bullough, 1995).

The Hebrew Bible (the Old Testament) is replete with sexual themes. For example, the first book, Genesis, contains over thirty stories dealing with sex (Haffner, 1997). Sarah describes sexual intercourse as a "pleasure," and Isaac is said to be "fondling his wife Rebekah." Genesis also contains numerous references to incest, rape, and prostitution. There are multiple references in the Hebrew Bible to sexual intimacy in relationships, including "Let your fountain be blessed, and rejoice in the wife of your youth, a lovely deer, a graceful doe. May her breasts satisfy you at all times; may you be intoxicated always by her love" from the book of Proverbs (5:19). Note that, consistent with the cultural norms that prevailed when they were written, the books of the Hebrew Bible are male-oriented and endorse sexuality only in the context of marriage. Homosexual relations are prohibited, as is sexual intercourse during menstruation.

The most explicitly erotic book of the Hebrew Bible is the Song of Solomon, which celebrates sex and love with passages such as "My beloved thrust his hand into the opening, and my inmost being yearned for him" (5:4). Finding this eroticism in conflict with their restrictive views, some early Christian writers challenged the authenticity of the Song of Solomon or argued that it was an allegory rather than a celebration of sexual love (Haffner, 1997). It is not surprising that this book of the Bible was censored for many centuries and was one of the last to be translated into English.

The New Testament includes fewer references to sex, although the teachings there are consistent with those found in the Hebrew Bible. The human body and sexual relationships in marriage are sacred. Prostitution and homosexual behavior are condemned, as is sex outside of a married relationship. In the context of marriage, there are no prohibited sexual behaviors. Extramarital sex, or adultery, is condemned throughout the Bible, and not only sexual intercourse but also sexual fantasies or urges toward someone other than one's spouse. Jesus is quoted in the book of Matthew as cautioning that "whoever looks on a woman to lust after her, has already committed adultery with her in his heart." A woman convicted of adultery under Jewish law was to be killed by stoning. Jesus demonstrated a more forgiving attitude, cautioning a woman caught in the act of adultery to "sin no more."

Looking At . . .

. . . Thinking About

Some Islamic teachings require women to wear veils in order to preserve their purity. How do Westerners react to these guidelines?

Islam

Islam, the predominant religion in most Middle Eastern cultures and one of the fastest growing religions in the United States (Sands, 2000), draws on both Jewish beliefs and traditional Arabic views. The teachings are even more male-centered than those espoused by Judaism (AbuKhalil, 1997). Sexual intercourse is considered one of the pleasures of life to be enjoyed in marriage, especially for men. Contemporary Islamic attitudes recognize the sexual desires of men but ignore women's sexuality, which is assumed to be nonexistent (at least among Muslim women). The Islamic holy text, the Koran, contains only one section on the rights of women. Islamic law permits polygamy, and men can have concubines, women who serve in the role of a wife but with lower status. All Islamic women are expected to remain pure, including in their appearance. In some countries, women are expected to wear clothing that covers their entire body, including veils, to ensure their purity.

Islam is viewed as a more tolerant belief system than Christianity because virtually every offense can be forgiven (AbuKhalil, 1997; Bullough, 1995). Many followers of Islam, for example, are relatively tolerant of homosexuality. As AbuKhalil (1997) observed, "violence against homosexuals, which is still common in Western societies, is quite rare among the Arabs" (p. 100). In contrast, violence against women remains a pervasive problem. The Koran permits husbands to beat rebellious wives (Kassam, 2000).

1.4 on the web

The religion of Islam is based on knowledge of Allah, believing in His place as Lord of the Universe and affirming His place as the One to be worshiped. Visit **www.ablongman.com/mcanulty2e** to learn more about this religion. Read the article on women in Islam to learn more about gender roles in this religion.

What does the Qu'ran (the Koran) dictate about a woman's place in society? How do the teachings of the Qu'ran compare to views of gender roles in other religions?

Hinduism

Hinduism, the main belief system in many Eastern regions, is actually a collection of belief systems (Bullough, 1995). Because of this diversity, no single set of beliefs will accurately describe Hinduism. In general, Hindu teachings regard love and sex as of divine origin. In contrast to Christian, Jewish, and Islamic beliefs, some Hindu sects view the pursuit of sexual pleasure as a form of worship (Lipner, 2000). The best illustration is found in the *Kama Sutra,* written in the 3rd century by Vatsyayana. This "love text" offers detailed information on courtship, dating, and positions for sexual intercourse. The book contains explicit advice for achieving sexual pleasure and satisfying a partner.

Members of the tantric sects of Hinduism believe that sexual intercourse allows practitioners to be united with God (Bullough, 1995). Sexual pleasure is believed to offer a taste of the divine by transcending the ordinary. In order to maximize and extend the spiritual experience, Hindu lovers are taught to delay orgasm. One popular strategy for extending the experience is to pause in the midst of intense feeling. "Through techniques of strengthening and lengthening sexual pleasure, both mind and body become bathed in bliss, opening the possibility of realizing the nature of the fundamental state," which involves rising above the physical to experience the spiritual (Martin, 2000, p. 279).

Buddhism

An offshoot of Hinduism, Buddhism comprises two main branches. The Theravada, which is dominant in Thailand and Burma, is the more conservative approach, and it advocates self-discipline. The Mahayana branch, found mainly in China, Japan, and Korea, promotes more liberal practices and love. In both cases, Buddhist monks practice a celibate lifestyle characterized by restraint and self-discipline. Tantric Buddhism, practiced in Tibet, shares many of the teachings of tantric Hinduism (Hopkins, 2000).

Religious teachings continue to shape sexual attitudes and practices in the United States. Being affiliated with any religion is related to sexual attitudes and sexual behavior (Brewster, Cooksey, Guilkey, & Rindfuss, 1998; Thornton & Camburn, 1989). People who report strong religious beliefs and who attend church regularly are more sexually conservative in their attitudes and sexual practices. However, church attendance per se is not necessarily a good predictor of a person's religious devotion (Beck, Cole, & Hammond, 1991). After all, no doubt many people attend church regularly because of pressure from parents and peers or because of family tradition. The religious factors that are more strongly related to a person's sexual values and behaviors are the particular religion's doctrinal teachings regarding sex and the person's commitment to and investment in those teachings (Beck et al., 1991). If a person's religious background emphasizes conservative sexual values and behaviors and the person is committed to that religion's teachings, his or her sexual attitudes and actual sexual behavior are very likely to be conservative. Sexual values alone, however, do not necessarily determine a person's sexual practices. A person may regularly engage in behaviors, sexual or otherwise, that he or she has been taught are unacceptable or sinful. As one student aptly put it, "I have good values, but I don't always practice them."

The Family

The family is the primary socializing agent in all cultures. First and foremost, the family is the context in which most people form their beliefs about relationships. The relationship between parents (or, increasingly in the United States, between one parent and a significant other) provides a model for children who are learning about love, intimacy, and communication. Children learn from parental example as well as from the sexual knowledge, attitudes, and values that parents impart verbally. Yet, the influence of parents' communication about sexuality on their children's sexual behavior is complex. Parents are often uncomfortable discussing sexuality with their children, thereby conveying the implicit message that the subject is taboo. Parental norms about sexual behavior also influence children's attitudes and values. Parental sexual permissiveness, for example, is related to adolescent sexual behavior. Sexually permissive parents are more tolerant of adolescent sexual activity, and this permissiveness tends to contribute to an earlier age of sexual initiation in the children (Calhoun & Friel, 2001).

The timing of parental communication about sexuality is also important. Adolescents who talked to their mothers about sex prior to initiating sexual intercourse are

IN YOUR own words

Stacey Cantwell
Central Michigan

My parents never talked to me about sex, nor did my school ever talk about what sexuality was. I learned what sex was through my peers when I was 13 years old.

three times more likely to use condoms than those who did not communicate with their mothers (Miller, Levin, Whitaker, & Xu, 1998). Parent-teenager discussions about sexual risks and precautions are only helpful, though, when parents are open and comfortable about having these talks (Whitaker, Miller, May, & Levin, 1999).

Family context—which includes the quality of the mother-child relationship, the nature of family interactions, and maternal attitudes toward sex—also seems important in shaping adolescent sexual activity (Calhoun & Friel, 2001). In close families, parents are very involved in the lives of their children, and this involvement extends to sharing information about sex and dating. In fact, family context is more influential than family structure in the process of sexual socialization. In other words, being reared in a traditional two-parent family instead of a blended family (one that includes a stepparent) seems to have little impact on sexual development. In single-parent families, however, girls tend to initiate sex earlier (Calhoun & Friel, 2001; Miller & Moore, 1990).

Although most people agree that sexual socialization is a parental responsibility and duty, there is plenty of evidence that many families do not live up to this obligation. Those that do often do so selectively or inconsistently. In U.S. families, mothers are expected to share sexuality information with the children, with daughters in particular (DiLorio, Kelley, & Hockenberry-Eaton, 1999; Miller, 1998). Discussions tend to be selective, however, as mothers are most likely to discuss topics related to reproductive health and functions and least likely to talk about eroticism. Pregnancy, sexually transmissible infections, and menstruation are viewed as essential topics by many parents, but orgasm and masturbation are usually not discussed (Daniluk, 1998; Jordan, Price, & Fitzgerald, 2000). As might be expected, many teens perceive their mothers' messages as moralistic and overly restrictive. Consequently, many teens are secretive and withhold information about their sexual activity from parents, and this is especially common among Hispanic American families (O'Sullivan, Meyer-Bahlburg, & Watkins, 2001). Fathers, as a rule, are less involved in sharing sexuality information with their daughters. Fathers are likely to adopt the role of protecting their girls from "being used" by boys (Daniluk, 1998). Despite major changes in the double standard, girls are still not given the same freedom for sexual experimentation afforded to boys (Milhausen & Herold, 1999).

In the United States, mothers are expected to be the ones to share information about sexuality with children, especially daughters. Unfortunately, many teens perceive their mothers' messages as moralistic and restrictive.

As you will see in Chapter 11, most adolescents in the United States receive very limited sexuality education in school. Consequently, it is not surprising that most U.S. teenagers are ill-equipped to express their sexuality responsibly as they go through puberty and initiate dating. For many teens, learning about sexuality is a process of trial and error, during which they haphazardly try to apply whatever they have learned from the media, their peers, and perhaps their parents (Jordan et al., 2000; O'Sullivan et al., 2001). Research confirms that adolescents whose parents do not share sexuality information with them are more likely to turn to peers for information (Whitaker & Miller, 2000). In a relative vacuum of information, the media play a larger than ideal role in answering children's and teenagers' questions about sex (Steele, 1999).

HISTORICAL PERSPECTIVES ON SEXUALITY

The evolution of contemporary views on sex did not follow a simple or direct route. Throughout history, periods of relative openness about sex have alternated with times of intolerance. Furthermore, during any particular historical period, different cultures have demonstrated widely varying attitudes and practices. This historical overview will necessarily be selective, focusing on those eras and cultures that have been most influential and are best documented.

The Earliest Records

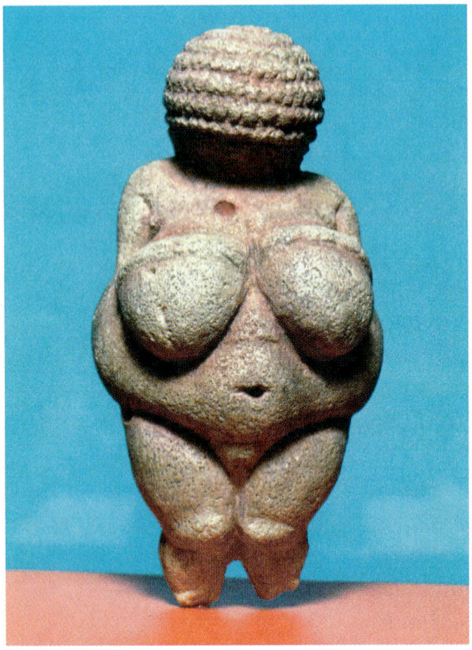

Ancient statuettes such as this Venus figurine were probably fertility symbols depicting pregnant women.

Prehistoric tribes must have been intrigued with the mysteries of the natural world (Dening, 1996). They most likely observed and pondered the phases of the moon, seasonal changes, and other regular natural occurrences. They must have also marveled at the cyclical bleeding of menstruation, the physical changes during pregnancy, and childbirth. Stone Age cave drawings and artifacts dating back over 20,000 years include primitive depictions of sexual intercourse and reproduction. Many early civilizations worshiped a female deity that was believed to have created the world. In ancient Mesopotamia, the creator-goddess Mammu (literally, "the sea") was said to have given birth to heaven and earth. Similar beliefs were held in ancient Egypt, Babylon, and Japan. Following that tradition, we still refer to "Mother Nature."

Fertility rituals and symbols are documented in various ancient cultures. Ancient statuettes, known as *Venus figurines,* are characterized by their oversized proportions, which accentuate breasts, bellies, and buttocks, and by their well-defined genitals. Although the significance of these figurines remains uncertain, it is widely believed that they were fertility symbols depicting pregnant women (Dening, 1996). As the role of males in reproduction became more understood, **phallic worship** evolved in several cultures. Phallic symbols were prominently displayed in worship ceremonies in ancient Egypt. In ancient Greece, giant penises made of wood were carried in religious processions, and *herms,* which are statues consisting of a human head on a pillar (a phallic symbol), were erected in various places to offer protection and to promote fertility. Similarly, penis symbols were worn around the neck as good-luck charms in ancient Rome.

Classical Greece

Modern understanding of ancient Greek views is derived from that culture's mythology and art. Greek culture was sexually explicit and, at least for men, sexually tolerant. Ancient Greece was very much a male-dominated, or patriarchal, society (Powell, 1998). The ideal roles for women were those of mother and housewife (the Greek word for "woman," *gyne,* means "bearer of children"). As was customary throughout much of the ancient world, Greek women received no education, had no political or legal rights, and entered into arranged marriages (Dening, 1996).

The Greeks believed that men and women were inherently bisexual, although they disapproved of exclusive homosexuality, which represented a threat to the institution of the family. Greek writings and frescos depicted male homosexual acts, including anal intercourse. Male bisexuality is common in Greek mythology. The god Zeus was characterized by his seemingly insatiable sexual appetite as he seduced both gods and mortals. His attentions were not limited to females; he was enamored of a Trojan youth, Ganymede, whom he carried off to Olympus. Another Greek hero, Heracles (known to the Romans as Hercules), was heralded for having deflowered 50 virginal women in a single night. Like Zeus, Heracles also had sexual relationships with men.

The Greeks prized physical beauty and the human body, irrespective of age and gender (Dover, 1989). This explains in part the widespread practice in ancient Greece of pederasty, an intimate relationship between an older man and an adolescent boy. The older man served as a mentor, educator, and guardian. Certain writings and paintings of the time suggest that the relationship might also have involved sex (Powell,

PHALLIC WORSHIP
Worship of the male genitals as a way of ensuring agricultural success and fertility.

1998). Although the custom was widespread, it was not universally accepted, as Aristotle and others were openly critical of it.

Prostitution thrived in Greece. Brothels were found in all the larger cities. High-class courtesans, the equivalent of today's call girls, were well-regarded; in fact, they were the only women to have leading roles in social and intellectual circles (Dening, 1996). Aphrodite, the goddess of sexual love, was also the patroness of prostitutes. Temples dedicated to her worship featured their own prostitutes. Women temporarily served the goddess by selling their services to men, thereby ensuring a long and prosperous life for themselves (Powell, 1998).

Contemporary ambivalence about sex can be traced in part back to ancient Greek beliefs (Bullough & Bullough, 1995). Plato, for example, distinguished between earthly (or profane) love and heavenly (or sacred) love. The former originated from the body, and the latter from the mind. Plato believed that happiness derived only from sacred love. Profane love lowered men and women to the level of other animals. Other Greek writers, such as Democritus and Epicurus, agreed that sexual desire was risky at best because it distracted humans from seeking higher spiritual good. These views were influential among early Christian writers.

Herms and other types of phallic symbols were prominently displayed or worn in ancient Rome and Greece. Such symbols denoted fertility or virility and were believed to offer protection from evil forces.

Ancient Rome

Roman attitudes toward sex have been characterized by many historians as decadent. In fact, these historians attribute the fall of the Roman empire, in part, to the sexual mores of its citizens. The Romans adopted and renamed the Greek gods, and there are many other parallels between the two cultures. Roman society was a highly structured hierarchy in which male citizens of Rome were most important, followed by female citizens and their children. Upper-class women were allowed some measure of freedom and were able to exercise some control over their lives (Dening, 1996). At the lowest level of Roman society were slaves of both sexes and those involved in what were considered disgraceful occupations, such as prostitutes, gladiators, and actors (Edwards, 1997). As in Greece, women were the property of first their fathers and later their husbands. Divorce was not commonly practiced in Rome until the end of the first century C.E. Prostitution was, however, a thriving business in ancient Rome.

The ancient Romans did not recognize the concepts of homosexuality and heterosexuality. People were classified not on the basis of their sexual partners but instead on the basis of whether their sexual behavior was active or passive (Parker, 1997). A male in the active role was the dominant partner, and he was the one who penetrated the passive partner. It would not matter what gender his partner was or what type of penetration was involved (anal, oral, or vaginal). Male citizens of Rome, holding the highest social status, were always active partners; it was unimaginable that they could ever be passive partners (Walters, 1997). For a male Roman citizen to allow himself to be penetrated, either anally or orally, would be to play the part of a woman, and such loss of status was totally unacceptable (Parker, 1997).

One major cult of Roman society was devoted to Bacchus (known to the Greeks as Dionysus), the god of ecstasy and wine. His Roman followers effectively transformed him into the god of drunkenness, and the festivals in his honor eventually degenerated into large-scale drunken orgies (Dening, 1996). The government eventually intervened and prohibited these festivities under penalty of death. Nevertheless, sexual exploits continued to be trademarks of several Roman rulers. Julius Caesar was openly bisexual, and later emperors were reported to have engaged in a variety of sexual practices. Caligula sponsored orgiastic parties that included bestiality and sadomasochism. He is said to have opened a brothel in his own residence (Edwards, 1997).

The Roman influence on contemporary sexuality is perhaps most evident in sexual terminology. Many English terms can be traced back to their Latin roots. *Cunnilingus* derives from the Latin *cunnus,* which means "vulva," and *lingere,* meaning "to lick." *Fellatio* is from the Latin *fellare,* which means "to suck." Fornication, a legalistic term for sexual intercourse between unmarried persons, derives from *fornix,* or "arch." The term originates from the practice of Roman prostitutes of conducting business in the darkened archways of public theaters, stadiums, and coliseums.

The influence of Christianity rose steadily in the centuries following the decline of the Roman empire (from the 5th century C.E.), Christianity was the leading religious, intellectual, and political force in Western cultures, and, as discussed earlier, it greatly influenced attitudes about sexual behavior.

The Medieval Period

For a thousand years—from the end of the Roman empire through the end of the 15th century—the Catholic Church was the dominant institution responsible for governing morality in Western Europe. The church established a rigid code of sexual morality (Brundage, 1982a). Those who committed sexual sins, such as fornication, lust, and homosexual relations, were required to perform acts of penitence. Marriage was supposed to be monogamous, and sex outside of marriage was to be punished. Sins called for confession, acts of devotion, and self-denial. Depending on the severity of the sin, a monetary fine might be imposed. Fornication called for a small fine, while adultery brought a heavy fine along with public humiliation, such as shaving of the adulterers' heads (Brundage, 1982b).

Medieval ideals of sexuality were drawn from interpretations of Christianity by church fathers such as Augustine, a bishop in northern Africa in the 4th century C.E. (Bullough, 1982). As a result of his own struggles to avoid what he viewed as the temptations of sex, Augustine became a leading denouncer of sexuality. To Augustine, sexual intercourse was a threat to spiritual growth. Recognizing that the Bible justified sex in marriage, Augustine reached a compromise by arguing that only sex for procreation was acceptable. "It was only through procreation that the evil act became good" (Bullough & Bullough, 1995, p. 23). To Augustine, however, the only permissible sex act was vaginal intercourse with the man on top. Marital intercourse in this so-called missionary position, then, was a necessary evil, to be tolerated only because it was necessary to produce offspring. Any other sexual activity was sinful and unacceptable. Augustine's views became the official doctrine of the Catholic Church through the Middle Ages.

The extent to which Catholic doctrine shaped the sexual practices of the common person in the Middle Ages is unknown. At the very least, church teachings instilled tremendous guilt by emphasizing the sins of sex. Eroticism essentially went underground during this era, although some surviving sculptures depict couples engaged in a variety of sexual activities, including oral sex (Webb, 1975). Prostitution remained a thriving commercial enterprise in large cities. Paradoxically, several religious writers, including Augustine and Thomas Aquinas, voiced a relatively tolerant attitude toward prostitution. The sex trade was viewed as a necessary evil, since it helped preserve the chastity of decent women (Bullough & Bullough, 1995).

The Victorian Period

No history of sex would be complete without a discussion of sexual morality during the reign of Queen Victoria of England. Although the sexual norms during this era, from 1837 to 1901, are remembered as being repressive and rigid, they were probably not as extreme as they have been portrayed (Miller & Adams, 1996). As is true today, there was a marked discrepancy between the sexual ideology of the time and the practices of real people (Degler, 1974).

Major social and economic changes occurred in both North America and Europe during the Victorian period. The role of the church in regulating social norms was decreasing, and the family became the preferred agent for maintaining social order and convention (D'Emilio & Freedman, 1997). A prudish attitude was evident in every aspect of society. Women's clothing was designed to cover every part of the body, from neck to toes. The roles of men and women in promoting societal values were explicitly formulated. Women had very few political or social rights but had clear domestic and maternal roles. Sexuality was not entirely suppressed but was tightly controlled, and women were designated as the gatekeepers. They were also supposed to be models of sexual purity in order to fulfill their roles and to help curb their husbands' sexual appetites.

The Victorians held a conflicted view of women. The ideal woman was virtuous, devoted, delicate, motherly, and chaste. The other extreme was the "fallen girl," who had forsaken her womanly duties and turned to a pleasure-seeking and immoral lifestyle. She was a prostitute, a threat to the institution of marriage, and a disgrace to her gender. Despite the Victorian ambivalence about sex, prostitutes continued to do a brisk business in Europe and in the United States. Larger cities such as New York and San Francisco reportedly supported several thousand prostitutes. The first erotic novels were published in the United States in the 1840s, and dance halls, which were the forerunners of striptease clubs, gained popularity (D'Emilio & Freedman, 1997).

During this time, a new sexual message was being spread by both physicians and nonprofessional reformers, under the guise of health advice. The message was that sexual indulgence could be detrimental to one's health. This doctrine, known as *degeneracy theory,* was popularized by a French physician, Samuel A. D. Tissot. In an influential book, Tissot warned readers that sexual indulgence depleted the body of essential resources and compromised both mental and physical health. Tissot and many other health professionals believed that sexual excess, especially masturbation, quite literally caused madness, blindness, and a host of other problems (Bullough & Bullough, 1995). Contemporary writers, such as the German physician Richard von Krafft-Ebing, produced detailed case studies that claimed to document the dreadful consequences of masturbation, including sexual perversion. (For a closer look at the history of masturbation, see Health Matters: Does Masturbation Cause Blindness?)

Looking At . . .

. . . Thinking About

The most striking similarity between contemporary views and those of the Victorian era is in the two eras' ambivalence about sex. Although most Americans at least recognize sex as a fundamental human need, many are still very uneasy with the topic. Like the Victorians, contemporary Americans may see sex as a potentially dangerous force that must be harnessed. How is this discomfort with sex manifested? How does it affect you personally?

Fortunately, much of this advice was being challenged by the end of the Victorian period. Medical writers began to revise their views on sex. Nonetheless, sexuality was still viewed as an instinct to be controlled, and marriage provided the only legitimate context for sexual experimentation. In a departure from earlier views, medical writers noted that sexual activity in marriage could promote health, increase marital intimacy, and even enhance personal happiness (D'Emilio & Freedman, 1997). These changes, along with increased availability of some forms of contraception, ushered in a new era in the history of sexuality. The rapidly changing norms paralleled unprecedented social and economic developments at the end of the 19th century.

HEALTH Matters

Does Masturbation Cause Blindness?

In 1760, French physician Samuel A. D. Tissot wrote a classic medical text, *Onanism, Dissertation on the Maladies Brought on by Masturbation* (Bullough & Bullough, 1995). Tissot believed that sexual activity of any sort caused blood to rush to the brain, thereby starving the nervous system. Masturbation was the sexual activity most damaging to the nervous system. Tissot's ideas received wide acceptance among European and American medical communities at a time when semen was viewed as a vital substance that, when lost through orgasm, was not replaced, resulting in physical and mental deterioration. In 1842, Alfred Hitchcock (not the film producer) wrote in the *Boston Medical and Surgical Journal* that physicians should be honest in blaming masturbation for most illness suffered by Americans; to illustrate his point, he told of a 23-year-old man who died after six years of excessive masturbation. Allen W. Hagenbach published a report in 1879 concluding that masturbation led inevitably to homosexuality and was a "cause of insanity" among 800 "insane men" at Cook County Hospital in Chicago.

By the late 19th century, the term *masturbation* encompassed all nonprocreative sexual activities, especially between same-sex partners, and was viewed by educators as responsible for most of society's problems. It was thought that excessive masturbation ultimately led to insanity. In the 1850s and 1860s, several American journals published cases claiming successful treatment of such "insanity" by castration, clitoridectomy, circumcision, blistering (with heat) of the thighs, vulva, or prepuce, and severe beatings (Bullough & Bullough, 1995; D'Emilio & Freedman, 1997). Not all physicians, though, wholeheartedly accepted the belief that masturbation produced permanent and damaging effects. In spite of the stigma, German physician Oskar Berger boldly remarked in 1876 that 99% of men and women masturbate and the other 1% lie about it.

Two antimasturbation activists, Sylvester Graham and John Harvey Kellogg, created a lasting impression in the United States. Each believed strongly that a rich diet overexcited the physical senses and promoted masturbation (Bullough, 1994). Graham believed that the loss of an ounce of semen was equivalent to the loss of several ounces of blood, and, therefore, ejaculation diminished vital life fluids. To reduce sexual desire and ejaculation, he recommended a diet of rye meal, hominy, and unbolted wheat, which he fashioned into crackers and sold under his name. To the same end, Kellogg introduced a bland breakfast cereal of corn flakes at his Battle Creek Sanitarium in Michigan and later sold that cereal to the general public. In 1882, Kellogg published a popular sexual hygiene manual, which listed physical signs of masturbation, including general sickness, sudden changes in disposition, insomnia, weakened mental abilities, love of solitude, extremes in shyness or boldness, confusion, homosexuality in boys and promiscuity in girls, small breasts in women, acne, shifty eyes, bed-wetting, fingernail-biting, and epileptic fits.

During the late 1880s, recognition of adolescence as a stage between childhood and adulthood prompted a national campaign to protect young people from the dangers of masturbation and its harmful effects. The prominent and well-respected psychologist G. Stanley Hall wrote in his landmark book *Adolescence* (1904) that masturbation was encouraged by a number of events, which were to be avoided if possible and which included a change of seasons, wearing improper clothing, eating rich food, overeating, indigestion, sleeping late, intense concentration, perfumes, pockets, rocking chairs, and bicycle riding. Well into the early 20th century, antimasturbatory devices for adolescents were sold to worried parents to prevent "self-pollution," particularly at night (Bullough, 1994). One such device for boys consisted of a leather strap worn around the penis. Other parents tied their children's hands to the bedposts or pinned them to the outside of the blankets and away from their genitals. For the incorrigible adolescent masturbator, castration was proposed as the final solution.

This short history of attitudes toward masturbation reveals the basis of several modern myths, including the belief that orgasm before an athletic competition saps one's strength, that masturbation indicates a lack of interest in heterosexual intercourse and may even suggest homosexuality, that excessive masturbation will make you go insane, and that certain foods excite (or inhibit) sexual desire. In fact, all of these myths are unfounded. Masturbation is a healthy and safe sexual practice, one that the majority of people in the United States engage in regularly (Laumann et al., 1994).

The 20th Century

Through the second half of the 19th century and into the 20th, Western culture witnessed developments that dramatically changed most people's lives. Changes in economic realities, in social customs, and in gender roles were transforming life in Western Europe and in the United States. Rapid economic growth was fueled by major discoveries and by industrialization, which also provided new employment opportunities (D'Emilio & Freedman, 1997). For the first time, women were going to work in factories, offices, and stores or attending college to pursue professional careers.

These departures from tradition also brought changes in sex norms and gender roles. Increasingly, dance halls drew a "predominantly young, unmarried crowd of both genders, without the chaperonage of adults" (D'Emilio & Freedman, 1997, p. 195). Dance halls and clubs provided a forum for dating and close physical contact. Sex was discussed more openly, young people were more free of parental control, men and women could interact openly in public settings, love became a legitimate pursuit, and leisure became an acceptable goal for hard-working adults. By the 1920s, many of these changes were well established in North America.

Not everyone enthusiastically supported these changes, however. The unprecedented freedom of middle-class youth was a threatening development to an older generation largely accustomed to Victorian values. The improvement in and consequent increased use of birth control methods were most controversial, because these developments signaled a shift away from sex for procreation toward sex for pleasure. Older generations lamented what they perceived as assaults on traditional values and on such institutions as marriage, the family, and religion. Prostitution, which flourished in large cities, was partly blamed for the breakdown of traditional moral values "because so many evils seemed related to it: exploitation of children, pornography, disease, and crime" (Bullough, 1994, p. 97). Prostitutes became a symbol of degradation and sinfulness, and this association was only strengthened by advances in medical understanding of sexually transmissible infections, or "social diseases," as they were euphemistically called. All of these changes challenged existing sexual norms and signaled the beginning of a new era—the rise of "sexual liberalism" (D'Emilio & Freedman, 1997, p. 241). This trend culminated in the "sexual revolution" of the 1960s.

By the mid-1960s, cultural views of sex in the United States were characterized by a growing emphasis on openness, freedom, and experimentation. "Free love" became a rallying call for a generation of young adults disenchanted with traditional views. They challenged the existing rules and the government's authority and proclaimed the importance of love. Along with love, they heralded uninhibited sexual experimentation—which was made possible by advances in birth control methods after World War II. The growing accessibility and effectiveness of contraception reinforced the view that sex could be fun instead of just for creating a family. Other cultural trends, such as the greater freedom and independence of women, the increased availability of automobiles, and the improvement of economic conditions, also played a part in shifting sexual norms (D'Emilio & Freedman, 1997).

The 1960s are best remembered as spawning the birth of the "hippie" movement. Opposing materialism and the government, the "flower children" espoused an uninhibited, drug-oriented, and pleasure-seeking lifestyle. They protested the Vietnam War and dreamed of changing cultural values. Analysis of the media of that time, especially films, novels, and plays, reveals that for the first time "sex became a daily staple of American popular culture" (D'Emilio & Freedman, 1997, p. 288). The circulation of *Playboy* magazine reached 1 million copies by the late 1950s and peaked at 6 million by the early 1970s. On college campuses, students campaigned for an end to visiting hours in dormitories and against college policies that withheld contraceptives from unmarried students and that prohibited female students from living off-campus with males. Most universities eventually gave in, and it was during this time that coed dormitories were introduced. The double standard about acceptable sexual behavior for

did YOU know?

Former **Cosmopolitan** *editor Helen Gurley Brown's book* **Sex and the Single Girl** *(1962), which informed readers that men "were a lot more fun by the dozen," became a runaway best-seller in the 1960s.*

men and women began to shift toward equality. Surely, what was fair for men should be fair for women, too. Sexual standards were clearly changing (Reiss, 1967). A 1967 editorial in *Newsweek* concluded, "The old taboos are dead or dying. A new, more permissive society is taking shape."

Again, not everybody welcomed these changes with open arms (Heidenry, 1997). Conservative-minded groups deplored the disintegration of moral values and warned of the impending breakdown of society as a whole (Mathewes-Green, 1997). By the late 1970s and early 1980s, several disillusioned critics announced that the sexual revolution had ended. A 1982 *Time* magazine article attributed the end of the sexual revolution to a sexually transmissible infection, genital herpes, which was described as an epidemic on a par with the bubonic plague. The growing awareness of problems that can result from sex, such as HIV infection, sexual abuse, and unplanned teen pregnancy, has led some critics to describe the period from the 1980s to the present as the "sexual counter-revolution."

The extent to which sexual norms in the United States have reversed over the past few decades is debatable. Without a doubt, however, some things have changed: Sexually explicit materials are available from a variety of media, "safer sex" is a household phrase, and contraception is readily available to most adults. On the other hand, Americans have not experienced full sexual liberation: Sexuality education remains a controversial topic, there are still different sexual standards for men and women, sex is sometimes used to victimize women and children, and certain taboos surrounding masturbation and homosexuality have not completely disappeared.

THEORETICAL PERSPECTIVES ON SEXUALITY

So far, the chapter has reviewed present and past sexual trends and discussed sexual practices and controversies. But it has not offered explanations. Why do people do the things they do in bed? Why do most of us find some things sexually arousing? How do we learn the "rules" of our culture about what is acceptable and desirable? Why do we fantasize about certain people? Why are men and women different? Unfortunately, there is no simple, single answer to any of these questions. But there are possible, or even probable, answers to some of them. Theories of sexuality are tentative explanations that have received some support from research but are not yet fully accepted as complete and factual. Theories provide a framework that can be used to explore the intricacies of human sexual behavior.

The pages that follow will review four influential theories of human sexuality. Psychoanalytic theory is important, largely for historical reasons. It represents the first systematic attempt to explain sexuality in a coherent fashion. The learning perspective focuses on conditioning and the importance of the (social) environment in shaping behavior. Script theory emphasizes the importance of culture in shaping human sexual behavior. Finally, the theory of evolutionary psychology attempts to trace human sexual practices to the evolution of *Homo sapiens*. Other theoretical perspectives will be introduced in later chapters.

Psychoanalytic Theory

Sigmund Freud's psychoanalytic theory has had a great influence on Western culture. The eminent physician's theory on sexuality was controversial at the time it was introduced, and it remains so today. Although highly influential, the theory has fallen out of favor in recent decades, because research has provided very limited support for certain aspects of it.

At the core of psychoanalytic theory is the idea that human beings are engaged in a constant struggle to fulfill their own needs and desires in the face of the demands and constraints imposed by society (Person, 1987). Freud saw internal conflict as inevitable and as a critical aspect of the human mind. To him, virtually everything people do is somehow related to this conflict and to their ongoing efforts to resolve or cope with it. Well-being in adulthood is largely determined by how successfully this conflict is managed early in life.

Austrian physician Sigmund Freud developed a comprehensive theory of personality in which he proposed that sex is the most powerful human drive.

According Freudian theory, the *libido*, or sex drive, is the driving force in personality development. The notion that childhood sexuality is a normal part of human development was quite controversial in the late Victorian period, when Freud first promoted his views. Nevertheless, Freud believed that the sexual instinct is present at birth. The libido and other basic biological urges such as hunger form a distinct part of the mind, the *id*. As an instinct, the libido causes a buildup of sexual tension, an uncomfortable state that motivates a person to seek release through gratification. The idea that the id always seeks to gratify instinctual urges is labeled the *pleasure principle*. The ways a person experiences sexual tension and seeks to relieve it change throughout development, in a series of biologically determined stages. This progression begins in infancy with the *oral stage*, centering on the stimulation provided by breast-feeding and thumb-sucking, and culminates in the *genital stage* of adolescence, in which genital sexuality is achieved. (Freud's stages of psychosexual development are reviewed in Chapter 11.) According to Freud's theory, the developmental transitions in sexuality are anything but smooth and uneventful. From infancy on, the individual faces several obstacles in the quest for relief of sexual tension.

According to Freud, the major obstacle each person must contend with during development is the conscience, which he dubbed the *superego*. This component of personality represents the internalization of the constraints imposed by society. The superego consists of values, rules, and the consequences of breaking these rules, all of which are assimilated from sources such as parents and teachers. The superego may counter sexual urges with feelings of guilt, shame, and fear (such as worrying about getting caught or getting a "bad reputation").

This ongoing struggle between the libido, seeking immediate gratification, and the superego, with its moralistic overtones, is mediated by a part of personality called the *ego*. The ego is rational and realistic, playing the role of referee between sexual urges and conscience. The ego is said to operate according to the *reality principle*. According to psychoanalytic theory, the components of the personality may operate at different levels of consciousness. The id, with its primitive instincts, is almost completely unconscious; that is, it operates outside of conscious awareness. The other two components, ego and superego, act at a more conscious level. Feeling guilty about masturbating, for example, is a conscious feeling that originates in the superego.

One of the more controversial aspects of psychoanalytic theory centers on its views of the differences between males and females. Freud portrayed women as envious of men's penises, a feeling he called *penis envy*. (In reality, women of the era were probably envious of men's roles and rights rather than of their anatomical organs—remember that women had virtually no legal or political rights at the time Freud was formulating his views.) To Freud, a significant experience in the life of all children is

1.5 on the web

Sigmund Freud remains one of the most controversial yet influential thinkers of the 20th century. For a closer look at the life of Freud and an overview of his psychoanalytic theory, go to **www.ablongman.com/mcanulty2e**.

How did Freud's background influence his theory of human behavior? What factors led him to give such a prominent role to sex in his theory? Which aspects of the theory do you find most intriguing?

the realization of the anatomical differences between the sexes—namely, that boys have penises and girls don't. Young boys experience the *Oedipus complex,* feeling an attraction to their mother while viewing their father as a hostile rival (Person, 1987). Fearing that his father may punish his incestuous longings by castrating him (a fear that Freud called *castration anxiety*), a boy renounces his attraction to his mother and identifies with his father. The young boy believes that by imitating daddy, he too can someday have a female partner like mommy. A similar experience, the *Electra complex,* occurs for girls. Realizing that she has no penis and blaming her mother for this, the girl becomes attracted to her father. Soon she discovers that she cannot compete with her mother, and eventually she comes to identify with her. By forming a feminine gender identity, the young girl hopes to eventually find a man like daddy. For Freud, resolving these respective complexes is essential to the formation of gender identity in boys and girls.

In sum, Freud saw sexuality as the fundamental motive for human behavior from birth to death. He also saw sexual development as a difficult and lengthy process, whose major challenge is to find a balance between the id (selfish and pleasure-seeking) and the superego (moralistic and guilt-prone). Recall that Freud developed his theory in a male-oriented Victorian society, one that was indeed sexually conflicted. Psychoanalytic theory has been criticized for its treatment of female sexuality. Freud's view that women can achieve a "mature" orgasm only through vaginal intercourse has since been refuted (see Chapter 4). Freud's theories have also been criticized for an overemphasis on sex and a relatively negative portrayal of human nature, and for being nonscientific (Fisher & Greenberg, 1977; Holt, 1989).

The Learning Perspective

The learning perspective comprises several viewpoints that stress the importance of conditioning. According to these viewpoints, much of human behavior is learned through interactions with the environment. Instead of focusing on unobservable processes such as thoughts, feelings, and motives, the learning perspective deals primarily with observable behavior, which is why it is often referred to as **behaviorism.** This emphasis on observable units of study has its basis in the scientific tradition of relying on observable and measurable phenomena, a topic we will revisit in Chapter 2.

The idea that much human behavior is learned, rather than biologically determined, is no doubt neither new nor foreign to most of you. Indeed, most people agree that behavior, including sexual behavior, is shaped by learning. Humans, for example, do not innately know how to kiss passionately, caress sensually, or perform other complex behaviors. Our early attempts, beginning with our first kiss, are clumsy and awkward, but practice (or *rehearsal,* as the behaviorists call it) and feedback allow us to sharpen our skills. These very ideas apply to most behaviors, from making conversation to mastering erotic techniques such as oral sex.

There are variations in the types of learning processes emphasized by the various theories. **Classical conditioning** describes fairly automatic and nearly reflexive conditioning principles by which one stimulus becomes associated with another one that already triggers some response. By association, the new stimulus comes to elicit a similar reaction. There are many real-world illustrations of this type of conditioning, such as the process by which a smell or scent (say, perfume or cologne), a sound (such as a song), or a sight (an article of clothing or a location) may become connected with a romantic or sexual partner. By association, the smell, sound, or sight may become a conditioned cue that triggers a response similar to the one the partner evokes. The scent or song elicits feelings of arousal by being paired with the arousing partner. You may remember the original research on this type of phenomenon by Ivan Pavlov, who conditioned dogs to salivate at the sound of a bell by repeatedly pairing the bell with food. Through repeated pairings, the bell became a conditioned stimulus that triggered con-

BEHAVIORISM
A scientific approach that emphasizes the study of observable behavior rather than unobservable processes such as thoughts and emotions.

CLASSICAL CONDITIONING
A form of automatic or reflexive learning in which one stimulus becomes associated with another one that already triggers some reaction. By association, the new stimulus comes to elicit a conditioned response.

ditioned salivation, much the way food (an unconditioned stimulus) triggers salivation (an unconditioned response).

Whereas classical conditioning is useful for explaining the process by which people learn to appreciate some stimuli and to find others distasteful, **operant**, or **instrumental, conditioning** explains how consequences affect people's responses. Quite simply, according to this theory, people are more likely to engage in actions that have previously been rewarded or reinforced in some fashion. Reinforcement is the process of strengthening a response by rewarding it with a desirable consequence (a positive reinforcer) or by removing some undesirable or aversive stimulus (negative reinforcer). Treating an acquaintance with kindness, for example, may be reinforced positively if that person returns your kind gesture or ceases to treat you aversively—for example, no longer criticizing you as he used to. In either case, the consequence is favorable, and you are likely to continue to be kind to that person because being kind "paid off."

There are numerous examples of operant conditioning in people's interpersonal exchanges. Interpersonal actions, from smiling at someone to caressing a partner, that produce a favorable outcome (such as a smile or a caress in return) are reinforced or strengthened. In the same situation, you are therefore likely to repeat the same actions. In fact, you are likely to try these very same behaviors in similar scenarios, such as with a new partner, a process called *generalization*.

A more recent extension of conditioning theories, the social cognitive perspective, is essentially a conglomeration of the views of theorists who share some common assumptions about human behavior (Hogben & Byrne, 1998). Social cognitive theories stress the importance of life experiences and learning in shaping human behavior. As the term **social cognitive theories** implies, most life experiences occur in a social context—in families, peer groups, neighborhoods, and the culture at large. Each of these social environments shapes behavior. In the context of social interactions, the most important form of learning is observational learning, or learning by imitation (Bandura, 1986). Social cognitive theorists also emphasize the importance of information processing in human behavior. In explaining sexual development, social cognitive theorists emphasize how various role models in people's lives influence their sexual attitudes and behaviors. Such models include parents, siblings, peers, and media celebrities, among others. The learning of sexual skills is also facilitated by the availability of prospective partners in one's environment. Further, such learning is more likely to occur in a society that permits or even encourages sexual experimentation. For example, among the Canela tribe of South America, adolescent sexual activity is openly encouraged and expected (Crocker & Crocker, 1994). Open sexual experimentation is viewed as fostering community well-being. Clearly, the sexual norms in U.S. culture are very different, and this difference explains some of the variation in sexual attitudes and customs across the two cultures. These observations are also consistent with the tenets of script theory (discussed next).

Another important determinant of human behavior is cognition. Individuals have varied beliefs, attitudes, and values about sexuality. Especially important are expectancies and personal values (Mischel, 1999). Based on their individual experiences, people develop different expectations that influence their reactions to life experiences. The individual who expects to be successful in a dating relationship will behave very differently on a date from one who believes he or she will fail. And personal values—including sexual values—often guide many decisions about sexuality. People's values determine their priorities, their tolerances and intolerances, and their choices. As Bandura (1986) noted, people's cognitions are influenced by both social context and life experiences. In turn, cognitions influence reactions to context and experiences. Thus, all of these factors are interrelated and largely inseparable.

One key aspect of learning theories is their empirical, or scientific, basis. Unlike the psychoanalytic viewpoint, learning theories are supported by much research. For

OPERANT (INSTRUMENTAL) CONDITIONING
A form of learning in which responses are controlled by their consequences.

SOCIAL COGNITIVE THEORIES
Conditioning theories that stress the importance of life experiences and social learning in shaping human behavior.

Looking At . . .

. . . Thinking About

Social cognitive theory is useful for understanding safer sex practices among adults. What factors influence decisions to use condoms? How do beliefs about their effectiveness and partner reactions to them affect your likelihood of using condoms?

example, social cognitive theories effectively predict condom use among college students (Wulfert & Wan, 1995) and among crack cocaine users (Bowen, Williams, McCoy, & McCoy, 2001). A particularly important aspect of social cognitive theories is their insistence that no single influence can fully explain human behavior. Rather, a combination of interactive influences, including the environment, life experiences, and cognitive factors, must be considered. (This perspective is similar to the one used throughout this book.) One unfortunate limitation of original conditioning theories is that they minimize the influence of biological factors. Like other forms of human behavior, sexual behavior is the product of a myriad of influences. Several biological factors, including sex hormones and heredity, play critical roles in shaping sexuality. Social cognitivists and learning theorists, however, generally emphasize the impact of the environment and life experiences.

A Sociological Perspective: Script Theory

In contrast to psychoanalytic theory, the sociological perspective on sexuality takes quite a broad view, attempting to explain human sexuality by examining society and its rules and norms. This approach rests on three main assumptions: (1) Each society shapes the development and expression of sexuality among its members; (2) social rules governing sexual behavior are tied to basic social institutions, primarily family, religion, and government; and (3) the culture determines what is sexually acceptable and normal or unacceptable and abnormal in any situation or context (DeLamater, 1987; Gagnon et al., 2001). According to this approach, people do not necessarily follow the cultural "rules" for sexual behavior, but they are usually aware of them and may adjust them to suit their personal needs or desires.

Within any culture, there are smaller units, or subcultures, that may be extraordinarily diverse in their sexual norms. These subcultures may be based on socioeconomic class, racial or ethnic background, religious affiliation, or sexual orientation (Kon, 1987). A subculture that holds a consistent set of beliefs or values about sex that readily identify it as distinct from the culture at large is viewed as a sexual minority (as are gay men and lesbians today) or as a sexually deviant subculture (as are fetishists and sadomasochists today).

According to script theory, sexual behavior is not a special or unique class of behavior. Sexual behavior, like any other form of behavior, is social behavior, and sex only takes on special meaning when it is defined as special by society or by the individual based on his or her experiences in society (Gagnon & Simon, 1973). Script theory, then, is most concerned with explaining "with whom people have sex, when and where they should have sex, what they should do sexually, and why they should do sexual things" (Laumann et al., 1994, p. 6).

According to script theory, there are three levels of scripts (or *scenarios*, as they are often called):

1. *Cultural scripts* include all of the rules and norms for sexual behavior in a culture. Cultural scripts specify appropriate partners (for example, in the United States, partners should be of approximately the same age and of opposite sexes), appropriate times and places for sexual activity (such as after dark and in privacy), and appropriate context (usually meaning that the partners should have some degree of emotional

involvement). People learn these rules and norms not from a single source but from multiple sources. The mass media, peers, parents, schools, religious institutions, and others provide instructions about the "what, where, why, and when" of sex and gender. There are scripts about gender roles, about flirtation and dating, about physical intimacy—about anything and everything having to do with sex (Sandelands, 2001). The cultural script about casual sex, for example, specifies rules that vary according to gender, age, and relationship status. Casual sex is most permissible for young unmarried men and least permissible for older married women. Thus, an older married woman will experience more disapproval than her younger male partner for the very same behavior, solely because she broke more of the "rules." In sum, cultural scripts are "roadmaps for sexual conduct" (Simon & Gagnon, 1987, p. 365). Often, though, these roadmaps may be confusing, contradictory, or incomplete. Therefore, individuals must adjust them to fit or fill in the gaps.

As highlighted in Close Up on Culture: Global Sex in Perspective, there are wide differences in cultural scripts in different societies. Also, cultural scripts can and do change over time in a given society. If there is one near-universal script, it is that sex within marriage is preferable to sex outside of marriage in virtually every society (Davenport, 1987). In other words, that is the ideal in most cultures. There are, however, differences across cultures in the extent to which the ideal is practiced and in how violations are punished.

2. *Interpersonal scripts* draw on cultural scripts and consist of people's responses in the real world. Interpersonal scripts are representations of how the cultural scripts are to be played out in actual interpersonal situations. These scripts help individuals figure out what their sexual partners want and expect, and even what their partners probably do not desire. For example, one interpersonal script describes "making the first move" in a sexual situation (Simon & Gagnon, 1987). The first move communicates intention, while also serving as a way of getting feedback from a partner. According to the cultural script in the United States, the meaning and appropriateness of making the first move depend on the situation, whether with a new partner or a regular partner. The actual sequence of sexual behaviors is scripted (Geer & Broussard, 1990). Kissing and then deep passionate kissing are usually the first steps, followed by fondling over the clothing. Fondling under clothing and genital fondling usually occur next. Actual sexual intercourse occurs last or near the end of the sequence (DeLamater & MacCorquodale, 1979). To understand the effects of scripts on sexual behavior, try to imagine your reaction to a partner who insisted on no kissing or fondling until after you had had sexual intercourse. You would probably find this preference very disconcerting, because it deviates from the accepted script. Similarly, most people would think it highly inappropriate for a stranger to touch their genitals, unless that stranger happened to be a gynecologist or a urologist. U.S. culture defines a great many interpersonal sexual scripts for such situations as "the one-night stand," "falling in love," "living together," and "having an affair" (DeLamater, 1987).

3. *Intrapsychic scripts* include the plans, fantasies, and motives that guide a person's past, current, and future sexual behavior. This level includes private thoughts, feelings, values, body image, and one's sense of identity as a man or a woman. The individual differences that make each person a unique sexual being are evident at the level of the intrapsychic script. Intrapsychic scripts are shaped but not completely determined by cultural scripts. Personal experiences, both rewarding ones and disappointing ones, play important roles in writing and rewriting intrapsychic scripts.

From the viewpoint of script theory, sexual behavior is the result of the interplay between these three levels of scripts. People learn general guidelines or rules from the cultural scripts, and these combine with individual beliefs, values, and desires embodied as intrapsychic scripts. An interpersonal script, such as that for "a one-night stand," results from an interplay between personal desires, values, and experiences and what the culture or subculture deems acceptable or permissible. Also, according to this viewpoint, no sexual behavior is truly spontaneous, since all behavior is scripted (Simon & Gagnon, 1987). Like actors in a play, people learn their parts and enact them at the proper times. Sexual scripts spell out the plot, the actors, and the parts they will or should play (Reiss, 1986). However, there is not always a prepared script for a given situation. In ambiguous sexual situations, a person may try to fill in the gaps or make things up as the situation evolves (Abelson, 1981). When two people bring different scripts to a situation, they may experience discomfort. If one person sees the situation as more intimate than the other, for example, neither may have a script for what to do. At this point, some trial and error may be involved, and the outcome may cause both parties to revise their interpersonal scripts for such cases in the future.

Script theory departs from psychoanalytic theory in arguing that rather than constraining sexual behavior, society actually defines it. Society essentially teaches the ABCs of sex and creates a framework within which personal sexuality develops and is expressed. Script theory emphasizes the social and interpersonal nature of sexual behavior. One major strength of this sociological approach is that it can explain the rich diversity in sexual practices across cultures and within a culture. This, however, has also been a criticism of script theory—that it may overemphasize cross-cultural differences while effectively ignoring similarities in sexual behavior across the world. That very point is a key tenet of evolutionary psychology, the last theory we will examine.

Evolutionary Psychology

As the name implies, evolutionary psychology was inspired by the work of Charles Darwin on evolution. According to evolutionary psychologists, current human sexual practices can be understood in light of the history of the species. Certain sexual practices made sense in the past because they were adaptive for survival. A basic tenet of this theory is that the primary force underlying human sexual behavior is the desire to successfully reproduce and thereby pass on one's genes. According to evolutionary theory, sexual practices that offer reproductive benefits are more likely to be passed on—that is, genetically transmitted—whereas practices that are not beneficial in that way will probably not be passed on. *Sexual selection* refers to the evolutionary process by which human sexual practices and preferences that provide reproductive advantages tend to become established (Buss, 1994a, 2001).

Sexual selection has been used to explain commonalities among peoples around the world in partner preferences and in strategies used to attract a partner. Sexual strategies are those practices for choosing and attracting a partner that have proven successful over the course of the evolutionary history of the human species. Humans use these strategies without being aware of the underlying motives behind their sexual choices (Buss, 1994a, 1999).

According to evolutionary psychology, gender differences in sexual behavior exist because males and females have encountered different reproductive challenges over the course of evolutionary history. Consequently, they have evolved different sexual strategies. For males, the minimum parental investment is contributing sperm, and they have a large window of opportunity for doing so, since a man can produce sperm even at an advanced age. The reproductive challenge for males, then, is to have multiple partners, since this maximizes the chance of reproductive success—the successful passing on of the male's genes and the survival of one or more of the offspring. Females, on the other hand, have a minimum investment of a 9-month pregnancy and often the responsibility of nursing the child after birth (Buss & Schmitt, 1993). For females, a larger number of offspring would not increase reproductive success and might actually decrease it, since females must make a greater investment of effort and time than males in bearing and raising children (Symons, 1987). Therefore, based on this theory, for females it is more adaptive to have fewer children. Additionally, because they are capable of bearing children for only a certain number of years, the window of opportunity for reproduction is much narrower for females than it is for males. Females, consequently, must be more selective than males in choosing partners.

Table 1.1 summarizes men's and women's reproductive challenges. Solutions to these challenges helped our ancestors survive and produce offspring. According to evolutionary psychology, males and females use different sexual strategies, depending on whether short-term or long-term mating is the goal. Men have evolved a desire for multiple short-term sexual partners (Symons, 1979). Men, therefore, are more willing to pursue casual sexual encounters with women whom they would probably not consider for a long-term relationship. Likewise, men prefer a short-term partner who is obviously willing to have sex (Schmitt, Shackelford, & Buss, 2001). Even in a short-term relationship, men favor women who are potentially fertile, that is, who might be impregnated. Cues for female fertility are youth, physical health, and the absence of major blemishes. Finally, in short-term relationships, men shy away from women who want commitment, since this would limit the options for casual sex. Women, on the other hand, want something different from their short-term partners. They prefer males who can prove that they can provide immediate resources, such as gifts of food, jewelry, and entertainment. Short-term mating therefore helps a woman judge

TABLE 1.1 Challenges for Women and Men in Selecting Short-Term and Long-Term Mates

	SHORT-TERM MATING	LONG-TERM MATING
Men's Reproductive Challenges	Finding a number of partners	Establishing confidence in paternity
	Identifying women who are sexually accessible	Assessing a woman's reproductive value
	Minimizing cost, risk, and commitment	Identifying women with good parenting skills
	Identifying fertile women	Finding women with high-quality genes
Women's Reproductive Challenges	Gaining material resources	Identifying men who are able and willing to invest in a relationship
	Evaluating short-term mates as possible long-term mate	Gaining physical protection from aggressive men
	Finding men with high-quality genes	Identifying men who will commit to a relationship
	Cultivating potential backup mates	Identifying men with good parenting skills
		Finding men with high-quality genes

SOURCE: Buss & Schmitt, 1993

whether a man has long-term potential. Not only can she learn more about his intentions, but she may be able to decide what he may be like as a husband and father. Women also favor men with "high-quality" genes, a sign of evolutionary fitness. High-quality genes are inferred from a man's physical condition and health. A man who looks healthy and whose physique looks normal will probably have a better genetic makeup than one who looks sickly or who has physical deformities. Finally, women are inclined to keep backups—other mate prospects—to ensure that they have one long-term relationship (Buss, 1994b).

Men and women also differ, according to evolutionary psychology, with regard to long-term mating—meaning marriage or an equivalent relationship. Men face the problem of paternity confidence: They need to be sure that the children they are supporting are their own, and not another man's. Therefore, in contrast to what they look for in a casual partner, men want a long-term partner who is sexually faithful, rather than promiscuous (Buss, 1994b). Furthermore, men seek wives who will be good mothers and who are physically fit and able to have children. For long-term partners, women favor men who are able and willing to commit to them and to invest in the future of a family. Like men, women prefer a long-term mate who has good genes and who will be a good parent (Buss & Schmitt, 1993).

In an ambitious test of the hypotheses of evolutionary psychology, David Buss and colleagues surveyed the mating preferences of more than 10,000 people from 37 countries (Buss et al., 1990). They concluded that their findings across all of those cultures confirmed the predictions of evolutionary psychology. Men consistently reported that they desired more sex partners than did women, and men were less discriminating than were women in these choices. The average man expressed a desire for 18 partners in his lifetime, compared to 4 or 5 for women (Buss, 1994b). Men found promiscuity to be mildly desirable in a short-term partner but not in a long-term partner; women did not find promiscuity desirable in either case. More than their female counterparts, "men throughout the world placed a high value on physical attractiveness in a partner" (Buss, 1994b, p. 245), a finding consistent with the prediction that men would be attracted to signs of fertility even in short-term partners. With respect to long-term mate selection, men in most countries favored chastity more than women did; a wife's infidelity is more likely than a husband's to lead to divorce (Buss, 1994b). Finally, women, as predicted, preferred long-term partners who could provide resources for their offspring. As expected, women ranked a man's ambition, financial prospects, and social status as essential factors to be considered in long-term mate selection.

The notion that men and women are biologically programmed to pursue different sexual strategies is one of the most controversial aspects of evolutionary psychology. One criticism of results such as Buss's is that such differences are actually the products of socialization rather than of biological heritage. With few exceptions, men in most cultures have more power than women do, and many differences in sexual practices may be more a function of that power imbalance than of evolution (Burns, 2000). In a female-dominated society, women might prefer to have multiple short-term partners. Furthermore, if most women did not have to depend on men for the survival of their offspring, women might place less emphasis on their partners' financial prospects and security. Another criticism is that the theory is not as universally applicable as it claims to be. For example, it cannot adequately explain the culture of the Nazaré, a small Portuguese fishing community that is female-dominated and where men are expected to take a "back seat" in all aspects of society (Brøgger, 1992). Additionally, evolutionary psychology is an explanation that relies on correlational studies for evidence (see Chapter 2). Simply put, these research strategies cannot show cause and effect, but only that there is (or is not) some kind of relationship between two or more phenomena. One final criticism is that evolutionary psychology may support the status quo in society, thereby perpetuating gender inequity and the double standard. However, according to some theorists, evolutionary psychology is "not a prescription for how things 'ought' to be" but rather an attempt to explain why they are as they are (Allgeier & Wiederman, 1994, p. 249).

An Integration of the Theories

Rather than trying to decide which of these theories is right, you should be asking which one best explains which part of human sexuality in a given context. Rather than seeking one "true" theory, this book uses each as a lens through which to catch a glimpse of some facet of human sexuality. Viewing sexuality through the various lenses may actually provide a better view of the bigger picture.

Psychoanalytic theory may be most useful for understanding the often conflicted nature of human sexuality. In addition, it emphasizes the fact that sexuality is not something that magically appears at puberty but rather is part of a lifelong, internal developmental process. Script theory, on the other hand, richly illustrates the ways in which society shapes individual sexuality. Society defines sexual meanings and the "what, when, where, why, and how" of sex. Script theory is useful for examining how sexual behavior varies according to social norms and cultures. Evolutionary psychology highlights the view that human sexual practices are strategic rather than random. Additionally, this theory of sexuality is grounded in a research-oriented approach; it does not rely on descriptions of traditions and personal belief systems. Evolutionary psychology also emphasizes that there is a biological substrate to sexual behavior, a point we will revisit in following chapters as we discuss the anatomy and physiology of sex.

IN YOUR own words

Jeanne McFeaters
Virginia Commonwealth University

If I knew the things back in school that I am now learning at almost 20 years old in my human sexuality class, life would have been easier. Yes, I knew the basics, but I feel very naïve about sex and sexuality.

HEALTHY DECISION MAKING

The purpose of this chapter's introduction to sexuality is to provide some perspective on current sexual attitudes and practices in the United States. Understanding various cultural and historical trends may be helpful as you examine your own sexual attitudes and values. As a college student, you will be exposed to diverse attitudes and norms, some of which may be quite different from those you were brought up with. Going to college affords many people an unprecedented degree of freedom and independence as they achieve some distance from the influence of parents and family. As a consequence, many college students begin to critically evaluate their attitudes and beliefs about many things, including sex.

Hopefully, this book will help you not only in mastering the facts about human sexuality but also in applying the findings to your own life and relationships. To that end, each chapter ends with a section called Healthy Decision Making, designed to provide applications of the facts and to recapitulate some of the issues and controversies reviewed in the chapter. These sections may lead you to ask yourself, "How does this apply to me?" Even if you are married, have children, or are returning to school after pursuing a career, there is likely to be room for personal growth in your life. This book's information may be helpful not only to you but also to others who are or will be important to you.

This chapter has highlighted the mixed feelings about sexuality that many people experience. Controversy surrounding sexuality, though, is not a new phenomenon—it can be traced to antiquity. Clearly, advances in science, medicine, and technology have led to dramatic changes in many sexual norms and practices, but the issues largely remain the same. Sex has always been an important aspect of life, and that is unlikely to change any time soon (nor should it!). As you examine your own thoughts about contraception, dating, sexual diversity, and other topics, adopt an open perspective. How did your upbringing, life experiences, and cultural heritage shape your attitudes and practices? How might these differ had you been reared in another culture, with a different religion, or under a different political system?

summary

CONTEMPORARY TRENDS

- The topic of sex elicits mixed feelings in many people. Yet, sexuality is pervasive in U.S. society.
- Sexuality refers to the sensations, emotions, and cognitions that are associated with physical sexual arousal and that usually give rise to sexual desire or behavior.
- Recent trends reveal that Americans are more open about sex but still believe that, ideally, sex belongs in some form of a committed relationship. Americans are more tolerant of sexual diversity than they have ever been. Nonetheless, a number of taboos, prejudices, and fears linger.
- Young adults are increasingly postponing marriage until they are older, but they are not postponing their first sexual experience. Differences in sexual practices are related to gender, ethnic or racial background, and relationship status.

SEX AROUND THE WORLD

- Worldwide sexual customs and practices are diverse. Yet, a trend toward globalization has led to some blending of sexual views and practices across cultures. In each culture, individuals must learn to balance their own needs with cultural guidelines.
- European sexual customs can be traced to countries' religious heritages. As a consequence of dramatic social and political changes, many Russians are exploring sexuality in unprecedented fashion. The Netherlands is viewed as a model for progressive views of sexuality. The French prize commitment in their romantic relationships.
- Africa is marked by extreme diversity in sexual attitudes and practices. Traditional beliefs promote procreation, marriage, and gender-based sexual norms. Sub-Saharan Africa suffers from high rates of sexually transmissible infections, including HIV.
- Asian countries draw upon centuries of tradition. Chinese attitudes toward sex remain very restrictive. Japanese men and women are taught to value self-control and moderation in all areas, including their sex lives. Premarital sex is tolerated as long as it is discreet. Thailand has a thriving sex industry. As in other Asian cultures, men in Thailand are afforded privileges few women enjoy.

MAJOR SOCIOCULTURAL INFLUENCES

- The mass media disseminate a range of sexual messages that shape sexual views. In some instances, the media have challenged cultural boundaries; more often, they perpetuate stereotypes, sometimes in a sensational manner. Sexual messages permeate all of the media, including television programming such as soap operas and talk shows. Popular magazines promulgate information about sex and relationships. Advertising and popular music present stereotyped messages about sex and gender. The Internet offers sexual materials on an unprecedented scale.
- All religions teach moral rules, although these vary significantly. In one way or another, all religions have tried to control sexual behavior. The dominant religious influence in Western cultures is the Judeo-Christian tradition. Islamic beliefs are male-centered, but more tolerant than Christianity in some respects. Hindu teachings see love and sex as having a divine origin. Buddhism consists of a conservative branch that promotes self-discipline and a more liberal one that advocates tolerance, including in matters of love and sex.
- The family is the primary socializing agent in all cultures. Many parents, however, do not communicate effectively with their children about sex. Relationships with parents, the nature of family interactions, and parental attitudes about sex all contribute to teens' sexual development.

HISTORICAL PERSPECTIVES ON SEXUALITY

- Historical records reveal that the modern fascination with sex is not unique. Virtually all cultures have created records and artifacts that illustrate their sexual views and practices. Classical Greece and ancient Rome were male-dominated societies in which men enjoyed sexual freedoms that were not afforded women. Early Christian beliefs were reactions to what were viewed as the sexual excesses of the Roman empire. The Catholic church became the dominant moral influence throughout the Middle Ages. Although the Victorian era is remembered as being repressive and antisexual, sexuality was not completely suppressed, just tightly controlled.
- The sexual revolution of the 1960s is remembered as a time when tradition was challenged and a permissive view of sex was promoted.

THEORETICAL PERSPECTIVES ON SEXUALITY

- Theories of sexuality represent attempts to understand sexual practices.
- Psychoanalytic theory proposes that sex is the most important human drive, leading to a continuous struggle between pleasure-seeking instincts and internalized inhibitions.

- The learning perspective comprises theories that emphasize the role of conditioning and the influence of the environment in shaping sexual attitudes and practices.
- Script theory explains human sexuality as socially defined rather than socially controlled. Society provides roadmaps for sexual behavior.
- Evolutionary psychology attempts to trace the origins of current sexual practices in human evolution. Sexual strategies that offered reproductive benefits to early humans were passed on. These strategies may explain existing gender differences in the selection of sexual partners.

CHAPTER 2

Research Methods in Sexuality

Influence of stimulants—The use of stimulants of any kind is a fruitful cause of the vice [masturbation]. Tea and coffee have led thousands to perdition in this way. The influence of tobacco is so strongly shown in this direction that it is doubtful if there can be found a boy who has attained the age of puberty, and has acquired the habit of using tobacco, who is not addicted to this vile practice. Candies, spices, cinnamon, cloves, peppermint, and all strong essences powerfully excite the genital organs, and lead to the same result.

J. H. Kellogg, *Plain Facts for Old and Young: Natural History and Hygiene of Organic Life* (1888)

Tea and coffee have led thousands to perdition.

The history of sex research provides a fascinating glimpse of many issues and problems that affected society at different points in time and that still do so. Cultural and personal beliefs and values continue to shape people's perspectives on human sexuality. This chapter considers the assumptions, methods, and dilemmas that characterize the scientific approach to studying human sexuality. The greatest promise of this approach is the emphasis on objectivity in seeking answers to questions. Scientists seek the "truth" instead of relying on personal biases and popular ideas. Objectivity, of course, is a matter of degree. No method, no matter how precise and rigorous, can be completely objective. The scientific method, though, is more systematic than other approaches in striving for objectivity.

As you saw in Chapter 1, people have sought to understand the mysteries of human sexual behavior throughout history. Until the early part of the 20th century, most information was derived from personal experiences, superstitions, mythology, and religious teachings or writings (Bullough, 1994). Much of what was assumed to be true of human sexuality was passed on by word of mouth and based on traditional beliefs. Rarely was there any type of proof that the information was accurate. Many notions about sexuality were blindly accepted because there were no established methods for verifying or rejecting them. For example, beliefs about the harmfulness of masturbation, as illustrated in the chapter epigraph, were widely accepted. At the time of Kellogg's writing, attitudes toward this practice were very repressive: Masturbation was described as unhealthy, immoral, unnatural, and socially reprehensible. These attitudes were perpetuated by "authorities"—among whom were religious figures, medical professionals, educators, politicians, and other public figures responsible for shaping cultural beliefs.

Best known for his cereal (corn flakes), J. H. Kellogg wrote about the dangers of masturbation, which he believed to be the cause of many mental and physical problems. Like many of his contemporaries, Kellogg held repressive views of sexuality. His cereal was originally intended to help curb consumers' sexual appetites, although its effectiveness was never systematically evaluated.

THE SCIENTIFIC APPROACH

Science is best described as a process of inquiry, a method of obtaining information and answers to questions (Wiederman, 2001).

2.1 on the web

The list of professional journals devoted to sex research and related topics is constantly growing. For a comprehensive listing, visit **www.ablongman.com/mcanulty2e.** Print out this list and visit your library. *Which of these journals does your local or regional library subscribe to? Print a list of your library's holdings for future reference.*

TABLE 2.1 Some Major Journals Devoted to Sexology

AIDS Education and Prevention	*Journal of Psychology and Human Sexuality*
Annual Review of Sex Research	*Journal of Sex Education and Therapy*
Archives of Sexual Behavior	*The Journal of Sex Research*
The Canadian Journal of Human Sexuality	*Sex Roles*
Child Abuse and Neglect	*Sexuality and Disability*
Journal of the History of Sexuality	*Sexual Abuse: A Journal of Research and Treatment*
Journal of Homosexuality	

There are many methods for seeking answers to questions, but what sets the scientific method apart are its assumptions and rules. For example, the earliest attempts to explain natural phenomena, such as reproduction, were derived from beliefs in supernatural forces. In the 4th century B.C., the Greek philosopher Aristotle wrote extensively about sexual behavior and reproduction in animals (Bullough, 1994). Derived from his personal observations and from popular superstitions, Aristotle's ideas were dominant influences for many centuries. He believed that animals reproduced by sexual or asexual means or by spontaneous generation. The latter explanation was his default option for animals that he had not been able to observe. For example, according to Aristotle, hermit crabs grew spontaneously out of soil and slime. It was not until the 17th century that the concept of spontaneous generation was challenged (Bullough, 1994).

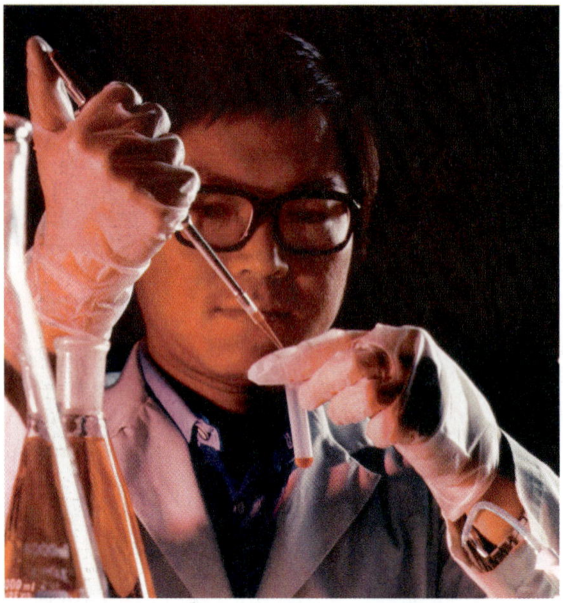

A scientist is committed to collecting information in an unbiased manner. Scientists rely on systematic observation and measurement to ensure accuracy and objectivity.

Although his idea about spontaneous generation was both inaccurate and unscientific, Aristotle's reliance on personal observations to obtain knowledge foreshadowed the scientific commitment to empiricism. **Empiricism** is the practice of relying on direct observation and measurement to obtain answers to questions (Liebert & Liebert, 1995). Rather than blindly accepting personal beliefs or popular folklore, scientists seek observable facts. This reliance on objective observation and measurement is a defining feature of the scientific method. The commitment to empiricism also separates science from common sense. As an approach to seeking answers, common sense does not involve a systematic effort to verify one's conclusions (Kerlinger, 1973). By insisting on proof, scientists hope to avoid false conclusions (such as that animals can reproduce by spontaneous generation).

Sexology has emerged as an interdisciplinary field dedicated to the scientific study of sexuality. An advantage of its emergence as a separate discipline is that "different angles of the same phenomenon (sexuality) are being examined by experts who are adept and trained at studying their own piece of the pie" (Orbuch & Harvey, 1991, p. 11). Elizabeth Osgood Goodrich Willard coined the term *sexology* in her 1867 book *Sexology as the Philosophy of Life.* (Ironically, Willard held repressive attitudes toward sex, viewing a sexual orgasm as "more debilitating to the system than a hard day's work" [Bullough, 1994, p. 26].)

SCIENCE
A systematic method of inquiry that follows certain rules.

As the field of sexology gained status, there was significant growth in the number of organizations, books, and journals devoted to the study of sexuality. Today, several professional organizations, such as the Society for the Scientific Study of Sexuality, number their members in the thousands. In addition, over a dozen professional journals publish sexological research findings (see Table 2.1).

did YOU know?

Although sexology is now an interdisciplinary field, early sex researchers came from such diverse disciplines as gynecology (William Masters), neurology (Sigmund Freud), and biology (Alfred Kinsey).

GOALS OF SCIENTIFIC RESEARCH

We may think broadly of science as a set of tools for studying the world. Scientific research may be carried out to achieve widely varying goals. In some cases, the goal is simply to understand some phenomenon; in others, the goal may be to solve some societal problem. Scientific research in the behavioral sciences is intended to fulfill four interrelated purposes: to describe behavior, to understand or explain behavior, to predict behavior, and to control or change behavior. We will consider each of these in turn.

Describing Behavior

Some research is simply descriptive by nature; the goal of such research is not to offer explanations but simply to describe. With few exceptions, survey research is descriptive. For example, if researchers were to survey a group of college students about their attitudes toward teenage pregnancies, they would be conducting descriptive research. Likewise, if they surveyed a group of adolescents to determine what percentage of them had ever experienced an unwanted pregnancy, they would be conducting descriptive research. The goals of these surveys are to describe attitudes toward pregnancy and actual experiences of unplanned pregnancy. The researchers may obtain precise descriptions of attitudes and experiences, but they will not be able to offer explanations. Descriptive research cannot explain why students have specific attitudes or why some teenagers had unplanned pregnancies.

Looking At . . .

. . . Thinking About

If you had to answer the question "Why do some teenagers have unplanned pregnancies?" how would you respond? One important goal in science is to provide cause-and-effect explanations of human behavior.

Explaining Behavior

A fundamental purpose of much research is explanation. In fact, explanation is often viewed as the most important of the four purposes of scientific research. When scientists seek answers to questions such as "What are the causes of teenage pregnancy?" they are trying to explain behavior. In trying to explain a phenomenon, they ask "Why?" Once scientists have explained a behavior, they have identified its cause or causes.

Predicting Behavior

Many scientists, especially those in the behavioral sciences, are interested in predicting behavior. They might ask, "What predicts whether a teenager will become pregnant?" Although it is commonly assumed that understanding and predicting behavior are the same goals, this is not necessarily so. Scientists may sometimes be able to make accurate predictions without having complete explanations. For example, if asked to predict risks of unplanned pregnancy for a group of adolescents, researchers would want to know what factors are associated with such pregnancies. If socioeconomic status and low rates of contraceptive use were known to be strongly associated with unplanned pregnancy, they could use this information in making their prediction.

EMPIRICISM
The scientific practice of relying on direct observation and measurement when seeking answers to questions.

SEXOLOGY
An interdisciplinary field devoted to the scientific study of sexuality.

Although their prediction might be accurate, they would not have explained the behavior. Thus, explanation and prediction are separate goals in science.

Controlling or Changing Behavior

A final purpose of scientific research is to control or change behavior in order to solve or prevent a problem. For example, researchers interested in preventing teenage pregnancies are striving to control, or change, adolescents' behavior. This type of scientific study is generally described as *applied research,* or research designed to solve a current problem. Generally, scientists must first explain behavior before they can modify it. Thus, only after identifying the risk factors for unwanted pregnancy could researchers attempt to prevent the problem. Similarly, as Health Matters: Epidemiology explains, scientists must identify a new disease before they can devise ways to prevent it.

HEALTH Matters

Epidemiology

Have you ever wondered how new diseases or epidemics are discovered? Obviously, some professionals are involved in tracking and reporting diseases. These professionals are epidemiologists. **Epidemiology** is the field concerned with public health and disease prevention. Originally, epidemiologists were concerned with studying epidemics, but the field has broadened its scope over the years. Today, epidemiology may be described as the discipline devoted to the study, control, and prevention of health problems and communicable diseases.

The epidemiological method includes four phases:

1. *Surveillance* consists of the ongoing collection and examination of public health information. While continuously monitoring changes in health conditions, epidemiologists search for trends in the occurrence of diseases. Surveillance requires the systematic collection of health information (such as mortality statistics and health department and hospital records), the evaluation and description of the information (see, for example, a recent issue of the Center for Disease Control's *Morbidity and Mortality Weekly Report*), and the dissemination of results to relevant governmental health officials.
2. *Investigation* involves in-depth examination of an identified health threat or disease. In the investigative phase, the existence of a health threat is confirmed, numbers of cases are identified, and the specific signs or symptoms are carefully described. Additionally, risk factors for contracting the disease (such as age, gender, and lifestyle risks) are tentatively identified. Finally, some preliminary speculations (or hypotheses) about the causes and modes of transmission of the disease are offered.
3. The next step, *analysis,* is the systematic examination of the information derived in the investigation phase. In the analysis phase, efforts are devoted to identifying precisely the causes and transmission modes that were proposed in the previous phase. The analysis phase goes beyond mere observation and description to explanation.
4. In the final phase, *evaluation,* all efforts to control or prevent a health threat are carefully examined to assess their efficacy. (This phase corresponds to the fourth purpose of science discussed in the text.)

Epidemiological methods have been instrumental in identifying certain diseases and in searching for their causes. For example, hepatitis B and human immunodeficiency virus (HIV) are life-threatening viruses that are often contracted through sexual activity (see Chapter 14). The identification of these diseases and the eventual discovery of their causes were accomplished through the application of epidemiological methods. In the case of HIV, in the mid-1980s, an observant epidemiologist in the Los Angeles County Health Department noted five reports of a then-rare disease (*Pneumocystis carinii*) over a short period of time. These observations, along with subsequent reports from other epidemiologists in other regions of the country, marked the beginning of the identification of the AIDS epidemic. The historical account of this identification provides a fascinating illustration of the methods and importance of epidemiology in the study of public health and disease prevention.

MEASUREMENT IN SCIENCE

The type of information gathered in scientific research and the methods for collecting the information vary significantly in objectivity, practicality, and validity. Three types of measures are used to obtain sexual information: self-report, behavioral, and medical/physiological measures (Orbuch & Harvey, 1991).

A behavioral self-report is a detailed record of one's own behavior, much like a diary. This is one of the most useful sources of self-report information on sexual behavior.

Self-Report Measures

Self-report measures include responses to questionnaires and interviews. Such measures have been used extensively in studying sexual attitudes and values, emotions, and sexual behaviors and experience. Information from self-reports is considered subjective and highly susceptible to *response bias,* such as voluntary distortion (lying, exaggerating, or minimizing) and unintentional distortion (forgetting).

Although self-report measures suffer from these limitations, they have been used most extensively in sex research for several reasons. First, they are usually the easiest measures to obtain. Second, for some research questions, self-report is the only feasible strategy for obtaining information. In his critique of sex survey findings (entitled "Sex, Lies, and Social Science"), Lewontin (1995) acknowledged that there seems to be no practical way of learning what people do "in the bedroom" other than to ask them. Third, ethical and legal issues may preclude the use of other measures. (The importance of ethics in sex research is considered in detail in a later section.)

Most self-report information in sexology is gathered using questionnaires completed by research participants. Alternatively, participants may be interviewed by a researcher. Another common source of self-reported information in sex research is a behavioral self-report, which usually consists of a personal record or diary describing sexual activity over a period of time (Minichiello et al., 2000; Morrison, Leigh, & Gillmore, 1999). For example, Berk, Abramson, and Okami (1995) had heterosexual men and women keep daily records of their frequency of vaginal intercourse, cunnilingus, and fellatio over a 2-week period. After turning over the diaries to the researchers, participants completed a questionnaire that asked them to recall the frequency of the same sexual acts over the same time period. The study findings suggested that the behavioral self-report measures were more accurate than the questionnaire responses. Although behavioral self-reports seem preferable to the traditional self-report measures in many instances, they have been used infrequently in sex research (Catania et al., 1993). One possible reason is that behavioral self-reports require sustained record-keeping by participants, whereas responding to a questionnaire usually requires a one-time interaction.

Another variation of the self-report, the *external observer report,* consists of having another person, usually a sexual partner, report the sexual behavior under study. In other words, a partner is asked to verify a research participant's self-reported sexual behavior. This is usually done to assess the **reliability** of a person's self-report. Presumably, if both partners report the same frequency of sexual activity, researchers can assume that each person's reported information is accurate. Unfortunately, this approach also has some limitations. First, it requires that each participant in a study recruit the participation of a partner, which may be difficult, especially if there are multiple partners. Second, in the case of a discrepancy, there is no way of knowing the source of error. If partners disagree on how often they had sex in the past week, it is entirely possible that both are wrong. Each couple's self-reported sexual behavior would still need to be checked against some objective measure of their actual sexual activity (Catania et al., 1993). Thus, this method may provide more a measure of agreement between partners than a sensitive way of measuring reliability in reports of sexual behavior. Perhaps it is for this reason that external observer reports have been used infrequently in sex research (Ochs & Binik, 1999).

EPIDEMIOLOGY
The discipline devoted to the study, control, and prevention of health problems and infectious diseases.

RELIABILITY
The accuracy or consistency of results of a scientific study.

Direct Behavioral Measures

Direct behavioral measures are generally viewed as more objective than self-reports. These measures are less dependent on participants' accuracy and openness. Direct behavioral measures are recordings of actual behavior as it occurs. The researcher may either take notes while observing the behavior or use videotaping equipment to record it. Direct behavioral observation can occur in either the natural environment or the laboratory. As an example, consider the question "How do dating couples express physical intimacy?" Self-reports would require individual participants to describe what they habitually do with their dating partners. Behavioral self-reports would require having participants keep a record or diary of what they did with their dating partners over a specified period of time. Direct behavioral measures could be obtained by videotaping couples or otherwise recording their behaviors in actual dating situations.

Although direct behavioral measures raise a number of practical and ethical questions, they are considered more objective than self-reports because they are relatively unaffected by such factors as memory. However, direct behavioral measures may be impractical, controversial, and costly. Imagine the logistical problems in following participants on their dates. Consider the controversy that might ensue if a researcher attempted to videotape physical intimacy. Even with participants' full cooperation and consent, some legal and ethical questions are raised when scientists observe and measure sexual behavior. (As you will see, this is exactly what the eminent sexologists William Masters and Virginia Johnson did in their laboratory.) Videotaping equipment and the required technical support may be prohibitively expensive. A final drawback to the use of direct behavioral measures in sex research pertains to people's reactions to being observed. As you might imagine, the mere awareness that one is being observed can affect behavior.

did YOU know?

A change in people's behavior that occurs merely because they are aware that they are being observed is a phenomenon known as the **Hawthorne effect.** *Studies conducted at the Hawthorne industrial plant in Cicero, Illinois in the late 1920s revealed that employees began to work more productively solely because they knew they were participating in a study and being observed.*

Medical/Physiological Measures

Medical/physiological measures are preferred for some sex research questions (Rowland, 1999). For instance, medical tests reveal sexually transmissible infections more accurately than do self-reports. Understandably, many people are reluctant to disclose information about their diseases; others may be unaware of having a disease. Similarly, scientists could study sexual arousal by asking people who are sexually aroused to describe what they are feeling. However, individuals' accounts of their emotional and physical states are subjective and inherently subject to error. More objective results can be obtained by precisely measuring bodily changes during the experience of sexual arousal. With the proper equipment, scientists can measure changes in multiple body systems, including heart rate, blood pressure, breathing, perspiration, and muscle tension. Information obtained from direct measurement of physiological changes is objective and precise. Physiological recording equipment can detect changes that are so small that an individual isn't even aware of them.

Limitations of medical/physiological measures are that they require intrusive and costly equipment and are therefore often impractical. Additionally, for many research questions in sexuality, there is no medical or physiological measure. There is no known physiological measure of attitudes, beliefs, or values. Further, there is no way to measure sexual history (for example, number of partners in one's lifetime) other than via self-report.

Genital measures have been used extensively in research and clinical settings to assess sexual problems such as erection difficulties, atypical and criminal sexual behavior, and sexual orientation. Genital measures are taken using special instruments that measure physiological changes in the penis or vagina to gauge sexual arousal. The rationale for using these devices is that they are less susceptible to measurement error (such as self-presentation bias) and thus more objective and reliable than self-reports (McAnulty & Adams, 1992).

With males, **penile plethysmography** involves attaching a measurement device known as a *transducer* to the penis and obtaining measures of changes in blood flow, or erection, while the person is exposed to sexual stimuli (films, color slides, or audiotaped sexual scripts). There are two types of transducer: circumferential and volumetric. A circumferential device is placed on the shaft of the penis to detect changes in circumference. As blood flow increases during penile erection, the circumference of the penis expands. A volumetric transducer is placed over the entire penis and measures erection in terms of displacement of air in a calibrated cylinder. As erection increases, more air is displaced, and the changes in air pressure in the cylinder are measured. Although the volumetric device is reportedly more sensitive and precise, it is also more cumbersome and prone to give false readings if the participant moves.

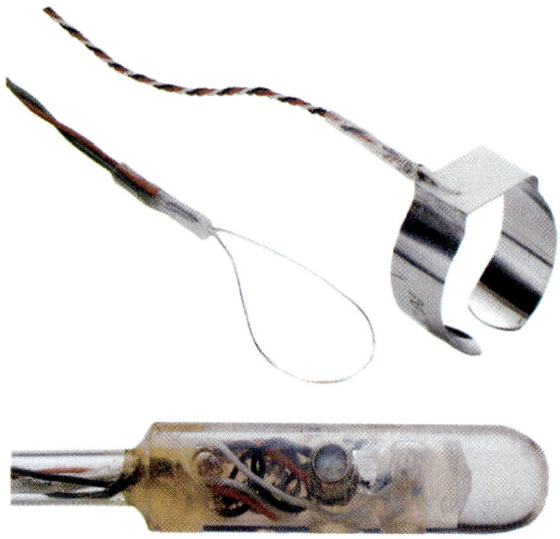

The penile plethysmograph (above) and vaginal photoplethysmograph (below) measure changes in blood flow in the genitals. They are considered the most precise devices for physiological measurements of sexual arousal.

A similar methodology is used with females: A **vaginal photoplethysmograph** provides a measure of blood engorgement in the vaginal walls, which is directly related to sexual arousal. The tampon-shaped photoplethysmograph emits a light inside the vagina. As blood flow increases, more light is reflected, so sexual arousal can be quantified in terms of amount of light being reflected. The degree of genital blood engorgement provides an estimate of the individual's sexual arousal to different types of sexual stimuli.

Although it might seem unlikely that participants could bias genital measures of sexual arousal, several studies reveal that some participants can successfully "fake" results of plethysmograph studies. For example, McAnulty and Adams (1991) found that up to one-third of the gay and heterosexual men they studied could fake a nonpreferred sexual orientation. That is, some of the gay men could suppress their erections in reaction to films depicting homosexual activity while enhancing their genital responses to heterosexual films. The same pattern was found with some of the heterosexual men, who produced a gay profile when tested using a plethysmograph. Similar results were obtained with heterosexual women (Beck & Baldwin, 1994).

Other studies reveal that it may be easier for men to suppress erections in response to preferred sexual materials than to generate erections in response to nonpreferred stimuli (Adams, Motsinger, McAnulty, & Moore, 1992). In other words, it seems more difficult for men to appear "turned on" when they are not, than the reverse. Presumably, people can control their genital arousal by the use of mental imagery and cognitive activity—visualizing something unattractive or engaging in mental distraction, such as thinking about math problems (Beck & Baldwin, 1994; McAnulty & Adams, 1991). Conversely, to appear aroused by a nonarousing stimulus, participants attempt to imagine something they find sexually desirable.

Genital measures of sexual arousal illustrate a creative attempt to overcome some limitations of other methods of measuring human sexuality. Further, research findings demonstrate that sexual arousal is multifaceted. Being sexually aroused includes multiple components—not only physical arousal but thoughts, emotions, and behaviors (McAnulty & Adams, 1992; Rowland, 1995).

PENILE PLETHYSMOGRAPH
An instrument used to estimate a male's degree of sexual arousal by measuring changes in blood flow to the penis.

VAGINAL PHOTOPLETHYSMOGRAPH
An instrument used to estimate a female's sexual arousal by measuring changes in vaginal blood flow.

RESEARCH DESIGNS IN SCIENCE

A research design specifies exactly what is done to answer a question scientifically. Scientists use a number of research designs, which differ in their usefulness in providing conclusive answers, in their practicality, and in their overall merit. The most com-

TABLE 2.2 Research Designs in Science

APPROACH	STRENGTHS	WEAKNESSES
Experiment	Manipulation of variables to control outside influences; best method for identifying causal relationships	Laboratory environment is artificial; limited generalizability of findings; manipulation of some variables is unethical or impractical
Case study	Extensive evidence gathered on a single person	Lack of generalizability of findings; time-consuming
Observational methods	Behavior is relatively unaffected by a researcher	Little opportunity to control variables; time-consuming
Survey methods	Effective means of measuring actions, attitudes, opinions, preferences, and intentions of large numbers of people; allows a wide range of responses; follow-up questions are possible	Lack of explanatory power; validity of findings limited by sample; reliability difficult to determine; self-report possibly inaccurate or biased; inability to draw conclusions about causal relationships; time-consuming

monly used designs are controlled experiments, case studies, observational methods, and survey methods (see Table 2.2). We will consider each in some detail.

CONTROLLED EXPERIMENT
An experiment involving the systematic application or manipulation of one variable and observation of its impact on another while other factors are held constant.

HYPOTHESIS
A predicted relationship between two or more variables that will be tested with an experiment.

VARIABLE
In a scientific experiment, anything that can vary or change, such as attitudes, behaviors, or physiological responses.

INDEPENDENT VARIABLE
In an experiment, the presumed causal factor that is manipulated or changed in some way.

DEPENDENT VARIABLE
In an experiment, the presumed effect, which is measured as the independent variable is manipulated.

EXPERIMENTAL GROUP
The group to which the independent variable in a controlled experiment is administered.

CONTROL GROUP
In an experiment, the comparison group that is treated identically to the experimental group, with the exception that the independent variable is withheld.

Controlled Experiments

A **controlled experiment** is the method of choice for discovering scientific explanations. Only through experimentation can cause-and-effect relationships be identified. An experiment begins with a **hypothesis**, which is a prediction or a guess about a cause-and-effect relationship. The experiment is carried out to test the hypothesis—to determine whether the predicted relationship exists. In its simplest form, an experiment includes two variables. A **variable** is anything that can vary or change, such as attitudes, behavior, or feelings. In an experiment, the presumed cause of a change is called the **independent variable;** this is the variable that is manipulated. The presumed effect is called the **dependent variable.** When conducting an experiment, researchers somehow apply or change the independent variable (the "cause") and then observe the impact, if any, on the dependent variable (the "effect").

A controlled experiment is conducted so as to render any alternative explanation for the findings implausible. In other words, all conditions are held constant, or are controlled, for all participants. Ideally, every participant in an experiment receives the same instructions or treatment from the same experimenter and in the same setting. In a typical experiment, there are two groups: an **experimental group** and a **control group.** The control group serves as a standard of comparison. Participants in the control group are treated identically to those in the experimental group with one exception: They are not exposed to the independent variable. Thus, any observed group differences with respect to the dependent variable can be attributed to the independent variable.

As an example, consider the application of the experimental method in studying the effects of viewing pornography. The hypothesis is that exposure to sexually explicit materials (the "cause") makes men more prone to perpetrate violence against women (the "effect"). Participants—male college students—are randomly assigned to the experimental condition (in which they view a sexually explicit film) or the control condition (in which they view a film without sexual content). Afterwards, all participants complete a questionnaire measuring acceptance of rape myths (for example, that victims are responsible for being raped). If the participants in the experimental group report more acceptance of rape myths and if it can be shown that the only difference between the two groups is the content of the films participants viewed, researchers could conclude that results are consistent with the starting hypothesis.

The experimental method has some limitations, including restrictions on the generalizability of results and concerns that the laboratory environment is artificial. The first of these limitations refers to whether the findings in an experiment apply to other participants, in other settings, and at other times. The primary way to assess generalizability is through replication; every time the same results are obtained with different participants and in different settings, scientists gain confidence in their generalizability. As for the second limitation, the more tightly controlled a laboratory experiment is (the more completely everything except the independent variable is held constant so as not to "contaminate" the results), the more artificial it may appear. A laboratory is not the natural environment, and it is always possible that research participants would react differently in the outside world. Is showing a film and having participants complete a rape myth questionnaire analogous to observing sexual violence in the natural environment? One solution to the problem of the artificiality of laboratory settings is to try to conduct studies in the natural environment. Naturally, the use of more natural settings and real-life variables can raise important ethical questions. How could a scientist conduct an experiment on the effects of viewing sexually explicit materials in a natural setting in a practical, ethical, and legal manner? There is no easy and obvious answer, which is why such a study has yet to be conducted.

2.2 on the web

Everyone (even textbook writers) occasionally has questions about sex. A multitude of sources can provide answers—however, not every source is necessarily reliable and factual. Two of the most reliable Web sites devoted to offering answers to questions about sex are one sponsored by the Kinsey Institute at Indiana University and another called Go Ask Alice, sponsored by Columbia University. Go to **www.ablongman.com/mcanulty2e** and find links to these two sites.

Familiarize yourself with the sites, as you may want to consult them in the future.

Correlational Designs

Because of practical and ethical limitations, the majority of studies in sex research are not true experiments but **correlational designs** (Wiederman, 2001). In a correlational design, the researcher does not manipulate one variable to observe its effect on another variable. Rather, the goal of a correlational study is to investigate the extent to which two (or more) variables co-vary, or change together. Essentially, correlational studies are designed to investigate the interrelationships among variables. Are measures of one variable associated with measures of another variable, and, if so, what is the extent or strength of this relationship? Are religious views, for example, associated with attitudes toward premarital sex? What is the strength of the relationship between these two variables?

Correlational designs allow researchers to investigate the extent to which two or more variables are related, but the results do not indicate the direction of the relationship. In other words, correlations do not permit researchers to conclude that one variable *causes* the other. For example, high self-esteem and frequency of sexual activity are correlated (Baumeister & Tice, 2001). However, the correlation does not indicate whether one variable causes the other, because some third variable may actually be responsible for both. High self-esteem may give people the confidence to secure many sexual partners, or, alternatively, having many partners may be a boost to one's ego and may inflate one's self-esteem. Perhaps a third variable, such as self-acceptance or being socially skilled, is actually responsible for both level of self-esteem and frequency of sex. Correlational designs cannot be used to determine causality; they show only that two or more variables are somehow related.

CORRELATIONAL DESIGN
A study whose goal is to investigate the extent to which two (or more) variables co-vary, or change together; unlike a true experiment, no independent variable is manipulated.

CASE STUDY
A scientific method that relies on an in-depth analysis of a single case or person.

Case Studies

Whereas a controlled experiment involves studying groups of people, a **case study** is essentially a detailed examination of a single case. A case study resembles a biographical account of a person's life. (In some instances, researchers may collect a series of related case studies.) The case study is most appropriate for providing descriptions of rare or complex cases and, therefore, is commonly used in medicine and in psychiatry. This method has been especially popular in clinical research on sexuality, where a detailed account of an unusual or rare condition is often desired. For example, eminent sexologist John Money has provided numerous detailed descriptions of individuals with rare or unique sexual problems (Money, 1986; Money & Lamacz, 1989). Money offered one insightful portrayal of the life history and erotic fantasies of a man with a sexual preoccupation with female amputees (women who were missing a limb). Such atypical sexual preferences could not readily be examined by any other research method.

Although case studies may generate a wealth of descriptive information, they do not allow conclusions about cause and effect. The case study method is generally viewed as unsystematic and uncontrolled because it provides no definitive answers. A detailed description of the life history of one individual may be a rich source of information about his or her case but does not permit any conclusions about causation. For instance, finding that a person suffered a troubled childhood does not prove that the experience caused his or her problems in adulthood. A myriad of other explanations is feasible. Another major limitation of the case study is the inability to assume that it represents the experiences of other individuals. That is, impressions from a case study cannot be generalized. Nonetheless, the case study method may be useful for describing rare phenomena and deriving questions that will subsequently be answered via some other research design.

Observational Methods

Observational methods allow scientists to witness the behavior of animal species, including humans, directly and to draw tentative conclusions from these observations. The major strength of observational methods is that they permit objective descriptions of behavior. Of all research designs, observation is the least susceptible to response biases. Observational methods allow researchers to avoid worrying about errors or bias caused by untruthful or forgetful participants.

2.3 on the web

Masters and Johnson's research ushered in a new era of sophistication in sex research. They were not, however, the first to attempt to collect scientific information about sex. For a chronology of sex research, go to **www.ablongman.com/mcanulty2e** and go to the History of Sexology link. Note that although people searched for answers to questions about sexuality as far back as antiquity, systematic inquiries did not begin until the 19th century.

Observational methods include (1) controlled observation, (2) naturalistic observation, and (3) participant observation. In sex research, controlled observation involves observing and recording sexual behavior as it occurs in a controlled setting, usually a laboratory. Naturalistic observation occurs in a participant's natural environment, as opposed to a laboratory. The third observational method, participant observation, involves researchers' actually participating in events while taking notes or recording their observations. An important difference between participant observation and the other two observational methods is that the former is unobtrusive; other participants do not know that one "participant" is actually an observer conducting a study. Obviously, an element of deception is involved in this form of observation. As an example, Enck and Preston (1988) studied topless dancers and their customers via the observations of one of their students, who secured a waitress job in a topless club. As an insider, the student was able to observe the interactions between dancers and their customers directly, without anyone knowing she was doing so. Other researchers have used participant observation to study anonymous sexual behavior in public restrooms (Humphreys, 1970) and "swinging," the practice by some couples of agreeing to have extramarital sex (Bartell, 1970).

The most important application of controlled observation to sex research was the pioneering work of William Masters and Virginia Johnson (1966). In 1954, Masters and Johnson launched a study that provided the first systematic observations and recordings of sexual behavior. The study began with careful interviews of 155 male and female prostitutes. Because of the tendency of prostitutes to move frequently and concerns over the generalizability of findings from prostitutes to the general population, this study had inherent limitations. Masters and Johnson eventually broadened their pool of participants by recruiting people from the community, especially from Washington University in St. Louis, where the two researchers worked. Over an 11-year period, the pair observed the sexual behaviors of nearly 700 married and unmarried individuals ranging in age from 18 to 89. Over the course of the study, Masters and Johnson made precise observations of over 10,000 sexual acts, resulting in the most complete body of information on human sexual arousal ever compiled. (Their findings are summarized in Chapter 4.)

Perhaps the most important innovation by Masters and Johnson occurred with respect to measurement technologies (Bullough, 1994). They obtained measures of changes in respiration, heart rate, muscle tension, blood pressure, perspiration, and blood flow in the course of their observations of sexual behavior. For example, they constructed an artificial penis whose rate and depth of penetration could be controlled by the participant. This device was made of transparent plastic and equipped with an internal light and miniature camera that permitted unprecedentedly complete and precise recordings of physiological events in the vagina during sexual activity.

Eminent sexologists William Masters and Virginia Johnson pioneered the application of controlled observation to the study of sexual behavior. Their research contributions to scientists' knowledge of human sexual arousal and sexual problems have as yet been unmatched.

Survey Methods

A **survey** is the systematic collection and analysis of information from people in a particular group. Because surveys, in all their forms, are more practical than other methods and are the only feasible approach for some studies, they remain popular in all of the social sciences and are the most widely used design in sexology. There are two general survey methods: interviews and questionnaires. Interviews may be conducted in person (*face-to-face interviews*) or over the telephone. Questionnaires are generally self-administered and therefore provide more privacy than interviews. Literally hundreds of questionnaires have been devised to measure virtually every imaginable aspect of sexuality, including sexual attitudes, emotions, sexual behaviors, sexual experiences, and sexual health (for a comprehensive overview, see Davis, Yarber, Bauserman, Schreer, & Davis, 1998). A number of studies have compared the various survey methods, but it is still unclear which yields the most accurate information (Catania et al., 1993).

A major limitation of survey methods is **measurement error** (Catania et al., 1993), which refers to an error that prevents researchers from obtaining accurate information (Laumann, Gagnon, Michael, & Michaels, 1994). In sexology, measurement error can be caused by any factor that produces inconsistencies between people's actual sexual behavior and what they report in a survey. Failure to obtain accurate measurements may be due to problems with the interviewer, the questionnaire, or the participants (Groves, 1987). Some steps, such as providing training, may minimize measurement error due to the interviewer. Laumann and colleagues (1994) provided three to five days of training for interviewers to ensure that they were able to discuss sexuality in a neutral, nonjudgmental, and professional manner. To minimize measurement error due to the questionnaire, researchers must address a number of aspects, including its length (number of questions), the type of language used (slang as opposed to technical terms), and the format of the questions (fixed or open).

A common source of measurement error in survey research is self-presentation bias. *Self-presentation bias* refers to respondents' attempts to present themselves in a favorable light (Catania, 1999). This bias may take the form of underreporting behaviors viewed as negative or overreporting behaviors viewed as socially desirable. What is viewed as socially desirable will vary according to the context, such as the respondent's culture

SURVEY
The most popular method in sexuality research, which involves interviewing a number of people or having them complete a questionnaire.

MEASUREMENT ERROR
Error caused by problems with the interviewer, participants, or questionnaires that result in inaccurate information.

and subculture. For instance, Catania, Gibson, Chitwood, and Coates (1990) suggested that young adults in contemporary Western cultures may find it difficult to admit to a researcher that they are sexually inexperienced. In a study of heterosexual women, Bolling and Voeller (1987) found that participants readily reported their experience with vaginal intercourse; however, only after repeated personal interviews did they openly discuss their experience with anal intercourse. And, since the AIDS epidemic, gay men may be less likely to report having unprotected anal intercourse (Catania et al., 1990).

One finding from sex surveys that has intrigued researchers is that men consistently report having more lifetime sexual partners than women do (Oliver & Hyde, 1993; Wiederman, 1997). Is this an accurate finding or a result of a self-presentation bias, a product of the cultural double standard that dictates that women are to be more sexually restrained than men? We take a closer look at this question in Close Up on Gender: Do Men Lie More about Their Sex Lives?

A number of strategies may be useful in reducing self-presentation bias. Efforts to ensure privacy, for example, enhance respondents' openness. Anonymity—the extent to which participants believe that their answers are not identifiable—also promotes openness. Participants are more likely to admit to sexual activities that might be viewed negatively if they do not have face-to-face contact with a researcher (Catania et al., 1993). Thus, telephone interviews and self-administered questionnaires may provide more valid information (Siegel, Krauss, & Karus, 1994). Computer-assisted interviewing is a relatively new method of obtaining sensitive self-reported information. This method seems helpful in reducing response bias to questions about behaviors that are stigmatized, illegal, or embarrassing (Gribble, Miller, Rogers, & Turner, 1999; Sharp, 2002). Computer-assisted interviewing has been used to assess children who may have been sexually abused (DeVoe & Faller, 2002) and in the National Survey of Sexual Attitudes and Lifestyles conducted in Great Britain (Johnson et al., 2001). Although computer-assisted interviewing may promote more candor in responses than face-to-face interviewing, it has not been proven superior to self-administered anonymous questionnaires (Johnson et al., 2001).

The use of nonjudgmental terms and familiar wording in questions may also reduce self-presentation bias (Blair, Sudman, Bradburn, & Stocking, 1977; Bradburn & Sudman, 1979). Finally, the credibility of the researcher is important. Respondents are more open and honest when they believe that they are participating in a legitimate study (Catania et al., 1993). Therefore, how a study is presented to potential participants is critical. For example, in one national survey (Laumann et al., 1994), prospective participants were initially sent a letter explaining that the survey was designed to help "doctors, teachers, and counselors better understand and prevent the spread of diseases like AIDS and better understand the nature and extent of harmful and healthy sexual behavior in our country" (p. 55). The intent was to convince those being recruited that the study was legitimate and that it served a socially useful purpose. The researchers hoped that this would promote participation and candor—which apparently it did, since nearly 80% of those who were contacted agreed to participate.

A relatively new and innovative approach to sex surveys involves administering questionnaires over the Internet. This medium allows a multimedia format and is accessible to a vast audience, including those in hard-to-reach places (Stern & Handel, 2001). Additionally, the Internet affords more anonymity than virtually any other survey method, which may facilitate openness and honesty in answering sensitive and personal questions. Although the Internet has been heralded as "an exciting new frontier for the collection of sexuality data" (Mustanski, 2001, p. 299), the anonymity and accessibility of the Internet are not without risk. Some of the limitations of all survey research, such as self-presentation bias and selective forgetting, are still problems for Internet surveys. Internet-based research also presents additional potential problems,

IN YOUR own words

Libby Tyner
Western Michigan

I read all of the surveys on sexuality (*Cosmo, Glamour, Mademoiselle,* etc.). When I was in middle school, I thought they were very accurate and took the content very seriously. However, now that I am more educated in the area of human sexuality, I read the surveys for entertainment purposes, not so much for informative reasons.

Do Men Lie More about Their Sex Lives?

If there is one consistent finding across all sex surveys, it is that heterosexual men report having more sexual partners in their lifetime than heterosexual women do. This finding has been observed in surveys of adolescents and college students, and in surveys from such diverse countries as the United States (Laumann et al., 1994), France (Spira et al., 1993), Norway (Sundet, Kvalem, Magnus, & Bakketeig, 1988), and Great Britain (Wellings, Field, Johnson, & Wadsworth, 1994). Statistically, this finding is troubling (Reiss, 1995). Shouldn't men and women drawn from the same sample have the same average number of sexual partners? How can the observed discrepancy be reconciled? Several possibilities have been suggested, all of which relate to either sampling bias or self-presentation bias (Baumeister & Tice, 2001).

One possible sampling bias is that men in the sex surveys were having sex with women who were not included in surveys, possibly younger women or women living outside of the country where the survey was conducted. Another possibility is that a small number of women were having sex with a large number of men. Finally, since there are more women than men in some populations, including the U.S. population, there may be fewer prospective partners for women and, hence, a lower average number of lifetime sexual partners. Several researchers have analyzed these potential sampling biases statistically. They all concluded that none of the proposed sampling biases can explain the gender discrepancy in reported numbers of lifetime sexual partners (Einon, 1994; Wiederman, 1997).

Can self-presentation bias account for this finding? Several researchers have proposed that men and women may differ in their definitions of "sexual partner." Men may define a sexual partner on the basis of any shared sexual contact, whereas women may restrict their definition to partners with whom they had vaginal intercourse. This seems unlikely, however, since large-scale sex surveys employ very precise definitions of who qualifies as a sexual partner. Alternatively, because of the cultural double standard, women may be reluctant to include in their estimates sexual partners with whom they did not have a long-term relationship. Men, on the other hand, may feel more comfortable including casual partners, or "one-night stands." That is, owing to a cultural script, men may be inclined to overreport, or boast, whereas women may tend to underreport, or minimize, their sexual experiences (Davis & Smith, 1991; Laumann et al., 1994).

One researcher, Michael Wiederman (1997), set out to test the last explanation. In his study, Wiederman found that the majority of men and women do in fact tend to include casual partners as well as committed partners in their estimated lifetime numbers of sexual partners. When questioned, only 6% of men and 7.5% of women later indicated that they had not included casual partners in their estimates. Weiderman also found that the difference in the numbers of men and women in his sample did not fully account for the men's higher reported number of partners. He did find that men were twice as likely as women to admit later that they had been somewhat inaccurate in reporting their lifetime number of sexual partners. Eliminating those men who admitted to inaccuracies from the sample essentially removed the gender discrepancy in number of partners.

The tendency for men to overreport their lifetime sexual partners is not necessarily a conscious deception. More than women, men who have had multiple partners may tend to use "ballpark" figures or to "round up" in estimating numbers of partners (Brown & Sinclair, 1999; Wiederman, 1997). Because of cultural factors, women may be more likely to try to provide precise estimates or even to underreport.

Because men report more sexual partners than women even in such sexually permissive cultures as Finland (where there is presumably less of a double standard about sex), it seems unlikely that self-presentation biases alone can explain the gender discrepancy. Undoubtedly, self-presentation biases do play a role, and this should be considered in conducting any sex research. Procedures that ensure anonymity and privacy should be used. Additionally, questions should be phrased in simple, nonjudgmental terms (Weinhardt, Forsyth, Carey, Jaworski, & Durant, 1998). Perhaps the best solution is to eliminate the cultural influences that lead some men to overestimate their sexual exploits and some women to underestimate theirs.

such as multiple submissions by the same individual and a lack of control over materials delivered over the Internet. A person could fill out a survey many times without being discovered, which would contaminate the results. Researchers have no control over the setting in which participants complete the surveys. Some may access it from

Looking At . . .

. . . Thinking About

A new approach to self-report methods involves administering surveys by computer. Computer-assisted interviewing offers confidentiality and privacy. It has been used to study such sensitive topics as past abuse and risky sexual practices. Would you be more inclined to participate in a sex survey if you could respond via computer?

a noisy, distracting environment; others may answer the questions in the middle of the night when they are half-asleep, and so on. Because the researcher has no control over the setting in Internet-based research, potential differences in mood and attention could introduce measurement error. Additionally, sampling bias could be a problem, since Internet-based research always relies on convenience samples (Mustanski, 2001). Much more research is needed to evaluate the limitations of Internet-based sex surveys.

Conducting National Surveys of Sexual Behavior

By far, the most ambitious application of survey methods is the attempt to obtain accurate information about sexuality for an entire population. National surveys are designed to provide a description of the sexual attitudes, behaviors, and histories of a country's whole population by studying a smaller representative group, or **sample.** There are two general approaches to selecting a survey sample: probability sampling and convenience sampling. In **probability sampling**, participants are recruited in such a way that every single member of the population has the same chance of being selected for the survey. (One problem with random telephone sampling procedures is that people who do not have a phone will never be selected.) Probability sampling is the preferred but less practical of these two approaches. A survey using probability sampling provides the most accurate, or least biased, description of the population under study (Dooley, 1995). As the term implies, **convenience sampling** involves recruiting participants on the basis of their availability, not because they are typical of the population at large (although the researcher usually hopes that they are). Most survey and experimental research relies on convenience samples, such as college students or prison inmates (a captive audience, quite literally).

A potential major problem with convenience sample is **sampling bias,** any systematic error that renders the sample nonrepresentative of the population. A simple example illustrates this problem. Suppose that you want to study the sexual practices of individuals in your hometown (the population under study) by interviewing 200 of the inhabitants (the sample). Imagine that you plant yourself on a street corner and interview the first 200 people to walk by, a sample of convenience. If you unwittingly locate yourself near a district where prostitutes and their customers congregate, you will obtain a disproportionately high number of these participants. In all likelihood, your findings will not be applicable to, or representative of, all inhabitants of your hometown. In this example, even if there is no measurement error (that is, even if all participants answer all your questions with complete accuracy and reliability), your sample is atypical. Therefore, your results will be biased. Unfortunately, it is usually difficult if not impossible to estimate how much sampling bias may have occurred in a survey or an experiment. Researchers can get only an indirect measure of the results' accuracy—either by comparing them to those of similar surveys or by attempting to replicate them with a new survey. The only way to avoid sampling bias is to use probability sampling. In the example, you might divide your hometown into neighborhoods or city blocks and interview a certain number of people chosen at random from each of these blocks. This

SAMPLE
A smaller group that is selected to represent a larger group, or population.

PROBABILITY SAMPLING
A method of recruiting research participants in which each person has the same chance of being selected.

CONVENIENCE SAMPLING
A method of obtaining research participants solely on the basis of their availability.

SAMPLING BIAS
A systematic error in obtaining research participants that renders the sample unrepresentative of the population.

approach would render it unlikely that an atypical group would be overrepresented in your sample.

A form of sampling bias that has been studied extensively by sexologists is **volunteer bias**, which arises from the fact that individuals who volunteer to participate in sex research have unique characteristics that may differentiate them from nonvolunteers in important ways (Strassberg & Lowe, 1995). As a result of volunteer bias, the findings of a survey may not be applicable to the larger population. Several studies have compared sex research volunteers to nonvolunteers, and a number of significant differences have been reported. Overall, volunteers are more likely than nonvolunteers

Alfred Kinsey, shown here with his research team, was a pioneer in sex research surveys. During his lifetime, Kinsey personally interviewed over 7,000 people about their sexual experiences and practices.

- To be males (Catania et al., 1990; Wiederman, 1999; Wolchik, Braver, & Jensen, 1985)
- To be more sexually experienced (Catania et al., 1986; Wiederman, 1999; Wolchik, Spencer, & Lisi, 1983), including experience with unusual sex (Morokoff, 1986)
- To have more positive attitudes about sexuality (Farkas, Sine, & Evans, 1978; Strassberg & Lowe, 1995), including attitudes toward masturbation (Morokoff, 1986) and pornography (Strassberg & Lowe, 1995; Wiederman, 1999; Wolchik et al., 1983)
- To have less sexual anxiety and guilt (Strassberg & Lowe, 1995; Wolchik et al., 1985)
- To have higher self-esteem (Catania et al., 1990; Wiederman, 1999)

The major concern about volunteer bias pertains to representativeness, or the extent to which study results may be generalized to a larger population. Volunteer bias may explain some problems in replicating findings across studies (Strassberg & Lowe, 1995). A prudent sexologist should investigate how much volunteer bias occurred in any study he or she conducted. As we discuss next, concerns over potential sampling biases are at the heart of the controversy over national surveys of sexual behavior.

Kinsey's Surveys

Alfred Kinsey remains one of the best-known sex researchers, despite the fact that he died almost 50 years ago. Kinsey earned his reputation from two landmark surveys of sexual behavior in the United States. His survey findings were reported in books on male sexuality (Kinsey, Pomeroy, & Martin, 1948) and female sexuality (Kinsey, Pomeroy, Martin, & Gebhard, 1953). Both became best-sellers almost overnight. Kinsey had planned to complete 100,000 interviews, but he died long before reaching this ambitious goal. However, by 1953, he had personally interviewed over 7,000 people, an average of approximately 1,000 a year!

Kinsey firmly believed that only a face-to-face interview provided accurate information. He believed that only when facing a participant could a researcher detect self-presentation bias and omissions and try to address them (Pomeroy, Flax, & Wheeler, 1982). The Kinsey interview included multiple checks for accuracy and consistency, and the speed at which questions were asked and the amount of detail required rendered it difficult for respondents to lie with consistency (Bullough, 1998). The number of questions ranged from 350 to 521, depending on the amount and type of sexual experience

VOLUNTEER BIAS
A form of sampling bias that occurs when people who volunteer for a study are shown to differ systematically from people who do not volunteer for the study; a common concern in sex research.

reported by a participant. The interview required an average of 90 minutes. In the end, Kinsey's interview style and system perhaps constituted his major contribution to sexology.

Kinsey relied on convenience sampling, using a method known as the **snowball technique.** Essentially, this technique consists of approaching an organization or a social group (such as a prison, college fraternity, or church congregation) and attempting to convince every member of the group to participate. Kinsey firmly believed that this strategy was more feasible and effective than random (probability) sampling. However, fewer than 30% of his participants were actually recruited in this manner. Unfortunately, because exact records were not kept, we do not know what percentage of all potential participants in Kinsey's surveys refused altogether. Thus, it is not possible to estimate the degree to which volunteer bias may have distorted his results.

Kinsey's survey of males included 5,300 individuals, all of whom were Caucasian and most of whom were married. The majority of participants were young to middle-aged adults residing in urban areas. Fewer than 100 participants were over 40 years of age. Participants were recruited from such diverse settings as universities, churches, professional organizations, psychiatric hospitals, and even prisons. The inclusion in the survey of males in such institutions as college dormitories and prisons has led some to question the representativeness of the sample (Gebhard & Johnson, 1979). Persons of lower socioeconomic status were underrepresented.

Kinsey's survey of females included 5,940 white, nonincarcerated females (Kinsey et al., 1953). A group of 915 women who had served criminal sentences and a group of 934 "non-white" women were excluded from the study because these groups were too small or too atypical. Participants in the final female sample ranged in age from 2 to 90, with the majority between 16 and 50.

As illustrated in Figure 2.1, several regions of the United States appear to have been oversampled relative to other areas. The Northeast was highly represented, whereas the Southwest was relatively undersampled. Kinsey and colleagues (1953) admitted that their survey findings for women were least likely to apply to those over 50, those with less education, those who had been married more than once, those of Catholic or Jewish faith, and those in rural areas, among others. African Americans were also excluded from the Kinsey reports. These limitations in the representativeness of the samples were in fact the bases of the major criticisms of Kinsey's surveys (Cochran, Mosteller, & Tukey, 1953; Lauman et al., 1994). Critics expressed two major concerns: The sample was not random, and the study relied completely on volunteers (Bullough, 1998). Thus, two potential problems exist: sampling bias and volunteer bias. Kinsey stubbornly defended his method to the end, insisting that more random methods of selecting participants were neither feasible nor warranted (Kinsey et al., 1953). Other criticisms were also leveled at Kinsey, many of them personal in nature (Bullough, 1994; Reisman & Eichel, 1990; Simon, 1992), but none as damaging as the concern over representativeness. Nevertheless, Kinsey's findings remain historically important as pioneering survey research in sexuality. His surveys revealed that this type of research was not only feasible but worthwhile (Bullough, 1998).

2.4 **on the web**

The influence of Alfred Kinsey's work cannot be overstated. His research culminated in the establishment of the Kinsey Institute at Indiana University, which is still conducting research today. Visit the Kinsey Institute's Web site at **www.ablongman.com/mcanulty2e** and review the key findings of Kinsey's landmark surveys.

Which of the findings are most surprising? Which still seem to be applicable today?

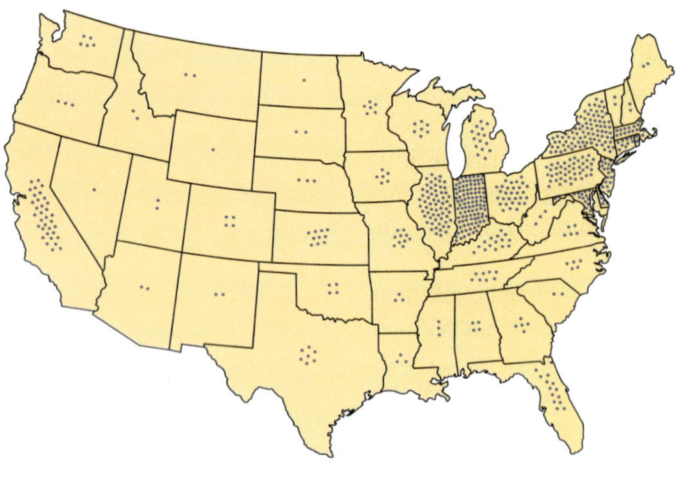

Figure 2.1 Geographic Sources: Total Female and Male Sample

The National Health and Social Life Survey

The National Health and Social Life Survey (NHSLS) was completed in 1994 by Edward Laumann, John Gagnon, Robert Michael, and Stuart Michaels under the auspices of the University of Chicago. Described as the "most comprehensive nationally representative study of sexuality" (Reiss, 1995), this survey included questions about a broader range of sexual experiences than are covered by most other major sex surveys.

The NHSLS involved interviews of 3,432 men and women between the ages of 18 and 59. The probability sample was drawn from English-speaking households. Therefore, people who did not live in households (such as those in college dormitories, military or correctional institutions, or shelters) and those who did not speak English fluently were excluded. The authors estimated that 138 million people, or 95% of the total U.S. population between 18 and 59 years of age, were eligible for sampling; therefore, this is the population that the survey was intended to represent. Perhaps the most impressive aspect of the NHSLS was the response rate: 79% of those recruited elected to participate. This high rate was achieved by sending an initial letter to establish credibility, multiple reminders via mail and telephone, and cash incentives for participation. The survey had two components, a face-to-face interview and a self-administered questionnaire for the more "sensitive" questions (such as whether respondents had ever paid for sex or experienced group sex). After completing the questionnaire, participants returned it in a "privacy envelope"; ensuring participants' privacy in this way was an effort to promote candor. The interview and questionnaire required approximately 90 minutes to complete.

From left to right: Stuart Michaels, John Gagnon, Robert Michael, and Edward Laumann, the authors of one of the most recent national sexual behavior surveys, involving over 3,000 respondents. Although the project was carried out rigorously, it suffers from the limitations of all survey methods. Respondents often underreport, or minimize, their experience of socially sensitive sexual behaviors.

Do you think a "privacy envelope" would make a difference to you? Think about that as you read Reflect on This: Would You Volunteer for Sex Research?

Despite the impressive nature of the NHSLS, it does have some limitations. As the authors themselves concluded (Laumann et al., 1994, p. 284), the reported rates of "socially stigmatized sexual behaviors and feelings, whether [. . .] masturbation, homosexual relations, anal sex, or extramarital affairs, are no doubt lower-bound [minimal] estimates." In other words, respondents probably underreported their experiences of such sexual behaviors. Finally, the results are potentially representative of only U.S. residents who speak English and reside in a household.

Other Sex Surveys

Several other sex surveys followed Kinsey's. Although each survey was described by its authors as a major contribution, most suffered from serious methodological problems. Several surveys of magazine readers have been conducted, often with extremely impressive sample sizes. For instance, the *Redbook* survey (Tavris & Sadd, 1987) boasted over 100,000 respondents! The *Psychology Today* survey (Athanasiou, Shaver, & Tavris, 1970) had 20,000 respondents. However, these respondents represented fewer than 10% of the readership of these magazines. Thus, the findings may not even be representative of the larger readership, let alone of the whole U.S. population. For example, the majority of readers of *Redbook* are women. Similarly, when the Playboy Foundation randomly selected over 2,000 people from the telephone directories of several large cities (Hunt, 1974), only individuals with telephones and listed numbers were contacted. More troublesome is the fact that 80% of those contacted refused to participate.

The reports by Shere Hite (1976, 1979, 1981, 1987) received a great deal of media attention when they were released. Hite obtained her respondents through social

SNOWBALL TECHNIQUE
A sampling method used by Kinsey that involves approaching a group or organization and trying to recruit the participation of every member.

reflect ON THIS

Would You Volunteer for Sex Research?

A recurring criticism of sex research is that the results may not be representative of the population at large. Volunteer bias is a potential problem if it can be shown that sex research volunteers are atypical (Catania et al., 1990). If volunteers are found to be more permissive about sexuality, for example, this could result in overestimates of sexual behaviors, whereas having participants who are unusually inhibited about sexuality may lead to underestimates. Finding individuals willing to participate in sex research studies, however, can present many obstacles.

Imagine that you were asked to participate in a study on sexuality. What would be your reaction? If you are like many people, you would request additional information about the nature and purpose of the study. One common concern is the legitimacy of the study: Is it a genuine study or a practical joke? What is the purpose of the study? Will it provide useful information, either to participants or to society at large? Recognizing these potential concerns, sexologists are very careful about how they present a study to prospective participants. Laumann and colleagues (1994), for instance, repeatedly stressed their professional affiliations in their contacts with prospective participants. Their initial contact letter was signed by Dr. Robert Michael, dean of the Irving B. Harris Graduate School of Public Health Policy Studies of the University of Chicago, also one of the investigators. Additionally, a hotline to the research office of the University of Chicago was established so that potential participants could easily broach any concerns they had. Finally, the original contact letter explained the purpose of the study: to understand and prevent diseases like AIDS and, more broadly, to understand sexuality.

Having accepted the legitimacy and value of the study, you might wish to know exactly what you would be asked to do. Assess your personal degree of comfort with each of the following possible research situations:

1. You will be asked to fill out several anonymous questionnaires concerning your personal sexual attitudes and experiences.
2. You will undergo a 30-minute personal interview, during which the researcher will ask you a standard set of questions about your sexual attitudes and experiences. (Imagine and rate two variants, one with a same-sex interviewer and one with an opposite-sex interviewer.)
3. You will be asked to sit in a room and watch a sexually explicit film (an X-rated, or "hard-core," pornographic film). Afterwards, you will complete a series of questionnaires about your reactions to the film.
4. Measurement equipment will be attached to your genitals to gauge your degree of arousal while watching a sexually explicit film.
5. You will be asked to come to a laboratory for a study on orgasms, conducted according to one of these scenarios:
   a. Males will attach a vibrating device to the penis and experience a vibrator assisted orgasm (see Rowland & Slob, 1992).
   b. Participants will consume a specified quantity of alcohol prior to masturbating to orgasm in the laboratory (see Malatesta, Pollack, Crotty, & Peacock, 1982; Malatesta, Pollack, Wilbanks, & Adams, 1979).
   c. Females will be manually stimulated to orgasm by either a male or female experimenter (see Alzate & Londono, 1987).

After evaluating your personal degree of comfort with the various situations, consider several consistent findings that have emerged from studies on this topic: First, the more intrusive the experimental situation, as in scenarios 4 and 5, the less likely a person is to volunteer for participation. Individuals who do volunteer for invasive studies of sexuality tend to have more sexual experience, less sexual guilt, fewer sexual inhibitions, and more exposure to sexually explicit materials (see Catania et al., 1990, for a review). For noninvasive situations, as in scenarios 1 through 3, there are fewer differences between volunteers and nonvolunteers, although some studies found volunteers to have more positive sexual attitudes and experiences.

Although some, perhaps many, individuals would be reluctant to participate in a study like that in scenario 5c, involving the experimenter's manual stimulation of their genitals, Alzate and Londono (1987) found that nearly 80% of their participants rated the experience as positive, and nearly 92% stated that they would be willing to participate in a similar experiment in the future. Asked to give their reasons for participating, most (88%) of the participants said that they wished to contribute to the scientific study of female sexuality; two-thirds reported an interest in better understanding their own sexuality; and one-fourth volunteered out of curiosity. Was volunteer bias a factor in this study? Unfortunately, the authors did not report the number of women who refused to participate after learning the nature of the study.

organizations, magazines, and newsletters and used an anonymous essay-type questionnaire. Her first survey was distributed to 100,000 women, of which 3,000 responded, a response rate of 3%. Her survey of men produced results from 8,000 men, with a response rate of 6%. Her final survey of women yielded a 4.5% response rate, or 4,500 out of 100,000 contacted. Thus, 94–97% of people contacted refused to complete the surveys.

More recently, the Janus report (Janus & Janus, 1993) was touted as a comprehensive survey of U.S. sexual attitudes and practices. The study included 2,765 individuals and had a response rate of 61%. Although little information on the sampling method was provided, apparently convenience sampling was used (Davis, 1993). The Janus report has been criticized for not specifying the sampling method and for apparently overestimating the sexual behaviors it reported (Greely, 1994). The report's estimates are sometimes 50–100% higher than those obtained with probability samples. For example, Janus and Janus found that 72% of men and 58% of women have had 10 or more partners in their lifetime. Other surveys report more modest percentages: 35% for men and 15% for women (Davis & Smith, 1991). In the NHSLS, 33% of men and 9% of women reported having had more than 10 partners since age 18. Failures to replicate the Janus findings cast doubt on their accuracy (Baumeister & Tice, 2001).

The National Longitudinal Survey of Adolescent Health, known as Add Health, is a large-scale study of teenagers' health behaviors, including sexual practices. Launched in 1994, the original sample included over 90,000 students from grades 7 through 12 who completed questionnaires at school. From that group, a sample of nearly 12,000 teens were interviewed at home. Additionally, 18,000 parents completed questionnaires about their teenagers. Most of the teens were re-interviewed in 1996 and again in 2000. Add Health is a unique survey of adolescent health behaviors that is unprecedented in size and magnitude (Bearman, Jones, & Udry, 1997). The researchers went to great lengths to ensure that teenage members of minority groups were represented. Another survey of adolescent health, the Youth Risk Behavior Surveillance System (Grunbaum et al., 2002), surveyed a nationally representative sample of over 13,000 students in grades 9 to 12. This national survey has been conducted in alternate years since 1991 by the Centers for Disease Control and Prevention (CDC). Despite sharing the limitations of all surveys, these studies do provide important estimates of adolescent sexual behavior. The Youth Risk Behavior Surveillance System, for example, found that 46% of students in the 9th through 12th grades had had sexual intercourse and that almost 7% had initiated intercourse before age 13. We will revisit these findings as we explore adolescent sexual behavior.

did YOU know?

According to the Youth Risk Behavior Surveillance System survey (CDC, 2002d), 46% of high school students have had sexual intercourse, but fewer than half of them reported using a condom during their last sexual encounter.

Administering sex surveys has become a popular enterprise. You have only to examine recent issues of popular magazines to discover self-administered surveys designed to help readers learn about their sexuality. The availability and popularity of sex surveys reveal that they are more socially acceptable now than they were prior to Kinsey's pioneering work and that learning about the sex lives of others, perhaps as a way of evaluating one's own sexuality by way of comparison, has a certain fascination. Remember, however, that although it is quite simple to devise a questionnaire for large-scale dissemination, conducting a scientifically sound survey is a major undertaking. When reading about the findings of the latest sex survey, you should maintain a healthy skepticism while searching for information about the survey's sampling method, refusal rates, and other potential sources of measurement error.

ISSUES AND CONTROVERSIES IN SEXOLOGY

Researchers adhere to guidelines designed to foster objectivity and to protect research participants. Ethical guidelines delineate the proper steps for carrying out research in a manner that is unbiased and that ensures the welfare of participants. Ethical guidelines for conducting research are based on relevant laws, professional principles, and the individual researcher's own conscience. In this section, we review ethical principles in science and address the question of whether science is truly value-free. Although scientists pride themselves on their commitment to objectivity, they also generally recognize that they are imperfect. No scientist is completely free from personal biases, and all researchers operate in a cultural context. Various components of a culture, such as the political climate, may exert some influence on research practices.

2.5 on the web

The Tuskegee Syphilis Experiment remains one of the darkest pages in the annals of medical research in the United States. You can find links to sites that offer detailed descriptions of this tragic experiment at **www.ablongman.com/mcanulty2e.**

What are your reactions to this kind of deception? What are your arguments against such deception in scientific experiments?

Ethics in Sex Research

From 1932 to 1972, the United States Public Health Service conducted the Tuskegee Syphilis Study in Alabama. The study consisted of withholding medical treatment from 412 African American men afflicted with syphilis, a potentially fatal sexually transmissible infection (syphilis and other sexually transmissible infections are discussed in Chapter 14). The stated goal of the study was to discover the effects of the disease in its final stages. The study was a disaster for all of the agencies involved when the press exposed the details. (An out-of-court settlement of a lawsuit filed once the study was reported produced $37,500 for each survivor.) Most disturbing was the fact that the people who planned and carried out the study were willing to allow the participants to suffer and even die. This experiment illustrates several unethical, or unacceptable, practices: Participants and their partners were placed at great risk of serious illness and death; none of the participants were informed of the nature of the experiment; and participants could in no way be considered "volunteers."

Ethics refers to right and wrong actions in conducting research. Science offers researchers powerful tools, but scientists must guard against misusing these tools. Researchers' major area of ethical concern is the protection of research participants. Scientists are committed to searching for facts and ultimately to contributing to the welfare of society. However, scientists must also respect the dignity and well-being of those who participate in research. After all, scientists are indebted to the individuals who volunteer to participate in research, thereby placing their trust in the researchers. Researchers have an ethical obligation to do the following:

- Protect research participants from physical and psychological harm
- Ensure the anonymity or confidentiality of participants, by not allowing disclosure of personal information they provide
- Obtain **informed consent** from participants by fully describing the nature of the study to them and ensuring that their participation is completely voluntary

INFORMED CONSENT
Consent given by research participants who are fully informed of the nature of a study and whose participation is completely voluntary; ethical principles require that participants give informed consent before participating in a study.

DEBRIEFING
Informing participants in a scientific study of any deception used and its purpose once they have fulfilled their part in the study; ethical principles require that participants be debriefed at the conclusion of a study.

In addition, when a study requires an element of deception, such as withholding information about the true goals of the experiment, participants must undergo **debriefing**—that is, they must be informed of the deception and its purpose once they have completed their role in the study.

Although the majority of studies on sexuality do not raise concerns about ethical conduct, some have been criticized. For example, Laud Humphreys's (1970) study of anonymous sexual activity in public restrooms raised some ethical questions. Many researchers find the observation of anonymous sexual activity ethically objectionable. Also, although many of the individuals he observed knew that Humphreys was conducting an observational study, others probably did not know. Thus, it is likely that not all "participants" truly consented to participate. Furthermore, Humphreys was observing activity that would be considered criminal in many locations. In Humphreys's defense, there were few other ways to investigate the topic, other than possibly interviewing practitioners. However, how would one recruit such participants?

In order to safeguard participants, professional organizations have developed sets of ethical guidelines to be used in conducting research. The American Psychological Association originally offered its guidelines in 1972 (a sampling from its more recently updated guidelines is given in Table 2.3, on page 60) and has established an ethics committee to review complaints. Medical organizations, such as the American Medical Association, have issued ethical guidelines for medical research. Congress has passed laws, including the 1974 National Research Act, to prevent harmful research practices. Additionally, all agencies and organizations (including colleges and universities) have institutional review boards that serve as internal watchdogs to protect research participants. All university studies that involve human participants or animals must be approved and overseen by such boards.

Values in Science

Historically, scientists took pride in viewing their work as objective, neutral, and value-free. In other words, scientists described their empirical approach as free from personal biases. Such a view was generally accepted until it was challenged by several writers. Thomas Kuhn (1970) argued persuasively that even the scientific method rests on some assumptions or beliefs. Researchers' personal beliefs influence what they choose to study and may affect their interpretation of findings. According to Reiss (1993), it is impossible to be completely value-free; the most a scientist can do is to strive to be "value-aware" (p. 7). To illustrate his point, Reiss listed three assumptions, or personal values, that influenced his recommendations in a study of sexually transmissible infections (Reiss & Leik, 1989):

> 1) sexuality in all its freely chosen forms can and usually is pleasurable and good; 2) people can and should learn to avoid, for themselves and their partners, the unwanted outcomes of sexuality such as disease, pregnancy, and psychological distress; 3) the basis for judging sexual morality should be the amount of honesty, equality, and responsibility in a relationship and not the number of such relationships a person has had. (p. 7)

Based on these assumptions and on the results of their study, Reiss and Leik (1989) recommended that to reduce risks of infection, people use condoms with all partners rather than reduce the number of partners. Other researchers with different values were critical and favored reducing the number of partners as the only safe strategy (Reiss, 1993). Thus, when considering the same results, individuals with different values may make different interpretations and recommendations.

Reiss's (1993) points are highly relevant to the study of human sexuality. Topics such as homosexuality and extramarital sex are controversial to some individuals. To maintain a degree of objectivity and credibility, scientists must be aware of their personal assumptions and values. Scientists who make their assumptions clear will help others evaluate the objectivity of their reported results. As consumers of science, our awareness of our own values and biases may help us avoid jumping to conclusions and may encourage us to consider alternative views. Clearly, both scientists and consumers of science must strive for objectivity if science is to be meaningful and useful.

Politics and Sex Research

The topics of study in sexology have often been viewed as taboo, reprehensible, or, at the very least, private. As a consequence, sex researchers have commonly been at the center of social and political controversy. For example, despite the significance of his work, Alfred Kinsey was subjected to criticism, harassment, and scrutiny. One congressman's worry that Kinsey's sex research would "pave the way for a Communist

TABLE 2.3	Excerpts from the APA Ethical Guidelines
Principle B Fidelity and Responsibility	. . . Psychologists uphold professional standards of conduct, clarify their professional roles and obligations, accept appropriate responsibility for their behavior, and seek to manage conflicts of interest that could lead to exploitation or harm. Psychologists consult with, refer to, or cooperate with other professionals and institutions to the extent needed to serve the best interests of those with whom they work. . . .
3.10 Informed Consent	(a) When psychologists conduct research or provide assessment, therapy, counseling, or consulting services in person or via electronic transmission or other forms of communication, they obtain the informed consent of the individual or individuals using language that is reasonably understandable to that person or persons except when conducting such activities without consent is mandated by law or governmental regulation or as otherwise provided in this Ethics Code. (b) For persons who are legally incapable of giving informed consent, psychologists nevertheless (1) provide an appropriate explanation, (2) seek the individual's assent, (3) consider such persons' preferences and best interests, and (4) obtain appropriate permission from a legally authorized person, if such substitute consent is permitted or required by law. When consent by a legally authorized person is not permitted or required by law, psychologists take reasonable steps to protect the individual's rights and welfare. . . . (d) Psychologists appropriately document written or oral consent, permission, and assent.
8.02 Informed Consent to Research	(a) When obtaining informed consent as required in Standard 3.10, Informed Consent, psychologists inform participants about (1) the purpose of the research, expected duration, and procedures; (2) their right to decline to participate and to withdraw from the research once participation has begun; (3) the foreseeable consequences of declining or withdrawing; (4) reasonably foreseeable factors that may be expected to influence their willingness to participate such as potential risks, discomfort, or adverse effects; (5) any prospective research benefits; (6) limits of confidentiality; (7) incentives for participation; and (8) whom to contact for questions about the research and research participants' rights. They provide opportunity for the prospective participants to ask questions and receive answers. (b) Psychologists conducting intervention research involving the use of experimental treatments clarify to participants at the outset of the research (1) the experimental nature of the treatment; (2) the services that will or will not be available to the control group(s), if appropriate; (3) the means by which assignment to treatment and control groups will be made; (4) available treatment alternatives if an individual does not wish to participate in the research or wishes to withdraw once a study has begun; and (5) compensation for or monetary costs of participating including, if appropriate, whether reimbursement from the participant or a third-party payor will be sought.
8.05 Dispensing with Informed Consent for Research	Psychologists may dispense with informed consent only (1) where research would not reasonably be assumed to create distress or harm and involves (a) the study of normal educational practices, curricula, or classroom management methods conducted in educational settings; (b) only anonymous questionnaires, naturalistic observations, or archival research for which disclosure of responses would not place participants at risk of criminal or civil liability or damage their financial standing, employability, or reputation, and confidentiality is protected; or (c) the study of factors related to job or organization effectiveness conducted in organizational settings for which there is no risk to participants' employability, and confidentiality is protected or (2) where otherwise permitted by law or federal or institutional regulations.
8.07 Deception in Research	(a) Psychologists do not conduct a study involving deception unless they have determined that the use of deceptive techniques is justified by the study's significant prospective scientific, educational, or applied value and that effective nondeceptive alternative procedures are not feasible. (b) Psychologists do not deceive prospective participants about research that is reasonably expected to cause physical pain or severe emotional distress. (c) Psychologists explain any deception that is an integral feature of the design and conduct of an experiment to participants as early as is feasible, preferably at the conclusion of their participation, but no later than at the conclusion of the data collection, and permit participants to withdraw their data.
8.08 Debriefing	(a) Psychologists provide a prompt opportunity for participants to obtain appropriate information about the nature, results, and conclusions of the research, and they take reasonable steps to correct any misconceptions that participants may have of which the psychologists are aware. (b) If scientific or humane values justify delaying or withholding this information, psychologists take reasonable measures to reduce the risk of harm. (c) When psychologists become aware that research procedures have harmed a participant, they take reasonable steps to minimize the harm.

takeover of the United States" (Reinisch & Beasley, 1990, p. xviii) led to an investigation of Kinsey and his work by the government in 1954. The Rockefeller Foundation, the major source of funding for Kinsey's surveys, withdrew its support when Congress elected to investigate all of Kinsey's financial backers (Bullough, 1994). William Masters had intended to engage in sex research as soon as he completed medical school. However, his medical school mentor, George W. Corner, advised him first to establish a reputation as a researcher in a more legitimate field, to obtain the sponsorship of a medical school, and to wait until he was at least 40 years old before embarking on sex research (Bullough, 1994). Masters followed most of this advice in an effort to establish credibility and respectability. Other researchers have had their research materials confiscated by law enforcement agencies and have been threatened with arrest and imprisonment (Sonenschein, 1987).

More recently, the Secretary of Health and Human Services and Congress, under pressure from some political and religious figures, canceled a major research project on adolescent sexual behavior. The project had already been approved and funded by the National Institutes of Health (Udry, 1993). However, two politicians orchestrated an attack on the legitimacy of the study. Essentially, they charged that such a project was intended to erode traditional sexual values and morality. Similarly, funding for the original NHSLS survey was eliminated. That survey was to involve 10,000–20,000 participants. However, when funding was withdrawn, the project directors sought financial support from private foundations and had to settle for a much smaller budget and, consequently, the reduced sample size of 3,432 participants.

Some political and religious leaders have vehemently opposed all sex research out of concern that it may promote sexual behavior they find objectionable. Critics fear that reporting the national frequency of certain sexual acts may "sway public attitudes in order to liberalize opinions and laws regarding homosexuality, pedophilia, anal and oral sex, sex education, teenage pregnancy and all down the line" (*Congressional Record,* September 12, 1991, pp. S12861–S12862). Curiously, the same line of reasoning has not been applied to studies of substance abuse and crime. If national studies of sexual behaviors serve to promote those behaviors, wouldn't studies of adolescent drug abuse and violent crime encourage increased acceptance and tolerance of these illegal acts? Yet, there have apparently been no governmental interventions concerning research on those topics. Although sexuality remains a very sensitive topic in U.S. society, the position of this book is that we stand to lose more by knowing too little than by knowing too much. Only through the application of the scientific method can we hope to understand and prevent such problems as sexually transmissible infections (including HIV), sexual aggression, and unwanted pregnancy.

HEALTHY DECISION MAKING

The general public is seemingly bombarded with information on how to improve their sex lives. The news media disseminate recent findings on sex. Magazine articles boast the latest insights on how to be a better lover. Medications to improve sexual functioning are mass-marketed. Unfortunately, much of the information being spread by these diverse sources is incomplete or even inconsistent. How can you decide whether such information is valid or useful? By answering the following questions, you will be in a better position to evaluate the applicability of any information to your personal decision-making.

1. *What is the source of the information?* The soundest sex research findings are disseminated in peer-reviewed professional journals (some of which are listed in Table 2.1 on page 40). The peer review process is a form of rigorous quality assurance that requires each article submitted for publication to be carefully reviewed by other

experts on the topic, usually at least three of them. Popular books and magazines do not typically use a peer-review process.

2. *Who participated in the study?* Popular publications frequently publish reader surveys on a variety of sexual topics. But how representative are these findings? The question of representativeness of findings should come to mind any time a study relies on a small or narrow sample, such as magazine readers or college students.
3. *How was the information obtained?* Closed questions, such as those in multiple-choice format, are simpler to answer but yield less information than open-ended or short-answer questions.
4. *What research design was employed?* Only through a controlled experiment can cause-and-effect relationships be detected. Evaluating the quality of an experiment requires knowing which variables were investigated, how they were measured, and the extent to which they changed as a result of the experimental manipulation.
5. *Are the findings reliable?* In other words, have the reported findings been replicated independently? The more times a finding is independently replicated, or confirmed, the more likely it is to be valid.

The next time you hear or read about some new research findings, try to apply each of these questions to them. The answers should help you determine whether the findings are valid and, therefore, whether they might be relevant and useful to you.

summary

THE SCIENTIFIC APPROACH

- As a process of inquiry, science relies on empiricism, the practice of using direct observation and measurement to obtain answers to research questions.
- Sexology is the discipline devoted to the scientific study of sexuality. It relies on the scientific method of inquiry.

GOALS OF SCIENTIFIC RESEARCH

- The purposes of scientific research are description, explanation, prediction, and control of behavior.

MEASUREMENT IN SCIENCE

- Sex research employs three types of measures: self-reports, behavioral measures, and medical/physiological measures. Because they are easiest and most feasible to obtain and avoid many legal or ethical problems, self-report measures in various formats are used most extensively.

RESEARCH DESIGNS IN SCIENCE

- The major sex research methods are controlled experiments, case studies, observational methods, and survey methods. Each method offers unique features but also suffers from distinctive problems. Experimentation is the preferred method for studying cause-and-effect relationships. Correlational designs are employed to measure the extent to which two or more variables change together, or are correlated. Observational methods do not rely on participants' self-reports, but they are impractical. Surveys remain popular as methods of studying sexual attitudes and behaviors. Surveys are susceptible to measurement errors arising from self-presentation bias and memory distortion. For some research questions, however, surveys are the only feasible method. Case studies yield a wealth of information but are uncontrolled, and the information is not always generalizable.
- National surveys of sexual behavior are ambitious attempts to describe the sexual behavior of the population of an entire country. Probability sampling is the preferred way of selecting a sample. A major limitation of other kinds of samples, such as convenience samples, is sampling bias. Research shows that sex research volunteers differ in several ways from people who decline to participate.
- Alfred Kinsey's pioneering surveys of sexual behavior set the stage for later, improved surveys, including the National Health and Social Life Survey, published in 1994. Other popular sex surveys, such as the Hite Reports, were based on less than impressive response rates.

ISSUES AND CONTROVERSIES IN SEXOLOGY

- Scientists are ethically bound to protect research participants. All researchers are expected to adhere to specific guidelines in conducting research.
- Although science is touted as a value-free and objective approach to seeking answers to questions, in reality, even scientists have personal biases. The only way for scientists and consumers to minimize the impact of their personal biases is to be aware of their personal values.
- Sex research remains controversial because sex is still a sensitive topic in U.S. society. The controversy is evident in many contexts and has led to governmental intervention and cancellation of research or loss of funding.

CHAPTER 3

Sexual and Reproductive Anatomy

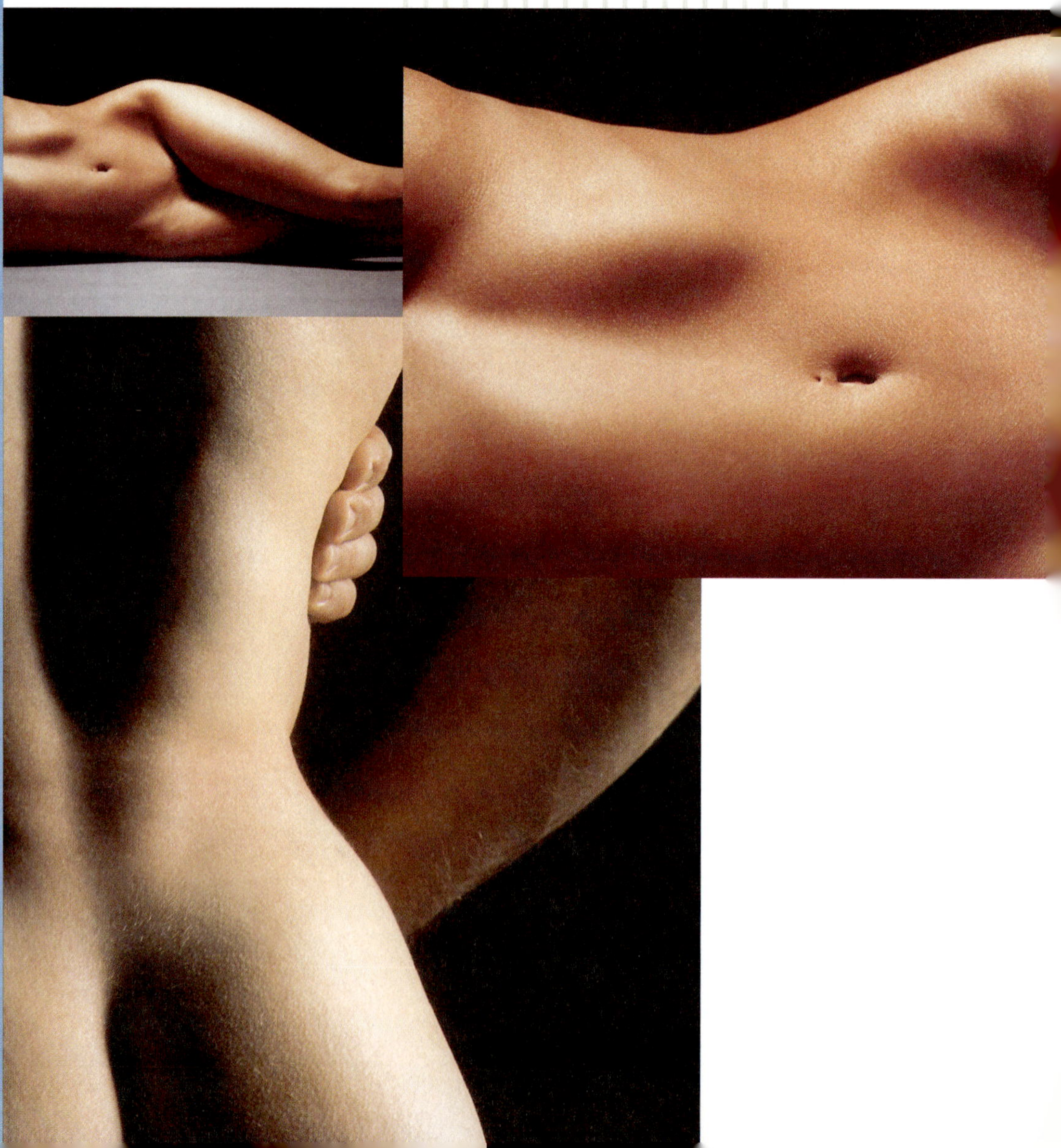

When someone first said to me two years ago, "You can feel the end of your own cervix with your finger," I was interested but flustered. I had hardly ever put my finger in my vagina at all and felt squeamish about touching myself there, in that place reserved for lovers and doctors. It took me two months to get up my nerve to try it, and then one afternoon, pretty nervously, I squatted down in the bathroom and put my finger in deep, back into my vagina. There it was, feeling slippery and rounded, with an indentation at the center through which, I realized, my menstrual flow came. It was both very exciting and beautifully ordinary at the same time. Last week I bought a plastic speculum so I could look at my cervix. Will it take as long this time?

I was interested but flustered.

The Boston Women's Health Book Collective, *The New Our Bodies, Ourselves* (1992, p. 241)

The anatomical structures collectively known as reproductive organs, or sex organs, interact in an extraordinary manner to produce intense pleasure and new life. Understanding what these organs are and what they do—and being comfortable talking about them—can benefit you tremendously, for knowledge is the key to sexual health, both psychological and physical. Familiarity with your sex organs can make you more comfortable with yourself as a sexual being and help you (and your partner) derive maximum enjoyment and satisfaction from your sexual experiences. In addition, understanding your sexual anatomy and how it works can guide you in protecting your reproductive health and knowing when you need medical care. As you read, consider how the anatomical structures work together to accomplish reproductive functions as well as to provide sexual pleasure. The functions of the major organs are summarized in Table 3.1 on page 66.

FEMALE SEXUAL AND REPRODUCTIVE ANATOMY

The female sexual anatomy includes both external and internal genitalia. Although a female's external genitals are not as prominent as a male's are, the external structures of the female genitals serve critical functions in reproduction, provide protection for the internal structures, and contribute to a woman's pleasure during sexual stimulation.

The External Genital Structures

All of the external genital structures in the female are collectively referred to as the **vulva**, or *vulval area.* It is common to hear people refer to this area as the vagina. (We hear parents telling their little girls this all the time!) However, the vagina is an internal organ; only the opening to the vagina is part of the external genitals. The external genitals are highly innervated—richly supplied with nerves—and are responsive to touch, which allows them to play an important role in sexual arousal. Refer to Figure 3.1 on page 67 as you read to note the appearance and location of each structure.

VULVA
All of the external female genital structures; the vulval area.

TABLE 3.1 Functions of the Major Sexual Organs

FEMALE ORGANS	FUNCTION	MALE ORGANS	FUNCTION
Cervical os	Passage to and from uterus	Cowper's gland	Production of discharge to neutralize acidity of male urethra to protect sperm
Clitoral hood	Stimulation and protection of clitoris	Ejaculatory duct	Allows passage of sperm and seminal fluid into the vas deferens to form semen
Fallopian tube	Passage for ovum from ovary to uterus, site of conception	Foreskin	Possible stimulation and protection of glans penis
Clitoris	Sexual stimulation and arousal	Corpora cavernosa	Erection of penis
Corpora cavernosa	Erection of clitoris	Corpus spongiosum	Erection of penis
Glans of clitoris	Sexual stimulation and arousal	Glans of penis	Sexual stimulation and arousal
Labia majora	Protection of vulva, sexual stimulation	Penis	Sexual stimulation, intercourse, and urination
Labia minora	Protection of vaginal opening, sexual stimulation	Perineum	Sexual stimulation
Mons veneris (mons pubis)	Sexual stimulation	Prostate gland	Production of semen
Ovaries	Production of ova	Scrotum	Holds testes, protects and regulates their temperature
Perineum	Sexual stimulation	Shaft of penis	Sexual stimulation
Uterus	Fetal development	Testes	Sperm production and storage
Vagina	Sexual intercourse, menstruation, vaginal delivery		

MONS VENERIS
The mound of fatty tissue covering the female's pubic bone; also called the *mons pubis.*

LABIA MAJORA
Two folds of fleshy tissue extending from the mons veneris to below the vaginal opening; also called the *outer lips.*

LABIA MINORA
Two relatively small, hairless folds of tissue located within the labia majora; also called the *inner lips.*

VESTIBULE
Area between the labia minora where the urethral and vaginal openings are located.

Mons Veneris

The **mons veneris**, also called the *mons pubis,* is a mound of fatty tissue covering the female's pubic bone. After puberty, the mons is covered with hair, which varies from sparse to dense across individuals.

Labia Majora and Labia Minora

The **labia majora**, also called the *outer lips,* are two folds of fleshy tissue extending from the mons veneris to below the vaginal opening. The labia majora are covered with pubic hair after puberty. When a female is unaroused, these structures protect the vaginal and urethral openings by closing over them. When she becomes sexually aroused, these structures engorge with blood, which causes them to open out so that the vaginal and urethral openings are exposed. After childbirth, even when a woman is unaroused, the labia majora no longer close completely (Slupik & Allison, 1996).

The **labia minora**, also known as the *inner lips,* are two, relatively small, hairless folds of tissue located within the labia majora. The labia minora join below the mons veneris to form the clitoral hood. They also cover and protect the vaginal and urethral openings when the female is not aroused. When the female is sexually aroused, the labia minora engorge with blood and open outward to expose the vaginal and urethral openings. These lips are rich in blood vessels, which accounts for their deep red tint

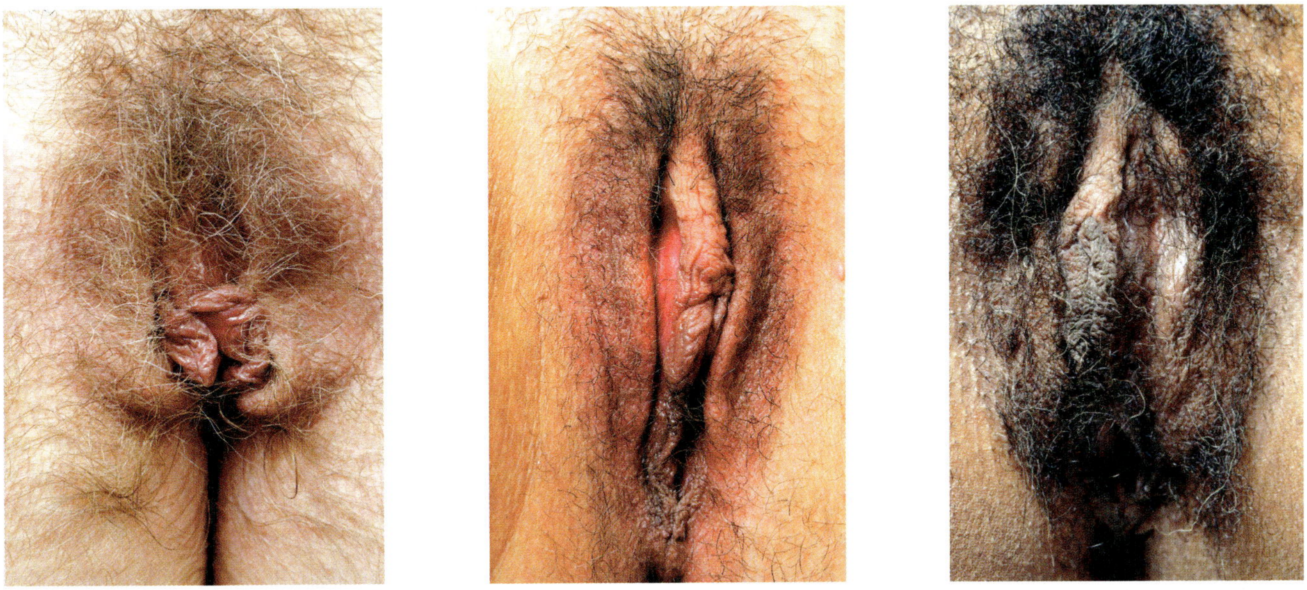

Healthy Female External Genitals

when they are engorged. The area between the labia minora where the urethral and vaginal openings are located is sometimes referred to as the **vestibule.** The appearance of the labia and other external organs differs considerably across individuals.

Clitoris and Clitoral Hood

The **clitoris** is a cylindrical structure composed of shaft and glans, which is found just below the mons veneris and under the clitoral hood. The **glans** is the visible tip of the clitoris, and the **shaft** is the body of the clitoris. The size of the clitoris varies considerably across individuals. It usually appears to be about the size of a pea. However, the average clitoris measures 1 inch in length and ½ inch in diameter. Much of the length of the clitoris is below the surface and is not visible. Its internal structure consists of two cylindrical spongy bodies (erectile tissue) collectively referred to as the **corpora cavernosa** (the singular is *corpus cavernosum*). During arousal, the spongy bodies become

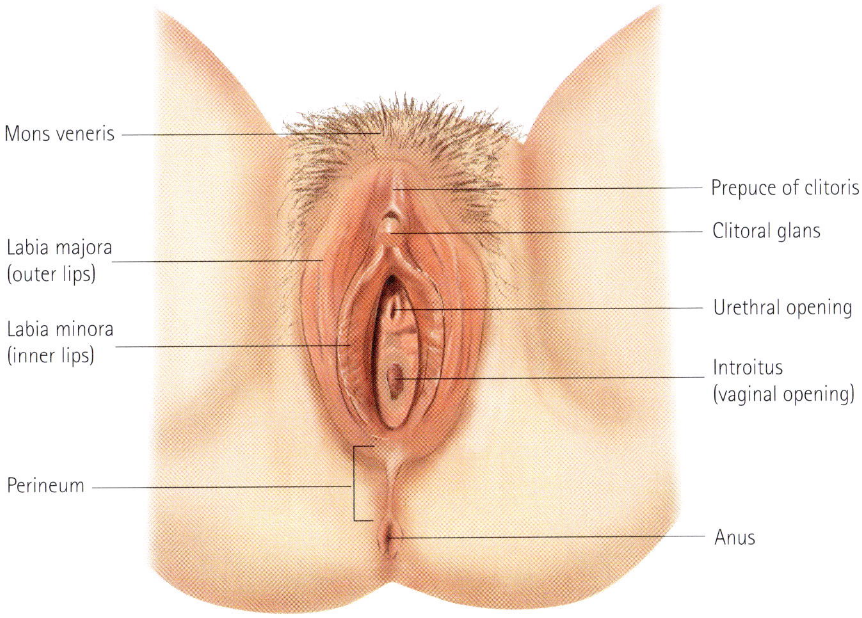

Figure 3.1 External Female Genital Structures

CLITORIS
A cylindrical structure composed of shaft and glans, found just below the mons veneris and under the clitoral hood.

GLANS
The visible tip of the clitoris.

SHAFT
The body of the clitoris.

CORPORA CAVERNOSA
Two cylindrical, spongy bodies of erectile tissue that are bound in thick membrane sheaths, are located within the shaft of the clitoris and the penis, and become engorged with blood during sexual arousal.

engorged with blood, resulting in an increase in the size of the clitoris. Many people wrongly assume that the vagina should be the focus of sexual stimulation. In fact, the glans of the clitoris has a high concentration of touch and temperature receptors and should be the primary center of sexual stimulation and sensation in the female.

The joining of the labia minora forms the **clitoral hood**, the tissue that covers the clitoris. It is believed that the hood provides stimulation during intercourse by moving back and forth across the highly sensitive clitoris. The clitoral hood protects the clitoris from overstimulation when the clitoris retracts under it at a certain point during sexual response. Direct stimulation of the clitoris is uncomfortable or even aversive to some women. The amount of direct clitoral stimulation that is pleasurable varies considerably from person to person.

Vestibule

The upper, smaller opening within the labia minora shown in Figure 3.1 (on page 67) is the opening of the **urethra**, through which the female urinates. The larger, lower opening is the **introitus**, or vaginal opening. The introitus is the entry to the vaginal canal and the opening through which a woman menstruates, gives birth, and has vaginal intercourse. The vaginal opening varies greatly in shape and appearance, mainly because of variations in the **hymen**, a thin ring of tissue partially covering the vaginal opening. Figure 3.2 shows some possible variations in the hymen. The hymen usually has one or more openings. However, occasionally, there is no opening, a condition called an *imperforate hymen*. To allow for menstrual flow, an imperforate hymen must be surgically opened before or at puberty.

Other than a possible protective function, the purpose of the hymen is not clear. A relatively intact hymen might tear when a penis is inserted into the vagina, resulting in some bleeding. Many women do not experience bleeding the first time they have vaginal intercourse, either because the hymen stretches and does not tear or because it was ruptured earlier in life from, for example, insertion of a tampon, rigorous exercise, or a minor accident (such as falling on the bar of a boy's bicycle).

Interestingly, the hymen has been given great religious and cultural significance. People in many cultures believe that the condition of the hymen is indicative of a female's virginity. The "tokens of virginity" referred to in the Bible (Deuteronomy 22:13–17) are the bride's garments stained with blood from the rupturing of the hymen during first intercourse on a couple's wedding night. The parents of the bride would keep these garments as proof of virginity in case the husband ever wanted to accuse his wife of not being a virgin prior to marriage. This custom is still observed in many places.

Perineum

Another area of the external genitalia is the **perineum**, the muscular region covered with skin that extends from the vaginal opening to the anal opening. This is the area

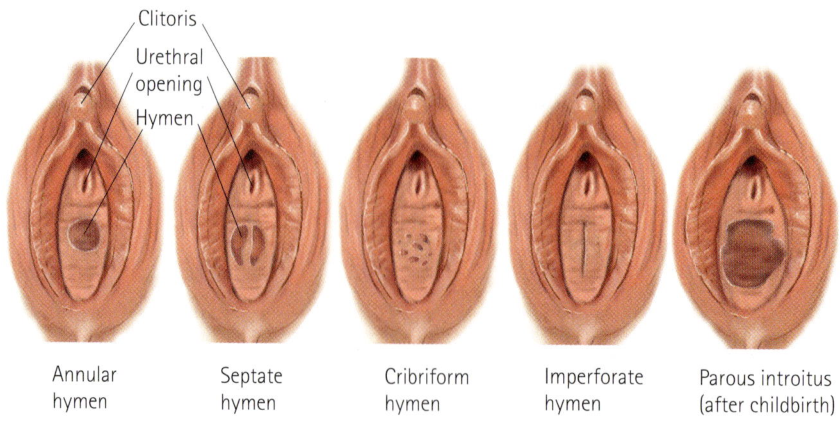

Figure 3.2 The hymen has many different forms.

CLITORAL HOOD
Tissue that covers the clitoris and is formed by the joining of the labia minora.

URETHRA
The passage through which urine flows out of the bladder; in the female, the urethral opening is just above the vaginal opening.

INTROITUS
The opening to the vaginal canal, through which the female menstruates, gives birth, and has vaginal intercourse.

HYMEN
A thin ring of tissue partially covering the vaginal opening.

PERINEUM
The muscular region covered with skin that extends from the vaginal opening to the anal opening in the female, and from the scrotum to the anal opening in the male.

FEMALE GENITAL MUTILATION
The removal of part or all of the external female genitalia.

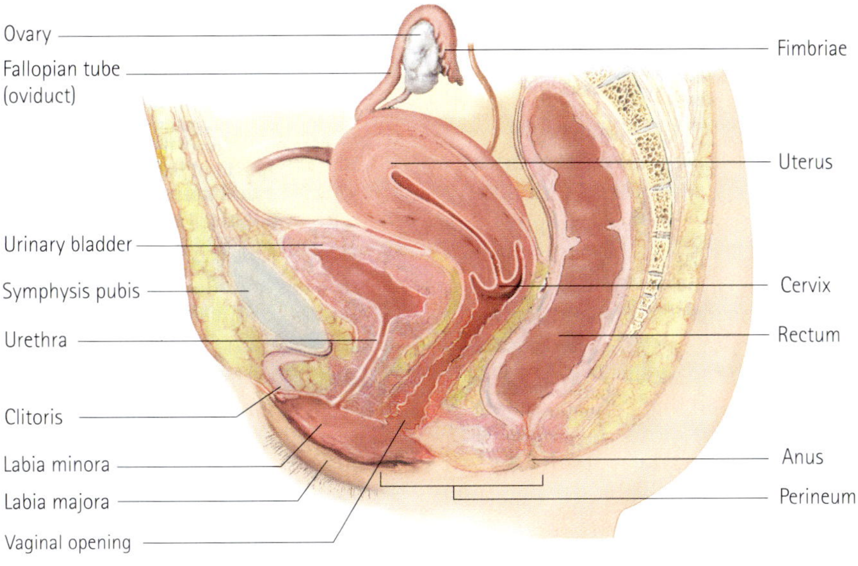

Figure 3.3 Female Reproductive Structures, Cross-Section

that may be cut open during a vaginal delivery to prevent tearing, a procedure referred to as an *episiotomy*. The perineum is sensitive to touch, and stroking the area can be sexually stimulating.

The female external genitals are the structures that are sometimes subjected to female circumcision, which is usually referred to in Western cultures as **female genital mutilation**, a ritualistic removal of some or all of the vulval structures that is practiced in some cultures. We discuss this topic in more detail in Close Up on Culture: Female Genital Mutilation.

The Internal Genital Structures

The internal genital structures primarily serve a reproductive function; however, the responses of these structures during sexual stimulation also contribute to sexual pleasure. We will consider the internal female genital structures from outermost to innermost, beginning at the vaginal opening, and moving on to the cervix, the uterus, and the fallopian tubes; this is the journey the sperm takes to unite with the egg. Refer to Figures 3.3 and 3.4 as we review these structures.

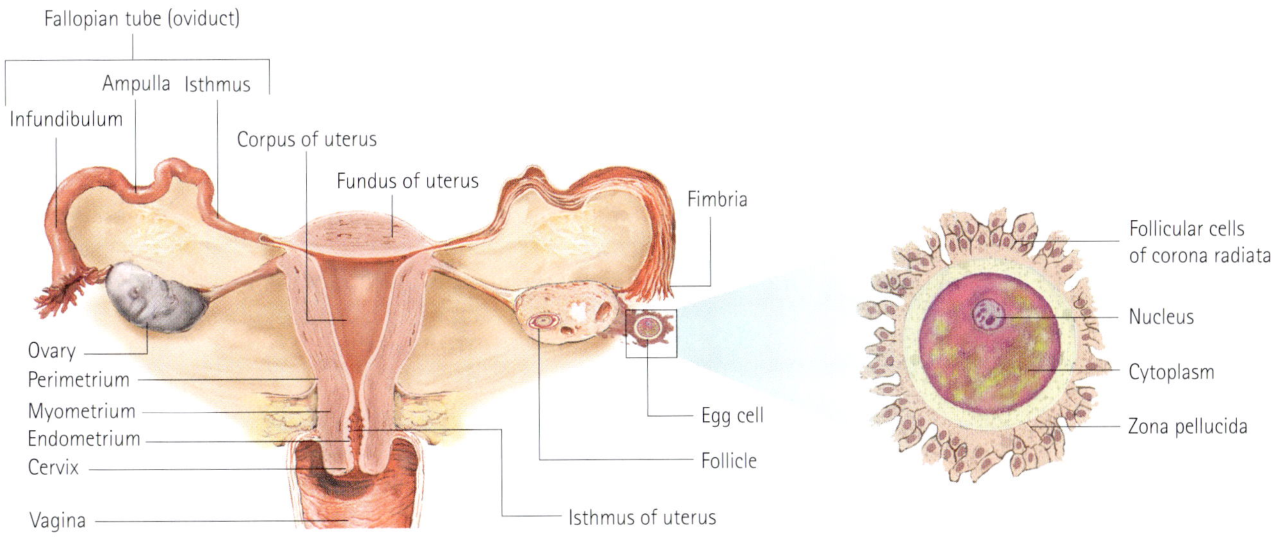

Figure 3.4 Female Internal Reproductive Organs

CLOSE UP ON culture

Female Genital Mutilation

Female genital mutilation (FGM) refers to the removal of part or all of the external genitalia for cultural, religious, or other nontherapeutic reasons. There are three primary types of FGM. *Sunna* is removal of the clitoral hood with or without some or all of the clitoris. *Excision,* or *clitoridectomy,* is the removal of all or part of the clitoris and labia minora; everything within the labia majora is cut or scraped away. This procedure accounts for about 80% of all FGM around the world. The most extreme form of FGM, *infibulation* (also called *Pharonic circumcision*) accounts for 15% of FGM (World Health Organization [WHO], 2000). It involves cutting or scraping away of all external genitalia, after which the remaining parts of the labia majora are pinned together with thorns or sewn together.

FGM is most commonly practiced in Africa and the Middle East, but because of immigration, it occurs all over the world. Muslims are the dominant religious group practicing FGM, but Catholics, Protestants, and Copts (members of a Christian sect primarily found in Egypt) practice it as well. Thus, it is a cross-cultural and cross-religious practice. It is estimated that 100–140 million women have experienced FGM and that 2 million girls (6,000 per day) are at risk of undergoing this mutilation each year (WHO, 2000).

The ritual is performed as part of a larger celebration just before or at the time of puberty. The World Health Organization (2000) suggested five categories of reasons for practicing FGM:

1. *Psychosexual.* It is believed that FGM decreases female sexual desire by reducing or entirely removing sensitive tissue, ensures chastity and virginity before marriage and fidelity afterward, and increases male sexual pleasure (via the made-to-fit opening after infibulation).
2. *Sociological.* FGM is seen as a rite of passage into womanhood and a way of maintaining a female's identification with her culture, which contributes to cohesion within the culture.
3. *Hygienic and aesthetic.* Female genitals are often considered unattractive and dirty. In some cultures, it is considered not only dangerous but even deadly if a woman's intact clitoris touches a man's penis (Sarkis, 2001). Still other cultures believe that if the clitoris is not removed, it will continue to grow until it hangs between a woman's legs. Removal eliminates these potential "risks."
4. *Religious.* Some religious groups believe that their faith demands FGM.
5. *Other.* Some cultures believe that FGM promotes fertility and survival of offspring.

Whatever the rationale for FGM, it poses a significant health threat to women around the world, which is the primary reason many individuals and groups have become activists trying to

Vaginal Canal

The **vagina** is a tubular structure, approximately 4 inches long (in an unaroused state), that has the vaginal opening at one end and the cervix at the other. When the female is unaroused, the vaginal walls touch each other. The walls have a layer of muscle with many folds in it, allowing it to stretch tremendously to allow passage of a baby during childbirth. The vagina also accommodates the penis during vaginal intercourse and functions as a passageway for menstrual flow from the uterus. The outer third of the vagina is responsive to physical stimulation; however, the inner two-thirds is not well innervated and does not function as a site of sexual stimulation. Because of the relatively sparse innervation in the inner two-thirds of the vaginal walls, a woman will not feel a tampon or a diaphragm once it is properly in place. Some experts claim that there is an area on the wall of the vagina near the front that is particularly richly supplied with nerves and thus, when stimulated, produces intense arousal and orgasm. The actual existence of this area, called the Grafenberg spot (G-spot), is controversial among sex researchers. The G-spot is discussed further in Chapter 4.

The interior of the vagina stays moist from constant secretions. The secretions increase during sexual arousal to

did YOU know?

Some women have an area, called the Grafenberg spot (G-spot), on the anterior, or front, wall of the vagina, between the vaginal opening and the cervix, which is often found to be extremely sensitive to stimulation. It is about 2 inches up from the entrance to the vagina toward the front of the body. To find it, put your fingers inside your vagina with the fingertips toward your front and move the fingers up and down. You might feel a raised spot or series of ridges (but you might not). Do you have a G-spot?

eliminate it. Immediate health threats from any form of FGM include extreme pain, shock, inability to urinate, ulcers on the genitalia, and injury to surrounding tissue. Excessive bleeding and infection from the unsanitary conditions also occur and can result in death. Over time, abscesses and cysts as well as large scars (*keloids*) may form. Loss of control of urination sometimes results from damage to the urethra, and painful intercourse and sexual dysfunction are certainly major risks. A major concern is HIV transmission from using one instrument for multiple procedures (WHO, 2000).

Those who defend FGM point to practices in Western cultures involving physical alterations, and it is interesting to note that clitoridectomies were practiced in the United States during the 19th century in an effort to squelch the desires of women who showed any interest in sex (they were referred to as *nymphomaniacs*). Even as recently as 1979, a physician in Ohio claimed that clitoridectomies actually increased a woman's sexual sensitivity. He performed these so-called love surgeries for 10 years before he was exposed (Sarkis, 2001). Western cultures also include many rites of passage into womanhood, such as shaving the legs, using makeup, and wearing a bra. While these are as unnecessary as FGM, they differ in that they generally do not pose any health threat or rob women of their sexual potential. Parallels have also been drawn between FGM and male circumcision, which is practiced in some Western cultures. We discuss the controversy over male circumcision elsewhere, but we point out here that both procedures are unnecessary and alter one's natural appearance. Furthermore, neither takes into account the individual's autonomy, as they are imposed by others. However, most forms of FGM are more analogous to removal of the penis than to circumcision (Sarkis, 2001).

Regardless of how much FGM offends the sensibilities of Westerners and raises concerns as a worldwide health risk, it is entirely inappropriate and most likely fruitless for "outsiders" to impose their judgment on cultures that practice FGM. Grassroots efforts by members of these cultures constitute the best hope for educating people about the dangers of FGM (WHO, 1997). Some countries, such as Egypt, have sought to combat the problem through making FGM practices illegal. However, legal solutions are not likely to have the desired impact, since these practices often occur in remote areas and many women (including many in Egypt) are supportive of them (Chelala, 1998). Kenya is working on a program to encourage rural communities to substitute an alternative celebration called *Ntanira Na Mugambo* ("circumcision through words") for FGM. This rite involves a week of seclusion for pubescent girls, whose mothers educate them about reproductive anatomy, physiology, and hygiene, gender issues, respect for adults, self-esteem, and avoiding peer pressure. The rite culminates in the receipt of a certificate, gifts, the granting of special wishes, and a public celebration in which the girl gets to be the center of attention (Chelala, 1998). Kenyan officials hope that, by not strong-arming their people into compliance and by offering an attractive alternative, they can eventually bring an end to FGM.

provide lubrication for intercourse. The moist environment supports "friendly" bacteria, which help to maintain a healthy level of acidity in the vagina. Because of the presence of the secretions and the bacteria, all women have some vaginal discharge. If the discharge causes irritation, smells strong or unpleasant, or seems to increase significantly in volume, a woman should consult a doctor to rule out infection (Slupik & Allison, 1996). Otherwise, daily bathing with a mild soap should be adequate self-care. Douching is not necessary and can even cause irritation, especially if a commercial douche containing deodorants and other chemicals is used. Douching does not protect against sexually transmissible infections or pregnancy. Antibiotics can cause the vaginal environment to become too basic (nonacidic) by killing off the "friendly" bacteria; when this happens, a yeast infection is likely to result. The acidity level of the vagina is hostile to sperm. However, the alkalinity of semen and emissions from a man's Cowper's gland protects the sperm from the acidic environment of the vagina. Mother Nature thought of everything!

VAGINA
A tubular structure that has the vaginal opening at one end and the cervix at the other.

Cervix

The **cervix**, or *uterine cervix,* is located at the innermost end of the vagina and is the narrowest and outermost part of the uterus. The **cervical os**, the opening in the cervix, is the passageway between the vaginal canal and the uterus. Sperm must get through it to make their way through the uterus to fertilize an egg cell. Menstrual flow also passes through the cervical os from the uterus. Glands in the cervix produce cervical mucus. The cervical mucus forms a plug in the cervix that keeps bacteria out of the uterus. The

CERVIX
Structure that is located at the innermost end of the vagina and is the narrowest and outermost part of the uterus; also called the *uterine cervix.*

CERVICAL OS
The opening of the cervix.

consistency of the plug thins during ovulation to make it possible for the sperm to pass through. The plug also dissolves during menstruation to allow the blood to pass out of the uterus. Around the cervix is a recessed area called the **fornix.** The contraceptive diaphragm fits snugly in this fornix (see Chapter 10).

The greatest health threat to the cervix is **invasive cervical cancer**, which occurs when abnormal cells grow beyond the outer tissue surface and into the cervix itself. Cervical cancer has a survival rate of nearly 100% if it is detected early, but this rate can drop significantly if the cancer remains undetected or untreated. Because the early stages of cervical cancer usually do not produce any symptoms, regular Pap tests are essential (National Cancer Institute, 2002).

Women of all ages and ethnic backgrounds are at risk for cervical cancer. Women of color, including Hispanic Americans, Native Americans, and African Americans, have a higher than average risk of contracting this disease—the death rate from cervical cancer among African Americans is twice the average national rate in the United States (American Cancer Society, 2001a). Lack of access to adequate health care probably accounts for racial and ethnic differences in mortality risk (Carlson, Eisenstat, & Ziporyn, 1996).

Women who start to have intercourse at an early age (before age 16) and who have multiple male sex partners also have a heightened risk of getting cervical cancer. The human papillomavirus (HPV) (discussed in Chapter 14 on sexually transmissible infections) is a major risk factor for cervical cancer. Thus, postponing first sexual intercourse and practicing safer sex are ways to reduce one's risk of cervical cancer; women who are sexually active should use barrier forms of contraceptives (diaphragm or condoms). Cigarette smoking is also associated with a greater risk of cervical cancer and should be avoided. In addition, some research suggests that deficiencies of vitamins A and C increase the risk of this disease (American Cancer Society [ACS], 2001a; Carlson et al., 1996).

did YOU know?

Cervical cancer is the third most common cancer of the female reproductive organs; it claims 4,600 lives annually in the United States (American Cancer Society, 2000).

Symptoms of invasive cervical cancer include vaginal bleeding after intercourse or between periods, bleeding after menopause, odorous or pinkish vaginal discharge, or pain during intercourse. Treatment of cervical cancer requires surgery to remove the cancerous tissue and might require removal of the entire uterus (including the cervix). Depending on how far the cancer has spread, the upper portion of the vagina, the ovaries, or some lymph nodes might have to be removed. Surgery is followed by radiation therapy to the pelvic region and chemotherapy if the cancer has spread (American Cancer Society, 2001a).

Uterus

The **uterus** is a hollow, muscular, pear-shaped organ measuring approximately 3 by 2 inches. The *uterine corpus* is the central part of the uterus, and the narrower portion between the corpus and the cervix is the *uterine isthmus*. The rounded, domelike top is called the *uterine fundus*. Like the vaginal canal, the uterus has tremendous capacity to stretch to many times its original size. When a woman becomes pregnant, the fertilized egg attaches itself to the wall of the uterus and eventually becomes a full-grown fetus. After delivery of the baby, the uterus shrinks back to its original size and shape. Housing the developing fetus is not the only function of the uterus. The uterus may also play a role in sexual response, which we discuss in some detail in Chapter 4.

The uterine fundus and corpus are composed of three layers. The thin external membrane is called the *perimetrium*. The middle layer, or *myometrium,* contracts powerfully during labor. Finally, the inner layer is called the *endometrium*. In a woman who is not pregnant, hormonal changes in the uterus cause a portion of the endometrium to shed regularly, producing menstrual blood flow. The endometrium is rebuilt after menstruation, and the cycle repeats itself. If the woman is pregnant, the endometrium nourishes and supports the fetus.

FORNIX
Recessed area around the cervix.

INVASIVE CERVICAL CANCER
Disease resulting when abnormal cells grow beyond the outer tissue surface and into the cervix itself.

UTERUS
The hollow, muscular, pear-shaped organ in which a developing fetus grows.

In most women, the uterine corpus is angled toward the front of the body, or *anteflexed,* as in Figure 3.3. However, some women have what is commonly referred to as a "tilted uterus," one that is *retroflexed,* or tilted backward toward the rectum and tailbone. In the past, it was believed that a retroflexed uterus put a woman at risk for infertility and menstrual cramps. Today, however, doctors know that a tilted uterus presents no such risks.

did YOU know?

Uterine fibroids are extremely common but often undiagnosed. In one study of women between the ages of 35 and 49, 72% of the African American women and 50% of the white American women had them. Forty-four percent of the African Americans and 69% of the whites were previously undiagnosed (NIEHS, 2001).

Uterine fibroids (*myomas*) are benign (noncancerous) solid tumors that form on the inside or outside of the uterus or within the uterine walls. Fibroids are common but become cancerous only rarely, usually in postmenopausal women. Fibroids can be as small as a pea or as large as a grapefruit, and in rare cases even larger. Fibroids do not generally produce any adverse symptoms. Some women with fibroids, however, experience abnormal bleeding, heavy periods, pain, urinary problems, and pregnancy problems such as infertility, miscarriage, or premature delivery. The causes of uterine fibroids are not known, but advancing age, early onset of menstruation, African American ethnicity, use of birth control pills, and possibly obesity put women at greater risk for developing them (National Institute of Environmental Health Sciences, [NIEHS] 2001).

Fallopian Tubes

The openings to the oviducts, or **fallopian tubes,** are located at the top and on either side of the uterus. The narrow portion of each fallopian tube adjacent to the uterus is called the **isthmus,** and the wider part is called the **ampulla.** The cone-shaped end of the fallopian tube is called the **infundibulum.** The **fimbriae,** found at the end of the infundibulum, are fingerlike projections that partially surround the ovary. The **egg cell,** or **ovum** (the female reproductive cell), comes out of the ovary, is coaxed by the waving fimbriae into the fallopian tube, and moves through the tube assisted by the movements of the **cilia,** tiny, hairlike structures inside the tube. Assuming that both egg and sperm are present at the same time, fertilization occurs in the fallopian tube. This process will be described in greater detail in Chapter 9 on conception, pregnancy, and childbirth.

Ovaries

The **ovaries** are two solid, egg-shaped structures located near the ends of the fallopian tubes. They are not connected to the fallopian tubes; instead, they are held in place by the pelvic wall and by ovarian ligaments, which attach to the uterus. Each ovary is approximately ¾ to 1½ inches long. The primary function of the ovaries is production of egg cells. The ovaries also produce hormones important to the female reproductive process, including the estrogens and progesterone. We will discuss these hormones in detail in the section on the menstrual cycle.

Each ovary contains approximately 1 million immature eggs, or ova. Over the course of a female's reproductive lifespan, between puberty and menopause, some of these eggs mature and are released during the monthly menstrual cycles. Each egg matures within a fluid-filled capsule (follicle) in the ovary. At a certain point each month, one follicle ruptures to release its egg; once it does so, the follicle is referred to as the *corpus luteum.* Occasionally, an **ovarian cyst,** an abnormal fluid- or gel-filled sac, forms on an ovary, either because a follicle failed to rupture and is continuing to grow, becoming a *follicular cyst,* or because a corpus luteum keeps growing, forming a *corpus luteum cyst.* These two types of cysts are called *functional cysts* because they result from normal cyclical changes. Functional cysts are usually painless and disappear on their own after a few menstrual cycles. A corpus luteum cyst sometimes causes discomfort between days 20 and 26 of the menstrual cycle (Slupik & Allison, 1996).

UTERINE FIBROIDS
Myomas; benign, solid tumors that form on the inside or outside of the uterus or within the uterine walls.

FALLOPIAN TUBE
A tube that runs from each ovary to the uterus; also called *oviduct.*

ISTHMUS
Narrow portion of a fallopian tube adjacent to the uterus.

AMPULLA
The wider section of a fallopian tube.

INFUNDIBULUM
Cone-shaped end of each fallopian tube near the ovary.

FIMBRIAE
Fingerlike projections at the end of the infundibulum that partially surround the ovary and help to guide the egg cell into the fallopian tube.

EGG CELL (OVUM)
The female reproductive cell.

CILIA
Tiny hairlike structures inside each fallopian tube whose movements guide the egg cell down the tube.

OVARIES
Two solid, egg-shaped structures that are located near the ends of the fallopian tubes and that produce egg cells and some female hormones.

OVARIAN CYST
An abnormal fluid- or gel-filled sac that forms on an ovary.

IN YOUR own words

Krista Price
University of Delaware

I refer to the vagina as "vagina" and the penis as "penis." Frankly, nicknames make me more uncomfortable than proper names.

Ovarian cancer results from the growth and spread of abnormal cells in an ovary. It is the second most common cancer of the reproductive organs, second only to endometrial cancer; however, more women die from ovarian cancer than from any other reproductive cancer (ACS, 2002a). If this cancer is detected early, before it spreads to other organs, patients have a 5-year survival rate of 95%. Unfortunately, ovarian cancer produces few symptoms and is difficult to detect; thus, only about 25% of cases of ovarian cancer are detected before it spreads (ACS, 2001b). When symptoms are present, they usually include bloating, a feeling of fullness, abdominal pressure or pain, back pain, and fatigue (Olson et al., 2001). Overall, just over half of women diagnosed will survive more than 5 years (ACS, 2001b).

New tests designed to detect various substances found in high amounts in the bloodstreams of women with ovarian cancer are currently under investigation. However, further research is needed to determine whether these detection methods are adequate (Kim et al., 2002; Mok et al., 2001). Close to 10% of ovarian cancers are caused by genes called BRCA1 and BRCA2. Experts now recommend that women who inherit these genes consider preventive surgery to eliminate their risk of ovarian cancer (ACS, 2002b). The best defense against ovarian cancer seems to be an annual gynecological exam. Women at high risk for this type of cancer might have annual ultrasounds to increase the chances of detecting the cancer early. However, the only way to determine whether a woman actually has ovarian cancer is a biopsy of the tissue (ACS, 2001b).

Ovarian cancer is most common in postmenopausal women, especially women who go through menopause after the age of 50. Women who have a family history of ovarian cancer are at increased risk of developing the disease. It also occurs at a higher rate in women who have never been pregnant or who had their first child after age 30, women who have a history of other cancers (especially breast), women who use talcum powder (talc is known to be a *carcinogen* or cancer-causing substance) in the genital area, and women who were on hormone replacement therapy or took fertility drugs (ACS, 2001b).

Like many cancers, ovarian cancer can be treated with a combination of surgery and chemotherapy or radiation therapy. In a woman who is young and wishes to have children, and whose cancer has been detected before it could spread, the surgeon might remove only the affected ovary and wait until after the woman has had children to remove the remaining ovary and other reproductive organs. In most cases, however, both ovaries, the uterus, and the fallopian tubes must be removed. The fatty lining of the abdominal cavity might also be removed, as well as some of the intestine, depending on how far the cancer has spread. Surgery is followed by either radiation therapy, using a radioactive liquid that is injected into the abdomen, or chemotherapy (Slupik & Allison, 1996; Twelve Major Cancers, 1996).

Other Internal Genital Structures

There are a few other internal genital structures with which you should be familiar (see Figure 3.5). The **pubococcygeus muscle**, which surrounds the vaginal and urethral openings, is important for bladder control and helps to maintain the tautness of the vaginal opening. **Kegel exercises**, which strengthen the pubococcygeus muscle, are recommended to reduce urinary incontinence and possibly to increase sexual pleasure. Arnold Kegel, a gynecologist who prescribed them to improve bladder control, first described these exercises. A woman learns the exercises by first identifying the muscle to contract by stopping urination in midstream. Once she has identified the muscle, she can perform the exercises by tightening it for up to 10 seconds and then releasing it. This sequence should be done 10 times and should be repeated several times a day.

The **vestibular bulb** is a body of tissue on either side of the vaginal opening, beneath the surface tissues. Engorgement of this bulb during sexual arousal contributes to the narrowing of the outer third of the vaginal canal. The **Bartholin's glands**, located just inside the vaginal opening, have no known function. They secrete a small

OVARIAN CANCER
Disease resulting from the growth and spread of abnormal cells in an ovary.

PUBOCOCCYGEUS MUSCLE
Muscle that surrounds the vaginal and urethral openings and is responsible for controlling the flow of urine and the tautness of the vaginal opening.

KEGEL EXERCISES
Exercises to strengthen the pubococcygeus muscle in order to reduce urinary incontinence and possibly increase sexual pleasure.

VESTIBULAR BULB
Body of tissue on either side of the vaginal opening beneath the surface tissues that becomes engorged during sexual arousal.

BARTHOLIN'S GLANDS
Glands located just inside the vaginal opening that secrete a small amount of fluid during sexual arousal; the function of this secretion is unknown.

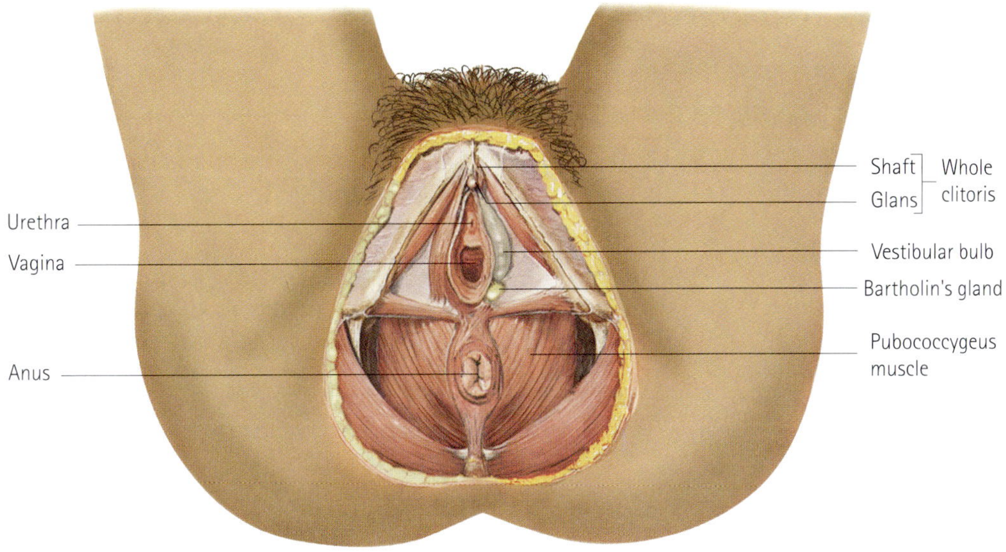

Figure 3.5 Pubococcygeus Muscle and Vestibular Bulb

amount of fluid during arousal but not enough to serve any purpose. Despite their apparent uselessness, we mention them here because they tend to get clogged and infected. When this happens, the woman experiences pain and may notice swelling just inside her vagina. While it might be frightening, the problem is easily treated by a medical professional. To the sides of the urethral opening are two glands called the **Skene's glands.** These glands also secrete a small amount of fluid and might play a role in female ejaculation (discussed in Chapter 4).

Being familiar with her own sexual anatomy can help a woman feel more comfortable about herself, sexually and otherwise. Some women are not so comfortable, as discussed in Reflect on This: For Women—Increasing Comfort with Your Sexual Anatomy.

did YOU know?

"Normal" menstrual cycles last anywhere from 21 to 35 days (Taffe & Dennerstein, 2002).

The Menstrual Cycle

A woman's internal genital structures carry out the **menstrual cycle,** a process by which the body produces a mature egg cell, or ovum, that is capable of being fertilized by a sperm. Reproduction in its natural form can occur only as a result of this cycle. The menstrual cycle has two phases: the follicular phase and the luteal phase. These phases are separated by ovulation. If a sperm does not fertilize the ovum, pregnancy does not occur, and **menstruation** begins, marking the end of a luteal phase and the onset of another follicular phase. Menstruation is bleeding that occurs as the body sheds the inner lining, or **endometrium,** of the uterus. Menstruation marks the end of a sequence of hormonal and physical changes in the ovaries and uterus that prepare the woman's body for pregnancy. However, because the onset of menstruation is the most obvious marker of the cycle, it is generally regarded as day one of the menstrual cycle. For 65% of women, the menstrual cycle lasts 28 days, plus or minus 3 days, and menstruation lasts 5 days, plus or minus 2 days. When a woman menstruates, she sheds anywhere from less than an ounce of blood to several ounces; the average woman sheds about 2 ounces, or 4 tablespoons, of blood at about the rate of a slow faucet drip. Refer to Figure 3.6 as you read about the phases of the menstrual cycle.

The Follicular Phase

A female is born with approximately 2 million immature eggs in her ovaries. Each month, one egg matures and is released from an ovary. (Occasionally, more than one

SKENE'S GLANDS
A pair of glands located at the sides of the urethral opening, which secrete a small amount of fluid and might play a role in female ejaculation.

MENSTRUAL CYCLE
The process by which the female body produces a mature egg cell, or ovum, that is capable of being fertilized by a sperm.

MENSTRUATION
Bleeding that occurs as a woman's body sheds the inner lining of the uterus if an egg has not been fertilized and implanted there.

ENDOMETRIUM
The inner lining of the uterus.

reflect ON THIS

For Women—Increasing Comfort with Your Sexual Anatomy

Some women are perfectly comfortable with their physical selves, but many women experience discomfort or dissatisfaction with their bodies. The intensity of this discomfort varies considerably. Some women don't especially like what they see in the mirror or have a particular problem with a certain body part such as their breasts or thighs. But many women have rather intense, adverse feelings about their bodies, particularly their genitalia, arising from their early learning experiences. Even though U.S. culture has made serious attempts to indoctrinate both females and males against the evils of touching their own genitals and masturbating in particular, males have a slight advantage in learning to be comfortable with their genitals. For one thing, male genitals are visible and easy to reach. In addition, at a very young age, little boys learn how to hold their penises when they urinate. Touching the genitals becomes a daily part of life that, at least when done for purposes of urination, is not punished by parents or other caretakers. In contrast, girls have no obvious reason to touch their genitals, except with a washcloth or toilet tissue. In addition, girls often receive strong, negative messages about their genitals. Many women who seek therapy because of sexual concerns share early memories of being scolded when very young for touching and exploring their genitals. A primary message that has often been transmitted to them by their parents is that their genitals are filthy. For example, one woman was taught to use two sets of washcloths and towels—one for cleaning and drying her genitals and one for the rest of her body. It was no surprise to find that she had a terrible perception of her body and that she developed difficulties in her sexual relationships as an adult.

A lack of familiarity and comfort with one's genitals can lead to problems. First and foremost, it can affect personal feelings of self-worth; it can also affect sexual ease and expressiveness. If you have any of these feelings or concerns, you may want to try to address them. Many good self-help guides are available; one of the better ones is entitled *Becoming Orgasmic,* by Julia Heiman and Joseph LoPiccolo. Such guides generally recommend that a woman increase her comfort level by first visually inspecting, then touching her genitals while she is relaxed. By doing this, a woman can learn to feel more comfortable with her genitals and discover what types of touches are sexually stimulating to her. If you think your discomfort is serious and needs professional attention, seek the advice of a trained sex therapist. (Some techniques used in sex therapy are described in Chapter 13.)

3.1 on the web

Many but not all women experience cramping and other physical symptoms during menstruation. Such symptoms are usually perfectly normal. Visit "My Body: My Period" at **www.ablongman.com/mcanulty2e.**

Describe the normal changes in a woman's body during menstruation that cause cramping. Also, describe the many approaches to reducing these symptoms.

egg is released and fertilized, which leads to the birth of fraternal twins or triplets.) The first phase of the menstrual cycle is called the **follicular phase**, because this is when a structure called an *ovarian follicle* develops in one of the ovaries; the follicle ultimately produces a mature ovum. This phase has also been called the *proliferative phase,* because the endometrium "proliferates," or becomes thicker, during it, or sometimes the *preovulatory phase,* because it occurs just prior to ovulation. This phase starts at the onset of menstruation and lasts for approximately 13 days. The onset of menstruation coincides with a drop in estrogen and progesterone in the woman's body, which signals the hypothalamus to stimulate the pituitary gland (both of which are structures in the brain) to release **follicle-stimulating hormone** (**FSH**). FSH stimulates the growth of several ovarian follicles, only one of which ultimately matures and releases an ovum. As the follicle matures, it begins to secrete estrogen, one of a group of hormones called **estrogens** that regulate the menstrual cycle. In response to the presence of estrogen, the endometrium of the uterus thickens and prepares to support a fertilized ovum. In addition, the cervical mucus becomes clear, thin, and watery, allowing sperm to pass through the cervical opening.

Ovulation

The increasing levels of estrogen during the follicular phase inhibit production of FSH, and this hormone drops to low levels. High levels of estrogen also signal the hypothalamus to produce another hormone called **GnRH**, or **gonadotrophin-releasing**

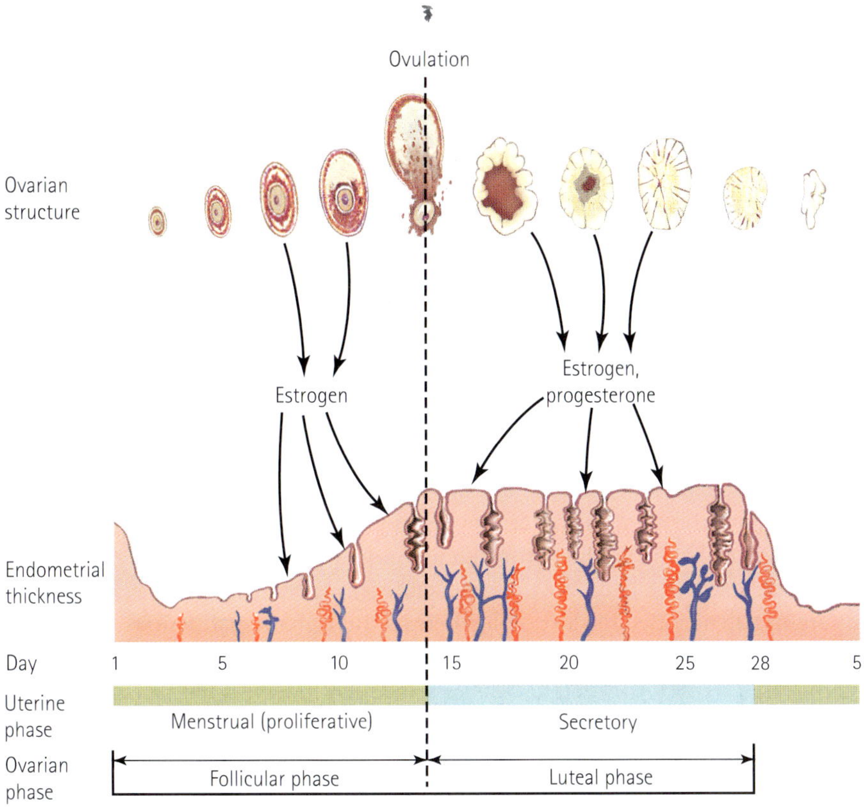

Figure 3.6 Phases of the Menstrual Cycle

hormone. The GnRH signals the pituitary gland to produce a third hormone, **luteinizing hormone** (LH). The surge in LH stimulates **ovulation,** or the release of an ovum from the ovarian follicle and into the fallopian tube (see Figure 3.6). Generally, ovulation occurs around the 14th day of a 28-day menstrual cycle. Each ovum released at ovulation contains 23 **chromosomes,** one-half of the number usually found in a living cell. The chromosomes transmit genetic factors from the mother to the baby.

The Luteal Phase

The **luteal phase** starts at ovulation and continues to the onset of menstruation. During this phase, LH stimulates the ovarian follicle to grow until it bursts and releases the egg; once it bursts open, the follicle is called the *corpus luteum.* The corpus luteum produces the hormone **progesterone,** which acts to make the uterine wall capable of accepting and implanting the fertilized egg. In yet another feedback loop, the high levels of progesterone inhibit production of LH; the decrease in LH eventually results in the disintegration of the corpus luteum. If fertilization does not occur, estrogen and progesterone levels drop, and the endometrial lining is shed once again. The luteal phase has also been called the *secretory phase,* because during it the corpus luteum secretes large amounts of estrogen and progesterone, or sometimes the *postovulatory phase,* because it occurs after ovulation.

The Menstrual Experience

Menstruation has been surrounded by myth and taboo for centuries. Judeo-Christian and Islamic teachings, which viewed women as unclean and dangerous during menstruation, survive in contemporary Western culture. Women's uncleanliness is still used by some churches as a justification for prohibiting women from being leaders in church activities. (No wonder many women still call menstruation "the curse"!) Such views of menstruation have not always existed, however, nor are they embraced by all

FOLLICULAR PHASE
The phase of the menstrual cycle that starts at the onset of menstruation and ends with ovulation, during which an ovarian follicle develops in an ovary; also known as the *proliferative phase* or the *preovulatory phase.*

FOLLICLE-STIMULATING HORMONE (FSH)
A hormone that is released by the pituitary gland during the follicular phase of the menstrual cycle and stimulates the growth of several ovarian follicles.

ESTROGENS
A group of hormones that regulate the menstrual cycle and are responsible for producing secondary female sexual characteristics; also found in males in small amounts.

GONADOTROPHIN-RELEASING HORMONE (GRH)
A hormone that is produced by a woman's hypothalamus and signals the pituitary gland to produce luteinizing hormone.

LUTEINIZING HORMONE (LH)
A hormone produced by the pituitary gland that stimulates ovulation.

OVULATION
The release of an egg cell, or ovum, from an ovarian follicle.

CHROMOSOMES
Rod-shaped structures within each cell nucleus that carry genetic material.

LUTEAL PHASE
The phase of the menstrual cycle that begins at ovulation and continues to the onset of menstruation; also known as the *secretory phase* or the *postovulatory phase.*

PROGESTERONE
The hormone that is produced by the corpus luteum and is responsible for preparing the uterine lining for impregnation.

cultures. In ancient times, many cultures were matriarchal and dominated by positive views of womanhood. The ability of women to bring forth life and to bleed and not die were revered in these cultures. (Based on cave paintings and other artifacts, anthropologists believe that people did not know that men contributed to reproduction until about 20,000 years ago.) Today, some cultures still hold positive views of menstruation. Many Native American cultures refer to the *menses* (the menstrual flow) as "moontime" and think of it as a time when a woman is most open to prophetic visions. Women are honored for their ability to give life. Women who practice traditional Native American customs gather during their menstrual periods in a "moon lodge" to celebrate the menses as a time of renewal and a representation of fertility.

Save for a small minority, women in Western culture remain relatively uninformed about their ancient ancestors and their contemporaries around the world who actually celebrate menstruation. Americans, in particular, are bombarded with negative messages about menstruation. Tampon advertisements use themes that capitalize on women's fears that others will discover they are menstruating—touting compact tampons that women can carry to the bathroom without anyone noticing or emphasizing that tampons, unlike thick pads, are not detectable by others. Unfortunately, women's concerns about the negative reactions of others to their menstrual periods are not totally unfounded. At least one study showed that women thought to be menstruating are actually rated as less competent and less liked by peers (Roberts, Goldenberg, Power, & Pyszczynski, 2002).

Too often, negative views of menstruation have a negative impact on women's experiences of menstruation. Women report a number of unpleasant symptoms before and during menstruation—breast tenderness and swelling, abdominal pain and bloating, fatigue, irritability, depressed mood, sudden mood changes, and impaired social functioning. While such symptoms are certainly real and should not be discounted, women's expectations of menstrual discomfort appear to increase the severity of reported symptoms (Marvan, Vacio, & Espinosa-Hernandez, 2001; McFarland, Ross, & DeCourville, 1989). Feelings of embarrassment and shame are unfortunate and damaging side effects of cultural myths and taboos surrounding menstruation. The only way to combat these damaging stereotypes is through education. Interventions that increase positive expectations about menstruation also increase women's reports of experiencing positive changes during menstruation and their willingness to regard menstruation as a "natural event" (Aubeeluck & Maguire, 2002). As one woman on the Web site "Redspot" suggests, "I really think that young women need to educated about menstruation and how powerful this lifeblood is. Rather than try to hide it and have an adverse relationship to it, young girls should be taught that menstruation is nothing to be ashamed of and nothing to feel dirty about."

Premenstrual Syndrome

While more positive attitudes toward menstruation can moderate symptoms, they do not always eliminate the negative experiences some women report, such as premenstrual syndrome. **Premenstrual syndrome (PMS)** consists of a number of negative psychological and physical symptoms that arise during the luteal phase, or the week prior to menstruation, and that have an impact on a woman's daily functioning. Symptoms may include mood swings, tender and swollen breasts, bloated abdomen, headaches, fatigue, irritability, hostility, and depressed mood; however, researchers over 4 decades have never managed to agree on what symptoms constitute PMS, nor on whether such physical and, especially, psychological symptoms consistently occur during the luteal phase of the cycle (Stanton, Lobel, Sears, & DeLuca, 2002). In other words, premenstrual symptoms may not be pervasive or consistent enough within any individual or across all women to warrant being called a syndrome. In fact, these symptoms may occur during other phases of the menstrual cycle but not be noticed or labeled as problematic because they are not occurring during the luteal phase. Between 25% and 90% of women report some premenstrual symptoms, but only 2–15% report

PREMENSTRUAL SYNDROME (PMS)
Negative psychological, behavioral, and physical symptoms that arise consistly and predictably during the luteal phase of a woman's menstrual cycle, which are severe enough to interfere with some aspect of a woman's life.

that their symptoms are severe or debilitating (Marvan & Cortes-Iniestra, 2001; Stanton et al., 2002). Research has demonstrated that women who assume that most women experience PMS and who hold stereotypical negative beliefs about physical and psychological changes during the premenstrual phase report more negative experiences (Marvan & Cortes-Iniestra, 2001). These data are only correlational and do not show that attitudes actually cause women to have more severe symptoms; however, one study showed that women who had hysterectomies reported a reduction in premenstrual symptoms even though their ovaries, which control hormonal cycling, were left intact (Metcalf, Braiden, Livesey, & Wells, 1992). This study would suggest that expectations do indeed influence the experience of premenstrual symptoms.

Between 5% and 6% of women experience extremely severe and debilitating premenstrual changes, primarily psychological in nature, which has led to the inclusion of a psychiatric diagnosis in the American Psychiatric Association's *Diagnostic and Statistical Manual* (1994) called **premenstrual dysphoric disorder,** or **PMDD** (Sternfeld, Swindle, Chawla, Long, & Kennedy, 2002; Straneva et al., 2002; Wittchen, Becker, Lieb, & Krause, 2002). The causes of PMDD are unclear, but research suggests that a luteal phase drop in beta-endorphins, naturally occurring opioids that protect the body from pain, may precipitate both physical and psychological symptoms of PMDD (Straneva et al., 2002). In addition, women with PMDD may have a deficit of the neurotransmitter serotonin, which can result in depressed mood and other psychological symptoms (Parry, 2001). Antidepressants that alleviate this deficit are sometimes used to treat PMDD. Other approaches include dietary changes and aerobic exercise (Frackiewicz & Shiovitz, 2001).

Dysmenorrhea

Dysmenorrhea is cramping in the lower abdomen, just before and during menstruation. Some women also experience pain in their hips, lower back, and inner thighs. When cramps are severe, some women experience stomach upset, including vomiting and loose bowel movements (Cleveland Clinic, 2002a). In the most severe cases, women may become dizzy or faint. However, such severe reactions are rare.

Dysmenorrhea that occurs in the absence of any disease is called primary *dysmenorrhea.* Dysmenorrhea brought on by an infection or disease is called *secondary dysmenorrhea.* As many as 90% of women experience primary dysmenorrhea, which is caused by an increase in the production of **endometrial prostaglandins,** hormones that cause uterine contractions. These prostaglandins tend to be at their highest levels during the first two days of menstruation, when women typically report the most cramping (Coco, 1999). Common treatments for dysmenorrhea include antiinflammatory pain medications, use of a hot pad applied to the lower abdomen, massaging the back or abdomen, dietary changes, exercise, and oral contraceptives.

Secondary dysmenorrhea is caused by a number of physical problems, including endometriosis, pelvic infection, use of an intrauterine device (IUD) for contraception, and ovarian cysts. Endometriosis is perhaps one of the more common causes of secondary dysmenorrhea.

Endometriosis occurs when tissue from the lining of the uterus, the endometrium, migrates to other parts of the body. Some experts believe that migration of the endometrial tissues results from "reverse menstruation," a backing up of menstrual flow into the fallopian tubes and then the abdominal cavity. Migrating endometrial tissue attaches itself to other organs and tissues in the body, such as the ovaries, fallopian tubes, ligaments, bladder, intestines, or the lining of the pelvic cavity. The tissue can also travel to more distant locations, such as the lungs, legs, arms, and brain. Just like the intact endometrium, the migrated endometrial tissue builds up and breaks down monthly, in response to hormonal changes in the female's body. Because the buildup of blood and tissue cannot leave the body like normal menstrual flow, it irritates the organs around it, causing inflammation, scarring, adhesions (scars that connect two normally separate tissues), and blood-filled cysts.

PREMENSTRUAL DYSPHORIC DISORDER (PMDD)
Severe and debilitating primarily psychological changes during the luteal phase of a woman's menstrual cycle.

DYSMENORRHEA
Spasmodic cramping in the lower abdomen, sometimes spreading to hips, lower back, or thighs, during menstruation.

ENDOMETRIAL PROSTAGLANDINS
Hormones that cause uterine contractions.

ENDOMETRIOSIS
A disorder of the female reproductive organs in which tissue from the lining of the uterus migrates to other parts of the body.

Amenorrhea

Amenorrhea is the absence of a menstrual period. *Primary amenorrhea* is diagnosed when a young woman has not begun to menstruate by the time she is 16 years old. *Secondary amenorrhea* occurs when a woman who was previously menstruating stops having menstrual periods. In a woman of reproductive age, amenorrhea is usually a sign of pregnancy. Amenorrhea in an older woman who is clearly not pregnant is likely to be a sign that she is heading into or has reached menopause. These are the most common causes of amenorrhea. However, young women sometimes experience amenorrhea as a consequence of excessive exercise or malnutrition; malnutrition is often precipitated by the eating disorders anorexia and bulimia, which can cause a shutdown of estrogen production and subsequent cessation of menstruation (Pruthi, 2001). Women who experience amenorrhea as a result of these practices probably need help in moderating their exercise or treatment for their eating disorders.

Some women who wish to skip a menstrual period may actually inhibit it through the use of contraceptive pills. By skipping the inert pills and starting another pack (refer to Chapter 10 on contraception), women can prevent bleeding between cycles. Women have been known to do this when they were anticipating a special event, such as a honeymoon, when menstruation would be undesirable (Gorman, 2000). This practice appears to be relatively safe. In fact, new hormonal contraceptives that will soon be available are designed to reduce women's cycles to only four a year (Miller & Notter, 2001; Rigby, 2002).

Sexual Activity during Menstruation

The fact that many women wish to reduce the number of menstrual periods they have may in part reflect common taboos surrounding sexual activity during menstruation. It was once believed that a man who had intercourse with a menstruating woman would become contaminated, and some religious leaders believed sex during menstruation to be a mortal sin. It was also once believed that babies conceived during a woman's menstrual period would be adversely affected; they would be leprous, epileptic, hunchbacked, blind, feeble-minded, or even possessed by the Devil—the list was seemingly endless (Ranke-Heinemann, 2002).

Overall, 70% of women and 72% of men avoid sexual intercourse during menstruation. However, college-educated women and men are more likely to engage in sexual relations during menstruation than are less well-educated men and women (Barnhart, Furman, & Devoto, 1995). Myths and religious beliefs are likely to influence the timing and frequency of sexual intercourse, but other explanations are possible. For example, some people may simply object to the risk of getting bloodstains on bedding or other furnishings. However, bloodstains can be prevented simply by placing a towel underneath you and by keeping a damp washcloth handy. Female barrier methods of contraception, such as a diaphragm, can also be used to collect menstrual flow. Barrier contraceptive devices are discussed in more detail in Chapter 10.

Is sex during menstruation safe? Sex during menstruation poses no health threat to the woman or her partner. Some women report that sex during menstruation actually has health benefits. Orgasms, regardless of how they are achieved, appear to reduce menstrual cramping for some women. Another benefit is the added lubrication provided by menstrual flow (Gardos, 1999).

AMENORRHEA
Absence of a menstrual period.

MAMMARY GLANDS
The breasts.

AREOLA
Pigmented circular area surrounding the nipple of a breast.

NIPPLE
Raised area in the center of the areola of each breast, with an opening through which an infant obtains milk.

POLYTHELIA
Having more than the normal number of nipples or breasts.

ALVEOLAR GLANDS
Glands in a woman's breasts that are responsible for producing milk after childbirth.

LACTIFEROUS DUCT
Duct that connects the alveolar glands to the opening of the nipple and that stores and releases milk during lactation.

The Breasts

The breasts, or **mammary glands**, are constructed of a base of muscle called the *pectoralis major,* which is covered by *adipose tissue* (fatty tissue); within each breast are the alveolar glands and the lactiferous duct. The **areola** is the pigmented circular area on the external surface of the breast. In the center of the areola is the **nipple.** Each of these structures is depicted in Figure 3.7. Mammals can have several pairs of mammary glands. Humans generally have only one pair; however, there have been reports of women having as many as eight pairs, a condition known as **polythelia** (Jones, 1991).

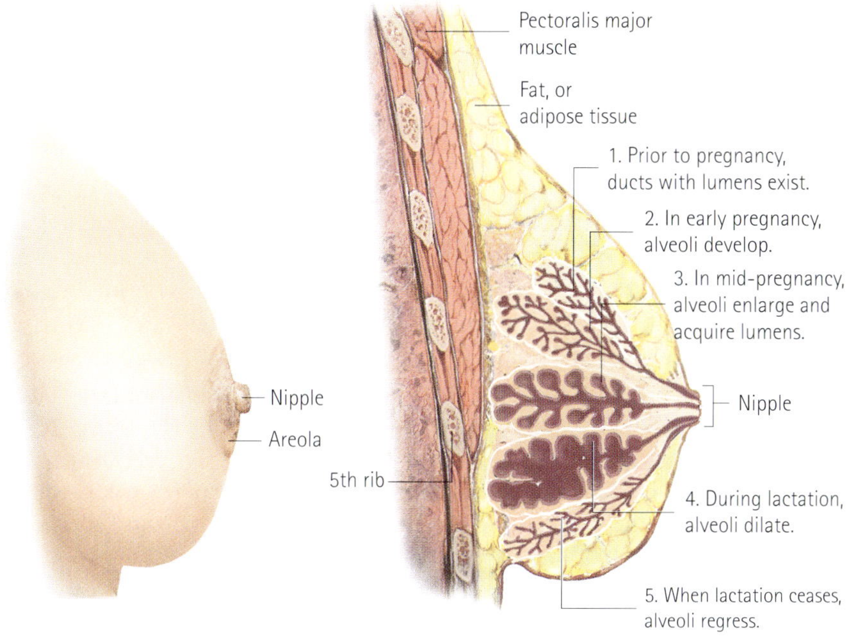

Figure 3.7 The Breast

The breasts are not genital structures, but they are functionally related to the genitals in that they serve as a source of sexual stimulus in some females as well as males, and they produce milk to nourish newborns. The **alveolar glands** (plural is *alveoli*) are divided into 15–20 lobes surrounded by adipose (fatty) tissue. They are responsible for producing breast milk after delivery of an infant. The alveoli resemble grape clusters and empty into the **lactiferous duct**, which opens into the nipple. The lactiferous duct stores and releases milk. An infant sucks on the nipple to stimulate release of milk.

Breast size and shape vary depending on the amount of adipose tissue and how it is distributed. The size of the breasts does not affect their ability to produce milk or their responsiveness to stimulation. Given the obsession with large breasts that characterizes U.S. culture, many people are dismayed to learn that breast size is largely genetically determined. But heredity does not stop many small-breasted women from having large ones. In fact, 206,354 women in North America had breast augmentation in 2001, a 56% increase from 1998 and a 533% rise from 1992 (American Society of Plastic and Reconstructive Surgeons, 2002). This trend reflects Americans' fascination with big breasts. Large breasts have not always been in vogue, however. In the 1920s, the 1960s, and the 1970s, small breasts (combined with a boyish look) were considered most attractive. Furthermore, people in many other cultures around the world find small breasts much more attractive than large ones, and in some cultures breasts are not considered erotic at all.

Why large breasts are admired in many cultures is not well understood. Small breasts are just as functional as large ones, so, from the perspective of human survival, it is not clear why an obsession with large breasts would

Looking At . . .

. . . Thinking About

In the 1920s small breasts were in. Today, large breasts are preferred, and women on popular TV shows, especially on channels such as MTV, are usually big-breasted. Do you think breast size matters? Why is breast size important?

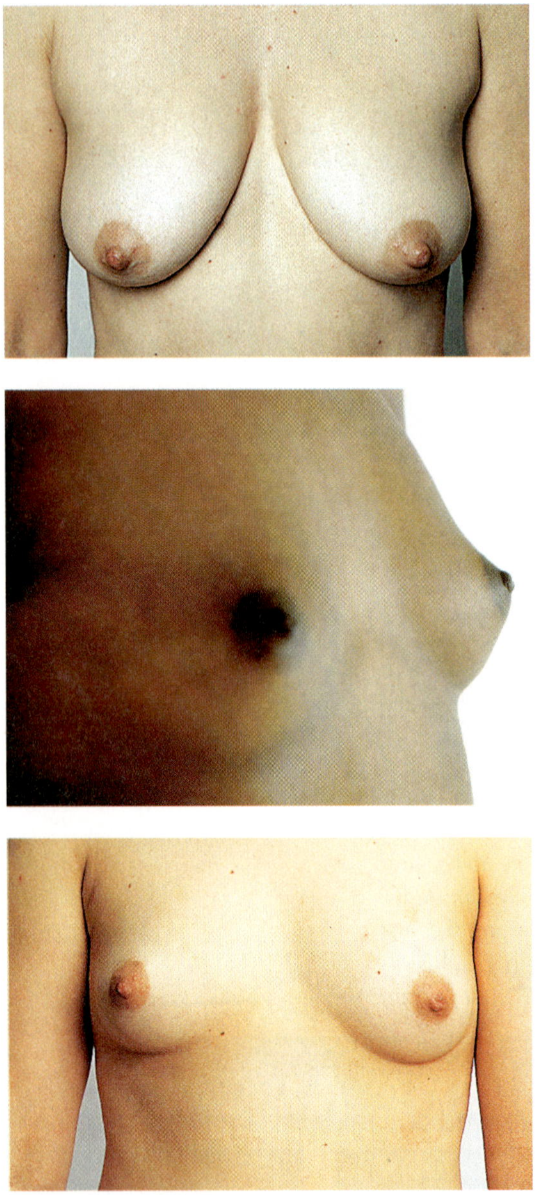

Variations of Healthy Breasts

develop. Scientists have offered many interesting theories about the evolutionary importance of breasts. However, Pulitzer Prize–winner and biology writer for the *New York Times* Natalie Angier has argued that the mere fact that breasts are so variable in size and appearance suggests that they serve no function in ensuring survival of the human species: "The woman's breasts . . . are . . . pretty, they're flamboyant, they're irresistible. But they are arbitrary, and they signify much less than we think. . . . They say little or nothing about a woman's inherent health, quality, or fecundity" (Angier, 1999, pp. 124–125). Whether or not this is true, breasts continue to have tremendous aesthetic and sexual value in many cultures.

The greatest threat to breast health is cancer. Breast cancer is the most common form of cancer found in women today. Because scientists have yet to find a way to prevent breast cancer, the key to getting adequate treatment and increasing the chance of survival is early detection. Table 3.2 shows the average female's risk of getting breast cancer at various ages; it does not take into account special risk factors such as family history.

The incidence of breast cancer in the United States increased during the 1980s but has since leveled off at about 0.5% (Alan Guttmacher Institute, 2002c). The increase was partly due to a higher detection rate resulting from increased awareness and improved detection methods. Another factor that accounts for the increased incidence of breast cancer is earlier onset of menstruation, resulting from better nutrition and other lifestyle changes. Early onset of menstruation means longer lifetime exposure to the hormone estrogen, which is linked to increased risk for breast cancer. Knowing that exposure to estrogen increases the risk of breast cancer raised concerns about use of oral contraceptives, but current evidence suggests that neither current nor past use increases the risk of breast cancer (Marchbanks et al., 2002). Other factors, such as the increasing prevalence of environmental toxins and the growing tendency for women to have children at an older age, also play a role in the increased incidence (ACS, 2002c). (Pregnancy causes a decrease in estrogen production, and thus early pregnancy is possibly beneficial in reducing the risk of breast cancer.)

Among various racial and ethnic groups, breast cancer is most common in white women. Although African American women have a lower risk of getting breast cancer, they have a slightly higher death rate from the disease. Asian American and Hispanic American women have the lowest risk of getting breast cancer. Lifestyle and access to adequate medical care probably account for differences across racial and ethnic groups (Alan Guttmacher Institute, 2002c).

Although women obviously cannot control all breast cancer risk factors (e.g., some women have a genetic predisposition), several that can be controlled have been implicated in increased risk of breast cancer. For example, women whose diets are high in fat are more likely to get breast cancer. In a woman already living with this disease, a high-fat diet also appears to influence the growth and spread of the cancer. Alcohol consumption has also been implicated in increased breast cancer risk; two drinks a day increases the risk by 25%. Research indicates that a drug called Tamoxifen, used to treat breast cancer, can reduce risk in high-risk women (ACS, 2002c).

The age at which lifestyle factors come into play is also important. It seems that women are most affected by cancer risk factors during adolescence and early adulthood. Engaging in regular physical activity, especially while young, seems to reduce the risk of breast cancer. Finally, there is some evidence that women who start smok-

TABLE 3.2 Breast Cancer Risk for U.S. Women by Age

AGE	RISK
From 30 to 40	1 in 22
From 40 to 50	1 in 68
From 50 to 60	1 in 35
From 60 to 70	1 in 27
Ever	1 in 8

SOURCE: National Cancer Institute, 2002.

ing before age 30 are at increased risk of developing breast cancer (Frazier & Colditz, 1995). Adequate nutrition combined with regular exercise, moderate alcohol intake, and no smoking goes a long way in preventing breast cancer and other cancers.

PREVENTIVE CARE OF THE FEMALE SEXUAL AND REPRODUCTIVE ANATOMY

Knowing about sexual and reproductive anatomy is the first step toward being able to recognize what is normal and what might be a symptom of a gynecological disorder. All women, young or old, need to take certain measures to take care of themselves. One key measure is to know the symptoms of the most common vaginal infections in order to be able to seek timely treatment if necessary. Regular breast self-examination and good physical hygiene, coupled with periodic pelvic exams, Pap tests, and professional breast exams, are also critical to self-care. Any woman who is sexually active or over the age of 18 is encouraged to have a pelvic exam, a Pap test, and a professional breast exam annually (Carlson et al., 1996; Slupik & Allison, 1996). Mammograms are usually recommended every 1 to 2 years for women aged 40–49 and every year for women aged 50 and over. There is a heated debate in the scientific community regarding whether women between 40 and 49 benefit from mammograms, but most experts agree that women over 50 should definitely have one annually (Maranto, 1996). In addition, women who have a strong family history of breast cancer or who are otherwise at significantly increased risk of breast cancer are encouraged to have mammograms starting before age 40 (Slupik & Allison, 1996).

Unfortunately, lesbian women are less likely than heterosexual women to get regular gynecological exams. There may be several reasons why this is the case. For instance, because cervical cancer is commonly associated with heterosexual intercourse, in which they do not currently engage, lesbian women do not always acknowledge their need to be tested for this cancer (O'Hanlon & Crum, 1996). Many physicians also adhere to this belief (Ferris,

Looking At . . .

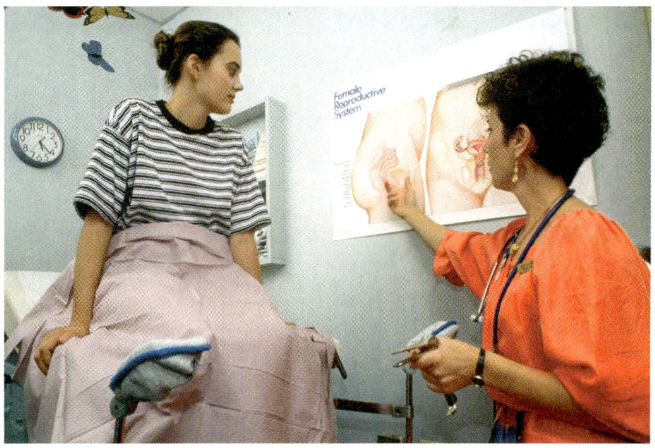

. . . Thinking About

Most medical professionals agree that "an ounce of prevention is worth a pound of cure"—that is, routine health care procedures can go a long way toward preventing significant illness. This is certainly true when it comes to reproductive self-care. Imagine that you are a sexual health educator and have only 5 minutes to convince a group of college-age women that physician's exams, Pap smears, and breast self-examinations are necessary. What would you tell them?

Batish, Wright, Cushing, & Scott, 1996), and they may discourage their lesbian patients from having regular Pap tests. Lesbian and bisexual women also cite as a reason they do not seek medical care their negative experiences with health care providers who are either unaware of or insensitive to issues of importance to them (Rankow & Tessaro, 1998). For example, health care providers may ask questions that are offensive or irrelevant to their lesbian patients. Another possible reason for not seeking health care is that lesbians do not use hormonal birth control methods and thus are not required to have regular checkups. Nonetheless, lesbians should have regular preventive testing.

Common Vaginal Infections

Knowing the warning signs of common disorders of the reproductive organs is an important step toward protecting your sexual health—knowledge is the first line of defense. *Vaginitis* is a general term for a variety of common vaginal infections and inflammations. A number of fungal, protozoan, and bacterial pathogens cause vaginitis in women and occasionally produce symptoms in men. These conditions are extremely common, although they appear to be on the decline (CDC, 2000f). And although these conditions are sometimes sexually transmitted, they can be acquired in a number of other ways.

Bacterial Vaginosis

Bacterial vaginosis (BV) is usually caused by an overgrowth of bacteria, usually *Gardnerella vaginalis* in combination with other anaerobic bacteria. Such bacteria are always present in the vagina, but an infection results when the normal balance of bacteria is upset. Exact figures on the prevalence of BV are not available, but it has been detected in 10–40% of women and is the most common cause of vaginal symptoms among women of child-bearing age (CDC, 2000a; McGregor & French, 2000).

did YOU know?

Between 100,000 and 150,000 women are rendered infertile each year as a result of PID brought on by a sexually transmissible infection (STI); about 15% of infertile women are infertile because they had PID from an untreated STI. Women who have PID are 6 to 10 times more likely to have an ectopic pregnancy (ASHA, 2001).

Vaginal odor is often the chief complaint of women suffering from vaginosis; an overgrowth of bacteria often produces a fishy-smelling, thin, milky discharge. BV might also cause itching or soreness around the vaginal area. About half of infected women have no symptoms at all (CDC, 2000a). The symptoms of BV are similar to those of other vaginal infections and must be confirmed through laboratory analysis. BV can lead to some serious complications if it is not detected and properly treated. First, it may increase a woman's risk of contracting other sexually transmissible infections (STIs), including HIV. Second, it is associated with many complications in pregnancy, including miscarriage and preterm labor. And finally, BV can infect the uterus and fallopian tubes, leading to an infection called **pelvic inflammatory disease (PID)** (CDC, 2000a; Ugwumadu, 2002). Symptoms of PID include disrupted menstrual cycle, pelvic pain, fever, nausea, vomiting, and headache, but some women are completely asymptomatic. Complications from PID, mainly caused by scar tissue that forms in the reproductive organs, are common, often irreversible, and sometimes fatal. The complications may include infertility, ectopic pregnancy, and chronic pelvic pain (American Social Health Association, 2001; CDC, 2001d). Unfortunately, most women with PID delay seeking medical treatment because they have few or no symptoms; but the longer treatment is postponed, the more ravaging the effects of the infection.

The causes of BV are not fully understood; it appears to be associated with sexual activity. Women who have never had sexual intercourse rarely develop it, and women who have a new sex partner, multiple sex partners, or other STIs are more likely to have BV (CDC, 2000a; Cleveland Clinic, 1997). Nonetheless, it is unclear whether BV is caused by sexual activity. Although men can exhibit symptoms of BV, treatment of

BACTERIAL VAGINOSIS (BV)
The most prevalent vaginal infection among women of childbearing age, characterized by a strong fishy odor and a grey or milky discharge; it was previously called *vaginitis*.

PELVIC INFLAMMATORY DISEASE (PID)
Inflammation of any of the organs in the pelvic region (the cervix, uterus, fallopian tubes, abdominal cavity, or the ovaries). The condition may cause abdominal pain, tenderness, nausea, fever, and irregular menstrual cycles and lead to infertility, ectopic pregnancy, ruptured membranes, and spontaneous abortions.

the infected male sexual partners of women with BV does not prevent its reoccurrence (CDC, 2002c). Thus, BV is not necessarily sexually transmitted. One study showed a strong association between BV and use of bubble bath, douching, and applying antiseptics to the vulva and the vaginal canal (Rajamanoharan, Low, Jones, & Pozniak, 1999). This finding seems to suggest that use of cleaning agents other than ordinary bath soap on the genitalia is unnecessary and may destroy beneficial bacteria that would ordinarily kill harmful bacteria, thereby upsetting the healthy balance of the various bacteria found in the vagina.

Candidiasis

Candidiasis, a vaginal yeast infection, is most commonly caused by the fungus *Candida albicans*. This vaginal infection is second only to bacterial vaginosis in prevalence in the United States and is believed to be increasing in frequency. About 75% of all women experience at least one episode of candidiasis during their lifetime, and 5–10% suffer repeated infections (Barousse et al., 2001; CDC, 2000f). *Candida albicans* is found in low concentrations in the vagina in about a third of healthy women. Vaginitis develops when there is an overgrowth of the fungus, thought to be due to changes in the normal balance of bacteria in the vagina or to disruption of the immune mechanisms that normally keep the fungus in check. Candidiasis is associated with a number of factors, including use of oral contraceptives, antibiotics, immunosuppressant drugs, and corticosteroid medications; use of tampons; diabetes; and wearing of tight-fitting undergarments. Candidiasis frequently results in irritation, inflammation, and itching of the vulva. The itching can be severe. A cottage-cheese–like vaginal discharge is sometimes evident. Men who are infected are usually symptom-free but may have a reddish rash and irritation or soreness of the penis, especially after intercourse. Candidiasis can be transmitted through sexual contact, but most cases are caused by other factors, including douching, use of scented soaps, use of underwear made from synthetic fibers, and chlorine in swimming pools. Sexual partners may infect and reinfect each other by passing the fungus back and forth during intercourse. Candidiasis of the mouth, throat, or anus may develop if the fungus is transferred through oral-genital or genital-anal contact. The condition is diagnosed by means of microscopic analysis or culturing of a smear taken from the vagina or the urethra.

Trichomoniasis

Trichomoniasis (commonly referred to as "trich," pronounced "trick"), is an extremely common cause of vaginitis; up to 48% of women making routine visits to family planning or university health centers have trichomoniasis (Cotch et al., 1997). Trichomoniasis is an STI caused by a pear-shaped, one-celled protozoan called *Trichomonas vaginalis*. It, too, is usually transmitted by sexual contact. The organism affects some 5 million people annually in the United States (CDC, 2000f). The prevalence among U.S. men is difficult to establish because the infection is often asymptomatic and self-limiting in men. If men do develop symptoms, these may include a slight penile discharge, pain with urination, irritation, or itching or tingling sensations along the urethra. Women typically experience a plentiful greenish-yellow, frothy vaginal discharge that is associated with irritation and soreness. Sexual activity and urination may be painful for women with trich infections. Trichomoniasis is diagnosed in women by microscopic examination or culturing of a specimen of vaginal fluids. Trich infection is more difficult to diagnose in men, since it often co-occurs with other diseases such as nongonococcal urethritis. Men are sometimes diagnosed after the fact—that is, if a particular medication clears up the problem, it must have been trich.

Diagnosis and Treatment

Vaginitis may be diagnosed when a woman seeks treatment for the symptoms or has a routine pelvic exam. To identify the type of infection, the health care provider first checks the vulval area, the vagina, and the cervix. In addition, a sample of vaginal discharge is obtained and examined under a microscope. Discharge from the cervical

IN YOUR own words

Terah Johnson
Virginia Commonwealth University

The first time I went to the doctor for an exam, I was terrified that something was going to be messed up in that area. Now, I do get regular exams, and as I am more comfortable with myself and my sexuality, I am also more comfortable with talking to my doctor.

CANDIDIASIS
A vaginal yeast infection, most commonly caused by the fungus *Candida albicans*. In women it results in vulval irritation, inflammation and itching, and sometimes a cottage-cheese–like discharge. Men are usually symptom-free.

TRICHOMONIASIS ("TRICH")
An STI caused by the protozoan *Trichomonas vaginalis*.

opening might also be cultured; confirmation of the source of a vaginal infection can take up to 2 weeks using this procedure.

Bacterial vaginosis is treated with antibiotics—for example, a 7-day oral dose of metronidazole or use of clindamycin cream or metronidazole gel. Trich is treated with a single oral dose of metronidazole. A yeast infection (candidiasis) is treated with any of a number of azole antifungal medications (CDC, 2002c), some of which are readily available over the counter. These therapeutic agents are in the form of creams, gels, tablets, or suppositories, all applied directly into the vagina.

3.2 on the web

Obtaining an abnormal result on a Pap smear can be very disturbing and confusing. However, an abnormal Pap smear does not necessarily mean that a woman has cervical cancer. Go to **www.ablongman.com/mcanulty2e** and click on Pap Smear Results: Atypical Cells.

What does it mean to have a low-level abnormality on a Pap test? Describe what happens if such an abnormality is found.

Pelvic Exam

A **pelvic exam** is an assessment of all the female reproductive organs. The physician visually examines the vulval area, the vagina, and the cervix for signs of infection (abnormal color, irritation, lesions, swelling, bumps, and unusual discharge). The Bartholin's and Skene's glands are also checked for lumps or unusual discharge indicative of infection. A **speculum**, a dual-bladed metal or plastic instrument, is inserted in the vagina (see Figure 3.8) to enable the physician to examine the cervix and vaginal walls for signs of infection or other disorders such as a **cystocele** (protrusion of the bladder into the vaginal wall). The physician then removes the speculum and conducts a **bimanual exam.** To conduct this exam, the physician inserts the index and middle finger into the vagina and simultaneously pushes down gently on the lower abdomen with the other hand. The physician checks the shape, size, firmness and position of the uterus and ovaries. A woman should report to her physician any tenderness she experiences during the exam.

Pap Test

Often a part of the pelvic exam, the **Pap test,** or *Pap smear* (named after physician George N. Papanicolaou, who first described the concept), is designed to detect abnormal cells on the surface of the cervix, which could become cancerous. The test can also detect some sexually transmissible infections, and it sometimes (though less reliably) detects endometrial cancer and tumors of the reproductive tract. A Pap test can be a lifesaver, since cancer is most likely to be cured if detected early. (It is important to understand, however, that abnormal cells do not necessarily develop into cancer. An infection can cause abnormal cell growth, which stops once the infection is treated. In addition, some abnormal cell growth will cease on its own and not progress to a cancerous condition.)

To conduct a typical Pap smear, a physician first places a speculum in the vagina to hold the vaginal walls open and then scrapes the surface of cervix and just inside the cervical os with either a small brush or a spatula to remove some of the surface cells (see Figure 3.8). The cells are smeared on a slide, "fixed" with a preservative, and examined microscopically for abnormalities.

Other techniques for carrying out a Pap test have been tested. One promising one, which is now approved by the FDA, is called a *thin-layer Pap test* (also *liquid-based cytology*). This technique preserves the entire cervical sample in a vial of liquid; the important cells (other than cells such as blood and mucus) are separated by a special machine and placed on a slide. Proponents of this technique argue that it is easier to accurately detect abnormal cells on this thin preparation, in which the irrelevant matter that appears on a traditional smear has been eliminated. Thin-layer Pap tests are more expensive than smears, and their use is controversial. Some research has shown that these tests are better and give fewer false results (Biscotti et al., 2002), but research findings have been mixed. Many researchers argue that more research is needed to demonstrate that this method is superior for cervical cancer screening and ultimately more cost-effective than a Pap smear (Mosely & Paget, 2002).

The Pap test is not perfect, in that it sometimes fails to detect abnormal cell growth that is present. Because the test is not perfect, women should be tested as frequently as their health care providers advise.

PELVIC EXAM
Medical assessment of all the female reproductive organs.

SPECULUM
A dual-bladed metal or plastic instrument that is inserted in the vagina during a pelvic exam to allow the physician to examine the cervix and vaginal walls.

CYSTOCELE
Protrusion of the bladder into the vaginal wall.

BIMANUAL EXAM
Medical procedure to check for abnormalities in the uterus and ovaries.

PAP TEST
A medical procedure designed to detect abnormal cells on the surface of the cervix; also known as a *Pap smear.*

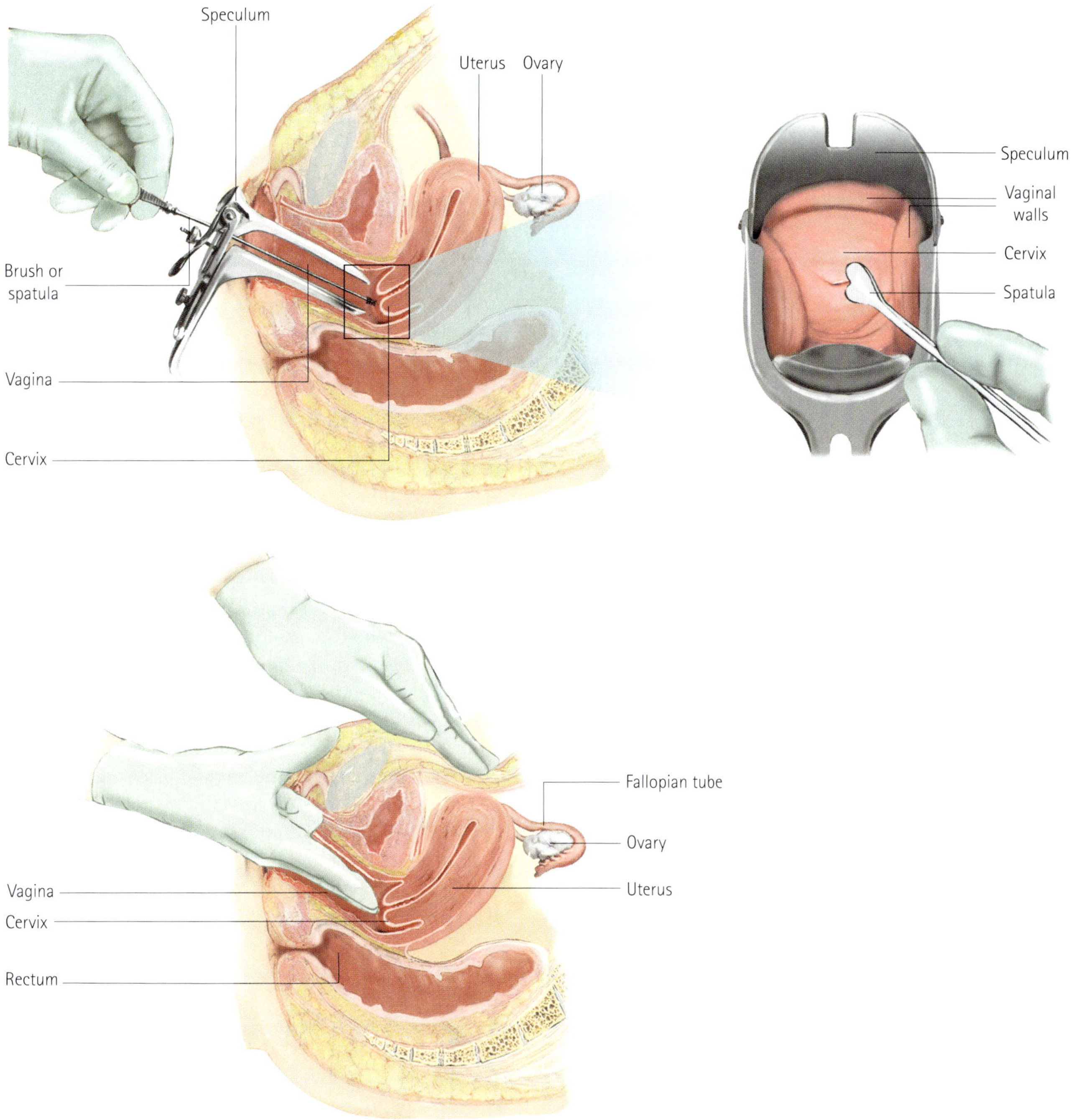

Figure 3.8 (Left, above) Pelvic Exam Using a Speculum; (Left, below) Bimanual Exam; (Right, above) Pap Test—Removal of Cervical Cells

Because most women have learned that their sexual anatomy is a private part of their bodies, a Pap test and pelvic exam can be both psychologically and physically uncomfortable. The circumstances under which the exam takes place are somewhat awkward and can make a woman feel ill at ease. The woman is usually instructed to wear a half-open gown (often made of scratchy paper), and she is required to place her heels in stirrups at the foot of the examining table and then slide her buttocks to the end of the table. While this situation can be emotionally stressful, the exam itself should not be physically painful. But if the woman is tense, she is likely to experience some discomfort. She can reduce discomfort by relaxing her abdominal and pelvic

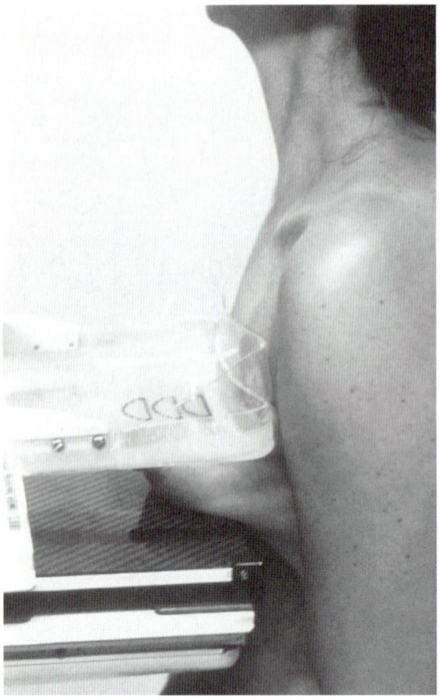

Mammogram: a few moments of discomfort can save a life.

muscles as much as possible; a few deep breaths before and during the exam can promote relaxation. A woman who is knowledgeable about her anatomy (see Reflect on This, page 76) and knows what to expect from the exam will be even more relaxed. The physician also plays a role in making the woman more comfortable. An empathic physician who explains what is happening during the exam and who attempts to be as gentle as possible can put the patient at ease. Some physicians even warm the speculum—or at least warn the patient that it is cold! If the examining physician is male, a female nurse must be present during the exam.

Breast Care

Breast care entails three routine self-care practices. All women should practice breast self-examination monthly and have a professional breast exam periodically; a physician usually does a breast exam in conjunction with the pelvic exam and Pap test. Finally women should have mammograms as advised by their physicians.

While breast self-examination (BSE) does not *prevent* breast cancer, it can lead to early detection, which reduces the chance that the cancer will spread to other parts of the body. Despite tremendous public health efforts to encourage monthly BSE, only about 18–27% of women examine their own breasts regularly. Some experts question the effectiveness of BSE for early detection of breast cancer; however, many agree that the better trained a woman is at conducting BSE, the better her chances of detecting a small lump (Wartik & Felner, 1994). Training in the proper technique is available at many local hospitals or clinics, the YWCA, or the American Cancer Society. Self-training kits are also available from Mammatech (1-800-626-2273), a company that provides silicone breast models on which a woman can practice detecting lumps.

A health professional conducting a breast exam uses techniques very similar to the BSE techniques shown in Figure 3.9. The physician has the woman place one hand behind her head and feels the breast for lumps. The same procedure is repeated on the other side. The physician also checks for discharge, nipple retraction, and dimpling, just as a woman does during her monthly self-exam.

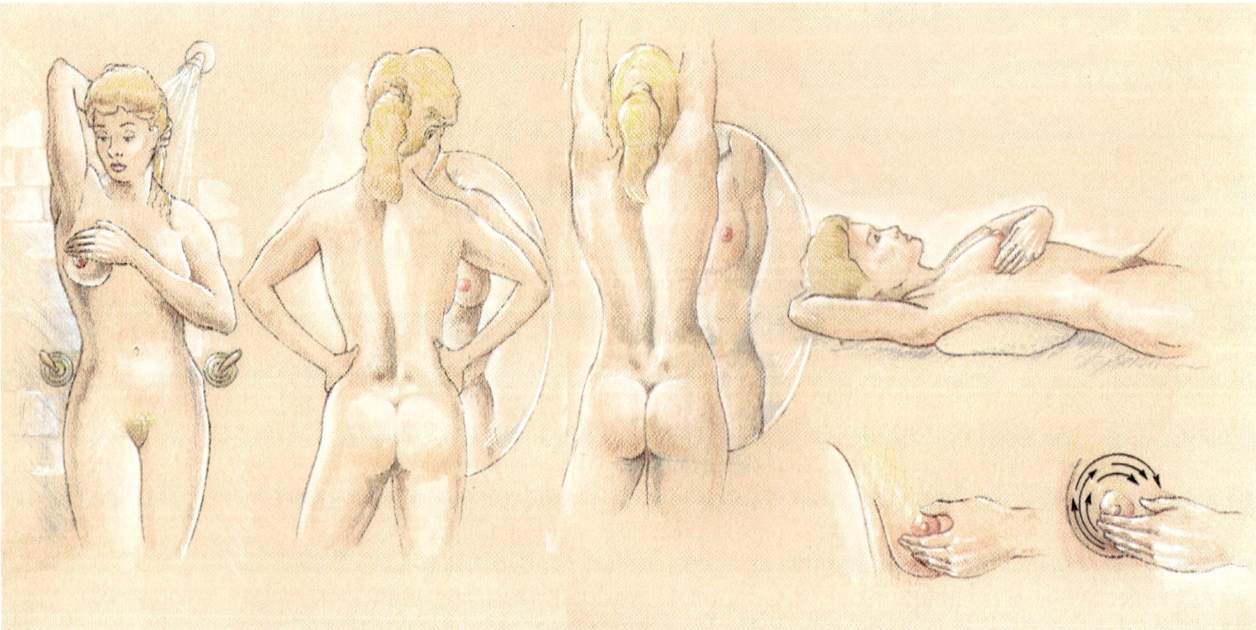

Figure 3.9 Techniques for Breast Self-Examination (BSE)

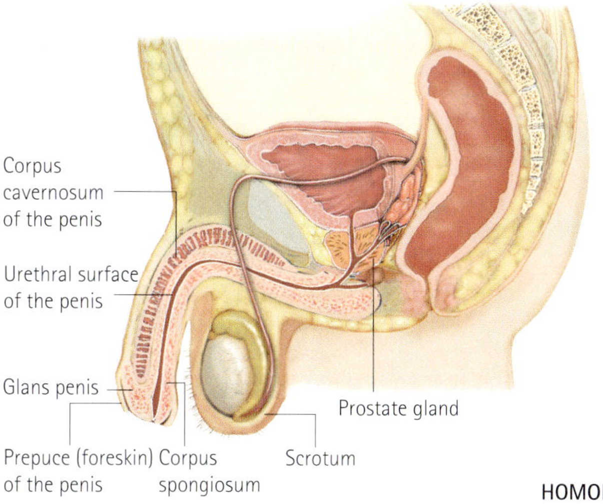

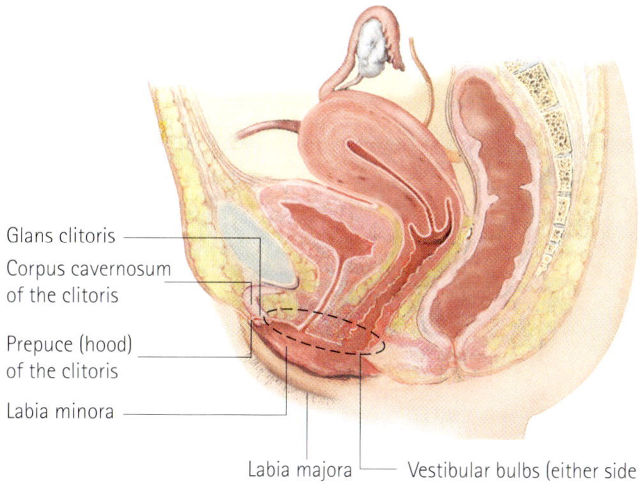

HOMOLOGOUS ORGANS

Male	Female
Glans penis	Glans clitoris
Penile prepuce (foreskin)	Clitoral prepuce (hood)
Corpus cavernosum of the penis	Corpus cavernosum of the clitoris
Urethral surface of the penis	Labia minora
Prostate gland	Skene's glands
Scrotum	Labia majora
Corpus spongiosum	Vestibular bulbs

Figure 3.10 Homologous Structures of Males and Females

A mammogram is usually performed at a center that has the necessary specialized equipment. During a mammogram, the breast is flattened between two plates in order to improve visualization of the breast cells. Low-intensity X-rays are used to obtain an image of the internal breast tissue; the image is later examined for signs of cancer or precancerous conditions. Because the procedure requires that the breasts be pressed and manipulated, the best time to have a mammogram is during the first week after a menstrual period, when the breasts are usually not tender or swollen (Slupik & Allison, 1996). If either manual examination or a mammogram reveals breast lumps, a woman should be reminded that many lumps (such as fibroadenomas or fibrocystic lumps) are benign. The woman and her doctor will determine the best treatment for both benign and cancerous lumps.

MALE SEXUAL AND REPRODUCTIVE ANATOMY

Each of the female sexual structures has a **homologous structure** in the male. *Homologous* simply means that the structures develop from the same cells in the developing fetus. All males and females have both "male" hormones (testosterone) and "female" hormones (estrogen and progesterone), but in the presence of a Y chromosome, the male hormones are produced in greater amounts. This male hormone production causes the cells in the fetus that will become the reproductive organs to develop into male organs. In the absence of a Y chromosome, every fetus would become a female. Figure 3.10 identifies the homologous structures of males and females.

The External Genital Structures

Like a female's, a male's sexual anatomy can be divided into external and internal structures. Also as in the female, the male's external genitals are richly supplied with nerve receptors, making them sensitive to touch and thus essential to the male's ability to respond sexually. The most prominent external structure is the penis (see Figure 3.11),

3.3 on the web

While women are more likely to have breast cancer, men can have it, too. Visit Male Breast Cancer: What Is It? at **www.ablongman.com/mcanulty2e.**

How common is male breast cancer? How does the prognosis for survival compare to that of women with breast cancer? What are the risk factors for breast cancer in men? What recommendations are made for early detection, and what are the symptoms that a man should look for? How are male and female breast cancer different, and how do these differences affect detection?

HOMOLOGOUS STRUCTURE
Any organ found in both male and female that developed from the same cells in the fetus.

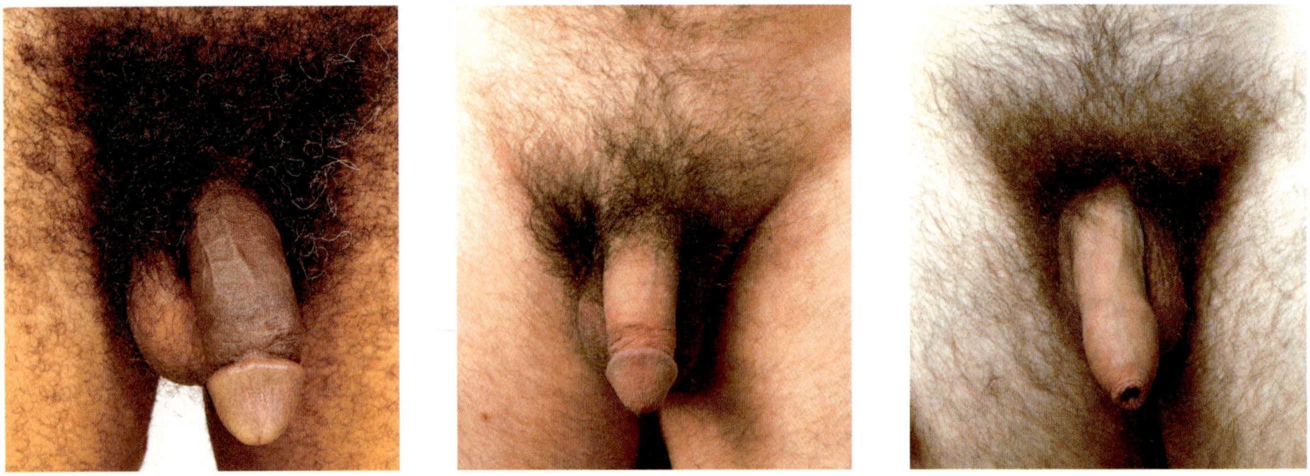

Healthy Male External Genitals

the actual prominence of which has often been the topic of jokes as well as true personal concern (see Reflect on This: Penis Envy for Men?).

did YOU know?

Less than 15% of boys around the world are circumcised, compared to 80% of boys in the United States. In Australia and Canada, only 40% of boys are circumcised, and the United Kingdom has the lowest rate of circumcision, only 6% (Kikiros, Beasley, & Woodward, 1993; Robson & Leung, 1992).

External Structures of the Penis

The **penis** is a cylindrical structure composed of a shaft and a glans. The glans and shaft of the penis are homologous to the glans and shaft of the clitoris. The tissue covering the underside of the penis is homologous to the labia minora in the female. A line, either faint or quite noticeable, runs along the underside of the penis where the tissue fused together during fetal development. The **shaft** is the area from the body wall to the glans. Not all of the penis is external; the penis extends beyond the body wall about half the shaft's length, and this portion, the **root**, serves to "anchor" the penis during an erection. The skin of the shaft is very

PENIS
External cylindrical structure composed of a shaft and a glans.

SHAFT
The portion of the penis between the glans and the body wall of the pelvis.

ROOT
The portion of the penis that extends into the body cavity and is anchored to the pubic bone.

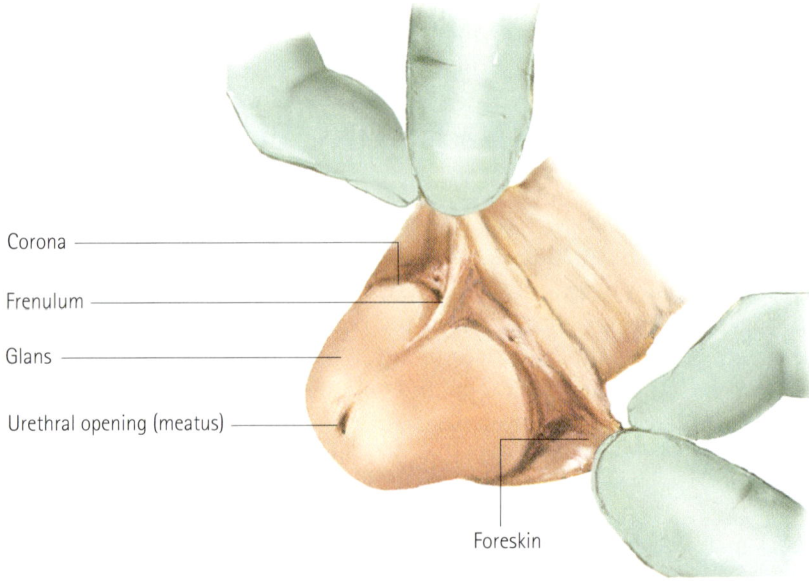

Figure 3.11 External Structures of the Penis

reflect ON THIS

Penis Envy for Men?

Did you know that some men undergo surgery to increase the length of their penises? The procedure, known as *penis augmentation,* is done by making an incision near the base of the penis and severing the ligament that attaches the penis to the pubic bone. Severing the ligament allows the root of the penis that is hidden within the body cavity to extend outside the body; thus, a man with a 4-inch penis may have a 6-inch penis after the surgery. One potential problem with this procedure is that it might change the angle of an erection; the erection might be horizontal or it might point down instead of up. A more serious problem might result if scar tissue reconnects the ligament—the penis can retract even further into the body cavity than it did before surgery. Nonetheless, a tremendous number of men have had or are considering penis augmentation.

What do you suppose motivates such a decision? The fact that so many men undergo penis augmentation is a strong indication that many men have grave concerns about the acceptability of their penises. Bernie Zilbergeld, an expert on male sexuality, says that he's never met a woman who wanted a penis (as Sigmund Freud proposed), but he *has* met a lot of men who suffer from penis envy or the desire to have a penis like someone else's.

It is true that some sex partners prefer large penises, but the vast majority think the size of a penis is less important than the overall attractiveness of the person and the quality of the sexual interaction. In fact, most women seem to prefer average-sized penises (5½ to 6 inches), and others report that they've had great lovers with smaller-than-average penises. Many "envied" men who have large penises have expressed a desire for a smaller penis because their lovers react with fear at the sight of their very large penises or they fear hurting their sex partners.

Are you a man with penis envy? Before you get out that measuring stick or start saving up for the operation to solve all your problems, consider for a minute whether you are being unduly influenced by a silly and potentially harmful cultural fantasy. What is more important is increasing your comfort with who you are as a sexual person and, if you're in a relationship, examining what is most important to your sexual partner.

SOURCES: Taylor, J. (1995, September). The long, hard days of Dr. Dick. *Esquire,* pp. 120–123. Zilbergeld, B. (1992). *The new male sexuality.* New York: Bantam Books.

elastic and can move freely across the underlying tissue. The skin is also hairless, as is the surface of the glans. The glans is aptly named for its shape; the word *glans* comes from the Latin word for "acorn." The **glans** is the cone-shaped structure at the tip of the penis; it ends at the rim called the **coronal ridge** (also called the *corona*). The **foreskin** (*prepuce*) is the fold of skin covering the glans, which is often removed in circumcision (see Health Matters: Circumcision—The Medical Controversy). The foreskin retracts slightly during urination and retracts all the way back to the coronal ridge during an erection. The **frenulum** is a band of tissue that connects the glans to the foreskin. It prevents the foreskin from retracting too far.

The glans is covered with a mucus membrane that is especially rich in sensory neurons, and thus, the glans is important in sexual stimulation. However, the frenulum and the coronal ridge have even greater concentrations of nerve endings and are thought to be even more sensitive to stimulation than the glans itself (Baldwin, 1993). This does not necessarily mean that all men prefer direct stimulation in these areas. Just like some women, some men find less direct stimulation of highly sensitive areas more desirable.

The penis houses the urethra, and the urethral opening, or **meatus**, is located at the tip of the penis. It is not unusual for the meatus to be located a few millimeters to the underside of the penis. This condition is called *glandular hypospadias* and is not a reason for concern. Other conditions, in which the meatus is on either the front or the back of the shaft or on the scrotum, are more serious, resulting in secondary problems

GLANS
The cone-shaped structure at the end of the penis.

CORONAL RIDGE
The rim of the glans; also called the *corona.*

FORESKIN
The fold of skin covering the glans of the penis; also called the *prepuce.*

FRENULUM
A band of tissue that connects the glans to the foreskin.

MEATUS
The urethral opening at the tip of the penis.

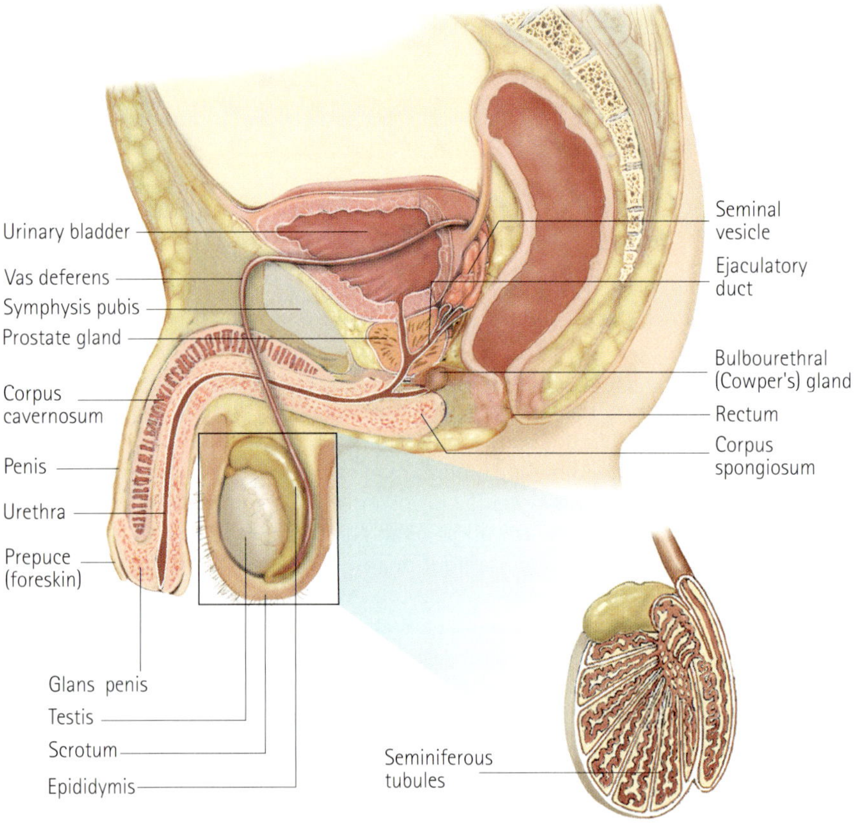

Figure 3.12 Male Reproductive Structures, Cross-Section

SCROTUM
Hairless or lightly hair-covered saclike structure with two separate chambers, each of which houses one of the testes.

PERINEUM
The muscular region covered with skin that extends from the vaginal opening to the anal opening in the female, and from the scrotum to the anal opening in the male.

CORPORA CAVERNOSA
Two cylindrical spongy bodies of erectile tissue that are bound in thick membrane sheaths, are located within the shaft of the clitoris and the penis, and become engorged with blood during sexual arousal.

CORPUS SPONGIOSUM
A cylindrical body located within the shaft of the penis, and consisting of spongy, erectile tissue bound in a thick membranous sheath; houses the urethra and becomes engorged with blood during sexual arousal.

URETHRA
In the male, a tube that runs the length of the penis in the center of the corpus spongiosum, through which urine flows and semen is ejaculated.

with urination, erections, and intercourse. These conditions are diagnosed and treated in childhood (Baldwin, 1993).

Scrotum

The **scrotum** is a hairless or lightly hair-covered saclike structure with two separate chambers, each of which holds one of the testes. The scrotum is homologous to the labia majora in the female. The skin covering the scrotum is very thin and moves loosely around the testes. The scrotum performs a critical function of regulating the temperature of the testes.

Perineum

The **perineum** is the area of skin between the scrotum and the anal opening. It contains many touch receptors, and therefore is highly responsive to physical stimulation.

The Internal Genital Structures

Like those of the female, the internal genital structures of the male have reproduction as their primary function; however, during sexual stimulation, they also contribute to the pleasurable sensations a man experiences.

Structures inside the Penis

Inside the penis and running its entire length are three cylindrical bodies consisting of spongy, erectile tissue bound in thick membranous sheaths. Two of the cylindrical bodies are collectively known as the **corpora cavernosa**, and the other is called the **corpus spongiosum** (see Figure 3.12). The corpora cavernosa of the penis correspond to the corpora cavernosa of the clitoris, and the corpus spongiosum is homologous to the vestibular bulb. The **urethra**, the tubelike structure through which the male uri-

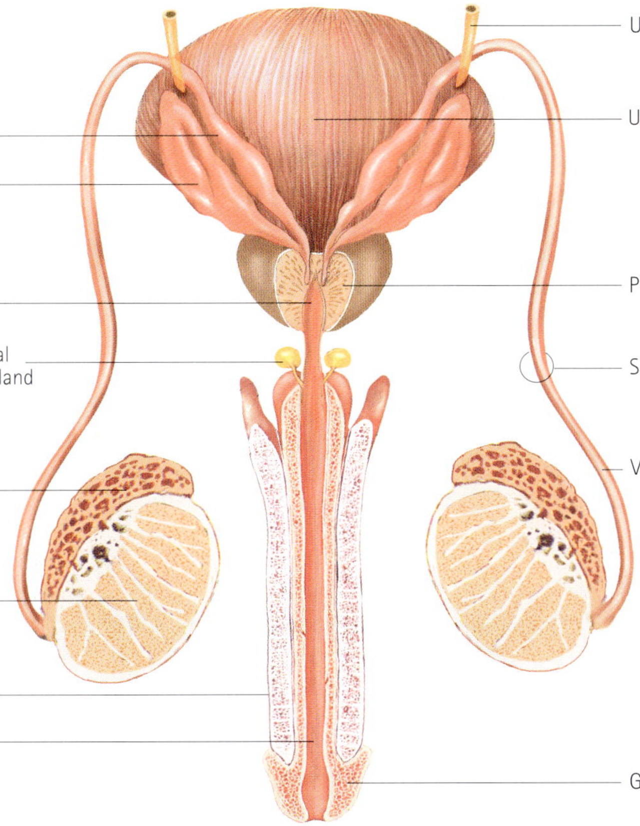

Figure 3.13 Male Internal Reproductive Organs

nates and ejaculates, runs through the center of the corpus spongiosum. The corpora cavernosa and corpus spongiosum are essential to male sexual functioning. When the male becomes aroused, these structures become engorged with blood, causing the penis to become erect. When the penis is erect, the spongy tissue squeezes the veins through which blood is drained from the penis; thus, most of the blood remains in these veins. A very small amount of blood (about 12 milliliters, or less than one-half ounce) does flow out of the veins in the penis during an erection but is replenished by the arteries (Baldwin, 1993).

Structures inside the Scrotum

The **testes** (singular is *testis*) are the organs responsible for production and storage of sperm. (Interestingly, because men in ancient times placed their hands over their genitals when taking an oath, the term *testis* is derived from the Latin word for "testify" and is also the root of a Latin word meaning "to witness.") These organs, located in the scrotum, are two oval structures measuring about 1 by 1.5 inches, although one testicle is often slightly larger than the other. They are homologous to the ovaries in the female. As Figure 3.13 illustrates, each of the testes is divided into lobes; inside each of the lobes are the **seminiferous tubules,** a mass of coiled tubes contained within a sheath called the **tunica albuginea.** The seminiferous tubules produce sperm in a process known as **spermatogenesis.** Lying among the seminiferous tubules are the **interstitial cells,** or **Leydig's cells.** These cells produce androgens, hormones important to male sexual functioning, and release them into the bloodstream. The sperm move from the seminiferous tubules to the **rete testis** (plural is *rete testes*), another network of tubes, and then to the **epididymis** (*epididymes* is the plural), where they continue to mature. The epididymis is a coiled tube lying against the back of the testis; this tube would be about 20 feet long if it were stretched out. If you roll a testis gently between

TESTES
The male organs that produce and store sperm, located in the scrotum.

SEMINIFEROUS TUBULES
Coiled tubes in the lobes of the testes that produce the sperm.

TUNICA ALBUGINEA
Sheath of tissue in the testes that surrounds the seminiferous tubules.

SPERMATOGENESIS
Process by which the seminiferous tubules produce sperm.

INTERSTITIAL CELLS
Cells in the testes that produce androgens and release them into the bloodstream; also called *Leydig's cells.*

RETE TESTES
Network of tubules within the testes through which the sperm travel to get from the seminiferous tubules to the epididymis.

EPIDIDYMIS
Long, coiled tube lying against the back of each testis, in which mature sperm are stored prior to ejaculation.

HEALTH Matters

Circumcision—The Medical Controversy

Have you ever wondered how a circumcision is performed? *Circumcision* is the removal of the foreskin from the penis. The foreskin, which completely adheres to the glans at birth, must first be torn away from the glans with a blunt, flexible object. Once the glans and foreskin are separated, the foreskin is cut and removed down to about the coronal ridge.

Medical professionals once assumed that circumcision was not a painful procedure for the newborn because development of the nerves in the penis was incomplete at birth. It is clear that this was a faulty assumption. Circumcision is painful, and infants display clear physiological and behavioral signs of pain during and after the procedure (American College of Obstetricians and Gynecologists, 2001). Although some physicians (but not all) now use anesthetics during circumcision, there is controversy regarding which pain management procedures are both effective and safe for newborns. The latest policy statement on circumcision from the American Academy of Pediatrics (AAP) states that analgesics (painkillers) are generally effective and safe and should be used if a circumcision is performed (American Academy of Pediatrics Task Force on Circumcision, 1999).

Is circumcision a medically recommended procedure? The medical literature reflects the differing viewpoints regarding whether male infants should be circumcised. In 1999, the AAP Task Force on Circumcision concluded that no scientific evidence suggests that circumcision should be recommended for the health of the child. That is, it is *not* a medically necessary procedure. The task force emphasized that parents should be properly informed of the risks and benefits, without exaggeration, prior to consenting to what is considered an optional procedure.

The primary potential health problem in an uncircumcised male infant is an increased incidence of urinary tract infection. Research has indicated an increased risk of such infection (Nayer, 2001), but the risk is still extremely low (less than 1% of noncircumcised males as opposed to 0.1% of circumcised males); also, the circumcision procedure itself is not free of complications (Lerman & Liao, 2001; Snyder, 1991; Thompson, 1990). The data suggest that from 2 to 40 of every 1,000 circumcised infants experience bleeding, infection, or other surgical trauma and that as many as 10 out of 1,000 require a surgical revision later in life (to correct a problem such as the remaining foreskin reattaching to the glans).

Many parents fear that not circumcising their sons will lead to (1) increased incidence of penile cancer, (2) increased risk of STDs and cervical cancer in female partners, and (3) increased risk of HIV infection. Penile cancer is a very rare disease, but it may occur at a higher rate in uncircumcised men. However, experts also believe that proper hygiene significantly reduces this risk (Lerman & Liao, 2001). Data on female cervical cancer indicate that there is some reason for concern that women who have intercourse with uncircumcised men are at higher risk of developing cervical cancer secondary to contracting the human papillomavirus (Castellsague et al., 2002). Once again, however, there is reason to believe that this risk is associated with improper hygiene by the male partners. The American Cancer Society does not support circumcision to prevent cancer (ACS, 1998). In 1996, the ACS re-

your fingers, you can feel the raised, crescent-shaped structure that is the epididymis. The sperm continue their maturation process and are stored in these tubes.

In order to survive, the sperm must be maintained at a temperature lower than normal body temperature (98.6 °F), at about 93 °F. The scrotum, because it hangs loosely outside the body, protects the sperm from changes in temperature. The **dartos muscle**, located under the skin of the scrotum, contracts to pull the scrotum closer to the body under cold conditions and relaxes to allow the testicles to hang farther from the body when the environment is too hot. The scrotum might also contract when the man feels fearful, an involuntary reaction designed to protect the testes (Baldwin, 1993).

Cryptorchidism occurs when one or both testes fail to descend into the scrotum during prenatal development. This problem occurs in about 3.4% of full-term and as many as 30% of premature male infants. The problem corrects itself in 80% of these children by the time they are 3 months old (Baldwin, 1993). The sperm-producing or-

DARTOS MUSCLE
Muscle under the skin of the scrotum that contracts and relaxes to raise or lower the scrotal sac.

CRYPTORCHIDISM
Failure of one or both testes to descend into the scrotum during prenatal development.

quested that the AAP not promote routine circumcision as a means of preventing cervical or penile cancer. The ACS pointed out that the data on cervical cancer risks that the AAP had been using were flawed methodologically and that the data on the relationship between penile cancer and circumcision were unconvincing. Furthermore, "fatalities caused by circumcision accidents may approximate the mortality rate from penile cancer" (Shingleton & Heath, 1996, p. 1). Research on potentially greater rates of transmission of HIV to males with foreskins suggests a relationship, but the finding is confounded by other factors such as hygienic practices (Bailey, Plummer, & Moses, 2001).

The issues surrounding circumcision are not just medical ones. In fact, the medically focused discussions involve many underlying social or personal biases regarding circumcision. One study showed that education about the potential risks and the AAP's position on circumcision had no effect on parents' decisions whether to circumicise (Binner, Mastrobattista, Day, Swaim, & Monga, 2002). Many parents want their sons circumcised because they want them to look like their fathers. Others are concerned that a boy with an uncircumcised penis will be laughed at in the locker room, because circumcised men are in the majority in the United States. There may also be concern that a man's sexual partners may find an uncircumsized penis undesirable. If these concerns have influenced you, please take a minute to ask yourself a few questions. First, should these concerns override the fact that circumcision is painful for the newborn boy? Do these concerns justify circumcision despite the absence of clear health benefits? Is it right to subject a baby to this procedure, given that he has no control over the decision? Some people who have joined this debate argue that parents should not circumcise newborns, especially when the potential health threat of not being circumcised can be managed through a healthy lifestyle (e.g., safer sex and good hygiene) (Hodges, Svoboda, & Van Howe, 2002).

If you haven't already, you might one day have to make a decision about circumcising a male infant. Reading the current scientific literature on circumcision can be an overwhelming experience. You may find it more helpful to seek out several informed opinions from pediatricians you trust. If you decide not to circumcise your infant, keep in mind that because so many infants are circumcised, your physician might not be able to give you the necessary information about proper care and hygiene of the uncircumcised child. Since proper hygiene appears to be the most critical factor in preventing many infections and cancer, you will want to make sure that you have such information and that you pass it along to your child as he grows. Information on proper care of the uncircumcised penis is readily available from the American Academy of Pediatrics in the pamphlet *Care of the Uncircumcised Penis* (1990), or at www.aap.org/family/uncirc.htm.

gans may be permanently damaged, resulting in infertility, if the testes have not descended by the time a boy is 5 years old. To avoid infertility, a surgical procedure (*orchiopexy*) to bring the testes down and stitch them into the scrotum is performed when the child is between 12 and 18 months old (Baldwin, 1993).

Testicular cancer is a relatively rare form of cancer, but its incidence is on the rise, currently at 7,500 cases annually in the United States (ACS, 2002). Despite the low overall incidence rate, men in the age range from 15 to 35 are more likely to die of this cancer than any other. The good news is that the 5-year overall survival rate for testicular cancer is 90% (ACS, 2001d). This high survival rate is the reason why self-examination is so important.

Not much is known about the causes of testicular cancer. However, about 10% of cases are found in men who have undescended testicles. Early detection of cryptorchidism can decrease the risk of developing testicular cancer later in life. Experts

Lance Armstrong, three-time winner of the Tour de France and still racing, is also a survivor of testicular cancer. He heads the Lance Armstrong Foundation, whose purpose is to support other cancer survivors.

have also suggested that environmental toxins disrupt normal hormone levels, causing abnormalities in the reproductive organs (ACS, 2001d).

Vas Deferens and Ejaculatory Ducts

Each testis is suspended in the scrotum from a **spermatic cord.** Each of these cords contains nerves and blood vessels supplying the testis as well as the cremaster muscle and the **vas deferens.** The **cremaster muscle** contracts and assists the dartos muscle in raising the scrotal sac closer to the body in colder temperatures and during sexual arousal. The vas deferens form the beginning of the path the sperm take when they are ejaculated. The vas deferens extend from the epididymes, into the inguinal canals (the openings in the abdominal wall for the spermatic cords), and up over the bladder. They continue behind and below the bladder, where they enter the prostate gland to join with their respective **ejaculatory ducts** (see Figure 3.13).

Seminal Vesicles

The **seminal vesicles** also open into the ejaculatory ducts within the prostate; these glands empty semen into the vas deferens through the ejaculatory ducts. The vas deferens then empty into the urethra. During ejaculation, the seminal vesicles, small and elongated structures, emit fluid, which makes up 70% of the semen. The semen mixes with the sperm as they move down the vas deferens. The alkalinity of the seminal fluid balances out the high acidity level of the vagina in order to provide an environment in which the sperm can survive. Seminal fluid also serves as a source of energy for the sperm.

At the opening of the bladder in the urethra is a wide sphincter muscle that relaxes to release urine during urination. When a man ejaculates, this muscle contracts, closing the bladder's opening to prevent ejaculate from entering the bladder instead of exiting through the narrow urethra. In some men, however, the sphincter does not contract, and the ejaculate goes into the bladder. This condition, called **retrograde ejaculation**, can cause infertility, since sperm are not ejaculated during orgasm. Retrograde ejaculation can be treated with over-the-counter decongestants, which act to tighten the sphincter muscle at the bladder's opening. Antidepressants have a similar effect and are sometimes prescribed to treat this condition. If neither of these treatments is effective, sperm can be retrieved from the urine for artificial insemination (see Chapter 9 for a discussion of infertility treatments). However, this procedure requires that the man drink a large amount of sodium bicarbonate in order to reduce the acidity of the urine so that the sperm can survive until they are extracted (Oppenheim, 1994).

Prostate Gland

The **prostate gland**, a walnut-sized structure roughly homologous with the Skene's gland in the female, is located beneath the bladder. The urethra passes through the prostate gland, which emits additional fluid that combines with the sperm and fluid from the seminal vesicles. This fluid makes up the other 30% of the semen and also helps to neutralize the acidity of the vaginal canal.

There are two benign forms of prostatic disease: prostatitis and benign prostatic hyperplasia (BPH). These conditions are sometimes detected when a man notices that he is having difficulty urinating; the swelling of the prostate compresses the urethra and limits or blocks urine flow. Ejaculation can also be impaired by these conditions.

Prostatitis is an inflammation of the prostate that can be either bacterial or nonbacterial in origin. The two types have similar symptoms. In addition to swelling and urinary difficulties, a man with prostatitis might feel itchiness and discomfort deep within the penis. He might notice a brown or yellowish stain on his underwear or

SPERMATIC CORD
A cord from which each testis is suspended in the scrotum; contains the nerves and blood vessels supplying the testes and the vas deferens.

VAS DEFERENS
Tubes running from each testis to an ejaculatory duct.

CREMASTER MUSCLE
Muscle located in the spermatic cord that assists the dartos muscle in raising and lowering the scrotal sac.

EJACULATORY DUCTS
Two ducts within the prostate gland through which the seminal vesicles empty into the vas deferens.

SEMINAL VESICLES
Small elongated structures located just outside the prostate gland that emit fluid into the vas deferens through the ejaculatory glands.

drops of clear liquid coming from his penis. He might also find the meatus "glued" shut by dried liquid (Salmans, 1996).

Benign prostatic hyperplasia (BPH), or an enlarged prostate, is actually a natural part of aging. When a male infant is born, his prostate is only about the size of a pea. Throughout childhood, the prostate grows slowly. During puberty, hormones cause rapid growth of the prostate to its adult size, about the size of a walnut. It remains this size until the man is between 40 and 45, when it begins growing again. It does not stop growing until the man dies. Thus, any man who lives long enough will develop BPH. By age 50, over 50% of men have BPH. Nearly all men have it by age 80 (Oppenheim, 1994; Salmans, 1996). Complications from BPH usually arise gradually. A man might first notice that his urine stream is weaker and that he has to strain more to urinate. He might also experience greater urgency and increasing frequency of urination (because the bladder gets irritated from not being emptied). BPH is often treated with medications such as alpha-blockers (commonly used to treat hypertension, or high blood pressure), which relax the smooth muscles around the urethra and bladder opening. Hormones to block production of male hormones can be used, but most also cause impotence and decreased sexual desire. The drug finasteride (its brand name is Proscar) promises to shrink the prostate without affecting a man's sexual functioning (Oppenheim, 1994). Ultimately, the most effective permanent treatment for BPH is surgery to remove the part of the prostate that obstructs the urethra.

Prostate cancer is of much greater concern than other diseases affecting the prostate because it is life-threatening. Prostate cancer is most common after age 50. In fact, 70% of men with prostate cancer are over the age of 65, and 80% of men age 80 and over have prostate cancer (ACS, 2001c; Cleveland Clinic, 2002b). Approximately 180,000 men are diagnosed with prostate cancer annually, and 40,000 will die from it. However, more than 90% of men survive prostate cancer for at least 5 years after being diagnosed. Prostate cancer generally progresses slowly; thus, many men with prostate cancer die of other causes (CDC, 2001e; Cleveland Clinic, 2002b).

African American males are far more likely than white American males to develop prostate cancer and more than twice as likely to die from it (CDC, 2001e). Hispanic American, Native American, and Asian American men are less likely than white men to get prostate cancer. The reasons for these racial and ethnic differences are not totally understood, but environmental factors, such as diet, appear to be significant. In fact, men who have diets that include a lot of red meat and dairy products are at increased risk, and men with diets high in tomato products have a lower risk of prostate cancer (Giovannucci, Rimm, Liu, Stampfer, & Willett, 2002; Michaud et al., 2001). Other factors, such as family history and exposure to cadmium, a heavy metal, also put men at greater risk for prostate cancer (Achanzar et al., 2001; CDC, 2001e).

Unlike BPH, prostate cancer is asymptomatic in the early stages, because cancerous tumors tend to grow on the outer surface of the prostate and often do not affect the urethra (see Figure 3.14). Prostate cancer usually presents as a very hard lump or irregular texture on the surface of the prostate gland. Therefore, the best defense against prostate cancer is regular rectal examination by a health professional. A newer diagnostic test measures how much prostate-specific antigen (PSA) is in the blood. High levels are indicative of prostate cancer. Unfortunately, this test has a high false-positive rate, and experts disagree as to whether its large-scale use would detect enough cases in the early stages to warrant the worry and risks of a biopsy for those men who test positive when they don't have prostate cancer (CDC, 2001e).

The extent of the cancer determines the type of treatment recommended. The three most accepted treatment approaches are "watchful waiting," radiation therapy, and surgery. Because some prostate cancer is not aggressive, the best option for older men may be to wait out the cancer in the hope that it does not advance. Surgery in the early stages of the disease can be quite successful. Because the surgery typically removes the prostate gland, seminal vesicles, and a portion of the spermatic cord,

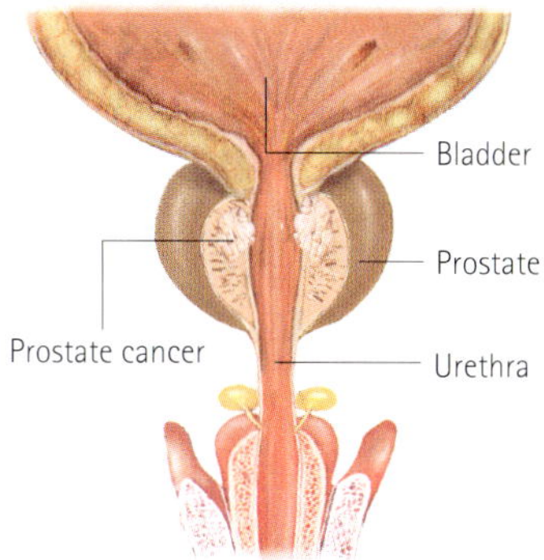

Figure 3.14 Prostate Cancer

RETROGRADE EJACULATION
A condition in which ejaculate backs into the bladder rather than moving out through the urethra, usually caused by failure of the sphincter muscle at the bladder opening to contract.

PROSTATE GLAND
Walnut-sized structure that is located beneath a man's bladder and emits fluid that combines with that from the seminal vesicles to form semen.

PROSTATITIS
Inflammation of the prostate gland that is bacterial or nonbacterial in origin.

BENIGN PROSTATIC HYPERPLASIA (BPH)
Enlargement of the prostate gland caused by the natural aging process.

PROSTATE CANCER
Disease characterized by the growth of abnormal cells in the prostate.

did YOU know?

Japanese men living in Japan are seven times less likely to die of prostate cancer than are American men. The mortality rate rises for Japanese men who immigrate to the United States, however, which implicates environmental factors (including diet) in prostate cancer.

however, permanent erectile dysfunction has been shown to occur in up to 91% of surgery patients. Temporary urinary incontinence and bowel urgency are other side effects. Radiation therapy is an effective alternative to surgery—it causes less erectile dysfunction and urinary incontinence but more bowel urgency (Madalinska et al., 2001). However, over time, quality of life appears to be about the same with either type of treatment (Lee, Hall, McQuellon, Case, & McCullough, 2001). In recent years, the medical profession has begun to focus not only on survival after prostate cancer but also on quality-of-life issues (Madalinska et al., 2001). Given the physical impairments resulting from treatment (and the emotional issues created by problems such as incontinence and erectile dysfunction), many doctors prefer watchful waiting to intervention to eliminate prostate cancer. As mentioned earlier, many men with untreated prostate cancer live full and happy lives to a natural end without the side effects of treatment.

Bulbourethral Gland

Just below the prostate lies the **bulbourethral gland**, or the **Cowper's gland**, homologous to the Bartholin's gland in the female. This pea-sized gland emits an alkaline fluid in response to sexual stimulation. This fluid may act to neutralize the acidity of the urethra prior to passage of the sperm as an added protective measure. The Cowper's gland emits fluid shortly before orgasm but not in sufficient amounts to function as a lubricant for sexual intercourse, as some might assume. The emissions of the Cowper's gland can contain thousands of stray sperm that found their way there during a previous ejaculation. Thus, if a barrier method of contraception (a condom or diaphragm, for example) is being used but is not in place before the Cowper's gland emits its fluid, pregnancy could occur. This is just one reason why it is so important to place a condom on the penis before there is any contact between the man's penis and his female partner's vulva.

Production and Structure of Sperm

You have already learned how an ovum develops, but, of course, sperm are equally essential to the creation of new life. The internal male genitalia play the critical role of forming the sperm. Sperm are produced in the seminiferous tubules of the testes. These tubules first generate germ cells, called **spermatogonia.** Each of these germ cells contains 46 chromosomes, the full number of a typical human cell. Through the process of spermatogenesis, spermatogonia develop into mature male reproductive cells, or **sperm** (also called **spermatozoa**). Spermatogenesis begins when the chromosomes of the spermatogonia double (in a process called *mitosis*); then each germ cell splits and half of the 92 chromosomes go to each cell that results from the division (a process called *differentiation*). These cells are called *primary spermatocytes,* and they also contain 46 chromosomes. These cells divide again, but this time, the chromosomes do not double; the result is the *secondary spermatocytes,* cells that contain only 23 chromosomes each. The secondary spermatocytes divide again to become immature sperm, the **spermatids.** Once a spermatid has matured, it is a sperm, with 23 chromosomes. When a sperm joins with an ovum, also having 23 chromosomes, the newly formed cell has the full complement of 46 chromosomes, half contributed by the mother and half contributed by the father.

A mature sperm cell consists of three parts: the head, the midpiece, and the tail (Figure 3.15). The head contains a nucleus that holds the chromosomes. The top of the head is covered by the **acrosome**, a vesicle (membrane) containing enzymes that enable the sperm to penetrate the ovum. The midpiece is the thicker section just below the head. It contains *mitochondria,* rodlike intercellular structures that provide energy

BULBOURETHRAL GLAND
A pea-sized gland that is located just below the prostate gland and emits an alkaline fluid in response to sexual stimulation; also called the *Cowper's gland.*

SPERMATOGONIA
Germ cells produced in the seminiferous tubules of the testes.

SPERM
The male reproductive cells; also called *spermatozoa.*

SPERMATIDS
Immature sperm.

ACROSOME
A membrane that covers the top of the head of a sperm cell and contains enzymes that allow the sperm to penetrate the ovum.

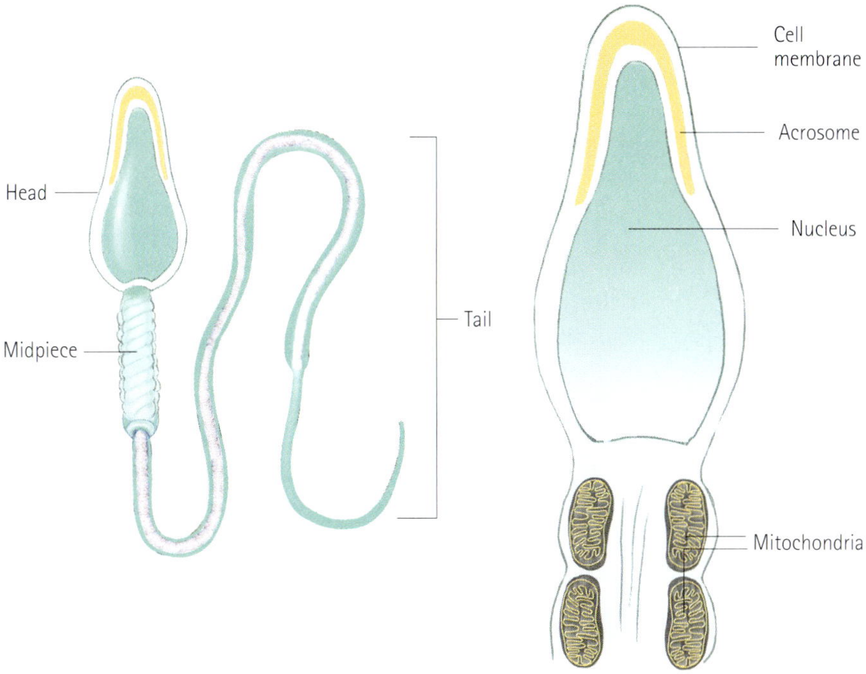

Figure 3.15 The Sperm

for swimming. The tail of the sperm is composed of filaments that contract to produce a whipping motion, called *flagellation.* The entire sperm is only about 0.05 millimeter, or 0.002 inch, long and is, therefore, not visible to the naked eye.

PREVENTIVE CARE OF THE MALE SEXUAL AND REPRODUCTIVE ANATOMY

Like women, men need to be aware of the signs of diseases in their reproductive organs so that they can apply an ounce of prevention in their sexual health care. Two exams, self-examination of the testicles and a rectal exam by a trained professional, are the preventive efforts that are most important for good sexual health in the male.

Testicular Exam

Regular testicular self-examination (TSE) is of particular importance for younger men. In general, a man should check his testicles for the presence of any small, hard mass, which could be an indication of testicular cancer. Testicular cancer can easily go unnoticed until it has spread to other parts of the body, because the tumors that form in the testes are generally painless. A man's best chance at early detection is to perform TSE regularly. The technique should be taught to all males around the time of puberty and should be carried out monthly. It is easy to learn and takes only about 3 minutes to perform. The best time to conduct TSE is just after a warm shower or bath, because the scrotal sac is relaxed and the testes are easier to examine. Here are the steps to follow in conducting TSE (see Figure 3.16) (Friman, Finney, Glasscock, Weigel, & Christophersen, 1986):

- Gently pull scrotum so that it hangs freely.
- Use fingers and thumbs of both hands to isolate one testicle.
- Locate the soft tender mass (the epididymis and spermatic cord) on top of and extending behind the testicle.
- Rotate the entire surface area of the testicle between fingers and thumbs.

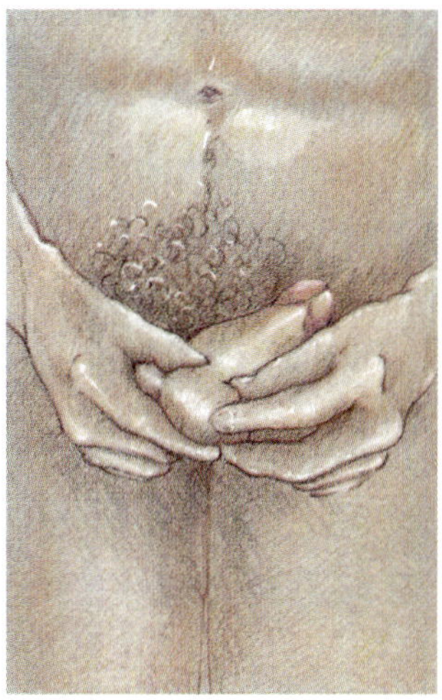

Figure 3.16 Testicular Self-Examination

Looking At . . .

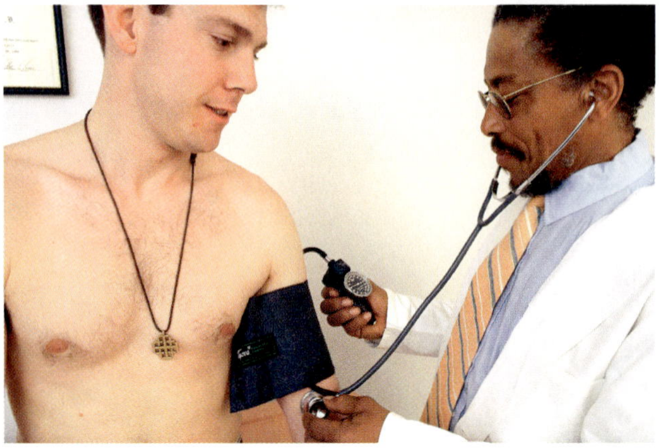

. . . Thinking About

Men do not seek preventive medical care as often as women, but they could greatly benefit from early diagnosis and treatment of medical conditions of the male reproductive organs. Why do you suppose some men don't seek preventive care when they should? Are there any men in your life who need to be encouraged to seek such care?

- Feel for a painless or uncomfortable lump, about the size of a pea.
- Repeat the examination on the other testicle.

Rectal Exam

Men are less likely than women to have a regular medical examination of their reproductive organs. Not only are their bodies not subject to menstruation and pregnancy, but they also tend to have fewer problems with genital irritation or urinary problems and are less apt to see a physician with concerns about fertility. Generally speaking, annual preventive exams are not necessary for otherwise healthy men until the age of 40 (Oppenheim, 1994). From age 40 on, however, every man needs an annual **rectal exam.** Men who are at high risk for developing prostate cancer are sometimes advised to start having rectal exams when they are in their late 30s (Salmans, 1996). During this exam, the man bends at the waist and leans over the examining table while a physician inserts a gloved and lubricated finger into the rectum and feels the prostate gland for inflammation or lumps or other irregularities on the surface. The physician also checks the rectum for signs of colon cancer, which becomes more likely in men after the age of 40. While a rectal exam might seem undignified, it can be life-saving.

HEALTHY DECISION MAKING

You can do much to protect your sexual health if you take care of yourself. Part of taking care of yourself is being educated about and aware of symptoms that might indicate the presence of an illness or infection that needs to be treated. Most ailments affecting the genitalia are minor and usually readily treatable. Sometimes, though, you might not be sure if a particular symptom warrants a doctor's visit. As guidelines to help you make healthy decisions about your sexual health, below are two checklists, one for women and one for men, of symptoms that should be reported to a health-care provider. However, do not rely solely on these lists. If you experience any symptom that concerns you, you should not hesitate to call a doctor to inquire about its significance.

For Her:

- ❑ Unusually increased vaginal discharge
- ❑ Vaginal discharge with an unpleasant or unusual odor or color
- ❑ Bleeding between periods
- ❑ Abnormal vaginal bleeding, especially if it occurs during or just after intercourse
- ❑ Persistent itching, burning, swelling, redness, or soreness in your vaginal area
- ❑ Sores or lumps in your genital area
- ❑ Pain or discomfort during intercourse
- ❑ Pain or pressure in your pelvis that differs from menstrual cramps
- ❑ Frequent and urgent need to urinate or a burning sensation during urination

Source: Slupik & Allison, 1996

For Him:

- ❑ One testicle that is considerably smaller than the other or any obvious change in the testes on examination
- ❑ A lump in the testicle

RECTAL EXAM
Medical procedure in which a physician feels the prostate gland through the rectal wall in order to assess for abnormalities.

- ❑ Pain and swelling that do not go away within an hour after injury by a blunt object or a fall
- ❑ Persistent urinary problems, including
  - Pain when urinating
  - Frequent or urgent need to urinate
  - Cloudy, smelly, or bloody urine
  - Difficulty beginning to urinate
  - Slow urination, dribbling, or inability to urinate at all
  - Inability to control urination most of the time
- ❑ Penile discharge
- ❑ Burning pain with ejaculation
- ❑ Swelling or irritations on the penis or surrounding area, including sores, redness, growths, or warts

Source: Larson, 1996

summary

FEMALE SEXUAL AND REPRODUCTIVE ANATOMY

- The external female genitals collectively form the vulva. These structures include the mons veneris, the labia majora, the labia minora, the clitoris, the clitoral hood, and the perineum.
- Within the labia lie the urethral and vaginal openings. All of these structures have a rich concentration of nerve endings, and stimulation of these structures can produce sexual arousal.
- The internal female genitals are responsible for the reproductive process.
- The vagina has a dual function. The outer third is sensitive to touch and, therefore, plays a role in sexual arousal, but it is also an important reproductive structure in that it accepts the penis during intercourse, is part of the passageway for sperm moving toward the egg cell, and is the birth canal. The cervix, uterus, fallopian tubes, and ovaries also play key roles in conception and pregnancy.
- The menstrual cycle is a process by which the body produces a mature egg cell, or ovum, that is capable of being fertilized by a sperm. Throughout the cycle, most of the internal organs undergo changes that ultimately make conception and pregnancy possible.
- Although menstruation is a normal, healthy function, it has been surrounded by myth and mystery for centuries. Women sometimes experience physical discomfort during the luteal and/or menstrual phases.
- The breasts are considered part of women's sexual anatomy because they sometimes function as sexual stimuli. They also provide nourishment for the newborn.

PREVENTIVE CARE OF THE FEMALE SEXUAL AND REPRODUCTIVE ANATOMY

- Women are advised to practice good preventive self-care and to seek medical care in protecting their sexual anatomy. Annual Pap tests, gynecological exams, regular breast self-exams, and professional breast exams are the key to sexual health.

MALE SEXUAL AND REPRODUCTIVE ANATOMY

- The penis, scrotum, and the perineum constitute the external male sexual anatomy. These structures, like the external genital structures of the female, are highly responsive to sexual stimulation. The penis plays a key role in sexual intercourse, and the scrotum holds the testes.
- The internal genital structures in the male include the corpora cavernosa and the corpus spongiosum, which allow the penis to become erect; the testes, which produce and store the sperm; the vas deferens, ejaculatory ducts, and urethra, which transport sperm and semen (collectively called *ejaculate*); and the seminal vesicles and prostate gland, which supply semen, the protective and energy-supplying fluid in which sperm are transported.

PREVENTIVE CARE OF THE MALE SEXUAL AND REPRODUCTIVE ANATOMY

- Men also need to take care of their reproductive organs. By practicing preventive care and responding quickly to unusual symptoms, men stand a good chance of protecting their sexual health into old age.

CHAPTER 4

Physiology of Sexual Arousal and Response

His hand gently brushes against her breast. She strokes his hair and chest. Slowly, they begin to undress. He kisses each part of her skin as it is revealed. Her hand touches his penis, which is now erect inside his pants. He unzips his fly. She runs her fingertips over the surface of his penis and kisses it lightly. They lie together gently kissing and caressing and delighting in each other's bodies, slowly but with increasing excitement. He strokes her back, buttocks, arms, neck, and her breasts. He kisses and sucks her nipples as she moans softly. Then his fingers gently play with her pubic hair and he touches her labia, which have grown quite moist. She begins fondling his penis and testicles in return. Finally, his fingers, moistened by her lubrication, play around her clitoris. First slowly, but as she responds his pace quickens. Their breathing becomes more rapid. . . . He enters her and thrusts—slowly at first, and then at a quickening pace. She too is thrusting in rhythm with him. They quicken their pace, he shudders and groans with pleasure as he climaxes. They lie quietly for a minute. Then he withdraws his penis and gently holds her in his arms while he stimulates her clitoris with his finger until she too tenses and writhes with her climax. Afterward, they lie together and caress each other's bodies with their fingertips.

Slowly, they begin to undress.

(Kaplan, 1979)

Many changes occur within the body throughout the sexual response cycle. These changes are produced by many different sources of stimulation. As the opening vignette suggests, stimulation by touch is a primary source of sexual arousal. However, other sources of stimulation activate the nervous system, which in turn produces sexual arousal. Visual cues, odors, and sounds, for example, can produce sexual arousal. In fact, arousal during sexual activities is highly dependent on all the senses. Furthermore, a person's emotional and mental status also help determine whether that person experiences arousal. Models proposed to explain sexual response all take into account at least some of these factors, but none of them fully account for the combined influence of all of these factors on sexual arousal and orgasm.

NEURAL AND HORMONAL CONTROL OF SEXUAL RESPONSE

Why can someone get aroused from smelling a sexual partner's cologne, having phone sex, or watching an erotic movie? How can a memory of a past event, or even more so, a fantasy about an experience you've never had, turn you on? You know that it happens, but have you ever wondered what causes you to respond the way you do? The functions of our bodies are indeed very complex.

Even scientists have a somewhat limited understanding of what causes sexual arousal. However, what they do know has led them to focus on two primary systems in the human body that appear to have a significant influence on sexual response: the nervous system and the endocrine system.

The Nervous System

The nervous system is composed of the **central nervous system (CNS)** and the **peripheral nervous system (PNS)** (Figure 4.1). The CNS consists of the brain and spinal cord, and the PNS includes all of the nerve pathways into and out of the spinal cord and the brain. The brain is the main control center for all body functions, coordinating everything from the development and release of hormones to the perception and evaluation of stimuli in the environment. Specific areas of the brain either directly or indirectly control various body functions, including sexual functions. The PNS becomes involved when messages from the CNS must reach other parts of the body, including the sex organs. In addition, messages from the external environment—whether tactile, olfactory, visual, or auditory—must move through the PNS pathways to reach the CNS.

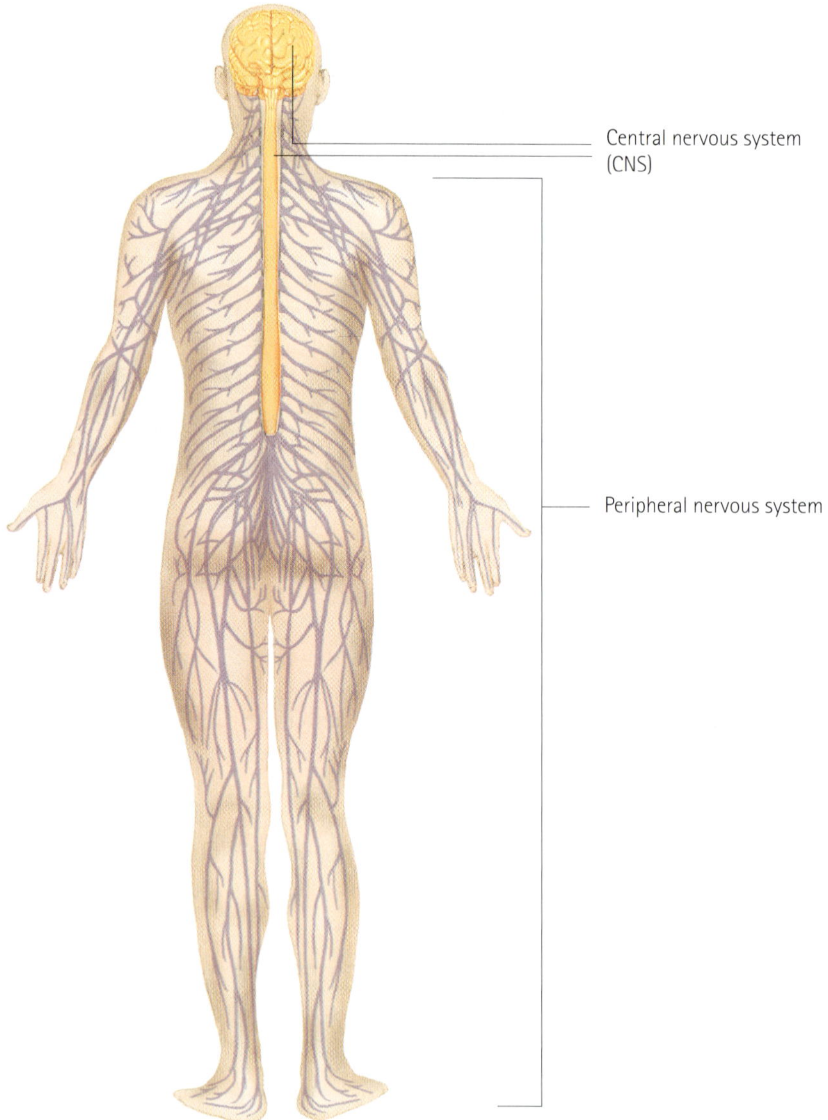

Figure 4.1 Divisions of the Central and Peripheral Nervous Systems

CENTRAL NERVOUS SYSTEM (CNS)
Division of the nervous system consisting of the brain and spinal cord.

PERIPHERAL NERVOUS SYSTEM (PNS)
All of the nerve pathways into and out of the brain and spinal column.

The PNS controls voluntary and involuntary muscle movements. The pelvic muscles surrounding the vaginal and urethral openings are under voluntary control. You can voluntarily contract certain pelvic muscles to stop the flow of urine. Voluntary tensing of the pelvic muscles may also enhance sexual pleasure. The PNS also controls involuntary sexual responses such as sweating and increases in heart rate and blood pressure.

Thus, both parts of the nervous system work together and independently to produce sexual arousal. Erections, for example, can result from direct genital stimulation (controlled by the PNS) as well as from the brain's response to stimuli such as memories, fantasies, and images (controlled by the CNS). However, it is not very useful to analyze sexual response using these two categories, since arousal and orgasm are generally produced through interaction of the two (Schiavi & Segraves, 1995). Images or fantasies usually work in concert with the right kinds of caresses, words, smells, and sights to cause sexual arousal.

On many parts of the body, touch can be sexually stimulating.

The Senses

We experience the world through sight, sound, smell, and touch. How each individual responds to these sources of stimulation is unique; however, all of them play a role in human sexual response.

Touch As was noted above, touch, or tactile stimulation, is of considerable importance in sexual arousal and orgasm. The focus of tactile stimulation is typically the clitoris or the penis, because these organs are so richly innervated. The clitoris has roughly the same number of nerve endings as the penis, albeit in a smaller area. You might assume that these two organs are reliably the most erogenous zones on the body. However, as you'll learn later in this chapter, some women achieve orgasm most easily through stimulation of an area on the front wall of the lower vagina, known as the *G spot*. It is possible that in such cases nerve endings on the other side of the vaginal wall, either in the pubococcygeus muscle, which is very sensitive to touch, or in the urethra and surrounding tissues, are being stimulated and are producing pleasurable sensations (Levin, 1992).

did YOU know?

It has been suggested that the most sensitive area on a woman's body is the area surrounding the urethra (Sevely, 1987).

The number and distribution of nerve endings in the pelvic region appear to vary from one individual to another. This variation may account for individual preferences as to the degree and location of touch stimuli (Bancroft, 1989). In fact, there are many areas of the body that, when touched or caressed, cause an individual to be sexually aroused. These areas are referred to as *erogenous zones*. The lips, mouth, and nipples are rich in nerve endings and, therefore, are highly erogenous. Other nongenital areas of the body may act as erogenous zones because of individual physical sensitivities and associations of sexually arousing experiences with stimulation of those areas of the body. In fact, almost any area of the body's surface has the potential to produce sexual arousal. Some people, for example, find gentle caressing of the skin much more arousing than direct stimulation of the genitals. In essence, erogenous zones have a biological basis in that they are typically areas of the body that are more densely innervated, but each person's prior learning and experiences determine what areas of the body are ultimately erogenous for that person. Touch appears to be the sense most crucial for sexual response, but input from other sensory systems also contributes to the experience of arousal.

Vision Our sense of vision allows us to experience many images that can trigger feelings of sexual arousal. In addition to the arousing aspects of seeing an attractive person or erotic image, some research suggests that when a man observes his own erect penis, his subjective feelings of arousal may be enhanced, resulting in increased levels

Looking At . . .

. . . Thinking About

How have criteria for what is beautiful changed over time?

of physiological arousal (Sakheim, Barlow, Beck, & Abrahamson, 1984). In addition, visual stimuli produced by fantasies or dreams can be sufficient to produce orgasms in both women and men.

The sexually arousing quality of visual stimuli may be primarily learned and subject to social and cultural influences. For example, current Western standards of female attractiveness emphasize unhealthy thinness, a trend that has increased over the past several years. Other cultures and times have held very different standards of female beauty or sexual attractiveness, as is illustrated by the robust figures painted by Peter Paul Rubens, a Flemish painter of the 17th century.

In a study on sexual attractiveness, Cowley (1996) found that women with waist-to-hip ratios around 0.7 (that is, a waist seven-tenths the size of the hips) seem to be considered most attractive, whether this ratio is on a robust or slender figure. These findings suggest that some universal human standard, possibly even genetic, by which attractiveness is measured persists over time and across cultures. Whether the sexually arousing quality of visual stimuli is innate or learned, vision can be a powerful source of sensory stimulation. Another potentially powerful source of sensory input is olfaction, or the sense of smell.

Smell (Olfaction) The role that odors play in sexual arousal is quite evident from the almost endless variety of fragrances available for both women and men. Many perfumes or colognes contain chemical substances that have been extracted from animal tissues (or synthetic versions of these chemicals) and can trigger sexual behaviors in the respective animals. These substances are called **pheromones.** Over the years, there has been considerable scientific debate about the existence of human pheromones and about the capacity of any such substances to trigger sexual responses in humans (Morris, 2000). This is a very active and exciting field of research.

In animals, many behaviors, including sexual behaviors, are controlled by pheromones that are detected by the vomeronasal organ (VNO), a set of tiny, tubelike structures just inside the animals' nasal cavities. Researchers have been uncertain about the existence of a VNO in adult humans; however, recent anatomical studies suggest that it does exist, but is located higher in the nasal cavity than in other animals (Bhatnagar & Smith, 2001; Smith et al., 2002). Another question has been whether the VNO functions in humans as it does in other animals—as a pheromone receptor. Although this question has not been resolved, the consensus appears to be that humans do "communicate" through chemicals. However, the VNO may not be the avenue through which humans detect pheromones (Meredith, 2001). Researchers have identified certain genes in humans that look remarkably like genes in other animals that are believed to control those animals' pheromone receptors. These human genes have been located in cells in the nasal mucosa, lungs, and brain (Rodriguez, Greer, Mok, & Mombaerts, 2000). So, VNO or no VNO, humans are likely to have receptors for pheromones.

The earliest and most consistent evidence supporting the effects of pheromones on humans was research on **menstrual synchrony.** Studies have repeatedly shown that women who live in close proximity (e.g., college roommates) or who simply have a high degree of interaction (e.g., mothers and daughters, sisters, close girlfriends) begin their menstrual periods at approximately the same time (Bartoshuk & Beauchamp, 1994; Weller & Weller, 1992; Weller, Weller, & Roizman, 1999). Do pheromones regulate menstrual synchrony? It appears so. A very interesting study conducted by a pioneer in pheromone research, Martha McClintock (Stern & McClintock, 1998), showed that ovulation was accelerated in a group of women after they breathed in odorless

PHEROMONES
Species-specific chemicals emitted by many animals that trigger mating behavior; human pheromones have not been conclusively identified and effects of pheromonelike substances on human sexual behavior have not been demonstrated.

MENSTRUAL SYNCHRONY
Similar timing of menstrual cycles that can occur among women who live in close proximity for extended periods.

compounds (basically sweat) from the armpits of women who were in the late follicular phase of the menstrual cycle (that is, just before ovulation). Furthermore, ovulation was delayed in these same women when they breathed in chemicals collected from women who were ovulating. These findings provide strong support for the effects of pheromones on humans and suggest potential ways to stimulate or inhibit ovulation in women.

Several studies have also provided support for pheromonal control of sexual behavior in humans. In one recent study (McCoy & Pitino, 2002), college-aged women wore either a perfume containing a chemical preparation (purported to be a pheromone) derived from fertile, sexually active, heterosexual women or a perfume containing a placebo. The women were unaware of which group they were in. Across three full menstrual cycles, significantly more pheromone wearers than placebo wearers increased their frequency of sexual intercourse, sleeping next to a partner, formal dates, and petting, affection, and kissing behaviors. Similar results have been demonstrated with men wearing synthesized male pheromones (Cutler, Friedmann, & McCoy, 1998).

The steroids androstadienone (a male hormone) and estratetraenol (a female hormone) are currently being studied as possible pheromones. To date, it appears that androstadienone reduces nervousness and tension and decreases negative mood states in women; no similar effects of estratetraenol have been observed in men (Grosser, Monti-Bloch, Jennings-White, & Berliner, 2000; Jacob, Hayreh, & McClintock, 2001; Jacob & McClintock, 2000). With current neuroimaging abilities, researchers can also study brain activity in men and women as they are being exposed to these odorless steroids. And, in fact, studies show that in both men and women, areas of the brain associated with smell, vision, emotion, and attention respond to the steroid from the opposite sex (Jacob, Kinnunen, Metz, Cooper, & McClintock, 2001; Savic, Berglund, Gulyas, & Roland, 2001). All the effects of these steroids observed so far may play a role in sexual attraction, but the connection is not yet clear.

While the debate regarding pheromones and human sexual behavior is likely to continue for some time, we should not overlook the general importance of smells in interpersonal relationships. As Comfort (1993) suggests, a number of natural odors (often masked by deodorants) can enhance the pleasure of a sexual encounter, and a variety of odors are produced throughout sexual activity. On the other hand, offensive odors (e.g., tobacco smoke and halitosis) are not conducive to sexual attraction or to sexual arousal.

Taste Although olfaction and taste are very closely related, taste does not appear to play a significant role in sexual arousal (Comfort, 1993). Although the taste buds may not be an important source of sensory input for arousal, touch receptors on the tongue may be. Tactile stimulation of the mouth and tongue, as various textures encountered during sexual activity produce sensations there, may be very important to sexual response. For example, many people may enjoy oral-genital contact not only because it stimulates the genitals, but also because it stimulates membranes in the mouth.

Hearing Auditory stimuli may also play an important role in sexual response. Hearing your lover's voice, the music you find sexy or romantic, and the sounds emitted in the heat of passion can intensify arousal and enhance the quality of a sexual encounter. On the other hand, unexpected or unpleasant sounds can terminate arousal or, at a minimum, create a temporary interruption.

Whatever the source of sensory input, sensations are transmitted through the PNS to the CNS. How those messages are interpreted there greatly influences their impact on sexual response.

The Brain and Spinal Cord—the CNS

Our perceptions and thoughts and our reactions to them may be among the most important factors in determining whether we exhibit a sexual response. In fact, you might say that the brain is the most important sex organ. Various structures in the brain contribute to sexual arousal (see Figure 4.2 on page 108).

IN YOUR own words

Sarah Weigman
Virginia Commonwealth University

In a potential mate, the most attractive quality is a good personality. Sounds like a cliché, but even if the guy is hot, if he's a jerk or can't keep me entertained, it's not going to keep me interested in him—physically or mentally.

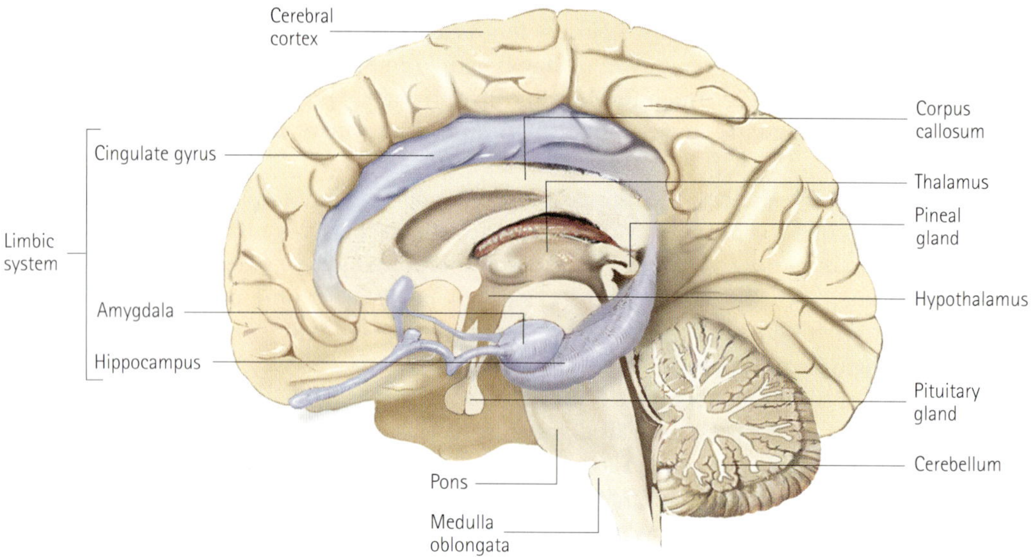

Figure 4.2 The Brain

The cerebral cortex is the part of the brain that responds to sensory input and interprets it as either sexual or nonsexual. Presumably, sensory input that is interpreted as sexual somehow activates the cerebral cortex to send messages through the spinal column to signal a sexual response, such as vasocongestion. However, brain signals are not required for sexual arousal to occur; sexual arousal can result from direct tactile stimulation even when connections to the brain have been severed. Animal research has shown that severing the spinal cord in monkeys actually *lowers* the "threshold for reflexive erections," suggesting that the brain and spinal cord play a role in normal inhibition of sexual response (Bancroft, 1989, p. 69). They may also be able to *activate* sexual responses independently of sensory input. For instance, paraplegics who are paralyzed in the genital region from spinal cord injury have reported orgasms as a result of dreaming. People have also experienced orgasms through hypnosis or fantasizing and during rapid eye movement (REM) sleep. Finally, in at least one case, direct stimulation of the brain resulted in orgasm (Levin, 1992). Thus, sexual responses can occur without sensory stimulation, such as touch.

Physical disabilities do not have to prevent people from enjoying love, affection, and sex.

The **limbic system**, an area of the brain that controls emotional behavior, appears to be critical to sexual function. It is made up of the *cingulate gyrus*, the *hippocampus*, the *amygdala*, and parts of the *hypothalamus*. Several studies have implicated the limbic system in the control of sexual function. Historic research conducted by Heinrich Klüver and Paul Bucy in 1939, in which the temporal lobes of monkeys were destroyed, revealed numerous behavioral changes in the monkeys. In addition to becoming quite docile, they displayed repeated sexual behavior such as masturbation and indiscriminate mounting of other monkeys (*and* the researchers, as well). This response is now referred to as the *Klüver-Bucy syndrome*. The scientists concluded that because the amygdala and the hippocampus were destroyed in the monkeys, these structures might be involved in controlling sexual response. Other animal research has also demonstrated that stimulation of multiple sites in the limbic system produces both erection and ejaculation in monkeys (MacLean, 1962). Similarly, human research, in which electrodes were inserted in several limbic structures, showed changes in brain activity in the limbic system during states of heightened sexual arousal and orgasm (Heath, 1972).

Numerous animal and human studies have suggested that the hypothalamus exerts control over sexual responses (Hart & Leedy, 1985; Kendrick & Dixson, 1986; Muller, Roeder, and Orthner, 1973; Perachio, Marr, & Alexander, 1979; Singer, 1968), perhaps indirectly through its regulation of many hormones, including sex hormones. Both disruption and stimulation of the hypothalamus are likely to produce changes in hormone regulation, and hormones, in turn, directly affect sexual response. The *preoptic area* of the brain has also been associated with sexual behavior in male monkeys (Robinson & Mishkin, 1966) and female rats (Singer, 1968). This area's involvement may be related to the fact it is functionally and anatomically tied to the hypothalamus.

did YOU know?

The impact of spinal cord injury on sexual function can be rather mild, depending on the extent and location of the injury. Also, willingness to employ a variety of activities and approaches to sexual expression—as opposed to limiting oneself to sexual intercourse—often leads to a very satisfying sexual relationship for the person with the injury and her or his sexual partner (Kreuter, Sullivan, & Siosteen, 1996).

The Endocrine System

The endocrine system (see Figure 4.3), like the nervous system, plays a key role in human behavior. The endocrine glands produce substances called *hormones* that are delivered to target organs through the bloodstream. Hormones can also affect behavior indirectly through their influence on the central or peripheral nervous system. The

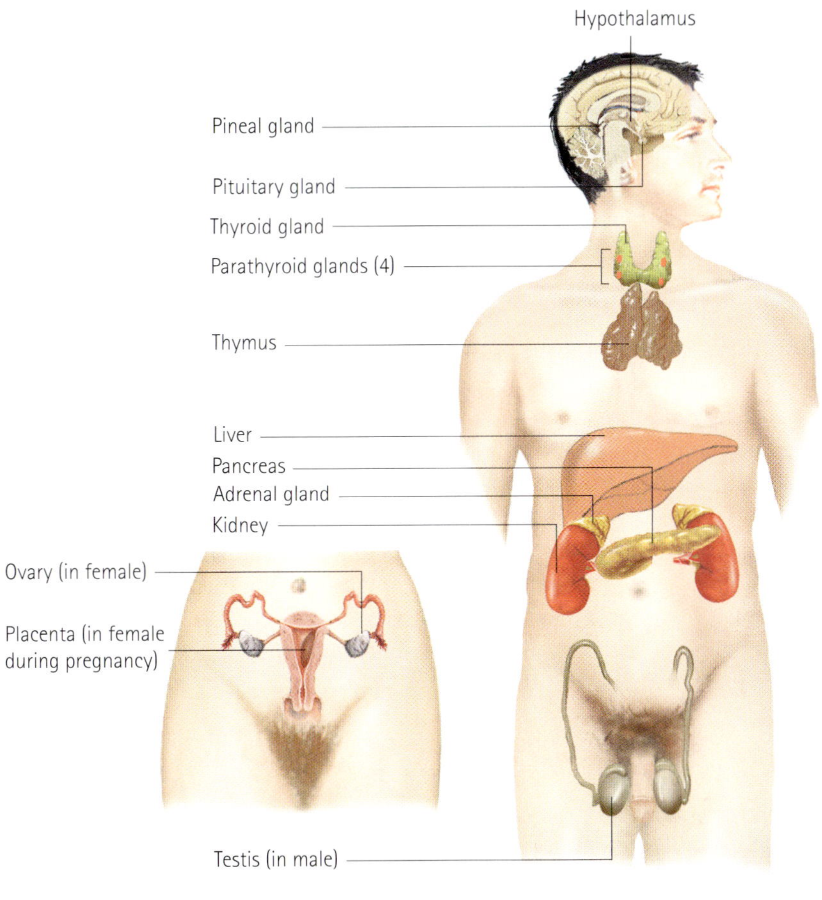

Figure 4.3 The Endocrine System

LIMBIC SYSTEM
Area of the brain that controls emotional behavior.

IN YOUR own words

Eddy Ameen
Northwestern University

When someone can be warm and inviting with their entire self—their body language, their tone of voice, and their words—that arouses me.

hormones that affect sexuality are referred to as *sex hormones*. Sex hormones have two distinct roles: First, during fetal development, they determine whether the infant will develop female or male genitalia and other sexual characteristics. Second, they temporarily modify behavior. This second role is most important to understanding hormonal effects on sexual response.

The hormones that affect sexual response the most are testosterone (an *androgen* produced by the adrenal glands), the *estrogens,* and progesterone. People generally think of testosterone as the "male" hormone and estrogens as "female" hormones. In reality, both of these types of hormones are present in women and men, although testosterone is present at much higher levels in men, and the estrogens are present at much higher levels in women. Progesterone, which serves an important role in pregnancy, is also typically at much higher levels in women.

Several other hormones are produced in the **pituitary gland**, the chief endocrine gland, located in the brain. These hormones influence the production of other sex hormones and include follicle-stimulating hormone (FSH), luteinizing hormone (LH), prolactin, and oxytocin. FSH increases the production of estrogen and also controls ovum maturation and sperm production. LH is responsible for increasing production of progesterone in women and of testosterone in men. Oxytocin is believed to play an important role in uterine contractions during orgasm as well as during childbirth and labor (see Chapter 9 for more detail). It might also trigger smooth muscle contractions of the penis during orgasm in men (Carmichael, Warburton, Dixen, & Davidson, 1994).

Hormonal Influences on Female Sexual Behavior

A link between fluctuations in sexual desire and the menstrual cycle has been reported by some women. A number of researchers have consequently seen the naturally occurring fluctuations in hormones across the menstrual cycle as a perfect focus for research on hormonal influence on sexual interest. This research has, however, produced inconclusive results. Some researchers report increased levels of desire coinciding with peak estrogen levels at midcycle (Clayton, Clavet McGarvey, Warnok, & Weiss, 1999; Regan, 1996); others report no variation in levels of desire across the cycle (Hoon, Bruce, & Kinchloe, 1982; Meuwissen & Over, 1992; Morrell, Dixen, Carter, & Davidson, 1984). A small proportion of women do report a peak in sexual interest around the time of ovulation (Bancroft, 2002). The research in this area has suffered from methodological difficulties, such as reliance on retrospective reports, inconsistent measures of sexual desire, and failure to determine the stage of the menstrual cycle reliably. Examination of postmenopausal women, who, by definition, have lower levels of estrogen, has also failed to demonstrate a relationship between estrogen levels and sexual desire or arousal (Bancroft, 2002; Cawood & Bancroft, 1996).

The influence of androgens—testosterone, in particular—on female sexual desire has received some attention but, sadly, has been studied considerably less than the effects of androgens on male sexuality. A correlation between testosterone levels in women and sexual desire has been demonstrated, largely through research on women who were given testosterone after surgery to remove their ovaries (Bancroft, 2002). One study of postmenopausal women demonstrated that testosterone therapy in addition to estrogen replacement led to improved sexual functioning. Perhaps the greatest concern about testosterone therapy for women is the possible masculinizing effects (e.g., excessive body hair) of male androgens (Padero, Bhasin, & Friedman, 2002; Redmond, 1999).

PITUITARY GLAND
The endocrine gland that controls the actions of all other endocrine glands.

Hormonal Influences on Male Sexual Behavior

The role of hormones in male sexual behavior has been studied much more than the role of hormones in female sexual behavior. In particular, research has repeatedly demonstrated the importance of testosterone in male sexual interest and ability to ejaculate (Bancroft, 2002). Testosterone levels are also associated with levels of sexual activity. Higher levels of testosterone in adolescent males appear to be associated with higher levels of sexual activity (Halpern, Udry, & Suchindran, 1998). In addition, administering testosterone to men with low sexual interest and erectile dysfunction increases their sexual activity (Schiavi, White, Mandeli, & Levine, 1997). The effects of testosterone replacement on older men are less positive. After about age 50, men show a decline in testosterone levels, which is often associated with a decline in sexual interest. However, testosterone replacement does not necessarily increase sexual interest in these older men. Experts suggest that older men's bodies may be less responsive to testosterone (Bancroft, 2002; Schiavi, 1999). The effect of testosterone on erections is not consistent across different situations. It appears that spontaneous erections, such as those that occur during sleep and without clear external stimulation, require a minimum level of testosterone if they are to occur. However, even men with low levels of testosterone may achieve erections in response to visual or tactile stimuli (Carani et al., 1990). In general, testosterone appears to have a fairly clear influence on sexual interest and behavior, but its effect on erections is unclear.

MODELS OF HUMAN SEXUAL RESPONSE

Efforts to understand just what happens during sexual arousal and orgasm—the series of events referred to as the *sexual response cycle*—have yielded various models describing the changes that occur. (A *model* is a conceptualization of a set of behaviors that helps organize them into easily understood components.) While the models are useful in research on sexual response, they are not necessarily accurate. In general, existing models of sexual response are based on the assumption that sexual response follows a cyclical pattern that is relatively predictable across time and situations, and from one individual to another. In truth, not all sex researchers agree that sexual responses universally follow an invariant sequence (Rosen & Beck, 1988). The lack of consensus on this issue is apparent in the various models of the sexual response cycle.

Ellis's Early Two-Stage Model

Havelock Ellis developed the first model of sexual response around the turn of the 20th century. He proposed a two-stage model, which included a period of tumescence and a period of detumescence (Ellis, 1906). In general, **tumescence** refers to the buildup of sexual tension and **detumescence** to the release of sexual energy, as in orgasm. Although we now associate these terms primarily with male sexual arousal and orgasm, Ellis applied them to both men and women. And although the terminology may seem to emphasize the physical aspects of sexual response, Ellis believed firmly that psychological factors also had an influence.

Ellis's model has served as a cornerstone for subsequent models. For example, one of the most influential and widely recognized models, Masters and Johnson's four-stage model, reflects the cyclical nature and the stage approach of Ellis's model. Their model differs from Ellis's, however, in being dedicated solely to physiological processes; it does not address psychological influences on sexual response.

Masters and Johnson's Four-Stage Model

William Masters and Virginia Johnson proposed their four-stage model in the mid-1960s, in a book entitled *Human Sexual Response* (Masters & Johnson, 1966). This book was soon followed by *Human Sexual Inadequacy* (1970), which described a model-based approach to the treatment of sexual problems. Publication of *Human Sexual Inadequacy* helped foster the idea that understanding sexual response is not only intrinsically valuable, but also useful for developing strategies to treat sexual problems.

Masters and Johnson's lasting contribution was to describe in detail the physiological changes, both genital and **extragenital** (not in the genitals), that occur at each stage of the sexual response cycle. In their research, this team described four stages of sexual response in both men and women, which they termed *excitement, plateau, orgasm,* and *resolution.* (These stages are discussed in greater detail later in this chapter.) Masters and Johnson suggested that because the timing of contractions is similar,

TUMESCENCE
The buildup of sexual tension in both men and women, according to Ellis's model.

DETUMESCENCE
The release of sexual energy, as in orgasm, in both men and women, according to Ellis's model.

EXTRAGENITAL
Occurring outside the genitalia.

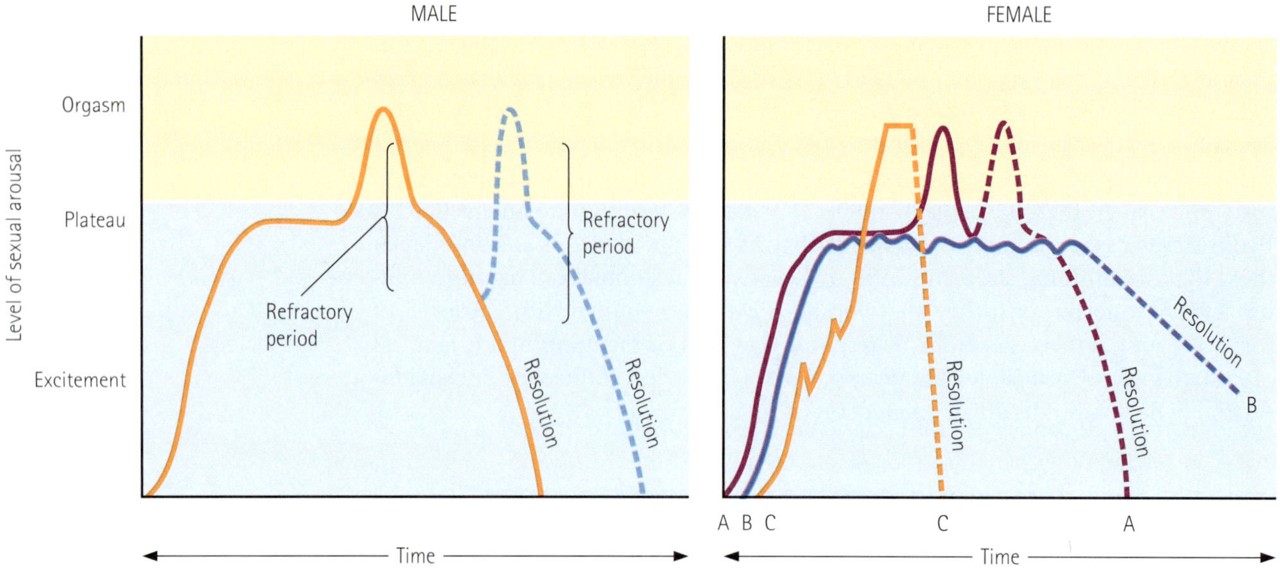

Figure 4.4 Masters and Johnson's Sexual Response Cycle: Variations in Response Patterns of Males and Females

orgasms in men and women are physically identical. However, they did acknowledge a variety of response patterns leading up to **orgasm** (Figure 4.4). Masters and Johnson (1966) stressed that their model provides only an arbitrary frame of reference. That is, describing the physiological changes that occur throughout arousal and orgasm as phases makes the overall process easier to understand, but the real events are not restricted to one sequence or confined to one stage.

Although Masters and Johnson's stage model has been important in advancing the understanding of human sexual response, sexologists have criticized it heavily. For example, Masters and Johnson focus too much on only one response pathway in women (namely, via the clitoris), when in fact sexual arousal may occur through several sources of stimulation, such as the muscles around the uterus (Whipple, 1995). Although Masters and Johnson allowed for some variation of sexual responding, the stages cannot be reorganized nor can stages be added to the cycle (Tiefer, 1991). Furthermore, psychological and motivational components of sexual desire are absent. Finally, the arbitrary division into stages imparts a fragmented view of the human body and does not indicate how the body's organs and systems interact during sexual response (Tiefer, 1991). This artificial fragmentation is reflected in clinical diagnoses of sexual dysfunction, which classify problems based on the part of the response cycle that is not functioning properly (e.g., arousal disorder, ejaculatory failure).

Some sexologists have noted biases in Masters and Johnson's research, including selection bias affecting their choice of participants. Tiefer (1991) argued that the research shows a favorable bias toward the male perspective on sexuality and that its emphasis on the similarities between men and women ignores differences and inequities in sexual socialization. Men are generally socialized to focus more on the physical aspects of sexuality, while women focus more on emotional closeness. Masters and Johnson intentionally selected participants who conformed to their own preconceived notions of what is meant by "sexually responsive." Women participants, for instance, had masturbated regularly for several years, had had experiences with sexual intercourse since adolescence, and were orgasmic nearly 100% of the time in the laboratory setting. These participants were not typical of the average female of the time—and probably not of today, either. In addition, Masters and Johnson considered a sexual response to be "successful" only when orgasm occurred. This assumption reflects a male-oriented bias, since, in general, males report orgasm during sexual activity at a higher rate than women do. Thus, application of the Masters and Johnson model to all individuals

ORGASM
A series of rhythmic contractions of the muscles around the vagina, anus, and uterus in women, and involving the testes, epididymes, vas deferens, seminal vesicles, and prostate gland in men. Orgasm occurs at the peak of sexual arousal.

might lead to the labeling of many women (or males who deviate from the model) as dysfunctional (Tiefer, 1991). Despite its shortcomings, Masters and Johnson's work made a tremendous contribution to the field of sex therapy, inspiring a multitude of research studies aimed at refining the model and applying it to the development of therapeutic approaches to sexual problems.

Kaplan's Three-Stage Model

Helen Singer Kaplan (1977) proposed a three-stage model that, like Masters and Johnson's, places heavy emphasis on the physiological aspects of sexual behavior. However, Kaplan includes sexual desire as a primary component of sexual response. Kaplan's three stages are *desire, excitement,* and *orgasm*. According to Kaplan, desire is the underlying or general level of sexual interest, or **libido**, which is a prerequisite for arousal and orgasm. According to Kaplan's model, desire is activated by the limbic system. While Kaplan placed control of desire in the brain, she proposed that peripheral reflex pathways, especially orgasm triggers located in the lower spinal cord, primarily control excitement and orgasm (see Figure 4.5).

The emphasis on the reflexive nature of orgasms reflects Kaplan's focus on the physiological aspects of the sexual response cycle. Kaplan's inclusion of the desire stage was an innovative attempt to address the motivational aspects and to explain how sexual behaviors are initiated. However, her model raised more questions than it answered. For example, Rosen and Beck (1988) noted that spontaneous desire is not required for achievement of arousal (excitement) and orgasm, a direct contradiction to Kaplan's model. Additionally, the model's relative neglect of the psychological aspects

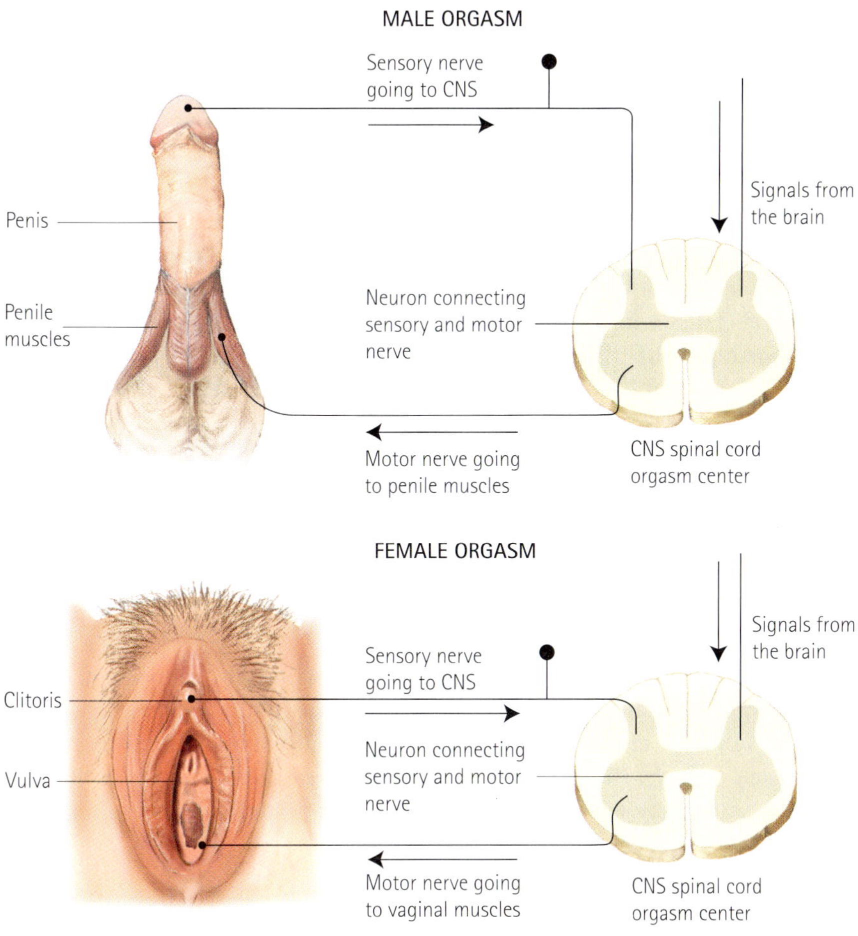

Figure 4.5 Kaplan's Orgasm Reflex Pathways

LIBIDO
The underlying or general level of sexual interest; the sex drive.

of sexual behaviors has left unanswered questions regarding the motivation and activation of these behaviors. Finally, desire is not well defined, and how it is linked to excitement and orgasm is not well described (Rosen & Beck, 1988). In spite of its limitations, Kaplan's (1977) model has resulted in some important changes in the treatment of sexual problems, such as the recognition that problems with sexual desire are a form of sexual dysfunction (see Chapter 13).

Cognitive Models

Several models that were developed in the 1980s and 1990s emphasize the primary importance of cognitive factors in the sexual response cycle (Bass & Walen, 1986; Janssen & Everaerd, 1993; Kothari & Patel, 1989; Palace, 1995). These models have many similarities. In general, they hold that sensory input must first be interpreted as sexual before sexual arousal can occur. Kothari and Patel (1989) refer to this cognitive process as *sexual grounding*. For example, a photograph in an art gallery of a naked woman reclining on a bed does not evoke sexual arousal, but a photograph in a pornographic magazine of a woman striking a similar pose might. A cognitivist would say that in the latter case, the stimulus was interpreted as sexual, whereas in the former case it was not. Once sexual grounding has occurred, the physiological process of sexual arousal is activated. Physiological changes occur, and those associated with sexual arousal (e.g., increased heart rate, increased respiration) also must be perceived, evaluated, and labeled as sexual for the response cycle to continue. Further, once sexual behavior has been initiated, the behavior must continue to be evaluated positively and labeled as sexual for the process of sexual response to advance.

According to these cognitive models, positive expectations, attitudes, values, and feelings toward sex augment sexual grounding. Alternatively, if sex is evaluated negatively, sexual grounding is impaired. Palace's (1995) research, in fact, has shown that increasing a person's expectations of sexual arousal increases physiological measures of arousal. Palace demonstrated the impact of cognitions on physiological arousal by providing false feedback to sexually dysfunctional women, suggesting that they were exhibiting high levels of sexual arousal. When the women received this feedback, their reported expectations of feeling sexually aroused increased, and their actual physiological arousal levels increased to the levels indicated by the false feedback.

Unlike the models put forth by Masters and Johnson (1966) and Kaplan (1977), the cognitive models stress the interrelationship of cognitive and other subjective factors and physiological changes in the activation and progression of arousal. This focus on subjective factors highlights the fact that descriptions of physiological changes alone do not completely account for the variability in human sexual response. The cognitive models are fairly recent attempts to address many of the factors that might account for observed patterns in sexual response. However, some of the cognitive models (e.g., Palace, 1995) are based on observations of sexually dysfunctional individuals; hence, the applicability of these models to "normal" or functional individuals is not clear. Like other models, cognitive models require further refinement to adequately account for the mechanisms of sexual response.

Interactive Models

Attempts to account for the wide variation among and within individuals, including occasional difficulties in achieving arousal or orgasm, have resulted in various interactive models of the sexual response cycle (Bancroft, 1989; Barlow, 1986; Byrne, 1983). Interactive models consider the combined impact on sexual arousal and orgasm of external events, cognitive and emotional factors, and physiological processes.

Byrne's and Barlow's Models

Donn Byrne's (1983) and David Barlow's (1986) models emphasize the role of emotions and cognitive appraisal in sexual response. Byrne's (1983) model, for example, proposed that sexual arousal is both physiological and subjective and is elicited by both external events (e.g., erotic visual or touch stimuli) and internal events (e.g., dreams and fantasies). However, Byrne emphasized that conditioned emotional responses play a role in determining one's actual response to sexual cues. That is, Byrne proposed that early emotional reactions to either symbolic or actual sexual stimuli or experiences become tied to those events through classical conditioning. When sexual cues elicit negative emotional reactions, evaluation of a current sexual situation is likely to be negative, and the individual is likely to avoid the situation. Alternatively, if sexual cues elicit positive emotional reactions, evaluation of a sexual situation is likely to be positive, and the individual is likely to approach the situation. Byrne called sexual avoiders *erotophobes* and sexual approachers *erotophiles*. For example, Byrne's model suggests that a child who is taught that sexual acts such as masturbation are "dirty" is more likely to be "erotophobic" as an adult. Alternatively, a child who is raised to view sex as a normal, healthy aspect of human behavior is more likely to be "erotophilic."

Like Byrne, Barlow emphasized the role that emotional responses, combined with an individual's cognitive appraisal of a sexual situation, play in sexual arousal. Most sex therapy experts have observed that anxiety contributes significantly to sexual dysfunction by inhibiting sexual arousal in many individuals (see Figure 4.6). However, Barlow demonstrated that although anxiety inhibits sexual responses in sexually *dysfunctional* men, it actually facilitates them in sexually *functional* men (Barlow, 1986). Thus, it is not the man's emotional reaction alone that determines whether a sexual response will occur. Barlow argues that cognitive processes play a significant role in

4.1 on the web

The models discussed in this chapter are only some of the sexual response models that have been proposed. Go to **www.ablongman.com/mcanulty2e** and find the discussion of David Reed's model.

How would you classify this model—is it physiological, cognitive, or interactive? What, if anything, does Reed's model add to your understanding of the sexual response cycle?

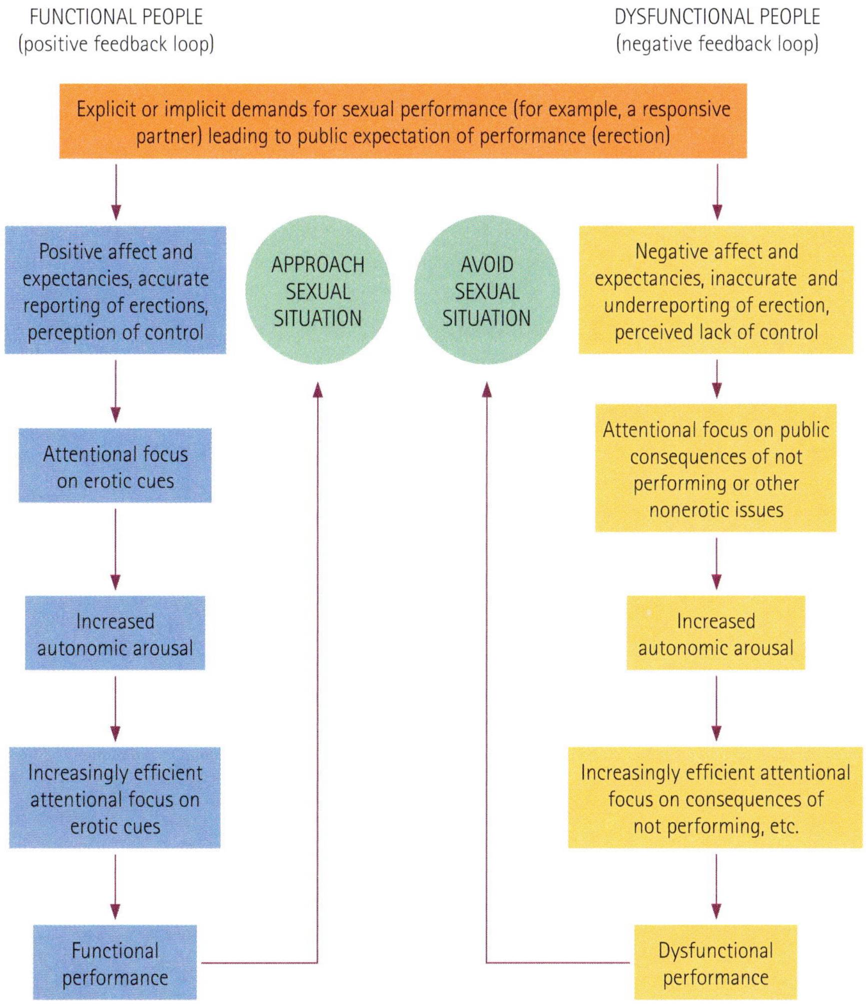

Figure 4.6 Barlow's Interactive Model of Sexual Function and Dysfunction

Looking At . . .

. . . Thinking About

Feelings of anxiety can both hinder and foster sexual arousal. In what ways might anxiety enhance sexual arousal?

determining when sexual arousal occurs in response to sexual cues. Men with erectile dysfunction, for example, focus on nonsexual stimuli and fears about their performance during sexual relations, whereas sexually functional men have erotic thoughts and focus on the sexual stimuli in their environment. Thus, there is good evidence that sexual response is heavily influenced by the *interaction* between cognitions and emotional responses, at least in men.

Bancroft's Model

John Bancroft's interactive model (1989) is more comprehensive than either Byrne's or Barlow's because it describes the interplay among cognitive, emotional, and physiological components of sexual response. Bancroft's model suggests that emotional factors play a role in the initial stages of sexual response. In addition, both cognitions and external stimuli directly influence centers in the CNS. Stimulation of the CNS leads to arousal of the PNS and controls genital responses. Orgasm is controlled by centers in the brain and spinal cord. Bancroft completes what he refers to as the *psychosomatic circle of sex* with cognitive processing of the physiological changes that occur. Like the models proposed by Byrne and Barlow, this model of sexual response assigns central roles to cognitive and emotional factors, but it also explains how these factors interact with the underlying physiological processes.

The various interactive models have contributed to the identification of specific components involved in sexual arousal but have not really clarified the interrelationships between and among those components. Questions about how the components interact to initiate sexual arousal and how they determine subsequent patterns of sexual response require additional attention.

All of the models just described provide important pieces of information regarding sexual response and the variations in response found within and across individuals. The model proposed by Masters and Johnson (1966) has considerably enhanced understanding of the physiological changes that accompany sexual arousal and orgasm. Their model and the other physiologically based models, however, did not account for variations in the response cycle or for the activation of sexual arousal. The interactive and cognitive models have made significant contributions to the identification of important nonphysiological components of sexual arousal, such as thoughts and emotions, but have not adequately explained how these factors interact with physiological processes.

THE SEXUAL RESPONSE CYCLE

The physiological components of arousal and orgasm were well delineated by Masters and Johnson's model, which is adequate for describing the *observable* effects of arousal and orgasm. Keep in mind, however, that the following general description based on that model does not fully take into consideration individual differences in sexual arousal and orgasm.

Female Sexual Response Cycle

The female sexual response cycle is arbitrarily divided into four phases: excitement, plateau, orgasm, and resolution. This section describes the responses that occur during each. Figure 4.7 depicts the changes that occur in the female during the sexual response cycle.

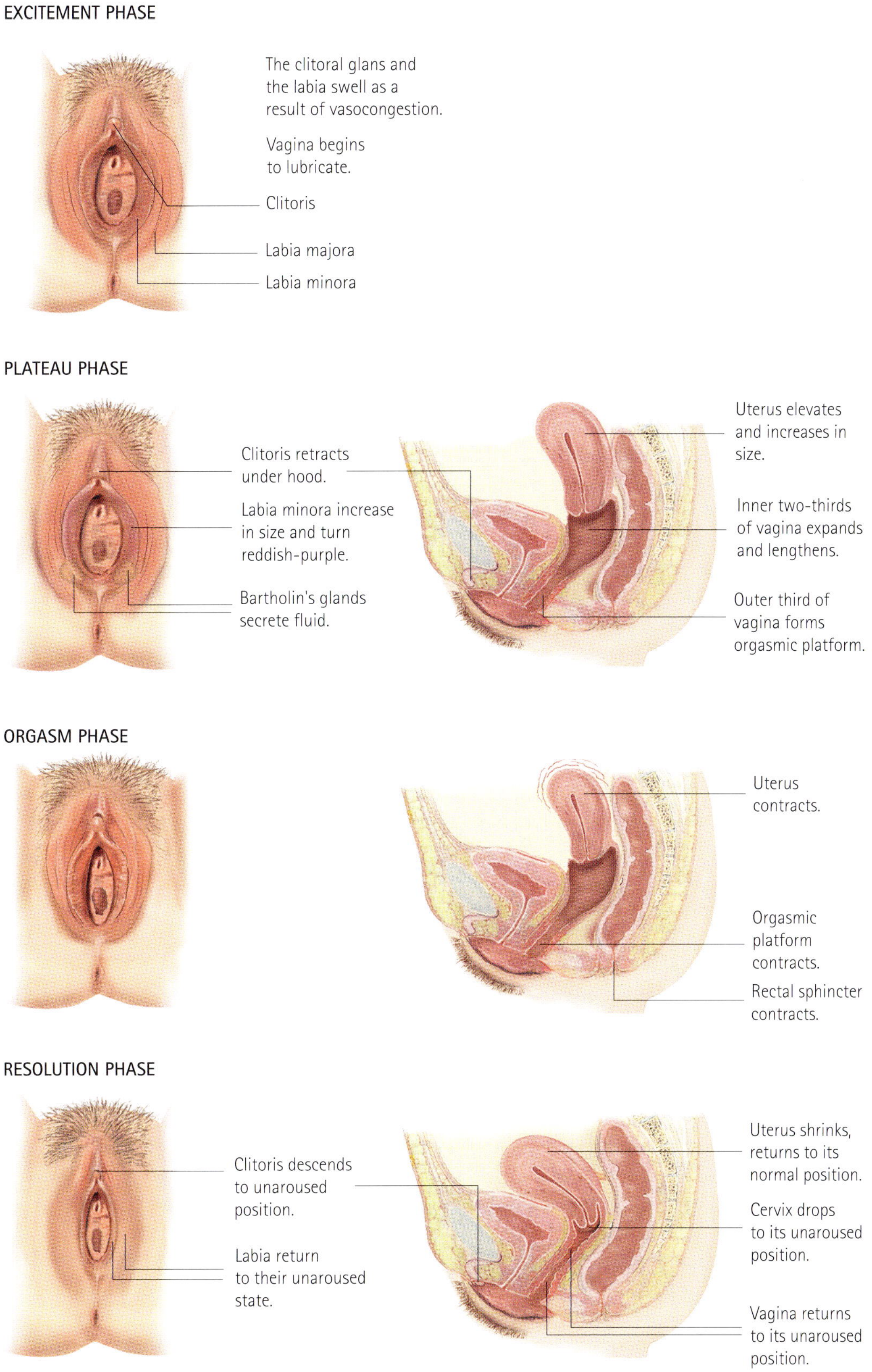

Figure 4.7 Genital Changes in the Female during the Sexual Response Cycle

Excitement

As the female becomes aware of sexually arousing stimuli and enters the *excitement phase,* her first response is vaginal lubrication, technically referred to as **transudation.** When a woman is aroused, more blood flows into the genital region than flows out, resulting in **vasocongestion**, or engorgement of the blood vessels. Transudation occurs when vasocongestion forces fluid through the walls of the vagina. Vasocongestion also causes vaginal walls to become dark red.

did YOU know?

Breasts increase in size by as much as 25% during sexual arousal.

The amount of vaginal lubrication may be small initially, but with adequate stimulation, it gradually increases until the vaginal opening and the labia become moist. The amount of lubrication and its consistency and odor vary across different women and in the same woman at different times, depending on multiple factors. How sexually stimulated a female is, for example, can affect the amount of lubrication, as does the amount of estrogen in her body. The consistency and odor of the lubricating fluid usually vary throughout the menstrual cycle. Women who have gone through menopause may find that they have less natural lubricant and may benefit from use of a commercial lubricant, such as KY jelly.

Recall from Chapter 3 that the vaginal walls are close together when a female is not aroused. During the excitement phase, the inner two-thirds of the vagina expands, so the vagina becomes wider and longer. In addition, the uterus moves upward, pulling the cervix up with it, resulting in what is referred to as the **tenting effect.** The uterus may also exhibit **fibrillations**—painless, rapid, and irregular contractions. Vasocongestion causes the uterus to increase in size somewhat as well.

The external genitalia also undergo many changes during the excitement phase. Vasocongestion of the labia causes the labia majora to flatten and move apart somewhat, and the labia minora to enlarge. The diameter of the clitoral shaft increases as the corpora cavernosa become engorged with blood; the glans also swells from blood engorgement. The breasts respond to sexual stimulation in several ways; most notably, the nipples become erect, the areolae widen and darken in color, and the breasts may increase in size.

In addition to changes in the genital region, increases in heart rate, respiration, and blood pressure occur during excitement. A majority of women experience a **sex flush** during this phase. This is a blotchy reddening or darkening of the skin, generally starting on the abdomen and throat, which results from dilation of the blood vessels. The sex flush may spread to the chest, face, and other parts of the body as well, such as the thighs, arms, and shoulders. A final important change that occurs during this phase is **myotonia**, an overall increase in muscle tension in both voluntary and involuntary muscles.

Plateau

In the *plateau phase,* the outer third of the vaginal wall becomes very engorged, resulting in a narrowing of the vaginal opening by 30% or more. This effect produces what is called the **orgasmic platform.** During heterosexual intercourse, the male may feel as though the vagina is actually gripping his penis. The labia minora become larger as a result of further engorgement, and become a deep pink or red color. According to Masters and Johnson, the change in color of the labia minora and the orgasmic platform directly precede orgasm. The clitoris retracts under the clitoral hood during the plateau phase so that it is protected from direct stimulation. The many changes that occur during excitement simply intensify during the plateau phase. The sex flush becomes more pronounced; heart rate, blood pressure, respiration rate, and myotonia increase; the breasts enlarge further; the nipples become more erect; and the color of the areolae deepens. The uterus continues to fibrillate and pulls up even further. As a result, the inner two-thirds of the vagina is quite expanded at this point. The **seminal pool**—a small pocket at the back of the vagina—forms from the combined effect of the

TRANSUDATION
Vaginal lubrication resulting from increased blood flow to the vagina.

VASOCONGESTION
Engorgement of the blood vessels from increased blood flow to the genital region without a reciprocal increase in blood leaving it.

TENTING EFFECT
Expansion of the upper portion of the vagina and narrowing of the outer portion of the vagina resulting from the pulling up of the uterus and cervix during high levels of sexual arousal.

FIBRILLATIONS
Rapid, irregular contractions of the uterus that are painless and occur during arousal and orgasm.

SEX FLUSH
Blotchy reddening or darkening of the skin, which occurs during the excitement phase of the sexual response cycle.

MYOTONIA
Overall increase in muscle tension in both voluntary and involuntary muscles, which occurs during the excitement phase of the sexual response cycle.

ORGASMIC PLATFORM
Narrowing of the vaginal opening due to engorgement of the outer third of the vaginal wall during the plateau phase of the sexual response cycle.

SEMINAL POOL
A pocket at the back of the vagina formed by the narrowing of the outer portion of the vagina in combination with the expansion of the inner portion during the plateau phase of the sexual response cycle.

narrowing of the outer part and expansion of the inner part of the vagina. When a male ejaculates into the vagina, the seminal fluid collects in the seminal pool.

Orgasm

When distention of the vagina from vasocongestion reaches a certain threshold level, a reflex stretch mechanism sets off simultaneous, rhythmic, muscular contractions of the outer third of the vaginal wall, the muscle around the anal opening (called the *sphincter*), and the uterus. This is called *orgasm*. Uterine contractions are believed to be produced by the release of the hormone oxytocin. A female may have as few as three to five contractions or as many as ten to fifteen, the first lasting 2–4 seconds and subsequent ones occurring about every 0.8 second (Jones, 1991). Other responses peak during orgasm, including the sex flush and heart rate, blood pressure, and respiratory rate. Involuntary muscle spasms result in contractions of the face, abdomen, hands, feet, and other parts of the body. If a female becomes highly sexually aroused but does not have an orgasm, she is likely to feel discomfort from the engorgement of her genital organs, until the blood gradually moves out of the genitals and her system returns to a pre-arousal state. This is analogous to the discomfort males sometimes experience when they become highly aroused but do not have an orgasm, a condition commonly referred to as "blue balls."

Until around the mid–20th century, it was commonly assumed that women were incapable of achieving orgasm. Of course, given adequate stimulation, most women are fully capable of achieving orgasm. However, the experience of orgasm varies considerably from one woman to another and from one sexual encounter to another. For example, some women experience multiple orgasms, while others do not. Multiple orgasms occur sequentially, without the woman's arousal falling to plateau levels. Another variation is that some women are orgasmic during masturbation but not with a partner, presumably because they are able to provide adequate stimulation for themselves, but a partner is not. Some women report that orgasms are not accompanied by any perceptible vaginal contractions, and some women do not have orgasms. In fact, many women report that they enjoy sex fully without having an orgasm (Ogden, 1999). Close Up on Gender: Types of Orgasms in Women and Men (on page 120) discusses two of the more distinct variations in the female orgasm.

Resolution

The *resolution phase* is the period during which the female's body returns to a nonaroused state. The orgasmic contractions cease, blood flows out of the genital region, the clitoris returns to its usual size and place, the vagina decreases in width and length, and the breasts decrease in size. Heart rate, blood pressure, and respiration rate also return to normal. In addition, the uterus moves back to its typical position. As it does, the cervix drops into the seminal pool, thereby making it more likely that sperm will enter the cervical os. Interestingly, this opening dilates after an orgasm, perhaps also to promote movement of sperm through the cervix and into the uterus.

Male Sexual Response Cycle

Like the female sexual response cycle, the male cycle includes four phases. The changes that occur during each phase of the sexual response cycle in the male are depicted in Figure 4.8 (on page 121).

Excitement

Upon exposure to sexual stimuli, the male's first observable response is penile tumescence, or an erection; the penis becomes stiffer, longer, and larger in diameter. An erection usually occurs within a few seconds of stimulation and results from engorgement of the corpora cavernosa and the corpus spongiosum. Thus, just like the female's, the male's sexual arousal depends on vasocongestion of the genital organs. Blood fills the corpora cavernosa, and the tunica albuginea (the membrane surrounding the spongy bodies) closes off the veins, preventing the blood from flowing out. In addition, the

CLOSE UP ON gender

Types of Orgasms in Women and Men

One of the earliest controversies regarding the female orgasm originated with Freud's assertion of the superiority of orgasms resulting from *coitus*—that is, penile-vaginal intercourse. Masters and Johnson (1966) attempted to minimize the distinction between orgasms produced through vaginal stimulation and those produced through clitoral stimulation by stating that the physiological changes during all orgasms are the same. Others have suggested that orgasms resulting from deep cervical or uterine stimulation are controlled by a different neural pathway and produce different subjective experiences than do those generated through clitoral stimulation (Whipple, 2000).

In fact, different patterns of vaginal changes have been observed when different forms of stimulation are used. As was mentioned in Chapter 3, the G-spot, or Grafenberg spot, is purported to be an area containing significantly more nerve endings than all other parts of the vaginal wall (Lundberg, 2001); see the figure. Researchers claim that orgasms achieved through stimulation of this area are different from orgasms achieved through clitoral stimulation. Such orgasms have been referred to as "A-frame" orgasms because of the shape of the vagina during them. The upper part of the vagina is compressed, and the uterus is forced downward; there is no formation of an orgasmic platform (Ladas, Whipple, & Perry, 1982). The A-frame is less common than the tenting effect, in which the uterus is pulled up, the upper portion of the vagina lengthens and expands, and the orgasmic platform is formed.

Recent research on the existence of the G-spot is contradictory. A Slovakian researcher described the G-spot in detail and reported that the tissue comprising it is the equivalent of the male prostate. Like males, he reported, females ejaculate prostate fluid into the urethra (Zaviacic, 2001). These orgasms in women are called "ejaculatory orgasms." At the same time, an American researcher published a paper claiming that there is not enough evidence to suggest that the G-spot even exists (Hines, 2001), and female ejaculate is said to be nothing but urine.

Despite the Freudian preference for vaginal orgasms, there is no clear evidence that one kind of orgasm is superior to another. Women have reported equal satisfaction from both types of orgasm, and multiple orgasms have been produced through both vaginal and clitoral stimulation. Thus, all orgasms are equally "good."

Do men have different types of orgasms as well? Although most aspects of female sexual response have received less attention than male sexual response, studies of types of orgasms have focused mostly on women. The common assumption has been that men have a single orgasm rapidly followed by ejaculation and a refractory period. It is generally assumed that the refractory period prevents a man from having multiple orgasms. However, some research challenging this assumption has suggested that at least some men are multiply orgasmic. According to Dunn and Trost (1989), male multiple orgasms occur in one of two ways. All the men they studied maintained full erections after orgasm. One group, however, experienced little or no refractory period. During continued penile stimulation, these men dropped only to the plateau phase and then went on to have another orgasm—however, only after a period of time. The other group of men experienced no refractory period—either for rearousal or for subsequent orgasm. One man in the study was able to experience as many as 16 orgasms during one sexual encounter! In another case study conducted in a laboratory setting, a 35-year-old male was able to experience six ejaculatory orgasms within 36 minutes, without ever losing his erection (Whipple, Myers, & Komisaruk, 1998).

There is a tendency for models of human sexual response to ignore the tremendous individual differences that exist, both from one sexual experience to another and from one person to another. The many different experiences of orgasm that both women and men report suggests that it is misguided to assume that sexual responses follow a uniform path. Thus, do not be alarmed if your experiences are physiologically, psychologically, and emotionally very different from what you might read about in magazines or textbooks or see in the movies. We are all different.

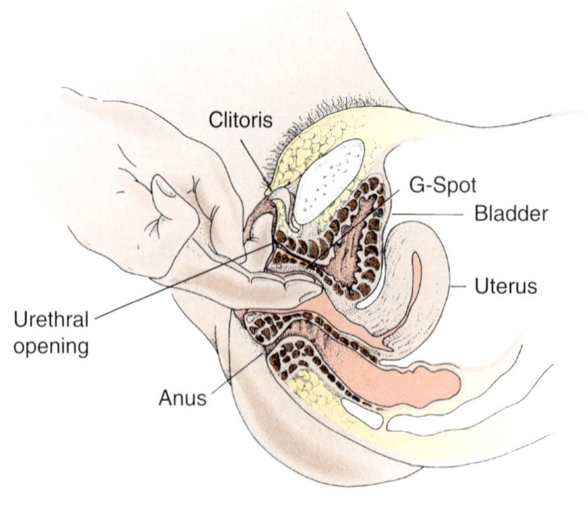

Locating the G-Spot

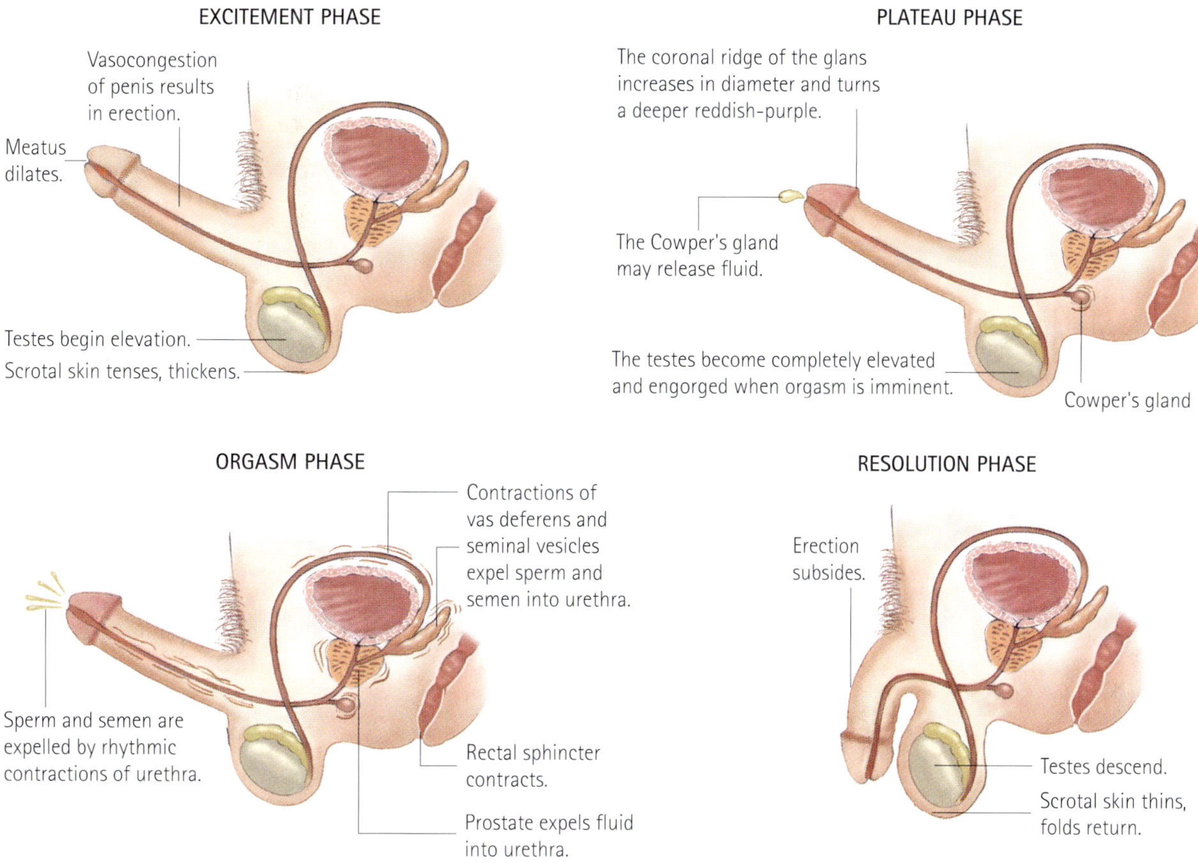

Figure 4.8 Genital Changes in the Male during the Sexual Response Cycle

urethral opening widens during the excitement phase. The scrotal sac thickens, causing its surface to smooth out, and the testes are drawn closer to the body by contractions of the cremaster muscle in the scrotum. Toward the end of this phase, the testes begin to enlarge. Other changes closely resemble those in the female—a skin flush appears and the nipples become erect in a majority of males; heart rate, blood pressure, and respiration rate increase; and myotonia occurs.

Plateau

Assuming adequate sexual stimulation continues, erection is maintained into the *plateau phase*. In addition, the diameter of the coronal ridge increases slightly, and the color of the penis darkens. The testes continue to enlarge until they are 50–100% larger than their original size. They also elevate further and rotate, so that the back surfaces are facing the perineum. Sex flush, myotonia, heart rate, blood pressure, and respiration rate all intensify. Also during the plateau phase, droplets of fluid from the Cowper's gland may appear on the tip of the penis. As explained in Health Matters: Cowper's Gland Emission and Pregnancy Risk (on page 122), although this fluid is not semen, it *can* cause a woman to become pregnant.

Orgasm

When all of the changes described above have reached a peak, a male's orgasm occurs, in two stages. First, the muscular walls of the testes, the epididymes, the vas deferens, the seminal vesicles, and the prostate gland contract, causing the ejaculate to collect in the **urethral bulb**, a part of the urethra near the prostate gland, which balloons out and

URETHRAL BULB
A part of the male's urethra, near the prostate gland, which balloons out and traps semen just prior to ejaculation.

HEALTH Matters

Cowper's Gland Emission and Pregnancy Risk

It is entirely possible for a woman to become pregnant even if her male partner is certain that he "pulled out in time." That is why "withdrawal" as a form of birth control is really not birth control at all! Recall that among the internal sex organs of the male is the bulbourethral, or Cowper's, gland. Combined fluids from the prostate gland, seminal vesicles, and Cowper's gland form the ejaculate. Droplets of fluid from the Cowper's gland generally leak out into the urethra in the plateau phase but prior to ejaculation. You might assume that because ejaculation itself has not yet occurred, this emission is "safe" and does not contain sperm. However, some sperm may have already found their way into the Cowper's gland emission. Therefore, pregnancy is a real possibility if appropriate measures are not taken.

It may be tempting to enjoy a few thrusts without a condom, assuming there will be no harm done. But if condoms are your only method of birth control and you do not want your partner to become pregnant, it is imperative that you put on a condom as soon as possible after becoming erect, well before any fluids that might contain sperm can be expelled.

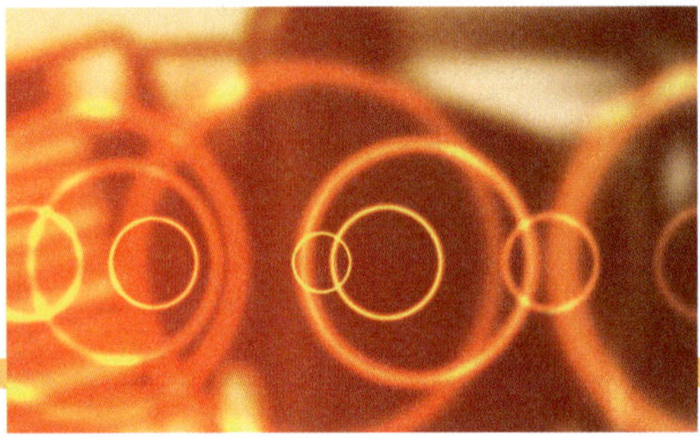

did YOU know?

There are exercises that men can do to learn to control ejaculatory inevitability, extend sexual intercourse, and achieve multiple orgasms (Chia, Arava, & Buck, 1997).

traps semen just prior to ejaculation. In addition, the muscle at the opening of the bladder contracts to prevent semen from entering the bladder and to prevent release of urine. These changes are referred to as the **emission stage of ejaculation.** At this point, the male reaches **ejaculatory inevitability**, or the point at which he cannot prevent ejaculation from occurring. In the second stage of orgasm, the **expulsion stage of ejaculation**, semen is forced out of the penis with the aid of contractions of the **bulbocavernosus muscle** at the base of the penis, the urethral bulb, and the urethra. Most of the semen may be released by the less intense contractions that follow. The contractions occur at about 0.8-second intervals (Jones, 1991).

EMISSION STAGE OF EJACULATION
The first stage of male orgasm, in which seminal fluid collects in the urethral bulb and the bladder sphincter closes to prevent release of urine and semen into the bladder.

EJACULATORY INEVITABILITY
The sensation that ejaculation is imminent and unpreventable, which occurs during the emission stage of ejaculation.

EXPULSION STAGE OF EJACULATION
The second stage of male orgasm, during which semen is expelled through the urethra.

Resolution

After orgasm, the male enters a period during which additional sexual stimulation will not produce an erection or other responses sufficient for another orgasm to occur. This is referred to as the **refractory period.** This period tends to be short in younger males but usually increases with age. There is evidence to suggest that some men may be capable of sequential orgasms; that is, some men may not experience any refractory period. This phenomenon is discussed in more detail in Close Up on Gender: Types of Orgasms in Women and Men.

As in the female, the resolution phase in the male involves the return of all body systems to a prearoused state. Heart rate, blood pressure, and respiration rate return to normal; the testes descend and decrease in size; the scrotum relaxes; and nipple erection disappears. The male's erection diminishes, but total loss of erection may take some time as the blood drains out of the corpora cavernosa and corpus spongiosum.

You should now have a better sense of the general changes that occur in both males and females during sexual arousal and orgasm. We turn now to some factors that can affect sexual response.

FACTORS AFFECTING SEXUAL RESPONSE

Factors that disrupt the normal functions of the nervous and endocrine systems can affect sexual response. Two major factors that have been researched and debated are the aging process and the use of pharmacological agents.

The Effects of Aging

Better health resulting from improved quality of life, advances in medicine, and better education has tremendously increased the average life expectancy of humans. Thus, an increasing proportion of the population can be classified as elderly, and accurate information about the effects of aging on sexuality is clearly of value to many people. Common cultural views of the elderly depict them as asexual. The stereotype might cause many aging individuals to view changes in their sexual responses as signs of failing sexuality. As a result, they might forgo sexual experiences prematurely. While it is true that several physiological changes occur as a result of the aging process, it is not clear that these changes consistently interfere with sexual behavior. Poor health or lack of a sexual partner may affect sexual expression; however, there is no reason to assume that the elderly cannot have very healthy sexual desires or satisfying sexual relationships. In fact, the lifestyle that many older adults enjoy may enhance sexual expression. Many older couples are no longer distracted by children or the stresses of work. Nor do they have to concern themselves with birth control. Slowed orgasm in an elderly male allows more time for an elderly female partner to enjoy extended stimulation and a greater opportunity to have an orgasm herself. Older couples who have shared many years together have typically worked out the "kinks" in their relationship, which means they are free to enjoy each other more fully.

4.2 on the web

When we are young, many of us have a difficult time imagining that people enjoy sex in old age. Read the article entitled "Older Women Talk about Sex" at **www.ablongman.com/mcanulty2e.**

Describe the overall findings regarding older women and sexuality discussed in this article and your reactions to them.

The Aging Female

You saw earlier that research on the correlation between natural fluctuations in estrogen levels and sexual arousal has been inconclusive. A naturally occurring decline in estrogen levels as women become menopausal does not interfere with sexual desire or with sexual satisfaction. In fact, some women's sexual interest increases after menopause, when estrogen is no longer present to oppose or inhibit the androgens, which are hormones that seem to enhance sexual responsiveness (Brackett, Bloch, & Abae, 1994). However, lower estrogen levels do result in some thinning of the vaginal walls and vaginal dryness, which might reduce sexual enjoyment. Dryness can be remedied by applying estrogen cream (or any other water-based lubricant) directly to the vagina. In addition, the "use-it-or-lose-it" philosophy appears to be relevant here: Older women who have sexual relations one to two times a week appear to lubricate more readily than those who do not have regular sexual relations (Brackett, Bloch, & Abae, 1994). Other changes that can occur with aging and that may alter a woman's sexual response are summarized in Table 4.1 (on page 124).

4.3 on the web

Like women, it appears that men go through a menopausal period between the ages of 45 and 60. Go to the article on male menopause at **www.ablongman.com/mcanulty2e.**

Describe the symptoms of male menopause and ways to cope with and treat it.

The Aging Male

Men, too, experience a decline in hormone production as they age (Schiavi, Schreiner-Engel, White, & Mandeli, 1991), but this decline does not appear to significantly affect their sexual functioning. The declines in testosterone resulting from aging may simply mean that the older man requires firm and direct stimulation to produce an erection. The declines in testosterone are not necessarily associated with decreased desire and certainly not with decreased satisfaction (Masters, Johnson, & Kolodny, 1994). However, lower testosterone levels may have a minor impact on the physiological responses of the aging male. For example, even erections produced by firm tactile stimulation may be delayed and may remain less firm until just prior to ejaculation. Sensations of ejaculatory inevitability may also be less distinct and may not last as long as when the man was younger. Other changes in sexual response experienced by older men are summarized in Table 4.2 (on page 125).

BULBOCAVERNOSUS MUSCLE
Muscle at the base of the penis that contracts to force ejaculate out through the urethra.

REFRACTORY PERIOD
In males, a period following orgasm during which additional stimulation will not produce an erection or result in orgasm.

TABLE 4.1 Normal Age-Related Changes in Women's Sexual Arousal and Orgasm

PHASE	CHANGES
Arousal	Foreshortening of vagina
	Delayed and less voluminous vaginal secretion
	Little or no Bartholin's gland secretion
	Delayed and reduced vaginal expansion
	Less constriction of introitus (vaginal opening)
	No enlargement and poor elevation of uterus during arousal
Orgasm	Fewer orgasmic contractions
	Occasional painful uterine spasms
Postorgasm	No dilation of external cervical os
	Possible vaginal irritation and clitoral pain due to friction
Extragenital effects	Less pronounced sex flush
	Less increase in breast volume during arousal
	Less areolar engorgement
	Longer postorgasmic retention of nipple erection
	Infrequent rectal sphincter contractions

Looking At . . .

. . . Thinking About

Old age does not have to be a death knell for sexual pleasure. Illnesses and some physical changes that occur with aging might force older men and women to adjust their approach to sexual relations, but changing life roles that bring more time and freedom to enjoy a sexual relationship may improve sexual responses. What are some life changes that might enhance sexual expression? What are some measures that can be taken during sexual activity to compensate for physiological changes resulting from aging?

In essence, aging does produce changes in the typical process of sexual response; however, aging couples can still gain tremendous satisfaction from sexual intimacy. Illness is probably the primary barrier to sexual activity, as many medications can impair sexual functioning. This, however, is true for everyone who uses such medications, whether young, middle-aged, or elderly.

The Effects of Pharmacological Agents

A variety of pharmacological agents can affect sexual responses. These agents may be derived from natural sources or synthesized.

Aphrodisiacs

Despite the popularity of numerous folk remedies for sexual difficulties over the centuries, few agents, when scientifically examined, show any ability to enhance sexual functioning. Although they have been considered **aphrodisiacs**, such substances as oysters, "Spanish fly," raw turtle eggs, rhubarb, goat testicles, and ground rhinoceros horn cannot, through any biochemical action, increase sexual desire or arousal. If any effect is observed, it is more likely that the person has become sexually aroused because of expectations regarding the effects of the substance. This placebo effect has been estimated at 50% (Yates & Wolman, 1991). Some of these substances do have a pharmacological effect that might lead people to believe that they

TABLE 4.2 Normal Age-Related Changes in Men's Sexual Arousal and Orgasm

PHASE	CHANGES
Arousal	Delayed and less firm erection
	Longer interval to ejaculation
	Less distinct sense of impending orgasm
	Shorter period of ejaculatory inevitability (sometimes longer, due to painful prostatic spasms)
Orgasm	Shorter ejaculatory event
	Fewer expulsive contractions of urethra
	Less forceful expulsion of seminal fluid
	Reduced volume of seminal fluid
Postorgasm	Rapid loss of erection
	Longer refractory period
Extragenital effects	Less discernible swelling and erection of nipples
	Absence of sex flush
	Absence of extragenital muscle spasms at climax
	Infrequent rectal sphincter contractions
	Reduced testicular elevation
	No gaping of urinary meatus during intense orgasm

are aphrodisiacs. "Spanish fly," for example, contains a toxic compound that is deadly in high enough doses. It was thought to be an aphrodisiac because it irritates the urethra, causing *priapism,* an abnormal and persistent erection (Royal Society of Chemistry, 1997).

Prescription Drugs

Many prescription medications interfere with sexual desire, arousal, and performance. The most notable are medications prescribed for psychiatric conditions, including many antidepressants. Some antidepressants, however, appear to have beneficial effects on sexual functioning. Buproprion and trazodone are two antidepressants that have produced positive changes in sexual desire and overall sexual functioning, in addition to the effects expected from improved mood (Rosen & Ashton, 1993). The effects are not reliably produced, however, and some individuals have suffered from painful engorgement of their genitals when being treated with these agents. Others have reported spontaneous orgasms that were not desired (Rosen & Ashton, 1993).

Other antidepressants, mood stabilizers, and **antipsychotic medications**, used to treat severe psychiatric conditions such as schizophrenia, are notorious for dampening either sexual desire or sexual responses (Schiavi & Segraves, 1995). **Anxiolytic agents** (drugs such as benzodiazepines that are used to treat anxiety) have also been associated with impaired sexual functioning.

Individuals treated with antihypertensive medications—especially alpha-agonists, beta-blockers, and diuretics—have frequently reported sexual difficulties. Anticonvulsants, ulcer medications, and a variety of cardiac medications have also been reported to have adverse effects on sexual responses (Rosen, 1991).

4.4 on the web

The list of substances purported to be aphrodisiacs is nearly endless. Go to **www.ablongman.com/mcanulty2e** and visit Johan's Guide to Aphrodisiacs (you are prompted to register, but it is not required).

Describe four or five aphrodisiacs listed at this site that the text does not mention.

APHRODISIAC
Any substance believed to stimulate or intensify sexual desire or arousal.

ANTIPSYCHOTIC MEDICATIONS
Drugs that are used to reduce or eliminate psychotic symptoms such as visual and auditory hallucinations or delusional beliefs and that reduce sexual functioning.

ANXIOLYTIC AGENTS
Drugs that are used to reduce anxiety and have been associated with impaired sexual functioning.

Not all drugs have been reported to have negative effects on sexual function. Yohimbine (derived from the bark of an African tree), for example, has been used to enhance sexual function. While this drug is not approved for medical use in the United States, it has been used in the treatment of erectile difficulties for many years. Yohimbine has been administered alone and in combination with trazodone and has produced some improvement in erections; however, fewer than 50% of the participants in these studies have seen clear improvements (Rosen & Ashton, 1993). Additionally, the side effects of yohimbine (nausea, tearfulness, sweating, and anxiety) may be quite unpleasant, detracting from possible positive effects.

L-dopa and other drugs in the dopamine family have also been associated with enhanced sexual desire and arousal in both men and women. However, the data on their effectiveness are mixed, and they have several negative side effects, including irregular heartbeat, mood changes, hallucinations, and confusion (Royal Society of Chemistry, 1997).

Another drug, Viagra (sildenafil citrate), has been widely touted as a cure-all for men who are impotent. Viagra increases a man's ability to have and maintain an erection by indirectly increasing blood flow to the penis. It enhances the effect of nitric oxide, which, when naturally released by the body during sexual stimulation, causes a chain of changes that ultimately causes blood to flow into the corpus cavernosa. Sexual stimulation is necessary in order for Viagra to have an effect, because nitric oxide must first be released naturally so that the drug can act with it (Lehigh Valley Hospital and Health Network, 1998). Viagra does not directly increase libido (sex drive). The assumption is that some men experience decreases in libido because of erectile difficulties, and once these problems are relieved, the libido will improve. Viagra has been reported to work in 80% of men. Viagra may also prove to be beneficial to women who experience sexual problems resulting from impaired blood flow, which can cause vaginal dryness, painful intercourse, and orgasmic difficulties. Several studies support Viagra's potential to aid women with sexual dysfunctions (Caruso, Intelisano, Lupo, & Agnello, 2001; Kaplan et al., 1999; Reuters, 1999), but the drug has not yet been approved by the FDA for use with women. It has also been shown to significantly reduce sexual problems in women who have antidepressant-induced anorgasmia (that is, inability to achieve orgasms) or delayed orgasm (Nurnberg, Hensley, Lauriello, Parker, & Keith, 1999) as well as in men with antidepressant-induced erectile dysfunction (Nurnberg et al., 2001).

did YOU know?

Viagra must be taken 1 hour prior to a sexual encounter in order to allow it to have an effect.

Unfortunately, Viagra does have some unpleasant side effects, including headache, facial flushing, upset stomach, and visual problems (i.e., not being able to distinguish blue from green). In addition, the FDA has released reports of multiple deaths among men using Viagra, but experts maintain that the drug is safe if used properly and by the right patients ("39 Viagra Deaths Confirmed," 1998). Theoretically, Viagra could cause priapism, which can lead to permanent tissue damage and impotence. Men who have sickle-cell anemia, leukemia, or inflammation of the urethra are advised not to take Viagra, because these conditions would exacerbate this effect of the drug. One of the greatest risks occurs when Viagra is taken by someone who is also taking nitroglycerine, used in the treatment of heart problems. Viagra itself can cause a sudden drop in blood pressure and, when combined with nitroglycerin or other blood-pressure medications, can cause a drop severe enough to cause fainting or even shock (Gorman, 1998).

In summary, it appears that drugs prescribed to treat a wide variety of medical and psychiatric conditions may impair sexual functioning. Any discussion of the sexual side effects of prescription medications must mention the possible negative effects of the conditions for which the medications have been prescribed. Since many psychiatric and medical conditions may be responsible for the development of sexual dysfunction, it can be difficult to determine whether sexual problems are related to the medical condition or to the treatment. Drugs created specifically to enhance sexual function seem promising, but their potential negative side effects must continue to be monitored.

Recreational Drugs

Individuals who use drugs for sexual purposes expect them to enhance the sexual experience. Unfortunately, the effects are usually quite the opposite. By far the most widely accepted and used recreational drug is alcohol, which is widely believed to enhance sex. Have you ever used alcohol to help you relax and enhance your desire to engage in sex? This common practice is based on a cultural myth that alcohol has aphrodisiac effects. It is true that small amounts of alcohol may make you feel more desirous and reduce your inhibitions and anxiety regarding sex. The reason for the disinhibiting effect is that alcohol depresses the CNS. Since inhibitions (whether conscious or not) and anxiety arise in the brain, they are minimized when the CNS is depressed. But the overall impact of alcohol consumption is to reduce the ability of information to be transmitted between the CNS and the PNS. Alcohol dulls the senses, reducing sensory input via the PNS regarding sexual stimuli. Another effect of alcohol is that hormone production is altered. Some studies have shown that a single drink (12 ounces of beer or wine or 1½ ounces of liquor) can lower the level of testosterone in the blood (Jones, 1991). As you learned earlier, testosterone seems to be important to sexual desire and arousal in both men and women.

Looking At . . .

. . . Thinking About

The overall impact of most drugs on sexual functioning is negative. Unfortunately, people do not always know the effects of the drugs they use, so problems with sexual performance may not be immediately attributed to the drugs. Imagine that you want to warn a friend who is a drug user about some of the adverse effects of drug use. What are at least four facts you would want your friend to know about the negative effects of drugs on sexual functioning?

Another substance commonly believed to possess sex-enhancing effects is marijuana. Although low doses can produce an increase in testosterone levels, higher doses cause these levels to fall below normal. Marijuana's effects, however, appear to be similar to those of alcohol in that they primarily influence cognitions and perceptions of events (Weller & Halikas, 1984).

Users of cocaine and amphetamines have attributed enhanced desire and orgasm to these drugs (Rosen, 1991). However, chronic use or high doses of these substances greatly interfere with sexual activity. Opiates (morphine, heroin, and methadone) are not usually associated with increased sexual behavior. Their effects are quite the opposite, and chronic users report decreased interest in and frequency of sexual behaviors.

MDMA, also known as Ecstasy, is a particularly popular drug, which has both stimulant and hallucinogenic effects (National Institute on Drug Abuse, 2002). It is often called the "love drug" or the "hug drug," because of its tendency to reduce social inhibitions and give people a sense of empathy and connection with others. Because of these effects, teens and young adults are taking the drug and engaging in high-risk sexual behaviors, including group sex and "gang bangs" (when a group of males have sex with one female). While many teens assume that MDMA is a safe and fun drug, it can produce multiple physical problems, including brain damage that affects thought and memory, and it can even cause death (National Institute on Drug Abuse, 2002).

The sex-enhancing effects of recreational drugs appear to be primarily cognitive. That is, these drugs alter a user's perceptions and evaluations of stimuli. They may enhance sexual desire; however, most of them actually interfere with the functioning of the peripheral nervous system. So the user may experience an increased desire for sex and impaired sexual performance at the same time.

Everyone wonders about his or her sexual performance at one time or another. Reflect on This: Concerns about Sexual Performance may help you address your own concerns.

reflect ON THIS

Concerns about Sexual Performance

For Him Have you ever been concerned about your sexual performance? If so, you are not alone. Concerns about sexual performance are widespread among men. These can range from concerns that inexperience will be obvious to fear that ejaculation will occur too quickly. Many men also wonder if their sexual desires, behaviors, and frequency are "normal." Is masturbating two times a day in addition to having intercourse three times a week normal? Are sexual relations once a month normal? What about not having sex at all? Bernie Zilbergeld (1992) suggests that what is normal covers a wide range of activities and frequencies. Frequency of sexual activity is a very personal choice—whatever feels right for you is normal. In addition, any activities that are pleasurable for both you and your partner, do not hurt anyone, and do not interfere with your relationship are acceptable.

Zilbergeld recommends that you consider the following questions to help you determine if your sexual practices are healthy:

- Is this activity something that feels good?
- Does my partner enjoy it?
- Is it interfering with my relationship?
- Is it hurting anyone?
- Does it interfere with other aspects of my life?

You may have other questions that stem from your personal situation. For example, perhaps religious or moral issues are of concern to you. If so, list your concerns, and then consider how your sexual practices are consistent or inconsistent with your belief system.

For Her Do you find it difficult to have an orgasm? Many women have never had an orgasm, and many more experience difficulties achieving orgasm at one time or another. Failing to be orgasmic can be a source of frustration and discomfort in a sexual relationship. However, it is important to remember that sex can be very fulfilling and enjoyable even without an orgasm. (Chapter 13 presents some relatively simple and straightforward steps that can help a woman become orgasmic.) Women are often taught at a young age to feel ashamed of their bodies and sexual urges. It is therefore not uncommon for them to feel uncomfortable about sex. Self-exploration of both your body and any psychological barriers to sexual expression is an important first step. Even if you are orgasmic, a little self-examination can help you improve your comfort with your sexual self. Take a moment to ask yourself these questions regarding sexual activity (Masters, Johnson, & Kolodny, 1994):

- What are my greatest concerns regarding sex (fear of pregnancy, disease, disappointment, other concerns)?
- What do I find most annoying or frustrating about sex (involving intercourse, masturbation, or any other sexual act)?
- What are the most pleasant aspects of sex?
- Which parts of my body are most sensitive or erogenous?
- Am I angry at or resentful of my partner?

For Him and Her Concerns about performance are not limited to men, and discomfort with one's sexuality and orgasmic concerns are not limited to women. Therefore, you might want to go back and read the section intended for the other sex.

HEALTHY DECISION MAKING

Let's assume for a moment that you are a sexually active adult. You are enjoying a romantic evening alone with a person you know well and care deeply for—someone you would like to have sexual relations with. The time is right, everything seems nearly perfect . . . but your physiological responses just are not cooperating. (If you are male, imagine that you cannot sustain an erection; if you are female, imagine that you are not becoming lubricated.) You start to worry: What is wrong with you? What are you going to do?

You should first take a deep breath and try to relax. This type of situation all too often results in a lot of needless worry and can even snowball into a real problem. Take a minute to examine the situation for factors that might be affecting you.

- Acknowledge that this is a high-demand situation—the moment you've been waiting for—and recognize your need for everything to be perfect.
- Consider other physical and psychological factors that you now know can impair sexual responses: Are you particularly fatigued? Have you had a lot of alcohol to drink? Have you taken any drugs or medications that might affect you? Are you worried about sexually transmissible infections and/or pregnancy? Are you truly ready to enter a new phase in your relationship with this person? Are you afraid he or she does not feel the same way about you?
- Try discussing your concerns with your partner before going any further. A healthy conversation with the person with whom you are about to be intimate can often reduce or eliminate any concerns that you have.

The most important message you can get from this chapter is that physiological sexual responses do not occur on their own. Humans are not machines, and many physiological and psychological factors can interfere with sexual responses. In most cases, a calm approach to problem solving can avoid exacerbating what is likely to be a passing condition. Only if you notice a persistent pattern of failing to respond sexually under prime conditions should you discuss your concerns with both a medical professional and a mental health professional who specializes in sexual problems.

summary

NEURAL AND HORMONAL CONTROL OF SEXUAL RESPONSE

- Numerous neural mechanisms underlie sexual responses. Both the CNS and the PNS control sexual response, but each can act independently to produce sexual arousal and sometimes orgasm.
- The senses of touch, vision, hearing, and smell can all provide sensory input that may produce a sexual response.
- Hormones may also influence sexual responses. Testosterone appears to be the only hormone that exerts a significant influence on sexual desire in both women and men. There is little evidence of a correlation between fluctuations in desire in women and estrogen levels.

MODELS OF HUMAN SEXUAL RESPONSE

- There are several major models of human sexual response. Ellis's two-stage model, Masters and Johnson's four-stage model, Kaplan's three-stage model, cognitive models, and interactive models are all efforts to describe and explain this phenomenon.

THE SEXUAL RESPONSE CYCLE

- Masters and Johnson's (1966) model first described the observable physical changes that occur from arousal through orgasm.

FACTORS AFFECTING SEXUAL RESPONSE

- Two factors known to affect the normal physiological mechanisms of sexual response are aging and the use of pharmacological agents.
- The effects of aging should not deter older individuals from having healthy sexual relations; however, some of these effects must be accommodated.
- There is no evidence that any substance acts as a true aphrodisiac; however, many recreational and prescription drugs inhibit normal sexual functioning.

CHAPTER 5

Gender Roles and Sexuality

On women, men, and sex—

This [sex] difference is reflected physiologically. The hormones in a man's body that are responsible for arousal quickly build up and then are quickly released after orgasm. For a woman, the pleasure builds up much more slowly and remains long after orgasm. (p. 15)

For a woman, arousal slowly builds long before it becomes a physical desire for sex. Before longing for sexual stimulation, a woman first feels warm, sensual, and attractive. She feels drawn to a man and enjoys sharing time together. It could be days before she wants to have sex. (p. 15)

When a man becomes aroused, it is immediately sexual. To wait days requires enormous restraint on his part. When a man returns home from a trip, he might want to have sex immediately, while his wife wants to take some time to get reacquainted and talk. (pp. 15–16)

A woman first feels warm, sensual.

Excerpts from John Gray's
Mars and Venus in the Bedroom (1997)

Are these statements true, or are they pure pop psychology? Although John Gray does not cite scientific data to support these points, they do represent the views of the majority of people. If these descriptions of differing male and female sexual needs are indeed *true,* are the differences biological, or are they imposed on the sexes by the culture? Whether we realize it or not, most of us are guided by a set of assumptions about what women and men are supposed to be like. When an individual is identified as male or female, an entire set of attributes is generally assumed to apply to that individual. Traditionally, males and females have been dichotomized into gender categories—masculine and feminine. But how many people actually fit perfectly into these categories? Are masculine and feminine characteristics real or perceived? These attributes can have a powerful influence on almost every aspect of life—including sexual relationships. Before we can explore the impact of these attributes on human sexuality, we must first understand them and where they come from.

PRENATAL SEX DIFFERENTIATION

The importance of biological factors in human sexual development is dramatically illustrated by prenatal sexual differentiation and particularly by abnormalities in this process. Before reading about the physiological processes that transform the embryo into a male or a female, you may find it useful to review Chapter 3 on sexual anatomy.

The prenatal differentiation of each individual into a male or a female depends on two processes: First, sex chromosomes determine whether the sperm and egg, upon joining, will produce a male or a female. The next step is dependent on hormones, particularly testosterone. The secretion of testosterone by the male fetus's testes programs the development of male genitals. In the absence of testosterone, female genitalia will develop (Money, 1980).

When they first form at about 5–6 weeks after conception, the gonads are undifferentiated—neither male nor female. Cells contain either XX or XY sex chromosomes, and these guide genital development during the prenatal period. If XY sex chromosomes are present, testes form from the gonadal ridge. If XX chromosomes are present, ovaries develop from the gonadal ridge. Hormones are also important during the prenatal period; they guide the differentiation of the gonads into male or female. The same hormones later set the stage for sexual maturation at puberty (Shepherd-Look, 1982).

5.1 on the web

The Johns Hopkins Children's Center maintains a Web site on abnormalities in sex differentiation. The site offers information for patients and families. Visit **www.ablongman.com/mcanulty2e.**

How common are these problems? What types of medical and psychological treatments are available?

Nature is predisposed toward female development. In contrast to male development, female development requires no added hormones. The ovaries, uterus, fallopian tubes, and the external structures (clitoris, labia, and vagina) will develop even in the absence of androgen or estrogen. For a male to develop, the testes must produce large amounts of testosterone between the 6th and the 12th week of the prenatal period. Secreted testosterone stimulates the growth of the Wolffian (male) ducts and the production of *Müllerian inhibiting substance (MIS)*. In turn, MIS causes the Müllerian (female) ducts to atrophy. Testosterone also stimulates the development of the internal structures (seminal vesicles, epididymes, and vas deferens) and external structures (penis and scrotum) of the male. Sex differentiation of males and females is illustrated in Figure 5.1.

For the vast majority of individuals, sex differentiation occurs flawlessly and normal genitalia develop. However, in rare instances problems may occur, resulting in abnormalities.

ABNORMALITIES IN SEX DIFFERENTIATION

Abnormalities in sex differentiation may result from problems with sex chromosomes or problems with hormones. Though these abnormalities are very uncommon, they can have dramatic effects on physical appearance and sexual adjustment. As you'll see, there are medical treatments for some, but not all, of these conditions. The treatments may help correct some of the defects but are not considered cures. Even with treatment, most individuals with chromosomal or hormonal abnormalities experience some chronic impairment.

Sex Chromosome Problems

Sex chromosome abnormalities occur when individuals have either an extra or a missing sex chromosome. There are reportedly over 70 different types of disorders associated with these sex chromosome problems (Levitan, 1988). We will discuss the most common and the best understood of these disorders.

Klinefelter's syndrome occurs in males who are born with an extra X (female) chromosome (XXY). Because of the additional female chromosome, individuals with Klinefelter's syndrome have incomplete masculinization and some female physical features. They generally have underdeveloped penises and testes, low testosterone production, and incomplete physical maturation at puberty. Because of these deficiencies, individuals with this syndrome are infertile; further, some show partial breast development at puberty. Some individuals with Klinefelter's suffer from mental retardation. Klinefelter's syndrome is estimated to occur at the rate of 1 in 500 to 1,000 live births. The only treatment involves administering testosterone at puberty. This treatment helps masculinize the body but does not correct the infertility.

KLINEFELTER'S SYNDROME
A sex chromosome abnormality that occurs in males who are born with an extra X chromosome. Their masculinization is incomplete, and they evidence some female physical characteristics, such as partial breasts.

TURNER'S SYNDROME
A sex chromosome abnormality that occurs in females who are born with only one X chromosome. They often are missing ovaries or have deficient ovaries, either of which interferes with sexual maturity and causes infertility.

Turner's syndrome occurs in females who are missing one X chromosome (X0). They usually have a female physical appearance but are missing ovaries or have deficient ones. Consequently, they are not capable of producing ova (eggs) or sex hormones. Because of the lack of sex hormones, these females do not mature physically at puberty unless they receive synthetic hormones. As a rule, females with Turner's syndrome are short, and they may have other physical defects. Webbed skin from the

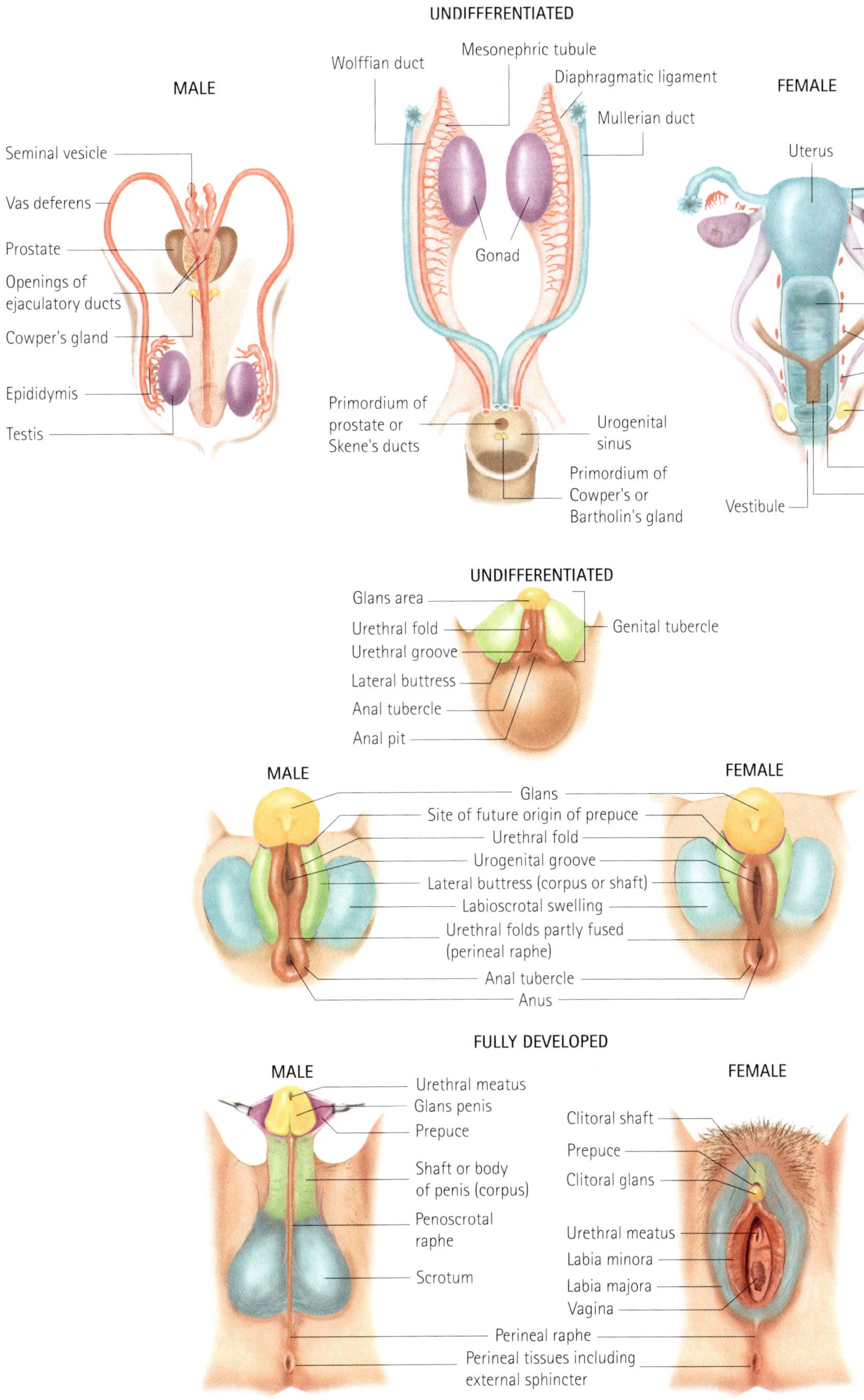

Figure 5.1 Sexual Differentiation during Fetal Development

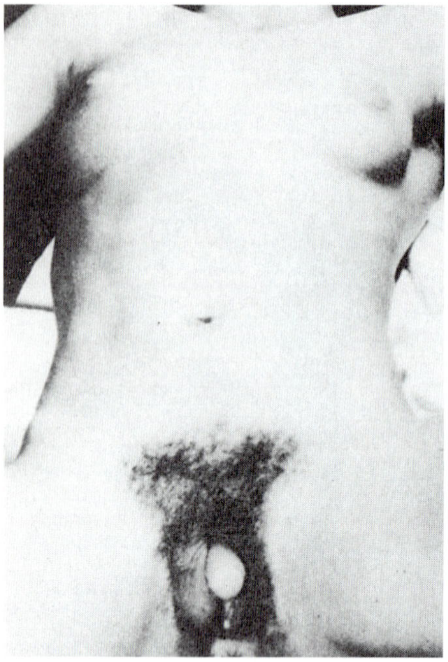

True hermaphroditism is a rare condition in which the person is born with partially male and partially female genitalia. They are usually genetic females who have a uterus and male external genitals.

neck to the shoulders occurs in some cases. Turner's syndrome is estimated to occur in from 1 in 2,500 to 1 in 5,000 live births. One out of 10 spontaneously aborted fetuses has a missing X chromosome. The medical treatment consists of administering estrogen and progesterone, which can trigger menstruation as well as breast and genital maturation.

In rare instances, some individuals with normal sex chromosomes experience abnormal sex differentiation. **Intersexuality**, or **hermaphroditism**, is a rare abnormality in sex differentiation that occurs during prenatal development. The defining feature of intersexuality is the presence of ambiguous genitalia at birth (Meyer-Bahlburg, 1994). True hermaphrodites are born with one ovary and one testicle, or with ovotestes. They are usually, but not always, genetic females, who have a uterus but whose external genitals may appear ambiguously male or female. At puberty, breast development and menstruation may begin. A similar condition, **pseudohermaphroditism**, is more common than true hermaphroditism, occurring in up to 1 out of 1,000 newborns. Male pseudohermaphrodites have XY sex chromosomes and testes, but their external genitals are female or ambiguous. Female pseudohermaphrodites have XX sex chromosomes and ovaries, with male or ambiguous external genitals. The causes of intersexuality are unknown.

Hormonal Problems

Problems with the production of hormones may also affect prenatal sexual development. Underproduction or overproduction of sex hormones during the prenatal period may alter the formation of the brain's hypothalamus. These changes in turn may cause abnormalities in the development of the reproductive system, including the genitals. Hormonal problems are sometimes due to abnormal hormone production by the embryo. At other times, these problems may be due to hormones produced or ingested by the mother during pregnancy, or to so-called hormone disruptions in the maternal environment.

did YOU know?

The term* hermaphroditism *is derived from the names of the Greek god and goddess of love, Hermes and Aphrodite.

Congenital adrenal hyperplasia (CAH), also known as **adrenogenital syndrome**, is caused by a genetic defect that causes the adrenal glands of the fetus to produce too much testosterone (androgen). For boys, this overproduction of testosterone results in precocious or premature puberty. There are reports of 5-year-old boys with CAH who have reached puberty. In girls, the overproduction of testosterone causes some masculinization of the genitals. To varying degrees, the clitoris is enlarged and has the appearance of a penis. The external labia may be fused and appear as a scrotum. The internal female sex structures are typically normal. Treatment for CAH in girls involves reducing testosterone production and surgically correcting the genitals. If the condition is detected early and treated, the child will mature normally (Hurtig & Rosenthal, 1987). If left untreated, the child's physical appearance will become increasingly masculine over time.

Androgen insensitivity syndrome (AIS) occurs in males whose bodies produce normal amounts of androgens (testosterone) but whose target cells—those cells that normally react to androgens—are unresponsive, because these males lack an androgen receptor gene. As a result, the Wolffian ducts are insensitive to androgens, and the male fetus's internal structures do not develop normally. Meanwhile, the Müllerian ducts are inhibited by MIS, as they are in all normal males. Consequently, the newborn lacks an internal reproductive system, either male or female.

Recall that nature is predisposed toward female development. Thus, being unresponsive to testosterone, males with AIS have what are apparently female external genitals. They usually have a normal-appearing clitoris and a shallow vagina. At puberty, they experience the breast development that is characteristic of normal female

INTERSEXUALITY
A rare sex differentiation abnormality in which the person has ambiguous genitalia at birth. These individuals typically show partially male and partially female genitalia; also known as *hermaphroditism.*

PSEUDOHERMAPHRODITISM
A sex differentiation abnormality that is more common than true hermaphroditism. In genetic males, it involves having XY chromosomes but female external genitals. In genetic females, it consists of having XX chromosomes but male external genitals.

maturation. Lacking internal reproductive structures, persons with AIS are incapable of reproduction.

Because they have the external genitals of a female, males with AIS are usually identified as girls at birth and reared as such. By undergoing surgery to lengthen the vagina and taking estrogen supplements, all of these individuals successfully adopt a female identity. One followup study of 14 cases revealed that the individuals exhibited traditional female gender roles. Several were adoptive parents (Money & Ehrhardt, 1972).

Looking At . . .

. . . Thinking About

Do you think U.S. culture is becoming more or less accepting of people who challenge traditional gender roles?

SEX, GENDER, AND CHALLENGES TO STEREOTYPES

The terms *gender* and *sex* are often used synonymously, but this usage is inaccurate. **Sex** refers to the biological differences of the sex chromosomes and sex organs of males and females. **Gender** refers to the psychosocial condition of being feminine or masculine—having particular behaviors, traits, and interests that are assumed to be appropriate for a given sex by the members of a society. Thus, a child whose chromosomal makeup includes two X chromosomes and whose genitalia include a clitoris, vagina, and labia is assigned the *sex* of female. But her behavior, personality, and general lifestyle will determine whether her *gender* is masculine or feminine.

Gender Roles

Almost everyone makes certain assumptions about what social roles men and women should play. These **gender roles** encompass behaviors, personality characteristics, and lifestyles that society expects of an individual based on that individual's sex. Have you ever noticed that people are more likely to ask you "What does your father do?" than "What does your mother do?" (Perhaps you do this, too!) Even at the beginning of the 21st century, most people still tend to think of men as providers and women as caregivers. A working woman is assumed to be in charge on the domestic front, and her job is usually considered secondary and of lesser status than the man's job. Gender-role expectations are not limited to family and career roles, however. Men are expected to be the initiators in dating relationships; women are expected to wait for men to make the first move. Women are assumed to be more concerned about their appearance than men are. Men are supposed to be sports-oriented. Individuals who adhere closely to the roles expected of their sex are said to engage in **gender-typed behavior.**

Today, traditional gender roles tend to be adhered to less rigidly, at least in the United States. Fathers are often much more involved in their children's lives than was true for preceding generations, and many women devote more time to career than to family. Women are more assertive in relationships, and many men are more concerned about their appearance than the average woman (as is obvious from the growth of the men's fashion industry). Furthermore, gender roles are not consistent across racial or ethnic groups. One study, for example, showed that on a measure of sex-role characteristics, African American women and men identified masculine traits *and* feminine traits as equally characteristic of themselves (Harris, 1996). These findings reflect the fact that gender-role socialization of African Americans is different from that of white Americans. African American culture dictates that girls learn to be self-reliant, strong, and independent (Harris, 1996). African American women are more likely to be heads

CONGENITAL ADRENAL HYPERPLASIA (CAH)
A hormonal abnormality resulting from a genetic defect that causes the adrenal glands of the fetus to produce excess testosterone. In boys, this results in premature puberty. In girls, the condition causes some masculinization of the genitals; also known as *adrenogenital syndrome.*

ANDROGEN INSENSITIVITY SYNDROME (AIS)
A hormonal abnormality that occurs in males whose adrenal glands produce normal amounts of testosterone but whose target cells are unresponsive. As a consequence, they lack an internal reproductive system, either male or female.

SEX
The biological state of being male or female.

GENDER
The psychosocial condition of being feminine or masculine; the collection of particular behaviors, traits, and interests that are agreed to be either masculine or feminine.

GENDER ROLES
Behaviors, personality characteristics, and lifestyles that a culture or society expects of an individual based on that individual's sex.

GENDER-TYPED BEHAVIOR
Behavior that adheres closely to the roles expected of a given sex.

of households than are white American women (Hyde, 1996). Nonetheless, cultural expectations regarding traditional roles persist in U.S. society.

Gender Stereotypes and Their Effects

Despite the fact that men and women in the United States enjoy more role flexibility than in the past, gender stereotyping is still common. **Gender stereotyping** occurs when an individual is assumed to possess certain characteristics or to perform certain tasks based on her or his sex, regardless of how closely the person actually adheres to gender-role expectations. Females are expected to behave in a stereotypic "feminine" fashion and males in a stereotypic "masculine" fashion. For example, we stereotype when we say that men hog the remote control or women try to change men in relationships. Even the popular phrases we adopt reflect these stereotypes; perhaps you have heard the phrases "It's a guy thing" and "a chick flick" (referring to a movie about relationships).

Perhaps one reason we tend to use gender stereotypes is that many men and women *do* have characteristics in common with other members of their sex; thus, at least some of the time, these generalizations are on target. Life is less complicated if we can predict what a person is like rather than having to discover each person's unique characteristics. A serious problem arises, however, when we are inflexible about stereotypes and do not accept people's individuality. Many stereotypes are not only inaccurate but also negative, and result in harm or oppression of the stereotyped group. **Gender bias** occurs when individuals of one sex are treated differently than are members of the opposite sex, based on assumptions about that sex. For example, consider the following:

> Every physiologist is well aware that at stated times, nature makes a great demand upon the energies of early womanhood and that at these times, great caution must be exercised lest injury be done. . . . It is better that the future matrons of the state should be without a University training than that it should be produced at the fearful expense of ruined health; better that the future mothers of the state should be robust, hearty, healthy women, than that by over-study, they entail upon their descendants the germs of disease. (From a publication issued by the University of Wisconsin, 1877)

Such highly inaccurate assumptions about women's physical capacities for many years prevented women from pursuing educational and career opportunities that would permit them to advance in society.

Despite the sometimes harmful effects of gender stereotyping, U.S. culture continues to require that "the sex of the body match the gender of the psyche" (Bem, 1993, p. 115). As a result, we tend to engage in **gender polarization**—assuming that males' and females' behavior patterns are completely different. Furthermore, people tend to view "any person or behavior that deviates from [gender-based] scripts as problematic—as unnatural or immoral from a religious perspective or as biologically anomalous or psychologically pathological from a scientific perspective" (Bem, 1993, p. 81). The dichotomy between genders is imposed on males and females despite the fact that most people's behavior falls along a continuum of masculine and feminine.

GENDER STEREOTYPING
Assuming that an individual possesses certain characteristics or should perform certain tasks, based on her or his sex, regardless of how closely the person actually adheres to gender-role expectations.

GENDER BIAS
Differential treatment of individuals of one sex, based on assumptions about that sex.

GENDER POLARIZATION
A cultural tendency to define "mutually exclusive scripts for being male and female" and to view a person who does not adhere to the script as unnatural, immoral, or mentally ill.

GENDER IDENTITY
One's view of herself or himself as female or male.

Gender Identity

We typically assume that an individual's concept of himself or herself as male or female is consistent with the individual's biological sex. This assumption is false. A person's **gender identity**, or view of herself or himself as female or male, does not always correspond with the biological condition of being female or male.

By studying the adjustment processes of persons with sex differentiation abnormalities, researchers have tried to evaluate the relative contributions of biological and psychosocial factors in shaping gender identity. Consider the case of a genetic female with congenital adrenal hyperplasia, or adrenogenital syndrome, who is born with male genitalia. Because her genitals appear to be male, this individual may be raised as a male even though she is a genetic female. What will her gender identity be as an adult? If biological factors, such as sex chromosomes and hormones, fully determine gender identity, the female will ultimately develop a female gender identity despite her upbringing. Conversely, if gender identity is completely shaped by environmental influences, she will accept the male gender role and develop a male gender identity. Studies of persons born with ambiguous genitals reveal that gender identity is shaped by the complex interplay of both biological and environmental factors (Diamond, 1982; Money, 1991).

Early research by Money and Ehrhardt (1972) revealed the important role of the environment in influencing gender identity. These researchers studied two genetic females with adrenogenital syndrome, one of whom was reared as a female and the other as a male. The first individual was accurately identified as a female at 2 months of age and underwent surgery to correct her ambiguous genitals. With hormone therapy, the girl developed a female gender identity and was described as feminine and attractive as an adult woman. The other individual was incorrectly identified as a male and reared as a boy. The child's genitals were surgically masculinized, and hormone therapy was initiated. In this case, a genetic female reared as a male adopted a male gender identity and reportedly adapted successfully to the male gender role. Though these two cases highlight the role of the environment in shaping gender identity, it is important to remember that biological factors also played a role, since both individuals underwent surgery and hormone treatments.

There is still considerable debate over the relative contributions of biological and environmental factors in shaping gender identity (Herdt & Nanda, 1994). Some researchers, such as Milton Diamond (1982, 1995), argue that biological influences are more significant; other experts, among them John Money (1991), believe that biological and environmental factors contribute equally. In either case, it seems clear that gender identity results from a complex interplay of many influences.

Children and adolescents with sex differentiation abnormalities commonly suffer from body-image problems associated with ambiguous genitalia. Traditionally, such problems were "corrected" through surgery in infancy to "normalize" the genitals—to make them look either male or female in order to prevent future distress and potential ridicule due to a different appearance. However, a growing number of intersexed individuals as well as doctors are opposing this process, and groups (e.g., The Intersex Society of North America, whose Web site is at www.isna.org) have formed in part to oppose surgical "normalization." Members of such groups argue that it is unethical to make a choice for a child, without his or her consent, because of the risk that the child may later regret having had the surgery. Why would an individual regret it? At least one reason is that these surgical techniques may cause damage to the genital region that often limits or destroys sexual function and may cause incontinence, painful scarring, and infertility as well (Creighton, 2001; Daaboul & Frader, 2001; Dreger, 2002). Instead of exposing children to these risks, intersex advocates emphasize the need to make U.S. society less bi-gendered and more open to the fact that even biological sex is not always easily classified as male or female.

Cultural standards play a powerful role in determining how well children with ambiguous genitalia will adjust, with or without surgery. Scientists who are concerned with the psychosocial adjustment of intersexed individuals suggest that there is a need to study those cultures that accept intersexuality as a normal condition (Kuhnle & Krahl, 2002).

Transgenderism

Intersexed individuals are not the only people who force us to question our tendency to dichotomize gender into masculine and feminine. **Transgendered individuals** are a highly diverse group who do not conform to traditional notions of how a person of a

IN YOUR own words

21-year-old female college student

I was not the traditional prissy girl that wanted to watch the boys on the playground—I wanted to get out there and play for myself. For that, they looked at me as a tomboy, and didn't want to have anything to do with me. Even now, at the age of 21, people are quick to call me "butch" or assume things about my lifestyle, just because I have short hair and don't feel comfortable in tight shirts and skirts. I am a human being—why can't people just accept me for who I am?

TRANSGENDERED INDIVIDUAL
A person whose appearance, behavior, or self-identification do not conform to traditional norms for his or her biological sex and gender.

given biological sex should look, behave, or identify himself or herself. In its broadest sense, the term *transgendered* can be used to refer to "all women who are less than perfectly feminine and all men who are less than perfectly masculine (i.e., almost all of us)" (Anonymous, 1999, p. 1). However, the most obviously transgendered individuals are cross-dressers, gay men in drag, lesbians who wear masculine clothing and hairstyles, and transsexuals (Bullough, 2000).

Cross-dressers comprise a diverse group, especially with respect to their motivations for cross-dressing. **Cross-dressers** are typically men who wear women's clothing, jewelry and/or makeup. There are women who cross-dress, but they are much more difficult to define and identify in our culture because it is more acceptable for women to wear men's clothing, and they often do so simply because it is fashionable. A true cross-dresser does not cross-dress as a fashion statement or for work (i.e., as a female impersonator). Lesbians who wear men's clothing and gay men in drag are not viewed as "pure" cross-dressers, although they do adopt the clothing of the opposite sex. Individuals who cross-dress for its own sake are generally motivated by a certain state or feeling that is achieved only by wearing the attire of the opposite sex. Some individuals cross-dress solely because they find it sexually arousing. This pattern of behavior has traditionally been called **transvestic fetishism** and is discussed in Chapter 6. Others cross-dress because doing so conjures up positive but nonsexual feelings, and some cross-dressers may be motivated by both sexual and nonsexual effects (Gilbert, 2000). In fact, for many cross-dressers, the motivation may be erotic at first, but later the behavior may become nonsexually motivated (Anonymous, 1999). Many male cross-dressers describe their experience of cross-dressing as satisfying the "yen to be feminine" (Gilbert, 2000, p. 5). In other words, these men wear the clothing of women because it creates a positive feeling of being feminine. This need can be satisfied through full or partial cross-dressing; cross-dressers may either completely deck themselves out in feminine garb or simply wear some women's clothing, such as undergarments under their usual "gender-typed" clothing. Some experts in the field question whether most cross-dressers are actually transsexuals who have simply not yet reached the point of identifying themselves as such (Anonymous, 1999).

5.2 on the web

Many Web sites offer support for transgendered individuals. Go to **www.ablongman.com/mcanulty2e** and take a few minutes to scan the articles and the discussion forums at the Transgender Boards.

Describe some of your thoughts and reactions to the information you read.

Transsexuals are people who view themselves as being of the sex opposite to their biological sex. Some transsexuals feel comfortable living as members of the opposite sex but have no desire to alter their biological sex. Some experts reserve the term *transgenderist* for those transsexuals who do not wish to change their biological sex through surgery but who live comfortably full-time in the gender role normally prescribed for the opposite sex (Richards, 1997). Indeed, individuals who live this way seem to have achieved transcendence over societal gender-role expectations. Many transsexuals, however, report significant distress from feeling like a "woman trapped in a man's body," or vice versa. A transsexual who experiences high levels of such distress may be diagnosed as having **gender identity disorder (GID).** Transsexuals who are distressed by their biological sex and physical appearance may choose to undergo hormone therapy and sex reassignment surgery in order to "become" the opposite sex. GID and sex reassignment are discussed in more detail in Close Up on Gender: GID (on page 140). Although many people view individuals who clearly defy societal gender-role expectations as abnormal or sick, many transgendered individuals are quite content with their lives, and perhaps those who are not happy are distressed less by their own gender identity than by the fact that they live in an environment that is hostile to them because they do not fit into preconceived gender categories.

The development of the transgendered individual in the face of a culture of nonacceptance is difficult to understand. In general, it is reasonable to assume that the causes of transgendered behavior are not the same either across types of transgendered individuals or among those of one type (e.g., no two transsexuals develop their identities via the same path). As you will learn in the next section, far more research has focused on normative gender-role development than on transgenderism.

CROSS-DRESSER
A person who gains sexual arousal or positive nonsexual feelings by dressing in the clothing of the opposite sex.

TRANSVESTIC FETISHISM
The behavior of a person who cross-dresses specifically to obtain sexual arousal and gratification.

TRANSSEXUAL
A person who views herself or himself as being the sex opposite her or his biological sex.

GENDER IDENTITY DISORDER (GID)
A psychological diagnosis based on a person's feeling as though he or she is trapped inside a body of the other biological sex and experiencing significant distress over this condition.

BIOLOGICAL AND SOCIAL THEORIES OF GENDER

The primary debate over how gender develops concerns the respective influences of nature and nurture. Numerous scientists have devoted their lives to determining the extent to which a person's biological makeup or physical and social environment programs gender-typed behavior patterns. Some experts argue that there is no single answer to this question. In fact, the contributions of heredity and environment are very complex and may vary depending on the time (in history) and the place (different cultures) (Sternberg, 1993). Each of the perspectives covered in this section emphasizes the contribution of either biology or environment. The first two viewpoints—behavioral genetics and the evolutionary perspective—are aimed at delineating the relative contribution of hereditary to the development of gender roles. The following three—the social learning, Freudian, and cognitive-developmental theories—are environmental models of gender-role development. Not much progress has been made toward integrating these models, but it will probably be apparent to you that these perspectives complement as well as contradict one another.

Behavioral Genetics

Behavioral genetics is an area of research that studies how inherited biological factors may determine, in whole or in part, certain behavioral characteristics. Traditional approaches used in this type of research focus on similarities and differences between adopted children and their adoptive and biological parents (Sherman et al., 1997). The assumption generally made is that if an adopted child shows characteristics more similar to those of the biological parents than to those of the adoptive parents, then those characteristics are likely to have been more greatly influenced by biological factors than by environmental factors.

Another approach is to look at similarities between monozygotic (identical) twins, who are genetically identical, relative to similarities between dizygotic (fraternal) twins, who share only about 50% of their genes. The assumption made in this type of research is that the influences of the environment are the same for both kinds of twins because they have shared the same environment since the womb. If a behavioral trait were controlled entirely by genetics, then monozygotic twins would show nearly 100% **concordance** on that trait—they would behave almost exactly the same. Dizygotic twins would show about 50% concordance on that trait.

Little behavioral genetics research has been conducted specifically to test the impact of genetics on gender-typed behavior (Jacklin & Baker, 1993). One study that explored the development of masculinity and femininity in preadolescents and early adolescents found only a modest correlation between parents and children with respect to gender-typed personality characteristics (such as assertiveness and nurturance) that could be accounted for by genetics. The effects of experiences outside the home (such as peer interactions) that were unique to the individual child seemed to be more influential than either genetics or parental influence (Mitchell, Baker, & Jacklin, 1989).

The Evolutionary Perspective

The evolutionary perspective suggests that the different behaviors and characteristics of males and females that present themselves across all cultures have been selected throughout evolutionary history to ensure survival of the species. Evolutionary psychologists claim that they can predict *similarities* between the sexes in those areas where both have been challenged by similar "adaptive problems" throughout history. Conversely, they say they can predict *differences* between males and females in those areas where different adaptive problems have been confronted (Buss, 1995). Proponents of this position argue that gender differences that are observed across the vast majority of cultures cannot be explained by environmental influences alone. If environment were

CONCORDANCE
Agreement.

CLOSE UP ON gender

GID

A person is diagnosed with gender identity disorder (GID) when his or her gender identity does not match his or her biological sex. A boy with gender identity disorder has the subjective sense of being a girl; a girl feels like she is really a boy. Signs of GID typically emerge in early childhood (Zucker et al., 1999); however, the condition sometimes develops after puberty (Doorn, Poortinga, & Verschoor, 1994). GID is rare, and males with the disorder outnumber females by a ratio of three or four to one. Adults with GID may be homosexual, heterosexual, or even asexual.

Individuals with GID often verbalize a desire to be the opposite sex and may also be fixated on the notion of eventually being transformed into that sex. Even a young child with GID is generally very clear about wanting to be the opposite sex. As the child matures into adolescence, he or she may express a desire to undergo sex-reassignment surgery. Children and adolescents do not always verbalize a clear desire to become the opposite sex, however. They may adopt many behaviors—for example, gestures, vocabulary, and speech patterns—that imitate those of the opposite sex. Cross-dressing is also common, and the child may actively resist wearing clothes deemed appropriate to his or her biological sex. Boys are obviously more likely to be ridiculed than girls for doing this, because our culture accepts "tomboys" more readily than it does "sissies." Parents should not be alarmed by any of these behaviors in a child, however, as many children grow out of them by about age 8. For the child with GID, in contrast, cross-gender dress and behavior generally become even more extreme as he or she reaches adolescence (Money & Lehne, 1999).

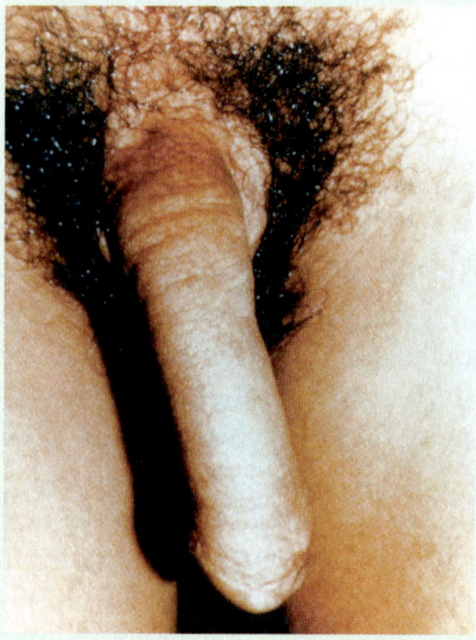
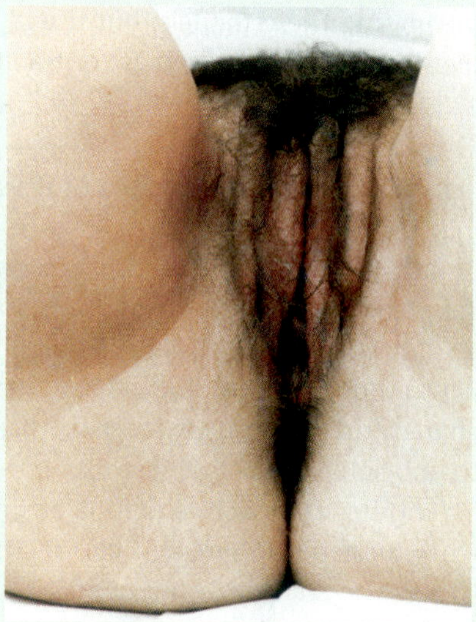

After sex reassignment. Left: female to male; Right: male to female.

the major influence, there would be much more variation in these characteristics across different cultures. As a case in point, in all cultures, women are less likely than men to commit murder or to reach high levels of social dominance and are less promiscuous than men and less likely to be polygamous (have multiple partners). In addition, women are more likely to seek out older partners, who have more material and social resources (Kenrick & Trost, 1993). Evolutionary psychologists argue that these behavior patterns persist across cultures because they ensure species survival.

David Buss, a psychology professor at the University of Texas–Austin, has contributed enormously to the evolutionary perspective. He identified a number of adaptive problems having to do with sex and mating and affecting men and women differently (Buss, 1999, 2001). For instance, Buss points out that one problem women, but not men, have had to face throughout evolutionary history is finding a mate who will not only father children but also invest in their care and support. Thus, women are much more selective than men are with respect to mating because the consequences of becoming pregnant are so great and the future investment is huge. If a woman had sex with a man who was not likely to stick around and help out, she could find herself struggling alone through pregnancy, not to mention through years of rearing a child, often with limited resources. Thus, finding a mate who will invest in a relationship and provide ongoing support is important for survival of the species. Men, on the other hand, are more likely to engage in casual sexual interactions because they can much

Many researchers have proposed a biological basis for GID; however, the evidence is mixed (Zucker, 1995). Some recent research has suggested that male transsexuals have certain brain structures that are more similar in shape and size to those of females than to those of males (Cohen-Kettenis & Gooren, 1999). Current research suggests that boys with GID tend to have more brothers and to be born later in the birth order than boys without the disorder (see Zucker, 1995; Zucker & Bradley, 1995). However, the meaning of these findings is unclear. It appears that parental tolerance or encouragement of identification with the opposite sex is common among individuals with GID. Difficulty identifying with the same-sex parent is another possible factor in this disorder (Zucker & Bradley, 1995). Finally, some researchers view GID as the result of a basic disturbance in the sense of self (Docter, 1988). According to this view, cross-dressing and cross-gender identification evolve from self-perceived identification with the opposite sex, beginning early in life. For some individuals with GID, the need to resolve *gender dysphoria* (distress about one's biological sex), may lead to living as a person of the opposite sex and even seeking sex-reassignment surgery.

Experts consistently agree that psychotherapy is generally ineffective in eliminating the distress associated with feeling trapped in a body of the "wrong" sex (Zucker, 1995). For many people, the preferred approach to "treating" GID is sex reassignment, primarily through surgical reconstruction of the genitalia. Sex-reassignment surgery has been controversial, although recent studies reveal that the vast majority of individuals who have undergone the procedure are pleased with the outcome. To ensure that they are ready, candidates for the procedure are typically required to live in the opposite-gender role and to undergo cross-sex hormonal treatment for 1–2 years. Biological males take estrogen therapy to produce some breast development, soften the skin, reduce muscle mass, and redistribute body fat somewhat. Biological females take testosterone to effect the growth of body and facial hair, deepening of the voice, and the elimination of menstruation. The male-to-female surgery involves removal of the penis and testes and the creation of an artificial vagina. Additionally, breast implants are sometimes offered. The female-to-male procedure consists of a hysterectomy (removal of ovaries and uterus), a mastectomy (breast removal), and sometimes the creation of an artificial penis, which is a complicated intervention. As you can see from the photos, surgically created genitals look no different than natural genitals.

One study found that 87% of those who had the male-to-female surgery and 97% of those receiving the female-to-male procedure were satisfied (Green & Fleming, 1990). Satisfaction with sex-reassignment surgery is related to level of personal adjustment prior to surgery, amount of social support, and effectiveness of the surgery (Blanchard, 1985; Ross & Need, 1989). Most benefits are associated with self-reports about the person's sense of well-being, with fewer benefits observed in other aspects of life (Kuiper & Cohen-Kettenis, 1988). Because the world at large is not accepting of those who change their sex, social support is essential, and many individuals seek therapy before, during, and after sex-change surgery to help with adjustment issues.

more easily walk away from these interactions without enduring lifelong consequences. Commitment is not necessary to achieving the ultimate goal of propagating the species. So why do men make commitments at all? Because men who will not commit do not attract women and, therefore, do not reproduce. In addition, men who commit are better off from an evolutionary standpoint because children from two-parent families are more likely to survive and eventually bear offspring (Buss, 1999). Thus, Buss argues that men might have a greater tendency to engage in casual sexual encounters, but evolution favors those men who commit to a relationship, at least for a period of time, because they are more likely to reproduce. Furthermore, women are more likely to have sexual relations in the context of a committed relationship.

Within the general context of these evolutionary forces, however, there is great individual variability in human behavior, and general tendencies are molded and modified by the cultural context in which they occur (Buss & Schmitt, 1993; Kenrick & Trost, 1993). Thus, genetic predispositions that have evolved throughout history indirectly influence, but do not control, sexual behavior. Experiences within the environment may either oppose or exaggerate genetic predispositions, and cultural influences can even change the course of evolution. For example, the very recent (in evolutionary terms) development of highly effective contraception is likely to have a tremendous impact on sexual patterns in females. Other recent developments, such as fertility drugs, sperm banks, and telephone sex, are likely to have an impact as well (Buss, 1994).

Looking At . . .

. . . Thinking About

According to evolutionary psychologists, why might a younger woman seek an older partner?

The evolutionary perspective on sex differences has been criticized in part because it is so speculative. Evolutionary scientists generally base their notions on observations of lower animals, so their conclusions are not necessarily applicable to humans. Another criticism, opponents would argue, is that evolutionary theory has been used to justify reprehensible behavior such as rape. Certain evolutionary scientists who have analyzed rape have identified it as an adaptive strategy for men who cannot attract a mate in other ways, such as through having high status (Thornhill & Palmer, 2000; Thornhill & Thornhill, 1983). According to this view, human males use three adaptive approaches to ensuring reproduction: cooperative bonding (marriage), manipulative courtship (seduce deceitfully, then leave), and forcible rape (Shields & Shields, 1983). Although men are not conscious of the evolutionary sexual motivation to reproduce and men who rape are most likely immediately motivated by anger and hostility, the conclusion reached by this perspective is "*all* men are potential rapists" (Shields & Shields, 1983, p. 119). Thus, the evolutionary perspective contends that any man might rape under the right circumstances.

Buss and other evolutionary psychologists contend that the view that sex differences evolve through natural selection does not imply that either sex is superior, that humans are unchangeable, or that the status quo is justified. Rather, they contend, if we learn from our evolutionary history, we can more effectively make desirable changes. "We are the first species in the known history of three and a half billion years of life on earth with the capacity to control our own destiny. The prospect of designing our destiny remains excellent to the degree that we comprehend our evolutionary past. . . . Only by understanding why these human [mating] strategies have evolved can we control where we are going" (Buss, 1994, p. 222).

So far, we have reviewed the perspective of behavioral genetics regarding gender roles, which implies that these differences are largely set in place at birth, and the evolutionary perspective, which sees them as predispositions dictated by evolution but influenced by environment. The next two perspectives generally assume that biological factors are of only minor significance and that the environment heavily dictates gender roles. Psychoanalytic theory and social learning theory are often held up as contrasting theories of human behavior, but both take an environmental approach to gender-role development.

Freud and the Psychoanalytic Viewpoint

Freud claimed that children learn to be "male" or "female" by observing and imitating the actions of the same-sex parent. He observed that children tend to go through a predictable sequence of developmental stages, of which the genital stage, which occurs between 3 and 6 years of age, is the most critical to gender development. During the genital stage, boys experience the Oedipal complex and girls experience the Electra complex. (The genital stage and the Oedipal and Electra complexes will be discussed in Chapter 11.) The boy emerges from the Oedipal complex by resolving to be more like his father so that he can one day have a woman of his own. Thus, the male child adopts a masculine gender role. By contrast, according to Freud, girls develop their feminine identities by emerging from the Electra complex and identifying with their mothers. Freud argued that in the process a girl develops self-hatred as the inferior sex, and because of her ambivalence toward being female, she does not adopt her mother's characteristics as thoroughly as a boy does his father's. Freud believed that because the girl's identification was incomplete, her superego, or her conscience, was poorly developed; therefore, women's values and morals are weaker than men's (Beal, 1994; Hoyenga & Hoyenga, 1993). For obvious reasons, Freud's theory has been criticized repeatedly for being quite sexist. It is important to note that Freud lived in a society and an era (Victorian Austria) that was extremely oppressive of women.

Social Learning Theory

Social learning theory proposes that children learn gender roles because such roles are shaped by events in the surrounding environment and primarily by the responses of others. Reinforcement, punishment, and role modeling are the primary modes through which gender-typed behavior is shaped. Social learning theorists argue that gender socialization begins at birth (and perhaps before, as parents prepare the environment in which the child will be raised), not between the ages of 3 and 6, as Freud argued. For example, even before birth, parents often prepare differently for boys and girls. They may paint and decorate the baby's room differently depending on the anticipated sex of their child (blue for boys and pink for girls). (For example, one mother-to-be was so convinced that she was having a girl that she decorated the nursery in a presumably "feminine" bunny rabbit motif. However, when the baby was a boy, the husband insisted that she completely redo the room with a more masculine theme!) Parents may purchase clothing in different colors and styles. Once the child arrives, they may give the child only certain kinds of toys to play with, such as trucks for boys and dolls for girls.

did YOU know?

Gender role socialization probably begins even before a baby is born.

Reinforcement and Punishment

Gender roles are learned and maintained throughout life by reinforcement and punishment. Reinforcement is simply a stimulus (or event) that follows a behavior and leads to an increase in the frequency of the behavior in the future. Reinforcement can also occur when an unpleasant stimulus is removed after a desired behavior takes place. Punishment works similarly. When an unpleasant stimulus (or the removal of a pleasant stimulus) follows a behavior, the likelihood of that behavior's occurring in the future is decreased.

In terms of gender-role development, a child who is reinforced for performing any gender-typed behavior is more likely to behave that way in the future. Gender-typed behavior patterns are usually established early in life; however, these behaviors are maintained by continued, periodic reinforcement throughout childhood and into adulthood. Thus, if a little boy plays with a doll at nursery school and the other boys make fun of him, he is unlikely to play with a doll again, at least not when other boys are around. Likewise, a college woman is less likely to participate in contact sports if peers and authority figures do not support her efforts or even frown on them.

Many parents today say that they have tried not to impose specific gender roles on their children. When their children persist in adopting gender-typed behavior, they often chalk the behavior up to biology or conclude that reinforcement does not work. However, the strength of a reinforcer relative to that of other reinforcers or punishers may influence its effect. For instance, in an effort to teach nurturance, parents may attempt to reinforce a son for playing with dolls. However, if this same behavior is more frequently punished by other powerful influences, such as

Looking At . . .

. . . Thinking About

If you observed these children playing with these toys, would you have a negative, positive, or neutral reaction to either scenario?

It can be difficult to encourage gender-neutral play when society places so much pressure on us to conform to expectations about boys and girls.

peers and teachers, the punishment may prevail. The boy may no longer play with dolls at all or may do so only in the presence of the parents and not in situations when it is likely to be punished.

You should also be aware that what constitutes a reinforcer or a punisher is not always clear. What is perceived as reinforcing or punishing varies considerably from person to person depending on the situation and the person's learning history. A smile of approval, for instance, may have no effect if it comes from a stranger and may even be perceived as a threat (an unpleasant stimulus) by a child. It is also clear that what might seem like an unpleasant stimulus may act as a reinforcer. If a child never otherwise gets a parent's attention, the parent's angry yelling may serve to increase undesired behavior because the child has succeeded in obtaining the much-desired attention! Thus, the parents may inadvertently reinforce the undesired behavior.

Role Modeling

In addition to being influenced by more direct forms of reinforcement, people learn through **role modeling**, or imitating the behaviors of someone they admire or like. Evidence suggests that children are most likely to imitate the behavior of someone of the same sex when several members of that sex demonstrate that behavior (Bussey & Bandura, 1984; Bussey & Perry, 1982). Thus, the availability of role models for various behaviors determines in part what behaviors members of each gender adopt. Changing trends in the occupations that men and women choose are, therefore, likely to influence the children of the future. It is probably safe to say, however, that more women have sought out the higher-status male roles than men have sought out traditional female roles.

ROLE MODELING
A learning process characterized by imitation of others' behaviors.

The Cognitive-Developmental Perspective

Social learning theory and the cognitive-developmental perspective are complementary in many respects; however, the cognitive-developmental perspective places greater emphasis on the role of cognitions (thought processes) in gender-role development. Cognitive-developmental theorists emphasize the active role that children take in their own gender socialization. These theorists agree with social learning theorists that behavior is shaped and reinforced by the environment, but they place special emphasis on a child's gender identity. They argue that once a child has identified herself or himself as female or male, the child tries to behave in a manner consistent with that sex; thus, the child takes on an active role in gender socialization. Once gender identity is established, the child seeks out role models from whom to learn behaviors that are appropriate for that gender. In addition to providing guidelines for a child's behaviors, gender identity guides the child in understanding and interpreting the behaviors of others (Beal, 1994; Cross & Markus, 1993). Similarly, Bem advanced the notion that children develop **gender schemas**, or internalizations of the culture's gender-based classification of social reality (Bem, 1981, 1993). As a result of early development of gender schemas, children become gender-typed in their behavior, incorporating only those actions that fit the culture's expectations of their particular sex.

Several studies have demonstrated that once children have developed **gender constancy**—that is, a sense of their own gender as unchanging—they are more likely to behave in a gender-typed manner. For example, Frey and Ruble (1992) demonstrated that boys with gender constancy were more apt to play with a relatively uninteresting toy preferred by other boys than with a much more appealing toy preferred by girls. Interestingly, girls did not demonstrate the same gender-typed response. Other research has demonstrated that girls are less apt to actively reject masculine objects than males are to reject feminine objects (Bussey & Perry, 1982). In these cases, socialization has likely already intervened in shaping behavior, in that it is less acceptable for a boy to demonstrate feminine behavior than it is for a girl to demonstrate masculine behavior.

Looking At . . .

. . . Thinking About

Condoleeza Rice stepped into a traditionally male position as President Bush's National Security Advisor in 2001. Can you think of any men who perform traditionally female jobs or roles, such as staying home to raise children?

A CLOSER LOOK AT ENVIRONMENTAL INFLUENCES

Exploring possible environmental influences on the development of gender roles has been of interest to many researchers over the years. Social determinants of behavior have been the focus of many studies, perhaps because they are more accessible and more amenable to manipulation and change than are genetic factors. Several sources of social influence on gender-role development—including parents, peers, schools, and the media—have been researched extensively.

Parents

What role do parents play in the development of gender-typed preferences and behaviors for boys and girls? Researchers have examined several areas in which parental treatment may differ, including encouraging achievement, fostering warmth and nurturance, encouraging gender-typed activities, and discouraging aggression. Lytton and Romney (1991) conducted an exhaustive review of the literature and examined quantitative data from 172 studies. The data were combined according to the type of socialization studied (e.g., discouragement of aggression). For a North American sample, Lytton and Romney found that only gender-typed activities (e.g., shoveling snow for

GENDER SCHEMA
An internalization of a culture's gender-based classification of social reality.

GENDER CONSTANCY
Knowledge that one's biological sex is unchanging.

IN YOUR own words

Jennifer Mason
Virginia Commonwealth University

The media totally reinforces gender stereotypes, but it is getting better. I think right now the music industry and the Internet are the mass communication sources that are the worst at reinforcing gender stereotypes.

boys and washing dishes for girls) were significantly influenced by both parents, and that fathers were more influential than mothers. Parents are especially likely to expect gender-typed behavior from boys and, in fact, evaluate boys with cross-gendered traits negatively. Girls are less pressured to conform but are expected to eventually grow out of "tomboyish" behavior (Sandnabba & Ahlberg, 1999).

The impact of parental influence on gender-typed behavior may be far-reaching. For example, Block (1978) pointed out that assignment of gender-typed chores leads to different experiences for girls and boys. Girls' chores tend to keep them in the home, while boys' chores often send them out of the home (Blair, 1992). Girls, therefore, spend more time with adults and infants in the home. Consequently, they tend to be more nurturing and responsible. Also, Block pointed out that toys may affect development; for instance, boys' toys facilitate inventiveness and manipulation more than girls' toys do. Thus, when boys and girls play with gender-typed toys, their skill development differs, often giving boys advantages over girls. Parents clearly gender-type children's toys (Campenni, 1999).

A couple of weaknesses in the research on parental influence should be noted. First, few studies take note of characteristics or predispositions that might affect a parent's tendency to foster gender-typed behavior. All parents are grouped together, regardless of the fact that parents who are relatively androgynous may influence their children very differently than those who adhere to more traditional roles. In fact, research (Blair, 1992) has shown that although daughters and sons perform gender-typed household chores in homes where fathers and mothers have egalitarian gender roles, daughters spend less time on female-typed chores. Also, sons of egalitarian fathers perform more household labor than sons of traditionally oriented parents do. Other studies have reported similar findings (Levy, 1989; Weisner, Garnier, & Louky, 1994). Thus, there is evidence that parents' gender-role orientations have an impact on their children's gender-role development.

Another weakness in studies of parental influences on children's gender-role development is that few studies have examined these influences beyond children's preschool years (Lytton & Romney, 1991). Certainly, there are endless opportunities for parents to have an effect on their children well beyond preschool. Research by Juni and Grimm (1993) demonstrated a high, positive correlation between mothers' and adult daughters' feminine characteristics and between fathers' and adult sons' masculine characteristics on the Bem Sex-Role Inventory. However, it is unclear whether these characteristics were formed in preschool or after. There is evidence that parental gender stereotypes with respect to an adolescent's aptitude in a particular area influence the adolescent's future success in or access to activities critical to development in that area. Eccles, Jacobs, and Harold (1990) reported on a number of studies that demonstrated that parents' perceptions of their child's performance in gender-typed activities, such as math and sports, are related to objective measures of the child's performance but are also biased by the gender of the child. For example, parents tend to perceive male children as more competent than female children in sports, because most sports have been gender-typed as "male" behaviors. In addition, parents often see different causes for the performance level of their son or daughter. Parents may attribute a male child's success in math to natural talent, but if a female child excels in math, they tend to attribute it to effort. Finally, children's self-perceptions and choices of activities are influenced by their parents' perceptions (Eccles, Jacobs, & Harold, 1990). Therefore, a child whose parents perceive her to be better at English than math might strive harder to excel in English than to do well in math.

Parents clearly have many opportunities to influence their children's gender roles. However, parental influence does not occur in a vacuum. Other outside factors influence children as well. Peers play an important part in gender-role development.

Peers

The most outstanding feature of peer relations from toddlerhood to middle childhood is that children segregate themselves by gender when adult supervision is absent. In other words, children are willing to play with members of the opposite sex when the play situation is structured by an adult, but when children are left to make their own choices, they generally choose to play with children of the same sex (Beal, 1994; Huston & Alvarez, 1990; Maccoby, 1990; Unger & Crawford, 1992).

Children tend to segregate themselves by sex when they play.

Why do children segregate themselves by sex? One explanation is that even in early childhood boys' and girls' interaction styles are different, and children prefer to interact with others who have similar styles. Furthermore, girls often initiate the segregation process because they find boys uncooperative and difficult to influence (Maccoby, 1990). Girls tend to comply when another child protects her belongings by saying "No!" or "Mine!" whereas boys generally ignore such admonitions (Beal, 1994). Boys also tend to play more roughly than most girls prefer (Beal, 1994; Maccoby, 1990), and girls' play tends to be more conversational and "boring" to most boys (Beal, 1994).

Within their sex-segregated groups, boys and girls differentially reinforce behavior, ignoring or punishing gender-inappropriate behavior and reinforcing gender-appropriate behavior (Hibbard & Buhrmester, 1998; Witt, 2000). Overall, boys' rules about adherence to gender roles tend to be much more rigid than girls' rules; therefore, boys are more likely than girls to imitate their friends and to criticize those who don't conform to gender roles. Boys often tease each other about liking a girl or hurl insults (e.g., "sissy," "fag") at each other to encourage conformity (Unger & Crawford, 1992). Both girls and boys tend to dislike boys who display cross-gender characteristics and girls who try to join in on the rough-and-tumble play of boys (Beal, 1994). In general, however, boys who engage in "feminine" activities are considered much more deviant than girls who engage in "masculine" activities. In other words, "tomboys" are more accepted than "sissies"—a judgment apparent in the fact that "sissy" has the more negative connotation. Many researchers hypothesize that this wider latitude for girls' behavior results from the higher status that males and masculine activities have in the culture (Unger & Crawford, 1992)—because they are considered more valuable or important, it is more important for males to adhere strictly to gender roles.

Teachers and Classroom Interactions

Children and young adults spend a large part of their lives in school. It should not surprise you, therefore, that teachers and classroom interactions are the focus of attention in many studies on gender-role development.

Some research on teacher/student interactions in the classroom suggests that girls are challenged less and given less attention than boys (American Association of University Women, 1994; Beal, 1994; Sadker & Sadker, 1994). For example, teachers communicate more with boys and praise their intellectual prowess and work quality; they show more approval to girls who work quietly in structured activities. In addition, teachers tend to evaluate girls' work for its appearance and orderliness rather than for its intellectual quality. Girls are often overlooked in favor of boys when they volunteer to participate in classroom demonstrations. Teachers tend to ask boys more open-ended questions and give them more detailed instructions on classwork. In contrast, they typically ask girls factual or yes/no questions and may finish a problem for a girl rather than challenging her to figure it out. Teachers tend to give boys more hints and second chances to answer questions but simply move on to another student or give the right answer when a girl provides an incorrect response. In addition, there is much greater tolerance for boys who speak out of turn and shout out answers to questions than there is for girls who do so. Girls are reprimanded when they call out but tend to be ignored when they sit quietly with hands raised. One might expect that because male teachers (at least at the elementary school level) are themselves in somewhat nontraditional

Gender inequality in schools appears to be less common today than it was only 10 years ago.

roles, they might be less inclined to treat male and female students differently. Studies suggest, however, that both male and female teachers treat students unequally in the classroom, but that male teachers have less egalitarian views than female teachers do (Massey & Christensen, 1990) and are less inclined to promote equal treatment through their own behavior, such as by using nonsexist language in the classroom (Poole & Isaacs, 1993). Thanks to the efforts of many enlightened teachers, schools, organizations, and the U.S. government, however, unequal treatment in the classroom appears to be less common today.

The impact of differential treatment is unclear. Many gender-role researchers as well as political groups have pointed out that during the elementary school years, girls test higher on standardized tests than boys and outperform boys in the classroom. However, around the middle school years, girls' scores on standardized tests begin to drop (Sadker & Sadker, 1994). This is cause for great concern because competition for academic scholarships and college admissions is usually heavily based on standardized scores. On the other hand, girls' achievement status has improved tremendously since the 1970s, when educators and researchers first began focusing on issues of gender equity in the classroom (Bae & Smith, 1997). Some data suggest that girls far exceed boys in other measures of achievement. For example, girls and women make better grades overall (Kersten, 1996), slightly more women than men complete at least 1 year of college, and at least as many women as men complete 4 or more years of college (Bae & Smith, 1997). One continuing problem, however, is that women's achievement in science and math, subjects that lead to degrees in fields commanding high status and good pay, is below that of men (Bae & Smith, 1997). Overall, however, the gender gap for standard test scores in math and science is narrowing (U.S. Department of Education, 2000). Nonetheless, it remains unclear whether differential interactions between teachers and male and female students account for existing gender differences in achievement (American Association of University Women, 1991; Sommers, 1994).

5.3 on the web

Increased sensitivity to differential treatment of boys and girls in schools has led to efforts to reduce bias. Go to **www.ablongman.com/mcanulty2e** and review the tips for reducing gender bias in the classroom.

Do you think these actions will address the problems described in this chapter? Why or why not?

Media

Like parents, peers, and schools, the media play an important role in gender-role development. Television is clearly the most powerful media influence on children in our culture [American Academy of Pediatrics, (AAP), 1999]. Therefore, this discussion of images of men and women in the media will be limited to those on television. However, research suggests that gender stereotypes are also found in newspapers, books, movies, and comics.

You only have to watch television for a few minutes to conclude that the media foster gender stereotypes. While the occasional commercial depicts a professional woman or shows a man putting detergent in the dishwasher, the majority of commercials portray women engaging in domestic chores or wondering which products to buy to maintain their youth and beauty. Men, on the other hand, are generally portrayed in situations involving work, alcohol, sports, or cars (Bartsch, Burnett, Diller, & Rankin-Williams, 2000; Beal, 1994; Huston & Alvarez, 1990). In addition, women are more likely to be portrayed as sex objects and as passive and deferential, while men are shown solving problems aggressively and being competent, autonomous, powerful, and active (Coltrane & Messineo, 2000; Huston & Alvarez, 1990). Past research has also shown that male characters dominate TV shows, repre-

did YOU know?

Children and adolescents in the United States watch about 25 hours of television per week or 3½ hours per day (National Institute on Media and the Family, 2000).

senting over two-thirds of all characters; women have been most often portrayed as secondary characters (Signorielli, 1989). This imbalance appears to be somewhat improved but persistent (Signorielli & Bacue, 1999). Today, more women are seen on television (Vande Berg & Streckfuss, 1992) and more often filling nontraditional roles, but few men are portrayed in traditionally female roles. For example, women play doctors (*ER*), detectives (*NYPD Blue*), judges (*Judging Amy*), White House advisors (*The West Wing*), and even vampire slayers (*Buffy the Vampire Slayer*)! But rarely are men shown as homemakers (one exception being the 1980s sitcom *Who's the Boss*). Examples of gays and African or Hispanic Americans in prominent roles are even more rare (although *Six Feet Under* actually has a gay African American character!).

Stereotypic images are found in all forms of TV programming, in children's as well as adult shows. In general, even cartoon characters adhere to stereotypic roles, with male characters being more numerous and talking much more than female characters (Thompson & Zerbinos, 1995). Even programs that have been shown to be beneficial to children in other ways adhere to these stereotypes. The characters on *Sesame Street,* for instance, are predominantly male. Miss Piggy, one of only a few female Muppets, conforms to extreme and negative stereotypes of feminine characteristics (e.g., giving excessive attention to her appearance). Even the female Power Rangers often find themselves having to be rescued by the male Power Rangers. Why are most characters male? Because in general, that's what sells. Boys prefer watching male characters, and girls will watch either (Beal, 1994). Television targeted at teens is equally stereotypic. Today, girls are shown more positive role models in the media, but media directed at adolescent girls continue to overemphasize beauty and thinness, romance and dating (National Institute on Media and the Family, 2000b). Music videos are particularly notorious for portrayal of women as sex objects (Beal, 1994).

Although television still depicts many stereotypes, today more women are being portrayed in traditionally masculine roles that nevertheless include a certain level of femininity, such as Jennifer Garner's character in the series Alias.

What is the impact on children of stereotypic media images? Many different approaches have been taken in studying this question; the majority of studies support the view that TV viewing encourages adherence to gender stereotypes. Since most people watch television, it is difficult to find a sample of nonviewers to use as a control group. One approach has been to make TV programming less stereotypic and to observe the effects. Probably the most impressive study of this type was a project sponsored by the National Institute of Education, which involved showing 13 half-hour episodes (one each week) of a program called *Freestyle* to children between the ages of 9 and 12 (Williams, LaRose, & Frost, 1981). All of the programs were designed to challenge pressures to adhere to stereotypes and to portray males and females in nontraditional roles. After viewing these programs, children expressed less traditional gender-role attitudes than they had before viewing them.

Research suggests that four very powerful sources of socialization—parents, peers, teachers, and the media—play tremendous roles in fostering and perpetuating adherence to traditional gender roles. While much of this socialization is blatant, even the most well-intentioned individuals can promote adherence to traditional gender roles through their actions. Good intentions can be overcome by the kinds of faulty assumptions discussed in Reflect on This: Are You Open-Minded about Sex Differences? on page 150.

GENDER ROLES AND WELL-BEING

A tremendous amount of research has focused on examining how masculine traits and feminine traits influence psychological well-being. Three models defining the basis of well-being have been proposed (Allgood-Merten & Stockard, 1991). The earliest model, called the *traditional model,* states that women who adhere to the feminine role and men who adhere to the masculine role are most likely to be psychologically healthy.

reflect ON THIS

Are You Open-Minded about Sex Differences?

As you read this chapter, keep in mind some common mistakes even experts make when drawing conclusions about sex differences. Remember: If the experts make these mistakes, you are probably prone to, as well. But to be a good student of human behavior, you should work to avoid drawing conclusions based on faulty assumptions. Here are just a few of the mistaken assumptions people make:

1. *If a sex difference is identified, all men and women will show this difference.* Let's assume for a moment that you just read a research report that concluded that women are more nurturing than men. From this finding, can you conclude that in any pair of male and female, the woman is more nurturing than the man? Of course not. When such a difference is found between two groups of individuals, it does not mean that *all* individuals in one group are different from *all* individuals in the other group. In fact, there is likely to be considerable overlap. The average nurturing ability of the group of women studied may have been higher than the average nurturing ability of the group of men studied, but you cannot conclude that a particular woman is more nurturing than a particular man (Caplan & Caplan, 1994). Look at the graph below. What you see is two hypothetical distributions, one depicting males' scores and one depicting females' scores on a particular trait. These distributions might actually lead you to conclude that *on average* males and females are significantly different on this trait. However, you can see that there is a substantial overlap, and therefore more similarity than difference between males and females.

2. *Sex differences are caused by either heredity or the environment,* and *if sex differences are biological, then they are unchanging and permanent.* These two statements are so closely linked that we will consider them together. First, you should understand that it is highly unlikely that any characteristic or behavior pattern a person possesses is completely determined by either heredity or the environment. In fact, heredity and environment are inextricably linked (Hoyenga & Hoyenga, 1993). While scientists can call on many techniques to estimate the relative contributions of nature and nurture, the link between the two will never be broken, for all organisms are constantly affected by biological makeup as well as experiences. For instance, researchers have observed higher testosterone levels in more aggressive males.

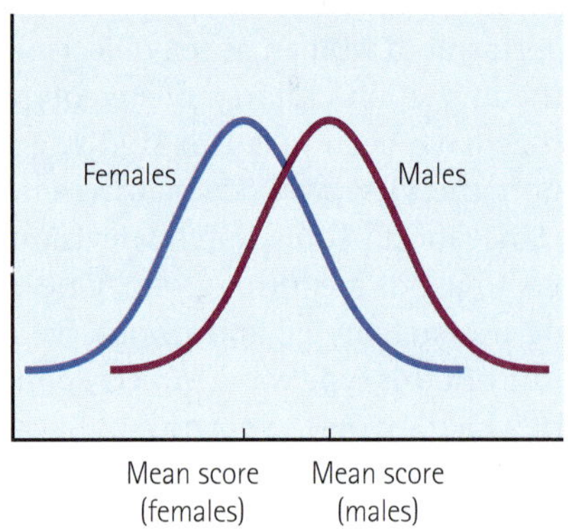

The *masculine model* states that because masculine traits are more highly regarded by society than feminine traits, both males *and* females possessing masculine traits will enjoy greater psychological well-being. The *androgyny model* states that individuals who possess a high number of both masculine and feminine traits (androgynous individuals) will be psychologically healthier than either strictly masculine or strictly feminine individuals, because androgyny allows for more flexibility across a range of situations. All of these theories support the notion that possession of masculine characteristics is healthy, at least for men if not for women. However, the studies in support of the theories generally defined masculinity as being characterized by high levels of self-efficacy, a positive trait. More recently, researchers have concerned themselves with less positive aspects of the male gender role, such as difficulty in expressing a range of emotions, and the impact on well-being of these traits.

GENDER-ROLE CONFLICT
The uncomfortable psychological state that arises in response to rigid, sexist, or restrictive gender roles and that may lead to maladaptive behavior.

Males and Gender-Role Conflict

Several researchers have studied gender-role conflict. **Gender-role conflict** occurs when "rigid, sexist, or restrictive gender roles, learned during socialization, result in

When testosterone levels in monkeys have been measured after a fight, the defeated monkey consistently had lower testosterone levels than the "winner" did. Such a finding has led many to conclude that testosterone level (a biological condition) *causes* aggression. In order to hypothesize about causal links, however, it would be necessary to also measure the monkeys' testosterone levels before the fight. In fact, other research has shown that male monkeys who are defeated in fights experience a sharp drop in testosterone levels. Thus, rather than a biological state causing greater aggression in monkeys, the environmental event (defeat) caused a change in the monkeys' biological state (Caplan & Caplan, 1994). Thus, in this case, environmental factors influence biological states.

Biology also influences environmental events. Few of us would dispute that a person's appearance influences how others behave toward that person. Attractiveness, skin color, height, size, and sex are likely to determine how one will be treated in the classroom, in a job interview, and by one's own parents.

3. *Feminine characteristics are inferior.* Over the years, many feminists sought to take on more masculine characteristics (e.g., aggressiveness) in order to prove they were equal to men. Why did they do that if they wanted to prove that women were equal? They did so because in U.S. society, characteristics considered feminine were also considered inferior to masculine characteristics. Women were more likely to achieve equality if they adopted those male characteristics most valued by society. One might say that it was a man's game, and women could only compete by learning the men's rules. Many terms used in the research literature on sex differences to describe feminine characteristics have negative connotations, whereas the masculine terms do not. For example, men are described as "independent" and women as "dependent" or "childlike." Can't women be characterized in more positive terms, such as "sensitive to others" (Hoyenga & Hoyenga, 1993)? Isn't it likely that many traits, both feminine and masculine, are valuable to all people? People seem to have difficulty seeing differences as good—or at least as not bad. This becomes clear when you reflect on the world's history of sex discrimination.

Some sex differences do exist, but that does not mean that men and women are not equal or that masculine characteristics are "better" than feminine characteristics. You will find that the relative utility of certain characteristics is often determined by situational factors and by how rigidly a person adheres to either a masculine or a feminine role. Finally, be careful about assuming that sex differences are etched in stone. Women and men have changed throughout history, different cultures display different gender-role patterns, and a single individual may vary in femininity and masculinity through time and in different situations. If you keep these things in mind, you are much more likely to draw objective and more accurate conclusions from what you read.

personal restriction, devaluation, or violation of others or self" (O'Neil, 1990, p. 25). For men, gender-role conflict results from societal pressure to fulfill the traditional male role, however contradictory and unrealistic it may be (O'Neil, 1990). Research has linked the male gender role with higher stress, high risk-taking and self-destructiveness, lack of concern for health, and a drive for power, money, and sexual partners (Cournoyer & Mahalik, 1995). Strict adherence to this gender role, therefore, may present a threat to well-being.

A scale developed by O'Neil and colleagues to measure gender-role conflict has been used to study the relationship between masculine gender-role adherence and well-being. Four groups of masculine characteristics emerged from this scale: (1) emphasis on success, power, and competition; (2) restrictive emotionality; (3) restrictive affectionate behavior between men; and (4) conflict between work and family (O'Neil, Helms, Gable, David, & Wrightsman, 1986). Research has shown that many of these characteristics are associated with depression, anxiety, poor self-esteem, and lack of intimacy. Of these groups of characteristics, however, the group consisting of success, power, and competition is least often associated with poor psychological health in college-aged

5.4 on the web

Adherence to a traditional masculine role may threaten a man's physical health in more ways than one. Review the paper on this topic found at **www.ablongman.com/mcanulty2e.** Describe the main points made in the paper. *What are your thoughts on these findings?*

did YOU know?

Despite the tendency in U.S. culture to place greater value on male characteristics, extremely gender-typed men tend to suffer from poor psychological adjustment.

men. In addition, as men age, they resolve many of their conflicts over their masculine roles, but difficulties with emotional expression continue to plague them into their older years (Cournoyer & Mahalik, 1995; Good and Mintz, 1990; Sharpe & Heppner, 1991).

In general, many so-called masculine traits, such as assertiveness and autonomy, predict psychological health for both men and women who show them. However, strict conformity to less desirable aspects of the male gender role produces many conflicts associated with poor psychological adjustment in men. Similarly, gender-role socialization may result in a number of unique conflicts for women.

Females and Gender-Role Conflict

Some women experience stress resulting from the demands of the female gender role. College-aged women, regardless of how strongly they identify with this role, are more likely than men to experience psychological stress in five categories: (1) fear of failing to develop emotionally close, trusting, intimate relationships; (2) fear of being physically unattractive, primarily overweight; (3) fear of being victimized; (4) fear of having to employ assertive behavior; and (5) fear of failing to be nurturant (Gillespie & Eisler, 1992). Depression is significantly associated with female gender-role stress in general and specifically with concerns about not meeting societal standards of attractiveness and fears of having to act assertively.

Self-assessment influences the effect of gender-role identification on psychological well-being in women as well as in men. Both female and male college students seem to value masculine traits more than feminine traits, and their psychological well-being is best predicted by the difference between ideal ratings and self-ratings on masculinity, not on femininity, as measured by the Bem Sex-Role Inventory (Grimmell & Stern, 1992). However, college women who assume a "womanist" identity tend to have higher self-esteem (one measure of psychological well-being) compared to women who do not (Ossana, Helms, & Leonard, 1992). Features of a "womanist" identity associated with high self-esteem include "questioning of previously held stereotypical views about gender and dawning awareness of alternative perspectives" and "active rejection of male supremacist values and beliefs and the search for a positive self-affirming definition of womanhood" (Ossana, Helms, & Leonard, 1992, p. 402). Thus, a woman who evaluates her female identity more favorably may actually be protected somewhat from the negative influence of a society that places less value on the female role.

Androgyny: A Picture of Health?

As was mentioned earlier in the text, most people's behavior falls along a continuum of masculine and feminine. People who possess a large number of both masculine and feminine characteristics are said to be **androgynous.** On the other hand, some individuals incorporate very few of those characteristics deemed either masculine or feminine by the culture. These people are said to be *undifferentiated.* In either case, traditional gender typing does not apply.

The recognition that people vary along a continuum of gender roles and characteristics emerged in the early 1970s in both psychology and literature (Bem, 1993). The movement away from the dichotomizing of gender challenged the assumption that non–gender-typed individuals were psychologically deviant (Bem, 1993). In fact, androgyny has often been held up as a model of well-being. The assumption is that an androgynous person is not compelled to "prove" her femininity or his masculinity. Rather, such a person has successfully integrated both masculine and feminine traits and perhaps even blends of these traits into her or his personality and ultimately benefits psychologically from this integration. For example, an androgynous business executive would know how to gain the competitive edge but would also be approachable by an

ANDROGYNOUS
Having both masculine and feminine characteristics.

employee who needed emotional support. Because they possess both feminine and masculine traits, androgynous individuals have a broader range of responses to draw from, and they can be flexible across a variety of situations. In other words, rather than being restricted to stereotypic behaviors, these individuals can choose from a broad repertoire of responses most appropriate to particular situations. One might assume, therefore, that an androgynous person is capable of functioning more effectively in the world (Kaplan & Sedney, 1980). On the other hand, people sometimes negatively evaluate a person who does not adhere to gender stereotypes. For example, a man who is used to taking the lead in relationships may not be receptive to a woman who calls him for a date.

The relationship between androgyny and psychological well-being has been studied extensively in adolescents, since adolescence is a time when young people are beginning to be influenced by societal demands to take on the roles expected of adults. In general, androgyny is associated with psychological well-being in male and female children and adolescents, but high masculinity is also associated with well-being (Allgood-Merton & Stockard, 1991; Markstrom-Adams, 1989). The association of well-being with high masculinity may be due to the higher value that society places on masculine traits; however, it is also possible that because of gender bias, the psychological constructs used to assess well-being measure primarily those positive traits associated with the male sex role (Markstrom-Adams, 1989).

Gender-role adherence affects more than just psychological well-being; physical well-being can also be affected. Close Up on Culture: The Influence of Gender Roles on Safe Sex Practices (on page 154) discusses one way that gender roles can affect physical health. In addition, both androgyny and strict adherence to gender roles may have an impact on interpersonal relationships, an important aspect of sexuality. Researchers have found that neither men nor women are necessarily satisfied in relationships when they play out traditional roles. Furthermore, being androgynous or having characteristics more common in the opposite sex seems to predict relationship satisfaction in several areas.

It is curious that societal pressures favor pairings between traditional men and women, when the evidence seems to suggest that these are not optimal relationships. An evolutionary perspective would argue that men seek out women who are feminine, exhibiting skills at nurturing and caregiving, and women seek out men with traits and

5.5 on the web

The impact of gender inequality is far-reaching. Read the report by the Alan Guttmacher Institute entitled "Global Concerns for Children's Rights: The World Congress against Sexual Exploitation," found at **www.ablongman.com/mcanulty2e.** Focus on the section on Gender Discrimination and Inequality.

Describe how acceptance of traditional views of women plays a role in the problem of sexual exploitation around the world.

Relationships between two androgynous individuals tend to be more rewarding than relationships between feminine women and masculine men.

CLOSE UP ON culture

The Influence of Gender Roles on Safe Sex Practices

Traditionally, gender-role socialization has carried different messages about sexuality for women and men. Women who are socialized in the traditional female role focus more on the relational aspects of sex and tend to view sex as a means to achieve emotional and psychological closeness. In addition, they generally view sex as appropriate only in committed relationships. In contrast, men who conform to the traditional male gender role focus on sex for pleasure and find casual sex more acceptable than do their female counterparts. Women who conform to traditional norms also do not talk very openly about sex, because that might make them appear "fast" or promiscuous, whereas men can discuss their sexuality more openly and may even increase their status with "the guys" in the process.

What is the impact on sexual health of adhering to traditional roles? First, consider for a moment the fact that the best protection against HIV and other sexually transmissible infections is consistent use of a condom. Until the female condom is more widely available and used, men must be willing to cooperate in condom use. (And even with a female condom, a man must agree to cooperate.) Furthermore, obtaining condoms requires that a woman acknowledge to herself that she intends to be sexually active. Women who are traditionally socialized might find it difficult to assert themselves enough to obtain condoms. Furthermore, they would likely find it difficult to bring up the topic of contraception, since it is not "appropriate" for them to even be thinking about having sex. Finally, you might assume that a woman's preference to wait until she knows a man well before having sex would reduce her risks, and this might be true in some cases. However, sometimes as a woman gets to know a man and desires to maintain a relationship with him, she may find it more difficult to insist on condom use. She may also be lulled into believing that because she "knows" him well, he is a "safe" sexual partner.

Such dangers of adhering to traditional gender norms have actually been demonstrated in research. One study showed that women who expressed as their ideal having only "relational" sex were less likely to use a condom and also delayed using any contraception longer than women who did not strongly value relational sex (Hynie, Lydon, Cote, & Weiner, 1998). Thus, traditional gender norms diminished women's inclination to practice safe sex and, therefore, put them at greater risk of contracting an STI or having an unwanted pregnancy.

Women from more traditional cultures, such as Hispanic cultures, may be at greatest risk. In fact, research has shown that Hispanic women adhere closely to traditional gender roles. Many Hispanic women believe that men have strong and uncontrollable sexual needs, that pleasing their partners sexually is an important part of the female role, and that men even have the right to pursue sexual relations outside of marriage if a woman does not preserve her sexual attractiveness (Gómez & Marín, 1996). And, in fact, Hispanic men are more likely than non-Hispanic white men to have extramarital relations (Marín, Gómez, & Hearst, 1993). Also, Hispanic women are less comfortable than non-Hispanic white women with various sexual behaviors (such as buying a condom, putting a condom on a sexual partner, or watching a sexual partner put on a condom). Furthermore, Hispanic women are less likely to negotiate the use of a condom or to use one with a steady sex partner (Gómez & Marín, 1996).

Similar findings have been noted in the African American population. One study showed that nearly half of all African American women never used a condom with their sexual partners, and their failure to use a condom was highly related to how they thought their partner would react (Wingood & DiClemente, 1998). The women who never used a condom were characterized as sexually nonassertive, which fits with the traditional female role. Additional research indicates that traditional gender roles still have a powerful influence in the African American culture (Fullilove, Fullilove, Haynes, & Gross, 1990).

skills enabling them to provide for a family. Such an arrangement would presumably promote survival of the species. Some evidence does support males' and females' expressed preferences for gender-typed partners (Buss, 1989). However, in today's world, both men and women must often contribute financially to a family, and there is a greater expectation that men will nurture their children. Thus, a paradox may result from the two conflicting factors. Humans' genetic makeup may dictate a preference for gender-typed partners, but current cultural context requires that at least one member of a couple possess both masculine and feminine traits (Green & Kenrick, 1994).

SIMILARITIES AND DIFFERENCES IN MALE AND FEMALE SEXUALITY

Many stereotypes concerning male and female sexuality persist even today. A widely held viewpoint (perhaps one you share) is that males are by nature more easily sexually aroused and generally more responsive to sexual stimuli than are females. There is a tendency in most Western societies to expect young men to behave sexually, and such behavior may even be implicitly encouraged. On the other hand, young women are often discouraged from engaging in sexual activity and may be watched more carefully (for example, by being given earlier curfews than males) to ensure that sexual activity is curtailed. Men with active sex lives, in fact, have traditionally been considered "studly," while women who have had several sexual partners have been labeled as "slutty." Furthermore, negative evaluations of sexually active females have gone beyond their sexual behavior alone—they have been evaluated more negatively than less sexually active females on factors such as likeability, intelligence, and adjustment (Garcia, 1982). However, this double standard appears to be waning. A study conducted in the mid-1990s showed that women are evaluated no more negatively than men are for having active sex lives (O'Sullivan, 1995). However, both women and men are judged most negatively if they have had numerous casual sex relations in uncommitted relationships, and women and men who have had few sex partners in committed relationships are viewed most positively. Cultural biases have tremendously influenced the assessment of female and male sexuality.

Sexual Responsiveness

Are males more sexually responsive than females? The earliest research on sexual responsiveness relied on self-reports of arousal. Most notably, Kinsey's interview data on females' and males' responses to visual erotic stimuli have commonly been cited as evidence that women are less arousable than men are (Kinsey, Pomeroy & Martin, 1948; Kinsey, Pomeroy, Martin, & Gebhard, 1953). In a sense, this conclusion is inaccurate. Kinsey did find that women were less likely to report being aroused by visual stimuli; however, he also showed that there was tremendous variability among the reported arousal levels of the women in his sample, and he noted that up to one-third of the women were just as responsive as the average man. Thus, some women are just as arousable as men are. In fact, research conducted in West Germany by Schmidt and colleagues found no differences in the responses of females and males to narrative erotic stimuli or to erotica in the form of film and slides (Schmidt & Sigusch, 1970; Schmidt, Sigusch, & Schafer, 1973; Sigusch, Schmidt, Reinfeld, & Wiedemann-Sutor, 1970).

More objective information on sexual responsiveness has been obtained using physiological measures of genital responses to sexual stimuli, sometimes combined with self-report measures. Figure 5.2 depicts the results of research by Julia Heiman (1977), who was the first to use an elaborate experimental design in which she exposed male and female college students to audiotapes of different sexual content and context, in different sequences. Tapes with erotic and erotic/romantic content effectively aroused males as well as females. Both sexes found female-initiated scenarios more sexually arousing than male-initiated scenarios. In addition, the self-reports and physiological measures of sexual arousal were highly correlated.

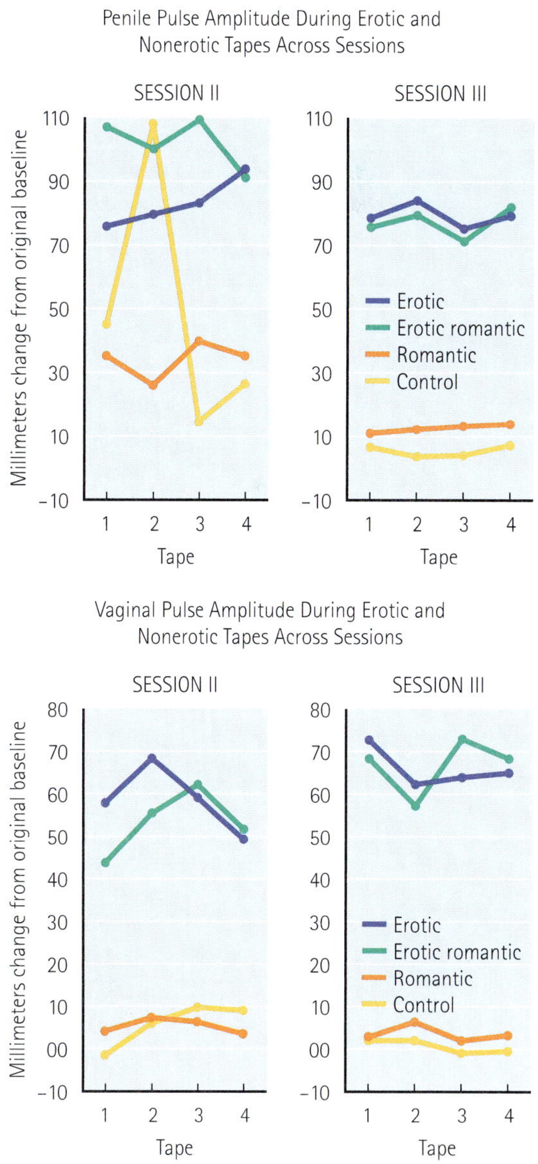

Figure 5.2 Heiman's research illustrates some surprising similarities in females' and males' sexual responses.

Heiman's findings suggested that romantic elements did not seem to enhance arousal in either males or females. These more objective findings contradicted Kinsey's interview results, which indicated that women were more sexually responsive to romantic stimuli and men were more responsive to sexually explicit stimuli. Several other studies have also contradicted Kinsey's conclusions (Jakobovits, 1965; Osborn & Pollack, 1977; Schmidt, Sigusch, & Schafer, 1973). Thus, it seems that, in general, women, like men, are most aroused by explicit sexual material, and it does not have to include a romantic element.

One dimension on which men and women do show differing patterns of arousal is in their responses to erotic films of varying content—heterosexual, male homosexual, lesbian, or group sex (Steinman, Wincze, Sakheim, Barlow, & Mavissakalian, 1981). First, men and women are similar in that heterosexual males and females are most highly responsive to group sex scenes and least responsive to male homosexual scenes. However, next to group sex, males found lesbian sex most highly arousing, followed by heterosexual sex, whereas females found heterosexual sex more highly arousing than lesbian sex.

Given Heiman's findings on female-initiated sexual scenarios, you might wonder whether contextual factors, such as which person is the initiator in erotic interactions, are important to sexual responsiveness. In recent years, female-made, female-initiated, and female-centered erotica has been produced to "address the needs" of women interested in sexually explicit material but turned off by male-made, male-initiated, male-centered erotica. One particularly interesting study (Laan, Everaerd, van Bellen, and Hanewald, 1994) assessed women's sexual responses to these two types of erotic films. The researchers expected to find greater arousal in response to the female-oriented films (Dekker & Everaerd, 1989). They found that the women's genital arousal was high and equivalent for both types of erotica. However, the women's reported feelings of arousal were much higher in response to the female-made films. Women also reported feelings of shame, guilt, and aversion to the male-made films. Thus, even though the women's bodies were certainly capable of responding to all erotic stimuli, their subjective preference was for female-made and female-centered erotica.

You can see that in contrast to stereotypes about sexuality, research suggests that women are definitely not sexually unresponsive, and women and men are not especially different in sexual responsiveness. It is also interesting to note that women experience greater subjective arousal when they view erotica showing a woman in charge, a role that contradicts traditional gender roles. Unlike sexual responsiveness, fantasies, attitudes, and overt sexual behaviors have been shown to differ between the sexes, but not always in ways that fit the stereotypes.

Fantasies, Attitudes, and Overt Behaviors

Early research on sexual fantasies characterized male and female fantasies very differently. Females' fantasies were thought to be more self-centered, passive, and sadomasochistic; males' fantasies were thought to be more active, aggressive, power-oriented, masochistic, and impersonal. However, some research has found that there are far more similarities than differences in males' and females' fantasies. For example, Rokach (1990) found that males and females described sexual fantasies that were very similar in content and that most of these fantasies fell into the traditional heterosexual category. This category was characterized as involving a "close, intimate, and possibly long-term heterosexual relationship" (p. 431). Interestingly, however, twice as many women's fantasies as men's fell into the categories of "uncommon, strange, or relatively rare sexual practices" (p. 434) and "fantasies wherein the fantasizer did not engage in sexual activity, or when an act was not realistically attainable" (p. 434). Thus, stereotypes about women being more restrictive in their sexual interests appear to be inaccurate.

By contrast, Ellis and Symons (1990) found several sex differences in responses to questions regarding fantasy content. They concluded that females fantasize less often and are less visually oriented than males and that males' visual images are more genitally focused. Furthermore, females tend to focus more on emotional context, their own physical and emotional reactions, the partner's responses, touching, and feelings; males' fantasies are more impersonal and more apt to involve imagined partners and partners as sex objects. In addition, males emphasize partner variety, but women focus on partners with whom they currently have or previously had a relationship. Finally, male fantasies move quickly to sexual acts.

did YOU know?

More than three times as many men as women (16.9% versus 5.8%) fantasize about foreplay, and more than two times as many women as men (5.8% versus 2.6%) fantasize about exhibitionistic behavior (Rokach, 1990).

The contradictory findings from these two studies are somewhat puzzling unless you consider the different ages of the groups of people these researchers studied. The participants in Rokach's study were in their early 30s for the most part, whereas over 54% of Ellis and Symons's participants fell into the 17–21 age range. Thus, it appears that sex differences in fantasies diminish as people age.

Oliver and Hyde (1993) found this age difference to be true of attitudes toward sex as well. They combined data from 177 studies to examine sex differences in sexual attitudes and behaviors. Studies included in the analysis dated from 1966 to 1990. The researchers discovered that males expressed more openness toward premarital intercourse, especially of a casual nature; much greater permissiveness toward sex in general; and greater acceptance of extramarital intercourse. Also, males reported less anxiety, fear, and guilt about sex than did females. However, males and females did not differ in their attitudes toward masturbation and homosexuality. Females surprisingly expressed greater acceptance of the double standard (the assumption that sexual promiscuity is acceptable for males but not for females). However, the researchers pointed out that the studies that assessed views toward the double standard were all conducted prior to 1977 and that the participants were young, 20 years old or under. Of all the attitudes examined, males and females differed most in their attitudes toward casual premarital intercourse.

Oliver and Hyde also found that more males than females had engaged in intercourse and that sexually active males had had intercourse more often than females had and with more partners. Males were younger at first intercourse, and more males than females had engaged in homosexual activities. Females masturbated much less often than males despite reporting equal acceptance of this activity.

The researchers also examined changes in sex differences over time. They found that the more recently obtained data revealed smaller differences between females and males, suggesting that the gap is narrowing. Differences diminished most for frequency of intercourse, number of partners, incidence of masturbation, attitudes toward homosexuality, and acceptance of premarital intercourse, particularly for engaged couples. Thus, the combined findings from 1966 to 1990 and the findings of other studies (Hsu et al., 1994; Person, Terestman, Myers, Goldberg, & Salvadori, 1989) indicate that there are differences in the sexual attitudes and behaviors of men and women. However, these differences are less distinct now than they were in previous years, and as females and males grow older, they become more similar in sexual attitudes and behaviors.

In summary, it appears that females and males show very few differences in biological sexual responsiveness; however, they do show at least some differences in sexual attitudes, fantasies, and behaviors, which are more likely to be influenced by environmental factors. The fact that these differences in sexuality diminish with age and are becoming less prominent supports the notion that they are influenced primarily by environmental factors. Another phenomenon likely to be affected by socialization is the nature of sexual interactions between females and males.

Sexual Interactions between Females and Males

Researchers have studied differences and similarities in females' and males' perceptions of sexual interactions, particularly perceptions of sexual intent and

In dating relationships, confusion may result from different expectations and perceptions about sexual intent.

initiation of sexual interactions, as well as their reactions to sexual interactions.

Heterosexual men and women interpret casual interactions with one another very differently. Males perceive much more sexual intent in casual, heterosexual interactions than do females. More specifically, during unstructured conversations, males see themselves and the female they are talking to as more seductive, promiscuous, and sexy than do their female counterparts. Males are also more likely to describe themselves as sexually attracted to the females. Females, on the other hand, are more likely to express an interest in becoming friends with the males (Harnish, Abbey, & Debono, 1990). Other research supports these general findings (Abbey & Melby, 1986).

Several reasons have been proposed for sex differences in perceptions of sexual intent. First, males have traditionally been responsible for initiating dating and sexual activity; thus, they may be more apt to look for signs of interest in females. Second, men have been taught the stereotypes that women avoid displaying sexual interest in males even when they are attracted to them and that women like men to be forceful and aggressive. Finally, as we discussed earlier, the mass media emphasize females' physical attributes and teach males to focus on a woman's sexual availability and physical qualities more than on other factors such as personality and character (Harnish et al., 1990).

Experts believe that males' and females' differing perceptions of sexual intent are important, in that a discrepancy between perceived versus actual intent may be one factor that leads to date rape. In fact, researchers have found that when participants are asked to evaluate various sexual scenarios, females are more likely than males to identify as unacceptable scenarios involving nonconsensual sex (Freetly & Kane, 1995). Furthermore, when these scenarios depict a couple who have previously been intimate, both males and females are less likely to rate the scenarios as entirely unacceptable, and as the level of prior intimacy increases, so does the acceptability of the scenario. However, males are still much more likely than females to rate depictions that include prior intimacy as acceptable. Interestingly, if an individual male or female has known a rape victim personally, he or she is much less likely to rate nonconsensual sex scenarios as acceptable. It appears that greater awareness of the negative impact of coercive sex may increase sensitivity to the inappropriateness of such behavior. (Related issues are discussed in detail in Chapter 16.)

> **5.6 on the web**
>
> Retrieve the list of first date ideas at **www.ablongman.com/mcanulty2e**. As you read them, jot down which suggestions you think were made by males and which by females.
>
> *What led you to draw the conclusions you did? Are your assumptions based on factual differences between males and females, or on inaccurate stereotypes?*

As was mentioned earlier, traditional gender roles dictate that males should be the initiators of sexual contact. Although nearly 93% of women report initiating sex at some time, males are more likely than females to report female initiation of sexual activity (Anderson & Aymani, 1993). Males are also more likely to infer motives such as "making someone else jealous" to female sexual initiation. In addition, it is generally assumed that the perpetrators of aggressive sexual acts are male. But males are more likely to report as coercive acts on the part of females such as "pressuring with arguments." These discrepancies imply differences either in male and female willingness to admit to certain acts or in male and female perceptions of their interactions. Perhaps females do not perceive themselves as coercive because they are influenced by the cultural stereotype that males are always primed to have sex.

In general, the research findings on heterosexual interactions suggest that many females and males adhere to socially expected gender roles. It is encouraging to see, however, that both males and females express more satisfaction with longer-term, more committed relationships and those that involve responsible behavior. Psychological health issues related to heterosexual interactions are discussed further in Health Matters: (Mis)Communication in the Bedroom.

HEALTH Matters

(Mis)Communication in the Bedroom

Just how far off are women and men when it comes to understanding what the other sex wants . . . between the sheets? Tapping into popular American culture, looking for what people know (or think they know) about men's and women's sexual desires by surfing the Internet, yields tons of information for heterosexual guys about what women want in a male sex partner. Interestingly, there isn't much available about what men want when they have sex. It seems that most people think that everyone already knows what men like, but women are a mystery. Is this true?

The following information on what men like and want in bed came mostly from a poll by *Redbook* magazine of 5,000 married men, which is at least a relatively sizable number (*Redbook,* 1999):

- Men want sex more often as well as sex that lasts longer than their current experiences.
- They want their partners to make the first move.
- Men would like more oral sex, but they feel like they have to beg for it. (Another source told us that men enjoy "hand jobs," too.)
- Men really enjoy performing oral sex on their partners.
- They wish their partners would pay more attention to other erogenous areas such as their nipples, earlobes, back, and neck.
- Their two favorite positions are with the woman on top and rear entry. Only 7% of the men preferred being on top.
- And what are their secret wishes? The top wish was to have a threesome with another woman. The next most common wish was to have anal sex with their wives.

What do women want from their male sexual partners? The following answers came from *Men's Health,* an online magazine (Men's Health Institute, 1999):

- Women do like orgasms, but they don't like feeling like they are being pressured or that a man is intent upon giving his partner an orgasm in order to fulfill *his* need to feel "successful" as a sex partner.
- Women like a man to make a connection with them by talking or using eye contact. Sexy talk is often desirable, but be careful to determine what is sexy talk and what is offensive. Furthermore, be natural and unrehearsed.
- Women like cunnilingus, but they often need signs that the man is enjoying it. (Some women fear the man won't like their taste or smell.) Making appreciative sounds or stopping to look in her eyes may set her at ease.
- They want men to focus on the whole breast, not just the nipple, when caressing their breasts. A man should ask his partner what is pleasurable. Pinching or biting can hurt—licking and sucking gently are better.
- Women would like men to pay attention to other erogenous areas—the scalp, lips, back, buttocks, and other areas.
- They like to take brief pauses every now and then. Stopping and starting can be highly arousing. Too much rubbing, stroking, or thrusting can make a woman's erogenous zones numb.
- Women say that trying new positions is good, but they don't want to be in bed with an overly enthusiastic gymnast.
- Women want more kissing.

From these lists, it seems clear that men and women *do* have some similar desires. For example, both would like their partners to pay more attention to their nongenital erogenous zones. Men like giving oral sex, and women like getting it. You probably found that you agreed with some of the suggestions above while others did not fit you.

These kinds of suggestions can probably help men and women understand each other's desires more, but not everyone is comfortable purchasing books on sex or surfing for sex tips on the Internet. Furthermore, these suggestions deal in generalities and may not be true for that special person with whom you want to make love. That is why communication is so important for closing any gaps in understanding that might exist between a couple. Learning to talk requires being comfortable enough with your sexual partner to talk about your likes and dislikes in a sensitive manner. Open, honest communication paves the way to a healthy and fulfilling sexual relationship.

HEALTHY DECISION MAKING

As you read this chapter, you may have pondered your own gender identity and your tendencies to either adhere or not adhere to traditional gender role expectations. Some traits that U.S. culture has traditionally viewed as typically feminine or masculine are listed below. Review each list and check those characteristics that you believe are true of you.

Feminine Characteristics	Masculine Characteristics
❑ Yielding	❑ Independent
❑ Cheerful	❑ Defends own beliefs
❑ Shy	❑ Self-reliant
❑ Affectionate	❑ Athletic
❑ Flatterable	❑ Assertive
❑ Loyal	❑ Strong personality
❑ Feminine	❑ Analytical
❑ Sympathetic	❑ Forceful
❑ Sensitive to the needs of others	❑ Has leadership ability
❑ Understanding	❑ Willing to take risks
❑ Compassionate	❑ Makes decisions easily
❑ Eager to soothe hurt feelings	❑ Self-sufficient
❑ Warm	❑ Dominant
❑ Soft-spoken	❑ Masculine
❑ Tender	❑ Willing to take a stand
❑ Gullible	❑ Acts as a leader
❑ Does not use harsh language	❑ Aggressive
❑ Childlike	❑ Individualistic
❑ Loves children	❑ Competitive
❑ Gentle	❑ Ambitious

The research reviewed in this chapter suggests that androgynous individuals are generally healthier psychologically and that relationships between two androgynous people tend to be healthier as well. Based on your evaluation of these characteristics, do you think you are androgynous? If you have a "significant other," is he or she androgynous?

Look at each characteristic you checked for yourself. Is this characteristic helpful or deterimental in your life in general and in your relationships with others? Consider what you might do to moderate those characteristics that you feel create problems in your life: What might you do to achieve a healthier balance in your life?

summary

PRENATAL SEX DIFFERENTIATION

- Sexual development begins before birth with the differentiation of the fetus into male or female, a process guided by sex chromosomes and hormones. In rare instances, chromosomal or hormonal problems may result in abnormal sex differentiation.

SEX, GENDER, AND CHALLENGES TO STEREOTYPES

- A person's sex is determined by her or his biological makeup. A person with an X and a Y chromosome who possesses a penis and testicles is male; a person with two X chromosomes and a vagina, uterus, ovaries, and other female structures is female.
- Gender roles do not always match biological sex.
- Regardless of the fact that not all women are highly feminine and not all men are highly masculine, common stereotypes assume that men and women possess traits typical of their sexes.
- Transgendered individuals are people whose appearance, behavior, or self-identification fall far outside of

traditional norms for their biological sex. These people include cross-dressers, gay men in drag, lesbians who wear masculine clothing and hairstyles, and transexuals.

BIOLOGICAL AND SOCIAL THEORIES OF GENDER

- Gender roles may in part reflect biological tendencies to be either masculine or feminine (whether the tendencies are due to genetics or to hormonal differences). Evolutionary theorists argue that men and women assume particular roles in society because, throughout evolution, members of the species who assumed these roles have survived and reproduced.
- Other theorists, such as learning theorists, argue that gender roles are learned.

A CLOSER LOOK AT ENVIRONMENTAL INFLUENCES

- Many environmental factors have been shown to influence and maintain gender roles. Social influences include parents, peers, schools and teachers, and the media.

GENDER ROLES AND WELL-BEING

- Many scientists have studied how adherence to masculine, feminine, or androgynous gender roles affects psychological well-being. In general, possession of masculine traits has often been shown to predict well-being in both men and women, as has possessing a mixture of masculine and feminine traits.
- Extreme adherence to the traditional male gender role, however, has been associated with psychological distress in men. Similarly, female gender-role expectations have been shown to affect women negatively. Women who identify themselves as more masculine are believed to enjoy greater psychological well-being. And women who challenge traditional views that maleness is more valuable have been shown to have high self-esteem. Androgyny has been associated with psychological well-being, and researchers hypothesize that possession of both masculine and feminine traits affords more flexibility and, therefore, greater adaptability across situations. Some research supports this notion.
- People in relationships with highly sex-typed partners are least likely to be satisfied. In general, androgynous people tend to fare better in intimate relationships and friendships. Some research suggests that similarity is the key to a good relationship and that couples in which at least one person is androgynous have more traits in common.

SIMILARITIES AND DIFFERENCES IN MALE AND FEMALE SEXUALITY

- Despite long-lived stereotypes, males and females do not differ with respect to their biological capacity to respond sexually or their arousal in response to different types of erotica. Male and female sexual fantasies, attitudes, and behaviors tend to differ and often conform to stereotypes, but these differences diminish with age. Men are more likely to infer sexual intent on the part of women in casual interactions. Contrary to popular belief, a large proportion of women report sometimes being the initiators of sexual interactions, although men initiate sex more often.

CHAPTER 6

Sexual Orientation

The world is not divided into sheep and goats. Not all black nor all things white. It is a fundamental of taxonomy that nature rarely deals with discrete categories and tries to force facts into separated pigeon holes. The living world is a continuum in each and every one of its aspects. The sooner we learn this concerning human sexual behavior the sooner we shall reach a sounder understanding of the realities of sex.

Alfred Kinsey, biologist (1948, p. 639)

The living world is a continuum.

Even a superficial look at other societies and some groups in our own society should be enough to convince us that a very large number of human beings—probably a majority—are bisexual in their potential capacity for love. Whether they will become exclusively heterosexual or exclusively homosexual for all their lives and in all circumstances or whether they will be able to enter into sexual and love relationships with members of both sexes is, in fact, a consequence of the way they have been brought up, of the particular beliefs and prejudices of the society they live in, and, to some extent, of their own life history.

Margaret Mead, anthropologist (1975, p. 6)

Heterosexual and homosexual is "an artificial division. . . . There's nothing in me that is not in everybody else, and nothing in everybody else which is not in me."

James Baldwin, novelist (1984, p. 14)

Each of these writers' perspectives challenges the traditional notion that sexual orientation is dichotomous—meaning that a person is either heterosexual or homosexual. To many heterosexual people, who take an "us and them" position on sexual orientation ("us" being "normal" heterosexuals and "them" being "abnormal" homosexuals), perspectives like those above can be discomforting. However disturbing they may be, the best scientific evidence available tends to support the position that sexual orientation falls along a continuum ranging from strictly heterosexual to strictly homosexual. We will revisit this notion and other challenges to stereotypic thinking as we explore the meanings, identities, characteristics, and sexual behaviors that comprise the range of human sexual orientation.

SEXUAL ORIENTATION: WHAT'S IN A NAME?

As you will soon see, it is very difficult to define sexual orientation precisely. Many people think of sexual orientation as defined exclusively by one's sexual attraction—whether to members of the opposite sex, the same sex, or both sexes. **Sexual orientation,**

SEXUAL ORIENTATION A person's erotic and romantic attraction to one or both sexes.

Like heterosexual couples, many gay couples enjoy a lifetime of love and commitment to one another.

however, means much more than that: Besides physical and sexual attraction, it includes emotional and romantic attraction. Western culture recognizes three types of sexual orientation: *homosexuality, bisexuality,* and *heterosexuality.*

Homosexual means having erotic and romantic feelings for members of the same sex. Men who are attracted to men are called *gay men,* and women who are attracted to women are called *lesbians;* however, *gay* is also used generally to refer to homosexual men and women. Most gay men and lesbians dislike the term *homosexual* because of its clinical and negative social connotations. **Heterosexual** means experiencing erotic and romantic feelings for people of the opposite sex; that is, male heterosexuals are attracted to females, and female heterosexuals are attracted to males. A person who feels erotic and romantic desires for people of both sexes is considered to be **bisexual.** Bisexuals are not generally equally attracted to men and women but may prefer one sex. Bisexuality is considered controversial in Western culture because of the prevailing view that sexual orientation is *either* heterosexual *or* homosexual. Some view bisexuals as people who are temporarily exploring their sexuality, and others see bisexuals as sexual opportunists who cannot control their sexual impulses. Not surprisingly, bisexuals often feel pressure from others to "choose" a sexual identity—that is, to identify themselves as heterosexual or homosexual (see Chapter 12). But although bisexuality is a temporary orientation for some, it is an enduring characteristic for many others.

did YOU know?

The word* lesbian *has a clear origin. Sappho, a famous female poet from the 7th century B.C.E., was born on the Greek Island of Lesbos. Sappho is known for her love poems to other women.

It is very difficult to classify individuals according to sexual orientation. Several experts in sexology have developed models that take into account various aspects of human sexuality. Two of these descriptive models are those developed by Alfred Kinsey and by Michael Storms.

Biologist Alfred Kinsey (Kinsey et al., 1948, 1953) was one of the first Western scientists to examine the prevalence of various sexual behaviors. He produced one of the first descriptive models of sexuality based on his empirical data. Defining sexual experiences as experiences leading to orgasm, Kinsey described the sexual behavior of individuals he interviewed using a linear 7-point scale, with 0 representing exclusive heterosexuality, 3 indicating equal amounts of heterosexual and homosexual experience, and 6 representing exclusive homosexuality. This scale is presented in Figure 6.1. According to Kinsey's model, sexual orientation is composed of varying proportions of same-sex and opposite-sex activity, which can change over a lifetime. Kinsey's description of sexuality as a fluid, continuous variable was extremely controversial and remains so today.

HOMOSEXUAL
Having erotic and romantic feelings for members of the same sex.

HETEROSEXUAL
Experiencing erotic and romantic feelings for people of the opposite sex.

BISEXUAL
Feeling erotic and romantic desires for both sexes.

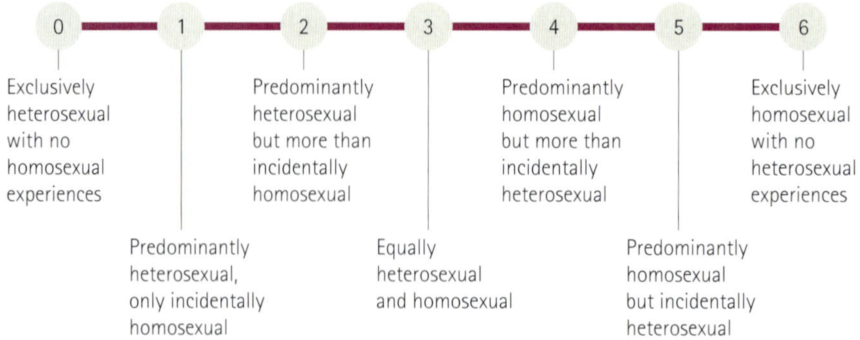

Figure 6.1 Kinsey Scale of Sexual Behavior

Furthermore, many found Kinsey's linear conceptualization too simplistic. For example, someone with mostly opposite-sex experiences but a few same-sex contacts might be categorized as a 1 or 2 on the Kinsey scale—but what if this person told you that he or she fantasized exclusively about members of the same sex? And where would you place a person with no sexual experience? In short, Kinsey's model failed to take into account anything other than behavior.

Michael Storms (1981) conceptualized sexual orientation on a two-dimensional grid, with the horizontal axis representing levels of heteroeroticism from high to low and the vertical axis representing levels of homoeroticism from high to low (see Figure 6.2). Eroticism encompasses sexual fantasy, romantic feelings, and sexual behavior. A person who is high on heteroeroticism and low on homoeroticism is heterosexual, and someone who is high on homoeroticism and low on heteroeroticism is homosexual. A person who is high on both heteroeroticism and homoeroticism is bisexual, and someone who is low on both axes is asexual. While fantasy, feelings, and behavior may conflict, this model provides a handy graphic representation of sexual orientation.

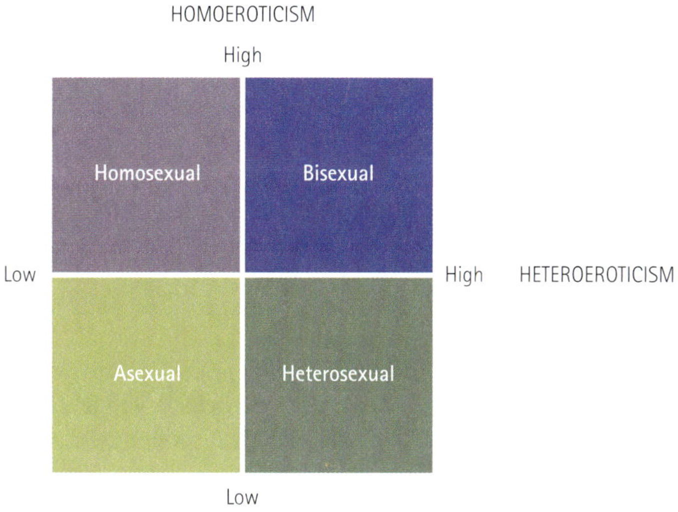

Figure 6.2 Storms's Model of Sexual Orientation

SEXUAL IDENTITY FORMATION

When an individual comes to identify herself or himself as heterosexual, homosexual, or bisexual, we say that she or he has formed a *sexual identity.* As a consequence of cultural views of same-sex behavior as odd, rare, sinful, or pathological, more information is available about homosexuality than about the other sexual orientations. In contrast, researchers tend to assume that heterosexuality does not need to be studied because everyone already understands it! Consequently, very little is known about heterosexual identity formation.

did YOU know?

Sexual identity—or the identification of oneself as heterosexual, bisexual, or homosexual—is a relatively new concept that was not used until the 20th century.

Heterosexual Identity Formation

Sigmund Freud (1905/1953) outlined the most comprehensive theory of heterosexual development available. In Freud's model of psychosexual development, all infants are **polymorphously perverse**, meaning that they are capable of erotic attraction to anyone or anything. However, at an early age, children must resolve either the Oedipus or the Electra complex and develop a male or female sexual identity (see Chapter 11). Although Freud did not see homosexuality as pathological and viewed bisexuality as inherent in every person, he portrayed heterosexuality as the outcome of successful psychosexual development. Thus, Freud's final stage of development consisted of adult heterosexual activity. Freud's conclusions regarding sexual identity formation, as you are aware, are limited because they were based on anecdotal evidence and observations of clients during the Victorian era.

More recently, one researcher attempted a more scientific approach to describing heterosexual identity formation (Eliason, 1995). Participants in this study were 14 heterosexual men and 12 heterosexual women, who wrote descriptions of their own identity development; the research then attempted to identify common themes or stages of development. Consistent with Freud's depiction of identity formation, most men in the study arrived at their heterosexual identity by *rejecting* a gay identity, while many

POLYMORPHOUSLY PERVERSE
According to Freud, being born with erotic desire that is neither heterosexual nor homosexual and can be directed by various objects.

of the women considered a lesbian or bisexual identity before identifying themselves as heterosexual. While men and women of color were more aware than whites were of their sexual identity formation, these participants viewed race as more relevant to their identity than sexual orientation.

The absence of data surrounding heterosexual identity formation should not suggest that development progresses easily or without conflict. Regardless of orientation, conflicts concerning sexual identity contribute to sexual dysfunction, relationship problems, low self-esteem, and anxiety and depression (Kaplan, 1974). Experts in sexology need to devote much more attention to this critical developmental process.

Gay or Lesbian Identity Formation

Vivienne Cass (1979) was one of the first experts on sexual orientation to propose a comprehensive model of gay and lesbian identity formation. She proposed a six-stage model of development. The first stage is *identity confusion: "Who am I?"* For many gay men and lesbians, awareness of same-sex feelings and identity uncertainty begin in childhood. With recognition of same-sex feelings comes an awareness of being different from others (Herdt, 1992), leading to social comparison and *identity comparison: "I may be gay."* By adolescence, heterosexual activities may seem unsatisfying and empty as same-sex peers become more attractive. For those brought up to believe that same-sex feelings are wrong or even sinful, realizing that they may be gay can produce a great deal of internal conflict. For those who do not adjust easily, denying part of themselves or pretending to be something they are not can carry a heavy psychological price. This struggle is discussed further in Health Matters: Gays and Lesbians—Easing the Burden.

6.1 on the web

Many Web sites, maintained by lesbian and gay youth, are designed to help other young people explore questions about their sexual identity. Go to **www.ablongman.com/mcanulty2e** to find two examples of such Web sites. Describe these sites and your reactions to them.

Would you recommend either of them to a friend who is having questions about his or her sexual identity? Why or why not?

The third stage of Cass's model is *identity tolerance: "I probably am gay."* In this stage, the individual accepts her or his same-sex desires. This may not happen until late adolescence or adulthood. Acknowledging that one is probably gay means viewing oneself as a member of a stigmatized minority (Dupras, 1994); if the person does not know anyone else in the same situation, she or he may feel even more isolated from peers, more alienated and self-deprecating (D'Augelli & Hershberger, 1993).

The next stage is *identity acceptance: "I am gay."* During this stage, secrecy about one's sexual identity increasingly interferes with self-acceptance and interpersonal relationships. More complete self-acceptance is sought through acknowledging and openly accepting one's same-sex feelings—that is, **coming out (of the closet).** *Being in the closet* and *being closeted* are terms used to describe gay men and lesbians who are not open about their homosexuality. Disclosure of a gay identity puts a person at risk of rejection, although most people eventually accept a friend's or relative's homosexuality. Being "out" is not an all-or-nothing proposition, however. For instance, some gay men and lesbians may be out to friends and even coworkers, but not to their parents. Furthermore, coming out is a lifelong process. As new friendships and relationships are forged over time, a gay man or lesbian must choose whether or not to come out to those people. Sexual exploration and social encounters with other gay people may coincide with an individual's coming out; some people even engage in same-sex activity before becoming aware of their sexual identity.

COMING OUT (OF THE CLOSET) Acknowledging and openly accepting one's same-sex feelings.

The fifth stage of identity formation, according to Cass, is *identity pride: "I'm good; you're bad."* Newly "out" gay men and lesbians relish their supportive gay family of friends and may even reject the heterosexual community as intolerant, hostile, and oppressive. The sixth and final stage is *identity synthesis: "Being gay is a part of who I am."* The individual pulls together his or her public and private identities into a single self-concept and behaves more consistently in all settings. In other words, the individual does not hide the fact that he or she is gay under any circumstances.

Several similar linear descriptions of gay and lesbian identity formation have been proposed (Coleman, 1985; Lewis, 1984; Troiden, 1989). Unfortunately, these linear models have undergone little empirical testing, and the studies that have been done

HEALTH Matters

Gays and Lesbians—Easing the Burden

Growing up homosexual in a heterosexual culture can be a tremendously painful process, as evidenced by the high rate of suicide and suicide attempts among gay and bisexual male youth. Suicide attempts among young gay men and lesbians are twice as common as suicide attempts among heterosexual females and ten times more common than suicide attempts among heterosexual males. Twenty-two percent of young lesbians and 23% of young gay men attempt suicide (Savin-Williams, 2001). The majority of these attempts are not life-threatening; their significance as markers of the distress experienced by these young people should not be minimized, however.

Fearing being identified as gay and wanting to protect themselves from a hostile society, men and women with same-sex feelings often learn to pass as heterosexual. They create for themselves a heterosexual *persona,* which may include a boyfriend or girlfriend, marriage, and even children. Other gays recognize and accept who they are and, in spite of a hostile world, manage to be comfortable with themselves.

It would be arrogant to think that your efforts alone could ease the pain of a gay or lesbian friend struggling to find peace in a hostile world. There are, however, things that one person can do to foster greater understanding and improve one-to-one interactions with lesbians and gay men. In general, putting oneself in another person's place can be an important step toward greater tolerance and understanding of differences. Here are a few other steps you can take to make ours a culture that supports the comfort and psychological health of all people, not just heterosexuals.

1. Acknowledge your own feelings, values, beliefs, and thinking about homosexuality, lesbians, and gay men.
2. Educate yourself about homosexuality.
3. Talk with lesbians and gay men you know and those who support them.
4. Identify community resources available to lesbians and gay men, so that you can offer a suggestion if someone asks for your help.
5. Provide an open and supportive atmosphere for your friends who think they might be homosexual. Be an impartial and supportive listener.
6. Make efforts to avoid language that implies that all people are heterosexual and either single, married, or divorced.
7. Remember that friends and acquaintances you associate with might be gay or lesbian.
8. Do not presume that all lesbians or gay men regret their orientation.
9. Do not presume that individuals who do regret their orientation necessarily need or want to change it.
10. Remember that societal oppression and discrimination create much of the unhappiness of many lesbians and gay men.
11. Remember that many lesbian or gay relationships fail because they receive no societal support.
12. Remember that the oppression directed at lesbians differs in many ways from the oppression suffered by gay men, and that nonwhite gay men and lesbians suffer in other ways.
13. Remember that stereotypical "gay" behavior or appearance does not mean that the person evidencing this behavior or appearance is necessarily gay or that gay men necessarily exhibit these traits.
14. Help people to help themselves by reinforcing their own expressions of self-worth, self-acceptance, and self-reliance so they can take charge of their own lives and integrate their feelings, thinking, and behavior in a positive way. Do not pity them.
15. Know when your knowledge has reached its limit. If you are not gay or lesbian, do not presume to know everything about it, no matter how well educated you are.
16. Know when your prejudices or negative feelings are interfering in your interactions with gay men or lesbians.
17. Consider working for civil rights for lesbians and gay men in order to create a more positive environment for everyone.

Adapted from a handout developed by the Office of Student Life, Western Michigan University, Kalamazoo, MI.

have methodological problems (McCarn & Fassinger, 1996). These models have also been criticized because they are based on white male samples and thus ignore possible differences between males' and females' gay identity formation.

Cass's model was recently tested on a sample of 12 white American lesbians (Degges-White, Rice, & Myers, 2000). The researchers found that well-adjusted lesbians did not necessarily move through Cass's stages sequentially, and they even skipped some stages altogether. However, for the lesbians studied, sexual identity formation did appear to be a multistage process, and many of the stages seemed relevant to healthy identity formation. Research has also found that young women's sexual identities can be quite fluid. In one study involving a group of young women (16–23 years old) who identified themselves as either lesbians or bisexuals or who could not apply a label to their sexual identities, half of the participants reported that they had changed their sexual identities more than once in the past (Diamond, 2000). In addition to not including lesbians in model development, researchers have done little to explore gay identity formation in people from racial and ethnic minority groups (McCarn & Fassinger, 1996). Models that have been proposed for lesbian identity formation (Chapman & Brannock, 1987; Sophie, 1985/1986) fail to take into account how the additional factor of societal oppression of females influences this process.

The linear models of sexual identity formation also fail to distinguish between a privately acknowledged identity and a public identity as a member of a larger group. In fact, an individual might *not* simultaneously identify herself or himself as gay *and* as a member of the greater gay and lesbian community. For example, a lesbian might choose not to come out at work despite the fact that she clearly identifies herself as a lesbian (McCarn & Fassinger, 1996). Among adolescents, the extent to which a gay or lesbian outwardly expresses his or her homosexual identity, for example, through membership in gay or lesbian groups, appears to depend on many external factors, among them parents' political ideologies, religion, and the importance of heterosexual friends (Waldner-Haugrud & Magruder, 1996). Finally, linear models imply that individuals must progress through the stages in order if they are to develop a healthy sexual identity, despite the fact that in reality, each person's experience can be unique. A phase model may be more appropriate, to illustrate how a person might be in different phases at different times, depending on her or his current life circumstances. McCarn and Fassinger (1996) proposed a model of lesbian identity formation that separates the process into two paths, *individual sexual identity development* and *group membership identity development;* their model acknowledges that sexual identity formation does not necessarily follow a rigid set of stages.

Bisexual Identity Formation

In their book *Dual Attraction,* Weinberg, Williams, and Pryor (1994) argued that people are naturally bisexual and learn through life experiences to be either heterosexual or homosexual. Inherent bisexuality could help explain why so many people persist in claiming same-sex attraction when the culture vigorously opposes it. However, one study found that most female bisexuals experienced attraction to and sexual interactions with men before same-sex attractions, although most male bisexuals experienced same-sex attractions earlier than or at the same time as other-sex behavior (Fox, 1995).

From interviews with 49 bisexual men and 44 bisexual women, Weinberg and associates (1994) identified four stages of bisexual identity formation: (1) *initial confusion,* when the person recognizes erotic feelings for both sexes and feels confused and uncomfortable; (2) *applying a label,* when the individual acknowledges that sex is pleasurable with both men and women and discovers the term *bisexual;* (3) *settling into an identity,* when the person becomes more self-accepting, which is usually associated with having a meaningful relationship; and (4) *continued uncertainty,* when the individual again feels confused about his or her identity because of pressures to have an exclusive relationship and difficulty managing multiple partners. Although 90% of bisexuals in this study thought their bisexuality was not a passing phase, 40% stated that their bisexual identity might change in the future. For bisexuals, sexual identity can be a fluid and unstable characteristic, perhaps much more so than for gays or lesbians; however, like many homosexuals, many bisexuals are quite comfortable with their sexual identity.

Little is known about bisexuals in Western culture, and those who do not publicly identify themselves as bisexual may differ substantially from those who do. The best available descriptive information regarding bisexuals comes from two studies by Weinberg, Williams, and Pryor (1994). The first study, in 1983, of 49 male and 44 female bisexuals in the San Francisco area, found that 90% of them saw their bisexuality as a fixed characteristic. Most of the participants in this study held very traditional views about gender and the roles that men and women play. About 60% of the men and 35% of the women preferred sexual relations with one sex, and both reported more lifetime male partners than female partners. When asked about their ideal relationship, the majority of these bisexuals said that they wanted two relationships, one with a man and one with a woman. Thus, although a large majority had a preference for one sex, most desired relationships with both men and women. These bisexuals appeared to base their sexual identity more on sexual desire or interest than on actual behavior. In fact, a recent follow-up of these bisexual participants showed that in mid-life, they tend to maintain bisexual attractions but become less involved in a bisexual lifestyle—they tend to have sexual relations with just one sex and to have less contact with the bisexual subculture, and their bisexual identity is less significant to them (Weinberg, Williams, & Pryor, 2001).

Looking At . . .

. . . Thinking About

Because gays, lesbians, and bisexuals must form their sexual identities within the context of the prevailing heterosexually oriented culture, coming to terms with their identities can be more difficult for them than it is for most heterosexuals. What is the importance of community in the development of a healthy sexual identity?

The AIDS epidemic appears to have pushed bisexuals toward limiting their sexual relations to one sex or the other. In their second study, Weinberg and colleagues (1994) returned to San Francisco to examine the potential impact of AIDS on bisexual identities and relationships. In general, bisexual men and women had significantly reduced their number of sexual partners and particularly avoided sex with bisexual men. The majority of participants in this study said their sexual behavior was becoming either more heterosexual or more homosexual, although their erotic and romantic feelings for both sexes had not changed. Most of the participants attributed the changes in their sexual behavior, including the increase in monogamy, to the fear of AIDS. One bisexual male stated:

> I'm married now and my wife really doesn't approve of me expressing my bisexuality. Because of AIDS, I'm not going to be promiscuous as I once was. I personally believe there's nothing wrong with having multiple partners, but marriage should be a thing of trust. I don't like to be unfaithful too because of the disease (AIDS) problem. (Weinberg et al., 1994, p. 222)

Cross-Cultural Trends

Cross-cultural observations make it clear that sexual identity and sexual expression are products of culture. In other words, culture dictates what is appropriate and what is not, what is possible and what is not. In East Asian cultures such as China, Japan, and Thailand, sexual expression is a private matter, and people are expected to fulfill the social function of producing a family irrespective of their sexual identity. Western cultures, on the other hand, place more emphasis on individual identity as opposed to social function. By Western cultural standards, gay people do not exist in those East Asian societies—which is not to say that same-sex desires and behaviors do not exist or are rare in those cultures. In fact, they do exist in most if not all cultures and are frequently considered normal. In 1951, Ford and Beach studied 76 societies around the world and found that 64% of them viewed same-sex behavior for some members of the community at certain times to be "normal" and appropriate. The role of same-sex behavior, however, may vary tremendously from one culture to the other.

In Melanesian and related cultures in the Pacific, same-sex behavior plays a dramatic social and developmental role, particularly for boys (Herdt, 1984). Boys are thought to be inherently infertile and unmasculine. Therefore, starting at about age 9 and continuing until marriage, around age 19, young boys perform fellatio on and ingest the semen of older men; members of this culture believe that this practice makes the young boys fertile. Young Sambian males of New Guinea participate in a similar fertility rite, which continues until they are around 30 years of age (Herdt, 1981). Observers have described the fertility rituals as erotic and have noted that the older and younger males form emotional attachments (Herdt, 1981, 1984). Aside from the fertility ritual, many (but not all) Melanesian and Sambian men maintain exclusive heterosexual relationships after marriage (Davenport, 1965). In both Melanesian and Sambian cultures, women are seen as inherently fertile, and same-sex relationships develop for other reasons.

Among the Lesotho of southern Africa, young women learn vital sexual and social information through same-sex intimate relationships (Gay, 1986). An adolescent Lesotho girl and an older woman may form a long-term relationship, called "Mummy-Baby," which includes casual sexual play and sometimes more intense genital contact. Such a relationship is not stigmatized in this culture as long as the young woman fulfills her social obligation to marry and produce children. Younger and older women also form same-sex relationships among the !Kung (Shostak, 1981) and Mombasa of South Africa (Shepherd, 1987) and the aboriginal Australians (Roheim, 1933). This practice appears to be most common in gender-segregated societies and in households where men have more than one wife or female partner (Blackwood, 1986). Mombasan boys and girls with limited economic means have intimate same-sex relationships with adults who can provide them with social and economic opportunities; young Mombasan boys in particular have little social status and often develop sexual relationships with older married men who can provide for them (Shepherd, 1987). The young boy, or *shoga,* takes a passive sexual role with his *basha* patron. After acquiring some personal resources, most but not all *shoga* males end their same-sex relationships and marry women. Mombasan girls have similar relationships with older women; however, these relationships may continue after marriage.

did YOU know?

People in most Latin American cultures do not approve of same-sex desires between women. Such cultures emphasize close family ties and marriage, and same-sex erotic encounters between women are seen as antifamily (Espin, 1993).

In many cultures, gender roles play a large part in the occurrence of same-sex behaviors. In the macho cultures of Central and South America, North Africa, and other Mediterranean countries, where male and female social roles are quite distinct, only passive recipients in same-sex acts between men are stigmatized (Carrier, 1980). Men who are penetrated are stigmatized and considered effeminate; the men who do the penetrating are not stigmatized and are considered masculine. In some Latin American and Mediterranean cultures, anal sex with a receptive male is an expected part of masculine sexual development. (The men prefer anal intercourse because it closely simulates penile-vaginal intercourse.) Interestingly enough, male-dominant societies that adhere rigidly to gender roles demonstrate the highest incidence of same-sex behavior (Reiss, 1986). Mexicans, for example, have terms for men who participate in same-sex encounters—*activos* to describe the dominant participant and *pasivos* to describe the recipient of anal penetration. The dominant male is generally viewed as normal, while the passive male is looked down on (Clausen, 1997).

Still other cultures with rigid gender roles identify individuals who feel same-sex desires and often exhibit cross-gender behaviors as a third gender, which is both male and female and is *not* identified as gay. Many cultures identify a third gender—examples are the *waria* of Indonesia (Adam, 1987), *hijra* of India, *mahu* of Tahiti, *xanith* of Oman (Mihalik, 1988), *washoga* of Muslim Mombasa in Kenya (Carrier, 1980), and male *berdache* and female *amazons* of Native American cultures (Williams, 1986). Among some Native American peoples, for example, boys and girls choose their gender during a ceremonial ritual by picking a gender-typed implement of daily life. A boy who chooses a bow is a "man" and then must dress and behave in male-identified ways. However, a boy who chooses a basket is a *berdache* and must wear some female clothing and perform traditional women's work. *Berdaches* are considered wise and spiritually gifted and are prized and protected by the community. Some *berdaches* marry men; others live alone or with their families and engage in sexual relations with married men. Interestingly, having sex with a *berdache* is thought to bring good luck. Female *amazons* are also spiritual leaders in their community, but it is unclear whether they have sexual relations with other women.

A berdache of the Zuni Indians: These men dress and live as women in the tribe.

Clearly, human beings are capable of a variety of sexual feelings and relationships. Sexuality does not appear to be fixed as Westerners perceive it, and exclusive heterosexuality is not universally practiced. In fact, the extent to which heterosexuality, homosexuality, and bisexuality are practiced varies considerably across and within cultures.

PREVALENCE OF HETEROSEXUALITY, HOMOSEXUALITY, AND BISEXUALITY

How common are heterosexuality, homosexuality, and bisexuality? The answers to this question largely depend on how and of whom it is asked. People in different cultures have very different perceptions of the various sexualities. Particular aspects of sexuality carry more weight for some people and in some cultures. And erotic desire, affectionate feelings, sexual identity, and sexual behaviors are not always consistent within an individual. So which should be used to define a person's sexual orientation? With respect to actual sexual behavior, are some sexual acts, such as vaginal intercourse, more powerful markers of sexuality than others, such as oral-genital sex or kissing? Finally, should recent or more frequent behaviors count more toward determining sexual orientation than past or infrequent behaviors? To understand the variety of sexualities, researchers (and you, as a consumer of research) must grapple with all of these questions.

During the 1940s, Alfred Kinsey and his colleagues interviewed thousands of men and women across the United States about their sexual activities. Using the criterion "activities and behaviors leading to orgasm," these researchers (Kinsey, Pomeroy, & Martin, 1948; Kinsey, Pomeroy, Martin, & Gebhard, 1953) found that 4% of men and 2% of women were exclusively homosexual, and 50% of men and 72% of women were exclusively heterosexual. Furthermore, 37% of men and 13% of women had at least one same-sex experience to orgasm in adulthood, while 13% of men and 10% of women experienced same-sex erotic fantasies but no sexual behavior. These data may surprise you, but imagine how shocked many people in the 1950s were to hear that half of all men and nearly a third of women had one or more same-sex experiences in their lifetime. Kinsey's research made it clear that same-sex behavior is not uncommon in U.S. culture. On the other hand, weaknesses in Kinsey's research methods led some researchers to conclude that the percentages he reported were higher than the actual prevalences of the same-sex behaviors (Laumann, Gagnon, Michael, & Michaels, 1994; Pomeroy, 1972).

Numerous other large-scale studies of sexual behavior in the United States have been conducted, including the Hite reports (1976, 1981); a reanalysis of the Kinsey data (Fay, Turner, Klassen, & Gagnon, 1989); the Janus Report (Janus & Janus, 1993); and the National Health and Social Life Study (Laumann et al., 1994). Some findings

TABLE 6.1 Prevalence of Sexual Identities among American Adults (18 or older)

	MEN			WOMEN		
	Exclusively Heterosexual	*Exclusively Homosexual*	*Bisexual*	*Exclusively Heterosexual*	*Exclusively Homosexual*	*Bisexual*
Fay et al. (1989)	—	3.3%	—	—	—	—
Hite (1976, 1981)	85.0%	11.0%	4.0%	79.0%	8.0%	13.0%
Janus & Janus (1993)	91.0%	4.0%	5.0%	95.0%	2.0%	3.0%
Kinsey (1948, 1953)	50.0%	4.0%	46.0%	72.0%	2.0%	26.0%
Laumann et al. (1994)	93.8%	2.4%	3.9%	95.6%	0.3%	4.1%

of these studies are summarized in Table 6.1. Although these studies suffered from some methodological problems, just as Kinsey's research did, they consistently show that (1) same-sex behavior crosses age, education, race, economic status, employment, occupation, religion, and political affiliation; (2) on average, 5% of adult American men and 3% of women regularly engage in same-sex activity; (3) same-sex desires and behaviors are more prevalent in men than in women; (4) a number of adults are attracted to both sexes; and (5) identifying oneself as heterosexual does not mean that same-sex desire or behavior is absent. Unfortunately, discrepancies between sexual identity and sexual desires and behaviors, often resulting from social pressures and the stigma attached to homosexuality, contribute to underreporting and misinterpretation of data. Thus, reported data may represent minimum proportions. For example, how would you categorize a woman who has been in a heterosexual marriage for many years, loves her husband, has three children, and experiences strong sexual fantasies about women? Or a gay man who on occasion has sex with a female friend whom he loves? Improved statistical methodology may strengthen the representativeness of the findings, but it cannot untangle complex human interpersonal behavior.

DETERMINING SEXUAL ORIENTATION: NATURE VERSUS NURTURE

What is the origin of sexual orientation? Is it learned, or is it genetically programmed at birth? It is possible that the answer to this question is "both." Perhaps humans are biologically predisposed to be heterosexual, homosexual, bisexual, or asexual, but their learning experiences ultimately determine whether their predisposition is expressed. The respective impacts of biological makeup and experiences in the environment are incredibly complex and nearly impossible to unravel. Nonetheless, many theorists have attempted to explain the origins of sexual orientation. Because homosexuality has been widely viewed as a pathological condition, many of these theories have focused mainly on heterosexual development—giving short shrift to homosexuality and almost no attention at all to bisexuality. A sound theory of sexual orientation would need to explain the full spectrum of sexual desires and behaviors.

Psychoanalytic Theory

One prominent theory about the development of sexual orientation is psychoanalytic theory. As was mentioned earlier, Sigmund Freud (1905/1953, 1920/1955) held that infants are *polymorphously perverse,* meaning that their erotic desire is neither heterosexual nor homosexual and can be directed in various ways. Pleasure fuels the erotic drive, or libido. In Freud's early writings on psychosexual development, homosexuality was described as the result of overidentification with the other-sex parent in the struggle for the affection of the same-sex parent (i.e., the Oedipal complex in boys and the Electra complex in girls). Freud later wrote that all people are inherently bisexual and that homosexuality is a normal condition.

Later psychoanalytical theorists rejected Freud's view of sexuality, however, and declared heterosexuality to be the only "normal" condition (Bergler, 1947). From case histories, these theorists hypothesized that men who desire men failed to separate from their mothers in early childhood (Socarides, 1968; Socarides & Volkan, 1990), grew up in dysfunctional families (Bieber et al., 1962; Rado, 1940; Wiedeman, 1974), had dominant and overprotective mothers and passive and distant fathers (Bieber, 1976), and evidenced more psychopathology than heterosexual men. Women who desire women were thought to have rejecting or indifferent mothers and distant or absent fathers (Wolff, 1971). Empirical studies have not supported these claims. In fact, most psychoanalytic research on sexuality is flawed by substantial methodological problems such as overreliance on anecdotal evidence from case studies, poorly controlled research design, circular reasoning, and confusion of gender identity with sexual orientation. These problems call into question many of the conclusions drawn from these studies.

Other studies have found that gay men and lesbians are no more likely than heterosexual individuals to come from dysfunctional families (Bell & Weinberg, 1978). Less than one-third of lesbians described their mothers as indifferent or negligent (Wolff, 1971), and gay men were only slightly more likely than heterosexual men to report poor father-son relationships (Saghir & Robins, 1973). Evidently, "bad" parents do not produce gay children.

Gay men and lesbians are also no more likely than heterosexuals to experience symptoms of psychiatric disorders. Evelyn Hooker (1956) conducted a clever experiment to see whether skilled clinicians could distinguish between responses of male heterosexuals and homosexuals to the Rorschach inkblot test, a personality measure and popular tool for diagnosing homosexuality. Hooker showed that the clinicians' identifications of homosexuals based on these responses were no more accurate than sheer guesses would have been. Her findings refuted the idea that homosexuals suffer from poor adjustment and debilitating psychological distress.

did YOU know?

As a result of studies confirming that homosexuals are no more poorly adjusted or distressed than heterosexuals, as well as pressure from gay rights activists, the American Psychiatric Association removed homosexuality from the list of disorders included in its Diagnostic and Statistical Manual of Mental Disorders *in 1973. At about the same time, many psychoanalysts moved away from the notion that homosexuality is an aberrant condition (Lewes, 1988).*

Learning Theory

Learning theorists believe that all behavior is learned, either by being paired with a reflexive response, in *classical conditioning,* or by being rewarded, in *operant conditioning.* Learning theorists generally assume that sexual orientation is just one of many learned behavioral patterns—that is, people learn to be gay, straight, or bisexual through various experiences. Among the explanations for homosexual orientation that have been offered are (1) accidental stimulation of an infant's genitals by the same-sex caregiver; (2) punishment following genital stimulation by the opposite-sex parent; (3) negative social messages about heterosexual relations; (4) attention from a same-sex person; (5) absence of an opposite-sex partner during sexual arousal; and (6) inadequate heterosocial skills, making heterosexual interactions unlikely (Barlow & Agras, 1973; Green, 1985, 1987; Greenspoon & Lamal, 1987). Most learning theorists, however, would argue that, rather than a single experience, an accumulation of experiences that reinforce same-sex attraction is necessary for homosexuality to be learned. For example, support for a learning model of homosexuality comes from one study that found that adolescents who learn to masturbate by being manually stimulated by someone of the same sex *and* experience their first orgasm during same-sex contact are more likely to have same-sex desires and a homosexual identity as adults (Van Wyk, 1984). What is not clear here is whether the same-sex desires preceded the sexual activities, or vice versa. Other support for a learning model

Looking At . . .

. . . Thinking About

Children of gay or lesbian parents are no more likely to be homosexual than are children of heterosexual parents. What are your feelings and thoughts on gay or lesbian parents?

comes from the high incidence of same-sex behavior in male-dominant societies with rigid gender roles, where contact between fathers and infants is minimal (Reiss, 1986). The lack of male parenting may make it difficult for young boys to learn how to be masculine, leaving them to socialize with women and to romanticize men.

Learning theorists assume that behavior precedes desire, that opposite-sex attraction is weakened and same-sex desire is highly reinforced by learning experiences (Feldman & MacCulloch, 1971; Greenspoon & Lamal, 1987). However, the most obvious error of learning theorists is their failure to explain how *anyone* in the United States—a strongly heterosexual society in which most families do not encourage but explicitly and implicitly punish same-sex tendencies—could experience enough competing reinforcing conditions to develop same-sex desire. Advertising, music, television, movies, and organized social functions constantly send the message that heterosexual behavior leads to the most rewarding lifestyle.

Furthermore, self-reports by gay men, lesbians, and heterosexuals indicate that same-sex feelings are not the outcome of unpleasant opposite-sex experiences or seduction by an older same-sex person (Bell, Weinberg, & Hammersmith, 1981). Also, gay men and lesbians do not lack sufficient social skills for heterosexual intimacy; in fact, many gay men and lesbians have a great deal of heterosexual experience (Bell and Weinberg, 1978; Kinsey et al., 1948, 1953), and bisexuals continue to have such experiences (Weinberg et al., 1994). Finally, even growing up in an environment with gay parents fails to make children gay (Green, 1978).

Biological Theories

Biological theorists view sexual orientation as a product of hormones, brain development, or genetics. Most biological studies focus on laboratory animals, assuming that all mammals develop similarly. Normal development is thought to produce heterosexual gender-role behavior: That is, males act masculine and are the instigators of sexual encounters with females, while females act feminine and are receptive to sexual activity with males. When these ideas of "normal" heterosexual gender roles are applied to nonheterosexuals, the result is as follows: Men who desire men are more like women, and women who desire women are more like men. Therefore, biological theorists speculate that gay men should be similar (biologically) to heterosexual women, and lesbians should be similar to heterosexual men. An interesting paradox for the heterosexual gender-role model is that men who desire men and take the active sexual role are seen as more masculine and, somehow, less gay. Because of this restricted approach, it is nearly impossible for biological theorists to explain bisexuality within their heterosexual gender-role model. Like most theories of sexuality, biological theories seem to focus more on explaining same-sex attraction than opposite-sex attraction.

Hormonal Studies

The premise of hormonal studies is that male heterosexuality and female homosexuality result from prenatal exposure to androgens, while male homosexuality and female heterosexuality result from an insensitivity to or an absence of androgens. Based on this explanation, gay men should show indications of androgen insensitivity or deficiency, and lesbians should have a history of prenatal exposure to androgens. However, literature reviews by Meyer-Bahlburg (1984) and Byne and Parsons (1993) found very few studies that reported evidence of hormonal abnormalities in gay men or lesbians. Nearly all studies found no significant hormonal differences between heterosexuals and homosexuals. Two studies that do support the hormonal argument (Dittman, Kappes, & Kappes, 1992; Money, Schwartz, & Lewis, 1984) concluded that a recessive genetic condition called *congenital virilizing adrenal hyperplasia* (CVAH), which masculinizes development in females, increases the likelihood of same-sex attraction. However, this condition also results in an enlarged clitoris and a shallow vagina, and the researchers failed to evaluate how their physical anomalies or their knowledge of their condition might influence these women psychosocially.

A related line of reasoning argues that prenatal exposure to estrogens produces same-sex desires in males. This is a curious hypothesis, since sexual differentiation of the brain is known *not* to be mediated by estrogens. Nevertheless, certain progesterone-related compounds, which are sometimes given to women during pregnancy to prevent miscarriage, have been investigated to test this hypothesis. Not surprisingly, most of the studies have failed to support the hypothesis (Byne & Parsons, 1993; Ehrhardt & Meyer-Bahlburg, 1981).

Neuroanatomic Studies

Some researchers have proposed that hormones determine sexual orientation indirectly via their influence on brain structure. The assumption underlying these hypotheses is that exposure to male or female hormones results in structural differences in the brain, which directs sexual behaviors and desires. Studies of several areas of the brain have produced mixed and uncertain results. Although it had methodological limitations, a promising study in this area was conducted by Simon LeVay (1991), who reported that brain structures called *interstitial nuclei* in the anterior hypothalamus are smaller in homosexual men and women than in heterosexual men. (The anterior hypothalamus is thought to function as a regulator of sexual behavior in humans.) Other researchers have found that other areas of the brain thought to affect sexual function differ in size in heterosexuals and homosexuals. For example, the anterior commissure tends to be larger in homosexual men than in women and heterosexual men (Allen & Gorski, 1992).

Studies of neuroanatomic differences between heterosexuals and homosexuals have intrigued scientists and are likely to continue. They are controversial, however, because some of the assumptions regarding the sexual relevance of certain areas of the brain are based on animal studies that may or may not be generalizable to humans. It is also important to understand that the existence of structural differences that correlate with sexual orientation does not necessarily imply a biological cause. Environmental factors such as nutrition, health, and social and cognitive stimulation alter the physiology and structure of the brain (Bhide & Bedi, 1984; Kraemer, Ebert, Lake, & McKinney, 1984; Turner & Greenough, 1985). Thus, even a strong biological disposition is shaped by environmental factors.

Genetic Studies

The most promising support for a biological origin of sexual orientation comes from genetic studies. Geneticist Dean Hamer and his colleagues (Hamer, Hu, Magnuson, Hu, & Pattatucci, 1993) recruited 40 gay men with gay brothers and compared the sibling pairs with respect to 22 genetic markers, or recognizable genes, on their X chromosomes. The researchers found that five consecutive genetic markers correlated highly for the sibling pairs. Seven of the sibling pairs (18%) showed no correlation on any of the markers, which could be a result of normal genetic variation. Although it is suggestive that most of the pairs of gay brothers showed similarity in certain genetic markers, it is not clear what mechanisms these genes might activate or influence to produce same-sex desires.

Supportive evidence for a genetic basis for sexual orientation also comes from two twin and family pedigree studies conducted by J. Michael Bailey and his colleagues. In the first study, Bailey and Pillard (1991) compared gay men and their twins or adopted brothers for concordance on homosexuality. Among the identical twins of the gay men, 52% were gay. Among the nonidentical twins of the gay men, 22% were gay. Only 11% of the adopted brothers said they were gay. Thus, sexual orientation is more likely to be

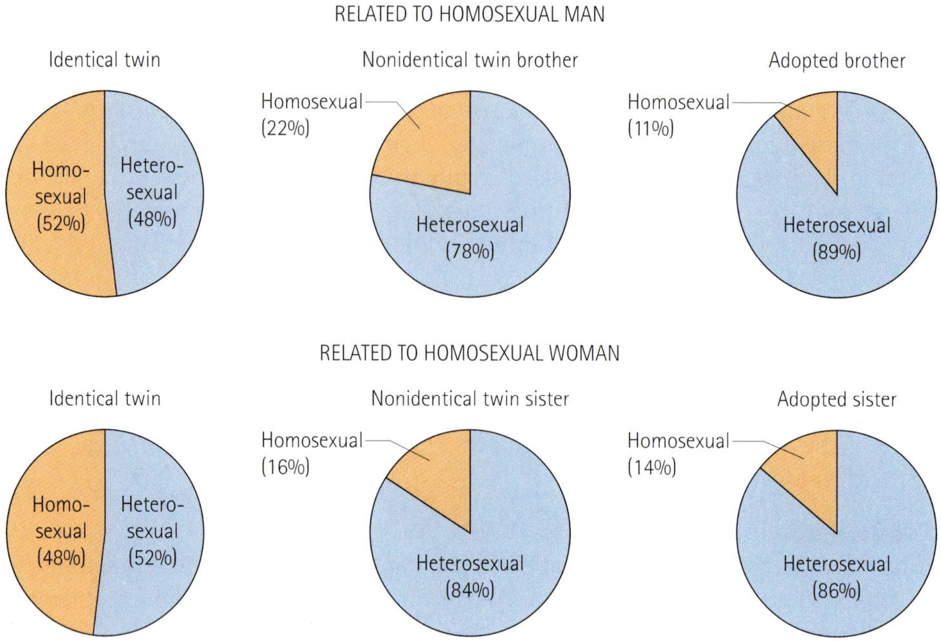

Figure 6.3 These findings by Bailey and colleagues suggest but do not confirm that sexual orientation is genetically determined.

similar for siblings who share identical genetic material. In the second study, Bailey and his colleagues (Bailey, Pillard, Neale, & Agyei, 1993) examined lesbians and their sisters for concordance on homosexuality. Consistent with the earlier study, 48% of the identical twins of the lesbians were also lesbians, and 16% of the nonidentical twins were lesbians. Six percent of adopted sisters of the lesbian participants said they were also lesbians (see Figure 6.3). Other researchers have found that gay men are four times more likely than heterosexual men to have gay brothers (Pillard & Weinrich, 1986). Interestingly, Hamer and his associates (1993) also noted that gay men in their study often reported that maternal uncles and sons of maternal aunts were gay.

The high concordance of homosexuality between identical twins supports, but does not establish with certainty, a genetic basis of sexual orientation. Less than 100% agreement in the sexual orientations of twins indicates that factors other than genetics influence same-sex desire. Furthermore, even identical twins, it can be argued, do not share identical prenatal or postnatal experiences.

Gender Nonconformity

Biologically oriented theorists observe that there is a strong relationship between gender-typed behavior in childhood and sexual orientation in adulthood, and they offer this as evidence for the heritability of sexual orientation. In short, prospective and retrospective studies have shown that gender nonconformity is more common in individuals who are homosexual as adults than in those who are heterosexual as adults. In other words, as children, homosexuals preferred toys, games, and clothing normally preferred by the opposite sex. Evidence of this association has repeatedly been found in the United States and has been observed in other countries as well, including Brazil, Peru, Guatamala, and the Philippines (Pillard & Bailey, 1998). Some researchers have surmised that this association is observed because hormones influence both sexual orientation and gender-typed behavior; however, this influence is complex and unclear (Berenbaum & Snyder, 1995), and many plausible arguments can also be made for socialization as the source of the influence (Bailey & Zucker, 1995). Furthermore, there is considerable within-group variability (Bailey & Zucker, 1995). In other words, a large number of homosexuals did *not* display gender-nonconforming behavior in childhood, and not all heterosexuals were gender-conforming in childhood.

Given the available research, it is unlikely that a single model can account for the origins of sexual orientation. In all likelihood, biology does not fully account for it; in fact, both biological and environmental theories appear to provide only partial explanations. It is most reasonable to assume that sexual orientation is guided by both biological and environmental factors. Indeed, there may very well be various heterosexuali*ties* and homosexuali*ties,* since individuals arrive at their sexual orientations via different biological and environmental paths. It is interesting how views of the origins of sexual orientation can affect judgments concerning those who do not "conform" to a heterosexual orientation.

Sexual Orientation as Choice: The Debate

The issue of "choice" arises often in discussions of sexual orientation, particularly in the political arena. Those who view sexual orientation as a choice assume that individuals make a conscious decision to be homosexual. Many assume that there is a right choice and a wrong choice—some people make "good" choices regarding their sexuality and some people make "bad" ones. Conservative moralists and anti-gay activists tend to hold this position: The "right" sexual orientation is heterosexuality, and all others are "bad" choices, for which those who make them are responsible. Furthermore, if someone has "chosen" to be gay, he or she could just as easily choose to be straight—the person who went astray, so to speak, could be "saved." The argument is sometimes even made that people who engage in unacceptable behavior should be punished. Unfortunately, many critics of homosexuality justify their views based on the perspective of learning theorists, that sexual orientation is learned. In a strict sense, however, learning theory holds that we have little control over our learning experiences through life. Just as a baby does not choose to be born into poverty, we cannot choose many or most of the circumstances into which we are born and reared—those very circumstances that may shape our sexuality.

The concept of a chosen sexual orientation tends to imply environmental causation and to refute the idea of a natural, or biological, sexuality. Viewing sexual orientation as inborn and determined before birth suggests that people have no choice about it. Because "choice" often opens the door to judgment and condemnation of gay men and lesbians, the biological explanation for sexual orientation is a viewpoint commonly held by liberal moralists and gay activists. Yet, an inborn characteristic is not necessarily acceptable to society. Some people with biological conditions such as albinism, sterility, cleft palate, and retardation have been condemned as defective or pathological. Furthermore, anti-gay people would argue that even those with inborn desires for the same sex can and should willfully violate their natural tendencies.

From another perspective, the idea that sexual orientation is a choice implies the freedom to select from a variety of possibilities, all being equally likely. This position suggests that a "good" informed choice requires trying out different kinds of relationships. The categorization of same-sex relationships as "right" or "wrong" then clearly becomes a matter of politics and cultural values. Anti-gay groups that argue that individuals do have a "choice"—at least to control their behavior—would certainly not like this particular "choice" perspective.

Like most phenomena, sexual orientation, whether a choice or not, can be politicized by efforts to regulate people's attitudes and behaviors. Consequently, the true origin of sexual orientation is less relevant than social beliefs about sexual orientation and behavior.

Gays and lesbians in all walks of life must still tread lightly if they want to be accepted in most segments of the mainstream culture. It is not surprising, therefore, that many gays and lesbians seek out their own "communities" in which they can relax and be themselves. Many gays and lesbians can feel more comfortable with their sexual identities if they are able to connect with a group of similar individuals. For decades, gay and lesbian activists have devoted their lives to creating communities with which homosexuals can identify.

CLOSE UP ON culture

Religion and Sexual Orientation

Nearly all religions condone procreative sex within heterosexual marriage—but there are vast differences among religions on most other matters of sexuality, such as sex outside of marriage, masturbation, oral and anal sex, and contraception. But one of the hottest topics of debate in religious organizations today is homosexuality. In recent years, nearly all Protestant sects of the Christian religion have created task forces to examine their positions on homosexuality and have argued the issue at denominational conventions. Other religions have been less interested in debating homosexuality, which is not to say that same-sex behavior is a non-issue for them.

Religious views on homosexuality and heterosexuality generally reflect one of four positions (Nelson, 1980): punitive, intolerant-nonpunitive, limited acceptance, or acceptance. Religions that take a *punitive* stance unconditionally reject same-sex behavior and believe that gay men and lesbians should be punished. The only acceptable sexual behaviors fall into a narrow range of acts within a monogamous heterosexual marriage. Procreation, not pleasure, is considered the goal of sexual activity. Religions that hold this view include Buddhism and fundamentalist sects of both Christianity and Islam (Bullough, 1995).

The *intolerant-nonpunitive* position condemns same-sex behavior as unnatural and a sin but does not reject the person. This position is sometimes expressed as "Hate the sin; love the sinner." Religions that take this stance may even support the civil rights of gay men and lesbians. Different forms of sexual activity within a heterosexual marriage are deemed acceptable. Examples of religions that hold this view are Judaism and moderate sects of Islam and Christianity (Baptists, Methodists, and Roman Catholics).

Religions that have a *limited acceptance* of homosexuality view same-sex behavior as a sin but acknowledge that the medical and psychological establishments accept same-sex desire as unchangeable. Therefore, the stance of religions in this group is that gay men and lesbians who cannot remain celibate should confine sexual behavior to fully committed monogamous relationships. This view allows that most sexual activities for the pursuit of pleasure are acceptable within the bonds of heterosexual marriage. Adultery is a sin, but divorce and remarriage are not condemned. Religions espousing this view are Taoism, Hinduism, liberal Judaism, and progressive Christian sects (Quakers, Presbyterians, Episcopalians, and Lutherans).

Acceptance of same-sex identity and behavior is more typical of liberal Christian sects (the United Church of Christ, the Unitarians, the Metropolitan Community Church, and some nondenominational churches). Sexuality is viewed as a vital and pleasurable part of romantic love. Ethical sexual relationships, whether between people of the same sex or of opposite sexes, are committed, trusting, tender, and respectful. Same-sex unions receive the church's blessing, and openly gay Christians are ordained as ministers. Consenting sexual acts within a loving relationship are not condemned.

SEXUAL COMMUNITIES

Who or what is a community? Is a community simply a place where people live? Or is a community a political or social group that holds meetings and sets agendas? A **community** can be defined as a collection of people who have similar beliefs, feelings, or behaviors and feel some degree of commitment to each other (although members of a community do not always see things exactly alike and may hold different views). Close Up on Culture: Religion and Sexual Orientation gives some examples of the diversity of views within one community. A community can be well-organized and activist or more loosely connected and apolitical. Examples of communities are retirees living in Florida, homeowners, people with AIDS, white supremacists, and left-handed chess players. To what communities do you belong?

We all belong to a sexual community, and our membership in that community is determined by our sexual orientation. You have no doubt heard reference to "the gay community," but heterosexuals belong to a community, too. Because heterosexuals control the dominant culture in most countries, including the United States, they may not be aware of the many signs of their community identification—boy-girl dating, proms, traditional marriages, debutante balls, and joint tax returns, to name just a few.

COMMUNITY
A collection of people with similar beliefs, feelings, and behaviors who feel a commitment to each other.

The existence of the heterosexual community is evident in the general public's reaction to gay marriage, a female couple raising a child, or a love song about two men. The 1996 Defense of Marriage Act, which defined marriage as a union between a man and a woman, is an example of the type of formal response often made by the heterosexual community when its traditions are challenged.

Actions to prevent gays, lesbians, and bisexuals from enjoying some of the privileges currently enjoyed by the heterosexual community can make it difficult for them to have their own sense of community, but it also makes building that sense even more important. The homosexual community in the United States is growing strong, establishing its own traditions and signs of togetherness. Most people tend to think of the gay community as existing primarily in urban centers such as San Francisco and New York City. Urban gay and lesbian communities once centered on gay bars, but they have grown into "mini-cities where one can work, play, pray, and sleep around without ever leaving the neighborhood" (LeVay & Nonas, 1995, p. 120). These are not the only gay and lesbian communities, however. Such communities can be found in rural areas, too. In Northern California and Oregon, for example, lesbian communities that originated in communes in the 1970s still thrive (LeVay & Nonas, 1995). And on the Internet, many Web sites promote a sense of community by offering support and encouragement and covering topics of interest to gay men and lesbians.

Gay-friendly towns, gay bars, bookstores that cater to gay men and lesbians, supportive businesses, and legal recognition all provide the sense of unity that symbolizes a community. Thus, there are really many different gay and lesbian "communities," some symbolic and some physical. The support that these communities provide is material, spiritual, and emotional. In essence, these communities, or subsets of them, often function as families. Such communities fly in the face of the stereotypes held by many Americans who see homosexual communities as places defined solely by the sexual activities of their members. In fact, gay and lesbian communities offer sanctuary from an unaccepting majority culture. Unfortunately, bisexuals seem to lack their own community in which to find such sanctuary.

6.2 on the web

To further your understanding of the diversity of viewpoints on homosexuality within religious groups, read the two different Christian perspectives at **www.ablongman.com/mcanulty2e.**

Describe how these views differ and explain how the issue of "choice" is incorporated into these groups' arguments.

Communities with large proportions of gay men and lesbians offer a sense of togetherness in a world that is often hostile toward them.

6.3 **on the web**

Several sites on the Internet provide community for gays, lesbians, and bisexuals. GLAAD, the Gay and Lesbian Alliance Against Defamation, is an organization that maintains such a Web site. Go to **www.ablongman.com/mcanulty2e** to read more about GLAAD. Describe the organization's primary mission.

Do you think organizations such as this one are beneficial? Why or why not?

Bisexuals and Community

Do bisexuals have a community? Where can a bisexual person look for companionship? Large metropolitan areas offer support groups, community centers, and social activities for identified bisexuals. However, few cities offer bars, clubs, bookstores, movie houses, or coffee shops that cater exclusively to bisexuals. And, since being bisexual may garner little support from either homosexual or heterosexual communities, many bisexuals do not label themselves and do not participate in gay or lesbian community events. People who engage in incidental, secondary same-sex behavior (because no partners of the opposite sex are available) or technical (for pay) same-sex behavior may not need to alter their sexual identities to make sense of their bisexual experiences (Ross, 1991). Likewise, men who view the "insertive" sexual act with same-sex partners as "not gay" do not feel compelled to change their heterosexual identities. Thus, it appears that bisexuals generally exist on the fringes of both the homosexual and the heterosexual community, and there appears to be no well-defined "bisexual community."

Gay and Lesbian Racial and Ethnic Minorities

Gays, lesbians, and bisexuals who are also members of racial or ethnic minorities often have an even more difficult struggle to find community. These individuals must develop self-acceptance of both their racial and ethnic heritage and their sexual identity in order to achieve a sense of community. Unfortunately, homosexuality is taboo or not even recognized in many racial and ethnic communities. In fact, there is no neutral descriptive term for *homosexual* in some languages. The only term that might be used to describe homosexuality in Arab languages translates to "perversion" (Peirol, 1997). Many Asian and African languages also lack a word for homosexuality (LeVay & Nonas, 1995; Macharia, 1997). However, the lack of a term does not mean that homosexuality does not exist in these cultures; it is simply not recognized. Homosexuality is perceived as a threat in many racial and ethnic groups, including African Americans, Asian Americans, Hispanic Americans, and Mexican Americans, because marriage and family are considered important to the cohesion of the minority culture. Same-sex desires and behaviors are considered antifamily and anticommunity. For Hispanic American women, for example, family and ethnic community support is critical for survival, so same-sex feelings and relationships are kept secret (Espin, 1993). Gay men and lesbians thus often experience a double identity stigma and often feel pressured to choose between their racial or ethnic community and the gay or lesbian community (Chan, 1993). Evidence suggests that African American females are less tolerant of homosexuality in their communities than are white American females, perhaps because male homosexuality contributes further to the diminishing availability of male African American partners (Ernst, Francis, Nevels, & Lemeh, 1991). The double identity stigma and the lack of acceptance within the racial or ethnic community may explain why African American and Hispanic American men are more likely than white men to maintain their heterosexual identity while engaging in same-sex behavior (Peterson & Marin, 1988).

Many minority gay men and lesbians feel marginalized by the mostly white gay and lesbian communities.

Minority gay men and lesbians not only feel that they receive little support from their racial or ethnic communities, but, as nonwhites, also feel marginalized by the mostly white gay and lesbian communities (Icard, 1986; LeVay & Nonas, 1995). The Gay and Lesbian Alliance Against Defamation (GLAAD), a major national gay/bisexual/lesbian organization, came under attack in the past for having a history of supporting mainly wealthy, gay white men to the exclusion of other groups, including racial and ethnic minorities (Che & Suggs, 1995). Because they feel they receive so little support, many minority gay men and lesbians have built their own communities, either by moving to larger cities to be near others in the same situation or by joining groups that represent them. Organizations that specifically represent gays, bisexuals, lesbians, and transgendered members of minority groups include Gay American Indians (GAI), Gay and Lesbian Latinos Unidos (GLLU), the National Black Lesbian and Gay Leadership Forum (NBLGLF), and the Gay Asian Pacific Alliance (GAPA), to name only a few. Internet sites devoted to issues of interest to minority gays and lesbians also abound. In general, it appears that being a member of both a racial or ethnic and a sexual minority creates a tremendous burden, but minority gays and lesbians are gradually finding supportive communities of which they can be a part.

6.4 on the web

A Web site maintained by an organization called Blackstripe offers support to gay, lesbian, and transgendered African Americans. Go to **www.ablongman.com/mcanulty2e** and read the article written by Blackstripe's founder about being African American and gay.

What are your reactions to this author's portrayal of his experiences?

RELATIONSHIPS

In many non-Western countries, such as India, Pakistan, and Thailand, romantic love is viewed as a threat to the family. In these countries, indulging in romantic love is seen as placing individual needs over group needs, which are considered of greater importance. By contrast, in Western countries, heterosexual romantic relationships are not only encouraged but also expected. Young people from Western cultures such as the United States, Brazil, England, and Australia, view love as the reason for beginning an intimate relationship, although not necessarily the only reason for remaining in one (Levine, Sato, Hashmoto, & Verma, 1995). However, sexual orientation also affects the nature of romantic and sexual relationships across cultures.

Finding Romantic or Sexual Partners

Heterosexuals in Western cultures can meet potential romantic or sexual partners in dozens of everyday situations—in the classroom, at church, at a football game, at a friend's wedding, or in the workplace. Singles' bars and clubs, Internet chat rooms, computer bulletin boards, and personal ads in newspapers are also popular ways for heterosexuals to meet other heterosexuals. However, the most popular places to meet a heterosexual partner are at school, work, a private party, or a bar (Laumann et al., 1994).

Men and women with same-sex desires have relatively less access to others like themselves. In urban areas, they can turn to gay or gay-friendly bars, clubs, restaurants, bookstores, social events, churches, support groups, and social organizations. Gay men and lesbians can also employ personal ads in newspapers, computer bulletin boards, and interactive chat rooms. Just as some straight men seek out prostitutes, some gay men seeking immediate sexual gratification might frequent bathhouses, sex clubs, public restrooms ("tearooms"), pornographic book and video stores, and "cruising" spots in parks and other public places. Many gay men find public solicitation for sex inappropriate and indecent, however.

did YOU know?

Like heterosexuals, bisexuals prefer vaginal intercourse to other activities, and 39% of bisexual men and 50% of bisexual women engage in vaginal intercourse one or more times a week. Oral sex was the second most popular activity among bisexuals (Weinberg et al., 1994).

Sexual Activities

Five decades ago, Kinsey and his colleagues (Kinsey et al., 1948, 1953) shocked the public when they described in clinical detail what people did sexually. One of the most surprising findings was that heterosexuals frequently engaged in behaviors that were thought to be uncommon, such as oral sex. Later researchers found that heterosexual men initiated sex more often than heterosexual women did (Blumstein & Schwartz, 1983) and that heterosexual men complained that women did not take an active role in initiating and experimenting sexually (Hatfield, Sprecher, Pillemer, Greenberger, & Wexler, 1988; Hite, 1981). Conversely, heterosexual women reported wanting men to be more tender and emotionally intimate during sex

(Halpern & Sherman, 1979; Hite, 1976). Interestingly, among same-sex couples, the more emotionally expressive partner tends to initiate sex (Blumstein & Schwartz, 1983). Masters and Johnson (1979) claimed that gay men and lesbians are more skillful as lovers than heterosexuals are, and Shere Hite (1976) noted that lesbian sexual encounters tend to be "longer and involve more all-over body sensuality" (p. 413). Some lesbians claim that women are better lovers because heterosexual men have poor knowledge of female anatomy and how to stimulate women.

Both other-sex and same-sex couples engage in similar sexual activities, with the exception of penile-vaginal intercourse, and for all couples, the longer they are together, the less frequently sex occurs. In fact, frequency of sex drops sharply after 10 years (Blumstein & Schwartz, 1983). Heterosexual men and women prefer vaginal intercourse (84% and 77%) to receiving oral sex (45% and 29%) or giving oral sex (34% and 17%). Thirty-five percent of men and women have sex with a partner two or more times a week (Laumann et al., 1994). Another 35% of heterosexuals have sex with a partner at least once a month, and the remainder have sex a few times a year.

Among lesbians, oral sex, manual stimulation, and rubbing of genitals against the partner's genitals or body are favored sexual activities (Laumann et al., 1994). Perhaps because society has taught women not to initiate sex (Loulan, 1984), lesbians have sex less frequently than heterosexuals do; this discrepancy increases over time. However, Kinsey (Kinsey et al., 1953) reported that lesbians more often had orgasms during sex than heterosexual women did. After 5 years of marriage, 55% of heterosexual women had orgasms during most or all sexual encounters, while 78% of lesbians had orgasms during most or all encounters over a 5-year period. Lesbians tend to form close, committed, sexually exclusive relationships of long duration, although one side effect of extreme togetherness is a dramatic decrease in frequency (but perhaps not quality) of sexual activity over time (Peplau, 1982; Saghir & Robins, 1969; Tuller, 1978). Other writers have noted that lesbians place greater emphasis on emotional expression and equality in their relationships than do heterosexual women (McCandlish, 1985; Peplau & Amaro, 1982).

For gay men, fellatio (oral sex) is the most frequent sexual activity, followed by mutual masturbation (Lever, 1994). In spite of popular myths, anal sex is the least common sexual activity for gay men, and most gay men (85%) prefer hugging, kissing, snuggling, and total body caressing to any other sexual act. Gay men typically have more lifetime sexual partners than heterosexual men, who in turn have more partners than heterosexual women (Laumann et al., 1994). Lesbians report the fewest lifetime sexual partners (Markowitz, 1993). Since the advent of AIDS, most adults, especially gay men, have reduced their number of sexual partners (Kelaher, Ross, Rohrsheim, Drury, & Clarkson, 1994).

Looking At . . .

. . . Thinking About

Heterosexual and homosexual relationships share many similar characteristics. Perhaps of greatest importance is the fact that all healthy relationships include mutual caring and respect. What is your perspective on same-sex marriage?

Typical Relationships

While no two couples are exactly alike, some typical relationship patterns exist within the heterosexual, gay, lesbian, and bisexual communities.

Marriage

Approximately 76% of American men and women marry at least once (U.S. Census Bureau, 1999), and 40% of all marriages are remarriages (Peck, 1993). In their national survey of sexual behavior, Laumann and colleagues (1994) found that over 60% of American men and women were married or living with someone. Similarly, an estimated 40–60% of gay men and 45–80% of lesbians are currently in same-sex relationships (Kurdek, 1995). Bisexuals and gay men are more likely than heterosexuals or lesbians to have a relationship outside of their primary one (Weinberg et al., 1994). Yet, whether it is the result of changes in society or of the threat of AIDS, many gay men report a preference for a single monogamous relationship (Kurdek, 1995).

The primary difference between heterosexual and gay and lesbian relationships is that same-sex couples cannot be legally married in the majority of states in the United States. Thirty-six states have passed laws banning same-sex marriages (Human Rights Campaign, 2002). As of 2002, Vermont was the only state that had passed legislation supporting a "civil union" between same-sex partners, which gives these couples the same legal benefits afforded opposite-sex married couples. Residents of other states can go to Vermont and have a civil union ceremony, but because of the Defense of Marriage Act (DOMA), signed in 1996 by then-President Bill Clinton, no other states are required to recognize these unions. (Chapter 12 discusses DOMA in more detail.) Same-sex American couples who want their relationship to be recognized officially may register as *domestic partners* in certain municipalities, hold special commitment ceremonies in which they pledge their love to each other, or participate in a religious ceremony called a *holy union* or *blessing,* which is conducted by several religious denominations.

did YOU know?

In September 2002, the* New York Times *became the largest U.S. daily newspaper to publish announcements of same-sex commitment ceremonies alongside traditional wedding announcements in its "Sunday Styles" section.

The United States is not alone in debating same-sex marriage, although other countries have evolved different approaches to the issue. Denmark and Norway allow same-sex couples to legally marry, and Sweden and Iceland recognize same-sex civil weddings, which carry most of the legal benefits of heterosexual marriage. Although Hungary does not permit same-sex marriage, a same-sex partner can inherit property or a pension from a deceased lover.

Gender Roles and Relationship Development

Within a stereotypic gender-role system, there is a strict division of labor between men and women: Men play active roles as breadwinners, protectors, and heads of households, while women are passive, expressive, and dependent. Heterosexual couples use gender roles to structure their relationships more often than same-sex couples do (D'Agostino & Day, 1991; Peplau, 1982). Same-sex relationships tend to be egalitarian, often resembling close friendships (Peplau, 1982). In egalitarian relationships, decisions are made by negotiation and by taking turns, not based on the authority of one partner. Egalitarianism among same-sex couples is made possible by the irrelevance of patriarchal gender roles that place women in subordinate positions. Furthermore, gay and lesbian partners often have dual careers, suffer a similar degree of discrimination in the workplace, and have similar earning potential (which eliminates a major source of conflict that affects many heterosexual couples).

Overall, heterosexual and gay and lesbian love relationships progress similarly (McWhirter & Mattison, 1984). The first year of the relationship is filled with erotic infatuation and constant togetherness. Living together focuses attention on creating a "home." Healthy couples learn to incorporate each other's shortcomings into the relationship and to view them as human differences. For a same-sex couple, being in a relationship makes it very difficult to deny or hide one's sexual orientation and pushes partners to come out. Yet, matched samples of heterosexual and gay and lesbian couples showed no differences in relationship satisfaction or in the love partners felt for each other (Peplau & Amaro, 1982).

IN YOUR own words

Ashley Logan
Virginia Commonwealth University

Same-sex marriages should be legal in the United States. By it not being legal, our country is saying "if we don't let it happen, maybe it will go away"—but it won't. A lack of legislation is not going to change who people love.

Celebrity Rosie O'Donnell is a powerful advocate for adoption rights for gays and lesbians.

Families and Parenting

For most heterosexuals, *family* refers to legal or blood relatives. For gay men, lesbians, and bisexuals in same-sex relationships, a *family* is any group of two or more people who are committed to caring about each other (Dahlheimer & Feigal, 1991). Especially for gay men and lesbians, close friends comprise an extended family, and sometimes the only family that is supportive (Ainslie & Feltey, 1991).

According to the 1990 U.S. Census, married couples made up 56% of American households, and traditional two-parent heterosexual families with children accounted for only 26% of all households (U.S. Census Bureau, 1990). Unmarried women head the majority of single-parent households. Coincidentally, while many heterosexuals are delaying first marriage, cohabiting instead of marrying, and having fewer children, a number of gay and lesbian couples are becoming parents. An estimated 2–8 million gay men and lesbians are parents, and approximately 4–14 million children have gay parents (Patterson, 1995). Most gays and lesbians had their children when they were in heterosexual relationships (Martin, 1993; Patterson, 1995). Other gay and lesbian couples adopt children or become foster parents where laws permit (Martin, 1993; Patterson, 1995). The laws are constantly changing, but in 2000, only Florida had a law that banned adoption by gays, and it was being contested in court (American Civil Liberties Union, 1999). In addition, a growing number of lesbians conceive via artificial insemination. To ensure the legal rights of both partners, lesbians often fertilize one partner's egg with sperm from a sperm bank or a male friend (*in vitro* fertilization) and implant it in the uterus of the other partner to carry to term (O'Hanlan, 1995). Gay men who want children sometimes contract with a surrogate mother to carry the child for a fee or inseminate a lesbian friend and share parenting responsibilities.

However, the legal rights of gay biological parents are not guaranteed. Custody laws usually favor the mother following a divorce, but this is not true if she is a lesbian (Allen & Demo, 1995), and gay mothers and fathers commonly lose visitation and custody rights based on the belief that their homosexuality will harm their children's development. Yet numerous studies show that children raised by gay parents demonstrate few if any differences from children with heterosexual parents in self-esteem, gender roles, sexual orientation, development, school problems, and general well-being (Bailey, Bobrow, Wolfe, & Mikach, 1995; Green, 1992; Patterson, 1995; Tasker & Golombok, 1995). Contrary to popular opinion, children reared in same-sex households are no more likely than children reared in other families to be gay.

While many gays, lesbians, and heterosexuals value similar things, such as enduring love relationships and parenting of children, gays and lesbians clearly do not conform to the heterosexual standards of American culture in many other ways. Indeed, until the 1970s, gays and lesbians were not a recognizable community within the United States. It was not until the late 1960s that the gay and lesbian movement brought them into the limelight.

THE LESBIAN AND GAY MOVEMENT

Though they are sometimes suppressed or rewritten, Western history includes numerous stories of same-sex attraction and behavior (Boswell, 1980). The modern concept of *homosexuality,* however, is little more than a hundred years old (Halperin, 1990). In

1869, the term *homosexual* was used for the first time by sex-law reformer Karl Maria Kertbeny to describe males attracted to other males, and especially men who enjoyed receptive anal intercourse (Feray & Herzer, 1990). People with same-sex desires had already begun drawing attention by forming collectives in large cities such as Berlin, Paris, Amsterdam, and New York.

The first pro-homosexual movement began in Germany in the late 19th century. One of the movement's most vocal leaders was sexologist Magnus Hirschfeld, who founded the Scientific Humanitarian Committee and advocated humane treatment of gay men and lesbians. Starting in 1897 and up until his death in 1935, Hirschfeld struggled to abolish the German sodomy law, which criminalized homosexual acts between men (women were not mentioned). Nonetheless, the late 19th and early 20th centuries represented a kind of "golden age" for homosexuals in Germany, with Berlin alone boasting 40 gay and lesbian bars by 1914. Lesbians, however, were usually married women and were less visible than the growing gay male community (Miller, 1995). One organization, the Committee of the Special, which formed in 1903, even went so far as to advocate sexual relations between younger and older men and to tout male supremacy. Despite this golden age, homosexuality remained controversial, and claims of homosexual activity were often used in political battles to weaken opponents' positions (Miller, 1995). By 1928, Germany's National Socialist Party referred to homosexuals as enemies of the state, and in 1933, Chancellor Hitler used Germany's sodomy law to place thousands of homosexual men under "protective custody" in concentration camps. Imprisoned homosexuals wore a pink triangle on their clothing and were singled out for harsh treatment and dangerous work details. An estimated 15,000 homosexuals died in Nazi concentration camps, and those who survived were detained as criminals by the liberation forces in 1944 (Plant, 1986).

The gay rights movement took root in the United States after World War II with the founding of the Mattachine Society in 1951 and the Daughters of Bilitis in 1955, both of which published national newsletters (Adam, 1987). In the 1950s and 1960s, only a handful of gay organizations and gay bars existed. Police harassment of the patrons of these bars was routine, and arrest could mean physical abuse and blackmail by officers, as well as public humiliation, loss of one's job, loss of social standing, breakup of one's marriage, and abandonment by friends. Gay men and lesbians had little legal recourse if threatened or assaulted. Then, on June 27, 1969, during a routine police raid of the Stonewall Inn in New York City, a core group of gay men, male prostitutes, transvestites, and drag queens fought back and started a 3-day riot. Overnight, several loosely organized gay groups solidified to demand recognition and protection from police harassment. The political force of the new gay movement was not fully appreciated until 1973, when angry activists successfully lobbied the American Psychiatric Association for removal of homosexuality from the list of psychiatric disorders in its diagnostic manual (Bayer, 1987).

By the late 1970s, the growing lesbian and gay movement faced renewed attack from fundamentalist religious

did YOU know?

In the 19th century, practitioners in medical science and psychiatry began to think of same-sex desires and behaviors not as sinful acts, but as personal characteristics or biological defects, the result of psychic and physical degeneration due to excessive masturbation (Krafft-Ebing, 1886/1936).

Looking At . . .

. . . Thinking About

Ruth Ellis, born in 1899, died at age 101. Known as the oldest "out" lesbian, Ellis and her partner, Ceceline "Babe" Franklin, opened their Detroit home to other gays and lesbians. Does she fit your image of a homosexual?

Gays and lesbians have fought hard to share the same freedoms as heterosexuals.

and conservative groups (Adam, 1987). In 1977, Anita Bryant led the national "Save Our Children" campaign against efforts in Florida to end discrimination against gays, while legislation in California attempted to ban gay teachers. The 1980s offered even less hope. In the early years of the decade, increasing numbers of gay men were contracting a mysterious "wasting syndrome," initially called *gay-related immune deficiency* (GRID) and later *acquired immune deficiency syndrome* (AIDS). As thousands of young men lost their lives to AIDS, the gay community observed the obvious lack of effort from the public health sector and the public in general to fight this disease, which was pigeon-holed as a "gay disease." In angry reaction to the apathetic or condemnatory responses from community and religious leaders, medical and elected officials, and the federal government, gay men, lesbians, and bisexuals soon formed their own AIDS prevention campaigns, AIDS support groups, and medical information networks. Coincidentally, the gay and lesbian community's constructive response to the AIDS epidemic made that community stronger, angrier, and more politically active.

Today gay men and lesbians are more visible in U.S. society. Most large cities hold Gay Pride marches in June to commemorate the Stonewall riot. The 30th anniversary of Stonewall in 1999 brought gay men and lesbians, along with many of their parents and other supporters, to cities such as New York and San Francisco to celebrate. Several well-known athletes and celebrities have openly declared their homosexuality, including tennis champion Martina Navratilova, Olympic diver Greg Louganis, swimmer Bruce Hayes, champion body-builder Bob Paris, billionaire David Geffen, rock star Elton John, Cher's daughter Chastity Bono, TV personality Rosie O'Donnell, former Minnesota Vikings star Esera Tualo, and movie director Gus van Sant. Today, TV sitcoms and movies are beginning to portray gay men and lesbians as ordinary people, rather than as villains, victims, or stereotypic characters for comic value. Gay men and lesbians have also achieved some measure of corporate and legal recognition. Several large companies and the Federal Civil Service Commission have adopted policies prohibiting discrimination against people on the basis of sexual orientation (Tuller, 1994), and a growing number of companies, including Disney and IBM, have extended domestic benefits such as spousal rights, medical and life insurance benefits, and bereavement leave to same-sex partners ("Benefits," 1996). And in 1996, the U.S. Supreme Court ruled in *Romer v. Evans* that states could not enact legislation to deny civil rights to gay men and lesbians or to exclude them from due process.

Yet greater visibility does not mean greater tolerance. For example, sodomy laws in many states are directed specifically and exclusively at homosexual acts of anal intercourse. In addition, groups opposed to gay rights have successfully portrayed gay men and lesbians as seeking "special rights," which would destroy heterosexual marriage and undermine society.

One arena in which resistance to gays and lesbians has been most evident is in the U.S. military, which has defended its right to exclude and expel homosexuals largely under the assumption that their presence will weaken the military (Herek, Jobe, & Carney, 1996). In truth, there are and have been many gay men and lesbians in the military, and national security has evidently not been weakened. Many homosexuals have served and continue to serve in the United States military with distinction, but not openly. The issue of gays in the military has been hotly debated. After months of dramatic testimony in congressional hearings, in September 1993, Congress and President Clinton agreed to the policy known as "Don't Ask, Don't Tell, Don't Pursue." Unlike the previous outright ban on homosexuals in the military, this policy prohibits asking recruits about homosexuality but views disclosure of homosexuality as misconduct worthy of discharge. The policy has been challenged repeatedly in the Supreme Court, but so far unsuccessfully.

6.5 on the web

Read the article at **www.ablongman.com/mcanulty2e** regarding harassment since implementation of the military's "Don't Ask, Don't Tell, Don't Pursue" policy.

Is this policy accomplishing what it was designed to? Why or why not? What is your view of gays in the military?

The military has put forth many arguments for excluding gay men and lesbians—including loss of morale and discipline, heterosexual discomfort, and negative impact on recruiting—but to date has produced no evidence to support its claims. In fact, considerable scientific data suggest that gay and lesbian personnel do not impair efficient military functioning (Herek et al., 1996; Kauth & Landis, 1994). Conduct is already regulated by existing codes of justice. However, extensive education and practical experience will be necessary to eradicate perceptions by heterosexual military personnel that their gay or lesbian comrades will view them as sexual objects and that homosexuality is emasculating to the military.

Several countries have policies that permit gay men and lesbians to serve in the military (or do not prohibit them from serving). These include Canada, Australia, Germany, France, Italy, Sweden, Denmark, Norway, the Netherlands, Spain, Portugal, Belgium, and Israel. However, actual practice often varies from policy; in Germany, for example, a member of the military who declares his or her homosexuality can be discharged. Other countries view same-sex behavior (but not sexual orientation) as sufficient grounds for discharge. Great Britain has a policy similar to that of the United States; it does not permit asking recruits about their sexual orientation but allows the military to discharge service personnel if they say that they are homosexual.

HETEROSEXISM AND HOMOPHOBIA

As the quotes at the beginning of this chapter reveal, a culture is a constructed reality. The dominant culture defines what is acceptable and what is vilified, what is considered natural and what is considered heinous. The dominant U.S. culture is largely heterosexual. "Conceptualizing human experience in strictly heterosexual terms and consequently ignoring, invalidating, or derogating homosexual behaviors and sexual orientation and lesbian, gay, and bisexual relationships" is referred to as **heterosexism** (Herek, Kimmel, Amaro, & Melton, 1991, p. 958). As a consequence of heterosexism, homosexuals are often stereotyped in a negative manner and are sometimes even viewed as dangerous to others.

Just as members of ethnic minorities are often stereotyped as "all the same," it is often assumed that all gays have the same characteristics and lifestyles. People refer to the "gay lifestyle" as if there is only one, and usually it is depicted negatively; for example, all gay men are assumed to bar-hop, use drugs, and have casual sex with multiple partners. And with respect to personal characteristics, of course, not all gay men are effeminate, and not all lesbians are masculine. In fact, some lesbians are ultrafeminine, the opposite of the stereotype. Most gay men and lesbians dislike the term *lifestyle* because it suggests that sexual orientation is an accessory, like a suit of clothes. If you were asked to describe the "heterosexual lifestyle," could you provide one single

HETEROSEXISM
Thinking of human experience in strictly heterosexual terms and consequently ignoring, invalidating, or derogating nonheterosexual behaviors, lifestyles, relationships, and sexual orientations.

IN YOUR own words

Bennett Barch
Northwestern University

Many times it is an insecurity in heterosexual males that causes them to be homophobic. I think it's very similar to racism.

description that fits all heterosexuals? In what way, if any, do gays and lesbians live differently from heterosexuals? Probably the one common thread is that gay men and lesbian women must contend with an oppressive social stigma. Gay people, like heterosexuals, vary widely in the expression of sexuality, depending on gender, racial or ethnic background, urban or rural setting, social class, religious beliefs, political views, education, occupation, personality, and other factors. There is no common "gay" way of life.

Heterosexism often takes the form of **homophobia**, or **homonegativism**—that is, an extreme discomfort, aversion, fear, anxiety, or anger toward gay people (Herek, 1984). Homophobia is evident when someone calls another a *faggot, sissy,* or *dyke;* views AIDS as a gay disease; discriminates against gay men and lesbians; or harasses or physically attacks gay people. Gay men are usually the targets of such physical assaults (Berrill, 1992). Gay men report higher frequencies of physical harassment and victimization by strangers than do lesbians, who are more likely to experience verbal harassment by their family members.

In his analysis of 24 studies representing eight U.S. cities, nine states, and six regional or national samples, Kevin Berrill (1992) found that 80% of adult gay men and lesbians had experienced verbal harassment. Furthermore, 44% of gay men and lesbians had been threatened with violence, 33% had been chased or followed, 25% had had objects thrown at them, 19% had had property vandalized, 17% had been physically assaulted, 13% had been spat on, and 9% had been assaulted with an object or weapon. Most gay adults (80%) expect to be targets of anti-gay violence in the future, and many attacks go unreported for fear of reprisal or police harassment or apathy. Data from 47 college campuses revealed similar findings: 40–98% of gay and lesbian students had been verbally harassed, and 15–26% had been physically assaulted (Berrill, 1992). Anti-gay violence has steadily increased in the United States since the mid-1980s, and it shows no sign of easing, even though violent crimes in general have decreased (Gallagher, 1996; National Gay & Lesbian Task Force, 1991).

Hate-motivated murders of gay men and lesbians are especially vicious and brutal (Berrill, 1992). One of the most highly publicized of such crimes occurred in Wyoming in 1998, when Matthew Shepard was abducted from a bar by two men, who beat, robbed, and tied him to a fence in freezing temperatures. He died 5 days after he was found. In addition to Shepard's murder, there was a similar crime in Alabama, where two men, aged 21 and 25, beat 39-year-old Billy Jack Gaither to death with an ax handle because he allegedly made a sexual advance toward one of them. Most perpetrators of anti-gay violence are young (in their 20s or younger) white men who act in pairs or groups (Berrill, 1992). Only 22% of anti-gay assaults involve a single attacker. Table 6.2

Fred Phelps, an anti-gay minister from Kansas, leads a protest against gays at the trial of those accused of Matthew Shepard's murder.

HOMOPHOBIA
An extreme discomfort, aversion, fear, anxiety, or anger toward gay people; also called *homonegativism.*

TABLE 6.2 Common Characteristics of People Who Are Intolerant of Gay Men and Lesbians

- Older
- Male
- Less well-educated
- Attend religious services frequently
- Conservative in religious beliefs (e.g., interpret the Bible literally)
- More likely to be Republican than Democrat or Independent
- Conservative in political beliefs
- Live in rural or Midwestern or Southern regions where anti-gay attitudes are common
- More likely to believe homosexuality is "freely chosen"
- Unlikely to have gay or lesbian family members or close friends
- Not sexually permissive
- Support traditional gender roles (especially traditional views of masculinity)
- More authoritarian

SOURCE: Herek, 1984, 2002; Kimmel, 2000

lists other characteristics commonly associated with (but not necessarily causing) gay and lesbian intolerance.

Henry Adams and his colleagues (Adams, Wright, & Lohr, 1996) conducted an interesting experiment that might help explain why some heterosexual men have strong negative reactions toward gay men. Adams asked 64 white heterosexual male college students to complete measures of homophobia and then to watch brief erotic videos of consensual adult heterosexual encounters, male homosexual activity, and lesbian activity. A penile plethysmograph (an instrument that records penile circumference) was used to assess participants' responses to the videos. While watching gay male erotic videos, 54% of strongly homophobic men showed definite erections, and 26% had moderate erectile responses. By comparison, only 24% of nonhomophobic men showed definite erections, and only 10% had moderate erections to the gay male erotic video. Self-reports of arousal were consistent with erection, except that homophobic men displayed more arousal than they reported while watching the gay male video. No differences were found between homophobic and nonhomophobic men in their erectile responses to heterosexual or lesbian erotic videos. Adams and his colleagues speculated that some homophobic men might be latent homosexuals who are unaware of or who deny their same-sex feelings. On the other hand, some homophobic men may simply be aroused by feelings of anxiety or threat associated with watching same-sex erotic activity.

Heterosexism is so pervasive and powerful that even many "out" gays and lesbians experience what many counselors and researchers call **internalized homophobia**, or "the internalization of society's antihomosexual sentiments by gay and lesbian people" (Huebner, Davis, Nemeroff, & Aiken, 2002, p. 327). Internalized homophobia affects gays, lesbians, and bisexuals in many ways. It can produce psychological conflicts ranging from insecurity about one's sexual identity to outright self-hatred. Internalized homophobia is also associated with HIV-related risky sexual behavior. Research has shown that gay men who experience a high degree of internalized homophobia are less likely to be aware of community-based HIV prevention services, to be comfortable

INTERNALIZED HOMOPHOBIA Psychological acceptance by a gay, lesbian, or bisexual person of the society's prevailing negative views of homosexuals, resulting in internal conflict.

reflect ON THIS

Analyzing Your Own Feelings and Attitudes

Whether you are gay or lesbian or heterosexual, homonegativism is a part of U.S. culture that influences your life. Are you aware of how anti-gay messages have shaped your thinking about yourself and others or how they affect your relationships with others? Consider your responses to the questions below. Even if you are (or think you might be) gay or lesbian, you should examine your responses to these questions, as even homosexuals can be homonegative in their thinking.

- Do you identify yourself as heterosexual, bisexual, gay, or lesbian?
- Refer back to the Kinsey Scale (Figure 6.1). Where would you place your erotic fantasies on this scale? Your romantic relationships? Do these scores differ? If so, what does that mean about you?
- Do you feel that you were you born with your current sexuality, or did you learn it? Explain your response.
- What experiences have you had that supported your sexual identity? That challenged it?
- Could you feel good about yourself even if your family and community did not accept you?
- Do you have any gay or bisexual friends?
- Would you go to a gay bar if people you knew were there?
- How would you feel if a same-sex friend told you that he or she found you attractive?
- What would you do if a same-sex friend kissed you on the cheek? On the lips?
- Would you tell anyone if you had an erotic dream about a person of the same sex whom you know?
- How would you feel if you found out that someone thought you were gay or bisexual?
- Do you ever find yourself consciously behaving in ways that are stereotypically heterosexual?
- What would happen if you refused to laugh at jokes about gays?
- If you are male, do you let people see you cry? If you are female, can you act assertive or "tough" without worrying that people will think you are a lesbian?
- How would you explain same-sex attraction to your young son or daughter?
- What would you do and how would you feel if your adolescent son or daughter said he or she was in love with someone of the same sex?
- If someone you respect confessed that he or she was gay, would this affect your opinion of the person?

Exploring your thoughts and feelings about sexuality can challenge many unexamined beliefs about how you want to live your life and promote greater self-confidence and freedom of expression. Following is a thought-provoking quiz for heterosexuals, intended to help them understand how it feels to be treated as homosexuals often are.

Heterosexuality Questionnaire

1. What do you think caused your heterosexuality?
2. When and how did you first decide you were a heterosexual?

6.6 on the web

Cultural bias against gays and lesbians can have far-reaching effects. Read the article entitled "The Effect of Bias on Lesbian Healthcare" at **www.ablongman.com/mcanulty2e.**

Describe how standards of health care for lesbians may be diminished by bias.

in group-structured HIV prevention classes, and to feel comfortable using a condom or asking a partner to use one (Huebner et al., 2002).

Many people have accepted the culture's prevailing beliefs and attitudes about same-sex desires and gay men and lesbians. You may find it interesting to analyze your feelings about homosexuality, as suggested in Reflect on This: Analyzing Your Own Feelings and Attitudes.

Fear that one's feelings will be misinterpreted or judged harshly can lead to intolerance of others or of one's own same-sex feelings—and intolerance and fear constrict emotions and expressiveness. In contrast, greater personal comfort and less concern about the perceptions of others contribute to increased intimacy with friends, family, and significant others. Everyone can benefit from a little perspective as well.

Accurate information about gay men and lesbians challenges commonly held stereotypes and replaces them with more positive and realistic images. Education about homosexuality in human sexuality courses, for example, has been found to increase tolerant attitudes among heterosexuals (Stevenson, 1988). Personal contact and positive interactions with gay men or lesbians under conditions of equal status and

3. Is it possible your heterosexuality stems from a neurotic fear of others of the same sex?
4. If you've never slept with a person of the same sex, how do you know you wouldn't prefer it?
5. Is it possible your heterosexuality is just a phase you may grow out of?
6. Isn't it possible that all you need is a good gay lover?
7. If heterosexuality is normal, why are a disproportionate number of mental patients heterosexual?
8. To whom have you disclosed your heterosexual tendencies? How did they react?
9. Why do heterosexuals place so much emphasis on sex? Why are you people so promiscuous?
10. Do heterosexuals hate and/or distrust others of their own sex? Is that what makes them heterosexual?
11. If you were to have children, would you want them to be heterosexual, knowing the problems they'd face?
12. Your heterosexuality doesn't offend me as long as you don't try to force it on me. Why do you people feel compelled to seduce others into your sexual orientation?
13. The great majority of child molesters are heterosexuals. Do you really consider it safe to expose your children to heterosexual teachers?
14. Why do you insist on being so obvious, and making a public spectacle of your heterosexuality? Can't you just be who you are and keep it quiet?
15. How can you ever hope to become a whole person if you limit yourself to a compulsive, exclusively heterosexual lifestyle and remain unwilling to explore and develop your homosexual potential?
16. Heterosexuals are noted for assigning themselves and each other to narrowly restricted, stereotyped sex roles. Why do you cling to such unhealthy role playing?
17. Even with all the societal support marriage receives, the divorce rate is spiraling. Why are there so few stable relationships among heterosexuals?
18. How could the human race survive if everyone were heterosexual like you, considering the menace of overpopulation?
19. There seem to be very few happy heterosexuals. Techniques have been developed that could help you change if you really wanted to. Have you considered trying aversion therapy?
20. Does heterosexual acting out necessarily make one a heterosexual?
21. Can't a person have loving friends of the opposite sex without being labeled a heterosexual?
22. Could you really trust a heterosexual therapist/counselor to be objective and unbiased? Don't you fear he or she might be inclined to influence you in the direction of his or her own preferences?
23. How can you enjoy a full, satisfying sexual experience or deep emotional rapport with a person of the opposite sex when the differences are so vast? How can a man understand what pleases a woman, or vice versa?

Attributed to Martin Rochlin, PhD, 1977

common goals also challenge homophobic beliefs (Herek, 1984). Cooperative, nonintimate interactions encourage homophobic people to view gay men and lesbians as being, for the most part, like them. Yet, tolerance does not mean acceptance. Many people are tolerant of gay men and lesbians, believing all the while that homosexuality is wrong.

HEALTHY DECISION MAKING

Despite the lack of acceptance by the mainstream culture, many gays and lesbians in the United States learn to cope well with being "different." However, accepting oneself as gay and gaining the acceptance of significant others can be a difficult and stressful process. Coming out to parents, other family members, and friends can be a great risk. Initially, significant others often react with anger and rejection to what amounts to the destruction of their image of the person who comes out to them. Parents may have a particularly difficult time, thinking that they caused their child to be gay

(Strommen, 1989) or that their child might be HIV-positive (Robinson, Walters, & Skeen, 1989). People who are moralistic and who value traditional gender roles are most likely to create an intolerant environment for gay family members and to have great difficulty accepting that a parent, child, or sibling is gay (Strommen, 1989). Even momentary rejection by people who claim to love the person "just as you are" can be very painful. The discomfort and internal conflict that some gays and lesbians experience while coming to terms with their identities might put them at risk for mental and physical health problems (Lock & Steiner, 1999).

If you are gay or bisexual, or think you might be, and are feeling conflicted about your identity, we encourage you to seek support. There are many resources such as gay and lesbian organizations and counseling services available today. Take advantage of them, and seek the support of those friends who are sure to be sensitive and caring. If you are hesitant to reach out to people in your community, consider seeking out support on the Internet. The Human Rights Campaign Foundation at **www.hrc.org** (click on "Coming Out") offers a wealth of information, including an extensive listing of political and religious organizations supporting gay, lesbian, bisexual, and transgendered people's rights. If you are not gay or lesbian, think about how your comments or actions might negatively affect someone who is. Sometimes even the most open-minded people make jokes or insensitive remarks about homosexuality. You might not be aware that a friend is being hurt. If you already have an accepting attitude about homosexuality, consider learning more about the experiences and perspective of a friend who is gay or bisexual; however, make sure the person is comfortable with your attempts to learn more so that you don't intrude on his or her privacy. Sometimes simply being a friend without making an issue of a person's sexual orientation is enough. And finally, remember that whether you "approve" of homosexuality or not, you can still choose to be respectful of others. There is nothing to be gained by harming others or causing pain.

summary

SEXUAL ORIENTATION: WHAT'S IN A NAME?

- Sexual orientation encompasses a person's sexual identity, sexual behavior, and erotic and romantic feelings for one or both sexes. In Western cultures, people typically identify themselves as heterosexual, homosexual, or bisexual.

SEXUAL IDENTITY FORMATION

- Little is known about heterosexual and bisexual identity formation in Western cultures, although existing evidence suggests that bisexuals view their sexual identity as fluid and unstable.
- Cross-cultural observations suggest that sexual identity and sexual expression are controlled by cultural scripts.

PREVALENCE OF HETEROSEXUALITY, HOMOSEXUALITY, AND BISEXUALITY

- The incidence of heterosexuality, homosexuality, and bisexuality is difficult to identify because of the difficulty in determining what behaviors, thoughts, and feelings qualify a person for any one of these categories.

DETERMINING SEXUAL ORIENTATION: NATURE VERSUS NURTURE

- Current data regarding sexual orientation suggest a biological influence on sexual orientation, which is shaped further by environmental events.
- Many interactive theories of sexual orientation attempt to account for the mixed data from biological and learning research and the variety of sexual identities and relationships observed across cultures.

SEXUAL COMMUNITIES

- Whether heterosexual, gay, or bisexual, every person lives in a community defined by sexual orientation. The dominant culture is controlled by heterosexuals, but gays, lesbians, and, to some extent, bisexuals have their own communities supported by businesses (e.g., bars and bookstores) that cater to them.

RELATIONSHIPS

- Heterosexuals, bisexuals, and gay men and lesbians vary somewhat in their kinds of sexual behavior and relationships. One of the primary differences between these groups in the United States is that gay people cannot marry and do not have protected civil rights. Heterosexual relationships are often structured by traditional gender roles, while same-sex relationships are more egalitarian.

THE LESBIAN AND GAY MOVEMENT

- The gay rights movement started in the United States in the early 1950s with the founding of two gay organizations, the Mattachine Society and the Daughters of Bilitis. However, the movement was not solidified until the Stonewall riot of 1969.
- Through the years, the movement has continued to grow despite resistance from political and religious conservatives.

HETEROSEXISM AND HOMOPHOBIA

- Cultural heterosexism and homophobia influence views of self, sexuality, same-sex feelings and friendships, and appropriate behavior. Most gay men and lesbians report experiencing anti-gay harassment and a few have experienced violent attacks.
- Some highly homophobic men respond sexually to homoerotic stimuli.
- In general, people who are intolerant of homosexuality are conservative, hold traditional gender roles, and have had little contact with gay people.

CHAPTER 7

Intimacy and Love

My definition of love would be someone who is your best friend, a person you could share anything with. I realized what love was when I had to spend a long time away from my girlfriend and when we dated other people. I realized then that we were meant to be together.

(A 23-year-old male college student)

Love is an extremely intense feeling of intimacy and caring for another person. It's unconditional. Love leads one to commit oneself physically and mentally to another individual, not because of any obligation but because of a genuine desire to be with that person.

(A 26-year-old female college student)

Love is the stage of fulfillment in a relationship. In one sudden instance, it will overcome you. It took a while to gain the trust and admiration of my girlfriend. When I felt relaxed and emotionally connected with her, I let myself go and felt free to give and receive love.

(A 22-year-old male college student)

Love is the stage of fulfillment.

Love is a deep, uncontrollable feeling that attracts people to each other and creates an attachment. It can be between friends, lovers, or family members. I don't think it was one particular thing that told me I was in love. It was more of a combination of wanting to be with this person all of the time, being very excited and happy with the person, and thinking that I would sacrifice anything for him.

(A 22-year-old female college student)

Imagine that you have been dating someone for several months. You get along well and usually have lots of fun together. You know that you really like this person, and you wonder, "Could this be love?" If it is love, how would you know? What is love, and how do you know when you have found it? Perhaps more important, once you have found love, how do you nurture it and make it last?

INTIMACY

Human beings have a fundamental need to connect with people, in order to feel cared for and valued. This need for a sense of connection leads most people to try to establish a meaningful intimate relationship—that is, to find the "right person." But what is intimacy? **Intimacy** refers to a state of closeness and familiarity. According to Brehm, Miller, Perlman, and Campbell (2002), intimate relationships differ from more superficial ones in several ways. Intimate partners readily share personal information, including such private matters as sexual likes and dislikes. Intimate partners also care about each other

INTIMACY
A state of closeness and familiarity with another person that is marked by mutual trust.

deeply. A core feature of intimacy is mutual trust, which allows intimate partners to be open with each other. Partners who have achieved intimacy show self-awareness, genuine interest and trust in one another, and little defensiveness. Additionally, their lives are interconnected in most respects, as each partner needs and influences the other. Intimate partners' lives are so interconnected that they often develop a shared identity in addition to their individual identities and refer to themselves as "us." In fact, the point in a relationship when partners begin to refer to themselves as a couple is an important transition that signals a significant degree of commitment (Agnew, Van Lange, Rusbult, & Langston, 1998). Having formed a bond, the two individuals are identified by themselves, by relatives, and by common friends as a couple. By definition, intimate relationships are characterized by some degree of commitment. Intimate partners expect that the relationship will last, and they invest time and energy to preserve it. For many people, the ultimate goal in an intimate relationship is long-term commitment.

Not all intimate relationships, however, have all of these qualities. Some intimate relationships, for example, may lack mutual trust. Psychological intimacy requires sharing one's inner experiences with another person. According to Levine (1998), there are three prerequisites to intimate sharing:

1. *The capacity to know one's own thoughts and feelings.* Because of socialization or parental models, some people—men in particular—may be out of touch with their feelings. For these people, self-disclosure is especially challenging.
2. *The willingness to share feelings.* Being in touch with one's true feelings is no assurance of being prepared to share them. A person may fear being rejected by a partner because of thoughts and feelings. Intimate sharing requires taking the risk of being rejected because of one's innermost thoughts and experiences.
3. *The interpersonal skills necessary for intimate sharing.* Once a person attains the self-awareness and motivation for intimate sharing, she or he must communicate effectively with a partner. The communication need not be eloquent or articulate, only sincere and direct. With persistence, the message eventually gets through.

Intimate sharing is a reciprocal process during which two people alternate between self-disclosure and listening. With true intimacy, listening goes beyond simply hearing and includes nonjudgmental acceptance. An intimate relationship offers security—the feeling of being important and needed—and acceptance. Intimacy also gives people a sense of belonging and offsets feelings of loneliness and depression. People who are involved in intimate relationships are more psychologically and physically healthy than

Adults seek an intimate relationship in order to share their dreams, goals, and interests with another person.

HEALTH Matters

Are Relationships Good for Your Health?

Ample research gives a clear answer to the question of whether relationships are good for one's health—a resounding yes. Intimate relationships and friendships are beneficial to both mental and physical health. Loneliness, on the other hand, has been shown to be detrimental to one's health. **Social support,** help and support received from one's social network, helps people cope with stressful events (Miller, Smerglia, Gaudet, & Kitson, 1998; Thoits, 1995). In its various forms, social support serves as a buffer, or protective factor, against the harmful effects of stress. People who have high levels of social support are more likely to survive a heart attack than those who lack such support (Farmer et al., 1996). People who have high levels of social support also have lower levels of depression and fewer medical problems (Thoits, 1995; Unger et al., 1998). Social support helps patients in advanced stages of cancer cope with their illness (Godding, McAnulty, Wittrock, Britt, & Khansur, 1995).

The effectiveness of social support depends on the type of support being provided and on its timing. Support from family members, for example, is most helpful in coping with the death of a spouse when offered immediately after the loss. As time passes, though, support from friends and peers becomes more important (Stylianos & Vachon, 1993). Social support may involve both practical support and emotional support. Practical support can be help with household chores and transportation, for example. Emotional support involves listening, offering advice, and comforting. A person's needs depend on the type of stressful event she or he is facing. Widows, for example, are more likely to need practical support, whereas divorced women need more emotional support (Miller et al., 1998).

Relationships help people cope with stressful experiences by providing a sense of belonging in addition to emotional support. Relationships provide a sense of security and the motivation to take care of oneself. Relationships help people overcome feelings of loneliness. High levels of intimacy and companionship in particular are most helpful (Stack, 1998).

Naturally, relationships can only provide these benefits if they are good relationships. Conflicted or abusive relationships only add to a person's problems, thereby exacerbating his or her stressful experiences. So, *good* relationships are indeed good for your physical and mental health.

those who are not (Berkman, 1995; Palosaari & Aroo, 1995), a topic discussed in Health Matters: Are Relationships Good for Your Health?

The need for intimacy seems to be universal. But what about the characteristics people seek in intimate partners? There are vast differences among cultures regarding which physical and personality traits are defined as desirable. In virtually all cultures, intelligence, a pleasant personality, and kindness are rated as highly desirable characteristics of an intimate partner (see Table 7.1 on page 198) (Buss, 1985, 1994). The importance of other characteristics (virginity, for example) varies tremendously across cultures, indicating that socialization plays a role in shaping at least some of people's preferences about sexual partners. In general, perceived similarities in attitudes, beliefs, and behaviors are important in interpersonal attraction. Finally, people tend to be attracted to people who are attracted to them.

As you might expect, intimacy is closely related to satisfaction with one's relationship. Married couples who report high levels of intimacy also report greater marital satisfaction (Greeff & Malherbe, 2001). Couples who enjoy high intimacy also tend to share personal information, express positive feelings, feel understood by their partners, and rate their interactions as pleasant (Lippert & Prager, 2001). In general, commitment and intimacy are closely related. Married couples report higher intimacy than cohabiting couples, who, in turn, tend to rate their level of intimacy as higher than dating couples do (Moore, McCabe, & Brink, 2001).

SOCIAL SUPPORT
Help and support received from family and friends.

TABLE 7.1 Characteristics Sought in Marriage Partners

Characteristics	RANK Women	RANK Men	Characteristics	RANK Women	RANK Men
Kindness/understanding	1	1	Good earning capacity	8	11
Intelligence	2	2	College graduate	9	9
Exciting personality	3	4	Desire for children	10	8
Good health	4	5	Good heredity	11	10
Adaptability	5	6	Good housekeeper	12	12
Physical attractiveness	6	3	Religious orientation	13	13
Creativity	7	7			

SOURCE: Adapted from Buss, 1985

THEORIES OF LOVE

Few topics have captured as much attention from poets, songwriters, philosophers, and authors as love. There are literally thousands of books, songs, and poems about it. Why is love such a hot topic? There are at least two reasons: First, humans are fascinated by love. Few, if any, people can truthfully say that they are not interested in finding love, or more specifically, a loving relationship. In fact, we tend to view a person who denies any interest in or desire for love as maladjusted. We assume that all people have an intrinsic need for a loving relationship. Indeed, research suggests that the need for love may have a biological basis just like other fundamental and essential needs such as the need for food, water, and sleep. Second, so much has been written about love because the definitive answers are elusive. There are multitudes of suggestions for finding love and explanations of what love is—but no consensus. This lack of consensus is due in part to the subjectivity and diversity of the definitions of love (Brehm et al., 2002). "Being in love" can take on different meanings for different individuals. For the same person, the meaning of love can change over time. As you will see, this is usually the case in a long-term loving relationship. Furthermore, we generally recognize different forms, or types, of love. The love we have for our parents is different from the love we feel for an intimate partner or spouse. And we have all said at one time or another we love an article of clothing, a song, or a certain food, but clearly this is not the same kind of love we have for people! Yet, this usage of the word *love* conveys one aspect of what we mean by "being in love." All uses of the word *love* denote positive feelings and desirability.

Love is a topic that has fascinated poets, songwriters, and novelists for centuries.

The scientific study of romantic love is still a fairly new endeavor. It has been hampered by the subjectivity and variability in the meanings of *love*. The only common thread in the various definitions of romantic love is that it involves wanting to be intimate with another person, a specific motivation that is accompanied by a variety of behaviors, thoughts, and feelings (Brehm et al., 2002). This chapter will focus on scientific findings about love and intimate relationships. Keep in mind as you read that most theories of love and the related research are based on a Western perspective. Men and women from different cultures may have different attitudes toward love (Hatfield & Rapson, 1996). Passionate love may very well be a near-universal ideal, but there are cultural differences in the extent to which people are willing to settle for less. In traditional Chinese culture, for example, duty and obligations to one's parents are much more important in choosing a spouse than are feelings of love and compatibility

(Pimentel, 2000). Thus, in different cultures, men and women have different expectations of love and intimate relationships.

Triangular Theory of Love

The best-known theory explaining love is the *triangular theory of love* developed by Yale psychologist Robert Sternberg (1986). Sternberg suggested that love is composed of three related yet distinct components. In any love relationship, one or both partners may feel different degrees of any of these three components. The relative strength of each component of love determines the kind of love a person experiences. When all three components are strong, the ultimate, or ideal, type of love is achieved (Sternberg, 1986).

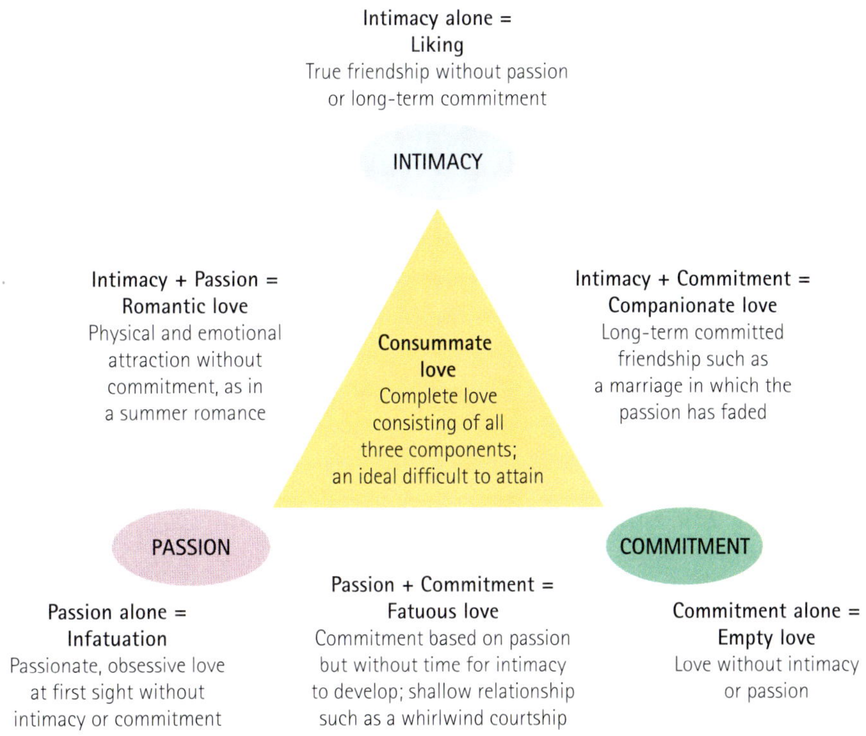

Figure 7.1 The Triangular Theory of Love

The first component of love in Sternberg's theory is intimacy. **Intimacy** corresponds to the emotional feeling of love. When we feel intimacy, we feel emotionally close to another person and desire to demonstrate our feelings to the loved one. In intimate relationships, we want to share our thoughts, our feelings, our time, and our possessions. The second component of love is passion. **Passion** provides a motivational dimension for love. We are driven by passion to be with the loved one or to think incessantly about the person, and this drive is coupled with emotional intensity and arousal. As you can imagine, it is passion that propels the sexual energy felt in a love relationship. The third component of Sternberg's theory of love is commitment. **Commitment** is a more conscious and cognitive dimension of love. When we choose to remain in a relationship, we have formed a commitment, which sometimes happens even if the other dimensions of love are absent. Whereas intimacy involves emotions and passion entails the sexual and motivational aspect of love, commitment is the decision to be in a relationship with another person and to work through problems that may arise, with the intention of sharing a life with that person.

These three components of love interact to produce unique types of love (see Figure 7.1). According to Sternberg (1986), any loving relationship can be characterized by the degree to which each of the three components is present. For example, friendship involves intimacy without passion or commitment. We feel close to a friend who shares many of our attitudes and interests, but there is no passion or any conscious decision to maintain a long-term relationship in most friendships. When we feel infatuated with another person, to the point that we almost can't think about anything else, we are experiencing passion in the absence of intimacy and commitment. And couples who are committed without feeling any intimacy or passion are experiencing what Sternberg refers to as **empty love.** This type of love may characterize a marriage in which two people stay together solely for their children or because of their religious beliefs. Outside of the decision to stay together, such couples do not have much of a loving relationship.

Just as individual components represent different types of love, pairs of components do as well. When we experience both intimacy and passion, we feel **romantic love.** This is a highly energized type of love, the kind that typically characterizes a developing relationship. Intimacy in combination with commitment results in **companionate love**, which characterizes very strong friendships and many marriages in which the passion has leveled off. Passion in combination with commitment is **fatuous love.** This type of love can be

INTIMACY
In Sternberg's triangular theory of love, the emotional component of love, which is often manifested through emotional sharing and feelings of closeness.

PASSION
The motivational aspect of love in Sternberg's triangular theory, providing emotional intensity and sexual arousal.

COMMITMENT
In Sternberg's triangular theory, the component of love that involves a conscious decision to remain in a love relationship.

EMPTY LOVE
A type of relationship in which both intimacy and passion have waned and only the commitment to stay together remains.

ROMANTIC LOVE
A love relationship in which intimacy and passion are strong but there is no significant commitment.

COMPANIONATE LOVE
In Sternberg's theory, a type of love that incorporates intimacy and commitment; it is characteristic of strong friendships.

FATUOUS LOVE
Love characterized by passionate feelings combined with commitment but little intimacy.

reflect ON THIS

Who Do You Love, and How Much?

Robert Sternberg's (1986) triangular theory of love is intuitively appealing to most people. People can understand and relate to his three distinct components: passion, intimacy, and commitment. So that you can better understand the triangular theory of love, complete the *Triangular Love Scale.* As you complete the scale, respond using the name of the person you love. If you are not currently in a love relationship, think about a past one—or try to imagine a future love relationship. If you are in a relationship, you may want to ask your partner to complete the scale so that you can compare his or her views with yours.

After scoring your answers using the key at the end of this feature, refer to the listing of types of love in the text and check which type of love most closely matches the one you described. Is it fatuous love? Romantic love? Perhaps you are fortunate enough to have attained what Sternberg describes as the ideal love—consummate love.

In evaluating your love style, keep in mind that the triangular theory is just one way of defining and measuring love—that's why it is called a "theory." Much research is still needed to evaluate the triangular theory of love. Despite its intuitive appeal, critics have argued that the theory does not explain the intricacies of love (Regan, 2000).

Sternberg's Triangular Love Scale

Which are the strongest components of your love relationship? Intimacy? Passion? Commitment? Perhaps two components are equally strong? All three?

To complete the following scale, fill in the blank spaces with the name of one person you love or care about deeply. Then rate your agreement with each of the items by using a 9-point scale in which 1 = "I disagree completely," 5 = "I agree moderately," and 9 = "I agree completely." Use points in between to indicate intermediate degrees of agreement. Then consult the scoring key.

Intimacy Component

____ 1. I am actively supportive of __________'s well-being.
____ 2. I have a warm relationship with __________.
____ 3. I am able to count on __________ in times of need.
____ 4. __________ is able to count on me in times of need.
____ 5. I am willing to share myself and my possessions with __________.
____ 6. I receive considerable emotional support from __________.
____ 7. I give considerable emotional support to __________.
____ 8. I communicate well with __________.
____ 9. I value __________ greatly in my life.
____ 10. I feel close to __________.
____ 11. I have a comfortable relationship with __________.
____ 12. I feel that I really understand __________.
____ 13. I feel that __________ really understands me.
____ 14. I feel that I can really trust __________.
____ 15. I share deeply personal information about myself with __________.

Passion Component

____ 16. Just seeing __________ excites me.
____ 17. I find myself thinking about __________ frequently during the day.
____ 18. My relationship with __________ is very romantic.
____ 19. I find __________ to be very personally attractive.
____ 20. I idealize __________.
____ 21. I cannot imagine another person making me as happy as __________ does.
____ 22. I would rather be with __________ than anyone else.
____ 23. There is nothing more important to me than my relationship with __________.

seen in relationships that form quickly, based on the passion the couple feels, and that often end once the passion wanes. In fatuous love, emotions are strong and passionate, but the relationship is often short-lived because the two people don't really know each other.

Sternberg also describes a type of love he refers to as consummate love. **Consummate love** represents an ultimate standard, the ideal type of love in which all three components—intimacy, passion, and commitment—are present. Although a couple may have phases of consummate love, maintaining this level of love requires considerable effort by both partners in the relationship. Although the Western cultural ideal holds that this type of love is readily available, the fact is that many couples do not experience consummate love. People who expect to feel consummate love but do not may

CONSUMMATE LOVE
In Sternberg's triangular theory, the ideal form of love that incorporates all three components: intimacy, passion, and commitment.

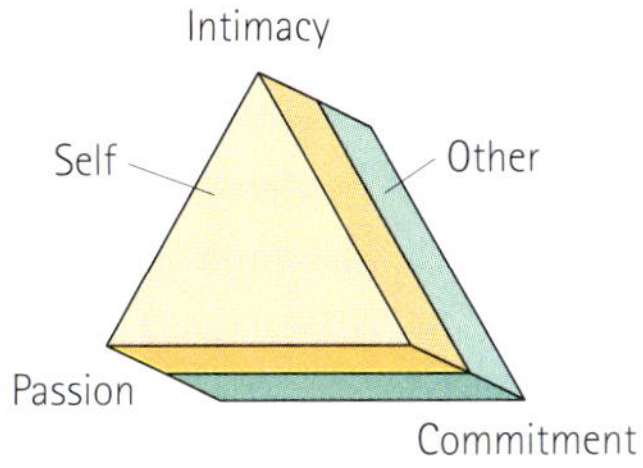

Perfectly matched involvements

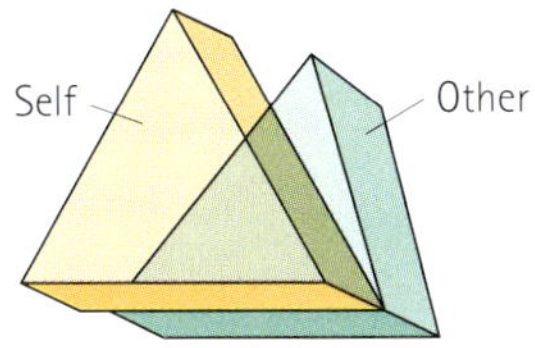

Closely matched involvements

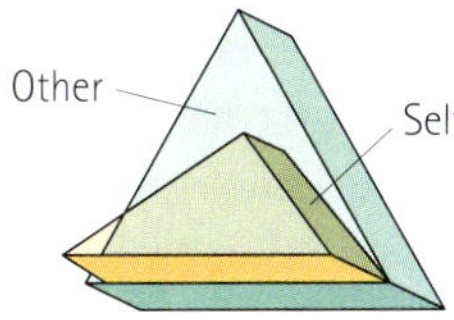

Mismatched involvements

____ 24. I especially like physical contact with __________.

____ 25. There is something almost "magical" about my relationship with __________.

____ 26. I adore __________.

____ 27. I cannot imagine life without __________.

____ 28. My relationship with __________ is passionate.

____ 29. When I see romantic movies and read romantic books, I think of __________.

____ 30. I fantasize about __________.

Commitment Component

____ 31. I know that I care about __________.

____ 32. I am committed to maintaining my relationship with __________.

____ 33. Because of my commitment to __________, I would not let other people come between us.

____ 34. I have confidence in the stability of my relationship with __________.

____ 35. I could not let anything get in the way of my commitment to __________.

____ 36. I expect my love for __________ to last for the rest of my life.

____ 37. I will always feel a strong responsibility for __________.

____ 38. I view my commitment to __________ as a solid one.

____ 39. I cannot imagine ending my relationship with __________.

____ 40. I am certain of my love for __________.

____ 41. I view my relationship with __________ as permanent.

____ 42. I view my relationship with __________ as a good decision.

____ 43. I feel a sense of responsibility toward __________.

____ 44. I plan to continue my relationship with __________.

____ 45. Even when __________ is hard to deal with, I remain committed to our relationship.

SOURCE: Sternberg, 1988. Reprinted by permission of Basic Books, Inc., New York.

Scoring Key for Sternberg's Triangular Love Scale First, add your scores for the items on each of the three components—Intimacy, Passion, and Commitment—and divide each total by 15. This will yield an average rating for each subscale. An average rating of 5 on a particular subscale indicates a moderate level of the component represented by the subscale. A higher rating indicates a greater level, a lower rating indicates a lower level. Examining your ratings on these components will give you an idea of the degree to which you perceive your love relationship to be characterized by these three components of love. For example, you might find that passion is stronger than commitment, a pattern that is common in the early stages of an intense romantic relationship. You might find it interesting to complete the questionnaire a few months or perhaps a year or so from now to see how your feelings about your relationship change over time.

feel that they have been cheated in a love relationship and may leave the relationship to seek a higher level of love in another. Attaining consummate love requires a strong commitment by both partners to nurture the relationship.

Despite the popularity of the triangular theory of love, there have been few studies to establish its validity. The theory does appear to conform to the intuitive view of love that is prevalent in Western culture (Aron & Westbay, 1996; Barnes & Sternberg, 1997). The Triangular Love Scale included in Reflect on This: Who Do You Love, and How Much? has been used to assess love based on this theory. One recent study found that married couples' scores on the three components were related to their relationship satisfaction (Lemieux & Hale, 2000).

Colors of Love

Psychologist John Alan Lee (1973, 1988) described six unique types of love, which are similar to the types described by Sternberg. Lee's first three types, the *primary love types,* are like primary colors in that they are pure and separate. Passionate love characterized by strong physical arousal, which drives one person toward another, is called **eros.** (You can readily see why Lee named this type of love for the Greek god of sexual love, whose name is the root of the word *erotic.*) This love is appetitive (insatiable) and is coupled with strong physical attraction. The second primary love type described by Lee is **ludus,** which is characterized by somewhat superficial game-playing devoid of commitment. Someone experiencing ludus enjoys being "in love" and the pursuit associated with falling in love. Love relationships based on ludus last only as long as the game of love continues. The third primary type of love is **storge** (pronounced STORE-gay), most similar to Sternberg's notion of intimacy. In storge, the critical dimension of the love bond is close friendship.

did YOU know?

According to one study, 44% of people in dating relationships described their romantic partner as their best friend (Hendrick & Hendrick, 1993).

Lee's theory proposes three secondary love types: pragma, mania, and agape. These secondary types are compounds of the primary types. **Pragma,** as the name suggests, is very practical. A love relationship involving pragma is based on a very practical and logical assessment of the advantages of being in the relationship. The ability to get along and feel emotionally connected with another person (the storge component) is important, as is the enjoyment of being in love (the ludus component). The person who feels pragma love has determined that being in that relationship is better, or more advantageous, than not being in the relationship. **Mania,** or manic love, is a possessive type of love. As a compound of eros and ludus, mania is characterized by a yearning for the feelings of love that can only be satisfied by the other person. When the manic lovers are not with their partners, they tend to be obsessed with thoughts of them. The final secondary type of love is **agape,** a form of selfless love characteristic of the person who puts the needs of his or her partner ahead of his or her own. As a combination of eros and storge, agape is expressed through selfless attention to the needs and wishes of the other person. According to Lee, this love type is an ideal that is rarely attained (Regan, 2000).

Relationships in which partners feel the same types of love are more rewarding (Hendrick, Hendrick & Adler, 1988; Morrow, Clark, & Brock, 1995). When partners differ in the type of love they feel, difficulties are likely to arise, which can compromise the relationship (Bailey, Hendrick, & Hendrick, 1987). Studies show that men and women may differ in the types of love they experience in a relationship: Men are more likely to feel ludus; women are more likely to experience pragma, mania, or storge (Hendrick & Hendrick, 1995). However, men and women are very similar in their personal definitions of love. The majority of people in U.S. culture define love as involving such qualities as trust, honesty, respect, loyalty, caring, acceptance, and support. Conversely, feelings of insecurity, dependency, and fear are incompatible with most people's definitions of love (Fehr, 1988). These core features of love are accepted by most Americans, regardless of age or sexual orientation (Regan, Kogan & Whitlock, 1998; Rousar, 1990).

Two-Component Theory of Love

Another theory of love is the *two-component theory of love* developed by Berscheid and Walster (Berscheid & Walster, 1974; Walster, 1971). The two components in this model are companionate love and passionate love. For Berscheid and Walster, **companionate love** characterizes a relationship built on trust and security. Their idea of companionate love is similar to Sternberg's companionate love (which entails intimacy and commitment) and to the storge type of love in Lee's model. **Passionate love** characterizes a relationship that is built on strong emotion and physical arousal. Passionate love provides the feeling of being "in love."

The two-component theory of love is based on Schachter's (1964) two-factor theory of emotion. According to the two-component theory of love, companionate love is based on

EROS
In Lee's colors of love theory, a primary type of love based on strong attraction and sexual arousal.

LUDUS
One of Lee's primary types of love that involves superficial game-playing.

STORGE
One of Lee's primary types of love, which consists of bonding and strong friendship.

PRAGMA
In Lee's theory, a secondary type of love that is based on logical and practical advantages; it combines ludus and storge.

MANIA
In Lee's theory, a secondary type of love that combines ludus and eros; it is an intense but possessive and obsessional type of love.

AGAPE
In Lee's theory, a selfless and ideal type of love that is rarely achieved; it combines eros and storge.

COMPANIONATE LOVE
Berscheid and Walster's term for a love relationship built on trust and security.

PASSIONATE LOVE
Berscheid and Walster's term for a love relationship built on intense emotions and strong sexual arousal.

mutual liking and equitable exchange in the relationship, whereas passionate love is based on the attribution—or misattribution—of the source of arousal. Passionate love is felt when one is aroused, for any of several reasons, while in the company of another person and that arousal is attributed to the presence of the other person. As an example, a couple on a date may experience physical arousal in response to a scene in a movie or a physical activity such as dancing. The excitement felt in response to the movie or the dancing (the circumstances) is then attributed to the other person. Referred to as **excitement transfer** (Zillman, 1978, 1984), this misattribution of arousal may lead to strong feelings of passionate love. This theory may explain why people become attracted to people they meet in bars or nightclubs (they are stimulated by socializing, drinking, music, and the like, as well as by someone they meet, but attribute all the arousal to the person) and why they often form strong feelings for people who assist them in times of fear or crisis. This effect is particularly strong when one is already attracted to the other person and thus experiences the combined effect of circumstantial arousal and excitement in response to the person's physical attractiveness.

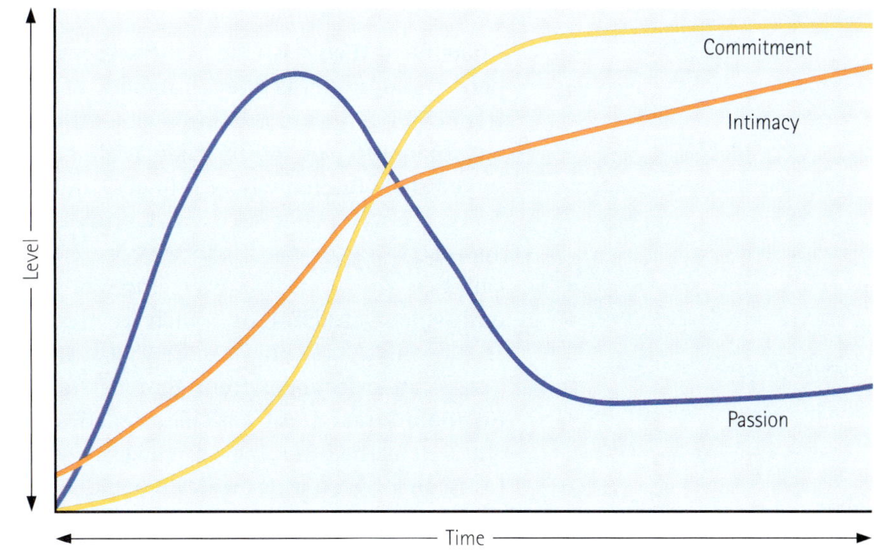

Figure 7.2 Expected Changes over Time in the Three Components of Love

"Till Death Do Us Part": Lasting Love

Most couples who enter a long-term relationship assume that they will live together "happily ever after." Love relationships, however, change. The passion that often characterizes a new relationship wanes over time. When partners in a relationship evaluate the current state of the relationship relative to the passion that existed in the beginning, they may feel frustrated and disappointed. Sternberg (1986, 1998) elaborated on his triangular theory of love by describing the changes that typically occur in a love relationship over time, as illustrated in Figure 7.2.

Love relationships often begin with a moderate level of intimacy, which increases rapidly as the relationship builds. After reaching a relatively high level, the intimacy returns to a moderate level. This decrease occurs as the novelty of the relationship begins to dissipate and as the partners begin to divide their attention between the relationship and other activities. Passion typically builds very rapidly in a love relationship and peaks at a higher level than intimacy, but it drops off sooner and more dramatically (Sprecher & Regan, 1998). The initial surge of passion typically lasts 18 months to 3 years, corresponding to the "honeymoon phase" (Fisher, 1992). The subsequent decline in passion can present a challenge to a relationship if passion is the sole criterion used to evaluate its quality. In fact, a decline in passion is part of the natural course of love relationships. This decline in passion may not be inevitable, however. Couples who regularly share novel experiences may enjoy a renewal of their passionate feelings (Aron, Norman, & Aron, 2001). As a rule, though, commitment is the only dimension of the triangular model that continues to build over time, eventually becoming the strongest dimension of a successful long-term relationship. For many couples, however, the relationship ends before commitment becomes strong. For others, the commitment builds but the other dimensions of love wane until the partners are left with empty love. In such unfortunate cases, the partners must wonder what happened to the relationship. What factors led to their original intimacy and passion? How did they become attracted to each other in the first place?

7.1 on the web

With so many different views of love, you may wonder how reliable any of them are. Go to the Love and Relationships link at **www.ablongman.com/mcanulty2e** and review the theories of love. You can follow the links to take the Love Test.

What is the test measuring? Which theory of love is it based on? Is the text useful?

EXCITEMENT TRANSFER
The misattributing of emotional arousal from nonromantic factors to the presence of another person.

Attachment Theory of Love

Attachment theory is based on the premise that individuals' early developmental experiences profoundly affect how they approach all intimate relationships. Borrowing from child psychiatrist John Bowlby's findings (1969), researchers reasoned that early attachment to parental figures may shape all close relationships in adults. Bowlby observed that children whose primary caregivers provided consistent and effective nurturance developed a **secure attachment**. These youngsters displayed a confident approach to the world, and they were trusting in their interpersonal interactions. Children whose caregivers were unresponsive and unpredictable developed an **anxious-ambivalent attachment**, which led them to be overly cautious and clingy in their relationships. As youngsters, they were visibly uneasy when separated from their caregivers, an insecure pattern that persisted into their adult relationships. Finally, **avoidant attachment** was characteristic of children who were actively rejected. These children learned that their caretakers were only reluctantly responsive to their needs. Consequently, children with an avoidant attachment were angry and resentful, and their relationships were permeated with distrust.

The relevance of early attachment style to adult relationships was uncovered by Hazan and Shaver (1987) in a landmark study. Their work, and other studies (Mickelson, Kessler, & Shaver, 1997), revealed that most adults, approximately 60%, describe themselves as securely attached. These adults are comfortable with intimacy, do not fear abandonment, and appreciate the give-and-take of close relationships. Another 25% of adults rate their attachment as avoidant; they acknowledge problems with closeness and trust and complain that their partners generally need more intimacy than they are willing to provide. The remaining adults, nearly 15%, can be categorized as having anxious-ambivalent attachment, based on their insecurities, clinginess, and excessive neediness. These individuals desperately crave intimacy but fear it will not last. These research findings marked the beginning of a productive line of research on attachment and love (see Cassidy & Shaver, 1999).

SECURE ATTACHMENT
Bowlby's terminology for a form of emotional bond that leads a person to approach the world confidently and to be trusting in interpersonal interactions.

ANXIOUS-AMBIVALENT ATTACHMENT
According to Bowlby, a form of emotional bond that leads a person to be insecure and needy in interpersonal relationships.

AVOIDANT ATTACHMENT
According to Bowlby, a form of emotional bond that leads a person to have difficulty forming intimate relationships.

PREOCCUPIED STYLE
Bartholomew's terminology for an attachment style that leads a person to be insecure and needy in interpersonal relationships; equivalent to Bowlby's anxious-ambivalent attachment.

FEARFUL STYLE
Bartholomew's term for an attachment style that leads a person to have difficulty forming intimate relationships; equivalent to Bowlby's avoidant attachment.

DISMISSING STYLE
Bartholomew's term for the attachment style shown by those who are indifferent to and uninterested in close relationships.

Subsequent research has expanded these findings. Attachment style, for example, was shown to influence not only people's approach to relationships, but also the manner in which they coped with negative emotions (Fuendeling, 1998). Under stress, securely attached people tend to remain calm, and they effectively enlist social support when needed. Avoidant people, on the other hand, tend to angrily withdraw from other people under these circumstances. Those with the anxious-ambivalent attachment style become overwhelmed with apprehension (Simpson, Rholes, & Nelligan, 1992).

Bartholomew (1990) argued that something was missing from the original formulation of attachment styles. Her reformulation retains the secure style but renames the anxious-ambivalent style, calling it the **preoccupied style.** Her **fearful style** is essentially the equivalent of Bowlby's avoidant style, characterizing people who avoid intimacy owing to their fear of rejection. Bartholomew's new category, the **dismissing style**, applies to individuals who appear indifferent to and uninterested in close relationships. In such people, a sense of self-sufficiency disguises their rejection of the demands of intimate relationships. The relationship between comfort with intimacy and fear of abandonment for each of Bartholomew's attachment styles is illustrated in Figure 7.3. Research confirms that people with a secure style tend to have higher self-esteem and to rate their overall adjustment higher than do people with the other styles (Diehl, Elnick, Bourbeau, & Labouvie-Vief, 1998). Couples who share secure attachment styles enjoy higher marital satisfaction (Feeney, 2002). Conversely, people who fear abandonment (those with fearful or preoccupied attachment styles) are prone to jealousy, and they tend to be distrustful and uncompromising (Feeney, 1999). Insecure attachment in either partner can be detrimental to a relationship (Jones & Cunningham, 1996).

It is important to note that these attachment styles are not absolute. It is possible to display a secure style in some relationships, such as with one's parents, while feeling insecure with a lover (Ross & Spinner, 2001). Furthermore, one's attachment style could vary from one romantic partner to the next (Cook, 2000). There is also some evidence of cross-cultural differences in attachment styles. One study, for example, re-

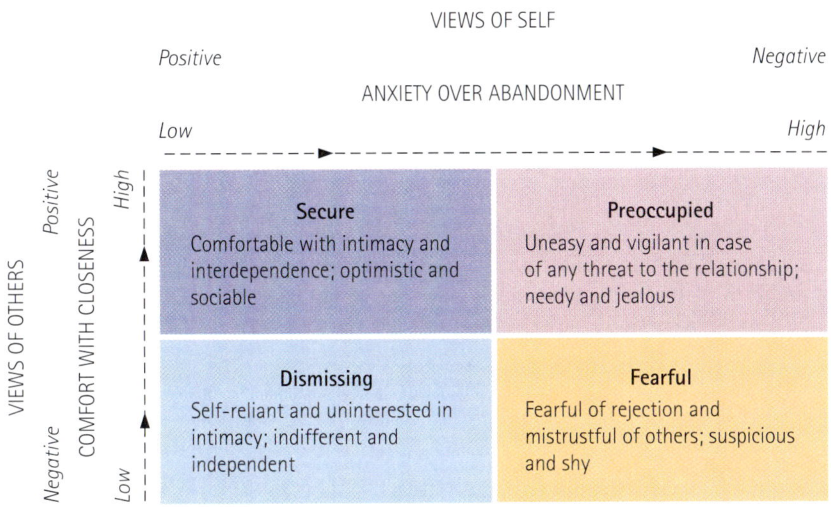

Figure 7.3 A Model of Adult Attachment (Adapted from Bartholomew, 1990, and Brennan et al., 1998)

vealed that Korean college students were more likely than white American students to exhibit a preoccupied attachment style (You & Malley, 2000).

Attraction Theory: Why We Love Who We Love

Research reveals that the drive to "belong" is a fundamental human drive (Baumeister & Leary, 1995). As social creatures, humans want to feel included in interpersonal relationships, to connect with other people. In fact, our very self-esteem is affected by the extent to which we feel attached to others and socially integrated (Leary & Downs, 1995). This drive to belong extends to our need to be involved in a loving relationship. But where do we find the right person for a loving relationship? It appears that most of us don't look very far to find that truly "right" person.

Proximity

One of the critical factors in determining who people fall in love with is **proximity**, or nearness: People are simply most likely to fall in love with someone they see frequently (Byrne, 1971). For instance, if you are a college student, you are likely to fall in love with someone you see regularly at social events on campus or in classes. Nonstudents tend to fall in love with people they meet at church or on the job. In a classic study, Festinger, Schachter, and Black (1950) found that students in a particular dormitory were far more likely to form close friendships with people living on the same floor than with people living on other floors. In another classic study, Bosard (1931) surveyed marriages in the Philadelphia area and found that a great proportion of the people getting married lived within one or two blocks of each other when they first met. As one researcher concluded, "cherished notions about romantic love notwithstanding, the chances are about 50–50 that the 'one and only' lives within walking distance" (Eckland, 1982, p. 16). Simply put, we tend to be attracted to people with whom we have regular contact, people who are available to us because of their proximity.

Looking At . . .

. . . Thinking About

Do opposites attract? Do couples who play together, stay together? Can novelty and adventure strengthen a couple's bond?

PROXIMITY
A determinant of human attraction—people are attracted to others with whom they interact on a regular basis.

CLOSE UP ON culture

Love and Attraction around the World

What do people really desire in a partner in a committed relationship? To answer this question, David Buss (1989, 1994) surveyed over 10,000 respondents in 37 cultures, spanning six continents and five islands, about what they considered desirable characteristics in a partner. These cultures were extremely diverse, ranging from those in which polygyny (one man having multiple wives) is common (such as Zambia and Nigeria) to such Western cultures as Canada and Spain. Some cultures openly condoned unmarried cohabitation (Sweden and Denmark, for example), whereas others were intolerant of such arrangements (Greece and Bulgaria, for example). Despite the cultural diversity, Buss discovered a remarkable consistency in characteristics desired in a partner. For men and women around the world, being in love is the single most important consideration in partner selection.

Love is truly universal, and each culture has its own terminology to refer to it. In a survey of 168 cultures, Jankowiak and Fischer (1992) found that nearly 90% had a concept of romantic love. In a survey of men and women from Japan, Russia, and the United States, Sprecher and colleagues (1994) found that over 60% of Russian men and 73% of Russian women, 53% of U.S. men and 63% of U.S. women, and 41% of Japanese men and 63% of Japanese women reported being in love. Mutual love, although key, is not enough. People want more from a relationship.

For both men and women in most cultures, dependability and emotional stability are essential characteristics of a partner. People in most cultures need to feel that their partners will be dependable and able to cope effectively with the stressors of life. Kindness and sincerity in a partner are also important to women and men around the world. Finally, women from diverse cultures rate their partners' financial prospects and social status as important. According to Buss, a sense of security is important to women.

Age is another consideration. In all 37 cultures that Buss surveyed, women tended to prefer that their male partner be older—approximately 3½ years older, on average. This, however, is not universal. In one small Chinese village, 18-year-old women sometimes married males who were 14 or 15, an exceptional finding, according to Buss. Men, conversely, have a universal preference for younger partners, although the preferred age differences vary across cultures. Men from Finland and Sweden prefer wives who are 1 or 2 years younger. In Zambia and Nigeria, a bride is preferably 6½ to 7½ years younger than her groom. Among the Tiwi of Northern Australia, powerful and influential men commonly find partners who are 20 to 30 years younger. Men around the world also rate physical beauty as important in partner selection. However, standards of beauty are highly culture-specific. Men of the Azande tribe of Eastern Sudan favor long, sagging breasts in their female partners, whereas men in many other cultures prefer large, firm breasts. Preferences in physical build

Similarity

Although proximity is a critical determinant of who we fall in love with, regular contact does not by itself lead to a love relationship. A second important determinant is **similarity.** We tend to have stronger feelings for people who share our attitudes, values, and interests. In fact, the more we have in common with another person, the more likely we are to develop strong feelings for that individual (Byrne, 1971; Sanders, 1982). Furthermore, there is no conclusive evidence that the popular notion that opposites attract is true. People actually tend to *avoid* interactions with people whom they view as opposite to them, and, therefore, they are unlikely to form intimate or loving relationships with them. The idea that opposites attract may stem from the observation that the similarities that initially attract two people to one another blind them to the host of differences that also exist. It is only after the novelty of a relationship begins to wane that the couple recognizes the differences that were present from the beginning. The fact that the two people often choose to stay together despite their differences might lead them to assume erroneously that the differences were responsible for the original attraction.

SIMILARITY
A determinant of human attraction—people like others whose personal attitudes, backgrounds, and interests are similar to their own.

RECIPROCAL LIKING
A determinant of human attraction—people like others who like them in return.

Reciprocity

After coming in contact with someone and finding that we share similar interests and attitudes, we are more likely to fall in love with that person if she or he reciprocates our feelings. The notion of **reciprocal liking** implies that people are likely to develop strong feelings for someone who shares these feelings, in part because doing so pays also vary. To the aboriginal tribesmen of Australia, a plump partner is most attractive; in contrast, thinness is generally preferred in female partners in Western cultures like the United States.

Preferences for sexual experience in one's marriage partner are also culture dependent. In some countries (for example, Iran, China, India, and Indonesia), virginity in a bride is highly valued or even expected by men. In cultures that are more tolerant of nonmarital sex and that advocate gender equity, previous sexual experience is accepted and sometimes expected. In France, Norway, Sweden, and the Netherlands, men rate virginity as irrelevant in their choice of a marriage partner.

In most cultures, love is viewed as a prerequisite for marriage. In some less developed Eastern cultures, however, people may be willing to compromise. In poorer Eastern cultures, it seems that "passionate love remains a bit of a luxury" (Hatfield & Rapson, 1996, p. 31). In such cultures, partner selection is more heavily influenced by practical concerns, duty, and family expectations than by personal feelings.

In summary, cross-cultural studies of love and attraction reveal that there are some partner attributes that are almost universally desired. Mutual love tops the list for most people in virtually all cultures. Emotional stability and dependability are also high on the list of desirable partner characteristics. Cultural scripts, however, influence standards of physical beauty. Most people want a partner who is physically attractive, although cultures shape people's views of beauty. These cross-cultural studies illustrate a recurring theme in human sexuality, which is that both biological and environmental forces interact to determine human sexual behavior.

off. Knowing the other person likes us offers us a sense of belonging and thus bolsters our self-esteem (Baumeister & Leary, 1995). However, if we develop positive feelings for another person and find that the person doesn't share our feelings, we tend to alter our initial positive feelings in a way that will serve to protect our self-esteem—by changing our positive feelings of liking to more neutral feelings. We may find ourselves settling for just being friends. Alternatively, if we initially form a neutral opinion of a person and then find that he or she has strong positive feelings for us, we are again inclined to alter our initial view, this time from neutral to positive.

Attractiveness

One other dimension of initial attraction often overrides the three just described. Although "love at first sight" may be a cliché, it is true that people are more likely to be attracted to people whom they find physically attractive. Perusing the personal ads in any newspaper illustrates the importance of physical attraction: Personal appearance is almost invariably mentioned—eye or hair color, height, weight, or an overall description of attractiveness. Although this emphasis may seem rather superficial, physical appearance is a factor that influences initial attraction in virtually all cultures, whether nonindustrial or modern (Buss, 1994). Factors that are considered important in love and attraction in various cultures are explored in Close Up on Culture: Love and Attraction around the World.

Fortunately, a natural selection process appears to govern the association between physical attractiveness and attraction. People involved in relationships are generally similar in their level of physical attractiveness (Feingold, 1988). The **matching hypothesis**

MATCHING HYPOTHESIS
The hypothesis that people tend to seek out partners whose physical, emotional, and social characteristics closely match their own.

Although we may find movie stars or models to be the prototypes of beauty, if we don't perceive ourselves as having the attributes to attract such a person, we adjust our ambitions.

(Berscheid, Dion, Walster, & Walster, 1971) suggests that people consider their own personal characteristics, including physical attractiveness and such factors as physical fitness and wealth, and seek romantic partners with similar characteristics (Buss, 1985). The matching of levels of attractiveness occurs in marriages, dating relationships, and even in friendships. Although movie stars or models may be the prototypes of beauty, if people don't perceive themselves as having the attributes to attract such a person, they adjust their ambitions.

While physical attractiveness is important when choosing a partner, it is not rated as equally important by men and women. Buss and Barnes (1986) found that women tend to judge the desirability of prospective partners by considering their financial resources and athletic ability in addition to their physical appearance. Men, on the other hand, tend to consider beauty and youth as most important (Buss, 1994). Although we may try to downplay the role of physical attractiveness in romantic relationships and to consider such concerns as superficial or frivolous, the fact is that physical attractiveness is important to most people. However, although women and men differ somewhat in their rankings of the desirable characteristics in a partner, they are remarkably similar in what they seek in relationships. In virtually all cultures, women and men want partners whom they find attractive, loyal, trustworthy, respectful, caring, devoted, and understanding (Buss, 1994; Hatfield & Rapson, 1996).

Some researchers have been critical of the evolutionary perspective on attraction just described. Borgia (1989) observed that the vast majority of participants for surveys on attraction were drawn from Western cultures, which may bias conclusions about the alleged universality of desirable traits in one's partner. Virtually every survey participant, even those from Eastern cultures, had been exposed to Western influences including media. As you saw in Chapter 1, globalization may shape individuals' preferences in a romantic partner. Dion and Dion (2001), for example, concluded that cross-cultural studies of attraction reveal more cultural differences than differences between the genders. In any culture, the extent to which women value financial resources in a partner may depend on their own economic status (Gowaty, 2001). A person whose very survival is in jeopardy would indeed value, and perhaps require, a partner with material resources.

did YOU know?

Although fewer than 4% of U.S. college students said that they would marry a person they did not love if he or she had all of the other desired qualities, nearly 50% of students from India and Pakistan stated that they would marry such a person as did nearly 20% of Thai college students (Hatfield & Rapson, 1996).

Gender Differences in Love Attitudes

According to a popular stereotype, men and women differ in their attitudes toward love, and research confirms this stereotype. For instance, male college students are more likely to view love in romantic terms, whereas college-aged women tend to view love in practical terms (Peplau & Gordon, 1983). College-aged males often believe that love will last forever. Many college women, however, are more realistic and understand that the emotional intensity of love will not last forever. College women are also more likely to view love as being based in part on factors such as financial security. This finding is consistent with research by Hendrick and Hendrick (1995), which found (to use Lee's terminology) that males tend to be more ludus-oriented in their feelings of love, while women tend to be more motivated by pragma and storge.

Men often tend to be less emotionally expressive than women, and many women prefer more self-disclosure from their male partners than they receive (Byers & Demmons, 1999; Peplau & Gordon, 1983). It has been demonstrated that the amount of self-disclosure in a heterosexual love relationship generally starts out being equal for both partners, suggesting that men and women reach a compromise in sharing feelings and personal information. As the relationship evolves, however, the amount of self-disclosure by men is more likely to decrease over time, (Antill & Cotton, 1987), which is often a contributing factor in communication problems later in the relationship (Markman, 1981; Markman & Floyd, 1980). Many men show a tendency to avoid discussing their frustrations and perceived shortcomings (Hacker, 1981; Peplau & Gordon, 1983).

did YOU know?

When touched briefly on the hand or arm by a stranger, women usually respond positively, but men generally don't. Perhaps because of these responses, men tend to touch women more than women touch men (Brehm et al., 2000).

For many women in committed relationships, love is heavily influenced by the amount and quality of communication they have with their partner, the extent to which chores and responsibilities are shared, and the amount of respect and appreciation they receive from their partner (Moranis & Tan, 1980; Patterson, 1974). Men, as a group, are more likely to define love by the degree to which they feel needed by their spouse and the extent to which they feel that they are being supported in their activities, such as work and recreation (Hatfield & Rapson, 1993). Consistent with one popular stereotype, men are also more likely than women to define love in terms of the sexual satisfaction they experience in the relationship (Fisher & Heesacker, 1995; McCabe, 1999).

Although there are some gender differences in attitudes toward love, remember that men and women are also very similar in their views of love and romantic relationships. In fact, men and women generally have the same basic needs and desires, although they sometimes differ in how they rank the relative importance of these. For men and women alike, the ingredients for a successful and rewarding relationship are essentially the same (Regan, 2000; Sprecher, Metts, Burleson, Hatfield, & Thompson, 1995). Intimacy, communication, and commitment are essential in love relationships, regardless of one's gender (Byers & Demmons, 1999; McCabe, 1999).

LOVE RELATIONSHIPS

After an initial attraction has been acknowledged and has led to a relationship, what characterizes the relationship that develops into a committed love relationship, in contrast to those that don't? In other words, what factors predict the success of a love relationship?

Love Schemas

Why are some people looking for love, ever so desperately, while others seem content to be alone or resigned to it? The question of such individual differences with respect to love is the chief concern of researchers who study love schemas. Schemas are basic beliefs or cognitive structures. **Love schemas** are the different views and expectations that people have for themselves and their partners in love relationships.

According to Hatfield and Rapson (1996), people's love schemas are determined by their level of comfort with closeness and independence and by the degree of their desire for a love relationship. These researchers describe those individuals who are relatively uninterested in romantic relationships as either (1) *casual,* meaning only interested in a problem-free and, therefore, low-maintenance relationship or (2) *uninterested,* meaning not interested in any type of romantic relationship. And individuals who are interested in a love relationship fall into one of four groups: (3) *secure,* or self-confident and comfortable with both closeness and independence, (4) *clingy,* meaning desiring closeness but having problems being independent, (5) *skittish,* or uncomfortable with too much closeness but comfortable with independence, and (6) *fickle,* or uneasy with both closeness and independence yet wanting a love relationship.

LOVE SCHEMAS
People's different views and expectations of themselves and their romantic partners.

IN YOUR own words

Laura Sell
Northwestern University

Unlike most things out there, love is not something you can learn or understand through books: There is no test for it, there is no empirical data or proof that it exists. How do you know when you're in love? You just feel it. There is no other way to describe it except to say you just know.

A number of studies of Hatfield and Rapson's schemas show that people categorized as secure tend to be well-adjusted, self-confident, and socially skilled. They generally are more successful in love relationships than people in the other groups. Not only are love schemas related to individuals' interest in relationships, they are also predictive of how people respond to breakups. Choo, Levine, and Hatfield (1996) found that people who are classified as secure, skittish, and uninterested feel more joy and relief after the dissolution of their romantic relationships than those with other kinds of love schemas. Those who are uninterested are less likely to feel any guilt over the end of a love relationship. People whose schemas are clingy, on the other hand, are more likely to feel angry, anxious, and sad after a breakup, and they are more likely to blame themselves for the relationship failure. The skittish and clingy are the most likely to use alcohol or drugs after a breakup to "drown their sorrows," and the secure are the least likely to do so.

These individual differences in love schemas are largely determined by early childhood experiences and, therefore, tend to be enduring patterns. There is some evidence, however, that love schemas can change over time as a result of actual experiences with love (Baldwin & Fehr, 1995).

Stages of Love

Many romantic relationships go through five distinct stages (Levinger, 1980), the first being *initial attraction*. As you have learned, initial attraction is influenced by such factors as proximity, similarity, reciprocal liking, and physical attractiveness. After two people become mutually attracted, the relationship may evolve through the stages of *buildup* and *continuation/consolidation*. Unsuccessful relationships typically go through a stage of *deterioration* prior to *ending*. Naturally, not every relationship goes through all of these stages, and certain features determine whether a couple will leave one stage and enter another.

In the buildup stage of a relationship, the two people are getting to know each other better. Over time, the initial excitement and novelty of the relationship begin to wane, and each partner's evaluation of the relationship is more rational and less emotional. Self-disclosure increases as partners feel more comfortable sharing private thoughts and feelings. As the relationship progresses, they discuss a broader range of topics in greater detail (Altman & Taylor, 1973). In addition, individual expectations for the relationship become clearer, and each partner begins to consider how well the other person will meet those expectations. Importantly, because the relationship is still very new, there is a tendency to overlook the negative characteristics and accentuate the positive, a pattern that is reflected in the cliché "love is blind."

Relationships that have the greatest likelihood of evolving into committed ones are those based on equity (Sprecher, 1986, 1988). As long as it appears to each partner that the benefits of remaining in the relationship outweigh, or are at least equivalent to, the benefits of leaving the relationship, the relationship will last. If, however, one or both of the partners begins to view the cost of being in the relationship as outweighing the benefits, the probability that the relationship will end increases substantially. Overall, dating and married couples who feel that their relationships are equitable tend to report more commitment and more satisfaction (Sprecher, 1988; Utne, Hatfield, Traupmann, & Greenberger, 1984). Of course, the cost/benefit considerations are different for each person and in each couple. Nonetheless, perceptions of equity play a critical role in determining whether a relationship progresses to the next stage.

In the continuation/consolidation stage of a relationship, the early excitement has diminished. At this point, the quality of the relationship is based more on both implicit and explicit agreements concerning the roles that each partner fulfills. The passionate feelings in the relationship have become more periodic than continuous, and both partners are more involved in individual activities than they were during the buildup stage. This is generally the nature of a committed relationship that has lasted for some time. However, in relationships that lack commitment, deterioration occurs.

If one of the partners begins to view the costs of the relationship as outweighing the benefits, the relationship commonly begins to deteriorate (Levinger, 1976). Deterioration occurs when one or both of the partners begin to consider life without the relationship as possible or even desirable. In this stage of a relationship, the partners are most vulnerable to developing a romantic interest in another person. Having an alternative intimate partner makes the prospect of leaving a deteriorating relationship less costly and, therefore, more acceptable. As the available alternatives to the relationship start to appear more positive, the rate of deterioration increases. Eventually one or both partners may conclude that life would be more rewarding if the relationship were to end so that other alternatives could be pursued. Thus, the relationship may enter the final stage—ending. Other factors certainly come into play as well. If the couple shares considerable financial investments, if there are young children involved, or if there are strong social inhibitions such as family and religious constraints, some people decide that the cost of leaving the union is too great and they opt to stay in what Sternberg refers to as an empty love relationship.

7.2 on the web

Ending a relationship can be quite painful. The University of New York at Buffalo sponsors a site through its counseling center offering information to college students. Visit **www.ablongman.com/mcanulty2e** and find the link to the SUNY Buffalo site.

What are common reactions to breakups? Which of these seem negative? What steps help people recover from the loss?

CONFLICT IN LOVE RELATIONSHIPS

Though some conflict is inevitable—and may even be crucial to the success of a relationship, as you'll read later in the chapter—too much conflict, of course, is destructive, and certain ways of dealing with conflict are harmful to a relationship.

Warning Signs: The Four Horsemen

In his book *Why Marriages Succeed or Fail* (1994), John Gottman identified four destructive ways of handling relationship conflict, which he dubbed the "Four Horsemen of the Apocalypse." These four horsemen are often critical warning signs of a troubled relationship. They are, in order of harmfulness, criticism, contempt, defensiveness, and stonewalling. Each horseman serves as a harbinger of the next, with the final horseman often rendering the final, fatal blow to the relationship. Basing their observations and conclusions on videotaped interactions between hundreds of couples, Gottman and his colleagues have been able to accurately predict which couples were heading for "marital meltdown" and divorce (Gottman & Silver, 1999).

Criticism

Criticism is different from complaining. Complaining is healthy for a relationship, because it provides a way of expressing anger and frustration and of identifying issues that need to be addressed and resolved. The problem is that in many relationships, instead of complaining, the partners criticize each other. Criticism involves "attacking someone's personality or character—rather than a specific behavior—usually with blame." (Gottman, 1994, p. 73). One way to differentiate between a complaint and a criticism is by listening to the message being articulated. When complaining, a person uses "I" statements, such as "I feel frustrated when I have to do your chores and mine also." Criticisms, on the other hand, are usually offered in the form of "you" statements. For instance, the statement "You never do any chores around the house" is likely to be taken as a personal attack and to put the recipient on the defensive, thereby making him or her unwilling to address the complaint—however justified it may be.

Contempt

Contempt is similar to criticism except that it goes further—it involves intentionally insulting the other person. Criticism may be little more than failing to see where responsibility for a problem lies or using a poor choice of words. Contempt is backed up by negative attitudes toward one's partner, which motivate personal attacks. Contempt involves an intention to cause emotional pain. Whether openly or in a subtle manner, contemptuous remarks convey the idea that the partner is inept, foolish, or disgusting. Contempt may be expressed verbally, in comments such as "You are a slob," or through actions, such as consistently and intentionally coming home later than expected without notifying one's partner. Contempt may take the form of name-calling, hostile humor, or sarcasm (Gottman & Silver, 1999). It may be expressed non-verbally through sneering, rolling one's eyes, or ignoring (the "silent treatment").

Without question, contempt erodes a relationship, masking all of its positive features. Partners who feel contempt rarely compliment or admire each other. Contempt fuels defensiveness in the recipient and does nothing to remedy the problems in the relationship. In fact, it creates new problems, such as resentment and anger.

Defensiveness

Once criticism and contempt appear on the scene, it is often only a matter of time before defensiveness follows. Defensiveness is a common response to feeling personally attacked or victimized and, thus, often a response to criticism. In such cases, the defensive partner feels obliged to put up a defense rather than attempting to resolve the problem. Defensiveness can take several forms, such as denying responsibility for the behavior or event in question, making excuses, "cross-complaining" (retaliating with an accusation, such as "I may be a slob but you're a nag"), or reflecting the complaint back onto the other person. None of these defensive reactions resolve the original conflict; rather, they typically lead to an escalation in negativity. Defensiveness elicits defensiveness, causing a cycle of conflict.

Stonewalling

Stonewalling occurs when one partner essentially decides that the situation seems hopeless and therefore there is no need for a response of any type. The stonewaller simply puts up a "stone wall" in response to criticism and refuses to engage in interaction. He or she may have concluded that the defensive strategies used in the past were ineffective, and that the partner is utterly unreasonable and unlikely to change. The stonewaller's message is "there's nothing that I can do or say to make you happy, so I might as well say nothing at all." Stonewalling communicates disapproval, distancing, and even smugness. Although most people may occasionally stonewall during an intense emotional exchange, it is a danger signal when it becomes a regular or habitual response in such situations. Stonewalling is often a reaction to feeling "flooded" or "shell-shocked" in response to overwhelming negativity from one's partner. A person who feels consistently flooded will gradually disengage and withdraw emotionally (Gottman & Silver, 1999).

According to Gottman (1994), a relationship is in trouble when the first horseman—criticism—arrives, and the relationship is in critical condition by the time the fourth horseman—stonewalling—appears. In subsequent research, Gottman and his colleagues identified a fifth horseman—belligerence (Gottman, Coan, Carrere, & Swanson, 1998). Belligerence entails a provoking attitude that is intended to challenge a partner's power and authority. Think of belligerence as a confrontational, "in your face" reaction to conflict (for example, "So what if I go drinking with my friends, what are you going to do about it?"). Not only do all five of these ways of handling conflict perpetuate tension and arguments, but more importantly, they interfere with communication. They create a cycle of conflict and negativity, resulting in increasing conflict and diminishing positive exchanges. Eventually, one or both partners may begin to question whether their investment in the relationship is paying off. Alternatives to the relationship may appear more and more appealing.

Jealousy

In his poem *Paradise Lost,* English poet John Milton referred to jealousy as the "injured lover's hell." The emotion jealousy is responsible for much heartache and conflict in love relationships. Jealousy involves feelings of fear coupled with anger (Berscheid, 1983; Sharpsteen, 1991). In the face of jealous emotions, lovers react with hurt and resentment, sadness and sorrow, anger and rage. What is the origin of this "green-eyed monster"?

Jealousy is a leading cause of conflict in an intimate relationship. Jealousy generally signals that one partner perceives a threat to the relationship because of an actual or imagined rival.

One of the reasons we enter into and remain in relationships is that they enhance our feelings about ourselves; that is, they bolster our sense of self-esteem. In many ways, we come to count on our partner to validate us and thus enhance our self-image. A love relationship is seriously threatened when one partner perceives an alternative—a new partner—as desirable. In other words, a relationship becomes unstable when one partner concludes that someone other than the current partner will do a better job of making him or her feel good about himself or herself. Jealousy may be the response of the other partner, who realizes that the relationship is in jeopardy and who feels threatened by the prospect of losing it (Boekhout, Hendrick, & Hendrick, 1999). The perceived threat may be real or imagined, past or present (White & Mullen, 1989).

Some people are more prone to jealousy than others. Individuals with low self-esteem may be especially likely to feel jealous. People who struggle with jealousy typically view themselves quite harshly and, as a result, are chronically insecure in their romantic relationships (White, 1981a, 1981b). The fact is, the more one needs another person to validate one's self-esteem, the greater will be one's fear that that person may find a better alternative (Berscheid & Fei, 1977). Constantly questioning a partner's loyalty takes a toll on feelings of intimacy. Partners who do not feel trusted and who are falsely accused of disloyalty may begin to question their investment in the relationship. As they feel more and more burdened by their partners' suspicions, they may begin to consider alternatives to the current relationship. Ironically, if the relationship does fail, the jealous partner's suspicions and fears will appear to have been confirmed. Jealousy can set up a self-fulfilling prophecy.

did YOU know?

Partner abuse and violence are serious problems in the United States. Each year, over 1 million women require medical attention for injuries inflicted by a partner.

A different perspective was offered by David Buss (2000), who argued that sexual jealousy serves the paradoxical purpose of increasing the likelihood that a committed relationship will survive. Recall that Chapter 1 discussed the basic premise of evolutionary psychology: Humans have an innate drive to have healthy offspring in order to pass on their genes. According to evolutionary psychologists, women want partners who will provide the stability and security necessary to raise offspring to adulthood, thus ensuring the passing of genes to the next generation. Jealousy in women, according to the theory, arises when there is a threat to their partner's commitment to the relationship (Allgeier & Wiederman, 1994). Women, that is, fear the potential loss of their mate's attention and resources (Daly & Wilson, 1983; Symons, 1987), and jealousy arises when there is competition for limited resources. Men, on the other hand, are more concerned about threats to paternity. Men want to be sure that their partner's offspring are actually their own, so that they do not waste their resources raising a competing male's offspring (Allgeier & Wiederman, 1994). Accordingly, men's jealousy is more likely to be aroused by sexual infidelity, whereas women's jealousy is triggered by the potential loss of the relationship. Several studies support these hypotheses (Buss et al., 1999). For example, Buss, Larsen, Westen, and Semmelroth (1992) found that male college students were more upset by imagining their partner having sex with

did YOU know?

According to one survey, 79% of lesbians, 75% of gay men, 65% of heterosexual women, and 58% of heterosexual men reported having had a sexual partner cheat on them (Harris, 2002).

7.3 on the web

Do men and women react differently to infidelity? Visit **www.ablongman.com/mcanulty2e** and read the article from the American Psychological Society to learn more about gender differences in feelings of jealousy. The article also explores the difference between emotional and sexual infidelity.

Do you think there is a difference between the two? Why or why not?

another male than by thinking about her falling in love with someone else. The opposite was true of female college students, who were more distressed by the prospect of their partner falling in love with a rival than by thoughts of his sexual infidelity.

More recent research, however, casts some doubt on these findings. Harris (2002) found no differences between the sexes when heterosexual and homosexual men and women were asked about their reactions to partner infidelity. Regardless of sexual orientation, both men and women were more distressed by a partner's emotional infidelity, although any form of infidelity was bothersome. This study was unique in that it asked participants about their reactions to actual partner infidelity rather than their responses to hypothetical infidelity. It seems that what people *imagine* they would do is different from what they actually *do* in reaction to a partner's infidelity: Approximately two-thirds of heterosexuals ended the relationship after learning of a partner's indiscretion (Harris, 2002). Furthermore, contradicting the predictions by evolutionary psychologists, women (94%) were more likely than men (43%) to end a relationship with an unfaithful partner.

Whether or not jealousy has an evolutionary basis, it signals a perceived threat in a committed relationship. Jealousy invariably causes anguish, bitterness, and conflict. Consequently, jealousy is a signal of potential danger, one that must be addressed directly and openly if the relationship is to survive and grow.

Neglect

Another common relationship problem is neglect. When two people settle into a committed relationship, it is easy for each to begin taking the other for granted. Someone who feels taken for granted feels unappreciated and as though her or his contributions to the relationship are not valued. Typically, early in a relationship when one partner does a favor (say, picking up the other person's dry cleaning), he or she receives profuse thanks, which has the effect of reinforcing the person's willingness to repeat the favor. As time passes, perhaps the recipient comes to expect the favor. Instead of being a gesture that signals caring, picking up the dry cleaning becomes just another chore to be performed. The net result is that one member of the couple starts feeling taken for granted, and this breeds resentment that can exacerbate existing problems or create new ones.

Another common source of neglect in a relationship comes from the universal limitations on time and resources created by work and children. During early adulthood, people tend to devote a great deal of attention to establishing a career. For some people, a relationship interferes with career plans. Those in established relationships may feel a conflict between the needs of their partner and the demands of their career. In the early stages of a relationship, the partner may take precedence; but once a couple has settled into a routine, the career may start becoming more prominent. Danger occurs when the job becomes more important than the relationship. In these cases, people may feel as if they are competing with their partners' careers. This competition for time and attention may be even worse for couples who have children—their time may be stretched to a critical limit. When partners reach the limits of time, energy, and emotional resources, they turn to each other for help and validation. If one person has little or no support or assistance to give, the quality of the relationship may deteriorate. Furthermore, children require a great deal of time and attention, and the time required to meet a child's needs diminishes the amount of time available to work on the relationship. Issues that would previously have been discussed and resolved may go unattended, fostering feelings of frustration and discouragement that can slowly erode the friendship and intimacy of the relationship.

Although the number of dual-career families continues to grow, Western cultural scripts dictate that women still have the primary responsibility for parenting and for managing the household chores. Thus, many women are busy meeting others' needs and are more vulnerable to feeling as though they are being neglected. Successful couples are able to balance the time spent dealing with occupational demands and the demands of parenting—but such balance does not arise by chance. A firm commitment by both partners to devote time and effort to nurturing the relationship is essential, especially when both face competing demands.

RESOLVING RELATIONSHIP CONFLICT

Fortunately, there are ways to break the cycle of negativity that may become entrenched in a relationship and to restore the feelings of love and respect. There are three strategies for handling conflict in a relationship so that the relationship lasts and remains mutually satisfying:

- Staying calm
- Using effective and nondefensive communication
- Practicing validation

Remaining Calm during Conflict

Learning to remain calm during interactions involving conflict is essential. First, remaining calm reduces the tendency to become defensive and to stonewall. Second, remaining calm may have a calming effect on one's partner, thereby reducing the chance that the argument will escalate. One of the most important reasons for remaining calm is to disrupt the cycle of negativity. Finally, remaining calm increases the likelihood of addressing the problem rationally and effectively.

Remaining calm during a disagreement requires having an awareness of the cues that signal that one's emotions are activated. A person must learn to recognize and to monitor such warning signs as increased heart rate and muscle tension. In fact, Gottman (1994) recommends that partners periodically check their pulse rates during difficult discussions. Few people can judge their actual heart rate accurately, but periodic checks of one's pulse rate can be helpful in determining if one is becoming overly emotional during a disagreement. Effective relaxation methods include calling a brief time-out to "cool down," lying down and concentrating on relaxing major muscle groups, and breathing deeply and slowly.

Another important component of calming down is learning to change your thinking during an emotional discussion, or "rewriting your inner script" (Gottman, 1994). Many thoughts people have during conflicts actually exacerbate the situation rather than leading to a solution to the problem. Such thoughts as "I'll show her," "I don't have to take this," and "He never thinks of my feelings" may seem legitimate and natural at the time. These thoughts, however, only intensify the conflict and perpetuate the cycle of negativity by leading to criticism, defensiveness, contempt, and stonewalling. Rewriting your inner script involves focusing on more constructive and calming thoughts, such as "No need to take this personally," "Although we are arguing now, we do love each other," and "Calm down and take some deep breaths." These calming thoughts will not come automatically during an emotional exchange. The upsetting thoughts people have during arguments generally are automatic and overlearned (repeatedly reinforced)—although a person may later regret acting on them. Therefore, successfully rewriting one's inner script requires an awareness of these thoughts, a commitment to changing them, practice (to be discussed in more detail later), and calmness.

Successful conflict resolution requires both partners to stay calm, to communicate nondefensively, and to validate each other's feelings.

Communicating Effectively

More has been written about communication than about any other relationship skill (McKay, Fanning, & Paleg, 1994). This extensive focus on communication arises out of observations by counselors, researchers, and couples that communication is a common problem area for many relationships (Cahn, 1990). The problem is generally *not* that people have deficiencies in communication skills, as was traditionally believed, but rather that people have a tendency not to use these skills during negative interchanges (Gottman, 1994). After all, most people who complain about being unable to communicate with their partners during arguments typically manage to communicate effectively with them in happier times, and with coworkers, friends, and even strangers. The key to success is learning to use communication skills during arguments, when we often seem less concerned with hearing our partners' complaints than with expressing our own dissatisfaction or hurt feelings (Nichols, 1995).

Effective communication has the impact you mean it to have, and what you intended to say is what the other person hears (Brehm et al., 2002). Therefore, good communication requires clear, nondefensive speaking and active, nondefensive listening. Nondefensive communication is helpful in countering the cycle of negativity that can be so harmful in relationships (Gottman & Silver, 1999).

Most of us think of communication as a process in which two people alternate speaking and listening. This is indeed part of communication, but there is another component that is just as important, if not more so: nonverbal communication. The fact is that much of what we say to our partners is unspoken and often subtle. Intonation, degree of eye contact, posture, and facial expressions all convey important messages. Gottman, Markman, and Notarius (1977), for example, found that the emotion displayed in conversations rather than the content of the discussion is what distinguishes happy from unhappy couples. Partners in troubled relationships are also more likely to interrupt each other (Margolin & Wampold, 1981).

did YOU know?

Women smile more than men do, even when they are not happy (Hecht & LaFrance, 1998).

Effective Speaking

Learning to speak with one's partner without eliciting defensiveness is an essential skill for long-term relationship satisfaction. By speaking nondefensively, you increase the likelihood that your partner will hear and understand your concerns, and, ultimately, you maximize the possibility of resolving the problem.

During difficult phases in relationships, there is a common tendency to focus on the problems while ignoring the positive aspects of the relationship. At such times, communication may be limited to airing complaints and criticisms. That is, virtually all expressed messages convey negativity. One of the most important tactics for nondefensive speaking is adopting a positive framework that allows praise and admiration to be reintroduced into the interaction. It is essential to remember that problems in the relationship and the negative characteristics of one's partner do not cancel out the positive attributes of either (Gottman, 1994). During conflicted periods in a relationship, it is especially important to remember the good times, to recall the characteristics of the partner that were initially so attractive, and to review the reasons for getting together in the first place.

Not only does reintroducing praise and admiration help restore the balance between positive and negative interchanges, it also helps disrupt the negativity cycle. A positive statement is more likely to trigger a positive response. Admiration is the opposite of contempt, and these two feelings are incompatible. Naturally, praise and admiration must be genuine; otherwise, they may have the opposite of the desired effect. Insincere praise may come across as sarcasm. Positive messages are strengthened by nonverbal signals such as sustained eye contact, smiling, and leaning toward the other person.

Another problem that may interfere with effective communication is the tendency to rely on "you" statements rather than "I" statements. When partners become frustrated with their relationship, each often assumes that his or her unhappiness is due to something the other person is doing and should stop doing or something the other person is not doing and should begin to do. Most "You should . . . " statements directed at one's partner during a conflict tend to generate anger and resentment. Such statements clearly imply that the other person is failing to live up to expectations. Inherent in these statements is unsolicited critical evaluation. When a person hears such a comment, the natural initial reaction is to become defensive and sometimes to counterattack. The net result is that each partner becomes more upset as the argument escalates, perpetuating a cycle of negativity.

When one partner perceives a problem in the relationship, an amiable resolution is far more likely if in presenting the complaint the person takes responsibility for his or her own feelings. This can best be done by using "I" statements. Although there is always a chance that the other person will be annoyed by the complaint, the probability of a defensive reaction is tremendously decreased if the speaker expresses the complaint from her or his own point of view. For example, "I feel frustrated when I have to clean up after you" is less accusatory than "You should learn to clean up after yourself."

In order for a relationship problem to be effectively resolved, the problem must be identified in specific terms. **Leveling** is the technique of communicating a concern in very clear, simple, and specific terms (Gottman, Notarius, Gonso, & Markman, 1976). Leveling requires the speaker to begin by focusing on his or her feelings rather than on the partner's behavior. The purpose of leveling is to clarify mutual expectations, to clarify what is acceptable and not acceptable, to sort the relevant from the irrelevant, and to identify the behaviors that strengthen the relationship and those that compromise it (Gottman et al., 1976).

For leveling to be effective, partners should remember to focus on a specific behavior rather than on global traits. For example, it is more effective to identify the problem as, say, a failure to ask for your opinion than to complain about your partner's "complete insensitivity." A reference to a particular behavior rather than to some general personality deficiency is less likely to be perceived as criticism. Furthermore, effective leveling requires focusing on behavior in a particular situation as opposed to making sweeping generalizations. It is more effective, for example, to say "I don't think you heard what I just said" than to complain about "selfishness." Specific behaviors in specific situations are easier to identify and to change. Finally, leveling is more constructive if one problem or complaint is addressed at a time, without bringing up a list of other concerns. Rather than complaining that "this whole relationship is going nowhere," pick one specific problem and explain your feelings about it to your partner.

Focusing on specific problematic behaviors one at a time increases the chances of effective communication. The speaker is more likely to express the concern accurately and clearly, and the listener, in turn, is more likely to hear and understand the identified problem. In fact, although many people assume that most communication problems are due to a failure to express one's views clearly, in reality the breakdown is more often due to a failure to listen effectively.

Effective Listening

All too often people become preoccupied with getting their point across rather than listening to their partners' viewpoints. What may start as a seemingly friendly conversation or as an innocuous statement by one partner may erupt into a storm of emotional, accusatory remarks as each partner becomes increasingly frustrated at the other's unwillingness to listen. The argument may escalate as the partners interrupt one another in an emotional attempt to be heard. In such a situation, effective communication is unlikely.

The most important component of any conversation is nearly always the role of the listener. By being an effective listener, one person can fully appreciate the other person's point of view before offering any reactions. Another benefit of good listening is that the other person feels understood and appreciated, and this minimizes the chance of defensiveness.

LEVELING
The communication technique of voicing a concern in a simple, clear, and specific fashion.

Looking At . . .

. . . Thinking About

Although thousands of books have been written about communication skills, the majority are misguided. Most communication problems are not due to lack of skills, as is usually implied. Rather, many people fail to use their skills when they experience relationship problems. The communication skill that is most important, yet most difficult to implement, is effective listening. What are the keys to effective listening? Think about the last time someone really listened to you. What did that person do that really made you feel he or she cared and understood?

Effective listening is not as easy as it may sound. It involves more than just closing one's mouth and opening one's ears (McKay et al., 1994). The essence of effective listening is empathy, the ability to understand a situation from another person's point of view (Nichols, 1995; Rogers, 1951). Empathy does not require the listener to agree with the other person's viewpoint, only to suspend any preoccupation with himself or herself and try to enter into the speaker's inner experience. Empathic listening means truly hearing what is being said *and* demonstrating that to the speaker.

Effective listening is an active process. It requires actively holding back what we have to say and resisting the urge to respond, clarify, or disagree. This is often the greatest obstacle to effective listening. When a speaker's statement or complaint strikes an emotional chord in the listener, it often creates a powerful urge to respond immediately. As Nichols (1995) noted, "the ability to listen rests on how successfully we resist the impulse to react emotionally to the position of the other" (p. 95). Empathic listening requires fully understanding the speaker's inner experience, and this cannot be done by responding or reacting. Therefore, the proverbial "biting your tongue" may sometimes be required for effective listening. Active listening involves suspending one's own thoughts and feelings in order to hear and to convey understanding to the speaker (Nichols, 1995).

One of the most effective means for conveying a deep level of understanding is **paraphrasing.** A person who paraphrases restates the other person's position in his or her own words, in the process asking for correction or confirmation. For example, if your partner commented that she feels frustrated when she has to clean up after you, you might paraphrase by saying, "So you feel that I am expecting you to clean up after me, as well as cleaning up after yourself." Accurately paraphrasing shows the speaker that the listener has truly listened and received the intended message. If the message was not accurately perceived, paraphrasing provides feedback to the speaker, who can then try to clarify the message. The fundamentals of effective listening are listed in Table 7.2.

PARAPHRASING
Rephrasing another person's statement as a way of showing that the statement has been understood.

TABLE 7.2 The Fundamentals of Effective Listening
• Paying attention to what the speaker is saying
• Listening without giving advice
• Listening without offering a personal opinion
• Listening without immediately agreeing or disagreeing
• Attending to how the speaker truly feels, then paraphrasing the speaker's words and asking him or her to confirm your impression
• Listening for feelings without pushing too hard to get the speaker to express them

Effective listening, then, is not simply a set of techniques. It begins with a sincere and determined effort to tune into the private world of one's partner. Effective listening requires a commitment to appreciating the other person's viewpoint. It often requires the listener to be silent, but never passive. Effective listening involves asking questions, requesting elaboration and clarification. Effective listening is not just taking turns talking.

Practicing Validation

When people are talking about something that is important to them, what they want more than anything else is to know that their feelings have been understood and respected. Offering validation is one of the most powerful tools for resolving relationship problems (Gottman, 1994). **Validation** is a problem-solving skill that consists of effective listening *and* acknowledging that the complaints may have some validity. In Gottman's (1994) words, "validation is simply putting yourself in your partner's shoes and imagining his or her emotional state" (p. 195). Validating a person's feelings means recognizing that the feelings are valid even if you don't share them.

Validation can be accomplished by saying such things as "I would feel the same way in this circumstance" or "I understand why you feel the way you do." Just knowing that one's feelings are understood and respected can be a powerful impetus for resolving relationship problems. Obviously, for validation to be effective, it must be sincere.

Several strategies are helpful in validating a partner's feelings. If one's actions have caused hurt feelings, taking responsibility is important. A statement as simple as "I can see that I really upset you" validates the other person's feelings while also communicating that the speaker accepts responsibility for the feelings. Apologizing is also a form of validation, as it communicates that the other person's complaint is legitimate and worthy of respect. Thus, if one bears any responsibility for an identified problem, it is important to accept and acknowledge that responsibility and express remorse sincerely.

Problem solving in relationships means looking for solutions that will best satisfy the needs of both partners. When each person takes responsibility for his or her own emotions, listens carefully to the other person, shows empathy and understanding, and validates the feelings of the other, problem solving in relationships is simpler. Perhaps most important, such techniques as empathic listening and validation are effective means of demonstrating love and respect as well as interrupting the cycle of negativity. In fact, effective listening and validation often encourage the partner to reciprocate.

An important component of good communication is not only knowing how to listen but knowing *when* to communicate. Like all interactions, communication occurs in a context. The context includes a time, a place (public or private), and a setting—including the mood and expectations of those who are trying to communicate. Communication is more likely to be effective if there are fewer distractions. For example, the end of the day is often a difficult time to have good communication; partners may feel frazzled, tired, and distracted. Effective communication involves selecting the right time, place, and setting for communication. Doing so communicates that you are making the other person a high priority—in other words, it communicates empathy.

For many, if not most people, remaining calm during conflict, communicating effectively, and validating the other person's feelings do not come naturally. Implementing these strategies takes practice. As with any new skill, rehearsal is required for mastery. Each time you rehearse nondefensive communication or validation, that skill becomes more familiar and you become more comfortable with it. Most important, such skills must be rehearsed even if you would prefer not to. By repeatedly and consistently practicing, the skills become natural and effortless parts of interactions.

VALIDATION
A problem-solving skill that consists of effective listening and acknowledging that the other person's complaints may have some validity.

TABLE 7.3 The Fundamentals of Effective Communication
• Take turns.
• Don't give unsolicited advice.
• Show genuine interest.
• Communicate your understanding.
• Take your partner's side.
• Convey a "we against others" attitude (remind your partner that the two of you are in this together).
• Express affection.
• Validate your partner's emotions.

SOURCE: From Gottman & Silver (1999)

Consistent and determined practice helps to ensure that the skills will be available when they are needed most—during a heated argument. The fundamentals of effective communication are listed in Table 7.3.

Problem Solving

Effective problem solving begins with empathic communication. People who can put themselves in a partner's shoes can comprehend that person's perspective on a given issue. Unfortunately, this is hard for most people, especially during emotional moments. Based on their research, Gottman and Silver (1999) identified these five components of successful problem solving:

1. Soft startup
2. Repair attempt
3. Time out
4. Compromise
5. Tolerance

Successful problem solving begins with a notable absence of criticism, contempt, defensiveness, and stonewalling. A *soft startup* involves bringing up issues without attacking one's partner in the process. This is critical, since "discussions invariably end on the same note they begin with" (Gottman & Silver, 1999, p. 161). Guidelines for soft startups are listed in Table 7.4. When a discussion does start off with too much tension, it is essential to de-escalate the conflict, through a process called a *repair attempt.* Repair attempts can range from taking a break to apologizing or using humor. By reducing tension, repair attempts make partners more receptive to compromise. Repair attempts can be thought of as damage control.

If repair attempts are not working, the argument is likely to escalate, which means it is time to take a break. Rather than allowing the conflict to build, couples who are not staying calm during an attempt at problem solving should take a brief *time out* to relax, distract themselves, and regroup.

Ultimately, effective problem solving inevitably requires some form of *compromise.* Negotiating a compromise, however, can occur only when partners are in a calm and cooperative frame of mind, which is why the previous steps are required. To arrive at a compromise, each partner must remain open to the other person's position and to being influenced by the other. Compromise requires each individual to remain open-

TABLE 7.4 Guidelines for Soft Startups
• Complain but don't blame.
• Make statements that begin with "I" instead of "You."
• Describe what is happening; don't evaluate or judge.
• Be clear.
• Be polite.
• Be appreciative.
• Don't store things up.

SOURCE: Gottman & Silver (1999)

minded while discussing different perspectives and preferences. Compromise is essentially an effort to find common ground.

A fundamental requirement in any close relationship is *tolerance*. Partners must learn to tolerate each other's faults and imperfections. Until a person accepts a partner's flaws, it will be impossible to compromise, because the person will devote time and energy to correcting these flaws. This strategy is not only ineffective, it is impossible. As Gottman and Silver (1999, p. 185) concluded, "conflict resolution is not about one person changing, it's about negotiating, finding common ground and ways that you can accommodate each other."

MAINTAINING LOVE RELATIONSHIPS

Couples in committed relationships have an explicit or implicit expectation that the relationship will last. What factors contribute to the longevity of relationships? What are the characteristics of relationships that work, those that make them fulfilling and satisfying? If the success of a relationship is judged solely in terms of its duration, commitment alone could provide the answer. As was noted earlier, commitment derived from concern for the welfare of children, religious constraints, and/or family concerns can make a relationship last. However, if we define success of a relationship as the ability to maintain intimacy and passion in addition to commitment, the formula for achieving it is more elusive.

In one study, researchers asked 60 widows to recall the factors that contributed to the longevity of their relationships (Malatesta, 1989). The participants had several interesting responses. Most common were comments such as "not expecting constant love from their husbands, or even wanting constant love," "maintaining their own private time, interests, and friends," "taking good care of themselves and their needs," "being able to compromise and apologize," and "keeping activities varied." The results of this survey highlight critical dimensions in successful long-term relationships: Partners must find a balance between dependence and independence, individual needs and the couple's needs, and freedom and responsibility (Nichols, 1995).

As was suggested in the discussion of love schemas, what some people call "love" may actually be a form of dependency. For some, the fear of not being able to function without their partner is what makes them think they love that person. Their feelings of love may hide the fact that they cannot count on themselves and must rely on another for fulfillment and validation. In happy and successful relationships, neither partner is overly dependent on the other, although each prefers to be with the partner as opposed to being alone. In his book *The Road Less Traveled* (1978), psychiatrist

When partners share the responsibility for decision making, the relationship is more likely to be built on mutual respect, a critical component of long-term success.

M. Scott Peck wrote that "two people love each other only when they are quite capable of living without each other but choose to live with each other" (p. 98).

Also, in successful relationships, each person has personal interests, yet is aware that individual choices will have an impact on the relationship. Because of this awareness, individuals in successful committed relationships try to make decisions that simultaneously sustain the relationship while also preserving their own sense of independence and individuality. Power is equally divided in these relationships as well. In fact, the greater the power imbalance in a relationship, the greater the likelihood that it will end (Felmlee, 1994). When partners share the responsibility for decision making, the relationship is more likely to be built on mutual respect, a critical component of long-term success.

Despite occasional disagreements and arguments, couples who have been in committed relationships with the same partner for 20–40 years show a distinguishing characteristic: Their interactions are typically characterized by mutual love and respect (Gottman, 1994). Their affection is displayed in their interactions—through their gestures, facial expressions, and eye contact. They take advantage of opportunities to brag about their partners' positive qualities. They are deeply interested in their partners' lives. When there are disagreements, they make a concerted effort to hear and understand their partners' views. In sum, for these couples, positive exchanges greatly outweigh negative interactions (Gottman, 1994).

Even the happiest couples, though, have differences of opinion and occasional conflicts. Research on loving relationships reveals that some amount of disagreement and conflict is inevitable. Based on his in-depth studies and observations of over 200 couples, John Gottman (1994) concluded that conflict is actually "crucial" to the long-term success of a committed relationship. Because every relationship involves occasional conflicts, expecting never to disagree or argue is idealistic and unrealistic. In fact, having a realistic expectation that the relationship will have to survive occasional hardships is essential for long-term success and mutual satisfaction. In comparing the interaction patterns of couples over time, Gottman and colleagues made a fairly dramatic discovery. As might be expected, couples in the early stages of a relationship who had some arguments reported less relationship satisfaction than couples who had virtually no arguments. A 3-year followup, however, revealed that the situation was reversed. Those couples who previously reported that they occasionally argued were *more* satisfied with their relationships. The couples who originally had no arguments were much more likely to be headed toward breakup. This seemingly paradoxical finding suggests that conflict in a relationship is not necessarily an omen of serious problems. Couples who never disagree may actually be ignoring problems that need to be addressed. Because the problems are never resolved, resentment and frustration build over time, often causing the partners to feel that they are drifting apart. Conflict in a relationship is crucial, therefore, because it often serves to help partners identify the issues that need to be addressed in order for the relationship to thrive.

HEALTHY DECISION MAKING

In successful relationships, the partners are intimately aware of the details of each others' lives. According to Gottman and Silver (1999) these couples have "richly detailed love maps" (p. 48). These partners remember the major events in each others' histories and in their shared past, and they keep updating their mental diaries. They know each others' likes and dislikes, including food and entertainment preferences and sexual preferences, and are aware of each other's life goals.

Partners who share such intimate knowledge of each other are better equipped to weather the inevitable storms in relationships. The demands of life and the distractions of daily routines are only minor glitches for partners who are in the habit of making time to catch up with each other. As Gottman and Silver (1999) noted, "the more you know and understand about each other, the easier it is to keep connected as life swirls around you" (p. 50).

You can gauge your current love map by completing the Love Map Questionnaire. This exercise will be most useful if you and your partner complete the questionnaire separately. After completing the questionnaire, remember that all couples have room for improvement in mutual knowledge. Getting to know your partner better should be fun. Find different ways to learn more about each other—and remember that this process takes time. In fact, in a long-term commitment, learning about your partner can take a lifetime.

Love Map Questionnaire

Read each statement and circle T for "true" and F for "false."

1. I can name my partner's best friends. T F
2. I can tell you what stresses my partner is currently facing. T F
3. I know the names of some of the people who have been irritating my partner lately. T F
4. I can tell you some of my partner's life dreams. T F
5. I am very familiar with my partner's religious beliefs and ideas. T F
6. I can tell you about my partner's basic philosophy of life. T F
7. I can list the relatives my partner likes the least. T F
8. I know my partner's favorite music. T F
9. I can list my partner's three favorite movies. T F
10. My spouse is familiar with my current stresses. T F
11. I know the three most special times in my partner's life. T F
12. I can tell you the most stressful thing that happened to my partner as a child. T F
13. I can list my partner's major aspirations and hopes in life. T F
14. I know my partner's major current worries. T F
15. My spouse knows who my friends are. T F
16. I know what my partner would want to do if he or she suddenly won the lottery. T F
17. I can tell you in detail my first impressions of my partner. T F
18. Periodically I ask my partner about his or her world right now. T F
19. I feel that my partner knows me pretty well. T F
20. My spouse is familiar with my hopes and aspirations. T F

Scoring: Give yourself one point for each "true" answer.

10 or above: Mutual knowledge is an area of strength for your relationship. You have a fairly detailed map of your partner's everyday life, hopes, fears, and dreams. You know what makes your spouse "tick." Try not to take for granted this knowledge and understanding of each other. Keeping in touch in this way ensures you'll be well equipped to handle any problem areas that crop up in your relationship.

Below 10: Your relationship could stand some improvement in mutual knowledge. Perhaps you never had the time or the tools to really get to know each other. Or perhaps your love maps have become outdated as your lives have changed over the years. In either case, by taking the time to learn more about your partner now, you'll find your relationship becomes stronger.

summary

INTIMACY

- Intimate relationships are characterized by mutual knowledge, sharing, and trust. Intimate partners' lives are often interconnected to the point that the two are identified as a couple rather than as individuals.
- The capacity for intimacy requires the ability and willingness to share one's private experiences with another person.

THEORIES OF LOVE

- Of all the terms in the English language, *love* may be the most misunderstood. The subjective nature of the concept of love has hampered scientific research on it.
- Several researchers have attempted to define love using theoretical models. Sternberg proposed the triangular theory of love, with the three components of intimacy, passion, and commitment. Lee proposed six love types: eros, ludus, and storge are primary types; pragma, mania, and agape are secondary types. Berscheid and Walster's two-component theory of love includes companionate love and passionate love.
- The experience and meaning of love change over time in relationships. Passion usually peaks early and drops off relatively quickly. Intimacy also levels off moderately over the course of a relationship, but commitment builds over time in successful relationships.
- Attachment styles describe individuals' levels of comfort with closeness and anxiety about being alone. People with secure styles value closeness and sharing, and they enjoy healthier relationships than people with insecure styles.
- Several important factors influence interpersonal attraction. Proximity plays a role, as does perceived similarity. A third factor is reciprocal liking. A person is more likely to be attracted to someone who reciprocates positive feelings. Finally, physical attractiveness is important. According to the matching hypothesis, people are more likely to be attracted to those who are comparable in physical attractiveness. In other words, we are more likely to fall in love with someone with whom we interact regularly, who is similar to us, who likes us, and whom we find physically attractive.
- Men and women often differ in their attitudes about sex, in their styles of communication, and in their views of love. Many of these differences are dictated by Western cultural scripts. For example, men are socialized to consider status and independence important, whereas women are socialized to consider intimacy and connection important.

LOVE RELATIONSHIPS

- Love schemas are individuals' views of and expectations for love relationships. These schemas differ based on a person's degree of comfort with closeness and independence and desire for a love relationship. Common schemas are casual, uninterested, secure, clingy, skittish, and fickle.
- Many romantic relationships go through five distinct stages: initial attraction, buildup, continuation/consolidation, deterioration, and ending. Initial attraction is marked by intense passion. Buildup begins as the initial excitement of the relationship begins to decrease; during buildup, self-disclosure increases and mutual expectations are clarified. Continuation is based on individual assessments of the relative costs and benefits of being in the relationship. If a person decides that he or she would be better off outside of the relationship, deterioration occurs. The ending comes

when one or both members of the couple terminate the relationship.

CONFLICT IN LOVE RELATIONSHIPS

- Conflict is not necessarily a sign of a troubled relationship. However, conflict may be a danger signal if it remains unresolved or if it is expressed through criticism, contempt, defensiveness, or stonewalling. These ineffective strategies usually perpetuate a cycle of negativity that is almost always destructive.
- Jealousy often stems from a perceived threat to self-esteem. Neglect can be a problem if the couple have many responsibilities (children, careers) or fail to nurture their relationship.

RESOLVING RELATIONSHIP CONFLICT

- The three critical skills for resolving relationship problems are staying calm, using effective communication, and practicing validation. Of all communication skills, listening is the most important, and often the most difficult to master. Practice is essential for long-term success.

MAINTAINING LOVE RELATIONSHIPS

- Long-lasting relationships are characterized by mutual love and respect. Expecting occasional conflict is essential for the long-term success of a committed relationship. Conflict can help couples identify the issues that they need to resolve.

CHAPTER 8

Sensual Communication and Techniques

I usually please him first. But he is more than willing to return the favor. Nothing gives an orgasm like a skilled tongue (and maybe a finger or two). Then when we have concluded those activities we can have great sex (he seems to last longer after an orgasm) and my body seems to be more responsive and orgasms better as well. I understand why some people might consider this taboo, but not much feels better. And I love the look on my man's face after I have pleased him.

(A 19-year-old female college student)

Whenever I asked my girlfriend about her self-pleasuring practices, she acted all bashful—which of course made it that much more fascinating. Finally, after a year, she let me watch her masturbate. She was shy about it; she kept her panties on.

(A 30-year-old male)

At first I just moaned when she did something right as far as pleasing me sexually—it took a matter of months to come right out and say, "Hey, touch me here, or use a softer/harder touch." I mean, you really don't see this kind of stuff in the media, so where was I going to learn?

(A 26-year-old female graduate student)

She acted all bashful.

Most of the time that I do masturbate, it usually follows reading an article or watching something a little racy, but that I can relate to—just looking at a naked man doesn't work. I have to imagine that maybe someone is watching me—almost like I am performing for a mystery audience. And of course, since I know what feels good, it takes much less time.

(A 23-year-old female college student)

In romantic relationships, sexual intimacy is closely linked with overall relationship satisfaction. As a rule, couples who rate their relationships as rewarding also tend to view them as sexually satisfying (Byers & Demmons, 1999; McCabe, 1999). This should not be surprising, since the skills that are essential for the success of a relationship also facilitate sexual interactions.

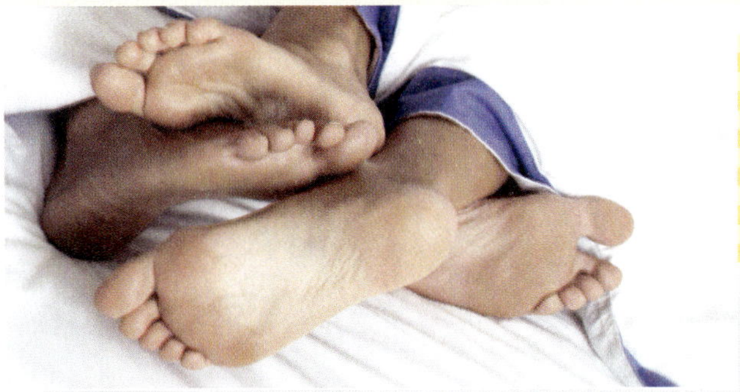

SEX IN LOVE RELATIONSHIPS

Most of us associate being in love with displays of physical affection. In virtually all romantic relationships, partners express their intimate feelings by kissing and hugging (Baumeister & Tice, 2001). There are, of course, many other intimate ways of expressing feelings for one's partner, and people may subscribe to different definitions of

Most of us associate being in love with displays of physical affection. In virtually all romantic relationships, partners express their feelings by kissing and hugging.

what constitutes sexual intimacy. But virtually everyone in most cultures agrees that sex belongs in the context of an intimate relationship.

Sexual Diversity

Historically, most people have thought of penile-vaginal intercourse as the standard sexual behavior. Even today, most heterosexuals mean penile-vaginal intercourse when they refer to "having sex" or "making love." Foreplay is viewed as a prelude, or warm-up, if you will, for the "main event" of sexual intercourse. This norm is reflected in existing laws about sexual behavior and in some religious writings. For example, some states still have laws that prohibit virtually any sexual behavior other than heterosexual penile-vaginal intercourse. Although the laws are rarely enforced, it is still technically illegal in some parts of the United States to engage in oral sex with any partner. Some early Christian writers condemned any form of sexual behavior other than penile-vaginal intercourse between married heterosexual partners (Bullough & Bullough, 1995). In some cases, they even stipulated that the only proper position for intercourse was the man on top of the woman.

Today, few people restrict their sexual behavior to penile-vaginal intercourse. Although heterosexual intercourse is still viewed as the norm in U.S. culture, alternatives are more widely tolerated, and sexual practices are extremely diverse. Although some Americans still display considerable ambivalence about such common practices as masturbation and oral sex, the fact is that most people have tried them, and many engage in them regularly. Nearly 70% of American men report having masturbated over the past year, as do close to 40% of women. Over one-quarter of men masturbate weekly. Yet, despite changes in social norms, approximately half of men and women who masturbate feel some guilt for doing so (Laumann et al., 1994). This cultural discomfort with masturbation was dramatically illustrated when U.S. President Bill Clinton forced Surgeon General Joycelyn Elders to resign in 1994. While attending a World AIDS Day conference, Dr. Elders affirmed her support for early sexuality education in the schools. In response to a question about the potential role of masturbation as a safer sex practice, she noted that it "is something that is part of human sexuality and it's part of something that perhaps should be taught" (Frankel, 1994, p. 1695). Anticipating heated controversy following those remarks, President Clinton dismissed Dr. Elders the very next day, citing a violation of his "policy decisions or personal convictions."

did YOU know?

Although most people have experienced oral sex, it is not the "main event" for most people. According to the National Health and Social Life Survey (NHSLS), fewer than one-third of American women and men report receiving or performing oral sex during their most recent sexual encounter (Laumann et al., 1994).

Like masturbation, oral sex is the focus of much ambivalence in the United States. It was not until the 1920s that it became a widespread sexual practice. Oral sex has become increasingly popular among men and women, both heterosexual and gay. *Fellatio,* oral stimulation of a man's genitals, is a practice that nearly 80% of men have experienced. Nearly 70% of women have performed fellatio. Also, nearly 75% of women have experienced *cunnilingus,* oral stimulation of their genitals. Eighty percent of men have performed cunnilingus (Laumann et al., 1994). Oral sex may be either a part of foreplay or an alternative to penile-vaginal intercourse. For some people, it is a preferred means of reaching orgasm. For many women, receiving oral sex produces a more reliable and intense orgasm than penile-vaginal intercourse does. A few heterosexual couples even replace intercourse with oral sex as a way of maintaining technical virginity (Carpenter, 2001; Gagnon & Simon, 1987; Remez, 2000).

Anal intercourse, or anal sex, entered the public spotlight in the mid-1980s when it was identified as a risk factor for transmission of HIV. Approximately one-quarter of heterosexual men and one-fifth of heterosexual women in the United States have experienced anal intercourse. Unlike oral sex, anal sex is not a regular practice for most heterosexual couples, although nearly 10% report having engaged in it during the past year (Laumann et al., 1994). Because of social ambivalence regarding this sexual practice, however, it seems probable that many people underreport their experience of it. Religious beliefs and values influence people's sexual behavior, and this is especially true of alternative practices like anal sex. People with no religious background report more experience with anal intercourse than do those who identify with Protestant and Catholic traditions (Laumann et al., 1994). Ethnic and racial factors also affect the practice of anal sex. As a group, Hispanic American men report more recent and lifetime experiences with anal intercourse than do members of other ethnic and racial groups in the United States. This pattern has been attributed to the Latin American cultural emphasis on female virginity and on machismo (an exaggerated sense of masculinity). The gender role specified by machismo emphasizes the masculine aspects of sexual penetration, whether vaginal or anal (Carrier, 1995; Parker, Herdt, & Caballo, 1991). Hispanic cultures tend to also have very negative attitudes toward homosexuality. As a consequence, "Hispanic men who have sex with men often do not self-identify as homosexual or bisexual because of the severe stigma attached to this behavior," and they tend to also have female sexual partners (Flaskerud, Uman, Lara, Romero, & Taka, 1996, p. 351). Interestingly, those with an Hispanic cultural perspective tend to view anal intercourse between two males as a homosexual act only on the part of the recipient.

Are We Having Sex Yet?

What do people mean when they talk about "having sex"? What specific sexual acts are included? Although most people would agree that sexual intercourse includes penile-vaginal intercourse, what about oral sex or anal intercourse? As was mentioned earlier, some heterosexual couples substitute oral sex for penile-vaginal intercourse as a way of maintaining technical virginity. In some Hispanic cultures that prize virginity, couples practice anal intercourse for the same reason. Does practicing oral or anal sex qualify as "having sex" to the majority of people?

According to Stephanie Sanders and June Reinisch (1999) of the Kinsey Institute, virtually every college student they surveyed considered penile-vaginal intercourse to constitute "having sex," and 81% agreed that anal intercourse also qualified. There was, however, much lower agreement among the students on whether engaging in other sexual practices qualified as "having sex." Approximately 60% did not consider oral sex to mean "having sex." Most of the students, about 85%, did not believe that fondling each others' genitals qualified as "having sex" (Sanders & Reinisch, 1999).

Other research shows that there is also considerable ambiguity in people's definitions of virginity. Whereas engaging in penile-vaginal intercourse always leads to loss of virginity, there is less agreement about whether a person can lose his or her virginity through oral sex or anal intercourse. Approximately 25% of respondents in one survey thought that a person could lose his or her virginity through oral sex alone, and over half (56%) believed that anal intercourse would lead to loss of virginity. Four out of five respondents believed that a person could lose his or her virginity through sexual activity with a partner of the same sex (Carpenter, 2001).

These studies are interesting for several reasons. First, they illustrate the variability in people's definitions of "having sex" and of virginity. Experiencing or performing oral sex counts as "having sex" for some but not for most college students; it is not surprising, then, that most students believe that a person cannot lose his or her virginity through oral sex alone. The studies did not fully address the factors that determine what meanings people assign to practices such as oral sex. According to a common cultural script, many sexual practices, including genital fondling and oral sex, represent foreplay that precedes "having sex," which refers to penile-vaginal intercourse for heterosexual persons. Anal intercourse is not viewed as foreplay or a prelude to penile-vaginal intercourse by most couples; it seems to be considered "having sex" (although it is not a regular practice in the sexual interactions of most heterosexual couples) (Laumann et al., 1994). Therefore, experiencing anal intercourse can lead people to label themselves "nonvirgins." The different meanings assigned to sexual practices must be considered in sex research, since these meanings influence people's estimates of the number of their past sexual partners. Sexual meanings also influence whether a person would volunteer for a study recruiting nonvirgins. Based on the Sanders and Reinisch (1999) survey, it seems likely that most research participants would not include in their tallies partners with whom they practiced only oral sex. Obviously, people may differ greatly not only in their actual sexual practices but also in what they consider to be sexual practices and in their definitions of virginity.

Sexual Relationships

Sexual activity is usually most intense when partners feel passionate love—the type of love that peaks early but declines more rapidly than intimacy and commitment. Younger couples who are happy with their relationships report higher rates of sexual activity and satisfaction than do older couples. Yet, even though feelings of passion may wane, the frequency of sexual activity does not inevitably decline. Age, length of the relationship, and relationship satisfaction are all related to sexual activity in a long-term relationship.

Most couples vividly recall their first sexual experience together. The first sexual encounter generally represents a turning point in the relationship, often leading to greater commitment (Baxter & Bullis, 1986). Sexual initiation for a couple typically follows one of the following patterns (Christopher & Cate, 1985):

- *Rapid-involvement couples* progress quickly into sexual involvement, often on a first date.
- *Gradual-involvement couples* report a more gradual transition to sexual activity over the course of the dating relationship.
- *Delayed-involvement couples* tend to postpone any sexual activity until they identify themselves as a couple and have a sense of commitment.
- *Low-involvement couples* are those who are sexually inactive even though they are in a committed relationship.

For nearly one-third of dating couples, sexual intimacy increases gradually over time, as partners become more com-

Looking At . . .

. . . Thinking About

Many students report having engaged in sexual activity with a person they knew only briefly. How do you feel about sexual encounters between people who have recently met?

fortable with each other and as they begin to feel some degree of commitment. The other common pattern is to delay sexual involvement until both people view themselves as part of a couple and their families and friends do as well. While having a sexual encounter on a first date is somewhat inconsistent with the current U.S. cultural script, over 45% of male college students and 33% of female college students reported having had a sexual encounter, or *hookup,* with a stranger or brief acquaintance (Paul, McManus, & Hayes, 2000), and 15% of males and 13% of females stated that they engaged in sexual intercourse with a new acquaintance while on spring break (Maticka-Tyndale, Herold, & Mewhinney, 1998).

did YOU know?

One-third or more of college students have had intercourse with a stranger or a recent acquaintance (Paul, McManus, & Hayes, 2000).

For most couples, the role of sex in the relationship changes over time. Early in a relationship, sexual activity is motivated primarily by passion, curiosity, and novelty. During the early stages of the relationship, partners are more open to sexual experimentation—trying different positions during sexual intercourse, having sex in different settings (such as outdoors or while bathing together) (Greeley, 1991). As a couple becomes habituated, there is often a decrease in sexual experimentation. Over time, as a couple becomes more committed, the level of sexual satisfaction often increases steadily before leveling off (Christopher & Sprecher, 2000).

8.1 on the web

Good communication is essential for a healthy sexual relationship. Go to **www.ablongman.com/mcanulty2e** and review the guidelines for communication and sexual behavior.

What are some effective ways to deliver criticism to an intimate partner?

Although novelty and experimentation typically diminish later in a relationship, a couple's sex life should not be allowed to become routine. Reintroducing novelty and nurturing the intimacy in the relationship are essential. Creating varied contexts for lovemaking, such as choosing unusual times or places, can restore novelty. Experimenting with different sexual techniques and positions is also recommended, no matter how long a couple has been together. In fact, the longer two people have been involved, the more essential it is that they remain committed to keeping the fun in their sexual relationship.

Couples' sexual satisfaction is heavily influenced by the extent to which partners agree on preferred sexual practices. Understanding one another's sexual preferences is associated with greater sexual satisfaction for both partners. Such understanding is essential in giving sexual pleasure to a partner (Byers & Demmons, 1999; Purnine & Carey, 1997). When their relationships end, married couples frequently cite unsatisfying sex as a reason (Cleek & Pearson, 1985), as do dating couples (Hill, Rubin, & Peplau, 1976) and homosexual couples (Kurdek, 1991). One or both of the partners may become dissatisfied with the sexual relationship and may harbor resentment and perhaps even begin considering alternatives to the current relationship. A satisfying sex life is important for maintaining the bond between the two people in a love relationship. For sex to remain a meaningful component of a long-term relationship, couples need to maintain realistic expectations and to nurture those aspects of the relationship that spurred the passion in the first place. In successful long-term relationships, sex is associated with feelings of strong friendship and shared intimacy (Regan, 2000). Like all of the other features of a successful long-term relationship, sexual interactions require attention, nurturing, commitment, and effective communication.

SENSUAL COMMUNICATION TECHNIQUES

For humans, sexual behavior occurs in an interpersonal context. Even solitary sexual behavior usually involves sexual fantasies of an idealized partner or recollections of a past sexual encounter. Cultural scripts, and most people's individual scripts, dictate that sexual activity belongs in the context of a relationship, preferably one that involves at least some emotional attachment. Although not invariably, sexual activity

CLOSE UP ON culture

Sex around the Globe . . . A World of Differences

Each culture has its own vernacular and euphemisms for sex. In Romania, for example, "Let me give you the hammer" is an invitation to sexual intercourse. In Brazil, "to drown the goose" means to have sexual intercourse. To a Spaniard, giving himself a "mushroom" is a reference to masturbation (Sevcik, 2001). There are also many colorful phrases to refer to having an orgasm. The Hungarian for "I left," the Croatian for "I'm finishing," and the Russian for "I am breaking up," are euphemisms for having an orgasm (Sevcik, 2001).

As fascinating as they are, cross-cultural comparisons of sexuality are difficult to make, for several reasons. Sex surveys have not been conducted in most countries because of political, moral, or logistical obstacles (Mackay, 2001). The few available international statistics mostly address matters of sexual health, such as pregnancy rates and the incidence of HIV infection. Most sexuality research has been conducted in Western cultures, particularly North America and Western Europe. In many Asian and Islamic cultures, sex is considered a private matter that is not open to public discussion or scientific inquiry.

The available data show that there are wide cultural variations in the age at first sexual intercourse. Intercourse tends to occur later among people in Asia and South America (usually when they are in their early 20s) than among those in Africa, Europe, and North America (who typically first experience intercourse while in their midteens) (Mackay, 2001). In cultures that prize female virginity, sexual activity before marriage is discouraged or prohibited. Officially, sex before marriage is denounced in China, although it is becoming increasingly common (Caron, 1998). In Korea, traditional beliefs restrict sexual activity prior to marriage. Consistent with their cultural norms, the vast majority of 18-year-old Koreans have not engaged in sexual intercourse (Youn, 2001). Officially, Japanese culture promotes sexual abstinence until marriage, especially for women. In actuality, Japanese sexual norms are quite ambivalent. The Japanese are apparently tolerant of premarital sexual behavior as long as it is discreet and does not interfere with social duties (White, 1993).

The frequency of sexual activity is also variable, from a high of 141 times per year for the average person in France to a low of 57 times per year for the average person in Hong Kong (Mackay, 2001). The French appear to enjoy more active sex lives than their American counterparts: approximately half of French men and women report engaging in sexual activity such as oral sex or intercourse two to three times per week, compared to one-third of respondents in the United States (Gagnon, Giami, Michaels, & de Colomby, 2001). As for Americans, the preferred context for sexual activity for French people is some form of committed monogamous relationship.

Many cultural differences are not related to geographical separation, since neighboring countries in the same continent may reveal dramatic differences. On most measures, Canadians' attitudes are more liberal and permissive than those of Americans (Widmer, Treas, & Newcomb, 1998). The majority of Canadians are tolerant of sex before marriage and of homosexual relationships. Most people in the United States are accepting of premarital sex, although one-third disapprove. The majority of U.S. respondents (70%) disapprove of same-sex relationships. Clearly, geography alone cannot explain cultural differences in sexual attitudes and practices. A host of factors, including history, politics, and religious influences, contribute to cultural norms regarding sexuality.

---

for the most part does occur in the context of a relationship, whether real or imagined, short-term or long-term, casual or committed. Cross-cultural variations in sexual activities and attitudes are explored in Close Up on Culture: Sex around the Globe . . . A World of Differences.

All of the factors that are helpful in nurturing a love relationship are important in sustaining a satisfying sexual relationship. For example, the amount of communication and understanding in the relationship is related to couples' sexual satisfaction (Byers & Demmons, 1999; Purnine & Carey, 1997). Couples' sexual satisfaction is also related to the compatibility between partners' sexual scripts (Rosen & Leiblum, 1988). Therefore, we refer to *sensual communication,* because any sexual encounter should involve communication about the partners' preferences.

Talking about Sex

Most couples need to negotiate a number of difficulties over the course of their relationship. Communicating about sex, however, poses unique problems for many peo-

Sexual communication is essential to sexual satisfaction.

ple whose upbringing and cultural heritage makes them uncomfortable talking about sex. This discomfort is evident on many levels, including sexual vocabulary (Braun & Kitzinger, 2001). Indeed, as was noted earlier, even the meaning of "having sex" is quite ambiguous in the United States (Carpenter, 2001; Sanders & Reinisch, 1999). Many euphemisms for sexual intercourse, such as "sleeping together" or "making love," betray the cultural discomfort with sexuality. (Curiously, most people are awake when they "sleep with" someone!) This ambiguity in language can create obstacles in sexual relationships by clouding communication.

Research confirms that both men and women find it easier to share nonsexual information about themselves than to communicate sexual information to their partners (Byers & Demmons, 1999). Marriage researcher and therapist John Gottman observed that "no other area of a couple's life offers more potential for embarrassment, hurt, and rejection than sex" (Gottman & Silver, 1999, p. 200). Consequently, clear and effective communication is a prerequisite to a satisfying sexual relationship (Purnine & Carey, 1997).

Communicating Sexual Needs

Effective sexual communication requires couples to share information about their sexual likes and dislikes and their desired levels of sexual intimacy. Over time, most couples in long-term relationships develop a shared sexual vocabulary and a set of "signals," both verbal and nonverbal, that they use to convey their sexual desire.

One of the first sexual decisions that dating couples face is the timing for the initiation of sexual activity. Disagreements over when to initiate a sexual relationship are common. Research shows that partners who agree on when to initiate sexual activity report better sexual adjustment (Purnine & Carey, 1997). Yet, most people have had the occasional experience of wanting sexual activity with a reluctant partner. Contrary to the popular stereotype, this experience is not restricted to males. More than half of the female college students in one study reported desiring sexual activity more than their male partners (O'Sullivan & Byers, 1993).

No matter how compatible two partners are, they will experience occasional disagreements, including discrepancies in their levels of sexual desire. Communication skills are important for resolving such differences. Communication that is obscure because it is imprecise or vague will detract from shared intimacy, both in the bedroom and out. Sexual desire can be communicated verbally or nonverbally. In fact, nonverbal communication of sexual interest is probably the most common form of sexual communication among couples (Metts, Sprecher, & Regan, 2000). More

8.2 on the web

Most people have some questions about the "best" techniques for pleasure. Reliable sources, however, are hard to find. Go Ask Alice is a Web site about sexuality, presented in a question-and-answer format and sponsored by Columbia University. You'll find a link to this site at **www.ablongman.com/mcanulty2e**. Review some questions about techniques. *Which are most common? Which of these have you wondered about?*

IN YOUR own words

Heather Redding
Northwestern University

The hardest thing about communicating my needs to my partner is being careful not to bruise his ego. When a guy believes he's "mastered" a certain move in sex, he wants to do it all the time. If it doesn't feel good, it's hard for me to say something because I'm afraid he'll stop doing *everything* because he'll be embarrassed, instead of simply "updating" his technique.

CLOSE UP ON gender

"Not Tonight Dear": Gender Differences in Sensual Communication

Historically, men have been viewed as more sexually oriented than women. In relationships, therefore, men are the ones who are expected to initiate and to orchestrate sexual encounters. Women, according to the traditional script, are the restrictors, or gatekeepers, of sex (O'Sullivan & Byers, 1992). And according to one stereotype, men are always ready for sex and never decline any opportunity.

Men and women sometimes do tend to interpret sexual situations differently. Men are more likely than women to perceive sexual content in objectively neutral situations. For example, compared to women, men are more likely to perceive a female's friendliness as flirtation. Men also perceive women as being more interested in sex than do other women (Abbey & Melby, 1986; Shotland & Craig, 1988). Research also confirms that men tend to initiate sex more often than women, but there are no differences in how often the sexes *consider* initiating sex. Therefore, the main difference is not in sexual desire but rather in acting on the desire: Women are more likely to refrain from pursuing a sexual encounter with their partner (Christopher & Sprecher, 2000). Similarly, women are more likely than men to be the unenthusiastic participant in a sexual encounter. For women in established dating relationships, giving in to a partner's sexual wishes is sometimes a way of preventing conflict or avoiding partner disappointment (O'Sullivan & Gaines, 1998).

Contrary to stereotypes, men are not always ready for sex, and there are times when men may decline a female partner's sexual invitation. Over half of women in dating relationships report having been turned down by a male partner (O'Sullivan & Byers, 1993). These subtle gender differences, however, mask the similarities between men and women. Here again, men and women are more alike than different. For example, the vast majority (80%) of sexual initiations by one partner lead to sexual encounters (O'Sullivan & Byers, 1992). Men and women are equally likely to consider initiating sex, to reject an initiation, and to use similar messages to initiate sex. There are some gender differences in reactions to being turned down when attempting to initiate sex: Women are more likely to desist, while men often try to persuade their partners to give in (O'Sullivan & Byers, 1993).

When it comes to sexual invitations, a partner may feel ambivalent and give mixed signals, a phenomenon known as putting up "token resistance" (Muehlenhard & Rodgers, 1998). The popular view is that women in the early stages of a relationship may resist a sexual invitation simply because they fear appearing "easy" or because they want to "play hard to get." Contrary to the stereotype, this behavior is not limited to women, as many men report putting up token resistance at least once. A study of college students in the United States, Russia, and Japan revealed that token resistance is reported in all three cultures, and it is more common among virgins than among nonvirgins (Sprecher et al., 1994). Muehlenhard and Rodgers (1998) noted that several explanations were given for engaging in token resistance: to alleviate guilt feelings about engaging in sex, to retain control in a relationship, to test a partner's reactions, and to retain some of the excitement in a sexual relationship. In any case, token resistance usually reflects some ambivalence about a sexual encounter or a relationship (O'Sullivan & Gaines, 1998). The phenomenon highlights the importance of open communication in all relationships. A prudent strategy is to follow the advice of Muehlenhard and Rodgers (1998), who concluded, "All refusals should be taken seriously. Engaging in sex with someone who does not consent is rape" (p. 462). If in doubt, check it out: Ask.

than half of couples report using direct nonverbal communication to initiate sex with their partners, such as passionate kissing or erotic touching (Brown & Auerbach, 1981). How do partners usually communicate a positive response to sexual invitations? Just as invitations tend to be nonverbal, so do responses. Rather than explicitly saying yes to a partner's sexual invitation, most people just don't say no and go along with the partner's intimate kissing or touching (Hickman & Muehlenhard, 1999). In this respect, there are few differences between men and women. Other differences and similarities between the communication patterns of women and men are explored in Close Up on Gender: "Not Tonight, Dear": Gender Differences in Sensual Communication.

Couples who are satisfied with their sex lives view their sexual interactions as shared intimacy. They recognize that no two people are identical, including in their sexual needs (Gottman & Silver, 1999). These couples learn to successfully compromise. Ideally, every sexual encounter is equally desired by both partners. In reality, though, this is rarely the case. As with any joint activity, there will be times when one partner wants sex and the other does not. Sometimes a reluctant partner will give in, whether to satisfy the needy partner, to enhance intimacy, or simply to avoid conflict (O'Sullivan & Allgeier, 1998; Shotland & Hunter, 1995). In cases where the discrepancy in sexual desire is more long-term, couples must negotiate an informal contract, often one that stipulates that the partner with the lower sex drive will occasionally accept sexual invitations (Shotland & Goodstein, 1992). The same informal contract dictates that sexual invitations can sometimes be declined without implying rejection. All successful sexual negotiations strengthen the bond between intimate partners (O'Sullivan & Allgeier, 1998).

IN YOUR own words

Travis Wright
Virginia Commonwealth University

My girlfriend was raised in a home where it's not a common thing to talk freely about any thought or issue, especially when it comes to sex. So it took a while for her to be free with me about what she wants to say about sex. I knew I had to be consistent in being open with her and asking her what she thinks or feels about the situation. Now if there is any issue, no matter what the subject, I feel that we can talk openly.

Sexual Self-Disclosure

Sexual self-disclosure, the ability to share one's sexual likes and dislikes, is easier in relationships characterized by openness about nonsexual matters as well (Byers & Demmons, 1999). Most people find it easier to open up when they anticipate that their partner will be accepting and understanding. Even under those conditions, however, some things are easier to share than others.

Byers and Demmons (1999) found that college students find it easier to share their sexual likes than their dislikes. Sharing one's sexual likes is helpful for guiding one's sexual partner in the desired direction during a sexual encounter. Conversely, sharing dislikes does communicate what one finds distasteful, but it does not necessarily convey what is desirable. Telling your partner, for example, that you do not enjoy oral sex does not necessarily convey what you *do* enjoy. Sharing likes rather than dislikes can also serve to minimize hurt feelings or to avoid conflict by helping couples focus on their similarities rather than their differences.

Effective communication is a two-way street, and sexual self-disclosure is much easier when a person feels that it is reciprocal rather than one-sided. As Byers and Demmons (1999) concluded, "Sexual self-disclosure occurs in the context of an overall disclosing relationship. That is, individuals self-disclose more about their sexual likes and dislikes when there is a high level of self-disclosure about other topics in the relationship, and when they perceive their partner [is self-disclosing about] his or her sexual likes and dislikes." (p. 186).

There are many ways of sharing sexual preferences with a partner. Frank discussions of one's sexual likes and dislikes is naturally effective, but there are other ways of self-disclosing. During a sexual encounter, partners can exchange verbal and nonverbal information. Guiding a partner's hand, body, or mouth can be effective. Moans and nonverbal gestures can effectively signal sexual enjoyment. In summary, sexual self-disclosure—the mutual sharing of sexual likes and dislikes—leads to greater sexual satisfaction. (Byers & Demmons, 1999).

This section of the chapter provides an overview of sexual techniques. Because of the wide range of sexual practices, the coverage is necessarily limited, focusing on those techniques that are most commonly practiced in the United States. Not all readers will find every technique presented here acceptable. Some readers, in fact, may find some information distasteful. The goal is to provide an informative summary of various common practices for educational purposes, in line with Reiss's (1993) philosophy that all decisions in a relationship, including decisions about acceptable sexual practices, should be based on honesty, equality, and responsibility. Health Matters: How to Have Great Sex with Your Partner (on page 236) provides additional information on strategies for enjoying a healthy sexual relationship.

HEALTH Matters

How to Have Great Sex with Your Partner

Knowing the "right" sexual techniques for pleasing one's partner is only a small part of a healthy sexual relationship. Attitude and communication with a partner are even more important than knowing what to do in bed. With a commitment to effective communication and an openness to listening nondefensively, anyone can learn how to satisfy and be pleased by a partner. Learning to please one's partner sexually is a process that may involve some trial and error and time—but building a healthy sexual relationship *always* requires effective communication.

The fact is that, sexually speaking, no two people are alike. A technique that is highly arousing to one person can be a complete turn-off to another. The only sure way to determine how to please one's partner is through open communication. As noted in Chapter 7, effective communication usually begins with effective listening and requires creating an atmosphere of openness that will facilitate the sharing of information about personal sexual preferences and dislikes. An open atmosphere may be created by such simple statements as "I really want to please you, so I need you to let me know what you want me to do." Listening also extends to observing a partner's behaviors, verbal and nonverbal, during a sexual encounter. A partner may signal what is pleasurable by guiding you with his or her hands, by demonstrating what to do, or simply by the sounds he or she makes.

Effective listening also means conveying to a partner that you will always try to be supportive, noncritical, and nonjudgmental. You want to make it easier for your partner to share preferences and dislikes, and this can be accomplished by making it clear that your partner is free to be as open as she or he is comfortable being. You should not expect that you and your partner will necessarily have the same likes or dislikes, but you should always *listen* and *hear* what your partner is saying. And you should not pressure a partner to share more than is comfortable at the time.

Sexual attitudes play a critical role in building healthy relationships. There are two common attitudes or approaches to sex that are particularly unhealthy:

- *Sex as competition.* Believing that you must outdo your partner's previous lovers will be detrimental. Men in particular are socialized to be competitive in social settings, including during sex (Zilbergeld, 1999). Remember that your partner chooses to be with you, and focus on enjoying your time together.
- *Sex as a performance.* Believing that you must know everything about sex and that you must prove it to your partner creates intense pressure. Worrying about your level of arousal or your desirability (Is my penis firm enough? Does he find me attractive? Are my breasts large enough?) will invariably detract from the sharing of pleasure and intimacy. As you'll learn in Chapter 13, performance anxiety is a problem associated with sexual dysfunction.

Rather than viewing a sexual encounter as competition or a performance, partners should focus on the moment, on the opportunity to share sexual pleasure and intimacy. Several suggestions may help you do that (Zilbergeld, 1999):

- Know your own sexual preferences, and be open to learning about your partner's needs and desires. Unrealistic expectations and the many myths about sexuality in our culture interfere with sexual fulfillment.
- Focus on the pleasure and fun of sex rather than on performance. Learn to concentrate on what feels good to you and to your partner.
- Foster the kind of relationship in which sex will be rewarding. Whether the relationship lasts a month or a lifetime, sex is most rewarding when there is an atmosphere of mutual respect, honesty, and equality.
- Be open to communicating verbally and nonverbally about sex. Again, it is impossible to overemphasize the critical importance of communication in *all* interpersonal exchanges, especially situations in which many people have little experience talking openly and frankly. Be open about your sexual preferences, and encourage your partner to do the same.

By following these relatively simple rules, you and your partner can develop the kind of rewarding sexual relationship that you both desire. Remember that great sex is not so much about techniques as it is about being open and willing to learn and share together. Communication is the most important part of the formula for success.

TABLE 8.1 Reasons for Masturbation, by Gender

REASONS FOR MASTURBATION	MEN (%)	WOMEN (%)
To relax	26	32
To relieve sexual tension	73	63
Partner unavailable	32	32
Partner doesn't want sex	16	6
Boredom	11	5
Physical pleasure	40	42
To get to sleep	16	12
Fear of AIDS/STI	7	5
Other	5	5
Total number of respondents	835	687

SELF-PLEASURING

Although masturbation is often viewed as solitary sexual behavior, many couples incorporate masturbation into their shared sexual activity—by masturbating their partner, masturbating simultaneously, or watching a partner masturbate. In fact, many individuals report being sexually aroused at the sight of a partner masturbating. Masturbation, then, is not necessarily a substitute for sexual activity with a partner, as Kinsey and his colleagues claimed (Kinsey, Pomeroy, & Martin, 1948; Kinsey, Pomeroy, Martin, & Gebhard, 1953). Men and women who report higher rates of self-pleasuring also report higher rates of sexual activity with a partner (Laumann, Gagnon, Michael, & Michaels, 1994). This finding suggests that persons who have a healthy sex drive and who are comfortable with their sexuality tend to enjoy expressing their sexuality in various ways, including self-pleasuring. As you can see in Table 8.1, men and women report diverse (and often multiple) reasons for masturbating, although it is usually engaged in for sexual relief (Laumann et al., 1994).

did YOU know?

Over 40% of men and 16% of women surveyed in the NHSLS report having used sex toys or viewed sexually explicit materials (Laumann et al., 1994).

Masturbation is often accompanied by sexual fantasy (Leitenberg & Henning, 1995; Reinisch, 1990). Some individuals use sexually explicit materials such as erotic videos or magazines during self-pleasuring in order to increase sexual arousal and to enhance sexual fantasy. Men are more likely to use sexually explicit materials during masturbation than are women (Laumann et al., 1994). Both men and women report that masturbation often produces intense orgasms (Masters & Johnson, 1966).

Sex toys are becoming increasingly popular, and not exclusively for self-pleasuring. One survey (Laumann et al., 1994) found that as many as 5% of Americans reported using such toys during sex with a partner as well as during masturbation. Among the toys most commonly used were dildos and vibrators. **Dildos** are penis-shaped objects that may be inserted into the vagina or anus. They are available in various sizes and may be made out of rubber, glass, or silicone (some ancient examples were made of wood!). During masturbation, the user of a dildo controls the speed and type of motion as well as the angle and depth of penetration. **Vibrators** are electrical or battery-operated

DILDO
A penis-shaped sex toy.

VIBRATOR
An electrical or battery-operated device used to massage erogenous areas.

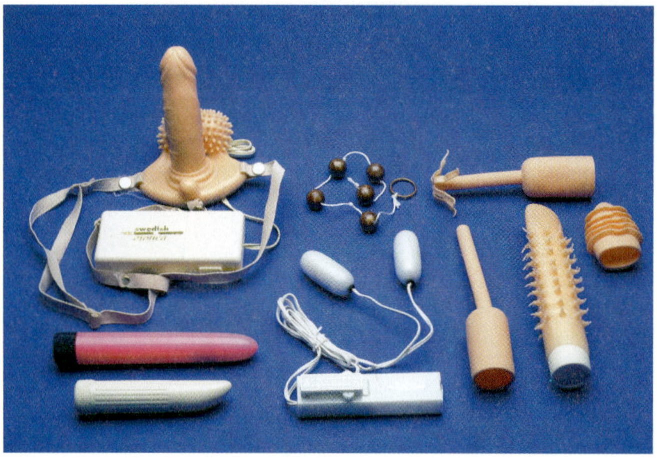

Sex toys, such as these vibrators and dildos, are used by individuals and couples to increase sexual pleasure. One survey found that up to 5% of couples used sex toys during sexual encounters.

devices used to massage erogenous areas of the body. Although vibrators come in various shapes and sizes, they all provide stimulation via their vibrating motion. Unlike dildos, which are primarily used for internal stimulation, vibrators stimulate the body's exterior surfaces such as the clitoris, vaginal lips, and mons. Women who use vibrators report that they produce more intense orgasms (Davis, Blank, Lin, & Bonillas, 1996).

Male Masturbation

Most males masturbate by stimulating the penis with the hand. A few men masturbate by rubbing their genitals against a soft object, such as a pillow or mattress (Kinsey et al., 1948). The man holds the shaft of the penis with his dominant hand and moves it up and down in a rhythmic, stroking fashion. Men generally begin masturbation with a steady pace, increasing the speed and the firmness of their grip as they sense that ejaculation is imminent (Masters & Johnson, 1966). Men differ in their firmness of grip and speed of stroking. Additionally, some men enjoy rubbing their scrotum before or during masturbation. It is also common for men to gently stroke the glans and frenulum, which may also be helpful in attaining an erection prior to masturbation.

The use of lubricants during male masturbation is not uncommon, since the penis produces little natural lubrication. Petroleum jelly or K-Y jelly, as well as other types of lotions, may be used to reduce friction during masturbation. Men also often find the added moisture to be sexually arousing, as it simulates the conditions of intercourse. Upon ejaculation, the man generally slows the speed and amount of stroking as the glans and coronal ridge are highly sensitized, and any further stimulation at this point may feel uncomfortable.

Male Masturbation

Female Masturbation

Masters and Johnson (1966) were the first to report that females use more varied masturbation techniques than males. The majority of women masturbate by stimulating the mons, labia minora, and clitoris (Hite, 1976), using either circular or back-and-forth stroking motions. Although some women may rub the clitoral glans directly early during self-stimulation, the glans quickly becomes hypersensitive. So women tend to shift their attention to the clitoral shaft as the clitoris becomes engorged. There are various methods for achieving clitoral stimulation during self-pleasuring, including stroking the shaft and gently pulling on the labia. While stimulating the clitoris, many women enhance their pleasure by rubbing their breasts or nipples with the other hand.

Despite a popular belief among men, few women choose to insert their fingers or objects like dildos into their vaginas during masturbation (Kinsey et al., 1953). Some women do, however, report that they enjoy vaginal insertion as a prelude to clitoral stimulation or as an adjunct to it. Other techniques might include pressing the genital region against an object, using water pressure from a shower for stimulation, crossing the legs and exerting pressure on the clitoris by rhythmically pressing the legs together, or using sex toys (Davis et al., 1996).

Female Masturbation

PLEASURING ONE'S PARTNER

The range of partner-pleasuring techniques is limited only by a couple's imagination and personal preferences. This section gives a brief overview of the most common sexual techniques for oral, vaginal, and anal sex. These techniques are usually preceded by a most fundamental form of stimulation—touching and caressing. Unlike the skin of most other species of mammals, human skin is not covered by thick hair; thus we have a large surface area for receiving sensuous caresses. Because of specialized sensory receptors in the skin covering the entire body, we humans enjoy being touched. Sensuous touching is not only a special way of increasing sexual arousal and exploring a partner's body, it is also a completely safe sexual practice.

The intimate kissing and caressing that are preludes to other forms of sexual stimulation are often referred to as *foreplay*. For many partners, foreplay represents a special opportunity for intimate sharing and serves to increase their arousal levels before they engage in penetrative sexual acts. Of course, foreplay need not be viewed only as a "warmup" for other activities; there may be times when it is sufficiently stimulating in itself.

Oral Sex

Oral stimulation of a partner's genitals is a popular way of giving sexual pleasure to a partner. Surveys reveal that the majority of adults have both performed and received oral stimulation. Oral sex is often viewed as one of the more pleasurable and intimate sexual practices. It is often part of foreplay, although it may also be an end in itself.

Derived from the Latin term for "to suck," *fellatio* involves oral stimulation of the penis by licking or sucking. A person performing fellatio may begin by licking the most sensitive areas of the penis, such as the frenulum, the glans, the underside of the shaft, and the base. Many men also find stimulation of the scrotum to be very pleasurable. Licking usually gives way to sucking—encircling the penis with the lips and moving up and down. The partner performing fellatio usually tries to find a position in which the angle of the penis and the angle of the throat are aligned. "Deep-throating" describes the practice of taking the penis into the back of the throat, which naturally stimulates the gag reflex. The gagging may be eliminated with repeated practice, during which the depth of penetration is gradually increased, effectively training the throat

Simultaneous Oral Sex, or "69"

Looking At . . .

. . . Thinking About

A satisfying sexual relationship involves much more than just knowing the right techniques. Effective communication and an openness to intimacy and sharing are more important. Whether short-term or long-term, sexual relationships based on responsibility, equality, and honesty are generally the most satisfying. What do you consider most important in a sexual relationship?

muscles to stay relaxed. To avoid the gag reflex, many people hold the base of the penis while performing fellatio in order to control the depth of penetration. While performing fellatio, a partner may choose to use the free hand to stimulate the scrotum or other erogenous zones.

One thing a couple must agree on is the question of ejaculating during fellatio. Some people enjoy receiving their partner's semen in the mouth; others find this practice distasteful. Another question is whether to swallow or spit out the semen. As in all consensual sexual behavior, these practices are matters of personal preference. In all cases, couples should talk openly about their sexual preferences in advance. As noted in Health Matters, communication is essential for clarifying individual expectations and making any sexual experience gratifying for both partners.

Cunnilingus is the term referring to oral stimulation of a female's genitals. Many women find cunnilingus to be one of the most pleasurable sexual experiences. It is not uncommon for women to report that it is the only method by which they consistently achieve orgasm. The oral stimulation may include licking or sucking the labia minora and vaginal opening. Directly stimulating the clitoris is almost always involved. Many women, though, prefer a gradual approach to oral clitoral stimulation that begins with kissing or licking the lower abdomen, inner thighs, and area surrounding the clitoris. As the woman becomes increasingly aroused, she may direct her partner to provide more direct stimulation of the clitoris. Some women desire rapid and direct stimulation of the clitoris, and others prefer slower oral caresses. At a certain point, some women may find the clitoris to be hypersensitive, and they may request that attention be directed to other erogenous zones. During cunnilingus, some women enjoy vaginal penetration by their partners' tongue, fingers, or a sex toy.

Simultaneous oral stimulation, or "69," is a technique whereby partners provide oral sex while also receiving it. It is most easily practiced in a side-by-side position or with one partner on top of the other. Aside from the possible awkwardness in finding a comfortable position, some couples complain that it is too distracting to receive oral sex while simultaneously performing it. They may prefer taking turns so that each partner may fully concentrate on the pleasurable sensations.

Vaginal Intercourse

Vaginal intercourse, or more technically, *coitus* (from the Latin *coire,* "to go together"), is the preferred sexual activity for the majority of people (Laumann et al., 1994). In fact, for the heterosexual majority, "having sex" is generally interpreted to mean engaging in vaginal intercourse, in which the penis is inserted into the vagina. There are numerous positions for vaginal intercourse—perhaps hundreds, according to some popular sex manuals. Perhaps only the participants' imaginations and acrobatic talents limit the possibilities. Nonetheless, the majority of these positions are variants of the male-superior, female-superior, and rear-entry positions.

Male-Superior Position for Vaginal Intercourse

Male-Superior Positions

Male-superior positions in a heterosexual relationship are those in which the man is on top of his partner during penetration. Male-superior positions allow easy entry (especially if the woman guides the man's penis into her vagina) and relatively deep penetration. The main drawback is that the woman's movements are restricted, and she may feel passive and that she has little control in this position. Couples may also find it difficult to use manual stimulation in these positions.

One of the most commonly used positions for vaginal intercourse in Western cultures is what is referred to as the **missionary position.** Frequently thought of as unadventurous and traditional, the missionary position, like other positions, has advantages and disadvantages. In this position, the man lies above the woman, usually using his arms and knees to support some of his weight rather than resting his full weight on his partner. If he remains in this position for a prolonged period of time, the man may experience muscle tension and fatigue, which could detract from his enjoyment. The position offers the advantage of full body contact, providing increased feelings of closeness and allowing the couple to kiss. The side-by-side posture is a variant for partners who enjoy face-to-face positions. In this position, the male penetrates the female's vagina while both partners lie on their sides. The primary advantage of the position is that it allows face-to-face contact without requiring either partner to bear the weight of the other. The position is favored by couples with health or weight concerns. Some couples also find it easier to stimulate a woman's clitoris and breasts in this position. A disadvantage is that penetration is relatively shallow.

Female-Superior Position for Vaginal Intercourse

Female-Superior Positions

Female-superior positions are those in which the woman is on top of her partner. Variations of these positions include the seated position and the female-superior position with the woman's back to her partner. One interesting variation is the female-superior position with both partners sitting up and holding each other in a close embrace. Partners may remain in this position without moving and enjoy the closeness as they kiss, talk, or look into each other's eyes. In the seated position, the woman faces her partner and straddles his penis. She controls the depth of penetration and speed of thrusting from her seated position. In this position, the man is comparatively less active, although female-superior positions make it easy for him to caress her breasts. The position also facilitates manual stimulation of the clitoris by either partner, something that is difficult to accomplish in the male-superior positions.

Masters and Johnson (1966) observed that female-superior positions provided the most direct clitoral stimulation of all positions for vaginal intercourse. Because of the ability to control the rhythm of thrusting and amount of clitoral stimulation, many women find these positions most effective for having an orgasm during intercourse.

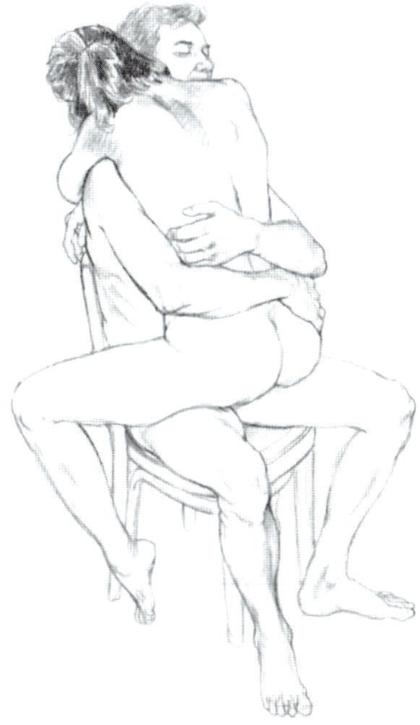
Sitting Position, Female-Superior

Rear-Entry Positions

Sometimes erroneously equated with anal intercourse (described later), rear-entry positions involve vaginal penetration; the man enters the woman's vagina from a position behind her. Popularly known as "doggy style," the position usually involves the woman positioning herself on her hands and knees with her partner kneeling behind her. The position affords more freedom of thrusting for the man than most other positions, and penetration occurs at a different angle than in the male-superior or female-superior positions. Because of the deep thrusting and different penetration angle, many women enjoy the unique sensations provided by rear-entry positions. Additionally, manual clitoral stimulation is easily accomplished by either partner in these

MISSIONARY POSITION
One of the most common positions for coitus, in which the man lies above the woman while supporting some of his weight with his arms and knees.

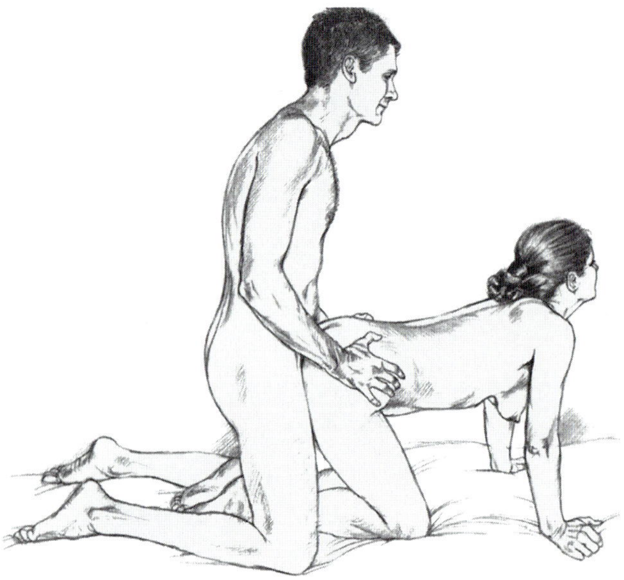

Rear-Entry Position for Vaginal Intercourse

positions. Men may enjoy the visual and tactile stimulation of their partner's buttocks pressing against their abdomen during penetration.

A variation is the chair position, in which the woman essentially sits on the man's lap with her back to him while he is seated comfortably. Thrusting is controlled by the female using her legs and arms for support. This position is especially suitable for men whose mobility is limited due to health problems or injury. Alternatively, rear entry can be accomplished with both partners lying on their sides. This may be especially comfortable for pregnant women or those who are unable to bear weight on their knees. The rear-entry position with both partners lying on their sides is referred to as "spooning."

Some people dislike rear-entry positions because they associate them with animal mating. Further, these positions may feel impersonal since partners do not face each other. Also, kissing is quite complicated in these positions, unless one is unusually limber. Finally, the rear-entry positions do not provide direct clitoral stimulation.

Anal Intercourse

Anal intercourse is penetration of the rectum with the penis, which may be accomplished in any of the positions previously described. It is probably most commonly done from the rear-entry position. Contrary to popular belief, gay men are not the only people who engage in anal intercourse. National surveys reveal that 20–30% of Americans in general (Billy, Tanfer, Grady, & Kepinger, 1993; Laumann et al., 1994) and up to one-third of U.S. college students (Seidman & Reider, 1994) have experienced anal intercourse. Approximately 10% of heterosexual couples report having engaged in anal intercourse during the past 12 months (Laumann et al., 1994; Voeller, 1991). Some individuals report having experimented with anal intercourse out of curiosity, but for others it is a regular and enjoyable sexual practice.

did YOU know?

For heterosexual men, group sex may enact fantasies of conquest and sexual prowess. Gay men tend to view it simply as "hot sex." Heterosexual women often view group sex as their male partners' attempt to exchange them for other men's sexual partners (Laumann et al., 1994).

The rectum has a rich nerve supply, making it sensitive to stimulation. Many couples engage in digital penetration of the anus (insertion of a finger) during sexual encounters. This may be particularly arousing prior to and during orgasm when the anal sphincter contracts rhythmically. Because the anal sphincter is a muscle that remains contracted most of the time, it must be relaxed during penetration. Anal penetration should proceed very slowly and gradually; otherwise, the receptive partner will experience significant pain.

Certain additional health precautions should be taken when practicing any form of anal stimulation. Oral-anal stimulation (also known as **analingus**) is especially risky. The intestinal tract, which extends to the anus, carries a variety of microorganisms that may cause hepatitis, intestinal infections, and other diseases. Additionally, as Chapter 14 will discuss, unprotected anal intercourse carries one the highest risks for HIV infection, and other STIs may be transmitted via anal stimulation. Because of these risks, couples practicing anal intercourse should always use a condom. Additionally, heterosexual couples should never proceed to vaginal intercourse or fellatio after anal intercourse without changing the condom. Inserting the penis or a finger into a partner's vagina or mouth following anal penetration also carries a high risk of transmitting infectious diseases.

ANALINGUS
Oral-anal stimulation.

Same-Sex Techniques

Lesbian and gay couples enjoy most of the same sexual practices as heterosexual couples. This is not surprising, since all persons, regardless of sexual orientation, have the same erogenous zones. So, like their heterosexual counterparts, same-sex couples enjoy kissing, intimate touching, various positions for intercourse, and oral sex. The only sexual activity they don't engage in, for obvious reasons, is penile-vaginal intercourse.

Lesbian Technique

Lesbian Techniques

Compared to heterosexual couples, lesbians tend to be less focused on genital sex (Fassinger & Morrow, 1995). Although lesbian couples report a lower frequency of sexual interactions than do heterosexual couples, many of them say that their encounters are quite passionate and lengthy (Frye, 1992). Lesbian couples spend comparatively more time snuggling, hugging, and kissing. Although lesbians in long-term relationships describe a decrease in their sexual frequency over time, they are more responsive and sexually satisfied than most heterosexual women. The vast majority of lesbians are orgasmic and sexually satisfied (Loulan, 1987; Nichols, 1990).

Over 80% of lesbians enjoy touching and kissing breasts, body-to-body contact, self-pleasuring, and inserting fingers in a partner's vagina. The majority also take pleasure in giving and receiving oral sex and in mutual masturbation (Loulan, 1987). **Tribadism**, the practice of rubbing the genitals together, is another lesbian practice. Between 10% and 30% of lesbians incorporate sex toys in their sexual encounters, but contrary to one popular stereotype, most lesbians do not require phallic substitutes during their sexual activities.

Gay Technique

Gay Techniques

Like heterosexual men, gay men enjoy a variety of sexual positions and activities. The stereotype that gay men favor either a "masculine" role (active partner, or inserter) or a "feminine" role (passive partner, or recipient) during sex is an oversimplification. Most gay men are versatile in their sexual practices and enjoy the variety of alternating sexual acts.

Compared to heterosexual and lesbian couples, gay men engage in oral sex more frequently. Fellatio is the most popular technique among gay men. Mutual masturbation and body rubbing are also popular. Contrary to a widespread belief, not all gay men practice anal intercourse regularly (Barrett, Bolan, & Douglas, 1998). One-third of gay men practice anal intercourse only rarely, if at all. Another third enjoy reciprocal anal intercourse, and the remainder have a clear preference for being either the insertive or receptive partner during the act (Blumstein & Schwartz, 1983). With the advent of the AIDS crisis, gay men have reported an overall decrease in anal intercourse. Among gay men who continue to practice anal penetration, a significant increase in condom usage has greatly reduced HIV infection rates (Rosenberg & Biggar, 1998). Finally, some gay men take pleasure in the practice of manually stimulating a partner's anus by inserting several fingers or even the entire fist (a practice known as "fisting"). As with any form of anal stimulation, manual-anal stimulation requires partners to be gentle, proceed slowly, and always use proper precautions.

TRIBADISM
Rubbing together of genitals by two women.

HEALTHY DECISION MAKING

If there is one key concept to be derived from this chapter, it is that communication is essential to a successful relationship. As Byers and Demmons (1999) discovered in their study of nearly 100 college students in dating relationships, people who feel that they communicate effectively with their partners are also better at sharing their sexual likes and dislikes. The following tips should help you improve sensual communication with your partner.

1. *Identify the barriers to effective communication.* Don't be hard on yourself for not having all of the answers. (Even "sexperts" who write textbooks don't know it all!) If you find it embarrassing to talk about your sexual preferences, practice giving your partner feedback while engaged in nonsexual touching, such as a backrub. Then gradually work up the courage to talk about your sexual relationship with your partner.
2. *Remember that communication, like all skills, requires practice.* Find opportunities to practice sensual communication with your partner. Begin by talking about things you like that you find easiest to talk about. Many people, for example, find it easier to start by describing how they like being kissed or held. As you become more comfortable, progress to sharing preferences that are more awkward for you to discuss.
3. *Remember that effective communication is a two-way street.* Find opportunities to share *and* opportunities to listen. Because people have busy schedules, they often must create opportunities to communicate by setting aside time and making sharing sessions a priority.
4. *If you don't succeed at first, try again.* Again, practice is the key. Nobody is born an expert communicator, but practice is the way to develop and polish your sensual communication skills.

summary

SEX IN LOVE RELATIONSHIPS

- Although heterosexual penile-vaginal intercourse is what most people mean when they talk of "having sex," sexual behavior in the United States is diverse. Masturbation and oral sex, which may generate feelings of guilt or shame, are nevertheless common practices.
- The meanings assigned to specific sexual phenomena (such as having sex and losing one's virginity) reflect cultural scripts.
- Like all other components of a relationship, sexual intimacy must be nurtured.
- The importance of sex in a long-term relationship may change over time.

SENSUAL COMMUNICATION TECHNIQUES

- Many couples find it difficult to talk openly about sex. Disagreements over sexual initiation and frequency are not uncommon. Open communication facilitates successful negotiation and compromise.
- Sexual self-disclosure is easiest in relationships characterized by openness and mutual sharing. Sharing sexual preferences is usually easier than discussing dislikes. Effective sharing involves both verbal and nonverbal communication.
- Relationship satisfaction is influenced by the quality of communication and sharing, both in the bedroom and elsewhere.

SELF-PLEASURING

- Masturbation is often viewed as solitary sexual behavior, although it can be incorporated into couples' shared activity as well.
- Both males and females report that masturbation can produce intense orgasms.
- Some individuals enjoy using sex toys to enhance their sensual pleasure.

PLEASURING ONE'S PARTNER

- The majority of adults have experienced oral sex. Many couples find the experience to be very intimate.

Openly communicating one's likes and dislikes makes the experience more enjoyable for both partners.

- Vaginal intercourse is the preferred activity for most heterosexuals. Male-superior positions are popular in Western cultures. Female-superior positions are often more satisfying for women. Rear-entry positions are common variations, although they may feel more impersonal.
- Anal intercourse is an experimental practice for a number of couples. It requires certain health precautions.
- Gay and lesbian couples enjoy most of the same practices as heterosexual couples. Lesbians tend to be less focused on genital sex. Many stereotypes about gay men's sexual practices are oversimplifications.

CHAPTER 9

Conception, Pregnancy, and Childbirth

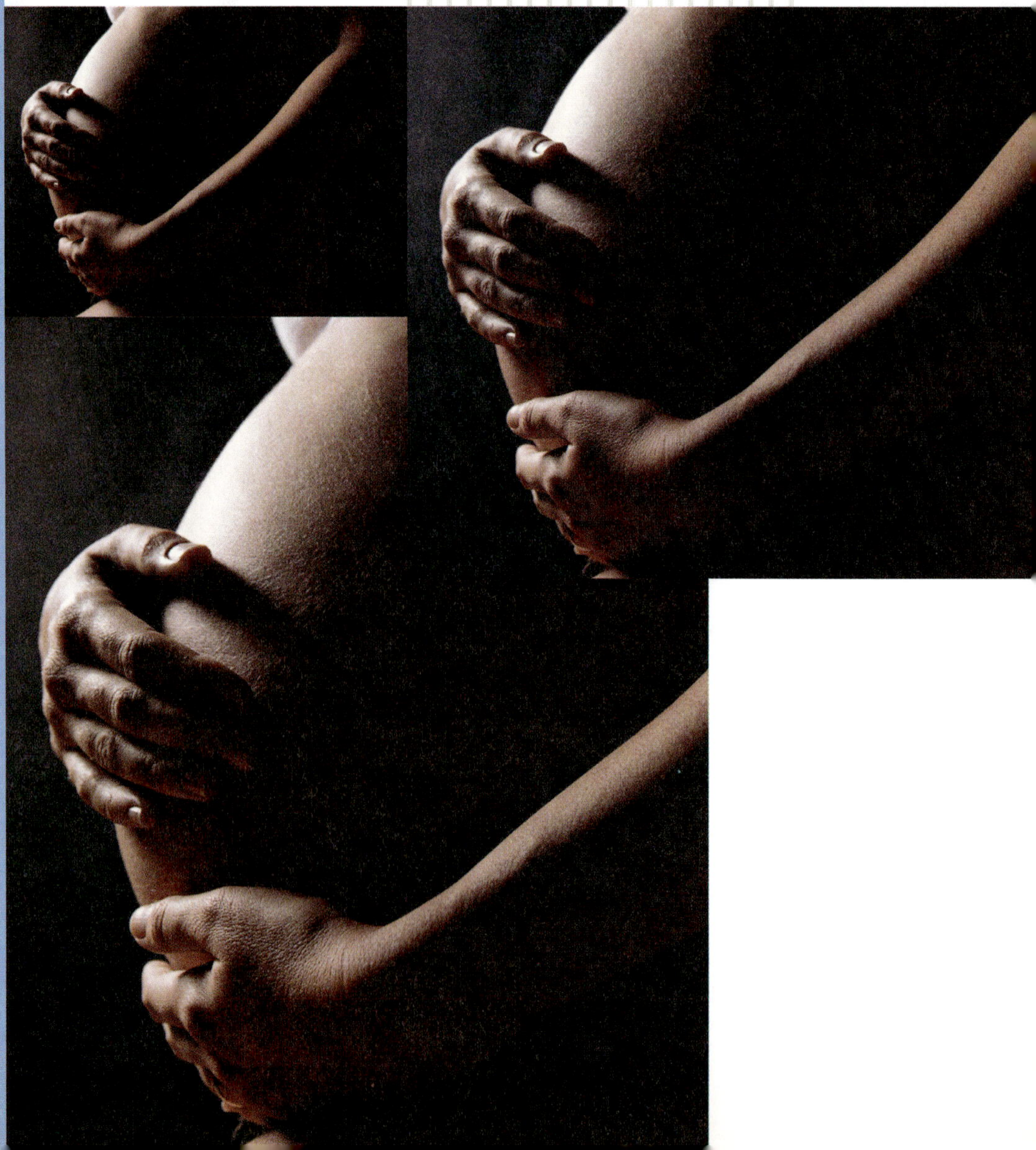

A story from a new mother:

I was in the grocery store with my 5-month old baby, and a kind woman came up to admire him. We began to chat, and I learned that she had *six* children of her own. As she leaned over the cart and cooed at my baby, I became filled with emotion. I looked at her with tears in my eyes and said, "I don't think I can have another baby." "Ah," she said, "that's because you don't think you could love another baby like you love this one." "That's right! How did you know that?" I replied. "Because I felt the same way," the woman said, "but, as hard as it may seem for you to believe right now, you will love all your babies just as you love this one."

I became filled with emotion.

CONCEPTION AND FETAL DEVELOPMENT

No text on human sexuality would be complete without a discussion of some of the most remarkable aspects of sexuality—the processes of conception, pregnancy, and childbirth. Whether you have been a participant or an observer, you probably agree that the birth of a child is truly miraculous. But the miracle does not begin at birth; it begins much earlier—40 weeks earlier, to be exact—at conception, when an egg and a sperm unite, and the new life begins to grow. Perhaps most miraculous of all is the fact that this life begins as a single cell, and despite a very complex developmental process with many opportunities for error, the outcome is almost always a perfectly formed, healthy baby. For the miracle of conception to occur, the timing of the release of an egg from an ovary and the movement of sperm into the woman's body must be perfect.

Once an egg has been released from a follicle, it is swept from the surface of the ovary by contractions of the fimbriae at the end of the fallopian tube. The movements of the cilia in the tube also coax the egg into the tube. After entering the tube, the egg moves quickly for a few moments as a result of the movements of the cilia and the contractions of the tube's smooth muscle. The muscle contractions quickly diminish, but the cilia continue to move the egg slowly toward the uterus. It takes the egg approximately 4 days to reach the uterus (Vander, Sherman, & Luciano, 1994), but fertilization generally occurs earlier than that, in the outer third of the fallopian tube closest to the ovary.

did YOU know?

On average, a sexually active, fertile woman, using no contraception, has an 85% chance of becoming pregnant within 1 year.

During intercourse, seminal fluid containing hundreds of millions of mature sperm is deposited in the vagina. Millions of sperm are produced and ejaculated because many of them are improperly formed, many die in the acidic vaginal environment, many do not survive the long-distance swim to the fallopian tube, and still others make a wrong turn into the other tube that contains no egg. Thus, only a few hundred sperm reach the tube containing the egg (Vander, Sherman, & Luciano, 1994). Finally, in order for the sperm to be capable of joining with the egg, they must

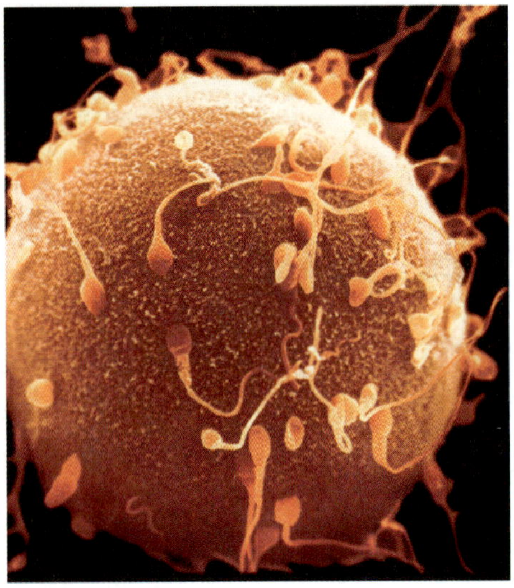

Only one sperm fertilizes the egg.

undergo a process called *capacitation*. Capacitation changes the way the sperm swim so that they lurch forward to come in contact with the egg; it also alters the outer membranes of the sperm so that they can join with the egg's membrane surface.

Fertilization

When the sperm reach the egg, several of them attach themselves to sperm receptor sites on the **zona pellucida**, which is the outer layer of the egg. These sperm are altered once again by this binding process. A reaction exposes enzymes in the acrosome, or tip of the sperm. These enzymes make it possible for the sperm to penetrate the zona pellucida. With the thrusting motions of their tails, the sperm begin moving through this layer until one penetrates it and reaches a space between it and the egg's plasma membrane. This sperm fuses with the plasma membrane and is pulled into the egg by contractions within the egg. As soon as one sperm reaches this point, vesicles around the egg secrete enzymes into the space between the zona pellucida and the plasma membrane. These enzymes deactivate the sperm receptor sites and cause the zona pellucida to harden. From that point on, no other sperm can penetrate the egg's plasma membrane.

The fertilized egg is now called a *zygote*. Assuming a normal developmental process, this single-celled organism will emerge from the womb as a fully developed human baby in about 266 days. First, however, it must progress through several developmental stages.

ZONA PELLUCIDA
Gelatinous outer layer of the ovum.

MONOZYGOTIC (IDENTICAL) TWINS
Two offspring deriving from a single fertilized ovum; these twins, therefore, have an identical genetic makeup.

DIZYGOTIC (FRATERNAL) TWINS
Offspring that develop from separate ova fertilized at the same time.

BLASTOCYST
A stage of a zygote in which it is a mass of developing cells surrounding a cavity.

EMBRYO
The prenatal organism from implantation on the uterine wall to the 8th week of pregnancy.

PLACENTA
A disk-shaped structure made up of tissues from both the prenatal organism and the mother that allows for exchange between their circulatory systems. The fetus is attached to the placenta by the umbilical cord, through which it receives nourishment and oxygen, and through which waste products pass.

UMBILICAL CORD
A flexible cord that contains two arteries and one vein. These vessels transport blood between the fetus and the placenta. Waste products and nutrients move from and to the fetus by way of the umbilical cord.

The Zygote

For 3 or 4 days after it is formed, the zygote travels down the fallopian tube to the uterus while dividing rapidly. The cells do not grow as they divide; thus, the resulting mass of cells is no larger than the fertilized egg when it reaches the uterus. With each division, the chromosomes—the structures within each cell that contain genetic material in the form of DNA—replicate themselves so that each cell has the same genetic material. Occasionally, the mass of dividing cells splits into two separate masses during the division process, resulting in **monozygotic twins**, or **identical twins**. Identical twins, therefore, have exactly the same genetic makeup. **Dizygotic twins**, or **fraternal twins**, in contrast, are no more similar genetically than any other pair of siblings, because they result from two eggs that have been fertilized by two different sperm.

As the zygote divides, it becomes a **blastocyst**, a mass of developing cells surrounding a hollow, fluid-filled cavity (see Figure 9.1). The blastocyst floats around in the uterus for about 3 days before implanting itself in the uterine wall (about 7 days after conception). Once implantation has occurred, the rest of prenatal development is divided into two phases: the *period of the embryo* and the *period of the fetus*. During the period of the embryo, all internal and external structures begin to form; during the period of the fetus, these structures grow and mature. Figure 9.2 summarizes the major changes that occur during embryological and fetal development.

The Embryo

The developing organism is referred to as an **embryo** from implantation until the 8th week of pregnancy. This 8-week embryonic period is especially critical, because the cells of the organism are differentiating into the various organs of the body at an astounding rate. In fact, the embryo's weight increases 10,000 times during the first month of pregnancy and an additional 74 times within the second month (Cherry, 1973). As we will discuss in more detail later, because of these rapid and dramatic developmental changes, the embryo is particularly vulnerable to the effects of poor nutrition and toxins.

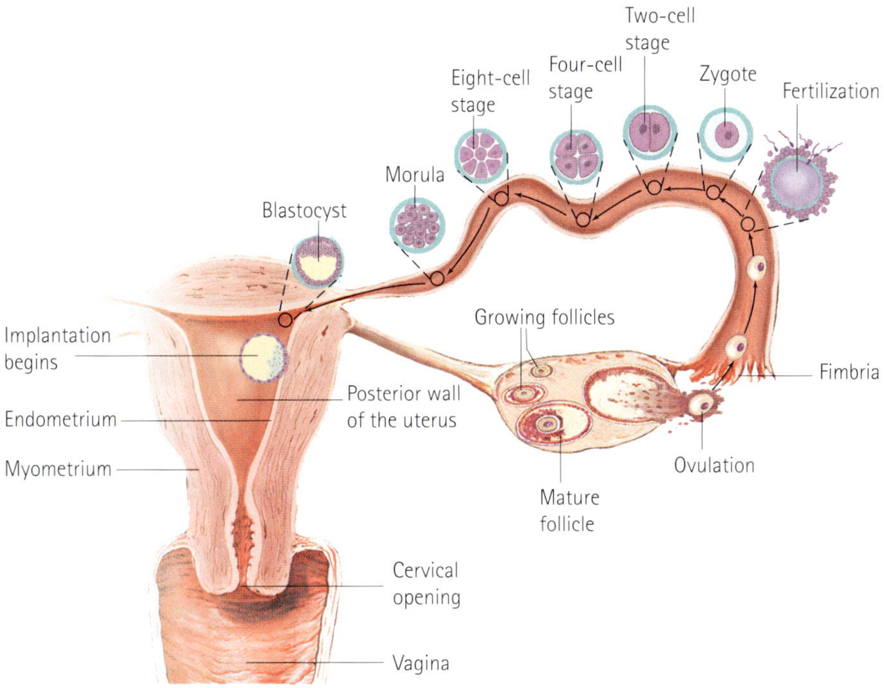

Figure 9.1 The Zygote/Blastocyst from Fertilization to Implantation

Nutritional Support and Protection

Early embryonic growth is aided by nutrients from the endometrium of the uterus. However, the placenta soon takes over nutritional support (see Figure 9.3 on page 250). The **placenta** is a disk-shaped structure that is made up of tissue from both the mother and the prenatal organism. At full size, it is about 7 inches in diameter and 1 inch thick. The placenta is connected to the mother via the uterine wall and to the embryo or fetus via the **umbilical cord.** The umbilical cord is a flexible structure that contains two arteries and one vein. These vessels transport blood between the fetus and the placenta.

The placenta allows exchange between the circulatory systems of the mother and the prenatal organism without any exchange of blood between the two. Thus, the placenta acts as a filter—important nutrients and oxygen are passed from the mother to the embryo or fetus, and waste products and carbon dioxide are passed from the embryo or fetus to the mother, but other harmful substances and many disease-causing bacteria and viruses are not allowed to pass into the embryo's or fetus's blood.

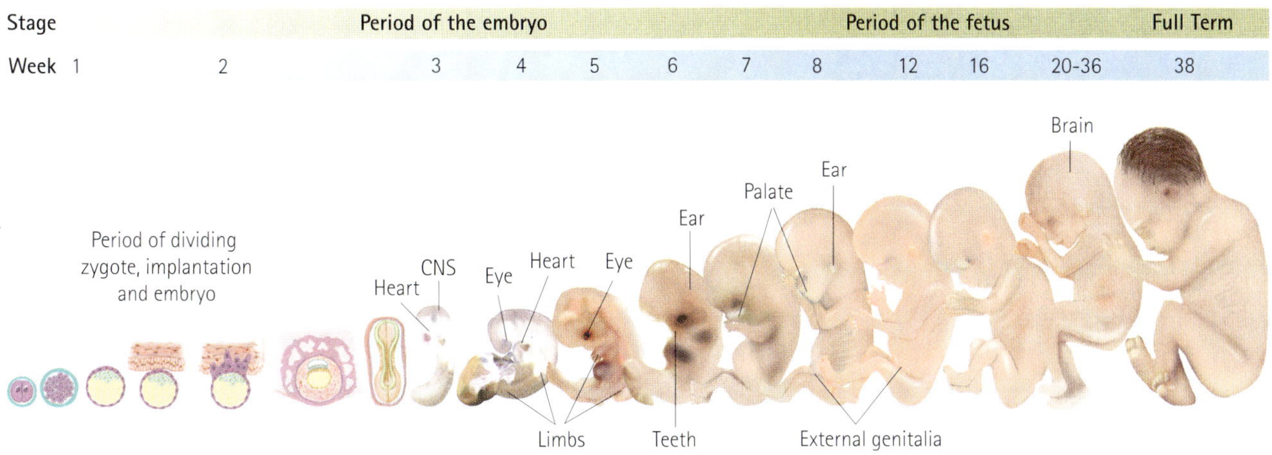

Figure 9.2 Changes during Embryological and Fetal Development

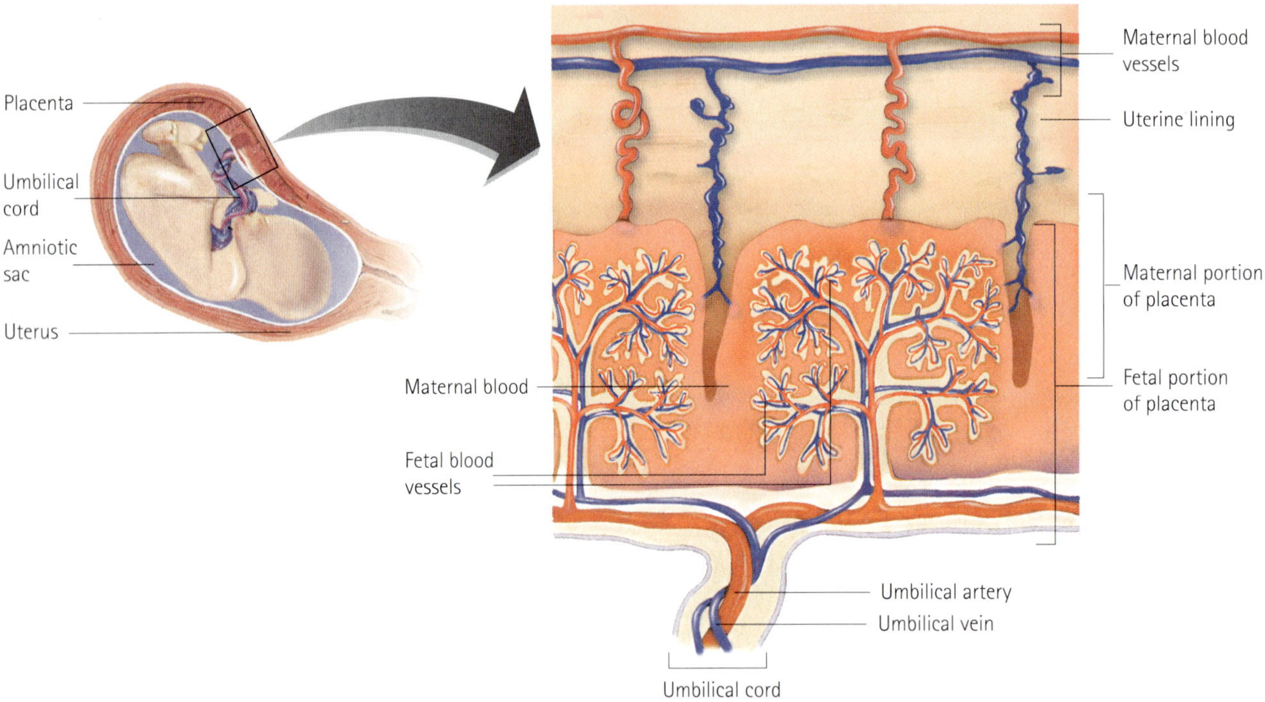

Figure 9.3 Life Support for the Fetus—Placenta, Umbilical Cord, Amniotic Sac

9.1 on the web

Go to **www.ablongman.com/mcanulty2e** and find the links to the articles on prenatal stimulation.

Would you recommend that a pregnant woman perform prenatal stimulation exercises, such as exposing the fetus to certain sounds or music or making an effort to eat a variety of foods to expand the food preferences of the child? Why or why not?

AMNIOTIC SAC
Fluid-filled membrane surrounding the fetus.

AMNIOTIC FLUID
Liquid inside the amniotic sac in which the fetus floats; it provides protection against jarring and bouncing and changes in temperature.

FETUS
The prenatal organism from the 8th week of pregnancy until delivery.

(Unfortunately, the placenta cannot filter out all harmful agents. For example, some microscopic organisms, such as the virus that causes AIDS, as well as harmful substances such as alcohol, aspirin, narcotics, and tranquilizers, can pass through.) The placenta also produces hormones that maintain the pregnancy, cause birth contractions, and prepare the breasts for breast-feeding.

Another support system, the **amniotic sac**, develops simultaneously with the placenta. This sac forms a protective membrane around the fetus. The **amniotic fluid** within the sac serves as a buffer against temperature changes as well as bumps and bouncing.

The Fetus

From the 8th week of gestation to delivery, at about 40 weeks, the developing human is called a **fetus.** The organ systems that first formed during the period of the embryo continue to mature during the period of the fetus. By the end of about the 16th week, the fetus has many human physical characteristics, including fingernails, eyelids, and genitals; thus, the sex of the child can be determined even though the fetus is less than 2 inches long.

Usually around 18 to 20 weeks, the pregnant woman begins to feel the fetus moving. (The fetus has been moving all along, but until this point it was too small for her to feel its movements.) The mother may notice that the fetus is more active at some times than others, which reflects its periods of waking and sleeping. The fetus also responds to sounds and is sensitive to light. The brain has developed considerably by this point, but if the fetus were to be born before the 28th week, it would be highly unlikely to survive. For one thing, the lungs are not yet prepared to extract oxygen from the air. By the 28th week, however, a fetus has a better chance of surviving if born early. By then, the lungs and heart are developed enough for life outside the womb, and the fetus has a layer of fat tissue under the skin to help regulate body temperature. Also, after the 28th week the fetus is much more responsive to stimulation from the environment, for example, becoming startled at the sound of loud noises such as an alarm clock. The mother may feel less movement from the fetus as the pregnancy nears term because the fetus is getting so large that there is not as much room to move around in the womb.

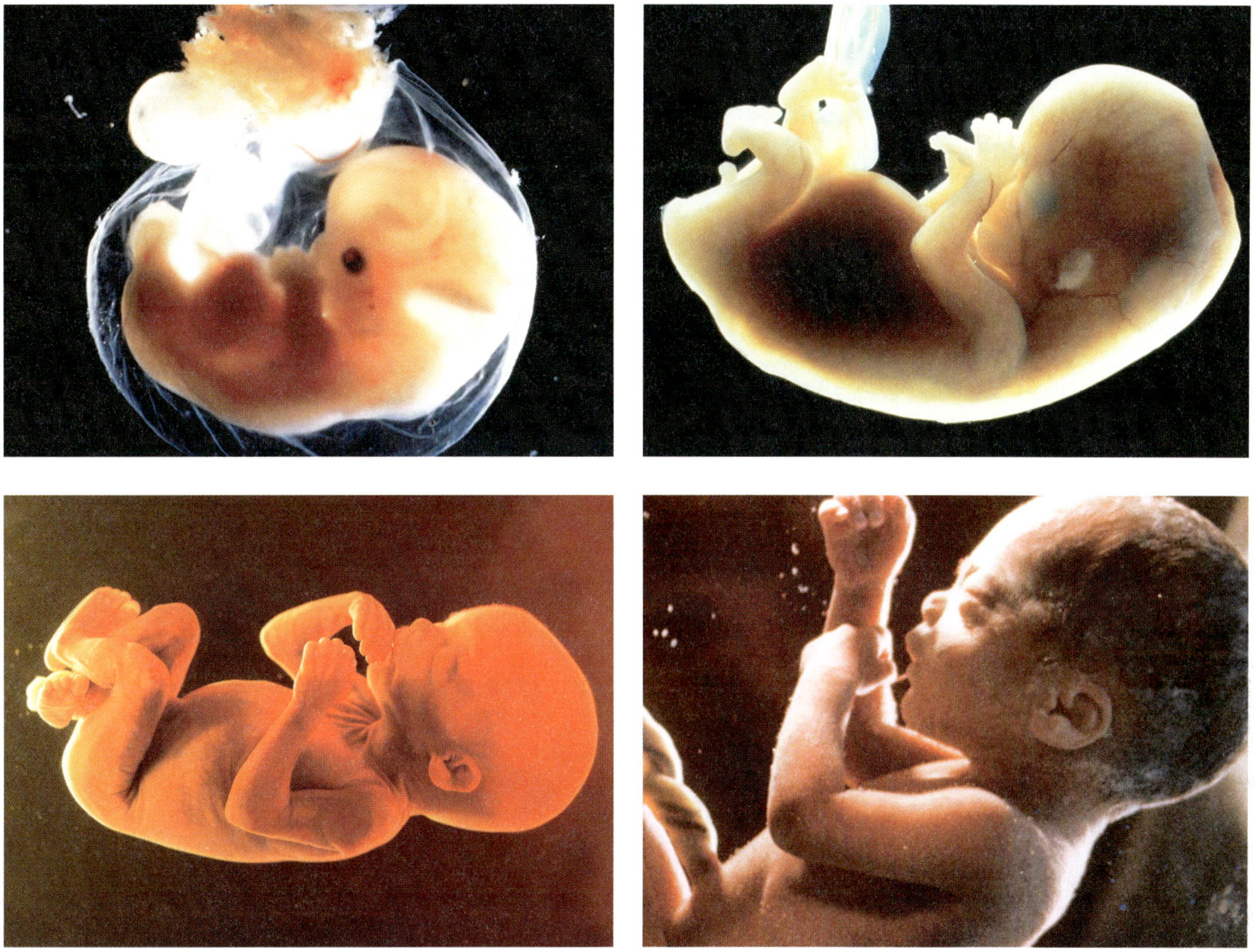

(Upper left) An Embryo at about 5–6 Weeks Gestation; (Upper right) A Fetus at about 11 Weeks Gestation; (Lower left) A Fetus at about 5 Months Gestation; (Lower right) A Fetus at Full Term

The fetus usually moves into a head-down position in the 7th month. If the fetus does not turn, it may reach the end of pregnancy in the **breech position**, which is when the buttocks or one or both legs are positioned in the pelvis first. If this position is detected in advance, a doctor can sometimes turn the fetus into the head-down position with external manipulation. Some breech babies are born vaginally, but many require a cesarean section.

THE EXPERIENCE OF PREGNANCY

In general, women experience many physical and psychological changes throughout pregnancy. Pregnancy is commonly divided into three trimesters. The *first trimester* is from conception to 16 weeks after the last menstrual period. The *second trimester* is from 16 to 28 weeks, and the *third trimester* is from 28 to 40 weeks. Each trimester is marked by unique changes.

Determining Pregnancy

Because early prenatal care is so critical to the health of the developing embryo and fetus, it is important that a woman confirm a pregnancy as early as possible. A woman's first clue that she is pregnant is usually a missed menstrual period. Of course, some women miss their periods for other reasons, and pregnant women sometimes bleed when their periods would normally occur. Swelling, tingling, or tenderness in the breasts may occur just days after conception. During the next few weeks, other

BREECH POSITION
Fetal position in which the buttocks or one or both legs position themselves in the pelvis first.

signs of pregnancy usually occur. These are not always pleasant symptoms—but to a couple anxiously awaiting pregnancy, they can bring much excitement and anticipation of a confirmed pregnancy. These signs indicate that the woman's body is making changes necessary to support the pregnancy. The woman may experience fatigue, frequent urination, food aversions, and nausea or vomiting. Nausea or vomiting experienced during pregnancy is generally referred to as **morning sickness**; however, these symptoms can occur at any time during the day or night and sometimes last all day. Other physical evidence later in the first trimester are food cravings, darkening of the areola, the appearance of blue lines on the breasts (a sign of increased blood supply), and changes in the color of cervical and vaginal tissue, detected during a medical exam.

The preceding signs are all considered *possible signs* of pregnancy. *Probable signs* of pregnancy include Hegar's sign. **Hegar's sign** is the softening of the uterus and cervix, which is detected by a physician during a bimanual exam (one hand on the abdomen and two fingers in the vagina). Enlargement of the uterus, another probable sign, is also detected in this way.

A positive pregnancy test is another probable sign of pregnancy. A woman can determine if she is pregnant in the privacy of her own home in only about 5 minutes. Several inexpensive home pregnancy tests are available. These tests are quite accurate and easy to use. Home pregnancy tests can detect pregnancy as early as 14 days after conception. The tests work by detecting **human chorionic gonadotrophin (hCG)**, a hormone secreted by the placenta and present in a pregnant woman's urine. These tests produce quick results and thus can allow for early prenatal care. However, if a woman gets a false negative result (that is, if the test wrongly indicates that she is *not* pregnant), she may dismiss her symptoms and not seek appropriate care.

Urine tests conducted in a laboratory or physician's office also detect hCG and with nearly 100% accuracy. These tests can be conducted as early as 7 to 10 days after conception. The physician may prefer to use a blood test, which not only detects the fact of pregnancy but also aids in determining how far the pregnancy has progressed by the amount of hCG detected (Eisenberg, Murkoff, & Hathaway, 1991). Signs that confirm pregnancy, or *positive signs,* include a fetal heartbeat, which can be detected anywhere between 10 and 20 weeks; visualization of the embryo via ultrasound, which can be done as early as 4 to 6 weeks; and feeling the fetus move, which occurs not earlier than 16 weeks. Table 9.1 summarizes the possible, probable, and positive signs of pregnancy.

The due date for a pregnancy has traditionally been called the EDC, or "expected date of confinement." The EDC is calculated by subtracting 3 months from the date of the first day of the last menstrual period, then adding 7 days and 1 year. For example, if a woman is pregnant, and the first day of her last menstrual period was June 28, 2003, she subtracts 3 months to get to March 28, then adds 7 days and 1 year. Her EDC is April 4, 2004.

did YOU know?

Pregnancy test manufacturers report over 99% accuracy when their tests are used correctly.

MORNING SICKNESS
Nausea or vomiting usually occurring in the morning, especially early in pregnancy.

HEGAR'S SIGN
Softening of the uterus and cervix, which is detected by a physician during a bimanual exam and is a probable sign of pregnancy.

HUMAN CHORIONIC GONADOTROPHIN (HCG)
A hormone secreted by the placenta. Pregnancy tests detect this hormone in urine as a way of indicating probable pregnancy.

The First Trimester

When it comes to the experience of pregnancy, no two women are alike. Some women have more symptoms than others. Similarly, psychological adjustments during pregnancy vary tremendously from one woman to another. In addition, many women tolerate the changes and symptoms well because the sheer excitement of being pregnant overrides any inconvenience or discomfort.

Physical Changes

Regardless of the severity of the symptoms or an individual's experience of them, every woman's body changes dramatically during pregnancy. The placenta is produc-

TABLE 9.1 The Signs of Pregnancy

POSSIBLE SIGNS	PROBABLE SIGNS	POSITIVE SIGNS
Missed menstrual period	Hegar's sign	Fetal heartbeat
Breast swelling, tingling, tenderness	Uterine enlargement	Visualization of fetus via ultrasound
Fatigue	Positive pregnancy test	Fetal movement
Frequent urination		
Food aversions		
Nausea and vomiting ("morning sickness")		

ing high levels of estrogen and progesterone, which may account for many of the early signs of pregnancy described above. As the first trimester progresses, these early symptoms may even heighten. The woman's breasts will become fuller and may be tender. She may experience faintness and dizziness as well as heartburn, bloating, indigestion, and flatulence. Later in the pregnancy, she might have to urinate more frequently because of hormonal changes and because the growing uterus puts pressure on the bladder. Many women develop food aversions as well as food cravings.

Virtually all of a pregnant woman's organ systems are undergoing changes and increased activity, but the cardiovascular system is probably affected the most. In fact, cardiac output, which is the amount of blood pumped out of the heart per minute, will increase by as much as 50% during pregnancy. Veins may become more prominent in the abdomen and legs as the blood flow increases to support the developing fetus. A pregnant woman may notice that the veins and capillaries on all surfaces of her skin are more prominent. This occurs because the fetus is generating about as much heat as a 15-watt lightbulb; thus, the body must increase its ability to cool the blood in order to regulate its core temperature and protect the fetus from overheating. By the end of the first trimester, the woman may notice that her clothes are getting snug, not just because the uterus and its contents are growing but because she has started to store a little fat as well. During the second trimester, the body breaks all the "rules" of the metabolic process: No matter how little the woman eats, her body begins to store fat to support the fetus.

Psychological Changes

The majority of pregnant women (and those who are close to them) experience many emotional ups and downs. These feelings can range from near-ecstasy to tremendous fear, sometimes all within the same day. The physical and hormonal changes a woman experiences during pregnancy can give rise to mood swings. Some women report general edginess and tearfulness, especially early in the pregnancy.

In the beginning, a pregnant woman and her partner may experience fears about the health of the baby, which is understandable: Although there may be few signs to cause alarm, there are also few signs to allay these fears. By the 3rd month, however, the couple can hear the baby's heartbeat using a monitor, which is a comforting sound. The first feelings of movement are often exciting as well. Medical tests such as chorionic villi sampling (at 10–12 weeks), amniocentesis (at around 16 weeks), and an ultrasound (at 20 weeks) can offer parents even more reassurance that all is well. (These tests are described later in the chapter.)

The Second Trimester

By the second trimester, many women report feeling much better, both physically and psychologically.

Physical Changes

Physically, the woman may be feeling less nausea (although some women are nauseous throughout pregnancy). She may also need to urinate less frequently, since there is less pressure on the bladder in the second trimester than in the first and third trimesters; during the second trimester, the fetus is floating in the amniotic fluid and is not yet heavy enough to press on the bladder. The breasts are still enlarged, but they may be less tender. Many women report feeling less fatigued, and still others report having more energy and feeling better than before pregnancy. This may be because their bodies are simply adjusting to the pregnancy; in addition, many women take better care of themselves during pregnancy, which contributes to feelings of well-being. Some women still experience unpleasant physical symptoms, however. For instance, gastrointestinal symptoms such as heartburn may continue, especially as the growing uterus puts pressure on the stomach. The woman may also develop swollen ankles and feet, varicose veins, hemorrhoids, and nasal congestion or occasional nosebleeds; increased body fluids create most of these symptoms. She may also have a little difficulty taking a full breath as the fetus grows and pushes up on the diaphragm. The best position for a woman to sleep at this time is on her left side. Sleeping on her back might allow the baby's weight to put pressure on an artery that carries oxygen to the baby. Sleeping on the left side rather than the right improves circulation because of the way blood is pumped out of the heart.

From about the middle to the end of the second trimester, the woman's breasts may occasionally secrete a yellowish substance called **colostrum.** This is an antibody- and nutrient-rich substance that the nursing baby will consume during the first 24 to 48 hours of life. Also, around the 20th week of pregnancy, the woman may begin to experience uterine contractions. These contractions, called **Braxton-Hicks contractions,** are not labor contractions; they are contractions that are thought to "prepare" the uterus for labor by strengthening the muscles in the uterine wall. They are generally experienced as uncomfortable but not painful, and they begin at the top of the uterus and work their way down, lasting about 30 to 120 seconds. Many women are excited to feel the Braxton-Hicks contractions, and since the abdomen becomes very hard, others can experience this event with her.

Psychological Changes

As the pregnancy progresses, many parents start to feel close to the unborn baby. Many people claim that a mother has an advantage over the father or partner because she can feel the baby moving inside her, which creates a special bond. For this reason, it is important that the father or partner be involved during the course of the pregnancy, perhaps by touching the mother's abdomen when the baby kicks, talking to the baby, attending parenting classes, attending a co-ed baby shower, and preparing the nursery. Such involvement minimizes feelings of being left out.

The Third Trimester

By the 28th week, pregnancy has become routine, and many women and their partners start growing impatient.

Physical Changes

As the woman continues to gain weight, she may find herself quite exhausted at times. As the abdomen stretches to accommodate the growing fetus, the woman's skin also stretches, causing itching. Moisturizers can help relieve any discomfort this causes. In the third trimester, the woman may find it difficult to find a comfortable sleeping position that supports the weight of the fetus. Sleeping on her left side with a large body pillow wedged between her knees and/or under her abdomen is often the solution.

IN YOUR own words

Diep Ly
Virginia Commonwealth University

If I could choose the sex of my unborn baby, I don't think I would. I think that every child, whether female or male, should be loved the same.

COLOSTRUM
A thin, clear or yellowish fluid secreted from the breasts in late pregnancy and for about 48 hours after birth. Colostrum contains many nutrients and antibodies that are valuable for the newborn.

BRAXTON-HICKS CONTRACTIONS
Uncomfortable but not painful contractions that occur around the 20th week of pregnancy that are thought to strengthen uterine muscles to prepare the uterus for labor. They are not part of labor.

Other factors can make sleep difficult as well. Increasing pressure on the bladder may force the woman to get up several times during the night to urinate (which can prepare her for the nights to come when the baby has to be fed throughout the night!). Also, the fetus often becomes more active at night and awakens her by kicking and squirming around. (Pregnant women and those who observe their experiences note that the fetus appears to sleep during the day because the woman's movements lull it to sleep, and when the woman becomes still, the fetus wakes up.) Of course, the excitement of feeling the fetus move may override the annoyance of being awakened by these movements. On the positive side is the fact that toward the end of pregnancy, the baby drops into the pelvis in preparation for childbirth; thus, the woman may notice less pressure on her diaphragm, so she can breathe more easily.

Psychological Changes

As the end of pregnancy draws near, the excitement mounts and expectations build, sometimes to the point of impatience. After 40 long weeks, the parents are usually eagerly anticipating the birth. One mother likened pregnancy to having a pen pal. She said she felt she had been getting to know this unseen little person throughout the pregnancy via a special form of communication, but she anxiously awaited getting to see and touch her or him for the first time. Despite the pressures of pregnancy and the ensuing life changes, most prepared parents will tell you that their overwhelming feelings at the birth of their baby are joy and elation.

Some women and men ease right into parenthood, but parents who do not should not feel guilty. Parenthood usually requires significant lifestyle adjustments. Increased financial burdens, restrictions on activities, and changes in work habits all require a shift of perspective. It is not unusual or wrong for one or both parents to feel some apprehension and even resentment over the demands of parenthood. One truly loving mother even confessed to feelings of wanting to give her baby up—a fantasy that has crossed many a parent's mind. Parenthood can be particularly stressful for the professional woman who is expected to shift her focus from career to baby. An equally involved father or partner, however, can reduce her burden.

Like so many aspects of human sexuality, the experience of pregnancy and childbirth varies not only from person to person but also from one culture to another. Close Up on Culture: The Experience of Childbirth across Cultures describes the variety.

Preparing for and anticipating a baby's birth together can make a couple feel very close.

CLOSE UP ON culture

The Experience of Childbirth across Cultures

The physiological processes of pregnancy and childbirth are very similar for all women, but varying social standards produce birth experiences that differ tremendously across cultures. Anthropologists have observed that the differences appear on several dimensions and are largely determined by the extent to which the medical establishment is involved in pregnancy and childbirth. Cultures differ with regard to the amount and type of birth preparation women receive, who is present to assist and support women during labor and delivery, where deliveries typically take place, and who controls the decision-making process during delivery.

Prepared childbirth and prenatal care are formal approaches to educating and preparing a woman (and her partner or support person) for birth. Such birth preparation is common in some cultures, whereas a more informal approach predominates in others. In the United States, the number of women who get prenatal care has increased tremendously over the last two decades. The incidence of prenatal care in the first trimester increased from 75.8% in 1990 to 82.5% in 1997 (although among racial and ethnic minority groups the rate was closer to 70%) (U.S. Department of Health and Human Services, 1999). In other developed countries such as Sweden and Holland, where prenatal care and education are readily obtainable and free, *all* women receive them. In these countries, prenatal preparation is largely guided by well-trained midwives, and only high-risk pregnancies call for the involvement of medical professionals. Physicians, nurses, and other medical professionals provide most of the prenatal care in the United States.

In the Mayan culture of the Yucatan region of southeastern Mexico and northern Central America, preparation does not occur until the woman is actually in labor and is provided by any of a number of individuals who are there to support and assist during the birth. However, because most women give birth at home, it is unlikely that a woman and her partner will not have observed many births throughout their lives. Thus, they are likely to be fairly well informed before the birth of their first child.

The individuals present at a birth may be either specialists or nonspecialists. The United States is unusual compared to other cultures in that, up until the 1970s, only medical specialists assisted women giving birth. Today, it is increasingly common for one or more family members or friends to be present and even to assist. However, the view of the medical professional as the "expert" who is present to "deliver a patient" has not disappeared entirely. This is a highly medicalized approach, which gives most of the control to the physician rather than to the woman and those who support her. In Holland and Sweden, the mother is attended by a midwife (a specialist) and a partner, mother, or anyone else she chooses (a nonspecialist). The general attitude in Holland and Sweden is that the woman is capable of delivering the baby by herself, and the midwife is there simply to assist, encourage, and watch for complications. An even stronger contrast to the U.S. culture is found in the Yucatan, where more nonspecialists than specialists attend and assist in childbirth.

The location of the birth also gives some indication of who is in control of the birth process. In the Yucatan, the woman remains in the familiar surroundings of her home. Only a blanket hung between the hammock in which she delivers and the rest of the living area separates her from everyday life. In Sweden and the United States, nearly all births take place in a hospital; in Holland, most births used to take place at home, but most now occur in hospitals. Birthing rooms within hospitals or birthing centers, which have cropped up in the United States over the years, are intended to create the feel of a home birth while offering ready access to high-tech interventions in an emergency. Although these are still unfamiliar environments with unfamiliar attendants, for the most part, women seem to feel more comfortable in them than in standard hospital rooms. Nonetheless, the medical personnel maintain ultimate authority over the birth process in these settings.

As noted, cross-cultural differences in birth processes are heavily influenced by who is assigned the role of decision maker. In the Yucatan, everyone present participates in the decision-making process via "negotiated consensus." In Holland, even hospital deliveries are attended by midwives, as long as there are no major complications; however, the midwives leave most of the decision making to the mother-to-be. Women are not instructed when to push, for example. Instead, they are asked if they feel ready to push. The view in the Dutch culture is that childbirth is a natural process, which should be allowed to take its own course. Drugs are not given for pain or to speed labor, even if the woman would like them. Swedes, too, assign control to the woman within the hospital system. The woman, for instance, is totally in control of the decision about using pain medication. As in Holland, midwives attend normal hospital deliveries. In the United States, decision making is largely assigned to the medical staff as soon as the woman enters the hospital. Although a woman may choose not to accept the recommendations of medical personnel, it is generally assumed that they are in charge of the birth process.

SOURCE: Unless otherwise indicated, the information above is from B. Jordan & R. Davis-Floyd, *Birth in Four Cultures,* 4th edition (Prospect Heights, IL: Waveland Press, Inc., 1993).

Sex during Pregnancy

Sexual intercourse during normal pregnancies is perfectly safe. Some women even report heightened sexual desire during pregnancy, especially during the second trimester, when the nausea is gone but they are not yet big enough to be uncomfortable during intercourse. Sometimes deep penetration may cause some bleeding of the cervix, which is engorged with blood during pregnancy. A pregnant woman who experiences bleeding should consult her doctor to rule out any threat of a miscarriage. With the doctor's okay, intercourse may resume, albeit less deeply. Most couples try different positions during the course of pregnancy in order to find those most comfortable for both partners. Each couple is different, but positions that allow the woman to control depth of penetration, such as woman on top, work best in general. On the other hand, as the pregnancy progresses, the woman may be more comfortable in a position that supports her belly; rear entry with the woman lying on her side, for example, both supports the woman's belly and reduces the man's ability to penetrate her too deeply. Some doctors recommend no intercourse during the last month to avoid the possibility of bursting the amniotic sac, which could lead to intrauterine infection.

PRENATAL CARE

Monitor your diet, exercise pattern, and use of medications and other drugs for a week or so after reading this section, and you will realize all the changes a pregnant woman needs to make to ensure the optimal health of her newborn. Of course, not all factors that might affect a developing fetus are under the mother's control, but many are. Good prenatal care can protect the mother's health and enhance the probability of having a healthy baby. Many substances known to have an adverse effect on unborn children, called **teratogens**, can be avoided if the mother alters her behavior; however, some, such as environmental toxins, may be difficult to avoid. The impact of the mother's behavior and of teratogens can be mild to life-threatening; thus, eliminating or at least reducing those factors that can have a negative impact during pregnancy is very important.

Looking At . . .

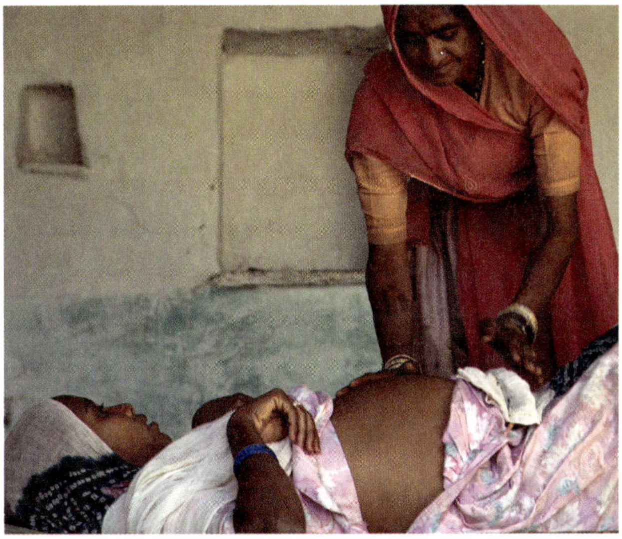

. . . Thinking About

The quality of prenatal care differs greatly from country to country. If you were developing a public health program to educate women in a country where the prenatal care is less than adequate, what three key points would you emphasize?

Maternal Health Practices

The list of things that women can do to influence the health of their newborns and the outcome of their pregnancies is growing as scientists learn more about the impact of maternal health on fetal development. Public health efforts to educate women about what science has learned are also on the rise. Public service announcements, other advertisements, news stories, and special features are common on television and in other media. These stress the importance of early checkups, good nutrition, exercise, and other prenatal factors.

Prenatal Checkups

The backbone of good prenatal care is regular visits to an obstetrician or midwife. Unfortunately, many expectant mothers fail to obtain prenatal care for a multitude of reasons, ranging from socioeconomic and cultural to highly personal. Some women are simply not aware of the importance of prenatal care or are told by important role models in their lives that it is unnecessary. Alternatively, they might be ambivalent about their pregnancy and might postpone getting care because they do not want anyone to

TERATOGENS
Substances that can be dangerous to the health of a fetus.

Pregnant women can exercise as strenuously as they did before pregnancy with a doctor's clearance. Exercise is vital self-care during pregnancy.

know that they are pregnant. Some women believe they cannot afford checkups, but because prenatal care is so important, mothers-to-be who have no health insurance or other means of paying for checkups can get assistance from various public service agencies.

The course of prenatal care with an uncomplicated pregnancy usually starts with monthly visits. As the pregnancy progresses, the visits become bimonthly, then weekly. At these visits, the woman's weight and blood pressure are checked, and her urine is screened for protein and sugar. Her hands and feet are checked for excessive swelling, and she is asked about unusual symptoms. The woman and her partner can hear the fetal heartbeat through a monitor placed on her abdomen, and the doctor will measure from the woman's pelvic bone to the top of the uterus, a measurement known as **fundal height**, to make sure the fetus is growing properly. These regular exams may be critical to early detection and treatment of complications.

Exercise

You may have noticed that pregnant women are often treated almost like invalids. People grab heavy objects from their hands, open doors for them, and even help them stand up and sit down. Pregnancy is not an illness, however, and women with normal pregnancies can and should exercise regularly. Safe, moderate aerobic exercise increases the movement of nutrients and oxygen to the fetus. Pregnant women are now advised to engage in moderate exercise for a minimum of 30 minutes daily or at least on most days. In addition, women athletes and women who engaged in vigorous exercise prior to pregnancy can continue that level of activity during pregnancy (American College of Obstetricians and Gynecologists, 2001). Medical professionals were once concerned that blood needed by the developing fetus would be diverted into exercising muscles, resulting in poor fetal growth. Some research has shown that exercise has no impact on the growth of the fetus (Sternfeld, Quesenberry, Eskenazi, & Newman, 1995); other research has shown that babies of exercising mothers do weigh less but fall within the normal weight range. In addition, these "exercised" babies have less body fat and continue to be leaner than other children through at least age 5 (Clapp, 1996).

The pregnant woman also benefits from exercise, which reduces fluid retention, hemorrhoids, and varicose veins (Eisenberg et al., 1991). Toning strengthens the back and other parts of the body that are placed under strain during pregnancy and also may be good preparation for childbirth. Squats may increase the size of the pelvic cavity, making delivery easier. In fact, the more women exercise throughout pregnancy, the fewer perceived discomforts they report in late weeks (Sternfeld et al., 1995).

The wrong kind of exercise can be unhealthy for the mother and developing fetus. Walking, cycling, and swimming are generally considered safe; however, pregnant women should avoid activities that may expose them to hard falls, such as downhill or water skiing, diving, rollerblading, and horseback riding. A pregnant woman should discuss the type and extent of exercise with her doctor or midwife, and strenuous exercise in high heat and high humidity should always be avoided because it can cause the fetus to become overheated.

FUNDAL HEIGHT
The measure from a woman's pelvic bone to the top of the uterus, used to assess whether the fetus is growing properly.

Stress in Pregnancy

As if a pregnant woman does not already have enough to worry about, she also has to worry about being stressed! Growing scientific evidence suggests that women should take measures to moderate their stress levels during pregnancy for the protection of the growing fetus. For example, job stress has been associated with pre-eclampsia, a medical complication in pregnancy, and the greater the job stress, the greater the risk (Klonoff-Cohen, Cross, & Pieper, 1996). High stress and anxiety in pregnancy have been repeatedly associated with miscarriage, premature birth, and low birth weight (Hamilton-Boyles et al., 2000; Lobel, DeVincent, Kaminer, & Meyer, 2000; Sandman, Wadhwa, Chicz-Demet, Dunkel-Schetter, & Porto, 1997). In addition, stress has been linked to nongenetically caused miscarriages as well as to temperamental difficulties in 6-week-old infants and to delayed development of motor and social skills and language comprehension and expression skills in 2- to 3-year-olds (Neugebauer, Kline, Stein, Shrout, & Warburton, 1996; Wadhwa, Herbel, Dunkel-Schetter, Chicz-Demet, & Sandman, 1998). It appears that maternal stress hormones that directly affect the developing fetus may be responsible for the negative effects of maternal stress on fetal and child development (DiPietro, Hilton, Hawkins, Costigan, & Pressman, 2002; Sandman et al., 1997; Wadhwa et al., 1998).

What can an expectant mother do to reduce stress? Although it might not be easy, she should make a point of taking time out to relax each day. If she finds it difficult to learn to relax on her own, she might consider attending a stress management or relaxation course, often offered by local hospitals or other community organizations. She might also look at ways to reduce stress at work and home, and she might increase her social support network, as the support of others can be a terrific moderator of stress. Exercise often helps to reduce the effects of stress as well.

did YOU know?

A woman should begin taking vitamin supplements containing 0.4 milligram of folic acid at least 1 month before becoming pregnant and through the first trimester to protect against neural tube defects, which can form in the first month of pregnancy (American Academy of Pediatrics, Committee on Genetics, 1999; March of Dimes, 2002).

Nutrition

Overall, a pregnant woman should have two dietary goals: getting adequate nutrition and gaining an appropriate amount of weight. A woman who is of average weight before pregnancy should aim to gain 25–35 pounds during pregnancy. Obese women are sometimes advised by their obstetricians to gain less than this amount.

Babies who do not receive adequate nutrition during fetal development are more likely to have a low birth weight, which is associated with increased postnatal problems and death (Luke, 1994). Women trying to become pregnant should start taking vitamins, especially folic acid, one of the B vitamins. Folic acid has been found to be crucial in preventing *neural tube defects* (brain and spinal cord defects). Research has shown that folic acid reduces the occurrence of two major spinal cord and brain defects, spina bifida and anencephaly, by 50–70% (American Academy of Pediatrics, Committee on Genetics, 1999; March of Dimes, 2002a). Even if a woman does not take vitamins before becoming pregnant, she should definitely take them during pregnancy. A prescribed prenatal vitamin supplement provides vitamins and minerals the mother needs for the developing fetus and for maintaining her own nutritional balance. In addition to taking vitamins, the woman should eat a balanced diet throughout pregnancy. This can be particularly difficult for the woman who is nauseous or who has strong food aversions; finding a balanced diet of foods she can eat may take some finesse.

Because caffeinated beverages are so popular, many women are concerned about caffeine consumption during pregnancy. Research has shown that moderate consumption of caffeine is generally not associated with preterm delivery or fetal malformations (Golding, 1995; Pastore & Savitz, 1995). However, consumption of large amounts of caffeine (over 30 mg, which is equal to over 2 cups of coffee or 7 cans of soda per day) may be associated with difficulty in conceiving a child, miscarriage, and **intrauterine growth retardation**, the failure of the fetus to grow at a proper rate (Golding, 1995; Stanton & Gray, 1995).

INTRAUTERINE GROWTH RETARDATION
Failure of the fetus to grow at the proper rate.

TABLE 9.2 Suggested Food Plan for Pregnant Women

FOOD GROUP	NUMBER OF SERVINGS PER DAY AND SERVING EQUIVALENT	EXAMPLES OF GOOD CHOICES	EXAMPLES OF POOR CHOICES
Fruits	3 to 4 servings A typical serving is one medium apple, one medium orange, or one-half banana, ½ cup orange juice, 2 tablespoons dried fruit	Citrus fruit, apple, banana, guava, mango, dried fruit, fruit juice	No poor choices, but drink only 100% fruit juice, not fruit "drinks"; choose fresh rather than canned fruit
Vegetables	3 to 5 servings A typical serving is 1 cup brussels sprouts, broccoli, collard greens, cabbage, etc.; ½ cup spinach, green pepper, sweet peas, green beans; 1 small sweet potato, ½ baked potato	Dark green vegetables such as broccoli, spinach, or kale are best; carrots, cabbage, squash, and white or sweet potatoes are good, too	No poor choices, but choose fresh rather than canned vegetables and do not overconsume starchy vegetables that are higher in calories
Milk and milk products	4 servings A typical serving is 1 cup milk, cottage cheese, or yogurt; two 1-inch cubes of cheese	Low-fat options	Whole milk and other high-fat milk products—fat content is unnecessary
Meat and other high-protein foods	2 to 3 servings A typical serving is 3 ounces of meat, poultry, or fish; 2 eggs; 1 cup dried beans, peas; 1 cup tofu	Lean meat, fish, poultry, beans, tofu—all low in fat	Hot dogs, sausage, bacon—all high in unneeded fat
Whole-grain (preferable) or enriched breads and cereals	6 or more slices A typical serving is 1 slice of bread, ½ cup oatmeal, 2 tortillas, ¾ cup cold cereal, ½ cup enriched brown rice	Whole grain or whole wheat (Note: Many supposedly whole wheat breads have little fiber—read the labels to pick those highest in fiber.)	No poor choices, except products loaded with saturated fat, such as many biscuits
Fats and sweets	Vary per calories needed	Limit all fats and sweets	Saturated fats

SOURCE: March of Dimes, 1993

Another nonnutritive substance that Americans tend to consume in excess is sugar. There is some evidence that babies born to women who eat a lot of sugar during pregnancy have low birth weights (Lenders et al., 1994). Thus, it is not enough to eat nutritious food; it is also important to avoid eating too much nonnutritious food. Table 9.2 provides suggestions for good nutrition during pregnancy.

Risks to Prenatal Development

In addition to following good health practices, pregnant women can eliminate behaviors that pose health risks for the developing fetus, primarily consumption of harmful substances. Another risk to fetal development is maternal illness, which is not so easily controlled by the mother.

Cigarette Smoking

Smoking may lower both a woman's ability to conceive and the quality of a man's sperm. In fact, smoking may decrease a woman's fertility by as much as 50%, even among women who smoke fewer than 9 cigarettes per day (Aldrete, Eskenazi, & Sholtz, 1995). Men who smoke also appear to be affected, in that their sperm are less dense and motile, less viable, have a shorter lifespan, and may be less able to fertilize an egg (Makler, Reiss, Stoller, Blumenfeld, & Brandes, 1993; Zavos, Correa, Antypas, Zarmakoupis-Zavos, & Zarmakoupis, 1998).

Smoking is not only hazardous to a smoker's reproductive health, it is also hazardous to the health of a fetus whose mother smokes or is even exposed to other's smoke. Smoking is the number-one risk factor for low birth weight in babies (Chomitz, Cheung, & Lieberman, 1995). In fact, a woman who smokes is almost twice as likely as a nonsmoker to have a low-birth-weight baby, and this risk increases the more a woman smokes. Nonsmoking women who are exposed to smoke also have lower-birth-weight babies (Eskenazi, Prehn, & Christianson, 1995; Shu, Hatch, Mills, Clemens, & Susser, 1995; Walsh, 1994). Cigarette smoking is associated with devastating events before, during, and after birth, including spontaneous abortion, stillbirth, preterm birth, and up to 25% of cases of sudden infant death syndrome (SIDS) (Action on Smoking and Health, 1999). Children born to smoking mothers also tend to have persistent respiratory problems, ranging from chronic coughing and excess phlegm to bronchitis, pneumonia, and bronchiolitis, and they are twice as likely to develop asthma (Action on Smoking and Health, 1999; Harding, 1995). Compared to children born to nonsmoking women, these children also suffer long-term problems with physical and intellectual development, including mental retardation in some cases (Drews, Murphy, Yeargen-Allsopp, & Decouflé, 1996; Fogelman & Manor, 1988). Pregnant women should not smoke or be around smokers.

Alcohol Consumption

How much alcohol, if any, is safe during pregnancy? This is a very difficult question to answer, but scientists do know that alcohol reaches the fetus through the placenta in about the same concentration found in maternal blood. You have probably heard stories of mothers who drank considerable amounts of alcohol with no apparent negative effects on their children. This may be true in some cases. However, there have also been cases in which maternal consumption of a very small amount of alcohol has had detrimental effects on a baby. In addition, alcohol has been shown to have more significant negative effects on babies born to older mothers (Jacobson, Jacobson, & Sokol, 1996). Thus, a relatively young mother might drink during pregnancy with few ill effects, but as she ages, drinking during subsequent pregnancies could have significant effects. Since no one can predict the effect that even light drinking will have on a fetus, the American Academy of Pediatrics urges women to avoid alcohol altogether during pregnancy (American Academy of Pediatrics, 2000).

One of the major effects of "excessive" alcohol consumption in pregnancy is **fetal alcohol syndrome (FAS).** Exactly how much alcohol must be consumed to produce FAS is unclear. FAS produces a specific pattern of physical abnormalities in children,

Looking At . . .

. . . Thinking About

Many maternal behaviors can have an effect on the developing fetus. Do you think women who take drugs that are known to have major negative effects on unborn fetuses should be punished? Why or why not? If so, how should they be punished? How might they be helped? Should pregnant women who smoke, drink alcohol, or eat a poor diet suffer consequences? If you answered yes to the first question but no to the last, where do you think the line should be drawn?

did YOU know?

Seventeen percent of pregnant women between the ages of 15 and 44 smoke (National Household Survey on Drug Abuse, 2001).

FETAL ALCOHOL SYNDROME (FAS)
Moderate to severe physical abnormalities in a child that are produced by the mother's regular bouts of heavy alcohol consumption during pregnancy.

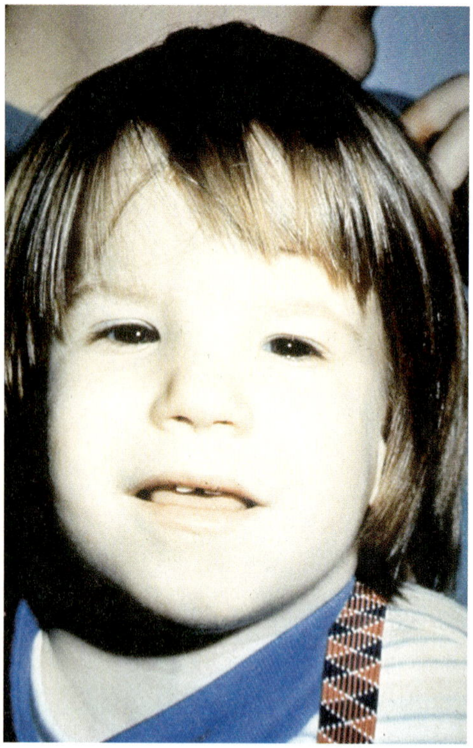

Alcohol consumption during pregnancy can have detrimental effects. Children born with FAS often have distinct facial characteristics.

marked by widely spaced eyes, small eye openings, small and upturned noses, and small upper lips. Physical defects of other organs such as the heart and genitals may be present as well. These children commonly experience intrauterine and postnatal growth retardation, failure to thrive, and a higher risk of perinatal death. In addition, they are generally mentally retarded and uncoordinated and may display symptoms of hyperactivity (Applebaum, 1995).

Drug Use

Every drug that a woman ingests during pregnancy crosses the placenta and reaches the fetus; thus, a pregnant woman must consider the effects of every medication she takes. Even aspirin might be harmful to the developing fetus. Because of the potential risks, a pregnant woman should always consult a physician who has up-to-date knowledge of teratogenic effects before she takes any over-the-counter or prescription medication.

Some prescription medications have been shown to have particularly detrimental effects, immediate or delayed. For example, a drug used for acne, Accutane, has been shown to cause birth defects in one out of five pregnancies. It can also increase the risk of miscarriage, defects of the nervous system, skull, and face, and cleft palate. In addition, nonsteroidal antiinflammatory medications such as ibuprofen may cause high blood pressure in the neonate's lungs if a woman takes them during her second or third trimester (Schneider, 1997).

Certain antibiotics present a risk to the developing fetus. Tetracycline is known to combine with calcium in the bones and teeth of the fetus if the mother ingests it from the middle to the end of pregnancy. It results in brown teeth, increased risk of cavities, and possibly retarded bone growth. Another antibiotic, streptomycin, may cause deafness.

Like some legal drugs, illicit drugs also pose specific risks to the developing fetus. Drug use during pregnancy has been associated with several conditions, including premature separation of the placenta, premature birth, intrauterine growth retardation, cerebral hemorrhage, and sudden infant death syndrome. Addicted babies tend to be hyperactive and developmentally delayed and to have attention deficits and other behavioral problems. In addition, the health and safety of a baby whose mother, father, or other household member is abusing or addicted to drugs, whether illegal or legal, may be at risk. Thus, both the specific physical effects of being exposed to drugs in the womb and the psychosocial implications of having a drug-abusing caregiver are grave concerns.

9.2 on the web

The effects of drug and alcohol exposure on the fetus are far-reaching. Go to **www.ablongman.com/mcanulty2e** to find a description of these effects. In addition, you can learn about strategies for managing a child who has lasting problems from drug or alcohol exposure.

Discuss these strategies and the difficulties that caretakers must endure.

Maternal Illness

There are several maternal illnesses that can affect the developing fetus. *Rubella,* or German measles, is a virus that was a much greater threat before the majority of children were immunized against it. However, it is still a primary cause of congenital anomalies. If a pregnant woman becomes ill with rubella, the virus is capable of causing malformations, hearing problems, cataracts, mental retardation, and other complications in her baby, especially if her illness occurs in the first trimester during early cell differentiation (Ornoy & Arnon, 1993). A woman who knows she was never immunized against rubella may wish to be vaccinated at least 3 months before becoming pregnant; vaccination during pregnancy can transmit rubella to the fetus (Eisenberg et al., 1991; Oster, 1999).

Sexually transmissible infections can also affect a fetus. *Human immunodeficiency virus (HIV)* can be transmitted to a baby from an HIV-infected mother. Transmission may occur through the placenta during pregnancy as well as during childbirth. A neonate who contracts HIV usually develops AIDS quickly and typically dies before age 2 (Berkow, 1992). Fortunately, researchers have made progress in decreasing the likelihood of transmission of HIV to newborns. *Herpes simplex virus (HSV)* can be passed to the newborn during childbirth if the mother has an active herpes lesion. Because the newborn's immune system is immature, HSV can have a much more severe impact on neonates than on adults. Although HSV-infected adults usually suffer only the annoying lesions, the virus can cause blindness in newborns and can even be fatal to them. However, the chances of a newborn's being infected are very low if no lesion is present. A *cesarean section*—removal of the baby through an incision made through the abdominal wall and uterus—may be necessary if an active herpes lesion is detected. *Chlamydia,* a sexually transmissible bacteria, has a high risk of fetal transmission, in part, because it often persists in women as a low-grade, undetected infection (Morell, 1995). If untreated, it may cause preterm labor and premature rupture of the amniotic sac. It can also cause pneumonia and eye infections in newborns.

PRENATAL MEDICAL COMPLICATIONS

Most women have relatively uncomplicated pregnancies. However, there are several medical complications that may threaten the health of the mother or the fetus, or both. A pregnant woman should know her risk for developing any of these conditions and should be alert for the signs and symptoms. A quick response can often reduce or eliminate their harmful impact.

Ectopic Pregnancy

An **ectopic pregnancy** occurs when the zygote becomes implanted somewhere other than in the uterus, usually in the fallopian tube (which is why such a pregnancy is often referred to as a *tubal pregnancy*) but sometimes on the surface of an ovary, on the cervix, or even in the abdominal or pelvic cavity. Between 2% and 6% of known first-trimester pregnancies are ectopic pregnancies (Gynecology Forum, 1997; Mol, Van der Veen, & Bossuyt, 2002). The misplaced implantation commonly occurs because the fallopian tube is blocked by scar tissue from a prior infection (such as pelvic inflammatory disease) or is twisted so that the zygote cannot pass into the uterus. An ectopic pregnancy that is undetected can be very dangerous because the fallopian tube will eventually rupture at the site of the zygote, causing severe abdominal pain and bleeding. A woman should see her doctor or midwife if she experiences any of these symptoms early in pregnancy: painful cramps on one side of the lower abdomen that radiate out into the abdomen, brown spotting or bleeding from the vagina, shoulder pain, or rectal pressure. Other symptoms include nausea, vomiting, dizziness, and weakness, although these are common to most pregnancies.

did YOU know?

Ectopic pregnancies account for 9% of all pregnancy-related deaths (Gynecology Forum, 1997).

Spontaneous Abortion and Late Miscarriage

Occasionally, an embryo or fetus is expelled from the uterus before it can survive outside the womb. The general term for this event is **miscarriage.** A miscarriage that occurs early in pregnancy (within the first trimester, usually between 6 and 10 weeks) is called **spontaneous abortion.** Spontaneous abortion is the most common form of miscarriage. Up to 20% of known pregnancies and up to 50% of all pregnancies end before the 20th week of pregnancy (Goldberg, 2002). Many women miscarry before they know they are pregnant. A spontaneous abortion may seem to the woman like an especially heavy and symptomatic menstrual period, since the most common signs are bleeding, cramping, and pain in the lower abdomen. The cause of a spontaneous abortion is often unknown but is typically a fetal abnormality, inadequate levels of

ECTOPIC PREGNANCY
Implantation of a fertilized egg somewhere other than in the uterus.

MISCARRIAGE
Expulsion of the embryo before it can survive outside the womb.

SPONTANEOUS ABORTION
A miscarriage that occurs early in pregnancy, within the first trimester but usually between 6 and 10 weeks.

hormones needed to support the pregnancy, or an immune reaction to the embryo (LebanonHealth, 2002).

A miscarriage that occurs after the first trimester and no later than the 20th week of gestation is called a **late miscarriage.** Poor maternal health, use of drugs or alcohol, poor uterine or cervical conditions, and environmental toxins are generally responsible for late miscarriages. A woman who has symptoms of a miscarriage should contact her physician immediately. Continuous pink or brown vaginal discharge sometimes signals an impending miscarriage. If heavy cramping and bleeding occur, a miscarriage is most likely. Unlike an early miscarriage, a late miscarriage may feel more like labor. A large gray and red clot is expelled. However distressing it may be for the woman, giving the mass of tissue to her physician may allow the cause of the miscarriage to be determined.

Once a miscarriage has occurred, a procedure called **dilation and curettage (D & C)** may be necessary to stop bleeding and prevent infection that sometimes occurs when tissue from the pregnancy has not been completely expelled. A D & C involves dilating the cervix and suctioning or scraping the uterus (using an instrument called a *curette*) to remove its contents. After the procedure the woman may experience some cramping and backaches and may pass small blood clots for a few days. She may continue to experience some bleeding for a couple of weeks, and she will be cautioned to refrain from having sexual intercourse, using tampons, or douching until the bleeding stops (Carlson, Eisenstat, & Ziporyn, 1996).

Prematurity and Postmaturity

Labor that begins between the 20th and 37th weeks of pregnancy is called **preterm labor.** If preterm labor is not stopped and delivery occurs, the neonate is referred to as a **premature infant,** and its birth is considered a **preterm birth.** (The birth is a **stillbirth** if the fetus is dead at birth.) The longer a baby remains in the womb, the better its chance of survival. Therefore, if preterm labor occurs, every effort is made to postpone delivery as long as neither the mother nor the fetus is in danger. The physician might prescribe bed rest and instruct the mother to limit her physical activity. Occasionally, medication may be given to relax the uterine muscles (Epps & Stewart, 1995). Factors commonly related to premature births are heavy smoking, poor nutrition, and poor maternal health; however, the cause of many premature deliveries is not known.

Thanks to modern medicine, many premature infants survive. They are usually kept in an incubator in a neonatal intensive care unit (NICU). Depending on whether the neonate's lungs are developed sufficiently, he or she may be placed on a respirator and other life supports. Human contact is believed to be helpful to the survival of premature infants, and parents and hospital staff are generally encouraged to touch and handle these babies to the greatest extent possible. Breast-feeding is encouraged if at all possible. A premature infant who lives through the first week has a good chance of surviving.

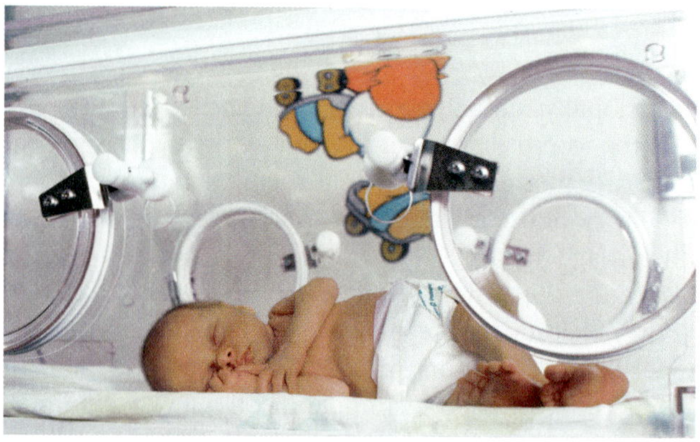

Scientific advances help medical professionals protect infants who are not quite ready for the world.

LATE MISCARRIAGE
Death of a fetus after the first trimester and no later than the 20th week of gestation.

DILATION AND CURETTAGE (D & C)
A procedure whereby the cervix is dilated and an instrument called a curette is used to scrape the uterine lining. This procedure is used following a miscarriage, as well as for abortions and to remedy other medical problems of the uterus.

PRETERM LABOR
Labor beginning between the 20th and 37th week of gestation.

PREMATURE INFANT
A baby delivered between the 20th and 37th week of gestation.

PRETERM BIRTH
Delivery of a fetus any time after the 20th week of gestation.

STILLBIRTH
Delivery of a dead fetus.

A baby is considered a **postmature infant** if the mother has not delivered by the 42nd week of gestation. After this time, the support system for the fetus, the placenta in particular, may begin to break down and not provide adequate nutrients and oxygen. In most cases, if a baby has not been delivered by 2 weeks past the woman's due date, labor is induced using a drug that causes contractions.

Pregnancy-Induced Hypertension

A woman with **pregnancy-induced hypertension**, also known as **preeclampsia**, experiences high blood pressure induced by pregnancy. Related symptoms include poor liver and kidney function, reduced urine output, protein in the urine, swelling of the hands and face and sudden weight gain (both caused by water retention), headaches, dizziness, blurred vision, itching, irritability, and stomach pain. Preeclampsia develops in from 7% to 12% of pregnant women (Chesley & Lindheimer, 1979; Sibai & Anderson, 1991). It is more common among African American women (Chesley & Lindheimer, 1979). Its exact cause is unknown, but poor nutrition is thought to be one factor. Drastic reduction of salt in the diet is generally recommended, and nutritional supplements, diuretics, and other hypertensive medications may be prescribed. Doctors commonly prescribe bed rest, and hospitalization may become necessary. In addition, relaxation therapy, hypnosis, and biofeedback have been used to help control high blood pressure in pregnancy (Little et al., 1984; Smith, 1989; Somers, Gervirtz, Jasin, & Chin, 1989). The condition of the fetus is monitored daily, and if there are signs of fetal distress, the baby is delivered prematurely by induction of labor or cesarean section. In the most severe cases, preeclampsia may develop into **eclampsia**, which involves the onset of one or more convulsions and can result in a coma. This condition is very rare (Cunningham, McDonald, & Gant, 1989) and usually does not develop until late in pregnancy. Once the immediate crisis is over, the woman will generally be kept in a darkened room to minimize stimulation from the environment. If the mother remains stable, the baby is usually delivered either by induction of labor or by cesarean section.

Rh Incompatibility

Rh is an antigen, or protein, on the surface of blood cells that is responsible for producing an immune response. **Rh incompatibility** can occur when the father of a baby is Rh positive (his blood contains the Rh antigen) and the mother is Rh negative (her blood does not have the Rh antigen). If the fetus is Rh positive like the father, and blood from the fetus makes contact with the mother's blood, her body begins to produce antibodies to the Rh antigen. Usually this is no problem for the first pregnancy, because the baby's blood generally only mixes with the mother's blood during delivery. During a subsequent pregnancy, however, the mother's body may produce antibodies in reaction to an Rh-positive fetus. These antibodies cross the placenta and attack the fetus's red blood cells, producing anemia in the fetus. If the mother has a high level of antibodies, the condition can be particularly threatening. Good prenatal care can prevent the dangerous effects of Rh incompatibility. With careful monitoring, several interventions can be used as needed to prevent complications. In the most severe cases, blood transfusion to the fetus or to the newborn immediately after birth may be necessary. Only about 15% of women are Rh negative, making the likelihood of Rh incompatibility very low (Eisenberg et al., 1991).

INFERTILITY AND TECHNOLOGICAL ADVANCES IN CONCEPTION

Some people who would like to become parents cannot do so without special assistance. These people are experiencing problems of **infertility.** Infertility is the inability to conceive after 1 year of unprotected sexual intercourse. In the United States, 18% of

POSTMATURE INFANT
A baby delivered after the 42nd week of gestation.

PREGNANCY-INDUCED HYPERTENSION (PREECLAMPSIA)
High blood pressure during pregnancy; can result in poor liver and kidney function, reduced urine output, protein in the urine, swelling of the hands and face and sudden weight gain (both caused by water retention), headaches, dizziness, blurred vision, itching, irritability, and stomach pain.

ECLAMPSIA
Severely high blood pressure during pregnancy that can cause convulsions and coma.

RH INCOMPATIBILITY
A complication of pregnancy that can occur when the father is Rh positive (his blood contains the Rh antigen) and the mother is Rh negative (her blood does not have the Rh antigen). If the fetus inherits Rh-positive blood from the father, and blood from the fetus makes contact with the mother's blood, her body begins to produce antibodies to the Rh factor. Her body, therefore, will attempt to reject the fetus containing the Rh factor.

INFERTILITY
The inability to conceive a child after 1 year of trying to become pregnant.

CLOSE UP ON gender

Pregnancy after Age 35

In recent years, Madonna, Iman, Susan Sarandon, Jane Seymour, and other celebrities over 40 have drawn much media attention by having babies—healthy babies, too. However, are their experiences with pregnancy and childbirth typical of women over 40? The experts are saying no. Many women today postpone parenthood primarily to focus on their careers. While many women do succeed in getting pregnant and having a healthy baby after age 35, biology definitely decreases the odds of such successes. In her recent book *Creating a Life: Professional Women and the Quest for Children,* Sylvia Ann Hewlett explained that in a survey she conducted of nearly 2,000 "high-achieving" women in U.S. corporations, 42% were childless at age 40—but most of them were not childless by choice.

Many of the businesswomen, as well as 90% of the college-educated women Hewlett interviewed, believed they could easily get pregnant after age 40 (Oxygen Media, 2002). The truth is that, on average, a woman over 40 has only about a 10% chance of having a baby using her own eggs. This figure includes those who undergo assisted reproduction. Unlike men, who produce sperm throughout their lifetimes, women have a finite number of eggs. They simply begin to run out of eggs as they age. The picture is even more complicated than that, however. A woman may still be producing a mature egg each month at age 40, but the eggs are 40 years old, and their quality has declined. And even if a woman makes efforts to protect her eggs through healthy lifestyle choices, "clean living" will not slow or stop the effects of the aging process on her eggs (Boyles, 2001). Consequently, as they age, women have an increasingly greater risk of having a baby with a genetic anomaly.

The most common genetic defect is Down syndrome (caused when the embryo has an extra 21st chromosome), which produces mental retardation as well as other physical problems (March of Dimes, 2002b). The table illustrates how rapidly the risk of Down syndrome increases after age 40. As we discuss later in the chapter, prenatal testing (e.g., amniocentesis or CVS) can detect the presence of Down syndrome early in pregnancy.

Chance of Having a Down Syndrome Baby

Age	Chance
25	1 in 1,250
30	1 in 1,000
35	1 in 400
40	1 in 100
45	1 in 30

Women who postpone pregnancy beyond age 35 are also more likely to have complications if they get pregnant; ectopic pregnancy, miscarriage (25% risk between ages 35 and 39 and a 50% chance by age 42), low birth weight, high blood pressure, diabetes triggered by pregnancy, and cesarean section are all more probable (March of Dimes, 2002b; Seoud et al., 2002; Ziadeh & Yahaya, 2001).

Does this mean that women should not attempt to have babies over the age of 35? Of course not—but they should be aware of the risks of postponing pregnancy and seek out advice and support from their health-care providers before attempting to start a family.

married couples who have no children are infertile, and approximately 8% of all couples in which the woman is of childbearing age are infertile (Mosher & Pratt, 1990).

Approximately 40% of infertility problems in couples are caused by male factors, and another 40% are explained by female factors. Approximately 10% of infertility problems result from a combination of male and female factors, and the remaining 10% are of unknown origin (Meyers et al., 1995). Age is a factor when considering fertility, as you'll read in Close Up on Gender: Pregnancy after Age 35.

Male Factor Infertility

SPERM PENETRATION ANALYSIS
A test of infertility that assesses the ability of sperm to penetrate an ovum. A sample of sperm is incubated with numerous hamster eggs from which the zona pellucida has been removed. The number of sperm successfully penetrating the eggs is then analyzed. Thus the test is also called the *hamster egg test.*

Male factor infertility is generally caused by low sperm count, inability of the sperm to move properly or to survive, or structural abnormalities in the sperm (Nusbaum & Schwarz, 2000). The first step in evaluating sperm for such problems is to obtain a sample of ejaculate and count the sperm. Any number under 20 million points to low sperm count as a possible cause of the infertility. In addition to sperm count, semen quantity and quality (including pH) are examined to determine if the semen is sustaining the life of the spermatozoa and supporting their movement. Finally, the sperm are assessed for adequate motility and for structural defects. The number of well-functioning sperm is perhaps more important than the actual sperm count (Corson, 1990). Occasionally, a **sperm penetration analysis**, also known as the **hamster egg test**, is conducted to determine if the sperm can penetrate an egg. A sample of sperm is incubated with numerous hamster eggs from which the zona pellucida has been removed. The number of sperm successfully penetrating the eggs is then analyzed. This test is somewhat controversial, particularly because scientists disagree as to whether hamster egg penetration is comparable to human egg penetration (Harkness, 1992).

Because poor sperm production may result from hormonal imbalances, a man's levels of testosterone, FSH, and LH may be analyzed. Structural abnormalities or damage from previous infection may also account for male infertility problems. Ultrasound is sometimes conducted to rule out blockage of or damage to the vas deferens or spermatic ducts due to such causes. The man is also checked for a *varicocele,* a mass of varicose veins in the scrotum thought to affect sperm count and quality (Redmon, Carey, & Pryor, 2002). Environmental factors that affect male fertility include cigarette and marijuana use, heavy alcohol consumption, illegal drug abuse, and use of some prescription medications (Nusbaum & Schwarz, 2000). These factors also need to be addressed in assessing male infertility.

did YOU know?

For women, fertility peaks in the early 20s and begins to decline significantly around age 35. By age 40, the chance of pregnancy has dropped by 30–50% (Greenhouse, 2001).

Female Factor Infertility

Infertility in the female primarily arises from blocked fallopian tubes, ovulation disorders, or, to a lesser extent, endometriosis (Healy, Trounson, & Andersen, 1994). Fertility in women is reduced by cigarette smoking (Jelovsek, 2000). In addition, drinking more than one alcoholic beverage per day has been shown to decrease ovulation by 60%. Depending on the condition suspected, any of a number of tests may be conducted to assess female factor infertility. Levels of hormones, including estrogen, progesterone, LH, and FSH, are analyzed. The woman may also be tested for an abnormally high level of naturally occurring sperm antibodies that kill the sperm before they can reach the egg cell. A postcoital test may also be conducted by extracting a small amount of cervical mucus and analyzing it for surviving sperm. An infertile woman is typically asked to record her basal body temperature to check for signs of ovulation. More invasive laparoscopic methods may be used, to allow the physician to view the physical condition of the uterus, fallopian tubes, and ovaries. Tubal and uterine damage or defects may be assessed using a technique called *hysterosalpingography,* which involves injecting a dye through the cervix into the uterus, then viewing it with X-rays. If the uterus is unobstructed, the dye will move from the uterus to the fallopian tubes and spill out of the tubes and into the abdominal cavity (Advanced Fertility Center of Chicago, 2002).

9.3 on the web

For the couple with fertility problems, any emotional upset can be compounded by the lack of understanding exhibited by friends and family. Click on the link for RESOLVE'S Infertility Myths and Facts page at **www.ablongman.org/mcanulty2e.**

Have you heard (or even repeated) any of these myths before?

Interventions for Infertility

Reproductive technology has advanced in recent decades, but the techniques are still being refined, vary widely in terms of success rates, and can be very expensive. Nevertheless, every year many thousands of couples seek out medical interventions for their infertility problems.

Artificial Insemination

Artificial insemination (AI) is commonly used in cases of male factor infertility. This procedure involves obtaining a sample of ejaculate, selecting only the most motile sperm through a method called "washing," and inserting the ejaculate into the woman. Two methods of insertion are common. One involves putting the sperm sample into a cap that fits tightly over the cervix. This procedure protects the sperm against the hostile vaginal environment and gives them a better chance of survival. Intrauterine insemination (IUI), involving injection of "washed" sperm into the uterus, is also used. Some evidence suggests that IUI is more effective than the cervical cap method in achieving pregnancy (Williams et al., 1995). Artificial insemination may be conducted with the husband's or partner's sperm (AIH) or with donor sperm (AID).

ARTIFICIAL INSEMINATION (AI)
Process whereby sperm are collected from a donor and deposited in a woman's uterus.

Drug Therapy

When infertility is the result of the woman's inability to produce an egg, clomiphene citrate (trade name Clomid or Serophene) or preparations of human LH and FSH (trade name Pergonal or Menotropin) can be given to induce ovulation. Both of these drugs, however, have numerous negative side effects. First, because they induce the maturation of several egg cells at once, multiple gestations are common. Clomiphene also can cause enlargement of the ovaries, and Pergonal can produce large ovarian cysts (Corson, 1990). Finally, clomiphene has been associated with increased risk of ovarian cancer in several studies (Harris, Whittemore, Itnyre, & Collaborative Ovarian Cancer Group, 1992; Horn-Ross, Whittemore, Harris, Itnyre, & Collaborative Ovarian Cancer Group, 1992; Whittemore, Harris, Itnyre, & Collaborative Ovarian Cancer Group, 1992).

Assisted Reproductive Technologies (ART)

More complicated techniques are available to couples who fail to conceive using AI or drug therapy. **In vitro fertilization (IVF)** involves the harvesting of eggs from the woman's or a donor's ovary using ultrasound and aspiration (suctioning out) of the eggs. Fertility drugs such as clomiphene are often used prior to harvesting to promote egg development. The eggs are combined with the partner's or donor's sperm in a petri dish in order that fertilization can take place. One or more fertilized eggs are removed from the dish 2 to 3 days later and inserted into the uterus through the cervix. The woman is given a pregnancy test about 10 days after the procedure to determine if implantation occurred (Harkness, 1992).

Several refinements of IVF are increasingly used. **Gamete intrafallopian transfer (GIFT)** is one such procedure. GIFT involves the harvesting of eggs from the ovary just as in IVF. But in this case, the eggs are combined with sperm, and both are injected into the fallopian tubes to foster natural fertilization and subsequent implantation. **Zygote intrafallopian transfer (ZIFT)** is like IVF except that the ovum is fertilized outside of the woman's body and then inserted into the fallopian tube instead of the uterus. Yet another technique is called **frozen embryo transfer (FET)**. As the name implies, frozen embryos developed from eggs previously harvested and fertilized are inserted into a woman's uterus. Finally, a technique known as **intracytoplasmic sperm injection** seems to be particularly useful in cases where few sperm are available or the sperm have functional abnormalities. This process involves injection of the sperm directly into the cytoplasm of the ovum (Palermo, Cohen, Alikani, Adler, & Rosenwaks, 1995).

Surrogate Motherhood

Surrogate motherhood is an option available to a woman whose uterus is incapable of carrying a fetus. The Ethics Committee of the American Fertility Society (1986) defines a **surrogate mother** as "a woman who is artificially inseminated with the sperm of a man who is not her husband; she carries the pregnancy and then turns the resulting child over to the man to rear" (p. 62). In most cases of surrogate motherhood, a couple contracts with another woman to produce a child for them using the man's sperm. In such cases, the woman of the couple is not genetically related to the baby and so must adopt the child after the birth. However, if she is capable of producing an egg but cannot carry the baby herself, IVF can be performed with her egg and her partner's sperm. The resulting zygote is inserted into the uterus of another woman who has agreed to carry the fetus for the biological parents. Alternatively, IVF may be used with a donor's egg and the man's sperm. In both of these cases, the surrogate mother is not genetically related to the fetus she carries.

In U.S. culture, we tend to hold sacred the bond between mother and infant and find it difficult to understand how a woman could deliberately become impregnated, nurture the baby through the pregnancy, and then part with the baby immediately after delivery. The media attention given to cases in which surrogate mothers changed their minds about giving the baby away seems to indicate that a surrogate mother is traumatized by the loss of the infant and cannot easily relinquish the child. Such cases have been highly publicized, but, in fact, there have been about 4,000 surrogate pregnancies, and few of them have ended in legal hassles (Bromham, 1992; Hanafin, 1996). In addition, when a surrogate has been properly screened, no controversy has ever arisen (Litz, 1996). Furthermore, most surrogates report being very satisfied with their experience (Kleinpeter & Hohman, 2000).

IN VITRO FERTILIZATION (IVF)
A procedure involving the harvesting of eggs from a woman's ovary using ultrasound and aspiration of the eggs, combining them with sperm in a petri dish to foster fertilization, and then inserting one or more fertilized eggs into the uterus through the cervix 2 to 3 days later.

GAMETE INTRAFALLOPIAN TRANSFER (GIFT)
A procedure involving harvesting eggs from an ovary, combining them with sperm, and injecting them into the fallopian tubes to foster natural fertilization and subsequent implantation.

ZYGOTE INTRAFALLOPIAN TRANSFER (ZIFT)
A procedure involving harvesting eggs from a woman's ovary, combining them with sperm in a petri dish to foster fertilization, and inserting them into the fallopian tube 2 to 3 days later.

FROZEN EMBRYO TRANSFER (FET)
A procedure in which frozen embryos are injected into a woman's uterus in an attempt to impregnate her.

INTRACYTOPLASMIC SPERM INJECTION
A procedure involving injection of sperm directly into the cytoplasm of an ovum to foster conception. This procedure is particularly useful in cases where few sperm are available or the sperm have functional abnormalities.

SURROGATE MOTHER
A woman who is artificially inseminated with the sperm of a man who is not her husband; she carries the pregnancy to term and then turns the child over to the sperm donor.

SEX SELECTION

Although most people would be happy with a healthy boy *or* girl, couples commonly prefer to have a baby of one sex or the other, to have their children in a particular order (e.g., boy first, girl second), or to have a certain number of boys and girls (e.g., one of each). Some couples feel so strongly that they attempt to select the sex of their unborn child. Personal preference is not the only reason for selecting the sex of a child, however. Some families are at risk for producing children with rare genetic disorders that occur only in a particular sex. For example, hemophilia and Duchenne muscular dystrophy are both carried by females but affect only male offspring. Sex selection may thus be practiced to prevent the appearance of a disorder that is sex-linked.

Sex selection, especially when its purpose is simply to ensure a baby that suits parents' personal preferences, is controversial. Parents in many societies, particularly those in which a bride must bring a dowry of money or property to her husband at marriage, prefer male to female offspring. An advertisement for a company that conducts sex tests and abortions in Bombay, India, read "Invest 500 rupees now, save 50,000 rupees later." In other words, people can spend a relatively small amount for an abortion and avoid having to pay a large dowry to a future husband ("Killing girls," 1993). In India and China, the ability to determine the sex of a fetus through the use of amniocentesis and chorionic villus sampling has resulted in abortions of female fetuses and the birth of more males than females (Marteau, 1993). Thus, it appears that the majority of couples in those countries who opt for sex selection show a preference for boys. This finding has raised concerns that widespread sex selection will lead to an unbalanced sex ratio or to sex discrimination (Wertz & Fletcher, 1993). However, others argue that few people in the general population would wish to predetermine their baby's sex, making the overall impact of sex selection techniques insignificant ("Jack or Jill?" 1993). In fact, one study of British couples showed that 75% of those surveyed were opposed to sex selection (Green, Wray, & Baluch, 1993). It is not clear what the impact of sex selection practices will be should they become more prevalent.

Looking At . . .

. . . Thinking About

Some couples attempt to select the sex of their child because of a strong preference for a male or female. Do you think this is a reasonable practice? Why or why not?

ADVANCES IN TESTING FOR AND TREATING FETAL PROBLEMS

Just as medical advances have improved fertility options for potential parents, so too have they affected the health of the developing fetus. In this section we will discuss several medical techniques used to detect genetic or physical defects in the fetus. In addition, we will discuss advances in prenatal surgical intervention.

Maternal Serum Alpha-Fetoprotein Testing

Alpha-fetoprotein (AFP) is a substance produced by the fetus and found in the mother's blood. Levels of AFP are routinely tested during pregnancy to identify potential problems. A relatively simple blood test on a pregnant woman at around 16–18 weeks can indicate if further testing is necessary. High levels of AFP are indicative of neural tube defects (Canick & Saller, 1993). Such defects include spina bifida, a spinal cord deformity, and anencephaly, a condition in which most or all of the fetus's brain is absent. Very low levels of AFP point to an increased risk of Down syndrome. The test is not a precise indicator of any disorder, however; thus, if a woman tests abnormally high or low, a retest

ALPHA-FETOPROTEIN (AFP) A substance produced by the fetus and found in the mother's blood. High levels of AFP in the mother's blood indicate the possibility of fetal neurological abnormalities, and very low levels of AFP are indicative of an increased risk of fetal Down syndrome.

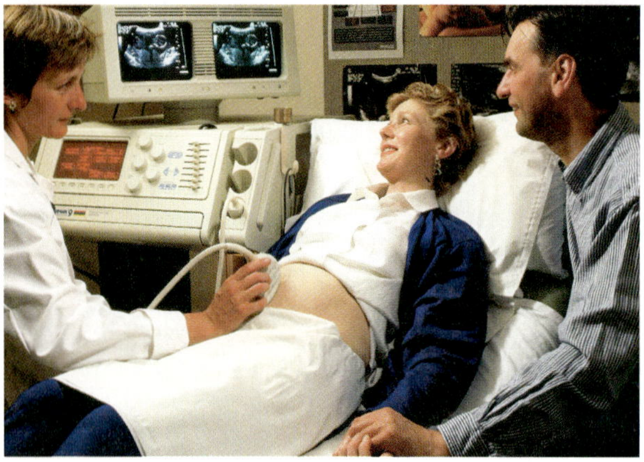

An ultrasound allows parents to see their growing fetus at different stages of development. It also allows medical professionals to assess for proper development and complications.

followed by ultrasound, amniocentesis, and genetic counseling is advised to determine if any abnormal condition exists.

Ultrasonography

Ultrasound technology has had a tremendous impact on obstetrics as well as on other areas of medicine. *Ultrasound* is sound that is inaudible to human ears. The diagnostic use of ultrasound waves is technically called *ultrasonography.* This technique allows a visualization of the developing fetus. A *transducer* (a device that emits sound waves and detects the echoes of the sound waves bouncing off objects) is either placed on the abdomen or inserted into the vagina. As the transducer is moved around, different areas are displayed on a videolike screen and recorded. The transducer is moved until an image of the fetus can be seen. The resulting picture is called an *ultrasonogram,* or simply a *sonogram.*

An ultrasound screening may be conducted as early as 5 weeks into a pregnancy. It is used for several purposes: (1) to determine fetal age (by size) and therefore verify a due date; (2) to check for ectopic pregnancy or other causes of spotting or bleeding; (3) to look for multiple fetuses; (4) to determine the sex of the fetus; (5) to identify physical abnormalities; (6) to detect signs of genetic abnormalities; and (7) to guide amniocentesis and CVS procedures (described below) (Eisenberg et al., 1991; Sanders, 1993).

The use of ultrasound has no known risks to the mother or fetus; thus, some obstetricians routinely order sonograms. However, some physicians are reluctant to use them unnecessarily because risks might be discovered in the future.

Amniocentesis

In **amniocentesis,** amniotic fluid, which contains fetal cells, microorganisms, and chemicals, is extracted by inserting a needle through the abdomen and into the amniotic cavity (see Figure 9.4). This process is guided by the use of ultrasound. The test is performed between 14 and 20 weeks of gestation and is used to determine the genetic makeup as well as the age of the fetus. Neural tube defects can be detected by this method as well. Fetal death from amniocentesis may be as high as 0.5%; thus, it should only be performed when the benefits are believed to outweigh the risks (Shulman & Elias, 1993).

Amniocentesis is generally recommended for pregnant women over the age of 35 because of the significant increase in genetic abnormalities in babies born to women

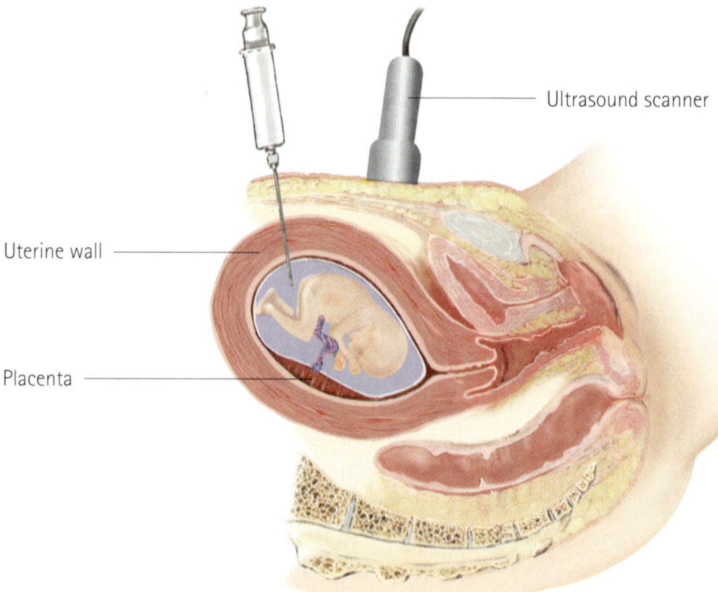

Figure 9.4 Amniocentesis

ULTRASOUND TECHNOLOGY
A technique that uses sound waves to produce a two-dimensional image of internal body structures, including fetuses; the resulting image is called a *sonogram.*

AMNIOCENTESIS
A diagnostic procedure in which amniotic fluid is removed from the amniotic sac to test for some fetal defects.

above this age. Couples who have already had one child with a chromosomal abnormality or who have a child or close relative with a neural tube defect are advised to have amniocentesis, possibly coupled with genetic counseling. Couples known to be at risk for other genetic disorders or detectable diseases such as Huntington's chorea or Tay-Sachs disease are also advised to be tested. Amniocentesis is often used as a follow-up to confirm the findings of other less invasive tests such as AFP or a sonogram. Amniocentesis tends to be highly accurate; however, because errors are possible, a second amniocentesis or other diagnostic tests may be recommended to confirm findings (Shulman & Elias, 1993).

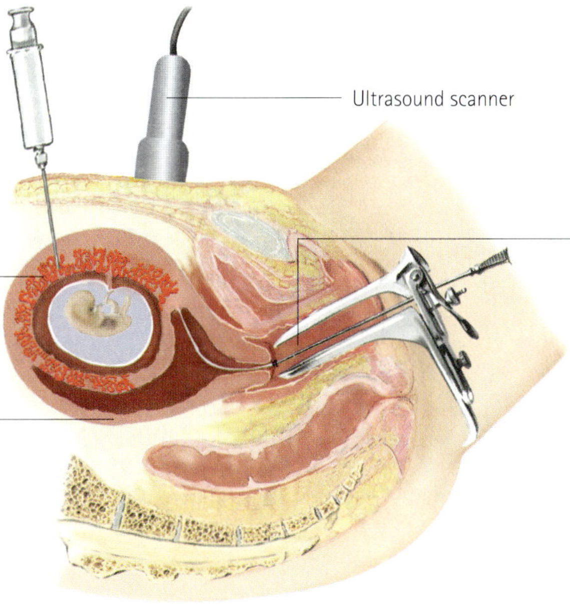

Figure 9.5 Chorionic Villi Sampling

Chorionic Villi Sampling

Because many parents want results of genetic testing as early in the pregnancy as possible and because some conditions can only be treated if detected early in the pregnancy (Shulman & Elias, 1993), researchers are exploring the use of amniocentesis before the 14th week of gestation. However, there is often not enough amniotic fluid available that early to do that procedure. Another procedure, known as **chorionic villi sampling (CVS)**, can be performed early in pregnancy and is becoming more popular as it becomes more refined and more readily available. CVS can be conducted in the first trimester, when the pregnancy is not apparent to others and when a first-term abortion is still an option. CVS involves sampling the chorionic villi, which are fingerlike projections of the *chorion,* or the membrane on the fetal side of the placenta. A long tube is inserted either through the cervix (a transcervical procedure) or into the abdomen (a transabdominal procedure), and chorionic tissue is either suctioned or cut off and retrieved through the tube (see Figure 9.5).

CVS is performed between 9 and 12 weeks of gestation and is no more risky than amniocentesis (Shulman & Elias, 1993). Reports on relatively small numbers of CVS recipients indicated that CVS might have a higher fetal death rate than amniocentesis and might cause malformations in the fetus's arms and legs (Froster & Jackson, 1996). However, other research has shown that limb defects are no more likely in fetuses tested by CVS than in those not tested (Froster & Jackson, 1996; Kuliev et al., 1996). CVS is less useful than amniocentesis, in that it cannot be used to detect neural tube defects and anterior abdominal wall defects (Shulman & Elias, 1993).

Embryoscopy or Fetoscopy

Embryoscopy and **fetoscopy** involve the insertion of an *endoscope* (a device that contains a light source and lenses) into the amniotic sac so that the embryo or fetus can be visualized and photographed. Embryoscopy and fetoscopy is the same procedure; the different names reflect the different gestational ages at which the procedure is done (Quintero, Puder, & Cotton, 1993). The endoscope is inserted either through tiny incisions made in the abdomen and uterus (transabdominally) or through the cervix (transcervically). This procedure has a 3–3.7% fetal death rate, making it much riskier than other available diagnostic tools. However, it is still used for research purposes and in certain medical cases. Improved methods may lead to an increase in use of this procedure, especially because the clarity of visualization possible is much greater than with ultrasonography (Quintero et al., 1993; Reece, 1999).

CHORIONIC VILLI SAMPLING (CVS)
A diagnostic procedure in which tissue from the chorion of the placenta is removed and tested for certain fetal abnormalities.

EMBRYOSCOPY
The insertion of an endoscope that contains a light source and lenses into the amniotic sac so that the embryo can be visualized and photographed.

FETOSCOPY
The insertion of an endoscope that contains a light source and lenses into the amniotic sac so that the fetus can be visualized and photographed.

Fetal Surgery

Perhaps even more amazing than the fact that doctors can photograph a fetus in the womb is the fact that some fetal abnormalities can be corrected in utero. Fetal surgery is used to correct life-threatening abnormalities of fetal organs so that they can develop normally. Because the surgery itself creates risks to the mother and the fetus, it is done only if (1) the diagnosis is clear, (2) the defect is well understood, (3) the risk to the mother is low, (4) animal studies have shown success with the intervention, and (5) the prognosis for the fetus would be poor without intervention (Sullivan & Adzick, 1994).

LABOR AND DELIVERY

As the end of pregnancy approaches, a pregnant woman is often simultaneously excited in anticipation of the big event and more than a bit weary, owing largely to the extra weight she is carrying. Along with feelings of excitement, anticipation, and even irritability, physical changes begin to signal that she is ready to go into labor. Labor involves a series of changes that occur over varying lengths of time and that ultimately prepare the body for the delivery of the newborn. The experience of labor is different for each woman, and not all women go through each of the changes of the typical labor and delivery, as described in the following sections.

9.4 on the web

The possibilities for correcting fetal abnormalities are astounding. Go to **www.ablongman.com/mcanulty2e** and read the article on fetal surgery. Then click on "See the most asked-for photos on the Web," which takes you to two photos taken during fetal surgery. Click on each of these and read the stories behind them.

What is your position on fetal surgery for conditions like spina bifida? Should parents risk the life of the fetus to reduce or eliminate the crippling effects of spina bifida?

Preparing for Labor

Several changes take place before labor actually commences. First, many women report feeling a burst of energy and an increase in activity level just before they go into labor. One of the first physical signs that the body is preparing for labor and delivery is **lightening and engagement**, or the descent of the fetus into the pelvic region. First-time mothers usually experience this event between 2 and 4 weeks prior to onset of labor; in subsequent pregnancies, lightening and engagement may not occur until labor has begun. A good sign that lightening and engagement has occurred is that the woman finds she can breathe better, because the pressure on her diaphragm has decreased. The fetus's movement downward may increase pressure on the bladder, however, causing the woman to have to urinate more frequently. Many women also report pressure in the rectum and pelvis and lower back pain after lightening and engagement has occurred.

Another change that occurs late in pregnancy is cessation of weight gain; some pregnant women even lose a couple of pounds in the final weeks. Vaginal secretions increase and become thicker, and as the cervix thins out (a process called **effacement**) and begins to dilate in preparation for delivery, a woman may notice a pinkish discharge, called a **bloody show.** The blood comes from capillaries in the cervix, which burst as the cervix effaces and dilates. Not every woman experiences or notices this change, but a woman who does should be prepared to go into labor within the next 24 hours. Also, as the cervix dilates, a **mucus plug** that sealed its opening may be discharged. If the amniotic sac ruptures, clear liquid gushes from the vagina; this event is commonly referred to as "the water breaking." Because amniotic fluid continues to be produced, a woman whose water has broken continues to experience leakage until delivery. Labor generally begins within 12 hours after a woman's water breaks. The longer the time between the rupturing of the protective membrane and delivery, the greater the risk of infection; thus, most physicians induce labor within 24 hours of the water breaking if it does not begin spontaneously during that period. Also, if the amniotic sac fails to rupture naturally, the physician breaks it once labor has started.

LIGHTENING AND ENGAGEMENT
The descent of the fetus into the pelvic region, usually occurring between 2 and 4 weeks prior to onset of labor in first pregnancies. Lightening may not occur until onset of labor in subsequent pregnancies.

EFFACEMENT
Thinning of the cervix that occurs just before labor.

BLOODY SHOW
Pink-tinted vaginal discharge caused by the bursting of capillaries in the cervix as it effaces and dilates.

MUCUS PLUG
A viscous substance that blocks the cervix during pregnancy and that is expelled as the cervix dilates in preparation for delivery.

Stages of Labor and Delivery

As soon as a woman starts to feel contractions, she should time them to determine their frequency. When contractions come every 5 to 20 minutes, last 30 to 60 seconds and become stronger, longer, and increasingly close together, the woman most likely is in labor.

Labor and delivery are divided somewhat arbitrarily into the stages described below (see Figure 9.6).

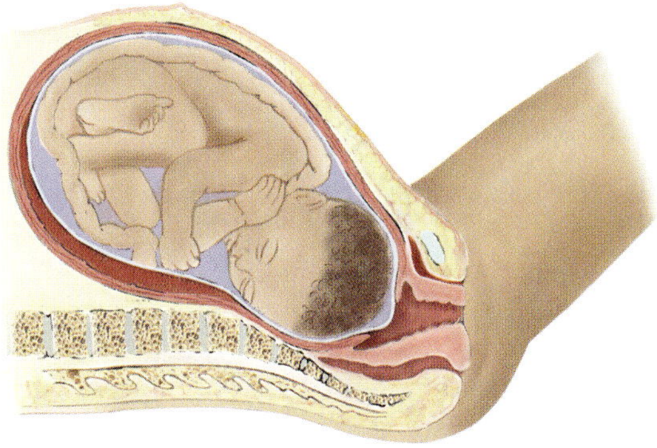

1. The second stage of labor begins.

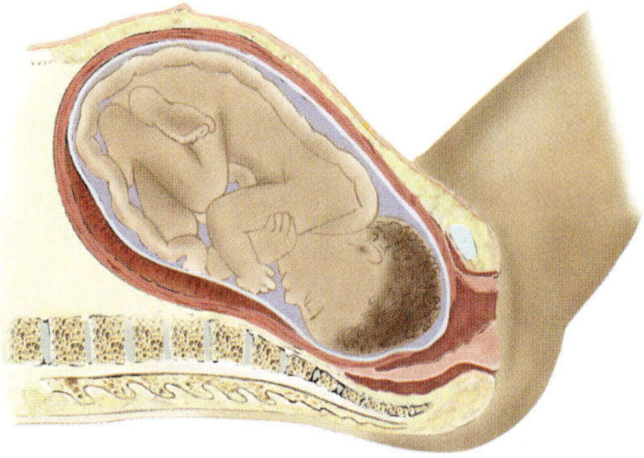

2. Further descent and rotation

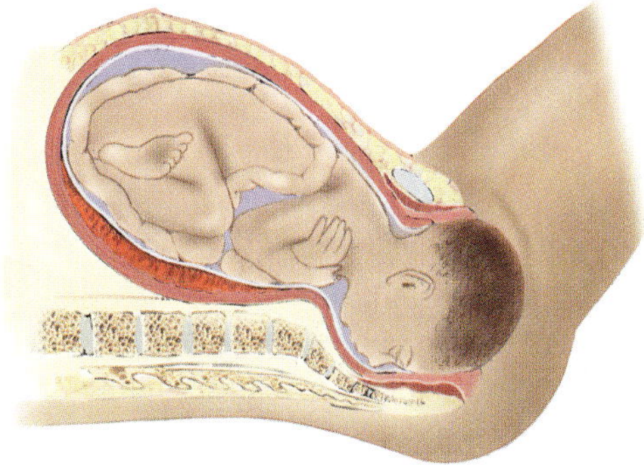

3. The crowning of the head

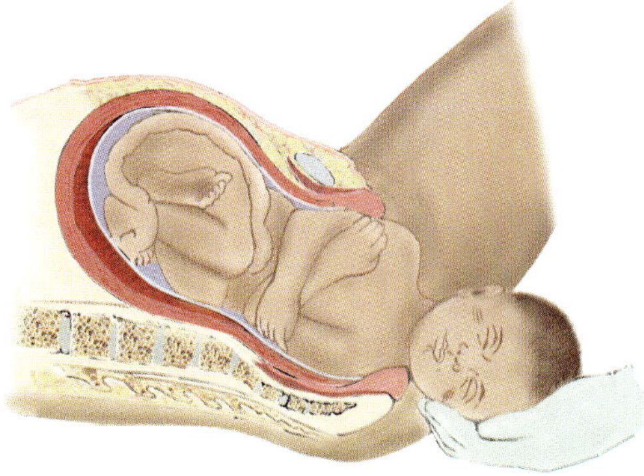

4. Anterior shoulder delivered

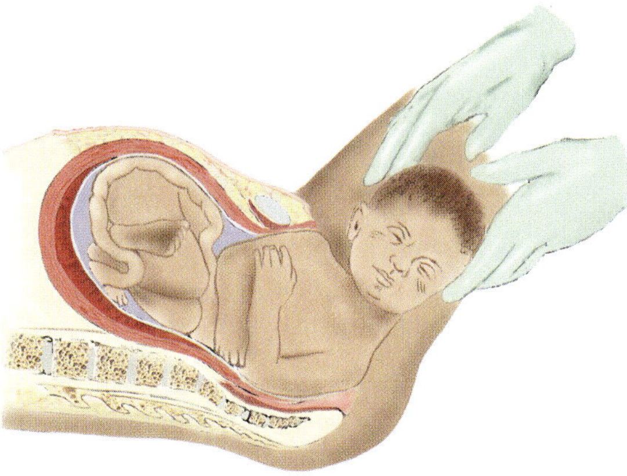

5. Posterior shoulder delivered.

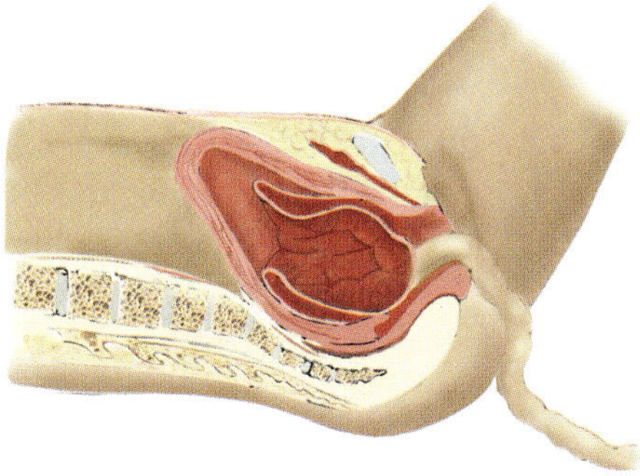

6. The third stage of labor begins with separation of the placenta from the uterine wall.

Figure 9.6 The Stages of Labor

Stage I

With a first baby, the first stage of labor lasts, on average, about 12 hours and is divided into three phases. During the *early phase,* the cervix dilates from 0 to 3 centimeters, which takes about 7 or 8 hours, on average. Contractions last anywhere from 30 to 60 seconds, are of mild to moderate intensity, and occur every 5 to 30 minutes. Some women experience nausea and vomiting and either constipation or diarrhea during this phase. Even a woman who plans to deliver in a hospital or birthing center will spend much of this early phase at home. Most doctors tell women not to come to the office or hospital until their contractions are about 5 minutes apart. The *active phase* of Stage I lasts about 5–7 hours, during which the cervix dilates from 3 to 7 centimeters. Moderately intense contractions occur about 2–4 minutes apart and last

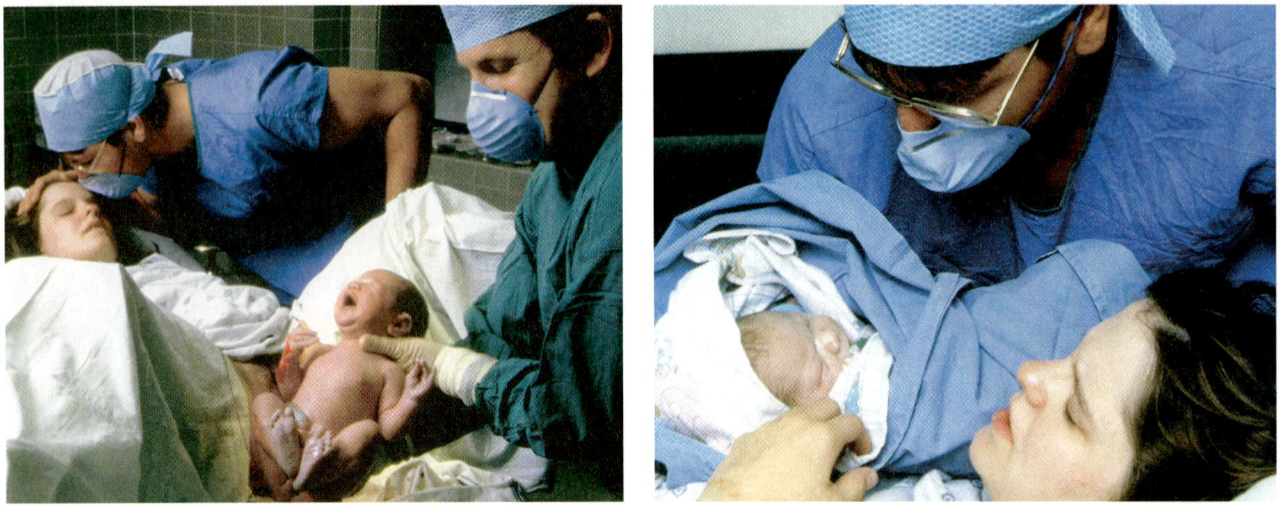

The birth of a baby is truly a miraculous event.

from 45 to 90 seconds. The woman is likely to experience increased discomfort in her back as the baby's head moves downward in the pelvis. The next phase of Stage I is called *transition;* this phase typically lasts from 30 to 90 minutes. The cervix dilates from 8 to 10 centimeters; intense contractions occur every 1–3 minutes and last up to 2 minutes. The woman may experience nausea, vomiting, hiccups, and belching; she may alternate between feeling hot and cold, and she may have the urge to push. At this point, her entire body is likely to shake, and she is very fatigued. Labor is far from over, however.

Stage II

Once the cervix is dilated 10 centimeters, it is time to start pushing. At this point, some women receive an **episiotomy**, a procedure involving cutting the perineum to allow more room for the baby to be delivered. Stage II can last anywhere from 20 minutes to 3 hours in a first delivery. It is also divided into three phases. Some women have an *early,* or *rest, phase* that is marked by a brief lull when they no longer feel an urge to push. During the *active,* or *descent, phase,* the woman pushes during contractions, which moves the baby down the birth canal. During *transition,* or the *crowning and birth phase,* the baby's head is delivered, followed by the baby's body.

Stage III

Stage III is also known as the *placental phase,* because this is when the placenta is delivered. The placenta may be delivered within 5 minutes after the baby or up to 30 minutes later. At this point, the woman is exhausted. Contractions continue at a rate of 4–8 minutes apart until the placenta is expelled; the woman also experiences vaginal bleeding as the contents of her uterus are expelled.

Stage IV

Stage IV is the *recovery phase.* The woman and baby are watched closely for the first hour after birth and checked for complications. The woman may experience chills, shakes, hunger and thirst, and exhaustion. She may also feel her uterus contracting.

Once delivered, the baby is generally placed on the mother's abdomen and chest to comfort both of them. After a few minutes (the timing depends on the practices followed in the facility where the baby is born), the delivery staff clean off the baby and check the vital signs. Often the partner assists in this process. Then the baby is wrapped and returned to the parents. Breast-feeding mothers should nurse their babies as soon after delivery as possible.

The labor and delivery process can be very uncomfortable and even painful and can place quite a strain on the woman. Fortunately, there are some strategies a pregnant woman and her partner can use to make the process less stressful.

EPISIOTOMY
An incision in the perineum sometimes made during delivery.

Prepared Childbirth Methods

With all the developments of modern science surrounding conception, pregnancy, and childbirth, it is easy to lose sight of the fact that having a child is not just a medical procedure; it is a highly personal event. **Prepared childbirth** is any method designed to allow the woman and her partner to maintain control of the birth process, rather than relying solely on instructions from medical personnel. Perhaps you have heard of the two most popular of these methods, the Lamaze and Bradley methods, which are named for the individuals who developed them. Prepared childbirth methods are based on the philosophy that knowledge and social support can help eliminate fear, tension, and pain during childbirth. Relaxation exercises and breathing techniques are the primary tools of these methods.

Prepared childbirth was once more commonly referred to as *natural childbirth,* implying childbirth without use of modern medical technologies (especially pain medication). Today, many hospitals offer prepared childbirth classes and have birthing suites (rooms that look like standard bedrooms) within the hospital setting, where high-tech interventions are available if needed. Birthing centers (often located near a hospital) that promote an all-natural option are available as well. Many couples train for and use prepared childbirth procedures to help the woman (and her partner) cope with labor but will opt for use of a regional painkiller (called an *epidural*) at a particular stage of labor. Thus, couples can now choose the extent to which they want to "go natural" in their birthing experience. In more urban communities, at least, the options are nearly limitless, and options are the key to giving women, and their partners, control over the childbirth experience. Anesthesia is certainly one of those options.

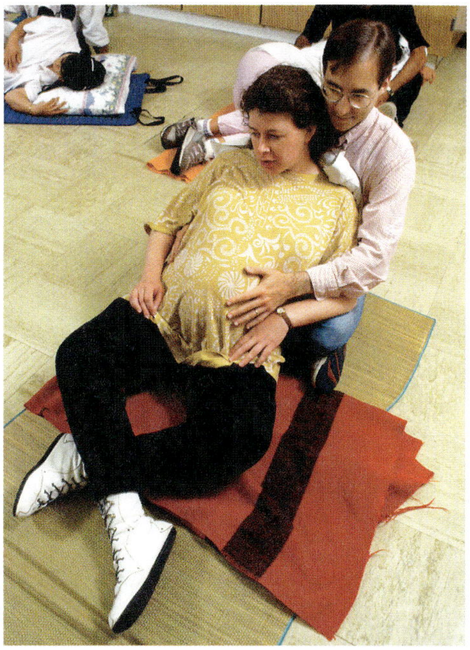

Prepared childbirth can teach a woman and her partner how to proceed through delivery using nondrug pain-management strategies.

Drugs during Labor

Both analgesics and anesthetics are commonly used during labor. Analgesics, or tranquilizers and narcotics, help the woman to relax and give some pain relief. A woman receiving an analgesic is not allowed to walk around, in case she becomes dizzy or faint. In addition, analgesics cause the woman to feel drowsy and, thus, less in control of the labor process. Nausea is also a side effect of these drugs. All side effects subside as the medication wears off.

While the use of anesthesia in childbirth is almost standard in obstetrics, it is a hotly debated topic among medical professionals. Although general anesthesia (which puts the woman to sleep) is no longer used, local and regional anesthetics are. Local anesthetics may be used to numb the vulval area before a woman is given an episiotomy. The most common regional anesthetic is a lumbar epidural, which eliminates sensation from the belly down. A catheter is placed into the woman's back so that anesthesia can be continuously administered. The woman can no longer feel her contractions; thus, they must be monitored so that she can be told when to push. A major problem with epidurals is that the loss of sensation is sometimes so severe that labor is prolonged or even stops. As a result, medications to induce labor may be necessary. These medications produce more pain and the potential need for more pain medications (Morales & Inlander, 1991). In addition, cesarean sections and forceps deliveries (the use of large tongs to pull the baby from the birth canal) are thought to be more common among women given epidurals (Bradley, 1996; Cohen & Estner, 1983); however, this issue remains unresolved.

The greatest risk of giving drugs to a pregnant woman arises from the fact that they cross the placental barrier to the baby (Boston Women's Health Book Collective, 1992). Babies whose mothers receive medications during labor often show side effects, such as irregular or slowed heartbeat, higher rates of jaundice, breathing and temperature regulation problems, and reduced muscle strength, but these are usually temporary (Bradley, 1996). Because of the potential adverse effects of medications on the mother and the baby, a pregnant woman and her partner should discuss the risks and benefits of using drugs with her doctor well in advance so that they can make informed choices.

PREPARED CHILDBIRTH
Birth guided by skills learned to ease and control the labor process, using techniques such as breathing exercises, focusing on an object, and support by a labor coach.

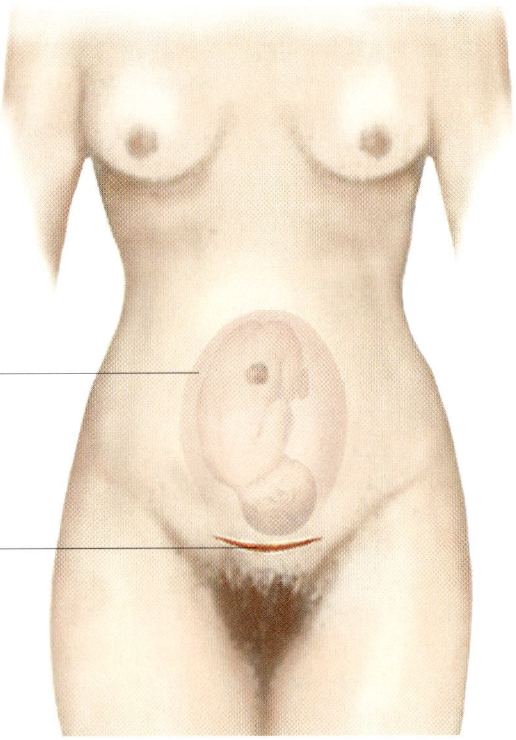

Figure 9.7 Location of a C-Section Incision

The woman and her partner should also be prepared for the possibility that her physician will recommend a cesarean section. They should be well informed in advance, so that they can make the best choice for her and the baby.

Cesarean Section

Cesarean sections are most commonly performed when one of the following occurs: (1) The baby is a breech (buttocks first) presentation; (2) labor is difficult or abnormal, a condition called **dystocia;** (3) the fetus is distressed (e.g., has an abnormal heartbeat); or (4) the woman has had a previous cesarean section. The doctor performs a cesarean section, or c-section, by cutting through the abdominal and uterine walls to remove the baby. The woman is generally given a regional anesthetic and may also be given an analgesic. A catheter is placed into her urethra to empty the bladder. After the pubic hair is shaved and an antiseptic solution is applied to the abdomen, an incision is made horizontally at the "bikini line" (Figure 9.7), and the baby is removed. Once the baby's nose and mouth are cleared and vital signs have been checked, the parents can usually hold the baby, just as they would following a vaginal delivery.

The United States has one of the highest cesarean birth rates in the world (CDC, 1993; Stolberg, 1994). This rate increased significantly during the latter part of the 20th century, from 5.5% in 1970 to 21.2% in 1998, and it has remained over 20% for more than a decade (CDC, 2000b; Ventura, Martin, Curtin, Mathews, & Park, 2000). The current rate of c-sections in the United States is in sharp contrast to the rate recommended by the World Health Organization (WHO) of between 5% and 15% (World Health Organization, 1999). According to WHO, if a country's c-section rate falls below 5%, it indicates that some women die in childbirth because they do not have access to a surgical intervention. If the rate exceeds 15%, this indicates that c-sections are being performed unnecessarily.

did YOU know?

Research has found that hospitals with c-section rates of 10–12% had the lowest rates of maternal mortality and poor outcomes as well as the lowest infant mortality rates and the highest scores on measures of infant health and illness (Joffe, Chapple, Paterson, & Beard, 1994; Rooney, Thompson, Schauberger, & Pearse, 1996). Thus, an optimal c-section rate might be around 10–12%—half the rate currently reported in the United States.

So controversial is the overutilization of c-sections that organizations (e.g., the Cesarean Prevention Movement, or CPM) have been formed to educate women and prevent unnecessary use of this procedure (Boston Women's Health Book Collective, 1992). Many opponents of c-sections claim that physicians are motivated to perform them for reasons other than the safety of the mother or fetus. These reasons include the convenience of scheduling a c-section rather than delivering a baby at any time of the day or night and the erroneous belief that c-sections reduce risk of complications and subsequent malpractice suits. Despite the controversy, there are times when a c-section is a medical necessity.

Birthing Options

Pregnant women and their partners have numerous choices about where they deliver, how they deliver, and who assists their delivery. A woman once told us that she had had great difficulty making it to the hospital to deliver her first two children—she ei-

DYSTOCIA
Abnormal or difficult labor.

ther had a very short labor or did not identify full labor until it was almost too late. She decided that trying to make it to the hospital was not the best strategy. The night she delivered her third child, she had just finished preparing dinner for her parents (her father was a doctor) and a friend who was a pediatrician. She finished her dinner preparations just in time to go to her bed and deliver her son with the help of her father, her friend, and her husband. Afterwards, they all enjoyed the dinner she had prepared.

Certainly, labor and delivery are rarely that easy, but home birth is still a viable alternative to a hospital delivery for many women. Even home birth advocates will tell you, however, that a woman should deliver wherever she feels most comfortable, and that it should be a well-planned process. Western cultural beliefs hold that hospital delivery is safest, but this is not necessarily true. With an uncomplicated pregnancy, home birth under the care of a well-trained midwife or a physician is at least as safe as hospital birth and may, in fact, be better than hospital births for women who are not having their first child. In addition, it reduces medical interventions (Olsen, 1997; Wiegers, Keirse, van der Zee, & Berghs, 1996).

Underwater birth is an interesting twist on delivery options. During an underwater birth, the woman is immersed in a birthing pool filled with warm water. The room is usually dimly lit and quiet. The water helps to relax the woman during labor and reduce the pain of contractions. The woman can be accompanied in the water by whomever she wishes. During delivery, the mother or helper reaches into the water and gently pulls the baby to the mother's chest. As the baby makes contact with the air, it begins to breathe. Babies born in water have been known to remain underwater for several minutes before floating to the surface to take their first breaths of air. Proponents of this method call it a *gentle birth* because it is soothing to the mother and allows the infant to have a gradual and calm introduction to the world. Moving through the birth canal into a familiar fluid environment is thought to be comforting to the newborn.

A woman may opt to use a midwife instead of (or along with) a physician, especially if the pregnancy has been free of complications. More than 70% of births worldwide are attended by a midwife (Sonnenstuhl, 1996). Midwives provide care and advice to women throughout the pregnancy, during labor and delivery, and after the delivery. U.S. laws vary somewhat from state to state, but generally midwives must receive formal training and certification or licensure to legally practice their trade. Midwives view pregnancy and birth as normal life events that should be under the power and control of the pregnant woman. The goal is to educate the pregnant woman so that she is empowered to make informed choices and decisions about her pregnancy and birth.

9.5 on the web

Support is very important during pregnancy, birth, and after birth. Go to **www.ablongman.com/mnanulty2e** and find the link for Doulas of North America to learn about trained professionals who provide supportive services to couples during and after pregnancy. Read the Doulas of North America position paper, which tells you more about the physical and emotional benefits of employing a doula.

Describe some of these benefits. Would you consider employing a doula's services? Why or why not?

THE POSTPARTUM PERIOD

After the birth of the child, the mother and her partner enter into the postpartum period, a time of tremendous change. Even the most well-prepared mother or couple will find that while the postpartum period is an exciting time, it requires many adjustments.

Physical Adjustments

Having gone through the tremendously exhausting experience of childbirth, the mother's body must begin to return to its prepregnant state. The mother still has a considerable amount of extra weight, in the form of fat and excess fluid. Blood volume decreases by about 30% within the first 2 weeks after delivery (Boston Women's Health Book Collective, 1992). In addition, the mother expels a bloody discharge from her vagina for up to 6 weeks. This discharge, called **lochia,** is the contents of the uterus. The uterus also begins to contract and return to its prepregnancy size. Breast-feeding facilitates uterine contractions because it causes the release of the hormone responsible for producing those contractions; thus, the mother usually feels some cramping as her baby nurses.

Breast-feeding can also produce discomforts of its own, at least at the outset. During the first 48 hours, the mother's breasts produce colostrum but no milk. Once the milk "comes in," she is likely to experience painful engorgement of her breasts. If a woman does not wish to breast-feed, binding her breasts tightly will help reduce the pain and

LOCHIA
Discharge of the uterine contents that occurs for up to 6 weeks after delivery of a baby.

stop milk production. For women who do choose to breast-feed, frequent nursing helps reduce engorgement, and over time, milk production will decrease and become more consistent with the demands of the newborn. In addition, the mother's nipples might become sore from the infant's suckling. Unfortunately, many mothers who wish to breast-feed soon abandon it because of the discomfort they experience. Proper support

HEALTH Matters

Is Breast Milk Best?

Most babies around the world are nourished with breast milk. In the United States, however, breast-feeding has a rocky history. At the start of the 20th century, more than 90% of U.S. mothers breast-fed their babies. However, technological advances, including refrigeration, pasteurization, and the ability to alter cow's milk to be easily digested by newborns, brought about a tremendous decrease in breast-feeding. By the 1960s, only about 25% of U.S. mothers breast-fed, and by the early 1970s, the rate fell to 22%. Public health efforts targeted at health care providers and women of child-bearing age brought about a reverse in this downward trend. By 1984, 62% of U.S. mothers were breast-feeding. Unfortunately, the rate dropped again throughout the 1990s (Losch, Dungy, Russell, & Dusdieker, 1995).

Why is this decrease unfortunate? Because breast-feeding provides great health advantages over the use of formula. In fact, the American Academy of Pediatrics (1997) recommends exclusive breast-feeding for the first 6 months of life, with no supplementation; breast milk is the only source of nutrition a newborn needs for the first 6 months. Unlike formula, which is always the same, the nutritional composition of breast milk changes over time to meet the changing needs of the growing infant. In addition, there are hundreds of substances in breast milk whose functions scientists have yet to discover. Given these two facts, it is impossible to duplicate breast milk. Even when formula contains certain substances, such as iron, that are found in breast milk, it is difficult to make these substances as "bioavailable" (readily absorbed and used by the infant's body) as they are in breast milk (Lawrence, 1994).

Following are some of the major advantages of breast-feeding. These result from breast milk's unique chemical composition, but also in part from the experience of breast-feeding.

1. Breast milk is highly digestible, so breast-fed babies rarely suffer from constipation or diarrhea (Dewey, Heinig, & Nommsen-Rivers, 1995; Popkin et al., 1990).

2. Breast-fed babies are less likely than formula-fed babies to be fat as children or as adults.
3. Breast-feeding enhances brain growth. In general, breast-fed babies score higher on mental development tests (Taylor & Wadsworth, 1984; Uauy & De-Andraca, 1995).
4. Breast-fed babies have enhanced visual development (Lawrence, 1994).
5. Breast-fed babies might have fewer problems with high cholesterol as they grow older (Lawrence, 1994).
6. Babies who breast-feed may have better jaw formation and straighter teeth than babies who don't (Dermer, 1995). Suckling, contrasted with nursing on a bottle, requires more exercise and different movements of the jaw.
7. Breast-feeding is associated with a lower incidence of chronic diseases and acute infections in childhood and adulthood (American Academy of Pediatrics Work Group on Breastfeeding, 1997; Dermer, 1995; Duncan et al., 1993; Shu et al., 1995; Virtanen et al., 1991; Wright, Holberg, Taussig, & Martinez, 1995). In general, breast-fed babies are sick less often and make fewer visits to the doctor (Eiger & Olds, 1987).
8. Breast-fed babies have fewer allergies (Lucas, Brooke, Morley, Cole, & Bamford, 1990; Saarinen & Kajosaari, 1995).
9. Breast-fed babies are three times less likely to die of sudden infant death syndrome, or SIDS (Ford et al., 1993; Sears, 1995).

Breast-feeding also provides advantages for parents. Breast milk is about $855 cheaper per year than formula (American Academy of Pediatrics Work Group on Breastfeeding, 1997). In addition, breast-feeding does not require the hassle of bottle preparation and cleaning. Imagine planning for a trip lasting several hours and having to figure out how to safely prepare (sterilize bottle and nipple), store (refrigerate), and feed formula (heated to proper temperature) to your baby. And what of the unexpected event such as and advice, which is now offered by most hospitals, can help reduce the problems and address a new mother's concerns about breast-feeding; she can receive such support and advice from her local lactation consultant or La Leche League. If the mother can minimize and withstand the temporary discomforts, the soreness does subside over time. The pros and cons of breast-feeding are examined in Health Matters: Is Breast Milk Best?

car trouble? As long as the mother and baby are both there, a breast-fed baby will not go hungry. And breast-fed babies' bowel movements and spit-up do not smell as bad as those of babies fed with formula!

In addition to being good for the baby, breast-feeding can be a wonderful bonding experience. Many women express great joy at the closeness that breast-feeding produces: "The satisfaction I get from nursing my baby overwhelms me. I feel like we are almost molded into one as my infant sucks on my breasts, pats me with his tender little hand, reaches for my face, and pauses to smile or laugh, or takes a quick look around before resuming the dance." Breast-feeding mothers may also benefit from a health standpoint. They experience less postpartum bleeding, and their uteruses return to normal more quickly; they return to prepregnant weight more rapidly; their bones, which lose minerals during pregnancy, remineralize better, leading to fewer postmenopausal hip fractures; and they have a reduced risk of ovarian cancer and premenopausal breast cancer (American Academy of Pediatrics Work Group on Breastfeeding, 1997).

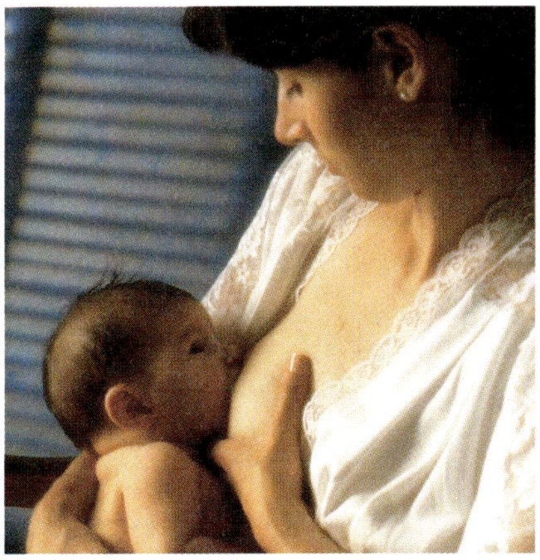

Despite all the advantages of breast-feeding, it is important to understand that it is not for everyone. Breast-feeding is not recommended for infants with a genetic condition called *galactosemia* (which prevents an infant from digesting the mother's milk), nor is it recommended if the mother uses illegal drugs, has untreated and active tuberculosis, and in most cases if the mother is HIV-positive (American Academy of Pediatrics Work Group on Breast-feeding, 1997). Women have personal reasons not to breast-feed as well. The most common reasons women give for not breast-feeding are that they are embarrassed, they fear the discomfort of breast-feeding, they think it will limit their freedom and social life, and they want the father to be involved in feeding the baby. They also see formula feeding as more convenient (Losch et al., 1995). Early on, breast-feeding *can* be difficult and painful; sometimes the baby and mother have trouble learning how to start the feeding process (called "latching on"), and the mother's nipples might get sore, crack, and bleed. Once a mother has started breast-feeding, getting through this adjustment phase is the toughest part. A middle-of-the-road option is to express milk (that is, to pump it from the breasts with a breast pump) so that the baby can still get the health benefits even if the mother does not actually nurse the baby.

Many mothers return to work within a few weeks of delivery, and breast-feeding can present a challenge for them. They may find it difficult to find time or privacy to express milk for the caregiver to feed the baby. High-tech pumps and storage systems are available that allow a woman to pump and store milk quickly and relatively easily (see White River Concepts, at www.whiteriver.com, for an example).

Social support—from the baby's father, the woman's mother, or another relative or friend—is a key determinant in maintaining breast-feeding (Losch et al., 1995). Unfortunately, many women do not receive such support. Even physicians fall short in educating and supporting women who might otherwise breast-feed. The health care industry is making efforts to enhance support for breast-feeding because it is so good for the baby (Dermer, 1995), and employers are being charged with the responsibility of making the workplace "breast-feeding-friendly" (American Academy of Pediatrics Working Group on Breastfeeding, 1997).

In the end, breast-feeding is a very personal decision, and a woman who decides not to breast-feed should not feel guilty or be judged. Indeed, the development of formula has given women the freedom to choose whether to make the commitment to breast-feeding. A woman's choice should be respected either way. While breast milk has enhanced health effects, formula is an acceptable and nutritious alternative, and scientists are hard at work to make it even more like the real thing.

The mother is likely to experience some physical discomfort after a delivery. If she has had a vaginal delivery, application of an ice pack to the external genitalia during the first day may reduce swelling, and warm sitz baths on subsequent days relieve the pain. Women who have had c-sections sometimes find it necessary to use pain medication; however, it is important to get up and move around as soon as possible to reduce stiffness and to help the digestive system to function normally again. Exercise restrictions are necessary for the first few weeks, especially after a c-section, which usually requires 6 weeks of limited activity.

Most new mothers find that they are very fatigued. As if all the postpartum demands on the body are not enough, newborns eat about every 2 hours for the first few months; therefore, at least one caregiver must get up for night feedings. Breast-feeding mothers find it helpful if someone else gets up and brings the baby to them to nurse at night so that they can continue to rest while feeding. Caregivers are well advised to take naps while the baby is sleeping during the day.

Psychological Adjustments

New parents often describe their postnatal experience as a smorgasbord of emotions. Most parents are thrilled and at the same time overwhelmed—they are fearful that they may not be competent caregivers for a helpless little baby. New parents also face having less time for intimacy and privacy. They can no longer run out for dinner or to a movie on a whim. These and other changes may be difficult for some people and may even cause feelings of resentment.

The Mother's Experience

Many women experience some disruption of mood in the weeks that follow delivery. Most commonly, they report feeling the **postpartum blues** (also called the "baby blues" or the postnatal blues), a state of short-term dysphoria (increased emotionality, tearfulness, mood swings, even anxiousness) that may accompany the feelings of happiness and excitement that follow the baby's birth (Kumar, 1994). Up to 70–85% of women in the United States report postpartum blues (American College of Obstetricians and Gynecologists [ACOG], 2002). These feelings generally disappear in a few days. They appear to be associated with drops in estrogen and progesterone, but they may also be related to the psychosocial adjustments the mother is going through. For instance, she may have left a demanding and exciting job to stay home with the baby for awhile. The isolation from other adults may be a difficult adjustment for her. She may miss the interaction with other adults and may also feel that she has lost her old identity and that her friends and coworkers view her differently now that she is a mother. In addition to struggling with her identity, the new mother who takes time away from work may also face the stress of losing her income while off work.

A more severe form of mood disturbance, **postpartum depression**, is reported in about 10% of new mothers in the United States (ACOG, 2002); it affects 26% of adolescent mothers (Troutman & Cutrona, 1990). Postpartum depression is more severe than the blues. The mother experiences extreme sadness and feelings of worthlessness and inadequacy as a mother and may become suicidal. She may also experience insomnia, digestive problems, and unusual weight loss (Epps & Stewart, 1995). Postpartum depression may require psychological intervention; however, most women tend to improve on their own within 3–6 months (Kumar, 1994). It appears that psychosocial factors play an important role in the development of postpartum depression (Murray, Cox, Chapman, & Jones, 1995). In addition, women are more likely to experience postpartum depression if they are also experiencing marital dissatisfaction and if the couple has traditional beliefs about marital and gender roles (Hock, Schirtzinger, Lutz, & Widaman, 1995). In addition, women who take only a short maternity leave (defined as 6 weeks or less) and who have other risk factors (e.g., marital concerns) are

POSTPARTUM BLUES
Mild depressive symptoms occurring for only a short period just after the birth of a baby.

POSTPARTUM DEPRESSION
Feelings of extreme sadness, worthlessness, and inadequacy as a mother, possibly combined with suicidal thoughts, insomnia, digestive problems, and unusual weight loss occurring after the birth of a baby. Postpartum depression may require psychological intervention; however, it tends to resolve itself within 3 to 6 months.

more likely to get depressed (Hyde, Klein, Essex, & Clark, 1995).

Even more rare is postpartum psychosis, which is marked by extreme highs and lows. The mother may become extremely agitated and paranoid and may experience delusions and hallucinations. Postpartum psychosis is a serious disorder that probably has underlying physiological causes (Kumar, 1994); it definitely requires psychological evaluation and treatment.

The joy of parenting is not only reserved for women.

The Partner's Experience

Mothers tend to get all of the attention at the birth of a new baby, and too often the partner's experiences are ignored. Obviously, the biological factors direct people's attention to the mother, since she has carried the baby for 9 months and can breast-feed it. Beyond those functions, however, partners can provide as much caregiving as mothers do. But societal and cultural pressures usually dictate that mothers are the primary caregivers. As a result, the partner may feel excluded from many of the pleasures of childrearing and, hence, find it more difficult to bond with the baby. They may even experience feelings of jealousy over the relationship between the mother and the newborn (Greenberg, 1985). One father, asked to describe some of the feelings he was having since the birth of his first child, replied:

> I feel a strong sense of responsibility for my baby, yet my wife and baby are so insulated by what seems to be a natural connection between mother and child. My wife nurses him, sleeps with him, and is very protective of him. I don't have the level of caretaking skills that she does because I was never taught them as a child. I even feel distrusted. At the hospital, the nurse would not leave the baby with me if my wife was in the bathroom, and even though I make a point of going along to the pediatrician, the doctor ignores me and directs her instructions to my wife. (Personal communication to author, 1997)

While little research has been published on fathers' experiences with parenthood (and even less on the experiences of partners who are not the child's father), one study showed that an overwhelming majority (84.2%) of new fathers rated the experience of fatherhood as wonderful. Despite adjustments to a changing lifestyle, sleep loss, difficulties in calming the baby, and concerns about other factors related to parenthood (relational and financial issues), the majority reported feelings of pride, happiness, excitement, and being loved (Chalmers & Meyer, 1996). Overall, new fathers' experiences are extremely positive.

Sexual and Partner Relations

Advice to new parents on when to resume sexual intercourse ranges from the general "when the woman feels comfortable with it" to the more specific "after 6 weeks." Even after any genital and vaginal trauma heals, a woman may experience some discomfort during sex. Discomfort can result from tenderness around an episiotomy. Breast-feeding women, in particular, may experience some vaginal dryness because of the hormones they produce while nursing. A lubricant can help with this problem. It is important for the couple to avoid sexual intercourse as long as it is painful, because negative experiences may make the woman less comfortable with having sex in the future (see Chapter 13 on sexual dysfunctions).

When a couple brings a new baby home, the dynamics of their relationship inevitably change. So much energy and time are necessarily given to the care and comfort of the baby that the couple's interpersonal relationship is likely to take a back seat. If at all possible, the couple should set aside time to nurture their relationship. If someone is available to care for the newborn, they might try scheduling short outings alone, even just a trip to the grocery store to pick up more diapers.

The process of conceiving, carrying the pregnancy to term, and giving birth is an extraordinary one, but it is not something to embark on without first examining very carefully your readiness for it and for the many, many years of parenthood to follow. Now that you have read this chapter, take time to read Reflect on This: To Be or Not to Be a Parent and to examine your thoughts on becoming a parent.

reflect ON THIS

To Be or Not to Be a Parent

Many of us learn during childhood that people (implying *all* people) grow up, get married, and have a family (two kids and a dog, to be exact)—in that order. Despite the fact that many people do not opt for this path in life, it is still generally assumed to be "normal" to do so, and people who opt not to have children are often questioned or pressured by family and friends. Think about your own situation: If you are already a parent, did you *assume* that parenthood was in your future, or did you recognize it as a choice, not a given? If you do not have children yet, what are your assumptions about becoming a parent?

If you haven't already had children or if you are considering having another child, you might want to think about the questions below. Keep in mind that your answers to these questions can change dramatically in the future, and you might want to assess yourself again sometime (such as the next time you decide to forgo using contraception!).

1. How do I rate my energy level and general health?
2. Could I handle the demands of both a job and a child?
3. How do I define personal freedom? How important is it to me?
4. Is doing what I want when I want to important to me?
5. How flexible am I? How do friends and family rate my flexibility? Am I able to change directions and plans easily with little fuss?
6. How much of my social life am I willing to curtail in order to care for a child?
7. Have I fully considered what it will mean to my own growth and development to devote the greatest portion of my time to a child for the next 18–20 years? Is this the way I want to spend a good part of the next two decades of my life? If not, what is?
8. Am I happy now? In what ways would a child make me happy?
9. Do I feel as if I am incomplete without children? If so, is this a good reason to have a child?
10. Do I feel pressure to have children from friends, family, the culture in general? Would I feel like I fit in if I had children? Are these good reasons to have children?
11. Do I enjoy being with children? Do I like children?
12. Am I patient by nature?
13. Do I have a temper that is difficult to restrain?
14. Is control a major issue for me?
15. Am I critical or judgmental by nature?
16. What is my history with intimate relationships? Divorce?
17. Is loving someone easy for me? Am I affectionate?
18. Do I enjoy teaching or explaining things?
19. What is my view of discipline? How well could I discipline a child?

SOURCE: Adapted from Lafayette, 1995

HEALTHY DECISION MAKING

Anyone who chooses to have a baby wants a healthy one. Therefore, it is surprising to find that so many pregnant women and their significant others persist in behavior that could potentially harm the developing baby. Why? There are probably countless explanations—cultural standards or a woman's feelings of powerlessness and lack of influence over people around her. One obvious possibility is that many women simply do not know that their behavior can have an impact on their baby, or they have been wrongly advised. Alcohol consumption is a case in point. Many pregnant women may have been advised by their doctors that it is acceptable to have an occasional alcoholic beverage during pregnancy. Research, however, suggests that it is a gamble—even small amounts of alcohol have been shown to have detrimental effects. Why gamble with your baby's health or life? What might you do to be sure you get the best possible advice if you or your partner decide to have a baby?

Whether you are a woman or a man, if you think you might ever become a parent, now is the time to learn about the influence of your behaviors on fetal and child health. If you do have children in the future, you will have to make decisions about how to put what you have learned into practice. What habits do you currently have that you would need to change if you or your partner became pregnant? Pregnancy can be a stressful and difficult time; therefore, pregnant women need support in practicing good health behaviors. A family member or significant other can help by not smoking, by preparing nutritious meals, by not bringing temptations (nonnutritious foods, alcohol, cigarettes) into the home environment, by setting a good example by eating well and exercising, and by helping the mother-to-be get plenty of rest. Which healthy behaviors do you think would be the most difficult for you to practice? You cannot control everything that influences the health of a developing baby, but you can certainly make healthy decisions regarding those factors that you can control.

summary

CONCEPTION AND FETAL DEVELOPMENT

- The miracle of life begins with the joining of a sperm from the male and an egg cell, or ovum, from the female. The fertilized egg is a single cell that divides and differentiates into a full-grown human being.
- Once conception has occurred, the cell is called a zygote. It begins to divide, forming a blastocyst. The blastocyst moves down the fallopian tube and into the uterus, where it implants itself into the uterine wall.
- During the next 8 weeks, known as the period of the embryo, the cells differentiate into the major organ systems of the body. The placenta, umbilical cord, and amniotic sac also form.
- From the 8th to the 40th week, the period of the fetus, the organ systems that were established in the first 8 weeks grow and mature.

THE EXPERIENCE OF PREGNANCY

- A woman begins to suspect she is pregnant when she misses a menstrual period. She might also notice other changes such as fatigue, nausea, and vomiting. As early as 7–10 days after conception, pregnancy can be detected through a change in the level of hCG in the woman's urine.
- Pregnancy is confirmed by detection of a fetal heartbeat and often by visualizing the fetus in a sonogram.
- Women experience multiple physical symptoms throughout pregnancy. In the first trimester, heartburn

and increased urination are common as the woman's internal organs shift to make room for the growing fetus; sensations of bloating and tender breasts from hormonal changes are also common. The second trimester is often easier. The woman may feel renewed energy as her body adjusts to the pregnancy. In the third trimester, the woman may begin to feel more fatigued, but her fatigue may be tempered by anticipation of delivery.

- A pregnant woman and her partner also go through many psychological adjustments. The emotional responses to pregnancy vary considerably, and emotional ups and downs are perfectly normal.
- Sex during pregnancy is usually perfectly safe. Certain positions might make sexual intercourse more comfortable for a pregnant woman.

PRENATAL CARE

- Good prenatal care is imperative. Such care includes regular prenatal checkups and good self-care, such as good nutrition; use of vitamin supplements; appropriate exercise; and good stress management.
- Women should also avoid cigarette smoke, alcohol, drugs, and excessive weight gain.

PRENATAL MEDICAL COMPLICATIONS

- Some pregnancies involve medical complications, such as ectopic pregnancy, miscarriage, or premature birth. With modern technology, many premature babies survive. The older the fetus, the greater the chance of survival. Some babies are postmature, which can be dangerous since the placenta may begin to break down.
- Other rare but potentially fatal complications in pregnancy are pregnancy-induced hypertension, preeclampsia or eclampsia, and Rh incompatibility.

INFERTILITY AND TECHNOLOGICAL ADVANCES IN CONCEPTION

- Only about 8% of all couples in the United States fail to get pregnant after 1 year of trying. Infertility can be caused by a number of reproductive problems affecting either the woman or the man.
- Infertile couples have many options today, including artificial insemination, drug therapies to promote ovulation, and various assisted-reproduction technologies. One such technology is in vitro fertilization.
- Surrogate motherhood is another option pursued by some infertile couples, particularly when the woman is unable to carry a child. Generally, the man's sperm are used to impregnate another woman who has agreed to carry the fetus and then relinquish the baby to the couple after it is born.

SEX SELECTION

- Some couples use special techniques to choose the sex of their child. Sex selection is used more frequently by couples when at least one of them carries a sex-linked genetic disorder.

ADVANCES IN TESTING FOR AND TREATING FETAL PROBLEMS

- Technological and medical advances have greatly increased the odds that fetal problems will be detected. Some conditions can then be treated through fetal surgery.

LABOR AND DELIVERY

- As labor approaches, the woman's body begins to undergo changes in preparation for the event. The woman may experience a bloody show (a pink discharge) as her cervix begins to change. A mucus plug that once blocked the cervical opening may also be discharged. If her amniotic sac bursts, she experiences a gush of liquid from her vagina. Once labor begins, the woman experiences contractions in her back and lower abdomen.
- Labor occurs in four stages. In Stage I, the woman experiences contractions, the cervix begins to dilate, and the fetus moves lower in the pelvis. Stage II starts when the cervix is dilated to 10 centimeters. The woman begins to push with contractions until the baby is delivered. Stage III is the delivery of the placenta, and Stage IV is the recovery phase.
- Many couples undergo training in prepared childbirth. All methods of prepared childbirth have a common goal of giving the couple more control over the delivery process and providing a natural method of controlling labor pain.
- Whether or not prepared childbirth is used, a woman can opt to receive a number of different pain medications. Long before doing so, however, she and her partner should investigate all the risks inherent in using drugs during labor and delivery.
- Occasionally, a baby cannot be delivered through the vaginal canal, and a physician performs a cesarean section—delivery of the baby through an incision in the abdominal and uterine walls. C-sections are most common where there is a breech presentation, difficult or abnormal labor, fetal distress, or a previous c-section.

THE POSTPARTUM PERIOD

- The days and weeks following the birth of a baby can be a tremendous adjustment for both the mother and her partner. Lack of sleep especially can take a toll.
- Many new mothers experience a brief period of postpartum blues as they adjust physically and emotionally to having a child. These blues usually go away on their own.
- Fathers and partners must also adjust to changes in their lives. Unfortunately, their needs often go unnoticed, and they may experience feelings of jealousy and neglect.

CHAPTER 10

Contraception and Abortion

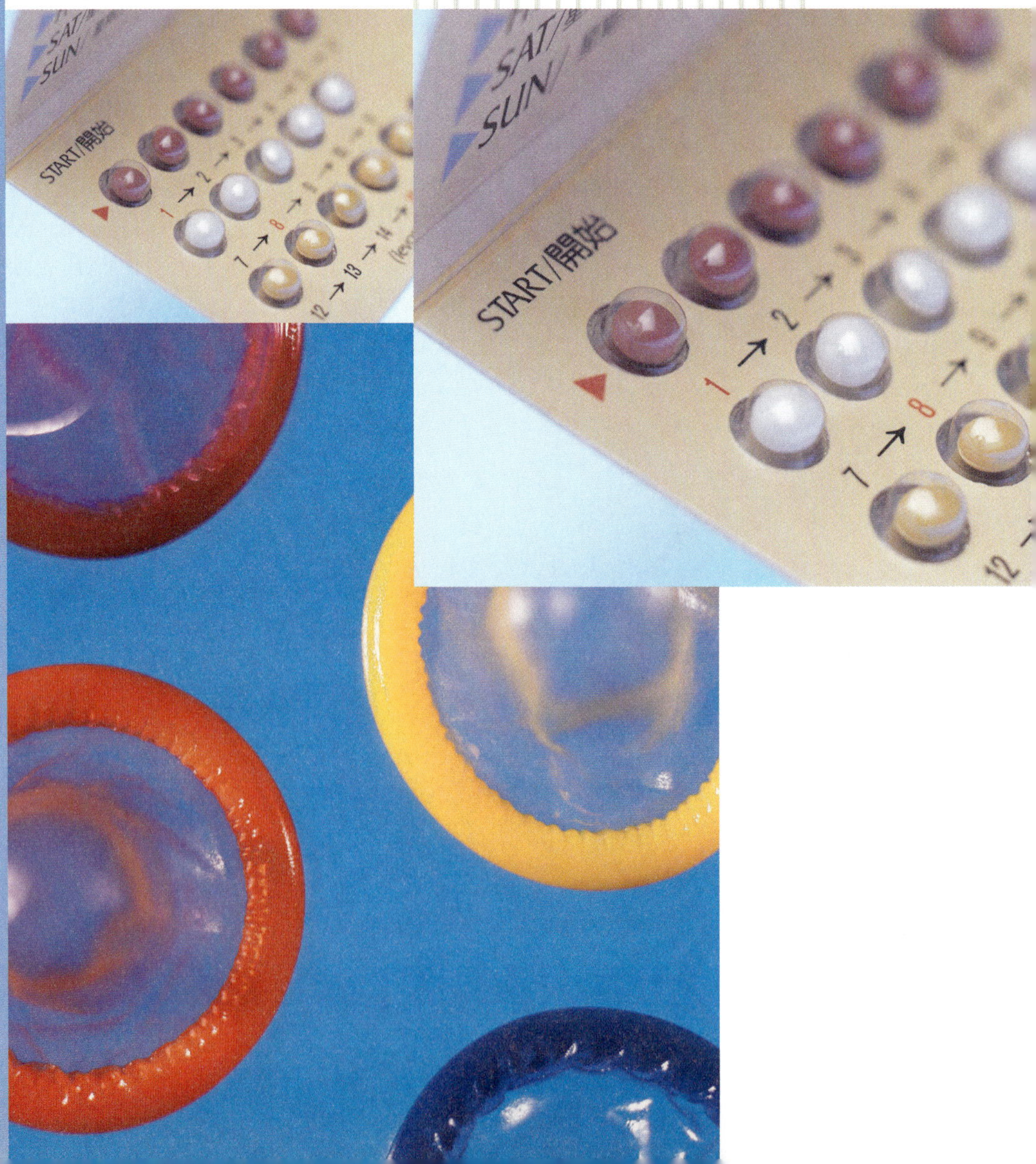

From a woman's journal:

It was the seventies—the fact that we were riding the wave of "sexual revolution" escaped me completely. I was young and naïve—no one had ever talked to me about sex, much less birth control methods. I am sure my mom assumed I would never have sex until I was married, so why warn me? I had not *planned* to be sexually active either—I was "saving myself for marriage." My friends saw me as a bit of a "goody two shoes." I was a good student, I didn't drink or smoke, and God forbid, I would never have sex! But *it* happened anyway. I was not at all prepared, but my boyfriend pressured me until I finally just "let it happen." Over Christmas vacation, my period didn't start, and I knew the worst possible thing had happened. My mother somehow read it on my face. We discussed it very little—she just handed me the money, and when I returned to college, I sneaked away to a nearby town to one of the few abortion clinics around in those days. The clinic staff treated me like dirt. I wondered why they would work in a place like that if they were going to sit in judgment. As I waited my turn for "the procedure," I pondered fleeing and killing myself instead. Nobody asked me how I was doing, how I got pregnant, what I was thinking. Just before I left, they simply threw birth control pills into my lap without explanation. When I attempted to reject the pills (thinking I would never be sexually active again, of course), the nurse scoffed at me. I felt like I had "slut" written on my forehead. I accepted the sentence—in my heart, I was branded for life.

It happened anyway.

Now that I am grown, I wonder how a woman as smart as I am ended up in a situation like that. I exercised little "choice" in the course of those events. I did not "choose" to have sex—I just let my boyfriend dictate to me. I did not "choose" to have an abortion—I just followed my mother's hints and went and did it. I did not "choose" to take birth control—I just silently accepted it.

Author's client files

So many women throughout the years have found themselves in exactly the same situation as this woman. What would have happened to her if she had had ready access to information, resources, and, perhaps most important, support? Would she have gotten pregnant? If she had, would she have chosen to have an abortion? No one will ever know. Fortunately, women *and* men have much more information available to them today and are now freer to address contraception and abortion issues openly.

You have the good fortune of having free and readily available information about both contraceptive choices and abortion options. You may even find that you have access to free contraceptives through your university health center or a local public health agency. Thanks to dedicated research and freedom of speech, you can also learn the facts about psychological and physical concerns related to the many types of birth control. This chapter provides a comprehensive review of all of this information as well as the many social, ethical, and moral aspects of birth control. We will consider some statistics on contraceptive use, the history of contraception, and the worldwide perspective on the subject of birth control.

CONTRACEPTION

Contraception literally means "the prevention of conception." However, some techniques referred to as contraceptives may actually be **abortifacients,** which act after conception to terminate a pregnancy. Birth control pills, for example, may act as contraceptives or as abortifacients. Throughout this chapter, we will point out the methods that act as abortifacients, since people who are opposed to abortion may wish to avoid using these methods.

About 64% of all U.S. women between the ages of 15 and 44 use some form of contraception. Of the women not using contraceptives, the vast majority are not at risk for unintended pregnancy because they are unable to become pregnant, are already pregnant, are trying to become pregnant, are abstinent, or have given birth within the previous 2 months. In fact, only 5% of all women at risk for unintended pregnancy are not using contraception (Alan Guttmacher Institute, 2002a). This general finding is not necessarily a cause for optimism, however. The U.S. *teen* population is not as conscientious as the general population—about 20% of young people between the ages of 15 and 19 who are at risk for pregnancy used no contraception at all the last time they had intercourse (Darroch, Singh, Frost, & The Study Team, 2001). Thus, a significant number of teens (as well as adults) are still not consistently protecting themselves from unwanted pregnancy. The motivations and decisions of young women and men regarding contraceptive use are addressed in detail in Chapter 11. Here we will discuss in more general terms the many factors that have influenced humans to develop and use contraception.

Looking At . . .

. . . Thinking About

Many sexually active teens do not use contraception during their first experiences with intercourse and are, therefore, at great risk of unintended pregnancy. Given what you know from talking to your friends or from your own personal experience, what do you think can or should be done to either increase contraceptive use or encourage abstinence among teens?

The Development of Contraceptive Use

Birth control is not a modern invention. Since ancient times, people have searched for methods that would make it possible to separate sex from procreation. As early as 1850 B.C.E., for example, women inserted plugs of crocodile dung or fermented dough in the vagina close to the cervix to serve as barriers to sperm (McCleskey, 2000). Cotton soaked in lemon juice was also employed; sperm cannot live in such an acidic environment (McCleskey, 2000). The Greeks and Romans employed various strategies to control reproduction. Men used withdrawal—removing the penis from the vagina just prior to ejaculation—and women continued breast-feeding for long periods of time to inhibit ovulation. Greek and Roman women also used wool plugs soaked in honey or cedar gum (McLaren, 1991). In more recent times, a reported favorite of the Victorians was a square wood block. However, this method was condemned as an "instrument of torture" in the early 1930s (Petrick, 1995). Various potions, such as herbal mixtures, that were thought to prevent pregnancy have also been popular through the centuries (Brodie, 1994). Queen Anne's Lace (also known as wild carrot) was described by Hip-

CONTRACEPTION
Any technique designed to either prevent the release of an ovum, prevent fertilization of an ovum, or prevent a fertilized ovum from implanting in the uterine wall.

ABORTIFACIENT
A method or substance that causes a fertilized ovum that has implanted in the uterine wall or a fetus to be expelled.

pocrates for use as an oral contraceptive (McCleskey, 2000). Condoms, of course, have also been popular for centuries. Casanova, an 18th century Italian adventurer known for his romantic intrigues with women, fashioned his out of fine linens. Almost every object imaginable, including precious jewels, has been inserted into the vagina in an attempt to prevent pregnancy (Petrick, 1995). Of course, the exact mechanisms by which many of these methods worked were not necessarily understood, so their use probably evolved through trial and error.

People have had many motives for controlling reproduction throughout history. One obvious motivation for contraception (and probably the most common one) has been to make it possible to have sex simply for the pleasure of it and not for reproductive purposes. Another motivation is that pregnancy and childbirth represent a health risk to women. This risk was especially great prior to the many medical and technological advances of the 20th century. Two motivations for contraception that have emerged fairly recently are the increasing world population and the desire of women to control their own fertility—that is, their desire for *reproductive autonomy*.

10.1 on the web

Is breast-feeding an effective form of birth control? Go to **www.ablongman.org/mcanulty/2e** and read the American Medical Association's discussion of this topic.

When is breast-feeding an effective form of contraception, and how can this effect be maintained?

World Population Concerns

Most experts agree that we are facing a major world population crisis. There are over 6 billion people in the world today, and some researchers estimate that, at the current rate of population growth, this number will reach between 7.9 and 12 billion by the year 2050 ("Battle of the bulge," 1994). The rapid growth of the world's population is a major concern for several reasons. First, experts are concerned that the earth cannot supply enough resources (e.g., water, topsoil, and land for food production) for so many people. Others argue that the earth could supply enough resources, but an unimaginable leap in technology would be necessary to do so while also protecting the environment from irreparable damage (Budiansky, 1994, p. 58). Another reason why population growth is of serious concern is the threat to public health. Many diseases flourish only in conditions of overpopulation and crowding. Furthermore, population growth leads to declines in certain parasite-killing organisms in the environment, which in turn facilitates the proliferation of various disease-carrying parasites. Overcrowding also means that people move into previously unpopulated areas, where they come into contact with new diseases. Lyme disease, transmitted by the deer tick, is a good example of this (Ehrlich & Ehrlich, 1990). Finally, overpopulation leads to a shortage of means to make a living and, therefore, higher poverty levels, which in turn are closely associated with malnutrition, illness, and premature death.

did YOU know?

Various animal membranes, and even snakeskins, have been used as condoms over the years (Petrick, 1995).

Completing a vicious cycle of poverty and overpopulation, families in impoverished, underdeveloped countries tend to be large. It may make little sense at first that very poor families should have more children, but there is a good reason why they do. Because underdeveloped countries have no social security system (government aid) for the elderly, parents depend on their children to support them in their old age. The infant death rate in such countries is high, and, because of their low status, women are rarely educated and have no means to earn a living. Therefore, impoverished couples have large numbers of children to ensure that they will have enough surviving sons to support them in their old age (Ehrlich & Ehrlich, 1990). Ultimately, however, large families mean more mouths to feed, and the cycle of impoverishment continues.

In September 1994, the United Nations' International Conference on Population and Development was held in Cairo, Egypt, to seek solutions to the world population problem. At the top of the agenda was population control. The plan proposed at the conclusion of the conference favored family planning and worldwide availability of contraceptives. The availability of contraceptives is key to population control. The goal of global efforts to control the population is not to *impose* limitations on reproduction but to make the means of contraception available to those who want it. Surveys have shown that as many as 120 million married women around the world want but cannot obtain safe and effective contraceptives. Making contraceptives available to these women would produce dramatic decreases in population growth rates. Furthermore, there would be a substantial reduction in the 50 million abortions performed worldwide each year (MacFarquhar, 1994). The fact remains, however, that many women around the world lack the status and power to control their own fertility.

did YOU know?

Margaret Sanger spent time in jail for opening an illegal birth control clinic in Brooklyn and fled the United States to avoid the possibility of a 40-year prison sentence arising from charges that were later dropped.

Reproductive Autonomy

Although they still experience some restrictions based on their sex, women in the United States enjoy many more freedoms than do women in many other areas of the world. Numerous advances in contraceptive technology grew out of women's efforts to control their reproductive capacity. Having witnessed tragic endings to botched abortions when she was a nurse on the Lower East Side of New York, reproductive pioneer Margaret Sanger dedicated her life to helping women exercise their right to reproductive freedom. She was the founder and first president of the American Birth Control League and the first president of the International Planned Parenthood Federation, and she was the primary force behind the birth control movement in this country.

By gaining control over reproduction, women are able to make choices regarding timing and spacing of pregnancies, number of children, or whether to have children at all. Therefore, contraception has made it possible for women to enjoy sex for pleasure without fear of unwanted pregnancy. Contraception also allows women to avoid having children when it might injure their health to do so. Estimates are that simply fulfilling current demands for contraceptives worldwide would reduce the annual maternal death rate by 30% (MacFarquhar, 1994). Since women have generally been the primary caregivers of children, reproductive control also influences a woman's freedom to get an education, work, and obtain financial independence. The availability of contraception, therefore, can have a tremendous impact on the autonomy of women.

10.2 on the web

Did you know that though many insurance companies pay for Viagra, used largely to improve sexual performance in men, most do not cover the costs of most contraceptives for women? Go to **www.ablongman.com/mcanulty2e** to find a discussion of the issues surrounding failure to cover the costs of most contraception.

Do you think insurance companies should cover the cost of contraceptives? Why or why not?

Choosing a Birth Control Method

Numerous factors must be considered when choosing a birth control method. One option is not to have any sexual relations at all or to limit physical expressions of intimacy to strictly "safe" activities. If you do choose to have sexual relations that call for birth control, there are many psychological and physical factors that you should consider.

Abstinence or Outercourse

The surest method of contraception is not to have intercourse at all—that is, to practice abstinence. Couples who are not ready to take the risk of pregnancy or do not want to have intercourse for other personal or religious reasons may consider **outercourse** the most viable option. There are many physical and nonphysical ways to share one's sexuality—hugging, holding, kissing, massaging or light touching, hand-genital stimulation, talking, laughing, looking—in fact, the possibilities are almost endless. Although we are socialized to believe that having sex inevitably means intercourse, couples who want to feel close and be intimate have many options.

OUTERCOURSE
Any sexual behavior except penile-vaginal or penile-anal contact.

For those who are ready for heterosexual intercourse but not ready for pregnancy, it is important to be well informed about contraceptive methods, to discuss the options with one's sexual partner, and to choose a method *in advance*. Communication with one's partner is particularly important. In fact, research has shown that the primary factor underlying effective contraceptive use for both men and women is partner support. It appears that the nature of the relationship also heavily influences effective contraceptive use—women in particular are more likely to use effective contraception in a stable and intimate relationship (Whitley, 1990).

Physical and Psychological Considerations

In choosing a contraceptive, it is essential to consider the characteristics of each method and how each method would affect both partners *personally*. As you read about contraceptive methods, you will learn that they vary in effectiveness and that each one has certain physical and psychological side effects and risks. Research suggests that assessment of risks and effectiveness is the major determinant of contraceptive choice (Beckman & Murray, 1991). In addition, side effects most certainly affect the consistent use and therefore the reliability of the various methods, particularly those that require substantial action on the user's part.

Physical side effects and risks of contraceptives vary from person to person. The hormonal methods, for example, affect different women differently. Some women find the side effects intolerable; others experience almost no negative effects at all. And depending on a woman's health status, the risks associated with the birth control pill may completely prohibit its use. Another consideration is the extent to which the contraceptive method protects against sexually transmissible infections, or STIs (see Chapter 14). If this is a concern, a condom or vaginal pouch should certainly be the contraceptive choice, because they are the only methods that reliably provide such protection.

From a psychological standpoint, too, there are certain risks, in that some people are less likely to use particular methods consistently or effectively because they are uncomfortable with them. Using a diaphragm, for example, requires that the woman feel comfortable touching her genitals. If she isn't comfortable, she is less likely to use the method consistently or correctly. Also, men may be resistant to using condoms because they believe that condoms reduce sensitivity to sexual stimulation. Methods that require action during foreplay may also be problematic for some. For example, a condom cannot be used until the male has an erection. If a couple is not comfortable discussing contraceptive use openly, the condom is less likely to be used when the time comes.

The skill required to use a particular contraceptive method is another consideration. In order to achieve a high rate of effectiveness, some methods, such as the natural family planning methods, require much more skill and practice than others. The method requiring the least skill is probably the intrauterine device, or IUD, since it is inserted into the woman's body by a health professional. On the other hand, it requires consultation with and assistance from a professional, which some woman may be unlikely to seek.

Simply gaining access to contraception can be a psychological stressor for some individuals. Having to ask a store clerk or pharmacist for a nonprescription method might be embarrassing for some; even discussing contraception with one's physician is sometimes uncomfortable. In recent years, nonprescription contraceptives have become readily available over the Internet, at sites such as Condom Country (www.condom.com), which features Prophylactic Pete, the Condom Cowboy, and Latex the Horse. Today, buying a condom is as simple as making a few keystrokes in the privacy of your home!

In general, choosing a contraceptive method requires thoughtful analysis of your personal circumstances. The more informed you are about contraceptive options and the more comfortable you are with contraception, the more likely you are to make a good choice. Certainly, the advice of a trusted health professional or an experienced friend or family member can make this decision easier.

10.3 on the web

Go to **www.ablongman.com/mcanulty2e** and find the link for Condom Country. Browse through this site to see the many different forms of condoms and other contraceptives available.

Were you aware of the varieties that exist? Would you be more comfortable ordering online or going to a store to purchase contraceptives? Why?

CONTRACEPTIVE METHODS

Many people are unaware of the many contraceptive methods available, how they are used, and their relative effectiveness. In the pages that follow, we will provide the following information about each available method: (1) how it prevents pregnancy; (2) how it is used; (3) its advantages and disadvantages (including side effects, risks, and its effectiveness in protecting against STIs); and (4) its cost. In addition, Table 10.1 provides information on each method's **typical use failure rate** (meaning, the percentage of typical users who get pregnant within 1 year when using the method) and its **theoretical use failure rate** (which represents the percentage of women who get pregnant within 1 year when using the method perfectly *each time*). Obviously, no one is perfect, so the theoretical use failure rates should be viewed as a way of comparing the different methods; typical use rates are more realistic indicators of contraceptives' relative effectiveness.

The perfect contraceptive would be 100% effective, safe, foolproof, free of side effects, under the user's control, reversible, long-acting, useful in preventing HIV and other STIs, discreet, spontaneous, and acceptable. (It would also be decided on by *both* the man and the woman; see Close Up on Gender: Who Is Responsible for Contraception? on page 294.) Unfortunately, no contraceptive is perfect. Every method has advantages and disadvantages. The contraceptive methods most commonly used by women across all age groups are, in order of preference, female sterilization, birth control pills, male condoms, and male sterilization (Alan Guttmacher Institute, 2002a). The pill is the most popular method in the teenage and college-age groups. However, in a significant trend, condom use has nearly doubled in these and all other age groups since the early 1980s, while use of the pill has decreased somewhat (Piccinino & Mosher, 1998). Thus, there is increased use of a contraceptive method that provides protection against both pregnancy and HIV and other STIs. Because both forms of protection are critical, we present the contraceptive options in order of effectiveness in preventing pregnancy, starting with the least effective, but we also evaluate them for effectiveness against STI transmission.

Chance

Chance is not a "method" of birth control at all. A woman who engages in intercourse with no contraceptive method at all for 1 year has an 85% chance of getting pregnant (Hatcher et al., 1994). It is also important to know that **douching** is not a birth control method. When a woman douches after intercourse, thousands of sperm have already traveled far enough into the vaginal canal and beyond to escape being washed away or killed. In addition, urination after intercourse is not a birth control method; a clear understanding of a woman's sexual anatomy should make the reasons apparent (review Chapter 3 on sexual anatomy).

TYPICAL USE FAILURE RATE
The percentage of typical users of a contraceptive method who will get pregnant within 1 year while using the method.

THEORETICAL USE FAILURE RATE
The percentage of users of a contraceptive method who will get pregnant within 1 year while using the method perfectly each time.

DOUCHING
Cleansing the vaginal canal by squirting a liquid into the vagina.

COITUS INTERRUPTUS
Also called *withdrawal;* a birth control method that requires a man to remove his penis from the vagina and away from the woman's genital area just before ejaculation.

Withdrawal—The "Nonmethod" of Birth Control

The technical term for withdrawal is **coitus interruptus**, or intercourse that is interrupted prior to ejaculation. Coitus interruptus is practiced as a formal birth control method by only 2% of U.S. couples (Winikoff & Wymelenberg, 1992). Sexual health educators on college campuses often refer to withdrawal as a "nonmethod" of birth control, because its proper use requires a significant amount of practice and self-control. In reality, withdrawal is often used by ill-prepared couples who simply did not plan to have intercourse or discuss the use of alternative contraceptive methods. Under such circumstances, this practice is certainly not an effective contraceptive measure.

Don't be lulled by the rather favorable theoretical use failure rate shown in Table 10.1; this rate is only achievable with perfect use of this method—and *perfect use* requires a high degree of awareness and control of one's sexual responses, as well as planning and practice. The man must ensure beforehand that no stray sperm are left

TABLE 10.1 Effectiveness of Various Contraceptive Methods

METHOD	THEORETICAL USE FAILURE RATE[a]	TYPICAL USE FAILURE RATE[b]	PROTECTION FROM STIs
Chance	85	85	No
Withdrawal	14	19	No
Natural Family Planning (all)	1–9	20	No
Calendar method	9		
Temperature and cervical mucus methods combined	2		
Cervical mucus charting	3		
Spermicides alone	6	18–21	Some
Male condom alone	3	12	Some
Male condom with spermicide	3–5	5	Yes
Sponge			
Parous women[c]	20	36	Some
Nulliparous women[c]	9	18	Some
Diaphragm	6	18	Some
Cervical cap			
Parous women	26	36	Some
Nulliparous women	9	18	Some
Female condom	5	21	Yes
IUD	0.1–1.5	0.1–2.0	No
Pill	0.1–0.5	3	No
Norplant	0.09	0.09	No
Depo-Provera	0.3	0.3	No
Morning-after hormone therapy	25	25	No
Female sterilization	0.4	0.4	No
Male sterilization	0.15	0.1	No

[a]The percentage of women who become pregnant within 1 year when using the method perfectly every time
[b]The percentage of typical users who become pregnant within 1 year while using the method
[c]A *parous* woman has given birth to one or more children. A *nulliparous* woman has never given birth.

in the urethra from a previous ejaculation. If any sperm are present, they may be carried into the vagina by the fluid emitted by the Cowper's gland prior to ejaculation (remember, a man can neither detect nor prevent this emission). Therefore, the man must urinate just prior to intercourse and clean the tip of the penis in order to attempt to eliminate any stray sperm. During intercourse, the man must detect that he will ejaculate soon and remove his penis from the vagina, completely away from the vaginal opening. At that point, it is safe to ejaculate.

Withdrawal requires a great deal of self-control on the part of both partners—but particularly the man. He must be able to both detect when he is about to ejaculate and exercise sufficient control to remove his penis and move away from his partner. Certainly, this method is not recommended for couples who do not know each other well or who are not comfortable discussing its proper implementation.

The advantages of withdrawal are that it has no unpleasant side effects and that it is free and available at all times. Its disadvantages are that, in addition to its heavy

CLOSE UP ON gender

Who Is Responsible for Contraception?

A continuing question concerns which person, male or female, should be responsible for providing contraception and protection against STIs and ensuring that contraception is used properly. In general, this responsibility has traditionally been placed in the hands of women, which is why the majority of contraceptives have been developed for them. The justification for this may be that it is an effort to empower women to protect themselves from unwanted pregnancy, since they ultimately have the higher price to pay if they get pregnant.

Society's tendency to place responsibility for contraception on women is probably also influenced by gender stereotypes, such as the belief that women are sexual "gatekeepers" and can better control their sexual impulses—a stereotype that has clearly been challenged by gender research (Lever, 1995). Research indicates that professionals and sex educators have, until recently, repeatedly targeted women when teaching safer sex practices (Edwards, 1994). Even advertisements for male condoms target women (Lever, 1995).

Educational and decision-making models used to promote safer sex and to prevent unwanted pregnancy aim to arm women with an understanding of the risks of unprotected sex and the benefits of protection, with the expectation that this knowledge will lead them to practice safer sex. However, this approach ignores the sociocultural context—specifically, the expectations and roles of men and women. For example, if a woman purchases or carries a condom with her, she may develop a reputation of being "loose." In many cultural settings, "good" women are expected to at least feign ignorance of and take a passive role in sexual interactions. Men, on the other hand, have greater sexual freedom, and they are usually expected to take control in sexual encounters (Gage, 1998).

In addition, men wield greater sexual power in most cultures (Wingood & DiClemente, 1998) and may resist women's attempts to control sexual decision-making. Particularly in more "macho" cultures, if a woman attempts to enforce her will with respect to contraceptive use, she may threaten her male partner's manhood, give him the impression that she does not trust him, or inadvertently incite a violent reaction. Men sometimes have reactions like the following when women attempt to control contraceptive decision making:

> *Mark:* Sometimes I'll be getting serious with a girl and she'll say, in a low whisper, "Do you have protection?" When she does, you get the picture that you have to stop, you have to do all the stuff. And if it's the only way you're gonna get something, you might as well do it. I have it on me, and I have it just for that use, but it kind of pisses me off. It's like, "Do you think I'm dirty, or what?"
>
> *Nathan:* I'd be very uncomfortable, 'cause girls aren't supposed to do that.

Other gender-specific factors that may play a role in determining whether a woman takes precautions against pregnancy are the high value that some cultures place on childbearing and motherhood and the bond that parenting a child together is expected to create in a relationship. These factors may have a particularly strong influence among African Americans as well as in rural settings, where there is greater social acceptance of childbearing at a young age (Cochran & Mays, 1993; Wingood & DiClemente, 1992).

Researchers, medical professionals, and sex educators need to take these and other gender-related issues into account when trying to influence contraceptive use. It is important not to strip women of a sense of power and personal self-efficacy, but it is equally vital to influence male decision making, especially among men in subcultures that place heavy emphasis on traditional gender roles. Both parties *should* take responsibility for preventing an unwanted pregnancy. In addition, both parties can potentially pay a high price for not taking responsibility. Condoms for protection against STIs serve a dual function of protecting both men and women from this risk.

reliance on the awareness and skill of the couple (the man in particular), it offers no protection against STIs, including HIV.

FERTILITY AWARENESS
A birth control method requiring familiarity with changes in bodily functions during ovulation; abstinence is practiced when the woman is ovulating.

Fertility Awareness

Fertility awareness, also called the *cycle-based method, natural family planning,* or the *rhythm method,* may be used both to prevent pregnancy and to try to get pregnant. Using this method to avoid pregnancy involves knowing when the woman is ovulating and abstaining from sex (or using another contraceptive method) during that time.

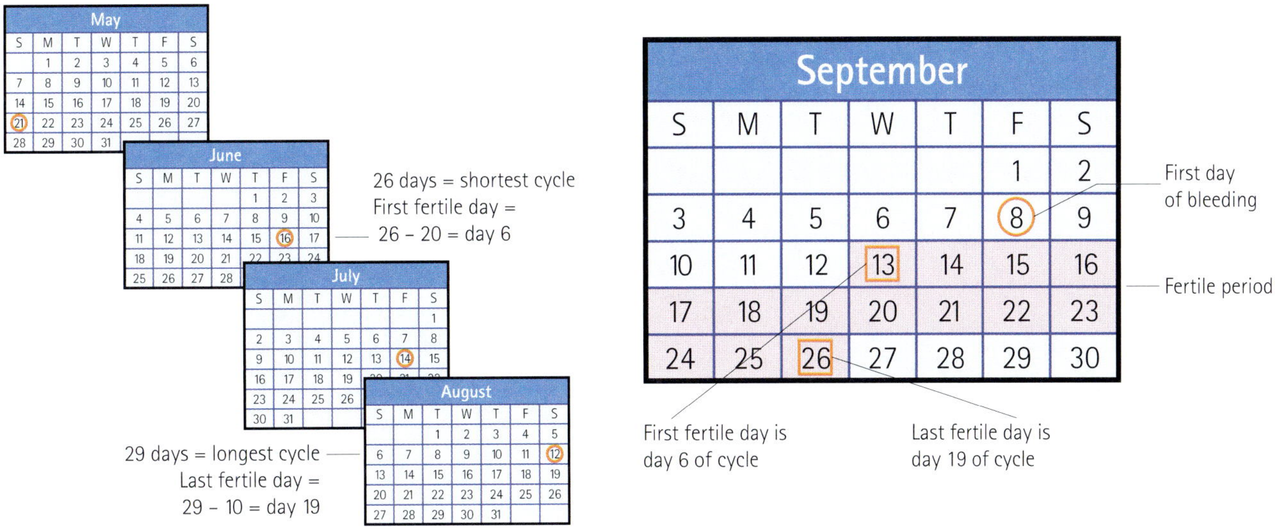

Figure 10.1 Calendar Method of Birth Control

Fertility awareness actually encompasses several methods used alone or in combination: calendar charting, basal body temperature charting, and cervical mucus charting. The most common strategy, symptothermal charting, combines charting of body temperature and cervical mucus with recording of other symptoms of ovulation, such as feelings of heaviness, lower abdominal pain or discomfort, and spotting (Boston Women's Health Book Collective, 1992).

Calendar Charting

Calendar charting requires that a woman keep a record of her menstrual cycles for several months. Once she has done this, she finds her longest and shortest cycles (a menstrual cycle begins on the first day of bleeding and ends on the day before the next menstrual cycle begins). The first fertile day is determined by subtracting 20 from the length of the shortest cycle, and the last fertile day is determined by subtracting 10 from the length of the longest cycle.

Figure 10.1 shows examples of menstrual cycle records. Based on the examples, the couple should abstain or use another birth control method from day 6 (September 8) through day 19 (September 26) of the woman's menstrual cycle (Hatcher et al., 1994). Different sources (Winikoff & Wymelenberg, 1992) recommend slightly different calculations for determining the fertile period. Because there is not 100% agreement regarding how to calculate the fertile period, it is especially important to seek expert assistance.

Basal Body Temperature

The **basal body temperature (BBT) method** is a birth control method that relies on determining time of ovulation based on basal (average resting) body temperature. A woman determines her BBT by taking her temperature immediately after awakening. There is sometimes a drop in BBT 12–24 hours prior to ovulation and a subsequent rise for 10 or more days afterward; however, this pattern is not observed in all ovulating women and may be disrupted by environmental factors, such as travel and stress. This method also requires several months of record keeping; BBT must be taken daily with a special thermometer, using the same site (rectum, mouth, or vagina) each time. A special chart is used to record BBT (as shown in Figure 10.2 on page 296), with a dot representing each daily temperature. The dots for a complete cycle are then connected so that the

BASAL BODY TEMPERATURE (BBT) METHOD
Birth control method that relies on identifying a drop in body temperature that occurs just prior to ovulation.

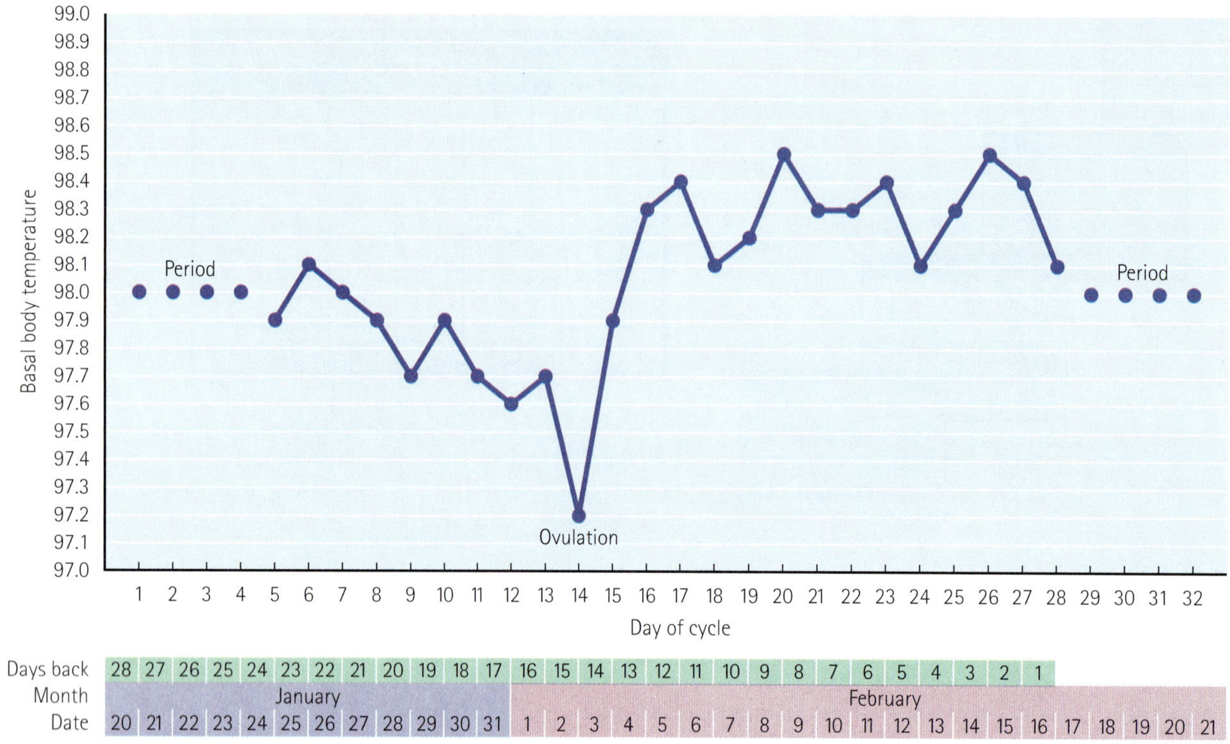

Figure 10.2 Basal body temperature charts like this one are used for detecting time of ovulation. Notice the drop in basal body temperature marking the time of ovulation.

woman can see the temperature pattern. Because small changes are significant, changes as small as 0.10 °F are recorded (Winikoff & Wymelenberg, 1992). An increase of approximately 0.4–0.8 °F following a drop in temperature is evidence that the woman probably has ovulated. Because many women do not show the characteristic drop in temperature, however, it may be impossible to predict ovulation accurately. Furthermore, sperm can survive in a woman's body for up to 5 days. Thus, the safest approach when using this method is to avoid intercourse or use a backup contraceptive method from the beginning of the menstrual cycle through the 3rd consecutive day of elevated temperature.

Cervical Mucus Charting

The **cervical mucus charting method** is based on the fact that vaginal mucus secretions change throughout the menstrual cycle. During ovulation, there tends to be more mucus, and it tends to be slippery, clear, and elastic—it will stretch 2 or more inches between the forefinger and thumb (Hatcher et al., 1994). This mucus discharge makes the woman's vagina more friendly to sperm, promoting sperm survival in an environment that would otherwise be too acidic. The woman must check the mucus daily and record its characteristics. The fertile period generally lasts from the first day of sticky mucus secretions to 4 days after the last day on which slippery mucus is observed. Women using this method are typically advised to avoid intercourse from the beginning of the menstrual cycle to the end of the fertile period. The accuracy of this method may be reduced by discharge from vaginal infections and by use of contraceptive jellies and creams (Winikoff & Wymelenberg, 1992).

CERVICAL MUCUS CHARTING METHOD
Birth control method that relies on identifying changes in mucus secretions that are associated with the fertile period.

Commercial Ovulation Detection Tests

Several kits are commercially available for determining fertile periods, either by detecting temperature increases during ovulation (e.g., Rite Time or The Rabbit) or by detecting hormone changes. The hormone detection kits (e.g., First Response or Ovu-stick Self-Test) work by detecting a rise in hormones that occurs during the fertile period. To use most of these tests, a woman holds a special stick in the stream of her first morning urine. If the stick turns a particular color, the woman knows she is ovulating. These kits tend to be expensive (about $18 to $30). In addition, they are not recommended for contraceptive purposes and are best used by couples who are trying to get pregnant, because they can only confirm ovulation rather than predict it. However, research is currently underway to develop similar tests that can predict ovulation as well as devices designed to measure factors such as water content of cervical mucus (which becomes more watery during ovulation) (Hatcher et al., 1994).

Obviously, using fertility awareness for birth control requires quite a bit of skill. Thus, its primary disadvantage is that the typical use failure rate is fairly high. The perfect use failure rate varies depending on the method or methods used, with calendar charting being the most unreliable. Women employing these methods are strongly advised to obtain training from another woman who has successfully practiced fertility awareness (The Boston Women's Health Book Collective, 1992). Its advantages are that it is inexpensive and has none of the unpleasant side effects that other methods may have. It is also considered acceptable to some religious groups that otherwise do not approve of contraceptive use.

Spermicides: Foams, Films, Suppositories, Gels, and Creams

Spermicides are chemicals that kill sperm. Spermicides come in various forms: foams, films, suppositories, tablets, gels, and creams. Also, many condoms are coated with spermicides. The most commonly used spermicide in the United States is nonoxynol-9, which has become virtually a household word. While there is some laboratory evidence that nonoxynol-9 kills organisms that cause many STIs, it does not do so reliably. HIV, for example, inserts itself into the cells it infects, which protects it from contact with the spermicide. Spermicides used alone, therefore, should not be considered protective against STIs. One other occasional problem with spermicides containing nonoxynol-9 is vaginal irritation.

All spermicides take about 6–8 hours after intercourse to effectively eliminate all the sperm; therefore, when using a spermicide, douching is ill-advised until 8 hours after intercourse. It is most important to remember that one application of a spermicide is good for only one act of intercourse. Another application is necessary for each act of intercourse.

Each spermicidal preparation comes with instructions on proper use. In general, if a couple plans to use a spermicide alone, foam is the best choice. Foam works by providing a barrier over the cervical opening in addition to killing the sperm. The bubbles capture the sperm, and the spermicidal agent kills them. The foam, inserted by an applicator, should be used no earlier than 30 minutes before intercourse to ensure maximum protection. Creams and gels are typically and best used along with a diaphragm or condom (Boston Women's Health Book Collective, 1992). They are also inserted with an applicator. Oval-shaped suppositories are inserted manually into the vagina and positioned as close to the cervix as possible. The couple should wait at least 10 minutes before having intercourse to allow the suppository to dissolve and become effective. Vaginal contraceptive films are also inserted manually and pushed as close to the cer-

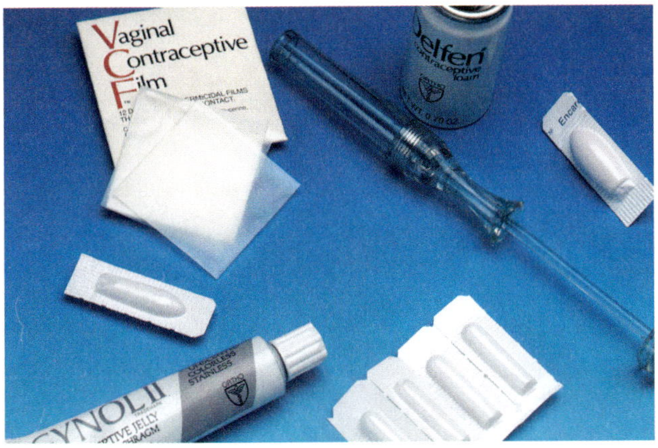

Spermicide is available in many different forms to meet the particular needs of the individual user.

SPERMICIDES
Substances known to kill sperm on contact.

vical opening as possible. The couple must allow 5 minutes or more before having intercourse in order to allow the film to melt.

The primary disadvantages of spermicides are that (1) the couple must preplan their use and have them readily available, (2) they must be used with every act of intercourse, (3) they may taste funny, (4) they may be messy, and (5) the user must feel comfortable touching her genitals during application. Rarely, some women experience an allergic reaction to a spermicide.

The advantages of spermicides are that they are easily obtained without a prescription, relatively easy to use, and relatively inexpensive (depending on frequency of use, of course). They may act as a lubricant, increasing coital pleasure and comfort, and they do not require the involvement of the woman's partner. However, if the partner is encouraged to be involved, spermicides can become a part of and even enhance the enjoyment of lovemaking.

The failure rates shown in Table 10.1 for spermicides used alone are estimates. Research on spermicides has shown that failure rates for spermicides used alone range from 0% to 50%. Unfortunately, research on spermicides has been less than adequate (Hatcher et al., 1994). The effectiveness of spermicides used in combination with a condom approaches 100% (Boston Women's Health Book Collective, 1992).

Condoms—The Male Barrier Method

Barrier contraceptive methods, such as the condom, are methods that provide a mechanical block between the semen and the cervix in order to prevent sperm from reaching the egg cell. The condom is the only male-controlled contraceptive method available today. A **condom** (also called a *rubber* or a *prophylactic*) is a sheath that is placed over an erect penis to form a barrier through which sperm (and infectious agents) cannot pass. Most condoms are made of latex. Some are natural membrane (sheep intestine), but these are not recommended because they contain pores through which many STIs, such as HIV, herpes, and hepatitis B, may pass. Condoms may be either lubricated or dry. The ideal lubricant contains nonoxynol-9, which provides additional protection against pregnancy and possibly against transmission of STIs. Condoms also come in different styles. Some have a reservoir tip, a space at the closed end to catch the seminal fluid. Some condoms have adhesive at the base to hold them on (although users complain that the adhesive is uncomfortable). Condoms also come in a variety of colors, scents, textures, and even shapes. Such variety may serve to increase the appeal of condoms by allowing for individual preferences.

did YOU know?

In the United States alone, at least 450 million condoms are sold per year ("How reliable are condoms?" 1995).

Condoms are a very popular form of contraception with numerous advantages. They are relatively easy to obtain, are inexpensive, and are considered the best method for preventing STIs when used correctly. (The female condom, discussed below, may be even more effective against STIs.) Interestingly, sales of condoms increased by over

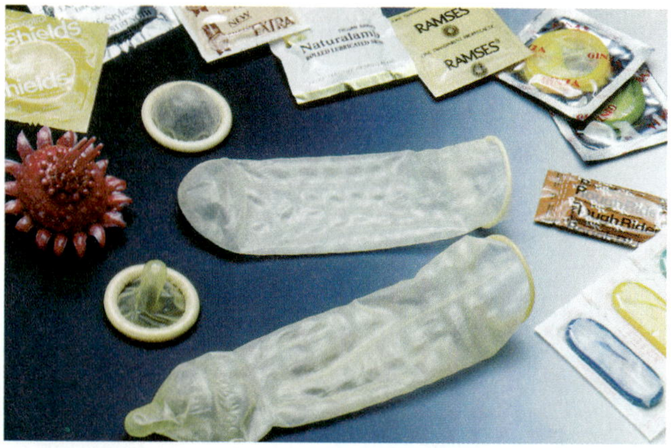

The vast array of condom options may increase the appeal of this contraceptive method.

BARRIER CONTRACEPTIVE METHODS
Birth control methods that provide a mechanical block between sperm-containing seminal fluid and the cervix.

CONDOM
A barrier method of birth control; a sheath that covers the penis to prevent expulsion of seminal fluid into the vaginal canal.

60% from 1987 to 1989—this increase seems to have corresponded to the increase in awareness about HIV infection ("Can you rely on condoms?" 1989).

Other advantages of condoms are that they increase male participation in contraceptive practices, and they may allow some males to maintain their erections longer by reducing stimulation to the penis ("Can you rely on condoms?" 1989). Furthermore, use of condoms empowers men to take control of their own fertility. Condoms can be a highly effective contraceptive method if used properly (see Figure 10.3). Some users like condoms because they eliminate the leaking of semen from the woman's vagina after intercourse. Finally, condoms are easy to carry; however, it is important not to store them in a warm environment (such as in a wallet carried in a back pocket) because heat can cause the latex to break down.

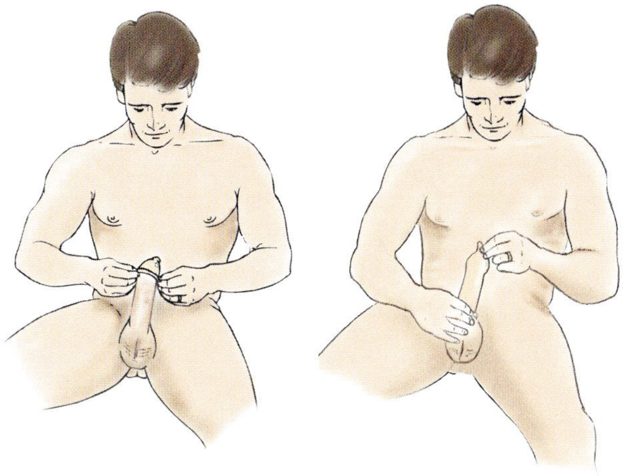

Figure 10.3 To put on a condom: Pinch off a half-inch space at the top, leaving no air inside. Hold the condom on the head of the penis and unroll to base of penis. Add a non–oil-based spermicidal lubricant if the condom is nonlubricated. After ejaculation, move away from your partner's genitals and from breaks or cuts in the skin. Hold the condom at the rim and withdraw the penis while it is still erect. Wrap the condom in tissue and dispose of it in a trash can. Wash your hands or body wherever semen spilled before returning to your partner.

Condoms do have some disadvantages. Some men, for example, complain that wearing a condom reduces sensitivity of the glans. Men who complain of this problem, however, may find that purchasing a different size or shape or switching to a textured or very thin condom will eliminate the problem. Likewise, some women report that they enjoy intercourse less when a condom eliminates direct vaginal-penile contact. Their diminished pleasure may result from the fact that condom use can produce friction that irritates the vaginal walls. The addition of a lubricant may eliminate this problem. Some men experience erectile difficulties when using a condom, and some couples complain that putting on a condom is disruptive. Incorporating condom use into foreplay may eliminate both of these problems and may actually increase arousal. In addition, repeated practice may reduce the awkwardness of using a condom. A potentially serious but uncommon problem with condoms is that they occasionally break. Research indicates that only 2–5% of condoms do so, however, and the overall risk of pregnancy or transmission of an STI is very slim ("How reliable are condoms?" 1995). Finally, some men and women are allergic to latex, of which the great majority of condoms are made.

A polyurethane condom is now available. The polyurethane condom has several advantages over the latex condom: It is thinner than latex, allowing for better sensation, including heat, and it can be used by men and women with latex allergies. In addition, polyurethane is nonallergenic (Solanki, Potter, Brown, & Ewan, 1996). A polyurethane condom is also less likely than a latex one to break or degrade from heat, oily lubricants, or light. In addition, some men find a polyurethane condom more comfortable because it fits more loosely than a latex condom. Unfortunately, polyurethane condoms cost about twice as much as latex condoms and tend to break or slip during intercourse or withdrawal more often than latex condoms, which break or slip only 1.6% of the time. The polyurethane condom is being tested extensively and will undoubtedly be improved, reducing or eliminating many of its disadvantages. One recently proposed improvement is the bidirectional polyurethane condom, called eZ•on. It is supposed to be quicker and easier to apply because it can be unrolled in either direction—either side of the condom can be placed against the penis. Mayer Labs, its developer, boasts that it is the first new design in condoms in 125 years (Mayer Labs, 2002). The fact that men are more likely to use a condom that is more comfortable to wear and diminishes sensitivity less makes the polyurethane condom promising as a contraceptive and STI preventative.

Female Barrier Methods

Female barrier methods of contraception are the contraceptive sponge, the diaphragm, the cervical cap, and the female condom. These share several advantages. First, they allow a woman to have control over contraception and not to have to rely on her partner. However, if her partner wants to participate, their use can become a part of

HEALTH Matters

A Note on Toxic Shock Syndrome

Because toxic shock syndrome (TSS) is a risk to women using barrier methods of contraception, it is important to be aware of its symptoms:

1. Sore throat, aching muscles and joints
2. Sudden high fever
3. Vomiting and/or diarrhea
4. Dizziness, faintness, or weakness
5. Rash (resembling a sunburn)

All of these symptoms may be signs of some other condition. However, if you are using a barrier contraceptive *and* you have a high fever and one or more of the other symptoms listed above, you should see a doctor immediately.

lovemaking. Such methods may also promote sexual self-awareness, since the woman must be familiar and comfortable with her anatomy to employ them. Furthermore, none of these methods presents any physiological side effects. They are especially good for women who have sex only occasionally, because they can be stored until they are needed. Finally, unlike the male condom, all of these devices can be inserted prior to foreplay if desired, making their use less disruptive.

Contraceptive Sponge

The **contraceptive sponge** is a polyurethane disk measuring 2¼ inches in diameter and ¾ inch thick, with a dimple in the middle and an attached cloth strap that is used to remove the sponge. The dimple side of the sponge is inserted against the cervical opening to provide a barrier. Prior to insertion, the sponge is moistened with water and compressed to activate the spermicide contained within it; it is then inserted by hand. One advantage of the sponge is that it provides 24 hours of protection no matter how many times intercourse takes place. It can be purchased over the counter—it does not have to be fitted by a physician, as the diaphragm and cervical cap, described below, do. To be effective, the sponge has to remain in the vagina for 6 hours after intercourse. A rare side effect of sponge use is toxic shock syndrome (see Health Matters: A Note on Toxic Shock Syndrome for a description of symptoms of this condition). To

The sponge is easy to use and can be purchased over the counter, but its reliability is not ideal.

CONTRACEPTIVE SPONGE
A barrier method of birth control; a polyurethane disk containing spermicide, which is placed over the cervix to prevent movement of sperm into the cervical os.

Figure 10.4 To insert a diaphragm, first wash your hands. Apply 1 tablespoon of spermicide to cup and spread around the edges. Pinch the sides of the diaphragm together and insert; tuck front of rim up behind public bone; feel for cervix under cup. To remove the diaphragm, place the index finger behind the front rim of the diaphragm. Pull down and out. Squatting and pushing down with the abdominal muscles makes this process easier.

avoid this complication, the sponge should not be left in the vagina for more than 24–30 hours and should not be used during menstruation (Hatcher et al., 1994). Other disadvantages include problems removing the sponge, accidentally expelling the sponge, and an unpleasant odor after intercourse. These complaints are infrequently reported, however.

Failure rates for the contraceptive sponge vary considerably, depending on whether a woman has ever given birth; failure rates among women who have had children can be quite high. Thus, the tradeoff for this method's convenience and accessibility is a less-than-ideal reliability.

Diaphragm

Another common female barrier method is the **diaphragm**, a dome-shaped rubber cup with a flexible rim. Any of several different styles of diaphragm may be recommended, depending on vaginal muscle tone and ease of use for the particular individual. A diaphragm works both by stopping sperm from entering the cervix and by holding spermicide against the cervix, so that any sperm that do make their way around the diaphragm will be killed before they can swim into the cervical opening. Insertion of a diaphragm requires several steps, which are outlined in Figure 10.4.

Diaphragms come in different sizes and can be obtained only by prescription from a physician, who must examine the woman to make sure she gets the right fit. This may be viewed as a disadvantage by some because it limits access to the device. Some other disadvantages of the diaphragm are that it cannot be used during menstruation, owing to risk of toxic shock syndrome; that using it requires preplanning, skill, and comfort with touching one's genitals; and that it may become dislodged during

Spermicide is applied to the cup and along the rim of the diaphragm.

DIAPHRAGM
A barrier method of birth control; a dome-shaped rubber cup with a flexible rim, which is placed over the cervix to prevent movement of sperm into the cervical os.

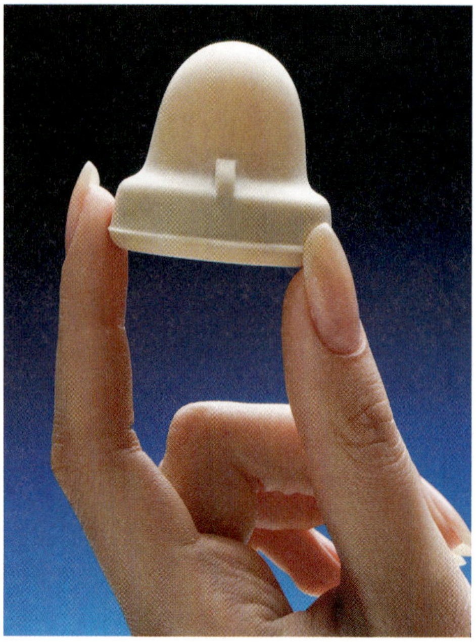

The cervical cap is smaller and fits more snugly against the cervix than a diaphragm.

intercourse with the woman on top or by deep penile thrusting. Finally, diaphragm use has been associated with increased incidence of urinary tract infections (Foxman et al., 2000). However, research suggests that this problem may be avoided by urinating after intercourse (Foxman & Chi, 1990).

Cervical Cap

Like the diaphragm, the **cervical cap** is designed to fit snugly over the cervix, but it is considerably smaller and deeper than the diaphragm (see Figure 10.5). Some advantages are that it can be worn longer than the diaphragm (48 hours) and does not require application of additional spermicide with each act of intercourse. A user should follow the 48-hour rule carefully to avoid risk of toxic shock syndrome. To insert the cap, the woman first fills it about one-third full of spermicide. She locates her cervix with her finger; then she folds the cap and pushes it into the vagina against the back wall. The rim of the cap is then pushed into place around the cervix. The woman checks the placement by feeling the dome and around the edge of the cap to make sure the cervix is completely covered.

The cervical cap was approved for marketing in the United States in 1988, but not many are manufactured and so it is not easily obtained. Cervical caps come in four different sizes, and a physician must determine which size, if any, will be effective for a particular woman. Thus, a disadvantage of the cervical cap is that the limited number of sizes available precludes its use by some women. Additionally, if the woman's cervix is angled so that the male's penis hits the side rather than the dome of the cap, the cap may become dislodged during intercourse. Most users appear to be satisfied with the cervical cap. Only a few complain of vaginal irritation or infections, and the primary complaint is that the cap is difficult to remove (Shitata & Gollub, 1992).

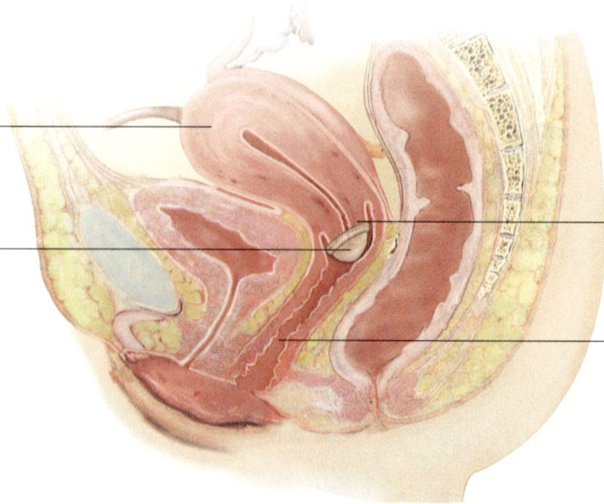

Figure 10.5 A Cervical Cap in Place

CERVICAL CAP
A barrier method of birth control, similar to a diaphragm but smaller; designed to fit snugly over the cervix to block the passage of sperm.

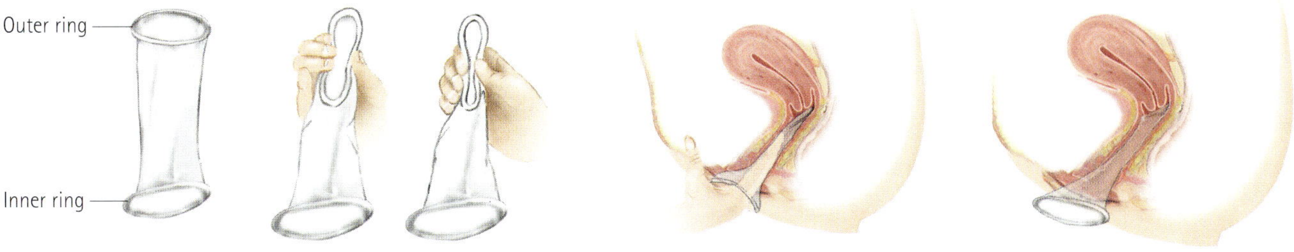

Figure 10.6 To insert a female condom: Rub the sides of the condom together to distribute lubricant. Pinch inner ring; insert the ring into vagina and push it up behind the pubic bone. Check placement and that pouch is not twisted. After intercourse, squeeze the outer ring of the condom together and twist the condom to keep the semen inside. Pull the condom out gently and discard it in a trash can.

The Female Condom

Relatively new to the contraceptive market is the **female condom**, a thin, lubricated, disposable polyurethane pouch with a flexible polyurethane ring at either end. As aptly put by one writer in the *Washington Post* (Blumenfeld, 1992), it looks like a condom "on steroids." The woman inserts the closed end into the vagina and fits the internal ring under the pubic bone, much like a diaphragm, so that the cervix is covered by the end of the sheath. The ring at the open end remains outside of the vagina, and the sheath covers and protects the labia and perineal area. Therefore, the entire penis is protected as well. A female condom can be used in conjunction with spermicide for added protection. For a better understanding of how the female condom works, see Figure 10.6.

did YOU know?

The tear rate for the female condom is less than 1%.

The polyurethane sheath of the female condom is stronger than the latex of male condoms and does not deteriorate as readily during storage or on exposure to oil-based products. The female condom may be an option for women and men who have allergic reactions to latex. Another advantage is that the condom can be inserted up to 8 hours prior to intercourse (although we question whether anyone would want to walk around with it in place). The biggest advantage of the female condom, which makes it surpass all other female-controlled contraceptive methods, is that it protects against STIs. (There is some evidence that other barrier methods reduce risk of STIs, but this is controversial.) Because it covers more contact surface, the female condom may provide even more protection than the male condom. It can also be used when a man refuses to use a male condom.

The general disadvantages of the female condom are similar to those of other barrier methods, such as the psychological discomfort some women experience with inserting the device. Other anecdotal complaints have been that it is noisy, cumbersome, and uncomfortable and causes bruising (Blumenfeld, 1992). Researchers, however, have found that there is no "significant trauma" resulting from its use (Soper, Brockwell, & Dalton, 1991).

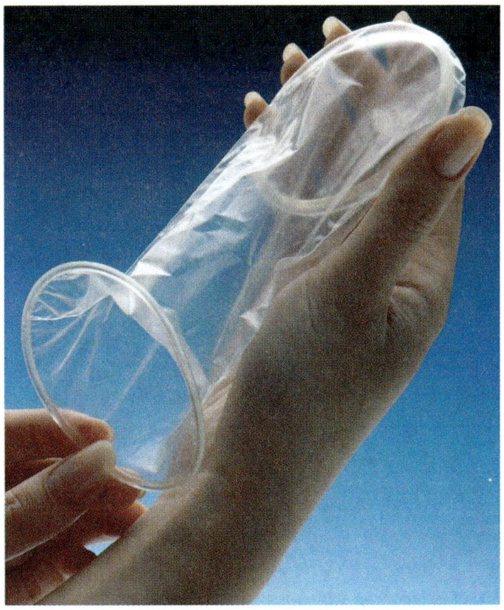

New to the contraception market is the female condom, which, like the male condom, protects against sexually transmissible infections.

FEMALE CONDOM
A barrier method of birth control; a thin, lubricated polyurethane pouch with a flexible polyurethane ring at either end, which is inserted into the vagina to prevent movement of sperm into the cervical os.

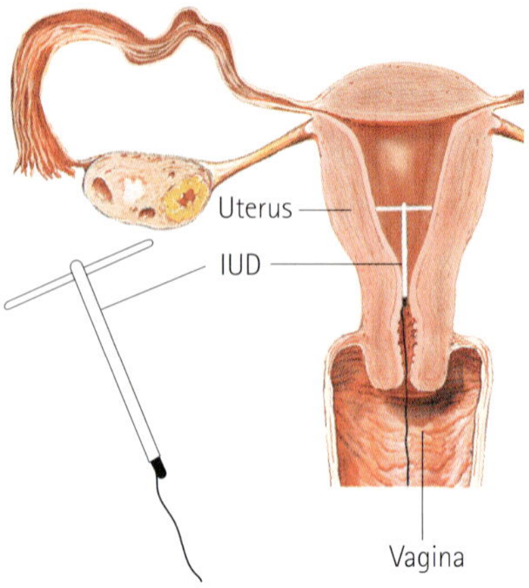

Figure 10.7 An IUD remains in a woman's uterus permanently unless removed by a physician.

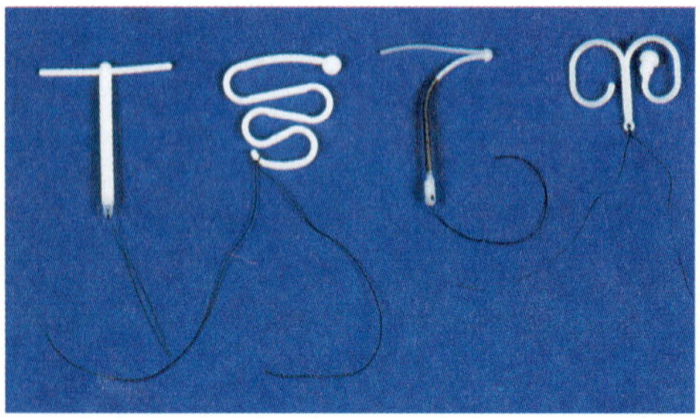

Several types of IUDs are available.

The Intrauterine Device

The **intrauterine device (IUD)** is a small plastic and copper object inserted into the uterus by a physician (Figure 10.7). A string attached to the IUD extends into the vagina; the string allows the woman to periodically check to see if the IUD is still in place.

There is little understanding of exactly how an IUD works. It may inhibit either fertilization or implantation in the uterine wall. There is some indication that the IUD immobilizes sperm, preventing them from moving into the fallopian tube to fertilize the egg cell. There is also some evidence that the egg cell moves through the fallopian tubes more rapidly in a woman with an IUD, thus shortening the time frame for fertilization. Finally, chemical changes produced by the presence of the IUD in the uterus may affect the uterine wall so that a fertilized egg cannot be implanted. In this case, the IUD works as an abortifacient. Some forms of IUD release progesterone. The progesterone, like that found naturally in a woman's body, thickens the cervical mucus to block the passage of sperm.

A primary advantage of an IUD is that, once it is inserted, the woman does not have to concern herself with contraception each day or each time she has intercourse. It is also relatively inexpensive; it may cost several hundred dollars to have one inserted at a public clinic, but there are no recurring costs once the IUD is in place (Hatcher et al., 1994). An IUD does not offer protection against STIs, however. It also has an expulsion rate of 2–10%. Furthermore, IUD users are at increased risk of pelvic inflammatory disease (PID), which is an infection of any of the female reproductive organs (refer to Chapter 3). Rarely, the IUD may perforate the uterus or the cervix or become embedded in the uterine wall. Some women with IUDs report increased menstrual pain and bleeding. Finally, there is a high risk of complications if a woman becomes pregnant with an IUD in place (Hatcher et al., 1994).

Hormonal Methods

Hormonal birth control methods involve the ingestion or injection of estrogen or progestin or a combination of the two. Introducing varying levels of these hormones into the body has one or more of several effects that reduce the chance of pregnancy. First, these hormones inhibit production of LH and FSH, the hormones responsible for ovulation. Second, progestin may cause the cervical mucus to become too thick for the sperm to penetrate. Third, these hormones may affect the contractions of the fallopian tubes, thereby disrupting the movement of the egg cell through the tube. Fourth, enzymes in the uterine lining may be altered, making implantation of a fertilized egg cell impossible. (Opponents of abortion should note that the pill may act by essentially aborting the **conceptus**, that is, the zygote or fetus.) Finally, the presence of these hormones may disrupt the actions of the corpus luteum (Ferin, Jewelewicz, & Warren, 1993). (You may wish to review the menstrual cycle, described in Chapter 3.)

Combined Oral Contraceptive

The **combined oral contraceptive**, also known as "the pill," contains a combination of estrogen and progestin. In order to work effectively, the pill must be taken at the same time daily. There are either 28 or 21 pills in a pill pack. In a 28-pill pack, the first 21 pills are active (they contain hormones), and the last 7 are inert (placebo pills). The woman takes them in order, and during the last 7 days, she has a period much as she would if she were not on the pill. The last 7 pills are basically reminders to keep the woman on track. In the case of a 21-pill pack, the woman takes all 21 pills, waits 7 days, and then begins a new pack. If a woman forgets to take one or more pills, she should follow the manufacturer's instructions to avoid pregnancy.

INTRAUTERINE DEVICE (IUD)
A small plastic and copper object inserted into the uterus by a physician to prevent pregnancy.

CONCEPTUS
A zygote or fetus.

COMBINED ORAL CONTRACEPTIVE
A pill that contains a combination of estrogen and progestin, hormones that prevent ovulation and have other contraceptive effects.

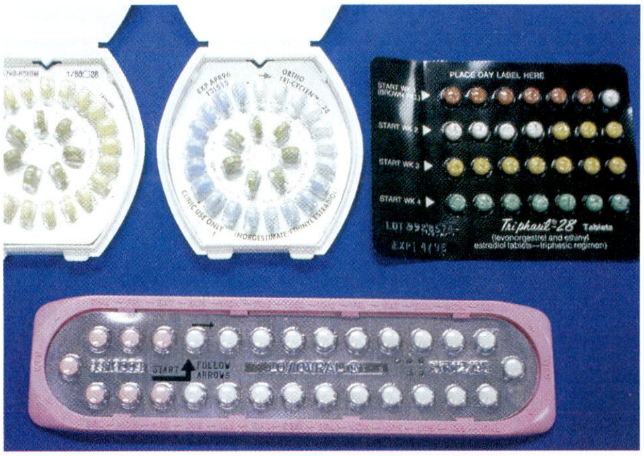

Several brands of oral contraceptive are available. Some women may try two or three different brands before finding one that creates the minimum number of side effects for them.

Women using the pill must remember that antibiotics may interfere with its action. If a woman is prescribed an antibiotic, she should consult with her physician regarding whether it could alter the effectiveness of her birth control pills. If so, she will need to use a backup contraceptive method until she has completed her prescription.

The health risks associated with use of the pill are highest in women who are heavy smokers and over the age of 35. These women have a significantly increased risk of stroke, clotting, and myocardial infarction (heart attack). In general, about 40% of women on the pill experience side effects, which are generally minor and disappear in about 3 months. These side effects include fluid retention, weight gain, breast tenderness, headaches, depressive symptoms, decreased sex drive, and nausea. If a woman experiences persistent side effects, switching to a different formulation of the pill might eliminate or reduce them. The pill does not offer protection against STIs. Depending on a woman's health status and age, the pill may not be an appropriate contraceptive option. Because of the many possible considerations, a woman should decide to use oral contraceptives only after thorough consultation with a health care provider. One common concern regarding the pill is discussed in Health Matters: Do Oral Contraceptives Cause Cancer?

HEALTH Matters

Do Oral Contraceptives Cause Cancer?

A common assumption is that taking the pill is associated with a higher risk of cancer. The medical community's current understanding of the risk of various kinds of cancer for women taking the pill is summarized here:

Breast cancer. It is possible that there is a subgroup of women who may be at increased risk of breast cancer as a result of using the pill. Likewise, there may be a subgroup of women for whom the pill provides a protective effect against breast cancer. In other words, the effects of oral contraceptive use with respect to breast cancer are inconsistent.

Ovarian and endometrial (uterine lining) cancer. The pill offers some protection against these cancers, even up to 10 years after a woman has ceased taking it.

Cervical cancer. Some research (but not all) has indicated a relationship between pill use and cervical cancer. These findings may be confounded in two ways, however: First, pill users may obtain pap smears more regularly than nonusers, allowing cervical cancer to be more readily detected in them. Second, pill users tend to have more sexual partners; this, too, is associated with increased risk of cervical cancer. Additional research is needed.

Melanoma (skin cancer). Research has failed to find a relationship between pill use and melanoma.

Liver cancer (hepatocellular carcinoma). Although liver cancer is very rare, there is some evidence of its increased incidence among women who used the pill for more than 8 years.

You'll find a more extensive discussion of this topic in *Contraceptive Technology: Sixteenth Revised Edition* by Hatcher et al. (1994).

There are numerous advantages to using the pill. If taken properly, the pill is a highly effective form of contraception. It can be taken safely for several years, and it may decrease menstrual cramps and bleeding. The pill may also provide some protection against severe forms of PID, reduce the occurrence of benign breast lumps, and relieve acne. Some women even report an increase in sexual enjoyment, perhaps because the pill lessens the fear of becoming pregnant (Hatcher et al., 1994).

Hormonal Alternatives to Oral Contraceptives

The last few years have seen remarkable advances in hormonal contraception for women. The primary advantage of these new options is that they free a woman from the need to remember to do anything to prevent pregnancy for periods ranging from 7 days to 5 years. In addition, they are highly effective against pregnancy (98–99%), and they may provide relief from conditions such as painful menstrual cramps (Brink, 2002). The primary disadvantage of these alternatives is that none provides protection against STIs. Like the pill, these hormonal methods should be thoroughly researched and discussed with a health care provider before being used.

Implants In 1991, the FDA approved Norplant for use in the United States. **Norplant** consists of six slender silicone-rubber capsules containing progestin, which are implanted under the skin and protect against pregnancy for 5 years ("Food and Drug Administration," 1991). The implants slowly release progestin. The major advantage of this method is that it prevents pregnancy without the woman's having to take any further action. The contraceptive effect is also readily reversible by removal of the capsules. Norplant can be used while breast-feeding, as early as 6 weeks after delivery. Finally, women who cannot take birth control pills can sometimes tolerate Norplant (Planned Parenthood Association of Utah, 1996). Norplant costs over $500 for the exam, the capsules, and the insertion, and up to $200 more to remove the capsules.

10.4 on the web

Not all contraceptive methods are recommended for college-age women. Go to **www.ablongman.com/mcanulty2e** and find the link to the Williams College Peer Health organization. Read about the four contraceptive methods listed.

Why is each method not recommended for women in this group?

Norplant has been criticized primarily for causing menstrual disturbances (e.g., long or short cycles, heavy or no menstruation, spotting in the first 6 months of use), for being difficult to insert or remove, and for leading to scarring due to insertion and removal of the rods ("Etonorgestrel Implant," 2001; Roan, 2002). Norplant was removed from the U.S. market in 2002 because of these problems, but a new implant, Implanon, is available in other countries (Australia and the United Kingdom) and may soon be available in the United States (Meckstroth & Darney, 2001; Roan 2002). Implanon is a single rod that can be inserted or removed in just a couple of minutes and offers 3 years of contraception. It is expected to have fewer side effects than Norplant (Roan, 2002).

Injections **Depo-Provera**, on the market since 1992, provides contraception via an injection of hormone given every 3 months. Costs for the injections and a physician's exam vary, with clinics often charging according to income (Planned Parenthood Association of Utah, 1996). Unfortunately, Depo-Provera is associated with delayed fertility

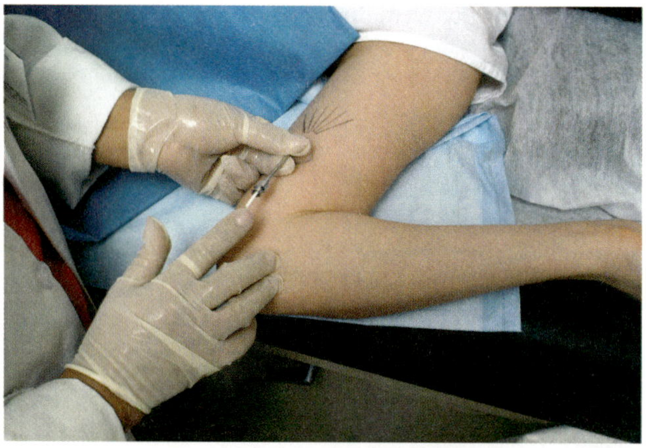

Norplant capsules are usually implanted into the upper arm. The capsules leave small raised areas on the skin.

NORPLANT
A birth control method that involves the implanting of six slender, silicone-rubber capsules under the skin; the capsules release a synthetic hormone, progestin, into the woman's system.

for up to 18 months after a woman stops using it, and it causes irregular bleeding. A new monthly injection, Lunelle, is now available, which boasts mild side effects no different from low-dose oral contraceptives (Shulman, 2000) and a return to fertility after only 2 to 4 months (Schultz, 2001).

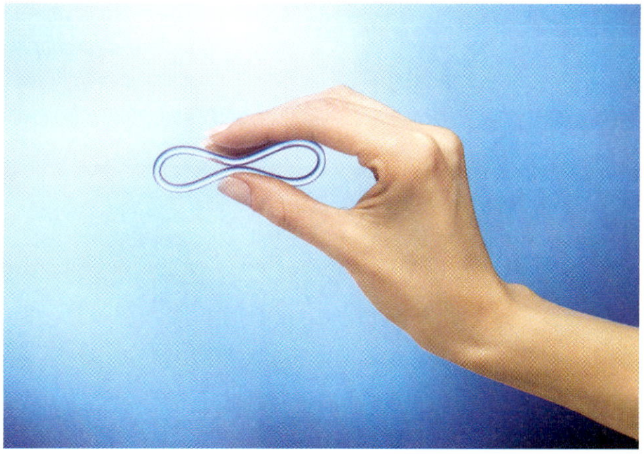

NuvaRing offers convenience, as it provides contraception for 3 weeks at a time.

The Vaginal Ring NuvaRing, a soft, flexible, hormone-releasing ring inserted around the cervix, was approved by the FDA in 2001 ("FDA approves," 2002). The hormone dosage is lower than that provided by low-dose oral contraceptives ("Today's new," 2001). A woman can insert the vaginal ring herself and leave it in for 3 weeks. She removes it during the 4th week, and then inserts a new one after menstruation. A vaginal ring cannot be used in combination with a diaphragm because the ring would interfere with placement of the diaphragm. Side effects of use of the vaginal ring can include vaginal discharge, infection, and irritation ("FDA approves," 2002).

The Modern IUD Mirena is a T-shaped intrauterine device (resembling earlier IUDs), which contains hormones that can prevent pregnancy for up to 5 years ("Women's choices," 2002). Overall, this modern IUD offers increased effectiveness (nearly equal to sterilization) and decreased side effects compared to earlier IUDs. Although Mirena causes increased spotting and bleeding in the initial months of use, it notably decreases the amount and length of menstrual flow in the long run. In addition, return to fertility and side effects are similar to those occurring with the other hormonal contraceptives. Rare complications include PID, perforation of the uterine lining, and expulsion, which is most likely to occur in the first month (Hidalgo et al., 2002; LNG IUS, 2001).

The Patch Ortho Evra, introduced to the U.S. market in 2002, provides contraceptive hormones via a skin patch. A woman applies a new patch each week for 3 weeks. She then skips a week for menstruation and starts a new series of three patches (Brink, 2002). She may place the patch on her lower abdomen, buttocks, upper body, upper outer arm,

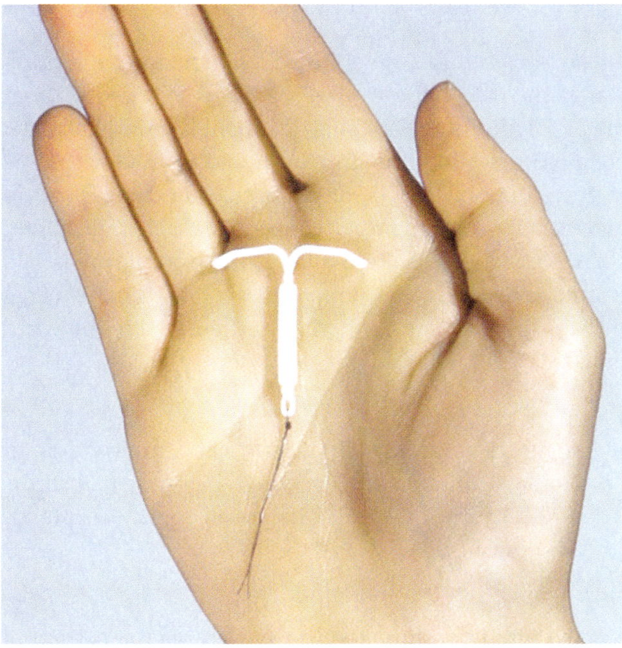

Mirena is the modern IUD. It can be left in place and creates few side effects.

DEPO-PROVERA
A birth control method involving injection of synthetic hormones every 3 months to prevent ovulation.

The patch is very easy to use—you simply place it on your skin and leave it for a week.

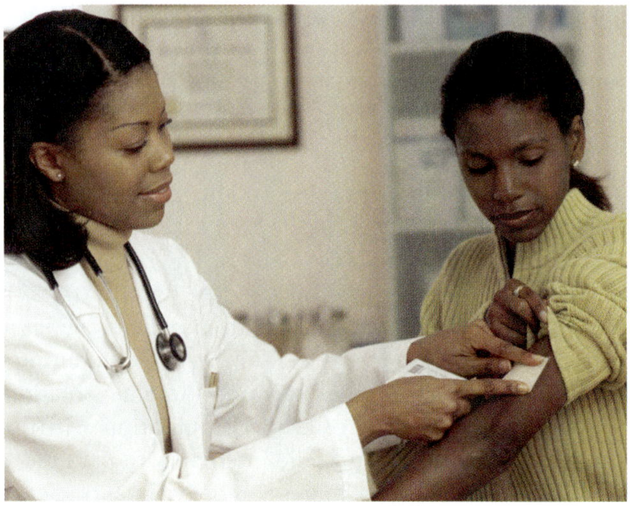

did YOU know?

Emergency contraception could potentially reduce the number of unintended pregnancies by 1.7 million (from the current 3.5 million) and the number of abortions by 800,000 per year in the United States alone.

or wherever is most comfortable. Women sometimes experience skin irritation at the site of application; therefore, it is best to apply the patch to a different site each week. The patch rarely comes off, but a backup prescription for one replacement patch is available. Side effects are similar to those experienced with low-dose oral contraceptives, but users of the patch tend to be more conscientious about applying it than are users of oral contraceptives about taking the pill (Burkman, 2002; Dittrich et al., 2002; Sibai et al., 2002).

Emergency Contraception

Try as they may, people fail in their efforts to prevent pregnancy. **Postcoital contraception** ("morning after" therapy) may provide an effective solution to an unwanted pregnancy. This treatment involves taking two large doses of ordinary oral contraceptives (from two to five pills, depending on the type of pill), generally 12 hours apart. An emergency contraceptive kit (called PREVEN), containing the pills along with a pregnancy test, is available by prescription, and toll-free hotlines (for example, 1-888-NOT-2-LATE) are available to direct women in need to clinicians who can prescribe it.

The effectiveness of postcoital contraception, determined by comparing the number of pregnancies that occur after the treatment to what would be expected without treatment, is about 85% (Grimes & Raymond, 2002). This treatment is most effective if used within 12–24 hours after intercourse, and it definitely should be used within 72 hours (Hatcher et al., 1994). Depending on the type of pill used, side effects may include nausea and vomiting, abdominal pain, fatigue, sleepiness, headaches, dizziness, breast tenderness, and vaginal discharge; the treatment may also disrupt the menstrual cycle. The most common symptom is nausea; other symptoms are rare (Hatcher et al., 1994). Overall, emergency contraception is a safe method for preventing an unwanted pregnancy (Turner & Ellertson, 2002).

POSTCOITAL CONTRACEPTION
A method of contraception whereby a woman takes substantial doses of hormones after intercourse to prevent possible pregnancy.

TUBAL LIGATION
Sterilization technique; severing of the fallopian tubes to permanently prevent a woman from becoming pregnant.

Surgical Contraception

Because of its permanence, people most commonly choose surgical contraception, or sterilization, when they wish not to have children at all or when they have had all the children they want. Improved surgical technology and increased social acceptance have greatly enhanced usage of this option.

Tubal Ligation

Sterilization of a woman, also called **tubal ligation,** involves preventing the passage of sperm and egg cells through the fallopian tubes. Although *ligation* means "tying off" or "binding," there are a number of ways to obstruct the fallopian tubes. Whatever the

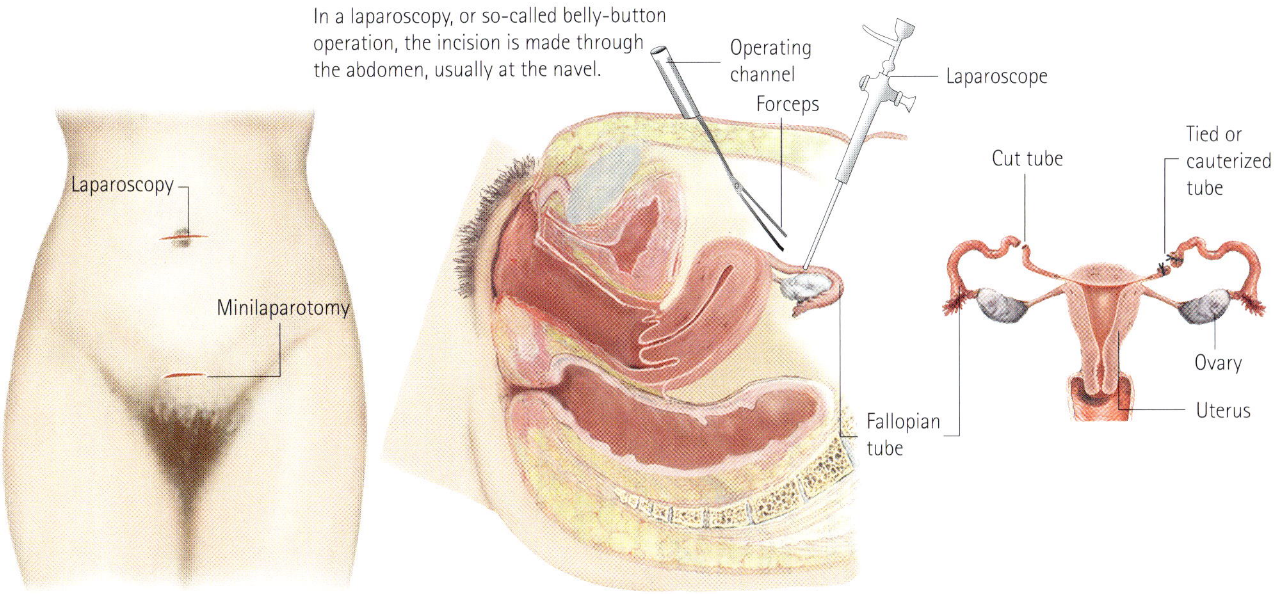

Figure 10.8 The drawing depicts the locations of incisions for the two female sterilization techniques, laparoscopy and minilaparotomy, or "minilap."

technique used, the doctor gains access to the tubes either through minilaparotomy or laparoscopy. Tubal ligation using **minilaparotomy** involves making a single 2–5 cm incision just above the pubic hairline (Figure 10.8). The uterus is elevated to make it easier to gain access to the fallopian tubes. The tubes are grasped and pulled to the incision with a hook or forceps; the surgeon then blocks the tubes, usually by tying them off. Tubal ligation using **laparoscopy** generally involves two incisions, which are smaller than the single incision of a minilaparotomy, so small that stitches may not be required. An incision is made at the navel, and a laparoscope is inserted to permit a view of the fallopian tubes (Figure 10.8). Next, a pubic hairline incision is made, through which an operating channel is inserted. Forceps are inserted in the operating channel to grasp the tubes for ligation. A single-puncture laparoscopy is also a possibility; it is accomplished by inserting the operating instrument just next to the laparoscope (Hatcher et al., 1994).

Tubal ligation is a relatively safe surgical procedure, generally performed under local anesthetic. Laparoscopy appears to be safer than minilaparotomy, and it appears to result in less cramping and pain (Boston Women's Health Book Collective, 1992). Assuming that a woman is certain that she does not want children in the future, this contraceptive method offers many advantages over other methods: It is cost-effective in the long run; it does not require remembering to use a contraceptive; lovemaking is uninterrupted; partner compliance is not necessary; and there are no long-term side effects. Tubal ligation was generally considered to be highly effective. However, a large-scale study of 10,000 women over a 10-year period revealed that almost 1 in 50 tubal ligations was a failure, and for women under the age of 28, the failure rate was 1 in 20 (Painter, 1996).

Some disadvantages of female sterilization are that, if a woman changes her mind about wanting to have a baby, reversal has a low success rate and is expensive to attempt. Furthermore, this method does not offer protection against STIs, is expensive in the short run, requires surgery, and, if it fails, increases a woman's risk of ectopic pregnancy. (The tube grows back together but scarring where the tubes were severed may prevent the fertilized egg from moving to the uterus so that it implants in the fallopian tube instead.)

Vasectomy

Male sterilization, or **vasectomy**, involves preventing passage of sperm through the vas deferens by severing them. Typically, a vasectomy requires two incisions, one on

MINILAPAROTOMY
A surgical technique used in performing a tubal ligation to permanently prevent pregnancy.

LAPAROSCOPY
A surgical technique used in performing a tubal ligation to permanently prevent pregnancy.

VASECTOMY
Sterilization technique; severing of the vas deferens to permanently prevent a man from impregnating anyone.

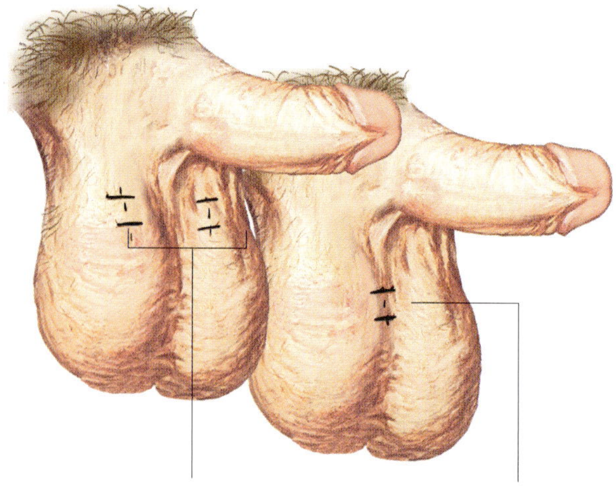

Figure 10.9 A vasectomy may be performed with one or two incisions.

either side of the scrotum (Figure 10.9). Alternatively, one incision is made, through which both vas deferens are pulled and cut. Another procedure, the *no-scalpel method,* involves grasping the vas deferens through the skin of the scrotum, puncturing the surface of the scrotum with a sharp dissecting forceps, pulling the vas deferens through the opening, and cutting them. Usually, a small length of each tube is removed or the ends are cauterized to ensure permanence of the occlusion. After this procedure, a backup contraceptive method is used until all stray sperm are out of the man's genitourinary tract (Boston Women's Health Book Collective, 1992). Typically, the man returns to the doctor 2 weeks after a vasectomy to test a sample of semen for the presence of sperm.

A vasectomy is performed under local anesthetic in a doctor's office. It is a popular option for men who are certain they do not want more children. There are many false assumptions about vasectomy, such as that it reduces a man's sex drive or that the man ceases to ejaculate. No functions are interrupted by this procedure other than the passage of sperm. Seminal fluid is still produced and ejaculated; it simply contains no sperm. There are no long-term side effects of a vasectomy. It has all the advantages listed for tubal ligation; among its drawbacks are that it is expensive in the short run and that it is a highly technical procedure requiring surgical expertise. There have been some reports of increased risk of cardiovascular disease and prostate cancer in men with vasectomies. However, the findings are mixed and have not led to changes in the practice of vasectomy (Hatcher et al., 1994).

10.5 on the web

Go to **www.ablongman.com/mcanulty2e** and find the link to myths about male contraception. Read each myth and its accompanying "reality."

Did you subscribe to any of these myths? Do you think men can and will take responsibility for contraception if they have more options available to them? Why or why not?

Experimental Methods

Researchers are investigating improvements in existing contraceptive methods as well as developing new methods. New contraceptives generally require 10–20 years of development before they are put on the market (Alexander, 1995).

Methods for Men

Perhaps one of the most exciting areas of current research on contraception is the investigation of male contraceptive options. For several years, researchers have been working on combinations of hormones that will significantly reduce sperm production without causing too many side effects. The combinations generally contain testosterone and progesterone or progesterone and estrogen (Gonzalo et al., 2002; Meriggiola, Costantino, & Cerpolini, 2002). Male hormonal contraceptives are most likely to be made available in a long-acting form, such as injection or implant (Wang & Swerdloff, 2002). Unfortunately, this method of contraception has faced many cultural barriers. In fact, the FDA has been accused of sex bias because it has been reluctant to approve male hormonal contraceptives, citing their side effects, although female hormonal methods have been marketed heavily and prescribed widely, despite their side effects. Furthermore, research on male hormonal methods has been hindered by lack of financial backing (Hair & Wu, 2000); however, as these contraceptives become more popular, they are likely to receive more attention. Interest in male hormonal contraception varies worldwide but is generally favorable (Glasier et al., 2000; Martin et al., 2000).

Nonhormonal methods for men are also under investigation. For example, several strategies to block passage of sperm through the vas deferens are being investigated and are currently in use in other countries. These methods generally involve the use of "plugs" that are injected into the vas deferens. The plugs are either preformed of rubber or are injected as silicone or polyurethane liquid, which hardens in the vas deferens. One type of preformed plug must be sutured into place. All of these methods are reversible (www.malecontraceptives.org, 2002).

did YOU know?

Publicly funded contraceptive services reduce the number of unintended pregnancies by 1.3 million per year—pregnancies that would otherwise result in 165,000 miscarriages, 534,000 unwanted births, and 632,000 abortions (Alan Guttmacher Institute, 1997).

Another experimental method is to inject a chemical into the vas deferens; the chemical coats the walls of the tube and ruptures the membranes of sperm as they pass. Thus, rather than blocking the tube, the chemical renders the sperm incapable of functioning properly. When the man wishes to reverse his infertility, the chemical can be washed from the vas deferens (www.malecontraceptives.org, 2002). Finally, two other options use the "old-fashioned" method of heating the scrotum enough to inhibit or significantly reduce sperm production. One way a man can do this is to wear a special pair of briefs that secures the testes up against (and even partially inside) his body. Another method involves a heated scrotal sack, equipped with thermometer, timer, and power source. However, neither of these methods has been scientifically tested (www.malecontraceptives.org, 2002)—and you should not try to "cook" your testes and then assume you have successfully inhibited sperm production!

Methods for Women

During the 1990s, there was such a boom in the introduction of new contraceptives for women that there is currently little in the works. Primarily, researchers continue to improve and perfect the methods that are already available. In addition, researchers are working on a pill (mentioned in Chapter 3) that can be taken continuously for 3 months, reducing menstrual periods to only four a year.

Contraceptive developers are concerned about ease of use, health risks, and side effects. The more reliable, safe, free of negative effects, and user-friendly contraceptive methods are, the more likely they are to be used effectively.

ABORTION

Although the availability of contraception significantly reduces the incidence of unwanted pregnancy, 9–12% of women using contraception become pregnant within 1 year of starting to use it. Millions of abortions still occur each year. Nearly one-half of all pregnancies are unintended, and one-half of unintended pregnancies end in abortion (Alan Guttmacher Institute, 2002b). Obviously, many more pregnancies are prevented by contraceptives purchased out-of-pocket or by private insurance.

In contrast to *spontaneous abortion,* **induced abortion** involves a deliberate decision to terminate a pregnancy. Worldwide, abortion is the primary form of contraception. Approximately 46 million abortions are performed per year; 20 million of these are illegal. Induced abortion is no less likely to occur in countries where it is illegal or restricted than in countries where it is legal (Alan Guttmacher Institute, 2002b). Two factors seem

INDUCED ABORTION
Surgical removal of a fetus and supporting tissues from the uterus.

to act in combination to produce the highest abortion rates: the desire for a small family, and low or ineffective contraceptive use. Furthermore, even among countries where abortion is safe and legal, abortion rates are lowest where couples use contraceptives effectively (Dailard, 1999).

did YOU know?

Nearly 26 out of every 100 pregnancies in the United States are aborted, totaling nearly 1.3 million abortions each year (Alan Guttmacher Institute, 2002b; Henshaw, Singh, & Haas, 1999).

Overall, African American women are about three times and Hispanic American women are two and a half times more likely than white American women to have an abortion (Alan Guttmacher Institute, 2002b). However, because of their greater numbers in the overall U.S. population, the majority of women who get abortions are white (59%), unmarried (81%), and young. In fact, 52% of women who obtain abortions are under 25 years of age. Women between 20 and 24 years old have 32% of all abortions, and teens obtain 20% of all abortions (Herndon et al., 2002). Of women having abortions, 43% report that they are Protestant, and 27% say they are Catholic (Alan Guttmacher Institute, 2002b).

Women give many reasons for having abortions. Seventy-five percent of women state that pregnancy and motherhood would interfere with work, school, or other responsibilities; about 66% cannot afford to raise a child; and 50% cite problems with a partner or concerns about single parenting as reasons for having an abortion. Pregnancies resulting from rape or incest account for at least 13,000 abortions a year (Alan Guttmacher Institute, 2002b).

Approximately 88% of all abortions occur in the first 12 weeks of pregnancy; 55% of these occur within the first 8 weeks of pregnancy (Alan Guttmacher Institute, 2002b). Figure 10.10 gives a breakdown of U.S. abortions according to the point in the pregnancy when they occur.

Physical and Psychological Considerations

Physically, a *legal* abortion presents significantly fewer risks to a woman than carrying a pregnancy to full term. The earlier the abortion, the lower the risks and the greater the probability of survival. Legal abortion carries only very minor risks of excessive bleeding, infection, intrauterine blood clots, or damage to the cervix or uterus—all of which are potential risks of pregnancy or childbirth. And only 1 out of every 150,000 legal abortions ends in death, which is only one-tenth of the deaths from childbirth (Alan Guttmacher Institute, 2000). We emphasize *legal,* because methods used in illegal abortions are dangerous and often deadly.

There is no doubt that most women who experience an unwanted pregnancy go through a difficult and painful process while deciding whether to have an abortion. Many women experience a range of negative emotions about the actual abortion and during the postabortion period as well, and some women have a more difficult time adjusting after an abortion than others (Major, Richards, Cooper, Cozzarelli, & Zubek, 1998). The emotional strain that these women experience should be acknowledged, and appropriate psychological support should be available to them. However, an expert panel appointed by the American Psychological Association reviewed the findings

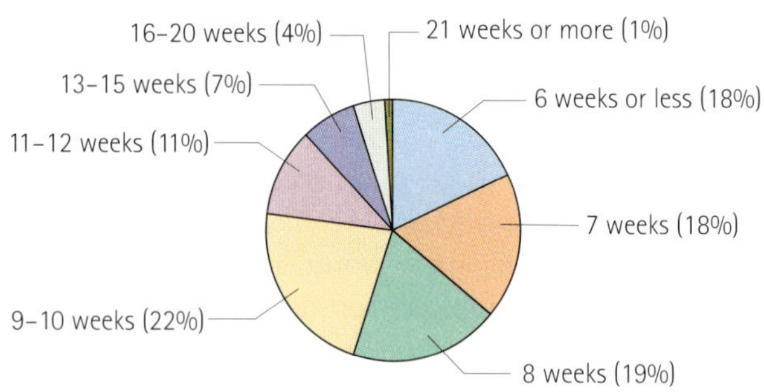

Figure 10.10 When Women Obtain Abortions (SOURCE: Alan Guttmacher Institute, 2002b)

from an exhaustive collection of sound, empirical studies on emotional responses to legal abortions (Adler et al., 1992). This review revealed that, although some women report both immediate and long-term negative emotional responses to an abortion, significant negative emotional responses are unusual. The panel also found that negative emotions are much more common prior to an abortion, and when negative emotional responses do occur after an abortion, they are typically no stronger than responses to other, typical life stresses. Furthermore, these findings were found to apply to women for up to 8 years following an abortion. It is not known if negative emotional responses ever emerge after this length of time, but the panel concluded that it is unlikely that a woman would have such a delayed reaction to an abortion. Women who do experience distress after an abortion tend to be those who wanted the pregnancy, lacked support from others, were ambivalent about the decision, blamed themselves for the pregnancy, or waited until the second trimester to abort. From both physical and psychological standpoints, therefore, it is fortunate that most women in the United States who want one have access to legal, safe, early abortions. Unfortunately, little information is available on how men who are involved in their partners' decision to have an abortion are affected.

Surgical Methods

Most abortions in the United States are accomplished using surgical methods. The most common of these is vacuum aspiration, which is performed early in pregnancy.

Vacuum Aspiration

The vast majority of abortions in the United States are performed before 12 weeks of gestation by **vacuum aspiration**, also called *vacuum curettage*. Only a local anesthetic is required to perform this procedure. The cervix is first dilated using graduated metal dilators. Alternatively, *Laminaria*, a highly absorbent seaweed, is used. It is placed in the cervical opening and, as it absorbs moisture, it expands, causing the cervix to dilate. Although using *Laminaria* is less painful and safer, 12–24 hours are required to achieve maximum dilation with this method. Once the cervix is sufficiently dilated, the actual abortion takes place in about 10 minutes. A thin tube connected to a suction pump is inserted through the cervix into the uterus (Figure 10.11). The tube is then used to suction (aspirate) the uterine lining. The fetus is removed with the lining.

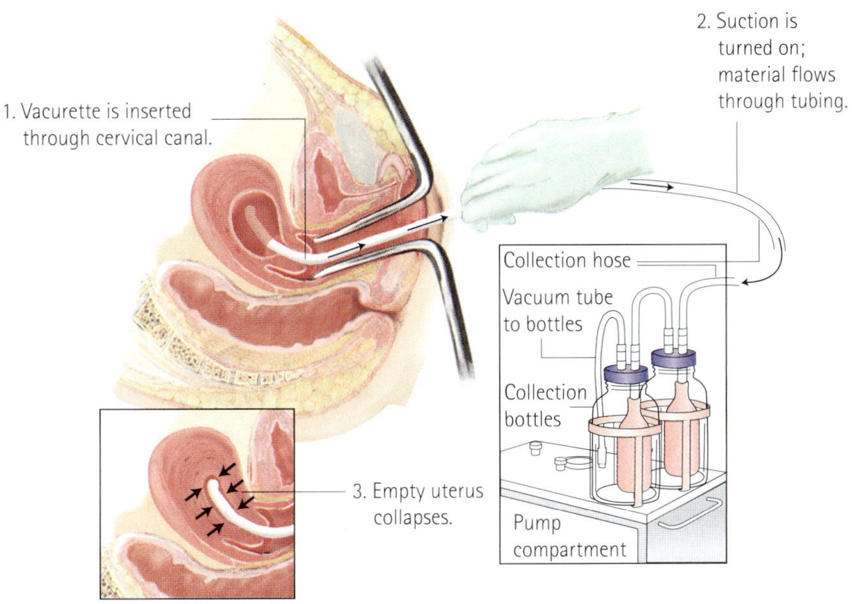

Figure 10.11 The Most Common Abortion Method, Vacuum Curettage

VACUUM ASPIRATION (VACUUM CURETTAGE)
An abortion procedure performed at any time up to 12 weeks of pregnancy, which involves enlarging the cervical opening and aspirating the contents of the uterus.

Dilation and Evacuation

Dilation and evacuation, also referred to as **D & E**, is conducted on women who are in the early portion of the second trimester (13–16 weeks). As with vacuum aspiration, the cervix is dilated and the contents of the uterus are aspirated; however, the inner walls of the uterus are then scraped with a metal curette to ensure complete removal of the contents.

10.6 on the web

Dilation and extraction is a controversial procedure. Go to **www.ablongman.com/mcanulty2e** and click on the Planned Parenthood link.

Discuss the many legal issues surrounding this controversy.

Early Surgical Abortion

A recently introduced form of surgical abortion permits a woman to obtain an abortion as early as 8 days after conception. Ultrasound imaging is used to identify the location of the amniotic sac; the sac is then extracted with a hand-held syringe (Planned Parenthood Federation of America, Inc., 1997). Early surgical abortion takes only about 2 minutes (Davis, 1997) and apparently offers minimal risks.

Late Surgical Abortion

An extremely controversial technique has been in the forefront of the abortion debate for the last few years. Its technical name is **dilation and extraction (D & X)**, or *intact dilation and evacuation*. Its opponents, however, have termed it "partial-birth abortion." This technique is so controversial and has been the subject of so much rhetoric that separating fact from fiction is somewhat difficult. Apparently, dilation and extraction is most commonly performed on women in the third trimester of pregnancy, but occasionally it is used for late second-trimester abortions, when the fetus is too large for other techniques. It involves dilation of the cervix and removal of the fetus through the vaginal canal, feet first, until all but the head is in the vaginal canal. The head size of the fetus must be reduced to allow delivery; thus, fluid or brain tissue is extracted through an incision at the base of the skull.

No data on the frequency of use of this technique are available. Since only 1% of abortions occur after 20 weeks, estimates of the numbers of abortions performed by this technique are low—but not low enough, according to abortion foes. We will address this procedure and the political controversies surrounding it in the section on abortion and the law.

DILATION AND EVACUATION (D & E)
An abortion procedure that can be conducted when a woman is between the 13th and 16th weeks of pregnancy, which involves enlarging the cervical opening, aspirating the contents from the uterus, and scraping the uterine lining.

DILATION AND EXTRACTION (D & X)
An extremely controversial abortion technique, also called *intact dilation and evacuation.* The technique involves dilation of the cervix to the extent possible and removal of the fetus through the vaginal canal, feet first, until all but the head is in the vaginal canal. To reduce the size of the head, fluid or brain tissue is extracted by way of suction through an incision at the base of the skull; then the fetus is delivered.

MIFEPRISTONE
A drug that induces an abortion; also known as RU 486.

Drug-Based Methods

Until recently, the only "abortion drug" the American public ever heard about was a drug known as RU 486, used in Europe and parts of Asia. The development of drug-based abortion methods, however, is proceeding rapidly, and despite protests from abortion opponents, these approaches are currently being tested in the United States.

Mifepristone (RU 486)

Mifepristone, as it is known in the United States, or *RU 486,* as it is known in Europe, induces an abortion when used alone or in combination with another drug, *misoprostol,* a prostaglandin that is approved in the United States for coating the stomach of people who take stomach-irritating antiinflammatory drugs. Mifepristone prevents progesterone from making the uterine lining hospitable for implantation of the zygote. If the fetus is already implanted, mifepristone causes the woman's uterus to shed its lining and, along with it, the fertilized zygote. Thus, a woman takes mifepristone shortly after intercourse to safely terminate an unwanted pregnancy or to prevent a pregnancy from occurring. The drug can generally be administered within 7 weeks of the first day of the woman's last menstrual period. Treatment occurs in two stages: Mifepristone is administered first, usually by injection, and a couple of days later misoprostol is given to cause the uterus to contract and expel its contents. Research assessing the relative effectiveness of administering prostaglandins orally or vaginally has shown that vaginal administration more readily and effectively induces an abortion (El-Refaey, Rajasekar, Abdalla, Calder, & Templeton, 1995). After she receives the misoprostol, the woman is observed for about 4 hours, during which time 60% of women abort (U.S. News Online, 1997).

Mifepristone is considered safer and less painful than surgical methods of abortion (Callum & Chalker, 1993). Despite the fact that it was legal in several other countries, abortion foes fought hard to prevent legalization of mifepristone in the United States. However, the FDA did approve it in September 2000 (Alan Guttmacher Institute, 2000). Anti-abortion activists are fighting its use by lobbying to limit its availability (Boonstra, 2001).

Legal Drugs Used in Combination

Methotrexate, a drug approved for treatment of ectopic pregnancy, cancer, arthritis, and psoriasis in the United States, produces an abortion with a single injection. Methotrexate stops the placenta and the embryo from developing by preventing cell division and multiplication. It may produce some mild side effects, including dizziness, vomiting, headache, sleeplessness, and vaginal bleeding. It, too, is used in combination with misoprostol, which ensures that the embryo is expelled from the uterus. Four misoprostol pills are inserted vaginally within about 6 days after a methotrexate injection. If an abortion is not induced within 48 hours, another four pills are inserted. Misoprostol has side effects similar to those of methotrexate; in addition, it induces cramping and bleeding, which are to be expected. A physician using a combination of methotrexate and misoprostal must be careful to confirm that the abortion is complete; otherwise, the woman could carry the pregnancy to term and give birth to a baby with severe deformities. Fortunately, the combination of methotrexate and misoprostol is 90% effective; however, an abortion using this method must be conducted within 49 days from the first day of the woman's last menstrual period (Planned Parenthood of Southeastern Pennsylvania, 1996).

Looking At . . .

. . . Thinking About

Imagine that you or your partner is pregnant. You want to have the child, but you have just been told that the fetus has major congenital defects. In fact, the doctors are certain that if the pregnancy reaches full term, the child will not survive outside the womb. Would you have an abortion (or want your partner to have one)? Discuss the factors you would consider in making your decision. Would it make a difference if you (or your partner) were 12 weeks, 20 weeks, or 30 weeks along in the pregnancy? If so, why?

Other Medical Abortion Procedures

Some abortion methods that are used between 16 and 24 weeks of gestation involve the injection of prostaglandins, saline, or urea directly into the amniotic sac. Such an injection stimulates uterine contractions and delivery of the uterine contents. Sometimes combinations of these three substances are used. Because there are restrictions on the availability of second- and third-trimester abortions and they are not frequently done, these abortion procedures are rarely used; they account for only about 1% of all abortions (Hatcher et al., 1994).

Historical Perspectives

Abortion, induced through ingestion of herbs or manipulation of the uterus, was practiced in many ancient societies as a form of birth control. Archeologists have uncovered ancient Egyptian prescriptions for herbal mixtures to induce abortion dating back to around 1500 B.C.E. The Greeks, including Hippocrates (about 460–377 B.C.E.), the father of modern medicine, practiced abortion. In fact, Greek medical texts have been uncovered that give case histories and prescriptions. Some of the great philosophers, including Aristotle and Plato, recommended abortion as a form of birth control. The Romans discouraged abortion because their birth rates were low and they wanted to increase their population, but they did not ban the practice.

As you'll read later in the discussion of the anti-abortion position, Jewish and Christian laws have never universally opposed abortion. Abortion is addressed but not forbidden in the Talmud, a book of Jewish laws. Even Pope Innocent XI stated in 1679 that abortion was permissible before the point of *ensoulment* (when the soul enters the body)—a point in the pregnancy that has been the subject of debate. Up until the late 19th century, abortion before *quickening,* the point at which fetal movement is felt, was legal, according to both English and American common law. The movement against abortion was actually spearheaded by the American Medical Association (AMA), not the church, as many might assume. In the early 20th century, the AMA became concerned about abortions, not for medical reasons, but because of bigotry on the part of some of its members—they were concerned that more and more Protestants were limiting reproduction through contraception and abortion and that Catholics would "take over" (Tanith, 2000).

Abortion and the Law

> It is nothing less than grim, driven desperation which can impel a woman to insert an unbent coat-hanger into her most sensitive parts, to place her body in the hands of a strange man with unverified credentials, or to lie down without anaesthesia on a filthy kitchen table, knowing that in so doing she risks illness, grilling by the police, and death. An illegal or self-induced abortion is no casual experience. It is painful, dangerous, and cloaked in the guilt of criminality. (A. Rich, from Freeman, 1997)

The 1973 Supreme Court decision *Roe v. Wade* guaranteed American women's right to limit childbearing. In essence, the decision states that first-trimester abortions cannot be regulated by states, and the decision to abort is between a woman and her physician. Second-trimester abortions are permitted only under circumstances in which the health (mental and physical) of the woman is at risk, but the right of a woman facing such risks to choose whether to have an abortion is maintained. Third-trimester abortions are allowed only if the life of the mother is at stake. This final ruling was made because, during the third trimester, it is possible to abort a fetus that is capable of surviving outside the womb.

Although the *Roe v. Wade* decision was intended to give *all* women unrestricted access to first-trimester abortions, many court battles have ensued to restrict access to abortion, and women under the age of 18 have been targeted. In 1992, in a case called *Planned Parenthood v. Casey,* the Supreme Court gave states the right to place restrictions on abortion as long as the regulations did not create an "undue burden" on women seeking abortions. Among the most common restrictions are those involving parental notification and consent; such restrictions now exist in 32 states (Alan Guttmacher Institute, 2002b). Parental consent laws require that one or both parents of a minor (a woman 18 years old or younger) provide consent to an abortion provider before an abortion can be performed. Parental notification laws require only that the minor's parents be notified that the young woman is going to have an abortion. Some states have judicial bypass clauses that allow a minor to go before a judge to obtain permission for an abortion. The minor must demonstrate either that the abortion is in her best interest or that she is mature enough to make a decision on her own. Opponents of judicial bypass argue that judges are often heavily influenced by their own moral positions, and therefore parental consent is merely replaced with judicial consent (Center for Population Options, 1995).

Proponents of parental consent and notification laws argue that they encourage communication and family involvement in abortion decisions (Center for Population Options, 1995). However, opponents argue that most young women do consult their parents prior to an abortion, and those who are not inclined to consult their parents are no more likely to as a result of a law. They will either petition the court or go to a neighboring state that does not require parental consent. Thus, family communication is not increased by these laws, and parental notification laws result in delays leading to later abortions and increased health risks for the young women (American Association of University Women, 1990). In fact, a clinic in Minnesota revealed that 63% of young women reported delaying an abortion on account of that state's parental notification law. In addition, Massachusetts and Minnesota saw a substantial increase in late abortions since enactment of these laws (Center for Population Options, 1995). Some young women have risked and even lost their lives in order to avoid telling their parents. Becky Bell, a 17-year-old from Indiana, died from a self-induced abortion she attempted in an effort to avoid hurting her parents by telling them she needed an abortion. As a result of this tragedy, Becky's parents became outspoken opponents of parental notification and consent laws (American Association of University Women, 1990).

Looking At . . .

. . . Thinking About

Many people have very strong views on abortion. Would you ever be a protestor on this issue? If so, which side would you be on?

Other types of restrictions have been placed on access to abortion as well. For example, many states require mandatory counseling and a waiting period before an abortion can be performed. Limitations on public funding have also been a major source of regulation. Congress passed the Hyde Amendment in 1977 to prohibit Medicaid funding of abortions except when the mother's life is in jeopardy. In addition, most states have restricted their funding of abortion (Fried & Ross, 1995). Opponents argue that these efforts restrict access to abortions for the poor, of whom a disproportionate number are minorities. Thus, cutting off state and federal funds for abortions denies many women the right to a safe and legal abortion.

Another particularly controversial ruling was the "gag rule" instituted by the U.S. Department of Health and Human Services in 1988, which prohibited federally funded health services agencies from providing information about abortion as an option for unwanted pregnancy or discussing abortion with their clients. This policy was later upheld by the Supreme Court in *Rust v. Sullivan* in 1991 (Trager, 1992). President Clinton repealed this rule immediately upon his inauguration in 1993. Many legal battles continue to ensue over reinstituting the gag rule, despite the fact that 71% of citizens think abortion should be legal (Clements, 1992).

A huge political debate is continuing over the D & X abortion technique. In 1997, Congress sought to ban this procedure except when necessary to save the life of the mother, but President Clinton vetoed the ban. Pro-choice advocates argue that there are cases when preservation of a woman's life is not at issue but D & X is nonetheless appropriate. For example, some argue for its appropriateness if a baby is found late in pregnancy to have a biological condition that would prohibit life outside of the womb, and any other options for terminating the pregnancy would threaten the mother's health or ability to conceive and carry a fetus in the future. President Clinton and others urged that the ban include an exception whenever the mother's "health" is at risk. Anti-abortionists find such an exception to be too broad because, according to the Supreme Court, "health" includes social, psychological, financial, and emotional concerns. Thus, according to this view, a case could be made for a D & X under almost any circumstance (Family Research Council, 1997).

Pro-choice advocates also fear that the provisions of the ban are vague and could easily be extended beyond this particular procedure to other safe procedures such as D & E. Ultimately, this would threaten a woman's constitutional right to reproductive freedom. Proponents of the ban argue that the legislation would affect only the D & X procedure, which they claim is *never* medically necessary.

Even medical professionals, who generally object to government interference in decisions that are generally viewed as part of the patient-doctor relationship, have involved themselves in efforts to ban D & X. In fact, in 1997, the American Medical Association issued a letter to the United States Senate expressing its support for the ban (First Breath Alliance, 1997). However, the American College of Obstetricians and Gynecologists has maintained that the ban would prevent physicians from recommending and using the D & X procedure when it might be the best option for a patient (Planned Parenthood Federation of America, Inc., 1998).

The debate about the D & X procedure also includes disagreements over the frequency with which this procedure is actually used and for what reasons. Opponents of banning the procedure maintain that it is used rarely and only when a physician, in concert with a patient, decides that it is absolutely necessary to protect the mother's life or health. However, supporters of the ban argue that the technique is used frivolously, when neither the mother nor the fetus has a life-threatening condition. As this debate rages, public support seems to be increasing for early abortions, in order to decrease the use and perhaps abuse of late-term procedures, which apparently most people (even those who are pro-choice) find disturbing. Pro-life advocates are troubled by this trend, since they generally want all abortions banned (Garrow, 1998).

The Abortion Controversy

You may not completely understand the pro-life and pro-choice positions on abortion. This may be because there probably isn't *one* position for each group. People who identify themselves as either pro-life or pro-choice probably differ tremendously along a continuum of positions. Others who identify themselves as one or the other—perhaps because their parents or peers do—may not have given the controversy much thought or understand many of the issues surrounding it. Still others may remain altogether undecided. Here we provide a brief synopsis of the general positions held by each group.

The Anti-Abortion Position

At the forefront of the anti-abortion (or "pro-life") movement are fundamentalist religious organizations. The pro-life position is based on the belief that human life begins at conception, and each fetus is entitled to full human rights. Interestingly, there have been times in history when some religious authorities held that a conceptus was not a person until after either 40 days for males or 80 days for females. This position was based on the belief that it was at these points in development that the conceptus gained a soul. At other times, abortions were considered acceptable up until the point of quickening. So, religious doctrine on "when life begins" has varied through time. Nonetheless, the current pro-life position is that the conceptus is a person at conception and thus has a right to life. Of course, there are differences of opinion among pro-lifers. Some people take an extreme stance and object to abortion even if the mother's life is at stake; others say that it might be necessary to abort a fetus if the mother's life is at stake.

IN YOUR own words

Beth Samuelson
Trinity College

I am pro-life, simply because there is no reason a child should be punished for his parents' behavior.

Other religious and political ideologies guiding some pro-lifers are that sex is for procreation only and that a woman's place is in the home raising children. According to this perspective, if people were to adhere to these two beliefs, no one would have a need for an abortion. The only time sex would occur would be when a couple was trying to have a baby, and the woman would remain at home to care for it. Clearly, not all abortion opponents endorse all of these beliefs.

The Pro-Choice Position

Pro-choice advocates also hold that everyone should have respect for human life, but they argue that the issues are complex and morality cannot be legislated. In particular, they advocate considering the effect on all concerned of continuing a pregnancy *and* the effect of terminating it, and take into consideration *quality* of life. Thus, if a child is born into a life of poverty and neglect or even abuse, is that better than having never lived? Another issue concerns the rights of the woman over those of the fetus: When a woman becomes pregnant, do her rights supersede those of the fetus? Pro-choicers are not necessarily "pro-abortion." The pro-choice camp includes people with many differing positions. Some may believe that women should have access to therapeutic abortions but not abortions on demand. Others may take the more extreme position that abortions are acceptable in all cases. Individuals who are pro-choice see the moral and ethical issues surrounding abortion as highly personal. Neither medical science nor the Supreme Court can answer the question of whether a fetus is a person or at what point it becomes a person. This is a matter of each individual's religious or philosophical convictions. Religious views vary from person to person; thus, pro-choicers argue that a decision to have an abortion must be a personal decision that each individual makes.

On the more pragmatic side of the discussion, pro-choice advocates have argued repeatedly that making abortion illegal does not decrease the rate of abortions. In fact, as noted earlier, abortion rates are the same or higher in countries where abortion is illegal as in countries where it is legal. Furthermore, illegal abortions are much more likely to end in illness or death of the woman. Thus, keeping abortions legal keeps them safe, and other approaches, such as sex education, should be used to reduce abortion rates.

IN YOUR own words

Kara Berrini
Emerson College

I am pro-choice. . . . It's a women's prerogative to handle herself and her pregnancy in the manner she sees fit.

Has the Anti-Abortion Movement Gone Too Far?

In May of 1994, an organization calling itself the Pro-Life Action League held a meeting in Chicago to discuss whether killing abortion doctors is justifiable homicide. Participants represented the more radical anti-abortion groups. Of the 60 participants, about 40 supported, on moral grounds, the position that murdering abortion doctors is justifiable. David Trosch, a Catholic priest, offered the following analogy: "If a person with a shotgun happened upon the scene of massive butchering of innocent children, and failed to act with deadly force, as quickly as possible, he would be committing a grave offense against God." Similarly, *Capital Area Christian News* editor Michael Bray believes in stoning abortion providers to death (Rochman, Tippit, & Peterzell, 1994). It appears that the few crusaders who have acted on this viewpoint are not alone in their views. In fact, a 1995 *Time/CNN* poll revealed that about 5.2 million Americans believe that murdering doctors who provide abortion services is justifiable homicide (Yankelovich Partners, 1995).

So, *has* the anti-abortion movement gone too far? If you read headlines, you might say yes. In the 1990s, there were numerous tragic instances of men opening fire and murdering people whom they considered to be murderers because of their association with abortion clinics. In March 1993, Michael Griffin strode up to Dr. David Gunn, a physician in Pensacola, Florida, as he got out of his car in his clinic parking lot and shot him three times in the back. Paul Hill shot and killed Dr. John Britton along with his escort, Lt. Colonel James Barrett, at another clinic in Pensacola just over a year later in September 1994. In January 1995, John Salvi III attacked three clinics in Massachusetts and Virginia, killing two clinic workers. In the fall of 1998, Dr. Barnett Slepian was murdered in Amherst, New York, by a bullet fired through his kitchen window.

10.7 on the web

Although they do not represent the majority, many people with pro-life views believe that murdering those who provide abortion services is justified. Go to **www.ablongman.com/mcanulty2e** and find the link to the declaration signed by many leaders in the Christian community who support this position.

Would you sign your name to such a document? Why or why not?

The murdered doctors are not the only victims of anti-abortionists; several other individuals have been injured in assaults by anti-abortionists. Furthermore, such assaults represent only a minority of the violent acts that have been committed against abortion clinics and the people who work in them. Clinics providing abortion services have been bombed, set on fire, and doused with butyric acid, an extremely foul-smelling chemical that can be harmful or fatal in high concentrations. From 1977 to 1996, at least 1,900 such attacks took place (National Abortion Federation, 1996). Many people associated with the clinics have been injured in these attacks. The worst was in 1998, when Robert Sanderson, a police officer who worked nights as a security guard at the All Women Health Care Clinic in Birmingham, Alabama, was killed when a bomb exploded outside the clinic. (A full listing of the many reported attacks against abortion service clinics and their workers can be found in an online newsletter called "The Abortion Rights Activist" at www.overvoice.com/agm/main.)

Many mainstream anti-abortion leaders have consistently spoken out against violence of any kind. Michael Andreola, Director of Organizational Development for the Pennsylvania Pro-Life Federation, finds it disturbing that the pro-life movement in general is being held accountable for these murders. "Let's set the record straight from the outset. Mainstream pro-life groups, representing millions of Americans . . . have always opposed the use of violence by anyone opposed to abortion" (Andreola, 1994). But the statements of other pro-life leaders cannot be ignored: "The shooter is a hero" stated Pro-Life Virginia's director, Reverend Donald Spitz, describing Dr. Slepian's killer; and "We have shed the blood of the innocent in the womb, and we are now reaping it in the streets" said "Flip" (Philip) Benham, Operation Rescue's national director, also in reaction to Dr. Slepian's murder (NARAL, 1998).

Pro-choice advocates claim that actual violence against others is not the only problem. The rhetoric employed by even mainstream anti-abortion groups—such as referring to doctors providing these services as "murderers" and "killers"—encourages and incites violence (NARAL, 1998). Several pro-life leaders have conceded that some members of the pro-life movement incite violence. The president of Texans United for Life, Bill Price, agreed that "there has been a philosophical or even moral groundwork laid for assassinating abortionists by certain people in the pro-life movement, and I think they bear some of the blame" (Barringer, 1993). Furthermore, a majority of Americans believe that pro-life advocates encourage violence (NARAL, 1998).

Pro-choice groups recently went to court against anti-abortion groups responsible for a Web site called "The Nuremberg Files" and for "wanted posters" featuring photos of abortion-clinic physicians. The defendants were charged with inciting murder and violence. A federal jury fined the defendants $107 million in damages (Associated Press, 1999). The Web site contained a "baby butchers" list of abortion doctors, along with data on the doctors' personal histories, property, physical appearances, and wedding anniversary dates. Readers were encouraged to send in photos of the doctors (as well as of their cars, houses, friends, and children) to the Web site. Dr. Slepian's name was crossed off with a dark line soon after he was killed.

Those who murder abortion doctors often call on religious doctrine and beliefs to justify their actions. When interviewed about his chance meeting with David Gunn at a gas station one morning, Gunn's murderer, Michael Griffin, said "I thought it was Providence. . . . I knew he was getting ready to go kill children that day. I asked the Lord what he wanted me to do. And he told me to tell him that he had one more chance." Griffin approached Dr. Gunn and told him that God was going to give him one more chance. Griffin then waited outside Gunn's workplace until Gunn left the building at the end of the day. He then asked Gunn if he planned to continue to perform abortions the next day, and Gunn said yes. Believing he was acting as God instructed him, Griffin killed Gunn 5 days later.

Take a minute to consider your views on abortion by reviewing the questions in Reflect on This: Where Do You Stand on Abortion?

reflect ON THIS

Where Do You Stand on Abortion?

Read the following questions and jot down your responses to each. After doing that, ask yourself, "Am I pro-choice, pro-life, or a mixture of the two?" Explain why you selected the position you did.

1. At what point does human life begin: at conception, at quickening, at viability, at birth?
2. When does the fetus become a person?
3. How should the definitions of "human life" and "personhood" enter into decisions regarding the legality of abortion?
4. Should abortion remain legal? Why or why not?
5. If it remains legal, should any restrictions be placed on it?
   - Should abortions be only therapeutic, or should they be available on demand? (If therapeutic only, how does one determine when abortion is essential for a woman's physical or emotional health?)
   - Timing of the abortion? First trimester only? When would a second- or third-trimester abortion be justifiable?
   - Parental consent?
   - Consent of the man?
6. How should the following circumstances affect the right to and/or the decision to abort, if at all?
   - The pregnancy results from a rape.
   - The woman is an unwed teenager.
   - The woman is on Medicaid and has several children.
   - The fetus is severely deformed at 5 or 6 months gestation.
   - The woman is a high school senior with aspirations to go to college and have a career.
   - The fetus is determined to have Tay-Sachs disease, which will cause death by the time the child is 4 or 5.
   - The parents are a separated or divorced couple, and the man wants the woman to have the child.
   - A 17-year-old woman was molested by her own father, and she must gain consent for an abortion from a judge who is anti-abortion.

Some individuals who are adamantly opposed to abortion are also adamantly opposed to educating people about contraception and providing contraception to teens. Discuss this issue and your views, and propose solutions to the problem of teen pregnancy.

HEALTHY DECISION MAKING

If you haven't already, you will no doubt at some point in your life have to make a decision about contraception: whether to use it or not, and what kind to use. And just when you think you have made your choice and are comfortable with it, your life situation will change, and you will have to start the decision-making process all over! And, depending on circumstances, you might at some point find yourself having to make a decision about whether you or your partner should have an abortion.

In going through these decision-making processes, the primary objective should be to protect your (and any sexual partner's) psychological and physical health. The best way to accomplish this objective is to be well-informed about your options and to make your choices deliberately and not while under pressure to do so. First and foremost, use of a contraceptive device usually implies anticipation of becoming sexually active—are you ready to be sexually active? Once you have decided that you are emotionally ready for an intimate relationship, you will want to evaluate all available contraceptives. If one of your objectives is to protect yourself from STIs as well as to prevent pregnancy, your choice of primary protection should be either a male or a female condom; however, you may want a second form of contraception (e.g., oral contraceptive pill) as added protection against pregnancy. It may help in making an

TABLE 10.2 Choosing the Right Contraceptive

QUESTIONS TO ASK ONESELF	EXAMPLE RESPONSES
Am I comfortable touching my own body in the way that this method requires?	Using a diaphragm or sponge may not be right for me, because I am not comfortable putting my fingers in my vagina.
Will I use a method that interrupts lovemaking?	Stopping to insert a diaphragm or apply a condom is not a problem for me.
Does this method protect me from STIs?	Because I have multiple partners who also have multiple partners, I should always use a male or female condom.
Does my partner have an STI?	My partner has herpes—I will always use a condom in addition to the pill.
Can I afford this contraceptive?	My insurance covers any prescription contraception I choose, so cost is not an issue.
Will I feel too shy or embarrassed to use this method?	I don't want to have to tell my partner that I have to insert a diaphragm or sponge. I would prefer to use a hormonal contraceptive with a condom.
Do I or does my partner plan to have more than one sexual relationship at a time?	We are mutually monogamous and have both been checked for STIs. A condom may not be necessary for us.
Do I ever want to have children?	No, I have all the children I want. I am going to get a vasectomy.
How often do I plan to have sexual intercourse?	Often! I need an easy and reliable method.
Can I remember to take a pill at the same time every day?	Yes. An oral contraceptive will work for me.
Can I remember to do something about contraception once a week?	No, after a week I might forget about it. The patch is not for me.
Would I be willing (and able to remember) to visit my doctor's office once a month for a shot?	My doctor gives me a reminder, and shots don't bother me. I can handle this.
Would I be willing (and able to remember) to visit my doctor's office once every 3 months for a shot?	I don't like shots. I am likely to put off going back. Shots won't do for me.
Am I allergic to latex?	Yes, I need to use a polyurethane condom.
Do I smoke?	Yes. Hormonal contraceptives are not for me.

informed choice to review Table 10.2, which gives examples of questions you might want to ask yourself about contraception and examples of possible responses that might guide your decision making. We also encourage you to seek advice from a well-informed professional or even a trusted friend. However you go about making your decision, we urge you to adopt a deliberate approach. Save the spontaneity until after that contraceptive is in place!

Making a decision about whether you or a partner should have an abortion is likely to be much more daunting than any choice you make about contraception. If faced with an unplanned pregnancy, seek the advice of someone who knows you well and who can help you sort out your views on abortion. Some of the questions in Reflect on This might help you with this process. Keep in mind that other options (keeping the child or giving the child up for adoption) are available. Don't rush to have an abortion before considering your options. If you take the time to make a conscious choice to have an abortion, you are less likely to look back on it with regret.

summary

CONTRACEPTION

- Throughout history, people have searched for methods to effectively eliminate the risk of unwanted pregnancy. They have been motivated by the desire to have sex for pleasure only, to eliminate the health risks of pregnancy, to control overpopulation, and to provide women with control over their own fertility.
- When deciding to use contraceptives and when choosing the exact method to use, you must consider your personal needs as well as each method's physical and psychological risks and benefits. You should consider the method's effectiveness, potential side effects, ease of use, and your comfort with and skill in using it. You should also consider if the method provides protection against sexually transmissible infections (STIs).

CONTRACEPTIVE METHODS

- A vast array of contraceptive methods is currently available. Each method has advantages and disadvantages; the expense and effectiveness of the methods also vary.
- The effectiveness of a contraceptive method depends on whether it is used appropriately; some methods require more skill than others and therefore tend to be less effective.
- Several new and improved methods of contraception have appeared on the market over the last few years.

ABORTION

- Legal and moral debate over the issue of abortion continues. While abortion is still legal in the United States, several federal and state laws restrict access to abortion, particularly for teenagers, who in some states must either inform or obtain consent from their parents.
- Pro-life and pro-choice advocates continue to debate the morality of abortion. Much of this argument focuses on the issues of when life begins and whether the woman's health and preferences take precedence over the life of the fetus.
- In deciding to have an abortion, a woman must first consider the physical and psychological risks and benefits. In general, abortion is less dangerous to a woman's health than is pregnancy, but complications such as infection and bleeding can occur. Some women suffer psychological distress after an abortion; however, long-term negative reactions are rare.
- Several abortion methods are available; the most common method, performed during the first trimester of pregnancy, is vacuum aspiration. Another method, performed in the second trimester, is dilation and evacuation. Controversy surrounds the use of drugs that induce abortion, which can make the procedure very private and relatively simple.

CHAPTER 11

Sexual Development from Birth through Adolescence

At the age of 5, with three friends who were sisters, we ended up behind the furnace playing doctor with a boy. No matter what he would say his symptoms were, we were so fascinated with his penis that it was always the center of our examinations. I remember giggling as I pinched it and as I dunked it in some water we used as medicine

(A female American college student; adapted from Martinson, 1994)

I knew for a long time about how the bodies of girls and boys weren't the same. But we ought to know about it all much earlier . . . when you are a small child. I'd like to know the real names now.

(A 9-year-old Australian boy)

It's silly all this secrecy. A man's penis and a girl's vagina need special care. I'm told that if you don't keep them clean, you can get a disease. We need telling all about that.

(An 11-year-old American girl; adapted from Goldman & Goldman, 1988)

My best friend and I engaged in sex play between 5 and 10 times during the fifth through the seventh grade. We would examine each other's genitals and occasionally engage in oral-genital contact. Playing doctor usually ended up by agreeing to perform oral sex on each other.

(A male college student)

It's silly all this secrecy.

She dared me to touch her breasts. I was very afraid and repulsed by the idea, but I did it because I didn't want her to see I was afraid. When she touched my breasts, I really enjoyed it. I felt a tingling all over my body that I had never felt before.

(A female college student; adapted from Martinson, 1994)

Childhood sexuality remains one of the last frontiers in sex research (Money, 1976). In large part, the lack of research in this area is due to taboos surrounding childhood sexuality. In the United States, especially, children are considered innocent, and we tend to view sexuality and innocence as incompatible. Floyd Martinson's book *The Sexual Life of Children* (1994) is one of the few books devoted to childhood sexuality, but it took the author 20 years to find a publisher for it. Most other studies of childhood sexuality focus on problems, such as sexual abuse, rather than on normal development. Thus, we know more about abnormal sexual development in children than we do about normal sexual development. Although there has been strong resistance to studying childhood sexuality,

Contrary to what many parents believe, children are not typically ignorant about sexuality. (© 1982, Jimmy Margulies/Journal Newspapers)

understanding it is clearly necessary for understanding adult sexuality.

The study of adolescent sexuality has been more acceptable in our culture. Adolescents are viewed as nearly adult, and, therefore, their sexuality is viewed as a more legitimate topic for research. As a result, studies on this topic abound. Furthermore, some problems of adolescence, such as unplanned teenage pregnancies and sexually transmissible infections, have added a sense of urgency to the study of sexuality in this phase of development.

In this chapter, we will review biological, behavioral, and social changes that are related to sexuality and occur from birth through adolescence. We will begin with a review of several major theories of sexual development. Next, we discuss sexuality during three phases of development: early childhood, preadolescence, and adolescence. Adolescence extends from the early to the late teens, and even into the early 20s, for some. For the sake of simplicity, we categorize adolescence as the stage ranging from puberty (usually ages 12 or 13) to the end of high school (ages 17 or 18). Sexuality throughout the rest of the lifespan is discussed in Chapter 12.

THEORIES OF SEXUAL DEVELOPMENT

Before reviewing the various explanations of sexual development, we should note that of the three major approaches, only Freud's psychoanalytic theory specifically emphasizes sexuality. The other two prominent approaches—psychosocial theory and social cognitive theories—attempt to explain human growth and development with little reference to sexuality. Although Freud's theory has been criticized for overemphasizing sexual motivation, the other theories err in the opposite direction, by underemphasizing sex. Nonetheless, all three approaches have made important contributions to our understanding of sexual development and human development.

Psychoanalytic Theory

We introduced the basic aspects of psychoanalytic theory in Chapter 1. In this section, we focus on the psychoanalytic perspective on sexual development. Freud believed that the **libido**, or sexual energy, was the driving force behind most human behaviors. Basically, he thought that most everything people do somehow ties in with sexuality. Every human is born with powerful biological urges, and the sexual instinct is the most important of these, according to the psychoanalytic viewpoint. One component of personality, the id, is evident at birth. The id is impulsive, self-centered, and irrational. It is governed by the pleasure principle and driven to seek immediate gratification. This component of personality provides the energy, or motivation, for most behaviors.

LIBIDO
Freud's term for the sex drive, which he claimed was the driving force behind most human behavior.

PSYCHOSEXUAL STAGES
In psychoanalytic theory, developmental stages during which the sexual instinct focuses on a particular body part. Healthy development requires the mastery of each stage and a transition to the next stage and culminates in genital sexuality.

To Freud, the nature of the sexual instinct changes over the course of development. As a child matures, the focus of the libido shifts from one body part to another, finally centering on the genitals at puberty. Healthy sexual maturity is achieved when an individual's sexual energy focuses on her or his genitalia. In his **psychosexual stages**, Freud identified the specific bodily sites associated with pleasure at different stages of development. According to Freud, successfully progressing through each stage is necessary in order to fully enter the next stage. A child could become partly stuck, or *fixated,* in a stage if he or she experiences extremes in stimulation. Receiving too much or too little stimulation at any stage has long-term consequences for personality development, because some of the person's sexual energy remains directed at that unresolved developmental conflict. Freud theorized that everyone passes through the following psychosexual stages.

The Oral Stage (Birth to 1 Year)

The oral stage is characterized by the derivation of pleasure from the mouth. Infants seek to explore their environment by sucking, chewing, and biting. During this stage, an infant needs adequate stimulation, which is mostly obtained through feeding. Inadequate or excessive stimulation prevents a child from entering the next stage.

The Anal Stage (1 to 3 Years)

The anal stage is marked by the expectation that the child will master toilet training. At this stage, the child experiences pleasurable sensations by developing control over bowel movements. For the first time, the child recognizes that other people, usually the parents, are making demands, and the child can no longer be completely self-centered and impulsive. For the first time, society is setting limits on the child's behavior. Toilet training, if too harsh or too lenient, can have a lasting impact on the individual's behavior.

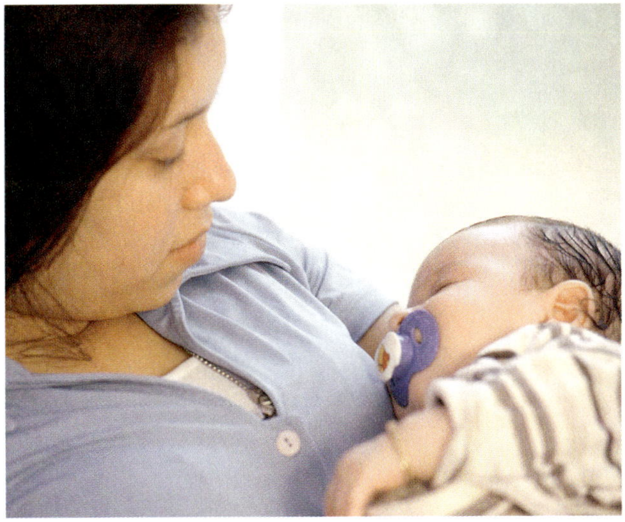

According to psychoanalytic theory, infants derive pleasure from the stimulation of their mouths that they experience as they explore the world through sucking, chewing, and mouthing.

The Phallic Stage (3 to 6 Years)

The phallic stage marks the first time that the child derives pleasure from genital sensations. It is during this phase that children can often be observed exploring their genitals with their hands and showing curiosity about the genitals of the opposite sex. This stage has been one of the most controversial parts of Freud's theory for several reasons. First, notice the source of the name for this stage: the phallus, or penis. Freud believed that the penis was critical to the sexual development of girls and boys at this stage. Second, Freud claimed that all children experience incestuous desires for the parent of the opposite sex during this phase. He introduced two concepts to explain the developmental challenges faced by toddlers in the process of identifying ultimately with the opposite-sex parent. The *Oedipus complex* (named after the legendary Greek king who killed his father to marry his mother) begins when a boy develops an erotic attraction to his mother. At the same time, he experiences jealousy and fear of his chief rival—his father. These feelings culminate in the boy's fear that his father may remove his penis, a fear referred to as *castration anxiety.* The threat is eliminated when the boy suppresses his incestuous desires and begins identifying with his father. The identification is exemplified by the child's imitation of his father's attitudes, appearance, behaviors, and sex role. The counterpart experience for girls is called the *Electra complex.* The young girl notices that she lacks a penis and blames her mother for this deficit. She turns her affection to the father and envies him for possessing a penis. Recognizing the impossibility of having her father, a girl ultimately identifies with her mother, who does possess the father. Ultimately, both girls and boys learn that by identifying with the same-sex parent, they will some day find a partner like the opposite-sex parent.

The Latency Period (6 to 12 years)

The latency period is a relatively asexual stage. During this stage, the sexual instinct is subdued, and the libido is redirected toward social activities and achievements. The calm of the latency period allows the child to recover from the extensive anxiety generated during the previous stage. The ego and superego also strengthen their influence on the child's behavior during the latency period. This stage, has, however, been likened to the "calm before the storm" of adolescence.

The Genital Stage (12 Years and Up)

The genital stage is the final stage of development in Freud's theory. This stage represents mature sexuality, because the libido is fully centered on genital pleasure with a partner. The guiding instinct is the urge toward biological reproduction through sexual intercourse. For most teenagers, this period is characterized by a growing interest in dating that corresponds with puberty.

You may react with skepticism to Freud's views on sexual development. A similar reaction occurs among many experts on human development, who reject some of Freud's more controversial concepts (Shaffer, 1999)—primarily the notions of the Oedipus and Electra complexes, for which there is little support. As you'll see in the next section, young children do have a natural curiosity about their genitals, but there is no evidence that they experience incestuous longings. Also, as we noted in Chapter 1, the male-centered perspective of psychoanalysis has been extensively criticized. Finally, researchers do not agree with the notion of a latency period in development, during which sexuality is temporarily "turned off."

To his credit, Freud helped legitimize the study of human sexuality and pioneered the notion that sexuality is an intrinsic part of the human psyche. Sexuality is not suddenly and dramatically activated in adolescence. Other theories of human development, however, have taken issue with Freud's emphasis on the predominance of the sexual instinct. One of these is Erikson's psychosocial theory, which has been more widely accepted by experts in the field of child and adolescent development.

Psychosocial Theory

Although he was originally a follower of Freud, Erik Erikson disagreed with Freud's insistence on the predominance of the sexual instinct. Erikson (1982) believed that sociocultural motives were most important in human behavior. Additionally, he stressed that children actively shape their social environment. Furthermore, rather than viewing humans as irrational and impulsive, Erikson (1963) viewed them as rational creatures.

According to Erikson's theory, children encounter several predictable social challenges during development. These challenges offer the potential for growth and enhanced emotional health. Each challenge can lead an individual to reexamine his or her views of the world, relationships, and the self. Should a particular psychosocial challenge prove overwhelming, however, it could have long-term effects on the individual's social and emotional growth. Erikson proposed that life presents eight major psychosocial challenges. Each of these challenges—listed in Table 11.1 along with Freud's corresponding psychosexual stages—must ultimately be mastered for successful adjustment in life. Although sexuality received limited emphasis in Erikson's theory, his stages readily incorporate sexual development because sociocultural factors play a major role in shaping human sexual behavior. In fact, this theory has been applied to such diverse aspects of human development as emotional development, peer relations, and self-concept formation.

Because they provide a useful framework for describing human development, we will be referring to Erikson's psychosocial stages as we cover sexual development throughout the lifespan. The first five psychosocial stages are discussed in this chapter; and the final three are reviewed in Chapter 12. Although most students of human behavior favor Erikson's views over those of Freud, psychosocial theory has been criticized. The most serious criticism is that the theory is more descriptive than explanatory in nature. Although it seems to accurately describe the psychosocial challenges we face during our lives, it does not explain why these challenges arise. Why do preschoolers, ages 3 to 6, struggle with establishing a sense of personal initiative? Why do teenagers face the challenge of finding a sense of identity in life? Do individuals in all cultures encounter the same psychosocial challenges? If the challenges have a social (or sociocultural) basis, shouldn't there be variations across diverse cultures? Unfortunately, these questions remain unanswered. However, similar social challenges are encountered in many Western cultures, making psychosocial theory useful for understanding development in those cultures, at least.

Social Cognitive Theories

The social cognitive perspective is not a single theory but rather a conglomeration of the views of theorists who share some common assumptions about human behavior. Social cognitive theories stress the importance of life experiences and learning in shaping human behavior. As the term *social cognitive theories* implies, most of our life expe-

IN YOUR own words

Beth Lee
Brown University

I was five years old and in kindergarten when I was first attracted to another person. I believe, looking back now, that I was just mimicking what I saw all around me. I have two older sisters who were always talking about their crushes on people in our Korean church community. I was also allowed to watch a lot of soap operas after school, which also fed into my idea of love and attraction to men.

TABLE 11.1 Stages of Development

APPROXIMATE AGE	ERIKSON'S PSYCHOLOGICAL CHALLENGES	ERIKSON'S VIEWPOINT: SIGNIFICANT EVENTS AND INFLUENCES	CORRESPONDING FREUDIAN STAGE
Birth to 1 year	Basic trust versus mistrust	Infants must learn to trust others to care for their basic needs. If caregivers are rejecting or inconsistent in their care, the infant may view the world as a dangerous place filled with untrustworthy or unreliable people. The primary caregiver is the key social agent.	Oral
1 to 3 years	Autonomy versus shame and doubt	Children must learn to be "autonomous"—to feed and dress themselves, to look after their own hygiene, and so on. Failure to achieve this independence may force the child to doubt his or her own abilities and feel shameful. Parents are the key social agents.	Anal
3 to 6 years	Initiative versus guilt	Children attempt to act grown up and will try to accept responsibilities that are beyond their capacity to handle. They sometimes undertake goals or activities that conflict with those of parents and other family members, and these conflicts may make them feel guilty. Successful resolution of this crisis requires a balance. The child must retain a sense of initiative and yet learn not to infringe on the rights, privileges, or goals of others. The family is the key social agent.	Phallic
6 to 12 years	Industry versus inferiority	Children must master important social and academic skills. This is a period when the child compares him- or herself with peers. If sufficiently industrious, children will acquire the social and academic skills to feel self-assured. Failure to acquire these important attributes leads to feelings of inferiority. Significant social agents are teachers and peers.	Latency
12 to 20 years	Identity versus role confusion	This is the crossroad between childhood and maturity. The adolescent grapples with the question "Who am I?" Adolescents must establish basic social and occupational identities, or they will remain confused about the roles they should play as adults. The key agent is the society of peers.	Early genital (adolescence)

riences occur in a social context—in families, peer groups, neighborhoods, and the culture at large. Each of these social environments shapes our behavior. In the context of social interactions, the most important form of learning is **observational learning**, or learning by imitation (Bandura, 1986). In explaining sexual development, social cognitive theorists emphasize how various role models in our lives influence our sexual attitudes and behaviors. Such models include our parents, siblings, peers, and media celebrities, among others. The learning of sexual skills is also facilitated by the availability of prospective partners in one's environment. Further, such learning is more likely to occur in a society that permits or even encourages sexual experimentation. For example, among the Canela tribe of South America, adolescent sexual activity is openly encouraged and expected (Crocker & Crocker, 1994). Open sexual experimentation is viewed as fostering community well-being. Clearly, the sexual

OBSERVATIONAL LEARNING Learning by observing and imitating other people. Social cognitive theories theorize that observational learning is the most influential process in human development.

norms in U.S. culture are very different, and this difference explains some of the variation in sexual attitudes and customs across the two cultures. These observations are also consistent with the tenets of script theory, discussed in Chapter 1.

Another important determinant of human behavior is cognition. Individuals have varied beliefs, attitudes, and values about sexuality. Social cognitive theorists emphasize the importance of information processing in human behavior. Especially important are expectancies and personal values (Mischel, 1999). Based on our individual experiences, we develop different expectations that influence our reactions to situations in life. The individual who expects to be successful in a dating relationship will behave very differently on a date from one who believes he or she will fail. And our personal values—including our sexual values—often guide many of our decisions about sexuality. Our values determine our priorities, our tolerances and intolerances, and our choices. As Bandura (1986) noted, our cognitions are influenced by both social context and life experiences. In turn, our cognitions influence our reactions to context and experiences. Thus, all of these factors are interrelated and largely inseparable.

One key aspect of social cognitive theories is their empirical, or scientific, basis. Unlike the psychoanalytic and psychosocial theories, social cognitive theories are often supported by research findings. For example, social cognitive theories effectively predict condom use among college students (Wulfert & Wan, 1995). Another important aspect of social cognitive theories is their insistence that no single influence can fully explain human behavior. Rather, a combination of interactive influences, including the environment, life experiences, and cognitive factors, must be considered. (This perspective is similar to that used throughout this book.) One unfortunate limitation of social cognitive theories is that they minimize the influence of biological factors. Like other forms of human behavior, sexual behavior is the product of a myriad of influences. Several biological factors, including sex hormones and heredity, play critical roles in shaping sexuality. Social cognitivists, however, generally emphasize the impact of the environment and life experiences.

Looking At . . .

. . . Thinking About

Parents often serve as role models for children's sexual attitudes and skills development. How did your parents or other significant adults influence you?

Finally, our discussion of theories of sexual development would be incomplete without a reference to the contribution of evolutionary psychology. To date, this theory has not focused on the developmental aspects of sexuality. Buss (1994), however, discussed sexual experimentation in adolescence. According to Buss, having several short-term partners during this transitional period in life serves adolescents as a "means of assessing their value in the mating market, experimenting with different strategies, honing their attraction skills, and clarifying their own preferences" (p. 93). According to this view, adolescent sexual experimentation represents rehearsal for long-term mating or marriage.

CHILDHOOD SEXUALITY: BIRTH TO 8 YEARS

From infancy through childhood, major changes occur in cognitive, social, and emotional development. Development in these areas has profound effects on a child's relations to others, self-concept, and sexuality. Healthy adult sexuality depends in part on normal development in all of these areas.

Psychosocial Development

Among the developmental stages of childhood, stages of cognitive development have been studied extensively. During the first 2 years of life, children learn to coordinate sensory information with their motor capabilities in what child psychologist and researcher Jean Piaget termed the **sensorimotor stage** of development (Piaget, 1952). Rapid changes occur in the infant's ability to solve problems, imitate others, and understand the basic features of the world. At the same time, children are learning to communicate and developing an attachment to parent figures and a sense of basic trust in others.

As the child grows, his or her cognitive abilities become more flexible, adaptable, and complex. The child becomes able to think logically and symbolically in the **preoperational stage** of development (Piaget, 1952). Symbolic thought is most evident in language development; a word represents, or symbolizes, a concept. At this stage, children's thoughts are egocentric; they have difficulty recognizing others' perspectives and view the world solely from their own perspective. At the same time, children are learning to function autonomously and are developing a sense of personal initiative. Successfully acquiring a sense of autonomy and personal initiative fosters healthy self-esteem.

Sexual exploration in preschoolers is usually playful and motivated by curiosity and novelty.

Sexual Behavior

Freud challenged the myth that children are born asexual creatures. Freud's notion of "sexuality" in infancy uses the term in a different sense from its usual meaning. As Freud used it in this context, the term refers to the ability and need to obtain pleasure from bodily stimulation. According to Freud, genital sexuality does not occur until puberty, although children derive pleasure from nongenital stimulation before that age. This view is supported by observations that newborns are capable of experiencing genital arousal; children less than 24 hours old may have penile or clitoral erections; and newborn girls are capable of vaginal lubrication. At this age, these responses are reflexes and are quite different from the sexual arousal experienced by adolescents and adults.

Although many of Freud's notions have been discredited, his belief that sexuality is a normal aspect of life beginning at birth is widely accepted. Preschool children demonstrate much interest in their genitals and have great sexual curiosity. Young children's curiosity about sex usually peaks around age 5 and decreases after that until they approach puberty (Friedrich, Fisher, Broughton, Houston, & Shafran, 1998). We will examine the various aspects of childhood sexuality—including self-stimulation and sexual rehearsal play—in the following sections. It is important to understand that collecting data on very young children is difficult, since researchers cannot question children but instead must rely on the observations of caregivers or adults' reports of their memories from childhood. Thus, children's sexual behaviors may go undetected much of the time.

Self-Stimulation and Orgasm

The manipulation of one's own genitals is often referred to as masturbation; however, in this discussion of young children's behavior, we will refer to it as *self-stimulation*. Masturbation implies orgasm-oriented behavior, whereas self-stimulation may involve pleasurable sensations but does not necessarily result in orgasm.

Self-stimulation is readily observed in most infants of both sexes. There are even reports of male fetuses manipulating their penises, observed on ultrasound! Solitary genital play is noted in many boys by 6 or 7 months of age and in girls by 10 or 11 months (Galenson & Roiphe, 1974). At these ages, because the children lack motor coordination, the self-stimulation appears more or less random. The rhythmic stimulation of the genitals for masturbation, on the other hand, requires fine muscle control that does not develop until 2 or 3 years of age. Therefore, the very young sometimes rely on indirect methods of self-stimulation. One case report, for example, described a 4-year-old

SENSORIMOTOR STAGE
In Piaget's theory of cognitive development, the first 2 years of life, during which children learn to coordinate sensory information with their motor capabilities.

PREOPERATIONAL STAGE
The second stage of Piaget's theory of cognitive development, during which young children learn to think logically and symbolically, as evidenced by language development.

girl who from the age of 1 was regularly observed clutching her abdomen just above the pubic area to achieve clitoral stimulation (Couper & Huynh, 2002). The mother mistakenly interpreted this behavior, combined with the daughter's face turning red, as a reaction to abdominal pain! In another report, a 7-month-old girl was observed regularly pressing her body against her rag doll while making rhythmic pelvic movements (Yates, 1978).

Self-stimulation becomes more intentional and less random as children mature. Children as young as age 2 have been observed using their hands to stimulate their genitals (Friedrich et al., 1998). Rubbing the penis against a surface or an item such as a pillow is also common. Girls are likely to use a wider range of techniques such as thigh pressure, manual stimulation of the clitoris or labia, or rubbing of the genital area against a soft object. Many children who self-stimulate discover the practice accidentally. Boys are more likely than girls to report that a peer explained or demonstrated it to them (Martinson, 1994).

did YOU know?

Surveys report that as many as 20% of preschool boys have experienced orgasm (Langfeldt, 1990).

Because self-stimulation is a private act and is often considered taboo, it is difficult to estimate how many children manipulate their genitals during early childhood. However, many schoolteachers report having occasionally observed young children masturbating (Larsson & Svedin, 2002b). Over 60% of boys and nearly 45% of girls between the ages of 2 and 5 have been observed by a parent occasionally touching their genitals (Friedrich et al., 1998). Although prepubertal boys are not physically capable of ejaculation, boys and girls are able to experience orgasm at an early age. According to Kinsey, many preschool boys have achieved orgasm (Kinsey, Pomeroy, & Martin, 1948). Reports by teachers and parents confirm that some young children show behavioral and physical signs of experiencing orgasm.

Childhood self-stimulation is a healthy aspect of sexual development. Unfortunately, in our culture, most parents are conditioned to have negative attitudes toward their children's genital self-stimulation. Up to 25% of mothers openly caution their daughters that self-stimulation is a harmful practice; others choose to ignore their children's self-stimulation (Gagnon, 1985). Very few parents in the United States openly discuss masturbation with their children, despite the fact that masturbation is a normal part of sexual development that entails no harmful short-term or long-term consequences.

Sexual Rehearsal Play

> She often let me watch her urinate, but I always refused to let her watch me because, as a boy, I was "different." Later I became bolder, and we ran back to the woods and undressed in front of each other. I suggested that we touch each others' genitals, but she refused. (A male American college student)

Preschool children reveal interest not only in their own genitals but also in those of other children, of both the same and the opposite sex (Martinson, 1994). Overall, boys show more interest than girls, and both boys and girls are more interested in boys' genitals. This sexual curiosity often involves mutual exploration in the form of games (such as "playing doctor"); the exploration is usually spontaneous rather than goal-oriented, or sexually motivated. Because young children are "not sure what they are looking for or what they will find" (Martinson, 1994, p. 37), it is the novelty of these experiences that is exciting to them. Their curiosity about the body is not just limited to peers; nearly half of preschool boys and girls also show a fascination with the breasts of adult women, including their mothers (Friedrich et al., 1998).

11.1 on the web

Most children have a natural curiosity about sex, often to the discomfort of their parents. The Mayo Clinic offers information to help parents address sexuality with their children. **Go to www.ablongman.com/mcanulty2e** to find the link to the Mayo Clinic's article "Discussing Birds and Bees."

What information is offered on the sexual behavior of preschoolers and school-age children? What kind of sexual information should parents give children, according to the American Academy of Pediatrics?

Sexual rehearsal play is a universal experience reported in virtually all cultures. In a comparison of children from the United States, England, Canada, Australia, and Sweden, on average 10% of children recalled engaging in sex play before age 6, and 40% had experienced such exploration between the ages of 6 and 9. Despite the fact that nearly 75% of the children described the experience as interesting or pleasurable, the

reflect ON THIS

Memories of Early Sexual Thoughts and Feelings

Few of us can clearly recall our earliest sexual thoughts and feelings, mainly because these probably occurred when we were small children. Most people do remember feeling curious about anatomical differences between boys and girls, and many have memories of childhood mutual exploration, all of which are normal and healthy developmental experiences.

In some cultures, parents openly discuss sexuality with young children and provide accurate answers for such common questions as "Where did I come from?" In the United States, parents often react to such questions with fear and embarrassment, reflecting our cultural ambivalence about sexuality, especially childhood sexuality. Receiving accurate answers to their questions about sexuality is actually a positive experience for children, one that appears to cause no problems whatsoever. Countries that mandate sexuality education in elementary school for all children foster a healthier sexual climate. Consistently, such countries report fewer sexuality related problems, including unwanted pregnancies, sexually transmissible infections, and sex crimes.

Because of the discomfort many parents experience, few U.S. adolescents and adults recall open and candid discussions of sexuality with their parents. Many people can vividly recall the embarrassment, unease, or even anger with which their parents reacted when the topic was raised. What reactions from your parents to the topic of sexuality do you recall? What message did their reaction provoke in you? Sometimes parental embarrassment suggests that the topic is off-limits or even shameful. If you were fortunate, your parents discussed sexuality openly and positively, setting the stage for positive feelings and thoughts. However, if you are in the majority, your parents delayed discussing sexuality, probably until you already knew more than they realized. For many adolescents, parental discussions of sexuality are limited to warnings of the potential risks of sexual behavior, with little if any mention of the positive aspects.

Some children learn about sexuality accidentally—often by witnessing their parents involved in sexual activity when they wander into the parents' bedroom at night. Freud believed that exposure to one's parents' sexuality, or a "primal scene experience" as he called it, was invariably traumatic and the source of psychological problems later in life. In fact, research reveals that this is not true. From his review of relevant studies, Paul Okami (1995) concluded that up to half of adults recalled accidentally hearing or seeing their parents engaged in sexual activity. There is no evidence that such exposure is traumatic or has long-lasting negative consequences. Young children usually react with amusement or do not understand what is occurring. Adolescents are likely to experience embarrassment or discomfort, but there is no evidence that they suffer long-term consequences, as Freud predicted.

majority never told their parents about it. Most children feared a negative reaction from parents (Goldman & Goldman, 1988). Reflect on This: Memories of Early Sexual Thoughts and Feelings discusses the benefits of accurate responses to young children's questions about sexuality.

Contrary to the fears of many parents, some sex researchers (e.g., Money, 1986) believe that suppressing sexual rehearsal play in children may have detrimental effects on adult sexuality. Depriving children of sexual play prevents the gradual learning of sexual and emotional intimacy, leaving sexual development up to chance. According to Money (1986), many adult problems of sexuality, including sexual dysfunctions and paraphilias (discussed later in this book), may stem directly from a deprivation of sexual rehearsal play in infancy and childhood.

PREADOLESCENT SEXUALITY: 8 TO 12 YEARS

Preadolescence is the transitional period between childhood and adolescence. Preadolescents gradually experiment with autonomy without straying too far from their parents. In other words, preadolescents still look and act like children, but they are starting to resemble teenagers.

Looking At . . .

. . . Thinking About

If adolescence is viewed as a tumultuous phase of development, preadolescence might be likened to the "calm before the storm." This is why Freud referred to this period as the latency stage of development. As the text shows, however, sexuality is not completely suppressed at this stage. What might account for the perception of preadolescence as an asexual phase of development?

Psychosocial Development

In the preadolescent phase of development, a child faces new challenges. According to Erikson, preadolescent children are expected to master several social and academic tasks. At this stage, which Erikson dubbed the stage of **industry versus inferiority** (Table 11.1), children increasingly compare themselves to peers. Those who successfully meet the new challenges will feel more self-assured; those who fail will suffer feelings of inferiority.

According to Piaget's theory, between the ages of about 8 and 12, children are in the **concrete-operational stage.** During this phase, cognitive development evolves rapidly. Children are able to think more logically about real problems and the world. They are increasingly able to appreciate others' viewpoints and are able to understand many basic facts of life. Accordingly, during this stage, children begin asking more realistic questions about human anatomy, reproduction, and sexuality. Whereas young children may be satisfied with simply observing that boys and girls are different, preadolescents want to know why (Goldman & Goldman, 1988). Furthermore, most preadolescents know that babies are not delivered by storks, nor do they come from "mother's tummy."

Preadolescent children's knowledge of sexuality tends to increase gradually. However, tremendous differences exist across cultures. By age 9, 100% of Swedish children can describe sexual intercourse, as can 48% of English and 40% of Canadian children. However, only 17% of 9-year-old children in the United States can discuss sexual intercourse. By age 11, the figures rise to 95% for Australians, 80% for English, and 50% for Americans (Goldman & Goldman, 1988).

Sexual Behavior

Preadolescent sexual behavior is more purposeful and pleasure-oriented than sexual behavior in early childhood. This progression toward more adultlike behavior is evident in solitary sexual behavior and in interactions with peers.

Masturbation

Because self-stimulation is less random and more orgasm-oriented for preadolescents than it is for younger children, we refer to this behavior in preadolescents as masturbation. Nearly 20% of U.S. boys and girls report having masturbated by age 10. By age 13, over 50% of boys and 25% of girls have begun masturbating (Janus & Janus, 1993). In Kinsey's survey of women, 15% had masturbated by age 13, and 12% of the women in the survey had had an orgasm from masturbating by that age (Kinsey, Pomeroy, Martin, & Gebhard, 1953). In a recent Swedish study, in which young adults were asked to recall sexual behaviors in childhood, over 6% of males and 7% of females recalled masturbating to orgasm between the ages of 6 and 10, and nearly 43% of males and over 20% of females recalled masturbating to orgasm between the ages of 11 and 12 (Larsson & Svedin, 2002a).

Because of differences in the dates of surveys and in the nature of samples studied, the findings on preadolescent masturbation are quite variable. Nonetheless, several consistent findings have emerged. As children approach adolescence, the numbers who report experience with masturbation increase steadily. Likewise, there is a steady increase in those who report masturbating to orgasm as they approach puberty. Overall, more boys than girls report masturbating to orgasm in preadolescence. Finally, since Kinsey's research in the 1940s and 1950s, an increasing number of preadolescent

INDUSTRY VERSUS INFERIORITY
In Erikson's psychosocial theory of development, the stage during which preadolescents are challenged to become self-confident in social and academic settings.

CONCRETE-OPERATIONAL STAGE
In Piaget's theory of cognitive development, the stage during which preadolescents become increasingly capable of thinking logically about real problems and the world. At this stage, their questions become more realistic.

girls and boys acknowledge having masturbated. Many adults recall that their preadolescent masturbation and other solitary sexual exploration elicited mixed feelings. Some report feelings of confusion, fear, and guilt, although many more report feeling excited and silly or giggly (Larsson & Svedin, 2002a).

Sexual Interactions

Parents often notice their preadolescents' growing interest in opposite-sex peers. Nearly 25% of boys and about 30% of girls between the ages of 10 and 12 are described by parents as "very interested in the opposite sex" (Friedrich et al., 1998). Most sexual activity between preadolescents is characterized by playful curiosity and mutual exploration (Goldman & Goldman, 1988). In this age group, sexual activity consists mostly of mutual showing of genitals, kissing, and fondling. Penetrative acts such as attempted intercourse and oral sex are less common. Only 3% of boys and 2% of girls have had sexual intercourse by age 10 (Janus & Janus, 1993; Larsson & Svedin, 2002a). However, one survey of nearly 1,400 6th grade students found that nearly one-third had initiated sexual intercourse (Kinsman, Romer, Furstenberg, & Schwarz, 1998). Similarly, the Youth Risk Behavior survey, conducted by the U.S. Centers for Disease Control, revealed that 22% of high school students reported initiating sexual intercourse before age 13 (CDC, 1999a).

did YOU know?

Masturbation is one of the sexual topics least likely to be addressed when parents talk about sexuality with their children (Martinson, 1994).

In another study, 82% of boys and girls under age 13 reported having mutual sexual experiences other than intercourse. The most common activities include kissing and hugging, talking about sex, and looking at pornographic pictures together. As with masturbation, these young people reported mixed feelings about these activities, but their reactions were largely positive. Seven percent of boys and 18% of girls reported nonconsensual sexual activity before the age of 13, which involved some form of trickery, bribery, persuasion, threat, or force (Larsson, & Svedin, 2002a).

Sexual activity with same-sex partners is also common among preadolescents. At this age, same-sex sexual play is usually periodic rather than showing a consistent pattern, is typically limited to one or two other children, and generally occurs over a limited period of time (Martinson, 1994). This seems to be especially true of females. By age 9, 25% of the women in Kinsey's sample had experienced same-sex sexual activity. In Kinsey's survey of men, 60% recalled same-sex sexual activity in preadolescence. Same-sex sexual activity usually consists of mutual genital examination and fondling. Mutual masturbation and oral sex are more common among preadolescent boys than girls. Among boys, same-sex sexual play often has a competitive quality. So-called circle jerks involve several boys masturbating in a group, often with the competitive goal of reaching climax first.

SEXUALITY IN ADOLESCENCE: 12 TO 18 YEARS

Adolescence has historically been characterized as a period of rapid growth involving dramatic change. This stage of development begins with puberty and involves many physical, cognitive, and emotional changes. We will discuss the important physical changes that relate to sexuality after summarizing the cognitive and psychosocial developments of adolescence.

Psychosocial Development

Adolescence represents the transition from childhood to adulthood. Adolescents enter what Piaget called the **formal operational stage** of cognitive development. Like adults, teenagers are able to think rationally and systematically about abstract concepts (Shaffer, 1999). Rather than merely accepting the world as it is, adolescents can imagine hypothetical alternatives. They are able and willing to question authority, rules, laws, and customs. They recognize that there are often different solutions to problems, different

FORMAL OPERATIONAL STAGE
In Piaget's theory of cognitive development, the stage at which adolescents are capable of rational and abstract thought. Consequently, they often challenge authority and tradition, as they can imagine alternative viewpoints.

philosophies of life, and different sources of information. Many adolescents will, for the first time, question and challenge their parents' viewpoints. Understandably, parents often describe their adolescent children as stubborn and rebellious.

As is evident in Table 11.1, adolescents face several psychosocial challenges. In Erikson's stage of **identity versus role confusion**, adolescents grapple with the basic question "Who am I?" Adolescents begin to attempt to establish a sense of who they are, where they fit into their peer group, and what their goals in life will be. An adolescent may ponder many questions pertinent to sexuality, having to do with sexual orientation, gender role, and sexual values. Identity formation is a lengthy process, and many college-age individuals are still trying to forge their identities (Waterman, 1982). In fact, many adults struggle with identity issues related to career goals, gender roles, and personal values (Waterman & Archer, 1990).

In general, puberty has only modest effects on self-concept, and the effects are largely dependent on the social context in which puberty takes place (Brooks-Gunn & Reiter, 1990). The effects that are observed also seem to depend in part on the timing of maturation relative to that of peers. In general, boys and girls who mature early tend to be more popular with their peers than late maturers (Petersen, 1985; Simmons, Blyth, & McKinney, 1983); however, boys' and girls' self-images are affected differently by early maturation. Early-maturing boys tend to evaluate themselves positively—presumably because they are larger, more muscular, and stronger than late-maturing boys and thus have an advantage in sports (Alsakar, 1992; Richards & Larson, 1993). However, early-maturing girls often have low self-images relative to their peers. There are two possible reasons for this. First, because girls develop, on average, 2 years before boys do, early-maturing girls are larger than both the girls and the boys in their age group. In addition, these larger girls are less likely to fit our culture's preference for thin, prepubescent-looking females (Brooks-Gunn & Reiter, 1990).

Early maturation has several disadvantages, in that it is associated with more problem behaviors in both boys and girls. Of particular interest is the fact that early maturers initiate sexual activity earlier than their peers; this finding has been consistently observed across many cultures (Lam, Shi, Ho, Stewart, & Fan, 2002; Magnusson, 2001; Rosenthal, Smith, & de Visser, 1999). Self-esteem may be a moderating variable. A recent study showed that boys with high self-esteem are *more* likely to initiate sexual intercourse, but girls with high self-esteem are *less* likely to engage in sexual intercourse (Spencer, Zimet, Aalsma, & Orr, 2002).

Physical Development

Physical development in adolescence often begins with a growth spurt characterized by significant bone and muscle growth, which is associated with weight gain and the maturation of several systems, such as the brain, heart, and lungs. The hallmark of adolescent development is puberty, which entails growth and maturation of the reproductive system. For boys, the penis and testes increase in size, and the testes begin producing semen, an event sometimes referred to as **spermarche.** For girls, the vagina becomes longer, the breasts grow, and **menarche**, the first menstrual period, occurs. The physical changes of puberty are listed in Table 11.2.

Pubertal development begins when a part of the brain, the hypothalamus, signals the release of hormones known as **gonadotrophins.** In turn, these hormones direct the production of testosterone by the testes and of estrogen by the ovaries. A sixfold increase in estrogen occurs in girls at puberty, and boys experience a twentyfold increase in testosterone levels (Moore & Rosenthal, 1993). Girls reach puberty approximately 12 to 18 months earlier than boys do (Nottelmann, Inoff-Germain, Susman, & Chrousos, 1990). The age range for the beginning of puberty is 9.5–13.5 years of age in boys and 8–13 years for girls.

The hormonal changes that mark the beginning of puberty are influenced by a number of biological and psychosocial factors. For instance, genetic and racial factors are involved in the onset of puberty. African American girls experience menarche a few months earlier than white girls, on average. Additionally, socioeconomic status,

11.2 on the web

There are several excellent Web sites dedicated to adolescent sexuality. We recommend George Mason University's Online Resources for Developmental Psychology, which you can access with a link at **www.ablongman.com/mcanulty2e.** Pay special attention to the sections on Puberty and Sex Education and Identity Development.

From your own experience, which of these issues seems most important in understanding the psychosocial challenges of adolescence?

IDENTITY VERSUS ROLE CONFUSION
According to Erikson's psychosocial theory, a developmental stage during which the major challenge for adolescents is to establish a sense of personal identity.

SPERMARCHE
The beginning of production of semen by the testes; akin to females' first menstrual period.

MENARCHE
A female's first menstrual period.

GONADOTROPHINS
Hormones released by the brain that direct the production of the sex hormones. In boys, these hormones cause the testes to produce testosterone; in girls, they direct the ovaries to produce estrogen.

TABLE 11.2 The Development of Sex Characteristics in Boys and Girls

AGE (YEARS)	BOYS	GIRLS
8 to 10		Breast buds begin to appear
10 to 12		Pubic hair begins to grow Vagina, ovaries, uterus, and labia grow rapidly Breasts enlarge Growth spurt occurs
12 to 13	Testes and scrotum grow Pubic hair begins to grow	Menarche occurs Underarm hair grows
13 to 16	Penis enlarges Voice begins to change First ejaculation of semen occurs Underarm and upper lip hair begin to grow Growth spurt occurs	Breasts continue to fill out Ova mature and conception is possible (1 year after menarche) Voice deepens
16 to 18	Hair grows on cheeks, chin, and body Noticeable changes in voice occur	

health, and nutrition also affect the timing of puberty (Hopwood et al., 1990). Interestingly, the age of onset of menarche has decreased steadily in Western societies for the past century. On average, girls today reach puberty 1 year earlier than girls did in the early part of the 20th century. The declining age at menarche has been attributed to improvements in health, diet, and body weight (Moore & Rosenthal, 1993), but it is also possible that exposure to hormones and other chemicals (in food, pharmaceuticals, or cosmetics) plays a role (Blanck et al., 2000; Partsch & Sippell, 2001; Tielmann, Juul, Skakkebaek, & Toppari, 2002).

There is a wide range in the age at puberty, a developmental event that marks the onset of many physical, cognitive, and emotional changes in adolescents.

11.3 on the web

Puberty is usually viewed as the event that defines adolescence. There are many useful sites for understanding the processes involved in puberty. Visit **www.ablongman.com/mcanulty2e** to find links to some of these sites.

What age-related emotional and physical changes are to be expected as girls and boys progress through puberty?

CLOSE UP ON culture

Adolescent Sexuality across Cultures

Puberty is a biological event. The onset of puberty is marked by obvious physical changes, including the development of secondary sex characteristics for both boys and girls and menarche for girls. Adolescence, on the other hand, is a socially defined phase of life. Puberty marks the beginning of adolescence, the beginning of the physical capacity for reproduction (Schlegel, 1995). However, the timing of the end of adolescence and the beginning of adulthood is defined by the culture. Various cultures have different views on the length of adolescence. In the United States, adolescence is defined as a period spanning about seven years. In some parts of the world, adolescence is defined as a much shorter period, only a few years, or even months in some cases (Hotvedt, 1990). In several cultures, adolescence ends when the person is married, and adolescents are expected to marry shortly after reaching puberty.

Anthropologists study practices, customs, and beliefs across diverse cultures, and their findings can help us better understand our own culture. By learning about the diversity of sexual practices, values, and beliefs around the world, we gain a better understanding about how our own culture shapes our sexuality. Anthropologists have been especially interested in nontechnological cultures, societies in which people are sustained by hunting, gathering, or small-scale agriculture. Anthropological studies often examine how industrialization and modernization influence cultural beliefs and practices.

In nonindustrial cultures, puberty is usually viewed as a special event. The transition from childhood to adulthood is often marked with puberty rituals or initiation rites. Such ceremonies are intended to prepare the adolescent for adult roles and to reinforce loyalty to the family or tribe (Hotvedt, 1990). For boys, puberty rituals often celebrate the adolescent's expected future contributions to the tribe or society. For girls, fertility is the most common theme in puberty rituals across cultures. These ceremonies are usually major public events, especially for boys. In nearly one-third of nonindustrial cultures, genital operations such as circumcision or subincision are performed. In more developed countries like the United States, special events to mark the beginning or end of adolescence are relatively rare (Schlegel & Barry, 1991). Perhaps the closest we come to a celebration of the end of adolescence in the United States are high school graduation ceremonies.

Cultural attitudes toward unmarried adolescent sexual behavior are diverse. In a large-scale study of over 150 nonindustrial societies, Schlegel and Barry (1991) found that over 60% of adults expected and approved of sexual behavior between unmarried adolescents. In nearly 20% of the sexually permissive cultures, female adolescents were the ones who initiated sexual activity with male peers. However, virtually all cultures try to exert some controls over adolescent sexuality by prohibiting incest and restricting the available partners to other adolescents.

An examination of views of adolescent homosexual behavior in 70 nonindustrial societies revealed that 21% of the cultures accepted or tolerated it, 41% were strongly disapproving, and 12% reportedly had no concept of homosexuality (Herdt & Nanda, 1994). A few tribes practice ritualized homosexual behavior, usually involving only males. The best-known example occurs among the Sambia, a Melanesian tribe (Herdt, 1987). Among the Sambia, younger boys practice ritualized fellatio on adolescents. The practice is designed to provide younger boys with semen, which is believed to promote physical growth and maturity, to "strengthen your bones" (Herdt, 1987, p. 150). After marrying, male adolescents continue nourishing younger boys with semen until their wives' first pregnancy. Upon the birth of the first child, adolescent males are expected to become exclusively heterosexual for the rest of their lives. Apparently, only very few men continue practicing homosexual activities after becoming fathers (Herdt, 1987).

The extraordinary diversity in adolescent sexual behavior is not only evident across cultures. Within the United States, adolescents reveal significant differences in their sexual values and practices. As we have noted throughout this book, cultural heritage, racial or ethnic background, religious values, gender roles, and life experiences are among the many influences that interact to shape individual sexual behavior.

Girls' reactions to menarche depend mostly on their advance preparation. For those who have been told to expect it as a normal phase in their development, the experience may be positive (Goldman & Goldman, 1988).

> My mother and elder sister told me all about it well in advance, told me what to expect. Mom and Dad talked about it openly when it happened, saying it was great to see me growing up. The next weekend, we had a party to celebrate. I think it was great help for my younger sister and brother to hear about. (Goldman & Goldman, 1988)

Adolescent girls who are unprepared often experience surprise and fear at their first menstrual period. As noted in Close Up on Culture: Adolescent Sexuality across Cultures, there are wide differences across cultures in reactions to menarche. Some cultures view it as a positive developmental transition, but in the United States it often has a negative connotation. Many teenagers—both girls and boys—have a negative image of menstruation (Stubbs, Rierdan, & Koff, 1989). For many, menstruation conjures images of uncleanliness and contamination; "the curse," as it is sometimes called, is rarely viewed in a positive light in this culture (Delaney, Lupton, & Toth, 1988). Most ways of referring to menstruation (such as the slang "being on the rag" or the more polite references to "feminine hygiene") do not present it as a normal physiological process that is experienced by over half of the population around the world.

For some boys, maturation of the reproductive system is signaled by a **nocturnal emission**, or wet dream. Although not all boys recall experiencing a nocturnal emission, it may be the first sign that sperm production has started and that ejaculation is physically possible.

> It happened one night. I don't know exactly when but I may have been in my early teens. There was this nasty sticky mess on the bedclothes and on my pajamas. I got into a panic and tried to wash the sheets and my nightclothes in the bathroom when no one was around. I thought I had a disease or something. (A male college student) (Goldman & Goldman, 1988)

While many boys are surprised by their first ejaculation, most regard it as a positive experience psychologically. Over half seem to feel more mature, and very few report a negative reaction to their first ejaculation (Gaddis & Brooks-Gunn, 1985). Boys who are ignorant about sexual maturation are more likely to be upset by this event.

Sexual Behavior

Adolescence marks a turning point in most people's lives, especially with respect to sexuality. Adolescents increasingly experience more of the range of adult sexual practices.

Masturbation

For most adolescents, masturbation is the most common form of sexual behavior. In the United States, 88% of boys and 62% of girls have masturbated by age 16 (Janus & Janus, 1993). The trends reported for younger age groups continue in adolescence. An increasing number of teens admit to masturbation, with boys more likely to admit to it than girls. Nonetheless, the majority of adolescents have experienced masturbation.

Similar trends are reported in other countries. Among Australian youths, 51% learned to masturbate between the ages of 14 and 15, and 76% had discovered masturbation by age 16 (Goldman & Goldman, 1988). Frequency of masturbation increases during adolescence; among teens 16 to 19 years old, over two-thirds of boys and half of girls masturbate once a week or more (Hass, 1979).

Although most adolescents masturbate, most still experience feelings of guilt and shame. Only one-third report being completely free of guilt about masturbation, and 20% report a "large amount" or "great deal" of guilt (Coles & Stokes, 1985). Teenage girls in particular are likely to feel guilty about this activity (Smith, Rosenthal, & Reichler, 1996). By the time they reach adulthood, two-thirds of women have apparently overcome their guilt feelings about masturbation (Davidson & Darling, 1993).

Sexual Interactions

Adolescent boys and girls progress through a similar sequence of sexual behavior. The characteristic progression begins with hugging and kissing ("making out"), followed by fondling ("petting"), rubbing genitals together while dressed, and sexual intercourse. DeLamater and MacCorquodale (1979) reported that oral sex occurs

NOCTURNAL EMISSION
A nighttime ejaculation, or "wet dream," that sometimes signals the maturation of the male reproductive system.

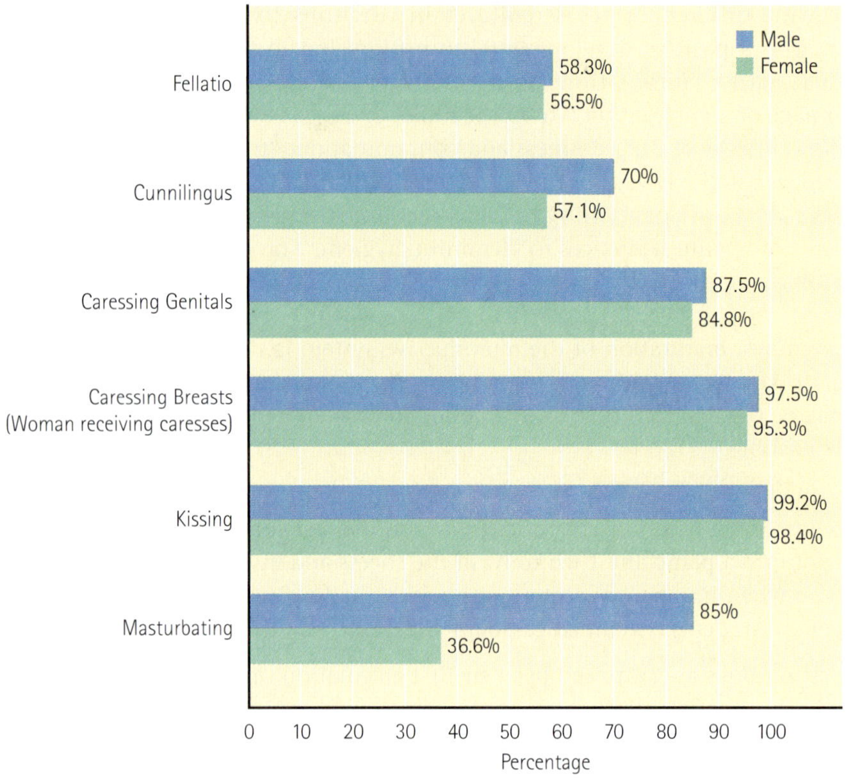

Figure 11.1 Percent of College Students Engaging in Heterosexual Precoital Activities (Source: Schwartz, 1999)

later in the sequence; however, more recently Schwartz (1999) found that the majority of college students recalled experiencing oral sex prior to first intercourse. Schwartz's findings on precoital sexual behavior among college students are summarized in Figure 11.1.

Overall, the percentage of high school students who have ever had sexual intercourse has dropped by nearly 10% in the past 10 years (CDC, 2000). However, the age at first intercourse has been declining over the decades for both males and females. Sex differences with respect to experience with intercourse are narrowing, but boys still tend to start younger than girls. Beginning in the 1960s, a greater proportion of female adolescents were having intercourse. In Kinsey's study, fewer than 6% of the women who were born before 1911 had had intercourse by age 19; over 40 years later, 74% of women in one study reported having sexual intercourse by age 19 (Spitz et al., 1996). Recent data indicate that over 9% of boys but only 4% of girls engage in sexual intercourse before the age of 13 (Grunbaum et al., 2002). Figure 11.2 shows the percentage of 9th through 12th grade females and males who have ever had sexual intercourse. As you can see, the percentage of high school

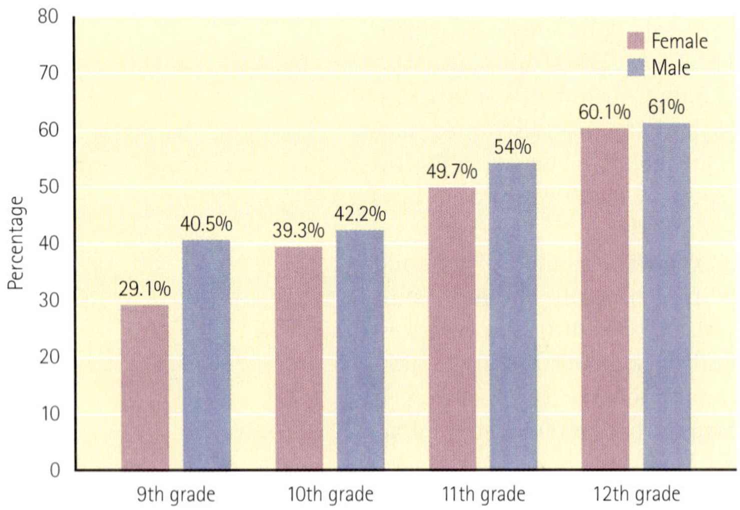

Figure 11.2 Percent of High School Students Who Have Ever Had Sexual Intercourse (Source: Grunbaum et al., 2002)

students who have had intercourse increases with age. In addition, at each age more males than females have had sexual intercourse, but these differences decrease with age.

Ethnic and racial differences in timing of first intercourse are also diminishing. It appears that more white Americans are having intercourse at earlier ages, whereas more African Americans are delaying intercourse. For example, compare data from 1980, which showed that 31% of white American and 63% of African American females experienced sexual intercourse between the ages of 15 and 19 (Zelnik & Kantner, 1980), to data from 2002 (depicted in Figure 11.3), which show an increase in sexual intercourse among white American females but a decrease among African American females. Still, significantly more African American males have intercourse in their teens, and they start earlier than any other group (see Figure 11.4 and Table 11.3).

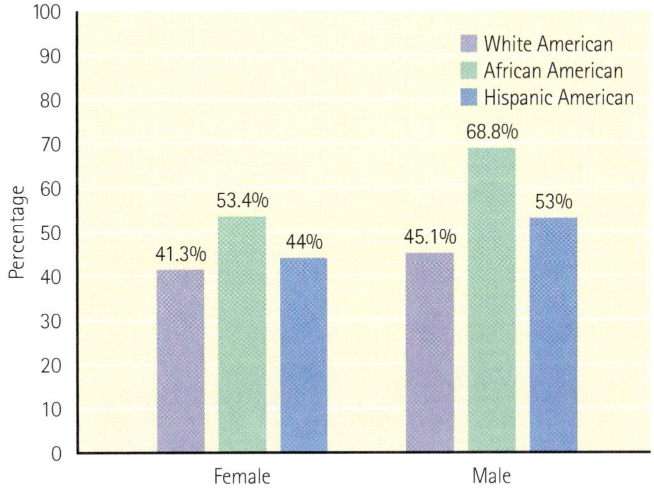

Figure 11.3 Percent of High School Students Who Have Ever Had Sexual Intercourse by Race/Ethnicity and Sex (SOURCE: Grunbaum et al., 2002)

Factors Contributing to Early First Intercourse

Because of potential problems associated with precocious and unprepared sexual behavior in adolescents, there is much interest in understanding why some teens begin having sexual intercourse much earlier than others. Early-maturing adolescent males and females report more sexual experience than late-maturing peers (Flannery, Rowe, & Gulley, 1993). Increases in testosterone levels in both adolescent males and adolescent females are positively associated with timing of first sexual intercourse (Halpern, Joyner, Udry, & Suchindran, 1998; Halpern, Udry, & Suchindran, 1997). However, it is clear that several social and environmental factors moderate these effects.

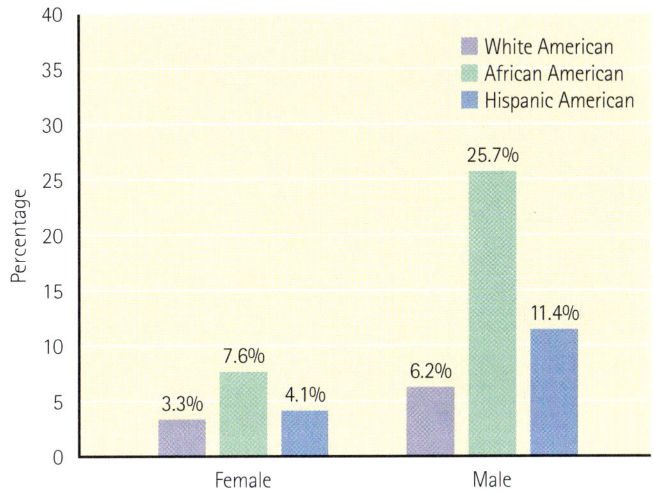

Figure 11.4 Percent of High School Students Who Have Ever Had Sexual Intercourse before Age 13 by Race/Ethnicity and Sex (SOURCE: Grunbaum et al., 2002)

Perceived peer norms and peer pressure play a role in timing of first sexual intercourse. Adolescents who perceive that their peers are having or approve of having sexual intercourse are more inclined to do so themselves (Bearman & Brückner, 1999; DiIorio et al., 2001; Whitaker & Miller, 2000). Direct peer pressure from friends or from a partner also influences the decision to have sexual intercourse for the first time (Kaiser Family Foundation/ABC Television, 1998). However, it appears that peer influence is overcome somewhat by parental communication about sex (Whitaker & Miller, 2000). In fact, teens who report high levels of communication with their parents delay sexual intercourse longer than teens with poor parental communication (Karofsky, Zeng, & Kosorok, 2001). In addition, teens who feel highly satisfied with their relationship with their parents are more likely to postpone sexual intercourse, and those who perceive that their mothers disapprove of sexual intercourse are less likely to engage in it (Dittus & Jaccard, 2000).

TABLE 11.3 Average Ages for Initiation of Sexual Intercourse

	AVERAGE AGE	
Ethnicity or Race	*Males*	*Females*
African American	14.3	16.8
White	16.3	17.4
Mexican American	16.3	17.6

SOURCE: Day, 1992

General intelligence and academic achievement are also related to timing of sexual intercourse. In one study, 7th through 12th graders who were rated high in intelligence were more likely to postpone sexual activity than those rated lower in intelligence (Halpern, Joyner, Udry, & Suchindran, 2000). The relationship between academic achievement and sexual initiation appears to be bi-directional. Low academic achievement and low educational goals for achievement are related to earlier initiation of sexual intercourse. In addition, those adolescents who become sexually active early tend to show a decline in their goals and achievements (Schvaneveldt, 2001).

Athletic involvement appears to influence age at first intercourse for girls. Girls who participate in sports have been shown to be half as likely as girls not involved in sports to experience first sexual intercourse between the ages of 10 and 13. However, at least one study showed that male athletes tend to be initiated into sexual intercourse at a younger age then their nonathlete counterparts. (Another study showed this to be true only for African American male athletes.) Female athletes in grades 9 through 12 were also more likely than nonathletes to be virgins, whereas male athletes were no more likely than nonathletes to be virgins (Women's Sports Foundation, 1998).

Looking At . . .

. . . Thinking About

Adolescence is a period of self-discovery and learning about dating. For many teenagers, it is also the period of initiating sexual interactions with a partner. What factors influence whether or not a teen becomes sexually active?

Religion is another factor that might influence timing of first sexual intercourse. Studies suggest that adolescents who consider religion to be important to their lives and/or have friends who are religious or spiritual are less likely to be sexually active (Dillard, 2002).

Finally, opportunity to have sexual intercourse is certainly another important factor in early initiation of sexual intercourse. Research shows that being in a steady dating relationship predicts early initiation (Whitbeck, Yoder, Hoyt, & Conger, 1999), whereas dating very little is associated with later initiation in girls (Meschke, Zweig, Barber, & Eccles, 2000). In addition, girls are more likely than boys to be initiated into sexual intercourse in a dating relationship (Sprecher et al., 1995). Reactions of boys and girls to first intercourse differ, as revealed in Close Up on Gender: "Was It Good for You?"

Same-Sex Sexual Behavior

As overall sexual experience increases through adolescence, so does same-sex sexual behavior. Same-sex sexual activity is difficult to report on accurately because it is still stigmatized in many cultures, and it is likely that some youth underreport their experiences. However, the Safe Schools Coalition of Washington (Reis & Saewyc, 1999) recently reported on several state studies, representing a total of 83,000 youth in grades 7–12, that assessed same-sex sexual behavior. Across these different population samples, from 1% to 5.3% of students reported engaging in same-sex sexual activity. Engaging in same-sex sexual activity does not necessarily mean that a youth is gay, lesbian, or bisexual. Many youth engage in these activities but identify themselves as heterosexual, while others who have never had same-sex experiences identify themselves as gay, lesbian, bisexual, or undecided. In a sample of youth in Seattle, 8.5% of the respondents described themselves as gay, lesbian, bisexual, or unsure of their sexual orientation. Clearly, adolescence is a time when many individuals begin to struggle with issues of sexual orientation.

CLOSE UP ON gender

"Was It Good for You?" Reactions to First Intercourse

Most people with sexual experience have vivid memories of their first sexual intercourse. In many cultures, first intercourse is an important rite of passage, a major life transition from being a virgin to having sexual experience. In the United States, first sexual intercourse generally follows a cultural script. The script delineates the expected circumstances for sexual initiation. For instance, first intercourse generally occurs in the context of a dating relationship with a same-age partner, is unplanned, occurs in the home of one partner, and does not consistently involve contraceptive use (because the experience is spontaneous rather than planned) (Sprecher et al., 1995). Additionally, first intercourse follows a sexual script that involves a progression over time from kissing, to breast fondling, to genital fondling, and finally to actual intercourse (DeLamater & MacCorquodale, 1979).

Studies of gender differences in reactions to first intercourse reveal two consistent findings. First, males generally rate their sexual initiation more positively than females do. Second, there are wide differences in reactions to first intercourse among males and among females. In an article entitled "Was It Good for You, Too?" Sprecher and colleagues (1995) asked over 1,600 college students to report their memories of first intercourse. The emotion reported most frequently by both genders was anxiety, with men recalling more fear than women. Both genders reported fears about personal performance and about possible negative consequences of intercourse, such as pregnancy. Though men recalled more fear during first intercourse than women did, they also reported more pleasure and less guilt. Men recalled more pleasure because they were more likely to have had an orgasm during first intercourse: Nearly 80% of men but fewer than 10% of women had an orgasm during first intercourse. Finally, the researchers found evidence for a "love effect." Participants recalled more pleasure during sexual initiation if they were still romantically involved with that partner at the time of the study. The "love effect" is part of a cultural script for sexual activity, the expectation that "love and sexual pleasure do go together—that sex is more pleasurable when there is love or commitment" (Sprecher et al., 1995, p. 13). Consistent with that finding, both men and women recalled more pleasure and less guilt if their first intercourse occurred in a committed relationship rather than in a casual one. Somewhat unexpectedly, both men and women also reported more anxiety if their first intercourse occurred in a committed relationship, perhaps because they had more at stake and were more concerned about potential negative consequences. Thus, once again, we see that cultural scripts play an important role in shaping sexual behavior, including how males and females react to the "first time."

ISSUES IN ADOLESCENT SEXUALITY

Many teenagers seem unprepared for sex and, consequently, may experience health and social complications as a result of sexual activity. The following sections review various strategies for resolving problems arising from sexual unpreparedness in adolescence.

Sexually Transmissible Infections

Over 3 million teens in the United States contract one or more sexually transmissible infections (STIs) each year (Alan Guttmacher Institute, 1994a). Although overall rates of syphilis, gonorrhea, and chlamydia have declined over the past decade, these bacterial infections disproportionately affect adolescents and young adults. In developed countries, between one-third and one-fifth of all infections by these three diseases occur in adolescents, and the United States has one of the highest rates of infection (Panchaud, Singh, Feivelson, & Darroch, 2000). This is alarming, because these diseases are highly contagious and, if left untreated, can cause long-term health problems. For example, untreated gonorrhea can cause permanent damage to the heart and brain and infertility in women. In addition to these curable diseases, teens are also susceptible to incurable viral infections. For example, studies have shown that between

did YOU know?

Approximately one in four sexually active adolescents will contract a sexually transmissible infection.

28% and 46% of young women are infected with the human papillomavirus (HPV), and 15% to 20% of young women and men are infected with herpes (CDC, 2000f).

Teenage girls seem especially vulnerable to STIs. Adolescent girls have the highest rates of all age groups for certain types of STIs. They are twice as likely as adolescent boys to contract some types from an infected partner (Harlap, Kost, & Forrest, 1991; Panchaud et al., 2000). For example, in a high school screening program of 9th through 12th graders, 12% of girls but only 6% of boys tested positive for chlamydia (CDC, 2000f). Additionally, an adolescent female is more susceptible than an adult woman to some STIs because her cervix is still immature and because her body still lacks certain antibodies that could protect against some STIs (Alan Guttmacher Institute, 1994b; CDC, 2000f).

Because of these findings, the rising rates of STIs among teenagers have been likened to an epidemic (Genuis & Genuis, 1995). Most troubling is the fact that rates of infection by human immunodeficiency virus (HIV), the virus that causes AIDS, are increasing among adolescents. AIDS is the seventh leading cause of death among 15- to 24-year-olds in the United States (CDC, 1998a; 1999a). Given the relatively long incubation period for HIV, disease specialists believe that many adults who are currently HIV-positive were infected in adolescence. Recent predictions suggest that the rates of STIs and HIV infection among teenagers will continue to increase.

Given the potentially life-threatening nature of these diseases, it is important to consider why STIs are reaching epidemic proportions among adolescents. The main reason is that most teenagers do not practice safe sex. Adolescent males and females do not consistently use condoms (the most effective form of protection against STIs and HIV among people who are sexually active), and up to one-quarter of teens rarely or never use any form of contraception (Rodgers, 1999). Among teenagers, condom use tends to be highest at the beginning of a relationship and to gradually decline over the length of the relationship (Ku, Sonenstein, & Pleck, 1994). It seems that after a period of sexual activity, regular partners decide that they are uninfected, and they use condoms less and less regularly (Rodgers, 1999). Unfortunately, many diseases, including HIV, do not produce visible signs of infection, especially in the early stages of infection.

Other adolescents feel that asking a partner to use a condom is threatening; they worry that it signals a lack of trust or love. Some males complain that condoms reduce the sensitivity of the penis during intercourse. Finally, some teenagers feel invincible, believing that "it could never happen to me." Unfortunately, current statistics show that this is not true.

Overall, condom use among sexually active teenage women more than doubled between 1982 and the mid-1990s (Piccinino & Mosher, 1998; Santelli, Lindberg, Abma, McNeely, & Resnick, 2000). This is an encouraging sign—you'll remember that many adolescents do not use condoms regularly. Risks of contracting an STI from a single act of intercourse without protection when one's partner is infected are quite high (Alan Guttmacher Institute, 1994b). As shown in Figure 11.5, a woman has a 50% chance of contracting gonorrhea and a 40% chance of developing chlamydia if her partner is infected and the couple does not use proper protection. For a man, the corresponding numbers are 25% for gonorrhea and 20% for chlamydia.

Adolescents who begin having sexual intercourse when they are younger than 15 are at higher risk for contracting STIs. They are less likely to use condoms, have more partners, and have sexual intercourse more often than their older peers (Seidman & Reider, 1994). All three of these patterns increase risks for sexually transmissible infections, including HIV. We'll discuss sexually transmissible infections more thoroughly in Chapter 14.

The increase in sexual activity among adolescents, combined with inconsistent condom usage, is the root of another problem of teenage sexuality—unplanned pregnancy.

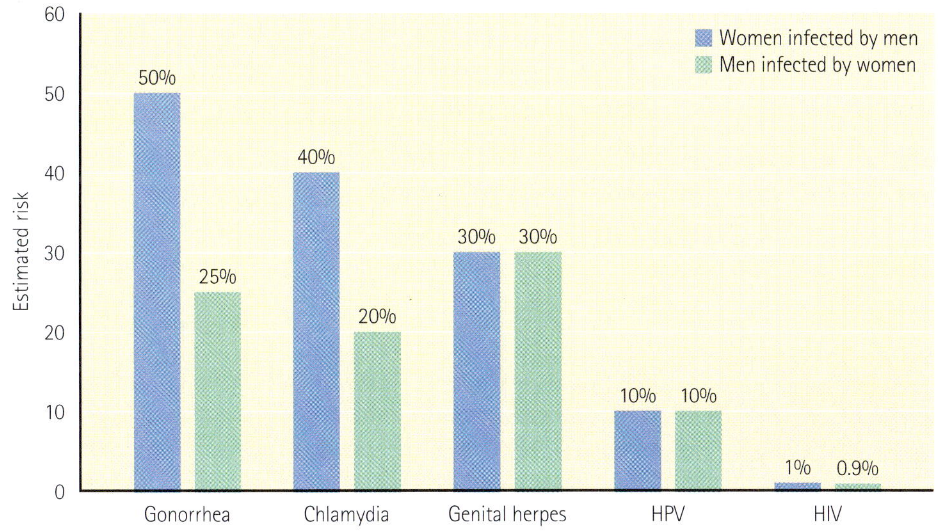

Figure 11.5 Estimated Risk of Contracting an STI from a Single Experience of Sexual Intercourse with an Infected Partner (SOURCE: Adapted with permission from *Sex and America's Teenagers,* Alan Guttmacher Institute, 1994a.)

Unplanned Pregnancy

Each year in the United States there are over 800,000 pregnancies among women under the age of 20, and 80% of these are unintended. What these data mean is that over 7% of adolescents experience an unplanned pregnancy each year (Boonstra, 2002; Henshaw, 2001).

Prevalence of Teenage Pregnancy and Births

Overall, the teenage pregnancy rate has declined 19% since 1990. In addition, in 2000 the rate of childbirth hit an all-time low of 49 out of every 1,000 teenage girls in the United States, a 22% reduction since 1990. Because abortion rates among teens are also down, we know that abortions are not accounting for the decline in childbirths to teens. So, why are these rates down? Simply put, fewer teens are getting pregnant; however, they are not having less sex. Instead, they are using contraceptives, and more effective ones, more often (Boonstra, 2002; Ventura, Mathews, & Hamilton, 2002).

While the recent trends are encouraging, adolescent pregnancies continue to be of concern in the United States because they are virtually always unplanned and unwanted. Unintended pregnancies often place the adolescent mother and her child at a disadvantage economically, socially, and financially. Most teenaged mothers are economically disadvantaged; most come from poor or low-income families, and because of their age and background, they have few financial resources. Teenaged mothers are also less likely to complete high school or to obtain vocational training and less likely to attend college, which further restricts their earning potential. Teenaged mothers are more dependent on public assistance for financial support than are other teenagers (Furstenberg, Brooks-Gunn, & Chase-Lansdale, 1989). Compared to their peers, teenaged mothers are more likely to have failed marriages and other unintended pregnancies. Finally, adolescent mothers have more difficult pregnancies and are less likely than older women to receive good prenatal care. The inadequate medical care often leads to health problems in their infants. The younger the mother, the more likely the baby is to have health problems. Premature birth and low birth weight are the most common complications affecting the newborns of teenaged mothers; these problems increase the risk of complications such as infant death, blindness, deafness, and mental retardation (Annie E. Casey Foundation [AECF],

11.4 on the web

Teen pregnancy is associated with many negative life outcomes. Go to **www.ablongman.com/mcanulty2e.** Read the article from *Social Work Today* and describe the relationship among teen pregnancy, poverty, and marital status.

What does the author suggest as a solution to teen pregnancy?

HEALTH Matters

Health Risks of Unplanned Teenage Pregnancy

From a purely biological perspective, middle to late adolescence represents an optimal age for child-bearing. However, a healthy pregnancy and delivery require high-quality prenatal care and services. Quality prenatal care includes regular medical checkups, proper diet and nutrition, and a healthy lifestyle. Unfortunately, one-third of pregnant adolescents do not receive proper prenatal care, thereby increasing the risks of problematic pregnancies and deliveries (Alan Guttmacher Institute, 1994). Furthermore, many pregnant teenagers smoke cigarettes (Ventura, Martin, Curtin, & Mathews, 1999), which is a known risk factor for problems during pregnancy.

Younger teens need more intensive prenatal care but are less likely to receive such care than older adolescents. Younger teenaged mothers may be unaware of the resources that are available for prenatal care. An additional obstacle to obtaining prenatal care is the stigma associated with being an unmarried adolescent parent. Because of inadequate prenatal care, teenagers are likely to have problematic pregnancies and deliveries. Low birth weight and premature birth are more common among infants of teenagers than among those born to women in their 20s. Infants born to women younger than 15 are twice as likely to have low birth weight and nearly three times as likely to die within the first month of life (American Academy of Pediatrics, 1999; Stevens-Simon & White, 1991). Low birth weight is an important risk factor for infant mortality and later health problems. Newborns who weigh less than 2 pounds at birth have a low survival rate, and those who do survive almost always have permanent neurological problems. Overall, babies born to young mothers have more health problems and spend more time in the hospital than babies of adult mothers. Various respiratory, digestive, and neurological problems are common in premature infants, because many of their organs are not fully developed at birth. Fortunately, some of these problems can be resolved with proper medical care. In the long term, children of teenaged mothers have more problems with school performance.

In order to improve conditions for teenaged mothers and their children, a number of family planning centers and school-based programs have been developed. By providing day care and special courses, some programs offer teenaged mothers the opportunity to complete school or receive job training. The most comprehensive programs offer classes on prenatal care, infant care, and parenting skills (Solomon & Liefeld, 1998). These programs enhance prenatal care among pregnant teenagers, reduce risks of low-birth-weight infants, and increase the mother's economic prospects (Alan Guttmacher Institute, 1994). Such programs have also been shown to reduce risks of future unplanned pregnancies and to decrease school dropout rates (Solomon & Liefeld, 1998).

2002; Coley & Chase-Lansdale, 1998; Kunz, 2002; Washington State Department of Health, 2002). These issues are explored in Health Matters: Health Risks of Unplanned Teenage Pregnancy.

Adolescent pregnancy rates vary by race and ethnicity. African American teenagers, on average, have a higher pregnancy rate than either Hispanic American or white American youths. This difference may be a consequence of variations in contraceptive usage. Some African American youths are less likely than members of the other groups to use birth control methods (Alan Guttmacher Institute, 1994b). It may also be because more African Americans are impoverished and adolescent girls from lower-income families are at greater risk for an unplanned pregnancy than are those from higher-income homes. For girls from disadvantaged backgrounds, the perceived costs of early motherhood may seem much lower than they do to girls from families that are better off (Coley & Chase-Lansdale, 1998; Kirby, Coyle, & Gould, 2001). In other words, a girl who has grown up in poverty and who sees few educational or economic opportunities in her future may feel that she has less to lose from an unintended pregnancy than a girl who sees many options in her future.

Outcomes of teenage pregnancies vary. Approximately half of unintended adolescent pregnancies end in abortion (Henshaw, 1998). Teenagers from higher-income families are more likely to have an abortion than those from poorer families. Feeling too young and too financially unprepared for children are the two most common reasons that adolescents give for terminating a pregnancy (Alan Guttmacher Institute, 1994b).

Looking At . . .

. . . Thinking About

Teens from economically disadvantaged backgrounds are more vulnerable to unplanned pregnancies, in part because of the lower perceived costs of motherhood among teens who have few opportunities and limited hope. What interventions might be helpful in addressing this sense of hopelessness among disadvantaged teens?

Explaining Teenage Pregnancy

Because the rate of unintended teenage pregnancy is higher in the United States than in most other industrialized countries in the world, we must ask why so many adolescents in this country have unplanned pregnancies. According to Caldas (1993), six explanations have been offered by those who have studied the problem:

1. The reproductive-ignorance hypothesis attributes the high adolescent pregnancy rates to a lack of knowledge about conception and contraception.
2. The psychological-needs hypothesis explains adolescent pregnancy on the basis of the mother's psychological needs. According to this view, some adolescents feel a need to be a mother.
3. The welfare hypothesis explains the teen pregnancy problem as a result of adolescent mothers' desire to receive public assistance funds.
4. The parental-role-model explanation proposes that pregnant adolescents are essentially imitating their mothers, who are themselves single parents.
5. The social-norms hypothesis attributes teenage pregnancies to a desire to fit in with a peer group in which unplanned pregnancy is common and even reinforced.
6. The physiological hypothesis explains the phenomenon as the direct result of pubertal hormones.

With regard to the first explanation, there is a relationship between knowledge of sexuality and sexually responsible behavior. As we'll discuss in the next section, adolescents who have had sexuality education classes tend to use contraception more effectively (Alan Guttmacher Institute, 2002). However, most sexually active adolescents know enough about pregnancy and contraception to prevent pregnancy. Therefore, a lack of knowledge alone does not totally explain the problem; rather, a lack of motivation seems most important. According to the second and third explanations, unintended pregnancies serve a purpose, either psychological or financial, for adolescents. Yet, given all the challenges of single parenthood, it seems unlikely that adolescents become pregnant simply to fulfill some need, whether conscious or subconscious. In support of the fourth explanation, it is true that teenagers who grew up in single-parent homes are more likely to experience unplanned pregnancies. Growing up with a single parent may signal to the adolescent that being a single

did YOU know?

Annually, adolescents account for one-fourth of all abortions in the United States.

Peer pressure and media messages that emphasize sexual experimentation without concern for detrimental consequences may encourage adolescents to take sexual risks.

mother is the norm. Further, a single parent is often less able to supervise a daughter's dating, which may lead to earlier pregnancy (Newcomer & Udry, 1987). The social-norms, or peer-influence, explanation seems unlikely, because most adolescents do not view unplanned pregnancies as desirable. Although there may be tremendous peer pressure in U.S. culture to engage in sexual behavior (Kinsman et al., 1998), there is very little pressure to get pregnant. In fact, having a pregnant sister is not associated with earlier initiation of sexual intercourse among teenagers, whereas having a mother who was pregnant as a teenager is (Crockett, Bingham, Chopak, & Vicary, 1996). Peer pressure is, however, the single most important reason cited by adolescent females and males for becoming sexually active (Kinsman et al., 1998). Likewise, adolescents are exposed to many media messages that promote sexual experimentation but rarely address the potential negative consequences (Kunkel, Cope, & Biely, 1999; Ward & Rivadeneyra, 1999). Finally, the physiological hypothesis proposes that hormonal changes are responsible for unintended pregnancy. This explanation is incomplete for two reasons: First, hormonal levels are important for predicting sexual activity of males but not of females. Second, hormonal influences cannot explain the extreme variability in teen pregnancy rates across cultures. Adolescents in all cultures undergo the hormonal changes of puberty. However, in some industrialized countries other than the United States, unplanned teenage pregnancies are quite uncommon.

We concur with Caldas (1993) that no single explanation is likely to fully explain the problem of unintended teenage pregnancies. Rather, a consideration of several interacting influences will provide a more complete understanding. Obviously, the pleasurable sensations of sex are a prime motive for sexual experimentation. People—including teenagers—have sex because it feels good! The timing of the consequences also plays a role in sexual behavior. The pleasurable sensations are immediate, beginning the moment a person merely anticipates a sexual encounter. The negative consequences, however, are delayed. Symptoms of STIs may not emerge until weeks, months, or even years after intercourse; pregnancy takes days to weeks to become evident. Many teenagers and adults are essentially playing the odds when having unprotected sex. Pleasure during sex seems almost guaranteed, with nearly 100% probability—whereas the probability of unpleasant consequences appears low, especially to an adolescent who feels invincible. Although a lack of knowledge about contraception may not be enough to explain why nearly 10% of sexually active teenage women become pregnant, a lack of motivation to use birth control consistently is obviously part of the explanation. Feeling invulnerable and wanting to become an adult may lead adolescents to have sex without proper planning. Growing up in a family and among peers who condone unintended pregnancy may also facilitate a lack of planning and caution among sexually active teens. Finally, cultural factors enter into play, since teenage pregnancy is more acceptable in some cultures. Furthermore, peer pressure and media messages that emphasize sexual experimentation without concern for detrimental consequences may encourage adolescents to take sexual risks. Because multiple factors underlie the adolescent pregnancy problem, multiple interventions will be required to resolve it.

Adolescent Sexuality Education

Although virtually everyone agrees that something must be done to address the problems associated with adolescent sexuality, there are major disagreements on what should be done and how to do it. There appears to be a consensus that education is part of the answer, but sexuality education remains one of the most controversial topics of public policy debate. Here are the major questions that arise concerning sexuality education:

1. *What should sexuality education encompass?* Some people advocate unrestricted coverage of all topics related to sexuality; others claim that only certain topics should be presented. An evaluation of early studies on the effectiveness of sexuality education revealed that the actual content of the courses often was not examined (Jacobs & Wolf, 1995).

2. *What are the benefits of sexuality education?* There is disagreement on the perceived benefits and risks associated with sexuality education. One critical concern is whether education alone modifies adolescents' actual sexual practices.

3. *Who is responsible for providing sexuality education?* Although many (including parents and teachers) believe that the family should be primarily responsible for providing sexuality education, few families seem actually to provide it. Many, if not most, parents feel uncomfortable discussing sexuality with their children.

4. *What is the most effective format for sexuality education?* Questions persist about the age or grade level at which sexuality education should begin, the best format (lecture, films, peer teachers), how long sexuality education should last (single course versus continuous throughout school years), and whether classes should be separated by gender or combined.

Overall, the vast majority of Americans support comprehensive sexuality education (see Figure 11.6). Furthermore, the majority of parents of teenagers favor sexuality education. Even in communities described as religiously conservative, almost 90% of parents support school-based sexuality education (Welshimer & Harris, 1994). In fact, most parents favor teaching about STIs, birth control, safe sex, and delaying sexual activity, as well as other topics listed in Figure 11.7 (on page 350) (Dailard, 2001; Hoff, Greene, McIntosh, Rawlings, & D'Amico, 2000). But controversies persist over the proposed content of

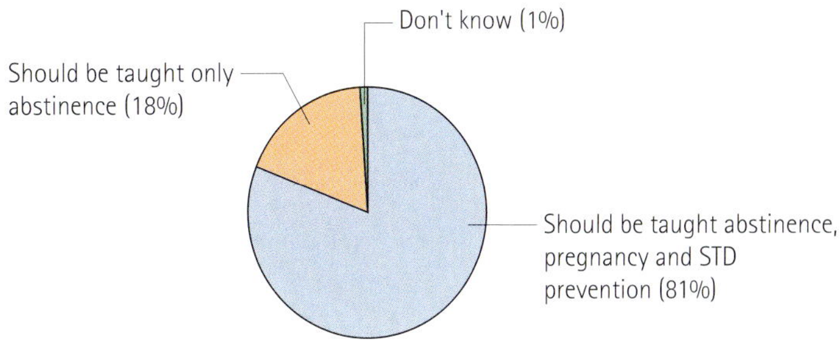

Figure 11.6 The vast majority of Americans support comprehensive sexuality education in school. (SOURCE: Adapted with the permission of the Alan Guttmacher Institute from Dailard, C., Sex education: Politicians, parents, teachers, and teens. *The Guttmacher Report on Public Policy,* 2001, 4(1), 9–12.)

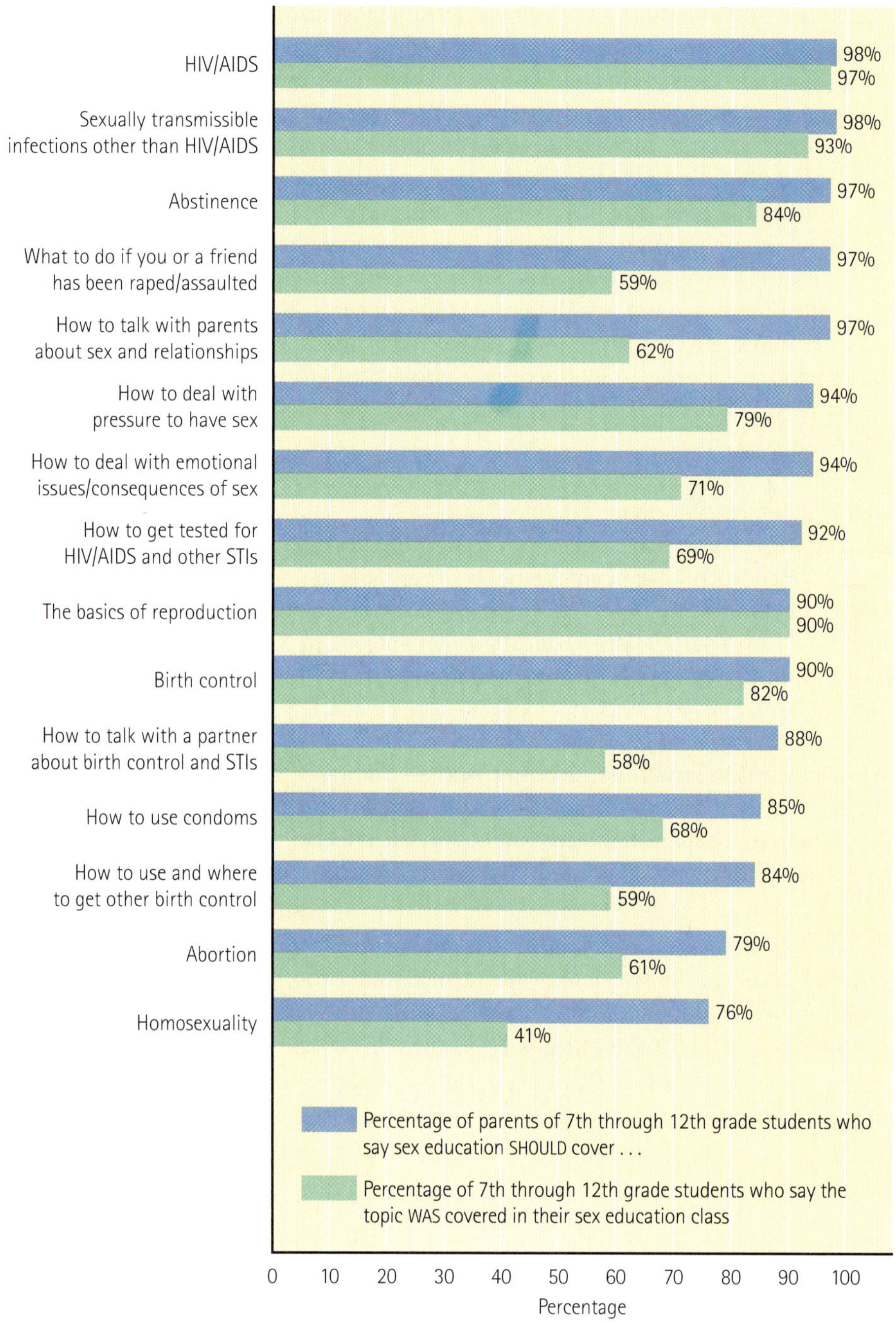

Figure 11.7 Sexuality Education: What Parents Want To Be Included and What Students Actually Receive (Source: Kaiser Family Foundation, 2000)

sexuality education courses. Most parents oppose the inclusion of topics such as masturbation, sexual orientation, and prostitution (Welshimer & Harris, 1994).

In some regions, most parents also support making condoms available in the schools. The small minority of parents who elect to keep their children out of sexuality education courses and who strongly oppose condom availability are those who consider themselves "very religious" (Guttmacher et al., 1995). Apparently, some parents fear that condom availability will increase sexual activity among their teenaged children. This fear seems unfounded: The lack of condoms does not seem to deter sexual activity among teenagers, and condom distribution programs have not been shown to increase sexual behavior in adolescents (Furstenberg, Geitz, Teitler, & Weiss, 1997; Kirby et al., 1999).

Educators in particular recognize the importance of sexuality education. Most high school teachers support such programs and feel a personal responsibility for providing some instruction, and at least half believe that contraception should be included in sexuality education and taught in grade 7 or earlier. However, one-fourth of high school teachers are told not to teach about sexuality (Dailard, 2001). In addition, many teachers feel inadequately prepared to provide sexuality education, and most want additional training before presenting such material. Over half of high school teachers who offer sexuality education have had no formal training in the subject (Gingiss & Basen-Engquist, 1994). Similar findings are reported in northern Europe, where most principals and teachers support offering sexuality education in the schools (Van Oost, Csincsak, & De Bourdeaudhuij, 1994).

Over one dozen different sexuality education curricula have been implemented in school systems in the United States (Kempner, 1998; Klein, Goodson, Serrins, Edmundson, & Evans, 1994). Most of these programs may be categorized as emphasizing either comprehensive sex education or abstinence from sexual activity. In reality, all programs share the common goal of encouraging adolescents to postpone sexual intercourse until they are prepared for responsible decision making regarding sexual activities. However, there is a fundamental ideological difference between abstinence-based and safer sex–based, or comprehensive, curricula. Abstinence-based sexuality education programs generally stress that there is no acceptable alternative to postponing sexual intercourse. Such programs are based on traditional values and often promote conservative religious doctrine. The goal of such programs is to encourage adolescents to postpone sexual intercourse until marriage to an opposite-sex partner.

Looking At . . .

. . . Thinking About

While most Americans want comprehensive sexuality education, a loud minority oppose it. What is your position on sexuality education in schools? At what age should it be provided, if at all?

The comprehensive sexuality education programs advocate postponement of sexual intercourse but recognize that not all adolescents will adopt this recommendation. Thus, they also emphasize birth control and safer sex practices. Many teenagers who are receiving sexuality education are already sexually active, and others will elect to become active despite recommendations to wait. Therefore, comprehensive educational programs also encourage adolescents to adopt practices that will minimize risks of STIs and unwanted pregnancy. Additionally, comprehensive sexuality education programs do not invariably assume that all teenagers have traditional values. They generally offer information to all, including those for whom heterosexual marriage is not necessarily a personal preference or goal.

Conservative social and political groups have effectively influenced some legislative bodies as well as school policymakers to bow to their concerns. In these cases, the sexuality education programs adopted on a state or local level are restrictive and reflect only the traditional beliefs of these very vocal conservative groups (Richards & Daley, 1994). As part of the 1996 Welfare Reform Act, new guidelines prohibited the awarding of any federal monies to sexuality education programs other than those promoting abstinence until marriage. Now, in order to qualify for federal funds, sexuality education programs must articulate the view that a "monogamous relationship in the context of marriage is the expected standard of human sexual activity" and that any variation

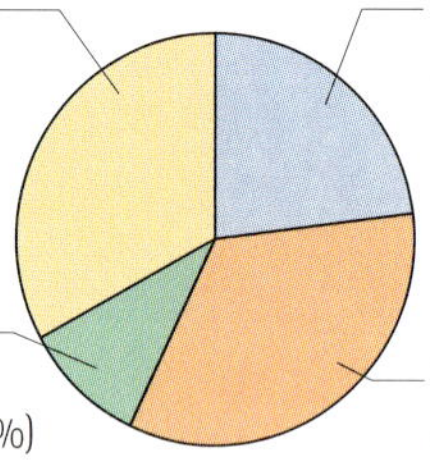

Figure 11.8 School District Sex Education Policies (Source: Alan Guttmacher Institute, Sexuality Education, *Facts in Brief,* New York: Alan Guttmacher Institute, 2002.)

thereof, including nonmarital sex, is likely to be harmful (Kempner, 1998, p. 16). Figure 11.8 shows a breakdown of school policies on sexuality education.

The debate over sexuality education has made its way into the courtroom. Several recent legal challenges to sexuality education and condom availability programs reflect the ongoing controversy over appropriate content, goals, and format. In one decision, the Supreme Judicial Court of Massachusetts concluded that "parents have no right to tailor public school programs to meet their individual religious or moral preferences" (Podgers, 1996, p. 44). As Collins (1997) noted, "politics rather than scientific evidence is driving the debate" over sexuality education. The controversy surrounding sexuality education was vividly illustrated when Surgeon General Jocelyn Elders was fired in 1994 because she openly recommended that masturbation be taught in sexuality education curricula as a means of reducing problems with adolescents' sexual health.

Cross-cultural comparisons are helpful in examining the effects of sexuality education on adolescent sexual behavior. Overall, countries in which attitudes are most open about sexuality and in which sexuality education is incorporated in the school curriculum have lower rates of unwanted pregnancies and STIs (Boonstra, 2002; World Health Organization, 1993). In Sweden, where comprehensive sexuality education is offered in every school beginning in the elementary grades, rates of unplanned pregnancies and STIs are much lower than in the United States. In fact, rates of teen pregnancy are higher in the United States than in most Western cultures—seven times higher than in the Netherlands, six times higher than in France, and four times higher than in Germany (Berne & Huberman, 1999). In some countries where HIV infection rates have soared, such as Thailand and Zimbabwe, mandatory and aggressive sexuality education programs, beginning in elementary school, were implemented in an effort to curb the spread (Cotton, 1994). Because of such programs, rates of HIV and STI infections have started to decline. In the United States, sexuality education is not mandatory in all school systems, and most programs emphasize abstinence as the only acceptable behavior. Our cultural ambivalence toward sexuality is manifested in many sectors of our society, including the educational system.

In the following sections, we'll look at some existing sexuality education programs, along with research findings on their effectiveness. We'll focus on the scope of the programs, benefits and risks, format, and context and setting. In examining the sexuality education programs, we'll refer to the *Guidelines for Comprehensive Sexuality Education* developed by the Sexuality Information and Education Council of the United States (SIECUS, National Guidelines Task Force, 1991). In 1990, this task force of twenty professionals from various disciplines established proposed guidelines for sexuality education. The guidelines suggested that every sexuality education program include the six key concepts and related topics listed in Table 11.4. The SIECUS guidelines are the standard against which existing programs are evaluated by many sex educators and researchers (Goodson & Edmundson, 1994; Klein et al., 1994).

Comprehensive Sexuality Education

Safer Choices, one of several comprehensive sexuality education curricula, is designed to encourage teenagers either to delay sexual intercourse or to increase condom use if they are already sexually active. The program addresses attitudes and beliefs, social skills, knowledge, social and media influences, peer norms, and parent-child communication (Coyle et al., 1996). The principles used in *Safer Choices* are derived from social cognitive theories. One important aspect of *Safer Choices* is the emphasis on skills

TABLE 11.4 SIECUS's Six Key Concepts and Topics To Be Included in a Comprehensive Sexuality Education Program

Key Concept	Topics	Key Concept	Topics
Key Concept 1: Human Development	Reproductive anatomy and physiology Reproduction Puberty Body image Sexual identity and orientation	Key Concept 4: Sexual Behavior	Sexuality throughout life Masturbation Shared sexual behavior Abstinence Human sexual response Fantasy Sexual dysfunction
Key Concept 2: Relationships	Families Friendship Love Dating Marriage and lifetime commitments Parenting	Key Concept 5: Sexual Health	Contraception Abortion Sexually transmissible infections and HIV infection Sexual abuse Reproductive health
Key Concept 3: Personal Skills	Values Decision making Communication Assertiveness Negotiation Finding help	Key Concept 6: Society and Culture	Sexuality and society Gender roles Sexuality and the law Sexuality and religion Diversity Sexuality and the arts Sexuality and the media

development. Using such strategies as modeling and role playing, students rehearse such skills as negotiation, assertiveness, and refusal. Students practice reading condom labels, obtaining condoms, and putting them on. To increase peer acceptance of safer sex and delayed sexual initiation, the program employs peer educators. Popular students are recruited and trained for this position. These peer educators can influence peer norms for sexuality more effectively than adults can because other students more readily identify with them (Ferguson, 1998). A related component of the program involves saturating the school environment with events, information, and services that reinforce the classroom topics. *Safer Choices* (and several other safer sex curricula) also provides information to help parents talk more openly about sexuality with their children.

Programs such as *Safer Choices* follow most of the guidelines recommended by the SIECUS task force. They are quite comprehensive in coverage, include skills building, and attempt to increase peer acceptance of safer sex practices (Coyle et al., 1996). Studies suggest that sexuality education alone may not be sufficient for changing adolescents' sexual risk taking. The most effective programs seem to be those that incorporate additional resources. For example, one study reported that sexuality education combined with a free in-school health clinic that provided contraceptives, pregnancy testing, and sexual health counseling led to a 30% decrease in pregnancy rate over a 2-year period (Zabin, Hirsch, Smith, Streett, & Hardy, 1986). The program did not encourage students to become more sexually active. Compared with students who did not participate in the program, those who received the sexuality education and access to the clinic tended to delay initiation of sexual intercourse by 7 months, on average. Additionally, access to the education program and the clinic increased contraceptive use among sexually active students. Therefore, sexuality education combined with sexual health resources may have a desirable effect on adolescent sexual health.

11.5 on the web

Sexuality education remains a controversial but critically important issue in the United States. A number of agencies and organizations address issues related to sexuality education. We recommend visiting the site sponsored by Planned Parenthood, which you can access through a link at **www.ablongman.com/mcanulty2e.**

What is the mission of the organization? Click on the Research Information link to find articles on sexuality education. What are the organization's views on sexuality education? What are the benefits of comprehensive sexuality education?

IN YOUR own words

Tina Rae Sparks
Trinity College

I think that abstinence should be encouraged much more highly than contraception and condom usage. We have gotten so far away from morality that some people do not even see it as an answer to many of the problems so prevalent in our society today.

Abstinence Education

Abstinence-based sexuality education programs were originally developed in reaction to so-called value-free programs. Essentially, the label "value-free" was used as a criticism of sexuality education programs that did not exclusively promote sexual abstinence prior to heterosexual marriage. There are several abstinence-based curricula. Among the best known is a curriculum named *Sex Respect.* This program is widely used and has received some government funding through the United States Office of Adolescent Pregnancy Programs.

The *Sex Respect* curriculum consists of eleven lessons designed to help students "realize that true sexual freedom includes the freedom to say 'no' to sex outside of marriage" (Mast, 1990). Most notable about *Sex Respect* are its imbalanced coverage, exclusions, and gender stereotypes (Goodson & Edmundson, 1994). For instance, although there are drawings of male genitals, there are no illustrations of female genitals. The labia and the clitoris are not even mentioned. Contraception is conspicuously omitted. The curriculum manual claims that teaching contraception increases sexual promiscuity and does not reduce pregnancy or abortion rates. Several gender stereotypes are perpetuated by *Sex Respect.* Males are described as "more readily excitable" and as often feeling "pressured to go further than they want to sexually (by girls who want to have sex)." Females are stereotyped as less impulsive, more levelheaded about sex, and having a "natural tendency" for more emotional warmth and closeness than males.

Sex Respect does not meet the recommended standards of the SIECUS guidelines for sexuality education. This and other abstinence-based sexuality education programs have been shown to contain medical misinformation, to exclude important facts, and to promote gender stereotypes. Abstinence-based programs are much less comprehensive in coverage than safer sex curricula (Klein et al., 1994). The most important question is the effectiveness of these programs. Unfortunately, there have been very few systematic efforts to evaluate their effectiveness (Jacobs & Wolf, 1995). Although students who participate in abstinence-based sexuality education later report more favorable attitudes toward sexual abstinence (Olsen, Weed, Ritz, & Jensen, 1991), it is unclear how these attitudes are enacted in their actual sexual practices. In one study of the effectiveness of abstinence-based sexuality education, participants actually reported an *increase* in sexual behavior following the program (Christopher & Roosa, 1990). In summary, the effectiveness of abstinence-based sexuality education curricula remains unknown.

One serious problem with abstinence-based sexuality education is that it usually does not serve the needs of adolescents who need such education most—those who are already sexually active. Because of the exclusive emphasis on abstinence, sexually active teenagers may tend to ignore what is being taught. Further, because most abstinence-based sexuality education curricula do not cover contraception, potentially lifesaving information is withheld from the students at highest risk for unwanted pregnancy and STIs, including HIV.

Sexuality Education in Perspective

The controversy over sexuality education reflects our cultural ambivalence about sexuality, especially childhood and adolescent sexuality. Curiously, most parents and teachers support sexuality education, but a significant minority rigidly insist that these programs be abstinence-based and that they avoid presenting topics that have historically been sensitive, such as masturbation, contraception, and homosexuality. Although questions about the effectiveness of sexuality education in reducing high-risk sexual behavior remain unanswered, several consistent findings have emerged:

1. Contrary to the fears of individuals who espouse traditional values, sexuality education does *not* promote sexual activity. In fact, sexuality education programs

assist in reducing teen pregnancy. In addition, comprehensive programs do not increase the chance that teens will have sex at an earlier age or more frequently or with more partners. They do, however, increase the probability that teenagers will use contraception when they do have sex (Kirby, 2001).

2. Sexuality education may not be sufficient to change sexual behavior among sexually active teenagers. The best results are often obtained when such education is combined with increased availability of contraceptives (usually condoms), reproductive counseling, and sexual health services, such as STI screening. Additionally, programs that use peer counselors and teach skills useful for sexual decision making (such as assertiveness) are generally more effective (Ku, Sonenstein, & Pleck, 1992; Mahler, 1996). Finally, culturally sensitive pregnancy prevention programs seem advisable. The most effective peer counselor programs employ counselors who share the ethnic and cultural background as well as the sexual values of the targeted students (Ferguson, 1998).

3. The most effective sexuality education curricula involve the parents of participating students. In fact, parents may be much more influential in shaping adolescent sexual behavior than any school-based sexuality education course. Students who are able to discuss sexuality and their related concerns openly with parents have fewer sex partners and are less likely to engage in unsafe sexual practices (Holtzman & Rubinson, 1995). Again, timing is critical. Adolescents who talked to their mothers about sex prior to initiating sexual intercourse are three times more likely to use condoms than teens who did not communicate with their mothers (Miller, Levin, Whitaker, & Ku, 1998). Parent-teenager discussions about sexual risks and precautions are only helpful, though, when parents are open and comfortable about having these talks (Whitaker, Miller, May, & Levin, 1999).

Ultimately, the most effective intervention to increase adolescent sexual health is one that combines school-based sexuality education with open communication about sexuality between parents and their children. Only when they receive safer-sex messages from all possible sources, including the media and their peers, will adolescents significantly reduce their sexual risk taking.

In summary, we concur with Kirby (1999), who concluded, after devoting 20 years to the study of sexuality education, that curricula that focus on reducing sexual behaviors, strengthen students' communication and refusal skills, use interactive teaching methods, are age-appropriate and culturally sensitive, employ trained teachers or peers, and are theory-driven are effective in reducing unintended pregnancies and STIs. Several programs have been shown to reduce adolescent sexual risk taking and pregnancy and birth rates. Kirby cautions, however, that "rarely is anything as simple as we initially perceive it to be, especially when it comes to adolescent sexual behavior" (1999, p. 92).

11.6 on the web

A teen's willingness to discuss sexuality issues with a parent can be vital to her or his sexual health. Go to **www.ablongman.com/mcanulty2e** and click on Sexual Health Communication and Summary Findings. Summarize what you learn about teen communication with parents and doctors.

As a teenager were you able to discuss sexual matters with your parents or a health care provider? If so, what do you think helped make communication possible? If not, why not?

HEALTHY DECISION MAKING

By now it should be clear that sexuality education is one of the keys to healthy sexuality. Realizing that many of us did not have the benefit of receiving information about our bodies, the reproductive process, risks of STIs, and pregnancy when we were young, we can try to ensure that the children of the future profit from what we have learned. One way to do so is to be prepared to discuss sexuality with your children, should you decide to become a parent. Parents should start talking about reproduction and sex by the time their children are about 5 or 6 years old—*but it is never too late!* Remember, children are sexual beings from birth and are introduced to messages about sexuality very early—through friends, television, music, and the culture at large. If you want to encourage your child to have a healthy perspective on sexuality, you need to be prepared to take an active role in her or his education. Here are some tips on talking with children about sex.

- Acknowledge that because sexuality is a private matter, you both may feel a little embarrassed to discuss it. Admit your own embarrassment to your child and acknowledge her or his possible embarrassment. Laugh together if laughing relieves tension—but emphasize that sex organs and sex are perfectly normal.
- Prepare by reading a book or two on the topic. Learn proper terms for body parts, and encourage your child to use them.
- Practice your discussion with another adult, preferably one with a little experience, who can offer support and advice.
- Remember that one talk is not enough. Think of sexuality education as a process that should involve deeper conversations and more detailed information as your child grows.
- Find "teachable moments"—while watching television, when you notice your child staring at someone who is nude, when a pet is giving birth, or when you or another customer at the drug store is purchasing tampons or sanitary napkins. These are all good times to address issues of sexuality in ways that are relevant to your child at that moment.
- It is okay to tell your child too much. Children will take in what they can and forget the rest. A good sign that you have said enough is when the child loses interest. Many facts will have to be repeated over time.
- Use and encourage your child to read age-appropriate books on sexual topics.
- If you don't have an answer to your child's question, tell the child that you don't know, but make sure you look up the answer and discuss it with your child later.
- If you discover you made a mistake, don't worry about it—just make sure you correct it later.

(SOURCE: Adapted from De Freitas, 1998)

summary

THEORIES OF SEXUAL DEVELOPMENT

- Psychoanalytic theory views human sexual development as a conflicted process requiring progression through several psychosexual stages. In contrast, psychosocial theory describes healthy development as requiring mastery of and progression through different social challenges. Social cognitive theories of sexual development stress the importance of life experiences, learning, and personal beliefs and values.

CHILDHOOD SEXUALITY: BIRTH TO 8 YEARS

- Sexual development continues after birth through the childhood years. Contrary to beliefs prevalent in our culture, childhood is a period of natural sexual curiosity and exploration. Despite parental concerns, sexual rehearsal play is a normal and healthy part of development.

PREADOLESCENT SEXUALITY: 8 TO 12 YEARS

- During preadolescence, children are increasingly concerned with peer acceptance and have a more realistic understanding of sexuality. This is the period in which sexual exploration becomes more purposeful and pleasure-oriented. Many preadolescents engage in sexual behavior, which often includes masturbation, heterosexual experimentation, and same-sex activity.

SEXUALITY IN ADOLESCENCE: 12 TO 18 YEARS

- By adolescence, a majority of individuals in the United States have some sexual experience. This developmental stage is characterized by the dramatic physical changes of puberty and the struggle to establish one's sense of identity. In general, teenagers view the experience of puberty as a positive change.

- The vast majority of adolescent males and most females have experienced masturbation. Most teenagers begin dating and have increasing experience with sexual behavior. By high school graduation, most males and females report having had sexual intercourse.

ISSUES IN ADOLESCENT SEXUALITY

- Although sexuality is problem-free for most teenagers, nearly one in four sexually active adolescents contracts a sexually transmissible infection, and up to one in ten teenaged women has an unplanned pregnancy. Many in the United States are increasingly concerned about these problems, but there is much controversy over the best solution.
- The majority of people in the United States favor providing sexuality education in the schools, but there are major disagreements on what to teach and how best to present it. Despite the fears of some parents and lawmakers, sexuality education does not make teenagers more sexually active and may help reduce some of the problems associated with adolescent sexuality.

CHAPTER 12

Sexual Development in Adulthood

I don't quite remember when I really felt like I was an adult. I guess probably first as a teenager, but not totally till I started college. I was finally on my own and free. It was really exciting but also kind of scary. I was away from home, from my friends, from high school. It was like starting over in a sense. The girls in college, well, they were intimidating. They too were adults. . . . The way they acted, the way they dressed, even the way they walked and looked at guys was different.

(A 21-year-old male college student)

I would never marry someone without knowing them inside and out, and I think you can only do that if you live together for a while. My parents probably would not approve but I am not going to take any chances on something as important as marriage. I know a lot of people who are living with their boyfriends.

(A 23-year-old female college student)

Getting married to my partner was the most important decision I ever made. Although we both had to make some changes in the beginning, we are totally happy together. In fact, I could not imagine going through life without my wife.

(A 54-year-old married male)

I remember getting married and thinking that we would be together always, forever happy together. After 12 years of marriage, I see things a little differently. Not that I regret marrying my husband, but our relationship has changed. For one thing, I never really anticipated how much work a marriage would be! I am happy, more than less. Would I do it again? Yes, probably. Would I do it differently? Yes, definitely.

(A 38-year-old married female)

Divorce? No, it could never happen to me.

Divorce? No, it could never happen to me. That's what I thought until one winter evening, out of the blue, my wife told me she thought we should separate. At first, I didn't believe it. But when she said she thought I should sleep in the guest bedroom that night, I realized she was serious. Sure, we had had our problems but who hadn't? I was devastated for almost 1 year and a half. Now, I am happier than I ever was during the 10 years we were married. At first, dating again made me feel uncomfortable. But I have had the time of my life, and I have met some interesting women who tell similar stories to mine.

(A 41-year-old divorced male)

PSYCHOSOCIAL CHALLENGES OF ADULTHOOD

Most young adults like to think that they have put their teenage years behind them and that they are ready to face the challenges of adulthood. However, for the majority of young adults, the developmental challenges of adolescence have yet to be completely resolved. The psychosocial challenges faced in adolescence continue for many years, and new ones

CLOSE UP ON culture

Sexual Attitudes around the World

The diversity of sexual attitudes across cultures has fascinated sexologists for years. Historically, researchers categorized cultural attitudes as either sexually permissive or nonpermissive. Sexually permissive cultures were those that espoused tolerant and liberal attitudes toward sexuality education, nonmarital sexuality, homosexuality, and media depictions of eroticism and nudity. Nonpermissive cultures held restrictive and more conservative viewpoints. Such cultures were believed to oppose sexuality education, homosexuality, sex outside of marriage, and virtually all portrayals of sexuality. Recent research, however, reveals that these classifications of cultural sexual attitudes are overly simplistic.

Widmer, Treas, and Newcomb (1998) compared attitudes toward "premarital sex, teenage sex, extramarital sex, and homosexual sex" in 24 countries. A total of 33,590 people were asked the following questions:

1. Do you think it is wrong or not wrong for a man and woman to have sexual relations before marriage?
2. What if they are in their early teens, say, under 16 years old?
3. What about a married person having sexual relations with someone other than his or her husband or wife?
4. What about sexual relations between two adults of the same sex?"

For each question, the answer choices were "always wrong," "almost always wrong," "wrong only sometimes," or "not wrong at all."

Overall, some basic similarities across cultures were uncovered. In all 24 cultures, 61% of people believed that sex before marriage was acceptable. Nearly the same number, however, believed that sex between young teenagers was wrong. Extramarital sex drew even stronger disapproval, as 96% of respondents rated it as "wrong." There were some differences across cultures in acceptance of sexual practices. From the answers of participants, six distinct viewpoints, or "sexual regimes," each advocating different sexual standards, emerged:

1. *Teen permissive cultures,* which included Germany, Austria, Sweden, and Slovenia, expressed relatively high levels of acceptance of adolescent sex and nonmarital sex.
2. *Sexual conservative cultures* expressed fairly strong disapproval of virtually any form of sex outside of traditional marriage, including teen sex, extramarital sex, and homosexual sex. These cultures, including the United States, Ireland, Northern Ireland, and Poland, were more ambivalent in their attitudes toward sex before marriage. Some members of each culture disapproved, but a sizable group believed that sex before marriage was acceptable.
3. *Homosexual permissive cultures,* such as the Netherlands, Norway, the Czech Republic, Canada, and Spain, express "high levels of acceptance of homosexuality." Like most of the other cultures, these cultures were fairly tolerant of sex before marriage, but intolerant of teen sex and extramarital sex.
4. *The Philippines* was unique with respect to sexual standards. Essen-

appear in early adulthood. The single major developmental challenge of adulthood is the formation of intimate relationships. For the majority of people, this means finding a long-term partner, probably starting a family, and planning for the future. In the search for that "special person," though, we must also continue to find ourselves.

Sexual Identity

From adolescence into early adulthood, one ongoing developmental challenge is the formation of a **sexual identity** (Levine, 1998). Sexual identity consists of gender identity, sexual orientation, and erotic intention (that is, personal preferences regarding specific sexual activities). Sexual identity is one's sexual self-view, or self-concept. A healthy, positive sexual self-view helps you enter relationships more freely and with fewer inhibitions. It also helps you clarify the type of persons you find sexually attractive. People with positive sexual self-views have more varied sexual experiences, are more open about sex, and show many more positive emotions in sexual relationships than people with negative sexual self-views (Andersen & Cyranowski, 1994).

Forming a sexual identity depends not only on your personal views and beliefs but also on your experiences with past and current sexual partners and on the cultural messages you are exposed to during development. Sexual identity can be understood as the process of acquiring **sexual meanings**, or internalized interpretations of sexual experiences and cultural norms (Daniluk, 1998). Sexual meanings are created through interactions with the environment. These sexual meanings are highly individual, since they are shaped by personal experiences, but they are also subject to some constraints because

SEXUAL IDENTITY
A person's sexual self-view, made up of gender identity, sexual orientation, and specific sexual preferences.

SEXUAL MEANINGS
Internalized interpretations of sexual experiences and cultural norms that contribute to one's sexual identity.

tially, Filipinos' answers to the four questions revealed "extremely conservative attitudes toward all kinds of nonmarital sex." The consensus in this culture was that sex outside of traditional heterosexual marriage is always wrong.

5. *Japan,* too, earned the distinction of a separate category, mostly because of the unique tendency of Japanese respondents to rate sex before marriage as "wrong only sometimes." Other than this apparent conditional acceptance of premarital sex, the Japanese culture was similar to other cultures in disapproving of teen sex and extramarital sex. It was the most disapproving of homosexual sex of all the cultures examined.
6. *Moderate residual cultures* were mostly indistinguishable from the average across all cultures. As a whole, these cultures tended to discourage nonmarital sex, with the exception of sex before marriage between adults. Essentially, this category included the cultures that did not fit into any of the other five: Australia, Great Britain, Hungary, Italy, Bulgaria, Russia, New Zealand, and Israel.

This study is unique in demonstrating differences in sexual attitudes across diverse cultures. As the authors expected, simply categorizing countries as sexually permissive or nonpermissive does not capture the diversity of sexual attitudes. People within a culture may have permissive views toward some sexual practices but restrictive views toward others. We must remain cautious of overgeneralizations and stereotypes. Even within a given culture, some diversity is evident. Consider, for example, the United States and the other sexual conservative cultures, which are quite divided in their attitudes toward sex before marriage; a large number of people oppose any sex before marriage, yet most young adults have had sex before marriage. Perhaps it would be more accurate to describe U.S. sexual attitudes as ambivalent with respect to premarital sex.

Widmer and his colleagues acknowledged that their results are mostly descriptive of Western cultures, since only two Asian cultures—Japan and the Philippines—were included in the comparison. These two Asian countries were very different from Western cultures and from each other, each representing a unique sexual regime. Other research shows that Middle Eastern and Asian cultures prize female virginity much more than Western cultures do. In some Middle Eastern cultures, such as Jordan, Egypt, Syria, and Lebanon, female chastity is a matter of family honor, and a woman who initiates sexual intercourse before marriage "is worse than a murderer, affecting not just one victim, but her family and her tribe" (Jehl, 1999). The woman who has dishonored her family by losing her virginity may be murdered in what is called an "honor killing." By some estimates, several hundred women are killed each year for this reason in Arabic cultures. The prohibition of sex outside of marriage is so intense that some of these countries have laws exonerating any man who has murdered a female relative who was caught having sex either before or outside of marriage.

Both survey findings and dramatic case reports show that sexual attitudes are heavily influenced by cultural standards. Cultural norms are extremely diverse with respect to sexual behavior, and they may vary over time within a given culture. Only by appreciating the diversity in cultural scripts can we truly understand the various sexual meanings that people assimilate and how these meanings shape sexual practices throughout life.

each of us is born into a "pre-existing sexual world with its own laws, norms, values, and meanings" (Daniluk, 1998, p. 11). Sexual meanings, then, depend not only on personal experiences but also on the cultural context. Consider, for example, views of first sexual intercourse. First sexual intercourse for boys is a step in the transition from childhood to adulthood, often euphemistically referred to as having "scored." In other words, for boys, the sexual meaning of first intercourse is competitive and denotes winning (that is, "scoring"). For girls, the sexual meaning is different; many feel they have "lost" their virginity and surrendered their most precious commodity. Some cross-cultural differences in sexual meanings are explored in Close Up on Culture: Sexual Attitudes around the World.

Sexual meanings are influenced not only by culture and gender but also by sexual orientation. "Having sex" takes on different meaning for gay men and lesbians, for whom heterosexual intercourse is definitely not the norm. In her humorous essay entitled "Are We Having Sex Now or What?" Christina (1992) grappled with the ambiguous meanings inherent in what our culture views as "having sex." She recalled that she had never included one particular male partner in her count of sexual partners because he never penetrated her vagina with his penis. That was nonetheless "one of the best" sexual encounters for her. Her counting problem became especially vexing when she started having sex with women. Was that "having sex" or something else? American culture has established a few sexual absolutes—for example, penile-vaginal intercourse always counts as sex—but these leave much room for ambiguity. Recall from Chapter 8 the concept of *technical virginity.* Some couples may engage in a variety of sexual acts other than penile-vaginal intercourse in order to maintain technical virginity. Do those acts count as "having sex"? Within our own cultural context and based on our own life experiences, we all seek sexual meanings as we form our sexual identities.

The unfolding of sexual identity, or sexual self-concept, is a lifetime process of self-discovery in which a person may be forced to review and redefine earlier interpretations. The sexual self-concept is composed of relevant self-knowledge related to sexuality. It involves awareness of one's physical attributes and body image, beliefs and emotions, needs and desires. It is shaped by sexual history, current circumstances, and expectations and hopes for the future. The sexual self-concept is a product of private thoughts and public messages, of personal experiences and social context, of individual views and experiences with partners. It is shaped by social identification—one's views of oneself as Christian, husband, lesbian, middle-aged, pregnant, and so on.

Unlike physical attributes, which change very slowly in a lifetime, the sexual self-concept is fluid and evolving. Sexual identity formation begins in childhood and continues into the adult years. Sexual identity development often involves experimentation—a kind of "trying on" of experiences. Many gay men and lesbians, for example, are involved in heterosexual relationships before discovering and accepting their homosexual orientation (Ettorre, 1980). And many bisexual women do not completely form their sexual identity until well into their adult years (Fox, 1996). As sexual meanings change, so may the sexual self-concept, and many sexual meanings are learned or modified within the context of intimate relationships.

12.1 on the web

SIECUS maintains an extensive list of sources on adult sexuality. Visit **www.ablongman.com/mcanulty2e,** find the link to the SIECUS Web site, and review the titles.

We recommend that you visit a library and check out some of these titles to supplement the information found in this chapter.

Phases of Adult Sexual Development

Each phase of adult development offers special challenges and opportunities. For most people, successful adjustment and personal growth in adulthood begin with the search for intimacy. The next challenge is negotiating the various roles that adults are expected to master. These roles may involve being a spouse or a partner in a long-term relationship, being a parent, having a career or trade, and being a member of a community. Many people find themselves trying to adapt to roles for which they feel unprepared, such as being divorced, remarried, or single. Late adulthood involves multiple life changes. Retirement signals the end of one's working life. Older adults must learn to adjust to the physical changes that accompany aging. Health problems may develop. These changes are not inevitably undesirable; older couples often reach new levels of satisfaction with their lives and relationships.

Early Adulthood

Recall from Chapter 11 that Erik Erikson theorized that people go through various psychosocial stages. Table 12.1 lists Erikson's adult stages. Beginning in early adulthood, one major psychosocial challenge involves developing a meaningful intimate relationship—that is, finding the "right person." The challenge, labeled **intimacy versus isolation** by Erikson (1963), marks a transition in the lives of most people. By early adulthood, most people have distanced themselves from their parents and are seeking to establish an intimate and committed relationship with another person. According to Erikson's theory, this transition is made possible by the identity formation that occurred during adolescence. After an individual establishes a sense of identity, personal goals, and values, the next challenge is finding a partner who will share these goals and values. In other words, we must find ourselves before we can find someone for ourselves.

As we enter our 20s, we continue our search for sexual identity, establish sexual meanings, and clarify our sexual selves. This process is affected by the quest for an intimate relationship, which affords further opportunity for self-discovery. Once we meet that special person, we attempt to establish an equilibrium—a relationship that will be mutually satisfying, both sexually and emotionally (Levine, 1998). Relationships that are sexually and emotionally satisfying in the beginning do not necessarily remain so, however. Steps must be taken to preserve the balance of the relationship. At this stage, couples must learn to negotiate conflict while also nurturing the relationship.

INTIMACY VERSUS ISOLATION
The stage described in Erikson's psychosocial theory of development during which young adults are faced with the challenge of finding a meaningful intimate relationship; if the challenge is not met, a person faces the prospect of loneliness.

Other psychosocial challenges face us in our 20s, including clarifying and pursuing vocational choices, establishing financial and emotional independence from parents,

TABLE 12.1 Erikson's Adult Stages of Development

APPROXIMATE AGE	ERIKSON'S PSYCHOSOCIAL CHALLENGES	ERIKSON'S VIEWPOINT: SIGNIFICANT EVENTS AND INFLUENCES
20 to 40 years (young adulthood)	Intimacy versus isolation	The primary task at this stage is to form strong friendships and to achieve a sense of love and companionship (or a shared identity) with another person. Feelings of loneliness or isolation are likely to result from an inability to form friendships or an intimate relationship. Key social agents are lovers, spouses, and close friends (of both sexes).
40 to 65 years (middle adulthood)	Generativity versus stagnation	At this stage, adults face the tasks of becoming productive in their work and raising their families or otherwise looking after the needs of young people. These standards of "generativity" are defined by one's culture. Those who are unable or unwilling to assume these responsibilities become stagnant and/or self-centered. Significant social agents are the spouse, children, and cultural norms.
Old age	Ego integrity versus despair	The older adult looks back at life, viewing it as either a meaningful, productive, and happy experience or a major disappointment full of unfulfilled promises and unrealized goals. One's life experiences, particularly social experiences, determine the outcome of this final life challenge.

and expanding social networks. During this decade, and into our 30s, many of us learn new roles: spouse, parent, working person, and member of the community and of diverse social organizations. As Levine (1998) noted, for many of us, the 30s are about ambition, success, and fatigue, or the process of learning about our potential as well as our limitations, whether emotional, social, or physical. Many young women must juggle multiple roles. Besides social and vocational challenges, they must learn to adapt to the new role of mother, experiencing changes in self-image and in relationships with significant others (Daniluk, 1998). They must cope with changes in their appearance and their body image that are induced by pregnancy and childbirth. Some may also continue striving to live up to the culture's standards of feminine beauty, personified as a young woman who is attractive and care-free. Perhaps it is no surprise, then, that young adult women are the major consumers of cosmetics, health-care products, dieting aids, and cosmetic surgery (Hesse-Biber, 1996; Seid, 1994; Tantleff-Dunn & Thompson, 1995).

Historically, young adults have been viewed as being in their sexual prime. This is perhaps true if we accept a performance-oriented view of sexuality. Sex drive is higher and fantasies are more frequent in young adults. Young males experience near-automatic erections and require minimal stimulation, and their refractory period after orgasm is often quite brief (see Chapter 4). Growing up in a culture that tends to suppress female sexuality, young women may take longer to overcome their inhibitions and to reach their "prime" (Daniluk, 1998). For both sexes, young adulthood is a period of sexual experimentation and learning, although the cultural rules are different for women and men.

For many people, though, the decade of the 30s is also about starting over. Relationship breakups, career changes, and new relationships require many individuals to revise and adjust their goals, their expectations, and even their sexual meanings. These major life changes may add to the other challenges of midlife, the 40s and 50s.

Being single at midlife is not inevitably problematic. Some midlife women, for example, find distinct advantages to "flying solo" as they enjoy freedom and independence.

Midlife

According to Erikson (1959), the major midlife psychosocial challenge involves **generativity versus stagnation.** Middle-aged persons must assume responsible adult roles in a variety of settings, such as the workplace and the family, and must prepare the next generation for productive lives. The failure to master these varied roles leads to feelings of personal stagnation and self-centeredness (McAdams & de St. Aubin, 1992). Midlife also requires individuals to adjust to the inevitable physical changes of aging, which become increasingly obvious. Thinning hair and receding hairlines, slowed metabolism, weight gain and loss of muscle tone, decreased endurance, and greater vulnerability to illness are increasingly common as people progress through midlife. In women, the 50s mark the end of their reproductive years. Such changes naturally influence individuals' sexual self-view and may even lead some to question their sexual desirability (Greer, 1992; Levine, 1998). For women, in particular, "getting old" denotes a changing body image and a reduced feeling of sexual attractiveness (Bachmann, 1995). Men in their 40s and 50s typically notice a change in sexual functioning as their performance becomes less predictable. Erections, for example, become less automatic. For some men, this slowing in sexual functioning is particularly threatening and can lead to a host of negative emotions. The popular stereotype of a "midlife crisis" refers to the middle-aged man who desperately tries to compensate for his fears of age-related inadequacy. Fearing that he is "losing it," the man strives to regain his youth by altering his lifestyle and by choosing a younger partner. Middle-aged women in our culture may notice that men pay less attention to them (Bell, 1989). As one middle-aged mother noted, "I was walking down the street with my daughter the other day and a couple of men stopped and looked. Suddenly I became aware that they were looking at *her* and not me. It was a little hard on me. I felt proud of her, but at the same time, I felt bad for myself" (Barbach, 1993, p. 95).

Sex, fortunately, does not end in early adulthood (Hällström & Samuelsson, 1990). Although some middle-aged men and women struggle with their changing sexual functioning, many actually find that their sex lives improve. By this time in their lives, men and women are often more comfortable with sex, as their sexual selves are more clearly defined. Many feel that they have nothing left to prove and that they have learned more effective ways of achieving mutual sexual satisfaction. Some women even experience an increase in sexual desire as they enter midlife (Koster & Garde, 1993).

The natural slowing of sexual responsiveness may encourage middle-aged individuals to discover novel ways to enjoy sex, and their sexual encounters may last longer and be more fulfilling. Additionally, many partners who have been together a long time have developed resilience and effective problem-solving skills, and these may generalize to their ability to work out problems in the bedroom. Heterosexual women who have passed their childbearing years are no longer affected by fears of unwanted pregnancy. In fact, for women, changes in sexual activity in midlife are more directly related to such factors as whether they have an available partner who is healthy and emotionally supportive than to age-related physical changes (Gannon, 1994). Suffering from depression or having an alcoholic partner is associated with decreased sex drive in middle-aged women (Hällström & Samuelsson, 1990).

Couples who have been together in a long-term relationship have often achieved a high level of emotional and sexual intimacy. Couples whose grown children have left home often experience a renewed satisfaction in their relationship afforded by increased privacy and reduced parenting demands. Other adults, however, are starting over as they enter midlife. Because almost one-third of divorces occur in midlife (Clarke, 1995), many persons become single again at this age. The prospects of dating after being married for many years may appear daunting to many middle-aged men and

GENERATIVITY VERSUS STAGNATION
According to Erikson, the stage of midlife, during which the major psychosocial challenge is to assume responsible adult roles in multiple settings; if the challenge is not met, a person faces the likelihood of experiencing a sense of self-centeredness and feeling nonproductive.

INTEGRITY VERSUS DESPAIR
According to Erikson, the psychosocial challenge of late adulthood, in which individuals review their lifetime accomplishments and either find a sense of satisfaction or struggle with a sense of despair over lost opportunities.

women, particularly if they are already struggling to adjust to their changing physical appearance, body image, and sexual functioning. Being single at midlife is not inevitably problematic, however. Some midlife women, for example, find distinct advantages to "flying solo" as they enjoy greater freedom and independence (Marks, 1996).

did YOU know?

Less than half of the 280 midlife women Mansfield, Koch, and Voda (1998) studied reported changes in their sexual responding. Nearly 25% of those who did described improvements in their sex lives, including a stronger sex drive and a greater enjoyment of sex.

Late Adulthood

Late adulthood is characterized by multiple life changes. Older people encounter the final psychosocial challenge, which Erikson dubbed **integrity versus despair**, as they evaluate their lives, finding either a sense of satisfaction in their accomplishments or despair because they cannot find meaning (Erikson, 1959). From age 60 onward, individuals must deal with changes in occupation as they approach retirement. Those who derive a large measure of their identity from their occupation will find retirement threatening (Smolak, 1993), but most retirees do not find the change traumatic. The adjustment to retirement is complicated for those older adults who experience financial problems, a relatively common experience for older widowed women in particular (Daniluk, 1998). Health problems are more common among older adults, who may have multiple health complaints, including partial disability. With the exception of health concerns, though, the majority of older adults report as much satisfaction with their lives as younger adults do (Smolak, 1993).

Older adults who have solid social support networks, including a spouse, children, and friends, usually enjoy a better quality of life than do those who are socially isolated (Smolak, 1993). Retired individuals have more time to spend together. Older couples report higher levels of companionship, emotional closeness, and marital satisfaction than do younger couples (Giordano & Beckman, 1985). Couples who have been together for many decades usually know each other very well and are dedicated to each other. However, like their younger counterparts, older couples must maintain some separateness in their relationship in order not to feel emotionally crowded (Butler & Lewis, 1993).

According to Levine (1998), the best predictor of sexual activity in people who are 60 and older is the degree of sexual adjustment achieved in midlife. Individuals who stay physically healthy can enjoy a rewarding sex life well into their advanced years. They do, however, have to make adjustments in their sex lives. Lacking the stamina of their youth, older persons need to communicate freely and to be open to experimenting with varied positions, in order to learn which ones provide optimal pleasure while reducing fatigue. Some couples find that having sex in the morning is best because they are well rested, and older men tend to have firmer erections in the morning (Butler & Lewis, 1993).

For older adults—as for people at any age—a relaxing and stimulating atmosphere is most conducive to sexual intimacy. A gradual approach to lovemaking that involves prolonged gentle touching and foreplay is often beneficial. Finally, older adults may need to remember that sex is not about performing and that there are many ways to have sex other than penile-vaginal intercourse. Manual or oral stimulation is an effective way of pleasing one's partner when a firm and sustained erection is lacking. Older couples who are able to achieve emotional and sexual intimacy may indeed view this phase of their relationship as the "golden years."

IN YOUR own words

Jason Maravelias
Trinity College

I believe people are staying single longer because they want to reach their goals and dreams and don't want anyone or anything to stand in their way.

SINGLEHOOD

Historically, a single person was someone who had never married. According to the prevailing cultural script, being single is a temporary state that precedes marriage. Singles in our culture are expected to eventually find the "right" person, marry, and settle into a domestic life. The expectation is that the transition into married life will eventually be followed by establishing a family. As you will see, recent trends suggest that more and more people are challenging this cultural script.

TABLE 12.2 Marital Status by Race or Ethnic Origin: 1970 and 1998 (percentage of total U.S. population)

MARITAL STATUS	WHITE		AFRICAN AMERICAN		HISPANIC	
	1970	*1998*	*1970*	*1998*	*1970*	*1998*
Married	73%	59%	64%	39%	72%	55%
Unmarried						
Never married	16%	24%	21%	43%	19%	35%
Widowed	9%	7%	11%	7%	6%	3%
Divorced	3%	10%	4%	11%	4%	7%

SOURCE: Lugaila, 1998; Saluter & Lugaila, 1996

Never-married singles represent a growing segment of the adult population in the United States (Lugaila, 1998; Saluter & Lugaila, 1996). Some singles have simply decided to postpone marriage, an increasingly common trend in American culture over the past three decades. Others have elected never to marry. Yet another group of singles is single again. Since nearly half of marriages end in divorce, this group is sizable. Finally, many singles can be categorized as nontraditional. Nontraditional singles include all adults who are unmarried for legal, social, or professional reasons. For example, gay men and lesbians are not permitted to marry in the United States; thus, they can be described as nontraditional singles. Members of the clergy in some religious sects cannot marry for doctrinal reasons. In summary, the category of singlehood is varied and growing.

did YOU know?

Never-married persons represent the largest proportion of single adults—nearly 60% (Lugaila, 1998; Saluter & Lugaila, 1996).

Since the contemporary societal expectation is that all people will eventually marry, singlehood should be a temporary rather than a permanent state. Recent studies, however, reveal that this cultural script has been slowly but steadily changing. Consider the following findings: The number of 20- to 24-year-old women who had never married doubled between 1970 and 2000, from 36% to 73%. The corresponding percentages for men are 55% in 1970 and 84% in 2000. The percentage of never-married adults in the total U.S. population grew from 16% in 1970 to over 31% in 2000 (Fields & Casper, 2001). As you can see in Table 12.2, this trend is most pronounced for African-Americans, among whom the percentage of never-married adults doubled between 1970 and 1998 (Lugaila, 1998; Saluter & Lugaila, 1996).

What accounts for this apparent increase in the percentage of never-married adults in the United States? First, men and women are delaying the decision to marry. The average age at first marriage has increased over the past decade. Second, an increasing number of people view singlehood as an acceptable lifestyle. Given that the cultural script still emphasizes heterosexual marriage as the norm, what explains the increasing numbers of single adults? We'll examine some facts and fictions about singlehood prior to exploring patterns of dating and singlehood sexuality.

Singlehood: Myths, Misconceptions, and Facts

In the early 1970s, there was a change in attitude toward singlehood (Stein, 1975). The stereotype changed from "lonely losers" to "swinging singles." This change coincided with the so-called sexual revolution of the 1960s and 1970s (see Chapter 1). In general, though, the popular stereotype of singles has been fairly negative. Terms used to refer to adult singles, such as "old maid" for a woman, often carry a negative connotation. (Our culture views singlehood as more acceptable for men than for women.) Singles have been portrayed as lonely, immature, socially inept, unattractive, or otherwise undesirable persons. In other words, the stereotype implies that singles are people who want to be married but are unable to attract a partner (Cargan & Melko, 1982; Gordon, 1994). In fact, the Internet is full of sites for singles on how to find love and "cope" with singlehood, with little or no emphasis on the advantages of being single (e.g., www.singlesfaq.com).

As with all stereotypes, there may be a kernel of truth to those about singles, although they are mostly unfounded. It is true that, as a group, singles tend to report being less happy with their personal lives than married persons (see Figure 12.1). However, the majority of singles, up to 85%, report being very happy or generally satisfied with their personal lives. In this respect, single individuals tend to fare better than those who are divorced, separated, or widowed (Glenn & Weaver, 1988; Laumann, Gagnon, Michael, & Michaels, 1994). The most common complaint from singles concerns loneliness; up to 40% of singles identify loneliness as the major challenge of singlehood (Janus & Janus, 1993). However, almost the same percentage of singles report no major problems with being single.

Old stereotypes of singles as lonely and socially inept are changing. The majority of singles are happy and satisfied with their personal lives, especially if they enjoy a well-developed social network.

One flaw in most studies is that they lump a variety of singles into the same category. We should not expect the experience of singlehood to be the same for everyone. A divorced 40-year-old man, an unmarried 21-year-old female college student, and a never-married 55-year-old woman all qualify as single. However, they may share very little beyond that label. Singles who have a small but carefully maintained network of close friends tend to be satisfied with their lives (Barrett, 1999). In fact, the quality rather than the quantity of friendships and relationships seems most important. Singles who have a limited number of close and affectionate relationships report being better adjusted than those who have many superficial friendships (Fischer & Sollie, 1993). Many singles are able to meet their needs for intimacy through close personal friendships. The experience of being single is affected by other factors such as financial security. Single women who struggle financially tend to be more dissatisfied with their status than single women with steady incomes (Gordon, 1994).

In general, there are both advantages and disadvantages to being single. Besides loneliness, perhaps the greatest disadvantages stem from the cultural bias in favor of marriage—a single person often feels out of place at social gatherings, which are predominantly couple-oriented, and may have to endure questions from friends and family about why she or he is not married. These pressures have lessened in recent years, and singlehood has grown more acceptable. In fact, many popular prime-time television shows—*Friends, Scrubs, Will & Grace*—reflect this change by revolving around the lifestyles of single adults. With less pressure to be married, many people today *choose* singlehood because of the attractive benefits. Singles have complete freedom to direct their own lives without having to compromise. They are free to pursue educational and career developments and advancements. They have more time for personal growth and fulfillment. Singles also tend to be economically independent and self-sufficient. Finally, they have the freedom to pursue a variety of romantic possibilities and friendships. For some, reaping the benefits of singlehood may be an extended but temporary state, but others choose to be single permanently.

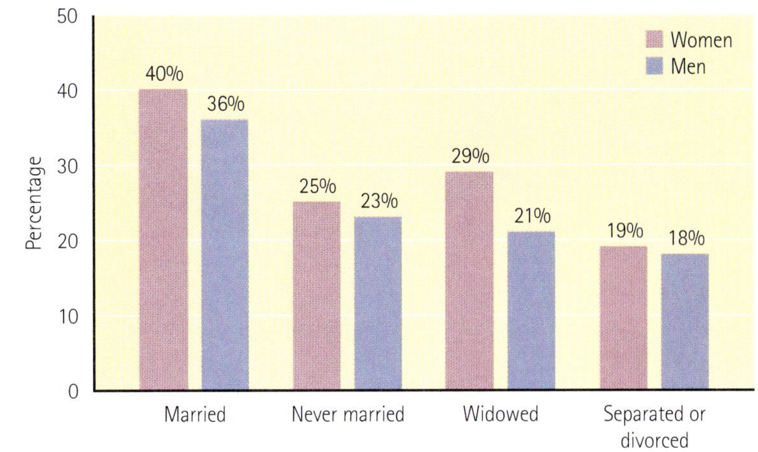

Figure 12.1 Reported Happiness, by Marital Status (Copyrighted 1988 by the National Council on Family Relations, Minneapolis, MN. Used by permission.)

As well as being a form of recreation, dating allows people to learn about themselves, to practice relationship skills, and to meet their needs for intimacy. Dating is also a way of finding a long-term partner.

Dating

In contemporary U.S. society, most people begin dating in adolescence. However, dating as we know it today is a relatively new social phenomenon. Only after World War I did dating become popular on college campuses. Dating became widespread among high school students during the 1950s (Gordon, 1978). Beginning in the 1960s, changing roles and opportunities allowed women more equality and freedom, including the freedom to ask men out (Hareven, 1977). Technological advances such as automobiles and telephones revolutionized dating in Western cultures. To understand how these technologies have influenced contemporary dating practices, try to imagine doing *without* them. Clearly, dating opportunities would be restricted. More recently, personal ads, computer networks, and dating services offer creative ways of meeting prospective dating partners.

According to various studies, dating serves several functions, including recreation, socialization, meeting personal needs, improving peer group status, and partner selection (Davidson & Moore, 1996). For most singles, dating usually serves more than one of these functions. Also, as people age, the functions of dating may change. For adolescents, dating may serve primarily to improve peer group status and as a socialization experience, whereas young adults may be seeking a partner.

The traditional dating process occurs in stages. At first, a person engages in casual dating, dating different people, simultaneously or sequentially, without expectations of commitment. As a couple spends more time together, dating implies more commitment. And as emotional commitment increases, so does the expectation of exclusive dating. The final stage of dating involves a mutual understanding of long-term commitment. At this stage, heterosexual couples are not formally engaged to be married, although they may intend to marry eventually.

Overall, men and women tend to be more accepting of sex in committed than in casual relationships, reflecting our culture's view that sex should be associated with emotional attachment, or love (Buss, 1994; DeLamater, 1987). Similar scripts have been reported in other cultures as well, including those of Russia, Japan, and Sweden (Sprecher & Hatfield, 1996; Weinberg, Lottes, & Shaver, 1995).

IN YOUR own words

Brian Kramer
University of Vermont

I believe cohabitation before marriage should be encouraged. It enables the couple to envision what life will be like once they are married.

Today, many young people's practices for establishing intimate relationships no longer follow this typical pattern. Casual dating, once called "playing the field," has been replaced with "hooking up." Hooking up involves sexual activity of one kind or another—it can mean anything from making out to a casual sexual encounter, with no expectation of any further involvement or commitments. The vast majority of college students think of hooking up as the latter (Raspberry, 2001). These encounters often originate in bars and clubs, where groups of young men and women go to meet. But that is not the only way young people meet these days. Another approach is through personal ads on the Web—sometimes called "cyberdating." The matchmaking Web sites and chat rooms on the Internet are too numerous to count. Young people today view surfing the personal ads as entertainment. And cyberdating is often done at "hyperspeed"—one personal ads user reported going out on 70 dates over just a few months by making Internet contacts (St. John, 2002). Safety issues associated with meeting Internet dates in person are discussed in Health Matters: Cyberdating Safety Advice.

Another interesting fad in dating is "speed dating," or "pre-dating." A dating service sets up an event where a group of men and women who don't know one another meet and engage in several 6-minute "pre-dates." Each person completes a form, listing only those individuals he or she would like to see again. The service matches up the lists and provides each person with the names of those between whom there is mutual interest ("How pre-dating works," 2002).

In general, it appears that dating has taken on a much faster pace, as young singles work and go to school longer hours and have less leisure time. Services like personal

HEALTH Matters

Cyberdating Safety Advice

Many young people today find the Web a great resource for meeting potential love interests. Internet communication can be very useful in getting to know someone, especially because there is no pressure to have a physical relationship. In addition, people often feel less shy and can act more assertive when communicating with others because they feel they have nothing to lose. Getting to know a person you have met over the Internet can feel easier than getting to know someone face-to-face. Unfortunately, this feeling can lead you to think you know that person better than you do and that you can trust them. You may find the following guidelines helpful if you get involved in cyberdating.

- Use a remote email service, not one provided by your Internet service provider, from which someone might be able to obtain personal information.
- Don't give out any personal information until you know the person very well—preferably only after you have been able to verify the person's identity.
- Have a photo and all the facts about the person before agreeing to meet him or her.
- Make sure a friend knows where you are going if you decide to meet this person.
- Check in with that friend during your date.
- Let your date know that your friend knows where you are and that you are checking in with him or her.
- Meet your date in a very public place. Never go to a private location, even if you have a friend with you.
- Be suspicious of someone who asks for financial assistance—e.g., asking you for airfare or hinting that you should purchase expensive gifts. He or she may be scamming you.
- Be suspicious of someone who asks to take photos or video footage of you in more intimate moments—this may be a scam to obtain pictures and video to sell.
- Use common sense!

SOURCE: Adapted from Dating Safely at www.cyberdatinghomepage.com/safe.html

ads and speed dating make it easier for people to meet a lot of potential love interests in a short amount of time.

Sexuality of Singles

By far, most research on sexuality among singles has been conducted with young adults, usually college students. This is because of the availability of this sample—for sex researchers, college students are conveniently accessible research participants. Consistent with the cultural script for sexual behavior, most studies of singles' sexuality refer to "premarital sex." Such references imply that although a person is engaging in sexual behavior, she or he will eventually marry and have marital sex. (People do, of course, sometimes have sex with partners other than their spouses; this is referred to as *extramarital sex* and is discussed in a later section of this chapter.) As noted earlier, however, many individuals elect to remain single, and others delay marriage. Therefore, we will not use the term "premarital sex" for sexual activity by singles.

Masturbation

The patterns of masturbation reported among adolescents remain fairly stable through young adulthood. The frequency of masturbation is slightly higher among never-married single men than among married men. Approximately half of single men report masturbating once a week or more often, compared to 44% of married men. Twenty-three percent of single men deny ever masturbating, as do 20% of married men. Approximately one-third of never-married single women masturbate weekly or more often, but only 16% of married women masturbate at this frequency (Janus & Janus, 1993). Similar findings were reported for the men who participated in the National Health and Social Life

Our personal sexual scripts specify how much intimacy we view as acceptable in relationships. A common script in Western cultures permits sexual activity between unmarried people if they are in love.

Survey (NHSLS) (Laumann et al., 1994): 41% of single men who were not cohabiting masturbated weekly or more often. However, the corresponding rate among women in the survey was only 12%. In this survey, married men and women consistently reported lower frequencies of masturbation (16% and 5%, respectively) (Laumann et al., 1994).

In discussing their findings, Laumann and colleagues (1994) concluded that "masturbation has the peculiar status of being both stigmatized and fairly commonplace" (p. 81). Enduring negative attitudes about masturbation may lead some individuals to underreport this activity. In support of this suggestion, 50–60% of men and women in the NHSLS admitted to feeling guilty after masturbation, regardless of marital status. It seems very likely, then, that percentages underestimate the frequency of masturbation for all groups.

Sexual Interactions

Each person has general and specific attitudes concerning what constitutes acceptable sexual activity. Individual sexual standards or sexual scripts guide sexual behaviors (Gagnon & Simon, 1973; Reiss, 1989). Sociologist Ira Reiss (1964) proposed four sexual scripts that influence the sexual interactions of singles. Reiss called these scripts forms of "premarital sexual permissiveness."

1. **Abstinence script.** The abstinence script prohibits any form of sexual behavior prior to marriage. This is described as the traditional and conservative standard for sexual behavior. Prior to the 1960s, abstinence was the normative sexual script. The following quote illustrates the abstinence script:

> I know it's old fashioned, but I believe in saving myself for the right person. To me, giving my virginity to my husband is the greatest gift I can offer. Having sex before marriage is a waste. It is not supposed to be that way. I am doing this because it is right for me, like my mother and grandmother did. (A 19-year-old female college student)

2. **Permissiveness with affection script.** According to this script, sex in an unmarried relationship is permissible if the partners have an emotional bond, if they are in love. This sexual script is the dominant one in most Western cultures, including the United States (DeLamater, 1987; Sprecher & Hatfield, 1996). The following quotes illustrate this script:

> I have a tremendous need for closeness and caring, someone to love and to love me. It is more than physical pleasure, not just sex. To me sex without love is unfulfilling. (A 21-year-old female college student)
>
> I realize that everybody is doing it [having sexual intercourse]. But I have decided to wait until I meet the right person. The only right way for me is to meet someone and fall in love. Anything less would be wrong. (A 23-year-old male college student)

3. **Permissiveness without affection script.** This script specifies that sex is acceptable without an emotional bond or commitment as long as both partners consent. According to this view, sex on a first date and "one-night stands" are acceptable.

> The first time, when I lost my virginity, was with a guy I barely knew. I was 15 at the time. He was a football player, and I only knew his name. It was purely physical attraction. I don't regret it. (A 21-year-old female college student)

4. **Double standard script.** According to this script, different standards apply to men and women. Historically, sexual standards for men have been more lenient. Women are judged more negatively than men are for having sex early in a relation-

ABSTINENCE SCRIPT
A set of sexual standards that prohibit sexual activity prior to marriage.

PERMISSIVENESS WITH AFFECTION SCRIPT
A common Western sexual standard that views sexual activity between unmarried persons as acceptable as long as there is an emotional bond between them.

PERMISSIVENESS WITHOUT AFFECTION SCRIPT
The sexual standard that specifies that sexual activity without emotional involvement is acceptable under certain circumstances, as in casual sex.

DOUBLE STANDARD SCRIPT
The viewpoint that different sexual standards apply to the sexes, and the expectation that women will be more sexually restrained than men.

TABLE 12.3 Men's Frequency of Sexual Intercourse for the Past 12 Months, by Marital Status

MARITAL STATUS	NOT AT ALL	A FEW TIMES PER YEAR	A FEW TIMES PER MONTH	TWO OR MORE TIMES PER WEEK
Never married (without cohabiting partner)	22%	26%	25%	27%
Never married (with cohabiting partner)	0	9%	36%	55%
Married	1%	13%	43%	43%
Divorced/Separated/Widowed (without cohabiting partner)	24%	22%	29%	25%
Divorced/Separated/Widowed (with cohabiting partner)	0	8%	36%	56%

SOURCE: Laumann et al., 1994

ship (Sprecher, McKinney, & Orbuch, 1987). A double standard is evident in the amount of sexual permissiveness desired in a dating partner. Women prefer dating a male who is low in sexual permissiveness, whereas males prefer a female who is more sexually permissive (Sprecher, McKinney, & Orbuch, 1991). The double standard is carried a step further in that males prefer a sexually permissive dating partner but a less permissive marriage partner (Buss, 1994). Over the past several decades, the double standard sexual script has become less prevalent, although it still exists and influences the sexual behaviors of many people, as the following quote illustrates:

> It's OK for a guy because they can't get pregnant. Girls have more to worry about so they have to be careful. Also people think differently about a girl who is promiscuous. For a guy, it's expected. (A 36-year-old college male)

These sexual scripts still apply today and are reflected in some of the self-reported sexual behaviors of single men and women (see Tables 12.3 and 12.4). Never-married singles who have a live-in partner report higher frequencies of sexual activity than never-married singles who lack a live-in partner and than married individuals (Laumann et al., 1994). Cohabiting singles often tend to accept the permissiveness with affection script.

TABLE 12.4 Women's Frequency of Sexual Intercourse for the Past 12 Months, by Marital Status

MARITAL STATUS	NOT AT ALL	A FEW TIMES PER YEAR	A FEW TIMES PER MONTH	TWO OR MORE TIMES PER WEEK
Never married (without cohabiting partner)	30%	24%	26%	20%
Never married (with cohabiting partner)	1%	7%	32%	60%
Married	3%	12%	46%	39%
Divorced/Separated/Widowed (without cohabiting partner)	34%	23%	22%	21%
Divorced/Separated/Widowed (with cohabiting partner)	0	9%	40%	51%

SOURCE: Laumann et al., 1994

More than just offering opportunities for sex, a trusting and intimate relationship provides a safe place for individuals to explore their sexuality. Having a trusted partner can facilitate learning about one's own sexual likes and dislikes. As we explored in Chapter 8, one key to enjoyable sexual interactions with one's partner is the ability to communicate effectively. Couples who can discuss sex openly are free to explore their mutual sexual interests and to experiment with novel sexual acts and positions. Over time, as regular sexual partners become more comfortable with each other, they learn to communicate and please each other more effectively (McCabe, 1999). As you might expect, partners are more sexually satisfied and pleased with the relationship when they openly and regularly disclose sexual likes and dislikes (Byers & Demmons, 1999). Feelings of trust and intimacy, combined with good communication, are essential components of a rewarding sexual relationship.

did YOU know?

In a survey of unmarried college students, 60% of males and 59% of females reported having sexual intercourse one or more times per week (Weinberg et al., 1995).

Not everyone, though, chooses to have a sexual relationship prior to marriage. A significant percentage of singles adhere to an abstinence sexual script. In a survey by Weinberg and colleagues (1995), 10% of females and 8% of males denied any form of sexual interactions over the past year. In a unique study of college virgins, Sprecher and Regan (1996) surveyed 97 men and 192 women who denied any previous experience with sexual intercourse. For men and women, the major reason for sexual abstinence was not feeling enough love for any particular person to justify sexual intercourse, or not having met the right person. The women placed more importance than the men did on their personal beliefs as reasons for remaining sexually inactive. Men, on the other hand, were more likely than women to list shyness or embarrassment as explanations for sexual abstinence. Gender differences in the students' emotional reactions to virginity were discovered. Women reported more positive feelings about their virginity, including pride and happiness. Men, however, reported more negative feelings, including embarrassment and guilt. These different meanings assigned to virginity by men and women are consistent with the cultural double standard referred to earlier. There is an expectation that men will be sexually active, and men who do not conform to this script may feel inadequate. For women, there is still pressure to be less sexually active than men are, so sexual abstinence is more socially acceptable, or even expected, for them. As Muehlenhard (1988) noted with respect to sex, "nice girls" are supposed to say no, and "real men" are supposed to say yes.

COHABITATION: AN ALTERNATIVE TO MARRIAGE?

Anthropologist Margaret Mead provoked controversy with an article she wrote for *Cosmopolitan* magazine in 1966. Mead proposed a two-stage marriage system, with stages she called "individual marriage" and "parental marriage." Although both stages would require a marriage license, individual marriage included the option to end the relationship in relatively easy fashion. Parental marriage required long-term commitment and allowed childbearing. Although Mead's proposal never caught on, her notion of individual marriage is akin to cohabitation as currently practiced in the United States.

12.2 on the web

Go to **www.ablongman.com/mcanulty2e** and read the information about the Alternatives to Marriage Project.

What is the purpose of the project? Do you support these efforts? Why or why not?

In the early 1990s, Cherlin (1992) observed that although young adults were postponing marriage, they were less likely to postpone living with a partner. Over 50% of persons who were married in the late 1980s had previously cohabited with a partner (Bumpass & Sweet, 1989). In 2000, nearly 4 million unmarried couples were cohabitating, compared to half a million in 1970 (Fields & Casper, 2001). Rates of cohabitation are even higher among the formerly married; the majority live with a partner prior to remarrying.

Cohabitation has been viewed two different ways by researchers. One view is that it represents an alternative to marriage, a semipermanent or permanent but "looser" status. This definition corresponds to what is called a "paperless marriage" in Denmark (Moore, 1986). The other view is that cohabitation is a stage of courtship that often precedes marital commitment, a definition similar to Mead's proposed individual marriage. In reality, though, cohabitation may have different meanings based on cultural norms, couples' expectations and needs, and local laws and regulations. For many young heterosexual couples, cohabitation seems to represent a trial form of a permanent relationship (Brown & Booth, 1996).

Cohabiting couples enjoy high levels of emotional and sexual intimacy compared to couples who are not living together.

Approximately half of all couples who are cohabiting either break up or marry within 2 years, and 90% end the relationship or marry within 5 years (Cherlin, 1992). For others, cohabitation represents commitment—an arrangement that is often called a **domestic partnership.** Gay and lesbian couples in the United States may cohabit and live in marriagelike relationships, although these are not legally recognized. For them, cohabitation may be equivalent to—or the next best thing to—legalized marriage. There are, however, some signs that the legal status of such relationships may be changing. In December 1999, the Vermont Supreme Court ruled that the state was required to extend the same benefits and protections to gay and lesbian couples as those afforded to heterosexual married couples (Adriano, 2000). The section on same-sex marriage will revisit this topic.

Cohabitation allows couples to meet their needs for intimacy and sexuality, often without the requirement of long-term commitment. As you saw in Tables 12.3 and 12.4, cohabiting couples, whether never-married or previously married, report higher frequencies of sexual activity than any other group (Call, Sprecher, & Schwartz, 1995; Laumann et al., 1994). Additionally, never-married cohabiting singles report more physical and emotional satisfaction with their partners than never-married singles who are not cohabiting (see Table 12.5). The same pattern is evident for divorced, separated, and widowed persons; those who are cohabiting report more sexual and emotional satisfaction.

TABLE 12.5 Satisfaction with Relationship, by Marital Status

	PHYSICALLY SATISFIED		EMOTIONALLY SATISFIED	
Marital Status	*Men*	*Women*	*Men*	*Women*
Never married (without cohabiting partner)	39%	40%	32%	31%
Never married (with cohabiting partner)	44%	46%	35%	44%
Married	52%	41%	49%	42%
Divorced/Separated/Widowed (without cohabiting partner)	35%	36%	23%	27%
Divorced/Separated/Widowed (with cohabiting partner)	58%	42%	53%	37%

SOURCE: Laumann et al., 1994

DOMESTIC PARTNERSHIP
A marriagelike relationship that is not legally recognized.

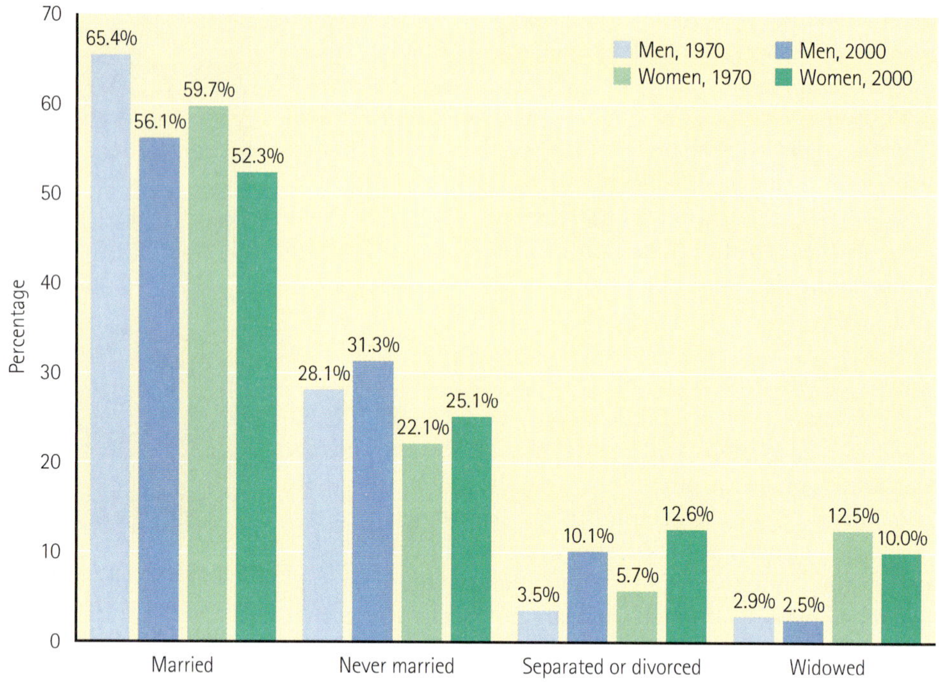

Figure 12.2 Marital Status of Americans Aged 15 and Over, by Sex: 1970 and 2000 (SOURCE: Fields and Casper, 2001; U.S. Bureau of the Census, 2000)

MARRIAGE

Although the institution of marriage has undergone dramatic changes in the past few decades, the majority of young adults in the United States will eventually marry. This section reviews trends in marriage and then addresses marital satisfaction, same-sex marriage, marital sexuality, problems that may develop in married relationships, and extramarital sexual relations.

did YOU know?

The current median age of first marriage for women is 25; for men it is nearly 27.

What is marriage? To use a definition borrowed from Davidson and Moore (1996), **marriage** is a legally binding contract between two people that confers certain rights and privileges and imposes certain responsibilities. Generally, marriage involves emotional commitment, shared economic and domestic responsibilities, and the expectation of sexual exclusivity. Other common characteristics of marriage are a public ceremony or wedding to mark its beginning, a license issued by a governmental agency, and the expectation of procreation (having children). Because no states currently recognize same-sex marriages, marriage in the United States is a contract between heterosexual adults, a point discussed later in this section.

Most young adults regard marriage as a major goal in life, and national statistics support this observation. As Figure 12.2 shows, despite modest declines in marriage rates over the years, in 2000 only one-quarter of men and one-third of women aged 15 and older had never married (Fields & Casper, 2001). Marriage rates vary according to race. Over half of African Americans aged 25–34 have never been married.

MARRIAGE
A legally binding contract between two people that confers certain rights and privileges, imposes certain responsibilities, and is based on expectations of emotional commitment, shared responsibilities, and sexual exclusivity.

Recent trends suggest that between 70% and 80% of all Americans will be married at least once (CDC, 1995; Day, 1996). Thus, marriage remains a very popular goal for the vast majority of Americans. However, as noted, the institution of marriage has undergone dramatic changes. The following are the most significant changes in U.S. marriage patterns:

1. Over the past 30 years, young adults have steadily postponed marriage. As illustrated in Figure 12.3, since the 1970s, the average age at first marriage for men and women has steadily increased.

2. Although the majority of people eventually marry, nearly half of all marriages are temporary. Beginning in the 1960s, annual rates of divorce rose sharply; they remained fairly constant through the 1990s (Cherlin, 1992; Goldstein, 1999). Although divorce rates dropped somewhat in the mid-1990s, the drop was misleading; it occurred simply because fewer people were getting married (CDC, 1995).

3. Most divorced persons eventually remarry. Today, in an unprecedented number of marriages, one or both partners were previously married, and blended families, including both partners' children from former marriages, are more common than ever.

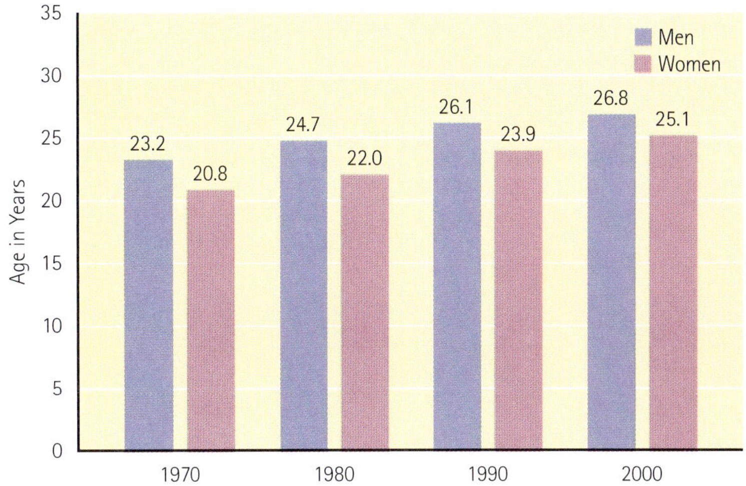

Figure 12.3 Median Age at First Marriage of Americans Aged 15 and Over, by Sex: 1970 to 2000 (SOURCE: Fields & Casper, 2001; U.S. Bureau of the Census, 2000)

4. Alternatives to traditional marriage are becoming increasingly popular and more acceptable in our society. Although young adults frequently delay marrying, they are more likely than in the past to live with a partner in an unmarried relationship. Cohabitation rates have steadily risen since the 1970s (Abma, Chandra, Mosher, Peterson, & Piccinino, 1997; Cherlin, 1992). Today, more than half of couples who marry had a live-in relationship before marrying. For most, cohabitation is a temporary arrangement rather than a permanent one.

These statistics reveal that the idealized depiction of marriage does not materialize for many people. Today, fewer people subscribe to the idea of meeting the perfect partner, being swept off one's feet, and living happily ever after.

Marital Satisfaction

Overall, people select marriage partners with whom they share certain fundamental similarities. Parents and society as a whole encourage individuals to select marriage partners from within their own social, economic, age, racial or ethnic, and educational group. For example, parents generally encourage their children to look for a mate who will share their religious views. There are exceptions, however. Although heterosexual partners who are married or cohabiting tend to be similar in age, income, education, and job prestige, partners in gay and lesbian couples tend to be more diverse, especially in incomes, careers, and education. Gay men and lesbians have a smaller pool of partners to choose from and, therefore, may be more likely to select a partner who is different with respect to age, income, and other characteristics (Kurdek & Schmitt, 1987).

For most people, personal values and the basic beliefs that guide many life decisions are important considerations in selecting a long-term partner. Shared values promote communication and satisfaction within close relationships. On the other hand, conflicts over personal values can lead to instability and marital disagreements. Happily married couples report that their ability to resolve conflicts, their communication patterns, and their agreement level in dealing with friends and families are most important to the success of their relationship (Fowers &

Looking At . . .

. . . Thinking About

What are the ingredients of marital satisfaction? Since satisfaction is a subjective state, couples' ratings of it vary widely and often change as the relationship changes. Having children, for example, may lower satisfaction, especially for wives. What other life changes and relationship challenges may alter marital satisfaction? What factors may influence the marital happiness of men and women differently?

Olson, 1986). Whether to have children, whether both will pursue a career, and where to live are decisions that most married couples must negotiate early in their relationship.

What factors contribute to marital satisfaction? Once a person has found a partner with whom he or she shares fundamental characteristics, what determines whether the couple will be happy? Communication skills are essential to marital adjustment and happiness (Tannen, 1990). Individuals' ratings of their marital satisfaction vary according to age and gender. Younger couples report greater marital satisfaction than do older couples. There is a tendency for couples to report a decline in marital satisfaction over the length of the marriage. However, marital satisfaction tends to remain stable for men, while women experience more variability in their ratings of marital happiness. Overall, men tend to report higher levels of marital happiness than women do (Mroczek & Kolarz, 1998; Stack, 1998). The presence of young children in the family is associated with lower marital satisfaction for women (Belsky & Rovine, 1990). Marital satisfaction often increases for women when grown children leave the home.

did YOU know?

Marriage is generally associated with better health and greater longevity, especially for men and when the marriage is happy. Unhappy marriages are associated with greater health problems and shorter-term survival of life-threatening illnesses.

Adjustment to marriage is a continuous process, but the first few years seem to be especially challenging for many couples. Half of all divorces occur within the first 7 years of marriage (Cherlin, 1992). At the end of the "honeymoon phase," which may last up to 1 year, a number of relationship issues must be addressed and negotiated. At this point, individual expectations regarding marital roles, duties, and lifestyle may be sources of conflict. Common areas of disagreement include social and leisure activities, financial and career decisions, and relations with relatives, especially in-laws (Blumstein & Schwartz, 1983; Boss, 1987). Sexuality may also be a problem area for married couples. Conflicts may arise over the desired frequency of sex, types of acceptable sexual activity, and expectations regarding initiating as well as declining sexual activity (Byers & Heinlein, 1989).

Perhaps most important in predicting marital satisfaction is not *what* couples disagree about, but *how* they disagree. Relationships in which one or both partners regularly inject positive emotions into disagreements—whether through humor, expressions of affection, or simply showing interest in their partner—are more stable and happy (Gottman, Coan, Carrere, & Swanson, 1998). Contrary to popular views, anger and conflict are not inevitably associated with marital dissatisfaction. Power and control imbalances, though, *are* predictive of relationship problems. Marriages in which the husband refuses to share power with his wife are more likely to end in divorce (Gottman et al., 1998). Such men often tend to be hostile, competitive, and dominating. Relationships in which partners compromise, negotiate, and share power are more stable and happier in the long run.

In most cultures of the world, married couples report being more happy than unmarried couples (Brown & Booth, 1996; Stack & Eshleman, 1998). For many couples, marriage offers benefits that are not found in other types of relationships. Perhaps because of a greater degree of commitment to the relationship, married couples enjoy more reciprocal emotional support, higher levels of perceived physical health, and more financial security. These findings seem to hold up for men and women in most cultures, as they were documented in 16 of the 17 industrialized countries studied (Stack & Eshleman, 1998).

Same-Sex Marriage

Nearly 80% of Americans marry at least once (Day, 1996). Marriage remains a goal for most of the U.S. population, yet the option of marrying is withheld from a significant segment of that population: gay men and lesbians. An estimated 40–60% of gay men and 45–80% of lesbians are involved in a committed same-sex relationship (Kurdek, 1995). Like most heterosexual men and women, a large number of gay men and lesbians express interest in being in a legally binding relationship, with all the responsibilities and commitment that go with marriage. Some countries, such as Denmark and Norway, recognize same-sex marriages. In Iceland and Sweden, same-sex civil weddings, which carry most of the legal benefits of heterosexual marriage, are formally recognized. Hungary does not permit same-sex marriage, but a gay or lesbian partner can inherit property and pension from a deceased lover. In October 1999, France passed a domestic partnership law that guarantees such benefits as inheritance, housing rights, and tax deductions to unmarried couples. Additionally, domestic partners, who are required to register as a couple to qualify, are liable for each other's financial debts (Gutierrez, 2000). Same-sex marriages are not recognized in the United States, although a growing number of American corporations allow employees to assign spousal benefits, such as health insurance coverage, to a same-sex partner.

The controversy surrounding same-sex marriage was highlighted in the early 1990s, when three homosexual couples (one gay and two lesbian couples) appealed to Hawaii's Supreme Court for the right to obtain marriage licenses. In May 1993, the Hawaii Supreme Court ruled in a 3–1 vote that the state's refusal to grant same-sex marriage licenses might represent sex discrimination and, therefore, be unconstitutional. The decision stirred major controversy and heated debate, because federal law required that all states recognize a marriage license issued by any state. In anticipation of the Hawaii Supreme Court ruling or afterwards, nearly 40 states introduced legislation banning same-sex marriages. In 1996, President Bill Clinton endorsed the Defense of Marriage Act (DOMA), which legally defined marriage as the union between a man and a woman. DOMA gave each state the power not to recognize any same-sex marriage licenses issued by another state. Additionally, DOMA denies spousal benefits for same-sex couples in which one partner is an employee of the federal government. In contrast to the position of the majority of states, the Vermont Supreme Court ruled on December 20, 1999 that the state must extend the same benefits and protections provided to married heterosexual couples to gay and lesbian couples. Although advocates of gay rights and civil rights leaders applauded the ruling, other commentators lamented what they viewed as an attempt by the court to dictate matters of "social, legal and moral policy" (Thomas, 2000, p. 9).

Homosexuality remains one of the most sensitive and controversial topics relating to human sexuality, and state laws pertaining to sexual orientation remain the most restrictive and unsupportive of all laws relating to sexuality (SIECUS, 1998).

Marital Sexuality

According to the standard cultural script, marriage is the preferred context for sexual activity. However, as Greenblat (1983) noted, sexuality in marriage "remains more the topic of jokes than of serious social scientific investigation" (p. 289). Fortunately, this situation has started changing, and several large-scale surveys of marital sexuality have been completed. The majority of these studies have focused on the frequency of sexual activity among married couples.

Several consistent findings have emerged from studies of marital sexuality. First, as Kinsey's landmark surveys established, the average frequency of sexual interactions among married couples is approximately twice per week (Blumstein & Schwartz, 1983; Kinsey et al., 1948, 1953; Laumann et al., 1994). Second, the reported frequency of sexual activity declines with age or the length of the marriage. Couples who are older or have been married for longer periods of time show a decline in frequency of sexual activity (Call, Sprecher, & Schwartz, 1995). Marital satisfaction is the second most important factor in explaining the decline in marital sexual interactions (Call et al., 1995). The greatest decline in sexual activity apparently occurs between the ages of 50 and 60 (Greeley, 1992), a phenomenon that will be discussed in more detail later in this chapter. Finally, for most couples, pregnancy is associated with a decline in sexual activity, especially during the third trimester (Hyde, DeLamater, Plant, & Byrd, 1996). Parenthood causes a change in roles and requires married partners to devote time and energy to child care, which decreases time spent together (and stamina!) and may interfere with opportunities for sexual interactions. Having young children especially seems to interfere with the sexual interactions of married couples (Call et al., 1995).

did YOU know?

Married couples under 30 years of age have sex two to three times per week. By age 65, the average frequency among sexually active couples is down to three times per month (Call et al., 1995).

Sexually Inactive Marriages

Since it is generally assumed in our society that married persons have sex, very little research has been conducted on sexually inactive marriages. In one exception, Donnelly (1993) studied the characteristics of married couples who reported no sexual activity during the preceding month. Overall, sexually inactive couples tended to view their marriages as unhappy, shared few activities, and were likely to have considered separation. Interestingly, such couples did not tend to have arguments over their sexual inactivity; it was as if these couples had reached an agreement or understanding about *not* having sex. Age and length of marriage were also related to sexual inactivity. Older couples who had been married longer tended to be less sexually active. Finally, for males at least, poor health was associated with being sexually inactive.

Sexual inactivity may lead to relationship problems. Discrepancies in sexual desire are a common complaint of couples seeking marriage counseling, a topic that is addressed in Chapter 13. Sometimes the partner who desires more sexual activity will come to question his or her sexual performance:

> If I were to believe in miracles, I would have to say that the conception of my four children was miraculous. We had intercourse so infrequently—she always had headaches, periods, and stomachaches—that it is amazing she conceived at all. I used to think there was something wrong with me because I couldn't get her turned on. (A 47-year-old man; adapted from Janus & Janus, 1993)

Contrary to the popular stereotype, men are not the only ones to feel dissatisfied with the frequency of sex in their marriages. One review of pertinent studies reported that the husband was the sexually inactive partner in nearly 60% of couples requesting sex therapy (Wincze & Carey, 2001).

In summary, sexual inactivity in a marriage is often a sign of unhappiness and dissatisfaction with the relationship. In our culture, satisfaction with the relationship and sexual satisfaction are closely related for most married couples. As Donnelly (1993) concluded, sexual inactivity is a danger signal for many couples because "when marriages suffer outside the bedroom, they may suffer inside it as well" (p. 177).

Sexually Active Marriages

In sexually active marriages, cultural scripts affect marital sexual interactions in a number of ways. Men are generally more likely than women to initiate sexual interactions and less likely to decline an invitation to have sex (Blumstein & Schwartz, 1983). In one study, 77 married or cohabiting couples kept behavioral records of their sexual initiations and their partners' responses to initiations over a 1-week period. Overall, men initiated sex more frequently than their wives did and considered initiating sex more often. Additionally, over twice as many wives (23%) as husbands (10%) made no sexual overture to their spouses during that period of time. Thus, husbands conformed to the cultural script that men should take the role of sexual initiator for the couple. Overall, partners of either sex were receptive to sexual initiations three out of four times. When one of the partners declined a sexual overture, it was more likely to be the wife. Several factors were related to the level of sexual activity among couples. Consistent with other studies, age, length of the relationship, and relationship satisfaction were related to sexual activity. The most common reasons given for declining a sexual overture were being too tired or not having enough time. Positive responses to sexual initiations were usually expressed by physical contact, whereas negative responses were expressed verbally (Byers & Heinlein, 1989). For example, a positive response to a sexual overture might con-

Approximately 40–50% of married men and women report being sexually and emotionally satisfied with their partners. Similar findings were reported by Janus and Janus (1993), who found that 60% of married couples rated their partners as "sexually sophisticated" and 56% described their marriages as good or great.

sist of a sensuous touch; a negative response was more likely to be a statement, such as "I am just too tired tonight."

The majority of married couples report being sexually active. Eighty-six percent of married men and 85% of married women report having sexual interactions from several times per month to several times per week (Laumann et al., 1994). Sexual intercourse is the preferred method for achieving orgasm for the vast majority of married couples, with oral sex being a distant second preference (Janus & Janus, 1993).

did YOU know?

Of people of all marital statuses, married couples are the least likely to report having recently masturbated. Nearly 43% of married men and 63% of married women denied having masturbated during the 12-month period prior to being surveyed for the NHSLS.

Extramarital Sexuality

Marital infidelity, or cheating, is nearly universally condemned (Widmer et al., 1998). Yet, despite widespread disapproval, many married persons have been unfaithful to their spouses. Extramarital sexual involvement usually takes the form of a clandestine affair. There are couples who agree to have sex outside of marriage, but this is much less common.

Infidelity

Extramarital sex means having a sexual interaction with a person other than one's current spouse at any point in the marriage. One of the most controversial findings reported by Kinsey and colleagues (Kinsey et al., 1949; Kinsey et al., 1953) was that 50% of married men and 26% of married women admitted to having had an extramarital sexual encounter by age 45. These findings caused quite a stir for two reasons: First, at the time, most people strongly disapproved of extramarital sexual relations. Second, the rates reported by Kinsey were much higher than anyone would have guessed. There is still strong societal disapproval of extramarital sexual interactions. Nearly 80% of people surveyed in the early 1990s viewed extramarital sexuality as unacceptable under any circumstance (Davis & Smith, 1994; Laumann et al., 1994).

Newer studies reveal that Kinsey's estimates of the frequency of extramarital sex were unusually high. Results of the NHSLS suggest that less than 25% of men and 10% of women have had extramarital affairs (Laumann et al., 1994). Findings from other studies suggest that at most 25% of married individuals have been involved in extramarital sexual encounters.

What are the reasons for being involved in sexual activity that is disapproved of by the majority of people in most Western societies? Four major reasons for extramarital sexual involvement have been described (Glass & Wright, 1992):

1. Sex—the desire for novelty, variety, or increased sexual activity
2. Romantic love—falling in love with a person other than one's spouse
3. Emotional intimacy—becoming involved sexually with another person in order to meet emotional needs for closeness and intimacy
4. External reasons—being involved in an extramarital affair to gain a job promotion, a business opportunity, or some other benefit

Among men, sex is the most commonly reported motivation for extramarital sexuality. Women are more likely to cite the search for emotional intimacy or romantic love as the justification for an extramarital affair (Glass & Wright, 1992). Generally, women involved in extramarital relationships are dissatisfied with most aspects of their marital relationships. Surveys of married persons reveal that having an unhappy marriage is associated with more permissive sexual attitudes. Unhappily married individuals are more likely than happily married ones to view extramarital sexuality as justified (Smith, 1994). Infidelity, whether verified or suspected, is the most common cause of relationship breakups worldwide (Beitzig, 1989). In any case, infidelity is usually a sign of a troubled relationship, and it may be the final blow for a compromised marriage. This seems especially true when the woman is the one who has the affair (Reibstein & Richards, 1993). Men feel especially threatened by their partners' sexual indiscretions and are therefore much less forgiving.

12.3 on the web

With recent technology, the scope of infidelity has changed. Visit **www.ablongman.com/mcanulty2e** to learn more about the Internet and infidelity.

Is a married man or woman who participates in cybersex or creates a relationship with another person online cheating on his or her significant other? What makes an online relationship an "affair"?

The most common reaction on learning of a partner's infidelity is a profound sense of hurt and betrayal. Infidelity is seen as a breach of trust, one that may have long-lasting effects. Couples who eventually recover recall that much time is required to heal the wounds and that trust returns slowly. In the interim, the partner who feels betrayed may experience great jealousy and the urge to periodically check up on the other partner. He or she may be suspicious and question the other about any departure from the usual routine. Returning home from work late or not answering the telephone may fuel the wounded partner's suspicions, which, in turn, may add to existing conflict. Infidelity need not be the *coup de grâce* for a marriage, however. The following steps can help any couple trying to recover from infidelity:

1. *Realize that the relationship has temporarily changed.* After the crisis triggered by the infidelity, the partners' roles, ways of interacting, and expectations will be affected for some time. The relationship is strained, and it is important for both partners to acknowledge that fact.

2. *Understand that one partner feels betrayed, hurt, and rejected as well as inadequate.* This understanding is critical, because the hurt partner's actions are direct reactions to those unpleasant emotions. The partner who feels betrayed will need frequent reassurances of the other partner's honesty, love, and respect. Also, the hurt partner can be expected to have numerous questions about the affair as he or she tries to make sense of it. Essentially, the partner who was involved in the extramarital affair must expect and accept the close scrutiny and monitoring that will follow.

3. *Show your commitment to your partner every chance you get.* Ultimately, the betrayed partner wants to know that the other partner is committed to the relationship and will do anything to ensure that there will be no future indiscretions. Commitment can be demonstrated in various ways, from giving small gifts to regularly phoning or sending notes to more public ways of showing devotion such as holding hands and hugging more frequently.

4. *Identify and resolve the factors that led to the infidelity.* When infidelity stems from dissatisfaction with aspects of the relationship, these need to be addressed eventually. If a couple has been unable to resolve these problems, couples counseling with a professional may be necessary. Getting help is often essential if couples are to negotiate the emotional minefield that results from infidelity. (This is true not only for married couples but for cohabiting couples as well.)

Swinging

Although most extramarital sexuality is clandestine, some couples agree that it is permissible for each partner to have sex with other people under certain circumstances. Relationships in which the partners have such an agreement are commonly referred to as **open marriages.** Some married couples are involved in **swinging,** the practice of meeting other couples for sexual interaction, which usually involves partner swapping. Blumstein and Schwartz (1983) reported that 15–26% of the married couples they surveyed allowed extramarital sexual involvement under some circumstances. In a 5-year followup of married couples, Rubin and Adams (1986) found few differences between those couples who permitted extramarital sex and those who did not; the majority of all couples were still married. The authors concluded that there appeared to be no differences between sexually open and sexually exclusive married couples. In his review of the literature on swinging, Jenks (1998) concluded that swingers were most likely to be white, middle- to upper-class, above average in income and education, with prestigious occupations. Perhaps not surprisingly, swingers were also found to be fairly liberal in their attitudes toward sexuality. Yet, there are no apparent personality differences between swingers and nonswingers.

OPEN MARRIAGE
An agreement between married persons that extramarital sex will be permitted under certain circumstances.

SWINGING
The practice in some open marriages of swapping partners with other couples.

Overall, open marriages appear to be less common than they were in the 1960s and 1970s. However, personal ads in newspapers and magazines and on computer bulletin boards reveal that some couples still practice swinging and sexual openness. Jenks (1998) estimated that up to 2% of married couples have experimented with swinging, although he noted that this percentage might be inaccurate because of a lack of recent studies. In any case, the practice of swinging is controversial, and practitioners tend to be secretive about this aspect of their sex lives, as illustrated by the following quote:

> We met some lovely people and we've become good friends. You'd be surprised at the type of people, and how many very successful people swing. It's amazing how you can get close to people who are not family, and yet you experience the most intimate things with them, but when you see them at the supermarket you act as if nothing happened. (A 45-year-old married woman; adapted from Janus & Janus, 1993)

DIVORCE

Because nearly half of all marriages end in divorce, marriage has been described as a "weakened institution" (Cherlin, 1992). Divorce rates in the United States began climbing in the mid-1960s, before leveling off in the mid-1980s (Goldstein, 1999). In 1998, approximately 10% of adults were divorced (Lugaila, 1998). More than half of divorcing couples have children living in the home (National Center for Health Statistics, 1995). Divorce rates vary across races and ethnic backgrounds. African American women are more likely than white women to divorce and less likely to remarry (Cherlin, 1992).

Reasons for Divorce

Researchers classify the factors that influence rates of divorce into two broad categories: sociocultural and individual. Sociocultural factors include changing societal attitudes toward divorce, changing gender roles, and widening economic opportunities for women. Individual factors are characteristics of the individuals and the marriage that increase risks of divorcing, such as marital dissatisfaction, sexual difficulties, infidelity, and age at first marriage.

Over the past 20 years, societal attitudes toward divorce have become more tolerant (Cherlin, 1992). For example, 48% of the respondents in the 1994 General Social Surveys agreed that divorce is the best solution for couples who cannot resolve their marital problems. Nearly 70% of respondents felt that having children was not an acceptable justification for staying in an unhappy marriage (Davis & Smith, 1994). Because of the decreased stigma associated with divorce, unhappy couples may find it a viable solution to their problems. Other commonly listed sociocultural factors that influence divorce rates are changing gender roles and increased vocational opportunities for women (Cherlin, 1992). Because women have more career and job choices today, they are less dependent on a husband for financial support. The ability to secure employment and a growing sense of independence and empowerment allow women who are unhappy with their marriages to terminate them. Support for this view comes from recent employment and divorce statistics. Younger women, who are more independent and career-minded, are more likely to divorce than older women. Women who are employed are more likely to divorce than married women who do not work. As Cherlin (1992) noted, changing gender roles and increased financial independence have provided more freedom for many women, including the freedom to terminate an unhappy marriage.

Some people have speculated that more relaxed divorce laws contribute to the rise in divorce rates—because it is easier to get a divorce, people are perhaps more apt to do so. In response to this, some states now offer couples the option of a *covenant marriage,* which is more difficult to dissolve, instead of the current *no-fault* marriage, which permits couples to end their marriage without cause (and typically with a short waiting period). Louisiana was the first state to enact this option in 1997, but other states have followed suit or have proposals to do so.

Most covenant marriage laws require that the couple participate in premarital counseling and training as well as counseling before a divorce is granted. They also stipulate longer waiting periods to get a divorce than under the no-fault option. All of these requirements are aimed at encouraging a couple to take marriage seriously and

IN YOUR own words

Angela Furman
University of Houston

I think cohabitation before marriage is acceptable and often helpful. A couple can see how they truly click before deciding to get married. If more people lived together for about two years before getting married, I think the divorce rate would go down!

12.4 on the web

A number of organizations have come together to start a covenant marriage movement.

Go to ***www.ablongman.com/mcanulty2e*** *and describe the goals and activities of this movement.*

to work toward saving their marriage before they end it. These laws may allow a divorce in a shorter period of time under certain circumstances, such as if one spouse commits a felony or adultery or physically or sexually abuses a child or spouse (Crouch, 2002; Walker, 2002).

A number of individual and relationship factors correlate with divorce risk. Marital dissatisfaction is the most obvious reason for seeking a divorce. The typical pattern starts with high marital dissatisfaction, followed by considerations of dissolving the relationship, and eventual separation and divorce (Gottman & Levenson, 1992). What factors are associated with marital unhappiness so severe that it leads to divorce? Growing apart is the reason most frequently given for divorcing. Other commonly cited reasons include not feeling loved, having sexual problems, and feeling that one's needs are not being met (Gigy & Kelly, 1992). A number of factors make some couples more vulnerable to marital conflict and unhappiness and thus to divorce. Parental divorce and marrying at a young age are risk factors for marital problems (Feng, 1999; Reiss & Lee, 1988). Women who marry in their teens or who marry because of a pregnancy are more than twice as likely as other women to divorce (London & Wilson, 1988). Thus, divorce generally results from serious marital unhappiness, for which there are multiple risk factors.

Looking At...

...Thinking About

It is misleading to claim, as some do, that high divorce rates in the United States are due to a permissive attitude toward dissolving relationships. No couple on their wedding day anticipates divorce as the likely eventual outcome of their marriage. Divorce results from relationship problems that appear unsolvable to one or both partners. Because of changes in cultural norms, divorce is an option today that was unimaginable a century ago, when immense negative stigma was attached to being divorced. What cultural factors have affected divorce rates in the United States?

Adjusting to Divorce

Divorce is one of the most stressful of life events. Regardless of how unhappy a marriage was, separation and divorce are painful experiences. Initial emotional reactions include anger, fear, sadness, and anxiety. The adjustment to divorce is akin to the grieving process. A pervasive sense of loss and mourning generally follows a marital breakup. Because one or both partners may feel unable to let go, prolonged distress is common (Masheter, 1991).

The most commonly identified worries of divorcing persons are concerns over the impact of divorce on children, financial worries, and loneliness. These concerns may be greatly exacerbated in couples undergoing a hostile separation. In such cases, the emotional suffering is prolonged for everyone involved. Unfortunately, amicable divorces are the exception rather than the rule (Ambert, 1988).

In general, divorce is more emotionally and financially stressful for wives than for husbands. This is especially true in older couples (Choi, 1992). Wives who are employed fare better than those who are completely dependent on their husbands for financial support. Coping with divorce is especially difficult if a person lacks social support. Receiving support from relatives and friends may facilitate the coping process. Divorced persons cope better if they have a close friend who will listen to their personal problems (Miller, Smerglia, Gaudet, & Kitson, 1998). However, not all divorcing people find support. In one study of men and women in the process of divorcing, almost half reported that their own parents were not supportive of them (Lesser & Comet, 1987). Another challenge stems from changes in social activities. A divorced person may have been accustomed to a couples-oriented social life, but she or he must adjust to life as a single person. When in the company of couples, the divorced individual may feel out of place or somewhat of a misfit. Loneliness is a common problem for divorced persons, as discussed in Reflect on This: The Lonely Hearts Club. Finally, divorce is stressful not only for emotional health but for physical health as well. In summary, divorce is a very stressful experience that may have detrimental effects in many areas of life.

12.5 on the web

Adjusting to divorce is a stressful process, both for the partners and for children. Go to **www.ablongman.com/mcanulty2e,** find the link to The Divorce Source, and explore this site.

Describe ways in which parents can minimize the impact of a divorce on their children. What are some negative effects that are not easily controlled?

reflect ON THIS

The Lonely Hearts Club

Loneliness is a common experience, affecting millions of people. Not only is loneliness a negative experience in and of itself, but it is also linked with other problems such as depression, low self-esteem, and anxiety (Snodgrass, 1989). Fortunately, for most of us, loneliness is a temporary experience.

The *UCLA Loneliness Scale* (to the right) is often used to measure loneliness. Answer the questions and compute your loneliness score.

In one survey of college students (Russell, 1996), the average score was 40 points, with two-thirds of students scoring between 30 and 50. Scores above 50 suggest that you may be experiencing more loneliness than the average college students in that survey; scores below 30 suggest less loneliness than average.

If loneliness is a problem for you, consider these recommendations.

1. Discover the source of your loneliness. If you are living alone, consider getting a roommate. If you just ended a relationship, giving yourself time to adjust is probably a big part of the answer. If shyness is the cause, practice meeting people with a close friend and taking some risks. Remember that being turned down is not catastrophic—it happens to everyone.
2. Join a group or take up a hobby that will put you in contact with people who share those interests. Shared interests and similarity are part of the formula for any successful relationship. Hobby groups, church singles programs, fitness centers, and team-oriented sports organizations are all possibilities. Singles bars are *not* the place to start. Try different interest groups and organizations until you find the right one for you.
3. Set realistic goals. Try to make friends and pursue a few close relationships rather than many superficial ones. Try to make friends of both sexes. And remember, don't act desperate. People who are especially needy are a turn-off because they seem so demanding and "high maintenance."

Instructions: The following statements describe how people sometimes feel. For each statement, please indicate how often you feel the way described by writing a number in the space provided. Here is an example:

How often do you feel happy?

If you never felt happy, you would respond "never"; if you always feel happy, you would respond "always."

NEVER	RARELY	SOMETIMES	ALWAYS
1	2	3	4

*1. How often do you feel that you are "in tune" with the people around you? ______

2. How often do you feel that you lack companionship? ______

3. How often do you feel that there is no one you can turn to? ______

4. How often do you feel alone? ______

*5. How often do you feel part of a group of friends? ______

*6. How often do you feel that you have a lot in common with the people around you? ______

7. How often do you feel that you are no longer close to anyone? ______

8. How often do you feel that your interests and ideas are not shared by those around you? ______

*9. How often do you feel outgoing and friendly? ______

*10. How often do you feel close to people? ______

11. How often do you feel left out? ______

12. How often do you feel that your relationships with others are not meaningful? ______

13. How often do you feel that no one really knows you well? ______

14. How often do you feel isolated from others? ______

*15. How often do you feel that you can find companionship when you want it? ______

*16. How often do you feel that there are people who really understand you? ______

17. How often do you feel shy? ______

18. How often do you feel that people are around you but not with you? ______

*19. How often do you feel that there are people you can talk to? ______

*20. How often do you feel that there are people you can turn to? ______

Scoring: Items with asterisks should be reversed (i.e., 1 = 4, 2 = 3, 3 = 2, 4 = 1), and the scores for each item then summed together. Higher scores indicate greater degrees of loneliness.

Sexuality and Divorce

Most divorced persons must adjust to the loss of a regular sexual partner and to dating again. Most divorced persons do resume dating—one study revealed that over half of divorced women and men were dating 2 years after divorcing, and one-fourth had remarried (Maccoby & Mnookin, 1992). For divorced persons, resuming dating and living as a single person again can be challenging experiences that require adjustment, as the following quote illustrates:

> One of the toughest things for me after the divorce was the thought of dating again. After 25 years of marriage, I did not know where to start. It also felt strange to think of being with another man. I often felt undesirable and worried that nobody would be interested in dating me. In time, I was able to start dating and learned that some men still found me interesting. Of course, most of the dates were pretty dull, sometimes dreadful. But I have since had several good dating relationships. I guess I didn't lose it all after all. Kinda like riding a bicycle, it comes back to you. (A divorced 48-year-old woman)

In the Janus and Janus (1993) survey, divorced men and women reported higher rates of masturbation than married and never-married men and women. The reported frequencies of sexual activity for divorced persons were the same as those for never-married men and women but were consistently lower than the rates for married persons. Janus and Janus studied a varied group of divorced persons, some of whom were not dating at all, which may account for the comparatively lower rates of reported sexual activity. Divorced persons who have a cohabiting partner report higher rates of sexual activity than divorced persons who lack such a partner (Laumann et al., 1994) (see Tables 12.2 and 12.3). In the NHSLS survey, those in the divorced/separated/widowed group who had a cohabiting partner reported rates of sexual activity that were equal to those reported by married persons and by never-married individuals with a cohabiting partner.

Most of the early studies of sexuality among divorced persons relied on nonrandom samples (e.g., Hunt, 1974; Kinsey et al., 1948, 1953). In a more representative study of 340 divorced people, Stack and Gundlach (1992) discovered lower rates of sexual interactions than those revealed by the nonrandom studies. Over one-fourth of respondents had had no sexual interactions over the past year, and 43% had sexual intercourse once or more per week. The authors of the study examined two measures of sexual activity: number of partners over the past year and frequency of sexual activity over the same period of time. Several factors were predictive of sexual activity in this sample. Age, gender, religiousness, political views, and opportunities for sex were related to number of sex partners over the previous year. Divorced men were more sexually active than divorced women, and younger persons reported more sex partners than older divorced individuals. Other factors, such as a low level of religiousness, liberal political attitudes, and the absence of children in the home, were associated with higher numbers of sex partners. Only two variables were predictive of frequency of sexual activity: age and gender. Males and younger adults had sex more frequently than females and older persons. For the entire sample, the average frequency of intercourse was twice per month, a much lower rate than was reported in previous studies. Remember, however, to be cautious of relying too much on averages, which can be misleading. Recall that for the entire sample, nearly one-fourth had no sexual interactions at all and nearly one-half had sex weekly. In summary, sexuality among divorced persons is quite variable. Younger divorced persons who have a regular partner are more sexually active than older divorced individuals. Younger divorced males report more sexual partners than do younger divorced females. These patterns of sexual behavior are consistent with those reported for never-married singles.

SEXUALITY AND AGING

As most sexuality educators know, asking people to imagine their own parents or grandparents having sex generates much discomfort (Kyes, 1995). Such a reaction is typical among college students (Pocs & Godow, 1977). Why is it difficult for many people to envision sexuality in older persons? The answer lies in stereotypes about aging and in cultural sexual scripts. In many cultures, aging is equated with illness, infirmity, helplessness, and unattractiveness. Consider the images of aging that are depicted in advertising. Older people are featured in ads for such products as vitamins, laxatives, health insurance, and various illness remedies. Young and attractive models are used in advertising for colognes and cosmetic products. The cultural message is that old, wrinkled, and gray are undesirable, and therefore incompatible with sexuality.

In reality, aging is not inextricably associated with deteriorating health and mental abilities. Although some health problems, such as heart disease, are more common among older individuals, these problems are not inevitably associated with aging. Many older persons are physically fit and healthy. Likewise, memory loss is not invariably associated with aging. In fact, only 5% of the elderly population suffers from serious memory problems, or "senility," as it is popularly known. (The term used by medical and psychological professionals for serious impairment in cognitive functions is *dementia*.) Another stereotype of aging is that most elderly people live a socially isolated existence, usually because they are widows. A related stereotype is that of an elderly person who depends on adult children for care or who resides in a nursing home. The reality is that most elderly people reside with a spouse in their own residence (Spitze & Logan, 1989). Older couples actually report higher levels of companionship, emotional satisfaction, and marital satisfaction than do younger couples (Giordano & Beckman, 1985). As a rule, older persons are just as happy as, if not happier than, younger persons (Mroczek & Kolarz, 1998).

Sexual Functioning in Older Persons

Masters and Johnson (1966, 1970) conducted the seminal work on the changes in sexual functioning associated with aging. Their findings documented several consistent physical changes that affect sexuality in older people. Overall, advancing age is associated with a slowing or decrease in most of the physical responses during the sexual response cycle.

Changes in Women

In women, the most significant physical changes follow **menopause.** Menopause is the time in a woman's lifespan when the ovaries cease producing estrogen. As discussed in Chapter 9, estrogen is the hormone that regulates the menstrual cycle and ovulation. Thus, menopause represents the end of a woman's reproductive capability. Women notice the onset of menopause when they cease having menstrual periods, usually between the ages of 48 and 52. One of the most obvious changes associated with menopause is a decrease in the elasticity of the skin. Most internal sexual structures, including the uterus and the cervix, undergo some shrinkage. Additionally, the vaginal walls become thinner, and there is a decrease in blood pooling in the vaginal walls during sexual arousal. The length of the vagina decreases, sometimes to the point that a woman suffers discomfort during sexual intercourse. Postmenopausal women commonly experience a decrease in vaginal lubrication during sexual arousal. The resulting increased friction during penetration can cause pain. Postmenopausal women still experience all of the physical changes during the sexual response cycle, although less intensely and for shorter periods of time (Masters & Johnson, 1966).

Interestingly, women who remain sexually active report fewer problems with age-related changes in sexual functioning. They experience fewer problems with vaginal lubrication and show less shrinking of the vaginal muscles than postmenopausal women who are less sexually active (Masters & Johnson, 1966). Although

12.6 on the web

There are several sites devoted to sexuality and aging. Go to **www.ablongman.com/mcanulty2e** and find links to the Sexual Health Info-Center and to the College of Wooster's information on sexuality and aging.

What "harmful attitudes" about sexuality and aging are discussed? What facts about sexuality and aging are listed? Which of these are you familiar with? What can be done to dispel the various myths about sexuality and aging?

MENOPAUSE
The phase in a woman's life, usually around age 50, when the ovaries cease producing estrogen, marking the end of her reproductive years.

Contrary to the stereotype, many older couples enjoy fulfilling sex lives.

it is tempting to conclude that having active sex lives prevented the age-related changes in sexual functioning, it is entirely possible that the older women Masters and Johnson studied maintained active sex lives *because* they did not experience the age-related changes. The correlational nature of the research does not permit a cause-and-effect conclusion.

Some age-related problems with sexuality are easily remedied. The use of artificial lubricants usually eliminates the friction stemming from insufficient lubrication. Taking female hormones (estrogen alone or combined with progesterone), known as *hormone replacement therapy* (HRT), may decrease or prevent the physical changes that follow menopause. However, recent evidence has called the safety of HRT into question, especially with long-term use (Nelson, 2002).

Changes in Men

Although men do not experience menopause, their bodies also undergo predictable changes with age. With advancing age, men experience a decrease in firmness of erection. Additionally, they require more direct and prolonged stimulation in order to attain an erection (Rowland, Greenleaf, Dorfman, & Davidson, 1993). According to Masters and Johnson (1966), younger males may achieve full erection in 3–5 seconds, but males in their 50s require two to three times longer. During sexual activity, older men require more stimulation in order to ejaculate. This delay in reaching orgasm is a welcome change for many men and their partners because it prolongs sexual activity. Older men also experience a decrease in the intensity of ejaculation. Semen seeps out during ejaculation rather than being forcefully expelled, as is typical in younger men (Schiavi, 1990). Another consistently reported change is an increase in the length of the refractory period that follows orgasm. As men age, the time required to achieve another erection after orgasm increases steadily. Men in their 30s may require 30 minutes to an hour, and men in their 50s may have a refractory period of several hours. After age 60, some men are incapable of a second orgasm for a 24-hour period.

Advancing age brings a decrease in testosterone production; by age 70, men experience a 30% decline in testosterone levels (Cowley, 1996). Despite this decrease, testosterone levels typically remain in the normal range (Metz & Miner, 1998). A few elderly men do have abnormally low levels of testosterone, which may cause a sharp decrease in sex drive and erectile difficulties (see Chapter 13). The majority of men experience a gradual decline in sex drive with advancing age, which coincides with lowered testosterone production. However, as the next section reveals, the majority of healthy elderly men maintain a regular and satisfying sex life, especially if they have an available partner.

Sexual Behavior and Aging

Older people are rarely portrayed as having romantic interests, much less as having sexual needs. However, just as sexuality does not begin abruptly at puberty, it does not end suddenly upon retirement. As noted in Chapter 11, taboos surround childhood sexuality. Because of similar taboos surrounding sexuality in elderly persons, serious scientific inquiry into sexuality and aging is a relatively recent development. The few existing studies reveal that "sexuality is not the exclusive property of the young" (Hodson & Skeen, 1994, p. 219).

The landmark surveys by Kinsey and colleagues documented a decline in the overall frequency of sexual activity among older males and females in comparison to younger and middle-aged adults. Call and colleagues (1995) reported that the frequency of sexual activity among married couples decreased from two to three times per week for those under 30 years of age to three times per month by age 65. They reported that age per se, rather than length of marriage, accounted for the decline. In other words, the decline in sexuality for older couples is not due to boredom or lack of novelty but to being older. Similarly, the older adults surveyed by Laumann and colleagues (1994) reported rates of sexual activity lower than those of younger adults. Men and women aged 50–60 reported a significant decrease in the frequency of masturbation and of sexual intercourse. By age 70–74, over 70% of the women were sexually inactive, as were 35% of the men. These figures seem to provide some support for the popular view that elderly persons have little interest in sex. However, these findings are not universal. Some elderly individuals maintain active and fulfilling sex lives, as illustrated in Figure 12.4, and healthy and happily married couples tend to be the most sexually active (Hawton, Gath, & Day, 1994).

Overall, studies of sexuality and aging consistently reveal a decline in sexual interests in older persons. However, advancing age does not eliminate sexual needs and behaviors. Many elderly persons maintain regular, if less active, sex lives (Morokoff, 1988). In fact, many elderly couples report that the quality of their intimate and sexual relationship has improved over the years, as the following quote illustrates:

> I am seventy-four years old and have been married for 52 years. We are fortunate to have good mental as well as physical health. . . . In our 52 years together we have had a lot of laughs. A sense of humor is as important as food, especially within the confines of marriage. For us the sharing that comes with having a warm and loving sex life over so many years deepens our joy in one another. (Adapted from Boston Women's Health Book Collective, *The New Our Bodies, Ourselves,* 1992, p. 535)

Although older couples may have sexual interactions less frequently, they often experience more satisfaction from those encounters. With advancing age, many men and women learn to experiment with novel ways of pleasing their partners, are less worried about performance, and derive more pleasure from touching, holding, and cuddling. Many older individuals feel that they no longer need to prove their adequacy as sexual beings. They can truly enjoy the experience of sexuality unencumbered by worries and inhibitions. For many older persons, having sex reaffirms their sexual selves and adds a sense of vitality to their lives (Adams & Turner, 1985).

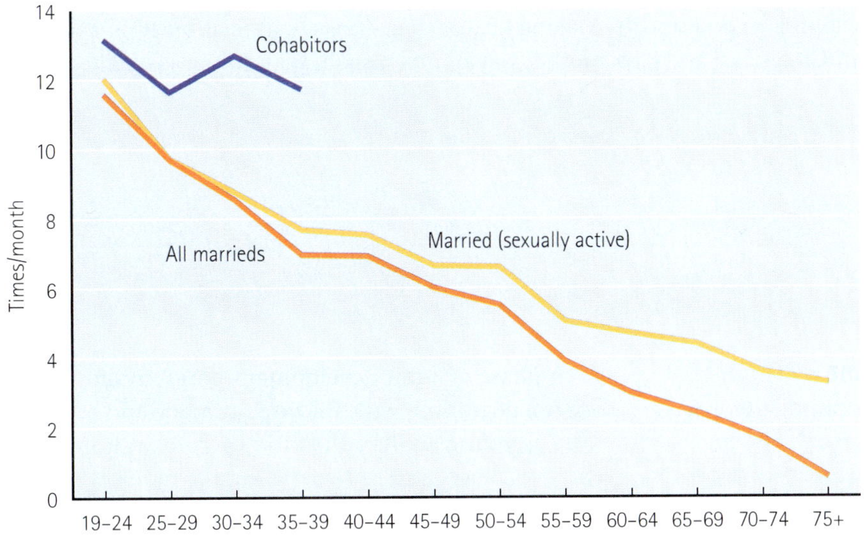

Figure 12.4 Frequency of Sex Last Month by Age and Marital Status

Contrary to popular stereotypes, sexuality and aging are not incompatible. A number of factors influence rates of sexual activity in older persons, including health, partner availability, and relationship satisfaction. As a rule, men and women who had active sex lives as younger adults continue to have sexual needs and interests into their advancing years. As Rothberg (1987) noted, "The potential for sexual expression continues until the day we die" (p. 4). All of us—including older people themselves—must overcome the popular stereotype that aging and sexuality are incompatible.

HEALTHY DECISION MAKING

As we progress through adulthood, our bodies change, and along with physical changes come changes in sexual functioning. Contrary to popular belief, though, these changes need not inevitably be problematic. People who are in good physical and emotional health and who have a sexual partner can expect to maintain rewarding sex lives. The odds of enjoying a long sexual life are greatly increased by being well-informed and making healthy decisions throughout life. The following recommendations may be helpful.

1. Educate yourself about the normal changes associated with aging. The material in this chapter and the preceding one will help you understand the normal sexual changes that people experience from childhood into their elderly years. If you are in a long-term relationship, you may find it beneficial to share this information with your partner.

2. Expect that both you and your partner will experience age-related changes in your sexual functioning. Anticipating some changes will make it easier to accept them. It is easier to cope with changes that are expected rather than unexpected.

3. Adjust to age-related changes as they occur. As noted earlier, many changes, such as the slowing in sexual responsiveness that can begin at midlife, can be welcome ones if both partners understand and accept them. Needing more time to become sexually aroused is conducive to spending more time kissing, cuddling, and caressing. In turn, this increased amount of foreplay can increase sexual enjoyment for both partners.

4. Make healthy decisions. One of the best ways to ensure a long and satisfying sex life is to adopt a healthy lifestyle today. Avoiding excessive use of alcohol, not smoking, and staying physically fit will make you feel better, in addition to reducing your risk of future health problems that could interfere with sexual functioning (see Chapter 13). The earlier in life that you adopt a healthy lifestyle, the better your chances are of maintaining a good sex life. Making healthy decisions about relationships, as discussed in Chapters 7 and 8, is another way of investing in your future sexual health.

summary

PSYCHOSOCIAL CHALLENGES OF ADULTHOOD

- As individuals enter adulthood, they continue to form their sexual identity and their overall sexual self-concept. Sexual meanings, which shape sexual identity, are derived from personal experiences and from cultural messages.
- Each phase of adult development poses unique challenges, beginning with finding intimacy and continuing as young adults adjust to new roles at home, in the workplace, and in society. Midlife requires individuals to adjust to changing physical appearance and increased responsibilities. For many people, late

adulthood is a period of contemplating one's lifetime accomplishments and finding meaning.

SINGLEHOOD

- In contrast to popular stereotypes, most singles are fairly comfortable with their lives. For many singles, dating affords opportunities to fulfill psychological, social, and sexual needs. According to the prevailing cultural script in the United States, sex "belongs" in a committed relationship, although exceptions to this rule are sometimes allowed.
- Sexual permissiveness is correlated with age, education, religiousness, gender, socioeconomic status, and relationship status. Overall, younger persons with more education, low levels of religiousness, and middle to upper income levels are more permissive. Men are generally more permissive than women.

COHABITATION: AN ALTERNATIVE TO MARRIAGE?

- Cohabitation is becoming an increasingly popular alternative to marriage, usually as a trial permanent relationship.

MARRIAGE

- Marriage is the preferred context for sexual intimacy in virtually every culture in the world. In recent decades in the United States, however, people have been postponing first marriage until later ages. Nearly half of all marriages end in divorce, yet most divorced persons eventually remarry.
- Men and women, regardless of sexual orientation, select partners with whom they share basic characteristics. Marital satisfaction varies over the course of a relationship, especially for women. Marital satisfaction is higher among couples who share power and learn how to negotiate their differences with humor and affection.
- Same-sex marriage is a controversial topic. Like heterosexual couples, most gay and lesbian couples wish to form a lifelong intimate relationship.
- Sexual inactivity in a marriage may be a sign that the relationship is troubled. Fortunately, half or more of married couples are sexually satisfied with their relationship.
- Infidelity is the single most commonly cited reason for marital breakups around the world. People have extramarital affairs for different reasons: sex, romantic love, emotional intimacy, or external reasons. Infidelity can hurt a relationship, but it need not inevitably end it. It is important, however, for couples to address the factors that led to the infidelity. Swinging, or partner swapping, is an uncommon and controversial practice.

DIVORCE

- Divorce rates in the United States have remained stable since the mid-1980s. Divorce does not carry the stigma it once did. Marital unhappiness, sexual problems, infidelity, and getting married too young are all risk factors for divorce. Adjusting to divorce is usually a lengthy process.

SEXUALITY AND AGING

- Contrary to popular stereotypes, older adults are able to maintain rewarding sexual relationships. Health problems or the unavailability of a partner may interfere with an older person's ability to maintain a healthy sex life.
- For women and men, aging brings a slowing in sexual responsiveness. Women also have to adjust to menopause. Many older couples who have spent many years together are deeply satisfied with their relationships.

CHAPTER 13

Sexual Dysfunctions

Greta was a 39-year-old single woman who was a virgin. She described a severe, lifelong aversion to sex. She was even disgusted by the thought of kissing a man. She was filled with dread at the prospect of meeting a man who might make a sexual advance, and she had avoided all dating opportunities. Greta had no difficulty using sexual fantasy and masturbating to orgasm when alone.

(Adapted from Kaplan, 1995)

Marjorie, age 44, and her partner of 10 years, Cheryl, age 47, were referred for sex therapy. They described a history of frequent and satisfying sex in the beginning of the relationship. Over the past few years, the frequency of sexual encounters had decreased to three to four times per year. The relationship was also characterized by frequent and sometimes volatile arguments. They originally agreed that Marjorie, labeled the "sexually repressed one" because of her upbringing, was the source of the sexual problem. In therapy, however, they came to recognize that the relationship dynamics were the main problem.

(Adapted from Nichols, 1995)

Max and Rita, an attractive couple in their early 40s, were referred for treatment of his long-standing problem with premature ejaculation. Although the problem dated back to Max's first sexual encounter at age 19, his loss of control had worsened significantly over the past 5 years. Over the past 6 months, the couple attempted sexual intercourse only three times, and he ejaculated prior to penetration on two of these occasions. Max felt frustration and shame, and he had essentially stopped initiating all sexual contacts with his partner. Rita was angry and resentful that he had waited so long before seeking professional help.

(Adapted from Rosen, 1995)

Max felt frustration and shame.

OVERVIEW OF SEXUAL DYSFUNCTIONS

What do Greta, Marjorie and Cheryl, and Max have in common? In clinical terms, all can be described as suffering from a sexual dysfunction—a problem with sexual performance. Experiencing a few isolated instances of problems with sexual performance is not a sexual dysfunction. All women and men experience occasional changes in their sexual performance. A temporary change in sex drive, an occasional problem in becoming sexually aroused, or even periodic difficulty

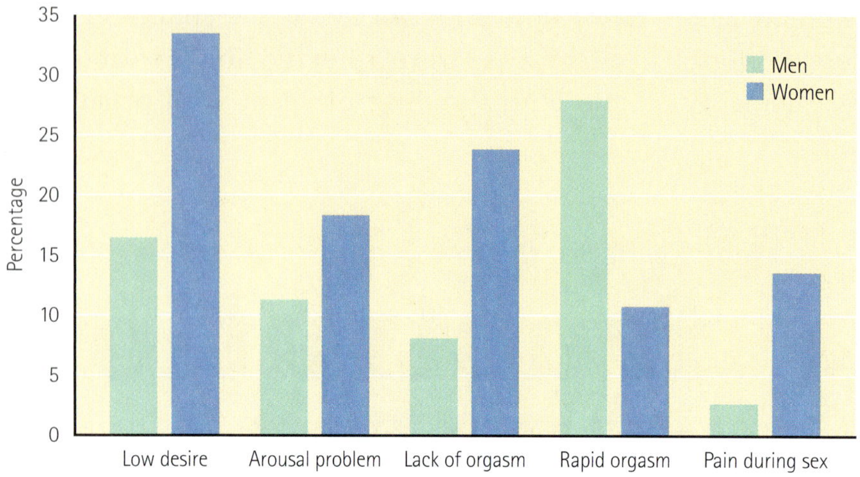

Figure 13.1 Prevalence of Sexual Problems from the NHSLS

in achieving orgasm are not uncommon experiences. **Sexual dysfunctions** are performance problems that are persistent or recurrent and distressing to the person with the problem and his or her partner.

Research shows that sexual dysfunction is common. Masters and Johnson (1970) reported that half of all married couples were affected by some form of sexual dysfunction, a finding that was originally met with much skepticism. Other studies, however, have confirmed that sexual dysfunctions are indeed common. In one well-known study, Frank, Anderson, and Rubinstein (1978) interviewed 100 happily married couples. The goals of the study were to determine the prevalence of sexual dysfunctions in this sample and to examine the relationship between couples' marital and sexual satisfaction. Although over 80% of the couples rated their marital and sexual adjustment as happy and satisfying, a significant number of the participants—approximately 40% of the men and 63% of the women—reported problems with sexual performance. Perhaps more surprising was the finding that having sexual problems was not strongly associated with couples' overall sexual satisfaction. This finding confirms that sexual satisfaction hinges on much more than performance. As you learned in Chapter 8, sexual satisfaction is also a function of such relationship factors as communication, intimacy, mutual respect, and trust (Wincze & Carey, 2001).

A recent reanalysis of the National Health and Social Life Survey (NHSLS) (Laumann, Paik, & Rosen, 1999) of over 3,000 adults indicated that 43% of women and 31% of men admitted to having a sexual dysfunction. These problems were more common in younger women and in older men. They were also often linked with poor emotional and physical health. Sexual dysfunctions are not limited to heterosexual persons; as the chapter opening vignette indicates, they also affect lesbians and gay men (Reece, 1987, 1988). One consistent finding is that sexual dysfunctions are common in the United States. Figure 13.1 illustrates some of the sexual problems reported by American men and women.

This chapter's overview of sexual dysfunctions draws on information from Chapter 4, which discussed the normal phases of sexual arousal and sexual response. A sound knowledge of the normal aspects of sexual arousal and response is essential to understanding how sexual dysfunctions manifest themselves and how they develop, as well as how to overcome them.

13.1 on the web

To learn more about sexual dysfunctions, visit **www.ablongman.com/mcanulty2e** and enter the key terms "male sexual problems," "female sexual problems," or "sexual dysfunction."

Which sexual problems are discussed the most? What treatments are described? What information do you find on the prevalence of such problems?

TYPES OF SEXUAL DYSFUNCTIONS

As Figure 13.1 suggests, sexual dysfunctions may involve difficulties with desire, arousal, or orgasm, or they may involve pain during sex. The American Psychiatric Association recognizes nine different sexual dysfunctions, based on the problem in question. Table 13.1 lists and describes these nine dysfunctions, which are described in the APA's DSM-IV-TR (2000).

The necessity for avoiding personal biases and subjectivity is recognized in the APA classification of sexual dysfunctions. Clinicians are advised to consider a number of

SEXUAL DYSFUNCTION
A recurrent sexual problem that interferes with normal performance and causes distress for the individual and his or her partner.

TABLE 13.1 List of Sexual Dysfunctions from DSM-IV-TR

DYSFUNCTION	DESCRIPTION
Hypoactive Sexual Desire Disorder	Persistently or recurrently deficient (or absent) sexual fantasies and desire for sexual activity
Sexual Aversion Disorder	Persistent or recurrent extreme aversion to, and avoidance of, all (or almost all) genital sexual contact with a sexual partner
Female Sexual Arousal Disorder	Persistent or recurrent inability to attain, or to maintain until completion of the sexual activity, an adequate lubrication-swelling response of sexual excitement
Male Erectile Disorder	Persistent or recurrent inability to attain or maintain until completion of the sexual activity, an adequate erection
Female Orgasmic Disorder	Persistent or recurrent delay in, or absence of, orgasm following a normal sexual excitement phase
Male Orgasmic Disorder	Persistent or recurrent delay in, or absence of, orgasm following a normal sexual excitement phase during sexual activity
Premature Ejaculation	Persistent or recurrent ejaculation with minimal sexual stimulation before, on, or shortly after penetration and before the person wishes it
Dyspareunia	Recurrent or persistent genital pain associated with sexual intercourse in either a male or a female
Vaginismus	Recurrent or persistent involuntary spasm of the musculature of the outer third of the vagina that interferes with sexual intercourse

factors such as the age and experiences of the individual, frequency of the problem in question, amount of distress it causes, and frequency of sexual activity. These considerations are very important in preventing professionals and affected individuals from erroneously labeling normal sexual variations as dysfunctions. Again, remember that an occasional decrease in sex drive or problem with performance does *not* constitute a dysfunction.

Sexual Desire Disorders

By definition, sexual desire is a subjective emotional state (Beck, 1995; Leiblum & Rosen, 2000). This state may be triggered by external cues, such as the sight of a sexually attractive partner, or by internal cues, such as memories of a previous sexual experience or sexual fantasies. The state of sexual desire may or may not lead to actual sexual behavior.

The essential problem in sexual desire disorders is that the person has an abnormally low or absent interest in sexual activity. This diagnosis implies that healthy sexuality includes a regular desire for sexual activity and that individuals will take advantage of opportunities for sexual interactions that they find desirable. Individuals who are persistently uninterested in sexual activity, who experience few if any sexual

Looking At . . .

. . . Thinking About

In the Victorian era, the ideal woman was a wife and mother, pure in her thoughts and chaste. Because sexual urges were viewed as impure, it was considered improper for women to have an interest in sex. Do you think such attitudes have lingering effects today? How have views of normal sexual desire evolved in U.S. culture?

fantasies, and who consistently avoid opportunities for sexual interaction are described as suffering from a sexual desire disorder (Carey & Gordon, 1995).

Hypoactive Sexual Desire Disorder

Hypoactive sexual desire disorder involves a persistent deficiency in sexual fantasies and desire for sexual activity; in some cases, the person reports a complete absence of sexual urges and fantasies (APA, 2000). The lack of desire causes distress to the individual or problems in intimate relationships. Individuals with this problem rarely initiate sexual activity with a partner and may go to great lengths to avoid sexual interactions. Although they may occasionally have sex with a partner, they usually do so to reduce conflict and please the partner.

Defining what constitutes hypoactive sexual desire can be difficult and subjective. Sexually "normal" people vary tremendously in the frequency and intensity of their sexual desire and fantasies. Some individuals of both sexes experience daily sexual thoughts and fantasies, while others report experiencing few such urges and fantasies. Men, as a group, report fantasizing about sex more frequently than women do. For example, one survey found that 54% of men and 19% of women reported daily thoughts about sex (Laumann, Gagnon, Michael, & Michaels, 1994). Although men generally report more frequent sexual fantasies and urges than women, there is considerable variability among members of both sexes (Baldwin & Baldwin, 1997; Renaud & Byers, 1999).

Because there are no definitive statistics that can establish the norm for sexual desire, a number of potential contributing factors must be considered (Tolman & Diamond, 2001). The person's age, life situation, and cultural background, as well as the quality of the relationship, must be taken into account. A decrease in sexual desire in the context of a divorce or other personal crisis does not constitute a desire disorder. Likewise, individuals whose cultural scripts prohibit them from expressing their sexual feelings are not labeled as suffering from a disorder. In their cultural context, the absence of sexual feelings is considered normal.

Couples seeking counseling for relationship problems commonly complain of discrepancies in their sex drives. However, just because one partner desires sex more frequently than the other does not mean that a sexual desire disorder is responsible. It is entirely possible that one partner has an excessive need for sexual interactions. Although most sex researchers and clinicians agree that hypoactive sexual desire disorder exists, the *DSM-IV* classification does not include hyperactive sexual desire disorder, and there is tremendous controversy over the concept of hypersexuality (see Health Matters: Too Much of a Good Thing?). Finally, it is also possible that two people with different degrees of sex drive are both normal but simply different (Wincze & Carey, 2001).

Over half of all people seeking sex therapy in recent years suffer from sexual desire disorders. Contrary to cultural stereotypes, these disorders do not occur exclusively in women. Males represent 50–60% of all cases seen in clinics (Kaplan, 1995; Spector & Carey, 1990). Although some researchers have disputed these figures (Letourneau & O'Donohue, 1993), there has definitely been an increase over the years in the number of males suffering from hypoactive sexual desire disorder. Hypoactive sexual desire disorder occurs in 15% of adult men (Laumann et al., 1999) and is the presenting com-

HYPOACTIVE SEXUAL DESIRE DISORDER
A sexual dysfunction involving a persistent deficit in sexual fantasies and desire for sex.

HEALTH Matters

Too Much of a Good Thing?

S*exual addiction, hypersexuality, sexual compulsivity, nymphomania, sexual impulsivity*—all are terms that have been used to describe what some writers view as pathologically excessive sexual desire. Essentially, "excessive" sexual desire is at the other end of the continuum from hypoactive sexual desire disorder. (Hyperactive sexual desire disorder is not among the *DSM-IV* classification of mental disorders.)

As conceptualized by such writers as Patrick Carnes (1983) and Aviel Goodman (1993), sexual addiction is similar to alcoholism and drug addiction. According to Carnes (1983), sexual addiction involves four key symptoms: a preoccupation with sex, ritualized sexual behavior (such as cruising for anonymous sex or visiting prostitutes), sexual compulsivity (loss of control over one's sexual behavior), and feelings of shame and despair resulting from sexual behavior. Goodman (1993) emphasized "a pattern characterized by recurrent failure to control the behavior and continuation of the behavior despite significant harmful consequences" (p. 226). Addictive behaviors, according to this view, simultaneously provide pleasure and an escape from unpleasant emotions such as boredom, anger, depression, and tension—but at a cost, because they are self-destructive.

In ancient Greek mythology, satyrs were part animal and part human. They were companions of Dionysus, the god of wine and fertility. Satyrs pursued nymphs, young and beautiful maidens who lived in nature, for sexual purposes. The term nymph *comes from the same root as* nymphae, *a reference to the inner labia of the vulva.* Nymph *is the root of the term* nymphomania.

The addiction model has been criticized as an oversimplification that is not supported by research (Coleman, 1990; Rinehart & McCabe, 1997). For example, some writers have grouped men who are preoccupied with pornography, compulsive masturbators, and child molesters in the same "sexual addict" category, implying that all have the same fundamental "disease." Additionally, there is no identifiable physical addiction or withdrawal reaction associated with sexual addiction. Finally, the label implies that the condition is permanent. This "disease model" has nonetheless been influential; it has spawned self-help groups such as Sexual Addicts Anonymous and Sex and Love Addicts Anonymous, all patterned after the 12-step program of Alcoholics Anonymous (AA).

More recently, the terms *hypersexuality* and *compulsive sexual behavior* have been used to denote an exaggerated sex drive. These terms, however, present the same problems as those encountered in trying to define hypoactive sexual desire. Because of these problems with definitions, there are wide differences in estimates of the prevalence of hypersexuality. Some researchers (Kaplan, 1979a; Leiblum & Rosen, 1988) argue that it is rare; others propose that it is a relatively common problem, especially in men (Carnes, 1983). Unfortunately, very few studies of hypersexuality have been conducted. Quadland (1985) compared a group of 30 gay or bisexual men who requested treatment for compulsive sexual behavior to a group of gay or bisexual men who had no such problems. The sexually compulsive men were no more neurotic than the comparison group, although they reported fewer long-term relationships, more sexual experiences in public settings, and more lifetime sexual partners. The groups did *not* differ in their desired number of partners or desired frequency of sex. Malatesta and Robinson (1995) concluded that this suggested a problem with sexual compulsiveness rather than hypersexuality, since the groups differed in their *actual* number rather than in their *desired* number of sexual partners.

Until scientists have a better understanding of excessive sexual desire and potential problems associated with it, there is a danger in using labels such as "sexual addiction" or "hypersexuality." These labels are stigmatizing and suggest pathology—a disease or disorder of some sort—when none to date has been uncovered (Rinehart & McCabe, 1997). There is no consensus on what excessive sexual desire is or even as to whether it should be labeled at all. Recall the controversy over masturbation described in Chapter 1. Will sexual addiction have a similar history?

13.2 on the web

According to some sources, online sexual addiction is a growing problem. To learn more about this problem, go to **www.ablongman.com/mcanulty2e,** find the link for online sex addiction, and review the information.

How does online sexual addiction relate to hypersexuality? What questions are asked in the online sexual addiction questionnaire? What research evidence is there to support claims that this is a serious problem?

13.3 on the web

Go to **www.ablongman.com/mcanulty2e** and find the link for panic disorders to learn more about the effects of various medications on sexual functioning.

Which seem to interfere with sex drive? Which might be useful in restoring sexual functioning? What are common side effects?

plaint of 30–40% of women seeking sex therapy (Hawton, Catalan, Martin, & Fagg, 1986). The NHSLS survey revealed that over 33% of women in the general U.S. population reported a lack of desire in sex (Laumann et al., 1999).

Most studies on the medical causes of hypoactive sexual desire disorder have concentrated on the role of sex hormones. It has long been known that abnormally low levels of testosterone cause a sharp decrease in a man's sex drive. For example, Bancroft (1984) found that men who had their testicles surgically removed because of cancer experienced a marked decrease in sex drive and in sexual behavior within 2–3 weeks of surgery. Testosterone injections restored normal sex drive in these men (Heiman, 2002b).

Other hormonal studies of individuals with hypoactive sexual desire disorder, however, have yielded mixed results (Wincze & Carey, 2001). One investigation suggested that men with hypoactive sexual desire disorder have lower levels of testosterone than men with normal sex drives (Schiavi, Schreiner-Engel, White, & Mandeli, 1988). The actual difference in levels of testosterone between groups was, however, very modest. As noted in Chapter 4, there is a growing consensus that testosterone is the major sex hormone associated with sex drive in males and females. However, the role it plays in hypoactive sexual desire disorder remains uncertain (Wincze & Carey, 2001). Only a minority of individuals with deficient sexual desire show measurable abnormalities in levels of testosterone and other sex hormones. One possibility is that these individuals may have a normal level of testosterone but an abnormally low number of receptors for that hormone in the brain (Kresin, 1993). Lacking a normal number of brain receptors, these individuals are not able to process testosterone normally.

In addition to possible hormonal factors, numerous causes for sexual desire disorders have been identified. Deficits in sexual desire can be triggered by some medical conditions, certain drugs and medications, emotional problems, negative feelings about sex, and relationship conflicts. Additionally, most people experience a decline in sex drive when they feel overwhelmed by stress. A later section of this chapter will examine the general causes of desire disorders and the other sexual dysfunctions.

Sexual Aversion Disorder

A **sexual aversion disorder** involves extreme aversion to virtually all sexual contact with a partner. The intensely negative feelings about sexual interactions may lead to avoidance of any type of intimacy with another person. An individual with this problem may go to great lengths to avoid situations that could lead to sexual activity—even neglecting his or her personal appearance or becoming overinvolved in work or other activities (APA, 2000). In more severe cases, the person may avoid dating altogether, as illustrated by the case of Greta in the opening vignette. Sexual aversion disorder is often described as a sexual phobia, because of the accompanying avoidance behaviors and the fear of sex (Gold & Gold, 1993). This disorder may be generalized or situational (Kaplan, 1987). A person with a generalized form of sexual aversion disorder, like Greta, avoids any and all sexual activity with a partner. A person with a situational sexual aversion disorder experiences feelings of disgust or fear in connection with one particular sexual act, such as oral sex, but otherwise functions adequately with a sexual partner (Everaerd, Laan, Roth, & van der Velde, 2000). Some researchers believe that sexual aversion and hypoactive sexual desire disorders are related, representing different points on a continuum of sexual avoidance (LoPiccolo & Friedman, 1988; Wincze & Carey, 2001).

SEXUAL AVERSION DISORDER
A sexual dysfunction characterized by extreme aversion to any form of sexual contact with a partner.

As currently defined, sexual aversion disorder occurs mostly in women (APA, 2000). There has been surprisingly little research on this disorder, however. Consequently, there are no reliable estimates of its prevalence. Over 21% of women in the NHSLS reported that sex was not pleasurable for them, but this does not necessarily mean that they suffered from sexual aversion disorder. Heiman (2002b) reported that it is a "rather rare" disorder.

Sexual Arousal Disorders

Sexual arousal entails the various physiological, cognitive, and emotional changes that a person undergoes in a sexual situation in preparation for sexual behavior. The sexual arousal disorders are characterized by problems with the process of sexual arousal. Women experience difficulties with vaginal lubrication; men have recurrent problems attaining or sustaining an erection. In both cases, the sexual dysfunction interferes with sexual activity. In women, sexual arousal difficulties make sexual intercourse painful if not impossible because of insufficient lubrication. In men, erection problems interfere with penetration. An occasional lapse in sexual responsiveness is not uncommon; the problem is not considered a disorder unless it becomes persistent.

Female Sexual Arousal Disorder

Female sexual arousal disorder involves a persistent inability to become sexually excited or to maintain an adequate level of arousal (APA, 2000). Most characteristically, it involves failure to experience vaginal lubrication and swelling of the outer labia in a sexual situation. Female sexual arousal disorder may be viewed as a lack of physiological or psychological responsiveness to adequate sexual stimulation. A deficit in mental excitement is the defining feature of this disorder (Basson et al., 2000).

In their classic text on sexual dysfunctions, Masters and Johnson (1970) omitted female sexual arousal disorder, categorizing it instead as a problem with reaching orgasm. As a consequence, they overestimated the prevalence of orgasm problems (Wakefield, 1987), without recognizing that some women are capable of having orgasms despite having difficulty becoming sexually aroused.

did YOU know?

Nearly 15% of women participating in the NHSLS reported problems with vaginal lubrication during sexual encounters (Laumann et al., 1999).

The signs of failure to become sexually aroused may go unnoticed in women. By using a vaginal lubricant, a woman may be capable of sexual intercourse even if she is not physically aroused. Men, however, have difficulty with penetration if the penis is flaccid (nonerect). Because both personal and cultural attitudes toward female sexuality are still ambivalent, some women who have difficulty achieving sexual arousal may be reluctant to label it a problem.

Because female sexual arousal disorder has only recently been identified as a problem for some women, there have been few studies on its causes. Many of the risk factors that have been identified for sexual desire disorders may also apply here. Hormones, negative emotions, and relationship problems may contribute to difficulties with sexual arousal. Any physical condition that interferes with vaginal lubrication could cause such difficulties. Approximately one-third of women with diabetes, for example, complain of problems with vaginal lubrication (Enzlin, Mathieu, Vanderschueren, & Demyttenaere, 1998). As you saw in earlier chapters, pregnancy, menstrual cycle phases, and menopause all involve significant changes in hormone levels. Low levels of estrogen are known to decrease vaginal lubrication, an important component of physical arousal. Postmenopausal women who are not taking replacement estrogens often report a decrease in sexual arousal, and this seems to be due to their awareness that vaginal lubrication is reduced (Myers & Morokoff, 1986). Some (although by no means all) women report that menopause has a detrimental effect on sexual functioning (Morokoff, 1988). This may be especially true for women whose ovaries have been surgically removed. These women experience not only decreased levels of estrogens (especially estradiol) but also reductions in levels of testosterone. Such women may have difficulties with both vaginal lubrication and a diminished sex drive.

Male Erectile Disorder

As defined in *DSM-IV-TR,* **male erectile disorder** involves a "persistent or recurrent inability to attain, or to maintain until completion of sexual activity, an adequate erection." (APA, 2000). The problem involves more than just an occasional inability to

FEMALE SEXUAL AROUSAL DISORDER
A sexual dysfunction involving difficulties becoming sexually aroused, including deficient vaginal lubrication.

MALE ERECTILE DISORDER
A sexual dysfunction involving recurrent problems in achieving or sustaining an erection in a sexual situation.

CLOSE UP ON gender

Myths about Sex in the United States

Most of our beliefs and expectations about sex do not come from courses or books on sexuality. Instead, we derive them from the multitude of messages that we receive throughout our lives from various other sources, including jokes, TV shows, magazine articles, novels, and movies. According to Zilbergeld (1999), such sources create an unrealistic view of sex, what he calls the "fantasy model of sex." This model is a totally unreal picture of "how bodies look and function, how people relate, and how they have sex" (p. 16). This unrealistic model affects men and women alike, creating sexual pressures and contributing to sexual difficulties (Ravart, Trudel, Marchand, Turgeon, & Aubin, 1996; Zilbergeld, 1999). Following are some of the most common myths that spring from this model.

1. *Most people are liberated, open-minded, and comfortable with sex.* Characters in media portrayals approach sex openly and explicitly, without any inhibitions. In reality, everyone has some discomfort with sex. Knowing that most people are at least somewhat uncomfortable discussing sex can help us understand ourselves and our partners. This awareness in turn can improve our sexual relationships by making us more sensitive to our partners' feelings.

2. *Real men are not into feelings and communication.* Real men, we might believe, are too macho to talk about feelings, and they don't need to communicate about sex, since they presumably know everything anyway. In fact, nobody knows everything about sex (even people who write books about it!)—and communicating with one's partner is the single most effective way to improve one's sex life.

3. *Men are always ready to have sex.* The "ever-ready" view of male sexuality creates enormous pressure on men and women. Men find it difficult to decline a sexual invitation, and they may be viewed by their partners as insatiable. This is a very common myth among men and women. In one study of women with low sexual desire, nearly two of three participants believed this myth (Ravart et al., 1996). Not surprisingly, these women felt pressured sexually, which contributed to their sexual difficulties.

4. *Making love should not be planned; rather, it should always be natural and spontaneous.* In fantasyland, sex is completely spontaneous. Two partners, overwhelmed with desire, enjoy passionate lovemaking on the spot, without discussion or planning. In reality, spontaneous sex is often not possible or practical. We have no trouble planning other activities, even important ones, yet sex is supposed to be different. Of course, planning requires communication, something that many people are uncomfortable with.

5. *There can be no sex without an erection (preferably one that is hard as steel and lasts all night).* This myth reflects the American cultural obsession with penis size. As Zilbergeld (1999) noted, in fantasyland penises

have an erection, and it causes significant distress for the man and often for his partner. Different patterns have been described. Some men report an inability to experience erection during foreplay. Others have relatively normal erections but lose them during attempts at penetration. In some cases, the man may successfully penetrate his partner but then lose the erection without ejaculating.

Popular magazines regularly feature articles that offer tips for improving sexual performance, often perpetuating unrealistic views of sex and relationships.

There has been more research on male erectile disorder than on any other sexual dysfunction. This is due, in part, to a cultural script that views male sexuality as more important. It has also been suggested that men find sexual performance problems more threatening to their self-esteem than women do and, therefore, draw more attention to their problems. As Person (1980) noted, a man with erection problems "always feels that his masculinity, and not just his sexuality, is threatened" (p. 619). American culture places a good deal of emphasis on erections, as witnessed by the countless jokes, media messages, and advertised remedies that address erectile problems. This exaggerated and unrealistic emphasis on erections is one aspect of what Zilbergeld (1999) refers to as the "fantasy model of sex." The fantasy model of sex and other myths about sexual performance affecting men and women are discussed in Close Up on Gender: Myths about Sex in the United States.

come in three sizes, "large, extra large, and so big you can't get them through the door" (p. 26). The clear message is that a man who does not "measure up" is inadequate and ineffective. Of course, this is a false standard, but many men and their partners are affected by this myth and may unrealistically devalue their sexual performance.

6. *A good sexual experience must always end with orgasm.* Like the previous myths, this one equates sexual adequacy with sexual performance. The total experience is judged by the outcome, which detracts from the other positive aspects of sex, such as sharing, intimacy, closeness, and pleasurable sensations. People often evaluate their sexual competence based on frequency and intensity of orgasms. Women in particular are vulnerable to this myth, which may cause them to feel obligated to have orgasms during intercourse or to have multiple orgasms. Men in turn may evaluate their performance based on their partner's orgasmic responsiveness. This type of pressure leads some women (and even men) to fake orgasms.

7. *Simultaneous orgasm is the highest level of sexual achievement, and all couples should strive for it.* This myth extends the previous one by making simultaneous orgasm of paramount importance. Not only must sex lead to orgasms, but they must be perfectly synchronized. This myth can cause tremendous pressure on a couple and detract from shared intimacy.

8. *Sex means sexual intercourse.* To most people, "sex" means sexual intercourse. However, equating sex with intercourse greatly limits the range of sexual activities. Even the word "foreplay" implies that such activities as kissing and caressing are preludes to the main event. In reality, many couples find sexual satisfaction through other sexual activities such as oral sex and mutual masturbation. This myth reinforces the one about an erection being critical to sexual success and contributes to the tendency to approach sex as a performance.

9. *If people masturbate, it is because something is wrong with their sexual relationship.* Masturbation is a normal and healthy sexual outlet for most adults. Many people who are in relationships masturbate occasionally (Laumann et al., 1994), and this does not mean that the sexual relationship is inadequate. Both men and women report that the orgasms they achieve through masturbation are often more enjoyable. Thus, as long as it does not replace shared sexual activities, masturbation is a healthy and safe sexual outlet.

10. *Sex should be avoided during menstruation.* This myth relates to the cultural taboo associated with menstruation. Although some women and men may choose to avoid sexual intercourse during menstruation, intercourse is by no means unhealthy at this time.

In summary, these cultural myths about sex overemphasize performance. Consequently, they restrict sexual activity and create undue pressure on individuals. These myths are unrealistic and detract from sexual enjoyment. They are, unfortunately, pervasive in American society.

Review each myth, and ask yourself how much you believe each one. Simply being aware that these are myths may lessen their impact somewhat and help you enjoy greater sexual intimacy.

As a practicing sex therapist, Zilbergeld observed that many of his clients held unrealistic notions about normal sexual performance. For example, many men seemed to believe that "they needed a penis as big and hard as a telephone pole to satisfy a woman" (1999, p. 15). Although perhaps too dramatic, this statement does illustrate the intense pressure many men feel to achieve and maintain a full erection during sexual encounters. The term *impotence,* which means "powerlessness" or "ineffectiveness," conveys the idea that a man who can't get an erection is ineffective—which is why sexologists and sex therapists have abandoned the term. However, many medical professionals, including urologists, still use *impotence* (or *impotency*) to refer to erectile disorder.

Not surprisingly, because of the tendency to measure a man's sexual competence by his erection, most men with male erectile disorder are devastated by the problem. Men seeking treatment for erection problems almost invariably suffer from depression, fear, guilt, and shame. They are frustrated and feel helpless. They are commonly fearful of rejection and overly sensitive to their partners' reactions to their erectile failures (Barlow, 1986). If the problem has lasted for some time, a man often develops a fear of failure and engages in self-monitoring, or constantly checking the level of erection in sexual situations. (This corresponds to what Masters and Johnson labeled "spectatoring.") Many men experiment with various "home remedies" to solve the problem, such as drinking alcohol before having intercourse, viewing sexually explicit films, or even trying to have intercourse with someone other than the primary partner (Wincze & Carey, 2001). (In the latter case, the man's motivation seems to be an attempt to place the blame for his erection problems on his partner.) However, when these methods fail, as they almost invariably do, the individual feels more hopeless and distressed.

Numerous products promise to enhance one's sex life and to remedy sexual problems. This market illustrates the sexual performance pressure that is evident in the United States. Shown here are Jennifer Berman, Laura Berman, and Irwin Goldstein, who together are trying to develop a drug similar to Viagra for women.

For the majority of men, erection problems are temporary and associated with transient life stressors. Kaplan (1974) estimated that as many as 50% of men will experience problems with erection at some time. Anywhere from 3% to 9% of men have persistent and recurrent erectile difficulties (Spector & Carey, 1990). Rates of erection problems reported by men who participated in the NHSLS were similar; 10% agreed that they were "unable to keep an erection" (Laumann et al., 1999). The rates increase with age: Nearly 2% of 40-year-old men experience erection problems; as many as 25% experience the problem by age 65 (Krane, Goldstein, & de Tejada, 1989). Similar findings were reported in another survey of 1,700 men between the ages of 40 and 70 (Feldman, Goldstein, Hatzichristou, Krane, & McKinlay, 1994): Rates of male erectile disorder tripled from 5% at age 40 to 15% at 70, a finding that was replicated by Laumann and colleagues (1999).

Numerous studies have investigated the possible causes of male erectile disorder. Early research was plagued by the simplistic notion that erection problems could be traced to a single cause, either a medical or a psychological condition. More recently, professionals have recognized that erectile disorder is typically due to a combination of causes rather than a single factor. Deficient levels of testosterone have long been the leading medical explanation for erectile disorder. However, support for this as the cause has been equivocal at best. Recent studies suggest that testosterone deficiencies are sometimes responsible for low sexual desire but are only indirectly related to erection problems. For example, Schiavi, White, Mandeli, and Levine (1997) found that administering testosterone to men with erectile disorder did increase their sexual activity but had no measurable effect on erection capacity. Other studies have also documented an increase in sexual desire following testosterone injection without improvements in erectile function (Bancroft, 1988; O'Carroll & Bancroft, 1984). Hormonal factors are rarely the primary cause of male erectile disorder (Buvat & Lemaire, 1997; Schover & Jensen, 1988).

did YOU know?

Male erectile disorder is the most common reason why men seek sex therapy.

A host of medical conditions may affect erectile function; Table 13.2 offers a partial list of medical conditions that are known to interfere with erection. Essentially, any medical problem or any substance that interferes with the nerves or arteries of the penis is capable of causing erectile failure. The most common medical cause of male erectile disorder is diabetes mellitus (see Meisler, Carey, Lantinga, & Krauss, 1989 for a review). It has been suggested that over 2 million American men with diabetes suffer from erectile problems, leading some researchers to conclude that such problems are one of the most common symptoms of diabetes mellitus (Weinhardt & Carey, 1996). Diabetes interferes with arterial blood flow in addition to causing peripheral nerve damage in the penis, either of which could cause erection problems (Mulhall, 2000).

Injuries or diseases of the nervous system may affect erectile functioning. Spinal cord injuries (SCIs) can interfere with erections, although many patients with such injuries retain the ability to have reflexive erections. In such cases, the man may achieve a normal erection with direct genital stimulation but not through fantasy alone (Graber, 1993). Other neurological conditions, such as multiple sclerosis and temporal lobe epilepsy, may cause erectile difficulties as well (Blumer & Walker, 1967; Vas, 1969). Finally, since prostate surgery may compromise the nerves that regulate erection, erection problems are a common consequence of prostatectomy (Catalona & Bigg, 1990; Hauri, Knonagel, & Konstantinidis, 1989).

TABLE 13.2 Some Medical Causes of Male Erectile Disorder

CAUSE	SPECIFIC EXAMPLE
Aging	Anatomical defects of penis, curvature, hardening of penis (Peyronie's disease)
Congenital problems	Displaced opening of urethra, spina bifida, Klinefelter's disease, under-developed testicles
Drug abuse	Alcohol, heroin, cocaine, marijuana
Endocrine problems	Thyroid abnormalities (hyper- or hypothyroidism), pituitary insufficiency, adrenal dysfunction (Addison's disease), excess prolactin (a hormone secreted by the pituitary gland)
Infection	Inflammation of prostate, infection of skin on the penis
Neurological	Multiple sclerosis, advanced syphilis, brain tumor, spinal cord injury, severe anemia, Parkinson's disease
Organ system failure	Heart attack, kidney failure, chronic lung disease, high blood pressure (hypertension)
Pharmacological agents	Antipsychotic drugs, antidepressants, antihypertensives
Surgical complications	Lower back surgery, prostate surgery, lower abdominal surgery
Toxicological agents	Lead, herbicides
Traumatic injuries	Castration, pelvic fracture, penile trauma, ruptured disc
Urological problems	Peyronie's disease, tumor of scrotum, painful erection (priapism)
Vascular problems	Vascular disease, diabetes

Orgasmic Disorders

Like desire and arousal disorders, orgasmic disorders can be very frustrating and anxiety-provoking for both partners. Unlike disorders of desire and arousal, however, orgasmic disorders are not so much problems of performance as they are problems of completion. People with orgasmic disorders have the desire for intimacy and the ability to sustain an aroused state and to enjoy the sexual experience. What is missing is the ability to climax, to complete the sexual experience. In both men and women, orgasmic disorders include persistent difficulty reaching orgasm with a partner. Additionally, some men have a recurrent problem of climaxing too quickly with minimal stimulation.

Although orgasm problems might seem easy to define, most definitions are in fact subjective and, to a large extent, culturally determined. A given culture defines the parameters of "normal sexuality" and thereby determines what is pathological or disordered (Wakefield, 1987). As several sex researchers (Heiman & Grafton-Becker, 1989; Stock, 1993) have noted, female orgasm problems have been particularly difficult to define.

Western societies have historically viewed female sexuality with ambivalence at best. This explains in part why female sexual responsiveness has only recently been the subject of rigorous research. During the 19th century, Victorian values prevailed; reputable women (wives and mothers) were expected to be pure and, therefore, asexual. During this era, a woman's ability to have orgasms was viewed with suspicion, since sexual disinterest was expected of respectable women. To his contemporaries, Sigmund Freud's (1961) writings about female sexuality were controversial and even sacrilegious. Freud's distinction between vaginal orgasms, which he viewed as "genuine" and mature, and clitoral orgasms, which he considered immature and superficial, has been refuted by various researchers, including Masters and Johnson (1966). Freud's notions about female orgasm did, however, represent a significant transition from Victorian inhibitions to a more realistic, and therefore, progressive, view of female sexuality. His views were also a compromise, in a sense. By affirming the "superiority" of vaginal orgasms (which result from penetration), Freud reflected the Victorian belief that "proper" female sexuality is intended for procreation rather than recreation. The role of cultural factors in another sexual dysfunction is examined in Close Up on Culture: Genital Retraction Syndrome.

Genital Retraction Syndrome

Culture plays a powerful role in the origin of sexual difficulties. One example of a culture-bound sexual disorder is *Koro,* which is referred to as *genital retraction syndrome* (Chowdhury, 1998). It is most prevalent in cultures of Southern China and Southeast Asia such as Malaysia (Bartholomew, 1994). The typical case involves a male who experiences a panic reaction to the fear that his penis is retracting into his abdomen (Kovacs & Osvath, 1998). The individual is terrified that the disappearance of the penis will be fatal. In some cases, afflicted men use string, bands, or clamps—or even their friends—to hold on to their supposedly retracting genitals. The disorder tends to occur in epidemics like the one that swept through Hainan Island, China, in 1984 and 1985, affecting some 2,000 men. In that case, rumors had spread that spirits, which according to traditional cultural belief inhabited certain individuals, were stealing penises from the living. Other outbreaks of Koro have been reported in Thailand, India, China, and Singapore (Bartholomew, 1994).

Koro occurs in the context of cultural beliefs about spiritual forces that control physical and mental health (Azhar & Varma, 2000). Additionally, the disorder has been observed in cultures that subscribe to the belief that certain supernatural phenomena can affect the size and functioning of genital organs. One epidemic, for example, occurred in a region of China where men were socialized to practice sexual restraint for fear that sexual excess could cause genital shrinkage and eventual death. They also believed that ghosts wandered in search of penises that would revive them. Suggestibility played a role, as most of the afflicted men had witnessed another person having an attack prior to their own. The episodes typically began during the night with chills and the sensation of penile shrinkage. Fearing a fatal outcome and believing that they were possessed by an evil ghost, these men became panic-stricken and tugged at their penises while calling for help (Bartholomew, 1994).

Koro can also occur in females, in which case the symptoms include "sexual frigidity" and preoccupation with breast, and sometimes vaginal, shrinkage. According to Cheng (1997), Koro afflicts young people who are deprived of accurate knowledge about sexual development. An unrealistic body image is also believed to play a part in the origins of this sexual dysfunction (Chowdhury, 1998). Fortunately, the disorder is short-lived, as most people recover within a few days (Bartholomew, 1994).

Female Orgasmic Disorder

Female orgasmic disorder involves recurrent or persistent difficulty in reaching orgasm. In making this diagnosis, the clinician must have evidence that the woman consistently has problems with orgasm despite adequate erotic stimulation (APA, 2000). Yet, according to Kinsey's research (Kinsey, Pomeroy, Martin, & Gebhard, 1953), 30% of wives did not have orgasms when they were first married, and 10% remained unable to reach orgasm after 10 years of marriage. More recently, over 24% of women participating in the NHSLS complained of being "unable to come to a climax" during the previous year (Laumann et al., 1999). Forty-six percent of the "happily married" women in the study by Frank and his colleagues (1978) had difficulty reaching orgasm, and 15% complained of being unable to have an orgasm. The most commonly listed reasons were inability to relax (47%), partner choosing an inconvenient time for sex (31%), lack of foreplay (38%), and disinterest in sex (35%). Although one-fourth to one-third of women may have orgasm difficulties at some point in life, primary, or lifelong, female orgasmic disorder affects only 10–15% of women (Frank et al., 1978; Hite, 1976; Kaplan, 1974).

Simply being unable to reach orgasm during sexual intercourse does *not* warrant a diagnosis of female orgasmic disorder. For example, only 30% of the nearly 3,000 women surveyed by Hite (1976) reported that they consistently experienced orgasms through intercourse. Similarly, only 29% of women in the NHSLS reported that they always had an orgasm during sex with their regular partner. The majority of women in those surveys, therefore, were *not* consistently orgasmic during intercourse. Another problem in defining female orgasmic disorder is trying to judge whether the woman is receiving adequate stimulation. Many women require direct stimulation of their genitals, such as manual or oral stimulation, to achieve orgasm. As Heiman and Grafton-Becker (1989) concluded, orgasm problems in a woman may say more about her sociocultural context or her relationship than about her. In a sexually repressed culture or in a relationship with an insensitive or inept partner, anyone, male or female, is likely to have difficulties

FEMALE ORGASMIC DISORDER
A recurrent problem with reaching orgasm despite adequate erotic stimulation; the term should not be applied to women who occasionally do not reach orgasm through vaginal intercourse.

reaching orgasm. Other than for women who have never or rarely experienced orgasm through any means, the diagnosis of female orgasmic disorder should be used cautiously.

Cultural, psychological, and interpersonal factors interact in human sexuality, particularly in female orgasmic capacity. Physiological factors may also play a role, although little is known about their influence, except that certain drugs and medications are known to diminish or delay orgasm. Although several medical conditions and substances are known to affect orgasmic response in women (Morokoff, 1978), there is surprisingly little information on medical causes of female orgasmic disorder. Hormone deficits have been proposed as explanations for female orgasm problems, but the research is inconclusive. In one study, women who were given testosterone reported an improvement in their orgasmic capacity, in addition to the side effect of an enlarged clitoris (Bancroft, 1984). On the other hand, other studies of the effects of hormones have reported increases in sexual desire and arousal without any measurable change in orgasm (Sherwin, Gelfand, & Brender, 1985). If hormones do contribute to female orgasm problems, their role is complex and poorly understood (Kingsberg, 2002).

Men with orgasmic disorder often avoid touching and caressing, which is quite frustrating for their partners.

Male Orgasmic Disorder

Male orgasmic disorder is characterized by persistent or recurrent delay in, or absence of, orgasm during sexual activity. Here again, the orgasm difficulty occurs despite erotic stimulation that is judged to be adequate. The failure to achieve orgasm is usually limited to the inability to ejaculate during vaginal intercourse (APA, 2000). According to Apfelbaum (1989), in a typical case, the man has never had an orgasm during sexual intercourse. Most men with this problem, however, are able to reach orgasm through masturbation or oral stimulation.

The major challenge in making this diagnosis is determining how long a delay in reaching orgasm should be considered abnormal. The amount of time men need to achieve orgasm varies tremendously. Kinsey and colleagues (1948) estimated that 75% of men ejaculated within 2 minutes after penetration. Fisher, Pollack, and Malatesta (1986) reported an average ejaculation latency of 8 minutes for men who were masturbating while viewing an erotic film; two-thirds of the men in that study needed between 4 and 8 minutes to reach orgasm. Because of the difficulty in defining normal orgasmic latency, most clinicians determine that delayed orgasm is a problem only when a man complains that it regularly interferes with his sexual satisfaction and that of his partner.

There is a common misconception that inhibited male orgasm is desirable to a man and his partner, since he can "go on forever" (Dekker, 1993). In reality, over time, the problem interferes with the sexual satisfaction of both partners, who eventually begin to view their sexual encounters as work. Prolonged sexual intercourse may be painful. A man's inability to ejaculate during intercourse also tends to make both partners feel inadequate. If the only way the man can ejaculate is with manual or oral stimulation, the restriction of sexual activities may lead to monotony and a loss of spontaneity over time.

Male orgasmic disorder is believed to be uncommon. Across several studies, the prevalence ranges from 0% to 13% (Arentewicz & Schmidt, 1983; Dekker, 1993). Nathan (1986) estimated that less than 4% of men experience problems with delayed orgasm. From their review of existing studies, Wincze and Carey (2001) concluded that male orgasmic disorder is one of the least common male sexual dysfunctions. It is, however, apparently more common in gay men (Sandfort & de Keizer, 2001).

As might be expected, some of the same factors that lead to orgasm problems in women are also associated with orgasm disorders in men. A wide range of psychological explanations of male orgasmic disorder have been proposed, but research support for any of them is very limited (Dekker, 1993). Anxiety over performance and a fear of causing pregnancy or of contracting a disease may play a role. Sexual orientation issues may

MALE ORGASMIC DISORDER
A dysfunction involving a delay or inability to reach orgasm during sexual activity.

also contribute to orgasmic difficulties in men. Hostility has frequently been mentioned as a possible cause for this problem. According to this viewpoint, some men are unable to "let go" and climax because of anger and hostility directed at their sexual partners. One of the few medical explanations of inhibited orgasm in men suggests that spinal cord abnormalities may be involved (Brindley & Gillan, 1982). This hypothesis is speculative, however, since there have been no studies to investigate it.

Premature Ejaculation

Like male orgasmic disorder, premature ejaculation (or *early ejaculation*) involves a problem with the time it takes a man to reach orgasm. However, premature ejaculation is essentially the opposite of male orgasmic disorder. **Premature ejaculation** is "persistent or recurrent ejaculation with minimal sexual stimulation before, on, or shortly after penetration and before the person wishes it" (APA, 2000). Several factors must be considered in determining whether a man has this disorder. Age is important, since younger men typically require less stimulation before reaching orgasm. In fact, one sex therapist commented that virtually all males begin their sex lives as premature ejaculators (McCarthy, 1989). Novelty is another factor to consider. Having a new partner or trying a new sexual technique with a regular partner may lead to early ejaculation and, therefore, is not considered abnormal or unusual. Most men require longer to climax during masturbation than during sexual activity with a partner. Finally, frequency of sexual activity plays a role in the timing of ejaculation. Men who have sex infrequently generally require less stimulation to reach orgasm than men who have sex frequently.

did YOU know?

Grenier and Byers (1997) found that a majority of college males express some concern about ejaculating earlier than they desire.

Premature ejaculation is believed to be the most common of all sexual dysfunctions in males (Spector & Carey, 1990). Several surveys of nonclinical samples (men *not* seeking therapy) suggest that approximately one-third of men complain of early ejaculation (Frank et al., 1978; Laumann et al., 1999). It is interesting that similar rates are found among gay men (Sandfort & de Keizer, 2001); Bell and Weinberg (1978) reported that 27% of the gay men they studied felt that they had a problem with premature ejaculation. Like all sexual dysfunctions, premature ejaculation can be very distressing for the man and his partner. Studies indicate that this problem accounts for 15–25% of cases of men seeking sex therapy (Bancroft & Coles, 1976; Hawton, 1982; Masters & Johnson, 1970).

Like male orgasmic disorder, premature ejaculation may be difficult to diagnose for several reasons (O'Donohue, Letourneau, & Geer, 1993). First, there is currently no agreement on the normal range of time for ejaculation. At what point does ejaculation become premature? How soon is too soon? The normal range is indeed apparently very broad. Masters and Johnson (1970) defined early ejaculation as a problem when the man reached orgasm before his partner 50% of the time or more often. It is, however, not clear how they arrived at this particular number. Second, part of the *DSM-IV-TR* definition involves reaching orgasm "before the person wishes it." Some men may *wish* to be able to last for long periods of time before ejaculating, but the wish may not be realistic. At what point is the wish considered unrealistic and problematic? Finally, how persistent or recurrent must the early ejaculation problem be for it to qualify as a disorder? Virtually all men occasionally ejaculate before they or their partner desire.

The case of Max described in the chapter opening vignette illustrates several of the characteristics of premature ejaculation. Ejaculation prior to or shortly after penetration, an inability to control the timing of ejaculation, and sexual dissatisfaction in both partners are typical of many cases. Consistently ejaculating before or at the time of penetration is a problem regardless of how premature ejaculation is defined. Most men with the problem, however, report that they usually ejaculate after at least some thrusting. One study, for example, found that men suffering from premature ejaculation reported having an orgasm during intercourse after 2 minutes, on average, compared to an average of 12 minutes for men without the problem (Strassberg, Kelly, Carroll, & Kircher, 1987). There was a range of time to orgasm within both groups. For most men in the premature ejaculation group, time to orgasm during intercourse was

PREMATURE EJACULATION
A dysfunction characterized by persistent or recurrent ejaculation following minimal stimulation and before the person wishes it.

between 1 and 3 minutes. The majority of men in the normal ejaculation group reported having an orgasm between 2 and 22 minutes after penetration. These estimates, unfortunately, were purely subjective, and it is possible that men with premature ejaculation may underestimate their time to orgasm. (Alternatively, the men in the other group may have overestimated how long they lasted, as a form of sexual bragging!)

Virtually all men report occasionally using strategies to delay ejaculation during intercourse. Table 13.3 lists several orgasm-delaying techniques that are commonly used

TABLE 13.3 Strategies Men Use for Delaying Ejaculation

TECHNIQUE	AVERAGE EFFECTIVENESS[a]	PERCENT OF SAMPLE WHO HAVE USED TECHNIQUE
Withdrawing for a few moments	4.3	65
Ejaculating before intercourse	4.3	47
Taking drugs before intercourse	4.3	12
Drinking alcohol before intercourse	4.0	62
Applying an anesthetic to penis/glans	4.0	2
Thinking distracting/nonsexual thoughts	3.9	86
Using a different intercourse position	3.8	80
Using more than one condom	3.7	3
Slowing down thrusting	3.7	91
Making a few thrusts, then stopping	3.7	81
Alternating intercourse positions	3.6	82
Having a cold shower	3.6	10
Applying ice to penis	3.5	4
Using a condom	3.3	80
Contracting pelvic muscles	3.3	57
Relaxing pelvic muscles	3.3	53
Thrusting more shallowly	3.1	67
Talking during intercourse	3.0	59
Gritting teeth	3.0	20
Using oral sex as a "warm-up"	2.9	66
Thrusting in a circular motion	2.9	51
Taking deep breaths	2.9	35
Having intercourse at a specific time of day	2.9	16
Using more lubrication	2.7	23
Biting lip, tongue, or cheek	2.5	22
Thrusting more deeply	2.2	76
Speeding up thrusting	1.6	49
Thinking erotic/sexy thoughts	1.6	61

[a]Effectiveness of technique, ranging from 1 (*very ineffective*) to 5 (*very effective*). SOURCE: Grenier & Byers, 1997, The relationships among ejaculatory control, ejaculatory latency, and attempts to prolong heterosexual intercourse. *Archives of Sexual Behavior, 26,* 27–47.

(Grenier & Byers, 1997). None of the techniques, however, seem to be highly effective in the long run.

Sexual Pain Disorders

The **sexual pain disorders** are characterized by genital pain during sexual activity with a partner. For some individuals, the pain is mild and transient, whereas others experience intense sensations of tearing and burning during sexual intercourse (Binik et al., 2002; Fordney, 1978). Because of the nature of pain complaints associated with sexual pain disorders, it has been suggested that they are primarily pain syndromes (like chronic pain disorders) rather than true sexual dysfunctions (Meana, Binik, Khalifé, & Cohen, 1997). In other words, the underlying problem may not be sexual (Binik et al., 2002).

Dyspareunia

Dyspareunia is recurrent or persistent genital pain associated with sexual intercourse (APA, 2000). It occurs in both males and females, although it is far more common in females (Masters & Johnson, 1970; Wabrek & Wabrek, 1974). The problem is not limited to difficulty with lubrication, which qualifies as a sexual arousal disorder. Although the genital pain is typically experienced during sexual intercourse, it may also be experienced prior to penetration or after intercourse (Glatt, Zinner, & McCormack, 1990). In women, the pain is experienced as either superficial and occurring during penetration or as a deep pain during penile thrusting (APA, 2000; Fink, 1972). In severe cases, the pain may be excruciating and difficult to treat medically (Reid & Lininger, 1993).

Because they experience pain, most individuals with dyspareunia avoid sexual activity. The sexual avoidance may then cause conflict in the person's relationship with a partner or interfere with his or her interest in finding a partner. Over time, a person with dyspareunia typically becomes uninterested in sex and may develop hypoactive sexual desire disorder.

A number of sources suggest that dyspareunia is a common complaint. Kaplan (1974) and Masters and Johnson (1970) concluded that it was the second most common sexual dysfunction in women, after female orgasmic disorder. One survey of female college students found that over 33% complained of recurrent dyspareunia (Glatt et al., 1990). Women with this problem are most likely to report the problem to their gynecologists. One study found that nearly 20% of 100 women who were seeking help from their gynecologists complained of genital pain during intercourse (Plouffe, 1985). In another study of nearly 900 women undergoing gynecological examinations, 9% reported problems with dyspareunia (Bachmann, Leiblum, & Grill, 1989). There have been very few studies of dyspareunia in men. In the NHSLS survey, 3% of men and over 14% of women indicated that they experienced physical pain during intercourse. Curiously, the rates of dyspareunia in sex therapy clinics are quite low (Renshaw, 1988), possibly because men and women with the problem may tend to consult physicians rather than sex therapists.

Several medical conditions have been linked to dyspareunia (Binik et al., 2002; Reid & Lininger, 1993), including anatomic malformations of the vagina, vaginal scarring, and diseases such as pelvic inflammatory disease and endometriosis. Other possible physical causes of dyspareunia include remnants of the hymen and pelvic tumors. A condition known as **vulvar vestibulitis**, which causes intense superficial pain, presents many of the symptoms of dyspareunia (Bergeron, Binik, Khalifé, Pagidas, & Glazer, 2001) but is characterized by multiple tiny sores on or around the vulva. The cause of this condition remains unknown. Finally, complications during pregnancy, delivery, or abortion may also be risk factors for dyspareunia (Bachmann, 1986; Reamy & White, 1987).

According to Wincze and Carey (2001), dyspareunia in men is virtually always associated with a medical condition, the most common cause being a urinary tract infection. In such cases, the male experiences pain during ejaculation as well as during urination. Some uncircumcised men experience painful intercourse. Finally, Peyronie's disease, which involves a painful buildup of scar tissue in the corpus spongiosum and corpora cavernosa of the penis, sometimes causes pain when the penis is erect (Wincze & Carey, 2001).

SEXUAL PAIN DISORDER
A sexual dysfunction involving genital pain during sexual activity with a partner.

DYSPAREUNIA
A dysfunction involving recurrent genital pain during sexual intercourse.

VULVAR VESTIBULITIS
A medical condition characterized by tiny sores on or around the vulva that may be the cause of genital pain during intercourse.

Vaginismus

Vaginismus is characterized by persistent, involuntary spasms of vaginal muscles that interfere with sexual intercourse (APA, 2000). Cramping and vaginal spasms distinguish vaginismus from dyspareunia. The muscle spasms are strong enough to prevent penetration in most cases. The spasms not only interfere with penile penetration, but also make insertion of a finger or tampon difficult and painful for some women (APA, 2000). Gynecological pelvic examinations could also bring on the involuntary spasms.

The muscle contractions are the result of fear of painful penetration (Beck, 1993); thus, vaginismus has been described as a fear of penetration (LoPiccolo & Stock, 1986). Masters and Johnson (1970) described vaginismus as an involuntary reflex associated with "imagined, anticipated, or real attempts at vaginal penetration" (p. 250). Like sexual aversion disorder, vaginismus is similar to a phobia, and women with this problem typically avoid all sexual contact for fear that it could lead to sexual intercourse (or the partner's expectation of sexual intercourse). However, Binik and colleagues (2002) have questioned the current description of vaginismus, since the reported vaginal spasms have not been demonstrated in relevant studies. The hallmark of vaginismus, according to them, is a problem with penetration, which extends to sexual intercourse. A woman might develop a conditioned fear of penetration following one experience of painful penetration. The original painful experience could be the result of sexual trauma, as in rape or childhood molestation, an unusually painful experience with first intercourse, or even a painful pelvic examination. Because penetration of the vagina is associated with pain, a conditioned fear of penetration may develop, accompanied by vaginal spasms. The penetration phobia is then reinforced by repeated avoidance.

According to the *DSM-IV-TR* (2000), vaginismus is more common among younger women, among women with negative attitudes toward sex, and among women with a history of sexual trauma such as incest or rape. Women with vaginismus are capable of normal sexual arousal and orgasm through means other than penile-vaginal intercourse (Duddle, 1977; Stuntz, 1986).

Estimates of the prevalence of vaginismus are highly variable (Beck, 1993). Masters and Johnson (1970) reported a prevalence rate of over 8% among the 342 women who entered their clinic for sex therapy over an 11-year period. There are no reliable nonclinical estimates, although some of the 14% of women who complained of pain during sex in their responses to the NHSLS may have had vaginismus. The question asked in the NHSLS ("During the last 12 months, has there been a period of several months or more when you experienced physical pain during intercourse?") could apply to both sexual pain disorders, so it is not possible to tell if respondents suffered from vaginismus or dyspareunia.

Although it is not listed in *DSM-IV-TR* (2000), painful receptive anal intercourse is a recurring problem for some gay men. According to Rosser, Short, Thurmes, and Coleman (1998), as many as 12% of gay men who practice receptive anal intercourse report that the pain is so severe that they discontinue the practice. Feeling tense, a lack of stimulation, and inadequate lubrication are the most important predictors of painful anal intercourse in gay men. It is likely that the same problems would interfere with heterosexual anal intercourse.

13.4 on the web

Find the link to the Web site maintained by Professor Michael Gonzalez, a sexuality instructor, at **www.ablongman.org/mcanulty2e.** The site offers a thorough overview of the different sexual dysfunctions.

What controversies are addressed? Which of the case examples do you find most interesting?

GENERAL CAUSES OF SEXUAL DYSFUNCTIONS

A host of possible causes of sexual dysfunctions have been identified (O'Donohue & Geer, 1993; Rosen & Leiblum, 1995a). Unfortunately, early hypotheses were not systematically investigated, and only recently has sound research on the causes of sexual dysfunctions been conducted. Accumulating evidence shows that medical conditions and various drugs (legal and illegal) are often implicated. In virtually every case, though, psychological factors also play a role. Relationship difficulties are important in understanding sexual problems. Finally, cultural context is critical to understanding

VAGINISMUS
A dysfunction characterized by persistent involuntary spasms of vaginal muscles, which interfere with sexual intercourse.

13.5 on the web

Several Web sites are dedicated to offering medical information about sexual problems. We recommend visiting one of those that can be accessed through links at **www.ablongman.com/mcanulty2e** for an overview of the latest medical developments. Although some of the articles are technical, you should find most of them interesting.

What topics are addressed? What seem to be the "hot" topics? What research findings are reported?

human sexuality and its disorders. Rarely will a single cause fully explain a sexual dysfunction, as these disorders usually result from a complex interaction of multiple factors.

Medications and Illicit Drugs

A number of drugs—both prescription medications and other drugs—are known to interfere with sexual desire (Crenshaw & Goldberg, 1996; Wincze & Carey, 2001). Chronic use of alcohol and cocaine is associated with impaired sexual desire (Schiavi, 1990a). Medications for high blood pressure, or hypertension (antihypertensives), depression (antidepressants), and seizures (anticonvulsants) are among the most extensively studied. Antidepressants cause sexual side effects in a majority of persons who take them (Ellison, 1998; Rothschild, 2000). Several widely used antidepressants, including fluoxetine and paroxetine (trade names Prozac and Paxil), have been shown to inhibit sexual desire in 20–50% of people taking them (Hirschfeld, 1999). In these cases, it is sometimes difficult to determine if the suppression of sex drive is due to the medication, to the depression, or to a combination of both.

There has been growing interest in the role of various substances in erectile failure. In addition to having a sedative effect, alcohol causes changes in blood vessels that can interfere with erection. Chronic alcohol abuse has been linked with nerve damage and with hormonal imbalances (Schover & Jensen, 1988). In one study of men in rehabilitation programs for alcohol problems, over 40% of participants reported occasional or frequent problems with erection (Fahrner, 1987). Some medications can also cause erection problems. Antihypertensives have been linked with erection difficulties in a number of studies and case reports (Dunn, Croft, & Hackett, 1999). Bansal (1988), however, questioned the reliability of such findings, noting that erectile problems associated with antihypertensives could be attributable to the drug (a pharmacological cause), the condition (a physiological cause), or to the patients' reactions to the disease and treatment (an emotional cause). Nevertheless, it has long been part of clinical lore that antihypertensives compromise erectile ability in some men, and that some of these drugs are more likely to cause problems than others (Graber, 1993; Weiner & Rosen, 1997).

Drugs may interfere with orgasm as well as sexual desire and sexual arousal. Alcohol intoxication, for example, increases the time to orgasm and decreases the intensity of orgasms in women (Malatesta, Pollack, Crotty, & Peacock, 1982). A significant number of people taking antidepressants such as Prozac and Paxil have problems reaching orgasm (Gitlin, 1994; Shen & Hsu, 1995). Similar effects are reported with minor tranquilizers such as Valium and Xanax (Gitlin, 1994). Normal orgasmic capacity is restored when the medication use is discontinued. A number of drugs are known to interfere with ejaculation (Munjack & Kanno, 1979), mostly by reducing the sensitivity of the penis. Table 13.4 lists many commonly prescribed drugs that are known to contribute to sexual dysfunctions.

Psychological Factors

Several psychological factors are known to contribute to sexual dysfunction (Wincze & Carey, 2001). The role of anxiety in particular has been studied extensively. Other factors, such as negative beliefs, past sexual trauma, and relationship problems, have also been related to sexual dysfunction.

Anxiety

Sexual anxiety can stem from fear of performing poorly, fear of losing control, fear of pregnancy, or fear of intimacy and emotional vulnerability (Leiblum & Rosen, 2000; LoPiccolo & Friedman, 1988). Anxiety, coupled with self-critical thinking, has been linked to problems with desire, arousal, and orgasm (Wincze & Carey, 2001). Studies by David Barlow and his colleagues (Barlow, 1986), for example, have shown that, as a group, men with erection problems consistently underestimate the degree and firmness of their erections. As a consequence, these men become overly focused on their sexual performance at the expense of erotic feelings and sexual enjoyment. Some people with sexual desire problems also experience anxiety in the form of panic attacks (Kaplan, 1987). Anxiety is related to premature ejaculation (Dunn et al., 1999).

TABLE 13.4 Common Drugs That May Cause Sexual Dysfunction[a]

MEDICATION	DECREASED SEXUAL DESIRE	ERECTILE DYSFUNCTION OR VAGINAL DRYNESS	DIFFICULTY REACHING ORGASM	EJACULATION PROBLEMS
Antianxiety drugs				
Alprazolam *(Xanax)*	X		X	X
Diazepam *(Valium)*	X		X	X
Anticonvulsants				
Carbamazepine *(Tegretol)*	X	X		
Phenytoin *(Dilantin)*[b]	X	X		
Primidone *(Myidone, Mysoline)*	X	X		
Antidepressants				
Amitriptyline *(Elavil)*	X	X		X
Amoxapine *(Asendin)*	X	X	X	X
Clomipramine *(Anafranil)*	X	X	X	X
Desipramine *(Norpramin)*	X	X		X
Fluoxetine *(Prozac)*	X	X	X	X
Imipramine *(Norfranil, Tofranil)*	X	X	X	X
Paroxetine *(Paxil)*		X	X	X
Phenelzine *(Nardil)*	X	X	X	X
Sertraline *(Zoloft)*	X	X	X	X
Trazodone *(Desyrel)*[b]			X	X
Venlafaxine *(Effexor)*	X	X	X	X
Antihypertensives				
Atenolol *(Tenormin)*	X	X		
Chlorthalidone *(Hygroton, Thalitone)*	X	X		
Clonidine *(Catapres)*	X	X	X	X
Hydrochlorothiazide *(Esidrix, HydroDIURIL)*	X	X		
Labetalol *(Normodyne, Trandate)*[b]	X	X		X
Methyldopa *(Aldomet)*	X	X	X	X
Metoprolol *(Lopressor)*	X	X		
Propranolol *(Inderal)*	X	X		
Spironolactone *(Aldactone)*	X	X		
Enlarged-prostate drug: Finasteride *(Proscar)*[c]	X	X		
Heartburn drugs				
Cimetidine *(Tagamet, Tagamet HB)*	X	X		
Famotidine *(Pepcid, Pepcid AC)*	X	X		
Nizatidine *(Axid, Axid AR)*	X	X		
Ranitidine *(Zantac, Zantac 75)*	X	X		
Heart-failure drug: Amiodarone *(Cordarone)*	X	X		
Muscle relaxant: Baclofen *(Lioresal)*		X	X	X

[a]Does not include sexual dysfunction that may be caused by interactions between drugs.
[b]May cause prolonged, painful erections.
[c]Finasteride is also available as *Propecia* for treating hair loss.
SOURCE: © 2002 by Consumers Union of U.S., Inc. Yonkers, NY 10703-1057, a nonprofit organization. Reprinted with permission from the March issue of CONSUMER REPORTS ON HEALTH for educational purposes only. No commercial use or photocopying permitted. To learn more about Consumers Union, log onto www.ConsumerReports.org.

Disinterest in sex is commonly associated with depression (Schreiner-Engel & Schiavi, 1986). In one sample of 686 British men, depression was the main predictor of low sexual desire or "inhibited enjoyment" (Dunn et al., 1999). For women in the same study, depression and anxiety were both associated with arousal problems, orgasmic dysfunction, and a lack of sexual enjoyment (Dunn et al., 1999). Therefore, sexual dysfunction may be one manifestation of a more pervasive problem with anxiety or depression (Segraves, 2002).

Negative Beliefs

Other psychological factors can play a role in sexual dysfunction including rigid and puritanical views of sex, guilt about sex, and sexual ignorance. Negative beliefs about masturbation and false beliefs about sex can lead to inhibitions that make it difficult for women and men to relinquish control and "let go." Being unable to let go detracts from sexual interactions. Additionally, problems with self-esteem and poor body image make it difficult for some men and women to enjoy sexual interactions. Related to these difficulties, problems communicating about sex can interfere with individuals' ability to help their partners please them (Kelly, Strassberg, & Kircher, 1990). Individuals who have negative views of sex often feel awkward discussing their likes and dislikes with sexual partners and, in many cases, they may have difficulties with sexual functioning.

Similar negative attitudes are associated with sexual problems among gay men and lesbians (Sandfort & de Keizer, 2001). Internalized homophobia, in particular, is related to arousal problems (Shires & Miller, 1998), impaired sexual desire, and orgasmic difficulties. Like their heterosexual counterparts, gay men and lesbians may struggle with negative attitudes about sex, sexual misinformation, and religious, moral, or family taboos surrounding sexuality. Some gay men and lesbians, however, have the additional burden of dealing with sexual identity confusion and their own homophobia. The emphasis among some gay men on presenting a macho persona, for example, may add performance pressure and anxiety, which can detract from sexual enjoyment and interfere with erection (Sandfort & de Keizer, 2001).

Sexual Trauma

Traumatic experiences associated with sex also contribute to sexual difficulties. Males and females who experienced sexual abuse in childhood are two to three times more likely to suffer from sexual dysfunction than adults who were never sexually traumatized (Laumann et al., 1999). Because of their experiences, victims of childhood sexual abuse may associate sexual intimacy with emotional and physical pain; thus, intimacy may trigger fearful feelings that may lead to a conditioned fear of sexual contact. As you will see in Chapter 16, Sexual Coercion, sexual abuse by a caretaker can predispose a person to a pervasive problem with trust and intimacy later in life.

Studies reveal that adult victims of sexual assault often develop sexual problems that can persist for years (van Berlo & Ensink, 2000). Common sexual problems following rape or attempted rape include fear of sex, arousal dysfunction, and desire disorders. Researchers have found that factors such as the age of the victim, whether the victim previously had a relationship with the offender, and whether the victim was subjected to penetration during the assault are related to sexual problems. Ensuing sexual difficulties are more likely if victims blame themselves for the assault or if they experience shame and guilt. Having a loving and understanding partner seems to be a protective factor against sexual dysfunction following sexual trauma (van Berlo & Ensink, 2000). Relationship factors, therefore, can have a profound impact on sexual functioning, a topic that we examine next.

Relationship Problems

Relationship problems such as resentment, anger, and conflict detract from sexual enjoyment for many couples. Dunn and colleagues (1999), for example, found that having marital problems was the single best predictor of sexual arousal problems in a sample of 979 women in England. The same study found that marital difficulties were also strongly associated with orgasmic problems and inhibited sexual enjoyment for women. Other studies confirm that relationship factors probably play a role in most cases of hypoactive sexual desire disorder, as illustrated in the case of Marjorie and Cheryl in the chapter opening vignette. As a group, individuals with deficient sexual desire report lower rates of agreement, affection, cohesion, and satisfaction in their re-

Relationship problems, such as unexpressed anger and resentment, may be detrimental to a sexual relationship and can contribute to sexual dysfunction.

lationships. They often express dissatisfaction with the communication, intimacy, and conflict resolution in the relationship. Persons with hypoactive sexual desire disorder are especially likely to report less love for their partners and tend to be critical of their own listening skills (Stuart, Hammond, & Pett, 1987).

Sexual enjoyment is influenced not only by a person's own awareness of his or her sexual interests, but also by the extent to which a partner understands those sexual interests and shares them (Purnine & Carey, 1997). Relationship problems are important in understanding sexual difficulties in people who have previously enjoyed rewarding sexual interactions. Such situational sexual problems are best understood in the context of relationship conflict. For example, Metz and Pryor (2000) suggested that premature ejaculation could stem from hypersensitivity to one's partner, unrealistic relationship expectations, or distrust. Individuals who fear sexual failure or disappointing their partners may experience performance anxiety and subsequently feel a sense of failure, thereby starting a self-perpetuating cycle. Alternatively, sexual dysfunction may be a reaction to partner infidelity and distrust. In such cases, the onset of the sexual dysfunction coincides with problems in the relationship. Other relationship issues such as fear of intimacy, fear of losing control, and "clumsy male partners" (Leiblum, 1995), might also contribute to sexual dysfunction, such as vaginismus.

Of course, relationship problems are not unique to heterosexual couples. The very same relationship issues can affect same-sex couples. Erectile dysfunction, for example, can be a sign of conflict in a same-sex relationship, or an indication of fear of intimacy or fear of rejection. Intimacy issues, in fact, may be more prevalent in gay couples than among heterosexuals (Sandfort & de Keizer, 2001). Heterosexual men, on the other hand, may be more prone to performance anxiety in their relationships (Shires & Miller, 1998).

Sexual dysfunctions are generally experienced in the context of an intimate relationship, but they are also experienced in the context of a culture. Certain cultural beliefs may predispose some individuals to sexual difficulties.

Cultural Factors

As this book has pointed out, culturally determined scripts shape sexuality in important ways. Several scripts are especially relevant to female sexual functioning, including the "good girl" and "sleeping beauty" scripts (Daniluk, 1998; Stock, 1993). According to the "good girl" script, women are expected to be passive, obedient, and "nice." Throughout adolescence and into early adulthood, females are responsible for setting limits on male sexual behavior and for restraining their own sexuality (Daniluk, 1998). After suppressing her own sexual desires for years, a woman is then expected to become sexually

13.6 on the web

Although women's sexuality was largely ignored in the past, more attention is devoted to the topic today. Go to **www.ablongman.com/mcanulty2e** and find the link to Women's Sexual Health, a site devoted to women's sexual problems. Click on More to Read and visit one or more of the Related Sites.

Which issues in women's sexuality seem to be the most common topics of discussion?

Looking At . . .

. . . Thinking About

Eve Ensler, author and performer of "The Vagina Monologues," recounts often-humorous excerpts of her candid interviews with women about their genitals. A landmark of feminist theater, the show is designed to make women more comfortable with their sexuality. Challenging the taboos, Ensler asks such questions as "How would you dress your vagina?" ("Blue jeans and a straw hat") and "What would your vagina say?" ("Accept gifts!"). Why do you think "The Vagina Monologues" has been so popular with audiences across the United States?

responsive and to "let go" on meeting the "right person." At this point, a new script is called for, one for which the woman may be unprepared. Similarly, the "sleeping beauty" script emphasizes sexual passivity for the female until a male awakens her dormant sexuality. Women who are guided by this script are uncomfortable initiating sex, talking openly about their sexual preferences, masturbating, and taking an active role in sexual encounters. Because their sexuality has been suppressed, they are often unaware of their own sexual needs and preferences (Stock, 1993).

Males are not immune to the conflicting messages that are disseminated by cultural scripts. As Muehlenhard (1988) aptly observed, sexually speaking, in the United States, "nice women" don't say yes and "real men" don't say no. Miscommunication combined with the cultural double standard about sex can lead to confusion and pressure (Muehlenhard & McCoy, 1991). Whereas many women feel cultural pressure to inhibit their sexuality, the pressure on men is to prove their masculinity. The very terminology many men use for having sex—"scoring"—implies a competition. Not surprisingly, many men and women feel some anxiety surrounding sexual performance (Laumann et al., 1999).

The role of cultural factors in sexual dysfunctions is also illustrated by differences in the prevalence of disorders across cultures. Prevalence rates of vaginismus, for example, vary substantially across different cultures, with several reports of higher rates in Ireland, Eastern Europe, and Latin America (Wincze & Carey, 2001). In studies of Irish women with vaginismus, both O'Sullivan (1979) and Barnes (1986) reported that the women recalled their fathers as threatening, tyrannical, and sometimes violent. The women with vaginismus were also more likely than women without the problem to have negative attitudes about sex arising from religious teachings. Presumably, women who grow up in cultures in which males are domineering and female sexuality is suppressed may be more vulnerable to this disorder. These findings are interesting, although more research is needed to reveal the precise role of cultural factors in vaginismus and other sexual dysfunctions.

TREATMENT OF SEXUAL DYSFUNCTIONS

Masters and Johnson's landmark text, *Human Sexual Inadequacy* (1970), essentially established the field of sex therapy. For over 20 years, their innovative and unique approach to treating sexual dysfunctions was the standard. They advocated short-term (usually a matter of weeks) and intensive therapy that included educational and behavioral components (that is, homework assignments) and was conducted by a team consisting of a man and a woman. Their approach was problem-focused and looked at sexual dysfunction as a problem for the couple rather than for the individual alone. From the beginning, Masters and Johnson sought to enlist a partner's cooperation and assistance in addressing any sexual dysfunction. Finally, Masters and Johnson claimed that the vast majority of sexual dysfunctions were due to psychological rather than medical causes. Most important, their reported success rates were impressive and unprecedented; see Table 13.5.

TABLE 13.5 Sex Therapy Success Rates from Masters and Johnson (1970)

	N	FAILURES	SUCCESSES	SUCCESS RATE
Primary impotence	51	17	34	66.7%
Secondary impotence	501	108	393	78.4%
Premature ejaculation	432	17	415	96.1%
Ejaculatory incompetence	75	18	57	76.0%
MALE TOTALS	1,059	160	899	84.9%
Primary anorgasmia	399	84	315	79.0%
Situational anorgasmia	331	96	235	71.0%
Vaginismus	83	1	82	98.8%
FEMALE TOTALS	813	181	632	77.7%
COMBINED TOTALS	1,872	341	1,531	81.8%

SOURCE: Kolodny, 1981

The early enthusiastic appraisal of Masters and Johnson's sex therapy has been tempered by recent findings, however. Those who questioned Masters and Johnson's approach pointed out that the majority of their clients were good candidates for such an approach. They tended to be young, educated, healthy, and motivated (Rosen & Leiblum, 1995b). It was also common for men and women to be sexually misinformed or ignorant but eager to learn as they came of age in the sexual revolution of the 1960s. The past four decades have seen a veritable explosion of self-help manuals, TV programs, and articles in the popular press on sexual problems and solutions. Consequently, it is now less common for sex therapy clients to be sexually naive or inexperienced. It is also more typical for clients to be older and to have medical problems. In other words, contemporary sex therapy cases are usually more complex than those described by Masters and Johnson (1970). Perhaps it should not be surprising that more recent studies offer a more modest estimate of the effectiveness of sex therapy (Hawton, 1992; Rosen & Leiblum, 1995a).

A common problem with any form of therapy is *relapse*. Over time, many treatment gains may dissipate and the original problems may recur. Sex therapy is no exception. For example, several studies of therapy for erectile problems reported high relapse rates during the months following treatment. At 3-month followups, anywhere from 44% (Hawton, Catalan, & Fagg, 1992) to 90% (Levine & Agle, 1978) of sex therapy clients reported that the problem had returned. Nevertheless, a number of other studies reveal that most couples affected by a sexual dysfunction do benefit from sex therapy. For example, Sarwer and Durlak (1997) reported a 65% success rate in treating 365 married couples experiencing a range of sexual dysfunctions.

Several trends in sex therapy are noteworthy. First, there is a growing recognition that medical conditions often do play a role in sexual dysfunctions; therefore, medical treatments are becoming increasingly popular (Rosen & Leiblum, 1995b). As a result, effective treatment for sexual dysfunctions usually requires integrating medical and psychological interventions. As noted throughout this chapter, relationship factors must be considered in the treatment of sexual dysfunctions. Problems with communication, trust, control, or intimacy are often associated with sexual dysfunctions. Even when relationship problems are not part of the cause of a dysfunction, they could be obstacles to effective sex therapy. Therefore, most sex therapists routinely address relationship

IN YOUR own words

Laura Vaughan
Virginia Commonwealth University

When I was younger I felt very uncomfortable in a doctor's office, but now I am more at ease because I know the most important thing is a person's health. I would rather be confident that I am healthy than embarrassed about asking a doctor a question.

issues when working with clients with sexual dysfunctions. The Masters and Johnson format of using a male-female team has been largely abandoned; one therapist, regardless of gender, is now thought to be just as effective (Libman, Fichten, & Brender, 1985). Finally, as cases of sexual dysfunction have become more complex, so have treatments. Few clients today respond to a short-term, "quick-fix" approach to sex therapy. Relapse prevention—ensuring that treatment benefits are maintained over time—is now considered a critical component of sex therapy (Rosen, Leiblum, & Spector, 1994).

Medical Treatment of Sexual Dysfunctions

Medical treatments for sexual dysfunctions are becoming more common for several reasons. First, there have been major advances in medical treatments for some sexual problems. The introduction of oral medications has truly revolutionized the treatment of erection problems, and ongoing studies are evaluating the effectiveness of certain medications for the treatment of premature ejaculation and sexual desire disorders. Second, some medical treatments, such as medications, are simple to implement. Third, medical treatments are often more palatable for people who are experiencing a sexual problem. There is less stigma associated with having a medical problem, so most people would prefer to think of their problem as a physical rather than a psychological impairment. As Tiefer noted (1986), "a medical explanation for erectile difficulties relieves men of blame and thus permits them to maintain some masculine self-esteem" (p. 591). Attributing one's problem to a medical condition makes the problem less threatening, as it reduces a person's sense of responsibility. Clients in sex therapy often complain that their physician informed them that their sexual problems were psychological in origin—as if this meant they were only imagining the problem or implied that they suffered from deeper psychological disturbances. In reality, clients whose sexual dysfunctions have psychological origins are no more mentally unstable than those whose problems have medical origins. Unfortunately, misconceptions about psychological problems are still common in our culture, and these are compounded when the problem is sexual in nature. Finally, many individuals prefer to think of their sexual dysfunction as a medical problem because of the promise of a simple cure, such as taking a few pills. In reality, even when medical factors are responsible for a sexual dysfunction, "quick fixes" are rare.

Medical treatments are not available for all sexual dysfunctions, and several existing treatments are still considered experimental. For example, administering testosterone to increase sex drive in persons with hypoactive sexual desire disorder is not routinely done because of concerns about the possible long-term side effects. Until more research on their effectiveness and side effects becomes available, such experimental medical treatments are not widely offered.

Treatments for Female Sexual Dysfunction

Medical interventions for female sexual dysfunction are still in their infancy. This is not surprising, since male sexuality (both normal and dysfunctional) has received more attention than female sexuality (Segraves, 2002). Fortunately, the situation is starting to change, and female sexual dysfunction is now viewed as a legitimate topic of study in its own right (Berman & Berman, 2000; Heiman, 2002a). An index of developments in this area was the formation in 2001 of the International Society for Study of Women's Sexual Health.

The Food and Drug Administration recently approved the EROS clitoral therapy device, a small battery-operated vacuum pump that applies gentle suction to the clitoris, thereby increasing blood flow to the area. A preliminary test with 15 women who had sexual arousal problems revealed that it increased erotic sensations, produced more orgasms, and enhanced satisfaction for most of them (Josefson, 2000). Clearly, more research is needed on the effectiveness of the EROS pump.

There are no widely accepted medical treatments for women with hypoactive sexual desire disorder. A few studies have investigated the effectiveness of administering testosterone to women with hypoactive sexual desire disorder that is due to hormone deficits following either menopause or hysterectomy. Overall, women in these studies reported increased sexual desire and arousal compared to those who received a placebo treatment (Davis, 2000; Heiman, 2002a). However, the levels of testosterone used in these studies are usually above the normal range, which raises important questions about the long-term effects. It is very likely that side effects could ultimately include masculinization (Segraves, 2002), such as facial hair growth and deepening of the voice. Another development was reported by Segraves and colleagues (2001), who administered buproprion (a medication marketed as Wellbutrin for depression and as Zyban for smoking cessation) to a group of women with hypoactive sexual desire disorder. Nearly one-third of the women responded to the medication, as evidenced by increases in sexual arousal, sexual fantasy, and interest in engaging in sexual activity (Segraves et al., 2001). Buproprion is one of the few antidepressant medications that does not seem to interfere with sexual functioning, and it has no known long-term side effects. As the Segraves study reveals, buproprion may in fact be beneficial to some women with low sexual desire, but more large-scale research is needed.

Finally, we should note that researchers have investigated the use of sildenafil (trade name, Viagra) to treat female sexual dysfunction. Early findings suggest that it does increase vasocongestion and lubrication, but findings on its effectiveness with women are mixed (Segraves, 2002). One study reported that Viagra improved sexual functioning in a group of 51 young women with sexual arousal disorder (Caruso, Intelisano, Lupo, & Agnello, 2001), but a large-scale study of 538 post-menopausal women found no real benefits (Basson et al., 2000).

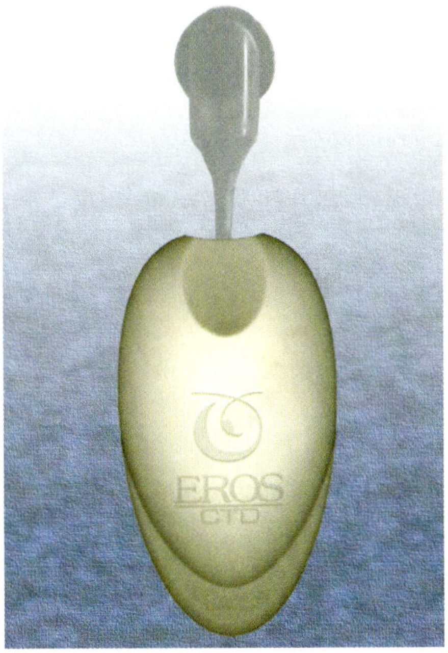

The EROS Clitoral Therapy Device is a battery-operated vacuum pump designed to apply gentle pressure to the clitoris and increase blood flow to the area. It is intended for use by women with sexual arousal problems.

Treatments for Erectile Disorder

Of all the sexual dysfunctions, male erectile disorder in particular has most often been treated medically in recent years (Rosen & Leiblum, 1995b).

Surgical Implants Several surgical approaches have been introduced to correct erection problems that originate in medical conditions. In some cases, a penile prosthesis is surgically implanted in the corpora cavernosa (Graber, 1993). The semirigid prosthesis consists of a pair of silicone rods that remain erect at all times, which tends to be awkward for the patient. A newer inflatable prosthesis requires more extensive surgery. Hollow cylinders are implanted in the corpora cavernosa, a reservoir of saline solution is inserted in the abdomen, and a pump to inflate and deflate the prosthesis is implanted in the scrotum. To achieve erection, the man presses the pump, which opens a valve, allowing saline to be pumped into the hollow cylinders; afterward he presses the pump again to reverse the process. Early versions of the inflatable prosthesis were fraught with problems such as mechanical failure, but newer models are more reliable (Rosen & Leiblum, 1995b).

Despite an estimated cost of $10,000 or more, over 25,000 men undergo penile prosthesis surgery in the United States each year. Long-term followup studies have found that the majority of these men and their partners were satisfied with the outcome (Pedersen, Tiefer, Ruiz, & Melman, 1988; Tiefer, Pedersen, & Melman, 1988). Common complaints among the men were that their sex lives did not improve as much as they expected and that they were limited to several positions for intercourse. Possible complications include postoperative pain and mechanical failure (Graber, 1993). Milsten and Slowinski (1999) estimated that 10% of men with a prosthesis experience a mechanical problem such as leakage of the pump. Pain may be due to infection, in which case the device must be surgically removed.

Vascular Surgery In cases in which erectile failure is due to abnormalities in blood flow to the penis, vascular surgery may be an option. Arterial (inflow) problems are due to a narrowing or blockage of the penile arteries that supply blood to the corpora cavernosa. Venous (outflow) problems occur when blood leaks back out of the corpora cavernosa so that erection is not maintained. Surgery for venous leakage is imperfect, and failure rates

The inflatable penile prosthesis is one medical treatment for erectile dysfunction.

are fairly high (Wincze & Carey, 2001). The evidence for the effectiveness of surgery in correcting arterial problems is mixed. In cases in which a specific arterial problem is identified, the surgery may be effective, but the procedure is costly and nearly always followed by complications. The chief advantage of vascular surgery over other medical treatments is that, when effective, it can restore a more normal sex life (Coleman, 1998). Despite fairly impressive satisfaction rates with surgical implants, nonsurgical approaches are likely to become the medical treatments of choice because they are less invasive.

Vacuum Constriction Devices Vacuum constriction devices offer men with erection problems an inexpensive alternative to surgery. Essentially, a tube that is connected to a hand-operated pump is placed over the penis. Pumping creates a vacuum within the tube, which in turn causes blood to flow into the arteries in the penis. Blood is then trapped in the penile vessels by a constricting band placed around the base of the penis. The band can be left in place for up to 30 minutes. The device is simple to use, and the majority of users and their partners are reportedly satisfied (Rosen & Leiblum, 1995b; Wincze & Carey, 2001). There are, however, some drawbacks associated with vacuum constriction devices. Pain and bruising of the penis are commonly reported, and many men report a loss of penile sensitivity and numbness when using the device (Graber, 1993). Also, ejaculation is blocked by the constrictive band.

Penile Injection Therapies Injections have become increasingly popular medical interventions for male erectile disorder (Graber, 1993). Essentially, this approach entails using a hypodermic needle to inject a muscle relaxant directly into the corpora cavernosa. The injected drug relaxes the smooth muscle of the corpora cavernosa and increases vasodilation (Althof & Turner, 1992). The most commonly used drugs for this purpose are papaverine, phentolamine, phenoxybenzamine, and prostaglandin E1, which are used either individually or in combination (Rosen & Leiblum, 1995b). Papaverine is one of the preferred agents because it becomes active within 15 minutes, and the erection may last for 1 to 4 hours when the proper dosage is administered. The first injection is administered in a physician's office as a demonstration so that the man can inject himself in the future.

Most men who use penile injections achieve an erection sufficient for sexual intercourse. The injections are less effective, though, for men with vascular problems that interfere with penile blood flow (Coleman, 1998). The effectiveness rate of injected vasodilators is estimated to be as high as 75–80%, and partner reactions are generally positive (Rosen & Leiblum, 1995b). As one might expect, however, some (perhaps most!) men are reluctant to stick a needle into their penis. A large number of men eventually discontinue the injections, up to 35% within 6 months of starting (Althof et al., 1989). Major side effects include prolonged erections (priapism), plaque buildup at the injection site, bruising, and liver function problems (Coleman, 1998; Rosen & Leiblum, 1995b). Penile injections may also encourage men to be overly focused on intercourse, to the detriment of foreplay (Wincze & Carey, 2001).

Oral Medications for Erectile Disorder The newest treatment for male erectile disorder is sildenafil citrate, better known by the trade name Viagra. This drug was approved for the treatment of erectile disorder by the U.S. Food and Drug Administration in March 1998. Demand for Viagra was immediate and extensive, making it one of the best-selling drugs in the history of medicine. It works by inhibiting an enzyme (PDE5) in the penis, which leads to decreased blood outflow, resulting in prolonged erection.

Studies of the effectiveness of Viagra have so far been quite encouraging (Goldstein et al., 1998; Werneke & Crowe, 2002). Reports by the pharmaceutical company that manufactures the drug suggest an effectiveness rate between 66% and 88%. In their review of

21 studies involving more than 3,000 men who took Viagra, Milsten and Slowinski (1999) concluded that between 63% and 82% were helped by the drug, depending on dosage. If this effectiveness rate is independently replicated, it is indeed impressive. Oral medications are preferable to other treatments, such as surgery or injections, because they are less invasive and more convenient. Drawbacks include cost (when introduced, Viagra cost over $10.00 per pill), limited availability, and uncertainty about the effects of long-term usage. Since the drug was approved by the FDA relatively recently, there are no studies on long-term effects in users. Short-term side effects such as headaches, nausea, facial flushing, and diarrhea are reported by 10% of men using the medication.

Shortly after the introduction of Viagra, a number of deaths of men using the drug were reported. The majority of the fatalities were men who suffered from cardiovascular problems. Although the actual number of deaths is very small in relation to the number of people using the drug, physicians must be extremely cautious in prescribing it for men with any of the following conditions (Milsten & Slowinski, 1999):

1. Coronary heart disease
2. Congestive heart failure and borderline low blood pressure
3. Conditions that require taking multiple blood pressure medications
4. Health conditions that may slow the body's metabolism, or breakdown, of Viagra, such as liver or kidney disease
5. Conditions that require the use of certain antibiotics, which can slow the metabolism of Viagra

The combination of Viagra and other medications that contain nitrates is especially dangerous (Viera, Clenney, Shenenberger, & Green, 1999). Nitrates are found in medications used to treat angina pectoris and in the amyl nitrates used by some men to intensify orgasms (so-called *poppers* were once popular among gay men). For these reasons, Viagra should only be prescribed by a competent medical professional who has thoroughly reviewed a candidate's medical history. Additionally, users are advised not to take more than one pill in a 24-hour period.

As noted earlier, the early success of Viagra in restoring erectile functioning in men led to questions about its possible use by women. Some preliminary findings revealed that it may be useful in increasing sexual desire and orgasmic responses in women, but more research is needed. Enthusiasm about medications for sexual problems must be tempered with evidence of their effectiveness and their limitations. One concern is the potential misuse of any medication that promises "better sex." One sign of the overemphasis on sexual performance is the public reaction to the introduction of an oral medication for erection problems. Some men with normal erections have reportedly attempted to obtain prescriptions for Viagra in the hope of improving their sexual performance. Clearly, this is an inappropriate use of the drug, and men who want to use it for this reason have fallen victim to the societal pressure to perform sexually. Viagra is not an aphrodisiac. A man still requires sexual stimulation to achieve an erection after taking this medication.

Looking At . . .

. . . Thinking About

The increasingly popular medical interventions for sexual dysfunctions do present some potential problems, and although researchers may seek a "magic pill" that will provide an instant cure, such a pill does not exist. Some sexual dysfunctions result from nonmedical causes such as relationship problems or performance fears, and these are not likely to be relieved by a medical intervention. Medical treatments for sexual dysfunctions are appropriate when a medical cause is discovered. These interventions are most effective when coupled with education and an emphasis on intimacy and communication rather than on performance. What do you think leads people to seek "quick fixes" for difficulties with sexual performance?

Treatment of Premature Ejaculation

As the success of Viagra has shown, oral medications for the treatment of sexual dysfunctions offer a promising alternative to surgery and prostheses. In recent years, there has been a growing interest in using medications to treat premature ejaculation (Metz & Pryor, 2000; Rosen, 1991). This interest derives from studies that show that a number of medications increase the latency to ejaculation (Hsu & Shen, 1995). Although this is viewed as a negative side effect for men with normal ejaculation, researchers reasoned that this effect could be used to the benefit of those who experience persistent early ejaculation (Assalian, 1994). The chief advantage of this approach is that oral medications are very simple to use—the man merely needs to remember to take the daily pill.

Most studies have investigated the use of antidepressants, such as fluoxetine (Prozac) and clomipramine (Anafril), to treat premature ejaculation. In one report (Assalian, 1988), five men with lifelong premature ejaculation were found to benefit from daily dosages of clomipramine. Two other studies (Althof, Levine, Corty, Risen, & Stern, 1994; Segraves, Saran, Segraves, & Maguire, 1993) also documented improved control of ejaculation in men who took antidepressants. The men taking the medication and their partners reported a significant improvement in their sexual satisfaction (Segraves et al., 1993).

Although the use of antidepressants to treat premature ejaculation seems promising, the treatment is not without problems. First, these drugs are relatively expensive. Second, the drugs have a number of adverse side effects, such as sedation, constipation, and dry mouth. Another side effect is that many people taking antidepressants experience a decrease in sex drive (Gitlin, 1994)—which obviously negates the initial intent. Finally, there is some concern that men who rely on an oral medication to improve their sexual functioning may become psychologically dependent on the drug, further compromising their threatened masculinity and self-esteem (McCarthy, 1995).

Sex Therapy

Sex therapy is a useful treatment approach for sexual dysfunctions. When the problem has a psychological origin, sex therapy is the treatment of choice. But even when a sexual problem is due to medical causes, sex therapy is an important adjunct to medical interventions (Wincze & Carey, 2001). Rosen and Leiblum (1995b) concluded that there is a great need for more research on the effectiveness of combined psychological and medical interventions for sexual dysfunctions.

The PLISSIT Model

Sex therapists usually employ a framework they call PLISSIT. PLISSIT is an acronym for

*P*ermission giving
*L*imited *I*nformation
*S*pecific *S*uggestions
*I*ntensive *T*herapy

This framework calls for increasingly intensive interventions *only* if less involved approaches are insufficient for helping people overcome sexual problems. The least intensive and most basic approach is permission giving, which involves providing a client with authoritative information about sexual functioning. Permission giving encourages a person to ask questions, to experiment with novel techniques and positions, and to realize that there is a huge range of sexual acts that are considered normal. For some couples, simply being told that it is okay to try different sexual behaviors and to enjoy them may be enough to eliminate a sexual problem.

If permission giving is not enough, limited information is offered next—most commonly in the form of readings on normal sexual functioning. Sometimes accurate information is enough to debunk myths and unrealistic expectations and can lead to improvements in a client's sex life. When permission giving and limited information are inadequate, specific recommendations may be necessary.

Specific suggestions by a sex therapist typically take the form of behavioral "homework." Such homework may involve step-by-step guidelines on ways to relax and perform sensual massage, along with communication guidelines. This homework is useful for lowering performance anxiety while increasing sexual arousal and communication. It also teaches partners to become attuned to each other's sexual likes and dislikes. Finally, behavioral exercises empower couples to implement change. Couples quite literally take the problem in their own hands.

Intensive therapy is the final option should the sexual problem be confounded by other issues. For example, serious relationship conflict calls for couples counseling, or, if depression is a problem, it must be addressed before any work on sexual difficulties can be accomplished.

Principles of Sex Therapy

Sex therapy encompasses a set of psychological techniques designed to alleviate sexual performance problems. The therapeutic techniques are based on several principles.

1. *Mutual responsibility is emphasized* in sex therapy. The sexual dysfunction is viewed as a shared problem rather than a deficit in or failure of one person. Both partners are therefore responsible for change. This emphasis helps minimize the common tendency to place blame on one partner, which is countertherapeutic.

2. *Information and education are integral components* of all sex therapy programs. Although sexual ignorance and misinformation are less common today than at the time of Masters and Johnson's (1970) writings, most clients with sexual dysfunctions lack important knowledge about sexual physiology and techniques. This ignorance can contribute to performance anxiety or lead to unrealistic expectations about performance. Being unaware, for example, of the normal effects of aging on sexual performance may cause unrealistic expectations. The need for increased direct stimulation and the longer refractory period in older men (discussed in Chapter 12) require partners to adjust their expectations, and a failure to do so may cause disappointment, frustration, and performance fears. Couples in therapy receive specific and detailed information, through discussions, readings, or educational films. Although providing information is not ordinarily sufficient for resolving sexual dysfunctions, it is considered a necessary step.

3. *Attitudes, expectations, and sexual scripts usually must be modified* to improve sexual functioning (Ravart et al., 1996). Negative attitudes and unrealistic expectations about sex may result from sexual ignorance or misinformation (as noted above), from a person's upbringing, from personal experiences, or from a combination of all three. The goal of therapy is to change the person's thoughts through a process known as **cognitive restructuring**, which is designed to modify negative attitudes and beliefs and to reduce thoughts that interfere with sexual performance and enjoyment (Carey, Wincze, & Meisler, 1993). Negative attitudes toward sex need to be changed in order to help individuals and couples become more open to sexual experimentation, to foster a healthier view of sex and intimacy, and to reduce negative emotions such as performance anxiety. Cognitive restructuring may require a therapist to directly challenge a couple's irrational or unrealistic beliefs and expectations. It may also be accomplished by having couples read positive material on sexuality, attend lectures or workshops, or consult a respected religious leader who has positive views about sexuality.

Dysfunctional sexual scripts may also contribute to sexual performance problems (Gagnon, Rosen, & Leiblum, 1982). Individuals with sexual dysfunctions often subscribe to rigid and inflexible scripts, which do not permit spontaneity and variety. This lack of flexibility and creativity may lead to monotony and boredom in their sex lives, ultimately hampering their interest in sex and leading to sexual dissatisfaction. In some cases, the problem may be a discrepancy between sexual scripts and sexual behavior, which leads to unrealistic expectations and a tendency to be overcritical of one's sexual performance. Some women, for example, may view being multiorgasmic during sexual intercourse as the ideal, and they may be dissatisfied with their inability to achieve orgasm repeatedly during sexual intercourse. The "good girl" and "sleeping beauty" scripts, described earlier, can be equally detrimental to sexual satisfaction for both partners.

4. *Eliminating performance anxiety is an essential outcome* in sex therapy (Bach, Wincze, & Barlow, 2001). The major focus of the therapist is reducing the many factors that lead to anxiety about sexual performance. Because of performance failures,

COGNITIVE RESTRUCTURING
A technique used in sex therapy to modify negative thoughts and beliefs that contribute to a person's sexual problems.

couples experiencing sexual dysfunction typically become overly focused on performance at the expense of sexual enjoyment and pleasure. In a sense, such couples "keep score," and are goal-oriented, focusing on erection or orgasm rather than on enjoying the sexual intimacy. Performance anxiety is eliminated by teaching couples to enjoy the moment regardless of how they are performing.

5. *Interpersonal factors are relevant* in most cases of sexual dysfunction. These factors include anger, poor communication, and problems with intimacy, trust, and control. For example, one study found that effective communication between partners was the single best predictor of success in therapy for erection problems (Hawton et al., 1992). Additionally, gender role conflicts can cause difficulties. A husband with rigid gender-role stereotypes may feel threatened by his wife's sexual assertiveness and openness. Sex therapy encourages couples to be open and expressive about their sexual desires, preferences, and expectations. Individuals are instructed to give their partners frequent feedback during sex, to demonstrate pleasurable sexual techniques, and to guide a partner's touches.

Even when relationship problems did not cause a sexual dysfunction, they can seriously jeopardize a couple's ability to overcome the problem. Prolonged relationship conflicts may lead a partner to avoid having sex and to sabotage attempts to improve the sexual relationship. Couples experiencing serious relationship problems are less likely to benefit from sex therapy (MacPhee, Johnson, & van der Veer, 1995). For all these reasons, it is becoming increasingly common to integrate couples counseling with sex therapy (Weeks & Hof, 1987).

Specific Techniques of Sex Therapy

The principles just discussed guide most clinicians' general approach to sex therapy. In addition, based on the specific dysfunction being treated, some specific techniques are used. The techniques discussed below were specifically developed for the treatment of male erectile disorder, premature ejaculation, and female orgasmic disorder.

Sensate Focus Developed by Masters and Johnson (1970) for the treatment of erectile problems resulting from performance anxiety, **sensate focus** is one of the fundamental techniques in sex therapy, designed to teach individuals and couples to focus

Couple Practicing Sensate Focus Technique

SENSATE FOCUS
One of the original sex therapy techniques, designed to teach couples to focus on pleasurable sensations rather than on sexual performance.

on sensations rather than on performance. Focusing on sensations during a sexual encounter reduces anxiety. To help reduce performance fear, couples are instructed to practice all sex therapy techniques in a comfortable and nonthreatening setting at a time convenient for both partners.

Sensate focus is a structured but flexible technique (Wincze & Carey, 2001). It begins with homework assignments designed to help couples learn to enjoy the touching and intimacy of erotic encounters. Sensate focus employs a gradual approach. Sexual intercourse is temporarily banned as couples learn, or relearn, to focus on nongenital pleasuring. Dressed in comfortable clothing, partners take turns providing nonsexual massages. As couples make progress, the assignments gradually become more sexual as genital pleasuring is introduced. At each step, couples are reminded to focus primarily on pleasurable sensations and are discouraged from being concerned with erection and orgasms. In the final phase, sexual intercourse is gradually reintroduced. At first, a man might be instructed to insert his penis into his partner but to avoid any thrusting and to concentrate on the pleasurable sensations. Sexual intercourse in the female-superior position with thrusting is often the next step. Intercourse in the female-superior position is usually less emotionally and physically straining and is therefore recommended before couples experiment with other positions.

Couple Practicing Stop-Start Technique

The sensate focus technique is valuable for several reasons. In addition to lowering performance fears, sensate focus encourages couples to communicate and to provide each other with frequent feedback. This feedback, in turn, can teach individuals what sensations their partners prefer. Finally, sensate focus, when it leads to improvements in sexual functioning, can be a strong confidence builder for couples.

Squeeze and Stop-Start Techniques Two techniques are intended to help men with premature ejaculation. A man using the **squeeze technique** (Masters & Johnson, 1970) masturbates almost to orgasm. Before reaching orgasm, as the man feels that ejaculation is imminent, he stops masturbating and squeezes the glans of his penis until the urge to ejaculate passes, usually for 20–30 seconds. Once the urge to ejaculate has subsided, he repeats the technique. In a typical squeeze technique session, a man may rehearse the process three to five times before allowing ejaculation to occur. This technique is practiced until the man gains some control over ejaculation (Wincze & Carey, 2001).

With the **stop-start technique** (Semans, 1956), which is similar to the squeeze technique, the couple engages in sexual foreplay and penile stimulation almost to the point of ejaculatory inevitability, at which point all stimulation is stopped. Once the man's sensation of imminent ejaculation subsides, the couple resumes stimulation until the man once again is on the verge of ejaculation. The process is repeated regularly until the man gains increased control over ejaculation. As the man achieves a longer latency to orgasm, the amount of stimulation is gradually increased and stimulation techniques are varied. After the man becomes better able to control ejaculation during manual stimulation, the same process is repeated with sexual intercourse, first without movement and later with thrusting (McCarthy, 1989).

Directed Masturbation Developed by LoPiccolo and Lobitz (1972), **directed masturbation** is the most commonly used technique for the treatment of lifelong female orgasmic disorder. Directed masturbation, like other sex therapy techniques, is

SQUEEZE TECHNIQUE
A technique aimed at solving the problem of premature ejaculation, whereby a man repeatedly masturbates almost to orgasm and then squeezes his penis to prevent orgasm.

STOP-START TECHNIQUE
A sex therapy technique used by couples to help the man gain ejaculatory control by ceasing stimulation as he nears orgasm. With repeated practice, the man gains increased control over ejaculation.

DIRECTED MASTURBATION
A technique aimed at solving the problem of female orgasmic disorder, involving several steps aimed at improving a woman's body image and sexual self-knowledge.

introduced gradually. It involves self-exploration, education, and communication and consists of several steps. In step 1, the woman is given reading material about female anatomy, body image, and female sexuality. In the next step, visual self-exploration helps the woman become more comfortable with her genitals. In step 3, self-discovery continues as the woman identifies areas of her body, including her genitals, where stimulation is pleasurable. In step 4, the woman is introduced to techniques for masturbation. She is encouraged to change the speed and amount of pressure used during masturbation, to learn more about what pleases her. In step 5, if a woman has not reached orgasm through manual masturbation, she is taught to use a vibrator to assist her in having her first orgasm. In step 6, the woman demonstrates to her partner what she has discovered about effective stimulation for her. She may guide his hand and control the speed and pressure of stimulation. This step is intended to teach her partner how best to please her. Finally, the woman and her partner have sexual intercourse, during which she or her partner stimulates her clitoris.

Several studies show that directed masturbation can be very effective in treating female orgasmic disorder (Heiman, 2002a; LoPiccolo & Stock, 1986). Like other sex therapy techniques, it is most effective when used with a cooperative and supportive partner and when the person seeking the therapy does not also suffer from other serious or chronic problems.

HEALTHY DECISION MAKING

As we have noted throughout the chapter, a host of problems can affect sexual functioning. Fortunately, most lapses in sexual desire, difficulty becoming aroused, or orgasm problems are only temporary and the result of the usual hassles we all encounter in life. Occasionally, the lapses become persistent problems that require attention.

In their book *Sex Matters for Women,* Foley, Kope, and Sugrue (2002) offer a self-assessment to assist women in addressing sexual problems and deciding whether to get help. Men can use the self-assessment just as effectively. Jot down your answers to the following questions:

1. What is the problem?
2. When does it occur?
3. When did it first happen?
4. If the problem is longstanding, what is guiding you to address it now?
5. What thoughts go through your mind when you are being sexual?
6. How comfortable are you with sex?
7. Do you avoid relationships or situations that could become sexual?
8. Do you have some attitude or beliefs that might interfere with your sex life?
9. Do you have accurate knowledge about sex and your body?
10. How is your problem affecting your partner and your relationship?
11. How is your relationship, both sexually and nonsexually?
12. How are things going in your life in general?
13. How is your emotional and physical health?

As you review your answers, you may feel reassured that your sexual health is basically okay. Perhaps you just need to find ways to simplify your life or reduce your stress level. You may need to consult your healthcare professional for a professional opinion; if so, bring these questions and your answers with you. Going to a professional you know and trust can facilitate the process. Together, you may decide that talking to a sex therapist may indeed be warranted.

Should you decide to see a professional sex therapist, be sure that the professional you consult is competent and adheres to ethical practices. You should verify that the professional has proper training and credentials. The major credentialing body for sex therapists is the American Association of Sex Educators, Counselors, and Therapists (AASECT). AASECT is an interdisciplinary organization of professionals devoted to promoting a better understanding of human sexuality and healthy sexual behavior. In order to be certified by AASECT, professionals must demonstrate proper education, training, and supervised practice. AASECT-certified sex therapists are bound to ethical guidelines intended to ensure competence, to protect the welfare of consumers, and to maintain the integrity of the profession. AASECT maintains a Web site at http://www.aasect.org/about.htm.

summary

OVERVIEW OF SEXUAL DYSFUNCTIONS

- Sexual dysfunctions involve recurrent difficulties with sexual performance. They include sexual desire disorders, sexual arousal disorders, orgasmic disorders, and sexual pain disorders.
- Sexual dysfunctions are common, affecting as many as 43% of women and 31% of men at some point in their lives.

TYPES OF SEXUAL DYSFUNCTIONS

- Sexual desire disorders involve absent or very limited interest in sex. Hypoactive sexual desire disorder is a near-complete lack of interest in sex. Sexual aversion disorder is characterized by sexual avoidance. Medical factors, such as low testosterone, certain medications (e.g., antidepressants), and psychological factors such as depression and sexual trauma may be responsible for problems with desire.
- Sexual arousal disorders include erection problems in men and problems with mental or physical arousal in women. Medical conditions and drugs may cause arousal disorders, as can performance fears and other cognitive and emotional factors.
- Orgasmic disorders include the inability to reach orgasm and, in men, premature ejaculation. Premature ejaculation is often associated with a hypersensitivity to sexual stimulation. Orgasmic disorders have been linked with false beliefs about sex, sexual inhibitions, and relationship problems.
- Sexual pain disorders involve either genital pain during intercourse or vaginal spasms during attempted penetration. Genital pain may result from medical conditions. Vaginismus is usually due to previous sexual trauma or to strong inhibitions.

GENERAL CAUSES OF SEXUAL DYSFUNCTIONS

- Medications and other drugs are common causes of problems with sexual functioning. Alcohol abuse is linked to several sexual dysfunctions. Antidepressants can lead to a loss of desire.
- Psychological factors are also associated with sexual problems. Anxiety has been consistently found to interfere with sexual functioning. Feelings of guilt and shame may also predispose some people to sexual difficulties.
- Relationship problems, including control issues, resentment, and fear of intimacy may contribute to sexual dysfunctions.
- Cultural beliefs, such as the sexual double standard, may lead to sexual inhibitions, conflict, and miscommunication, which can result in sexual difficulties.

TREATMENT OF SEXUAL DYSFUNCTIONS

- There are several medical interventions for erection problems, including surgery, injections, and use of vacuum constriction devices. Oral medications for erection problems are extremely popular treatments and can be effective. Medications may also be prescribed for men who experience recurring problems with premature ejaculation.
- Sex therapy involves techniques designed to provide education, correct faulty beliefs, reduce performance fears, and resolve relationship conflicts. To elicit partner support and cooperation, sexual dysfunctions are viewed as problems for the couple.
- Techniques such as sensate focus, stop-start, the squeeze technique, and directed masturbation are often useful for resolving sexual performance problems.

CHAPTER 14

Sexually Transmissible Infections

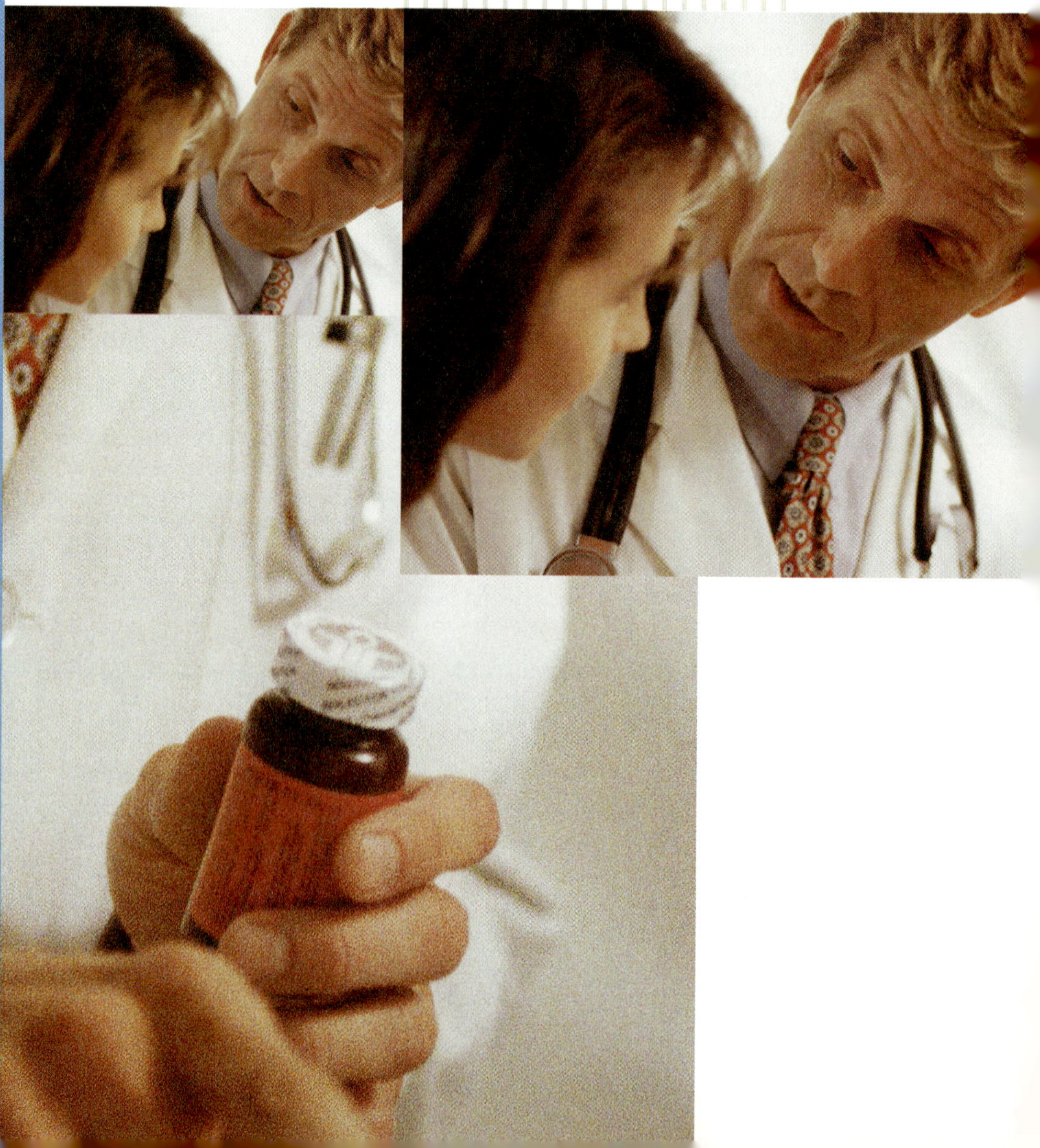

I was only 19 years old and was infected [with herpes simplex virus, HSV] through oral sex. I felt as though my world was crumbling. I was all alone; no one was there to really understand what I was going through; and I was too embarrassed to seek help beyond my doctor. It has been one of the toughest things I've ever had to deal with. In the beginning, the virus was on my mind every minute of the day. I cried and cried and asked "Why me?" Now, 6 years later, I am in a wonderful relationship and will be married this fall. My partner loves me for who I am, and HSV is a part of me for now, until one day when there is a cure. I've gone on with my life and don't dwell on the fact that I have herpes.

My partner loves me for who I am.

The things that can help you through this are time, patience, education, love and support.

(From *The Helper*, a newsletter published by the American Social Health Association)

This note that a reader of a newsletter for herpes sufferers wrote to comfort fellow sufferers aptly illustrates the progression from devastation to effective coping that so many people go through when they are diagnosed with a **sexually transmissible infection (STI)**, an infection that is spread through sexual contact. STIs can have physically and emotionally painful consequences for the sufferer. Unfortunately, the emotional pain of contracting an STI is worsened by the cultural tendency to stigmatize people with STIs much more than people with diseases that are not sexually transmitted. First and foremost, we want to help you to "destigmatize" STIs and to understand that STIs do not make people dirty, morally base, or otherwise less deserving of respect. We also want you to understand that although sexually transmissible infections are a significant public health problem, they are entirely avoidable. But in order to avoid them, you must know how they are contracted. We also want you to know how to treat or manage an STI, should you ever contract one. People are much more likely to take action to prevent or reduce the spread of STIs if they are both educated about them and comfortable discussing them. We hope that after reading this chapter you will have a realistic but not overly fearful perspective on STIs and that you will be well armed to protect yourself and others from these troubling infections.

The terminology in this chapter is somewhat different from what has been used traditionally. The older term *venereal disease (VD)* was abandoned in favor of *sexually transmitted disease* because it was imprecise. This book uses *sexually transmissible infections* instead, because the word "infections" more accurately characterizes these conditions, which are all acquired via invasion of the body by harmful agents, through sexual contact or other means. You may recognize the names of the most common STIs, such as gonorrhea, syphilis, and herpes. The human immunodeficiency virus (HIV) is the most threatening of the STIs and, therefore, probably the best known, but it will surprise you to know that there are more than 50 organisms that can be transmitted through sexual contact to cause infections and syndromes. Many STIs are epidemic, particularly among younger Americans; however, the vast majority of people are poorly informed about them. Very few Americans can name the two most rapidly spreading STIs—genital warts, caused by the human papillomavirus, and trichomoniasis, caused by a bacterium—and

SEXUALLY TRANSMISSIBLE INFECTION (STI)
Any of a number of parasitic, bacterial, or viral infections that can spread through sexual contact.

they grossly underestimate the prevalence of STIs and their personal risk of contracting an STI (Kaiser Family Foundation/*Glamour* Magazine, 1998). Obviously, everyone can benefit tremendously from learning about these infections.

Despite tremendous advances in research on STIs and the implementation of large-scale screening programs, health education, and behavioral interventions for their prevention, the United States continues to lead the industrialized world in the prevalence of these infections. In the United States alone, 65 million people are living with an incurable STI (CDC, 2000f). In addition, approximately 15.3 million Americans acquire an STI each year, half of which are incurable infections, and one in three sexually active Americans will have contracted one by age 24 (CDC, 2000f; Kaiser Family Foundation/American Social Health Association, 1998). Information on prevalence and costs of some of the most common STIs in the United States is presented in Table 14.1. It is obvious from these statistics that STIs constitute a huge personal and public health burden.

Adolescents (10–19 years of age), young adults (20–24), women, and minorities are disproportionately affected by STIs. Adolescents and young adults run the greatest risk of acquiring an STI, largely because they tend to have multiple sexual partners and to engage in more risk-taking behavior. Adolescents tend to deny being at risk, to have more spontaneous sex, and to use fewer preventive measures. But it is women and infants who suffer the most from STIs in the long term. These infections are associated with complications such as spontaneous abortions, fetal and neonatal (occurring in the first 4 weeks after birth) infections, premature labor, and gynecological cancer. The incidence (number of new cases within a defined period) of many STIs is much higher among racial and ethnic minorities than among whites. There is no biological explanation to account for this difference; however, social factors that are associated with race and ethnicity—such as poverty, use of illicit drugs, lack of access to quality health care, and health-care-seeking behavior—may account for these differences (CDC, 2000f). Ethnic and racial differences in STI transmission are discussed in more detail in Close Up on Culture: Ethnicity, Race, and Transmission of STIs.

TABLE 14.1 The Most Common STIs in the United States and Their Costs

STI	ESTIMATED NUMBER OF NEW CASES PER YEAR	ESTIMATED NUMBER OF CASES IN THE POPULATION	CURABLE?	ESTIMATED ANNUAL COSTS
All STIs	15.3 million	—	N/A	$8.4 billion (not including indirect costs*)
Chlamydia	3 million	2 million	Yes	$375 million (acute infection only; $2.1 billion including complications)
Trichomoniasis	5 million	N/A	Yes	$375 million
Gonorrhea	650,000	N/A	Yes	
HPV (genital warts)	5.5 million	24 million	No	$1.6 billion
Herpes†	1 million	45 million	No	$208 million
Hepatitis B	200,000	417,000	No	$51.4 million
Syphilis	70,000	N/A	Yes	$43.8 million
HIV/AIDS	20,000 (half through sexual contact)	560,000	No	$4.5 billion

*Indirect costs include costs such as loss of productivity/wages, out-of-pocket costs, and costs related to transmission to infants.
†HSV-2 rates only—would be higher if HSV-1 on genitals were counted.

SOURCES: (Most recent figures are used where available.) Kaiser Family Foundation/American Social Health Association, 1998; National Institute of Allergy and Infectious Diseases, 1998, July; American Social Health Association, 1995; CDC 2000f.

CLOSE UP ON culture

Ethnicity, Race, and Transmission of STIs

Race and ethnicity have long been established as factors related to the risk of transmission of STIs. In other words, some racial or ethnic groups have higher STI transmission rates than others. Unfortunately, singling out any one group for analysis sometimes results in stereotyping the group as a whole. It is important to remember that it is not ethnicity that puts someone at risk but rather high-risk behaviors associated with various social and cultural factors. There is *no* biological basis for these differences. The benefit of recognizing ethnic and racial disparities in STI transmission is that it allows efforts to reduce transmission rates to be tailored to meet the specific needs of each group. Early public health interventions to reduce high-risk sexual behaviors and, consequently, STI transmission tended to take a generic approach rather than taking into account cultural and social factors. Let's take a look at some differences in STI transmission rates among white Americans, African Americans, and Hispanic Americans and some cultural and social factors that might account for these differences.

Racial Disparity

Studies have found that certain STIs are much more common among Hispanic Americans and African Americans than among white Americans. Despite the fact that primary and secondary syphilis rates among African Americans declined 88% from 1990 to 1999 (CDC, 2000e), the 2000 rate of syphilis infection in this group was still 21 times greater than among white Americans. The rate among Hispanic Americans was three times that among white Americans (CDC, 2001f). Similarly, African Americans contract gonorrhea at a rate 30 times higher than that for white Americans, and Hispanic Americans contract it three times as often as white Americans (CDC, 2001f). AIDS also affects African Americans and Hispanic Americans at higher rates than it does white Americans. African Americans accounted for 38% of all AIDS cases through 2000, even though they make up only 12% of the U.S. population (CDC, 2002a). Hispanic Americans make up 13% of the U.S. population but represent 19% of all AIDS cases (CDC, 2002a).

The consequences of STI infections are also greater for African American women than for white American women. Because they are more likely to get treatment before pelvic inflammatory disease (PID) becomes severe, white American women are only one-third as likely as African American women to be hospitalized for acute PID and only half as likely to be hospitalized for chronic PID. In addition, African American women die from cervical cancer three times more often than do white American women.

Access to Health Care

The differences just discussed are probably largely attributable to minorities' relative lack of access to good preventive health care. The reasons for this disparity include financial and nonfinancial factors. From a financial standpoint, more members of racial and ethnic minorities lack funds to cover health care and are uninsured or on Medicaid than are white Americans. Among nonfinancial factors, institutionalized and personal stereotypes and biases may contribute to substandard care for ethnic and racial minorities. Research has shown that racial and ethnic minorities are more likely to seek treatment in hospital settings instead of in private clinics. They report having more difficulties getting an appointment and waiting longer during an appointment—disparities that exist regardless of the patient's socioeconomic or health status (Kaiser Family Foundation, 2002; Shi, 1999; Williams & Rucker, 2000).

Reporting Differences

It is important to point out that rates of infection for minorities may merely appear to be higher than those for white Americans as a result of reporting differences. As noted, African Americans, for example, are more likely than white Americans to go to a public clinic for diagnosis and treatment, and public clinics are more consistent than private clinics in reporting their rates to government agencies that track STI infections (Alan Guttmacher Institute, 1994a).

Sexual Attitudes

Several studies have attempted to assess behaviors and attitudes that may account for differences in STI transmission rates across ethnic groups. For example, research has shown that high-risk members of racial or ethnic groups are less likely to perceive themselves as "at risk" for AIDS than are high-risk white Americans. One factor that might contribute to this finding is that members of ethnic minorities report having greater concerns about aspects of immediate survival, such as employment, childcare, and crime, which take precedence over concerns about STI transmission (Kalichman, Hunter, & Kelly, 1992). This finding suggests that interventions aimed at ethnic and racial minority groups must take into account sociocultural factors that could interfere with the adoption of safer sexual practices.

Other research has shown that young white American women (51%) are more likely to use condoms than are young African American women (35%) or young Hispanic American women (41%) (Catania et al., 1992; Marin & Marin, 1992). One factor that might partially account for these differences is that white American women are more likely than Hispanic American women to be confident about and comfortable with condom use—that is, to feel a greater willingness to ask a partner to use a condom or to refuse to have sex if a partner rejects condom use (Gomez & Marin, 1996). Having multiple sexual partners is another risk factor that appears to differ among these groups. Young African American men are most likely to have multiple sexual partners. On the other hand, white American women are more likely than African American or Hispanic American women to have multiple sex partners (Dolcini, Coates, Catania, Kegeles, & Hauck, 1995), which is inconsistent with reported STI infection rates.

These research findings represent only the beginning of an exploration of factors that are correlated with race and ethnicity and that might influence differing rates of STI transmission. Learning more about these important factors may allow intervention programs to be tailored to meet the needs of people of various ethnic, racial, or cultural backgrounds.

did YOU know?

Every year in the United States, 1 out of every 4 sexually active teens gets an STI—a total of some 3 million young men and women a year (American Social Health Association, 2000).

Geographical differences also exist. The southern states have the highest rates of syphilis and gonorrhea of any area in the United States. It is not entirely clear why this is the case, but it may be related to social factors such as less access to quality health care and higher poverty rates in the South (CDC, 2000f). In any case, these findings highlight the need for screening and preventive measures within the South, particularly among poor, young minorities.

PARASITIC INFECTIONS

Parasites are organisms that live on or within a host. Pubic lice and scabies are two common parasites that infest the skin or pubic hair and can be sexually transmitted.

Pubic Lice

Pediculosis is an infestation of parasitic crab lice, *Phthirus pubis,* or **pubic lice.** Those infested with this parasite are commonly said to have "crabs." Somewhat resembling a miniature crab, the louse is a small (1.2 millimeters), flat-bodied, wingless parasite that grasps the pubic hair with its claws, anchors its mouth to the skin, and feeds off the blood of the host. Pubic lice are usually transmitted through sexual contact but may be contracted from using infested bedding, clothing, towels, or even toilet seats. The lice are somewhat difficult to detect, although they are visible to the eye, and may look like small scabs. Millions of cases of pediculosis are treated annually in the United States. The main symptom is itching, but irritation and reddened skin may develop. In exceptional cases, the infected person may experience fever, malaise (general sense of ill-being) and increased irritability. Pubic lice can survive only about 24 hours off the body; however, their nits (eggs) mature in 7–8 days and can hatch in bedding or clothing.

Scabies

Scabies is a contagious skin disease caused by the parasitic itch mite, *Sarcoptes scabiei.* Scabies has a long incubation period, which makes the source of an infestation difficult to determine. It is transmitted sexually when partners spend long periods of time together—for example, an entire night rather than a brief sexual encounter. It is also commonly acquired nonsexually through skin-to-skin contact or from shared clothing, bedding, and towels. If one individual becomes infected, his or her entire household often requires treatment. Outbreaks are not unusual in schools, child-care settings, nursing homes, and hospitals. Scabies causes intense itching, skin irritation, and sometimes a red rash that later develops into lesions (isolated patches of infection). Itching is usually worse at night or after bathing. Common sites of involvement are the hands, genitalia, buttocks, groin, armpits, and feet. The condition is diagnosed by its symptoms and signs and confirmed by microscopic examination of scrapings from the infected areas.

The pubic louse resembles a crab.

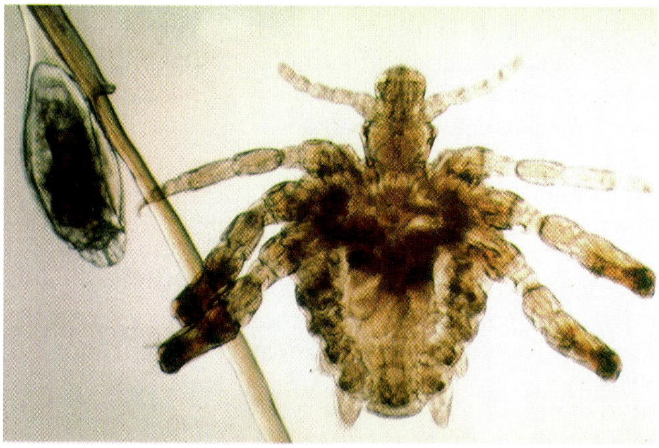

PEDICULOSIS
An infestation of parasitic pubic lice that causes itching.

PUBIC LICE
Parasitic biting lice that can be transmitted sexually.

SCABIES
An infestation of a tiny parasitic mite that results in itching.

Diagnosis and Treatment

An infestation of pubic lice or scabies may feel repugnant and may make a person feel unclean and create anxiety and embarrassment. However, while seeking treatment for a parasitic infection can be embarrassing, a cure is readily available. Prescription and nonprescription medications are available to treat pubic lice. Preparations are sold in the form of lotions, creams, or shampoos (some trade names are Kwell, Rid, A-200, and Triple X; some drug names are Permethrin and Lindane) (CDC, 1998c). The medications are applied directly to the areas of infestation to kill both adult lice and nits (eggs). Bedding and clothing should also be decontaminated by laundering with water at 125° F and drying with hot air or by dry cleaning. Sexual partners should be treated as well, whether or not they show signs of infestation. Like pubic lice, scabies is readily treatable with a Lindane cream or lotion (commonly, Kwell). All sexual and household contacts should also be treated. To effectively eradicate the parasite, clothing and bedding should be washed and dried in the hot cycle or boiled.

BACTERIAL INFECTIONS

Bacteria are single-celled microorganisms that do not have an organized nucleus, unlike many other cells. They reproduce by dividing, and if conditions are favorable, a single bacterium can yield a colony of more than a million cells in a day. As they grow, bacteria release toxins (poisonous substances), which make a person sick. The major bacterial STIs are gonorrhea, syphilis, chlamydia, and chancroid, all of which are curable.

Chlamydia

Chlamydia, one of the most prevalent of all STIs, is caused by the bacterium *Chlamydia trachomatis*. Symptoms of this infection closely resemble those of gonorrhea. Chlamydia is responsible for an increasing number and variety of clinical syndromes infecting men, women, and babies. The number of reported cases of chlamydia has increased substantially over the years, primarily in women (CDC, 2001g; see Figure 14.1); however, this increase is due in part to increased screening efforts, better reporting, and improved detection of asymptomatic infections, especially in women.

did YOU know?

Forty percent of all reported cases of chlamydia are in young people, aged 15–19. Seventy-five percent of women and 50% of men with chlamydia have no symptoms (CDC, 2000f).

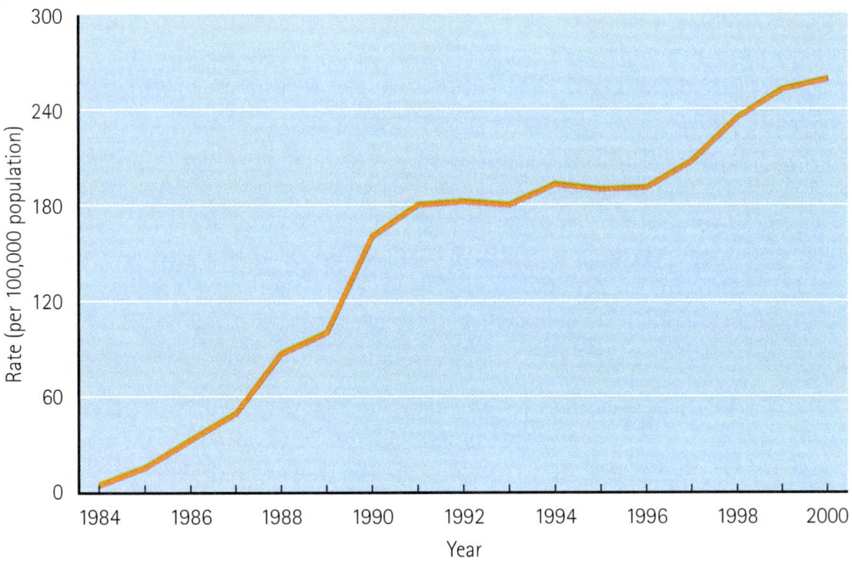

Figure 14.1 Chlamydia infection rates in the United States have continued to rise over the years, partly as a result of increased testing for asymptomatic infection. The graph represents U.S. infection rates from 1984 through 2000 (CDC, 2001g).

CHLAMYDIA
An STI caused by the bacterium *Chlamydia trachomatis.* It commonly causes abnormal vaginal and urethral discharge in women, eye disease and pneumonia in infants born to infected women, and may cause nongonococcal urethritis in men.

Women have nearly five times as many detected cases of chlamydia as men—but many infections continue to go undetected in both sexes.

Signs and Symptoms

Like the early stages of syphilis, asymptomatic chlamydia can be a significant problem, because the infection can still be transmitted to others and can result in serious health problems for the infected person. If symptoms are present, they may include mild itching or irritation in the genitals, burning sensations during urination, and sticky yellow or green cervical discharge. In women, urethritis and **cervicitis** (inflammation of the cervix) are the most common infections. If chlamydia goes untreated, it can progress to PID; up to 40% of women with chlamydia (about 1 million annually) develop PID (CDC, 2000f). Making the detection and treatment of chlamydial infections a standard of care for sexually active young women can be an important step in preventing PID.

Men usually develop symptoms of chlamydial infections between 7 and 28 days after intercourse with an infected partner. Symptoms may include mild pain or burning with urination, urethral discomfort, and a clear or pus-like discharge. Men may also experience pain, swelling and tenderness of the scrotum, and fever. With rectal infections, pain, bleeding, mucous discharge, and diarrhea have been reported. Infected men sometimes develop **nongonococcal urethritis** (inflammation of the urethra), which results in penile discharge, itching, and burning with urination. Chlamydial infections can also affect the testicles and prostate gland and may cause Reiter's syndrome (inflammation and arthritic symptoms). Like untreated chlamydial infections in women, untreated nongonococcal infections in men may result in infertility.

Transmission

Chlamydial infections are transmitted primarily through vaginal, anal, and oral-genital intercourse. The disease can also be transmitted to other areas of the body, for example, by touching the eyes after touching infected genitalia. Newborns can acquire the disease during birth (with both vaginal and C-section deliveries), in the form of infections of the eyes and/or lungs. Blindness and pneumonia are potential consequences if these infections are not detected and treated.

Diagnosis and Treatment

Many chlamydial infections are difficult to diagnose, especially among women, because symptoms are often limited or absent. Chlamydia is diagnosed by examining the infection site and by culturing urethral or cervical discharge. New tests that detect bacterial DNA in urine are faster, less invasive, and painless (Los Angeles County Department of Health Services, 1998). For women, a cervical smear is often used to verify the diagnosis in that region. Penile infections are identified by obtaining a specimen from the urethra. The two antibiotics most highly recommended for treatment of chlamydia are azithromycin and doxycycline. Alternatively, erythromycin or ofloxacin can be used, but erythromycin is less effective than azithromycin and doxycycline and may cause stomach upset, and ofloxacin, though as effective as the two preferred antibiotics, is more expensive. Patients treated with erythromycin might be retested for cure after 3 weeks, but azithromycin and doxycycline are so effective that retesting is unnecessary unless symptoms are still present or recur. Patients should also refrain from sexual intercourse until treatment is complete and all sexual partners have been treated (CDC, 2002c).

Gonorrhea

Perhaps you have heard people refer to "the clap" or "the drip"—they are referring to gonorrhea. **Gonorrhea** is a sexually transmissible infection caused by the bacterium *Neisseria gonorrhoeae.* As far as is known, gonorrhea is transmitted almost exclusively through sexual activity. People have suffered from this disease for thousands of years, as revealed by historical accounts in ancient Chinese, Egyptian, Roman, and Greek writings. Incidence rates in the United States began rising sharply in the 1950s. It is believed that the introduction of oral contraceptives and intrauterine devices in the 1970s led to greater sexual freedom and, along with decreased use of condoms and spermicides, gonorrhea rates rose rapidly. Gonorrhea peaked in 1975 and then de-

CERVICITIS
Inflammation of the cervix.

NONGONOCOCCAL URETHRITIS
An inflammation of the urethra in men, principally caused by chlamydial infections.

GONORRHEA
An STI caused by the bacterium *Neisseria gonorrhoeae.* The infection commonly results in abnormal vaginal or urethral discharge and can also cause eye disease in infants born to infected women.

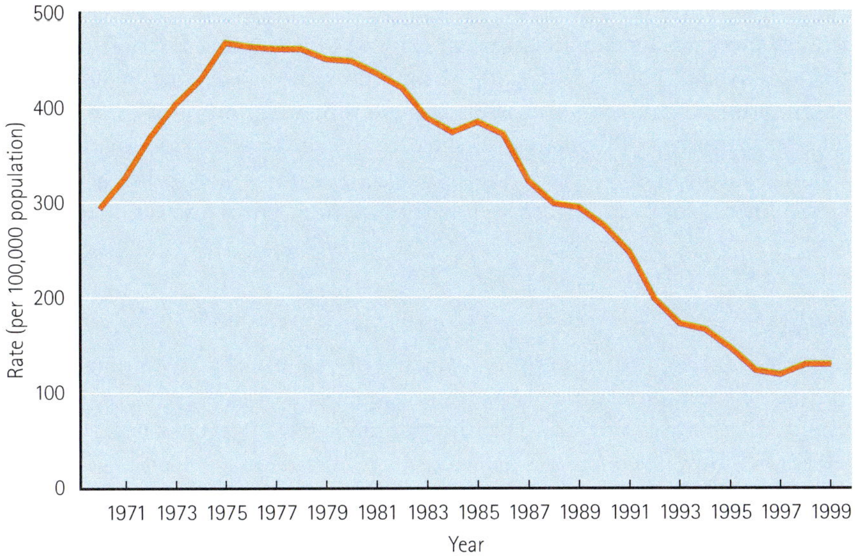

Figure 14.2 Gonorrhea rates in the United States have declined significantly over the past 30 years, but the disease is far from being eradicated (CDC, 2000f).

clined steadily until it stabilized between 1996 and 1997, as you can see in Figure 14.2. Unfortunately, it increased by 9% between 1997 and 1999 (CDC, 2000f). Like many other diseases, gonorrhea is most prevalent among adolescents, young adults, and minorities (CDC, 2000f; Kaiser Family Foundation/American Social Health Association, 1998). At one time, gonorrhea was more prevalent among men, but it decreased more rapidly among males than among females in recent years. Today, the prevalence rates for the genders are roughly equal and on the rise (CDC, 2000f).

Signs and Symptoms

The signs and symptoms of gonorrhea vary considerably from case to case. In men, symptoms usually appear within 2–7 days after contact. Mild discomfort in the urethra is the most common first symptom. This is followed by burning sensations that accompany urination and a pus-like penile discharge that is clear at first but yellowish later on. Increased frequency and urgency of urination, itching, and inflammation and swelling of the urethra are also common. Even without treatment, these symptoms frequently disappear; more than 95% of untreated patients become asymptomatic (showing no symptoms) in 6 months. Less frequently, the disease spreads to the prostate, bladder, kidneys, and testicles. Women typically report mild symptoms within 7–10 days, but these can become severe. The most common symptoms are increased vaginal discharge, pain with urination, increased frequency of urination, uterine bleeding, and menorrhagia (excessive menstruation). If gonorrhea is left untreated in women, it can increase the risk of contracting other infections and can result in serious and permanent obstetrical complications, such as infertility and ectopic pregnancy. Pregnant women infected with gonorrhea are also at risk for spontaneous abortion, rupture or acute infection of fetal membranes, and premature delivery. In rare cases in both men and women, the disease is associated with fever, chills, and inflammation of joints, tendons, skin, and the heart (Braverman & Strasburger, 1994; Hook & Handsfield, 1990; Soper, 1991).

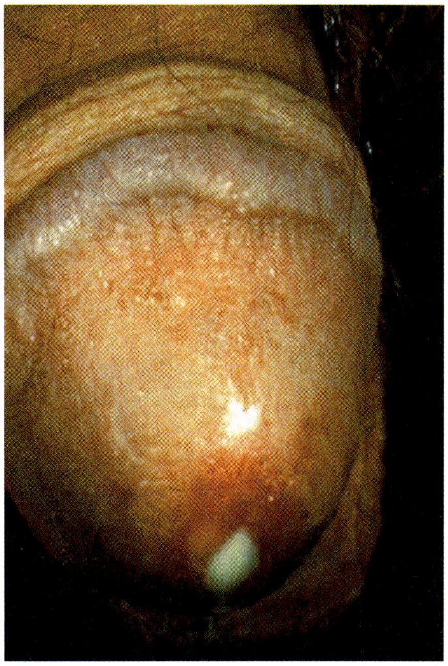

Gonorrhea causes a clear or yellowish discharge from the urethra.

Gonorrhea can also infect the rectum. Rectal gonorrhea is most common among women and homosexual men. Homosexual men are most likely to contract rectal gonorrhea through receptive anal sex, but women can also contract it through anal sex or if vaginal discharge containing the bacteria touches the rectum. Rectal infections are found in 35–50% of women with genital gonorrhea. Unfortunately, women with rectal infections are usually asymptomatic, yet they can still transmit the infection to others. Men with rectal gonorrhea tend to experience mild to severe anal itching, mucus-coated stools, rectal bleeding, and pain. Oral-genital contact can cause mouth and throat infections (pharyngeal gonorrhea), but these are not common. Over 90% of pharyngeal infections are asymptomatic, but symptoms can include inflammation of the throat and tonsils and fever. Women with rectal gonorrhea are not the only asymptomatic carriers—many men and women remain asymptomatic. Not only does being asymptomatic increase the risk of transmitting gonorrhea to others, but it also tends to cause greater harm to the infected person by allowing the infection to spread to other organs of the reproductive tract or by causing infertility.

Transmission

Gonorrhea is transmitted primarily through vaginal or anal intercourse or oral-genital contact. Newborns can contract the disease during vaginal delivery. It can also be contracted from using a warm, moist towel or sheet immediately after it has been used by an infected person. Despite common misconceptions, there is no evidence supporting the transmission of gonorrhea via toilet seats or other dry objects. This disease, however, is highly contagious, and women are more likely than men are to catch it from an infected person. In fact, the chances of acquiring the disease from one sexual contact with an infected person are about 60–90% for women and 30–50% for men (Sexual Health InfoCenter, 2001).

Diagnosis and Treatment

Gonorrhea can be rapidly diagnosed in men through microscopic examination of urethral discharge. Identification of gonorrhea in women generally requires swabbing the infected site and then culturing the specimen to determine if the bacteria are present. Gonorrhea is usually curable with antibiotics and changes in sexual practices to prevent reinfection. Penicillin, tetracycline, and ampicillin were once considered the best antibiotics to treat gonorrhea. However, strains of gonorrhea that do not respond to these antibiotics (antibiotic-resistant strains) have been surfacing in the United States and have become epidemic in other parts of the world (Bowie, Hammerschlag, & Martin, 1994; CDC, 2000c; Hook, Sondheimer, & Zenilman, 1995). Thus, newer antibiotics such as ceftriaxone, cefixime, ciprofloxacin, ofloxacin, azithromycin, and doxycycline are now recommended for gonorrhea. Because azithromycin and doxycycline are also effective in treating chlamydia, which co-occurs with 20–40% of gonococcal infections, the Centers for Disease Control encourages use of these drugs to treat gonorrhea (CDC, 1998c).

Syphilis

The name *syphilis* comes from the work of a 16th-century Italian physician and poet, Fracastoro of Verona. He wrote about a shepherd boy named Syphilius, who suffered the disease's symptoms as punishment from the god Apollo for not making sacrifices to him. **Syphilis** is a sexually transmissible infection caused by *Treponema pallidum,* a corkscrew-shaped bacterium that can affect any tissue or organ of the body. Complications of this infection can include skin lesions (*chancres,* pronounced "shan-kers"), rash, heart disease, blindness, mental illness, and death. Like gonorrhea, syphilis is an old disease. In fact, symptoms of syphilis were described in the Old Testament of the Bible and in ancient Chinese writings. The disease reached epidemic proportions in Europe in the late 15th century, as a result of urban growth and related unsanitary conditions and more widespread travel. Syphilis rates in the United States have been cyclical, with peaks in 1947, 1959, and 1990, when it reached a 40-year high (see Figure 14.3). However, U.S. prevalence rates have consistently declined since that time; in 1996, the rate fell below the goal established by the Centers for Disease Control for the year 2000 (CDC, 1998c, 2000f). The disease disproportionately afflicts African Americans and Hispanic Americans; rates among African Americans are over 30 times those of white Americans and among Hispanic Americans they are over 3 times those of whites (CDC, 2000f). As mentioned earlier, risk factors thought to account for the higher rates among ethnic minorities include poverty, low access to quality health care, and less health-care-seeking behavior. Some STI experts have associated the

SYPHILIS
An STI caused by the *Treponema pallidum* bacterium and that if untreated, progresses through several stages of development from a chancre to a skin rash to damage of the cardiovascular or central nervous system to death.

higher rates with the use of cocaine (Astemborski, Vlahov, Warren, Soloman, & Nelson, 1994; Coles, Hipp, Silberstein, & Chen, 1995; Rolfs, Goldberg, & Sharrar, 1990). It is thought that cocaine users have a higher probability of contracting the disease because they often engage in risky sexual practices, including having sex with multiple partners and exchanging sex for money or drugs.

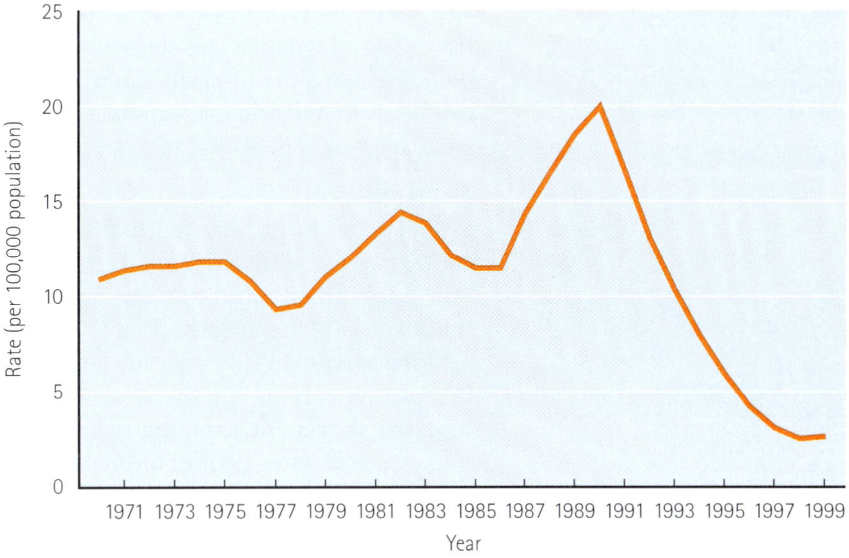

Figure 14.3 Syphilis rates in the United States have taken a downward turn since 1990, when rates of the disease were at their highest in years.

Signs and Symptoms

Left untreated, syphilis develops through three stages: primary, secondary, and late (or tertiary). An infected person is highly contagious in the first two stages of the disease, when the bacteria are shed in genital discharges, saliva, and blood, and from chancres (sores or ulcers). Primary symptoms usually appear within 3–4 weeks of becoming infected. A hard, round, painless sore, or chancre, is the first sign of infection and occurs at the site of contact. Chancres appear wherever the bacteria make contact with the body. In women, these lesions usually form along the vaginal wall or cervix or on the external genitalia, commonly the labia. Among men, the lesions typically form on the tip of the penis, the scrotum, or the penile shaft. Chancres can also be found on the lips, tongue, cheek, tonsils, and fingers. Furthermore, receptive anal intercourse with an infected man can result in ulcers of the rectum and anus.

The chancres disappear after the primary stage, usually within several weeks. Because the chancres are painless and disappear, the early symptoms of syphilis may go undetected. This fact, combined with the all-too-common tendency for denial, can lead to significant complications for the infected person and to a much greater chance of spreading the disease to others.

Skin rashes, which mark the secondary stage, usually appear within 6–12 weeks of contact. The rash is commonly located on the hands and feet. Also common are flu-like symptoms including fever, swollen lymph nodes, malaise, fatigue, headache, sore throat, aches in the bones, joint swelling, weight loss, and nausea.

After the secondary stage, the person may again become asymptomatic. Syphilis may remain latent for a few years or for the rest of the person's life. Left untreated, the bacteria continue to burrow into and multiply in the blood vessels, spinal cord, brain,

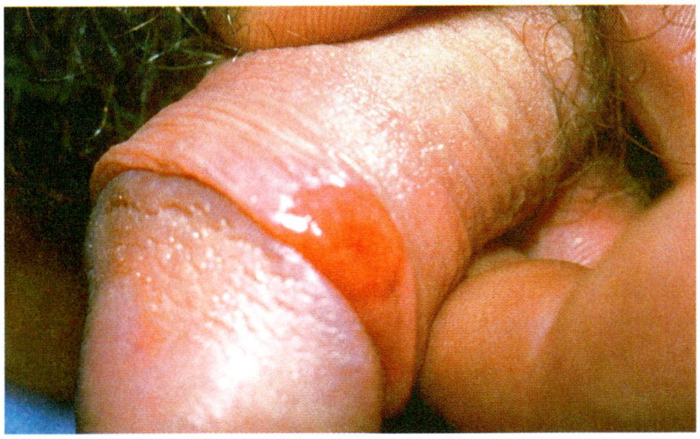

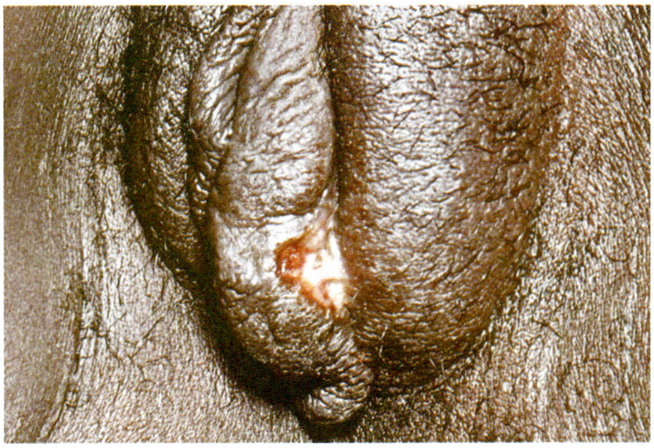

In the primary stage of syphilis, a hard, round, painless sore, or chancre, appears at the site of contact.

and bones; signs of this bacterial spreading may appear years later in the late, or tertiary, stage of syphilis. This stage is marked by lesions almost everywhere on and in the body, including the stomach, lungs, liver, testicles, eyes, muscles, and skin. The lesions can result in heart failure, ruptured blood vessels, loss of muscle control, disturbance of balance, blindness, deafness, severe mental disease, and, ultimately, death.

Transmission

Syphilis is primarily transmitted through vaginal and anal intercourse, oral-genital contact, or oral-anal contact. Like gonorrhea, syphilis is highly contagious. Transmission occurs when moist mucosal membranes or skin abrasions come in contact with the chancres of the infected person. The most common way this occurs is through sexual intercourse. However, because chancres can form anywhere in or on the body and because the bacteria can live in saliva, even kissing can result in contracting the disease. The chances of acquiring syphilis from one sexual contact with an infected person are one in three (Reinisch, 1990).

An infected and untreated pregnant woman can pass the bacteria on to her unborn baby. If she does, she may miscarry. However, 25% of such pregnancies end in stillbirths, and 40–70% result in a newborn who has the disease, called *congenital syphilis* in that case. These babies may have skin sores, rashes, fever, jaundice, anemia, and physical or mental disabilities (National Women's Health Information Center, 1998). Fortunately, antibiotic medications can be highly effective in preventing congenital syphilis if mothers are diagnosed and treated within the first months of pregnancy.

Diagnosis and Treatment

Syphilis can be diagnosed in its primary and secondary stages through physical examination, microscopic analysis of fluid from lesions, and blood analysis. When a diagnosis has been made, the implications of the disease are explained to the infected person, and any sexual partners from the past year are contacted for examination and possible treatment. Penicillin was first used to treat syphilis in 1943; use of this antibiotic led to marked declines in rates of syphilis infection. Penicillin, or doxycycline and tetracycline for those allergic to penicillin, continues to be the treatment of choice (CDC, 2002c).

NON-HIV VIRAL INFECTIONS

Viruses are simply microscopic capsules containing genetic material. They are incapable of reproducing on their own. Instead, they invade the cells of a host organism and substitute their genetic material for the host cells' genetic material so that the host cells pass on genetic instructions that will enable the virus to reproduce. Eventually the infected cells burst open and release the new viral particles, which in turn infect other cells. Viruses represent a major cause of disease in humans and other animals. New viruses develop every day as existing viruses mutate (change their genetic makeup). Because viruses are capable of mutating so readily, it is difficult to create drugs to eradicate them. Thus, as a rule, infections caused by viruses are incurable; only the symptoms can be treated. The human immune system is capable of attacking and killing some viruses, but many remain in the body indefinitely, among them viruses that cause a number of STIs, including genital herpes, genital warts, hepatitis, and HIV. Because these STIs must be endured for life, they have long-term physical and psychological consequences for individuals who contract them.

did YOU know?

In a study of adolescents, 10% of 17–20-year-olds and nearly 22% of 21–24-year-olds tested positive for HSV-2 (Standberry & Rosenthal, 1999).

Herpes Simplex Virus

Genital herpes, a sexually transmissible infection characterized by recurring painful, itchy blisters and lesions, is a major health problem worldwide. Diagnosed cases of this disease do not have to be reported to the Centers for Disease Control as do cases of gonorrhea, syphilis, and chlamydia; therefore, the exact prevalence rate is not known.

However, it is estimated that 45 million people in the United States have genital herpes (1 in 5 adults). Interestingly, only about one-third of these individuals are aware that they are infected, because many people with herpes have no detectable symptoms or do not seek a diagnosis for their symptoms (CDC, 2000f).

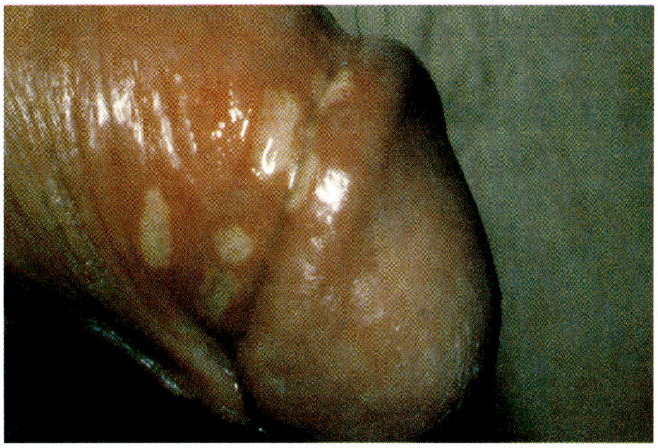

Genital herpes is caused by the herpes simplex virus (HSV). Herpes simplex viruses are a family of six different viruses that cause more disease and associated problems in humans than any other virus. Most common and of greatest concern are **herpes simplex virus 1 (HSV-1)** and **herpes simplex virus 2 (HSV-2).** These two types are virtually identical, but one primary difference is their so-called site of preference. HSV-2 is usually the cause of genital lesions and tends to reside in a cluster of nerve cells called the sacral ganglion at the base of the spine. HSV-1 is most commonly responsible for lesions in and around the mouth, known as cold sores, and tends to reside in the trigeminal ganglion near the ear. Despite the fact that these two types of HSV are virtually the same virus, much more social stigma has been attached to HSV-2 because it is more closely associated with the genitals. This is merely a social distinction, not a biological one. In fact, both HSV-1 and 2 can be contracted through sexual contact, and both can be transferred between the mouth and genitals through oral-genital contact (American Social Health Association, 2001b). When either HSV-1 or HSV-2 is contracted someplace other than its site of preference, it tends to cause less severe symptoms and to recur significantly less frequently than if it is in its favored location.

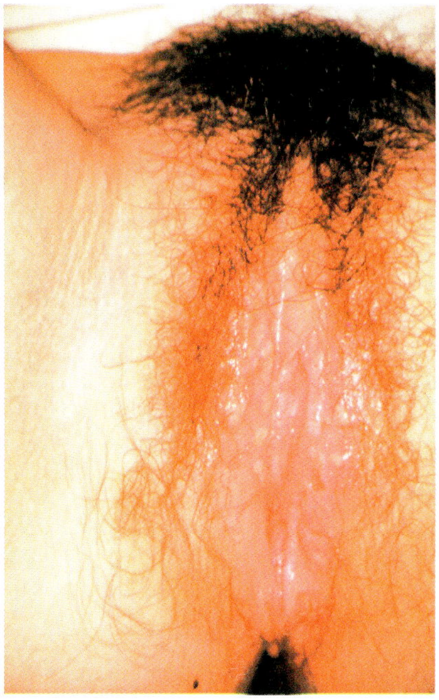

Initial herpes outbreaks can be extremely painful and itchy. Subsequent outbreaks may be less symptomatic but troublesome nonetheless.

HSV-2 infection is positively associated with certain factors: number of lifetime sexual partners, lower education level, increasing age (once you have it, you have it for life; therefore, it is increasingly prevalent in the aging population), being African American, and being female (CDC, 2000f, 2001a; Mbizvo et al., 2002).

Signs and Symptoms

The signs and symptoms of herpes vary greatly. Herpes simplex viral infections are classified as primary and recurrent. Primary infections follow the first exposure to the virus. These often involve multiple sites and are more severe and prolonged than recurrent infections. The disease may cause a range of body-wide symptoms and skin lesions. Ulcerative lesions are the primary signs of herpes simplex viral infections, whether on the genitals or the lips and mouth. Genital sores typically develop 2–12 days after sexual contact (International Herpes Management Forum [IHMF], 2002a). They may begin as painful blisters in the genital region. A small group of these blisters form and then open to become lesions. Pain and irritation often accompany the sores. In women, the sores usually appear on the labia, clitoris, vagina, or cervix; men typically have them on the glans or the shaft of the penis. Women and men may also have lesions on the perineum or around the anus and rectum if those areas have been exposed. The lesions heal, become scabs, and then disappear, generally within 20 days (IHMF, 2002a). Herpes infections may also cause generalized symptoms such as fever, swollen lymph glands, headache, malaise, joint pains, pain with urination, and vaginal discharge. An individual is more likely to have these symptoms during an initial episode of herpes than during a recurrence. Symptoms are similar during subsequent episodes but are often limited to mildly to moderately painful or irritable lesions.

The most common complication of herpes is recurrence. After the initial infection, the herpes virus remains inactive in the nerve ganglion cells and is periodically reactivated. About 80% of individuals with HSV-2 genital infections and 50% of those with HSV-1 genital infections experience at least one recurrence (IHMF, 2002a). As already noted, symptoms of recurrent herpes are generally milder and last 8–12 days or less. About half of persons with recurrent genital herpes have *prodromal symptoms* (symptoms that precede the appearance of lesions), which typically include mild tingling, itching, and radiating

HERPES SIMPLEX VIRUS 1 (HSV-1)
The virus that most commonly causes oral herpes, which is characterized by cold sores or fever blisters on the lips or mouth. The virus can also be transmitted to other areas of the body such as the eyes and genitalia.

HERPES SIMPLEX VIRUS 2 (HSV-2)
The virus that most commonly causes genital herpes.

pain in the groin, thighs, legs, or buttocks. Women tend to have more severe recurrent symptoms than men do. Recurrence rates vary greatly among herpes sufferers. It is most typical for someone with herpes to have about four outbreaks a year (IHMF, 2002a).

A variety of physical factors—diet, exposure to sun or wind, fever, menstruation, fatigue, and coital friction or other trauma to the site of infection—are believed to exacerbate herpes recurrences. Increased frequency, duration, and severity of recurrences have also been associated with psychosocial factors, including stress, emotional distress, and social support (Green & Kocsis, 1997; Shah & Button, 1998). These findings suggest that psychosocial factors play a role in recurrence; however, experts debate the exact role these factors play. Because the relationship between recurrences and psychosocial factors is correlational, researchers are not sure whether the psychosocial factors cause outbreaks or the recurrent herpes infections result in stress, emotional upset, and social isolation. It is possible that both of these hypotheses are true: That is, psychosocial factors both cause and result from herpes outbreaks. There is now strong support for the notion that psychosocial factors affect immune function (Kiecolt-Glaser, McGuire, Robles, & Glaser, 2002), but there is still no direct evidence that stress causes herpes outbreaks (Green & Kocsis, 1997). Nonetheless, since stress management strategies have been shown to reduce herpes recurrences (Burnette, Koehn, Kenyon-Jump, Hutton, & Stark, 1991) and levels of HSV-2 antibodies in the blood (Cruess et al., 2000; Lutgendorf et al., 1997), it seems important for a better understanding of the disease to address these psychosocial dimensions, regardless of the direction of causality.

Transmission

Initial herpes simplex viral infections occur when the virus passes through breaks in the skin or membranes of the mouth, vagina, penis, urethra, or anus. Herpes can be transmitted through any combination of oral, vaginal, and anal contact. Other means of transmission are highly unlikely but have occasionally been reported. Because the virus is readily deactivated at room temperature and through exposure to chemicals and soap and water, it is unlikely to be spread from toilet seats, hot tubs, swimming pools, or other objects. Therefore, close, intimate contact with an infected person is the most common and most likely means of transmission, and even then, the timing of contact in relation to the person's outbreaks is important.

Viral shedding (when the virus is active and contagious) is most likely to happen between the appearance of a lesion and crusting over, but some experts believe it can occur before a herpes sore appears and until the lesion is crusted over. The virus is most easily transmitted during this period. Experts also believe that the virus can become active (and, therefore, the person become contagious) without any noticeable symptoms; this condition is called *asymptomatic viral shedding.* Although the risk of transmission is much lower when no symptoms are present than when some are, most cases of sexually transmitted herpes infections are acquired when the infected person is asymptomatic (Koelle & Wald, 2000).

The most serious complications from herpes infections can occur during pregnancy. Infections in pregnant women can lead to miscarriages, premature rupturing of membranes, retarded fetal growth, and neonatal infection during delivery. Transmission of herpes during delivery can result in death of the newborn or blindness, mental retardation, and pneumonia. Fortunately, the incidence of neonatal herpes is low. In the United States, there is one case of neonatal herpes transmission in 1,800 to 5,000 live births (IHMF, 2002b). Herpes is most dangerous if an initial episode occurs during late pregnancy, because the mother has not yet built up antibodies against the virus to pass along to the baby. Pregnant women who are infected with the herpes simplex virus should inform their physicians so that the disease can be monitored and treated up to delivery. Vaginal deliveries are generally encouraged if there are no outbreaks at the onset of labor. Cesarean section used to be the standard procedure for delivery if a woman had an initial outbreak near the end of pregnancy, but now some doctors recommend that the woman take acyclovir (an antiviral medication used to control herpes outbreaks) in the days before delivery in order to prevent an outbreak (IHMF,

14.1 on the web

Genital herpes is a tough topic to discuss with a potential sex partner. Review the advice given at the American Social Health Association's Web site, which you can access through a link at **www.ablongman.com/mcanulty2e.**

If you had (or have) herpes, would you tell a potential sex partner about it? Why or why not?

2002b; Randolph, Hartshorn, & Washington, 1996). This approach is less costly and eliminates the risks associated with C-sections (see Chapter 9).

In general, the only direct health threat a person with genital herpes faces is an increased risk of becoming infected by HIV (Schacker, 2001). Genital lesions may predispose individuals to HIV infection by providing a point of entry for the virus. Before genital warts and HIV became so common, genital herpes was perhaps the most feared STI. Such fear was perhaps an overreaction, as the disease is not deadly and many people learn to live with it with minimal intrusion in their lives. Now that more is known about it, people generally respond to herpes with less trepidation.

Diagnosis and Treatment

Genital or oral ulcers, particularly if they are recurrent, should lead a person to suspect herpes. Herpes is diagnosed by conducting an interview to assess symptoms, examining the site of infection, and taking a culture from a lesion. A culture should be obtained within 48 hours of the appearance of a lesion; otherwise, there is a risk of a false negative test because the infection is already healing. A blood test can also be used, especially for those individuals who suspect they have the virus but have no signs or symptoms.

Currently there is no cure for or vaccine against herpes available in the United States. Researchers have been working to find a vaccine to stop transmission and possibly treat patients with genital herpes but have had only limited success (Morrison, 2002; Stephenson, 2000). Researchers are optimistic, however, because the experimental vaccines do alter the course of the herpes simplex infection (for example, making the outbreaks less frequent or less severe), and therefore may ultimately provide immunity to its effects.

A family of antiviral medications is available to help shorten the duration of outbreaks, decrease their severity, and suppress their recurrence. These antivirals also reduce asymptomatic viral shedding (Koelle & Wald, 2000). The most commonly used are acyclovir (Zovirax), valacyclovir (Valtrex), and famicyclovir (Famvir). These drugs are most commonly used in the form of a topical ointment or cream and a pill. Topical ointments are generally only effective in reducing the symptoms of an initial outbreak. Pills are most often prescribed for recurrent infections. People with severe and frequent outbreaks may take the antiviral medication daily to both decrease viral shedding and reduce the frequency of outbreaks. Those people who have very few outbreaks may only take it when they notice any prodromal signs (e.g., itching, tingling, pain, or blisters forming) to shorten the healing time and reduce viral shedding. Daily suppressive therapy reduces the frequency of outbreaks by 75% or more (Barton, Ebel, Kirchner, & Mertz, 2002; CDC, 1998c). However, some medical experts recommend that antiviral medications be discontinued after 1 year. The benefits of taking this medication must be weighed against its high cost, potential side effects, and inconvenience. Asymptomatic viral shedding has been found among persons taking suppressive doses of acyclovir; however, the degree of viral shedding is reduced in such cases, and thus the virus may be less likely to reach transmissible levels. A recent large-scale study showed that regular use of Valtrex reduced herpes transmission by 50%, from 4% to 2% (Bouchert, 2002).

Relaxation techniques such as meditation can help reduce HSV outbreaks.

A variety of personal measures have been found to alleviate herpes symptoms, promote healing, and reduce recurrences. Herpes sufferers are advised to keep the infected area as clean and dry as possible to allow healing and to wash the area with warm water and soap several times per day, followed by gently toweling dry or using a hair dryer on a low or cool setting. Loose-fitting clothing prevents moisture retention and reduces rubbing of the sores. Creams or ointments (other than acyclovir) are not advised because they may delay healing, and applying them may spread the infection. Herpes-related pain can be treated with analgesics (pain-killers such as ibuprophen or acetaminophin) and icepacks. Women in particular may suffer pain or

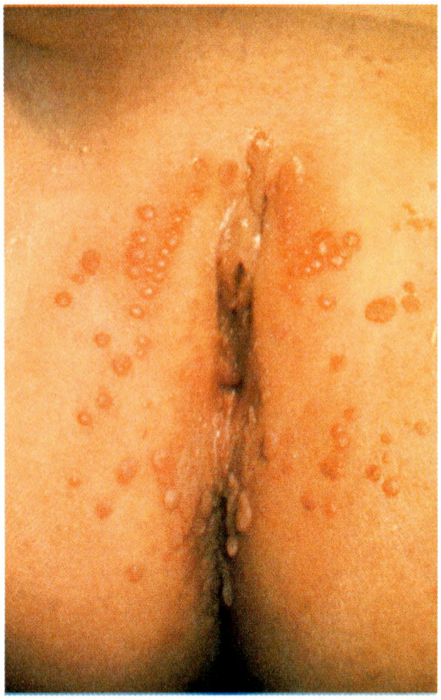

The human papillomavirus can cause warts, sometimes resembling cauliflower, at the infected site.

burning when they urinate. The discomfort can be reduced by urinating while sitting in a bathtub or while pouring water over the genital area, and by drinking plenty of fluids to dilute the uric acid that causes the stinging. Covering sores with petroleum jelly prior to urinating may help as well; however, it is important to wash the jelly off afterward, as it may slow the healing process. Fatigue and illness affect the immune system's ability to keep the herpes simplex virus in check; therefore, getting proper rest and remaining physically healthy are important for minimizing recurrences.

Herpes sufferers frequently report that stress and negative emotions trigger or exacerbate outbreaks. As mentioned earlier, research has yet to demonstrate that stress and negative emotional states *cause* herpes outbreaks, but a number of studies have documented the benefits of psychological interventions for individuals with herpes, both in reducing emotional distress and in reducing recurrences. It appears that successful treatment of herpes includes physical, psychological, and social dimensions.

Genital Warts

Genital warts infect the skin on and around the genitals or the mucous membranes of the urethra, vagina, and cervix. They are caused by the **human papillomavirus (HPV)**, of which between 30 and 35 types are known to infect the genital tract (Hildesheim, 1997). Thus, individuals with genital warts may be simultaneously infected with more than one type of HPV.

HPV infection rates are greater than rates for all other STIs. Based on 1999 data claiming that 20 million people are already infected with HPV and that about 5.5 million people in the United States are infected each year, we can assume that by the time of the publication of this book, around 40 million people were infected with HPV. About 1% of sexually active adults have genital warts (CDC, 2000f). Like other STIs, genital warts are most common among young adults between 20 and 24 years of age; in one study of female college students, 43% became infected with HPV over a 3-year period (Ho, Bierman, Beardsley, Chang, & Burk, 1998).

Signs and Symptoms

Genital warts usually appear as small, soft, moist, pink or red swellings that grow rapidly. They tend to cluster together in one area and may resemble cauliflower. If the warts develop on dry skin, they tend to be hard and yellow-gray. Genital warts may come and go or may remain permanently. Men with urethral HPV infections occasionally report bleeding or painful discharge, but most such men are symptom-free. Women may also be asymptomatic. Subclinical microwarts (flat lesions that are not visible to the naked eye) are especially problematic. They are found on the cervix and occasionally on the penis.

Genital warts have a variable incubation period. They may appear at any time from as early as 1 month to as late as 18 months after infection. However, they usually occur within 3 months of contracting the virus (National Institute of Allergy & Infectious Diseases [NIAID], 2001). In women, genital warts usually appear on the vulval surfaces, inner vagina, and cervix. They also appear on the perineum and/or around the anus. Men usually develop the warts in the urethra or on the glans, foreskin, or shaft of the penis. The warts are common in the anal region and the rectum in infected homosexual males. The warts can appear in nongenital areas, most commonly the anus and the rectum, but also the lips, tongue, mouth, eyelids, and nipples, depending on the type of sexual activity involved during transmission of HPV.

Genital warts cause few complications in infected individuals. Of greatest concern is the fact that a few types of HPV are associated with cancer of the cervix, vulva, penis, and anus (NIAID, 2001). We address this concern in more detail in Health Matters: HPV and Cancer. Rarely, genital warts can cause complications in pregnancy. Changes in hormones during pregnancy can cause genital warts to become quite large. Enlarged warts sometimes make urination difficult or, if they are in the vagina, can make the vaginal walls less elastic and obstruct delivery of the baby (NIAID, 2001).

GENITAL WARTS
An STI caused by the human papillomavirus and manifested by warts around the genitalia and anus.

HUMAN PAPILLOMAVIRUS (HPV)
The virus that causes genital warts.

HEALTH Matters

HPV and Cancer

Scientific findings that HPV causes cancer of the cervix and, to a lesser extent, of the penis have left infected women and men deeply concerned about the potentially dangerous impact of this STI. In 2002, about 13,000 cases of invasive cervical cancer were diagnosed in the United States, and about 4,100 women died from it (American Cancer Society, 2001). HPV has been found in 99.7% of women with this type of cancer (Walboomers et al., 1999). Furthermore, women whose husbands or regular male sexual partners are infected with HPV have a significantly greater risk of developing cervical cancer (Iversen, Tretli, Johansen, & Holte, 1997), although the reasons for this association are not clear. Several other factors associated with the development of cervical cancer include immunosuppression (lack of a normal immune response), smoking, possibly oral contraceptive use, other concurrent STIs, and nutritional factors (Schiffman & Brinton, 1995; Vittorio, Schiffman, & Weinstock, 1995). Thus, while HPV infection is not the only risk factor for developing cervical cancer, it is considered one of the most critical.

The role that HPV plays in the development of cervical cancer is not yet well understood. Some experts believe that the virus produces proteins that interfere with proteins in human cells that normally prevent excessive growth. This excessive growth results in abnormal cells that eventually become cancerous (National Cancer Institute, 2001). Two factors appear to promote cervical cancer in women with HPV. The first is the type of HPV a woman is exposed to. Not all types of HPV are associated with cervical cancer. In fact, only a few forms of HPV, primarily HPV-16 and 18, are associated with cervical cancer, and they are rare forms (Hildesheim, 1997; Ho et al., 1998). In fact, the types of HPV that cause visible warts (HPV-6 and 11) are not risk factors for cervical cancer (National Cancer Institute, 2001). The second factor is length of infection. HPV infections that persist over long periods of time are more likely to cause cervical cancer (Hopman et al., 2000). Fortunately, most types of HPV infections will go away without treatment and before they ever cause abnormal cell growth (National Cancer Institute, 2001). In fact, 90% of HPV infections in women disappear within 2 years (CDC, 2001b).

What do all these facts tell us? Although cervical cancer is almost always associated with HPV, having genital warts is not necessarily cause for alarm, because most HPV infections do not lead to cervical cancer.

Transmission

Unlike many of the other microorganisms responsible for STIs, HPV invades and resides in surface tissues, rather than in semen, vaginal secretions, and blood. Thus, surface-to-surface contact (at the point of infection) between an infected person and an uninfected person transmits this virus. Transmission is most likely to occur through vaginal or anal intercourse or oral-genital contact. Very rarely, HPV is transmitted from a woman to her baby during delivery. Research has shown that about two-thirds of sexual partners of individuals with visible warts develop genital warts within 3 months (NIAID, 2001). The disease is most contagious when the warts are visible because the HPV resides both in the warts and in the surrounding normal-looking tissue. As is true of those with gonorrhea, syphilis, and other STIs, however, infected individuals can shed the virus even if they are asymptomatic and have had no sign of warts for many years. In addition, an infected person may be unaware of the infection if the warts are located on the cervix or in the urethra, where they cannot be seen. The bottom line is that it is easy to transmit the virus unknowingly to a sexual partner.

14.2 on the web

Go to **www.ablongman.com/mcanulty2e.** Describe the 12 myths and misconceptions about HPV discussed at the American Social Health Association link.

Now that you are an expert, take the STI quiz created by Pfizer, Inc., which you can also find at ***www.ablongman.com/mcanulty2e.***

Diagnosis and Treatment

Genital warts are usually identified by their appearance. A colposcopy, a procedure using a special microscope, is conducted to examine the cervix, vagina, vulva, anus, and penis for the presence of infection. In addition, acetic acid (vinegar) or an iodine solution is applied to any presumed infected area; if the area turns white, the virus is present. This test is helpful in detecting asymptomatic HPV infections. In women, the presence of HPV sometimes causes an abnormal Pap smear, but a biopsy and microscopic analysis of lesions must be conducted to confirm the diagnosis.

Genital warts will often simply disappear over time. Thus, some individuals choose not to seek active treatment. If they do, however, the traditional method is to remove the warts using topical compounds and surgical procedures. More recently, biological-based strategies that directly affect the virus have been developed to treat genital warts. Common topical preparations include Podofilox, Imiquimid, and Trichloroacetic acid. The infected person or a health care provider applies the preparation to the warts, and they ulcerate, dry, and fall off. These procedures may cause pain, redness, itching, burning, swelling, and scarring. Warts can also be frozen off using liquid nitrogen (called cryotherapy) (CDC, 2002c).

Common surgical techniques include cutting, shaving, curretage, or electrosurgery techniques, which may be painful and often require anesthesia; also, the site can take months to heal. Laser surgery is also used, especially for patients who have not responded to more traditional approaches (CDC, 2002c). Possible complications of surgery include excessive bleeding, infection, and scarring. Surgical treatments, like topical ones, are designed to remove the warts; they do not eradicate the virus itself, and recurrences are common. Most recurrences occur within 3 months of the treatment. Furthermore, removal only reduces, but does not eliminate, the risk of transmitting the virus to others (CDC, 2002c).

A newer treatment using **interferon,** a biochemical produced by the human immune system to inhibit viral replication, is now being used for recurrent and resistant genital warts (CDC, 2002c). A number of studies have shown that it is effective against HPV (Friedman-Kien, 1995; Gall, 1995; Syed et al., 1995). Unfortunately, this treatment can be expensive, requires multiple visits to a physician, and can cause flu-like symptoms and pain. Consequently, it is recommended only for patients for whom other treatments have not been successful. Research is underway to test the safety and effectiveness of systemic approaches, such as vaccines designed to boost immunities to HPV (Key, Denoon, & Boyles, 1996; Slade, 1998).

Looking At . . .

. . . Thinking About

You have a friend who has just been diagnosed with genital warts. At this point, your friend is completely devastated but has little information on the disease. What information would you give her in order to allay some of her fears?

INTERFERON
A biochemical that occurs naturally in the human immune system and that inhibits reproduction of some viruses; interferon injections have been approved by the FDA as a treatment for genital warts.

VIRAL HEPATITIS
Hepatitis caused by one of several viruses. Hepatitis B is the most common form of viral hepatitis that can be transmitted sexually. The virus is found in blood, semen, vaginal secretions, and saliva. Most cases of viral hepatitis are asymptomatic, but those infected can have a wide range of symptoms.

Viral Hepatitis

Hepatitis is an inflammatory disease of the liver that can be caused by a number of factors, including alcoholism, exposure to toxins, and viruses. There are five types of **viral hepatitis:** hepatitis A, B, C, D, and E (CDC, 2002b). Not all types of hepatitis are sexually transmitted; hepatitis A, B, and, less often, D can be contracted through sexual activity—but none is transmitted sexually 100% of the time. Hepatitis B alone is estimated to infect 5% of the U.S. population. In addition, 200,000 hepatitis B infections occur each year in the United States, 120,000 of these through sexual contact (CDC, 2000f).

Signs and Symptoms

Many individuals with viral hepatitis are asymptomatic. When symptoms do appear, they can vary from minor flu-like symptoms to fatal liver failure. Flu-like symptoms include loss of appetite, nausea, diarrhea, muscle pain, skin rash, fatigue, and malaise. As the disease advances, fever, darkened urine, vomiting, and severe abdominal pain develop. Jaundice, a condition in which the person's eyes and skin become yellow, is a classic sign of liver damage from a hepatitis virus.

Transmission

Sexual transmission—primarily through anal intercourse—is believed to account for 60% of hepatitis B infections (CDC, 2000f). However, hepatitis B can also be transmitted by any kind of contact with infected body fluids (blood, saliva, semen, vaginal or nasal mucus), through sharing of contaminated needles by drug users, by needle-stick accidents among health care workers, and possibly by sharing of personal items such as razors and toothbrushes. Like other STIs discussed in this chapter, hepatitis can be transmitted even if the infected person is asymptomatic. Certain individuals appear to be chronic carriers of hepatitis B and can transmit the virus to others even after recovering from the acute stages of the disease.

did YOU know?

Non-HIV STIs cost about $8 billion each year to diagnose and treat (ASHA, 2001b).

Sexual practices involving oral-anal contact can spread the hepatitis A virus; however, hepatitis A is most commonly transmitted via food or water that is contaminated by infected fecal material. This is why food service workers are required to wash their hands after using the toilet. Eating uncooked, contaminated shellfish can also result in a hepatitis A infection.

Diagnosis and Treatment

Hepatitis is diagnosed by testing blood samples for *antigens* (substances that indicate that the body has been infected by the virus) and *antibodies* (specialized proteins produced by white blood cells in response to disease organisms; their presence indicates that the donor's body is defending itself from the disease). Rest and adequate intake of fluids to prevent dehydration are prescribed for the acute symptoms of hepatitis. Generally, acute symptoms resolve within weeks, and full recovery occurs in several months for severe cases. Chronic hepatitis B has been effectively treated in 40% of cases with an antiviral drug called interferon alpha-2b (CDC, 1998c). Research has explored the potential effectiveness of this interferon treatment to help prevent liver damage associated with hepatitis (Davis, Balart, Schiff, Lindsay, & Bodenheimer, 1989; Scheig, 1991; Wang, Cong, Dong, Chen, & Ma, 1991). Vaccines to prevent hepatitis B have been available since 1982 and were approved for hepatitis A in 1995. (Vaccinations offer no help to those who are already infected.) Individuals who are considered at high risk for contracting hepatitis A or B should be vaccinated. Since the virus is spread in all types of body fluids and excrement, high-risk individuals include anyone who comes in contact with others' body fluids or fecal matter or dirty needles—particularly health care workers, IV drug users and their sexual partners, individuals who engage in anal intercourse, individuals with multiple sexual partners, kidney dialysis and chronic liver patients, and people who travel abroad. Children and adolescents, and those who work with them, are also susceptible because of increased chances of being exposed in school. Therefore, the federal government and the American Academy of Pediatrics have recommended that all adolescents and young adults be vaccinated against hepatitis B. Some states made the vaccination mandatory for all school-age children starting in 2000.

THE HIV EPIDEMIC

Before AIDS, few young men and women died from STIs, few babies died from viral infections, there were no public service announcements on television urging people to use condoms, and no one had ever heard of "safer sex." At the beginning of the 1980s, it seemed that modern medicine was winning the war against infectious diseases; antibiotics cured most bacterial infections, and vaccines were overcoming many viruses. But then, in the spring of 1981, a few young men in New York City and Los Angeles became ill with what were at the time very rare conditions, caused by infections that were usually kept in check by a normal, healthy immune system. The only things that were clearly understood about this new disease were that young men were dying and that the victims had only two things in common: Their immune systems had failed, and they were gay. It was soon learned that this new disease afflicted more than just gay men and not only Americans. Men and women who used needles to inject drugs, people who received blood transfusions, hemophiliacs, and heterosexual men and women around the world were being diagnosed with this fatal condition. It was not until 1984, after the disease had killed hundreds of people in the United States alone, that scientists in France and the United States discovered that a single virus is responsible for the collection of fatal illnesses known as **acquired immunodeficiency syndrome (AIDS):**

- "Acquired" means that AIDS is not inherited and that it does not just develop on its own. The cause of AIDS is a virus that is contracted from a source outside of the body.
- "Immuno" refers to the body's disease-fighting system, which HIV damages.
- "Deficiency" reveals the type of damage suffered by the body's immune system—it becomes deficient or less effective.
- "Syndrome" indicates that AIDS is actually a group of symptoms and illnesses, not just a single disease.

Because it was simultaneously discovered by different researchers, the virus was originally given different names: lymphadenopathy associated virus (LAV), human T-cell lymphotropic virus type III (HTLV-III), and AIDS-associated virus (ARV). But it soon became known that these were all one virus that could simply be given one name: **human immunodeficiency virus (HIV):** "human" because it infects only human beings, and "immunodeficiency" to indicate its negative impact on the body's ability to fight off diseases.

HIV is a **retrovirus**, which is a type of virus that follows an uncommon biological process for reproduction. HIV attacks the body's immune system, rendering it defenseless against the virus itself and in turn against many other illnesses. How HIV affects the immune system is key to understanding HIV disease and AIDS.

The human immune system is made up of several types of cells found in the blood, all of which work in a coordinated fashion to protect the body from disease. One type of cell in the immune system is the T-helper cell. T-helper cells are the "generals" of the body's immune system army—they control and direct various branches of the immune system to fight disease. T-helper cells have what are known as CD4 receptors on their cell membranes. (Several other kinds of cells also have CD4 receptors; many of these are found in blood and other body fluids, others are found in the mucous membranes, and still others are in the brain. The CD4-carrying cells in the mucous membranes and in the blood are also quite susceptible to HIV infection.) When HIV attaches itself to the CD4 receptors, it gains entry into the T-helper cell and renders the infected cell defenseless against HIV. Over the long haul of HIV infection, T-helper cells are destroyed by HIV, causing a profound effect on the body's ability to fight off many diseases. However, even before they are killed, infected T-helper cells, as well as other infected immune system cells called monocytes and macrophages, do not function normally; they lose their ability to control infections and prevent disease. The immune system attempts to control HIV by producing antibodies against the virus. These efforts are futile, because the virus infects more and more of the immune system until it can no longer function.

Today, AIDS is considered the world's leading threat to public health. While it may seem that no one is immune from AIDS, HIV infection is entirely preventable.

ACQUIRED IMMUNODEFICIENCY SYNDROME (AIDS)
A condition caused by the human immunodeficiency virus (HIV) and characterized by destruction of the immune system, which leaves the infected person susceptible to a wide range of serious diseases.

HUMAN IMMUNODEFICIENCY VIRUS (HIV)
The virus that causes AIDS.

RETROVIRUS
A type of virus that follows an uncommon biological process for reproducton.

The HIV Pandemic

Cases of AIDS are now known in every country around the world. No one knows exactly where HIV first came from, but it is believed that the virus had its origins in the tropical rain forests of Africa, like many other viruses. Also like other disease-causing agents, HIV is most likely to have spread from continent to continent and country to country through international travel and immigration. Global air travel has made it particularly easy for new diseases to spread rapidly over great distances. Because it takes years for a person with HIV to develop AIDS, it is clear that people were becoming infected and passing the virus to others for a long time before anyone knew what was happening. The threat to public health of HIV infection is now a reality around the world, as Close Up on Culture: Worldwide and U.S. Trends in HIV/AIDS makes clear.

Worldwide and U.S. Trends in HIV/AIDS

By studying trends in infection and death rates, researchers gain a better understanding of any disease. Studying such trends for HIV and AIDS can provide invaluable information that can help slow the pandemic. This information can also be useful in evaluating the effectiveness of programs intended to reduce the risks of HIV infection.

International Trends

According to UNAIDS/WHO (2002a), nearly 42 million people are living with HIV worldwide. Of these, 2.7 million are children under 15. During 2002, HIV-related illnesses caused the deaths of 3.1 million people. In addition, rates of HIV infection among women have been steadily increasing. Half of the adults living with HIV worldwide are women.

Several continents have been especially hard hit by HIV. Sub-Saharan Africa has felt the brunt of the pandemic, accounting for over two-thirds of the world's cases of AIDS. Not surprisingly, AIDS is the leading cause of death in many African countries, responsible for 5,500 funerals per day (UNAIDS/WHO, 2001). For example, nearly 34% of Zimbabwe's adult population (ages 15–49) is living with HIV. An additional 200,000 people died of AIDS in 2001 alone. In fact, so many have died that in 2001, nearly 800,000 children were orphans as a result of AIDs. Like those in other parts of Africa, Zimbabweans infected with HIV are mainly heterosexual adults, and over half are women (UNAIDS/WHO, 2002b).

In Central Asia and Eastern Europe, rates of HIV infection have been soaring—rising faster than in any other area around the world (UNAIDS/WHO, 2002a). Asia now ranks second to Africa in the prevalence of HIV and AIDS, with over 7 million people infected with HIV. The main mode of transmission in Asia is heterosexual intercourse. In Asian countries such as Thailand and India, the commercial sex trade is largely responsible for the spread of HIV. In Thailand, the majority of sexually experienced men have sought the services of prostitutes and continue to do so, despite the threat of AIDS. For example, 40–90% of Thai men have had a sexual experience with a prostitute and over half of these men had done so in the 6 months prior to being surveyed (Maticka-Tyndale et al., 1997; VanLandingham, Grandjean, Suprasert, & Sittitrai, 1997). Yet, only 25–40% of these men always used a condom during their sexual encounters with the prostitutes. Related to this inconsistent practice of safer sex was the fact that many of the men had serious misunderstandings about HIV. Nearly half of them thought they could tell if a prostitute had AIDS merely by looking at her, and one-quarter of them thought that unprotected sex was safe if it occurred in a reputable establishment (VanLandingham et al., 1997).

So prevalent is HIV in South Africa that Sesame Street *is introducing a new female Muppet, who happens to be HIV-positive, to South African audiences. The character will address issues related to the impact of the AIDS epidemic in Africa on children and families.*

Up to 17% of married Thai men have purchased sexual services (Maticka-Tyndale et al., 1997; Morris, Podhista, Wawer, & Handcock, 1996). Married men who have unprotected sex with prostitutes and with their wives represent a "bridge population," serving as potential conduits for transmitting the virus from sex workers to their wives (Morris et al., 1996). Given these trends, it is not surprising that HIV infection rates are climbing in Thailand and similar Asian cultures. An encouraging fact is that the Thai government has implemented a massive campaign promoting safer sex among commercial sex workers. This intervention is paying off, as evidenced by increased condom use, declines in STIs, and a lower incidence of HIV among men and women (Hanenberg & Rojanapithayakorn, 1998).

U.S. Trends

Since the epidemic began, over 800,000 Americans have been diagnosed with AIDS (CDC, 2001h). Over half of these people have died. The estimated incidence (number of new cases) of AIDS has increased at a rate near 5% each year since 1992. In addition, the proportion of female adults and adolescents with AIDS increased from 7% of all cases in 1985 to nearly 30% in 2001 (CDC, 2001h). At least 40,000 Americans are infected with HIV each year (UNAIDS, 1999b). HIV infection rates among men have started to decline, whereas infection rates among women have been climbing. Most AIDS-related deaths occur among young and middle-aged adults, particularly those of ethnic and racial minorities (CDC, 1998b).

Because HIV infection is epidemic, causing disease and death across the globe, it qualifies as a *pandemic*. At the end of 2002, the Joint United Nations Programme on HIV/AIDS (UNAIDS) estimated that 42 million people were living with HIV. The majority of people with AIDS are believed to be living in Africa. More than 29 million people in Africa are living with HIV and over 2.4 million Africans died from AIDS in 2001 alone (UNAIDS/WHO, 2002). In 16 African countries, 10% or more of people aged 15 to 49 are infected. In southern Africa, at least 20% of people carry HIV. Worldwide, over 5 million people were newly infected in 2001, and over 3 million died of HIV-related causes in that year (UNAIDS/WHO, 2001). Figure 14.4 shows the estimated number of people with HIV infection for each continent.

Over 20 years, more than 800,000 Americans have been diagnosed with AIDS; close to 470,000 of these individuals have died (CDC, 2001h), and up to 1 million Americans are believed to have been infected with HIV (CDC, 2001h). HIV infection had been most concentrated in the cities where the U.S. epidemic first began, places referred to as *epicenters*. The majority of AIDS cases in the United States have therefore occurred in eight states (California, Florida, Illinois, Maryland, New Jersey, New York, Pennsylvania, and Texas) and Puerto Rico, but every state has felt the impact of HIV disease. States with large cities are likely to have been hit hardest by AIDS. That greater numbers of people with AIDS live in large cities is primarily because cities have dense and highly mobile populations, with a greater degree of transience, poverty, and illegal drug use, all of which help spread any disease, including HIV infection. But rural areas have not been spared; HIV disease is becoming increasingly common in nonurban communities.

did YOU know?

The AIDS epidemic in the world's most highly populated countries—China, Ethiopia, India, Nigeria, and Russia—is so widespread that military experts fear AIDS will pose a threat to these countries' national security. They fear loss of key military personnel to AIDS and manpower shortages. As many as one-third of army recruits in some countries are turned away because they are HIV-positive.

The people in the United States who have historically been and continue to be most affected by HIV and AIDS are gay and bisexual men (CDC, 2001h; UNAIDS, 1999). Men who had sex with men were the first victims of AIDS in the United States. It is believed that men who became infected with HIV overseas brought it back with them and unknowingly transmitted the virus to their sex partners. In 2001, over 40% of all new cases of AIDS occurred among men who had sex with other men. The incidence of cases of AIDS in gay men has decreased in all ethnic and racial groups over the years, but the decline has been slowest among Hispanic Americans and African Americans. As a result, men of color represent the greatest proportion (52%) of gay men with HIV/AIDS (CDC, 2000d). Another group with a high

Figure 14.4 Estimated Number of Adults and Children Living with HIV/AIDS as of the End of 2001 (UNAIDS, 2001)

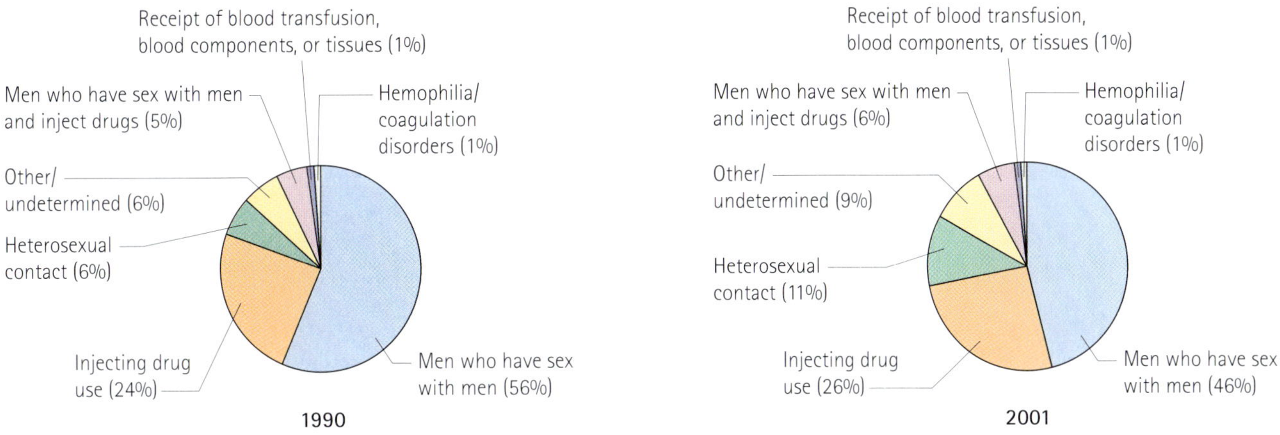

Figure 14.5 Changes in AIDS Cases by Exposure Category: 1990 and 2001

incidence of AIDS is composed of men and women who inject drugs and their sexual partners; these people represented one-fourth of the new cases in 1998. Although it has been common to associate AIDS with gay men and people who use drugs, the AIDS epidemic knows no boundaries. People of all sexual orientations, ethnic and racial backgrounds, and lifestyles can be at risk for HIV infection. Why? Because HIV transmission depends on specific *behaviors,* not on lifestyle or group membership. Figure 14.5 shows the percentage of Americans with AIDS who became infected through various means between 1990 and 2001. Most significant are the decline in the proportion of cases arising from men having sex with men (from 56% of cases in 1990 to 46% in 2001) and the increase in the proportion of cases among heterosexuals (up from 6% in 1990 to 11% in 2001).

did YOU know?

The majority of individuals in Africa with HIV acquired it through heterosexual contact.

From the early 1990s through 1996, AIDS was the leading cause of death among men aged 25–44, accounting for nearly 20% of all deaths in this age group. For women in the 25–44 age group, AIDS was the third leading cause of death. Women who use injectable drugs or have sex with men who either injected drugs or had sex with other men are at particularly high risk. Adolescents are also among those at greatest risk. AIDS is the seventh leading cause of death among 15- to 24-year-olds (CDC, 1999b). Because it takes many years for HIV to cause AIDS, it is likely that most young adults diagnosed with AIDS were infected as teenagers. Among certain ethnic and racial groups, AIDS has been devastating. For example, although African Americans constitute only 13% of the U.S. population, over 45% of new cases of AIDS in 1997 were diagnosed in African Americans. Hispanic Americans accounted for 20% of new cases of AIDS in 1997. AIDS has become the leading killer of African American males aged 25–44 (UNAIDS, 1998).

HIV Transmission

One piece of good news about AIDS is that HIV is not very easy to transmit, which means that HIV disease is definitely controllable. People become infected with HIV only if the virus gets into the body and if enough of the virus is exposed to infectable cells. A sufficient amount of the virus must come in contact with cells that have CD4 receptors on their outer membranes. The situations and behaviors that carry the greatest risk for HIV transmission are those that bring a sufficient amount of the virus in contact with CD4 receptors.

Blood Products

A large amount of HIV-infected blood must enter a person's bloodstream in order for a massive dose of the virus to have direct contact with infectable cells. Having a transfusion with HIV-infected blood is therefore very dangerous, because great quantities of the virus have direct contact with blood cells. Early in the AIDS epidemic, before there was a method for screening blood, people did become infected with HIV from blood transfusions. Fortunately, the risk of receiving HIV-infected blood during a transfusion in the United States has become extremely low. Donors are screened for past risky behavior, and donated blood is tested for HIV antibodies. The nation's blood supply is now considered safe. In fact, because the AIDS crisis called attention to the importance of screening blood for disease, the blood supply is possibly safer today than it was before the HIV epidemic. In some developing countries of the world, however, blood supplies are not properly screened for HIV, and blood transfusions remain a source of infection in such countries.

Sharing Instruments Used to Inject Drugs

The HIV virus can be transmitted by sharing instruments used to inject drugs. A person who uses a needle or syringe to inject a drug after it has been used by a person with HIV is at high risk for infection. Sharing needles and other instruments is characteristic of the drug culture. Like sex, needle sharing occurs in intimate relationships. There are economic aspects to needle sharing as well. Because drug use is illegal, injection equipment is usually difficult to obtain. Users therefore are often forced to use dirty needles and share equipment.

For these reasons, sharing of injection instruments has been a major factor in the AIDS crisis. Because injection needles are hollow, both the inside and the outside come into contact with the user's blood. In addition, it is common for users to draw blood up into the syringe, contaminating the entire set of injection instruments. If a contaminated needle or syringe is shared, HIV-infected blood can be passed directly from the bloodstream of one person to that of another.

Looking At . . .

. . . Thinking About

Is either or both of these couples at risk of contracting HIV? Is one couple at greater risk than the other? Even though AIDS has thus far affected some groups and some places more than others, it is essential to remember that it is what a person *does,* not who he or she is, that creates the risk. It is no longer relevant to discuss particular groups as being at risk for AIDS; rather, it is necessary to focus on the behaviors that allow for HIV infection. Both of these couples could be at risk if they don't practice safer sex.

Anal and Vaginal Intercourse

Almost all HIV infections among men who have sex with men result from anal intercourse. A large number of (although by no means all) gay men engage in anal intercourse; however, it is the anal intercourse rather than being homosexual that creates the risk of HIV infection. Gay men are not the only people who engage in anal intercourse (Erickson et al., 1995). Heterosexual anal intercourse is just as risky in terms of HIV infection if either partner has the virus. Anal intercourse with an HIV-positive partner and without the protection of a latex condom carries a greater risk for HIV infection than any other sexual act.

Several factors make anal intercourse risky. The walls of the anus and rectum are supplied with numerous blood vessels and are thin, making it easy for rips or scratches to occur during sexual penetration. Furthermore, the anal opening is narrow and constricts when stimulated, again increasing the chances for bleeding. HIV-infected semen has direct access to the bloodstream and lymph nodes when the walls of the rectum are damaged. Torn tissues in the rectum can also expose the mucous membranes of the penis to HIV-infected blood. But even when there are no openings in the rectal lining, anal intercourse carries a high risk for HIV infection because the mucous membranes contain Langerhans cells, which have CD4 receptors on their surfaces and are thus infectable. These cells transport foreign material to immune system cells that protect against infection (Schoub, 1993), so if the HIV virus binds to them, the Langerhans cells transport the virus to immune cells, making them vulnerable to HIV infection.

CLOSE UP ON gender

Women's Risks of HIV Infection

As you've learned, rates of HIV infection and AIDS among women have been steadily increasing in the United States and worldwide. Worldwide, the majority of women with HIV were infected by heterosexual intercourse with an infected partner.

What places women, especially those from ethnic minority groups, at risk for HIV infection? There are several explanations: First, women are at higher risk than men for anatomical reasons. HIV transmission occurs more efficiently from male to female than from female to male (Forrest, 1991). Some researchers believe that male-to-female HIV transmission is 20 times more efficient than female-to-male transmission (Billy, Tanfer, Grady, & Kepinger, 1993). The virus is found in higher concentration in semen than in vaginal secretions. During penile-vaginal intercourse, women's genital mucous membranes are proportionately more exposed than a man's penile membranes. That is, women have a greater surface area of mucous membrane exposed to potential infection than men do. Second, there are sociocultural reasons for women's greater vulnerability to HIV infection. Ziergler and Krieger (1997) argued that social inequality is the major reason for the increased risk of HIV infection among women in the United States. Worldwide, HIV-infected women are disproportionately economically and socially disadvantaged. For example, in some African and Asian countries, many women are being infected not because of their own risky behavior but because of that of their male partners, typically their husbands (Maticka-Tyndale et al., 1997; UNAIDS, 1999b). In such cultures, women lack economic and social bargaining power to negotiate safer sex or monogamy with their husbands (Laver, van der Borne, Kok, & Woelk, 1997). Such women face the prospect of rejection, abandonment, and even violence should they try to assert their rights.

Women in the United States, particularly minority women, also face social, cultural, economic, and political obstacles to taking control of their sexuality (Carovano, 1991; Fullilove, Fullilove, Haynes, & Gross, 1990; Stein, 1990). Minority women are more likely than white women to live in poverty and to require the economic support of their male partners, and they are therefore unwilling to jeopardize the support they receive, however limited it may be (Cochran, 1989). One cultural script stresses that women are to play passive and submissive roles in their intimate relationships. The same script specifies that men are to take charge of sexual encounters and are responsible for decision making. For many men, the use of condoms implies a lack of trust, a reduction in intimacy, and a decrease in sexual pleasure. Disadvantaged women often feel unable to counter these arguments and to stand up for their rights; they have been socialized to accept the inequality and powerlessness they encounter daily (Weeks et al., 1995).

Interventions to reduce HIV risk among minority women must be culture- and gender-sensitive (Gomez, 1999; Weeks et al., 1995). These interventions must be tailored to reach at-risk women in their own environments and to target women's partners to enhance their sense of responsibility for disease prevention. Issues of gender roles and relationships, reproduction, and financial dependence must be considered. For example, women need to be taught how to assert their desire for their male partners to wear condoms within a cultural context that might normally condemn such assertions. At-risk women must be empowered to exercise their rights and take control of their sexuality if they are to protect themselves from HIV infection.

More than 75% of HIV-infected people in the world became infected with the virus through penile-vaginal intercourse (Infectious Diseases Society of America, 2002), and this mode of transmission is a growing problem in the United States. No matter how a man or woman contracts the virus, he or she can infect subsequent sexual partners during penile-vaginal intercourse by not using a condom. HIV can be transmitted from woman to man or from man to woman. A growing number of men in the United States become infected through vaginal intercourse. Worldwide, most men with AIDS became HIV-infected though vaginal intercourse. However, women are more vulnerable to the virus via vaginal intercourse than are men, as discussed in Close Up on Gender: Women's Risk of HIV Infection. Most women who have AIDS were infected by having vaginal intercourse with an infected man; more than half of all women in the United States who have AIDS became infected during vaginal intercourse with a man who had sex with other men, used injectable drugs, or had sex with an infected woman. Thus, the risk of a woman's becoming infected from having sex with an infected male partner is greater than the risk of a man's becoming infected from a female partner.

IN YOUR own words

Dionne Burks
University of Northern Iowa

I personally feel that my health is way more important than any immediate gratification.

Oral Sex

Oral sex is practiced by the vast majority of adults. Oral sex has been the most controversial behavior in terms of possible sexual transmission of HIV. Of all the questions that people have about behaviors that put them at risk for HIV, the most common one concerns oral sex because of the ambiguities surrounding its risk (Kalichman & Belcher, 1997).

It is impossible to know how many people have been infected with HIV through oral sex. People who engage in oral sex usually also have vaginal or anal intercourse with their partners. Researchers have tried to examine the risk of HIV infection from oral sex by studying the past sexual behaviors of people who have been infected. These studies have shown that far fewer people have been infected from oral sex alone than from anal or vaginal intercourse. However, sexual contact that involves taking vaginal fluids or semen into the mouth or allowing contact between saliva and the genitals must be considered to pose some risk of HIV infection, though a fairly small one. There is evidence that enzymes and other chemicals in saliva inactivate HIV. The envelope that surrounds the core of the virus is very fragile and is easily damaged by substances found in saliva. However, the virus can remain protected inside infected immune system cells of the oral mucous lining. Nevertheless, the antiviral substances found in saliva surely reduce the possibility of its oral transmission. The best way to decrease the risk of HIV transmission during oral sex is to use a latex condom or other latex barrier, to completely avoid getting semen or vaginal fluids in the mouth.

Transmission of HIV from Mother to Child

In the United States, over 1.4 million children under 15 years of age were living with HIV at the end of 2000 (Brocklehurst & Volmink, 2002), and more than 90% of children with HIV contracted the virus from their mothers either during pregnancy, labor, or delivery or while breast-feeding (CDC, 1999c; Harris, Thompson, Ball, Hussey, & Sy, 2002). Transmission of HIV from mother to child occurs when the virus crosses the placenta, usually during the second and third trimesters, or when the newborn has contact with infected maternal blood and vaginal fluids during labor and delivery. During delivery, the risk of transmission increases 2% for each hour that a women is in active labor (International Perinatal HIV Group, 2001). In addition, HIV has been isolated from breast milk, making it possible for transmission to occur during breast-feeding. This is most likely to occur when the baby is breast-fed for more than 15 months, presumably because higher levels of the virus are found in breast milk after extensive breast-feeding. Transmission during breast-feeding is also more likely when the baby develops a mouth irritation called infant thrush and when the mother develops tears in the nipples or breast while breast-feeding (Embree et al., 2000).

Mother-to-child transmission is most likely to occur when the mother has high levels of the virus in her system. Remarkably, mother-to-child transmission has been reduced by 75% since 1992, owing to the now widespread use of the anti-HIV medication zidovudine (also known as ZDV or AZT) (Mofenson & the Committee on Pediatric AIDS, 2000). Use of ZDV for pregnant women has become routine, but researchers continue to examine long-term effects of exposure to this drug (Mofenson & the Committee on Pediatric AIDS, 2000). So far, the benefits appear to significantly outweigh the potential dangers. Obstetrical interventions (e.g., cesarean section if warranted) as well as early screening for HIV in pregnant women further help reduce the transmission of HIV to children. Proper interventions such as these can reduce mother-to-child transmission of HIV to about 2% (CDC, 2002c).

Not knowing the facts about HIV/AIDS can cause prejudice against people who are living with HIV. This link is explored in Health Matters: Myths about HIV Transmission.

Symptoms of HIV Infection

Once a person has been exposed to HIV, the virus can be found in lymph nodes within 2–5 days. Once it detects the virus, the immune system counterattacks, producing a decrease in the level of HIV. However, the virus is rarely, if ever, completely eradicated.

HEALTH Matters

Myths about HIV Transmission

The most common myth about AIDS asserts that HIV can be transmitted through casual contacts. Although few people believe that HIV can be transmitted through the air, like a cold or the flu, significant numbers erroneously believe that HIV can be transmitted from person to person through some types of physical contact, such as drinking from the same glass, sharing kitchen utensils, or kissing. Thus, despite widespread HIV/AIDS education programs, behaviors that pose no risk at all are wrongly perceived to be risky.

Fears of contracting HIV from common daily experiences such as work accidents, using a public phone, donating blood, or going to a dentist become exaggerated to the point that such risk-free activities appear more threatening than actual high-risk situations. Consider airline crashes, for example: These cause widespread fear, but the chances of dying in an auto accident are actually far greater than those of dying in a plane crash, even for a frequent flyer. It is a psychological fact that emotionally charged images, such as those presented by the media after an air accident, can make a remote risk seem threatening. Unfortunately, false impressions about HIV/AIDS risks lead to fear, stigma, and prejudice. There is no risk that a child with HIV could infect another child, but rumors fuel irrational fears, which in turn lead to prejudice. One of the great ironies of the AIDS epidemic is that many people worry about getting HIV from going to the dentist (virtually 0% risk), but the real risk of infection from having unprotected sexual intercourse is shrugged off by many others. It seems that focusing their attention on remote risks allows people to ignore real risks that are more difficult to cope with.

An equilibrium is reached as the virus reproduces itself and the immune system tries to rid the body of the virus (Graham, 1998). As HIV disease progresses over several years, the immune system is increasingly compromised by the virus. The level of the virus in the body, called the *viral load,* gradually and steadily begins to increase. During this equilibrium stage of HIV infection, which can last many years, the person is usually symptom-free and may not even realize that he or she is infected. Approximately half of all people who are HIV-positive develop AIDS within 10 years of being infected. A lingering question is why some HIV-positive individuals remain healthy and symptom-free for many years, while others develop symptoms within a relatively short time after contracting the virus. Researchers believe that a number of factors affect the progression of the disease, including overall health, heredity, and immune system function (Easterbrook, 1994; McDermott et al., 1998).

The most common early symptoms of HIV infection are chronic low-grade fever, persistent fatigue, diarrhea lasting at least 2 weeks, rashes or other skin conditions, unintentional weight loss of at least 10 pounds, night sweats, and thrush (an infection of the mouth or throat). These symptoms were once referred to as AIDS-related complex (ARC) because they were believed to precede AIDS. However, the term ARC is rarely used today because these early symptoms of HIV infection do not always mean that a person is about to get AIDS. Because these symptoms occur after the immune system has been run down, they can signal infections caused by bacteria, viruses, fungi, and parasites that, if not progressive, are not part of the AIDS diagnosis.

People with severely damaged immune systems can develop many infections and cancers. The illnesses that make up AIDS are rarely seen in people with healthy immune systems. Because they take advantage of the opportunity resulting from the body's inability to defend against them, AIDS-related illnesses are called *opportunistic.* Opportunistic illnesses, which include several bacterial, viral, and parasitic infections,

14.3 on the web

Go to **www.ablongman.com/mcanulty2e** to find Pfizer Inc.'s STD Risk Profiler and determine what your risk factors are for contracting HIV.

What are your reactions to the information? Will you have yourself tested for HIV? Why or why not?

as well as cancers, are the major cause of death among persons who are infected with HIV. In 1997, nearly 22,000 people with AIDS in the United States died, nearly all from opportunistic illnesses (CDC, 1999d). Opportunistic infections include *Pneumocystis carinii* pneumonia (PCP), a form of pneumonia common among AIDS sufferers, and Kaposi's sarcoma, a disfiguring type of cancer.

Even if he or she has not yet become ill with any opportunistic illness, a person who has HIV infection can be diagnosed with AIDS once the immune system itself has suffered significant damage, particularly the loss of many T-helper cells, and the number of T-helper cells drops to a very low level. The frequencies of opportunistic illnesses vary according to sex and mode of HIV exposure. Men who were infected through injecting drugs, for example, are more vulnerable to tuberculosis than are men who were infected in other ways (CDC, 1999d).

Diagnosis of HIV

It is impossible to know whether one has contracted HIV simply from the way one feels or looks. The only reliable way to know if a person has been infected with HIV is to test for the antibodies the immune system produces in response to the virus. Individuals who wish to be tested have a number of options, including confidential testing, anonymous testing, and home testing.

The standard procedure for HIV-antibody testing involves receiving the individual's written informed consent and then providing 30–90 minutes of pretest counseling, including an explanation of the test, discussion of limited confidentiality when the test is not anonymous, personalized risk assessment, and exploration of individual concerns. The test itself involves drawing blood and sending samples for laboratory analysis. Notification of results and post-test counseling usually occur about 2 weeks later.

Blood collected for testing is first analyzed by an **EIA (enzyme immunoassay) test,** which tests for antibodies to HIV. The EIA test is done first because it is sensitive to these antibodies. If an EIA test is negative, it is very unlikely that the person is infected with HIV. However, a positive EIA test must be repeated, because the test is not specific for HIV antibodies. After a blood specimen produces a repeated positive EIA test, the result is confirmed using a technique called the **western blot.** Like EIA, a western blot detects HIV antibodies, but it is highly specific for those antibodies (CDC, 2002c). Thus, both a positive repeated EIA screening test and a positive western blot confirming test are required for a diagnosis of HIV infection.

HIV-antibody testing is among the most accurate diagnostic tools in medicine. If a false negative result is obtained (the person is found not to be infected when he or she really is infected), the most common cause is that the blood sample was collected during the incubation period, before any HIV antibodies were produced. HIV antibodies are detectable after 3 months in 95% of people with HIV (CDC, 2002c). A person cannot be diagnosed as HIV-infected during the incubation period, although the virus can be transmitted to others during this time. The potential for obtaining a false negative result requires that all persons who receive a negative result get tested again 3–6 months later. People who test HIV-positive and have no identifiable risk factors should also be retested, although false positive test results occur only because of laboratory errors.

In the spring of 1996, the U.S. Food and Drug Administration approved the first HIV test for home use. Currently, the Home Access Express HIV-1 Test System is the only home test approved by the FDA. In 1999, the FDA evaluated several other kits and found that they produced false negative results. HIV home testing involves collecting blood specimens at home, but the actual tests for antibodies are still performed in a laboratory. The diagnostic function of a home test is essentially the same as that of a clinic-based test.

Home HIV testing allows the person to use a finger lancet to collect a few drops of blood on blotter paper, which is then mailed to a laboratory that performs the test. After waiting as little as 3 days, the person telephones the lab for the results. Post-test notification for people who test HIV-positive involves discussing the meaning of the test

EIA (ENZYME IMMUNOASSAY TEST)
A blood test for HIV antibodies. Two positive EIA tests indicate a high likelihood that a person is infected with HIV.

WESTERN BLOT
A blood test that is highly specific for HIV antibodies. This test is used to confirm positive results from an EIA test.

results over the telephone with a counselor, much like receiving post-test counseling in a clinic. In contrast, people who test HIV-negative receive their test results via an audiotaped telephone message, but are given the option of talking with a counselor afterward. By providing another way for people to get tested, home testing increases potential access to HIV-antibody testing. Many people with histories of high-risk behavior prefer home testing and may not be willing to get tested in a clinic (Branson, 1998; Phillips, Flatt, Morrison & Coates, 1995).

Additional HIV testing alternatives have appeared on the scene. Methods for detecting the HIV antibodies in saliva or urine are becoming increasingly available. Saliva and urine HIV-antibody tests make it unnecessary to draw blood and provide results that are just as accurate as those from blood tests. Being able to get tested for HIV without having blood drawn is likely to increase many people's willingness to undergo the test.

Kit for HIV Home Testing

Treatment of HIV/AIDS

There is at present no cure for HIV infection or AIDS. Medical researchers are actively pursuing an HIV vaccine. However, although several are being investigated and human trials are ongoing, to date, no effective vaccine has been found. The life expectancy for people living with HIV has doubled since the start of the epidemic, however, primarily because of an arsenal of medications that slow down the virus and prevent and cure the opportunistic illnesses that occur after the immune system declines. In addition to medical treatments, there have been many advances in psychological treatments to help people cope with HIV and AIDS.

14.4 on the web

As you know, the AIDS epidemic has reached unimaginable proportions in some areas of Africa. Go to **www.ablongman.com/mcanulty2e.** Describe U.S. efforts to help 24 countries in Africa and the rationale for doing so.

Do you agree with these efforts? Why or why not?

Medications for treating HIV infection have shown great promise in recent years. Deaths from HIV declined rapidly in the late 1990s following the introduction of potent antiviral drug combinations. Known as *highly active antiviral therapies* (HAART, also called "AIDS cocktails"), these medications have increased survival for many people infected with HIV (CDC, 2002c). These drugs, however, cause unpleasant and severe side effects and are quite costly.

Drugs that work directly on the virus to slow down its disease-causing processes are known as *anti-HIV medications*. These drugs include ZDV, ddI, 3TC, and several others. They work by inhibiting the enzyme called reverse transcriptase (RT), which plays a critical role in the early part of the process by which the virus replicates (reproduces) itself. A more recently developed type of anti-HIV medication acts by targeting a different enzyme, called protease, which is necessary at the end of the HIV replication process (NIAID, 2002). In 1996, Dr. David Ho was named Man of the Year by *Time* magazine for his pioneering work in developing protease inhibitor treatments. Today, researchers are still hard at work to develop more effective but less toxic RT inhibitors and protease inhibitors. In addition, new types of anti-HIV drugs are under development, including *fusion inhibitors,* which prevent HIV from entering cells, and *integrase inhibitors,* which prevent HIV from entering its genetic material into a cell's normal DNA. Scientists are also developing drugs to boost the immune system and to enhance the effectiveness of anti-HIV drugs (NIAID, 2002). Using combinations of anti-HIV medications in an "AIDS cocktail" has been shown to slow the progression of the disease and has brought more hope to people living with HIV. Such combinations of drugs hit HIV early and late in its replication process, delivering a double punch. These new treatments have led to the hope that HIV can be controlled and may one day be cured (Graham, 1998; NIAID, 2002).

People living with HIV can also benefit from drugs that prevent and treat the numerous opportunistic illnesses that arise as the immune system is slowly destroyed. For example, several drugs have now been shown to prevent *Pneumocystis carinii* pneumonia. There have been many other advances in the drug treatment of AIDS-related illnesses, both bacterial and viral. Thus, drugs can not only slow down the destructive onslaught of HIV infection but also reduce the accompanying opportunistic illnesses, allowing people with HIV to stay healthier longer and giving them reason to hope for further medical breakthroughs (CDC, 1999b; Palella, Delaney, & Moorman, 1998).

Drugs for treating HIV are expensive, and access to them is therefore extremely limited, preventing many people, particularly those living in poverty and in developing countries, from realizing their benefits. In fact, in 2002, only 230,000 of the 6 million people in poor and developing areas around the world had access to anti-HIV treatments. Fortunately, the World Health Organization has established guidelines aimed at increasing worldwide access to these drugs (WHO, 2002).

For individuals who do have access to anti-HIV drug treatments, these interventions are difficult to adhere to, requiring close attention to diet and to the specific times at which pills must be taken. Missing a daily dose can have devastating results and can cause the drugs to become ineffective when the person starts taking them again. Furthermore, many people living with HIV cannot tolerate the drugs' side effects, which can include nausea, intestinal distress, headache, and rashes as well as fatigue and depression.

Living with HIV Infection

People with HIV must learn to live with an infection that is truly life-altering. As might be expected, these individuals struggle with a host of emotions that escalate as their physical health becomes increasingly compromised (Siegel, Karus, Epstein, & Raveis, 1996). Fortunately, along with advances in medical treatments for HIV, there has been progress in the psychological care of people living with HIV. Research has also shown that many people living with HIV can benefit from group and individual counseling. Other research has shown that medications used to treat depression and anxiety can help people with HIV cope, without having adverse effects on the immune system (Rabkin & Harrison, 1990). Furthermore, psychological interventions such as stress management strategies reduce emotional distress in HIV-positive individuals as well as improve immune functioning (Antoni et al., 2000).

HIV-positive individuals have also been shown to benefit from exercise and other improvements in health habits, such as better nutrition. These changes in health habits can increase a person's sense of control and self-esteem. Researchers at the University of Miami have shown that exercise—for example, mild aerobics and bicycle riding—can help reduce stress and alleviate symptoms of depression and anxiety in those living with HIV (Antoni et al., 1991). It is unclear whether exercise and the consequent stress reduction can extend life expectancy, but the benefits in terms of quality of life are clear. Thus, people living with HIV have several options available to help them manage the stress of facing the long-term effects of this disease.

Medical treatment, combined with social support and a healthy lifestyle, can help change a person's focus from "dying from AIDS" to "living with HIV."

Persons living with HIV should use a latex condom during every act of sexual intercourse to reduce risks of STIs such as herpes and genital warts. They should also avoid any oral-anal contact to reduce risks of intestinal infections. Certain work settings are inadvisable because of the possibility of exposure to pathogens. Health-care settings and homeless shelters may expose an HIV-infected person to tuberculosis, and occupations involving contact with animals, including farm animals, also pose a risk of this infection. Child-care providers and parents of children in child care also run an increased risk of certain infections. Washing the hands after gardening or any contact with soil may reduce some infection risks.

Certain dietary restrictions are advised for persons living with HIV. Raw and undercooked eggs, meat, poultry, seafood, and unpasteurized dairy products should be avoided. Unfiltered and untreated water, such as that from lakes or rivers, should not be consumed. If unsure about the safety of a water supply, a person with HIV should boil the water or drink bottled water. Finally, certain travel limitations are recommended because risks of exposure to opportunistic pathogens are higher in many countries. In developing countries especially, risks of contamination of food and beverages are high. Fungi, parasites, and bacteria that should be avoided by persons with HIV are common in some places. Travelers with HIV should seek information about region- or country-specific risks.

As these recommendations reveal, living with HIV requires many adjustments and lifestyle changes. However, this fact is not cause for hopelessness and despair. Today, those with HIV who receive the proper medical treatment and who enjoy solid support from family and friends can enjoy relatively productive and normal lives. More than ever before, infected persons can change their mental outlook to learn to live with HIV, rather than dying of AIDS rather quickly.

REDUCING THE RISKS OF SEXUALLY TRANSMISSIBLE INFECTIONS

Effective control of STIs involves many factors. Ultimate success will require a range of efforts involving the health care system (e.g., physicians, STI clinics, college health services), the government (e.g., Centers for Disease Control, state health departments), and the public (e.g., demand for prevention programs); funding for any prevention and control efforts is also necessary (Cates & Meheus, 1990).

A major component of any preventive health care effort, and perhaps the most challenging, is changing personal behavior. If you have ever attempted to change some habit or develop a new one (quitting smoking, eating properly, exercising, or studying regularly), you know how difficult it can be. Changing sexual practices can be particularly problematic, because the unsafe practices are often rewarding in the short term and the potential negative consequences (symptoms of a disease) are delayed (not immediately associated with the unsafe practice). Furthermore, initiating safer sex practices, such as asking a sexual partner questions about past sexual activity, can be uncomfortable. A number of behavioral practices can help reduce or even prevent the transmission of STIs. These include remaining abstinent or monogamous, making a commitment to practice safer sex, using barrier methods of contraception, limiting the number of sexual partners and communicating with potential partners openly, avoiding alcohol and other drugs, avoiding certain high-risk sexual behaviors, seeking routine screening, and following treatment regimens. As you read earlier in Close Up on Gender: Women's Risks of HIV Infection, getting people to follow these practices requires paying attention to cultural, economic, and gender-role factors.

Abstinence and Monogamy

The only prevention method that is 100% effective is abstinence. Abstinence can mean several things. It is commonly used to mean avoiding any form of sexual activity forever. Actually, a person can be abstinent for a limited period of time—until committed to a single individual or until married to that person. In addition, abstinence does not need to mean avoidance of all sexual activity. Avoidance of penetrative genital, anal-genital, and oral-anal activity is recommended to prevent STIs. Other sexual activities, such as kissing, petting, masturbation, and use of sex toys, are generally considered safe and not likely to result in transmission of disease.

The second most effective prevention method is maintaining a monogamous relationship with an uninfected partner. *Monogamy* refers to two people having sexual relations (including intercourse) only with each other. For monogamy to be effective against STIs, both partners must be disease-free. Because many STIs can be asymptomatic and latent, it is difficult to determine visually whether a potential partner is in fact disease-free. Asking the person directly is effective only if he or she knows (has been tested recently and not subsequently exposed) and is honest. Thus, monogamy depends on trust. Serial monogamy, where partners have sex exclusively with each other during their relationship but have had previous sexual relationships with one person at a time, is risky. That is, if you have a partner who has had sexual relations before, you are at risk indirectly from all of that person's previous sexual contacts.

14.5 on the web

Revisit the issue of sex education by clicking on the link to Rethinking Schools at **www.ablongman.com/mcanulty2e.** Jocelyn Elders, former U.S. Surgeon General, discusses her views on abstinence-based sex education.

Do you agree with her views? If not, which points do you disagree with?

A Commitment to Practice Safer Sex

A major part of effective STI prevention programs has been encouraging people to make a commitment to practice safer sex. Prevention programs encourage people to identify personal goals and the strategies that would be necessary in order to achieve these goals. The strategies are seen as stepping-stones leading to the long-term goals. For example, a person's long-term goal might be to use condoms every single time he or she has sexual intercourse, and the strategies for reaching this goal would be to buy condoms, to keep condoms in places where sex is likely to take place, to talk with sexual partners about using condoms, and to use condoms more often.

As you know, condoms, diaphragms, and spermicides protect against most STIs (Stone, Grimes & Magder, 1986). However, barrier methods of contraception provide protection only to the degree that they cover genital areas and are used properly. For example, a diaphragm alone, which covers only the cervix, does not prevent infection of labial surfaces or the penis. STIs such as genital warts and herpes may infect sites not covered by a condom; therefore, that form of protection is not complete. However, latex condoms, when correctly and consistently used, provide an effective barrier to HIV, HSV, hepatitis B, cytomegalovirus, gonorrhea, and chlamydia. Latex condoms are poreless, in contrast to natural-membrane condoms (sometimes called "skins" or "lambskins"), which have pores that are large enough to allow microorganisms, particularly viruses, to pass through. Female condoms that are inserted into the vagina are now available. These are effective barriers to viruses, including HIV, but their overall success in preventing STI infections has not yet been established. Condoms should also be used when practicing anal and oral sex. Dental dams (square pieces of latex used during dental surgery and available at specialty shops) are designed to cover the vagina during cunnilingus and can help reduce the risk of transmitting STIs. Unfortunately, even if you choose to employ a barrier method, some sexual partners will be resistant.

14.6 on the web

Read the excuses a sex partner might give for not using a condom and the responses you might give at the Pfizer Inc. link at **www.ablongman.com/mcanulty2e.**

Would you use either the excuses or responses to them with a sex partner? Explain why or why not.

Scientists are hoping to make microbicides, sometimes referred to as "invisible condoms," available in the near future. Microbicides are vaginal preparations (perhaps in the form of foams, gels, creams, suppositories, film, sponges, and vaginal rings) designed to kill or block pathogens, or even to stop viruses from replicating once they have invaded the vaginal wall; some would also function as contraceptives. Microbicides hold great promise in that they would give women more control over protecting themselves and might not be met with the same resistance that condoms sometimes are. Furthermore, women with HIV-positive partners could get pregnant while also protecting themselves against HIV infection. More than 60 of these products are currently being investigated and some are being tested in other countries (Wulf, Frost, & Darroch, 1999).

Although surveys suggest that condom use is increasing among adolescents and adults (Murphy & Boggess, 1998; Sonenstein, Ku, Lindberg, Turner, & Pleck, 1998), there are still many people who do not consistently practice safer sex (Anderson, Wilson, Doll, Jones, & Barker, 1999; Moore & Halford, 1999). The greatest obstacles to using condoms are beliefs that they interfere with sexual pleasure, stimulation, and spontaneity. Some people complain that insisting on condom use conveys a lack of trust in one's sexual partner. A better understanding of condoms and their proper use can help people change their negative attitudes, which will make them more likely to protect themselves and their partners from HIV and other STIs. Availability of and positive attitudes toward condoms are associated with more consistent use (Anderson et al., 1999; St. Lawrence & Scott, 1996).

Communication about sexual decisions is essential to practicing safer sex.

Sexual Communication Skills

People can reduce their risk for STIs by communicating more effectively and assertively with their sexual partners. Sexual assertiveness includes initiating wanted or desired sexual ac-

HEALTH Matters

Telling Your Partner You Have Herpes

If you have herpes, telling your partner is important for your partner's health and for the health of your relationship. It also shows that you respect and care for your partner, and it is more likely to increase the trust and intimacy in your relationship than if you are deceptive—having to make up excuses not to have sex during outbreaks, and possibly transmitting the virus unknowingly, will only break down your relationship. Finally, telling your partner will also make it easier for your partner to be more open with you about her or his sexual history and sexually transmissible infections that he or she might transmit to you.

How?

1. Be prepared. Make sure you are well-informed about herpes, its risks and management. The American Social Health Association (www.ashastd.org) or the National Herpes Helpline (919-361-8488) can help you learn more about herpes.
2. Practice what you will say out loud to yourself or to someone else you have confided in.
3. Choose a setting that is neutral and that offers few distractions.
4. Be calm and act naturally; speak confidently without lecturing or sounding like you are at a confessional. Your partner is likely to take your lead on how to react. If you are calm and accepting of your condition, your partner is more likely to react with acceptance and support.
5. Make your comments simple and straightforward. Here is an example of what you might say:

   I have been feeling very close to you lately, and I would like to become intimate with you. But before we do, I need to tell you something very personal. I have genital herpes. It is like a cold sore or fever blister, but instead of being on the lip or mouth, it appears in my genital area. It is not as bad as some people think. If you like, I can tell you more about it.

What Will Your Partner Do?

Obviously, no one can predict exactly how a particular individual will react, but most people do not overreact. Most importantly, you should probably know sooner rather than later whether the person you are getting close to can handle the fact that you have herpes. If not, you might need to reconsider whether you want to be with this person. If the person cares for and respects you, he or she should respect and care for you even knowing that you have herpes.

SOURCE: Adapted from the American Social Health Association, www.ashastd.org.

tivities, refusing unwanted sexual activities, and discussing or insisting on using condoms (Grimley, Prochaska, & Prochaska, 1993). Communicating about condom use may be particularly important for men who engage in receptive anal intercourse and for women, who oftentimes are the ones who must ensure that their partners put on a condom. Naturally, safer sex is everybody's responsibility.

Being direct and honest with potential sexual partners can cut the risk of contracting an STI. You should ask explicit questions and volunteer information; Health Matters: Telling Your Partner You Have Herpes provides tips on how to go about this. Potential partners should be asked about symptoms of current infections, history of STIs, multiple partners, and exposure to previous partners with an STI. Specific risk behavior should also be assessed. For example, you should determine whether a potential partner has had unprotected anal sex, engaged in intravenous drug use, or has had sexual contact with prostitutes. Unfortunately, even honest answers to direct questions are not always enough. The person may be unaware of infections and even of personal risk factors. As has been noted, many STIs (including herpes, genital warts, chlamydia, and syphilis) can be transmitted when the infected person is symptom-free. Getting to know a person over a long period of time and routine testing are the best ways to reduce the chance of acquiring an infection.

Unfortunately, lack of experience in discussing sexual needs and concerns can interfere with initiating safer sex discussions. For example, women often find it difficult to discuss condoms with sexual partners, do not feel confident that they can persuade their partners to use condoms, and believe that men can easily persuade them to have sex without condoms even when they really do not want to (Moore & Halford, 1999; Sikkema et al., 1995). Some people find it embarrassing to talk about safer sex with potential sexual partners. Minority women, particularly low-income women living in urban areas, tend to be in power-imbalanced relationships in which they experience little control over their sexual interactions and feel ineffective at getting men to wear condoms (Sobo, 1993; Weeks, Schensul, Williams, Singer, & Grier, 1995). Similarly, gay men experience difficulties requesting that their sexual partners use condoms. Gay and bisexual men also sometimes report being coerced to engage in unprotected anal intercourse, indicating a possible lack of assertiveness in resisting partner pressure for unsafe sex (Kalichman & Rompa, 1995).

Aside from requests for condom use, sexual communication can also include a broader discussion of issues related to sexual health. Partners may discuss their sexual pasts and gain better understanding of each other's histories. They may also discuss HIV-antibody testing and the option of getting tested together. Once both partners test negative for HIV (confirmed by a repeated test), a couple may negotiate sexual safety within their relationship, such as not using condoms with each other but remaining monogamous. Partners may also agree to practice safer sex with other people if they choose not to be monogamous. Negotiated safety, however, is complicated by the fact that some people are dishonest in their relationships. For example, one survey found that HIV-positive men often do not disclose their status to sexual partners and that a significant number of men admit lying about their sexual histories (Cochran & Mays, 1990). Moore and Halford (1999) found that one-third of survey participants admitted that they were not always honest with a new sexual partner about their sexual history. The lack of honesty in some relationships, the frequency of serial monogamy, and infidelities in relationships make negotiated safety an uncertain risk-reduction option. Thus, unlike abstinence and condom use, sexual communication relies on assumptions of partner openness and honesty.

Looking At . . .

. . . Thinking About

Do you use condoms every time you engage in anal or vaginal intercourse? Women and men alike sometimes have trouble being assertive with potential sexual partners about using condoms to protect against STIs. What will you do the next time (or first time) you consider having sexual intercourse?

Avoiding High-Risk Behavior

Although alcohol and other drugs do not cause STIs directly, they are associated indirectly with high-risk sexual behavior (Santelli, Robin, Brener, & Lowry, 2001). Alcohol and drugs can be disinhibiting and can interfere with a person's judgment, resulting in increased risk of engaging in unsafe sexual activities. If you remain sober, you are more likely to practice safer sex. A commitment to safer sex requires good judgment, especially in high-risk situations. Certain sexual activities are considered especially high-risk; therefore, it may be best to avoid them altogether. Oral-anal contacts, or *analingus* (sometimes called "rimming"), and finger, hand, or fist-anal activity (sometimes called "fisting") are very risky behaviors. Fisting in particular can cause tears in the anal and rectal linings, through which bacteria and viruses can easily enter the bloodstream. Both of these sexual practices have also been associated with enteric bacterial infections such as hepatitis A and shigellosis. Anal intercourse is a clear risk factor for acquiring HIV.

Regular Medical Checkups

Early detection is critical to treating STIs and to preventing their spread. Some STIs, such as chlamydia and syphilis, can have few or no symptoms and, if undetected, can have serious consequences. If you are sexually active, you should routinely visit your physician or health center for STI screening. Routine means twice per year, whether symptoms are present or not. You, as well as your partner, should undergo such screening before you become sexually active. Many public health centers provide these services for free, at a low cost, or on a fee-for-service basis, adjusted for ability to pay.

After reading this somewhat overwhelming amount of information on STIs, you may still be thinking that it does not apply to you. This is a common tendency, especially among young adults who generally feel protected by their youth from tragic consequences such as serious diseases. Reflect on This: Are You at Risk for Acquiring an STI? offers a checklist you can use to assess your risk factors.

STI Risk Reduction: Does It Work?

Effective STI risk reduction strategies are those that reinforce positive attitudes toward condom use, encourage the use of condoms for contraception, promote the view that sexual partners should use condoms, and strengthen intentions to practice safer sex (Sheeran, Abraham, & Orbell, 1999). Interventions will be most effective if they are offered to adolescents prior to first intercourse, involve parental and community support, and teach the necessary skills for personal risk reduction. Such skills include sexual communication and assertiveness training (Kalichman, 1998). All prevention

reflect ON THIS

Are You at Risk for Acquiring an STI?

Many factors, both biological and behavioral, put people at risk for STIs. Here is a list of major risk factors, with a blank next to each one for you to check if the risk factor applies to you. After reading this list, take note of the number of factors you checked.

___ Are you a man? Men have more STIs than women.

___ Are you a woman? Women are more likely to contract an STI after one sexual contact. Also, women, and particularly young women, are biologically more vulnerable to acquiring an STI.

___ Are you an adolescent or young adult? Rates of STIs are highest among adolescents and young adults.

___ Do you already have an STI? A person with one STI is more likely to contract another.

___ Do you have multiple sexual partners? The risk of acquiring an STI increases markedly with multiple sexual partners.

___ If you have only one sexual partner, does that person have multiple sex partners?

___ Do you use condoms consistently? Consistent and proper use of latex condoms reduces the transmission of all STIs. A latex condom with spermicide is even more effective in preventing STI transmission. All sexual behaviors, even those that don't lead to pregnancy (such as oral and anal sex), call for condom use.

___ Do you use drugs and alcohol? Drugs and alcohol greatly affect an individual's ability to make healthy decisions about sexual activity.

___ Do you believe you are invulnerable to STI infection, for whatever reason? Depending on which of the above factors you checked, you may not be as invulnerable as you think.

As you know, abstinence is the best way to avoid infection with an STI; however, there are other behaviors that can significantly reduce your risk: choosing your partner carefully, evaluating how risky that partner is, using condoms at all times, and avoiding use of drugs and alcohol, particularly in situations where you might make impulsive judgments about sexual activity.

and risk-reduction efforts must be sensitive to characteristics such as cultural context and the gender, age, racial and ethnic background, and sexual orientation of the targeted group.

Research shows that people are most likely to practice safer sex consistently if they do so beginning at first intercourse (Sheeran et al., 1999). In a study of sexually active adolescents, Miller and her colleagues found that adolescents who had discussed safer sex with their parents were more likely to use condoms during first intercourse and to continue doing so in the future. The timing of the parent-adolescent discussion was critical; it was most effective if it took place prior to the teens' first sexual intercourse (Miller, Levin, Whitaker, & Ku, 1998). Subsequent research showed that not only the timing but the type of communication between adolescents and their parents was important in predicting condom use. Parental discussions were effective only if parents were open, skilled, and comfortable in having these talks with their teenagers (Whitaker, Miller, May, & Levin, 1999). Some school-based programs are now including parent-student interactive homework assignments and are leading to significantly improved communication with parents and intentions among adolescents to delay intercourse until after high school (Blake, Simkin, Ledsky, Perkins, & Calabrese, 2001).

Several large-scale HIV risk-reduction efforts have been investigated. The findings reveal that these interventions are efficacious, cost-effective, and usually well received (Kalichman, 1998). The NIH Multisite HIV Prevention Trial (NIH, 1998) is an effective risk-reduction intervention aimed at high-risk populations at 37 clinics across the United States. Over 1,800 participants recruited in STI or general medical clinics were assigned to small groups for an HIV risk-reduction intervention that involved seven sessions. The control group, of approximately the same size, participated in a 1-hour AIDS education program. Over a 12-month followup period, participants in the risk-reduction intervention reported fewer unprotected sexual acts, increased condom use, and fewer STI symptoms. Males recruited from STI clinics also had a lower incidence of gonorrhea compared to males in the control group (3.6% compared to 6.4%). Another study addressed women attending a family planning clinic in an area of New York City with high rates of HIV. Researchers found that an eight-session group intervention tailored specifically to women significantly reduced their number of unprotected sexual encounters and their number of sexual encounters (Ehrhardt et al., 2002). HIV risk-reduction programs have been shown to reduce the number of new HIV infections in several African communities. Grosskurth and colleagues (1995) offered treatment for STIs, condoms, and health education to Tanzanian women between the ages of 15 and 24. Over a 2-year period, this program achieved a 50% decrease in HIV incidence. Early in the HIV epidemic, the government of Senegal in western Africa implemented an education and condom promotion campaign, which was supported by political, religious, and community leaders. The effects have been impressive, as measured by young adults' postponement of sexual initiation, increased condom use, and lower rates of STIs, including HIV, than in neighboring countries (UNAIDS, 1999a). In conclusion, "preventive interventions are effective for reducing behavioral risk of HIV/AIDS and must be widely disseminated" (National Institutes of Health, 1997, p. 16). The NIH has now established a global network to study HIV prevention strategies, and numerous studies are in various stages of development and implementation (National Institutes of Health, 2000).

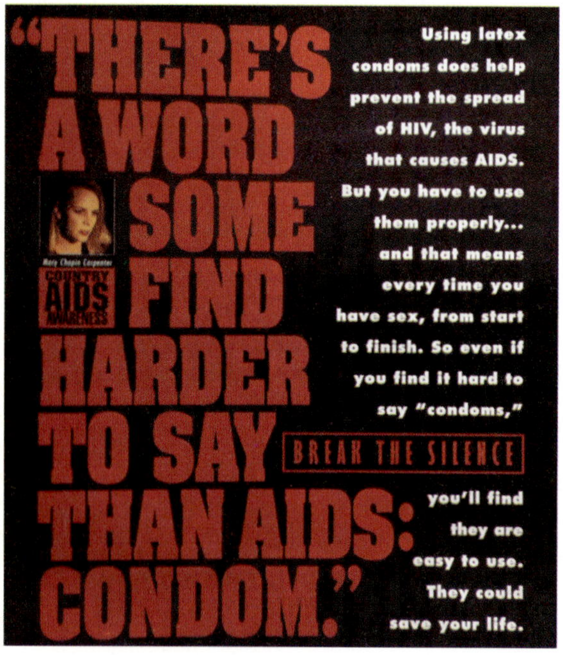

HIV/AIDS prevention programs have been shown to be effective at reducing risky sexual behavior.

With respect to modifying sexual risk taking, interventions that include education about STIs and skills training to further consistent condom use and successful negotiating of safer sex with sexual partners are most effective. Successful STI risk reduction also requires changes in legislation and government policy. This is particularly applicable to current U.S. policies on sexuality education, which dictate that only abstinence-based programs for at-risk adolescents qualify for federal funds. As an NIH panel concluded, "although sexual abstinence is a desirable objective, programs must include instruction in safer sexual behavior, including condom use. The effectiveness of these programs is supported by strong scientific evidence" (NIH, 1997, p. 16). Unfortunately, when it comes to sex, politicians tend to ignore research findings.

HEALTHY DECISION MAKING

We hope that by now you have learned that one of the most important aspects of preventing STI infection is the use of a condom. One impediment to this very critical part of prevention is resistance from a sexual partner. Here are several types of responses you might get from a potential sexual partner who does not want to use a condom, along with possible rejoinders you might offer (Grieco, 1987).

Partner: "I'm on the pill, you don't need a condom."
You: "I'd like to use it anyway. It protects us both from infections we may not realize we have."

Partner: "I know I'm clean. I haven't had sex with anyone in months."
You: "Thanks for telling me. As far as I know, I'm disease-free, too. But I'd still like to use a condom, since either of us could have an infection and not know it."

Partner: "I'm a virgin."
You: "I'm not—so this protects both of us and the relationship."

Partner: "I can't feel a thing when I wear a condom; it's like wearing a raincoat in the shower."
You: "I know there is some loss of sensation, and I'm sorry about that. But there's still plenty of sensation left."

Partner: "I'll lose my erection by the time I stop and put it on."
You: "I can help you put it on—I'll bet you'll find that erection again soon enough!"

Partner: "By the time you put it on, I'm out of the mood."
You: "I know it's distracting, but what we feel for each other is strong enough to keep us in the mood."

Partner: "It destroys the romantic atmosphere."
You: "It doesn't have to be that way. It may be a little awkward the first time or two, but that will pass."

Partner: "Condoms are unnatural, fake, and not very sexy."
You: "There's nothing sexy about a sexual infection either. Please let's try to work this out—either give the condom a try or let's look for alternatives."
Partner: "What do you have in mind?"
You: "Making out, using our hands. Or we could postpone making love altogether—even though I know we both want it."

Partner: "This is an insult! You seem to think I'm some sort of disease-ridden slut/gigolo."
You: "I didn't say or imply that. I care about both of us and our relationship. In my opinion, it's best to use a condom."

IN YOUR own words

Hollie Heither
University of Northern Iowa

If I were to even think about having a sexual relationship with someone, I would make sure that I am comfortable discussing everything with him or her, including STIs. I have personally been in that exact situation and have explained that before anything goes down we both need to be tested. My partner surprisingly didn't object and we both protected ourselves by doing the right thing.

Partner: "None of my other boyfriends use a condom."
You: "Please don't compare me to them. A real man cares about the person he is involved with, himself, and their relationship."

Partner: "I love you! Would I give you an infection?"
You: "Not intentionally, of course not. But many people don't know they are infected. I just think this is best for both of us."

Partner: "Just this once."
You: "Once is all it takes."

Partner: "I won't have sex with you if you're going to use a condom."
You: "Let's put it off then until we have a chance to work out our differences." Or, "Okay, but let's try some other things besides intercourse."

summary

- STIs are a major health problem around the world. STIs, of which there are more than 50, have had a tremendous impact on health in the United States.

PARASITIC INFECTIONS

- Parasitic infections, such as scabies and pubic lice, can also be sexually transmitted. Good hygiene practices can prevent these infections, and they are curable. While parasitic infections are a nuisance, they do not tend to have long-term health consequences.
- Parasitic infections are treated with preparations applied directly to areas of infestation. Clothing and bedding must also be decontaminated.

BACTERIAL INFECTIONS

- Many STIs are caused by bacteria. The most common bacterial STIs are gonorrhea, syphilis, and chlamydia.
- Bacterial STIs can be treated with antibiotics. Unfortunately, however, bacterial STIs are often "silent," meaning that they are not detected because the symptoms are mild or not present.
- There are different tests for diagnosing bacterial STIs, but all are treated with antibiotic medications. Recently, however, some antibiotic-resistant strains of gonorrhea have been reported.

NON-HIV VIRAL INFECTIONS

- Herpes presents as a painful blister that becomes an open sore, usually on or around the genitals. Many people with herpes are asymptomatic. Herpes is transmitted largely by skin-to-skin contact with these lesions.
- Genital warts, caused by the human papillomavirus, are cauliflower-like warts in the genital area. As with herpes, skin-to-skin contact with these warts is the primary mode of transmission.
- Hepatitis B is the most common form of the three varieties of hepatitis. The virus is found in blood, semen, vaginal secretions, and saliva. Not all forms of hepatitis are sexually transmitted. Many individuals are asymptomatic, but others experience flu-like symptoms.
- To date, viral STIs remain incurable. Treatment only provides relief of symptoms. Antiviral medications such as acyclovir often minimize symptoms and may reduce outbreaks of herpes. Genital warts are usually diagnosed by a visual examination. Traditional methods of removing the warts include use of topical compounds, surgery, and freezing. Viral hepatitis is detected in blood samples. Effective vaccines for hepatitis A and B exist.

THE HIV EPIDEMIC

- HIV infection is a global epidemic, or pandemic. Although most people with AIDS in the United States live in large cities, rural communities are increasingly becoming affected by AIDS.
- HIV transmission occurs when a sufficient amount of the virus comes into contact with cells that carry CD4 on their surface. Anal and vaginal intercourse, and to a lesser degree oral sex, carry high risk for transmitting HIV. In addition, babies born to HIV-positive mothers can also become infected, although this risk can be reduced by the mother's use of AZT and other anti-HIV medications.
- HIV causes disease by disrupting and destroying the human immune system, most importantly

the T-helper cells, which direct the actions of the immune system.

- A person can only know he or she has HIV by having an HIV antibody test. People can be tested confidentially, anonymously, or through home testing.
- Once a person tests positive for HIV, he or she is faced with decisions regarding treatment. There have been many advances in treating HIV infection, and there is reason to hope that some day there will be a cure. For example, anti-HIV medications (especially in combinations called "AIDS cocktails") have been shown to slow proliferation of the virus. Although these drugs are life-prolonging for most patients, they are costly and can produce many negative side effects.

REDUCING THE RISKS OF SEXUALLY TRANSMISSIBLE INFECTIONS

- Prevention remains the best way to deal with HIV and other STIs. HIV infection is prevented by remaining abstinent, practicing only safer sex, or maintaining an exclusive monogamous relationship with a partner who does not have HIV. Condoms also offer protection against transmitting the virus.
- STI risk reduction requires identifying personal risk, making a commitment to safer sex, using condoms, and practicing sexual communication skills. Other strategies that have proven beneficial include having regular checkups, limiting alcohol and drug usage, and being selective about one's sexual activity.
- Several studies show that various interventions—including education and skills training—can successfully reduce risks of HIV and other STIs.

CHAPTER 15

Atypical Sexual Behavior

As he grew into adolescence, he became much more interested in girls and their clothing. Being a rather shy teenager, he often found their clothes far more interesting than the girls themselves. Later he began trying on his mother's coats and skirts. As an adult, he periodically dressed as a woman in the privacy of his home and with his wife's full consent.

He periodically dressed as a woman.

(Adapted from Brierley, 1979)

Three dominant women were preparing a submissive man for a scene. His legs were tied together, and he was hoisted by the legs in the air, his upper body resting on a table. Two of the women asked in a barely audible whisper if he was uncomfortable. He nodded to reassure them that he was okay.

(Adapted from Weinberg, 1994)

As a college student, he recalled feeling inadequate, and he had little success with dating. One day, while looking out his apartment window, he noticed an attractive woman undressing behind her partially opened window-shades. After that sexually arousing experience, he actively sought out opportunities to watch unsuspecting women who were undressing. He fantasized about observing an attractive woman in the act of masturbating, and he remarked that he was amazed at what some women did behind closed doors.

(Authors' files)

WHAT IS ATYPICAL SEXUAL BEHAVIOR?

What sexual fantasies and behaviors qualify as atypical? And how does one decide whether atypical sexual behavior is unacceptable? Although you may consider the sexual fantasies and behaviors in the opening vignettes atypical, only a few sexual urges or behaviors are considered totally unacceptable.

It is a common tendency to label anything that seems different as problematic and even deviant (which means departing or deviating from an accepted norm). There is a long tradition of trying to prohibit sexual behavior deemed to be unusual. Historically in Western cultures, the acceptability of various forms of sexual behavior was established by religious authorities and traditions. Early Christian writers provided explicit guidelines for acceptable sexual behavior; for Augustine, only penile-vaginal intercourse between a husband and his wife in the missionary position was permissible (Bullough & Bullough, 1995). All variations, including oral sex and homosexuality, were condemned as sinful.

As medical science became more influential, behavior that was formerly labeled sinful came to be viewed as sick or pathological. The shift from a religious to a medical

TABLE 15.1 The Types of Paraphilias Recognized by the American Psychiatric Association (2000)

DISORDER	ACTIVITIES THAT PROVIDE SEXUAL AROUSAL
Exhibitionism	Exposing one's genitals to an unsuspecting person
Fetishism	Use of a nonliving object (not limited to cross-dressing)
Frotteurism	Rubbing one's genitals against a nonconsenting person
Pedophilia	Sexual activity with a prepubescent child
Sexual masochism	Being humiliated, beaten, bound, or otherwise made to suffer
Sexual sadism	Inflicting psychological or physical suffering
Transvestic fetishism	Cross-dressing
Voyeurism	Observing an unsuspecting person who is disrobing or having sex
Paraphilia not otherwise specified:	
Telephone scatologia	Achieving sexual arousal by making obscene phone calls
Necrophilia	Sexual activity with corpses
Partialism	Exclusive sexual focus on one part of the body
Zoophilia	Sexual activity with animals (bestiality)
Coprophilia	Sexual arousal in response to feces
Klismaphilia	Sexual arousal in response to enemas
Urophilia	Sexual arousal in response to urine

perspective on atypical sexuality is also evident in the history of psychiatry (McAnulty, 1995). In its original *Diagnostic and Statistical Manual of Mental Disorders (DSM),* the American Psychiatric Association (APA, 1952) proposed a category of disorders called "sexual deviations," which included such sexual behaviors as "homosexuality, transvestism, pedophilia, fetishism, and sexual sadism (including rape, sexual assault, mutilation)" (pp. 38–39). Other types of sexual deviations were subsequently added to the *DSM* list, including exhibitionism, voyeurism, and frotteurism (APA, 1968, 1980). These "disorders" were ultimately renamed *paraphilias,* meaning "abnormal" (*para*) "loves" or "attractions" (*philia*). The paraphilias were said to involve sexual arousal to sexual situations or acts that are not "part of normative arousal-activity patterns" (1980, p. 261) and to interfere with the person's ability to have a healthy sexual relationship. The most recent edition of the *DSM* (APA, 2000) lists eight specific types of paraphilias and one generic category that encompasses others (see Table 15.1).

As currently defined by the American Psychiatric Association (1994, 2000), the **paraphilias,** or sexual deviations, involve "recurrent, intense sexually arousing fantasies, sexual urges, or behaviors" that center on objects, suffering or humiliation, or nonconsenting partners, including children. To be considered paraphilias, the atypical sexual urges or behaviors must have been experienced for at least 6 months and must significantly interfere in one or more areas of life, such as relationships (Hilliard & Spitzer, 2002). The preferred erotic stimulus is often highly specific; shoe fetishists, for example, do not experience sexual arousal to any and all shoes, but only to some styles of women's shoes (high heels and open-toed sandals are common). Additionally, individuals may structure their lives to have access to the sexually arousing stimulus; a shoe fetishist, for example, may work in a shoe store.

Another important characteristic of paraphilias is that they are predominantly reported in men (APA, 2000). This important observation is considered more closely in Close Up on Gender: Female Perversions? It is also considered further later in the chapter, in the section on explanations of atypical sexuality. Paraphilic fantasies and urges commonly develop during adolescence and frequently show lifelong patterns. In one study of more than 1,000 men who were seeking treatment, over 40% reported that they were aware of their atypical sexual urges in adolescence, usually before reaching age 18 (Abel, Osborn, & Twigg, 1993). For individuals whose sexual behaviors are illegal, the possibility of arrest and associated difficulties cause significant distress. However, individuals with paraphilias rarely seek professional help voluntarily (APA,

PARAPHILIAS
Sexual disorders that occur primarily in males, are characterized by recurrent fantasies, urges, or acts involving objects, nonconsenting partners, or physical pain or humiliation, and are distressing to the person or cause problems in his or her life.

CLOSE UP ON gender

Female Perversions?

According to the American Psychiatric Association (2000), paraphilias other than sexual masochism are almost never reported in women. Is atypical sexual behavior really limited to men, or could other factors explain this finding? Hunter and Mathews (1997) assert that the finding largely reflects aspects of a female gender-role stereotype. Describing a woman as a sex offender is incongruent with the cultural stereotype of women as sexually passive and inhibited. In addition, female sexuality is widely considered to be dependent on love and commitment. It is, therefore, somewhat difficult to imagine a woman flashing her genitals at unsuspecting strangers or making random obscene phone calls. The stereotypical female gender role also encompasses nurturance and caretaking. Imagining a women molesting a child contradicts this stereotype. Finally, males are typically seen as aggressive and females as submissive in their intimate relationships. It may seem odd to think of a woman restraining and spanking or whipping a man for their mutual sexual pleasure.

Because of such cultural scripts, people often react very differently to identical behaviors by men and women. A man who exposes his penis to an unknown woman is likely to be charged with a crime. However, a woman's exposing her breasts or genitals to a stranger is unlikely to be viewed as a criminal act—in fact, many men would actually welcome such an experience. The double standard even applies to child molestation. A 30-year-old man who had sexual intercourse with a 15-year-old girl would be charged with a sex offense. Historically, society has been more tolerant if the teenager is a male and the adult a female. There are, however, exceptions, as illustrated by the widely publicized case of schoolteacher Mary Kay Letourneau, who had a sexual relationship with an 11-year-old student when she was 32 years old. She was charged with a criminal offense and given a 7-year prison sentence. The pair later collaborated on a book, *Forbidden Love,* that was published in 1999.

Although there are not many reports of atypical sexual behavior in women, a few case studies and surveys have documented that some of the same behaviors reported in males also occur in females. Grob (1985) described a 43-year-old woman who exposed her breasts and genitals to passing truck drivers from her car. She experienced intense sexual arousal and occasional orgasms from "flashing," but sought therapy because her driving became increasingly reckless as she tried to evade pursuing drivers. Mathews, Hunter, and Vuz (1997) described 67 adolescent girls who had molested younger children. Over half of them had only one victim, but several had molested over ten victims. Their sexual activities ranged from oral sex to vaginal or anal intercourse. Approximately 20% of these girls had used force on their victims, most of whom were relatives or acquaintances, often younger children the girls were babysitting. Of interest is the finding that nearly 80% of these girls were themselves victims of childhood sexual abuse.

According to Hunter and Mathews (1997), "the study of female sex offenders is a comparatively recent phenomenon and the field is still in its infancy" (p. 478). As you have seen throughout this book, female sexuality in all of its forms has received much less attention than male sexuality.

1994). Those who come to the attention of mental health professionals usually do so because of the insistence of the courts or family members.

Several problems arise when scientists attempt to describe atypical sexual behavior in psychiatric and medical terms. Because social norms for sexual behavior change over time, definitions of sexual disorders vary as well (Simon, 1994). For instance, consider "childhood masturbation disorder," an archaic medical diagnosis applied to children whose parents discovered that they masturbated (Engelhardt, 1974). As social acceptance of masturbation as a natural and typical sexual practice grew, this "disorder" was eliminated from medical textbooks. Similarly, over the course of 20 years, homosexuality went from being considered a sexual deviation, listed in the *DSM* classification of mental disorders, to being viewed as a normal variation in human sexuality. Furthermore, as you've learned, there are tremendous differences in definitions of acceptable sexual behavior across cultures; a given type of sexual behavior can be viewed as typical and normal in one culture but atypical and abnormal in another. Even within the United States, some sexual practices, such as oral sex, are still officially criminal offenses in some states, although they are by no means atypical or abnormal (Bhugra, 2000).

did YOU know?

The terms "sexual deviation" and "paraphilia" replaced an older term, "perversion." Although "perversion" was used by Sigmund Freud (1953) and other important psychologists in the past, it has largely been abandoned because of its pejorative connotation.

15.1 on the web

Many people have questions about whether their sexual interests are common. Several Web sites offer advice and provide candid answers to such questions. Visit one of the links at **www.ablongman.com/mcanulty2e.**

What are common questions and worries? What type of advice is offered? Is the advice based on research findings or common sense?

In sum, we must be cautious in labeling a sexual behavior as atypical or uncommon. Surveys reveal that some sexual behaviors that might be considered by some to be uncommon are actually commonly practiced. Heterosexual anal intercourse was once described as deviant, but more than 25% of men and 20% of women report having experience with this sexual act (Laumann, Gagnon, Michael, & Michaels, 1994). We must be especially careful not to categorize sexual behavior that we find unusual as abnormal. Unquestionably, sexual practices that involve another person who is nonconsenting qualify as unacceptable and illegal. However, many of the sexual practices discussed in this chapter can be viewed as atypical but not necessarily deviant.

This chapter categorizes the different forms of atypical sexual behavior into two groups: those that do not involve coercion and those that do. Noncoercive atypical sexual behavior consists of benign sexual urges and activities that, although seemingly unusual, are nonetheless harmless. If the activity involves a sexual partner, her or his participation is ordinarily fully consensual. In coercive sexual behavior, an individual derives sexual pleasure from activity that involves another person who does not consent to this activity. Coercive sexual behavior can range from exposing one's genitals to an unsuspecting stranger to sexual molestation.

NONCOERCIVE ATYPICAL SEXUAL BEHAVIOR

Noncoercive atypical sexual behavior can range from becoming sexually aroused by inanimate objects to cross-dressing. Some people enjoy sexual role-playing with a consenting partner that involves domination, humiliation, and even pain. In fact, most people with such sexual urges and fantasies desire a partner who is willing and eager to participate.

Fetishism

Fetishism involves sexual urges, fantasies, or behaviors centering on the use of objects. The fetish objects are usually associated with a person's body or a bodily function and commonly are articles of female clothing (APA, 2000). Because the fetish must be an object, individuals who are intensely aroused by nonsexual body parts, (such as feet, hair, or knees) are not technically considered fetishists. Such a preference is classed as **partialism** by the American Psychiatric Association (see Paraphilia Not Otherwise Specified in Table 15.1). Arousal in response to women's shoes is an example of fetishism; an erotic attraction to feet is officially described as partialism. In fact, the distinction between fetishism and partialism is subtle.

did YOU know?

The most common fetishes are items of women's clothing, including panties, bras, stockings, shoes, and boots.

In one survey conducted in the United States, 11% of men and 6% of women reported personal experience with fetishes (Janus & Janus, 1993). The study did not specify the extent of the women's involvement, but it appears that it typically consisted of having a male partner with a fetishistic preference. This confirms other reports that this paraphilia is rare in women. Although fetishism begins in adolescence, it is believed that the fetish often attains its special significance in childhood (Gosselin & Wilson, 1984). Fetishism is usually lifelong.

Because many men may experience sexual arousal at the sight of intimate apparel, the label "fetishist" is reserved for those who require the fetish to become sexually aroused or who consistently substitute the object for a human partner (Weinberg, Williams, & Calhan, 1995). Fetishes are selected for particular features such as texture (for example, silk and nylon), or smell (Money, 1986). Rubber and leather fetishes combine both texture and smell. In their classic study of 48 fetishists, Chalkley and Powell (1983) found that many were aroused by more than one fetish; approximately 60% preferred items of clothing, 23% were aroused by rubber items, 15% chose

FETISHISM
A paraphilia involving the use of an object (for example, articles of clothing) to obtain sexual arousal or satisfaction.

PARTIALISM
A paraphilia characterized by sexual arousal in response to specific parts of the human body that are usually not associated with sexual activity (for example, feet).

footwear, and 15% preferred body parts (i.e., partialism); other stimuli that were deemed sexually exciting ranged from leather to nylon garments. In this sample, 44% preferred to wear the item, 23% enjoyed seeing the item worn by another person, and 38% regularly stole fetish items.

The themes in the materials on the table illustrate the overlap between fetishism, sadomasochism, and transvestism.

Fetishists either use the arousing object during masturbation or have a partner wear the item during sexual activity to facilitate the fetishist's sexual performance. Commonly, the fetish is necessary for sexual arousal, and without it the fetishist may experience erectile failure (Gosselin & Wilson, 1984). During solitary sexual behavior, the fetish is held, smelled, or rubbed against the genitals.

Fetishism has been reported in heterosexual and homosexual men. Weinberg and colleagues surveyed 262 members of the Foot Fraternity, an organization for homosexual and bisexual foot fetishists. Clean feet were the most commonly reported fetish, followed by boots, shoes, sneakers, and smelly socks (Weinberg, Williams, & Calhan, 1994). The majority of respondents had a partner with whom they engaged in fetishistic and nonfetishistic sexual behavior. One-third of the respondents admitted that the fetish was necessary for sexual arousal. Only 30% of the respondents felt emotional distress because of their fetish, but approximately one out of four admitted to psychological problems including guilt, social anxiety, and difficulty with intimacy. These emotionally troubled fetishists were more likely to have had a sexually repressive upbringing and to have felt socially isolated in adolescence (Weinberg et al., 1995). The majority of fetishists in the survey denied that their sexual interest in feet caused any serious problems for them.

Fetishists most commonly come to professional attention after being apprehended for theft (McConaghy, 1993). The preferred item may be obtained from clotheslines or public laundries and, in some cases, by breaking and entering. Fetishists often collect the preferred object, amassing a large quantity of stolen items (Gosselin & Wilson, 1984). Men with a fetish such as panties prefer them already worn rather than purchased new in a store. The close association between the fetish and another person's body is essential for most fetishists. However, to the fetishist, the item is actually more sexually arousing than the woman or man who wore it (Money, 1984). Fetishists occasionally wear the fetish but, unlike transvestites, do not try to look like women; their gender identity is masculine (Docter, 1988).

In another classic study, Wilson and Gosselin (1980) surveyed 87 members of a society for rubber fetishists, 38 members of a similar club for leather fetishists, 133 members of a sadomasochists' club, and 285 members of an organization for transvestites and transsexuals. The most significant finding was the overlap across groups: 88% of the fetishists engaged in sadomasochistic activities, and over 60% were involved in transvestism. Approximately two-thirds of homosexual foot fetishists also report some interest in sadomasochism (Weinberg et al., 1994).

Transvestic Fetishism

The phrase *transvestic fetishism* was introduced as a replacement for the term *transvestism*. Transvestism, which means "wearing the clothes of the opposite sex," was introduced by the sexologist Magnus Hirschfeld in 1910. The recent change in terms was intended to clarify that transvestic fetishism shares many features with fetishism but not with transsexualism, which is a gender identity disorder. **Transvestic fetishism** essentially involves cross-dressing (dressing in women's clothing) for purposes of sexual excitement. This sexual variant is identified in a heterosexual male who experiences, for at least 6 months, recurrent and intense urges, fantasies, or behaviors involving cross-dressing that cause significant distress or impairment in social, occupational, or other important areas of

TRANSVESTIC FETISHISM
A paraphilia in which a heterosexual male achieves sexual arousal by wearing women's clothing, commonly known as "cross-dressing."

Transvestites are heterosexual men who become sexually aroused by dressing as women. Their gender identity, occupations, and hobbies are masculine.

functioning (APA, 2000). In some cases of transvestic fetishism, the person also experiences or eventually develops *gender dysphoria,* or persistent discomfort with gender role or identity (Doorn, Poortinga, & Verschoor, 1994).

According to Docter (1988), five characteristics identify a transvestite: (1) a heterosexual orientation, (2) sexual arousal in response to cross-dressing, (3) occasional cross-dressing only (in contrast, some transsexuals live full-time as the other gender), (4) no desire for sex-reassignment surgery, and (5) masculine gender identity except when cross-dressed. When cross-dressed, transvestites have fantasies of being female. Contrary to popular stereotypes, transvestites are not effeminate. Their careers and hobbies are masculine, and most are married and have children (Zucker & Blanchard, 1997).

The specification that transvestic fetishism occurs only in heterosexual males eliminates all gay men who cross-dress, including female impersonators and drag queens, from this group (Docter, 1988). If a man who cross-dresses also feels dissatisfied with his biological sex, then he has *gender identity disorder,* or *transsexualism.* The essential differentiation is that the cross-dressing is sexually arousing in transvestic fetishism but not in the other conditions. The fetishistic aspect of the activity to a heterosexual male is the defining feature. Admittedly, differentiating transvestic fetishism from other similar conditions can be quite challenging (Wise & Meyer, 1980).

In their study of 504 transvestites who were readers of the magazine *Transvestia,* which caters to this group, Prince and Bentler (1972) found that the majority of respondents (89%) were heterosexual. A total of 64% were married, and only 14% had no previous marital history; three-fourths had children. A vast majority of respondents preferred to cross-dress fully (rather than merely wearing one item of women's clothing). The favorite item during sexual intercourse, worn by one-third of the transvestites, was a nightgown. In 80% of cases, the wives were aware of their spouses' cross-dressing; approximately half of the wives accepted it. Fewer than one-third of the respondents had appeared in public while cross-dressed. Nearly three-fourths of them described themselves as men seeking to express a feminine side. A more recent survey of 1,032 "periodic cross-dressers" by Docter and Prince (1997) essentially replicated the previous findings, as illustrated in Table 15.2.

When cross-dressed, transvestic fetishists strive to look like women (Allen, 1989). They do not display exaggeratedly effeminate mannerisms but, to the typical observer, appear to be men dressed as women (Whitam, 1987). Transvestites report feeling more relaxed, confident, and outgoing when cross-dressed (Gosselin & Eysenck,1980). They may have an extensive wardrobe of clothing or may simply wear a single item of clothing under their regular masculine attire (McConaghy, 1993). Partial cross-dressing may progress over time to complete cross-dressing, including the use of cosmetics (APA, 2000).

Buhrich and McConaghy (1977) studied 35 members of a club of self-identified heterosexual transvestites, at their invitation. Club members met monthly in female attire for social, not sexual, interactions. The majority reported that their sexual arousal to cross-dressing had decreased over the years and their primary motivation for continuing was the aesthetic satisfaction and feeling of relaxation associated with cross-dressing. However, genital measures of arousal revealed that many continued to be sexually aroused by cross-dressing. This finding provides more evidence that transvestic fetishism and transsexualism are different conditions, the former a paraphilia and the latter a gender identity disorder.

As a group, transvestites report feeling more anxious, introverted, and neurotic than males who don't cross-dress (Docter, 1988). Initially, cross-dressing is done secretively to avoid the feelings of shame and guilt that would arise if this behavior were discovered. Over half of transvestites begin cross-dressing by age 10, and almost all by adolescence (Docter & Prince, 1997). The existence of clubs, Web sites, and publications catering to transvestites suggests that cross-dressing is not a rare phenomenon.

15.2 on the web

The Harry Benjamin International Gender Dysphoria Association developed recommendations for helping people with gender identity disorders. To review their recommended Standards of Care, visit **www.ablongman.com/mcanulty2e.**

What treatments are recommended? What eligibility criteria are listed? What are the guidelines for sex reassignment surgery?

TABLE 15.2 Some Characteristics of Transvestic Fetishists

SURVEY ITEM/RESPONSE	PERCENTAGE OF RESPONDENTS
Sexual orientation	
Heterosexual	87
Bisexual	7
Homosexual	1
Asexual or unsure	5
Some homosexual experiences	29
Sexual interest in women	
Above average	17
Average	57
Below average	26
Age began cross-dressing	
Before age 10	66
Between 10 and 20	29
After age 20	5
View of self when cross-dressed	
Express different part of myself	80
Just myself with different clothes	20
Cross-dressing brings sexual excitement and orgasm	
Nearly always	21
Often	19
Occasionally	32
Rarely	12
Never	9
Enjoy wearing feminine items when orgasm is not feasible	
Frequently	41
Often	24
Occasionally	24
Rarely	8
Never	2
Prefer complete cross-dressing	93
Frequency of public cross-dressing	
Frequently	14
Occasionally	48
Rarely	38
Have appeared cross-dressed in public	71
Activities while cross-dressed	
Ride on bus, train, etc.	10
Eat in restaurants	28
Plays, lectures, church	18
Tried on feminine clothing in stores	22
Used ladies' room	26
Seen by acquaintances who'd know me	17
Wife is aware of cross-dressing	83
Wife's acceptance or antagonism	
Completely accepting	28
Mixed view	47
Completely antagonistic	19
Wife knew of cross-dressing before marriage	
Yes	32

SOURCE: Doctor and Prince, 1997, Transvestism: A survey of 1032 cross-dressers. *Archives of Sexual Behavior, 26,* 589–605.

IN YOUR own words

Kari LaVecchia
Virginia Commonwealth University

As long as both parties follow the credo of safe, sane, and consensual, then it doesn't matter how atypical a particular behavior is. Safe means that they've taken all precautions necessary to make the activity as safe as possible. Sane means that they are not under undue influence or drunk or passed out cold. Consent is the backbone to kinky sex.

McConaghy (1993) estimated the prevalence of "marked transvestite behavior" at less than 1% of the population, but solid data on prevalence rates are not available because of the clandestine nature of cross-dressing.

Sexual Sadism and Sexual Masochism

Sexual sadism and *sexual masochism* are two distinct paraphilias in which the experience of pain or humiliation is associated with sexual gratification. Krafft-Ebing (1936) described sadism as the counterpart of masochism: What is arousing to the sadist, in the active role, is arousing to the masochist, in the passive role. By definition, **sexual sadism** entails recurrent and intense fantasies, urges, and behaviors that center on inflicting physical or psychological suffering, such as humiliation. **Sexual masochism** involves fantasies, urges, and behaviors involving being subjected to physical or mental suffering. The suffering or humiliation must be real, not merely simulation or role-playing. Further, the fantasies or acts must cause subjective distress or interfere in important areas of life for these to be considered disorders (APA, 2000). Physical pain is a common but not a universal or necessary component of sadomasochism (Weinberg, 1994). Extreme and dangerous forms of inflicting physical pain are, in fact, quite uncommon (Moser, 1988).

In the vast majority of instances, sadomasochistic sexual interactions are consensual in nature (Stoller, 1991). Gosselin (1987) described the implicit "sadomasochistic contract" that governs the sexual scripts of sadists and masochists. This informal contract specifies the limits of acceptable sexual behavior during a sadomasochistic encounter, or a "scene," as it is called. With rare exceptions, sadists do not derive pleasure from inflicting more harm or humiliation than is desired by a partner (Gosselin & Wilson, 1984). In fact, most sadists seek partners who are sexually excited by suffering or humiliation rather than those who do not enjoy these feelings (Gosselin, 1987). Masochists have very specific preferences for the type of pain or humiliation they seek; as Stoller commented, "no sadomasochist likes all kinds of pain. The distinctions, though fine, are precise" (1991, p. 16). Some individuals may alternate between administering and receiving the suffering (Stoller, 1991).

Sexual sadists and masochists are to be distinguished from sadistic rapists and sadistic murderers, who seek nonconsenting victims. According to the American Psychiatric Association (1994), such individuals exhibit severe sexual sadism and may be diagnosed as having a serious personality disorder, *psychopathy*. Psychopaths are self-centered, manipulative persons who have a history of violating the rights of other people for their own benefit. They are insensitive to the suffering they cause others and do not experience remorse. In contrast, sexual sadists are attuned to their partners' emotions, and they delight in controlling them.

Table 15.3 lists some practices of sexual sadists and masochists. Gosselin (1987) identified three common sadomasochistic practices:

- Beatings, which may vary drastically in intensity and duration (up to 200 strokes in some cases). The beatings may be administered by hand or with paddles, belts, or whips.
- Bondage, which is ritualistic and often associated with beatings. Bondage commonly involves the use of mouth gags, hoods, blindfolds, immobilization, handcuffs, and rope or leather restraints. In some less common instances, the binding is designed to cause partial asphyxiation. The essential aspect of bondage seems to be asserting dominance or control and experiencing submission (Ernulf & Innala, 1995).
- Humiliation, which may arise from bootlicking and crawling or the use of degrading costumes, and even urine, feces, and enemas. A majority of masochists report a strong preference for humiliation (Moser & Levitt, 1987); over two-thirds of male and female masochists admit to experiencing significant sexual arousal when they feel humiliated (Weinberg, 1994).

Sadomasochistic encounters often entail a prominent imbalance of power (e.g., master/slave roles). Power, control, and trust, rather than suffering, are at the core of sado-

SEXUAL SADISM
A paraphilia involving sexual arousal from inflicting real pain or emotional suffering on another person.

SEXUAL MASOCHISM
A paraphilia involving sexual arousal in response to being subjected to physical pain or humiliation.

TABLE 15.3 Sexual Interests Reported by Male and Female Sadomasochists

INTEREST	MALE (%)	FEMALE (%)
Spanking	79	80
Master-slave relationships	79	76
Oral sex	77	90
Masturbation	70	73
Bondage	67	88
Humiliation	65	61
Erotic lingerie	63	88
Restraint	60	83
Anal sex	58	51
Pain	51	34
Whipping	47	39
Rubber/leather	42	42
Boots/shoes	40	49
Verbal abuse	40	51
Stringent bondage	39	54
Enemas	33	22
Torture	32	32
Golden showers	30	37
Transvestism	28	20
Petticoat punishment	25	20
Toilet activities	19	12

SOURCE: Breslow, Evans, & Langley, 1985, On the prevalence and roles of females in the sadomasochistic subculture: Report of an empirical study. *Archives of Sexual Behavior, 14,* 303–317.

masochism. A number of other terms are used to refer to sadomasochism (or S & M, as it is often abbreviated): Dominance and submission (D & S) and bondage and discipline (B & D) involve subtle distinctions and denote specific sadomasochistic themes and practices.

Sadomasochists may be heterosexual, homosexual, or bisexual (Santtila, Sandnabba, Alison, & Nordling, 2002). Among practitioners, heterosexual men tend to prefer the dominant/sadistic role, whereas gay men and heterosexual women are more likely to prefer the submissive/masochistic role (Ernulf & Innala, 1995). Recent studies reveal that 20–30% of those in the sadomasochistic subculture are female, usually masochists (Levitt, Moser, & Jamison, 1994). Surveys report that consensual beatings (usually spanking), bondage, and fetishism are most common; more dangerous activities are quite rare. Few sadomasochists report being distressed by their sexual activities.

did YOU know?

Masochism is the most common form of atypical sexual behavior in women.

One extreme and dangerous form of masochism is known as *hypoxyphilia,* or *autoerotic asphyxiation,* which is the derivation of sexual pleasure and intensification of

Looking At . . .

. . . Thinking About

Because of the consensual nature of sadomasochistic interactions and the finding that it usually involves role-playing, some researchers have questioned whether it should be considered a paraphilic or deviant sexual practice (Baumeister & Butler, 1997; Lohr & Adams, 1995). What is your view? Do you think S & M should be considered a deviant sexual practice?

orgasm from oxygen deprivation (APA, 1994). Practitioners deprive themselves of oxygen through a variety of methods, including the use of nooses, plastic bags, chest compression, or even chemicals; a rope around the neck is most common. Although apparently rare, the condition is sometimes publicized after the person's escape mechanism from the self-strangulation fails (Resnik, 1972). In such cases, an unsuspecting spouse or relative discovers the body, and the incident may be erroneously explained as suicide (Innala & Ernulf, 1989). Although this is usually a solitary sexual practice, some people hire prostitutes for assistance. The majority of people who practice hypoxyphilia are unmarried, white males; most are adolescents or young adults (Milner & Dopke, 1997).

Sadistic fantasies are believed to develop in childhood, although they are rarely acted on until adolescence or early adulthood (Breslow, Evans, & Langley, 1985). One team of researchers (Person, Terestman, Myers, Goldberg, & Salvadori, 1989) reported that 4% of the college women in their survey had recently experienced being bound or sexually degraded during sexual activity. The corresponding estimate for males as the masochistic partner was 3%. Approximately 1% of participants of both genders had recently whipped or beaten a consenting sexual partner. Janus and Janus (1993) reported that 14% of males and 11% of females in their survey had personal experience with sadomasochism. The wide availability of sadomasochist publications, clubs, and Web sites also suggests that it is not a rare phenomenon. For example, London's Torture Garden is a club for individuals with sadomasochistic interests (Steele, 1996). There are also prostitutes who cater to clients who want sadomasochistic sex.

With few exceptions, sadomasochistic activities are safe and enjoyable for both partners. The majority of practitioners are "reasonably well-adjusted, successful individuals" (Baumeister & Butler, 1997, p. 227). Thus, although these sexual practices may be considered atypical, most do not qualify as deviant.

COERCIVE ATYPICAL SEXUAL BEHAVIOR

Coercive forms of atypical sexual behavior are problematic. When an individual imposes sexual acts on an unwilling person, a victim, the sexual activity is not only socially unacceptable but also illegal.

Exhibitionism

Exhibitionism involves recurrent and intense sexual fantasies and urges to expose one's genitals to an unsuspecting stranger. Individuals who expose themselves tend to engage in a prolonged series of behaviors: fantasizing about exposing, going to a preferred setting for exposing, choosing a victim, mentally rehearsing the act, exposing the genitals, and finally masturbating to orgasm (Abel, Levis, & Clancy, 1970). An exhibitionist usually seeks a secluded location, such as in a park or library, where he is likely to find one or more unknown women without male escorts. Some exhibitionists scout for potential victims from an automobile. They usually approach the potential victim and get her attention by asking an innocuous question before exposing their

EXHIBITIONISM
A paraphilia characterized by the exposing of one's genitals to an unsuspecting person.

genitals. While exposing themselves, exhibitionists are mentally and physically aroused, and they masturbate to orgasm during the act or afterwards, while fantasizing about the experience (Langevin, 1983).

Contrary to a popular belief, exhibitionists do not seek to shock or frighten their victims, but are aroused by the hope that the victims will be excited by the sight of the exposed penis or that they will reciprocate the genital exposure (Lang, Langevin, Checkley, & Pugh, 1987). Exhibitionists describe their behavior as a compulsion. Many exhibitionists actually prefer exposing their genitals to having sexual intercourse. Responses from two samples of exhibitionists indicated that less than one-third desired sexual relations with their victims (Langevin et al., 1979). In fact, exhibitionists rely heavily on masturbation for sexual gratification (Gebhard, Gagnon, Pomeroy, & Christenson, 1965), and this is particularly true of unmarried exhibitionists.

Exhibitionism is one of the most common of the paraphilias. For example, 30–50% of women report being victims of exhibitionists (Zverina, Lachman, Pondelickova, & Vanek, 1987). Exhibitionists often have a large number of victims. In a sample of 142 exhibitionists, the average number of reported victims was 514 (Abel et al., 1987). Exhibitionists have a greater than average number of both sexual and nonsexual criminal convictions, although the majority are for sexual offenses (Blair & Lanyon, 1981). *Indecent exposure,* the legal term for exhibitionistic behavior, accounts for approximately one-third of all sexual offenses in Europe and the United States (MacDonald, 1973; Rooth, 1972, 1973b), yet this crime is almost nonexistent in other regions (Rooth, 1973a). Because exhibitionists are usually arrested eventually, many of them are seen by mental health professionals for evaluation and counseling.

Looking At . . .

. . . Thinking About

Although this woman may be an exhibitionist, females who expose their genitals as nude models or strippers are not. Do you know why?

The age of onset of exhibitionism is usually the early to mid-20s, although it is assumed that exhibitionistic fantasies begin in adolescence (Blair & Lanyon, 1981). There is a consistent drop in the number of arrests with age, and very few exhibitionists are arrested after age 40 (Mohr, Turner, & Jerry, 1964). Most of the research on exhibitionism has involved males charged with indecent exposure. There have been very few reports of female exhibitionists; the reported cases have involved women who are mentally retarded or mentally ill (Hollender, Brown, & Roback, 1977).

The onset of exhibitionism is associated with interpersonal stressors such as beginning dating or getting married, poor marital or sexual adjustment, and difficulty in intimate relationships. Despite these interpersonal difficulties, a majority of exhibitionists are or have been married (Blair & Lanyon, 1981) and, paradoxically, report having satisfactory heterosexual relationships (Langevin & Lang, 1987). Exhibitionists do not appear to differ from the general population with respect to intelligence, educational level, or vocational interests (Blair & Lanyon, 1981). However, they often perceive themselves as inferior, are generally timid and unassertive, and have problems expressing hostility. Other studies have found exhibitionists to be self-centered and antisocial (Lang et al., 1987).

Several studies report that exhibitionism commonly occurs along with other paraphilias, especially voyeurism. In fact, Smukler and Schiebel (1975) claimed that all participants in their sample had engaged in voyeurism prior to the onset of exposing behavior. In another study, half of the sample of exhibitionists reported other paraphilias, primarily voyeurism (Freund & Blanchard, 1986). Because exhibitionists sometimes choose female children as victims, a relation between exhibitionism and pedophilia has been proposed (Langevin & Lang, 1987). However, studies using penile plethysmographs to measure sexual arousal indicate that exhibitionists show normal arousal in response to adult females and little arousal in response to children (Langevin et al., 1979). Some exhibitionists expose themselves to children because of the lower likelihood that a child victim will report the incident.

Voyeurism

Voyeurism—also known as *peeping*—is a pattern of repeatedly observing an unsuspecting person who is undressing or engaging in sexual activity. The peeping itself provides sexual gratification; the voyeur does not want actual sexual activity with the victim. Typically, the voyeur—who is male—masturbates while peeping or afterward while recalling the episode in fantasy. As defined by the American Psychiatric Association (2000), **voyeurism** involves recurrent and intense urges and fantasies about or the actual act of observing unsuspecting persons who are undressing or having sex.

Voyeurs commonly fantasize about having a sexual encounter with the person being observed, usually a woman. They also experience a thrill and sense of power from watching a woman who is unaware of being observed. Typically, a voyeur has a preferred neighborhood or series of houses that he approaches during an outing, which he has generally selected on the basis of previous success at peeping. Various strategies may be used to gain visual access and escape detection. One voyeur habitually took the family dog for evening walks and carried binoculars, presumably to watch birds. (His wife became suspicious when she realized the birdwatching was not possible in the dark.) Although peeping is a secretive act, some voyeurs attempt to attract the attention of their victims (Money, 1986). This inevitably terrifies the victim, and the voyeur hurriedly escapes.

As noted, a voyeur does not seek actual contact with the victim. The lack of victim consent is what distinguishes voyeurism from the viewing of pornography or adult entertainment. The lack of consent also separates voyeurism from **troilism**, in which a man watches his wife or regular partner engaging in sexual activity with another person. Troilism usually occurs with the consent of all parties. In addition, not all individuals who take advantage of an opportunity to observe a woman disrobing are considered voyeurs; a single instance of peeping reflects poor judgment, whereas voyeurs repeatedly seek out such experiences and regularly fantasize about them.

Voyeurism may occur together with other paraphilias, including exhibitionism, frotteurism, and pedophilia. Research supports an association between voyeurism and exhibitionism (Freund & Blanchard, 1986; Langevin & Lang, 1987), but the co-occurrence of voyeurism and other paraphilias is less common. The belief that voyeurism is associated with sexual aggression, especially rape, has not been confirmed. Individuals accused of both voyeurism and rape are probably more likely rapists who engaged in surveillance of prospective victims.

The vast majority of voyeurs are heterosexual and married or involved in a regular sexual relationship. Their level of sexual experience is above average, although they often report shyness and limited dating during adolescence (Langevin & Lang, 1987; McConaghy, 1993). Disturbed relationships with parents in childhood are common (Langevin, Paitich, & Russon, 1985). The pattern of sexual arousal in response to peeping begins in adolescence and is often lifelong.

Voyeurism is apparently a fairly uncommon sexual disorder. In fact, some researchers even question the existence of voyeurism as a separate disorder. In one sample of 600 paraphiliacs, no cases of exclusive voyeurism were identified (Langevin et al., 1985). In a survey of male college students, 4% admitted to having observed others engage in sexual activity (Person et al., 1989). A similar survey of 60 students found that 42% had secretly engaged in voyeuristic behaviors (Templeman & Stinnett, 1991). However, it is unclear how many, if any, of these students had intense and recurrent urges and fantasies of a voyeuristic nature—they may have simply been curious!

IN YOUR own words

Helena Kryuchkin
Northwestern University

Anything that involves another person who is unwilling (e.g., rape or voyeurism) I believe to be harmful. Someone who gets a kick out of shoe stores and goes home fantasizing is pretty harmless.

VOYEURISM
A paraphilia that involves observing an unsuspecting person who is undressing or engaging in sexual activity.

TROILISM
Observation by a male of his usual sexual partner engaged in sexual activity with another person; differentiated from voyeurism by the fact that all parties involved consent to the activity.

Web sites that allow viewers to view aspects of another person's intimate life attest to the prevalence of voyeuristic tendencies.

The same question arises with the recent reports of high-tech voyeurism. Small video cameras that are easily concealed have been used to make video recordings of people in the most private of settings, including restrooms and bedrooms (Hawaleshka, 2001). The tapes are later viewed by individuals with voyeuristic tendencies or even disseminated over the Internet. In some cases, women have even installed their own cameras in their residences or dormitories to broadcast the intimate details of their daily lives, usually to an audience that has paid a subscription fee. Would such women qualify as exhibitionists, or are they more akin to topless dancers who perform for a price? The popularity of Web sites that allow viewers into the privacy of another person's life suggest that many people have voyeuristic tendencies (Chen, Lindsay, & Maroney, 2000).

Frotteurism

Frotteurism (from the French *frotter,* "to rub") is characterized by recurrent urges and fantasies about or the actual behavior of rubbing one's genitals against a nonconsenting person, usually a woman. The frotteur—most often a man—generally rubs his penis against a victim's thighs or buttocks. The man typically fantasizes a sexual relationship with the victim during the act. Frotteurism begins in adolescence. The practice reportedly peaks between the ages of 15 and 25 and declines after that (APA, 2000). If so, frotteurism is significantly different from other paraphilias, which are usually lifelong.

A distinction is often drawn between frotteurism and **toucherism,** which is the fondling of a nonconsenting person (McAnulty, Adams, & Dillon, 2001). Toucherism involves the active use of the hands (Langevin & Lang, 1987). In either case, it is the physical contact, rather than the lack of victim consent, that is sexually arousing to the individual (APA, 2000). Frotteurs generally engage in this activity by positioning themselves next to an attractive woman in a crowded public transportation vehicle or elevator. The frotteur takes advantage of the proximity afforded by the crowding and swaying of the vehicle to rub his genitals against the victim. The frequent stops allow

FROTTEURISM
A paraphilia involving rubbing one's genitals against a nonconsenting person.

TOUCHERISM
The fondling of a nonconsenting woman; differentiated from frotteurism in that it involves use of the hands.

Frotteuristic behavior usually occurs in busy, crowded places such as nightclubs or on public transportation vehicles.

escape should the victim protest. Apparently, many victims allow the activity to continue out of fear and embarrassment. A frotteur may repeatedly board crowded subway cars during rush hour in order to find multiple victims in a short period of time.

Money (1986) claimed that it is the impersonal nature of the sexual contact that is essential to the frotteur. Some researchers consider the condition to be a form of sexual aggression, on the basis of the lack of consent from the victim (Langevin, 1983). They question whether frotteurism is a preferred sexual activity, believing instead that it represents a substitute for more desirable consensual sexual activity with a partner (Langevin & Lang, 1987).

In their large-scale study of men with paraphilias, Abel and colleagues (1987) examined 62 self-identified frotteurs. The average number of victims was 901 per person! After exhibitionists, frotteurs accounted for the largest percentage (18.1%) of the paraphilic acts carried out by the total sample of 561 admitted paraphiliacs. More than half of the 119 frotteurs participating in another study also admitted to having a problem with exhibitionism (Freund, 1990). Over 30% admitted to voyeuristic acts, and nearly 22% admitted to having raped a woman. Twenty-five percent of the college students in Templeman and Stinnett's (1991) survey admitted to having engaged in frotteuristic behavior. However, it seems unlikely that all of them would meet the criteria for the paraphilia, especially the requirement that the problem must be longstanding (lasting 6 months or longer).

15.3 on the web

The Child Abuse Prevention Network was created for professionals in the field of child abuse and neglect. Visit its site through the link at **www.ablongman.com/mcanulty2e.**

What are the network's key concerns? What are some recent statistics on the scope of the problem? What are the recommended procedures for reporting suspected child abuse?

Pedophilia

Pedophilia (literally, "love of children") is a paraphilia characterized by recurrent and intense sexual urges and fantasies involving sexual activity with a prepubertal child by a perpetrator who is at least 16 years old and at least 5 years older than the child. Specification of the preferred sex of the victim, the pedophile's relationship to the victim (incestuous or not), and whether the person is attracted only to children (exclusive pedophilia) or also attracted to adults (nonexclusive pedophilia) is important when describing this paraphilia (APA, 2000). Like most paraphilias, pedophilia is almost exclusively reported in males, although some cases of female pedophiles have been described.

Some writers refer to pedophiles who are attracted to boys as "homosexual" pedophiles and to those attracted to girls as "heterosexual" pedophiles. This book uses the terms "same-sex" and "opposite-sex" pedophiles instead. Opposite-sex pedophiles are more common than same-sex pedophiles. Pedophiles attracted to both sexes are uncommon. Several studies (Groth & Birnbaum, 1978; Lanyon, 1986) have reported significant differences between same-sex pedophiles and opposite-sex pedophiles. For example, same-sex pedophiles often have a large number of victims, whereas opposite-sex pedophiles typically molest only a few children (Abel et al., 1987). Opposite-sex and same-sex pedophiles also differ in that opposite-sex pedophiles typically know their victims and repeat the pedophilic acts with them for a number of months or years (Lukianowicz, 1972); same-sex perpetrators typically do not know their victims, and usually commit only one offense with each victim. The average age of the victim may also differ between opposite-sex and same-sex pedophiles: Same-sex pedophiles often choose older children as victims. In most cases, victims are between 6 and 12 years of age (Groth & Birnbaum, 1978). However, children of any age may be victimized. Table 15.4 compares characteristics of same-sex and opposite-sex pedophiles.

PEDOPHILIA
A paraphilia characterized by recurrent fantasies, urges, or acts involving sexual activity with prepubertal children.

The type of sexual activity between a pedophile and the victim ranges from fondling to oral-genital contact and actual penetration (Erikson, Walbek, & Seeley, 1988). Among opposite-sex pedophiles, fondling of the child is most common, although cunnilingus

TABLE 15.4 Characteristics of Opposite-Sex and Same-Sex Pedophiles

OPPOSITE-SEX PEDOPHILES	SAME-SEX PEDOPHILES
Fewer victims	Many victims (up to hundreds)
Offender knows victims	Offender does not know victims
Offenses repeated with victim for many months or years	Fewer offenses with each victim
Younger victims, on average	Older victims, on average
Offender is also attracted to adults	Offender has little or no sexual interest in adults
Offender is typically married	Offender is generally single
Offenses often begin in adulthood	Offenses begin in adolescence
Sexual activity tends to be impulsive	Sexual activity is planned
Offender often is of lower socioeconomic status and has lower IQ; offender often has other impulse-control problems	Offender usually has stable employment, is of higher socioeconomic status; offender has average IQ and is socially immature, prefers company of children

SOURCE: Adapted from McConaghy, 1993

and penile-vaginal contact are not rare. For same-sex pedophiles, fondling is also the most common activity, followed by performance of fellatio on the victim. Penile-anal contact occurs in about one-third of the cases of same-sex pedophilia.

In contrast to same-sex pedophiles, opposite-sex pedophiles are commonly married and show some sexual attraction to adult women (Groth & Birnbaum, 1978). Same-sex pedophiles are more likely to be single and typically do not show significant sexual arousal toward adults of either sex. For these pedophiles, pedophilic behavior usually begins in adolescence, whereas opposite-sex pedophiles' interest in children may not emerge until adulthood (Groth & Birnbaum, 1978).

did YOU know?

Contrary to popular belief, pedophiles are not "dirty old men"; the majority of incarcerated child molesters are in their mid-20s to mid-30s.

Researchers who study pedophilia commonly make a distinction between *preferential* and *situational* pedophilia (Lanyon, 1986). Preferential pedophiles are attracted primarily or exclusively to children, and they tend to be unmarried. Same-sex pedophiles are usually preferential molesters. Groth and Birnbaum (1978) characterized these individuals as unable to establish relationships with adults; thus, their sexual development is considered to be blocked. They tend to be more comfortable socially and sexually with children and to have poor heterosexual skills. Because of these social-skill deficits, same-sex pedophiles have higher recidivism (relapse) rates after incarceration or treatment (Marshall & Barbaree, 1990). Opposite-sex pedophiles tend to be situational molesters. Incestuous child molesters are primarily classified as situational. As mentioned earlier, these individuals are likely to be married and to have some sexual experience with adult partners. Situational pedophiles' sexual activity with children tends to be impulsive, whereas most preferential perpetrators' encounters with children are premeditated.

15.4 on the web

Can sex offenders be helped with treatment? Contrary to popular belief, treatment seems to help. Go to **www.ablongman.com/mcanulty2e** and review the summary of recent evidence. *Does treatment reduce recidivism rates? By how much? What seems to help?*

Many studies have focused on the patterns of sexual arousal of child molesters. Such research relies on the penile plethysmograph to measure offenders' sexual arousal in response to films or photographs depicting adult men and women or children of both sexes. Nonincestuous, or exclusive, child molesters often reveal a sexual preference for prepubertal partners by exhibiting more penile erection to stimuli involving children than to those involving adults (Marshall, Barbaree, & Butt, 1988). Incestuous pedophiles, however, tend to show patterns of arousal similar to those of

Defrocked Catholic priest John Geoghan watches as an alleged victim enters the courtroom to testify that Geoghan molested him sexually. Victims assert that Geoghan's bishop did nothing to prevent Geoghan from repeatedly molesting young children, and the case initiated a crisis in the Catholic church.

normal heterosexual adult men (Marshall, Barbaree, & Christophe, 1986; Quinsey, Chaplin, & Carrigan, 1979). Apparently, nonsexual motives play an important role in incest, and some incestuous child molesters may not be true pedophiles. In other words, these incestuous offenders may not show intense and recurrent fantasies and urges centering on immature children, as is typical of pedophiles. These findings reinforce some theorists' speculation that incest is best understood in the context of a dysfunctional family and a deeply troubled marriage.

Pedophiles are often described as shy, unassertive, and socially withdrawn. However, a review of the characteristics of some pedophiles concluded that there seems to be no "classic pedophile" profile (Okami & Goldberg, 1992). Studies attempting to construct personality profiles of pedophilic individuals using psychological tests have yielded mixed findings. Although many pedophiles report feeling significant social anxiety and unassertiveness and holding rigid stereotypes of women, not all of them do (Overholser & Beck, 1986). Many child molesters are alcoholics, but some are otherwise law-abiding citizens, as illustrated by several cases of priests who sexually molested children. It is increasingly clear that pedophiles are quite variable in most respects (McAnulty, Adams, & Wright, 1994).

Popular theories have suggested that the typical pedophile is a socially and perhaps mentally handicapped individual who seeks out children because they are emotionally and interpersonally similar to the perpetrator (Langevin, 1983). Pedophiles have also been popularly characterized as exhibiting the "village idiot" syndrome (Wilson & Cox, 1983), but research findings contradict this stereotype. The impression that pedophiles lack intelligence may have originated from samples of child molesters who were senile or mentally retarded. However, some pedophiles are educated professionals, and most have normal intelligence. Interestingly, one study found some pedophiles who claimed to have strong religious beliefs (McAnulty & Loupis, 1999).

The Internet has apparently become a popular forum for individuals with pedophilic tendencies. The Internet allows users an inexpensive, safe, and efficient means of transmitting and exchanging child pornography (O'Grady, 2001). Investigations have uncovered international rings devoted to exchanging sexually explicit materials involving children. In Great Britain alone, investigators found computer files containing three quarters of a million images of child pornography (Nordland et al., 2001). Many, if not most, individuals who collect and exchange child pornography are pedophiles. Internet chat rooms offer a convenient venue for some pedophiles who are seeking victims. Often posing as teenagers, offenders attempt to contact potential victims and form a cyber-relationship with them, in the hope of eventually meeting them. This is a fairly common strategy, as evidenced by the fact that as many as one in five teenagers who uses the Internet reports having received an online sexual solicitation. It is likely that some of these solicitations came from pedophiles.

Other Paraphilias

Table 15.1 lists a total of 15 paraphilias. However, it has been suggested that many other forms exist but rarely come to the attention of mental health or legal professionals. Renowned sexologist John Money (1986) listed over 60 different paraphilias, the majority of which are not included in the American Psychiatric Association's DSM-IV-*TR* (2000). Money has even coined his own terms to describe atypical sexual fantasies and urges. His views will be considered in the next section, on the explanations of atypical sexual behavior. This section discusses the other types of paraphilias recognized by the American Psychiatric Association. (Partialism was discussed under fetishism, with which it is usually associated.)

TELEPHONE SCATOLOGIA
A paraphilia in which sexual arousal is derived from subjecting another person to obscene or inappropriate sexual language over the telephone.

Telephone scatologia, or lewdness, involves deriving sexual pleasure from making obscene phone calls. It may represent a form of exhibitionism in which the victim is the listener and is exposed to obscene language (Alford, Webster, & Sanders, 1980). This is a common paraphilia. Approximately one-third of female college students and over 10% of male college students have received obscene phone calls (Matek, 1988; Murray & Beran, 1968). Such telephone services as caller identification and call tracing probably deter some would-be obscene phone callers.

Necrophilia entails sexual activity with corpses. Access to a morgue or funeral parlor is essential for a person with this paraphilia (Money, 1986). The primary motive for necrophilia is to have a nonresistant and nonrejecting sexual partner.

Zoophilia, or bestiality, is defined as sexual activity with animals. The preferred animal is usually one the person was exposed to during adolescence, as a family pet or farm animal. Although some young males may experiment with sexual activity with animals, this activity does not constitute a paraphilia unless the pattern is repetitive.

Coprophilia and **urophilia** involve sexual urges and acts associated with feces and urine, respectively. Although some sadomasochists and fetishists engage in these practices, they are believed to be quite uncommon. "Water sports" and "golden showers" are slang terms for urophilic practices.

Klismaphilia involves becoming sexually aroused from administering or receiving enemas. Although some individuals may use enemas as a sanitary practice prior to anal sex, this practice would not constitute a paraphilia unless it included sexual fantasies and urges centering on the enema itself. The majority of practitioners of klismaphilia are heterosexual men (Arndt, 1991).

EXPLANATIONS OF ATYPICAL SEXUAL BEHAVIOR

As this book has stressed, human sexual behavior is determined by a myriad of biological, psychological, and sociocultural factors that interact to shape sexual attitudes, fantasies, urges, and practices. This is also true of sexual fantasies and acts that are categorized as atypical.

Biological Factors

Early writers, such as Krafft-Ebing, believed that atypical sexual behavior was the result of physiological dysfunction—namely, defects in the nervous system. According to Krafft-Ebing, such abnormalities might be inherited or might develop later in life from damage to the brain. Such views seemed to be supported by case studies. More specifically, changes in sexual behavior, including the appearance of behaviors such as fetishism, exhibitionism, and pedophilia, have been reported following brain injuries (Cummings, 1985; Epstein, 1961; Langevin, 1990).

Changes in sexual behavior have also been reported in several men with epilepsy. Most commonly, the affected area of the brain is the temporal lobe (Cummings, 1985). Fetishism is the paraphilia most often associated with epilepsy, although some instances of pedophilia have also been reported to result from it (Regenstein & Reich, 1978). Dysfunction in the frontal lobes has also been found to be associated with some cases of sexual sadism. However, only limited support has come from more controlled studies that use sophisticated brain-imaging technologies (Langevin, Wortzman, Wright, & Handy, 1989). Furthermore, it should be noted that the majority of epileptics and other persons with neurological problems do *not* exhibit paraphilic behavior. Thus, if brain dysfunction plays a role in causing atypical sexual behavior, it is only relevant in some cases, perhaps only the most severe ones (Galski, Thornton, & Shumsky, 1990). In fact, brain dysfunctions may be more strongly associated with a propensity for violence than with atypical sexuality.

The possible role of heredity in atypical sexual behavior has largely been ignored by researchers, and so remains unknown. Research on abnormalities in sex hormones, especially testosterone, has produced conflicting results. If these hormones do play a role, it is likely to be a small one in only a limited number of cases (Hucker & Bain, 1990).

NECROPHILIA
A paraphilia characterized by sexual activity with a corpse.

ZOOPHILIA
A paraphilia that involves sexual activity with animals.

COPROPHILIA
A paraphilia involving sexual arousal in response to feces.

UROPHILIA
A paraphilia characterized by sexual arousal in response to urine; typically, a person has a desire to be urinated on ("golden shower").

KLISMAPHILIA
A paraphilia involving sexual arousal in response to giving or receiving enemas.

Psychological Factors

Psychological explanations of atypical sexual behavior have been most popular in recent years. According to such explanations, life experiences are critical in the development of atypical sexual fantasies, urges, and activities. In other words, sexual urges and practices are the product of learning.

How and why does a person develop unusual or deviant sexual urges? To find the answers, researchers usually study an individual or a group of people who admit to the sexual behavior in question or who have been charged with a sex crime. These studies rely on self-reports and, therefore, are susceptible to the limitations discussed in Chapter 2. Also, because of difficulties inherent in recruiting people who have unusual sexual interests, most studies have examined the more serious paraphilias, those involving nonconsenting partners. A few studies have surveyed members of organizations catering to "specialized interests" (for example, the members of the Foot Fraternity for gay and bisexual foot fetishists, mentioned earlier). Typically, individuals complete anonymous surveys for these studies. With few exceptions, the studies have had only male participants. Because of these research strategies, the generalizability of the findings is sometimes questionable. Studies of the causes of atypical sexual behavior have explored a number of developmental factors, which are examined next.

Childhood Family Environment

Child molesters commonly report familial chaos in their childhoods (Marshall & Marshall, 2000). Up to half of adolescent pedophiles report growing up in an unstable family characterized by parental neglect and marital conflict (Pithers, Kashima, Cumming, Beal, & Buell, 1988). A large number of adolescent sex offenders claim that they endured physical abuse and neglect; estimates of its prevalence range from 41% (Van Ness, 1984) to 75% (Lewis, Shankok, & Pincus, 1979). In particular, being physically abused by a father seems to increase the risk of sexual aggression in adolescent offenders; a lack of emotional bonding with the mother also increases this risk (Kobayashi, Sales, Becker, Figueredo, & Kaplan, 1995). Over two-thirds of rapists and half of child molesters report that their home environment was so unpleasant that they ran away from home as children (Davidson, 1983). A majority of rapists and child molesters state that their fathers abused alcohol and drugs, and this, undoubtedly, contributed to the physical and emotional abuse and neglect in their histories (Bard et al., 1987).

Like child molesters and rapists, many exhibitionists (nearly half of one sample) report that they felt emotionally rejected by their parents as children or adolescents (Marshall, Payne, Barbaree, & Eccles, 1991). Voyeurs also commonly report a disturbed relationship with their parents (Langevin et al., 1985). Mother-son conflict and separation from the mother are common childhood scenarios for males with transvestic fetishism (Zucker & Bradley, 1995). Growing up in a dysfunctional family, however, is not a universal experience for persons with paraphilias. Though many of these individuals recall growing up in an unpleasant and dysfunctional family environment, others report a normal family history.

Sexual Experiences and Attitudes

Because the formative years are critical in sexual development, early experiences with sexuality may have a great deal of influence. For instance, the period from ages 5 to 8 has been described as critical in the formation of sexual urges and fantasies (Money, 1986). Therefore, early sexual experiences—including sexual trauma, sex education, and exposure to parental attitudes toward sexuality—are important in understanding both normal and abnormal sexual development. Money introduced the concept of a *lovemap,* a person's mental representation of, or template for, the ideal lover and ideal romantic and erotic relationship. During the early years of life, this lovemap exists as mental imagery—urges and fantasies that are eventually translated into sexual activity with a partner, usually beginning in adolescence (Money, 1986).

In Money's (1986) terminology, a person's lovemap may be "vandalized" in childhood by sexual trauma or parental suppression or prohibition of sexual rehearsal play. In support of this view, being sexually molested in childhood is commonly reported by paraphiliacs. However, contrary to popular belief, not all sex offenders were themselves the victims of sexual abuse; it is a common, although by no means universal, experience. Among convicted child molesters, up to half report being sexually abused in childhood or adolescence (Weeks & Widom, 1998). The corresponding figure for rapists is approximately 25% (Bard et al., 1987). Being the victim of sexual abuse by another male has been associated with sexual aggression in adolescent sex offenders (Kobayashi et al., 1995). Overall, the rate of childhood sexual victimization among aggressive sex offenders is higher than it is among nonoffenders and nonviolent paraphiliacs. Therefore, early sexual abuse seems to be an important precursor of aggressive sexual behavior, and it is more commonly reported by pedophiles and rapists.

Indirect exposure to atypical sexual behavior is also common in the histories of convicted sex offenders. Approximately 20% of rapists and 30% of child molesters recall witnessing unusual sexual behavior in their families that did not directly involve them (Bard et al., 1987). Thus, observational learning, or modeling, may play a role in the development of paraphilias. Some individuals with paraphilias appear to have acquired their deviant sexual urges and fantasies through a process of imitation (Kobayashi et al., 1995).

In some cases, early sexual experiences may incidentally condition atypical sexual fantasies and urges (McGuire, Carlisle, & Young, 1965). For example, one male teenager was accidentally seen by a female while he was urinating in a public place. By later incorporating memories of this experience into his masturbation fantasies, and thereby mentally associating genital exposure with orgasm, he conditioned an association between exposing himself and sexual satisfaction. Thus, the exposing behavior was reinforced and became part of his lovemap. A similar pattern is reported in the histories of some foot fetishists. A majority of respondents in one study recalled having a sexually pleasurable experience with another person's feet in childhood or adolescence (Weinberg et al., 1995).

Looking At . . .

. . . Thinking About

As you learned in Chapter 11, sexual development begins at birth and is a lifelong process. Early experiences of intimacy, sexual rehearsal play, and parental models set the stage for the formation of a healthy identity and the building of meaningful relationships. Problems in any one of these areas can compromise healthy sexual development. How do such experiences as neglect and abuse jeopardize sexual development?

Exposure to sexually explicit materials has been proposed as a cause of deviant sexuality. Approximately one-third of child molesters and rapists report being exposed to sexually explicit materials in adolescence (Marshall, 1988). However, the amount of such exposure is no higher among these sex offenders than among nonoffenders. In a review of the existing findings, Murrin and Laws (1990) concluded

> it is not exposure to pornography per se that has an influence on sexual crime, but rather the nature of the person being exposed and the existing cultural milieu in which the exposure occurs. In a cultural environment where people are not considered sexual objects, pornography would have little effect on sexual crime. (p. 89)

It seems highly unlikely that exposure to sexually explicit materials alone could transform a person with normal sexual urges into a dangerous sex offender. However, for individuals predisposed to committing sexual offenses, such exposure may precipitate sexual aggression (Seto, Maric, & Barbaree, 2001). Predisposing factors may include a chaotic home environment during childhood, a history of significant abuse or neglect, and the presence of interpersonal inadequacies, which are considered next.

Social Skills Deficits

Social skills deficits, or difficulties in forming relationships, have traditionally been viewed as characteristic of paraphiliacs (Lee, Pattison, Jackson, & Ward, 2001; Segal & Stermac, 1990). According to this view, because of their social incompetence, men with paraphilias may be unable to build and maintain mutually rewarding relationships with other adults, especially women. Similarly, it has been suggested that many pedophiles seek the company of children because they feel less threatened by children than by adult women (Lanyon, 1986). In support of this view, studies show that pedophiles often have problems being assertive, hold rigid stereotypes about women, and report fears of being viewed negatively by others (Overholser & Beck, 1986). Further, pedophiles report feeling more social anxiety than do rapists (Segal & Marshall, 1985).

Indirect evidence of social skills deficits is found in retrospective studies of other types of atypical sexual behavior. For instance, many exhibitionists and voyeurs recall being shy as teenagers and have difficulty with dating. Up to 60% of exhibitionists and 72% of child molesters recall having no close friends as children (Saunders, Awad, & White, 1986). Similarly, over half of one sample of fetishists reported having few friends as teenagers (Weinberg et al., 1995). However, it is important to understand that not all persons with atypical sexual interests exhibit social skills deficits. And most people with social skills deficits probably do not experience atypical sexual urges and fantasies. Thus, although interpersonal and social difficulties play a role in the development of some paraphilias, other factors—such as sociocultural ones—also contribute to atypical sexual behavior.

Sociocultural Factors

The United States has one of the highest rates of sexual aggression in the Western world. What sociocultural factors account for this high rate of sexual coercion? Why are coercive paraphilias virtually nonexistent in other parts of the world?

In the United States, England, Germany, and Canada, exhibitionism is one of the most commonly reported paraphilias. It is apparently uncommon in Italy and France and is reportedly quite rare in South America and in most Middle Eastern, African, and Asian countries. However, it is commonly reported in Chinese populations, including in Hong Kong (Rooth, 1972, 1973a). Higher rates of sexual aggression against women are reported in cultures that condone male domination and the exploitation of women (Costin, 1985). Specifically, cultures that endorse rigid gender-role stereotypes tend to have higher reported rates of rape.

Cross-cultural differences in noncoercive atypical sexual behavior have also been reported. Sadomasochism, for example, is confined to Western cultures in which dominance and submission permeate gender roles and relationships, and in which aggression is socially acceptable or even valued. In such cultures, power imbalances are pervasive and the illusion of either taking or giving up control can be sexually arousing, depending on a person's status in that society. These cultures also tend to be affluent enough that some individuals can afford the luxury of playing games, including sexual role-playing. Finally, since simulated domination and control are essential to the sexual scripts of sadomasochists (Bullough & Bullough, 1995), sadomasochistic practices are more common in cultures that value creativity, imagination, and leisure.

The fact that paraphilias occur almost exclusively in males must be considered in any theory that attempts to explain them. Western culture seems to develop in males a highly sexualized view of the world (Marshall & Eccles, 1993). Additionally, males more than females are conditioned to perceive sexual aggression as acceptable in some

CLOSE UP ON culture

The History of Cross-Dressing

Throughout history, different cultures have attached different meanings to cross-dressing (Bullough & Bullough, 1993). In some cultures, cross-dressing had religious or ritualistic significance. Ancient Greek religious ceremonies often included rites in which men wore women's clothing. In addition, Greek actors dressed as women to play female roles because women were prohibited from acting on the stage. In contrast, Jewish tradition prohibited cross-dressing: "The woman shall not wear that which pertaineth unto a man, neither shall a man put on a woman's garment" (Deuteronomy 22:5). This admonition was apparently a reaction to the religious rituals of rival groups, including the Syrians and the Greeks (Bullough & Bullough, 1993).

Medieval authorities also disapproved of cross-dressing, especially by men. Because women held a low status in society, for a man to cross-dress would represent an unacceptable loss of social status. However, cross-dressing in women was more understandable, since it could result in significantly higher social status and privileges. As an exception, female impersonation on the stage continued to be an accepted practice in the 16th and 17th centuries. All dramatic productions featured cross-dressed men or boys playing the women's roles.

One basis for religious authorities' opposition to cross-dressing was its association with homosexuality. For example, Philippe d'Orléans, the brother of French king Louis XIV, was a notorious homosexual cross-dresser. He was occasionally seen in the king's palace in full female costume. The image of male cross-dressers as homosexual was bolstered by the establishment of cross-dressing clubs in 18th-century London. Known as "Molly clubs" (Trumbach, 1977), they are recognized as the first formal gay organizations in England. These clubs, along with a few highly visible and well-known cross-dressers, brought cross-dressing to a new level (Nixon, 1965); no longer was it only a theatrical performance.

Unlike transvestites, drag queens do not cross-dress to experience sexual arousal. They impersonate women to earn a living, to make a social or political statement, or simply for fun.

A significant change in the style of women's dress occurred in the 19th and 20th centuries in Western cultures. Fashions increasingly emphasized female shapes and sexual attractiveness. Contemporary writings increasingly revealed male fascination with such women's clothing items as underwear and high heels—in some cases to the extent of constituting fetishism. At the same time, fetishistic cross-dressing by heterosexual men was reported by several sources (Bullough & Bullough, 1993).

During the late 19th and early 20th centuries, pioneering sexologists such as Havelock Ellis and Krafft-Ebing began describing the phenomenon of cross-dressing. Their contemporary, Magnus Hirschfeld, coined the term "transvestism" in his book *The Transvestites: An Investigation of the Erotic Drive to Cross Dress,* published in 1910. By the time of Hirschfeld's writing, cross-dressing had come to the attention of many sectors of society, including medical professionals and the public at large, and the phenomenon was a crime in many European countries.

The observations of the early sexologists remain valid in many respects. There are multiple motives for cross-dressing, and the meaning of cross-dressing can vary tremendously, depending on a person's gender, social role, gender identity, and sexual orientation. Hirschfeld's ideas about transvestism are retained in the modern label "transvestic fetishism," which applies to heterosexual men, for whom cross-dressing is sexually arousing. Cross-dressing is also associated with gender identity disorder; in those cases, it is not usually associated with erotic desires. Rather, the opposite-sex clothing fits the person's gender identity. Homosexual cross-dressing can be a form of entertainment, a political statement, or even a job; drag queens, or female impersonators, are popular entertainers at some nightclubs (Newton, 1972).

In all likelihood, there are probably other, less common motives for cross-dressing. The persistence of this activity throughout history and across diverse cultures suggests that it meets important needs for some individuals. The phenomenon is not new, nor is it limited to a few deviant individuals—but many people still find it perplexing.

situations. Sources of these messages may include parental relationships, the media, and peer influences. As this book has emphasized, culture plays an important part in determining what is normal and acceptable sexual behavior. Society shapes our views of acceptable gender behavior and roles, and one example of how this happens is explored in Close Up on Culture: The History of Cross-Dressing.

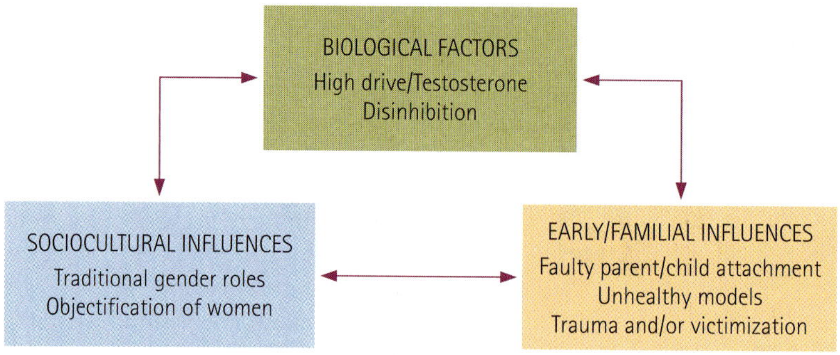

Figure 15.1 A Multifactor Theory of Coercive Paraphilia
(SOURCE: Marshall & Barbaree, 1990)

A Multifactor Theory of Coercive Paraphilias

One theory of coercive paraphilias takes into account biological, behavioral, and sociocultural factors, as illustrated in Figure 15.1 (Marshall & Barbaree, 1990). This model proposes an interaction among three factors: (1) a biological drive to be sexually aggressive, which may be exacerbated by hormonal changes at puberty; (2) early learning experiences, poor modeling, or dysfunctional parenting; and (3) negative sociocultural attitudes and beliefs, especially those relating to adult intimacy and relationships with women. According to this formulation, a lack of intimacy in adulthood and the resulting experience of loneliness predispose some individuals to sexually aggressive behavior (Garlick, Marshall, & Thornton, 1996). This deficiency in adult intimacy may interact with sociocultural influences, precocious sexualization, conditioning experiences, and biological factors to further the development and maintenance of atypical sexual behavior (Marshall & Eccles, 1993).

The developmental history of sex offenders may reflect inadequate parent-child attachment early in life, which may render them vulnerable to becoming sexually coercive (Marshall & Marshall, 2000; Smallbone & Dadds, 1998). The child with poor parental attachment is likely to lack the skills and self-confidence necessary for mastering the social challenges in the transition to adolescence. As a vulnerable male undergoes puberty, he experiences emerging sexual urges while feeling socially inept, especially with female peers. Thus, such an individual is believed to be especially susceptible to nonthreatening sexual scripts (Marshall & Eccles, 1993). Examples of nonthreatening scripts for a socially incompetent male might be child molestation, voyeurism, and fetishism. Likewise, for a male who fears intimacy, nonconsenting sexual activity, including rape, may be less threatening than consensual sex. Such an individual may also be influenced by cultural messages perpetuating gender-role stereotypes, such as the view that males are naturally aggressive and women are inherently passive. The presence of any disinhibiting influences, including drug abuse and brain damage, may further increase the risk that any existing deviant urges will be enacted. Table 15.5 lists some possible factors that may underlie the aggressive sexual behavior of pedophiles and rapists.

It appears that no single experience or biological or sociocultural factor fully explains why some individuals develop coercive paraphilias or why these are much more prevalent in men than in women. Undoubtedly, an interaction between psychological, biological, and cultural variables is responsible for shaping atypical sexual behaviors. Early childhood experiences seem to predispose some individuals; these experiences, combined with low self-esteem and social isolation, further increase risks

TABLE 15.5 Precursors of Sexual Aggression by Rapists and Pedophiles

PRECURSORS	PERCENTAGE OF SAMPLE *Rapists*	*Pedophiles*
Cognitive impairment (IQ < 80)	9	10
Divorce (more than 5 years before act)	14	15
Exposure to violent death of human or animals	22	2
Familial chaos	86	49
Late sexual experience (older than 25 at initial activity)	0	4
Limited education (< grade 9 completed)	44	26
Maternal absence/neglect	41	29
More than one prior sex offense	14	17
More than one known victim	30	60
Parental marital discord	59	45
Parental absence/neglect	59	54
Physically abused as child	45	7
Pornography use (habitual)	14	33
Precocious sexuality (< 12 years at time of first act of penetration not considered abuse)	14	30
Prior arrest for nonsexual offense	44	15
Sexual anxiety	39	58
Sexual dysfunction	11	11
Sexual victimization		
Prior to age 12	5	56
Between ages 12 and 18	11	6
Use of female prostitutes	30	8

SOURCE: Pithers et al., 1988

of developing unusual sexual urges after puberty. Exposure to significant abuse and to cultural norms that condone violence against women may contribute to the development of a propensity for sexual aggression.

TREATMENT OF PROBLEMATIC SEXUAL BEHAVIOR

There has been tremendous interest in developing strategies for treating paraphilias that are considered problematic—especially those that involve nonconsenting partners. Most treatments are designed to address atypical sexual behavior that is harmful to others, illegal, or distressing to the individual.

There is a common belief that coercive paraphilias cannot be successfully treated and that persons with these problems are therefore incapable of changing. But research does not support this belief. Although a review of studies on the topic concluded that recidivism (relapse) rates among sex offenders are near 55% (Heilbrun, Nezu, Keeney, Chung, & Wasserman, 1998), other studies have shown that treatment is in fact beneficial. From his review of treatment studies of sex offenders, Hall (1995) concluded that treatment produces a 30% decrease in recidivism. Rather than a cure, most researchers believe that treatment provides offenders with increased self-control, very much the way AA and similar programs help alcoholics refrain from drinking.

Two general intervention strategies have shown promise: cognitive-behavioral treatment and pharmacological approaches.

Cognitive-Behavioral Treatment

Cognitive-behavioral treatment is a collection of procedures, including social skills training, assertiveness training, and sex education, that aim to increase appropriate social and sexual interactions and decrease deviant sexual fantasies and behaviors (Marshall & Serran, 2000). These strategies also target the problems with adult intimacy and the sexual anxiety that are common in sex offenders. Other behavioral procedures are designed to decrease deviant sexual desires and fantasies (Barbaree, Bogaert, & Seto, 1995). One such procedure is *covert sensitization,* which consists of having offenders repeatedly visualize a deviant fantasy that is followed by a highly aversive consequence. Covert sensitization scenes include three components: (1) the buildup of a deviant sexual fantasy and urge, (2) an aversive consequence, and (3) an escape from the scene. Following is an actual example used by a male whose fantasies were of exposing himself to schoolgirls:

> As you see their young faces, you start to get hard. You can feel your penis stiffening as you rub it. They notice you! You call the girls over to your car. They don't know what's waiting for them. As they approach, you take it out and begin to jerk off violently. The girls are shocked. They don't know what to do. They're just staring at it as you're about to come, but suddenly there's pain—you've got your penis stuck in your pants zipper. You try to yank it free but it only catches more. It's starting to bleed and you go soft. The kids are laughing and a policeman is coming over . . . (from Maletzky, 1997, p. 54)

The advantages of covert sensitization are that it is simple to use, causes no side effects, and targets fantasies and urges that trigger the deviant sexual behavior. The procedure in its various forms may be a useful component of treatment for some paraphilias (Maletzky, 1997).

Cognitive components targeting distorted thinking and beliefs have also become essential in the treatment of sex offenders (Marshall & Barbaree, 1990). Cognitive therapy with child molesters involves confronting and modifying the common false beliefs that children desire sex with adults or that sex is not really harmful to children. In addition, a treatment approach used with addictive behaviors, termed *relapse prevention,* has been extended to paraphilias. Relapse prevention teaches sex offenders to identify and avoid situations that present a high risk of reoffending. Avoiding alcohol, learning strategies for controlling anger, and finding ways to delay gratification are common goals of this approach. These procedures have yielded success in decreasing recidivism rates among sexual offenders (Pithers & Cumming, 1989).

Drug Treatment

Another approach to treatment of coercive paraphilias involves the use of medication. The goal of this intervention is to reduce deviant sexual arousal and urges by eliminating the individual's overall sex drive or ability to act out the deviant behavior. Pharmacological treatments use antiandrogen drugs (such as medroxyprogesterone acetate, or Depo-Provera) that suppress the production of testosterone, drugs known as "erotic tranquilizers" (Money, 1986). Unlike surgical castration, the effects of testosterone-suppressing drugs are largely reversible when the drugs are discontinued. Some pharmacological treatment studies of pedophiles and rapists have yielded promising results (Bradford, 1997; Gijs & Gooren, 1996). Another pharmacological approach uses antidepressants such as fluoxetine (Prozac). Although a decreased sex drive is an undesirable side effect for many people who take antidepressants, this side effect is desirable for individuals whose sexual behavior is illegal. A drug that lowers sex drive may help these individuals gain some control over their sexual behavior. Abouesh and Clayton (1999), for example, reported successfully treating a voyeur and an exhibitionist with Prozac.

Unfortunately, pharmacological treatments are not problem-free. First, the long-term effects of taking antiandrogen drugs are unknown. In the short term, they may cause undesirable side effects such as weight gain, testicular atrophy (shrinkage), and hypertension. Second, if the person discontinues taking the medication, the deviant fantasies and urges usually return. Finally, pharmacological treatments require a high level of motivation and compliance on the part of the person being treated. Antidepressants must be taken daily, preferably at the same time each day.

The purpose of the various treatments for paraphilias is ultimately to reduce deviant sexual arousal, to modify social skills deficits, to enhance self-esteem, and to teach procedures for improving self-control. Pharmacological approaches can be useful in helping to treat some paraphilias, but they should not be used alone. For persons with serious, longstanding sexual disorders, pharmacological and psychological treatments are usually offered in combination.

HEALTHY DECISION MAKING

This chapter's coverage of atypical sexual behavior probably triggered a range of reactions—from surprise to shock and dismay. Now that you've finished the chapter, think again about the question of what is normal with regard to sex.

Adopting a purely biological stance, it is possible to argue, as some religious writers have, that only sexual acts that can lead to reproduction are natural. Therefore, only heterosexual intercourse qualifies as normal, and anything else is unnatural and atypical. Such a rigid standard would be impractical and unrealistic, since the vast majority of people engage in nonreproductive sex. If the majority of people engage in "unnatural" sex acts, then the acts are not atypical.

Another viewpoint defines normal sexual behavior based on morality. The problem with this viewpoint is that moral codes vary across cultures, over time, and according to one's interpretation of the many moral principles.

A third standard relies on social norms: Normal sexual behavior includes any activity that is socially acceptable. The obvious limitation of this standard is that it would be impossible to attain consensus among members of any society on any topic—let alone a topic as sensitive as sex. Therefore, the meaning of "normal sex" is highly likely to vary across cultures, age groups, social networks, regions, and so on. Clearly, this approach is also impractical.

The most appropriate and realistic standard is that used by many sex researchers and sex therapists: The desire for pleasurable sex is a fundamental human need, and normal and acceptable sex encompasses any consenting sexual activity that brings pleasure and satisfaction to both partners. With this standard, several forms of atypical sexual behavior are classified as problematic. Exhibitionism, voyeurism, and frotteurism do not involve consensual and mutually pleasurable sexual activity. Similarly, pedophilia is deviant and problematic because children are not capable of giving consent and because such activity usually has long-term harmful effects on the victims, as you will learn in Chapter 16. Many other forms of sexual behavior discussed in this chapter, however, do not qualify as problematic. Although fetishism, transvestic fetishism, and sadomasochistic sex in all of its forms are relatively uncommon and atypical, they usually do involve consensual and mutually pleasurable sex.

Outside of coercive paraphilias such as pedophilia, few sexual interests are absolutely abnormal. Sexually speaking, "normal" and "abnormal" are not separate and exclusive categories but rather different points on a continuum. The notion of a continuum emphasizes that what is normal is usually more a matter of degree than an absolute. For example, the majority of heterosexual men show some sexual arousal to sexy lingerie. Such interest falls in the normal range of the continuum—whereas a male who cannot function sexually without some women's lingerie to touch or wear and who actually prefers using lingerie to having a sexual partner is at the abnormal end of the continuum.

summary

WHAT IS ATYPICAL SEXUAL BEHAVIOR?

- Throughout history and throughout the world, societies have defined normal and abnormal sexual practices and have attempted to prohibit those deemed abnormal. Religious views shape many attitudes about what is normal and abnormal. In Western societies, medical and psychological professionals have provided definitions and terminology. Changing social norms for sexual behavior make definitions of sexual disorders vary as well.
- Paraphilias involve sexual interests that center on objects, suffering or humiliation, or nonconsenting partners. They are more commonly reported in males and often last a lifetime. They can be classified as either noncoercive or coercive.

NONCOERCIVE ATYPICAL SEXUAL BEHAVIOR

- Sexual attraction to objects, such as shoes or women's underwear, is characteristic of fetishism. Fetishists usually require the item in their sexual activity and may prefer it to a partner.
- Transvestic fetishism is a paraphilia that occurs in heterosexual males who derive sexual pleasure from cross-dressing. Most transvestites are married and have traditionally masculine interests.
- For sexual sadists and masochists, sexual pleasure is associated with the experience of pain or humiliation. The majority of sadomasochists are involved in consensual sexual activities that involve role-playing with the theme of control.

COERCIVE ATYPICAL SEXUAL BEHAVIOR

- Exhibitionism involves exposing one's genitals to unsuspecting strangers. A relatively common paraphilia, it often takes on a compulsive quality.
- Voyeurs, or peepers, seek out opportunities to observe unsuspecting people who are undressing or having sex. The secretive and forbidden nature of voyeurism is essential to the voyeur.
- Frotteurism involves the urge to rub one's genitals against a nonconsenting person. This activity usually occurs in a crowded setting, such as in a subway or an elevator.
- Pedophilia, sexual attraction to prepubescent children, has several subtypes. Child molesters can be classified based on the gender of their victims and on their relationship to the victim. Opposite-sex pedophiles are more common. They tend to know their victims and to act impulsively. Same-sex pedophiles tend to choose older victims and to plan their activity in advance.

EXPLANATIONS OF ATYPICAL SEXUAL BEHAVIOR

- Biological factors may play a role in sexual deviation. Brain dysfunction has been implicated in several paraphilias, although it is more strongly associated with aggression than with atypical sexual behavior.

- A host of psychological factors—including negative childhood experiences, distorted sexual beliefs, sexual trauma, and social skills problems—have been implicated in a number of paraphilias. Sociocultural influences, such as rigid gender roles, also contribute to these sexual disorders.
- A multifactor theory integrates biological, psychological, and sociocultural influences in explaining the origins of atypical sexual behavior.

TREATMENT OF PROBLEMATIC SEXUAL BEHAVIOR

- The two main approaches to treating coercive paraphilias are cognitive-behavioral treatment and drug treatment. Both show promise in helping individuals with these problems to control their deviant urges.

CHAPTER 16

Sexual Coercion

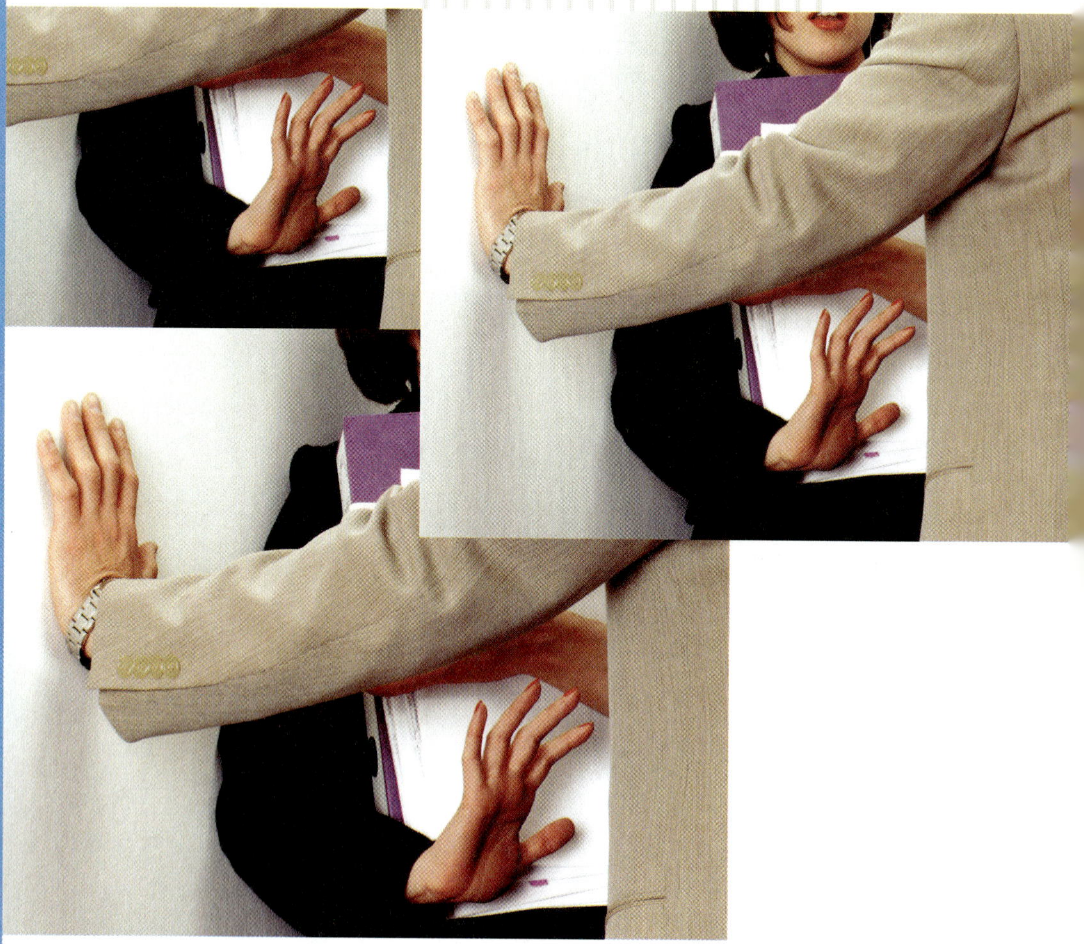

Jessica and Matthew were sitting on the couch watching a movie. Neither one had said much for the first part of the movie; they just ate popcorn and silently watched the movie. Occasionally, Matthew would crack a joke and Jessica would laugh.

About 20 minutes into the movie, Matthew put his arm around Jessica and kissed her. Jessica moved closer to Matthew, and they continued to watch the movie. Matthew slowly rubbed his hand along Jessica's arm and, after several minutes, moved his hand over her breast. He put both arms around Jessica, pulled her closer, and kissed her passionately, longer this time. Jessica and Matthew snuggled closer to each other. Matthew began rubbing his hand over the outside of Jessica's blouse and squeezed her breast. After several more minutes, he slipped his hand up under her blouse. As he pushed up her bra and began stroking her nipple, he kissed Jessica repeatedly. Matthew then unhooked her bra and began unbuttoning her blouse.

Matthew slid his hand down Jessica's breast and stomach. He whispered "You're so beautiful," as he slid his hand down to her thigh, pushed her skirt up, and gently stroked the outside of her panties along her crotch. Jessica took Matthew's hand and moved it away from her legs. She adjusted her skirt to cover herself. Matthew kissed her along the neck and cupped her breast in his hand, squeezing it softly. He moved his other hand down her thigh and toward her panties. Just as Jessica crossed her legs, Matthew took hold of her panties and pulled them down. Jessica again took Matthew's hand and attempted to adjust her skirt. He pulled her hand away and continued stroking her crotch. As Jessica held her legs together tightly, Matthew whispered, "Relax." Jessica whispered, "Matthew, please." He pressed his body up against hers and thrust his tongue between her lips.

He used force; she did not give her consent.

Matthew stroked her crotch with one hand and unzipped his pants with the other hand. Jessica was trembling and could not move under Matthew's weight as he pulled his jeans and briefs down. Matthew was breathing heavily, and Jessica could feel his hard penis against her. She squeezed her legs together tightly, locking them together. Matthew pushed her legs apart and thrust himself between her legs.

Adapted from R. Kenyon-Jump, *Detection of Sexual Cues: An Assessment of Nonaggressive and Sexually Coercive Males* (1992)

SEXUAL ASSAULT

Is the scenario described in the opening vignette an immoral and illegal act? It is a rather common scene, particularly among college-age adults. To some, it may appear to be a typical and acceptable initiation of sexual relations. However, most experts on the subject of sexual assault would

Looking At . . .

. . . Thinking About

Many people have misguided perceptions about what puts them at risk for rape. Which of these situations is more risky?

agree that Matthew's behavior is rape. **Rape** is generally defined as the occurrence of sexual intercourse by force or threat of force without the consent of the person against whom it is perpetrated (Benson, Charlton, & Goodhart, 1992). All the elements of this definition are found in the chapter-opening vignette: Matthew used force, Jessica did not give her consent, and intercourse occurred. Because he knew her, Matthew's actions are more specifically called acquaintance rape.

Acquaintance rape is the occurrence of nonconsensual sex between individuals who are acquainted. As the name implies, acquaintance rape often involves platonic friends, dating partners, marital partners, professional or academic colleagues, or family members. Two common forms of acquaintance rape are date rape and marital rape. **Date rape** refers specifically to nonconsensual sex between people who are dating or are on a date (Bechhofer & Parrot, 1991). **Marital rape** involves a husband forcing sexual intercourse on his wife. Less often, the assailant is someone that the victim does not know. This category of rape is referred to as **stranger rape.**

Statutory rape is a legally defined category of rape that involves sexual intercourse with a person who is under the legal age of consent. Unlike the other forms of rape, overt force or threat of force is not required, because individuals below a certain age are not considered capable of voluntarily giving their consent. Laws governing statutory rape vary across states and countries. In the United States, the age of consent ranges from age 14 to age 18. These laws once applied only to girls as victims, but today they are applied to male and female victims (Donovan, 1997).

Rape is one of many forms of sexual assault. **Sexual assault** is a broader term that refers to coercive sexual contact that does not necessarily involve penile-vaginal intercourse. Many states now prosecute several forms of sexual assault, including anal intercourse, oral-genital contact, and penetration of the vagina or anus by objects such as broom handles (Powell, 1991). Rape has traditionally been a highly "heterosexualized" concept—that is, until recently it was assumed that only females could be raped, and only by males. Rape of a woman by a man is still the most common type of sexual assault, but men are raped by women or other men, and women sometimes coerce other women into sexual activities (see Close Up on Culture: Coercive Sexuality in Same-Sex Relationships). All of these forms of sexual assault are now considered crimes.

RAPE
The occurrence of sexual intercourse by force or threat of force without the consent of the person against whom it is perpetrated.

ACQUAINTANCE RAPE
The occurrence of nonconsensual sex between individuals who are acquainted (for example, as relatives, friends, classmates, or coworkers).

DATE RAPE
A specific form of acquaintance rape that occurs in a dating situation.

MARITAL RAPE
A form of acquaintance rape that involves a husband forcing sexual intercourse on his wife.

STRANGER RAPE
Nonconsensual sex between individuals who do not know each other.

STATUTORY RAPE
Intercourse with an individual who is under the age of consent.

SEXUAL ASSAULT
Coercive sexual contact that does not necessarily involve penile-vaginal intercourse, but may include anal intercourse, oral-genital contact, or penetration of the vagina or anus by objects such as broom handles.

How Common Is Rape?

About 386,000 sexual assaults and attempted rapes and almost 141,000 completed rapes are reported by females and males combined to law enforcement agencies per year. However, only 36% of completed rapes, 34% of attempted rapes, and 26% of sexual assaults are ever reported to the police (Rennison, 2002). As you can see in the graph in Figure 16.1, the rate of reported rapes (including female and male victims) has generally declined since the late 1970s. In addition, a significant and steady decrease in reports of forcible rape has occurred since 1991.

Although most victims of rape do not report the rape to law enforcement authorities, they appear more willing to divulge to psychological researchers if they have ever been sexually assaulted. Research studies might, therefore, provide a more accurate indication of the true extent of rape. Overall, the lifetime prevalence of completed rapes in the United States has consistently remained around 15% for women since the mid-1980s, regardless of rape education and prevention efforts as well as legal interventions to reduce rape (Rozee & Koss, 2001). A study of college women alone showed that each year there are about 35 attempted or completed rapes for every 1,000 women on college campuses (Fisher, Cullen, & Turner, 2000). Much less is known about the prevalence of rape of men, but recent research

CLOSE UP ON culture

Coercive Sexuality in Same-Sex Relationships

Most of the attention given to rape has been directed at the most frequent form: the rape of females by heterosexual males. Much less attention has been given to coercive sexuality in same-sex relationships. The truth is that coercive sexual acts can occur in all types of relationships. Some reports suggest that both lesbians and gays have been forced or coerced to engage in sex more frequently than their heterosexual counterparts. One study, for example, found that 31% of lesbians reported having been forced to have sex (versus only 18% of heterosexual females). In addition, 12% of gay men (versus 4% of heterosexual men) reported having been forced to have sex (Duncan, 1990). The problem with this study and others, however, is that it does not separate out coercive heterosexual experiences of these lesbians and gays. It is especially common for lesbians to have had heterosexual relationships before coming out, and the reported numbers could easily include experiences in these prior relationships (Waldner-Haugrud & Gratch, 1997).

Waldner-Haugrud and Gratch (1997) conducted a study of coercive sexuality in same-sex relationships. These researchers expected that, consistent with theories on coercive heterosexual sexuality and male socialization, some form of sexual coercion would be found more frequently in gay relationships than in lesbian relationships. In addition, they expected to find that gay men would be more likely to experience more extreme and violent forms of coercion (e.g., being held down physically versus being lied to). The researchers found, however, that 57% of gay men versus 45% of lesbians had experienced some form of sexual coercion. The difference was not statistically significant. In addition, the forms of coercion experienced did not differ significantly between the two groups. For example, 33% of gay men and 32% of lesbians reported unwanted fondling, and 55% of gay men versus 50% of lesbians experienced unwanted penetration. The two groups also did not differ with respect to the types of coercive tactics used (e.g., guilt trips, alcohol, physical restraint, threats of force).

Although this study began to clarify some of the dynamics in coercive same-sex relationships, substantially more research is needed. The findings, which suggest that the gender differences found in heterosexual relationships are not found in same-sex relationships, require further analysis. Is it possible that gay men underreport coercive experiences as much as heterosexual men do? Are there particular dynamics in lesbian relationships that allow more coercive sexuality than one might expect to occur in a two-female relationship? As the culture increasingly acknowledges diversity in relationships, more research on some of these fascinating questions should be forthcoming.

reveals prevalence rates ranging between 2 and 3% (Coxell, King, Mezey, & Gordon, 1999; Rozee & Koss, 2001). About 36,000 cases of sexual assault, attempted rape, or completed rape are reported by males over the age of 12 in the United States each year (Rennison, 2002). In a British survey, 3% of the men reported being survivors of nonconsensual sex as adults (Coxell et al., 1999). This statistic is consistent with an

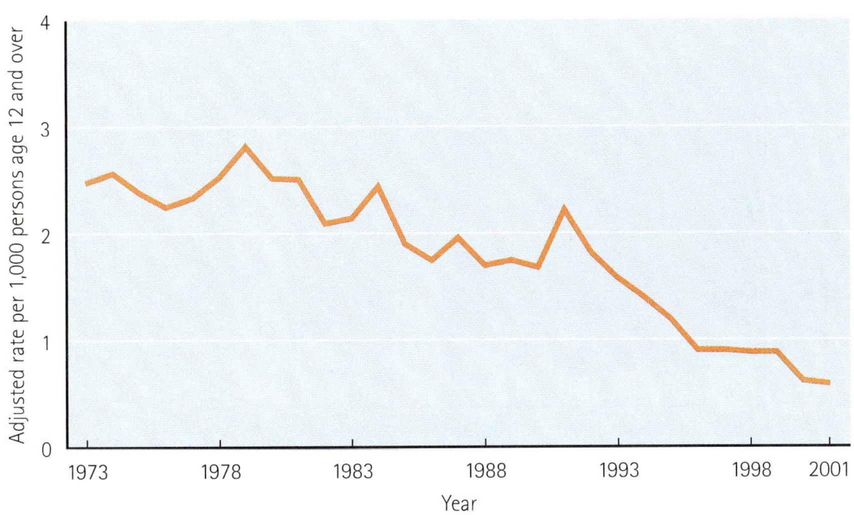

Figure 16.1 Change in Forcible Rape, 1973–2001
SOURCE: The National Crime Victimization Survey (NCVS), www.ojp.usdoj.gov/bjs

did YOU know?

Three out of every 100 adult men are victims of sexual assault.

estimate that 3% of U.S. men are victims of rape or attempted rape at some time in their lives (Tjaden & Thoennes, 2000).

Acquaintance Rape

Close to 86% of women know their rapists, and 40% of men know their rapists. Figure 16.2 provides a breakdown of rape and physical assault by relationship of victims to perpetrators. While these data do not separate out victims of rape alone, they do include data on males for comparison purposes, which is a rarity. In addition, they are consistent with other findings, and perhaps even underestimate the number of women who were raped by someone they knew. Laumann and his colleagues, for example, found that 96% of female victims knew their perpetrators (Laumann, Gagnon, Michael, & Michaels, 1994).

did YOU know?

Almost two-thirds of all rapes of women are committed by someone the victim knows well—a boyfriend, date, spouse, or ex-spouse.

Unfortunately, many victims of acquaintance rape fail to identify themselves as victims of a rape, largely because of their preexisting belief that most rapes are perpetrated by strangers—a belief that does not match the experience of being coerced into sex by an acquaintance (Hickman & Muehlenhard, 1997; Kahn, Mathie, & Torgler, 1994; Parrot, 1991). This belief, in conjunction with self-blame, fear of being blamed by others, concern for the consequences to the rapist, not wanting the rape to become public, and desire to forget the experience, may lead to underreporting of acquaintance rape (Kilpatrick, 2000; Parrot, 1991).

Date rape, especially on college campuses, has been studied extensively because it is so common. A landmark study of college women revealed that 57% of all sexual assaults reported occurred on dates (Koss, 1988a). In a recent study of college women, date rapes comprised 12.8% of completed rapes, 35% of attempted rapes, and 22.9% of threatened rapes on college campuses (Fisher, Cullen, & Turner, 2000). Little has been done to assess coercive sexuality in high school dating relationships; however, one study found that nearly 16% of high school females and over 4% of high school males reported being victims of sexual coercion in a dating relationship (Bergman, 1992).

Sexual coercion of men in dating relationships has been studied, although to a lesser extent than sexual coercion of women. Muehlenhard and her colleagues, over

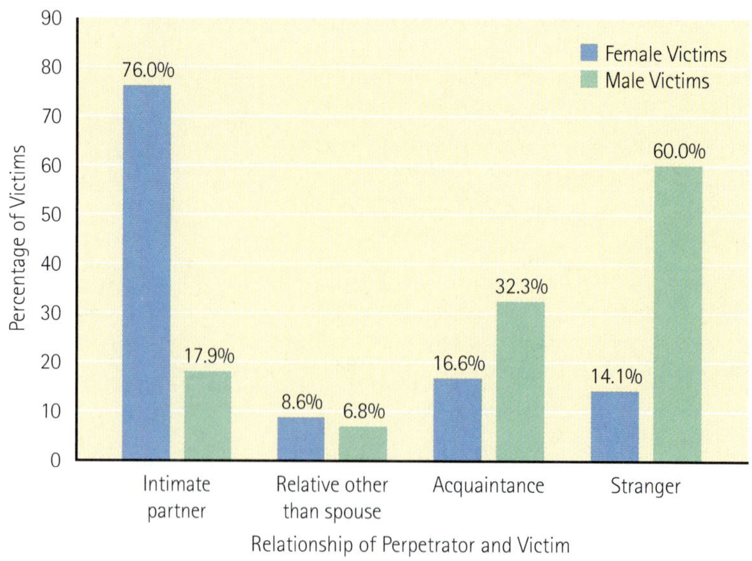

Figure 16.2 Identity of Rape Perpetrators
SOURCE: Tjaden & Thoennes, 2000

the course of several surveys, found that between 62.1% and 93.5% of men reported unwanted sexual experiences (Muehlenhard & Cook, 1988; Muehlenhard & Long, 1988). Results of more recent studies suggest that anywhere from 10% to 45% of high school and college men have experienced some form of coercive sexual contact, ranging from kissing to sexual intercourse (Struckman-Johnson & Struckman-Johnson, 1997).

The reasons for submitting to unwanted sexual activities appear to differ significantly for men and women. Women are more likely to report that they were forced to engage in such activities, while men rarely report that force was used. Women indicate that they engaged in unwanted sex because they felt they should satisfy their partner's needs, feared that the relationship would end, or were verbally coerced, or because their partner threatened self-harm. Men report engaging in unwanted sexual activities because their partner aroused them (e.g., touched or undressed them), because they wanted to build self-confidence or gain experience, because of peer pressure, or because they did not want to appear unskilled or inexperienced.

Many date rapes occur spontaneously, but it is important to recognize that some date rapes are planned for hours or days before they occur (Hughes & Sandler, 1987). A man who is determined to have intercourse with his date might plan to use whatever means necessary, including force, to obtain sexual contact. Recent research on acquaintance rape in colleges shows that nearly 60% of these rapes occur in the victims' dorm, apartment, or home, 31% occur in someone else's residence, and 10% occur in a fraternity house. Furthermore, women in their first few days of their freshman year at college are most vulnerable to date rape (Sampson, 2002).

Like date rape, marital rape is thought to go unrecognized as rape by most women and is rarely reported to authorities (Russell, 1982). In fact, until fairly recently, marital rape was not even recognized by the law as rape. A wife's sexual availability to her husband was considered a given part of the marriage contract—she was essentially considered his property, and in marrying him she gave him irrevocable consent to sex at any time. According to the most recent summaries available, all fifty states now have marital rape laws, but 33 of these states allow for certain exemptions, such as that a husband and wife have to be legally separated, to have filed for divorce, or to be living separately at the time the coercive act occurs in order for the husband to be prosecuted for rape (Bergen, 1999). In general, marital rape is not viewed as being as serious a problem as other forms of rape, and its incidence and the negative effects it has on the survivor are grossly underestimated (Auster & Leone, 2001; Kirkwood & Cecil, 2001). What little research has been done on marital rape in the United States suggests that approximately 13–14% of women report being raped by a husband (Painter & Farrington, 1998; Russell, 1982). One study compared a sample of heterosexual couples in the general community to a group of heterosexual couples seeking marital therapy with regard to certain measures of sexual aggression (Meyer, Vivian, & O'Leary, 1998). The researchers also compared wives' reports of sexual aggression with husbands' reports. They separated sexual aggression into two general categories: sexual coercion and threatened/forced sex. Sexual coercion referred to tactics such as applying psychological pressure or having sex with one's wife while she was asleep, drunk, or on drugs and continuing to engage in sex

Looking At . . .

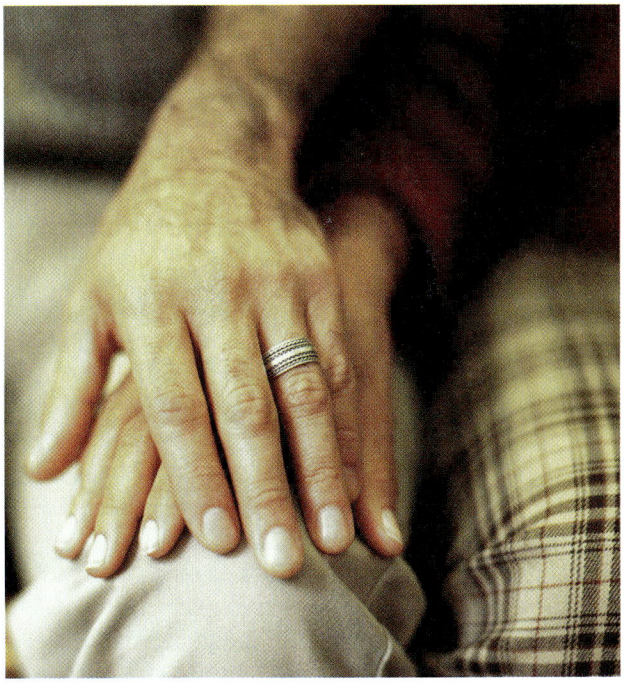

. . . Thinking About

Many women marry husbands who are very controlling and domineering, sometimes even subjecting them to unwanted sex. Why do you suppose these women enter into and often remain in these types of relationships?

TABLE 16.1 Couples in Therapy and in the General Community Who Report Acts of Sexual Aggression

	PERCENT OF COUPLES IN THERAPY	PERCENT OF COMMUNITY COUPLES
Sexual Coercion		
Wives	36.29	13.46
Husbands	35.02	22.92
Threatened/Forced Sex		
Wives	5.06	0
Husbands	0.46	0

SOURCE: Meyer, Vivian, & O'Leary, 1998

despite her objections; threatened/forced sex referred to verbal threats of physical force or the actual use of force. Table 16.1 shows the results of this study. The findings for the community sample are consistent with other reports, but the couples seeking marital therapy have a noticeably higher rate of sexual aggression.

Rape Survivors

Researchers who have examined the characteristics of survivors of rape have found only a few clear patterns; anyone could become a victim of rape. Furthermore, much less is known about male survivors than female survivors. Male rape has received minimal attention in the scientific literature as well as in society in general. The few studies that are available are generally uncontrolled case reports. Perhaps one of the major causes of this lack of attention is a set of myths about male rape that make it seem implausible. Like the rape of women, the victimization of men is often hidden behind a curtain of ill-founded beliefs, such as that men cannot have sex against their wills, when in fact they can, or that men are less psychologically affected by rape and, thus, less in need of consideration.

Rape of Men

Most commonly, male rape survivors are younger children or prison inmates, and the perpetrator is nearly always another male. One study revealed that 87% of male rapes were committed by at least one man, 6% by a man and a woman, and 7% by a woman (King & Woollett, 1997). In a groundbreaking study on male rape, Groth and Burgess (1980) identified three forms of attack used by rapists of males: First, males may experience entrapment, in which the perpetrator gets the victim drunk and then assaults him. The rapist may also use either physical force or threat of physical force or harm. These two forms of attack appear to be more common than entrapment. The most common motivations for male rape seem to be domination and control, revenge, and sadism. In addition, some males rape other males for status or affiliative purposes; for example, if an individual is a member of a group that commits a gang rape, he might participate in the rape in order to strengthen his identification with the group (Groth & Birnbaum, 1979).

Male rape most commonly involves forced penetration of the anus by the penis. One study showed that forced anal penetration occurred in 79% of cases, and forced anal or oral penetration was most common in victims under the age of 16 (King & Woollet, 1997). Alternatively, the male victim is often forced to endure fellatio, to perform anal sex, or even to be masturbated by his assailant (Scarce, 1997). Male rape usually occurs in the victim's home. Male rape survivors are more likely than female survivors to be threatened with a weapon, to suffer physical injuries, to be raped by multiple perpetrators, and to endure multiple assaults (Kaufman, Divasto, Jackson, Voorhees, & Christy, 1980; King & Woollet, 1997; Scarce, 1997).

The belief that women do not rape men is strengthened by the myth that men do not have erections in coercive situations. However, men have reported having erections while experiencing fear, anxiety, or embarrassment and feeling no sexual desire (Ledray, 1986). Sarrell and Masters (1982) described several cases in which women sexually assaulted men. In one case, two women raped a male victim at gunpoint. In another case, a man awoke in bed, gagged and blindfolded. He was then forced to have intercourse with four different women under threat of castration.

Rape of Women

Women of all races appear to be at risk for rape. People from the lowest socioeconomic group (annual incomes under $7,500 per year), those who never married and those who are divorced or separated, and people living in urban areas report being victimized at a higher rate (U.S. Department of Justice, 1998), although, again, reported crimes do not necessarily reflect actual rates. Research on females over the age of 12 shows that women from 18 to 21 are the victims of more than one-fifth of all rapes and sexual assaults, and 56% of all survivors are under the age of 25 (Perkins, 1997). A landmark study called the National Women's Study, which included females of all ages, found that in over 29% of all rapes the victims were under the age of 11, and in another 32% of rapes the victims were between 11 and 17 years old (National Victim Center, 1992). However, women of all ages are raped, not just the young.

So far we have examined the different types of rape, the prevalence of rape, and the characteristics of rape survivors. Now we turn to the important and complex issue of *why* rape occurs.

did YOU know?

Lifetime estimates of victimization from rape suggest that Native Americans are victimized far more often than African Americans, white Americans, or Asians/Pacific Islanders (U.S. Department of Justice, 1999).

Correlates and Causes of Rape

When studying rape, it is necessary to know facts and figures about the prevalence and methods of rape—but facts and figures fail to explain why rape occurs. One very controversial notion put forth by evolutionary scientists is that rape has evolved as an adaptive strategy for men that ensures that they can reproduce and pass on their genes (Thornhill & Palmer, 2000). Thus, it can be considered "natural" for a man to rape, and any man is a potential rapist. This is a hotly disputed notion, in part because the inferences people tend to draw from this theory often go beyond the scientific evidence. In addition, scientists have pointed out that the theory is weakened by the fact that few rapists actually impregnate their victims and that not all men rape (Standford, 2000). Evolutionary theorists do, however, allow that sociocultural factors interact with biological predispositions to determine whether a man rapes. Nonetheless, the prevailing viewpoint is that sociocultural, and not biological, factors influence rape behavior.

Most rape researchers agree that it is important to make a distinction between stranger rape and acquaintance rape, and studies illustrate that the factors that lead to these two types of rapes differ. Both feminist writers and psychological researchers have long argued that rape is not motivated by sex but rather by a desire for power and domination (Brownmiller, 1975; Darke, 1990). However, research studies that have distinguished between stranger and acquaintance rape suggest that while power issues are probably a component of both forms of rape, sexual gratification is also often an important motivator of rape. It is now generally believed that stranger rape is usually premeditated and that in such cases the sexual motive is secondary to motives of power and aggression. By contrast, sexual motives appear to be more prominent in the case of acquaintance rape, especially date rape. The two types of rapes are also often distinguished based on the perpetrators' perspective of the rape. In acquaintance or date rape, it is not uncommon for the perpetrator to perceive that no harm was done (Parrot & Bechhofer, 1991).

16.1 on the web

Many people still do not believe that males can be raped. Read the personal account at **www.ablongman.com/mcanulty2e** by a man who was raped. Describe the difficulties men face when seeking support after a sexual assault.

What can be done to increase understanding and support for men who are raped?

Cultural Factors

Cultural factors appear to play a role in the occurrence of rape, regardless of whether the perpetrator is a stranger or is known by the victim. Societies with higher incidences of rape are described as glorifying male violence, encouraging males to be aggressive and competitive, and seeing physical force as natural and valuable. In contrast, in societies with lower rates of rape, men and women share power and authority equally and contribute equally to the community welfare. In addition, males and females are taught to value nurturance and to avoid aggression (Lottes & Weinberg, 1997).

Cross-cultural research completed by anthropologist Peggy Reeves Sanday (1981) compared the incidence of rape in 95 societies. Her results indicated that women in the United States are several hundred times more likely to be raped than are women from some other societies. (It is also significant that the United States ranks higher than many countries on crime in general.) According to one report, the rate of reported rapes in the United States was 13 times higher than in Great Britain and more than 20 times higher than in Japan ("Women under assault," 1990). More recent reports of rape rates placed the United States ahead of all other industrialized countries, including England, France, the Netherlands, Switzerland, Germany, and Poland (Myers, 1995). One extensive cross-cultural comparison between the United States and Sweden, a country in which women have more institutional power and social benefits, revealed that U.S. women experience significantly higher rates of sexual coercion than do Swedish women (Lottes & Weinberg, 1997). These differences were attributed to a number of cultural factors, including the nature of relations between men and women, the status of women, and the attitudes that males are taught in youth.

Within the United States, different groups of women are differentially affected by rape. The U.S. Department of Justice (1999) reported that Native American women are raped and sexually assaulted more often than any other group of women. This would suggest that there are different factors, yet to be understood, operating in some sub-cultures but not others, that increase the prevalence of rape.

did YOU know?

Seven out of every 1,000 Native American females age 12 and older are raped or sexually assaulted each year. This compares to 3 of every 1,000 African Americans, 2 of every 1,000 white Americans, and 1 of every 1,000 Asian Americans.

Psychosocial Factors

In the United States, such factors as negative attitudes toward women, beliefs in **rape myths**—prejudiced, stereotyped, or false beliefs about rape—(discussed in Reflect on This: Rape Myths about Women), and ideology restricting women's roles are thought to contribute to the high rates of rape (Stermac, Segal, & Gillis, 1990; Warshaw & Parrot, 1991).

Traditional Gender Roles Traditional gender-role identification and male sexual dominance are hypothesized to play a direct role in determining the likelihood that an individual will engage in sexual assault, verbal sexual coercion, and rape (Parrot, 1991). It is possible, therefore, that the socialization process in U.S. culture, with its emphasis on social and sexual dominance for males, predisposes men to become rapists (Albin, 1977; Burt, 1980). Results of a number of studies have, in fact, suggested that date rapists hold pro-rape, adversarial, and violent attitudes and adhere to more traditional or stereotyped gender roles (Marx, Van Wie, & Gross, 1996). A 1996 study (Truman, Tokar, & Fischer, 1996) demonstrated that men who adhere to traditional gender roles tend to be more accepting of interpersonal violence, to believe that sexual relations are generally adversarial (e.g., "Men are out for only one thing"), and to believe that rape myths are true. Interestingly, women who hold to traditional gender roles are also more likely to accept rape myths (Anderson, Cooper, & Okamura, 1997). This finding is reasonable, given that many rape myths reflect the traditional notion that women are to be the "gatekeepers" of sex. Men who have antifeminist views (which represent women as inferior and devalued) and who feel hostility toward women in general are very likely to have attitudes that are supportive of rape (Anderson et al., 1997; Truman et al., 1996).

RAPE MYTHS
Prejudiced, stereotyped, or false beliefs about rape, rape survivors, and rapists.

reflect ON THIS

Rape Myths about Women

Research has shown that acceptance of rape myths is associated with gender-role stereotyping, adversarial sexual beliefs, and acceptance of interpersonal violence. Acceptance of rape myths is also associated with a greater likelihood of and acceptance of rape (Bohner et al., 1998; Morry & Winkler, 2001). Following are some common rape myths about women as victims and men as aggressors. Take a minute to think about why these beliefs are false and harmful.

Victims provoke rape by their appearance or behavior. Women do not ask to be raped through their appearance or dress. Even if a woman walked down a street naked, it would not give a man the right to assault her. Rapists are responsible for rape; the victim is not responsible.

Men cannot control their sexual urges. An interesting corollary to the myth that victims provoke rape is the notion that if a man is exposed to a sexually arousing situation, he will not be able to control himself. Implicit in this myth is, again, the notion that women are responsible for fending off potential rapists.

Women want sex but later falsely cry rape. The idea here is that a woman may fabricate rape charges against a man with whom she has had sex for any number of reasons—because she is angry at the man or regrets having had sex and wants to claim that she had no control over the situation. In truth, women are more likely not to describe a sexual assault as rape because of embarrassment or self-blame. Few women make up charges of rape.

A nonconsenting adult can't really be raped. This is the notion that any able-bodied person can fend off a potential rapist. Rape does occur against an individual's wishes, and often men are stronger than women. Fears of being hurt or killed and threats can prevent victims from stopping rape.

Women mean yes when they say no. As Burt (1991) has pointed out, many phrases from popular songs or day-to-day speech impart this myth—"Your lips say no, no, no but your eyes say yes, yes, yes" is just one example. It should be assumed that a woman does not mean maybe when she says no. If a woman has to be persuaded, the couple is not ready to have sex. No should be understood to mean no.

The sexual contact didn't do her any harm. Many people think of rape as simply sexual intercourse. They assume that if the woman was not hurt, there was no harm done. This notion is especially common when it is known that the victim was not a virgin—the underlying assumption being that a woman loses her value and the right to her own body once she has had intercourse. Of course, this is an invalid assumption. Rape has a number of negative consequences for victims, both initially and in the long term.

It could never happen to me. Rape can happen to anyone—either sex, any age, any race, any religion, any level of education, any physical appearance.

Most rapes are committed by strangers in a dark alley. As you have already learned, the majority of rapes are carried out by individuals known to the victim, and most rapes occur in the victim's or perpetrator's home.

Rape is primarily a sexual crime. While sexual gratification is one motivation for rape, it is generally agreed that rapists are motivated by the need for power, domination, and control.

Rough treatment is a sexual turn-on for women. The threat of force and the use of force are rarely sexually arousing to women. When a woman says no to sexual contact, playing rough will not make her change her mind.

All women want to be raped. While some media (soap operas, porno films) have traditionally portrayed rape as "sexy," women do not want to be humiliated, terrified, made powerless, and violated. In defense of this myth, some people point to the fact that many women have "rape fantasies." Rape fantasies, however, are a far cry from actual rape. They usually entail a man's becoming so impassioned and finding the woman so irresistible that he sweeps her off her feet and makes passionate love to her—like Scarlett O'Hara and Rhett Butler in *Gone with the Wind.* In addition, many people, men and women, fantasize about sexual acts that they would find distasteful or even aversive in real life.

Unfortunately, rape myths are accepted by many college males (Muehlenhard & Linton, 1987) and by men (and women) throughout U.S. culture. The most obvious evidence of societal acceptance of these myths is that they are often used by defense attorneys in rape cases and accepted by jurors. It is not unusual for the defense to raise the issue of what a woman was wearing at the time of the rape or her previous sexual history. In fact, in a case in Florida in which a woman was raped and physically mutilated, her assailant was acquitted based on the fact that she was wearing a midriff top and short skirt with no underwear.

Rape myths are outgrowths of broader cultural beliefs that it is acceptable to use force and violence in interpersonal, and especially sexual, interactions and that sexual relationships are by nature adversarial and exploitative, which justifies using manipulation to "get what one wants" (Burt, 1991). The overall message is that the victim is to blame and must take responsibility to prevent rape. Self-protection is important, but in order to eliminate rape, the problem must be attacked at the root. Combating false beliefs about rape is a step toward preventing it.

And men who have difficulty establishing intimate relationships with others—male or female—are more likely to behave in a sexually coercive manner. This relationship between intimacy deficits and sexual aggression suggests that such men feel entitled to have sex to satisfy a physical need, and in the absence of any desire for intimacy, they may seek sex without any regard for the other person (Hill & Fischer, 2001). Other studies have found correlations among difficulties with intimacy, hostility toward women, and acceptance of rape myths (Marshall & Hambley, 1996).

Miscommunication Confusion about whether certain behaviors signal sexual interest has also been associated with the occurrence of date rape. In general, men interpret women's behavior in a more sexualized way than women interpret men's behavior; men also tend to overestimate their dates' interest in sexual intimacy, while women underestimate men's interest in sexual activity (Goodchilds & Zellman, 1984; Patton & Mannison, 1995; Regan, 1997). For example, men interpret petting as a precursor to intercourse, whereas women see it as an endpoint. In fact, it is common for date rape to occur between men and women who have previously experienced some form of mutual intimacy, such as genital fondling (Koss, 1988a; Miller & Marshall, 1987). Results of one study, in which college students read fictional scenarios of dating situations and then provided their perspective on them, indicated that prior sexual activity between a man and a woman is associated with the belief that the woman is obligated to engage in further sexual behavior (Shotland & Goodstein, 1992).

When some sexual contact has occurred and a woman refuses to engage in more intimate levels of contact, some men may perceive "no" as "maybe," or even as a signal that the woman needs to be "convinced." This perception by men that women do not really mean it when they say no may lead to coerced sexual contact. The interaction between Jessica and Matthew in the chapter opening vignette illustrates how petting is often an endpoint for the woman and how the man may misinterpret signals. Matthew might have interpreted the fact that Jessica did not resist cuddling, kissing, and even breast fondling as interest in sexual intercourse. He also might have mistakenly interpreted her pushing his hand away as **token resistance**—mild resistance offered even though she actually intended to become sexually involved.

A woman's willingness to go to a man's dorm room or apartment might also represent another "miscue" for him, that she is interested in having sexual intercourse. Alternatively, Muehlenhard and Linton (1987) suggested that the higher rate of victimizations in a man's apartment or home may be related to the fact that he is on his own "turf" and may, therefore, feel more in control of the situation. All of these circumstances that lead to misunderstandings about one's intentions underscore the need to communicate explicitly about sexual contact.

Alcohol and Drugs One factor that is clearly associated with being a victim of sexual assault or other forms of violence is public drinking. From interviews of 52 women who drank regularly in bars, one study found that 48% had been sexually victimized and nearly 33% had been victims of an attempted or completed rape either while at a bar or after leaving a bar (Parks & Miller, 1997). Similarly, 24% of sorority members reported being survivors of alcohol- or drug-related sexual coercion. This research suggests that sorority women are more frequently in high-risk situations, especially where alcohol is involved (Tyler, Hoyt, & Whitbeck, 1998). The impact of alcohol use on a woman might be twofold: Use of alcohol might impair a woman's ability to resist a perpetrator's attack and/or her ability to perceive cues that would normally warn her of a potential sexual assault (Abbey, 1991; Abbey, Ross, McDuffie, & McAuslan, 1996; Norris, Nurius, & Dimeff, 1996). There are also at least two ways in which the effects of alcohol might increase the likelihood that a man will rape: Alcohol reduces a man's sense of responsibility for his behavior and decreases inhibitions against sexual coerciveness. In addition, it promotes the perception of a woman as "easy" or sexually available, thereby enabling a man to rationalize sexually coercive behavior (Abbey et al., 1996; Bernat, Calhoun, & Stolp, 1998; Gross, Bennett, Sloan, Marx, & Juergens, 2001). However, the relationship between alcohol and permissiveness toward sexual coercion is not

TOKEN RESISTANCE
Mild resistance to sexual advances offered by someone whose true intention is to engage in sexual behavior.

straightforward. Bernat and colleagues (1998) found that only men who report that they are sexually aggressive respond to alcohol consumption by a woman as a cue that signals that it's okay to pressure her into sex. Findings such as this underline the fact that sexually coercive behavior is influenced by a combination of factors.

Public drinking and consumption of excessive amounts of alcohol are two factors that have been found to contribute to rape.

The introduction of "date rape drugs," namely, Rohypnol (called "roofies" or "roaches") and the less common GHB (gamma-hydroxylbutyrate), into social drinking settings has significantly increased women's vulnerability to rape. Both drugs are odorless, colorless, and easily dissolved into the drink of an unsuspecting victim. These drugs produce multiple symptoms including drowsiness, disorientation, disinhibition, and ultimately amnesia, which makes them ideal rape drugs. Rohypnol has become so popular that its manufacturer, Hoffman-LaRoche & Company, is producing Rohypnol in a form that will turn blue and become clumpy when mixed with alcohol (About.com, 1998). In addition, drink coasters that detect date-rape drugs added to drinks are available to people who want to test the safety of their drinks before drinking them. The coaster changes color when the drug-laden drink is dripped on it (Villalon, 2002). Personal strategies for protecting oneself from date rape drugs are listed in Table 16.2

Group Affiliation Several researchers have examined the relationship between specific peer group affiliations and date rape; fraternities have been the most prominent targets of these investigations. Many studies have drawn a link between rates of membership in Greek organizations and rape rates on college campuses. One study showed that nearly 28% of sorority women and 21% of fraternity men were victims of unwanted sexual contact (Larimer, Lydum, Anderson, & Turner, 1999). However, more detailed analysis appears to link fraternities to rape via a common denominator: Excessive use of alcohol is strongly associated with rape, and excessive use of alcohol is also frequently observed in fraternities (Koss & Gaines, 1993). Other all-male peer groups might also perpetuate rape myths and, therefore, encourage rape. Schaeffer and Nelson (1993), for example, found that males in single-sex housing displayed greater acceptance of rape myths than did men in coeducational housing. In general, experts on rape agree that some fraternities do condone or even encourage date rape. However, not all fraternities are guilty of these practices and not all men who rape are fraternity members. Therefore, it is best not to abandon broad anti-rape efforts and focus only on fraternity men when there are many nonfraternity men who rape or condone rape (Schwartz & Nogrady, 1996).

TABLE 16.2 Protect Yourself against Date Rape Drugs

- Never accept a beverage that is not in a sealed container.
- Never leave your beverage unattended.
- Never go out with or go home with a person you do not know well.
- Never leave a friend who is displaying any effects of a date rape drug; be sure to help her or him get home safely.
- Report suspicious people or activity to campus or local police.

Looking At . . .

. . . Thinking About

Sorority women are more likely to become victims of date rape than are college women in general. Can you think of any possible explanations for this?

Sexually Violent Media Exposure to sexually violent films, books, magazines, and videos has repeatedly been shown to be associated with rape (Malamuth, Addison, & Koss, 2000). In studies of college men, men exposed to violent erotic movies were found to have much more accepting attitudes toward sexual violence than men exposed to consensual, nonviolent erotic material (Boeringer, 1994). It is possible that repeated exposure to sexually explicit material, especially material that links sex and violence, may desensitize men to violence toward women and, in turn, may decrease the likelihood that they will see rape as a crime (Donnerstein & Malamuth, 1997). But even exposure to nonviolent erotic material has been associated with the likelihood of committing rape (Boeringer, 1994; Check & Guloien, 1989). However, the link between any form of pornography and attitudes toward women has been heavily debated. Not all studies have supported this connection, and the methodology employed in studying it has often been criticized (Davies, 1997; Kimmel & Linders, 1996).

Characteristics of Rapists

What kind of man commits rape? The answer to this question is not a simple one. Overall, studies have suggested that male college students who have engaged in sexually coercive behavior are more irresponsible than other college males, lack a social conscience, and have values that legitimize aggression against women (Rapaport & Burkhart, 1984). As noted earlier, the need for dominance over sexual partners may also be related to rape (Malamuth, 1986). Research suggests that men who perpetrate severe sexual aggression are more likely to have had their first sexual experience at a younger age and to have reported more frequent childhood sexual experiences, both forced and voluntary (Koss & Dinero, 1989).

The majority of studies that have addressed the characteristics of rapists investigated samples of incarcerated rapists. These studies, therefore, are somewhat limited, because rapists who are convicted of the crime are probably not representative of all rapists. However, as a group, incarcerated rapists resemble other prison inmates in terms of criminal history, psychological adjustment, and background (Polaschek, Ward, & Hudson, 1997). Studies of convicted rapists do provide some impressions of the characteristics of rapists. However, although there appear to be some characteristics that may correlate with the likelihood of committing rape, there does not appear to be one type of rapist. The majority of men arrested for rape are relatively young—more than one-third of men arrested on rape charges are between 18 and 24 (Greenfeld, 1997). Furthermore, although a small proportion of men who rape could be classified as mentally ill based on their other behaviors, most appear basically normal (Ledray, 1986). Interestingly, rapists have been found to score *higher* on moral development scales than nonoffending college males, but they also score higher on measures of psychopathic deviance and paranoia (Valliant, Gauthier, Pottier, & Kosmyna, 2000). Studies have also found that convicted rapists are more likely to have been victims of recurrent physical and/or sexual maltreatment (Hamilton, Falshaw, & Browne, 2002).

Interpersonal skills deficits may also be related to the likelihood of committing rape. It has been suggested that rapists may lack the interpersonal skills necessary to form social and sexual relationships with women (Stermac et al., 1990). Studies that have investigated this theory have shown mixed results, however, which suggests that this factor alone is not sufficient to lead to rape.

Studies also suggest that the kind of stimuli men find to be sexually arousing is related to the commission of rape (Barbaree, 1990). One question that researchers have asked is whether rapists are more sexually aroused than nonrapists by scenarios depicting rape scenes or depictions of consensual sex. Abel, Barlow, Blanchard, and Guild (1977) exposed rapists and nonrapists to explicit audio descriptions of both rape and consensual sex and found that the rapists were sexually aroused by both kinds of scenarios, whereas the nonrapists found only the consensual scenarios sexually arousing. Other studies have also found that rapists are more aroused than nonrapists are by descriptions of rape and that rapists are more aroused by descriptions of rape than by descriptions of consensual sex (Quinsey, Chaplin, & Upfold, 1984; Seto & Kuban, 1996). However, not all studies consistently show such patterns of arousal; rapists often show greater arousal to descriptions of consensual sex (Barbaree, 1990). One study (Howes, 1998) found no differences between rapists and nonrapists in responses to various sexual stimuli. However, this study did find that the nonrapists could inhibit arousal to deviant sex stimuli, whereas the rapists could not. The possible inability of rapists to inhibit sexual arousal to depictions of rape should be examined further.

In an attempt to provide clarification of the motivations of rapists, researchers at one Massachusetts treatment center have identified five general types of rapists (Knight & Prentky, 1990), which are described in Table 16.3. These types of rapists can be further categorized on the basis of motivation for the rape, degree of social competence, and lifestyle impulsivity. Several studies have confirmed the utility of this classification of rapists (Barbaree, Seto, Serin, Amos, & Preston, 1994). Overall, such findings reveal that there are multiple motives for rape, and different offenders may be driven by different motives. Some rapists are primarily motivated by hostility and aggression; others seem to be enacting deviant sexual fantasies and urges.

Malamuth (1998) described a confluence model of coercive sexuality and discussed three characteristics that are common in men who are sexually coercive: (1) assertion

TABLE 16.3 Five Types of Rapists

TYPE	DESCRIPTION
Opportunistic Rapists	Display an impulsive, predatory lifestyle Sexual aggression is just one aspect of their antisocial behavior patterns. Commonly have extensive criminal histories and often fit the description of a psychopath Sexual assaults are usually unplanned and impulsive. The most common type of rapist
Pervasively Angry Rapists	Show generalized anger and tend to be very aggressive Often cause serious injury to victims An uncommon type of rapist (Barbaree, Seto, Serin, Amos, & Preston, 1994)
Vindictive Rapists	Primarily motivated by aggression; rape is an expression of rage and anger directed at women. Harbor deep resentment of women; the act of rape is intended to punish and degrade the victim.
Sexual Sadistic Rapists	Have prominent sadistic fantasies and preoccupations that motivate the sexual aggression
Sexual Nonsadistic Rapists	Aggression is instrumental in obtaining sexual compliance from a victim. Rape is associated with nonsadistic sexual fantasies.

of one's own interests at the expense of others, (2) orientation toward short-term mating that creates a conflict with females, and (3) combination of emotions and attitudes that sets the stage for using coercive approaches to deal with interference and conflict. Malamuth pointed out that while any one of these characteristics increases the likelihood that a man will be sexually coercive, a confluence, or convergence, of all three is most likely in sexually coercive men.

Female sex offenders have never been studied systematically, largely because so few have been identified (Travin, Cullen, & Protter, 1990). Also, reviews of cases of female sex offenders have tended to group together all kinds of sexual offenses, including child abuse and adult sexual assault, making it difficult to delineate factors that are related to each type of offense. Some research suggests, however, that many of these women were previously victimized themselves and have significant psychological problems. In other cases, the women were coerced by a man into victimizing someone else (Travin et al., 1990).

In general, researchers interested in the causes of rape have not been successful in identifying consistent characteristics of rape offenders (Stermac et al., 1990). Instead, theoretical models have tended to emphasize the social context of rape.

16.2 on the web

This chapter's discussion of rape and its causes has focused on the motivations of individual rapists. Are rapes committed by hundreds of people as acts of war something different? Review the accounts of the huge number of rapes that occurred during the war in Bosnia in the late 1990s at **www.ablongman.com/mcanulty2e.**

What do you think motivated Serbian men to rape and torture Bosnian women?

Preventing Rape or Taking Precautions?

Despite increased attention to the topic of rape, researchers still do not fully understand what combination of factors leads to rape or who is most likely to commit a rape. However, they have been able to identify some cultural, situational, and belief factors that may increase the risk of rape. Two approaches have been used in efforts to reduce the incidence of rape. One is to teach potential victims how to avoid conditions under which rape frequently occurs; the other is to attempt to prevent rape by changing potential rapists' attitudes and behaviors.

Unfortunately, most so-called prevention efforts have focused primarily on teaching women to take "precautions" against being raped—to monitor their behavior and to avoid situations that place them at increased risk for rape. To a certain extent, this focus on women's behavior leads to a false notion that women are responsible or to blame for being raped. For example, how a woman was dressed at the time of a rape is often raised by the defense in court, as if a man has a right to rape a scantily clad woman. In addition, even the most careful woman can be raped. Keep this caution in mind as you read the suggestions for avoiding rape in Health Matters: Taking Precautions against Being Raped. Education of women about factors that put them at risk is important but should not take the place of efforts to prevent rape, which means eliminating those behaviors that constitute rape.

Prevention programs have focused largely on education to reduce rape myths and facilitation of empathy for rape survivors. Men's organizations focused on ending rape have developed around the United States in recent years. One such organization is Men Can Stop Rape, which operates a Web site (www.mencanstoprape.org). However, most rape prevention programs have been introduced primarily in college settings. Many such programs use videotaped scenarios depicting date rape or the events that lead up to such rape (Hansen & Gidycz, 1993; Lenihan, Rawlins, Ebefiy, Buckley, & Masters, 1992). One innovative college program presented a play designed to reduce tolerance of date rape and the likelihood that students who saw it would become either victims or perpetrators of date rape (Lanier, Elliott, Martin, & Kapadia, 1998). The various scenes in the play communicated the following ideas:

- Alcohol can play a role in date rape.
- Explicit verbal communication in a relationship is the only way to consent to sex.
- Abstinence is a viable choice even in serious relationships.
- An individual's choice to set limits on sexual activity must be respected.
- Going to someone's home does not automatically mean that sex is forthcoming.
- Men can be concerned about date rape and can empathize with a victim.

HEALTH Matters

Taking Precautions against Being Raped

The only way to really prevent rape is to eliminate the act of raping—meaning that potential rapists should be the targets of prevention efforts. However, you can significantly reduce the chances that you will become a victim of rape by following certain guidelines.

To avoid stranger rape:

- Do not advertise that you live alone or that you are a woman (use initials on your mailbox and in the phone book).
- Lock your windows and doors and use peepholes on doors.
- Do not open the door to strangers. If a repairperson comes to your door, ask to see identification; call to verify that it is authentic.
- When you do interact with strangers, use body language that demonstrates self-confidence (e.g., stand up straight) and speak clearly and confidently.
- Lock your car while you are driving as well as when you are parked.
- Avoid dark or deserted areas, and always be aware of your surroundings. Do not approach others when you are alone, even when they ask for assistance or directions.
- Have your keys in your hand before you reach your car or door; check the back seat and floors of your car before getting in.
- If your car breaks down, tie a white rag on the antenna and then stay in your car with the doors locked. If someone stops to help, ask them to call the police or a garage, but do not leave your car.
- Do not pick up hitchhikers or hitchhike yourself.
- Consider carrying a whistle or alarm with you to use if you find yourself in an uncomfortable situation. If you are assaulted, shout and draw attention to yourself.

To avoid rape by an acquaintance:

- Choose a safe place for a first date, and consider going with a group of people. Avoid being alone with the person until you believe that trust is warranted.
- Consider providing your own transportation on the first few dates, or bring money for transportation in case it is necessary.
- Watch for behaviors that suggest that your date is overly controlling or dominating.
- Offer to share the expenses of a date. If your date feels that his or her paying puts you in the position of needing to reciprocate sexually, you may reduce such expectations if you help pay for the date.
- Avoid alcohol and drugs. Intoxication may inhibit your ability to protect yourself and may increase your date's likelihood to behave in a sexually coercive manner.
- Know your sexual desires and limits.
- Be aware that some people may misinterpret your behavior or dress. You do not have to change your appearance, but you should be aware that possible misunderstandings may occur.
- Communicate your expectations regarding intimacy directly to your date (e.g., if you invite him over to watch a video, let him know that you do not want him to misinterpret the invitation as being permission for any sexual contact).
- Trust your feelings. If you begin to feel uncomfortable, leave.
- If your date does begin to behave in a sexually coercive manner, respond immediately with direct refusal and even physical force if necessary. State clearly, "This is rape, and I'm calling the police." Do not merely plead with him.

SOURCE: Beal & Muehlenhard, 1987

Students who saw this play showed reductions in attitudes indicating acceptance of date rape. Unfortunately, these attitudes were only measured shortly after the play; thus, any long-term effects are not known. Furthermore, the impact of the play on actual behavior of the participants could not be assessed with these data.

Date rape education programs are also finding their way into high schools. One such program was empirically tested. It included dispelling rape myths, educating students about how to avoid potentially dangerous situations, increasing effective and assertive communication with dates, looking at media effects on attitudes about rape, and providing community resources for survivors. The researchers found that rape myths were prevalent in this high school population and that the intervention reduced students' acceptance of rape myths (Proto-Campise, Belknap, & Wooldredge, 1998). Some evidence supports the notion that educational programs moderate college students' rape-supportive attitudes (Hinck & Thomas, 1999). Unfortunately, the effectiveness of such programs in actually reducing the incidence of rape cannot be assessed because it is difficult, if not impossible, to establish whether a participant is subsequently less likely to rape. In the meantime, rape remains a significant threat, and it can have a devastating effect on a victim.

The Aftermath of Rape

While the physical injuries sustained by rape survivors might heal relatively quickly, the psychological effects of sexual assault are often long-lasting and pervasive. Immediately following a rape, many survivors respond intensely to the victimization. Inability to sleep, frequent crying, depression, eating problems, irritability, mood changes, and anxiety are common initial reactions. Confusion, shock, helplessness, and fear are also common (Gidycz & Koss, 1991), as are guilt and shame, and withdrawal from and distrust of others (McArthur, 1990). The most common reactions to rape are anger, sadness, and anxiety (Siegel, Golding, Stein, Burnham, & Sorenson, 1990). Fortunately, not all survivors of rape have significant problems afterward; some experience few difficulties (Calhoun & Atkeson, 1991).

In some cases, however, rape survivors do experience long-term problems. Despite what is commonly assumed, psychological symptoms are not limited to survivors of stranger rape; survivors of acquaintance rape—including date rape and marital rape—suffer similarly (Kilpatrick, Best, Saunders, & Veronen, 1988; Shapiro, 1997; Shapiro & Chwarz, 1997). Rape survivors have been found to experience health problems, disturbances in sexual functioning, reduced levels of sexual enjoyment, impaired relationships with friends and family (such as decreased intimacy, fear of abandonment), increased anxiety, and depression (Calhoun & Atkeson, 1991; Thelen, Sherman, & Borst, 1998; Waigandt, Wallace, Phelps, & Miller, 1990). Research has also demonstrated that women are at greater risk for developing **posttraumatic stress disorder (PTSD)** following rape. PTSD involves the reexperiencing of a traumatic event through involuntary intrusive thoughts, dreams, or flashbacks. These symptoms are accompanied by symptoms of increased arousal, such as difficulty falling or staying asleep, irritability, difficulty concentrating, hypervigilance, and an exaggerated startle response. PTSD also includes the avoidance of thoughts, feelings, places, people, or things associated with the trauma. Feelings of detachment from others, diminished interest in activities, and a restricted range of affect are consistent with this avoidance (American Psychiatric Association, 1994).

POSTTRAUMATIC STRESS DISORDER (PTSD)
The reexperiencing of a traumatic event through involuntary thoughts, dreams, or flashbacks, accompanied by symptoms of increased arousal and by avoidance of thoughts, feelings, places, people, or things associated with the trauma.

RAPE TRAUMA SYNDROME
A two-phase reaction following rape; the acute phase is characterized by feelings of disorganization, and the long-term process phase is the stage of reorganization.

SILENT RAPE REACTION
A pattern of response to rape in which a woman experiences many difficulties but does not disclose the occurrence of the rape to anyone, and therefore, is not able to obtain the support of others in coping with her experience.

The psychological effects of rape have been named **rape trauma syndrome** by Burgess and Holstrom (1974). These researchers have proposed that women experience two phases following rape: the acute phase, which is characterized by feelings of disorganization, and the long-term process phase, which is the time for reorganization. The acute phase is thought to last for several weeks after the rape and is a time of intense reactions to the assault. The long-term process phase follows and may last for many years. During this phase, women begin to come to terms with the experience of rape and its repercussions on their lives. Burgess and Holstrom also note that some women have a **silent rape reaction.** Women fitting this description may experience many of the difficulties described above, but they do not disclose the fact that they were raped to anyone.

The public health burden of rape is tremendous. One of the largest and best studies on rape reported that 1.3 million women currently suffer from rape-related posttraumatic stress disorder, and 211,000 more women develop it each year. Furthermore, they are 4.1 times more likely to have contemplated suicide and 13 times more likely to attempt suicide. Also, according to this study, rape survivors suffer 12.4 times more alcohol-related problems and 26 times more drug-related problems than other women do (National Victim Center, 1992). About 5% of rape survivors in the United States who come to rape crisis centers become pregnant from the rape. Rape has an indirect influence on the pregnancy rate as well, however. Women who were sexually assaulted as children are three times more likely to become pregnant by the age of 18 than are nonvictims (Koss, Heise, & Russo, 1994). Rape results in the transmission of sexually transmissible infections in 4–30% of cases (Koss & Heslet, 1992). After being victimized either sexually or physically, women make twice as many visits to their physicians as nonvictimized women do (Koss, Woodruff, & Koss, 1991). It is clear that the impact of rape goes far beyond the immediate physical and psychological pain. It is unfortunate that so many rape survivors do not seek out the support of others to help them cope with their experience.

Supportive counseling is often important for victims immediately following a rape. Special treatment programs for rape survivors are also available for those women who may continue to experience difficulties months after the victimization.

Given that many rape survivors experience significant difficulties following rape, it is fortunate that treatment for rape survivors is readily available. The approach to treating rape survivors during the period immediately following the rape differs from the approach used for long-term care. Crisis intervention, which occurs immediately following rape, focuses on providing the survivor with immediate assistance during the reporting process as well as support and education about the experience of rape. Survivors are encouraged to express their thoughts and feelings regarding their experience in a safe place. They are also assisted in developing coping strategies to deal with their experience. Survivors are urged to enlist the assistance of their friends and families and may be encouraged to join support groups sponsored by rape crisis centers. Assistance at this time is designed to help survivors deal with anxiety, fears, depression, and feelings of loss of control.

did YOU know?

Rape survivors are three times more likely than women in the general population to have had a major depressive episode.

Longer-term counseling may be needed to help some rape survivors reestablish relationships with partners that may have been disrupted by the rape, to help them regain a sense of self-worth and safety, and to help them cope with posttraumatic stress disorder (Foa, Rothbaum, Riggs, & Murdock, 1991; Resick & Schnicke, 1992). Partners of rape survivors might be included in treatment with the survivor to work on relationship issues, and might even be encouraged to seek separate counseling as well. Individual therapy may also be appropriate for some rape survivors who continue to experience difficulties.

SEXUAL ABUSE AND INCEST

Since the mid-1970s, mental health and child welfare workers have become increasingly aware of and attentive to the sexual victimization of children. Public agencies have seen a dramatic increase in reports of childhood sexual abuse since then. At the same time, public awareness of and media attention to this problem have escalated, with such nationally prominent figures as Anne Heche and Oprah Winfrey disclosing histories of victimization. With this increased attention, research on the sexual abuse of children has broadened, and much more is now known about the prevalence and effects of this type of victimization.

CHILDHOOD SEXUAL ABUSE
Any sexual experience between a child or adolescent and either an adult or a more knowledgeable child, which may or may not involve physical contact.

Childhood sexual abuse, broadly defined, refers to any sexual interaction between a child or adolescent and either an adult or a more knowledgeable child, which may or may not involve physical contact. This broad interpretation of sexual abuse includes the activities of individuals who expose their genitals to children or have children pose, undress, or perform some form of self-stimulation while being watched, filmed, or photographed. More conservative definitions of sexual abuse include only sexual experiences that involve actual physical contact between the child and the perpetrator. According to these definitions, activities that are considered sexual abuse include kissing, touching, and fondling a child's body, oral-genital contact between the perpetrator and child, penetration of the child's anus or vagina with fingers or objects, and vaginal and anal intercourse. Genital fondling is the most common type of abuse of children (Haugaard & Reppucci, 1988). Intercourse is reported more rarely and is most likely to occur with older children (Wakefield & Underwager, 1994). The most common form of abuse of male children is the performance of oral sex on the child, which is more often reported by male victims than by female victims (Gold, Elhai, Lucenko, & Swingle, 1998).

Sexual abusers sometimes use or threaten to use force or physical harm in order to get a child to comply with their wishes. In one report, 50% of childhood sexual abuse victims experienced some form of physical force (Becker, 1994). However, abusers might also take advantage of their authority over a child, offer rewards, trick the child, describe the experience as "educational" or "good" for the child, threaten the child with suspended privileges, or threaten to tell others about the activities to ensure the child's silence. Since an older child might be knowledgeable enough to employ some of these tactics, children can be as vulnerable to older children as to adults. It is important to remember, however, that not all sexual contact between similar-aged children should be considered abuse. Voluntary sexual exploration and play between children (what is often called "playing doctor") is common and is not typically labeled as abuse. Sexual contact between children that involves coercion or psychological manipulation, however, is likely to be labeled abuse. In addition, even in the absence of force, the contact can be labeled abuse if the children differ in age by 5 years or more (Finkelhor, 1986).

Incest refers to a more specific form of sexual abuse: sexual activities between a child and a relative, defined fairly broadly as a parent, stepparent, parent's live-in partner or lover, foster parent, sibling, cousin, uncle, aunt, or grandparent. Incest, like the broader category of childhood sexual abuse, includes both physical contact and noncontact activities and usually involves the same types of coercion and manipulation. While most child incest victims are abused by only one perpetrator, they are likely to be abused repeatedly (Long & Jackson, 1991). Both sexual abuse in general and incest in particular are probably more common than any of us imagine.

Prevalence of Sexual Abuse

Despite a large increase in the number of studies of childhood sexual abuse and incest, there is still little consensus regarding how many individuals in the population have been sexually abused. The variations in the estimates appear to be partly a function of how sexual abuse is defined (Roosa, Reyes, Reinholtz, & Angelini, 1998). Definitions vary on two primary dimensions: the presence or absence of physical contact, and the age of the child at the time of victimization. Whether surveys or interviews are used to collect information and whether college students, clinical samples, or community samples are examined also influence the estimates. Nonetheless, a 1997 survey showed that child protective service agencies throughout the United States received over 3 million reports of child maltreatment in one year. Of these reports, 9% were cases of sexual abuse (Wang & Daro, 1997). These are only reported cases, however; many cases of sexual abuse go unreported. A national survey of adults found that 20% of females and 5–10% of males had suffered sexual abuse as children (Finkelhor, 1994). Another survey found slightly higher rates: 32% of females and 13% of males (Elliott & Briere, 1995). Regarding actual rapes of girls, in 61% of all cases, the victim is younger than 18; 29% of the victims are younger than 11, and 32% are between 11 and 17 (National Victim Center, 1992).

INCEST
A more specific form of sexual abuse involving sexual activities between a child and a relative—a parent, stepparent, parent's live-in partner or lover, foster parent, sibling, cousin, uncle, aunt, or grandparent.

Patterns of Sexual Abuse

Studies on the nature of sexual abuse typically ask adults to think back to their childhoods and report any sexual experiences they recall. Such retrospective reporting has drawbacks, however. Individuals might forget experiences or might not recall specific aspects of their victimization accurately. Unfortunately, it is difficult for researchers to question samples of children in order to identify the prevalence of abuse. Although state laws vary somewhat as to what they specify as the age of consent, sexual activities between children and adults are illegal in every state, and ethical and legal standards require that identified cases of abuse be reported to appropriate governmental agencies. Given this fact and the nature of the questioning that would occur, many families—and especially families in which abuse is occurring—are unwilling to allow their children to participate in a study designed to investigate sexual abuse. Thus, most sexual abuse research continues to focus on retrospective reports by adults. Despite their limitations, these reports and other types of research do reveal some things about the nature of this crime and those who commit it.

Perpetrators of Sexual Abuse

Sexual abusers of children can be either men or women and are of various races, age groups, and social classes. Sex abusers are rarely strangers to their victims. They are family friends, neighbors, teachers, priests or ministers, and other people known to the victims. Ninety percent of child abusers are male (Finkelhor, 1994); however, women do abuse, and a higher number of female perpetrators are identified by male victims than by female victims (Fromuth, 1997; Haugaard & Reppucci, 1988). Some child abuse experts argue that there are many more female perpetrators than are reported. In a study of a small sample of male survivors of childhood sexual abuse, over one-half had been abused by a female, and one-half of the female abusers were the victims' mothers (Etherington, 1997). Another study surveyed female college students and found that 4% of them had performed acts with children that met the definition of sexual molestation. The majority of their victims were between the ages of 1 and 9, and the women committed these acts when they themselves were around 12 years old (Fromuth, 1997). In fact, approximately one-third of all sexual abusers of children are juveniles (Finkelhor, 1994).

did YOU know?

Seventy to ninety percent of sex abusers are either relatives of the child or are known by the child or the child's family.

Experts speculate that the sexual victimization of children may in many cases be motivated by atypical patterns of sexual interest. As you read in Chapter 15, pedophilia is a psychiatric disorder in which an adult has recurrent, intense sexual urges and sexually arousing fantasies involving sexual activity with a prepubescent child (13 years of age or younger) that persist for at least 6 months (American Psychiatric Association, 1994). While not all individuals who molest children meet the criteria for pedophilia, many do. However, other sexual abusers of children commit the abuse for a variety of reasons. For example, some experts speculate that some adults who sexually abuse children may do so as a reaction to high levels of stress.

Some professionals believe that incest offenders, as a group, are different from other sexual abusers of children. In particular, it is often assumed that incest is an expression of nonsexual needs. That is, incest is often seen not as a sexual disorder but rather as a family problem. This belief is also based on the assumption that the perpetrators of incest with children act out sexually in this way only in the home (Conte, 1986). However, half or more of incest offenders have also molested children outside of their own families (Abel, Becker, Cunningham-Rathner, Mittelman, & Rouleau, 1988; Abel et al., 1987).

Earlier research indicated that abuse by fathers, stepfathers, and other father figures appeared to account for approximately 24% of abuse cases within families (Russell, 1983). However, more recent research in New Zealand showed that other family members and friends were more often the abusers than were fathers and stepfathers (Romans, Martin, Anderson, O'Shea, & Mullen, 1996). However, fathers and stepfathers who do engage in incest with their children tend to commit frequent acts, sometimes for many years; although nonparental incest occurs more often, it may involve only one or a few episodes. Access to the victim may account for these differences (Allaboutcounseling.com, 1998; Romans et al., 1996). Father-child incest is the most frequently reported form of incest, comprising 75% of reported cases (Finkelhor, 1987; Kempe & Kempe, 1984). Sibling sexual abuse might occur more frequently (Finkelhor, 1980), but is often discounted as innocent "sex play" (O'Brien, 1991; Wiehe, 1998).

Estimates suggest that 6–33% of all acts of incest are committed by siblings (Pierce & Pierce, 1985; Thomas & Rogers, 1983). In addition, it has been estimated that as many as 23,000 out of every million women in the United States (that is, 2.3%) are sexually abused by a sibling before age 18 (Leder, 1991). Because sibling incest frequently goes unreported, these estimates may be low. Researchers have suggested that additional investigation of this type of victimization is needed, as adolescents who commit sibling incest may go on to commit other serious offenses as adults (Stenson & Anderson, 1987).

Abuse by mothers has been considered quite rare (Finkelhor & Russell, 1984). Wakefield and Underwager (1991), however, have suggested that sexual abuse of children by female adults often goes unrecognized. They suggest that women may disguise inappropriate contact as normal caretaking activities such as dressing and bathing the child, and children who experience incest may be unwilling to disclose the abuse because of their dependence on their mother. Females are more likely to victimize female children than female infants, male infants or children, or even adults (Mathews, Matthews, & Speltz, 1989). As more female sexual abusers are identified, researchers are able to learn more about them.

16.3 on the web

When Mary Kay Letourneau's case came to the public's attention, many people came to her defense. A Web site was even established anonymously to honor and support her. You can review the details of this case at **www.ablongman.com/mcanulty2e.** Then click on the link to the site established in her support.

Do you think Ms. Letourneau is a sex offender? Would you call her a rapist? A child molester? If she were a man, would people view her differently? Explain your answers.

Children Most at Risk for Sexual Abuse

Children of all ages are vulnerable to sexual abuse, but the average age of abuse appears to be slightly before puberty (Haugaard & Reppucci, 1988). Preadolescent children are both becoming more independent and requiring less supervision, which may expose them to more potentially abusive situations. Children usually know the meaning of sexual situations at this age, but they may not be able to avoid them (Finkelhor, 1979). Aside from age, other factors put some children at greater risk of sexual abuse than others.

Girls appear to be at greater risk for sexual abuse than boys are (Finkelhor & Baron, 1986). One study revealed that three times as many girls as boys are sexually abused (Sedlak & Broadhurst, 1996). Several other factors appear to place children, especially girls, at greater risk for victimization. These include the absence of a biological parent in the home, the mother's unavailability to the child (due to illness, disability, or employment out of the home), marital conflict or unhappiness between the parents, a poor relationship between the child and his or her parents (including being exposed to excessive punishment or physical abuse), and having a stepfather in the home (Finkelhor & Baron, 1986). Neither social class nor race appears to be related to the occurrence of childhood sexual abuse.

Looking At . . .

. . . Thinking About

If you had a child who was old enough to understand information regarding sexual abuse, what information would you give the child that might lessen the risk of her or his becoming a victim?

The Psychological Impact of Sexual Abuse and Incest

Significant problems can but do not always develop following victimization by sexual abuse or incest. Studies investigating the initial effects of sexual abuse, those that occur within the first few years after the abuse, have documented problems such as fear, anxiety, posttraumatic stress disorder, depression, anger, aggression, general behavioral problems, low self-esteem, and sexually inappropriate behavior (Browne & Finkelhor, 1986; Kendall-Tackett, Williams, & Finkelhor, 1993). Such problems are seen in both male and female survivors, with boys being somewhat more likely to respond by acting aggressively and girls being more likely to experience depression (Finkelhor, 1990). Sexually inappropriate behavior and PTSD symptoms, in particular, were more common in sexually abused children than in children referred to therapy for other reasons (Kendall-Tackett et al., 1993)

Many aspects of an abuse victim's functioning can be affected in the long term. Individuals with a history of abuse report psychological symptoms such as depression, anxiety, posttraumatic stress disorder, personality disorders, dissociation (disruption of consciousness, perceptions, memory, or identity), and poor self-esteem. They are also more likely to experience revictimization, self-destructive behavior, substance abuse, eating disorders, and sexual maladjustment in adulthood (Conners & Morse, 1993; Jackson, Calhoun, Amick, Maddever, & Habif, 1990; Linehan, 1993; Long & Jackson, 1993; Messman & Long, 1996; Saunders, Villeponteaux, Lipovsky, Kilpatrick, & Veronen, 1992). Both men and women who were sexually abused as children are more than twice as likely to have a current or past psychiatric disorder as those who were not (Stein, Golding, Siegel, Burnham, & Sorenson, 1988). However, women appear somewhat more likely to report problems with mood and anxiety, as well as alcohol abuse, whereas men report more problems with substance abuse. In addition to these findings, several studies have begun to link childhood and adolescent sexual abuse to higher rates of teen pregnancy. Teens who become pregnant are twice as likely as those who don't to have had prior sexual abuse experiences (Kenney, Reinholtz, & Angelini, 1997).

16.4 on the web

Some people have argued that in at least some cases of child abuse, the victim should be considered accountable for fostering a sexual relationship with an adult. Read the article on this issue at **www.ablongman.com/mcanulty2e.**

Discuss the main argument and the counter-arguments. What is your reaction to them?

Many of the findings on the severe consequences of childhood sexual abuse are based on studies of survivors who were involved in therapy or legal proceedings as a result of the abuse. When child abuse survivors from the general population are included (that is, those who may not have reported their abuse to a counselor or legal professional), it appears that some individuals are deeply affected by childhood sexual abuse, but not all are (Rind & Tromovitch, 1997). Children who have experienced less serious victimization, who do not have close familial ties to the abuser, and who have more parental support and coping skills display fewer problems following abuse (Finkelhor, 1990; Luster & Small, 1997; Rind & Tromovitch, 1997).

Researchers have studied the impact of various types of abuse in order to determine whether specific aspects of abuse may be associated with adjustment problems. Results of these studies are somewhat mixed, suggesting that no single factor is consistently associated with better or worse adjustment. However, there are a few factors that appear to worsen the impact of abuse. They include abuse by fathers or stepfathers; abuse that involves multiple incidents, genital contact, or force; abuse by a male; and abuse by an adult as opposed to a teenager (Beitchman et al., 1992; Browne & Finkelhor, 1986; Kendall-Tackett et al., 1993). No clear relationship has been found between the development of adjustment problems and the age of the victim at the time the abuse started, the duration of the abuse, or disclosure of the abuse.

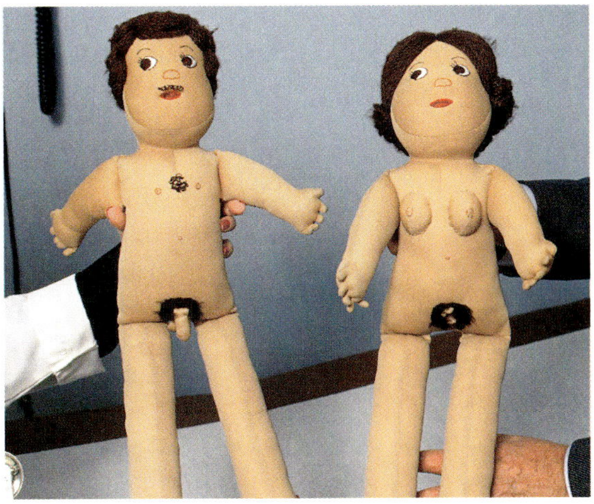

Many clinicians employ anatomically detailed dolls in an interview with a child to elicit accurate recall of abuse.

Treatment of the Survivor

Interventions following childhood sexual abuse are often multifaceted. Various kinds of individual and group therapy are often implemented with child survivors (Cohen & Mannarino, 1999). Intervention with the parents is often necessary to educate them regarding the effects of victimization and ways they may help their child cope with the abuse and to assist them with difficulties they themselves may experience. Siblings may be involved in individual or group therapy for these same purposes. Finally, the family may attend family therapy together to discuss issues related to the abuse and, in the case of incest, to facilitate the possibility of

IN YOUR own words

Christeen Roth
Virginia Commonwealth University

Sexually harassing behavior can be anything from an offensive offhand comment to physical touching.

family reunification if the perpetrator was removed from the home by a child protective agency. Some or all of these components may be involved in treatment, depending on the type and severity of abuse.

The first stage in the treatment of a child who is suspected of having experienced sexual abuse is determining whether such victimization indeed occurred. This is accomplished through interview procedures specifically developed to assess whether a child has undergone the experience. Given the legal implications of determining that a child has been sexually abused, these interviewing procedures must be carefully conducted so that their findings will be admissible in court (Goodman & Helgeson, 1988). For example, suggestive and leading questions must be avoided. Many clinicians also employ anatomically detailed dolls during the interview in an effort to elicit accurate recall regarding abuse without contaminating the interview with too many leading questions (Boat & Everson, 1996). However, use of these dolls has been questioned, because some research has suggested that using them results in inaccurate reporting of events (Bruck, Ceci, Francoeur, & Renick, 1995) and that some young children have trouble using the dolls as representations of themselves, which is necessary if the dolls are to be effective (DeLoache & Marzolf, 1995).

Because the initial effects of sexual abuse are quite varied and may involve a range of problems for any given child, an assessment of the types of problems that a survivor is experiencing is conducted. Treatment is then tailored to address the particular needs of the child. The child's developmental status and age are taken into account in deciding how therapy will proceed. A type of therapy called *play therapy* may be used with very young children, while some combination of talking, skills building, and play activities may be used with school-aged children and adolescents (Berliner & Wheeler, 1988). Cognitive-behavioral treatment programs have been developed for children experiencing posttraumatic stress disorder (which typically includes problems such as nightmares, avoidance of discussion of the trauma, irritability, and exaggerated startle response) (Deblinger, McLeer, & Henry, 1990). In addition, treatment professionals may discuss with the survivor her or his emotional response to the abuse and provide education about what constitutes abuse ("bad touch/good touch") and how to protect herself or himself from it (Cohen & Mannarino, 1999).

Because many cases of sexual abuse are not disclosed during childhood, many survivors do not receive treatment until they are adults. Like treatment of child survivors, treatment of adult survivors begins with an assessment of the specific problems experienced by the abuse survivor, and therapy is tailored accordingly. Frequently, adult survivors have problems that are tied directly to their experiences as victims—namely, difficulty establishing trust or feeling safe and problems with self-esteem (McCann, Pearlman, Sakheim, & Abrahamson, 1988). Therapy is designed to assist the individual in identifying how these problems are related to victimization and in resolving them. Both individual and group therapy may be appropriate for adult survivors of sexual abuse. Treatment programs originally developed for rape survivors have been modified for use with survivors of childhood sexual abuse who show problems such as posttraumatic stress disorder (Foa et al., 1991; Resick & Schnicke, 1992).

One problem that has arisen in recent years in the treatment of adult survivors of childhood sexual abuse or incest is called *false memory syndrome.* This problem arises when various therapeutic procedures are being used to uncover repressed memories of sexual abuse, and the therapist wrongly concludes that abuse occurred and influences the client to believe that as well. While many allegations of sexual abuse are true, many families and individual lives have been torn apart by these false allegations. Although some victims of sexual abuse might repress memories, this is a rarity; a more common characteristic of sexual trauma is intrusive recollections. Therapists who work with suspected victims of sexual abuse need to be very cautious not to "plant" memories. Recovered memories should always be supported with additional evidence before anyone is accused of abuse.

Sexual assault and sexual abuse can be silent crimes because survivors find it difficult to expose the truth for fear others will not believe them or will blame them or because it is just too painful to bring up. Sexual harassment is often not reported for similar reasons—and because the victim's job and livelihood may be at stake.

SEXUAL HARASSMENT

Sexual coercion in the workplace, commonly called *sexual harassment,* is a pervasive problem. As with childhood sexual abuse, the mass media have increasingly drawn the nation's attention to this problem in recent years. Anita Hill's charges of sexual harassment against Judge Clarence Thomas during the 1991 confirmation hearings on his Supreme Court nomination and the U.S. Navy's Tailhook scandal, in which investigators concluded that 83 women had been sexually harassed by naval aviators, made many people much more aware of the nature of this problem. Even more recent are the multiple charges of sexual harassment brought against soldiers and officers in the U.S. Army. In nearly every case, accusations of sexual harassment are controversial because of the difficulty in defining the act.

Anita Hill's charges of sexual harassment by Judge Clarence Thomas during confirmation hearings on his nomination to the Supreme Court in 1991 made many individuals much more aware of the nature of this problem.

What Is Sexual Harassment?

Sexual harassment in the workplace refers to any deliberate or repeated pattern of sexual advances that are unwelcome and/or other sexually related behaviors that are hostile, offensive, or degrading (Fitzgerald, 1993). Uninvited letters, emails, telephone calls, or materials of a sexual nature; uninvited and deliberate touching, leaning over, cornering, or pinching; uninvited sexually suggestive looks or gestures; uninvited pressure for sexual favors; uninvited pressure for dates; and uninvited sexual teasing, jokes, remarks, or questions all constitute sexual harassment (U.S. Merit Systems Protection Board, 1995).

Sexual harassment was identified as illegal by Title VII of the Civil Rights Act of 1964, which made various forms of workplace discrimination illegal, including sexual discrimination. It was not until 1980, however, that sexual harassment was more clearly defined in a set of guidelines issued by the U.S. Equal Employment Opportunity Commission (EEOC). The EEOC guidelines indicate that unwelcome verbal or physical conduct of a sexual nature is sexual harassment when (1) an individual's rejection of such conduct, or submission to such conduct, is used as a basis for employment decisions, or (2) the unwelcome conduct interferes with an employee's work performance or creates an intimidating, hostile, or offensive working environment. These guidelines have led to the recognition of two forms of sexual harassment: *quid pro quo* ("this for that") *harassment* and *hostile environment harassment* (U.S. Merit Systems Protection Board, 1995). In **quid pro quo harassment**, an employee is expected to exchange sexual favors in return for keeping a job or getting a promotion. This type of harassment is typically carried out by someone who has authority over the victim. An explicit demand for sexual favors is not required to establish quid pro quo harassment; rather, the behavior of the harasser must merely be reasonably interpreted as a demand for sexual favors in exchange for job benefits. The sexual activity being proposed must be unwanted by the victim.

Hostile environment harassment is often a more subtle form of behavior, but it is considered the more common of the two types. In this case, unwanted behavior of a sexual nature creates a hostile work atmosphere that may interfere with the employee's ability to complete his or her job. To establish this form of harassment, the offensive behavior must be judged to be pervasive enough to create a hostile work environment. Deciding whether behavior is pervasive enough to meet such a standard is typically done on a case-by-case basis. Generally, the more offensive the behavior, the less pervasive it needs to be to create a hostile work environment. For example, one rape would be considered sufficient to meet this criterion, as would unwelcome intentional touching of intimate body areas. However, less offensive behaviors would need to be more pervasive and to occur

SEXUAL HARASSMENT
Deliberate or repeated pattern of sexual advances that are unwelcome and/or other sexually related behaviors that are hostile, offensive, or degrading.

QUID PRO QUO HARASSMENT
A form of sexual harassment in which an employee is expected to exchange sexual favors in return for keeping a job or getting a promotion.

HOSTILE ENVIRONMENT HARASSMENT
A form of harassment in which unwanted behavior of a sexual nature creates a hostile or offensive work atmosphere that may interfere with the employee's ability to complete his or her job.

Sexual harassment may include unwelcome sexual advances, requests for sexual favors, and other verbal or physical conduct of a sexual nature that is made a condition of employment or that substantially interferes with work performance or creates a hostile or offensive working environment.

over a more extended period of time. For example, being asked for a date by one's supervisor on one occasion would not meet official criteria for a hostile environment, but repeated pressure to go out might.

In cases of both quid pro quo and hostile environment harassment, the sexually related behavior is illegal only when it is unwelcome, meaning that the employee did not invite the behavior and regarded it as undesirable or offensive. Whether or not the victim submitted to sexual activities with a harasser voluntarily is not the crucial factor in determining whether conduct is illegal (*Meritor Savings Bank, FSP v. Vinson,* 1986). Again, no explicit rules exist to determine whether a behavior was welcome or unwelcome, and harasser and victim may disagree on the extent to which a behavior was invited. The entire context of the behavior must be considered.

Since the implementation of Title VII of the 1964 Civil Rights Act and the issue of the 1980 EEOC guidelines, a number of court decisions have further delineated the concept of sexual harassment. For example, many courts have employed the reasonable person standard in determining whether a behavior is harassing. According to the **reasonable person standard,** a hostile environment is one that a reasonable person in a similar situation would find to be intimidating or abusive. More recently, courts have asserted that a **reasonable woman standard** should be applied instead in some cases (*Ellison v. Brady,* 1991). The Ninth Circuit Court of Appeals mandated that when the person who suffered harassment is female, the facts of the case must be viewed from the perspective of a reasonable woman, suggesting that behaviors that do not seem offensive to a man may be so to a woman.

Research in this area does support the idea that men and women label sexually related behaviors differently. For example, in a survey of over 8,000 federal employees, a consistently higher percentage of women than men classified a number of behaviors as sexual harassment (U.S. Merit Systems Protection Board, 1995). Virtually all the men and women agreed that pressure for sexual favors and deliberate touching constituted sexual harassment, but there was disagreement about more subtle forms of harassment.

Patterns of Workplace Harassment

Both men and women can commit sexual harassment, and victims can be of either sex. However, the majority of cases involve men harassing women. A number of studies reveal that sexual harassment in the workplace is far from uncommon. Reported rates of sexual harassment of women in the workplace range from 42% to 88% (Begany & Milburn, 2002). Since 1992, the proportion of sexual harassment charges made by men has risen from 9.1% of all sexual harassment charges to 13.7%. In 2001 alone, over 2,000 harassment cases were filed by men (Talbot, 2002). Although you might tend to assume that these cases are either men harassed by gay men or by women, most of these cases are filed against presumably heterosexual men who engage in acts such as grabbing the man's testicles (called "bagging"), calling him names such as "bitch," or barraging him with lewd or sexual themes.

Coworkers or other employees are more likely to be harassers than are individuals in the supervisory chain (U.S. Merit Systems Protection Board, 1995). Seventy-nine percent of men and 77% of women reported harassment by coworkers or other employees, compared to 14% of men and 28% of women reporting harassment by a supervisor. Employees who experience sexual harassment are likely to work exclusively or mostly with people of the opposite sex and to be supervised by members of the opposite sex. Furthermore, employees under the age of 35 have a somewhat greater chance of experiencing unwanted sexual attention compared to those who are older.

Fortunately, recent research suggests that current practices to reduce workplace harassment have worked. In a 2002 poll of 1,000 American workers, only 21% of women and 7% of men said that they had been sexually harassed (Hirschfeld, 2002).

REASONABLE PERSON STANDARD
A standard used in determining whether a behavior is harassing. According to the reasonable person standard, a hostile environment is one that a reasonable person in a similar situation would find to be intimidating, hostile, or abusive.

REASONABLE WOMAN STANDARD
A standard used in determining whether a behavior is harassing. According to the reasonable woman standard, when the person who suffered harassment is female, the facts of the case must be viewed from the perspective of a reasonable woman, not a reasonable man, as behaviors that do not seem offensive to a man may be traumatic for a woman.

Sexual Harassment in Academia

Sexual harassment is not limited to the work environment; in fact, it appears to be more prevalent in academic settings. Students may find themselves exposed to unwanted sexual advances or sexually demeaning remarks from instructors or professors. Like harassment in the workplace, harassment in the classroom can be directed at both men and women, but historically the most common form has involved male instructors or professors harassing female students. For example, a study limited to females in a university setting found that 30% of the staff, 22% of the faculty, 43% of the administrators, 20% of the undergraduates, and 19% of the graduate students reported being sexually harassed while at the university (Kelley & Parsons, 2000). However, males are subject to harassment as well. In a study of university students, 20% to 55% of females as well as 15% to 44% of males reported being subjected to harassment ranging from sexist remarks, humor, and language to unwanted physical contact. More men than women (15% vs. 12%) reported sexual advances from their faculty. These students also experienced a significant amount of harassment from fellow students, with 49% to 78% of both men and women reporting various kinds of harassment (Shepela & Levesque, 1998).

Harassment in academic settings is frequently viewed as less serious than harassment in the workplace. People often assume that a student who is harassed by an instructor or advisor can simply avoid classes taught by that person or choose another advisor, whereas employees are limited in their options and depend on the job for their livelihood. However, students do not always have the liberty to avoid a harasser—they may have to take a class taught by that individual, or they may not be able to choose their advisor. Furthermore, students often face pressures that force them to maintain a relationship with the harasser, such as the need to obtain a good grade, a letter of recommendation, or a work assignment (Riger, 1991). Instructors and professors often have considerable power over students' future career pursuits.

Some students who are subjected to sexual advances from their teachers may identify their discomfort quickly and recognize such behavior as harassing. In other cases, the students are not aware of the potential dangers involved in becoming sexually involved with an instructor or professor. The advances may be seen as flattering. It may be tempting to a young student to become intimately involved with an older, admired professor; however, the consequences can be costly. Professors are in a position of power that makes it easy for them to exploit students. Given this potential, a number of universities have adopted policies that ban dating or intimate relationships between students and professors. Such policies are based on the assumption that such relationships cannot be truly consensual, given the professor's power to assign grades and make decisions regarding the student's academic career. This power is thought to undermine the student's ability to make independent decisions throughout the relationship.

Harassment is also present in primary and secondary schools. In a national survey of students in 8th through 11th grades, 83% of girls and 79% of boys reported experiencing some form of sexual harassment (American Association of University Women, 2001). The most common forms this harassment took were sexual jokes, gestures, taunting, rumors, and graffiti, but physical acts, such as pulling off clothing or forced sexual acts, also occurred. Of the students who reported some form of harassment, only 7% said they had been harassed by a teacher. Peer-to-peer harassment constituted the majority of cases.

16.5 on the web

Which behaviors constitute sexual harassment in the workplace has been hotly debated for years. Go to the link to Feminists for Free Expression at **www.ablongman.com/mcanulty2e** and read the discussion of sexual harassment.

What is your reaction to their position that the courts have gone too far in defining hostile work environment?

Possible Causes of Sexual Harassment

Sexual harassment is generally considered an abuse of power or an attempt to establish power rather than an expression of sexual desire (Goleman, 1991; Maccoby, 1998). As noted earlier, the more prevalent form of sexual harassment is not direct requests for sexual favors or sexual contact but rather sexual remarks, teasing, jokes, or questions. The prevailing viewpoint among researchers in the field is that harassers (typically men) use sexual harassment as a power tactic, to frighten or control the victims (typically women). A recent study, in fact, demonstrated that men who harass tend to be highly authoritarian, a personality trait that is exacerbated by adherence to rape myths and a desire for male dominance (Begany & Milburn, 2002). Harassment may thus be used to keep women "in their place" and out of settings that have traditionally been predominantly male. It has also been suggested that sexual harassment is a reflection of the low status of women (Studd, 1996). Since men typically have greater power and authority within the workplace, they are often able to coerce women into sexual activities. In many cases, the men justify this harassment later by blaming the women.

Sexual harassment is probably related to the gender roles that are central to U.S. society. Nieva and Gutek (1981) proposed that expectations consistent with traditional gender roles affect women in the workplace. These researchers suggested that women are believed to be patient, nurturant, helpful, loyal, and submissive, among other things. Further, sexual scripts suggest that men should be sexually aggressive and women should be ready and willing sex objects. Harassment is thought to occur when these gender-role expectations and sexual scripts are brought into the workplace (Maccoby, 1998).

The Effects of Sexual Harassment

Despite the wide prevalence of sexual harassment, charges are unfortunately often ignored or minimized by coworkers, supervisors, and employers. Results of a survey of federal employees revealed that 63% of men and 50% of women believe that some people are too quick to take offense when someone expresses a personal interest in them through looks or remarks (U.S. Merit Systems Protection Board, 1995). In addition, the victim is often blamed for the harassment (Powell, 1991). Nevertheless, research does show that sexual harassment has serious consequences.

Sexual harassment in the workplace has significant emotional effects for the victims. In a study by Loy and Stewart (1984), emotional reactions such as anxiety, irritability, and anger were reported by 75% of victims of sexual harassment. Lowered self-esteem, self-blame, impaired social relationships, and lower life satisfaction have also been reported by women who were harassed (Gruber & Bjorn, 1982; Maypole, 1986). The experience of sexual harassment has been further described as being degrading and humiliating and producing shame and helplessness (Safran, 1976). Other signs of the psychological impact of sexual harassment on the job include greater absenteeism, higher turnover, and increased time spent thinking about quitting (Fitzgerald, Drasgow, Hulin, Gelfand, & Magley, 1997).

did YOU know?

Over one 2-year period, sexual harassment cost the federal government approximately $327 million (U.S. Merit Systems Protection Board, 1995).

Students who experience sexual harassment are frequently upset, feel less self-confident, and have lower self-esteem following the experience (Benson & Thomson, 1982). Results of a national survey of 8th through 11th graders revealed that 33% of girls and 12% of boys no longer wished to attend school because of sexual harassment (AAUW, 1993). Additional consequences included not wanting to talk as much in class, finding it harder to pay attention in school, making a lower grade on a test or paper, making a lower grade in a course, and finding it harder to study. Emotional consequences for both boys and girls included feeling embarrassed, feeling self-conscious, being less sure of themselves or less confident, feeling afraid or scared, doubting whether they could have a happy romantic relationship, feeling confused about who they were, and feeling less popular (see Figure 16.3).

Combating and Eliminating Sexual Harassment

Despite the very serious consequences of sexual harassment, victims of sexual harassment most often do nothing about it. Results of one survey of federal employees revealed that the most common response to unwanted sexual advances is to ignore the behavior or do nothing; 44% of individuals indicated that they reacted this way, with men and women being equally likely to respond in this manner (U.S. Merit Systems Protection Board, 1995). Other common reactions involved asking or telling the harasser to stop and avoiding the harasser. Unfortunately, although doing nothing is the most common response to harassment, it is not the response most likely to end the abuse. Only 22% of people who reported that they had done nothing when harassed said that this had made things better. The majority of victims who ignored the behavior, went along with it, or made a joke of it reported that their actions did not help. In fact, going along with the behavior reportedly led to more harassment, according to one-third of women who used this response (U.S. Merit Systems Protection Board, 1995). Table 16.4 presents information regarding the impact of different responses to harassment.

Victims rarely file formal complaints in response to sexual harassment on the job. Results from the survey of federal employees mentioned previously (U.S. Merit Systems Protection Board, 1995) revealed that while 76% of survivors knew the formal complaint channels, only about 6% took such action against their harassers. The most common reason given for not filing complaints was that victims did not think the offense was serious enough to warrant formal action. A number of other survivors reported that they believed that nothing would be done, that the situation would not be kept confidential, or that formal action would harm their careers. Similar patterns of responding have been found in other studies. Loy and Stewart (1984) found that most victims handled harassment by ignoring the harasser (32%) or by saying something to the harasser (39%), while some quit their jobs or obtained job transfers (17%). Only a few sought legal help (2%).

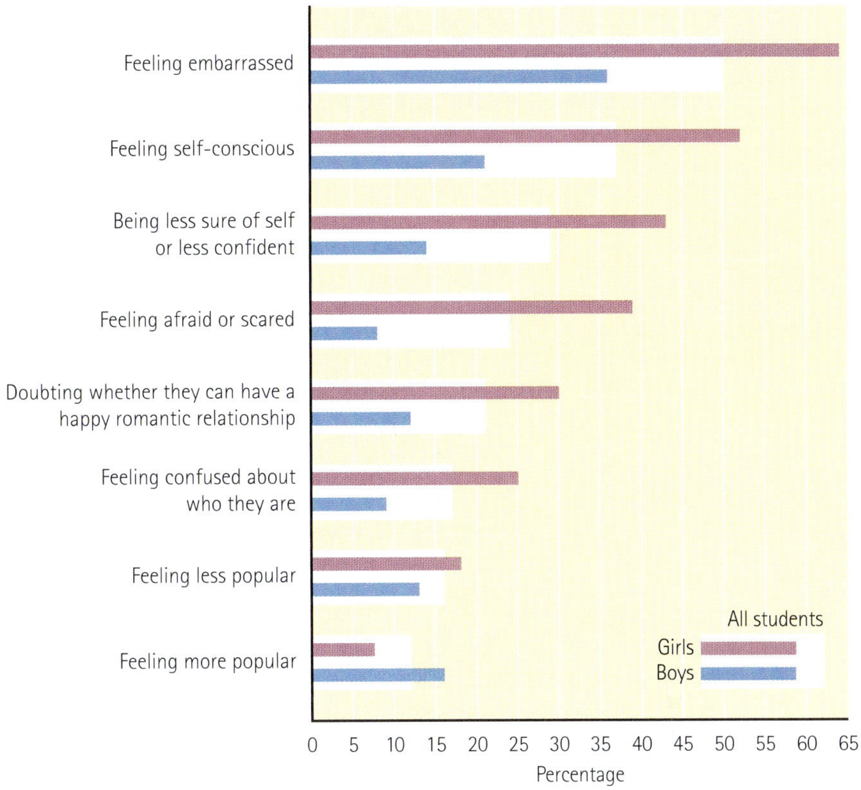

Base: the 81% of students who report some experience of sexual harassment in school.

Figure 16.3 Emotional Impact of Sexual Harassment
American Association of University Women Educational Foundation, 1993. Reproduced by permission.

TABLE 16.4 Success of Various Responses to Sexual Harassment (percentage of victims reporting the response)

RESPONSE	MADE THINGS BETTER		MADE THINGS WORSE		MADE NO DIFFERENCE	
	Men	*Women*	*Men*	*Women*	*Men*	*Women*
Asking or telling the person to stop	61	60	15	8	25	32
Reporting the behavior to a supervisor or other official	33	58	16	13	52	29
Avoiding the person	52	44	13	8	36	48
Threatening to tell or telling others	55	37	0	14	46	49
Making a joke of the behavior	29	29	3	16	68	55
Ignoring the behavior or doing nothing	32	17	6	10	62	73
Going along with the behavior	18	7	17	37	65	57

Note: Respondents could endorse more than one item.
SOURCE: U.S. Merit Systems Protection Board (1995)

HEALTH Matters

What You Can Do If You Experience Sexual Harassment

If you have not already you may, at some time in your life, find yourself being sexually harassed. Here are some guidelines you can follow if you ever find yourself in that situation.

- Interact with the harasser in a professional manner. Do not respond positively to any inappropriate humor or sexual comments. If a harasser continues the offensive behavior, you may wish to respond directly to any inappropriate requests or comments with something like "I'd prefer we keep our relationship strictly professional."
- Avoid being alone with the harasser when possible. If the harasser is a professor, talk to the person when there are other students present. Do not go to office hours alone; take a friend along.
- Keep a written record of all the incidents of harassing behavior. Indicate when the incident occurred and where, what happened (including the exact words that were used) how you felt, and the names of any witnesses.
- Talk with someone else about what is happening to you. Find someone you trust, either within the institution (a coworker, a supervisor, another faculty member) or one of your friends or family members, with whom to discuss the experience. These people can help by giving you support and advice.
- Inform the harasser that the conduct is unwelcome and must stop. Be as direct as possible.
- Consider writing a letter to the harasser describing the incident, indicating that you want the behavior to stop, and indicating that if it continues, you will file charges. If you write a letter, keep a copy for yourself and send a copy to the harasser by certified mail. Consider filing a formal complaint. Companies and organizations must respond to charges of sexual harassment with an appropriate investigation. Set up an appointment to find out about the grievance procedures in your organization and your right to confidentiality and to discuss your experience. In a work setting, you might speak with an immediate supervisor first, or you may wish to speak with an ombudsperson or an affirmative action officer. In an academic setting, you might speak with a department chair or head, a dean, or another university official. Government agencies, such as the federal Equal Employment Opportunity Commission and state Human Rights Commissions or Fair Employment Practices Agencies, may also be able to assist in filing formal charges.
- You may also want to consider taking legal action. Consult with an attorney familiar with sexual harassment issues to discuss the possibilities and the benefits to which you may be entitled.

SOURCE: Adapted from Lindsey (1977) and Powell (1991)

What should someone who is being harassed do? When federal employees were asked what they believed would be the most beneficial steps, they recommended the following three actions: (1) asking or telling the perpetrator to stop, (2) reporting the behavior to a supervisor, and (3) filing a formal complaint (U.S. Merit Systems Protection Board, 1995). When individuals who had actually been harassed were asked to indicate which actions were most helpful to them, they gave similar responses. Confronting a harasser and asking or telling him or her to stop was the action most often reported as helpful. Reporting the situation to a supervisor or telling someone else was also reported as being helpful, as was avoiding the person. Suggestions for what you can do if you experience sexual harassment are presented in Health Matters: What You Can Do if You Experience Sexual Harassment.

The U.S. government and courts have clearly established that sexual harassment is illegal. In fact, the Supreme Court ruled in 1998 (*Oncale v. Sundowner,* 1998) that same-sex sexual harassment is also illegal. Thus, victims of sexual harassment can seek assistance from governmental and other agencies to obtain compensation from employers for losses or hardships resulting from the harassment. Employers have a legal responsibility to maintain a working environment that is free of sexual harassment and to take any steps necessary to end any harassing practices in the workplace. Employers have been found liable for harassment when they knew or should have known of inappropriate conduct and failed to take appropriate actions (Collier & Associates & Huddleston, 1995). Today, most businesses and academic institutions have policies regarding such harassment. It is obvious, however, that harassment continues to be a problem, and continued research on ways to remedy it is necessary.

HEALTHY DECISION MAKING

There are so many forms of and opportunities for sexual coercion that many of you will find yourselves or close friends subjected to it at some time in your lives. Often victims feel ashamed and blame themselves for the abuse—whether it is rape, childhood sexual abuse, or sexual harassment. This self-blame is not justified. Instead, the healthiest response is to understand that the victim/survivor is not blameworthy and did not do anything to "bring on" the abuse. However, it is also healthful to seek ways to empower oneself in order to cope with and overcome the negative effects of the sexual coercion. Empowerment can result from many actions, such as seeking support from friends, family, or professionals who understand, taking legal action against the person who committed the sexual offense, and learning about ways to protect yourself from future abuse. Following are some practical guidelines to keep in mind if you have been raped:

- *Go to a safe place.* Go to a friend's or a family member's home, someplace where you don't have to be alone. This is a time to talk with someone else and get support as you make decisions. You may want to have a friend or family member go to the hospital with you. Or you may prefer to call a rape crisis center to talk to a counselor who could accompany you to the hospital.
- *Get medical attention.* Do not shower, bathe, wash your hands, brush your teeth, or use the toilet. Do not change your clothes. Semen, hair, and material under the fingernails or on your clothing may be helpful in identifying the rapist. Obtaining medical treatment will allow a physician to treat you for any injuries you may have sustained (which you may or may not be aware of). The hospital will also be able to collect evidence that can be used if you decide to press charges later. The medical treatment will include a test for sexually transmissible infections, and you may be given penicillin or other antibiotics to prevent infection from certain STIs. A pregnancy test will also be conducted to determine your preassault pregnancy status, and you can consider whether to take a medication to prevent pregnancy that could have resulted from the rape.
- *Report the rape.* Whether or not you plan to file charges against the rapist, you should report the rape to the police. Have someone go with you to do this. If you are going to file charges, you should be prepared to provide a description of the rapist and to identify the place where the assault occurred. You will probably be interviewed about the rape in order to help you remember any important details about what happened.
- *Decide if you would like to file charges.* Filing a rape report does not mean that you must file charges.
- *Get support and help from others.* You may want to seek counseling. Rape crisis centers can provide you with initial contacts, and many communities have sexual assault centers. Universities also often have counseling centers or student health centers that can be of assistance.
- *Remember that rape is a crime.* Many victims blame themselves for the rape. Remember: The person who raped you committed the crime. Do not blame yourself.

How can you help if someone you know has been raped?

- *Listen.* One of the most important things you can do is listen to a victim. Accept what the victim says. Be supportive, and encourage the victim to talk as much as she or he needs to. Distracting a victim may not be what is needed.
- *Do not judge the victim.* Accept the facts as the victim presents them. Do not make the victim feel as though you do not believe her or him or that you question her or his judgement (e.g., "You were where?").
- *Remind the victim that the rape was not her or his fault.*
- *Manage your own emotions.* It is not the victim's responsibility to take care of you. You should help comfort the victim. Do not make her or him reassure you. You can let the victim know that you are upset, but it is not fair or helpful to make her or him focus on your anger or sadness and comfort you. If you are upset, you should talk with others and get support as well.
- *Offer assistance.* The victim may need to talk to someone at "inconvenient" times—offer to be available. You may also offer to stay with the victim or invite the victim to stay with you. She or he may not feel safe or be comfortable being alone.
- *Support the victim.* Victims need support. This will be true for days, weeks, and even months following the rape. Continue to provide her or him with support and reassurance. Be patient, and understand that healing takes time.
- *Encourage the victim to get help.* Sometimes victims need more than help from friends and family. Encourage the victim to call a rape hotline or go to a crisis center and report the rape to the police. Short-term or long-term therapy might be beneficial. Respect the victim's decision if she or he chooses not to pursue all of these options right away.
- *Do not be overly protective.* Encourage the victim to make her or his own decisions in order to begin to feel control over her or his life again. You can act as a sounding board but should not make choices for the victim.
- *Accept the victim's decisions regarding the rape.* Even if you disagree with how the victim decides to cope with the rape, support and respect those decisions. Do not impose your view of what is "right" on the victim.

summary

SEXUAL ASSAULT

- Sexual aggression is a significant problem in U.S. society. The most extreme form of sexual assault is rape—sexual intercourse by force or threat of force without the consent of the person against whom it is perpetrated.
- Rape is extremely common, but barely one-third of all rapes are actually reported to the police.
- Acquaintance rape, rape committed by someone the victim knows, is by far the most common form of rape. Date rape and rape by a spouse are two common forms of acquaintance rape.
- While women are much more likely to be victims of rape, men are also victims, but society tends to minimize the problem and the pain men experience after an assault.
- Women of all ages and races are victims of rape, although women under 25 are most affected.
- Multiple social and cultural factors play a role in the occurrence of rape. For example, negative attitudes toward women, belief in rape myths, and ideas about gender roles are thought to contribute to high rates of rape in the United States. Miscommunication and use of alcohol and drugs most certainly contribute to occurrences of rape, and exposure to sexually violent media may also contribute.
- Although some characteristics appear to correlate with the inclination to rape, there does not appear to be one type of rapist.
- Prevention programs need to focus on the (potential) rapist and altering the sociocultural factors that are associated with rape.

- Many "prevention" programs focus on teaching women to monitor their behavior and to avoid situations that place them at increased risk for rape. While the survivor should never be blamed when rape does occur—rape *is* the rapist's responsibility—such programs are based on the idea that women may be able to take some precautions to avoid becoming victims of assault.
- Following a rape, many survivors experience reactions such as anger, sadness, anxiety, depression, and distrust of others. Long-term effects are not uncommon following a sexual assault and may include health problems, disturbances in sexual functioning, lower levels of sexual enjoyment, poorer relationships with friends and family, anxiety, and depression.
- Crisis intervention with rape survivors typically focuses on providing immediate assistance during the reporting process as well as support and education about the experience of rape. Longer-term counseling may be needed for some survivors to reestablish relationships with partners and friends and to recover from posttraumatic stress disorder.

SEXUAL ABUSE AND INCEST

- Childhood sexual abuse is any sexual experience between a child or adolescent and either an adult or a more knowledgeable child, whether it involves physical contact or not. For example, exposing one's genitals to children or having children undress or perform some sexual activity while being watched are included in this broad interpretation of sexual abuse. Incest is a type of sexual abuse that involves sexual activities between a child and a relative.
- In the majority of childhood sexual abuse cases, the survivor knows the abuser, who is usually male. Genital fondling is the most common form the abuse takes.
- Girls are at greater risk for sexual abuse than boys are, and preadolescents appear to be at greater risk than either older or younger children.
- Initial effects of abuse include fear, anxiety, posttraumatic stress disorder, depression, anger, aggression, and sexually inappropriate behavior. Long-term problems associated with abuse include depression, self-destructive behavior, dissociation, posttraumatic stress disorder, revictimization, substance abuse, eating disorders, and sexual maladjustment.
- Sexual victimization of children may in many cases be motivated by atypical patterns of sexual interest, or pedophilia. Some sexual abuse of children may occur in reaction to high levels of stress. Although incest has been conceptualized as being a family problem rather than a sexual disorder, men who commit incest often abuse children outside of their own families as well.
- Interventions following childhood sexual abuse are often multifaceted and can include individual and group treatment for the survivor, parents, siblings, and the entire family. A number of treatments are also available for adult survivors of childhood sexual abuse.

SEXUAL HARASSMENT

- Sexual harassment refers to any deliberate or repeated pattern of sexual advances that are unwelcome or other sexually related behaviors that are hostile, offensive, or degrading.
- There are two forms of sexual harassment. In quid pro quo harassment, an employee is expected to provide sexual favors in return for keeping a job or getting a promotion. Hostile environment harassment involves unwanted behavior of a sexual nature that creates a hostile work atmosphere that may interfere with the employee's ability to complete his or her job. Behavior is considered harassment (and thus illegal) only when it is unwelcome.
- Men commit most sexual harassment, and women are typically the victims. It is estimated that between 42% and 88% of women have experienced some form of unwanted sexual attention in the workplace.
- Sexual harassment can occur not only in workplaces but also in academic settings. Recent studies show that over half of college women have been harassed in some way—having to endure insulting remarks, come-ons, propositions, bribes and threats, or sexual assault—by their instructors or professors. Harassment is also common in primary and secondary schools.
- Sexual harassment is generally considered abusive. It has been suggested that harassers use sexual harassment as a power tactic to frighten or control the victims.
- The most common response to unwanted sexual advances on the job is to ignore the behavior and do nothing, despite the fact that doing nothing is not likely to end the harassment. Formal complaints are rarely filed.

CHAPTER 17

Commercial Sex

> I was a prostitute for 8 years, from the time I was 15 up until I was 23, and I don't know how you can possibly say, as busy as you are as a lady of the evening, that you like every sexual act, that you work out your fantasies. Come on, get serious! How can you work out your fantasies with a trick that you are putting on an act for?
>
> (Bell, 1987, pp. 49–50)

> Every night, between the peak hours of 9 P.M. and 1 A.M., perhaps a quarter of a million Americans pick up the phone and dial a number for commercial phone sex. The average call lasts 6 to 8 minutes, and the charges range from 89¢ to $4 a minute. . . . Three-quarters of the callers are lonely hearts seeking conversation with a woman.

Most calls are answered by "actresses."

> The sexual content of the call is often of secondary importance. . . . Most calls are answered by "actresses"—bank tellers, accountants, secretaries, and housewives earning a little extra money at the end of the day.
>
> (Schlosser, 1997, pp. 48–49)

Popular culture is replete with sexual images and messages. The entertainment industry, in particular, is seemingly "sizzling with sex" (Anderson, 2001, p. 225). The trend toward increasing openness and explicitness in portrayals of sexuality is evident in all media (Brown, 2002; Stern & Handel, 2001). Consider the following:

- It was estimated that as many as two-thirds of televised programs in the 1999–2000 season contained sexual content, ranging from harmless flirtation to sexual activity. As many as 1 in 10 televised programs included depictions of sexual intercourse, either explicit or implied (Kunkel, Cope-Farrar, Biely, Farinola, & Donnerstein, 2001). Sexual content is evident in 90% of all movies. As many as half of all music videos include sexual themes (Durant et al., 1997; Seidman, 1999).
- Advertising is also becoming increasingly explicit in its depictions of male and female models. As one commentator lamented, fashion ads now seem to show "more skin than clothing" (Anderson, 2001, p. 186). Content analyses confirm that print advertising increasingly depicts sexually explicit images of male and female models (Reichert, Lambiase, Morgan, Carstarphen, & Zavoina, 1999).
- The global pornography industry generates over $55 billion in revenues each year (Morais, 1999). Nearly half of that amount is derived from sexually explicit films; some 10,000 "adult films" are produced each year in the United States alone.
- The Internet is replete with sexually oriented sites and chat rooms. Virtually every imaginable sexual theme is available on the Internet (and a few that would shock those with even the most vivid imaginations). Entering the term "sex" into a search engine will yield links to over 10 million sites (Casanova, Solursh, Solursh,

IN YOUR own words

Jyoti Jain
Northwestern University

I think pornography is a legitimate form of entertainment that does not lead to violence or promote hatred toward women. There is some pornography that crosses the line, but more often than not, porn can show sexual acts from the perspective of the woman.

Roy, & Thigpen, 2000). Indeed, the word "sex" is searched more than any other term online (Pastore, 2001).

- Popular magazines such as *Penthouse* regularly feature articles intended to enhance readers' intimate relationships. The majority of articles address sex in one form or another (McMahon, 1990). Magazines oriented toward male audiences, such as *Maxim,* feature skimpily clad attractive models in every issue.

As sex is moving from the bedroom to the living room, the boundaries between tasteful depictions of sex and indecent portrayals are becoming blurred. And the increasingly explicit depictions of sex in popular culture are raising controversy. Where do we draw the line between decent and indecent depictions of sex? How much explicitness is required for an image to be considered pornographic?

This chapter considers commercial sex, or sex as a commodity. On one hand, sex can be a vehicle for selling other products, through sexually suggestive advertising and music videos. For some, however, the sale of sex provides a livelihood. Film producers and actors who specialize in making sexually explicit films offer vivid depictions of sex to millions of viewers. Millions of "adult magazines" are sold each month. Sexually explicit conversation is available to anyone who calls one of the many 900 numbers ("Dial-a-Porn" services). Video cameras transmit live sexual acts over the Internet as digital peep shows. Finally, sexual intercourse and virtually any other imaginable sexual service can be purchased in many places.

Of all the forms of commercial sex, pornography and prostitution have exceptionally long and controversial histories. Their longevity reveals that there have always been enough consumers to sustain the sex trade. Adult entertainment also has a long history, although entertainment for hire probably is a more recent phenomenon than pornography.

PORNOGRAPHY

The word *pornography* is derived from a Greek word meaning "the writing of [or about] prostitutes." According to Bullough and Bullough (1977), such writing was associated with erotic imagery and sexual arousal; it was a type of "psychological aphrodisiac." *Webster's New Collegiate Dictionary* defines **pornography** as the "depiction of erotic behavior (as in pictures or writing) intended to cause sexual excitement." The inclusion of intent in the definition introduces problems, because the intent of the person who created the depiction is not always clearly discernible.

Pornography defies definition for several reasons. First, some materials, such as books, that were once labeled pornographic have been later redefined as classic writing. For example, D. H. Lawrence's *Lady Chatterley's Lover* was highly controversial when it was published in 1929, and, until 1960, portions of the novel were cut whenever the book was printed in the author's homeland, Great Britain. In 1960—about 30 years after his death—Lawrence was charged with obscenity (Marcuse, 1965). His novel is now considered a significant literary achievement. Mark Twain's classic novel *The Adventures of Huckleberry Finn* was also once considered indecent. Thus, definitions of pornography can change over time. Second, cultures vary drastically in their attitudes about and tolerance for material with sexual content. For example, the same year that U.S. courts found Lawrence's novel not obscene, Japan reached the opposite conclusion and banned it. Similarly, the 1972 film *The Last Tango in Paris,* which featured actor Marlon Brando in relatively explicit sexual scenes, was ruled obscene in Italy but not in Great Britain (Randall, 1989). Finally, definitions of pornography tend to be highly subjective. The often quoted statement by U.S. Supreme Court Justice Potter Stewart—that although he could not define pornography in objective terms, he knew it when he saw it—illustrates the subjective nature of attempt-

PORNOGRAPHY
Term used to describe written or visual materials that are designed to be sexually arousing.

ing to define pornography. Pornography has even been classed as a literary genre that, although written at a low cultural level, is nonetheless art (Peckham, 1969). Without a universal and absolute definition of pornography, disagreement and controversy are inevitable.

Obscenity is a legal term derived from the Latin word for "filth" (Bullough & Bullough, 1995) and used to characterize sexually explicit materials that are deemed illegal. However, defining obscenity has proved no less formidable a task than explaining what constitutes pornography. The legal definitions and criteria have changed over the years. Most original definitions applied terms such as "indecent" and "immoral" to the material under consideration. Because of their highly subjective nature, these criteria were replaced with the criterion of "harmfulness." Sexually explicit materials that might deprave and corrupt minds open to such influences (generally meaning children's minds) were declared illegal. A more recent definition of obscenity states that it pertains to material that is without "redeeming social value" and that the average person, using contemporary standards, would judge as appealing to the "prurient interests." In this context, **prurient** (from a Latin word meaning "to itch" or "to crave") means "relating to lustful desire." (The intricacies of legal definitions of obscenity are considered in more detail later in the chapter.)

Looking At . . .

. . . Thinking About

Popular musicians such as Eminem court controversy because of their provocative attire and explicit lyrics. Where do you draw the line between artistic expression and obscenity?

Erotica is a newer term used to describe sexually explicit material that has artistic value (Mosher, 1988). In reality, the distinction between pornography and erotica is a matter of degree, and where the line is drawn is subjective. For sexually explicit films, the distinction is put in terms of "hard-core" versus "soft-core." In hard-core films, there is typically only a vestige of a plot, if any, and the film consists mostly of explicit sexual activity with graphic footage of genitalia and ejaculations. Soft-core films generally have more of a plot and leave more of the graphic detail to the viewer's imagination. Many popular men's magazines such as *Playboy* and *Penthouse* qualify as erotica, or soft-core. *Hustler* magazine is more pornographic, or hard-core, in the eyes of many. Interestingly, there seem to be few if any female-oriented hard-core magazines. The majority of explicit sexually oriented materials are designed for a male audience.

The blurred line between pornography and erotica was illustrated by the controversy that surrounded an exhibit of photographs by Robert Mapplethorpe in 1990. His exhibit stirred intense controversy because of the sexual content of several—but not all—of the photographs. Several erotic themes were represented, including homosexuality and sadomasochistic sexual activity. However, what viewers objected to most were the nude photographs of children. Although not explicitly sexual in nature, these photographs did display frontal nudity. The controversy culminated with the indictment in 1990 of the director of a gallery in Cincinnati, Ohio on charges of obscenity. Although the gallery director was eventually acquitted, the fact that there was legal action dramatically illustrates the difficulty in distinguishing obscene from artistic depictions of nudity and sexuality. Fashion clothing designer Calvin Klein was at the center of controversy over promotional photographs depicting very young-looking models in rather provocative poses that revealed the models' underwear. Facing threats of legal prosecution, the advertising photographs were

OBSCENITY
Legal term used to characterize sexually explicit materials that are judged to be illegal because of content that is harmful to viewers, without artistic merit, and that appeals to lustful desires.

PRURIENT
Appealing to or inciting lustful desire; from the Latin word meaning "to itch" or "to crave."

EROTICA
A newer term used to describe sexually explicit material that is more artistic in its content.

Popular music such as Janet Jackson's album All for You *often features explicit lyrics that blur the distinction between art and pornography. There has been a trend toward increased nudity and sexually explicit language in popular media over the past few years.*

withdrawn. Similar concerns have been expressed about *Showgirls* and *Striptease,* two mainstream films about topless and nude dancers, and about *Eyes Wide Shut,* late director Stanley Kubrick's last film.

This chapter employs the more neutral phrase *sexually explicit* to refer to materials that have been alternately described as pornographic, erotic, or obscene. Use of this phrase avoids any subjective judgments about the materials.

Sexually Explicit Materials and the Law

From the legal perspective, sexually explicit materials raise four basic questions: (1) What is obscene? (2) What effect does obscene material have on the viewer? (3) Should this material be controlled by the government? (4) If so, what form of control is preferable? (Donnerstein, Linz, & Penrod, 1987). Most censorship efforts have arisen out of concern that the materials in question were threats to public morality.

One of the first legal cases about obscenity occurred in England in 1868. The case of *Regina v. Hicklin* involved a pamphlet detailing the alleged sexual immorality of the Roman Catholic clergy (Randall, 1989). In that case, obscenity was defined as material that might "deprave and corrupt those whose minds are open to such immoral influences." The Hicklin rule defined obscenity on the basis of its potential harm to the reader. This vague definition was applied in England and the United States for nearly a century.

The first authoritative decision on obscenity by the U.S. Supreme Court was rendered in the case of *Roth v. United States* in 1957. The Court ruled that obscene material was not protected by the First Amendment to the Constitution, which guarantees the right to free speech. In this decision, obscenity was defined as appealing to "prurient interests." The Roth test further defined obscenity on the basis of "whether to the average person, applying community standards, the dominant theme of the material taken as a whole appeals to the prurient interest." However, the court failed to specify who the "average person" is and which community's standards are to be considered (the nation's? a state's? a city's?). "Patent offensiveness" (*Mishkin v. New York,* 1962) and the absence of any "redeeming social value" (the *Fanny Hill* case, 1966) were added as legal criteria for obscenity in subsequent rulings.

Throughout the 1960s, the Roth test was challenged and refined in U.S. courts. In 1968, a film based on D. H. Lawrence's novel, *Lady Chatterley's Lover,* was found not to be obscene using the Roth test. In the case of *Miller v. California* (1973), the Court clarified that local rather than national norms were to be considered in determining the offensiveness of the material. Additionally, the Miller standard established that obscenity referred to materials lacking "serious literary, artistic, political, or scientific value." However, the involvement of the government in determining the literary or artistic value of sexually explicit material has been questioned. Opponents of government intervention argue that the constitutional right to freedom of speech applies to sexually explicit materials. Opponents of censorship reason that, because of the subjective nature of eroticism, it is too risky to permit the government to decide what is art and what is obscene. Although the Presidential Commission on Obscenity and Pornography (1970) concluded that there was no link between exposure to sexually explicit materials and the commission of sex crimes and recommended that the government not interfere with individuals' rights to use sexually explicit materials, these recommendations were not adopted. Some argue that it is the government's responsibility to protect the public from harmful sexually explicit materials. Kristol (1999), for example, warned that "if you want to prevent pornography and/or obscenity from becoming a problem, you have to be for censorship" (p. 8). Other writers point to the lengthy history of dissemination of sexually explicit materials and note that attempts at censorship are futile, especially with the international access offered by the Internet (Maxwell, 1996). This controversy was ignited again in 1995 with the passage by the U.S. Congress of legislation that prohibited the dissemination of sexually explicit materials over computer networks. Various court cases have shown that there is indeed a very fine line between protecting the public from harm and preserving freedom of expression.

Currently, in obscenity cases, the jury must answer three questions: (1) Would the average person, applying local standards, find that the material appeals to prurient interests? (2) Does the material depict sexual acts offensively, as defined by state law? (3) Does the work lack literary, artistic, political, or scientific value? Because such concepts as "prurient interests" and "artistic value" are somewhat subjective, there is much variability across juries. Think about how you might respond as a juror to such questions as you read Reflect on This: Assessing Your Attitudes toward Sexually Explicit Materials.

reflect ON THIS

Assessing Your Attitudes toward Sexually Explicit Materials

Fisher, Cook, and Shirley (1994) found that a majority of respondents to their survey favored bans on violent sexually explicit films, but only a third supported a ban on nonviolent sexually explicit films. Factors that were found to correlate with support for censorship of sexual media included age, religious views, gender, sexual conservatism, adherence to gender-role stereotypes, and concern about the effects of pornography. Being older, female, and religious, having traditional views of gender roles, and being sexually conservative were associated with stronger support for censorship. Of all the variables, concern about the effects of sexually explicit materials on viewers was the most important predictor of support for censorship.

Take a few minutes to consider the following questions. Jot down your thoughts, and discuss them with someone (such as a classmate) who has different beliefs.

1. How would you define pornography?
2. What experience do you have with sexually explicit materials?
3. How would you define obscenity?
4. Based on your answers to the previous questions, which of the following would you consider sexually explicit or sexually suggestive?
   - Popular music videos
   - Advertising (such as fashion ads depicting near-nude models)
   - Erotic scenes in popular TV series
5. What are your thoughts about media depictions of violence?
6. Compare and contrast your attitudes toward media depictions of sex and of violence. Note similarities and differences in your attitudes.
7. How did your attitudes toward sexually explicit films and photos evolve? Which of the following most shaped your attitudes toward sexually explicit materials?
   - Sexual and religious values
   - Gender-role beliefs (your views of the roles of men and women in society)
   - Sources of information about pornography, such as parents, peers, and personal experience
8. What forms of censorship, if any, would you support? Why?

Nudity and sexuality were prominent themes in ancient Greek art.

Sexually Explicit Materials: A Brief History

Pornography is by no means a product of contemporary culture. The production of sexually explicit material probably dates back to the origin of the first social structures (Randall, 1989). Primitive drawings of human genitals, probably dating to the Cro-Magnon period (at least 10,000 years ago), have been discovered on cave walls in western Europe. Some carved representations of sexual intercourse are estimated to date back to 7000 B.C.E. Explicit sculptures of female genitalia and other symbols of fertility, such as "Venus" figurines, were common in the ancient world. Excavated potteries from pre-Columbian Peru displayed explicit sexual organs and acts, including fellatio and anal intercourse. In many such relics, the genitalia are disproportionately large, as if to accentuate their importance. Clearly, they were intended to be noticed by the observer.

Sexual themes have also been prominently addressed in the theater for centuries. Erotic themes and nudity were common and widely accepted in ancient Greek drama. In the play *Lysistrata* by Aristophanes, the women of Athens pledge to abstain from sexual activity with their husbands until peace with Sparta is restored. In ancient Greece, "ordinary words for sex organs and sex acts had not acquired an obscene significance" (Loth, 1961, p. 50). The genitals, especially the penis, were associated with fertility and religious rituals, such as spring prayers for abundant crops (Loth, 1961). Several cultures associated sexuality with religious worship. Therefore, explicit visual representations of sexual themes were common and accepted. Hindu temples were decorated with sculptures of characters in various sexual poses, many of which appear physically impossible. Genital symbols were the objects of worship in several sects of Hinduism (Bullough, 1995). The famous Indian sex manual of the 3rd century, the *Kama Sutra,* offered graphic illustrations and explicit instructions for achieving ultimate sexual pleasure.

Sex was not prominently addressed in ancient Hebrew writings, but several of these texts include sexual themes. For example, *Song of Solomon,* one book of the Hebrew Bible, has been described as erotic poetry (Randall, 1989). Several biblical passages were not translated from the Latin until fairly recently because of their sexual content (Bullough & Bullough, 1977).

A revolution occurred during the Renaissance era following Gutenberg's invention of the printing press in the 15th century. No longer did books have to be painstakingly inscribed by hand. As a result, sexually explicit writings became more widely available. Renaissance literature offered a broad array of such writings (Frantz, 1989). The Italian author Pietro Aretino, for example, produced explicit descriptions of such varied sexual

The ancient Hindu text the Kama Sutra *is one of the earliest sex education manuals. It offers candid and explicit advice for achieving ultimate sexual pleasure. Note that some of the illustrated sexual positions require unusual acrobatic talents.*

acts as masturbation, anal intercourse, and group sex. Shakespeare's *The Merry Wives of Windsor* has a plot based on marital infidelity, and sexually suggestive language is used throughout. Because some of its content was considered indecent, *The Family Shakespeare,* a ten-volume compilation printed in 1818, omitted the original language, which "cannot with propriety be read aloud in a family" (Loth, 1961, p. 124).

Most sexually explicit literature read in the United States was imported until 1846, when William Haynes began publishing such material in New York. Success was immediate, and it is estimated that, by 1870, he sold more than 100,000 publications annually, a significant number by any standard (Bullough & Bullough, 1977). Subsequent technological developments, such as the invention of motion pictures, further facilitated the distribution of all forms of information, including sexually explicit materials.

Today, the production of sexually explicit materials—especially magazines, books, computer files, and films (including videocassettes)—is a multimillion-dollar industry in the United States. Worldwide sales of such materials net approximately $56 billion annually (Morais, 1999). Since *Playboy* made its debut in 1953, the number of sexually explicit magazines in the United States has increased to over a dozen (Randall, 1989). Sexually explicit videocassettes are stocked by two-thirds of the country's video rental stores (U.S. Department of Justice, 1986). The *X-Rated Videotape Star Index* (Riley, 1994) boasts a listing of 17,000 films and 10,000 performers. Up to 23% of men and 11% of women report having purchased a sexually explicit (X-rated) movie in the past year (Laumann, Gagnon, Michael, & Michaels, 1994). In 1998, Americans rented nearly 7 million "adult" videotapes (Morais, 1999). Nearly three out of four adults in the United States have viewed at least one sexually explicit film (Bryant & Brown, 1989). In the United States alone, several thousand "adult" movies are produced annually, with sales and rentals in the millions of dollars. Some sexually explicit films, such as *Behind the Green Door* and *Debbie Does Dallas,* are considered classics. Demand for sexually explicit materials has steadily increased over the past several decades, in part because of the increased social acceptability of some forms of commercial sex. The majority of adults in the United States, for example, have fairly tolerant attitudes toward sex and nudity in the mass media (Winick & Evans, 1994). As you can see in Figure 17.1 and Table 17.1 (on page 530), sexual content is evident in a wide variety of

17.1 on the web

One organization that monitors online child pornography is PedoWatch. Visit their Web site through the link at **www.ablongman.com/mcanulty2e.**

What is the group's mission? How is the organization attempting to address the problem of "kiddie porn" online? How can individuals help in dealing with this problem?

did YOU know?

The movie* Deep Throat*, which brought fellatio into the national spotlight in 1972, has generated over $100 million in profits, making it one of the most profitable movies ever produced (Cook, 1978).

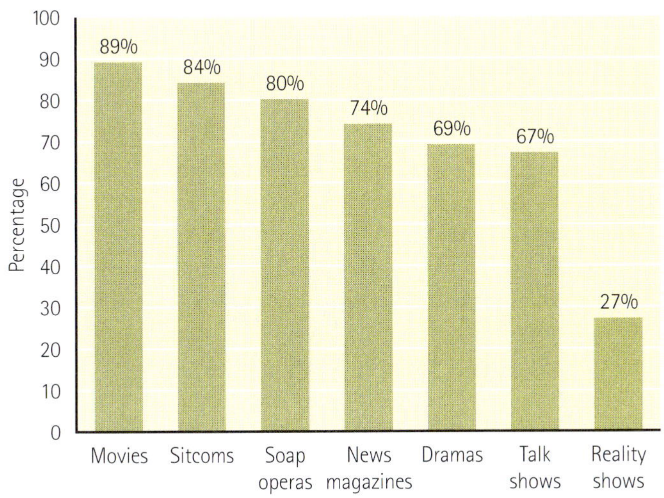

Figure 17.1 Percent of All Television Shows That Contain Sexual Content, by Genre

Source: Kunkel et al., 2001

TABLE 17.1 Sexual Content of Television Shows

TYPE OF SHOW	PERCENT OF ALL SHOWS ON TELEVISION	PERCENT THAT INCLUDE ANY REFERENCE TO SEXUAL RISKS OR RESPONSIBILITIES
Shows with any sexual content	68%	10%
Shows with sexual intercourse	10%	25%
Shows with any sexual content involving teens	9%	17%
Shows with teens talking about or engaging in sexual intercourse	3%	32%

SOURCE: Kunkel et al. (2001)

televised programs. However, most presentations of sexual content are unbalanced and unrealistic, because the potential risks associated with sexual behavior are not generally addressed (Kunkel et al., 2001).

Content of Sexually Explicit Materials

Virtually every imaginable sexual act and theme has been represented in one or more media. The explicitness of the content has varied tremendously across cultures and over time. Much of the sexually explicit material of the Victorian era is very mild by contemporary standards, but ancient sculptures and writings such as the *Kama Sutra* depicted explicit sexual behavior. Many of these offered graphic representations of sexual activities that are uncommon or even considered deviant, such as bestiality (sexual activity with animals). The content of modern sexually explicit materials has also changed over time. Bogaert, Turkovich, and Hafer (1993) documented changes in the content of *Playboy* centerfolds from 1953 through 1990. Degree of explicitness gradually increased before leveling off in the 1980s. The content of other publications, however, has become increasingly graphic over the years, perhaps because of the competition from movies.

Movies

The development of motion picture technology allowed a degree of sexual explicitness surpassing that provided by all earlier media, with the exception of live sexual performances. Because printed narratives and color photographs cannot match the visual and auditory realism offered by film, movies are the preferred medium for many contemporary consumers of sexually explicit materials.

Analyses of contemporary sexually explicit films reveal a fairly narrow range of themes and content. The majority of popular adult films focus almost entirely on sex, routinely representing "lesbianism, group sex, anal intercourse, oral-genital contact and visible ejaculation" (Hebditch & Anning, 1988, p. 7). Nonsexual interpersonal behavior is almost completely excluded. A content analysis of 50 randomly selected sexually explicit films revealed that fellatio was the most frequent sexual act, followed by vaginal intercourse. Cunnilingus was a distant third. Sexual scenes typically culminated with the male ejaculating on the partner's body. The characters depicted in the films were rarely portrayed in committed relationships (such as marriage). Brosius, Weaver, and Staab (1993) described a typical scene:

> With only a minimal preamble, the viewer encounters the characters. They are strangers, or perhaps only recent acquaintances, who—overcome by their desire for sexual pleasure and abandon—embrace one another eagerly. She is young and blond; he is older and has dark hair. Consumed by their passion, there is no time for persuasion or coercion nor time to voice concerns about contraception or "safer sex" practices. She seems to understand that their intercourse will be a hurried affair of less than 6 minutes and initiates the sexual actions by fondling his penis or kneeling before him to perform fellatio. With his urgent need readily apparent, they shun, or at least minimize, any reciprocal genital foreplay and quickly move to coitus. The camera focuses on her, providing only fleeting glimpses of him, except for his penis. She is enraptured by his sexual excitement and, ignoring her own sexual satisfaction, is very expressive as her utterances encourage him to climax. Then, almost as swiftly as it began, their rendezvous ends when, in the heat of their passion, he graphically displays his orgasm by depositing semen onto her belly. After the briefest pause to establish that the characters have been fulfilled and are content, the viewer is rapidly propelled into another context where some variation of the same script is enacted by innumerable other women and men. (pp. 168–169)

The depictions of human sexuality offered by most sexually explicit films have been criticized as "chauvinistically male or macho" (Crabbe, 1988). Because the overwhelming majority of sexually explicit materials, including films, are created for male audiences, this evaluation is not too surprising. A related concern is that these films degrade women, who are portrayed unrealistically. As Diamond (1985) noted, such material demeans women by depicting them as "malleable, obsessed with sex, and willing to engage in any sexual act with any available partner" (p. 42). The Presidential Commission on Obscenity and Pornography (1970) reported that sexually explicit materials characteristically involve "the degrading and demeaning portrayal of the role and status of the human female" (p. 239). Themes reflecting the subordination of women (for example, depictions of a man sexually dominating a woman) are rated as particularly degrading by both female and male viewers (Cowan & Dunn, 1994).

did YOU know?

Over 10,000 porn films were produced in the United States in 1999 alone.

Concerns about the objectification and degradation of women in male-oriented sexually explicit films led to a new genre—sexually explicit films intended for women, also called *femme films*. Former sex film star Candida Royale founded Femme Productions to offer sexually explicit films made by and for women. These productions have been described as being less focused on genitals, more focused on female sexual pleasure, and more sensual. Some studies confirm that women tend to find femme films more enjoyable and to feel less disgust and shame in response to them than in response to male-oriented films (Mosher & McIan, 1994). Laan, Everaerd, van Bellen, and Hanewald (1994) also found that female-centered films evoked more positive emotion, less negative emotion, and more subjective sexual arousal in female viewers than did male-centered films. However, there was no difference in genital arousal in response to the two types of films, as measured by vaginal pulse amplitude. Female viewers showed signs of physical arousal in response to both types of films but reported more psychological arousal while viewing femme films, a finding that illustrates the multifaceted nature of human sexual arousal.

Print

Interestingly, themes of female subordination, degradation, and bondage are most common not in pornography but in detective magazines. Dietz, Harry, and Hazelwood (1986) found that 76% of the covers of detective magazines depicted domination of women and 38% depicted women in bondage. However, these magazines have never been classified as pornographic or obscene (Linz, Donnerstein, & Penrod, 1987).

IN YOUR own words

Marina Trninic
University of Houston

Sexual desire, something that is essential and good, becomes distorted and tainted with pornography. Porn leads to the objectification of both men and women and desensitizes the immature viewer, so he or she doesn't take sex seriously.

Mass-circulation romance novels boast a predominantly female audience. These paperback novels, prominently displayed in many grocery stores, often depict a partially unclothed couple in a romantic embrace on their covers. The covers promote the often explicit erotic content of these books. A sample passage of one typical novel, *Forbidden,* conveys the sexual content:

> And when he moved over her, to satisfy her passionate need, she touched the swollen pulsing crest of his erection, her fingertips gentle, and guided him into her honeyed warmth. He filled her slowly, penetrating in measured degrees until his entire length was deep inside her. (Johnson, 1991, p. 419)

Although this erotic scene is sexually explicit, romance novels are not considered pornographic. There have been no official attempts to restrict the distribution of these books, and they are widely circulated. Few, if any, readers of these novels would be likely to describe themselves as consumers of pornography. Again, this situation illustrates the difficulty in defining pornography.

Online Pornography

The age of microchips and megabytes has introduced another medium for the dissemination of sexually explicit materials. Because the Internet permits near-instantaneous transmission of information to millions of users, special user groups and services focusing on sex are common. In contrast to other media, the Internet is global, readily accessible, affordable, and, perhaps most important, anonymous (Stern & Handel, 2001). The accessibility of the Internet, combined with the relative safety from detection that it provides, contributes to the bewildering range of sex-related topics one can find there—ranging from dating opportunities to such "specialized" interests as sadomasochism, bestiality, and other atypical behaviors (see Chapter 15). A recent search of sexually explicit postings revealed the following key words:

bondage (physical restraint)
domination (primarily psychological)
female-female (lesbianism)
group sex (threesomes and more)
sadomasochism (physical)
humor (sexual or "dirty" jokes)
incest and pedophilia (sex with children, both within and outside of the family)
male-female (conventional heterosexual sex)
male-male (gay sex)
rape (violent nonconsensual sex)
teen (consensual sex between teenagers)
cross-dressing (transvestism and/or transsexualism)

Although most of these topics are unusual, if not socially unacceptable, some involve illegal acts. For example, it is illegal to circulate sexually explicit materials that qualify as child pornography. America Online enlisted the aid of the Federal Bureau of Investigation after learning that computerized graphics of nude children were being posted on the Internet. Operators of Internet servers attempt to censor material that is illegal, but the sheer volume of submissions can be overwhelming. Although the majority of transmitted information is not illegal, some material is very explicit and has aroused controversy similar to that surrounding adult films. Compared to sexually explicit materials in print and videotapes, Internet porn is often more graphic and violent (Barron & Kimmel, 2000). For example, Gossett and Byrne (2002) studied several Internet rape sites, some of which include graphic depictions of violent rape. The images they sampled portrayed brutal torture rather than a romanticized depiction of forceful sex.

The controversy over online porn led to the passage in 1995 of the *Communications Decency Act,* which imposed penalties on users who transmitted to or solicited from a person under the age of 18 any information considered obscene or indecent. The American Civil Liberties Union (ACLU), with the support of computer software companies and Internet service providers, challenged the Communications Decency Act on the grounds that it violated the First Amendment right to free speech. Additionally, the ACLU argued that the term *indecent* was too vague for law enforcement and that the Internet is too large and complex to police effectively. A panel of federal judges agreed with the ACLU arguments and granted a preliminary injunction in June, 1996. The Communications Decency Act was eventually overturned by the U.S. Supreme Court on the grounds that it was vague and overly broad. The courts noted that Internet users are still subject to child pornography laws (Esposito, 1998). Congress subsequently passed the more narrowly written Child Online Protection Act in 1998, although it too was challenged.

Child Pornography

Child pornography usually consists of photographs of nude children as well as films involving adults having sex with children. Because the production and possession of such materials are prohibited by law, this trade, like child prostitution (discussed later in this chapter) is clandestine. Most of those who produce and purchase child pornography are *pedophiles,* men who are sexually attracted to prepubescent children. Some men, however, are involved in this business purely for financial reasons. In fact, child pornography and child prostitution represent the third most lucrative illegal trade in the world (Esposito, 1998); only the markets for illicit drugs and weapons generate more profit. Child pornography rings usually involve one or more pedophiles who entice or coerce children, sometimes their own, into being photographed or filmed. The photographs or films are then exchanged or sold to others with similar sexually deviant interests. One admitted child pornographer reported that a set of 200 photographs of nude children could sell for up to $25,000. Most disturbing was his revelation that the parents were often aware of his activities and received payment for offering their children as models for nude pictures (Burgess & Clark, 1984).

In recent years, the Internet has become a popular vehicle for transmitting and trading child pornography (Guttman, 1999). There are over 20,000 Web pages that include the phrase "kiddie porn," and a search using the term "child sex" can yield as many as 150,000 Internet sites (Casanova et al., 2000). By some estimates, 1,500 people regularly use chat rooms to exchange child porn. One in four teenagers who are regular Internet users reports having encountered unwanted sexual materials, and 20% have been exposed to sexual propositions or solicitations online (Finkelhor, Mitchell, & Wolak, 2000).

In contrast to producers of other forms of pornography, makers or users of child pornography can be prosecuted using the broadest definition of obscenity. The images do not have to be considered offensive, and artistic value is not a defense (Casanova et al., 2000). The Department of Justice prosecutes several hundred cases of child porn each year. The Federal Bureau of Investigation has a staff of over 150 agents devoted to eliminating child pornography. Yet, the clandestine nature of the trade and lack of enforcement in many countries allow child pornography to thrive. Although there is no question of the harmfulness of child pornography, there is ongoing debate over the effects on viewers of sexually explicit materials. The next section provides an overview of the intense debate about the effects of porn, along with a review of recent findings.

did YOU know?

The U.S Federal Bureau of Investigation has launched several undercover operations to target people who trade in child porn. Several hotlines for reporting potential illegal content on the Internet have been set up.

The Effects of Sexually Explicit Materials: An Ongoing Controversy

Although the majority of sexually explicit materials depict consenting partners, a number of books and films incorporate the element of violence or aggression into sex scenes. Some films present rape scenes in which a male forces an unwilling female into sexual acts. Brosius and colleagues (1993) reported this theme in 6% of the filmed scenes they examined. Although the Attorney General's Commission on Pornography (1986) concluded that violence in pornography had substantially increased since the 1970s, other sources have reported no change (Scott & Cuvelier, 1993). It is generally accepted that most sexually explicit films and magazines do not incorporate themes of sexual violence, but there is still significant controversy over whether these themes are becoming more prevalent (Fisher & Grenier, 1994).

17.2 on the web

People are divided on the issue of the harmfulness of pornography. There is even dissension among feminists, a group that has traditionally opposed pornography. Go to **www.ablongman.com/mcanulty2e.** *What viewpoints are discussed? What is the basis of each viewpoint? What does the author mean by "pro-sex feminism"?*

Linz and Malamuth (1993) identified three prevailing theories about the effects of sexually explicit materials on consumers: conservative-moralist, feminist, and liberal. The **conservative-moralist position** views these materials as threats to fundamental social institutions and religious values. According to this view, repeated exposure to such materials causes the reader/viewer to become desensitized and more accepting of sexually immoral acts. The **feminist position** is that sexually explicit materials degrade women and ultimately contribute to a variety of social injustices and problems, including the sexual coercion of women. In fact, some feminists, such as Andrea Dworkin and Catherine MacKinnon, broadly define pornography as "the sexually explicit subordination of women, graphically depicted, whether in pictures or in words" (Diamond, 1985, p. 41). In their view, any and all sexually explicit materials are inherently harmful to women. The **liberal position** stresses that sexually explicit materials are inherently harmless, just the depiction of fantasies. This view sees such material as a form of art, a source of sexual stimulation and sex education, and a potential means of liberation from inhibitions. The liberal position also invokes the basic right to freedom of speech.

The harmfulness debate revolves around two basic questions: (1) Do sexually explicit materials in general have detrimental effects on consumers? (2) Do violent sexually explicit materials in particular contribute to violence against women and to criminal behavior? These are distinct issues, which have been investigated separately in various research studies.

General Effects on Viewers

Zillman and colleagues have examined the general effects of sexually explicit materials on consumers. One focus of interest has been the **habituation effect**, or the tendency to show lower sexual arousal to a sexual stimulus with repeated exposure. The notion is that long-term consumption of (nonviolent) sexually explicit materials gradually causes the user to lose interest in their themes in favor of more deviant and violent themes, such as sadomasochism. According to Zillman and Bryant (1986), "the consumer of nonviolent erotic fare is likely to advance to less innocuous material . . . sooner or later" (p. 576). In his presentation to the Surgeon General's Workshop on Pornography and Public Health, Zillman (1986) suggested that censorship may be necessary in order to prevent an escalation to more deviant sexually explicit materials. Consistent with the conservative-moralist position, the concern is that regular users of sexually explicit materials may lose interest in more common sexual acts, which in turn might threaten the institutions of monogamy, marriage, and the family.

CONSERVATIVE-MORALIST POSITION
A viewpoint that condemns all sexually explicit materials as threats to such social institutions as the family and to moral values.

FEMINIST POSITION
A viewpoint that criticizes sexually explicit materials on the grounds that they degrade women and present them as objects and that argues that such materials promote sexual violence.

LIBERAL POSITION
A viewpoint that maintains that sexually explicit materials are not only harmless but educational and helpful for overcoming inhibitions.

HABITUATION EFFECT
The tendency to show lower sexual arousal after repeated exposure to a sexual stimulus.

In support of this view, Zillman and Bryant (1988) found that regular exposure (1 hour per week for 6 weeks) to nonviolent sexually explicit materials made viewers more accepting of premarital and extramarital affairs for both partners. Earlier studies, however, produced different results. Several researchers reported that habituation tended to be short-lived and that the most consistent consequence of regular exposure to nonviolent sexually explicit materials was a temporary increase in normal sexual behavior (Byrne & Lamberth, 1970; Mosher, 1970). These findings led the 1970 Presidential Commission on Obscenity and Pornography to conclude that the effects were temporary and usually consisted of an "increase in masturbation or coitus in individuals who habitually engage in these activities" (p. 194). More recently, Davies (1997) found that men who viewed sexually explicit films did not have negative attitudes toward women's rights, nor were they more accepting of marital or date rape. In an analysis of 30 laboratory studies of the harmfulness of sexually explicit materials, Allen, D'Alessio, and Brezgel (1995) concluded that exposure to pictorial nudity actually reduced sexually aggressive behavior. The same analysis, however, suggested that exposure to nonviolent sexually explicit films increased such behavior. Thus, the question of the effects of nonviolent sexually explicit materials remains open (Linz, 1989).

Harmful Effects of Sexually Explicit Materials

Several research strategies have been employed to assess the potential negative effects of sexually explicit materials. One type of study retrospectively examines the use of such materials by convicted sex offenders, such as rapists. Another strategy involves examining sex crime statistics in countries that have decriminalized pornography, as have most Northern European countries. Is there a systematic increase in sex crimes following the increased availability of sexually explicit materials? Both of these research strategies rely on correlational designs, which essentially involve determining whether there is a correlation (an interdependent relationship) between number of sex crimes and the availability of sexually explicit materials. A statistically significant positive correlation would mean that the number of sex crimes did increase when these materials became more widely available. The third research strategy for studying the potential harmfulness of sexually explicit materials has been the most popular of the three. In this approach, sexually explicit films with and without sexual violence are presented to research participants, usually male college students, in a laboratory setting. The effects of such materials are evaluated by examining changes in participants' attitudes toward women and rape and in their willingness to commit some analogue form of violence (such as administering a low-voltage shock to another person).

Looking At . . .

. . . Thinking About

The controversy over the potential harmfulness of sexually explicit materials revolves around the question of whether those who use them become more susceptible to sexual aggression and violence. Research reveals that the relationship between viewing sexual acts and behavior is complex. What factors might influence this relationship?

In examining convicted sex offenders' experiences with sexually explicit materials, Marshall (1989) concluded that they did not differ from those of other incarcerated males. Although one-third of rapists did report using sexually explicit materials immediately prior to assaulting a victim, several important points must be noted: First, the majority of viewers of sexually explicit materials do *not* have histories of sex offenses. Second, the majority of rapists commit their crimes without being aroused, or primed, by sexually explicit materials. Finally, some sex offenders may attribute their crimes to such materials in an effort to minimize their personal responsibility (Randall, 1989).

Kutchinski (1991) examined the incidence of rape in several societies that have lenient attitudes toward sexually explicit materials. He concluded that increased availability of such materials was not associated with increased reports of rape in Denmark, Sweden, West Germany, and the United States. A contradictory finding was reported by Baron and Straus (1984), who found a significant correlation between the circulation of adult magazines and the rape rate in all 50 states of the United States for the period between 1980 and 1982. There are a number of possible explanations for this finding, including a cause-and-effect relationship between pornography and rape (the feminist perspective) and the presence of a third variable, such as a *hypermasculine gender identity* (Baron & Straus, 1984). Such a gender identity may lead to both a strong interest in sexually explicit materials and a proclivity toward sexual violence. If this were the case, then the real cause of sexual violence would be the man's hypermasculine gender identity and not his exposure to sexually explicit materials. Although sexual violence and exposure to sexually explicit materials would be correlated, there would not be a cause-and-effect relationship. Clearly, this research did not resolve the harmfulness controversy.

Many laboratory-based studies of the harmfulness of sexually explicit materials have been conducted. Donnerstein, Berkowitz, and Linz (1986) compared reactions to three film conditions: nonviolent sexually explicit, violent but not sexually explicit, and violent sexually explicit. Prior to viewing the films, participants were treated in either an anger-provoking or a neutral manner by a female accomplice of the experimenters. The researchers found that both the violent sexually explicit and the violent but not sexually explicit conditions produced greater acceptance of rape myths among participants. The effects occurred regardless of how the participants had previously been treated by the female accomplice. These findings indicate that exposure to explicit violence, whether sexual or nonsexual, made research participants more accepting of rape myths.

A number of methodological criticisms have been directed at laboratory-based studies of the harmfulness of sexually explicit materials (Donnerstein et al., 1987). First, the aggressive behaviors shown by participants in the laboratory, such as administering shocks or aversive noise, are not equivalent to sexually assaulting a woman. Second, real-world punishments for sexual aggression, such as imprisonment, are not factors in these studies. Participants might be more reluctant to display aggressive behavior if they feared legal consequences. Third, these studies focus on a narrow segment of the population—male college students. The extent to which findings could be generalized to the entire population is unknown. Other concerns include problems in defining aggression, a publication bias (the tendency to publish only positive findings), and the possibility that participants respond to questionnaires in the way they think the researcher expects. Finally, the realism of the content of films shown in laboratory settings may vary tremendously. For example, many scenes of sexual assault depict the woman as initially resisting and ultimately being overcome by her own passion and enjoying the encounter. Clearly, this is a depiction in line with the rape myth, not a realistic portrayal of the brutality of rape. Some also question the ethics of exposing participants to materials that may lead to more sexually aggressive attitudes.

17.3 on the web

The debate over pornography has been extended to controversy over "cyberporn." Go to **www.ablongman.com/mcanulty2e** to review some recent articles on the controversy.

Which sides in the debate are represented? What are each side's arguments? Where do you stand?

From his review of the literature, Linz (1989) concluded that exposure to nonviolent sexually explicit materials does not seem to have adverse effects on attitudes toward rape and rape victims. The most consistent negative effects are observed "when subjects are exposed to portrayals of overt violence against women or when sex is fused with aggression" (p. 74). In addition, slasher films (which graphically depict nonsexual violence against women) consistently produce adverse effects in research studies. Therefore, Linz (1989) and other researchers (Donnerstein et al., 1987) have concluded that violence—not sex—is the toxic ingredient in violent sexually explicit materials, and that the "obscenity" in contemporary society is not sex but violence.

According to Intons-Peterson and Roskos-Ewoldsen (1989), exposure to violent sexually explicit materials leads to several consistent effects: (1) increased sexual arousal in normal and rape-prone males, (2) increases in rape fantasies, (3) desensitization to filmed sexual acts, (4) increases in aggression, (5) decreases in respect for women's rights, and (6) increased tolerance for rapists, rape myths, and violence toward women. More recently, Malamuth, Addison, and Koss (2001) concluded that exposure to pornography may indeed have harmful effects, depending on the individual. According to these writers, frequent exposure to pornography, especially porn with violent content, may elevate the risk of sexual aggression if the viewer is inclined to that behavior. Sexually aggressive men may interpret, and ultimately react to, pornography differently than do nonaggressive viewers.

Although controversy over the harmfulness of sexually explicit materials shows no signs of abating in the near future, there is near-unanimous agreement that exposure to sexual violence has negative effects on viewers (Allen et al., 1995; Linz & Malamuth, 1993; Malamuth et al., 2000). It seems clear that films depicting women being subjected to violence in any form have no redeeming value. Fortunately, although the degradation of women and sexual force are fairly common themes in sexually explicit films, extreme sexual violence is uncommon (Monk-Turner & Purcell, 1999).

ADULT ENTERTAINMENT

Adult entertainment is a broad term referring to a variety of products and services that have an "adult" theme, meaning that the content is sexually explicit. The term can refer to entertainment such as topless and nude dancing, to sexually explicit materials that are available in print (so-called adult magazines) or on film, or to services such as "phone sex" and Web sites that disseminate sexually explicit graphic images. Several Web sites offer interactive services that allow users to "converse" from their individual computers. Such interactive services make it possible for subscribers to exchange intimate personal information and even to develop relationships. Users may share sexual fantasies and even engage in simulated sexual activity.

The controversy over pornography spread to the Internet in 1995 with the passage of the Communications Decency Act. The act, which prohibits the dissemination of sexually explicit materials if they are potentially accessible by viewers younger than 18, was repealed on the basis of the First Amendment right to freedom of speech and on grounds of vagueness.

Cybersex

Online porn, or "cybersex," is one of the most profitable industries on the Internet. Annual sales reportedly range from $366 million to nearly $1 billion. On a given day, up to 4 million individuals visit one of the nearly 50,000 sites that offer sexually explicit materials (Webb, 2001). Nearly 44% of college students admit to having accessed sexually explicit materials on the Internet (Goodson, McCormick, & Evans, 2001). As noted earlier, the wide range of explicit materials and the anonymity afforded by the Internet make it a very attractive medium for many people.

The controversial side of cybersex has repeatedly made the news headlines in recent years. Internet users who compulsively visit sexually explicit sites are more likely to report psychological problems than are casual and typical users. In a survey of over 9,000 responses to an anonymous questionnaire posted on the Internet, Cooper, Scherer, Boies, and Gordon (1999) found that users who spent 11 or more hours per week visiting sexually oriented sites were more likely to admit to psychological distress and to agree that their Internet "surfing" caused problems in some areas of their lives. These compulsive surfers represent only a minority of visitors to sexually oriented sites. The majority of people logging onto such sites, some 92%, do so much less frequently, usually less than 1 hour per week, and they do not report any problems associated with their Internet use. In fact, the majority of Internet users do not even visit sexually oriented sites (Goodson, McCormick, & Evans, 2001). Those who access sexually explicit sites, usually males, list curiosity about sex as their main reason, followed by a desire to become sexually aroused or to enhance their sex lives. The majority of Internet users deny engaging in sexual activity online: 15% have masturbated while online and 12% had cybersex with an online partner (Goodson et al., 2001). Some gender differences in accessing Internet sex sites are reported. Men are more likely to seek visual materials than women, who tend to prefer chat rooms (Cooper et al., 1999). As might be expected, men are therefore more likely to report being sexually aroused by viewing sexually explicit materials online than are women (Goodson, 2000).

There are many noncontroversial sexually oriented uses of the Internet. Users can access any of several dating services, and there are countless examples of people meeting online and forming meaningful relationships. Many groups and organizations provide free educational information about sexuality and health. Also available is detailed information on STIs, safer sex practices, and medical treatments for various diseases. In addition to making this information available to a worldwide audience, the Internet protects users' anonymity, which encourages the more timid and inhibited to seek out sex-related information that they might not otherwise dare to obtain (Barak & Fisher, 2001).

Topless and nude dancing have become more popular in recent years. A recent survey found that nearly one out of four men had attended a club featuring this type of entertainment.

Topless and Nude Dancing

Entertainment featuring nude or topless dancing has gained popularity in recent years. In one survey, 16% of men and 4% of women reported having been to a club featuring nude or seminude dancers (Laumann et al., 1994). It is estimated that most major metropolitan areas have several dozen clubs that offer such entertainment, and these numbers seem to be steadily growing. The clubs offer acts consisting of performances by dancers in various stages of undress—from topless to completely nude, depending on local ordinances. These dancers have a variety of names, including "topless dancers," "strippers," "exotic dancers," and "adult entertainers." The last is apparently preferred by the dancers themselves because it carries less of a negative connotation than the others. Although live sex acts are illegal in the United States, some countries, such as Thailand, permit acts featuring sexual intercourse, heterosexual and lesbian, to be performed on stage (Manderson, 1992).

One of the first descriptions of such dancers was offered by Skipper and McCaghy (1970) who conducted a field study of 35 performers. Using semistructured interviews, the authors gathered information on the physical, social, and psychological attributes of "strippers." According to these researchers, the performers were typically the first born in a family in which the father was absent; they reached puberty early, had sexual experiences at an early age, and possessed the physical endowment (large breasts) desired in the trade. The dancers tended to demonstrate independence early, often leaving home when relatively young. The researchers suggested that this early departure from home represented an urge to escape an aversive environment and that the dancers' need for affection was met by their occupational choice; the public display of their bodies was a means of securing approval and recognition. In addition, the opportunity to dance for pay came at a time of financial need in these women's lives. The authors concluded that performers "became strippers more by chance than design, more by drift than aspiration" (p. 400). Thus, this description paints a picture of troubled childhood, early sexualization, and an opportunistic motivation for taking up the occupation. One finding that is consistently reported in studies of topless and nude dancers is that the primary motivation for pursuing it as an occupation is financial (McAnulty, Satterwhite, & Gullick, 1995; Skipper & McCaghy, 1970). The same finding has been noted for male strippers (Dressel & Petersen, 1982).

did YOU know?

According to the* Exotic Dancer Directory*, an industry publication, there are over 2,000 clubs offering adult entertainment in the United States.

Enck and Preston (1988) analyzed the nature of interactions between dancers and customers. Their conclusions were based on the observations of a student who secured a job as a waitress in a topless club. (She elected not to be listed as a coauthor with Enck and Preston because of the stigma associated with the topless dancing.) Enck and Preston (1988) emphasized the "counterfeit intimacy" that characterized the interactions between dancers and patrons. In their analysis, performances are orchestrated to provide an illusion of sexual intimacy, thus constituting a form of role-playing in which the actors have distinctive parts and goals. For dancers, the ultimate goal is to generate an income, by acting in a sexually provocative fashion. Several ploys used by dancers were identified, including making each customer feel special and sexually desirable and making themselves appear emotionally and/or sexually needy. For the customer, the primary goal is to obtain a "sexual experience." Customers' ploys included claiming an emotional attachment to a dancer, complaining of being lonely or deprived, and boasting of physical or financial resources. Despite their portrayal of the interactions as shallow and "counterfeit," Enck and Preston postulated that the dancing provided a source of fulfillment, for customers and dancers alike, which conventional or "legitimate" institutions had failed to offer them. Thus, adult entertainment is viewed by some as a useful and legal outlet for unmet needs.

In contrast to the negative portrayals of adult entertainers provided by earlier studies, a more recent study revealed a more positive picture. The personality profiles and background characteristics of 38 topless dancers were compared with those of a control group of restaurant waitresses (McAnulty et al., 1995). Overall, the dancers were not found to be more psychologically maladjusted. Both groups were above average in extraversion and openness to new experiences, and the dancers had higher incomes, earning four times as much as the waitresses. The dancers viewed themselves as more physically attractive, but they also reported greater preoccupation with body image than did the waitresses. No differences were found regarding criminal history. The vast majority of all participants reported a heterosexual orientation, and virtually all were in dating or committed relationships. Anecdotal information suggested that none of the dancers engaged in prostitution, which was strictly prohibited by the regulations of the particular club where these participants worked.

Although it is a newer form of adult entertainment, male stripping has increased in popularity. Interestingly, many who find this type of entertainment obscene do not object to the same degree of explicitness on national TV broadcasts.

Although many people consider adult entertainment to be a deviant occupation, topless dancers are not inherently maladjusted—although, undoubtedly, individuals attracted to such a job tend to be more uninhibited and more comfortable with their bodies than most. Some researchers have suggested that deviance is mostly in the eyes of the beholder. In other words, a career or lifestyle is deviant only if society labels it as such. This same issue arises in connection with another profession, prostitution. However, unlike topless and nude dancing, prostitution is almost always considered a deviant occupation.

PROSTITUTION

Prostitution is the indiscriminate exchange of sexual favors for economic gain, or the sale of sexual services, treating sex strictly as a commodity (de Zalduondo, 1991). Prostitutes are sometimes referred to as *sex trade workers*. For the prostitute, the sale of sexual services is a means of deriving or supplementing an income. In some cases, a prostitute may exchange sexual acts for illicit drugs; for example, so-called crack whores trade sex for crack cocaine (Fullilove, Lown, & Fullilove, 1992). A person who traded sexual favors for a job promotion would not be labeled a prostitute (at least not by law enforcement officers), although doing so would involve some of the same elements as in prostitution. What separates the prostitute from the person seeking a promotion is the repeated and indiscriminate selling of sexual services.

Historical Perspective

Prostitution has been called the "oldest profession." In reality, it is probably not any older than other social roles such as medicine man and priest. However, prostitution has always been and continues to be one of the most controversial occupations. Historically, there has been great ambivalence concerning the practice of selling sexual favors as an occupation. Although prostitution is often viewed as a deplorable practice, the fact that it has existed for millennia reveals that there has always been a demand for sex at a price. This longstanding ambivalence is illustrated by the writings of early religious authorities. Biblical texts refer to Mary Magdalene as a "woman of the city, a sinner," and many

PROSTITUTION
The indiscriminate exchange of sexual services for money.

references to harlots are found throughout the Bible. The 4th century Christian bishop Augustine viewed prostitutes as shameful, while also noting that they served as useful outlets for lustful desires. Similarly, during the Middle Ages, Italian priest and philosopher Thomas Aquinas believed that prostitutes helped prevent the spread of lustful sins (Bullough & Bullough, 1977). Napoleon Bonaparte is alleged to have said that "prostitutes are a necessity. Without them, men would attack respectable women on the street." In Victorian-era England, prostitutes were viewed as unfortunate but essential sexual outlets for men's needs; the existence of the trade prevented "worse offenses" such as having sexual encounters with other men's wives or with virgins (Taylor, 1970).

The ambivalence about prostitution is evident in various governmental policies and interventions. President Juan Perón of Argentina ordered the legalization of prostitution in 1954, and it has remained legal in Argentina since then. The Argentine government reasoned that legalizing the commerce of sex would help control the spread of STIs and would prevent men from engaging in sexually deviant behavior (Guy, 1991). One Argentinian, Dr. Nicolás V. Greco, wrote that banning prostitution led men to seek "artificial methods" (such as masturbation) or "sexual perversions" (homosexuality) for sexual release. Greco and others believed that prostitution encouraged heterosexuality and, therefore, reinforced the institutions of marriage and family. Lacking any scientific evidence to support these views, Greco quoted St. Thomas Aquinas and St. Augustine. Historical records suggest that prostitution has generally been viewed as a "necessary evil," one that might be tolerated to prevent worse evils.

Prostitution across Cultures

In most cultures, prostitution is viewed as a deviant occupation. This is clearly illustrated by the terms used to described prostitutes: "hooker," "whore," and other, perhaps less pejorative, terms such as "working girls," "ladies of the night," and *femmes fatales* (French for "deadly women"). The prevalence of prostitution varies widely across cultures, as do cultural attitudes toward the sale of sex. Many societies have quietly tolerated the practice; others are more openly accepting of it, within specified boundaries. In ancient Greece and Mesopotamia, temple prostitutes—both male and female—were common, and prostitution was associated with religious rituals. Having sex with a temple prostitute was considered a form of worship. Temple prostitution was also practiced in India. The Hindu temple of Samanâtha reportedly had over 500 "dancing girls" who provided music for the gods and sensual pleasure for male worshippers (Bullough & Bullough, 1978). Prostitution also flourished in medieval Europe.

17.4 on the web

Prostitution has a long history. For an idea of its prevalence in history, read the essay at **www.ablongman.com/mcanulty2e.**

What types of prostitutes existed in ancient Greece and Rome? Which issues were evident in those days? How did people of those days address these issues?

Some societies have banned prostitution outright, whereas it is regulated in others. In countries where prostitution is legalized, such as France and the Netherlands, prostitutes must be registered and must submit to periodic medical examinations. Prostitution is more prevalent in male-dominated, or patriarchal, societies in which women have a comparatively low status and are expected to cater to men's needs and desires. Prostitution is most prevalent in economically depressed countries that do not have severe sanctions for nonmarital sex, such as Mexico, Brazil, the Ivory Coast, and Thailand. Prostitution is least common in sexually open societies. Presumably, in an open and tolerant society, where both genders have equal rights and opportunities, there would be no need for a clandestine sex trade (Goode, 1990). However, note that even liberal countries such as Denmark report a thriving sex trade. And in a study of men in Norway (another sexually liberal country), 13% admitted to having paid for sex with a prostitute (Høigärd & Finstad, 1992).

Prostitution in the United States

Even in countries where prostitution is illegal, it exists and even thrives. Prostitution is illegal everywhere in the United States except a few counties in Nevada, where it is legal but regulated. (Each county in the state has the right to allow prostitution in designated areas). Janus and Janus (1993) estimated that 4 million women in the United States were involved in some form of prostitution. And this is probably an underestimate because of the clandestine nature of the profession and the tendency of some prostitutes to drift in and out of the trade. Potterat and colleagues (1990) pointed out that prostitution tends to be a short-term career, lasting 4 to 5 years for most. However, Freund and colleagues (1989) found that the prostitutes they studied had been in the trade for an average of 8 years. In their survey of sexual behavior, Janus and Janus (1993) found that 4% of the women surveyed admitted to having traded sex for money. In one study in New York City, 22% of gay and bisexual male adolescents admitted to exchanging sex for money or drugs (Rotheram-Borus et al., 1994). Interestingly, there seems to be no comparable survey of heterosexual male adolescents.

Although it is impossible to estimate accurately the number of prostitutes in the United States, survey results suggest that fewer men have experience with prostitutes today than did in the 1940s. Kinsey and colleagues (Kinsey, Pomeroy, & Martin, 1948) noted that two out of three white males they surveyed admitted to having had sex with a prostitute at least once, and up to 20% described themselves as regular customers. Later surveys suggested a significant decline in men's experiences with prostitutes. In the Janus survey (Janus & Janus, 1993), 20% of men admitted to having paid for sex. A similar pattern is noted for men who reported that their first sexual encounter occurred with a prostitute: Approximately 54% of high school graduates and 20% of college graduates who participated in Kinsey's survey were sexually initiated by prostitutes, compared to 10% of men surveyed over 20 years later (Hunt, 1974). A related pattern was more recently documented by Laumann and colleagues (1994), who found that 7% of 55- to 59-year-old men had their first sexual encounter with a prostitute, compared to 1.5% of 18- to 24-year-olds. The preferred explanation for this trend is the decline in the strength of the double standard in the second half of the 20th century, which made more women open to premarital sexual experimentation. The consequent increase in available sexual partners reduced men's inclination to pay a stranger for sexual activity (Edgley, 1989).

did YOU know?

The term **prostitute** *comes from Latin words meaning "to station in front of" or "to expose for sale." The word thus derives from prostitutes' advertising of the availability of their sexual services, whether through manner of dress, verbal propositions, or location. The corresponding legal term,* **solicitation,** *is a reference to offering sexual activity for a fee.*

The Prostitute

Throughout history and into modern times, the most common form of prostitution has involved women selling sexual favors to heterosexual men. The second most common form is carried out by homosexual male prostitutes catering to gay men. Male prostitutes who make themselves available to women are reportedly uncommon. Lesbian prostitutes are considered extremely rare. Despite what customers may believe, a prostitute does not engage in the practice for personal sexual satisfaction, but rather as a financial enterprise. Female prostitutes earn over 13 times the salary of nonprostitutes with comparable levels of education (Earls & David, 1989). Prostitutes do not generally derive pleasure from their encounters with customers and, in fact, generally resent those customers. By definition, the transactions are void of emotional involvement. The briefer the encounter, the sooner the prostitute can return to work and generate more income. One prostitute commented: "When I have intercourse, I move around just a little. Then the customers get more turned on, so it goes faster. Otherwise, it's so gross; besides, I get sore if it takes too long" (Høigård & Finstad, 1992, p. 68). Street prostitutes may have a dozen or more anonymous sexual encounters during the course of an evening (Cordelier, 1978; Heyl, 1979). One study of prostitutes found that the average number of customers per day was four, with some prostitutes reporting as many as ten (Freund et al., 1989).

Looking At . . .

. . . Thinking About

Although prostitution may not be the "world's oldest profession," it is one of the most controversial of all social roles. There has been a marketplace for the sale of sex throughout recorded history, but prostitution remains a deviant occupation in most cultures. What factors influence cultural attitudes toward this trade?

In some countries where prostitution is decriminalized and regulated, prostitutes work out of brothels. In these "houses of ill-repute," customers may choose from several prostitutes, who often pay the house a percentage of all earnings. In return, the prostitutes get a room, a steady clientele, and some protection from violence.

Female Prostitutes

There are different classes of female prostitutes. From society's perspective, the most deviant class is **streetwalkers**, who are also the most common and most visible. Streetwalkers are virtually indiscriminate in accepting customers, have relatively low fees, and generally have numerous customers in one night. Compared to other types of prostitutes, streetwalkers are more vulnerable to arrest and to abuse by customers. Most streetwalkers work for a pimp, usually a man who provides protection in return for a large percentage of the money the prostitutes earn.

Over 60% of the streetwalkers studied by Freund and colleagues (1989) engaged in fellatio and 23% had vaginal intercourse with customers. According to reports from female prostitutes, kissing is uncommon (Freund, Lee, & Leonard, 1991). As one prostitute stated: "Like most girls, I personally refuse to let a client kiss me on the mouth. . . . I make a distinction between my vagina and my mouth. I think it's only normal, we've got our dignity too" (Jaget, 1980, p. 167).

Streetwalkers advertise their services in several ways. They tend to wear provocative and revealing clothing and generally frequent areas known for prostitution. On gaining the attention of potential customers, they often make subtle ("Want to party?") or direct propositions ("I can show you a good time"). The cost of services is negotiated early in an encounter, and fees vary, depending on the type of sexual act requested; fellatio is often cheaper than intercourse (Winick & Kinsie, 1971).

Prostitutes who work in **brothels** (whorehouses), massage parlors, or clubs have higher status. Being employed by an establishment has some advantages for the prostitute: It is safer, and business is often more regular. However, arrest is also a risk if prostitution is illegal in the area where the brothel is located, since police vice squads periodically raid such facilities. In countries where prostitution is legal and regulated, brothel prostitution is prevalent. Typically, brothels are managed by a "madam," who collects a percentage of all earnings in the establishment (Heyl, 1979). Massage parlors are sometimes fronts for brothels. These typically do provide massages, but other services (often fellatio and masturbation) are available to clients for an additional charge. Such extra services are, of course, illegal in the United States. This association between prostitution and massage parlors has led many legitimate masseuses and masseurs to emphasize that they do not provide sexual services. One way to stress the legitimacy of massage services is to identify them as providing "therapeutic massage."

At the highest level of prostitution are **call girls**, who often operate through an escort service. Escort services advertise that they provide male or female escorts for social occasions. The advertisements stress that the services are confidential and discreet. In one large city in the southeastern United States, no fewer than 106 such escort agencies advertised their services. The advertisements made it clear that the agencies were thinly veiled covers for prostitution ("Fantasy Girls," "Wild College Girls," "Affairs of the Heart").

Call girls demand a higher price and are more selective than streetwalkers or brothel prostitutes, and they typically have a small clientele of regular customers (Greenwald, 1970). They often operate independently and live a luxurious lifestyle in comparison to other types of prostitutes (Winick & Kinsie, 1971). Unlike streetwalkers and brothel prostitutes, call girls do not usually have multiple encounters in one evening. Heidi Fleiss, "the Hollywood Madam," made the headlines in 1993 when it became known that she operated an exclusive call girl service that catered to wealthy men in California. This case was sensational not so much because it involved prostitution but because of allegations that Fleiss's customers included politicians and popular actors.

Roles equivalent to those of contemporary prostitutes were found in ancient Greece, where *pornoi* (a term meaning "the writing about [or by] prostitutes") made up the lowest class of prostitutes and *hetairae* (meaning "companion") were the higher-

STREETWALKERS
The most visible prostitutes, who have low status and are indiscriminate in accepting customers for comparatively low rates.

BROTHEL
An establishment that offers prostitutes a location for conducting their trade, with attendant benefits such as protection and a fairly stable clientele.

CALL GIRL
High-status prostitute who commands a higher fee and usually has a small clientele of regular customers.

class courtesans (Bullough & Bullough, 1978). The latter held high unofficial status, were educated and socially sophisticated, and commanded a high price for their services. Ancient Greek culture was characterized by rigid gender inequality: Wives were responsible for child-rearing and domestic duties, while hetairae served as social and sexual companions. In both cases, the woman was considered a man's property, for either his sexual enjoyment or his domestic comfort.

Male Prostitutes

Although both are old practices and probably have similar prevalence rates, male prostitution has received less attention than female prostitution. Prior to 1963, even less was known about male prostitution than is known today. That year, John Rechy published *City of Night,* a novel about a boy from Texas who becomes a prostitute and plies his trade throughout the United States. The novel portrayed the seamier side of male prostitution and increased public awareness about the "profession."

Male prostitutes tend to practice their trade intermittently in comparison to female prostitutes (Winick & Kinsie, 1971). The vast majority of male prostitutes offer their services to gay men. Interestingly, the majority of male prostitutes do not describe themselves as gay. In a study of 224 male street prostitutes, Boles and Elifson (1994) found that only 18% described themselves as homosexual, nearly 36% considered themselves bisexual, and 46% were self-described as heterosexual. These prostitutes' average age was 28, and most had been in the trade for close to 10 years. In a study of male prostitutes in London, West and de Villiers (1993) reported that the ages ranged from 16 to 21 years. This study found that fellatio and masturbation were the most commonly reported sexual activities performed by male prostitutes. Anal intercourse occurred somewhat less frequently and commanded a higher fee.

The types of services offered by male prostitutes vary as a function of their reported sexual orientation. Boles and Elifson (1994) found that heterosexual prostitutes were unlikely to participate in anal intercourse, whereas nearly 65% of homosexual prostitutes engaged in receptive anal intercourse. Twenty-three percent of bisexual male prostitutes participated in receptive anal intercourse (Boles & Elifson, 1994).

Like female prostitutes, male prostitutes cite making money as their primary motivation (Boles & Elifson, 1994). Some male prostitutes report being attracted initially by the excitement of life on the streets and the prospect of multiple sexual encounters. However, the novelty rapidly wears off, and the main reason for continuing in the trade is financial. As one male prostitute put it, "I'm hustling money—not sex" (Boles & Elifson, 1994, p. 44).

Several types of male prostitutes have been identified. **Hustlers** are viewed as the male counterpart of streetwalkers. Like streetwalkers, they tend to have multiple indiscriminate encounters during the course of a day or a night. These encounters may take place in public places, such as parks or restrooms, or in customers' automobiles. However, in contrast to streetwalkers, hustlers generally do not have pimps. A few gay or transgendered male prostitutes cross-dress while working (Weinberg, Shaver, & Williams, 1999). Some of their customers may mistake them for women, especially if the prostitute restricts his sexual activity to performing fellatio on the customer. **Call boys** are equivalent to call girls, in that they have a regular clientele and live a more comfortable lifestyle. **Kept boys** are financially supported by an older male, or "sugar daddy," in exchange for sexual favors. Finally, heterosexual males who are paid for sex by female customers are known as *gigolos,* but they are fairly uncommon. In comparison to female prostitutes, very little research has been conducted on the types of male prostitutes, with the exception of hustlers. This classification of male prostitutes is somewhat arbitrary, because some men adopt more than one of these roles over time (Earls & David, 1989).

HUSTLER
The male counterpart of a streetwalker.

CALL BOY
The male equivalent of a call girl.

KEPT BOY
Usually a younger man who is financially supported by an older "sugar daddy."

Customers of Prostitutes

Both researchers and the legal system have shown far more interest in prostitutes than in their customers. Prostitutes are more likely to be arrested than their customers, and the criminal charges filed against them are typically more serious (Boyle & Noonan,

1987). According to Margo St. James, a former prostitute and advocate for the rights of sex trade workers, few men are arrested on prostitution charges. Those few who are arrested are actually male prostitutes rather than customers (St. James, 1987). This pattern of prosecuting prostitutes more frequently than their customers is not new. In the 18th century, convicted male customers were fined, but the female prostitute was publicly flogged. The prostitute's crime has consistently been viewed as worse than the customer's. Prostitution remains the only sexual offense for which more women than men are convicted.

In the trade, customers are referred to as "johns" or "tricks." Their demographic characteristics cross all socioeconomic and racial strata. One study of the customers of an escort service, based on an address listing obtained during a raid, found that the majority of clients were white, married, and affluent (Adams, 1987). From interviews with 101 customers of New Jersey streetwalkers, Freund, Lee, and Leonard (1991) reported that 42% were married and most resided in the surrounding area. The average age of the customers was 40. Most of them were regular customers (93% made monthly visits and 63% reported weekly encounters) who had been visiting prostitutes for more than a year. Furthermore, 55% of the customers engaged in sexual activity with the same prostitute each time. Sex usually occurred outdoors, for example, in a back alley, or in the customer's car. The preferred sexual activity was fellatio; vaginal intercourse was the second most frequent activity (Monto, 2001).

Among the motives cited for using prostitutes are sexual variety, loneliness, sexual deviance, curiosity, and sexual deprivation (Xantidis & McCabe, 2000). Some customers cite the anonymous nature of sex with a prostitute. The encounters do not require emotional commitment or preliminary courting. The prostitute holds no expectation of the client other than financial remuneration. The customer may believe that he is unable to obtain sexual favors without paying for them. This might be the case for men whose wives object to certain sexual practices (such as fellatio), men who have serious physical deformities or are socially anxious, or men with deviant or kinky sexual proclivities. For example, some customers solicit from prostitutes unusual sexual activities that their regular partners find objectionable, such as bondage, spanking, or the use of unusual costumes or sex toys. Finally, some customers employ the services of prostitutes when their regular partners are unavailable because of travel or illness. In the 1930s and 1940s, prostitutes sometimes functioned as sex educators by initiating young men into sexual intercourse, but this role is much rarer in contemporary society.

The Life of Prostitution

In contrast to the fairly positive depictions of the lives of prostitutes in such films as *American Gigolo, Pretty Woman,* and *Moulin Rouge,* their actual existence is typically anything but glamorous. Studies and autobiographies frequently portray prostitutes as coming from dysfunctional backgrounds, suffering from psychological and medical problems, and living on the fringe of society (Dalla, 2000; Earls & David, 1989). Such findings bring up the question of why someone would choose this way of making a living. Do prostitutes select this stigmatized and often risky occupation in full appreciation of these factors, or is it a desperate choice when no other viable options present themselves?

Motives for Entering Prostitution

The social and personal dynamics that lead a person into prostitution have been the subject of study. Poverty and limited alternatives are commonly reported as underlying factors. In some Third World countries, impoverished parents sell their daughters to brothels. McCaghy and Hou (1994) reported that one-third of Taiwanese prostitutes entered the sex trade to provide financial assistance to their parents. Another third became prostitutes because of personal debts. The remainder entered the trade out of desperation or exploitation. As one prostitute reported, "I was sold to an illegal wine house by my foster father. That is the way I began my life as a prostitute. I was often beaten by him since I was 3. When I was sold, I did not have much choice" (p. 261).

A significant number of those entering the trade in the United States and Canada are adolescent runaways. It is estimated that several million children and adolescents are involved in prostitution (Willis & Levy, 2002). In the United States alone, more than 244,000 children are at risk of commercial sexual exploitation, which includes prostitution and child pornography (Estes & Weiner, 2001). Child prostitution has been reported throughout the world, from Boise, Idaho, to Bangkok, Thailand and London, England (see Figure 17.2). Both boys and girls are involved, and their ages range from 10 to 17. Many adult prostitutes started their careers in adolescence, when they ran away to escape physical, mental, or sexual abuse at home. According to Williard (1991), low self-esteem and a lack of marketable skills may lead some runaways to turn to prostitution as a means of survival on the streets. Most commonly, an adult—a pimp or even a parent—is involved in initiating an adolescent into the trade, often promising easy money as a lure. Campagna and Poffenberger (1988) described a pimp who recruited 12- to 14-year-old girls from a shelter for runaways and another who met desperate youths at bus stations. Providing them with illegal drugs is another common means of facilitating the sexual exploitation of children and adolescents.

Several million children and adolescents are involved in prostitution worldwide. Many enter the sex trade out of desperation, having run away from home after enduring sexual, physical, or emotional abuse (Kidd & Kral, 2002).

A history of childhood sexual abuse is commonly reported by prostitutes (Potterat, Rothenberg, & Muth, 1998; Simons & Whitbeck, 1991). In one study of 200 adolescent and adult female prostitutes, 67% reported being sexually abused by a father or father figure (Silbert & Pines, 1981a, 1981b). Typically, young prostitutes have escaped a troubled home and find themselves isolated with virtually no financial resources. Williard (1991) estimated that 75% of juvenile prostitutes are runwaways or "castaways" (youths who are actively encouraged to leave home by parents). In their study of adolescent runaways, Rotheram-Borus and colleagues (1992) found that 13% of males and 7% of females had provided sexual favors in return for money or drugs. For a number of these adolescents, prostitution is a readily available option when survival on the streets seems problematic (Earls & David, 1989). Vanwesenbeeck (2001) concluded that childhood abuse, homelessness, and substance abuse were common motives for entering prostitution. In non-Western cultures, such as Taiwan and Thailand, economic necessity is the primary reason for entering the sex trade. Rather than having an abrupt beginning, becoming a prostitute is usually a gradual, insidious process.

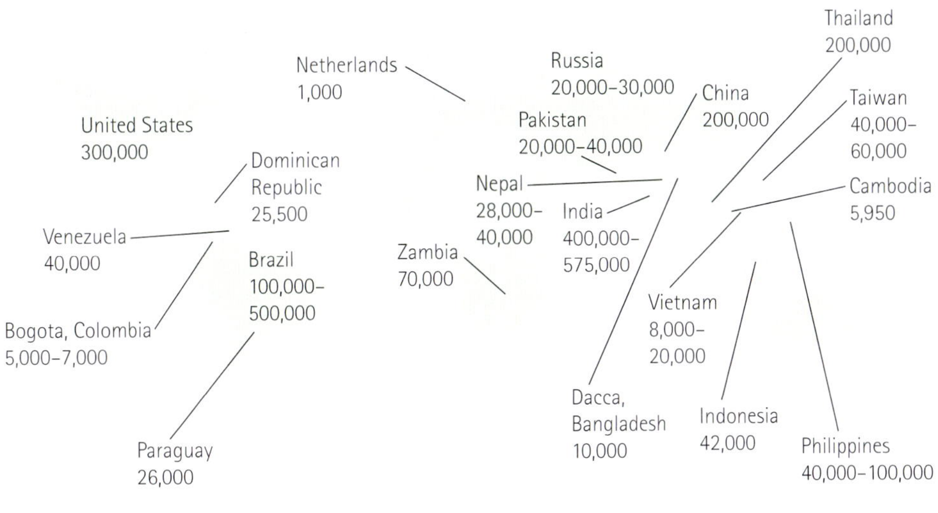

Figure 17.2 A Problem of Global Proportion: Number of Children Exploited through Prostitution
SOURCE: Willis and Levy, 2002

Risks of the Business

The lifestyle of prostitutes entails many risks, including violence from customers and pimps, criminal arrest, and STIs. According to Høigård and Finstad (1992), prostitutes' risk of assault by customers increases proportionately with the number of customers served. Nineteen of 26 prostitutes they interviewed had experienced violence from customers, ranging from "slaps to rape, from confinement to threats of murder" (p. 58). Nearly two-thirds of the 211 male prostitutes studied by Simon, Morse, Osofsky, Balson, and Gaumer (1992) feared violence by their customers. The risk of violence is especially high for female streetwalkers (Church, Henderson, Barnard, & Hart, 2001). Health Matters: HIV and Prostitutes details what may be the most dangerous risk of prostitution.

Substance abuse is another problem commonly reported by prostitutes. All of the male prostitutes studied by Simon and colleagues (1992) were users of drugs (primarily alcohol, cocaine, and marijuana), and 80% of them abused more than one drug. Boles and Elifson (1994) found that over half of the male prostitutes in their study were

HEALTH Matters

HIV and Prostitutes

The increased recognition of the role of prostitutes in the worldwide spread of HIV and other STIs has renewed efforts to study the sex trade. Although infection by a prostitute accounts for a relatively small percentage of total cases of HIV worldwide, in some countries prostitution represents the major avenue for the spread of this disease. In a study of 1,000 prostitutes in Kenya, 85% tested positive for HIV (Lambert, 1988). In some brothels in Thailand, up to 70% of prostitutes are infected (Gray et al., 1997; Manderson, 1992). In the United States, estimates of HIV infection rates among prostitutes range from none to 60%, depending on location and the number of years the prostitutes have been in the trade (Lambert, 1988). Rates of infection may be higher among male than female prostitutes in the United States. Simon and colleagues (1992) reported that nearly 18% of the 211 male prostitutes they studied tested positive for HIV. Boles and Elifson (1994) found that 35% of the 224 male prostitutes in their study carried HIV. Male prostitutes who identified themselves as homosexual had higher rates of HIV infection (50%) than those who described themselves as heterosexual (18.5%).

Prostitutes may be more likely to contract HIV because they often engage in two behaviors with high risk for exposure to HIV: having sex involving fluid exchange with multiple partners and injecting drugs (Vanwesenbeeck, 2001). Obviously, the nature of prostitutes' work puts them in frequent contact with bodily fluids. Prostitutes who practice unprotected receptive anal sex are especially vulnerable to HIV infection (Karim & Ramjee, 1998). Although there has been a trend toward increased condom use among prostitutes, it is by no means consistent and universal. In addition, a prostitute's lifestyle commonly involves injectable drug use. Many prostitutes who are not injectable drug users have regular sex partners who are. Therefore, the partner's behavior puts the prostitute at risk for HIV disease, since male and female prostitutes rarely practice safer sex with their regular partners (Albert, Warner, & Hatcher, 1998; Weir, Roddy, Zekeng, & Ryan, 1999).

Recognizing these problems, several programs have been implemented to reduce health risks among prostitutes and their clients. One such program, EMPOWER (Education Means Protection of Women in Recreation), was developed in Thailand to provide HIV testing, education, and health counseling. Preliminary results reveal that this and similar programs are effective in reducing rates of HIV and other STIs among prostitutes (Hanenberg & Rojanapithayakorn, 1998).

users of injectable drugs; 54–71% used crack cocaine and 16–20% had abused heroin. Cocaine was reportedly the drug of choice, with nearly 80% reporting a history of abuse. Similar trends are reported among female prostitutes. The vast majority (86%) of one sample of 237 female streetwalkers reported drug usage. One-half of the women had used injectable drugs (Potterat et al., 1998). In most cases, substance abuse preceded the women's entry into prostitution, suggesting that they entered the trade as a means of supporting their drug habits. Problematic substance abuse may therefore represent another motive for becoming a prostitute (Dalla, 2000).

Prostitution in Perspective

Sociologists and feminists have emphasized the gender inequality that is evident in prostitution. Most prostitution primarily benefits men: Male customers obtain sexual favors from prostitutes, who, in turn, often financially support their male pimps. As mentioned earlier, women who are most likely to enter the trade are economically disadvantaged, with limited education and skills, and commonly having a background of abuse (Bell, 1987). They take up prostitution because they believe they have few social or economic resources other than their sexuality. Prostitution is never fully accepted in any modern society. Prostitutes generally occupy the lowest rungs of the social ladder. Even where prostitution is legalized, legalization is "not an expression of society's acceptance of prostitution but instead epitomizes a policy of isolation and stigma toward the prostitute" (Hobson, 1987). In other words, policies and regulations in tolerant societies represent subtle attempts to control or segregate prostitutes. In a fair, egalitarian society, many other options would be available to disadvantaged women, and they would rarely select such a deviant occupation. As Hobson noted:

> A society that institutionalizes prostitution as a work option for the poor makes a statement about its position on inequality. One can see this in the policy toward prostitution in countries like Korea, and until recently, the Philippines. The governments have sought to legitimize prostitution as work, even elevated it to a patriotic endeavor, since sex commerce has brought in foreign tourism and reduced the national debt. (p. 235)

Within the feminist movement, there is disagreement over whether prostitution is degrading to women or an acceptable choice for independent women. Feminists have debated whether the prostitute is the "quintessential oppressed woman or the quintessential liberated woman" (Tong, 1984). The majority of feminists have argued that women would not choose to be prostitutes if they were offered better alternatives. With the proper education and economic opportunities, women would be free to select any career, and it seems unlikely that many would opt for such degrading, socially rejected roles as prostitute, topless dancer, and actress in sexually explicit films (Bell, 1987).

From the perspective of evolutionary psychology, prostitution and all forms of commercial sex are based on two factors: men's inherent desire for casual sex and sexual variety, and the willingness of some women to exchange sexual services for material resources (Buss, 1999). According to this view, men, whether viewing pornography or visiting a prostitute, are seeking sexual variety with minimal investment. Women, on the other hand, whether acting in a film or indiscriminately providing sexual favors, are motivated by the need for material resources. As Buss (1999) noted, "some women choose prostitution because it provides a quick and lucrative source of income and hence may be seen as a desirable alternative to a 9-to-5 job or a demanding husband" (pp. 341–342). Prostitutes, like other women who pursue sex without commitment, are controversial because they compete for men's resources by exploiting their desires for casual sex. In other words, "prostitutes may siphon off resources that might otherwise go to a man's wife or children" (Buss, 1999, p. 342).

17.5 on the web

Visit the Prostitution Research and Education (PRE) Web site through the link at **www.ablongman.com/mcanulty2e.** The purpose of PRE is to organize against the institution of prostitution and to advocate for alternatives to prostitution—including emotional and physical healthcare for women in prostitution. Read the article on prostitution and racism by Vednita Carter.

According to Carter, how does racism make black women and girls especially vulnerable to sexual exploitation?

From any perspective, the sex trade is flourishing and will continue to do so despite efforts to regulate or eliminate it. Clearly, commercial sex, in all its forms, represents one of the most controversial aspects of human sexuality.

HEALTHY DECISION MAKING

Part of the controversy surrounding commercial sex centers on the question of harmfulness. Does the consumption of sexually explicit materials pose social or psychological risks? Does the trade in such materials jeopardize the rights and freedom of women? Research provides some answers, but the answers to many questions remain elusive. Some of the issues are not readily addressed by research—they involve matters of personal beliefs and values. You've considered your attitudes toward sexually explicit materials as you've read this chapter. If your position on such materials is basically the conservative-moralist or the feminist one, your life is unlikely to include their use. But maybe you take a more liberal position. If so, the research findings summarized below may help you make healthy decisions.

- What is the medium? Most research has been concerned with the effects of exposure to sexually explicit films. Comparatively little research has been aimed at print and computer graphics. Soft-core films and photographs of nudes are not nearly as controversial as hard-core films.
- What is the content? Sexual violence depicted in any form has been shown to have potentially negative effects on viewers. Films involving consensual sexual activity, including women-centered films, are less controversial, and they appeal to a broader audience.
- How much exposure? The vast majority of consumers of sexually explicit materials are occasional users. The likelihood of potential harm is much lower than for the compulsive user, who may spend several hours per day viewing sexually explicit materials.
- What is the viewer's motivation? It is likely that occasional use of sexually explicit materials for entertainment or educational purposes is less problematic than regularly substituting such materials for an actual partner. Excessive reliance on sexually explicit materials could interfere with the formation or maintenance of a healthy sexual relationship.

Other considerations include local regulations and laws surrounding the possession of sexually explicit materials and one's partner's reactions to such materials. Partners who disagree about the use of sexually explicit materials should try to discuss their individual concerns, their reasons for enjoying such materials, and their personal values. Once again, open communication is the key to a healthy and rewarding intimate relationship.

summary

PORNOGRAPHY

- Technological advances have made sex more public than ever before in history. Commercial sex constitutes a lucrative industry worldwide.
- Definitions of what constitutes pornography have varied across cultures and changed over time. *Obscenity* is the legal term applied to material deemed indecent or immoral. *Erotica* refers to sexually explicit materials that are judged to have some artistic value.
- Several legal definitions of pornography have been used. Current legal standards hinge on whether the material in question is offensive, lacks artistic value, and appeals to prurient interests.

- Sexually explicit drawings can be traced back to the time of the earliest social structures. Primitive drawings, ancient figurines and carvings, and sexual themes in literature attest that pornography is not a product of modern culture. Technological advances, from the printing press to the Internet, have facilitated the large-scale production and dissemination of sexually explicit materials.
- The content of certain media has become increasingly graphic over the years. Motion pictures allowed an unprecedented degree of explicitness. Most sexually explicit films are male-oriented. Women-centered films are less graphic in their content. Magazines and books are generally less controversial than films. Online porn is readily accessible.
- The illicit production of child pornography is a growing problem. Those who are involved in distributing child porn are usually pedophiles.
- The question of the harmfulness of sexually explicit materials remains controversial. There is, however, a near-consensus that explicit depictions of sexual violence are potentially harmful. Studies suggest that exposure to such materials renders some viewers more accepting of rape myths and less empathetic toward rape victims.

ADULT ENTERTAINMENT

- The Internet provides access to a wide range of sexual materials and online relationships.
- Topless and nude dancing have become popular forms of adult entertainment. The notion that these dancers are psychologically maladjusted does not seem to be valid. The primary motivation for entering the occupation is financial.

PROSTITUTION

- Prostitution involves the indiscriminate exchange of sex for money. Prostitution has a long and controversial history. It is virtually always viewed as a deviant occupation. Societal attitudes vary from quiet tolerance to prohibition. Prostitution is more prevalent in male-dominated societies in which women have low status and in sexually restrictive cultures.
- Prostitutes usually have relatively short careers. Fewer men have their first sexual experience with prostitutes today than in the past.
- There are several types of prostitutes. Among female prostitutes, streetwalkers are the most common and most visible. The equivalent role among male prostitutes is the hustler. The customers of prostitutes have been studied infrequently. Most customers are regulars who solicit prostitutes for a variety of motives, ranging from loneliness to sexual deprivation. The anonymous and indiscriminate nature of sex with a prostitute is often essential to the customer.
- Common motives for entering the sex trade include financial need and previous exploitation. The lifestyle involves multiple risks, including violence, diseases, and substance abuse.
- Child prostitution is a tragic problem throughout the world. Some victims are coerced into the trade, but for others it is a survival strategy.
- The feminist perspective traces the roots of prostitution to gender inequality and sexual exploitation of women by men. Feminists are, however, divided on whether prostitution represents oppression or a free choice for its practitioners. From the viewpoint of evolutionary psychology, prostitution thrives because of men's inherent desire for casual sex and women's willingness to offer sex in exchange for money. From this perspective, prostitutes are stigmatized because they compete with other women for men's resources.

glossary

abortifacient A method or substance that causes a fertilized ovum that has implanted in the uterine wall or a fetus to be expelled.

abstinence script A set of sexual standards that prohibit sexual activity prior to marriage.

acquaintance rape The occurrence of nonconsensual sex between individuals who are acquainted (for example, as relatives, friends, classmates, or coworkers).

acquired immunodeficiency syndrome (AIDS) A condition caused by the human immunodeficiency virus (HIV) and characterized by destruction of the immune system, which leaves the infected person susceptible to a wide range of serious diseases.

acrosome A membrane that covers the top of the head of a sperm cell and contains enzymes that allow the sperm to penetrate the ovum.

agape In Lee's theory, a selfless and ideal type of love that is rarely achieved; it combines eros and storge.

alpha-fetoprotein (AFP) A substance produced by the fetus and found in the mother's blood. High levels of AFP in the mother's blood indicate the possibility of fetal neurological abnormalities, and very low levels of AFP are indicative of an increased risk of fetal Down syndrome.

alveolar glands Glands in a woman's breasts that are responsible for producing milk after childbirth.

amenorrhea Absence of a menstrual period.

amniocentesis A diagnostic procedure in which amniotic fluid is removed from the amniotic sac to test for some fetal defects.

amniotic fluid Liquid inside the amniotic sac in which the fetus floats; it provides protection against jarring and bouncing and changes in temperature.

amniotic sac Fluid-filled membrane surrounding the fetus.

ampulla The wider section of a fallopian tube.

analingus Oral-anal stimulation.

androgen insensitivity syndrome (AIS) A hormonal abnormality that occurs in males whose adrenal glands produce normal amounts of testosterone but whose target cells are unresponsive. As a consequence, they lack an internal reproductive system, either male or female.

androgynous Having both masculine and feminine characteristics.

antipsychotic medications Drugs that are used to reduce or eliminate psychotic symptoms such as visual and auditory hallucinations or delusional beliefs and that reduce sexual functioning.

anxiolytic agents Drugs that are used to reduce anxiety and have been associated with impaired sexual functioning.

anxious-ambivalent attachment According to Bowlby, a form of emotional bond that leads a person to be insecure and needy in interpersonal relationships.

aphrodisiac Any substance believed to stimulate or intensify sexual desire or arousal.

areola Pigmented circular area surrounding the nipple of a breast.

artificial insemination (AI) Process whereby sperm are collected from a donor and deposited in a woman's uterus.

avoidant attachment According to Bowlby, a form of emotional bond that leads a person to have difficulty forming intimate relationships.

bacterial vaginosis (BV) The most prevalent vaginal infection among women of childbearing age, characterized by a strong fishy odor and a grey or milky discharge; it was previously called *vaginitis*.

barrier contraceptive methods Birth control methods that provide a mechanical block between sperm-containing seminal fluid and the cervix.

Bartholin's glands Glands located just inside the vaginal opening that secrete a small amount of fluid during sexual arousal; the function of this secretion is unknown.

basal body temperature (BBT) method Birth control method that relies on identifying a drop in body temperature that occurs just prior to ovulation.

behaviorism A scientific approach that emphasizes the study of observable behavior rather than unobservable processes such as thoughts and emotions.

benign prostatic hyperplasia (BPH) Enlargement of the prostate gland caused by the natural aging process.

bimanual exam Medical procedure to check for abnormalities in the uterus and ovaries.

bisexual Feeling erotic and romantic desires for both sexes.

blastocyst A stage of a zygote in which it is a mass of developing cells surrounding a cavity.

bloody show Pink-tinted vaginal discharge caused by the bursting of capillaries in the cervix as it effaces and dilates.

Braxton-Hicks contractions Uncomfortable but not painful contractions that occur around the 20th week of pregnancy that are thought to strengthen uterine muscles to prepare the uterus for labor. They are not part of labor.

breech position Fetal position in which the buttocks or one or both legs position themselves in the pelvis first.

brothel An establishment that offers prostitutes a location for conducting their trade, with attendant benefits such as protection and a fairly stable clientele.

bulbocavernosus muscle Muscle at the base of the penis that contracts to force ejaculate out through the urethra.

bulbourethral gland A pea-sized gland that is located just below the prostate gland and emits an alkaline fluid in response to sexual stimulation; also called the *Cowper's gland.*

call boy The male equivalent of a call girl.

call girl High-status prostitute who commands a higher fee and usually has a small clientele of regular customers.

candidiasis A vaginal yeast infection, most commonly caused by the fungus *Candida albicans.* In women it results in vulval irritation, inflammation and itching, and sometimes a cottage-cheese–like discharge. Men are usually symptom-free.

case study A scientific method that relies on an in-depth analysis of a single case or person.

central nervous system (CNS) Division of the nervous system consisting of the brain and spinal cord.

cervical cap A barrier method of birth control, similar to a diaphragm but smaller; designed to fit snugly over the cervix to block the passage of sperm.

cervical mucus charting method Birth control method that relies on identifying changes in mucus secretions that are associated with the fertile period.

cervical os The opening of the cervix.

cervicitis Inflammation of the cervix.

cervix Structure that is located at the innermost end of the vagina and is the narrowest and outermost part of the uterus; also called the *uterine cervix.*

childhood sexual abuse Any sexual experience between a child or adolescent and either an adult or a more knowledgeable child, which may or may not involve physical contact.

chlamydia An STI caused by the bacterium *Chlamydia trachomatis.* It commonly causes abnormal vaginal and urethral discharge in women, eye disease and pneumonia in infants born to infected women, and may cause non-gonococcal urethritis in men.

chorionic villi sampling A diagnostic procedure in which tissue from the chorion of the placenta is removed and tested for certain fetal abnormalities.

chromosomes Rod-shaped structures within each cell nucleus that carry genetic material.

cilia Tiny hairlike structures inside each fallopian tube whose movements guide the egg cell down the tube.

classical conditioning A form of automatic or reflexive learning in which one stimulus becomes associated with another one that already triggers some reaction. By association, the new stimulus comes to elicit a conditioned response.

clitoral hood Tissue that covers the clitoris and is formed by the joining of the labia minora.

clitoris A cylindrical structure composed of shaft and glans, found just below the mons veneris and under the clitoral hood.

cognitive restructuring A technique used in sex therapy to modify negative thoughts and beliefs that contribute to a person's sexual problems.

coitus interruptus Also called *withdrawal;* a birth control method that requires a man to remove his penis from the vagina and away from the woman's genital area just before ejaculation.

colostrum A thin, clear or yellowish fluid secreted from the breasts in late pregnancy and for about 48 hours after birth. Colostrum contains many nutrients and antibodies that are valuable for the newborn.

combined oral contraceptive A pill that contains a combination of estrogen and progestin, hormones that prevent ovulation and have other contraceptive effects.

coming out (of the closet) Acknowledging and openly accepting one's same-sex feelings.

commitment In Sternberg's triangular theory, the component of love that involves a conscious decision to remain in a love relationship.

community A collection of people with similar beliefs, feelings, and behaviors who feel a commitment to each other.

companionate love Berscheid and Walster's term for a love relationship built on trust and security. In Sternberg's theory, a type of love that incorporates intimacy and commitment; it is characteristic of strong friendships.

conceptus A zygote or fetus.

concordance Agreement.

concrete-operational stage In Piaget's theory of cognitive development, the stage during which preadolescents become increasingly capable of thinking logically about real problems and the world. At this stage, their questions become more realistic.

condom A barrier method of birth control; a sheath that covers the penis to prevent expulsion of seminal fluid into the vaginal canal.

congenital adrenal hyperplasia (CAH) A hormonal abnormality resulting from a genetic defect that causes the adrenal glands of the fetus to produce excess testosterone. In boys, this results in premature puberty. In girls, the condition causes some masculinization of the genitals; also known as *adrenogenital syndrome.*

conservative-moralist position A viewpoint that condemns all sexually explicit materials as threats to such social institutions as the family and to moral values.

consummate love In Sternberg's triangular theory, the ideal form of love that incorporates all three components: intimacy, passion, and commitment.

contraception Any technique designed to either prevent the release of an ovum, prevent fertilization of an ovum, or prevent a fertilized ovum from implanting in the uterine wall.

contraceptive sponge A barrier method of birth control; a polyurethane disk containing spermicide, which is placed over the cervix to prevent movement of sperm into the cervical os.

control group In an experiment, the comparison group that is treated identically to the experimental group, with the exception that the independent variable is withheld.

controlled experiment An experiment involving the systematic application or manipulation of one variable and observation of its impact on another while other factors are held constant.

convenience sampling A method of obtaining research participants solely on the basis of their availability.

coprophilia A paraphilia involving sexual arousal in response to feces.

coronal ridge The rim of the glans; also called the *corona.*

corpora cavernosa Two cylindrical spongy bodies of erectile tissue that are bound in thick membrane sheaths, are located within the shaft of the clitoris and the penis, and become engorged with blood during sexual arousal.

corpus spongiosum A cylindrical body located within the shaft of the penis, and consisting of spongy, erectile tissue bound in a thick membranous sheath; houses the urethra and becomes engorged with blood during sexual arousal.

correlational design A study whose goal is to investigate the extent to which two (or more) variables co-vary, or change together; unlike a true experiment, no independent variable is manipulated.

cremaster muscle Muscle located in the spermatic cord that assists the dartos muscle in raising and lowering the scrotal sac.

cross-dresser A person who gains sexual arousal or positive nonsexual feelings by dressing in the clothing of the opposite sex.

cryptorchidism Failure of one or both testes to descend into the scrotum during prenatal development.

cystocele Protrusion of the bladder into the vaginal wall.

dartos muscle Muscle under the skin of the scrotum that contracts and relaxes to raise or lower the scrotal sac.

date rape A specific form of acquaintance rape that occurs in a dating situation.

debriefing Informing participants in a scientific study of any deception used and its purpose once they have fulfilled their part in the study; ethical principles require that participants be debriefed at the conclusion of a study.

dependent variable In an experiment, the presumed effect, which is measured as the independent variable is manipulated.

Depo-Provera A birth control method involving injection of synthetic hormones every 3 months to prevent ovulation.

detumescence The release of sexual energy, as in orgasm, in both men and women, according to Ellis's model.

diaphragm A barrier method of birth control; a dome-shaped rubber cup with a flexible rim, which is placed over the cervix to prevent movement of sperm into the cervical os.

dilation and curettage (D & C) A procedure whereby the cervix is dilated and an instrument called a curette is used to scrape the uterine lining. This procedure is used following a miscarriage, as well as for abortions and to remedy other medical problems of the uterus.

dilation and evacuation (D & E) An abortion procedure that can be conducted when a woman is between the 13th and 16th weeks of pregnancy, which involves enlarging the cervical opening, aspirating the contents from the uterus, and scraping the uterine lining.

dilation and extraction (D & X) An extremely controversial abortion technique, also called *intact dilation and evacuation.* The technique involves dilation of the cervix to the extent possible and removal of the fetus through the vaginal canal, feet first, until all but the head is in the vaginal canal. To reduce the size of the head, fluid or brain tissue is extracted by way of suction through an incision at the base of the skull; then the fetus is delivered.

dildo A penis-shaped sex toy.

directed masturbation A technique aimed at solving the problem of female orgasmic disorder, involving several steps aimed at improving a woman's body image and sexual self-knowledge.

dismissing style Bartholomew's term for the attachment style shown by those who are indifferent to and uninterested in close relationships.

dizygotic (fraternal) twins Offspring that develop from separate ova fertilized at the same time.

domestic partnership A marriagelike relationship that is not legally recognized.

double standard script The viewpoint that different sexual standards apply to the sexes, and the expectation that women will be more sexually restrained than men.

douching Cleansing the vaginal canal by squirting a liquid into the vagina.

dysmenorrhea Spasmodic cramping in the lower abdomen, sometimes spreading to hips, lower back, or thighs, during menstruation.

dyspareunia A dysfunction involving recurrent genital pain during sexual intercourse.

dystocia Abnormal or difficult labor.

eclampsia Severely high blood pressure during pregnancy that can cause convulsions and coma.

ectopic pregnancy Implantation of a fertilized egg somewhere other than in the uterus.

effacement Thinning of the cervix that occurs just before labor.

egg cell (ovum) The female reproductive cell.

EIA (enzyme immunoassay test) A blood test for HIV antibodies. Two positive EIA tests indicate a high likelihood that a person is infected with HIV.

ejaculatory ducts Two ducts within the prostate gland through which the seminal vesicles empty into the vas deferens.

ejaculatory inevitability The sensation that ejaculation is imminent and unpreventable, which occurs during the emission stage of ejaculation.

embryo The prenatal organism from implantation on the uterine wall to the 8th week of pregnancy.

embryoscopy The insertion of an endoscope that contains a light source and lenses into the amniotic sac so that the embryo can be visualized and photographed.

emission stage of ejaculation The first stage of male orgasm, in which seminal fluid collects in the urethral bulb and the bladder sphincter closes to prevent release of urine and semen into the bladder.

empiricism The scientific practice of relying on direct observation and measurement when seeking answers to questions.

empty love A type of relationship in which both intimacy and passion have waned and only the commitment to stay together remains.

endometrial prostaglandins Hormones that cause uterine contractions.

endometriosis A disorder of the female reproductive organs in which tissue from the lining of the uterus migrates to other parts of the body.

endometrium The inner lining of the uterus.

epidemiology The discipline devoted to the study, control, and prevention of health problems and infectious diseases.

epididymis Long, coiled tube lying against the back of each testis, in which mature sperm are stored prior to ejaculation.

episiotomy An incision in the perineum sometimes made during delivery.

eros In Lee's colors of love theory, a primary type of love based on strong attraction and sexual arousal.

erotica A newer term used to describe sexually explicit material that is more artistic in its content.

estrogens A group of hormones that regulate the menstrual cycle and are responsible for producing secondary female sexual characteristics; also found in males in small amounts.

excitement transfer The misattributing of emotional arousal from nonromantic factors to the presence of another person.

exhibitionism A paraphilia characterized by the exposing of one's genitals to an unsuspecting person.

experimental group The group to which the independent variable in a controlled experiment is administered.

expulsion stage of ejaculation The second stage of male orgasm, during which semen is expelled through the urethra.

extragenital Occurring outside the genitalia.

fallopian tube A tube that runs from each ovary to the uterus; also called *oviduct*.

fatuous love Love characterized by passionate feelings combined with commitment but little intimacy.

fearful style Bartholomew's term for an attachment style that leads a person to have difficulty forming intimate relationships; equivalent to Bowlby's avoidant attachment.

female condom A barrier method of birth control; a thin, lubricated polyurethane pouch with a flexible polyurethane ring at either end, which is inserted into the vagina to prevent movement of sperm into the cervical os.

female genital mutilation The removal of part or all of the external female genitalia.

female orgasmic disorder A recurrent problem with reaching orgasm despite adequate erotic stimulation; the term should not be applied to women who occasionally do not reach orgasm through vaginal intercourse.

female sexual arousal disorder A sexual dysfunction involving difficulties becoming sexually aroused, including deficient vaginal lubrication.

feminist position A viewpoint that criticizes sexually explicit materials on the grounds that they degrade women and present them as objects and that argues that such materials promote sexual violence.

fertility awareness A birth control method requiring familiarity with changes in bodily functions during ovulation; abstinence is practiced when the woman is ovulating.

fetal alcohol syndrome (FAS) Moderate to severe physical abnormalities in a child that are produced by the mother's regular bouts of heavy alcohol consumption during pregnancy.

fetishism A paraphilia involving the use of an object (for example, articles of clothing) to obtain sexual arousal or satisfaction.

fetoscopy The insertion of an endoscope that contains a light source and lenses into the amniotic sac so that the fetus can be visualized and photographed.

fetus The prenatal organism from the 8th week of pregnancy until delivery.

fibrillations Rapid, irregular contractions of the uterus that are painless and occur during arousal and orgasm.

fimbriae Fingerlike projections at the end of the infundibulum that partially surround the ovary and help to guide the egg cell into the fallopian tube.

follicle-stimulating hormone (FSH) A hormone that is released by the pituitary gland during the follicular phase of the menstrual cycle and stimulates the growth of several ovarian follicles.

follicular phase The phase of the menstrual cycle that starts at the onset of menstruation and ends with ovulation, during which an ovarian follicle develops in an ovary; also known as the *proliferative phase* or the *preovulatory phase*.

foreskin The fold of skin covering the glans of the penis; also called the *prepuce*.

formal operational stage In Piaget's theory of cognitive development, the stage at which adolescents are capable of rational and abstract thought. Consequently, they often challenge authority and tradition, as they can imagine alternative viewpoints.

fornix Recessed area around the cervix.

frenulum A band of tissue that connects the glans to the foreskin.

frotteurism A paraphilia involving rubbing one's genitals against a nonconsenting person.

frozen embryo transfer (FET) A procedure in which frozen embryos are injected into a woman's uterus in an attempt to impregnate her.

fundal height The measure from a woman's pelvic bone to the top of the uterus, used to assess whether the fetus is growing properly.

gamete intrafallopian transfer (GIFT) A procedure involving harvesting eggs from an ovary, combining them with sperm, and injecting them into the fallopian tubes to foster natural fertilization and subsequent implantation.

gender The psychosocial condition of being feminine or masculine; the collection of particular behaviors, traits, and interests that are agreed to be either masculine or feminine.

gender bias Differential treatment of individuals of one sex, based on assumptions about that sex.

gender constancy Knowledge that one's biological sex is unchanging.

gender identity One's view of herself or himself as female or male.

gender identity disorder (GID) A psychological diagnosis based on a person's feeling as though he or she is trapped inside a body of the other biological sex and experiencing significant distress over this condition.

gender polarization A cultural tendency to define "mutually exclusive scripts for being male and female" and to view a person who does not adhere to the script as unnatural, immoral, or mentally ill.

gender roles Behaviors, personality characteristics, and lifestyles that a culture or society expects of an individual based on that individual's sex.

gender schema An internalization of a culture's gender-based classification of social reality.

gender stereotyping Assuming that an individual possesses certain characteristics or should perform certain tasks, based on her or his sex, regardless of how closely the person actually adheres to gender-role expectations.

gender-role conflict The uncomfortable psychological state that arises in response to rigid, sexist, or restrictive gender roles and that may lead to maladaptive behavior.

gender-typed behavior Behavior that adheres closely to the roles expected of a given sex.

generativity versus stagnation According to Erikson, the stage of midlife, during which the major psychosocial challenge is to assume responsible adult roles in multiple settings; if the challenge is not met, a person faces the likelihood of experiencing a sense of self-centeredness and feeling nonproductive.

genital warts An STI caused by the human papillomavirus and manifested by warts around the genitalia and anus.

glans The cone-shaped structure at the end of the penis; the visible tip of the clitoris.

gonadotrophin-releasing hormone (GRH) A hormone that is produced by a woman's hypothalamus and signals the pituitary gland to produce luteinizing hormone.

gonadotrophins Hormones released by the brain that direct the production of the sex hormones. In boys, these hormones cause the testes to produce testosterone; in girls, they direct the ovaries to produce estrogen.

gonorrhea An STI caused by the bacterium *Neisseria gonorrhoeae.* The infection commonly results in abnormal vaginal or urethral discharge and can also cause eye disease in infants born to infected women.

habituation effect The tendency to show lower sexual arousal after repeated exposure to a sexual stimulus.

Hegar's sign Softening of the uterus and cervix, which is detected by a physician during a bimanual exam and is a probable sign of pregnancy.

herpes simplex virus 1 (HSV-1) The virus that most commonly causes oral herpes, which is characterized by cold sores or fever blisters on the lips or mouth. The virus can also be transmitted to other areas of the body such as the eyes and genitalia.

herpes simplex virus 2 (HSV-2) The virus that most commonly causes genital herpes.

heterosexism Thinking of human experience in strictly heterosexual terms and consequently ignoring, invalidating, or derogating nonheterosexual behaviors, lifestyles, relationships, and sexual orientations.

heterosexual Experiencing erotic and romantic feelings for people of the opposite sex.

homologous structure Any organ found in both male and female that developed from the same cells in the fetus.

homophobia An extreme discomfort, aversion, fear, anxiety, or anger toward gay people; also called *homonegativism.*

homosexual Having erotic and romantic feelings for members of the same sex.

hostile environment harassment A form of harassment in which unwanted behavior of a sexual nature creates a hostile or offensive work atmosphere that may interfere with the employee's ability to complete his or her job.

human chorionic gonadotrophin (HCG) A hormone secreted by the placenta. Pregnancy tests detect this hormone in urine as a way of indicating probable pregnancy.

human immunodeficiency virus (HIV) The virus that causes AIDS.

human papillomavirus (HPV) The virus that causes genital warts.

hustler The male counterpart of a streetwalker.

hymen A thin ring of tissue partially covering the vaginal opening.

hypoactive sexual desire disorder A sexual dysfunction involving a persistent deficit in sexual fantasies and desire for sex.

hypothesis A predicted relationship between two or more variables that will be tested with an experiment.

identity versus role confusion According to Erikson's psychosocial theory, a developmental stage during which the major challenge for adolescents is to establish a sense of personal identity.

in vitro fertilization (IVF) A procedure involving the harvesting of eggs from a woman's ovary using ultrasound and aspiration of the eggs, combining them with sperm in a petri dish to foster fertilization, and then inserting one or more fertilized eggs into the uterus through the cervix 2 to 3 days later.

incest A more specific form of sexual abuse involving sexual activities between a child and a relative—a parent, stepparent, parent's live-in partner or lover, foster parent, sibling, cousin, uncle, aunt, or grandparent.

independent variable In an experiment, the presumed causal factor that is manipulated or changed in some way.

induced abortion Surgical removal of a fetus and supporting tissues from the uterus.

industry versus inferiority In Erikson's psychosocial theory of development, the stage during which preadolescents are challenged to become self-confident in social and academic settings.

infertility The inability to conceive a child after 1 year of trying to become pregnant.

informed consent Consent given by research participants who are fully informed of the nature of a study and whose participation is completely voluntary; ethical principles require that participants give informed consent before participating in a study.

infundibulum Cone-shaped end of each fallopian tube near the ovary.

integrity versus despair According to Erikson, the psychosocial challenge of late adulthood, in which individuals review their lifetime accomplishments and either find a sense of satisfaction or struggle with a sense of despair over lost opportunities.

interferon A biochemical that occurs naturally in the human immune system and that inhibits reproduction of some viruses; interferon injections have been approved by the FDA as a treatment for genital warts.

internalized homophobia Psychological acceptance by a gay, lesbian, or bisexual person of the society's prevailing negative views of homosexuals, resulting in internal conflict.

intersexuality A rare sex differentiation abnormality in which the person has ambiguous genitalia at birth. These individuals typically show partially male and partially female genitalia; also known as *hermaphroditism.*

interstitial cells Cells in the testes that produce androgens and release them into the bloodstream; also called *Leydig's cells.*

intimacy A state of closeness and familiarity with another person that is marked by mutual trust. In Sternberg's triangular theory of love, the emotional component of love, which is often manifested through emotional sharing and feelings of closeness.

intimacy versus isolation The stage described in Erikson's psychosocial theory of development during which young adults are faced with the challenge of finding a meaningful intimate relationship; if the challenge is not met, a person faces the prospect of loneliness.

intracytoplasmic sperm injection A procedure involving injection of sperm directly into the cytoplasm of an ovum to foster conception. This procedure is particularly useful in cases where few sperm are available or the sperm have functional abnormalities.

intrauterine device (IUD) A small plastic and copper object inserted into the uterus by a physician to prevent pregnancy.

intrauterine growth retardation Failure of the fetus to grow at the proper rate.

introitus The opening to the vaginal canal, through which the female menstruates, gives birth, and has vaginal intercourse.

invasive cervical cancer Disease resulting when abnormal cells grow beyond the outer tissue surface and into the cervix itself.

isthmus Narrow portion of a fallopian tube adjacent to the uterus.

Kegel exercises Exercises to strengthen the pubococcygeus muscle in order to reduce urinary incontinence and possibly increase sexual pleasure.

kept boy Usually a younger man who is financially supported by an older "sugar daddy."

Klinefelter's syndrome A sex chromosome abnormality that occurs in males who are born with an extra X chromosome. Their masculinization is incomplete, and they evidence some female physical characteristics, such as partial breasts.

klismaphilia A paraphilia involving sexual arousal in response to giving or receiving enemas.

labia majora Two folds of fleshy tissue extending from the mons veneris to below the vaginal opening; also called the *outer lips.*

labia minora Two relatively small, hairless folds of tissue located within the labia majora; also called the *inner lips.*

lactiferous duct Duct that connects the alveolar glands to the opening of the nipple and that stores and releases milk during lactation.

laparoscopy A surgical technique used in performing a tubal ligation to permanently prevent pregnancy.

late miscarriage Death of a fetus after the first trimester and no later than the 20th week of gestation.

leveling The communication technique of voicing a concern in a simple, clear, and specific fashion.

liberal position A viewpoint that maintains that sexually explicit materials are not only harmless but educational and helpful for overcoming inhibitions.

libido Freud's term for the sex drive, which he claimed was the driving force behind most human behavior; the underlying or general level of sexual interest.

lightening and engagement The descent of the fetus into the pelvic region, usually occurring between 2 and 4 weeks prior to onset of labor in first pregnancies. Lightening may not occur until onset of labor in subsequent pregnancies.

limbic system Area of the brain that controls emotional behavior.

lochia Discharge of the uterine contents that occurs for up to 6 weeks after delivery of a baby.

love schemas People's different views and expectations of themselves and their romantic partners.

ludus One of Lee's primary types of love that involves superficial game-playing.

luteal phase The phase of the menstrual cycle that begins at ovulation and continues to the onset of menstruation; also known as the *secretory phase* or the *postovulatory phase.*

luteinizing hormone (LH) A hormone produced by the pituitary gland that stimulates ovulation.

male erectile disorder A sexual dysfunction involving recurrent problems in achieving or sustaining an erection in a sexual situation.

male orgasmic disorder A dysfunction involving a delay or inability to reach orgasm during sexual activity.

mammary glands The breasts.

mania In Lee's theory, a secondary type of love that combines ludus and eros; it is an intense but possessive and obsessional type of love.

marital rape A form of acquaintance rape that involves a husband forcing sexual intercourse on his wife.

marriage A legally binding contract between two people that confers certain rights and privileges, imposes certain responsibilities, and is based on expectations of emotional commitment, shared responsibilities, and sexual exclusivity.

matching hypothesis The hypothesis that people tend to seek out partners whose physical, emotional, and social characteristics closely match their own.

measurement error Error caused by problems with the interviewer, participants, or questionnaires that result in inaccurate information.

meatus The urethral opening at the tip of the penis.

menarche A female's first menstrual period.

menopause The phase in a woman's life, usually around age 50, when the ovaries cease producing estrogen, marking the end of her reproductive years.

menstrual cycle The process by which the female body produces a mature egg cell, or ovum, that is capable of being fertilized by a sperm.

menstrual synchrony Similar timing of menstrual cycles that can occur among women who live in close proximity for extended periods.

menstruation Bleeding that occurs as a woman's body sheds the inner lining of the uterus if an egg has not been fertilized and implanted there.

mifepristone A drug that induces an abortion; also known as RU 486.

minilaparotomy A surgical technique used in performing a tubal ligation to permanently prevent pregnancy.

miscarriage Expulsion of the embryo before it can survive outside the womb.

missionary position One of the most common positions for coitus, in which the man lies above the woman while supporting some of his weight with his arms and knees.

monozygotic (identical) twins Two offspring deriving from a single fertilized ovum; these twins, therefore, have an identical genetic makeup.

mons veneris The mound of fatty tissue covering the female's pubic bone; also called the *mons pubis.*

morning sickness Nausea or vomiting usually occurring in the morning, especially early in pregnancy.

mucus plug A viscous substance that blocks the cervix during pregnancy and that is expelled as the cervix dilates in preparation for delivery.

myotonia Overall increase in muscle tension in both voluntary and involuntary muscles, which occurs during the excitement phase of the sexual response cycle.

necrophilia A paraphilia characterized by sexual activity with a corpse.

nipple Raised area in the center of the areola of each breast, with an opening through which an infant obtains milk.

nocturnal emission A nighttime ejaculation, or "wet dream," that sometimes signals the maturation of the male reproductive system.

nongonococcal urethritis An inflamation of the urethra in men, principally caused by chlamydial infections.

Norplant A birth control method that involves the implanting of six slender, silicone-rubber capsules under the skin; the capsules release a synthetic hormone, progestin, into the woman's system.

obscenity Legal term used to characterize sexually explicit materials that are judged to be illegal because of content that is harmful to viewers, without artistic merit, and that appeals to lustful desires.

observational learning Learning by observing and imitating other people. Social cognitive theories theorize that observational learning is the most influential process in human development.

open marriage An agreement between married persons that extramarital sex will be permitted under certain circumstances.

operant (instrumental) conditioning A form of learning in which responses are controlled by their consequences.

orgasm A series of rhythmic contractions of the muscles around the vagina, anus, and uterus in women, and involving the testes, epididymes, vas deferens, seminal vesicles, and prostate gland in men. Orgasm occurs at the peak of sexual arousal.

orgasmic platform Narrowing of the vaginal opening due to engorgement of the outer third of the vaginal wall during the plateau phase of the sexual response cycle.

outercourse Any sexual behavior except penile-vaginal or penile-anal contact.

ovarian cancer Disease resulting from the growth and spread of abnormal cells in an ovary.

ovarian cyst An abnormal fluid- or gel-filled sac that forms on an ovary.

ovaries Two solid, egg-shaped structures that are located near the ends of the fallopian tubes and that produce egg cells and some female hormones.

ovulation The release of an egg cell, or ovum, from an ovarian follicle.

Pap test A medical procedure designed to detect abnormal cells on the surface of the cervix; also known as a *Pap smear*.

paraphilias Sexual disorders that occur primarily in males, are characterized by recurrent fantasies, urges, or acts involving objects, nonconsenting partners, or physical pain or humiliation, and are distressing to the person or cause problems in his or her life.

paraphrasing Rephrasing another person's statement as a way of showing that the statement has been understood.

partialism A paraphilia characterized by sexual arousal in response to specific parts of the human body that are usually not associated with sexual activity (for example, feet).

passion The motivational aspect of love in Sternberg's triangular theory, providing emotional intensity and sexual arousal.

passionate love Berscheid and Walster's term for a love relationship built on intense emotions and strong sexual arousal.

pediculosis An infestation of parasitic pubic lice that causes itching.

pedophilia A paraphilia characterized by recurrent fantasies, urges, or acts involving sexual activity with prepubertal children.

pelvic exam Medical assessment of all the female reproductive organs.

pelvic inflammatory disease (PID) Inflammation of any of the organs in the pelvic region (the cervix, uterus, fallopian tubes, abdominal cavity, or the ovaries). The condition may cause abdominal pain, tenderness, nausea, fever, and irregular menstrual cycles and lead to infertility, ectopic pregnancy, ruptured membranes, and spontaneous abortions.

penile plethysmograph An instrument used to estimate a male's degree of sexual arousal by measuring changes in blood flow to the penis.

penis External cylindrical structure composed of a shaft and a glans.

perineum The muscular region covered with skin that extends from the vaginal opening to the anal opening in the female, and from the scrotum to the anal opening in the male.

peripheral nervous system (PNS) All of the nerve pathways into and out of the brain and spinal column.

permissiveness with affection script A common Western sexual standard that views sexual activity between unmarried persons as acceptable as long as there is an emotional bond between them.

permissiveness without affection script The sexual standard that specifies that sexual activity without emotional involvement is acceptable under certain circumstances, as in casual sex.

phallic worship Worship of the male genitals as a way of ensuring agricultural success and fertility.

pheromones Species-specific chemicals emitted by many animals that trigger mating behavior; human pheromones have not been conclusively identified and effects of pheromonelike substances on human sexual behavior have not been demonstrated.

pituitary gland The endocrine gland that controls the actions of all other endocrine glands.

placenta A disk-shaped structure made up of tissues from both the prenatal organism and the mother that allows for exchange between their circulatory systems. The fetus is attached to the placenta by the umbilical cord, through which it receives nourishment and oxygen, and through which waste products pass.

polymorphously perverse According to Freud, being born with erotic desire that is neither heterosexual nor homosexual and can be directed by various objects.

polythelia Having more than the normal number of nipples or breasts.

pornography Term used to describe written or visual materials that are designed to be sexually arousing.

postcoital contraception A method of contraception whereby a woman takes substantial doses of hormones after intercourse to prevent possible pregnancy.

postmature infant A baby delivered after the 42nd week of gestation.

postpartum blues Mild depressive symptoms occurring for only a short period just after the birth of a baby.

postpartum depression Feelings of extreme sadness, worthlessness, and inadequacy as a mother, possibly combined with suicidal thoughts, insomnia, digestive problems, and unusual weight loss occurring after the birth of a baby. Postpartum depression may require psychological intervention; however, it tends to resolve itself within 3 to 6 months.

posttraumatic stress disorder (PTSD) The reexperiencing of a traumatic event through involuntary thoughts, dreams, or flashbacks, accompanied by symptoms of increased arousal and by avoidance of thoughts, feelings, places, people, or things associated with the trauma.

pragma In Lee's theory, a secondary type of love that is based on logical and practical advantages; it combines ludus and storge.

pregnancy-induced hypertension (preeclampsia) High blood pressure during pregnancy; can result in poor liver and kidney function, reduced urine output, protein in the urine, swelling of the hands and face and sudden weight gain (both caused by water retention), headaches, dizziness, blurred vision, itching, irritability, and stomach pain.

premature ejaculation A dysfunction characterized by persistent or recurrent ejaculation following minimal stimulation and before the person wishes it.

premature infant A baby delivered between the 20th and 37th week of gestation.

premenstrual dysphoric disorder (PMDD) Severe and debilitating primarily psychological changes during the luteal phase of a woman's menstrual cycle.

premenstrual syndrome (PMS) Negative psychological, behavioral, and physical symptoms that arise consistently and predictably during the luteal phase of a woman's menstrual cycle, which are severe enough to interfere with some aspect of a woman's life.

preoccupied style Bartholomew's terminology for an attachment style that leads a person to be insecure and needy in interpersonal relationships; equivalent to Bowlby's anxious-ambivalent attachment.

preoperational stage The second stage of Piaget's theory of cognitive development, during which young children learn to think logically and symbolically, as evidenced by language development.

prepared childbirth Birth guided by skills learned to ease and control the labor process, using techniques such as breathing exercises, focusing on an object, and support by a labor coach.

preterm birth Delivery of a fetus any time after the 20th week of gestation.

preterm labor Labor beginning between the 20th and 37th week of gestation.

probability sampling A method of recruiting research participants in which each person has the same chance of being selected.

progesterone The hormone that is produced by the corpus luteum and is responsible for preparing the uterine lining for impregnation.

prostate cancer Disease characterized by the growth of abnormal cells in the prostate.

prostate gland Walnut-sized structure that is located beneath a man's bladder and emits fluid that combines with that from the seminal vesicles to form semen.

prostatitis Inflammation of the prostate gland that is bacterial or nonbacterial in origin.

prostitution The indiscriminate exchange of sexual services for money.

proximity A determinant of human attraction—people are attracted to others with whom they interact on a regular basis.

prurient Appealing to or inciting lustful desire; from the Latin word meaning "to itch" or "to crave."

pseudohermaphroditism A sex differentiation abnormality that is more common than true hermaphroditism. In genetic males, it involves having XY chromosomes but female external genitals. In genetic females, it consists of having XX chromosomes but male external genitals.

psychosexual stages In psychoanalytic theory, developmental stages during which the sexual instinct focuses on a particular body part. Healthy development requires the mastery of each stage and a transition to the next stage and culminates in genital sexuality.

pubic lice Parasitic biting lice that can be transmitted sexually.

pubococcygeus muscle Muscle that surrounds the vaginal and urethral openings and is responsible for controlling the flow of urine and the tautness of the vaginal opening.

quid pro quo harassment A form of sexual harassment in which an employee is expected to exchange sexual favors in return for keeping a job or getting a promotion.

rape The occurrence of sexual intercourse by force or threat of force without the consent of the person against whom it is perpetrated.

rape myths Prejudiced, stereotyped, or false beliefs about rape, rape survivors, and rapists.

rape trauma syndrome A two-phase reaction following rape; the acute phase is characterized by feelings of disorganization, and the long-term process phase is the stage of reorganization.

reasonable person standard A standard used in determining whether a behavior is harassing. According to the reasonable person standard, a hostile environment is one that a reasonable person in a similar situation would find to be intimidating, hostile, or abusive.

reasonable woman standard A standard used in determining whether a behavior is harassing. According to the reasonable woman standard, when the person who suffered harassment is female, the facts of the case must be viewed from the perspective of a reasonable woman, not a reasonable man, as behaviors that do not seem offensive to a man may be traumatic for a woman.

reciprocal liking A determinant of human attraction—people like others who like them in return.

rectal exam Medical procedure in which a physician feels the prostate gland through the rectal wall in order to assess for abnormalities.

refractory period In males, a period following orgasm during which additional stimulation will not produce an erection or result in orgasm.

reliability The accuracy or consistency of results of a scientific study.

rete testes Network of tubules within the testes through which the sperm travel to get from the seminiferous tubules to the epididymis.

retrograde ejaculation A condition in which ejaculate backs into the bladder rather than moving out through the urethra, usually caused by failure of the sphincter muscle at the bladder opening to contract.

retrovirus A type of virus that follows an uncommon biological process for reproducton.

Rh incompatibility A complication of pregnancy that can occur when the father is Rh positive (his blood contains the Rh antigen) and the mother is Rh negative (her blood does not have the Rh antigen). If the fetus inherits Rh-positive blood from the father, and blood from the fetus makes contact with the mother's blood, her body begins to produce antibodies to the Rh factor. Her body, therefore, will attempt to reject the fetus containing the Rh factor.

role modeling A learning process characterized by imitation of others' behaviors.

romantic love A love relationship in which intimacy and passion are strong but there is no significant commitment.

root The portion of the penis that extends into the body cavity and is anchored to the pubic bone.

sample A smaller group that is selected to represent a larger group, or population.

sampling bias A systematic error in obtaining research participants that renders the sample unrepresentative of the population.

scabies An infestation of a tiny parasitic mite that results in itching.

science A systematic method of inquiry that follows certain rules.

scrotum Hairless or lightly hair-covered saclike structure with two separate chambers, each of which houses one of the testes.

secure attachment Bowlby's terminology for a form of emotional bond that leads a person to approach the world confidently and to be trusting in interpersonal interactions.

seminal pool A pocket at the back of the vagina formed by the narrowing of the outer portion of the vagina in combination with the expansion of the inner portion during the plateau phase of the sexual response cycle.

seminal vesicles Small elongated structures located just outside the prostate gland that emit fluid into the vas deferens through the ejaculatory glands.

seminiferous tubules Coiled tubes in the lobes of the testes that produce the sperm.

sensate focus One of the original sex therapy techniques, designed to teach couples to focus on pleasurable sensations rather than on sexual performance.

sensorimotor stage In Piaget's theory of cognitive development, the first 2 years of life, during which children learn to coordinate sensory information with their motor capabilities.

sex The biological state of being male or female.

sex flush Blotchy reddening or darkening of the skin, which occurs during the excitement phase of the sexual response cycle.

sexology An interdisciplinary field devoted to the scientific study of sexuality.

sexual assault Coercive sexual contact that does not necessarily involve penile-vaginal intercourse, but may include anal intercourse, oral-genital contact, or penetration of the vagina or anus by objects such as broom handles.

sexual aversion disorder A sexual dysfunction characterized by extreme aversion to any form of sexual contact with a partner.

sexual dysfunction A recurrent sexual problem that interferes with normal performance and causes distress for the individual and his or her partner.

sexual harassment Deliberate or repeated pattern of sexual advances that are unwelcome and/or other sexually related behaviors that are hostile, offensive, or degrading.

sexual identity A person's sexual self-view, made up of gender identity, sexual orientation, and specific sexual preferences.

sexual masochism A paraphilia involving sexual arousal in response to being subjected to physical pain or humiliation.

sexual meanings Internalized interpretations of sexual experiences and cultural norms that contribute to one's sexual identity.

sexual orientation A person's erotic and romantic attraction to one or both sexes.

sexual pain disorder A sexual dysfunction involving genital pain during sexual activity with a partner.

sexual sadism A paraphilia involving sexual arousal from inflicting real pain or emotional suffering on another person.

sexually transmissible infection (STI) Any of a number of parasitic, bacterial, or viral infections that can spread through sexual contact.

shaft The body of the clitoris; the portion of the penis between the glans and the body wall of the pelvis.

silent rape reaction A pattern of response to rape in which a woman experiences many difficulties but does not disclose the occurrence of the rape to anyone and, therefore, is not able to obtain the support of others in coping with her experience.

similarity A determinant of human attraction—people like others whose personal attitudes, backgrounds, and interests are similar to their own.

Skene's glands A pair of glands located at the sides of the urethral opening, which secrete a small amount of fluid and might play a role in female ejaculation.

snowball technique A sampling method used by Kinsey that involves approaching a group or organization and trying to recruit the participation of every member.

social cognitive theories Conditioning theories that stress the importance of life experiences and social learning in shaping human behavior.

social support Help and support received from family and friends.

speculum A dual-bladed metal or plastic instrument that is inserted in the vagina during a pelvic exam to allow the physician to examine the cervix and vaginal walls.

sperm The male reproductive cells; also called *spermatozoa*.

sperm penetration analysis A test of infertility that assesses the ability of sperm to penetrate an ovum. A sample of sperm is incubated with numerous hamster eggs from which the zona pellucida has been removed. The number of sperm successfully penetrating the eggs is then analyzed. Thus the test is also called the *hamster egg test*.

spermarche The beginning of the production of semen by the testes; akin to females' first menstrual period.

spermatic cord A cord from which each testis is suspended in the scrotum; contains the nerves and blood vessels supplying the testes and the vas deferens.

spermatids Immature sperm.

spermatogenesis Process by which the seminiferous tubules produce sperm.

spermatogonia Germ cells produced in the seminiferous tubules of the testes.

spermicides Substances known to kill sperm on contact.

spontaneous abortion A miscarriage that occurs early in pregnancy, within the first trimester but usually between 6 and 10 weeks.

squeeze technique A technique aimed at solving the problem of premature ejaculation, whereby a man repeatedly masturbates almost to orgasm and then squeezes his penis to prevent orgasm.

statutory rape Intercourse with an individual who is under the age of consent.

stillbirth Delivery of a dead fetus.

stop-start technique A sex therapy technique used by couples to help the man gain ejaculatory control by ceasing stimulation as he nears orgasm. With repeated practice, the man gains increased control over ejaculation.

storge One of Lee's primary types of love, which consists of bonding and strong friendship.

stranger rape Nonconsensual sex between individuals who do not know each other.

streetwalkers The most visible prostitutes, who have low status and are indiscriminate in accepting customers for comparatively low rates.

surrogate mother A woman who is artificially inseminated with the sperm of a man who is not her husband; she carries the pregnancy to term and then turns the child over to the sperm donor.

survey The most popular method in sexuality research, which involves interviewing a number of people or having them complete a questionnaire.

swinging The practice in some open marriages of swapping partners with other couples.

syphilis An STI caused by the *Treponema pallidum* bacterium that, if untreated, progresses through several stages of development, from a chancre to a skin rash to damage of the cardiovascular or central nervous system to death.

telephone scatologia A paraphilia in which sexual arousal is derived from subjecting another person to obscene or inappropriate sexual language over the telephone.

tenting effect Expansion of the upper portion of the vagina and narrowing of the outer portion of the vagina resulting from the pulling up of the uterus and cervix during high levels of sexual arousal.

teratogens Substances that can be dangerous to the health of a fetus.

testes The male organs that produce and store sperm, located in the scrotum.

theoretical use failure rate The percentage of users of a contraceptive method who will get pregnant within 1 year while using the method perfectly each time.

token resistance Mild resistance to sexual advances offered by someone whose true intention is to engage in sexual behavior.

toucherism The fondling of a nonconsenting woman; differentiated from frotteurism in that it involves use of the hands.

transgendered individual A person whose appearance, behavior, or self-identification do not conform to traditional norms for his or her biological sex and gender.

transsexual A person who views herself or himself as being the sex opposite her or his biological sex.

transudation Vaginal lubrication resulting from increased blood flow to the vagina.

transvestic fetishism A paraphilia in which a heterosexual male achieves sexual arousal by wearing women's clothing, commonly known as "cross-dressing." The behavior of a person who cross-dresses specifically to obtain sexual arousal and gratification.

tribadism Rubbing together of genitals by two women.

trichomoniasis ("trich") An STI caused by the protozoan *Trichomonas vaginalis*.

troilism Observation by a male of his usual sexual partner engaged in sexual activity with another person; differentiated from voyeurism by the fact that all parties involved consent to the activity.

tubal ligation Sterilization technique; severing of the fallopian tubes to permanently prevent a woman from becoming pregnant.

tumescence The buildup of sexual tension in both men and women, according to Ellis's model.

tunica albuginea Sheath of tissue in the testes that surrounds the seminiferous tubules.

Turner's syndrome A sex chromosome abnormality that occurs in females who are born with only one X chromosome. They often are missing ovaries or have deficient ovaries, either of which interferes with sexual maturity and causes infertility.

typical use failure rate The percentage of typical users of a contraceptive method who will get pregnant within 1 year while using the method.

ultrasound technology A technique that uses sound waves to produce a two-dimensional image of internal body structures, including fetuses; the resulting image is called a *sonogram*.

umbilical cord A flexible cord that contains two arteries and one vein. These vessels transport blood between the fetus and the placenta. Waste products and nutrients move from and to the fetus by way of the umbilical cord.

urethra The passage through which urine flows out of the bladder. In the female, the urethral opening is just above the vaginal opening; in the male, a tube that runs the length of the penis in the center of the corpus spongiosum, through which urine flows and semen is ejaculated.

urethral bulb A part of the male's urethra, near the prostate gland, which balloons out and traps semen just prior to ejaculation.

urophilia A paraphilia characterized by sexual arousal in response to urine; typically, a person has a desire to be urinated on ("golden shower").

uterine fibroids Myomas; benign, solid tumors that form on the inside or outside of the uterus or within the uterine walls.

uterus The hollow, muscular, pear-shaped organ in which a developing fetus grows.

vacuum aspiration (vacuum curettage) An abortion procedure performed at any time up to 12 weeks of pregnancy, which involves enlarging the cervical opening and aspirating the contents of the uterus.

vagina A tubular structure that has the vaginal opening at one end and the cervix at the other.

vaginal photoplethysmograph An instrument used to estimate a female's sexual arousal by measuring changes in vaginal blood flow.

vaginismus A dysfunction characterized by persistent involuntary spasms of vaginal muscles, which interfere with sexual intercourse.

validation A problem-solving skill that consists of effective listening and acknowledging that the other person's complaints may have some validity.

variable In a scientific experiment, anything that can vary or change, such as attitudes, behaviors, or physiological responses.

vas deferens Tubes running from each testis to an ejaculatory duct.

vasectomy Sterilization technique; severing of the vas deferens to permanently prevent a man from impregnating anyone.

vasocongestion Engorgement of the blood vessels from increased blood flow to the genital region without a reciprocal increase in blood leaving it.

vestibular bulb Body of tissue on either side of the vaginal opening beneath the surface tissues that becomes engorged during sexual arousal.

vestibule Area between the labia minora where the urethral and vaginal openings are located.

vibrator An electrical or battery-operated device used to massage erogenous areas.

viral hepatitis Hepatitis caused by one of several viruses. Hepatitis B is the most common form of viral hepatitis that can be transmitted sexually. The virus is found in blood, semen, vaginal secretions, and saliva. Most cases of viral hepatitis are asymptomatic, but those infected can have a wide range of symptoms.

volunteer bias A form of sampling bias that occurs when people who volunteer for a study are shown to differ systematically from people who do not volunteer for the study; a common concern in sex research.

voyeurism A paraphilia that involves observing an unsuspecting person who is undressing or engaging in sexual activity.

vulva All of the external female genital structures; the vulval area.

vulvar vestibulitis A medical condition characterized by tiny sores on or around the vulva that may be the cause of genital pain during intercourse.

western blot A blood test that is highly specific for HIV antibodies. This test is used to confirm positive results from an EIA test.

zona pellucida Gelatinous outer layer of the ovum.

zoophilia A paraphilia that involves sexual activity with animals.

zygote intrafallopian transfer (ZIFT) A procedure involving harvesting eggs from a woman's ovary, combining them with sperm in a petri dish to foster fertilization, and inserting them into the fallopian tube 2 to 3 days later.

credits

Chapter 1: p. 2: Creatas; p. 3: Getty—Digital Vision; p. 4: Tom Rosenthal/SuperStock, Inc.; p. 6: Mary Kate Denny/PhotoEdit; p. 9: Jacques Zorgman/Newsmakers/Getty Images; p. 10: Roger De La Harpe/Gallo Images/CORBIS; p. 12 (both): Photofest; p. 14: Photofest; p. 16: LWA—JDC/CORBIS; p. 17: Reuters NewMedia Inc./CORBIS; p. 19: Getty Images, Inc.—Photodisc; p. 20: Jim Cartier/Photo Researchers, Inc.; p. 21: Ellen Rosenbery/The J. Paul Getty Museum, Los Angeles, Workshop of Boethos, Herm, 100–50 B.C., Bronze/ivory inlay, 23.5" × 103.5"; p. 23: Courtesy of Estelle Freeman, from John D'Emilio & Estelle B. Freedman, *Intimate Matters: A History of Sexuality in America,* 1997. Published by University of Chicago Press, Chicago, Illinois; p. 27: National Library of Medicine; p. 30: Tomas Del Amo/Phototake NYC.

Chapter 2: p. 38: Getty—Digital Vision; p. 39 (top): Getty Images Inc.—Stone Allstock; p. 39 (bottom): Bettman/CORBIS; p. 40: R. Ian Lloyd/CORBIS; p. 41: David Young-Wolff/PhotoEdit; p. 43: David Young-Wolff/PhotoEdit; p. 45 (both): Courtesy of Behavioral Technology, Inc.; p. 49: Ira Wyman/Corbis/Sygma; p. 52: Getty Images Inc.—Image Bank; p. 53: Everett Collection, Inc.; p. 55: Bruce Powell/Library of Congress.

Chapter 3: p. 64: Creatas; p. 64: Getty Images/EyeWire, Inc.; p. 65: Corbis Digital Stock; p. 67 (all): Susan Lerner/Design Conceptions; p. 81 (left): CORBIS; p. 81 (right): Brenda Chase/Getty Images, Inc.—Liaison; p. 82 (top): Joel Gordon/Joel Gordon Photography; p. 82 (middle): Custom Medical Stock Photo, Inc.; p. 82 (bottom): Susan Werner/Joel Gordon Photography; p. 83: B. Daemmrich/The Image Works; p. 88: Ghislain & Marie David de Lossy/Getty Images Inc.—Image Bank; p. 90 (left): Susan Lerner/Design Conceptions; p. 90 (middle, right): Joel Gordon/Joel Gordon Photography; p. 96: AFP/CORBIS; p. 100: Dan McCoy/Rainbow.

Chapter 4: p. 102: Getty—Digital Vision; p. 103: Getty—Digital Vision; p. 105: Jeff Greenberg/PhotoEdit; p. 106 (left): Phil Ramey/Corbis/Sygma; p. 106 (right): Frank Trapper/Corbis/Sygma; p. 108: Kathy Ferguson/PhotoEdit; p. 115: Jose Luis Pelaez/CORBIS; p. 124: Esbin-Anderson/The Image Works; p. 127: David Lees/Getty Images, Inc.—Taxi.

Chapter 5: p. 130: Creatas; p. 131: Image Source/ElectraVision/Picturequest—Royalty Free; p. 134: John Money, *Sex Errors of the Body and Related Symptoms: A Guide for Counseling Children, Adolescents and Their Families,* Second Edition, Revised 1994, Published by Paul H. Brookes Publishing Company, Baltimore, MD; p. 135 (left): Tony Freeman/PhotoEdit; p. 135 (right): Bob Daemmrich/Stock Boston; p. 140 (both): Dr. Laub/Gender Dysphoria Program, Inc.; p. 142: Colin McPherson/Corbis/Sygma; p. 143 (left): Laura Dwight/Laura Dwight Photography; p. 143 (right): L. Morris-Nantz/Pearson Education; p. 144: Universal Press Syndicate; p. 145: Alex Wong/Getty Images, Inc.—Liaison; p. 147: Ellen Senisi/The Image Works; p. 148: Tom McCarthy/PhotoEdit; p. 149: Touchstone Televison/Getty Images, Inc.—Liaison; p. 153 (left): Bachman/The Image Works; p. 153 (right): Brian Haimer/PhotoEdit; p. 158: Michael Newman/PhotoEdit.

Chapter 6: p. 162: Stockbyte/Picturequest—Royalty Free; p. 163: Ron Chapple/Thinkstock/Picturequest—Royalty Free; p. 164: Joel Gordon/Joel Gordon Photography; p. 169: Ryan McVay/Getty Images, Inc.—Photodisc; p. 171: National Anthropological Archives/Smithsonian Institution; p. 174: Dan Callister/Getty Images, Inc.—Liaison; p. 179: Axel Koester/Corbis/Sygma; p. 180: Creatas; p. 182: James Wilson/Woodfin Camp & Associates; p. 184: Neal Preston/CORBIS; p. 185: Ruth Ellis photo by Clint Steib, courtesy of The Washington Blade; p. 186: Richard Pasley/Stock Boston; p. 188: AP/Wide World Photos.

Chapter 7: p. 194: Creatas; p. 195: Getty—Digital Vision; p. 196: Steve Prezant/CORBIS; p. 198: Brown W. Cannon III/Getty Images Inc.—Stone Allstock; p. 205: Lori Adamski Peek/Getty Images Inc.—Stone Allstock; p. 207 (left): Art Wolfe/Photo Researchers, Inc.; p. 207 (middle): Getty Images Inc.—Image Bank; p. 207 (right): Rob Lewine/CORBIS; p. 208: AP/Wide World Photos; p. 213: Jack Star/Getty Images, Inc.—Photodisc; p. 215: IT STOCK INT'L/Index Stock Imagery/PictureQuest; p. 218: Photo Researchers, Inc.; p. 222: Michael Newman/PhotoEdit.

Chapter 8: p. 226: Creatas; p. 227: Creatas; p. 228: Ryan McVay/Getty Images, Inc.—Photodisc; p. 230: Jana Birchum/The Image Works; p. 233: Dann Tardif/CORBIS; p. 238: Eric Fowke/PhotoEdit; p. 240: Steve Mason/Getty Images, Inc.—Photodisc.

Chapter 9: p. 246: Getty Images/EyeWire, Inc.; p. 247: Picturequest—Royalty Free; p. 248: David M. Phillips/The Population Council/Photo Researchers, Inc.; p. 251 (top left): Petit Format/Nestle/Photo Researchers, Inc.; p. 251 (top right): Gary Watson/Science Photo Library/Photo Researchers, Inc.; p. 251 (bottom left): James Stevenson/Science Photo Library/Photo Researchers, Inc.; p. 251 (bottom right): Petit Format/Nestle/Science Source/Photo Researchers, Inc.; p. 255: Cat Gwynn/CORBIS; p. 257: Viviane Moos/CORBIS; p. 258: Royer/Explorer/Photo Researchers, Inc.; p. 261: Will & Deni McIntyre/Photo Researchers, Inc.; p. 262: Fetal Alcohol & Drug Unit (FAS); p. 264: Bill Stanton/Rainbow; p. 269: Stephen Simpson/Getty Images, Inc.—Taxi; p. 270: Saturn Stills/Science Photo Library/Photo Researchers, Inc.; p. 274 (both): SIU/Photo Researchers, Inc.; p. 275: Lawrence Migdale/Photo Researchers, Inc.; p. 279: David A. Wagner/Phototake NYC; p. 281: Laura Dwight/PhotoEdit.

Chapter 10: p. 286 (top left): Creatas; p. 286: Getty—Digital Vision; p. 287: Creatas; p. 288: Tom & Dee Ann McCarthy/CORBIS; p. 297: Joel Gordon/Joel Gordon Photography; p. 298: Joel Gordon/Joel Gordon Photography; p. 300: Yoav Levy/Phototake NYC; p. 301: SIU/Photo Researchers, Inc.; p. 302: Joel Gordon/Joel Gordon Photography; p. 303: Joel Gordon/Joel Gordon Photography; p. 304: M. Siluk/The Image Works; p. 305: Tom Pantages/Phototake NYC; p. 306: Joel Gordon/Joel Gordon Photography; p. 307 (top): Courtesy of Organon, Inc.; p. 307 (bottom): Courtesy of Berlex Laboratories, Inc.; p. 308: Michael Keller/CORBIS; p. 315: Dann Tardif/CORBIS; p. 317: Joe Sohm/The Image Works.

Chapter 11: p. 324: Getty Images, Inc.—Photodisc; p. 325: Creatas; p. 327: David Young-Wolff/PhotoEdit; p. 330: Roy Morsch/CORBIS; p. 331: Cassy Cohen/PhotoEdit; p. 334: Bob Daemmrich/Stock Boston; p. 337: David Young-Wolff/PhotoEdit; p. 342: Bob Daemmrich/The Image Works; p. 347: Getty Images, Inc.—Taxi; p. 348: Sergio Perez/CORBIS; p. 351: Keith Dannemiller/CORBIS/SABA Press Photos, Inc.

Chapter 12: p. 358: Ron Chapple/Ben Kikuyama/Thinkstock/Picturequest—Royalty Free; p. 359: Creatas; p. 364: Billy E. Barnes/PhotoEdit; p. 367: Getty Images Inc.—Stone Allstock; p. 368: Bill Bachman/Rainbow; p. 370: Timothy Shonnard/Getty Images Inc.—Stone Allstock; p. 373: Getty—Digital Vision; p. 375: Arlene Collins/The Image Works; p. 378: Ryan McVay/Getty Images, Inc.—Photodisc; p. 382: Michael Newman/PhotoEdit; p. 386: Myrleen Ferguson Cate/PhotoEdit.

Chapter 13: p. 390: Getty—Digital Vision; p. 391: Creatas; p. 394: The Cumer Museum of Art and Gardens, Jackson/SuperStock, Inc.; p. 395: Dan McCoy/Rainbow; p. 398: Spencer Grant/PhotoEdit; p. 400: Courtesy of Klang Images/Creative Management Partners; p. 403: Labat/Jerrican/Photo Researchers, Inc.; p. 411: Gary Conner/PhotoEdit; p. 412: Robbie Jack/CORBIS; p. 415: Courtesy of UroMetrics, Inc.; p. 416: Mulvehill/The Image Works; p. 417: Jonathan Ferrey/Getty Images, Inc.—Allsport Photography.

Chapter 14: p. 424: Getty Images/EyeWire, Inc.; p. 425: Getty—Digital Vision; p. 428: R. Calentine/Visuals Unlimited; p. 431: Cutis Magazine; p. 433 (left): CNRI/Phototake NYC; p. 433 (right): C. James Webb/Phototake NYC; p. 435 (top): Biophoto Associates/Photo Researchers, Inc.; p. 435 (bottom): CORBIS; p. 437: Stewart Cohen/Getty Images Inc.—Stone Allstock; p. 438: Biophoto Associates/Photo Researchers, Inc.; p. 440: Mark Antman/The Image Works; p. 443: AP/Wide World Photos; p. 446 (left): Rolf Bruderer/CORBIS; p. 446 (right): Kent Meireis/The Image Works; p. 451: Home Access Health Corporation, www.homeaccess.com; p. 452: Rachel Epstein/PhotoEdit; p. 454: David Hanover/Getty Images Inc.—Stone Allstock; p. 456: Doug Menuez/Getty Images, Inc.—Photodisc; p. 458: David Young-Wolff/PhotoEdit.

Chapter 15: p. 462: CORBIS Digital Stock; p. 463: CORBIS Digital Stock; p. 467: Allan Tannenbaum/CORBIS/Sygma; p. 468: Doumic-Rouet/Getty Images, Inc.—Liaison; p. 472: Getty Images Inc.—Stone Allstock; p. 473: Lee Celano/CORBIS/SABA Press Photos, Inc.; p. 475: Paula Bronstein/Getty Images, Inc.—Liaison; p. 476: Robert Brenner/PhotoEdit; p. 478: AP/Wide World Photos; p. 481: Ariel Skelley/CORBIS; p. 483: Barry King/Getty Images, Inc.—Liaison.

Chapter 16: p. 490: Creatas; p. 491: Getty Images/EyeWire, Inc.; p. 492 (both): Getty Images Inc.—Image Bank; p. 495: ER Productions/CORBIS; p. 501: Andrew Lichtenstein/The Image Works; p. 502: Gary Walts/The Image Works; p. 507: R. Sidney/The Image Works; p. 510: Getty Images Inc.—Stone Allstock; p. 511: Jacques Chenet/Woodfin Camp & Associates; p. 513: Paul Conklin/PhotoEdit; p. 514: Richard Townshend/CORBIS.

Chapter 17: p. 522: CORBIS Digital Stock; p. 523: Creatas; p. 525: AP/Wide World Photos; p. 526: CORBIS; p. 528 (top): Erich Lessing/Art Resource, N.Y.; p. 528 (bottom): David Young-Wolff/PhotoEdit; p. 535: Getty Images, Inc.—Taxi; p. 537: Lisa Quinnoes/Black Star; p. 538: Richard Sobol/Stock Boston/PictureQuest; p. 539: Christopher Brown/Stock Boston; p. 541 (left): Adam Scull/Rangefinders/Globe Photos, Inc.; p. 541 (right): Robin Nelson/Black Star; p. 542: Sovfoto/Eastfoto/PictureQuest; p. 545: Lutte/Getty Images, Inc.—Liaison.

Health Matters boxes: Chad Baker/Getty Images, Inc.—Photodisc.

Reflect on This boxes: Getty Images/EyeWire, Inc.

references

Abbey, A. (1991). Acquaintance rape and alcohol consumption on college campuses: How are they linked? *Journal of American College Health, 39,* 165–169.

Abbey, A., & Melby, C. (1986). The effects of nonverbal cues on gender differences in perceptions of sexual intent. *Sex Roles, 15*(5/6), 283–298.

Abbey, A., Ross, L. T., McDuffie, D., & McAuslan, P. (1996). Alcohol, misperception, and sexual assault: How and why are they linked? In D. M. Buss & N. Malamuth (Eds.), *Sex, power, conflict: Evolutionary and feminist perspectives* (pp. 138–161). New York: Oxford University Press.

Abel, G. G., Barlow, D. H., Blanchard, E. B., & Guild, D. (1977). The components of rapists' sexual arousal. *Archives of General Psychiatry, 34,* 895–903.

Abel, G. G., Becker, J. V., Cunningham-Rathner, J., Mittelman, M., & Rouleau, J. L. (1988). Multiple paraphilic diagnoses among sex offenders. *Bulletin of the American Academy of Psychiatry and the Law, 16,* 153–168.

Abel, G. G., Becker, J. V., Mittelman, M., Cunningham-Rathner, J., Rouleau, J. L., & Murphy, W. (1987). Self-reported sex crimes of nonincarcerated paraphiliacs. *Journal of Interpersonal Violence, 2,* 3–25.

Abel, G. G., Levis, D., & Clancy, J. (1970). Aversion therapy applied to taped sequences of deviant behavior in exhibitionists and other sexual deviations: Preliminary report. *Journal of Behavior Therapy and Experimental Psychiatry, 1,* 59–69.

Abel, G. G., Osborn, C. A., & Twigg, D. A. (1993). Sexual assault through the life span: Adult offenders with juvenile histories. In H. E. Barbaree, W. L. Marshall, & S. M. Hudson (Eds.), *The juvenile sex offender* (pp. 104–117). New York: Guilford.

Abelson, R. (1981). Psychological status of the script concept. *American Psychologist, 36,* 715–729.

Abma, J. C., Chandra, A., Mosher, W. D., Peterson, L. S., & Piccinino, L. J. (1997). *Fertility, family planning, and women's health: New data from the 1995 national survey of family growth.* Atlanta: Centers for Disease Contol and Prevention/National Center for Health Statistics.

Abouesh, A., & Clayton, A. (1999). Compulsive voyeurism and exhibitionism: A clinical response to paroxetine. *Archives of Sexual Behavior, 28,* 23–30.

About.com (1998). Rohypnol and GHB: The popular "date-rape drugs." Retrieved February 27, 2002, from http://parentingteens.about.com.library/weekly/aa062398.htm?terms=Rohypnol%2C+blue

AbuKhalil, A. (1997). Gender boundaries and sexual categories in the Arab world. *Feminist Issues, 15,* 91–105.

Achanzar, W. E., Diwan, B. A., Liu, J., Quader, S. T., Webber, M. M., Waalkes, M. P. (2001). Cadium-induced malignant transformation of human prostate epithelial cells. *Cancer Research, 61*(2), 455–458.

Action on Smoking and Health. (1999). Fact sheet #7: Smoking and reproduction. Retrieved May 17, 2000, from www.ash.org.uk/papers/fact07.html

Adam, B. D. (1987). *The rise of the gay and lesbian movement.* Boston: Twayne Publishers.

Adams, C. G., & Turner, B. F. (1985). Reported change in sexuality from young adulthood to old age. *Journal of Sex Research, 21,* 126–141.

Adams, H. E., Motsinger, P. K., McAnulty, R. D., & Moore, A. L. (1992). Voluntary control of penile tumescence in heterosexual and homosexual males. *Archives of Sexual Behavior, 21,* 17–31.

Adams, H. E., Wright, L. W., & Lohr, B. A. (1996). Is homophobia associated with homosexual arousal? *Journal of Abnormal Psychology, 105*(3), 440–445.

Adler, N. E., David, H. P., Major, B. N., Roth, S. H., Russo, N. F., & Wyatt, G. E. (1992). Psychological factors in abortion: A review. *American Psychologist, 47,* 1194–1204.

Adriano, J. (2000). Vermont high court orders state to treat gay and non-gay couples equally. *Lesbian News, 25,* 18.

Advanced Fertility Center of Chicago. (2002). Hysterosalpingogram (HSG). Retrieved January 14, 2003, from www.advancedfertility.com/hsg.htm

Agnew, C. R., Van Lange, P. A. M., Rusbult, C. E., & Langston, C. A. (1998). Cognitive interdependence: Commitment and the mental representation of close relationships. *Journal of Personality and Social Psychology, 74,* 939–954.

Ainslie, J., & Feltey, K. (1991). Definitions and dynamics of motherhood and family in lesbian communities. *Marriage & Family Review, 17,* 63–85.

Alan Guttmacher Institute. (1994a, April). *Issues in brief—sexually transmitted diseases in the US: Risks, consequences and costs.* New York: Author.

Alan Guttmacher Institute. (1994b). *Sex and America's teenagers.* New York: Author.

Alan Guttmacher Institute. (1997). Issues in brief: Title X and the U.S. family planning effort. Retrieved May 15, 1998, from www.agi-usa.org/pubs/ib16/ib16.html

Alan Guttmacher Institute. (2000). Facts in brief: Induced abortion. Retrieved June 6, 2000, from www.agi-usa.org/pubs/fb_induced_abortion.html

Alan Guttmacher Institute. (2002a). Facts in brief: Contraceptive use. Retrieved October 6, 2002, from www.guttmacher.org/pubs/fb_contr_use.html

Alan Guttmacher Institute. (2002b). *Facts in brief: Induced Abortion.* New York: Author.

Alan Guttmacher Institute. (2002c). *Sexuality education: Facts in brief.* Washington, DC: Author.

Albert, A. E., Warner, D. L., & Hatcher, R. A. (1998). Facilitating condom use with clients during commercial sex in Nevada's legal brothels. *American Journal of Public Health, 88,* 643–647.

Albin, R. S. (1977). Psychological studies of rape. *Signs, 3,* 423–435.

Aldrete, E., Eskenazi, B., & Sholtz, R. (1995). Effect of cigarette smoking and coffee drinking on time to conception. *Epidemiology, 6,* 403–408.

Alexander, N.J. (1995, September). Future contraceptives. *Scientific American,* pp. 136–141.

Alford, G. S., Webster, J. S., & Sanders, J. H. (1980). Covert aversion of two interrelated deviant sexual practices: Obscene phone calling and exhibitionism. A single case analysis. *Behavior Therapy, 11,* 15–25.

Allaboutcounseling.com. (1998). Sexual abuse/trauma. Retrieved June 22, 1998, from www.allaboutcounseling.com/sexual_abuse.htm

Allen, K., & Demo, D. (1995). The families of lesbians and gay men: A new frontier in family research. *Journal of Marriage and the Family, 57,* 111–127.

Allen, L. S., & Gorski, R. A. (1992, August). Sexual orientation and the size of the anterior commissure in the human brain. *Proceedings of the National Academy of Sciences, 89,* 7199–7202.

Allen, M., D'Alessio, D., & Brezgel, K. (1995). A meta-analysis summarizing the effects of pornography II. *Human Communication Research, 22,* 258–283.

Allen, M. P. (1989). *Transformations: Crossdressers and those who love them.* New York: E. P. Dutton.

Allgeier, E. R., & Wiederman, M. W. (1994). How useful is evolutionary psychology for understanding contemporary human sexual behaviour? *Annual Review of Sex Research, 5,* 218–256.

Allgood-Merten, B., & Stockard, J. (1991). Sex role identity and self-esteem: A comparison of children and adolescents. *Sex Roles, 25,* 129–139.

Alsaker, F. D. (1992). Pubertal timing, overweight, and psychological adjustment. *Journal of Early Adolescence, 12,* 396–419.

Althof, S. E., Levine, S. B., Corty, E., Risen, C., & Stern, E. (1994, March). *The role of clomipramine in the treatment of premature ejaculation.* Paper presented at the annual meeting of the Society for Sex Therapy and Research.

Althof, S. E., & Turner, L. A. (1992). Self-injection therapy and external vacuum devices in the treatment of erectile dysfunction: Methods and outcomes. In R. C. Rosen & S. R. Leiblum (Eds.), *Erectile disorders: Assessment and treatment* (pp. 283–312). New York: Guilford.

Althof, S. E., Turner, L. A., Levine, S. B., Risen, C., Kursh, E., Bodner, D., & Resnick, M. (1989). Why do so many people drop out from auto-injection therapy for impotence? *Journal of Sex and Marital Therapy, 15,* 121–129.

Altman, D. (2001). *Global sex.* Chicago: University of Chicago.

Altman, I., & Taylor, D. (1973). *Social penetration: The development of relationships.* New York: Holt, Rinehart, & Winston.

Alzate, H., & Londono, M. L. (1987). Brief reports: Subjects' reactions to a sexual experimental situation. *Archives of Sexual Behavior, 23,* 362–400.

Ambert, A. (1988). Relationships with former in-laws after divorce: A research note. *Journal of Marriage and the Family, 50,* 679–686.

American Academy of Pediatrics. (1990). *Care of the uncircumcized penis.* Chicago: Author.

American Academy of Pediatrics. (1999). Adolescent pregnancy—Current trends and issues: 1998. *Pediatrics, 103,* 516–521.

American Academy of Pediatrics. (1999). *News release: Pediatricians join "better TV" coalition.* Washington: Author.

American Academy of Pediatrics Committee on Genetics. (1999). Folic acid for the prevention of neural tube defects (RE9834). *Pediatrics, 104,* 325–327.

American Academy of Pediatrics Committee on Public Education (2001). Sexuality, contraception, and the media. *Pediatrics, 107,* 191–195.

American Academy of Pediatrics Committee on Substance Abuse and Committee on Children with Disabilities. (2000). Fetal alcohol syndrome and alcohol-related neurodevelopmental disorders (RE9948). *Pediatrics, 106,* 358–361.

American Academy of Pediatrics Task Force on Circumcision. (1999). Circumcision policy statement. *Pediatrics, 103,* 686–693.

American Academy of Pediatrics Work Group on Breastfeeding. (1997). Breastfeeding and the use of human milk (RE9729). *Pediatrics, 100,* 1035–1039.

American Association of University Women. (1990). *Teen women and abortion: Myth vs. reality.* Rockville, MD: Author.

American Association of University Women. (1991). *Stalled agenda: Gender equity and the training of educators.* Washington, DC: Author.

American Association of University Women. (1994). *Shortchanging girls, shortchanging America. Executive Summary.* Washington, DC: Author.

American Association of University Women. (2001). Sexual harassment widespread in nation's schools, new AAUW report finds. Retrieved February 20, 2002, from http://www.aauw.org/2000/hostilebd.html

American Association of University Women Educational Foundation (1993). *Hostile hallways: The AAUW survey on sexual harassment in America's schools.* Washington, DC: Author.

American Cancer Society. (1998). Misleading information: Dispelling miscommunications. Retrieved June 26, 2002, from http://www.cancer.org/eprise/main/docroot/NWS/content/NWS_1_1x_Misleading_Information

American Cancer Society. (2000). *Cancer Facts & Figures—2000. Selected cancers.* Retrieved April 18, 2000, from www. cancer.org/statistics/cff2000/selected_toc.html

American Cancer Society. (2001a). All about cervical cancer. Retrieved June 26, 2002, from http://www.cancer.org/eprise/main/docroot/CRI/CRI_2x?sitearea=CRI&dt=8

American Cancer Society. (2001b). All about ovarian cancer. Retrieved January 14, 2003, from http://www.cancer.org/eprise/main/docroot/CRI/CRI_2x?sitearea=CRI&dt=33

American Cancer Society. (2001c). All about prostate cancer. Retrieved July 1, 2002, from http://www.cancer.org/eprise/main/docroot/CRI/CRI_2x?sitearea=CRI&dt=36

American Cancer Society. (2001d). All about testicular cancer. Retrieved July 1, 2002, from http://www.cancer.org/eprise/main/docroot/CRI/CRI_2x?sitearea=CRI&dt=41

American Cancer Society. (2001e). What are the key statistics for cervical cancer? Retrieved June 4, 2002, from http://www.cancer.org/eprise/main/docroot/CRI/content/CRI_2_4_1X_What_are_the_key_statistics_for_cervical_cancer_8?sitearea=CRI

American Cancer Society (2002a). *Breast cancer facts & figures 2001–2002.* Atlanta: Author.

American Cancer Society. (2002b). What are the key statistics for testicular cancer? Retrieved November 15, 2002, from http://www.cancer.org/docroot/CRI/content/CRI_2_4_1X_What_are_the_key_statistics_for_testicular_cancer_41.asp?sitearea&level=

American Civil Liberties Union. (1999, May 26). ACLU challenges Florida ban on lesbian and gay adoption. Retrieved June 25, 1999, from www.aclu.org/news/1999/n052699a.html

American College of Obstetricians and Gynecologists. (2001). ACOG news release: ACOG addresses latest controversies in obstetrics. Retrieved September 20, 2002, from www.acog.org/from_home/publications/press_releases/nr12-12-10.cfm

American College of Obstetricians and Gynecologists. (2002). ACOG news release: Answers to common questions about postpartum depression. Retrieved September 24, 2002, from www.acog.org/from_home/publications/press_releases/nr01-08-02.cfm

American College of Obstetricians and Gynecologists, Committee on Obstetrics Practice. (2001). ACOG committee opinion: Circumcision. Number 260, October 2001. *Obstetrics & Gynecology, 98*(4), 707–708.

American Psychiatric Association (1952). *Diagnostic and statistical manual of mental disorders.* Washington, DC: Author.

American Psychiatric Association (1968). *Diagnostic and statistical manual of mental disorders* (2nd ed.). Washington, DC: Author.

American Psychiatric Association (1980). *Diagnostic and statistical manual of mental disorders* (3rd ed.). Washington, DC: Author.

American Psychiatric Association. (1994). *Diagnostic and statistical manual of mental disorders* (4th ed.) (*DSM-IV*). Washington, DC: Author.

American Psychiatric Association (2000). *Diagnostic and statistical manual of mental disorders* (4th ed., text revision). Washington, DC: Author.

American Social Health Association. (1995). *Annual Report.* Research Triangle Park, NC: Author.

American Social Health Association. (2000). Get the facts! Retrieved February 28, 2003, from http://www.iwannaknow.org/

American Social Health Association. (2001a). Herpes: Get the facts. Retrieved May 15, 2002, from http://www.ashastd.org/hrc/educate.html

American Social Health Association. (2001b). Information to live by: Pelvic inflammatory disease (PID). Retrieved May 15, 2002, from http://www.ashastd.org/stdfaqs/pid.html

American Society of Plastic and Reconstructive Surgeons. (2002). *2001 cosmetic surgery trends.* Arlington Heights, IL: Author.

Amirkhanian, Y. A., Tiunov, D. V., & Kelly, J. A. (2001). Risk factors for HIV and other sexually transmitted diseases among adolescents in St. Petersburg, Russia. *Family Planning Perspectives, 33,* 106–113.

Andersen, B. L., & Cyranowski, J. M. (1994). Women's sexual self-schema. *Journal of personality and Social Psychology, 67,* 1079–1100.

Anderson, J. E., & Dahlberg, L. L. (1992). High-risk sexual behavior in the general population: Results of a national survey, 1988–1990. *Sexually Transmitted Diseases, 19,* 320–325.

Anderson, J. E., Wilson, R., Doll, T. L., Jones, S., & Barker, P. (1999). Condom use and HIV risk behaviors among U.S. adults: Data from a national survey. *Family Planning Perspectives, 31,* 24–29.

Anderson, K. B., Cooper, H., & Okamura, L. (1997). Individual differences and attitudes toward rape: A meta-analytic review. *Personality & Social Psychology Bulletin, 23,* 295–315.

Anderson, P. (2001). *Passion lost: Public sex, private desire in the twentieth century.* Toronto: Thomas Allen.

Anderson, P. B., & Aymani, R. (1993). Reports of female initiation of sexual contact: Male and female differences. *Archives of Sexual Behavior, 22*(4), 335–343.

Andreola, M. (1994, January 15). Pro-life means pro-life [Letter to the Editor]. *Pittsburgh Post-Gazette,* p. E1.

Angier, N. (1999). *Woman: An intimate geography.* Boston: Houghton Mifflin.

Annie E. Casey Foundation. (2002). When teens have sex: Issues and trends. Retrieved November 11, 2002, from www.aecf.org/kidscount/teen/overview/overview.htm

Anonymous. (1999). Transgender in the United States: A brief discussion. *SIECUS Report, 28*(1), 8–13.

Antill, J. K., & Cotton, S. (1987). Self disclosure between husbands and wives: Its relationship to sex roles and marital happiness. *Australian Journal of Psychology, 39,* 11–24.

Antoni, M. H., Baggett, L., Ironson, G., LaPerriere, A., August, S., Klimas, N., Schneiderman, N., & Fletcher, M. A. (1991). Cognitive-behavioral stress management intervention buffers distress responses and immunologic changes following notification of HIV-1 seropositivity. *Journal of Consulting and Clinical Psychology, 59,* 906–915.

Antoni, M. H., Cruess, D. G., Cruess, S., Lutgendorf, S., Kumar, M., Ironson, G., Klimas, N., Fletcher, M. A., & Schneiderman, N. (2000). Cognitive-behavioral stress management intervention effects on anxiety, 24-hr. urinary norepinephrine output, and T-cytotoxic/suppressor cells over time among symptomatic HIV-infected gay men. *Journal of Consulting & Clinical Psychology, 68*(1), 31–45.

Apfelbaum, B. (1989). Retarded ejaculation: A much-misunderstood syndrome. In S. R. Leiblum & R. C. Rosen (Eds.), *Principles and practice of sex therapy: Update for the 1990s* (2nd ed.) (pp. 168–206). New York: Guilford.

Applebaum, M. G. (1995). Fetal alcohol syndrome: Diagnosis, management, and prevention. *Nurse Practitioner, 20*(10), 24, 27, 31–33.

Arentewicz, G., & Schmidt, G. (1983). *The treatment of sexual disorders: Concepts and techniques of couples therapy.* New York: Basic Books.

Arndt, W. B., Jr. (1991). *Gender disorders and the paraphilias.* Madison, CT: International Universities.

Aron, A., & Aron, E. N. (1991). Love and sexuality. In K. McKinney & S. Sprecher (Eds.), *Sexuality in close relationships* (pp. 25–48). Hillsdale, NJ: Erlbaum.

Aron, A., Norman, C. C., & Aron, E. N. (2001). Shared self-expanding activities as a means of maintaining and enhancing close romantic relationships. In J. H. Harvey and A. E. Wenzel (Eds.), *Close romantic relationships: Maintenance and enhancement* (pp. 47–66). Mahway, NJ: Erlbaum.

Aron, A., & Westbay, L. (1996). Dimensions of the prototype of love. *Journal of Personality and Social Psychology, 70,* 535–551.

Assalian, P. (1994). Premature ejaculation: Is it really psychogenic? *Journal of Sex Education and Therapy, 20,* 1–4.

Associated Press. (1999, February 3). Abortion Web site loses case. Retrieved May 20, 1999, from www.tcpalm.com/news/national/0203absite.shtml

Astemborski, J., Vlahov, D., Warren, D., Soloman, L., & Nelson, K. (1994). The trading of sex for drugs or money and HIV seropositivity among female intravenous drug users. *American Journal of Public Health, 84,* 382–387.

Athanasiou, R., Shaver, P., & Tavris, C. (1970, July). Report to the readers of *Psychology Today* on the PT sex survey. *Psychology Today,* 39–52.

Aubeeluck, A., & Maguire, M. (2002). The Menstrual Joy Questionnaire items alone can positively prime reporting of menstrual attitudes and symptoms. *Psychology of Women Quarterly, 26*(2), 160–162.

Auster, C. J., & Leone, J. M. (2001). Late adolescents' perspectives on marital rape: The impact of gender and fraternity/sorority membership. *Adolescence, 36*(141), 141–152.

Azhar, M. Z., & Varma, S. L. (2000). Mental illness and its treatment in Malaysia. In I. Al-Issa (Ed.), *Al-Junun: Mental illness in the Islamic world* (pp. 163–186). Madison, CT: International Universities Press.

Bach, A. K., Wincze, J. P., & Barlow, D. H. (2001). Sexual dysfunction. In D. H. Barlow (Ed.), *Clinical handbook of psychological disorders* (3rd ed.) (pp. 562–608). New York: Guilford Press.

Bachmann, G. A. (1986). Dyspareunia due to obstetrical trauma. *Medical Aspects of Human Sexuality, 20,* 21–25.

Bachmann, G. A. (1995). Influence of menopause on sexuality. *International Journal of Fertility and Menopausal Studies, 40,* 16–22.

Bachmann, G. A., Leiblum, S. R., & Grill, J. (1989). Brief sexual inquiry in gynecologic practice. *Obstetrics and Gynecology, 73,* 425–427.

Bae, Y., & Smith, T. M. (1997). Issues in focus: Women in mathematics and science. From *The Condition of Education 1996.* Retrieved May 14, 1999, from http://nces.ed.gov/pubs/ce/c97005.html

Bailey, J. M., Bobrow, D., Wolfe, M., & Mikach, S. (1995). Sexual orientation of adult sons of gay fathers. *Developmental Psychology, 31,* 124–129.

Bailey, J. M., & Pillard, R. D. (1991). A genetic study of male sexual orientation. *Archives of General Psychiatry, 48,* 1089–1096.

Bailey, J. M., Pillard, R. D., Neale, M. C., & Agyei, Y. (1993). Heritable factors influence sexual orientation in women. *Archives of General Psychiatry, 50,* 217–223.

Bailey, J. M., & Zucker, K. J. (1995). Childhood sex-typed behavior and sexual orientation: A conceptual analysis and quantitative review. *Developmental Psychology, 31,* 43–55.

Bailey, R. C., Plummer, F. A., & Moses, S. (2001). Male circumcision and HIV prevention: Current knowledge and future research directions. *The Lancet Infectious Diseases 1*(4), 223–231.

Bailey, W. C., Hendrick, C., & Hendrick, S. S. (1987). Relation of sex and gender role to love, sexual attitudes, and self-esteem. *Sex Roles, 16,* 637–648.

Baldwin, D. (1993). *Understanding male sexual health.* New York: Hippocrene Books.

Baldwin, J. (1984, June 26). "Go the way your blood beats": An interview by Richard Goldstein. *Village Voice,* 13–14, 16.

Baldwin, J. D., & Baldwin, J. I. (1997). Gender differences in sexual interest. *Archives of Sexual Behavior, 26,* 181–210.

Baldwin, M. W., & Fehr, B. (1995). On the instability of attachment style ratings. *Personal Relationships, 2,* 247–261.

Bancroft, J. (1984). Hormones and human sexual behavior. *Journal of Sex and Marital Therapy, 10,* 3–21.

Bancroft, J. (1988). Sexual desire and the brain. *Sexual and Marital Therapy, 3,* 11–27.

Bancroft, J. (1989). *Human sexuality and its problems* (2nd ed.). New York: Churchill Livingstone.

Bancroft, J. (2002). Biological factors in human sexuality. *The Journal of Sex Research, 39*(1), 15–21.

Bancroft, J., & Coles, L. (1976). Three years' experience in a sexual problems clinic. *British Medical Journal, 1,* 1575–1577.

Bandura, A. (1986). *Social foundations of thought and action: A social cognitive theory.* Englewood Cliffs, NJ: Prentice-Hall.

Bansal, S. (1988). Sexual dysfunction in hypertensive men: A critical review of the literature. *Hypertension, 12,* 1–10.

Barak, A., & Fisher, W. A. (2001). Toward an Internet-based, theoretically driven, innovative approach to sexuality education. *Journal of Sex Research, 38,* 324–332.

Barbach, L. (1993). *The pause: Positive approaches to menopause.* New York: Dutton.

Barbaree, H. E. (1990). Stimulus control of sexual arousal: Its role in sexual assault. In W. L. Marshall, D. R. Laws, & H. E. Barbaree (Eds.), *Handbook of sexual assault: Issues, theories, and treatment of the offender* (pp. 115–142). New York: Plenum.

Barbaree, H. E., Bogaert, A. F., & Seto, M. C. (1995). Sexual reorientation therapy for pedophiles: Practices and controversies. In L. Diamant & R. D. McAnulty (Eds.), *The psychology of sexual orientation, behavior, and identity: A handbook* (pp. 357–383). Westport, CT: Greenwood.

Barbaree, H. E., Seto, M. E., Serin, R. C., Amos, N. L., & Preston, D. L. (1994). Comparisons between sexual and nonsexual rapist subtypes: Sexual arousal to rape, offense precursors, and offense characteristics. *Criminal Justice & Behavior, 21,* 95–114.

Bard, L. A., Carter, D. L., Cerce, D. D., Knight, R. A., Rosenberg, R., & Schneider, B. (1987). A descriptive study of rapists and child molesters: Developmental, clinical, and criminal statistics. *Behavioural Sciences and the Law, 5,* 203–220.

Barlow, D. H. (1986). Causes of sexual dysfunction: The role of anxiety and cognitive interference. *Journal of Consulting and Clinical Pyschology, 54,* 140–148.

Barlow, D. H., & Agras, W. S. (1973). Fading to increase heterosexual responsiveness in homosexuals. *Journal of Applied Behavior Analysis, 6,* 355–366.

Barnes, J. (1986). Primary vaginismus (Part 2): Aetiological factors. *Irish Medical Journal, 79,* 62–65.

Barnes, M. L., & Sternberg, R. J. (1997). *A hierarchical model of love and its prediction of satisfaction in close relationships.* New York: Guilford Press.

Barnhart, K., Furman, I., & Devoto, L. (1995). Attitudes and practice of couples regarding sexual relations during the menses and spotting. *Contraception, 51*(2), 93–98.

Baron, L., & Straus, M. A. (1984). Sexual stratification, pornography, and rape in the United States. In N. M. Malamuth & E. Donnerstein (Eds.), *Pornography and sexual aggression* (pp. 185–209). Orlando, FL: Academic Press.

Barousse, M. M., Steele, C., Dunlap, K., Espinosa, T., Boikov, D., Sobel, J. D., & Fidel, P. L. (2001). Growth inhibition of candida albicans by human vaginal epithelial cells. *Journal of Infectious Diseases, 184,* 1489–1493.

Barrett, A. E. (1999). Social support and life satisfaction among the never married. *Research on Aging, 21,* 46–73.

Barrett, D. C., Bolan, G., & Douglas, J. M., Jr. (1998). Redefining gay male anal intercourse behaviors: Implications for HIV prevention and research. *Journal of Sex Research, 35,* 381–389.

Barringer, F. (1993, March 12). Slaying is a call to arms for abortion clinics. *New York Times,* p. A1.

Barron, M., & Kimmel, M. (2000). Sexual violence in three pornographic media: Toward a sociological explanation. *Journal of Sex Research, 37,* 161–168.

Bartell, G. D. (1970). Group sex among mid-Americans. *Journal of Sex Research,* 6, 113–130.

Bartholomew, K. (1990). Avoidance of intimacy: An attachment perspective. *Journal of Social and Personal Relationships, 7,* 147–178.

Bartholomew, R. E. (1994). The social psychology of "epidemic" Koro. *International Journal of Social Psychiatry, 40,* 46–60.

Barton, S. E., Ebel, C. W., Kirchner, J. T., & Mertz, G. J. (2002). The clinical management of recurrent genital herpes: Current issues and future prospects. *Herpes, 9,* 15–20.

Bartoshuk, L. M., & Beauchamp, G. K. (1994). Chemical senses. *Annual Review of Psychology, 45,* 419–449.

Bartsch, R. A., Burnett, T., Diller, T. R., & Rankin-Williams, E. (2000). Gender representation in television commercials: Updating an update. *Sex Roles: A Journal of Research, 43*(9–10), 735–743.

Bass, B., & Walen, S. R. (1986). Rational-emotive therapy for the sexual problems of couples. *Journal of Rational-Emotive Therapy,* 482–494.

Basson, R., McInnes, R., Smith, M. D., Hodgson, L., Spain, T., & Koppiker, N. (2000). Efficacy and safety of sildenafil in estrogenized women with sexual dysfunction associated with female sexual arousal disorder. *Obstetrics and Gynecology, 95*(Suppl. 4), 554.

Battle of the bulge. (1994, September 3). *The Economist,* pp. 23–25.

Baumeister, R. F., & Butler, J. L. (1997). Sexual masochism: Deviance without pathology. In D. R. Laws & W. O'Donohue (Eds.), *Sexual deviance: Theory, assessment, and treatment* (pp. 225–239). New York: Guilford.

Baumeister, R. F., & Leary, M. R. (1995). The need to belong: Desire for interpersonal attachments as a fundamental human motivation. *Psychological Bulletin, 11*(7), 497–529.

Baumeister, R. F., & Tice, D. M. (2001). *The social dimension of sex.* Boston: Allyn & Bacon.

Baxter, L. A., & Bullis, C. (1986). Turning points in developing romantic relationships. *Human Communication Research, 12,* 469–493.

Bayer, R. (1987). *Homosexuality and American psychiatry: The politics of diagnosis.* Princeton, NJ: Princeton University Press.

Beach, F. A. (Ed.). (1977). *Human sexuality from four perspectives.* Baltimore: Johns Hopkins University.

Beal, C. R. (1994). *Boys and girls: The development of gender roles.* New York: McGraw-Hill.

Beal, G., & Muehlenhard, C. L. (1987, April). Decreasing miscommunication about sex: Approaches for getting men to stop their sexual advances. Paper presented at the Midcontinent Regional Meeting of the Society for the Scientific Study of Sex, Bloomington, IN.

Bearman, P., & Brückner, H. (1999). Power in numbers: Peer effects on adolescent girls' sexual debut and pregnancy. Washington, DC: National Campaign to Prevent Teen Pregnancy.

Bearman, P., Jones, J., & Udry, J. R. (1997). *The National Longitudinal Study of Adolescent Health: Research Design.* Retrieved January 14, 2003, from http://www.cpc.unc.edu/addhealth/design.html

Bechhofer, L., & Parrot, A. (1991). What is acquaintance rape? In A. Parrot & L. Bechhofer (Eds.), *Acquaintance rape: The hidden crime* (pp. 9–25). New York: John Wiley & Sons.

Beck, J. G. (1993). Vaginismus. In W. O'Donohue & J. H. Geer (Eds.), *Handbook of sexual dysfunctions: Assessment and treatment* (pp. 381–397). Boston: Allyn & Bacon.

Beck, J. G. (1995). Hypoactive sexual desire disorder: An overview. *Journal of Consulting and Clinical Psychology, 63,* 919–927.

Beck, J. G., & Baldwin, L. E. (1994). Instructional control of female sexual responding. *Archives of Sexual Behavior, 23,* 665–684.

Beck, S. H., Cole, B. S., & Hammond, J. A. (1991). Religious heritage and premarital sex: Evidence from a national sample of young adults. *Journal for the Scientific Study of Religion, 30,* 173–181.

Becker, J. (1994). Offenders: Characteristics and treatment. *The Future of Children, 4,* 179, 186.

Beckman, L. J., & Murray, J. (1991). Perceived contraceptive attributes and method choice. *Journal of Applied Social Psychology, 21,* 774–790.

Begany, J. J., & Milburn, M. A. (2002). Psychological predictors of sexual harassment: Authoritarianism, hostile sexism, and rape myths. *Psychology of Men and Masculinity, 3*(2), 119–126.

Beitchman, J. H., Zucker, K. J., Hood, J. E., DaCosta, G. A., Akman, D., & Cassavia, E. (1992). A review of the long-term effects of child sexual abuse. *Child Abuse and Neglect, 16,* 101–118.

Beitzig, L. (1989). Causes of conjugal dissolution: A cross-cultural study. *Current Anthropology, 30,* 654–676.

Bell, A. P., & Weinberg, M. S. (1978). *Homosexualities: A study of diversity among men and women.* New York: Simon & Schuster.

Bell, A. P., Weinberg, M. S., & Hammersmith, S. K. (1981). *Sexual preference: Its development in men and women.* Bloomington: Indiana University Press.

Bell, I. P. (1989). The double standard: Age. In J. Freeman (Ed.), *Women: A feminist perspective* (4th ed.) (pp. 236–244). Mountain View, CA: Mayfield.

Bell, L. (Ed.) (1987). *Good girls/bad girls: Sex trade workers and feminists face to face.* Toronto: The Women's Press.

Belsky, J., & Rovine, M. (1990). Patterns of marital change across the transition to parenthood: Pregnancy to three years postpartum. *Journal of Marriage and the Family, 52,* 5–19.

Bem, S. L. (1981). *Bem Sex Role Inventory professional manual.* Palo Alto, CA: Consulting Psychologists Press.

Bem, S. L. (1993). *The lenses of gender: Transforming the debate on sexual inequality.* New Haven: Yale University Press.

Benefits will go to partners of gay IBM workers. (1996, September 20). *The New Orleans Times-Picayune,* p. C-2.

Benson, D., Charlton, C., & Goodhart, F. (1992). Acquaintance rape on campus: A literature review. *Journal of American College Health, 40,* 157–165.

Benson, D. J., & Thomson, G. E. (1982). Sexual harassment on a university campus: The influence of authority relations, sexual interest, and gender stratification. *Social Problems, 29,* 236–251.

Berenbaum, S. A., & Snyder, E. (1995). Early hormonal influences on childhood sex-typed activity and playmate preferences: Implications for the development of sexual orientation. *Developmental Psychology, 31,* 31–42.

Bergen, R. K. (1999). Violence against women online resources: Marital rape. Retrieved October 18, 2002, from www.vaw.umn.edu/Vawnet/mrape.htm

Bergeron, S., Binik, U. M., Khalife, S., Pagidas, K., & Glazer, H. (2001). Reliability and validity of vulvar vestibulitis syndrome. *Obstretics and Gynecology, 98,* 45–51.

Bergler, E. (1947). Differential diagnosis between spurious homosexuality and perversion homosexuality. *Psychiatric Quarterly, 31,* 399–409.

Bergman, L. (1992). Dating violence in high school students. *Social Work, 37,* 21–27.

Berk, R., Abramson, P. R., & Okami, P. (1995). Sexual activities as told in surveys. In P. R. Abramson & S. D. Pinkerton (Eds.), *Sexual nature, sexual culture* (pp. 371–386). Chicago: University of Chicago.

Berkman, L. F. (1995). The role of social relations in health promotion. *Psychosomatic Medicine, 57,* 245–254.

Berkow, R. (Ed.). (1992). *The Merck manual of diagnosis and therapy* (16th ed.). Rahway, NJ: Merck Research Laboratories.

Berliner, L., & Wheeler, J. R. (1988). Treating the effects of sexual abuse in children. *Journal of Interpersonal Violence, 2,* 415–434.

Berman, L. A., & Berman, J. R. (2000). Viagra and beyond: Where sex educators and therapists fit in from a multidisciplinary perspective. *Journal of Sex Education and Therapy, 25,* 17–24.

Bernat, J. A., Calhoun, K. S., & Stolp, S. (1998). Sexually aggressive men's responses to a date rape analogue: Alcohol as a disinhibiting cue. *Journal of Sex Research, 35,* 341–348.

Berne, L., & Huberman, B. (1999). *European approaches to adolescent sexual behavior and responsibility.* Washington, DC: Advocates for Youth.

Berrill, K. T. (1992). Anti-gay violence and victimization in the United States: An overview. In G. M. Herek & K. T. Berrill (Eds.), *Hate crimes: Confronting violence against lesbians and gay men* (pp. 19–45). Newbury Park, CA: Sage Publications.

Berscheid, E. (1983). Emotion. In H. H. Kelley, E. Berscheid, A. Christensen, J. H. Harvey, T. L. Huston, G. Levinger, E. McClintock, L. A. Peplau, & D. R. Peterson (Eds.), *Close relationships* (pp. 110–168). New York: Freeman.

Berscheid, E., Dion, K., Walster, E., & Walster, D. (1971). Physical attractiveness and dating choice: A test of the matching hypothesis. *Journal of Experimental Social Psychology, 7,* 173–189.

Berscheid, E., & Fei, J. (1977). Romantic love and sexual jealousy. In G. Clanton & L. G. Smith (Eds.), *Jealousy.* Englewood Cliffs, NJ: Prentice-Hall.

Berscheid, E., & Walster, E. (1974). A little bit about love. In T. L. Huston (Ed.), *Foundations of interpersonal attraction.* New York: Academic Press.

Beyrer, C. (1998). War in the blood: Sex, politics, and AIDS in southeast Asia. In *Medical ethics, human rights, Asian values.* London: Zed Books.

Beyrer, C. (2001). Shan women and girls and the sex industry in southeast Asia: Political causes and human rights implications. *Social Science and Medicine, 53,* 543–550.

Bhatnagar, K. P., & Smith, T. D. (2001). The human vomeronasal organ. III. Postnatal development from infancy to the ninth decade. *Journal of Anatomy, 199*(Pt. 3), 289–302.

Bhide, P. G., & Bedi, K. S. (1984). The effects of a lengthy period of environmental diversity on well-fed and previously undernourished rats, II: Synapse-to-neuron ratios. *Journal of Comparative Neurology, 227,* 305–310.

Bhugra, D. (2000). Disturbances in the objects of desire: Cross-cultural issues. *Sexual and Relationship Therapy, 15,* 67–78.

Bieber, I. (1976). A discussion of "Homosexuality: The ethical challenge." *Journal of Consulting and Clinical Psychology, 44,* 163–166.

Bieber, I., Dain, H. J., Dince, P. R., Drellich, M. G., Grand, H. G., Gundlach, R. H., Kremer, M. W., Rifkin, A. H., Wilber, C. B., & Bieber, T. B. (1962). *Homosexuality: A psychoanalytic study of male homosexuals.* New York: Basic Books.

Bielay, G., & Herold, E. S. (1995). Popular magazines as a source of sexual information for university women. *Canadian Journal of Human Sexuality, 4,* 247–262.

Billy, J. O. G., Tanfer, K., Grady, W. R., & Kepinger, D. H. (1993). The sexual behavior of men in the United States. *Family Planning Perspectives, 25,* 52–60.

Binik, Y. M., Reissing, E., Pukall, C., Flory, N., Payne, K. A., & Khalife, S. (2002). The female sexual pain disorders: Genital pain or sexual dysfunction? *Archives of Sexual Behavior, 31,* 425–429.

Binner, S. L., Mastrobattista, J. M., Day, M. C., Swaim, L. S., & Monga, M. (2002). Effect of parental education on decision-making about neonatal circumcision. *Southern Medical Journal, 95*(4), 457–461.

Biscotti, C. V., O'Brien, D. L., Gero, M. A., Gramlich, T. L., Kennedy, A. W., & Easley, K. A. (2002). Thin-layer Pap test vs. conventional Pap smear: Analysis of 400 split samples. *Journal of Reproductive Medicine, 47*(1), 9–13.

Blackwood, E. (1986). *The many faces of homosexuality: Anthropological approaches to homosexual behavior.* New York: Harrington Park Press.

Blair, C. D., & Lanyon, R. I. (1981). Exhibitionism: Etiology and treatment. *Psychological Bulletin, 89,* 439–463.

Blair, E., Sudman, S., Bradburn, N. M., & Stocking, C. (1977). How to ask questions about drinking and sex: Response effects in measuring consumer behavior. *Journal of Marketing Research, 14,* 316–321.

Blair, S. L. (1992). The sex-typing of children's household labor: Parental influence on daughters' and sons' housework. *Youth and Society, 24*(2), 178–203.

Blake, S. M., Simkin, L., Ledsky, R., Perkins, C., & Calabrese, J. M. (2001). Effects of a parent–child communications intervention on young adolescents' risk for early onset of sexual intercourse. *Family Planning Perspectives, 33*(2), 52–61.

Blanc, A. K. (2001). The effect of power in sexual relationships on sexual and reproductive health: An examination of the evidence. *Studies in Family Planning, 33,* 189–213.

Blanchard, R. (1985). Research methods for the typological study of gender disorders in males. In B. W. Steiner (Ed.), *Gender dysphoria: Development, research, and management* (pp. 227–258). New York: Plenum.

Blanck, H. M., Marcus, M., Tolbert, P. E., Rubin, C., Henderson, A. K., Hertzberg, V. S., Zhang, R. H., & Cameron, L. (2000). Age at menarche and Tanner stage in girls exposed in utero and postnatally to polybrominated biphenyl. *Epidemiology, 11*(6), 641–647.

Block, J. H. (1978). Another look at sex differentiation in the socialization behaviors of mothers and fathers. In J. A. Sherman & F. L. Denmark (Eds.), *The psychology of women: Future directions in research* (pp. 29–87). New York: Psychological Dimensions.

Blumenfeld, L. (1992, March 9). The new sexual "reality": Now a condom for women. *Washington Post.*

Blumer, D., & Walker, A. E. (1967). Sexual behavior in temporal lobe epilepsy. *Archives of Neurology, 16,* 37–43.

Blumstein, P., & Schwartz, P. (1983). *American couples: Money, work, sex.* New York: Morrow.

Boat, B. W., & Everson, M. D. (1996). Concerning practices of interviewers when using anatomical dolls in child protective services investigations. *Child Maltreatment, 1,* 96–105.

Boddewyn, J. J., & Kunz, H. (1991). Sex and decency issues in advertising: General and international dimensions. *Business Horizons, 34,* 13–21.

Boekhout, B. A., Hendrick, S. S., & Hendrick, C. (1999). Relationship infidelity: A loss perspective. *Journal of Personal & Interpersonal Loss, 4,* 97–124.

Boeringer, S. B. (1994). Pornography and sexual aggression: Associations of violent and nonviolent depictions with rape and rape proclivity. *Deviant Behavior, 15,* 289–304.

Bogaert, A. F., Turkovich, D. A., & Hafer, C. L. (1993). A content analysis of *Playboy* centrefolds from 1953 through 1990:

Changes in explicitness, objectification, and model's age. *Journal of Sex Research, 30,* 135–139.

Bohner, G., Reinhard, M-A., Rutz, S., Sturm, S., Kerschbaum, B., & Effler, D. (1998). Rape myths as neutralizing cognitions: Evidence for a causal impact of anti-victim attitudes on men's self-reported likelihood of raping. *European Journal of Social Psychology, 28,* 257–268.

Boles, J., & Elifson, K. W. (1994). Sexual identity and HIV: The male prostitute. *Journal of Sex Research, 31,* 39–46.

Bolling, D., & Voeller, B. (1987). AIDS and heterosexual anal intercourse. *Journal of the American Medical Association, 258,* 474.

Boonstra, H. (2001). Voicing concerns for women, abortion foes seek limits on availability of Mifepristone. *The Guttmacher Report on Public Policy 4.* Retrieved March 5, 2002, from www.guttmacher.org/pubs/journals/gr040203.html

Boonstra, H. (2002). Teen pregnancy: Trends and lessons learned. In *The Guttmacher Report on Public Policy,* pp. 7–10. New York: Alan Guttmacher Institute.

Borgia, G. (1989). Typology and human mating preferences. *Behavioral and Brain Sciences, 12,* 16–17.

Bosard, J. H. S. (1931). Residential propinquity as a factor in marriage selection. *American Journal of Sociology, 38,* 219–224.

Boss, P. (1987). Family stress. In M. B. Sussman & S. K. Steinmetz (Eds.), *Handbook of marriage and the family* (pp. 695–724). New York: Plenum.

Boston Women's Health Book Collective (1992). *The new our bodies, ourselves.* New York: Simon and Schuster.

Boswell, J. (1980). *Christianity, social tolerance, and homosexuality.* Chicago: University of Chicago Press.

Bouchert, S. (2002). Valacyclovir halved transmission of genital herpes in study. *Internal Medicine News, 36*(21). Retrieved November 18, 2002, from www.einternalmedicinenews.com

Bowen, A. M., Williams, M., McCoy, H. V., & McCoy, C. B. (2001). Crack smokers' intention to use condoms with loved partners: Intervention development using the theory of reasoned action, condom beliefs, and processes of change. *AIDS Care, 13,* 579–594.

Bowie, W., Hammerschlag, M., & Martin, D. (1994). STDs in '94: The new CDC guidelines. *Patient Care, 28,* 29–53.

Bowlby, J. (1969). *Attachment and loss: Vol. 1. Attachment.* New York: Basic Books.

Boyle, C., & Noonan, S. (1987). Gender neutrality, prostitution, and pornography. In L. Bell (Ed.), *Good girls/bad girls: Sex trade workers and feminists face to face* (pp. 34–37). Toronto: The Women's Press

Boyles, S. (2001). Fertile—or futile? Retrieved September 24, 2002, from my.webmd.com/content/article/3606.738

Brackett, N. L., Bloch, W. E., & Abae, M. (1994). Neurological anatomy and physiology of sexual function. In C. Singer & W. J. Weiner (Eds.), *Sexual dysfunction: A neuromedical approach* (pp. 1–43). New York: Futura.

Bradburn, N., & Sudman, S. (1979). *Improving interview method and questionnaire design.* San Francisco: Jossey Bass.

Bradford, J. (1997). Medical interventions in sexual deviance. In D. R. Laws & W. O'Donohue (Eds.), *Sexual deviance: Theory, assessment, and treatment* (pp. 449–464). New York: Guilford.

Bradley, R. A. (1996). *Husband-coached childbirth.* New York: Bantam Books.

Branson, B. (1998). Home sample collection tests for HIV infection. *Journal of the American Medical Association, 280,* 1699–1701.

Braun, V., & Kitzinger, C. (2001). "Snatch," "hole," or "honey-pot"? Semantic categories and the problem of non-specificity in female genital slang. *Journal of Sex Research, 38,* 146–158.

Braverman, P., & Strasburger, V. (1994, January). Sexually transmitted diseases. *Clinical Pediatrics,* 26–37.

Brehm, S. S. (1992). *Intimate relationships* (2nd ed.). New York: McGraw-Hill.

Brehm, S. S., Miller, R. S., Perlman, D., & Campbell, S. M. (2002). *Intimate relationships* (3rd ed.). New York: McGraw Hill.

Brennan, K. A., Clark, C. L., & Shaver, P. R. (1998). Self-report measurement of adult attachment: An integrative overview. In J. A. Simpson & W. S. Rholes (Eds.), *Attachment theory and close relationships* (pp. 46–76). New York: Guilford.

Brentl, D. J., & Cantor, J. (1988). The portrayal of men and women in U.S. television commercials: A recent content analysis and trends over 15 years. *Sex Roles, 18,* 595–609.

Breslow, N., Evans, L., & Langley, J. (1985). On the prevalence and roles of females in the sadomasochistic subculture: Report of an empirical study. *Archives of Sexual Behavior, 14,* 303–317.

Brewster, K. L., Cooksey, E., Guilkey, D. K., & Rindfuss, R. R. (1998). The changing impact of religion on the sexual and contraceptive behavior of adolescent women in the United States. *Journal of Marriage and the Family, 60,* 493–505.

Brierley, H. (1979). *Transvestism: A handbook with case studies for psychologists, psychiatrists, and counsellors.* New York: Plenum.

Brindley, G. S., & Gillan, P. (1982). Men and women who do not have orgasms. *British Journal of Psychiatry, 140,* 351–356.

Brink, S. (2002, September 23). Beyond the pill: Four new devices aim to make contraception easier. *U.S. News and World Report,* pp. 54, 56.

Brocklehurst, P., & Volmink, J. (2002). Antiretrovirals for reducing the risk of mother-to-child transmission of HIV infection (Cochrane Review). Retrieved May 31, 2002, from http://www.update-software.com/abstracts/ab003510.htm

Brodie, J. F. (1994). *Contraception and abortion in nineteenth-century America.* Ithaca, NY: Cornell University Press.

Brøgger, J. (1992). *Nazaré: Women and men in a pre-bureaucratic Portuguese fishing village.* Fort Worth, TX: Harcourt Brace Jovanovich.

Bromham, D. R. (1992). Surrogacy: The evolution of opinion. *British Journal of Hospital Medicine, 47*(10), 767–772.

Brooks-Gunn, J., & Reiter, E. (1990). The role of pubertal processes. In S. Feldman & G. Elliott (Eds.), *At the threshold: The developing adolescent* (pp. 16–23). Cambridge, MA: Harvard University Press.

Brosius, H. B., Weaver, J. B., & Staab, J. F. (1993). Exploring the social and sexual "reality" of contemporary pornography. *Journal of Sex Research, 30,* 161–170.

Brown, H. G. (1962). *Sex and the single girl.* New York: Bernard Geis Associates.

Brown, J. D. (2002). Mass media influences on sexuality. *Journal of Sex Research, 39,* 42–46.

Brown, M., & Auerbach, A. (1981). Communication patterns in initiation of marital sex. *Medical Aspects of Human Sexuality, 15,* 105–107.

Brown, N. R., & Sinclair, R. C. (1999). Estimating number of lifetime sexual partners: Men and women do it differently. *Journal of Sex Research, 36,* 292–297.

Brown, S. L., & Booth, A. (1996). Cohabitation versus marriage: A comparison of relationship quality. *Journal of Marriage and the Family, 58,* 668–679.

Browne, A., & Finkelhor, D. (1986). Impact of child sexual abuse: A review of the research. *Psychological Bulletin, 99,* 66–77.

Brownmiller, S. (1975). *Against our will: Men, women, and rape.* New York: Simon & Schuster.

Bruck, M., Ceci, S., Francoeur, E., & Renick, A. (1995). Anatomically detailed dolls do not facilitate preschoolers' reports of a pediatric examination involving genital touching. *Journal of Experimental Psychology: Applied, 1,* 95–109.

Brundage, J. A. (1982a). Adultery and fornication: A study of legal theology. In V. L. Bullough & J. Brundage (Eds.), *Sexual practices and the medieval church* (pp. 129–134). Buffalo, NY: Prometheus.

Brundage, J. A. (1982b). Sex and canon law: A statistical analysis of samples of canon and civil law. In V. L. Bullough & J. Brundage (Eds.), *Sexual practices and the medieval church* (pp. 89–101). Buffalo, NY: Prometheus.

Bryant, J., & Brown, D. (1989). Uses of pornography. In D. Zillman & J. Bryant (Eds.), *Pornography: Research Advances and Policy Considerations* (pp. 25–55). Hillsdale, NJ: Erlbaum.

Budiansky, S. (1994, September 12). 10 billion for dinner, please. *U.S. News and World Report,* pp. 57–62.

Buhrich, N., & McConaghy, N. (1977). Clinical comparison of transvestism and transsexualism. *Australian and New Zealand Journal of Psychiatry, 6,* 83–86.

Bullough, B., & Bullough, V. L. (1995). Female prostitution: Current research and changing interpretations. *Annual Review of Sex Research, 7,* 158–180.

Bullough, V. L. (1982). Introduction: The Christian inheritance. In V. L. Bullough & J. Brundage (Eds.), *Sexual practices and the medieval church* (pp. 1–12). Buffalo, NY: Prometheus.

Bullough, V. L. (1994). *Science in the bedroom: A history of sex research.* New York: Basic Books.

Bullough, V. L. (1995). Sexuality and religion. In L. Diamant & R. D. McAnulty (Eds.), *The psychology of sexual orientation, behavior, and identity: A handbook* (pp. 444–456). Westport, CT: Greenwood.

Bullough, V. L. (1998). Alfred Kinsey and the Kinsey Report: Historical overview and lasting contribution. *Journal of Sex Research, 35,* 127–131.

Bullough, V. L. (2000). Transgenderism and the concept of gender. *International Journal of Transgenderism, 4*(3), NP. Retrieved July 22, 2002, from www.symposion.com/ijt/gilbert/bullough.htm

Bullough, V. L., & Bullough, B. (1977). *Sin, sickness, and sanity: A history of sexual attitudes.* New York: Garland Publishing.

Bullough, V. L., & Bullough, B. (1978). *Prostitution: An illustrated social history.* New York: Crown Publishers.

Bullough, V. L., & Bullough, B. (1993). *Cross-dressing, sex, and gender.* Philadelphia: University of Pennsylvania.

Bullough, V. L., & Bullough, B. (1995). *Sexual attitudes: Myths and realities.* Buffalo, NY: Prometheus.

Bumpass, L. L., & Sweet, J. A. (1989). National estimates of cohabitation. *Demography, 26,* 615–625.

Burgess, A. W., & Clark, M. L. (1984). *Child pornography and sex rings.* Lexington, MA: D.C. Heath.

Burgess, A. W., & Holstrom, L. L. (1974). Rape trauma syndrome. *American Journal of Psychiatry, 131,* 981–986.

Burkman, R. T. (2002). The transdermal contraceptive patch: A new approach to hormonal contraception. *International Journal of Fertility and Women's Medicine, 47*(2), 69–76.

Burnette, M. M., Koehn, K. A., Kenyon-Jump, R., Hutton, K., & Stark, C. (1991). Control of genital herpes recurrences using progressive muscle relaxation. *Behavior Therapy, 22,* 237–247.

Burns, A. (2000). Position statement on gender relations and gender differences. *Psychology, Evolution and Gender, 2,* 87–89.

Burt, M. R. (1980). Cultural myths and supports for rape. *Journal of Personality and Social Psychology, 38,* 217–230.

Burt, M. R. (1991). Rape myths and acquaintance rape. In A. Parrot & L. Bechhofer (Eds.), *Acquaintance rape: The hidden crime* (pp. 26–40). New York: Wiley.

Buss, D. M. (1985). Human mate selection. *American Scientist, 73,* 47–51.

Buss, D. M. (1989). Sex differences in human mate preferences: Evolutionary hypotheses tested in 37 cultures. *Behavioral and Brain Sciences, 12,* 1–49.

Buss, D. M. (1994a). *The evolution of desire: Strategies of human mating.* New York: Basic Books.

Buss, D. M. (1994b). The strategies of human mating. *American Scientist, 82,* 238–249.

Buss, D. M. (1995). Psychological sex differences: Origins through sexual selection. *American Psychologist, 50,* 164–168.

Buss, D. M. (1999). *Evolutionary psychology: The new science of the mind.* Boston: Allyn & Bacon.

Buss, D. M. (2000). *The dangerous passion: Why jealousy is as necessary as love and sex.* New York: Free Press.

Buss, D. M. (2001a). Cognitive biases and emotional wisdom in the evolution of conflict between the sexes. *Current Directions in Psychological Science, 10*(6), 219–223.

Buss, D. M. (2001b). Human nature and culture: An evolutionary psychological perspective. *Journal of Personality, 69,* 955–978.

Buss, D. M., Abbott, M., Angleitner, A., Asherian, A., Baggio, A., et al. (1990). International preferences in selecting mates: A study of 37 cultures. *Journal of Cross-Cultural Psychology, 21,* 5–47.

Buss, D. M., & Barnes, M. (1986). Preferences in human mate selection. *Journal of Personality and Social Psychology, 50,* 559–570.

Buss, D. M., Larsen, R. J., Westen, D., & Semmelroth, J. (1992). Sex differences in jealousy: Evolution, physiology, and psychology. *Psychological Science, 3,* 251–255.

Buss, D. M., & Schmitt, D. P. (1993). Sexual strategies theory: An evolutionary perspective on human nature. *Psychological Review, 2,* 204–232.

Buss, D. M., Shackleford, T. K., Kirkpatrick, L. A., Choe, J. C., Lim, H. K., Hasegawa, M., Hasegawa, T., & Bennett, K. (1999). Jealousy and the nature of beliefs about infidelity: Tests of competing hypotheses about sex differences in the United States, Korea, and Japan. *Personal Relationships, 6,* 125–150.

Bussey, K., & Bandura, A. (1984). Influence of gender constancy and social power on sex-linked modeling. *Journal of Personality and Social Psychology, 42,* 1292–1302.

Bussey, K., & Perry, D. G. (1982). Same-sex imitation? *Sex Roles, 8,* 773–784.

Butler, R., & Lewis, M. (1993). *Love and sex after 60.* New York: Ballantine.

Buvat, J., & Lemaire, A. (1997). Endocrine screening of 1,022 men with erectile dysfunction: Clinical significance and cost-effective strategy. *Journal of Urology, 158,* 1764–1767.

Byers, E. S., & Demmons, S. (1999). Sexual satisfaction and sexual disclosure within dating relationships. *Journal of Sex Research, 36,* 180–189.

Byers, E. S., & Heinlein, L. (1989). Predicting initiations and refusals of sexual activities in married and cohabiting heterosexual couples. *Journal of Sex Research, 26,* 210–231.

Byne, W., & Parsons, B. (1993, March). Human sexual orientation: The biologic theories reappraised. *Archives of General Psychiatry, 50,* 228–239.

Byrne, D. (1971). *The attraction paradigm.* New York: Academic Press.

Byrne, D. (1983). The antecedents, correlates, and consequences of erotophobia-erotophilia. In C. Davis (Ed.), *Challenges in sexual science* (pp. 53–75). Lake Mills, IA: Graphic.

Byrne, D., & Lamberth, J. (1970). The effect of erotic stimuli on sex arousal, evaluative responses, and subsequent behavior. *Technical reports of the Presidential Commision on Obscenity and Pornography* (Vol. 8). Washington, DC: U.S. Government Printing Office.

Cahn, D. D. (1990). Perceived understanding and interpersonal relationships. *Journal of Social and Personal Relationships, 7,* 231–244.

Caldas, S. J. (1993). Current theoretical perspectives on adolescent pregnancy and childbearing in the United States. *Journal of Adolescent Research, 8,* 4–20.

Calhoun, E., & Friel, L. V. (2001). Adolescent sexuality: Disentangling the effects of family structure and family context. *Journal of Marriage and the Family, 63,* 669–682.

Calhoun, K. S., & Atkeson, B. M. (1991). *Treatment of rape victims: Facilitating social adjustment.* New York: Pergamon.

Call, V., Sprecher, S., & Schwartz, P. (1995). The incidence and frequency of marital sex in a national sample. *Journal of Marriage and the Family, 57,* 639–652.

Callum, J., & Chalker, R. (1993). RU-486: Yes. *Ms., 3*(5), 34–36.

Campagna, D. S., & Poffenberger, D. L. (1988). *The sexual trafficking of children: An investigation of the child sex trade.* Dover, MA: Auburn House.

Campenni, C. E. (1999). Gender stereotyping of children's toys: A comparison of parents and nonparents. *Sex Roles: A Journal of Research, 40*(1–2), 121–138.

Can you rely on condoms? (1989, March). *Consumer Reports,* pp. 135–142.

Canick, J. A., & Saller D. N., Jr. (1993). Maternal serum screening for aneuploidy and open fetal defects. *Obstetrics and Gynecology Clinics of North America, 20,* 443–453.

Caplan, P. J., & Caplan, J. B. (1994). *Thinking critically about research on sex and gender.* New York: Harper-Collins.

Carani, C., Bancroft, J., Del Rio, G., Granata, A. R. M., Facchinetti, F., & Marrama, P. (1990). The endocrine effects of visual erotic stimuli in normal men. *Psychoneuroendocrinology, 15,* 207–216.

Carey, M. P., & Gordon, C. M. (1995). Sexual dysfunction among heterosexual adults: Description, epidemiology, assessment, and treatment. In L. Diamant & R. D. McAnulty (Eds.), *The psychology of sexual orientation, behavior, and identity: A handbook* (pp. 165–196). Westport, CT: Greenwood.

Carey, M. P., Wincze, J. P., & Meisler, A. W. (1993). Sexual dysfunction: Male erectile disorder. In D. H. Barlow (Ed.), *Clinical handbook of psychological disorders: A step-by-step treatment manual* (2nd ed.) (pp. 442–480). New York: Guilford.

Cargan, L., & Melko, M. (1982). *Singles: Myths and realities.* Beverly Hills, CA: Sage.

Carlson, K. J., Eisenstat, S. A., & Ziporyn, T. (1996). *The Harvard guide to women's health.* Cambridge, MA: The Harvard University Press.

Carmichael, M. S., Warburton, V. L., Dixen, J., & Davidson, J. M. (1994). Relationships among cardiovascular, muscular, and oxytocin responses during human sexual activity. *Archives of Sexual Behavior, 23,* 59–79.

Carnes, P. (1983). *Out of the shadows: Understanding sexual addiction.* New York: Bantam.

Caron, S. L. (1998). *Cross-cultural perspectives on human sexuality.* Boston: Allyn & Bacon.

Carovano, K. (1991). More than mothers and whores: Redefining the AIDS prevention needs of women. *International Journal of Health Services, 21,* 131–142.

Carpenter, L. M. (1998). From girls into women: Scripts for sexuality and romance in *Seventeen* magazine, 1974–1994. *Journal of Sex Research, 35,* 158–169.

Carpenter, L. M. (2001). The ambiguity of "having sex": The subjective experience of virginity loss in the United States. *Journal of Sex Research, 38,* 127–139.

Carrier, J. (1995). *De los otros: Intimacy and homosexuality among Mexican men.* New York: Columbia University.

Carrier, J. M. (1980). Homosexual behavior in cross-cultural perspective. In J. Marmor (Ed.), *Homosexual behavior: A modern reappraisal.* New York: Basic Books.

Caruso, S., Intelisano, G., Lupo, L., & Agnello, C. (2001). Premenopausal women affected by sexual arousal disorder treated with sildenafil: A double-blind, cross-over, placebo-controlled study. *British Journal of Obstetrics and Gynaecology: An International Journal of Obstetrics and Gynaecology, 108*(6), 623–628.

Casanova, M. F., Solursh, D., Solursh, L., Roy, E., & Thigpen, L. (2000). The history of child pornography on the Internet. *Journal of Sex Education and Therapy, 25,* 245–252.

Cass, V. C. (1979). Homosexual identity formation: A theoretical model. *Journal of Homosexuality, 4*(3), 219–235.

Cassidy, J., & Shaver, P. R. (1999). *Handbook of attachment: Theory, research and clinical applications.* New York: Guilford.

Castellsague, X., Bosch, F. X., Munoz, N., Meijer, C. J. L. M., Shah, K. V., de Sanjose, S., Eluf-Neto, J., Ngelangel, C. A., Chichareon, S., Smith, J. S., Herrero, R., Moreno, V., Franceschi, S., & The International Agency for Research on Cancer Multicenter Cervical Cancer Study Group. (2002). Male circumcision, penile human papillomavirus infection, and cervical cancer in female partners. *New England Journal of Medicine, 346*(15), 1105–1112.

Catalona, W. J., & Bigg, S. W. (1990). Nerve sparing radical prostatectomy: Evaluation of results after 250 patients. *Journal of Urology, 143,* 538–543.

Catania, J. A. (1999). A framework for conceptualizing reporting bias and its antecedents in interviews assessing human sexuality. *Journal of Sex Research, 36,* 25–38.

Catania, J. A., Coates, T. J., Kegeles, S., Fullilove, M., Peterson, J., Marin, B., Siegel, D., & Hulley, S. (1992). Condom use in multiethnic neighborhoods of San Francisco: The population based AMEN study. *American Journal of Public Health, 82,* 284–287.

Catania, J. A., Gibson, D. R., Chitwood, D. D., & Coates, T. J. (1990). Methodological problems in AIDS behavioral research: Influences on measurement error and participation bias in studies of sexual behavior. *Psychological Bulletin, 108,* 339–362.

Catania, J. A., McDermott, L. J., & Pollack, L. M. (1986). Questionnaire response bias and face-to-face interview sample bias in sexuality research. *Journal of Sex Research, 22,* 52–72.

Catania, J. A., Turner, H., Pierce, R. C., Golden, E., Stocking, C., Binson, D., & Mast, K. (1993). Response bias in surveys of AIDS-related sexual behavior. In D. G. Ostrow & R. C. Kessler (Eds.), *Methodological issues in AIDS behavioral research* (pp. 133–162). New York: Plenum.

Cates, W., & Meheus, A. (1990). Strategies for development of sexually transmitted disease control programs. In K. Holmes, P. Mardh, P. Sparling, P. Wiesner, W. Cates, S. Lemon, & W. Stamm (Eds.), *Sexually transmitted diseases* (2nd ed.) (pp. 1023–1030). New York: McGraw-Hill.

Cawood, E. H., & Bancroft, J. (1996). Steroid hormones, the menopause, sexuality and well-being of women. *Psychological Medicine, 26*(5), 925–936.

Center for Population Options. (1995). Laws should not require parental involvement in abortion decisions. In C. Cozic & J. Petrikin (Eds.), *The abortion controversy* (pp. 105–112). San Diego: Greenhaven Press.

Centers for Disease Control. (2001c). *Prostate cancer: The public health perspective 2001.* Atlanta: Author.

Centers for Disease Control and Prevention. (1993a, April 23). Rates of cesarean delivery—United States, 1991. *Morbidity and Mortality Weekly Report, 42,* 285–289.

Centers for Disease Control and Prevention. (1993b). Recommendations for the prevention and management of chlamydia trachomatis. *Morbidity and Mortality Weekly Report, 42*(RR-12), 1–39.

Centers for Disease Control and Prevention. (1998a). *HIV/AIDS surveillance report, 1998, 10 (No. 2).* Atlanta: Author.

Centers for Disease Control and Prevention. (1998b). HIV prevention through early detection and treatment of other sexually transmitted diseases—United States: Recommendations of the Advisory Committee for HIV and STD Prevention. *Morbidity and Mortality Weekly Report, 47* (RR-12).

Centers for Disease Control and Prevention. (1998c). *Sexually transmitted disease surveillance 1998.* Atlanta, GA: Author.

Centers for Disease Control and Prevention. (1999a, October). CDC Surveillance Summaries: Youth Risk Behavior Surveillance. National alternative high school risk behavior survey, United States, 1998. *Morbidity and Mortality Weekly Report, 48.*

Centers for Disease Control and Prevention. (1999b). *HIV/AIDS surveillance report, 1999, 11*(No. 1). Atlanta: Author.

Centers for Disease Control and Prevention (1999c). *Status of perinatal HIV prevention: U.S. declines continue.* Atlanta: Author.

Centers for Disease Control and Prevention. (1999d). Surveillance for AIDS-defining opportunistic illnesses, 1991–1997. *Morbidity and Mortality Weekly Report, 48,* 1–22.

Centers for Disease Control and Prevention (2000a). Bacterial vaginosis (BV). Retrieved May 8, 2002, from http//www.cdc.gov/nchstp/dstd/Fact_Sheets/FactsBV.htm

Centers for Disease Control and Prevention. (2000b). Cesarean deliveries as a percentage of all deliveries in U.S. hospitals, by year. *Public Health Surveillance Slide Set.* Retrieved May 22, 2000, from www.cdc.gov/epo/dphsi/phs/sld51.htm

Centers for Disease Control and Prevention. (2000c). Facts about drug-resistant gonorrhea. Retrieved May 14, 2002, from http://www.cdc.gov/od/oc/media/pressrel/fs2k0922a.htm

Centers for Disease Control and Prevention. (2000d). HIV/AIDS among racial/ethnic minority men who have sex with men—United States, 1989–1998. *Morbidity and Mortality Weekly Report, 49,* 4–11.

Centers for Disease Control and Prevention. (2000e). Syphilis elimination update: Syphilis rate declines among African Americans—Promising sign for CDC campaign to eliminate syphilis in U.S. Retrieved June 3, 2002, from http://www.cdc.gov/nchstp/dstd/Press_Releases/syphilisAfricanAmericans.htm

Centers for Disease Control and Prevention. (2000f). *Tracking the hidden epidemics: Trends in STDs in the United States, 2000.* Atlanta: Author.

Centers for Disease Control and Prevention. (2001a). Genital herpes. Retrieved May 15, 2002, from http://www.cdc.gov/nchstp/dstd/Fact_Sheets/facts_Genital_Herpes.htm

Centers for Disease Control and Prevention. (2001b). Genital HPV infection. Retrieved May 21, 2002, from http://www.cdc.gov/nchstp/dstd/Fact_Sheets/FactsHPV.htm

Centers for Disease Control and Prevention. (2001c). *HIV/AIDS Surveillance Report, 13 (No. 1).* Atlanta: Author.

Centers for Disease Control and Prevention (2001d). Pelvic inflammatory disease (PID). Retrieved May 15, 2002, from http://www.cdc.gov/nchstp/dstd/Fact_Sheets/FactsPID.htm

Centers for Disease Control. (2001e). *Prostate cancer: The public health perspective, 2001.* Atlanta: Author.

Centers for Disease Control and Prevention. (2001f). *Sexually transmitted disease surveillance, 2000.* Atlanta, GA: Author.

Centers for Disease Control and Prevention. (2001g). *Sexually transmitted disease surveillance 2000 supplement: Chlamydia Prevalence Monitoring Project.* Atlanta: Author.

Centers for Disease Control and Prevention. (2001h). *U.S. HIV and AIDS cases reported through December 2001: Year-end edition:* Atlanta: Author.

Centers for Disease Control and Prevention. (2002a). HIV/AIDS among African Americans. Retrieved June 3, 2002, from http://www.cdc.gov/hiv/pubs/facts/afam.htm

Centers for Disease Control and Prevention. (2002b). National Center for Infectious Diseases: Viral hepatitis. Retrieved May 30, 2002, from http://www.cdc.gov/ncidod/diseases/hepatitis/index.htm

Centers for Disease Control and Prevention. (2002c). Sexually transmitted diseases treatment guidelines 2002. *Morbidity and Mortality Weekly Report, 51*(No. RR-6): 1–84.

Centers for Disease Control and Prevention. (2002d). Youth Risk Behavior Surveillance—United States 2001. *Morbidity and Mortality Weekly Reports, 51,* 1–64.

Chalkley, A. J., & Powell, G. E. (1983). The clinical description of forty-eight cases of sexual fetishism. *British Journal of Psychiatry, 142,* 292–295.

Chalmers, B., & Meyer, D. (1996). What men say about pregnancy, birth, and parenthood. *Journal of Psychosomatic Obstetrics and Gynecology, 17,* 47–53.

Chan, C. S. (1993). Issues of identity development among Asian American lesbians and gay men. In L. D. Garnets & D. C. Kimmel (Eds.), *Psychological perspectives on lesbian and gay male experiences* (pp. 376–388). New York: Columbia University Press.

Chapman, B. E., & Brannock, J. C. (1987). Proposed model of lesbian identity development: An empirical examination. *Journal of Homosexuality, 14,* 69–80.

Che, C., & Suggs, D. (1995, December). Open letter to GLAAD. Retrieved October 7, 1999, from www.qrd.org/qrd/www/culture/black/discussion/letter.html

Check, J., & Guloien, T. (1989). Reported proclivity for coercive sex following repeated exposure to sexually violent pornography, nonviolent dehumanizing pornography, and erotica. In D. Zillman & J. Bryant (Eds.), *Pornography: Research advances and policy considerations.* Hillsdale, NJ: Erlbaum.

Chelala, C. (1998). An alternative way to stop female genital mutilation. *The Lancet, 352,* 126.

Chen, C. Y., Lindsay, G., & Maroney, T. (2000). We like to watch. *Fortune, 142,* 289.

Cheng, S. T. (1997). Epidemic genital retraction syndrome: Environmental and personal risk factors in southern China. *Journal of Psychology and Human Sexuality, 9,* 57–70.

Cherlin, A. J. (1992). *Marriage, divorce, and remarriage.* Cambridge, MA: Harvard University.

Cherry, S. H. (1973). *Understanding pregnancy and childbirth.* New York: Bobbs-Merrill.

Chesley, L., & Lindheimer, M. D. (1979). Pregnancy. *Report of the Hypertension Task Force.* (Vol. 9. NIH Publication #79–1631). Washington, DC: U.S. Public Health Service.

Chia, M., Arava, D. A., & Buck, T. (1997). *The multi-orgasmic man: Sexual secrets every man should know.* New York: HarperCollins.

Ching, L. (1997). Imaginings in the Empire of the Sun. In J. Treat (Ed.), *Contemporary Japan and popular culture.* Honolulu: University of Hawaii.

Choi, N. G. (1992). Correlates of the economic status of widowed and divorced elderly women. *Journal of Family Issues, 13,* 38–54.

Chomitz, V. R., Cheung, L. W., & Lieberman, E. (1995). The role of lifestyle in preventing low birth weight. *Future of Children, 5*(1), 121–138.

Choo, P., Levine, T., & Hatfield, E. (1996). Gender, love schemas, and reactions to romantic break-ups. *Journal of Social Behavior & Personality, 11,* 143–161.

Chowdhury, A. N. (1998). Hundred years of Koro: The history of a culture-bound syndrome. *International Journal of Social Psychiatry, 44,* 181–188.

Christenson, P. G., & Roberts, D. F. (1998). *It's not only rock 'n' roll: Popular music in the lives of adolescents.* Cresskill, NJ: Hampton Press.

Christina, G. (1992). Are we having sex now or what? In D. Steinberg (Ed.), *The erotic impulse: Honoring the sensual self* (pp. 24–29). New York: Jeremy P. Tarcher.

Christopher, F. S., & Cate, R. M. (1985). Premarital pathways and relationship development. *Journal of Social and Personal Relationships, 2,* 271–288.

Christopher, F. S., & Roosa, M. W. (1990). An evaluation of an adolescent pregnancy prevention program: Is "just say no" enough? *Family Relations, 39,* 68–72.

Christopher, F. S., & Sprecher, S. (2000). Sexuality in marriage, dating, and other relationships: A decade review. *Journal of Marriage and the Family, 62,* 999–1017.

Church, S., Henderson, M., Barnard, M., & Hart, G. (2001). Violence by clients toward female prostitutes in different work settings: Questionnaire survey. *British Medical Journal, 322,* 524–525.

Clapp, J. F. (1996). Morphometric and neurodevelopmental outcome at age five years of the offspring of women who continued to exercise regularly throughout pregnancy. *The Journal of Pediatrics, 129*(6), 856–863.

Clarke, S. C. (1995, March 22). Advance report of final divorce statistics, 1989 and 1990. *Monthly Vital Statistics Report 43* (No. 9, supplement).

Clausen, J. (1997). *Beyond gay or straight: Understanding sexual orientation.* Philadelphia: Chelsea House Publishers.

Clayton, A. H., Clavet, G. J., McGarvey, E. L., Warnock, J. K., & Weiss, K. (1999). Assessment of sexual functioning during the menstrual cycle. *Journal of Sex & Marital Therapy, 25*(4), 281–291.

Cleek, M. G., & Pearson, T. A. (1985). Perceived causes of divorce: An analysis of interrelationships. *Journal of Marriage and the Family, 47,* 179–183.

Clements, M. (1992, May 17). Should abortion remain legal? *Parade,* pp. 4–5.

Cleveland Clinic. (1997). Bacterial vaginosis. Retrieved November 3, 1998, from www.ccf.org/health/media_list. asap?Topicld=671

Cleveland Clinic (2002a). Prostate cancer basics. Retrieved July 1, 2002, from http://content.health.msn.com/content/article/1688.50844?z=1688_50814_6502_00_03

Cleveland Clinic. (2002b). Your guide to menstrual cramps. Retrieved June 27, 2002, from http://my.webmd.com/content/article/2953.496

Cochran, S. D. (1989). Women and HIV infection: Issues in prevention and behavior change. In V. M. Mayes, G. W. Albee, & S. F. Schneider (Eds.), *Primary prevention of AIDS: Psychological approaches* (pp. 309–327). Newbury Park, CA: Sage.

Cochran, S. D., & Mays, V. M. (1990). Sex, lies, and HIV [Letter to the editor]. *New England Journal of Medicine, 332,* 774–775.

Cochran, S. D., & Mays, V. M. (1993). Applying social psychological models to predicting HIV-related sexual risk behaviors among African Americans. *Journal of Black Psychology, 19,* 142–154.

Cochran, W. F., Mosteller, F., & Tukey, J. (1953). Statistical problems of the Kinsey Report. *Journal of the American Statistical Association, 48,* 673–716.

Coco, A. S. (1999). Primary dysmenorrhea. *American Family Physician, 60*(2), 489–496.

Cohen, J. A., & Mannarino, A. P. (1999). Sexual abuse. In R. T. Ammerman, M. Hersen, & C. Last (Eds.), *Handbook of prescriptive treatments for children and adolescents* (2nd ed.). Boston: Allyn & Bacon.

Cohen, L. L., & Shotland, R. L. (1996). Timing of first intercourse in a relationship: Expectations, experiences, and perceptions of others. *Journal of Sex Research, 33,* 291–299.

Cohen, N. W., & Estner, L. J. (1983). *Silent knife: Cesarean prevention and vaginal birth after cesarean.* South Hadley, MA: Bergin & Garvey Publishers.

Cohen-Kettenis, P. T., & Gooren, L. J. G. (1999). Transsexualism: A review of etiology, diagnosis, and treatment. *Journal of Psychosomatic Research, 46*(4), 315–333.

Coleman, E. (1985). Developmental stages of the coming out process. In J. C. Gonsiorek (Ed.), *A guide to psychotherapy with gay and lesbian clients.* New York: Harrington Park Press.

Coleman, E. (1990). The obsessive-compulsive model for describing compulsive sexual behavior. *Journal of Preventive Psychiatry and Neurology, 2,* 9–14.

Coleman, E. (1998). Erectile dysfunction: A review of current medical treatments. *Canadian Journal of Human Sexuality, 7,* 231–245.

Coles, F., Hipp, S., Silberstein, G., & Chen, J. (1995). Congenital syphilis surveillance in upstate New York, 1989–1992: Implications for prevention and clinical management. *Journal of Infectious Diseases, 171,* 732–735.

Coles, R., & Stokes, G. (1985). *Sex and the American teenager.* New York: Harper & Row.

Coley, R. L., & Chase-Lansdale, P. L. (1998). Adolescent pregnancy and parenthood: Recent evidence and future directions. *American Psychologist, 53,* 152–166.

Collier & Associates, & Huddleston, D. (1995). Defining and avoiding sexual harassment. *Letter of the Law.* Retrieved June 21, 2000, from http://www.aas.org/~cswa/sexhar.htm.

Collins, C. (1997, December). Do as I say . . . Should we teach only abstinence in sex education? Retrieved 1998, from http://www.epibiostat.ucsf.edu/capsweb/publications/abstinencemono.html

Coltrane, S., & Messineo, M. (2000). The perpetuation of subtle prejudice: Race and gender imagery in 1990s television advertising. *Sex Roles: A Journal of Research, 42*(5–6), 363–389.

Comfort, A. (1993). *The new joy of sex.* New York: Crown.

Commission on Obscenity and Pornography. (1970). *Report of the Commission on Obscenity and Pornography.* Washington, DC: U.S. Government Printing Office.

Conners, M. E., & Morse, W. (1993). Sexual abuse and eating disorders: A review. *International Journal of Eating Disorders, 13,* 1–11.

Conte, J. R. (1986). Child sexual abuse and the family: A critical analysis. *Journal of Psychotherapy and the Family, 2,* 113–126.

Cook, J. (1978, September 18). The X-rated economy. *Forbes,* 81–92.

Cook, W. L. (2000). Understanding attachment security in family context. *Journal of Personality and Social Psychology, 78,* 285–294.

Cooper, A., Scherer, C. R., Boies, S. C., & Gordon, B. L. (1999). Sexuality on the Internet: From sexual exploration to pathological expression. *Professional Psychology: Research and Practice, 30,* 154–164.

Cordelier, J. (1978). *"The life": Memoirs of a French hooker* (H. Matthews, Trans.). New York: The Viking Press.

Corson, S. L. (1990). *Conquering infertility: A guide for couples.* (Rev. ed.). New York: Prentice-Hall.

Costin, F. (1985). Beliefs about rape and women's social roles—a four-nation study. *Archives of Sexual Behavior, 14,* 319–325.

Cotch, M. F., Pastorek, J. G., Nugent, R. P., Hillier, S. L., Gibbs, R. S., Martin, D. H., Eschenbach, D. A., Edelman, R., Carey, J. C., Regan, J. A., Krohn, M. A., Klebanoff, M. A., Rao, A. V., & Rhoads, G. G. (1997). Trichomonas vaginalis associated with low birth weight and preterm delivery. The Vaginal Infections and Prematurity Study Group. *Sexually Transmitted Disease, 24,* 353–360.

Cotton, P. (1994). U.S. sticks head in the sand on AIDS prevention. *Journal of the American Medical Association, 272,* 756–757.

Couper, R. T., & Huynh, H. (2002). Female masturbation masquerading as abdominal pain. *Journal of Paediatrics & Child Health, 38*(2), 199–200.

Cournoyer, R. J., & Mahalik, J. R. (1995). Cross-sectional study of gender-role conflict examining college-aged and middle-aged men. *Journal of Counseling Psychology, 42,* 11–19.

Courtney, A. E., & Whipple, T. W. (1983). *Sex stereotyping in advertising.* Lexington, MA: Lexington.

Cowan, G., & Dunn K. F. (1994). What themes in pornography lead to perceptions of the degradation of women? *Journal of Sex Research, 31,* 11–21.

Cowley, G. (1990, June 3). The biology of beauty. *Newsweek,* 61–66.

Cowley, G. (1996, September 16). Attention, aging men. *Newsweek,* 128, 68–75.

Coxell, A., King, M., Mezey, G., & Gordon, D. (1999). Lifetime prevalence, characteristics, and associated problems of non-consensual sex in men: Cross sectional survey. *British Medical Journal, 318,* 846–850.

Coyle, K., Kirby, D., Parcel, G., Basen-Engquist, K., Banspach, S., Rugg, D., & Weil, M. (1996). Safer choices: A multicomponent school-based HIV/STD and pregnancy prevention program for adolescents. *Journal of School Health, 66,* 89–94.

Crabbe, A. (1988). Feature-length sex films. In G. Day & C. Bloom (Eds.), *Perspectives on pornography: Sexuality in film and literature* (pp. 44–66). London: MacMillan Press.

Creighton, S. (2001). Managing intersex. *British Medical Journal, 323,* 1264–1265.

Crenshaw, T., & Goldberg, J. (1996). *Sexual pharmacology.* New York: Norton.

Crocker, W., & Crocker, J. (1994). *The Canela: Bonding through kinship, ritual, and sex.* Fort Worth, TX: Harcourt Brace.

Crockett, L. J., Bingham, C. R., Chopak, J. S., & Vicary, J. R. (1996). Timing of first intercourse: The role of social control, social learning, and problem behavior. *Journal of Youth and Adolescence, 25,* 89–111.

Cross, S. E., & Markus, H. R. (1993). Gender in thought, belief, and action: A cognitive approach. In A. E. Beall & R. J. Sternberg (Eds.), *The psychology of gender.* New York: Guilford Press.

Crouch, J. (2002). The Marriage Movement: An introduction to divorce reform and other marriage issues. Retrieved November 16, 2002, from www.divorcereform.org/mmo.html

Cruess, S., Antoni, M., Cruess, D., Fletcher, M. A., Ironson, G., Kumar, M., Hayes, A., Klimas, N., & Schneiderman, N. (2000). Reductions in herpes simplex virus type 2 antibody titers after cognitive behavioral stress management and relationships with neuroendocrine function, relaxation skills, and social support in HIV-positive men. *Psychosomatic Medicine, 62,* 828–837.

Cummings, J. L. (1985). *Clinical neuropsychiatry.* New York: Grune & Stratton.

Cunningham, F. G., McDonald, P. C., & Gant, N. F. (1989). *Williams' obstetrics.* New York: Appleton-Century Crofts.

Cutler, W. B., Friedmann, E., & McCoy, N. L. (1998). Pheromonal influences on sociosexual behavior in men. *Archives of Sexual Behavior, 27*(1), 1–14.

Daaboul, J., & Frader, J. (2001). Ethics and the management of the patient with intersex: A middle way. *Journal of Pediatric Endocrinology and Metabolism, 14*(9), 1575–1583.

D'Agostino, J. V., & Day, S. K. (1991). Gender-role orientation and preference for an intimate partner. *The Psychological Record, 41,* 321–328.

Dahlheimer, D., & Feigal, J. (1991, January/February). Bridging the gap. *Networker,* 44–53.

Dailard, C. (1999, June). *Issues in brief: Abortion in context: United States and worldwide.* Alan Guttmacher Institute. Retrieved August 12, 1999, from http://www.agi-usa.org/pubs/ib_0599.html

Dailard, C. (2001). Sex education: Politicians, parents, teachers, and teens. *The Guttmacher Report on Public Policy, 4*(1), 9–12.

Dalla, R. L. (2000). Exposing the "pretty woman" myth: A qualitative examination of the lives of female streetwalking prostitutes. *Journal of Sex Research, 37,* 344–353.

Daly, M., & Wilson, M. (1983). *Sex, evolution, and behavior* (2nd ed.). Boston: Willard Grant Press.

Daniluk, J. C. (1998). *Women's sexuality across the life span: Challenging myths, creating meanings.* New York: Guilford.

Darke, J. L. (1990). Sexual aggression: Achieving power through humiliation. In W. L. Marshall, D. R. Laws, & H. E. Barbaree (Eds.), *Handbook of sexual assault: Issues, theories, and treatment of the offender* (pp. 55–72). New York: Plenum.

Darroch, J. E., Singh, S., Frost, J. J., and the Study Team. (2001). Differences in teenage pregnancy rates among five developed countries: The role of sexual activity and contraceptive use. *Family Planning Perspectives, 33*(6), 244–250, 281.

D'Augelli, A., & Hershberger, S. (1993). Lesbian, gay, and bisexual youth in community settings: Personal challenges and mental health problems. *American Journal of Community Psychology, 21*(4), 421–447.

Davenport, W. (1965). Sexual patterns and their regulation in a society of the Southwest Pacific. In F. A. Beach (Ed.), *Sex and behavior* (pp. 164–207). New York: John Wiley & Sons.

Davenport, W. H. (1987). An anthropological approach. In J. H. Geer & W. T. O'Donohue (Eds.), *Theories of human sexuality* (pp. 197–236). New York: Plenum.

Davidson, A. T. (1983). Sexual exploitation of children: A call to action. *Journal of the National Medical Association, 75,* 925–927.

Davidson, J. K., & Darling, C. A. (1993). Masturbatory guilt and sexual responsiveness among post-college-age women: Sexual satisfaction revisited. *Journal of Sex and Marital Therapy, 19,* 289–300.

Davidson, J. K., Sr., & Moore, N. B. (1996). *Marriage and family: Change and continuity.* Boston: Allyn & Bacon.

Davies, K. A. (1997). Voluntary exposure to pornography and men's attitudes toward feminism and rape. *Journal of Sex Research, 34,* 131–137.

Davis, C. M. (1993). A reader's guide to the Janus Report [review of the Janus Report on sexual behavior]. *Journal of Sex Research, 30,* 336–343.

Davis, C. M., Blank, J., Lin, H., & Bonillas, C. (1996). Characteristics of vibrator use among women. *Journal of Sex Research, 33,* 313–320.

Davis, C. M., Yarber, W. L., Bauserman, R., Schreer, G., & Davis, S. L. (1998). *Handbook of sexuality-related measures.* Thousand Oaks, CA: Sage.

Davis, D. M. (1990). Portrayals of women in prime-time network television: Some demographic characteristics. *Sex Roles, 23,* 325–332.

Davis, G., Balart, L., Schiff, E., Lindsay, K., & Bodenheimer, H. (1989). Treatment of chronic hepatitis with recombinant interferon alfa. *New England Journal of Medicine, 321,* 1501–1506.

Davis, J. A., & Smith, T. W. (1991). *General social surveys, 1972–1991: Cumulative codebook.* Chicago: National Opinion Research Center.

Davis, J. A., & Smith, T. W. (1994). *General social surveys, 1972–1994.* Chicago: National Opinion Research Center.

Davis, R. (1997, December 22). Method enables earlier abortion. *USA Today,* p. D1.

Davis, T. (2000). Testosterone and sexual desire in women. *Journal of Sex Education and Therapy, 25,* 2–33.

Day, J. C. (1996). *Projections of the number of households and families in the United States: 1995 to 2010.* Washington, DC: U.S. Government Printing Office.

Day, R. D. (1992). The transition to first intercourse among racially and culturally diverse youth. *Journal of Marriage and the Family, 54,* 749–762.

de Freitas, C. (1998). *Keys to your child's healthy sexuality.* New York: Barron's.

Deblinger, E., McLeer, S. V., & Henry, D. (1990). Cognitive behavioral treatment for sexually abused children suffering post-traumatic stress: Preliminary findings. *Journal of the American Academy of Child and Adolescent Psychiatry, 29,* 747–752.

Degges-White, S., Rice, B., & Myers, J. E. (2000). Revisiting Cass' theory of sexual identity formation: A study of lesbian development. *Journal of Mental Health Counseling, 22*(4), 318–333.

Degler, C. (1974). What ought to be and what was: Women's sexuality in the nineteenth century. *American Historical Review, 79.*

Dekker, J. (1993). Inhibited male orgasm. In W. O'Donohue & J. H. Geer (Eds.), *Handbook of sexual dysfunctions: Assessment and treatment* (pp. 279–301). Boston: Allyn & Bacon.

Dekker, J., & Everaerd, W. (1989). Psychological determinants of sexual arousal: A review. *Behavior, Research and Therapy, 27,* 353–364.

DeLamater, J. (1987). A sociological approach. In J. H. Geer & W. T. O'Donohue (Eds.), *Theories of human sexuality* (pp. 237–255). New York: Plenum.

DeLamater, J. D., & MacCorquodale, P. (1979). *Premarital sexuality: Attitudes, relationships, behavior.* Madison: University of Wisconsin.

Delaney, J., Lupton, M., & Toth, E. (1988). *The curse: A cultural history of menstruation.* Urbana: University of Illinois.

DeLoache, J. S., & Marzolf, D. P. (1995). The use of dolls to interview young children: Issues of symbolic representation. *Journal of Experimental Child Psychology, 60,* 155–173.

D'Emilio, J., & Freedman, E. B. (1997). *Intimate matters: A history of sexuality in America.* New York: Harper & Row.

Dening, S. (1996). *The mythology of sex.* New York: Macmillan.

Dermer, A. (1995). Overcoming medical and social barriers to breast feeding. *American Family Physician, 51,* 755–763.

DeVoe, E. R., & Faller, K. C. (2002). Questioning strategies in interviews with children who may have been sexually abused. *Child Welfare, 81,* 27–32.

Dewey, K. G., Heinig, M. J., & Nommsen-Rivers, L. A. (1995). Differences in morbidity between breast-fed and formula-fed infants. *Journal of Pediatrics, 126,* 696–702.

de Zalduondo, B. O. (1991). Prostitution viewed cross-culturally: Toward recontextualized sex work in AIDS intervention research. *Journal of Sex Research, 28,* 223–248.

Diamond, L. M. (2000). Sexual identity: Attractions and behavior among young sexual-minority women over a 2-year period. *Developmental Psychology, 36*(2), 241–250.

Diamond, M. (1982). Sexual identity, monozygotic twins reared in discordant sex roles and a BBC follow-up. *Archives of Sexual Behavior, 11,* 181–185.

Diamond, M. (1995). Biological aspects of sexual orientation and identity. In L. Diamant & R. D. McAnulty (Eds.), *The psychology of sexual orientation, behavior, and identity: A handbook* (pp. 45–80). Westport, CT: Greenwood.

Diamond, S. (1985). Pornography: Image and reality. In V. Burstyn (Ed.), *Women against censorship* (pp. 40–57). Vancouver, Canada: Douglas & McIntyre.

Diehl, M., Elnick, A. B., Bourbeau, L. S., & Labouvie-Vief, G. (1998). Adult attachment styles: Their relations to family context and personality. *Journal of Personality and Social Psychology, 74,* 1656–1669.

Dietz, P. E., Harry, B., & Hazelwood, R. R. (1986). Detective magazines: Pornography for the sexual sadist? *Journal of Forensic Sciences, 31,* 197–211.

DiIorio, C., Dudley, W. N., Kelly, M., Soet, J. E., Mbwara, J., & Potter, J. S. (2001). Social cognitive correlates of sexual experience and condom use among 13- through 15-year-old adolescents. *Journal of Adolescent Health, 29*(3), 208–216.

DiIorio, C., Kelley, M., & Hockenberry-Eaton, M. (1999). Communication about sexual issues: Mothers, fathers, and friends. *Journal of Adolescent Health, 23,* 181–189.

Dillard, K. (2002). *Adolescent sexual behavior. II: Socio-psychological factors. The Facts.* Washington, DC: Advocates for Youth.

Dion, K. K., & Dion, K. L. (2001). Gender and relationships. In R. K. Unger (Ed.), *Handbook of the psychology of women and gender* (pp. 272–288). New York: Wiley.

DiPietro, J. A., Hilton, S. C., Hawkins, M., Costigan, K., & Pressman, E. K. (2002). Maternal stress and affect influence fetal neurobehavioral development. *Developmental Psychology, 38*(5), 659–668.

Dittman, R. W., Kappes, M. E., & Kappes, M. H. (1992). Sexual behavior in adolescent and adult females with congenital adrenal hyperplasia. *Psychoneuroendocrinology, 17,* 153–170.

Dittrich, R., Parker, L., Rosen, J. B., Shangold, G., Creasy, G. W., Fisher, A. C., & Ortho Evra/Evra 001 Study Group. (2002). Transdermal contraception: Evaluation of three transdermal norelgestromin/ethinyl estradiol doses in a randomized, multicenter, dose-response study. *American Journal of Obstetrics and Gynecology, 186*(1): 15–20.

Dittus, P. J., & Jaccard, J. (2000). Adolescents' perceptions of maternal disapproval of sex: Relationship to sexual outcomes. *Journal of Adolescent Health, 26,* 268–278.

Docter, R. F. (1988). *Transvestites and transsexuals: Toward a theory of cross-gender behavior.* New York: Plenum.

Docter, R. F., & Prince, V. (1997). Transvestism: A survey of 1032 cross-dressers. *Archives of Sexual Behavior, 26,* 589–605.

Dolcini, M., Coates, T. J., Catania, J., Kegeles, S., & Hauck, W. (1995). Multiple sexual partnerships and their psychosocial correlates: The population-based AIDS in Multiethnic Neighborhoods (AMEN) study. *Health Psychology, 14,* 22–31.

Donnelly, D. A. (1993). Sexually inactive marriages. *Journal of Sex Research, 30,* 171–179.

Donnerstein, E., Berkowitz, L., & Linz, D. (1986). *Role of aggressive and sexual images in violent pornography.* Unpublished manuscript, University of Wisconsin—Madison.

Donnerstein, E., Linz, D., & Penrod, S. (1987). *The question of pornography: Research and policy implications.* New York: The Free Press.

Donnerstein, E., & Malamuth, N. (1997). Pornography: Its consequences on the observer. In L. B. Schlesinger & E. Revitch (Eds.), *Sexual dynamics of anti-social behavior* (2nd ed.). Springfield, IL: Charles C. Thomas Publisher.

Donovan, P. (1997). Special report: Can statutory rape laws be effective in preventing adolescent pregnancy? *Family Planning Perspectives, 29,* 30–34.

Donovan, P. (1998). School-based sexuality education: The issues and challenges. *Family Planning Perspectives, 30,* 188–194.

Dooley, D. (1995). *Social research methods* (3rd ed.). Englewood Cliffs, NJ: Prentice-Hall.

Doorn, C. D., Poortinga, J., & Verschoor, A. M. (1994). Cross-gender identity in transvestites and male transsexuals. *Archives of Sexual Behavior, 23,* 185–201.

Dover, K. J. (1989). *Greek homosexuality.* Cambridge, MA: Harvard University.

Dowsett, G., & Aggleton, P. (1999). Young people and risk-taking in sexual relations. In *Sex and youth: Contextual factors affecting risk for HIV/AIDS.* Geneva, Switzerland: UNAIDS.

Dreger, A. (2002). *Notes on the treatment of intersex.* Retrieved July 16, 2002, from www.isna.org/library/dreger-compare.html

Dressel, P. L., & Petersen, D. (1982). Becoming a male stripper: Recruitment, socialization, and ideological development. *Work and Occupation, 9,* 387–406.

Drews, C., Murphy, C., Yeargen-Allsopp, M., & Decouflé, P. (1996). The relationship between idiopathic mental retardation and maternal smoking during pregnancy. *Pediatrics, 97,* 547–553.

Drugs that can sabotage your love life. (2002, March). *Consumer Reports on Health, 14*(3), 1–6.

Duddle, C. M. (1977). Etiological factors in the unconsummated marriage. *Journal of Psychosomatic Research, 21,* 157–160.

Duncan, B., Ey, J., Holberg, C. J., Wright, A. L., Martinez, F. D., & Taussig, L. M. (1993). Exclusive breast-feeding for at least 4 months protects against otitis media. *Pediatrics, 91,* 867–872.

Duncan, D. (1990). Prevalence of sexual assault victimization among heterosexual and gay/lesbian university students. *Psychological Reports, 66,* 65–66.

Dunn, K. M., Croft, P. R., & Hackett, G. I. (1999). Association of sexual problems with social, psychological, and physical problems in men and women: A cross sectional population survey. *Journal of Epidemiology and Community Health, 53,* 144–148.

Dunn, M. E., & Trost, J. E. (1989). Male multiple orgasms: A descriptive study. *Archives of Sexual Behavior, 18,* 377–387.

Dupras, A. (1994). Internalized homophobia and psychosexual adjustment among gay men. *Psychological Reports, 75,* 23–28.

Durant, R. H., Rome, E. S., Rich, M., Allred, E., Emans, J., & Woods, E. R. (1997). Tobacco and alcohol use behaviors portrayed in music videos: A content analysis. *American Journal of Public Health, 87,* 1131–1135.

Earls, C. M., & David, H. (1989). Male and female prostitution: A review. *Annals of Sex Research, 2,* 5–28.

Easterbrook, P. J. (1994). Editorial comment: Non-progression in HIV infection. *AIDS, 8,* 1179–1182.

Eccles, J., Jacobs, J. E., & Harold, R. D. (1990). Gender role stereotypes, expectancy effects, and parents' socialization of gender differences. *Journal of Social Issues, 46,* 183–201.

Eckland, B. K. (1982). Theories of mate selection. *Social Biology, 29,* 7–21.

Eder, F. X., Hall, L., & Hekma, G. (Eds.). (1999). *Sexual cultures in Europe: National histories.* New York: Manchester University Press.

Edgley, C. (1989). Commercial sex: Pornography, prostitution, and advertising. In K. McKinney & S. Sprecher (Eds.), *Human sexuality: The societal and interpersonal context* (pp. 370–424). Norwood, NJ: Ablex.

Edwards, C. (1997). Unspeakable professions: Public performance and prostitution in ancient Rome. In J. P. Hallett & M. B. Skinner (Eds.), *Roman sexualities* (pp. 66–95). Princeton, NJ: Princeton University.

Edwards, S. (1994). The role of men in contraceptive decision-making: Current knowledge and future implications. *Family Planning Perspectives, 26,* 77–82.

Ehrhardt, A. A., Exner, T. M., Hoffman, S., Silberman, I., Leu, C. S., Miller, S., & Levin, B. (2002). A gender-specific HIV/STD risk reduction intervention for women in a health care setting: Short- and long-term results of a randomized clinical trial. *AIDS Care, 14*(2), 147–161.

Ehrhardt, A. A., & Meyer-Bahlburg, H. F. L. (1981). Effects of prenatal sex hormones on gender-related behavior. *Science, 211,* 1312–1318.

Ehrlich, P. R., & Ehrlich, A. H. (1990). *The population explosion: From global warming to rain forest destruction, famine, and air and water pollution—why overpopulation is our #1 environmental problem.* New York: Simon and Schuster.

Eiger, M. S., & Olds, S. W. (1987). *The complete book of breastfeeding.* New York: Bantam Books.

Einon, D. (1994). Are men more promiscuous than women? *Ethology and Sociobiology, 15,* 131–143.

Eisenberg, A., Murkoff, H. E., & Hathaway, S. E. (1991). *What to expect when you're expecting.* New York: Workman Publishing.

Eliason, M. J. (1995). Accounts of sexual identity formation in heterosexual students. *Sex Roles, 32*(11/12), 821–833.

Elliott, D. M., & Briere, J. (1995). Posttraumatic stress associated with delayed recall of sexual abuse: A general population study. *Journal of Traumatic Stress, 8,* 629–647.

Ellis, B. J., & Symons, D. (1990). Sex differences in sexual fantasy: An evolutionary psychological approach. *Journal of Sex Research, 27*(4), 527–555.

Ellis, H. (1906). *Studies in the psychology of sex* (Vols. 1–7). New York: Random House.

Ellison, J. M. (1998). Antidepressant-induced sexual dysfunction: Review, classification, and suggestions for treatment. *Harvard Review of Psychiatry, 6,* 177–189.

Ellison v. Brady, 924 F.2d 872 (1991).

El-Refaey, H., Rajasekar, D., Abdalla, M., Calder, L., & Templeton, A. (1995). Induction of abortion with mifepristone (RU 486) and oral or vaginal misoprostol. *New England Journal of Medicine, 332,* 983–987.

Elwin, V. (1968). *Kingdom of the young.* London: Oxford University.

Embree, J. E., Njenga, S., Datta, P., Nagelkerke, N. J. D., Ndinya-Achola, J. O., Mohammed, Z., Ramdahin, S., Bwayo, J. J., & Plummer, F. A. (2000). Risk factors for postnatal mother-child transmission of HIV-1. *AIDS, 14,* 2535–2541.

Enck, G. E., & Preston, J. D. (1988). Counterfeit intimacy: A dramaturgical analysis of an erotic performance. *Deviant Behavior, 9,* 369–381.

Engelhardt, H. T. (1974). The disease of masturbation: Values and the concept of disease. *Bulletin of the History of Medicine, 48,* 234–248.

Enzlin, P., Mathieu, C., Vanderschueren, D., & Demyttenaere, K. (1998). Diabetes mellitus and female sexuality: A review of 25 years' research. *Diabetic Medicine, 15,* 809–815.

Epps, R. P., & Stewart, S. C. (1995). *The American Medical Women's Association guide to pregnancy and childbirth.* New York: Dell Publishing.

Epstein, A. W. (1961). Relationship of fetishism and transvestism to brain and particularly to temporal lobe dysfunction. *Journal of Nervous & Mental Disease, 133,* 247–253.

Erickson, P. I., Bastani, R., Maxwell, A., Marcus, A., et al. (1995). Prevalence of anal sex among heterosexuals in California and its relationship to other AIDS risk behaviors. *AIDS Education and Prevention, 7,* 477–493.

Erikson, E. H. (1959). *Identity and the life cycle.* New York: International Universities Press.

Erikson, E. H. (1963). *Childhood and society* (2nd ed.). New York: Norton.

Erikson, E. H. (1982). *The life cyle completed.* New York: Norton.

Erikson, W. D., Walbek, N. G., & Seeley, R. K. (1988). Behavior patterns of child molesters. *Archives of Sexual Behavior, 17,* 77–86.

Ernst, F. A., Francis, R. A., Nevels, H., & Lemeh, C. A. (1991). Condemnation of homosexuality in the black community: A gender-specific phenomenon? *Archives of Sexual Behavior, 20*(6), 579–585.

Ernulf, K. E., & Innala, S. M. (1995). Sexual bondage: A review and unobtrusive investigation. *Archives of Sexual Behavior, 24,* 631–654.

Eskenazi, B., Prehn, A. W., & Christianson, R. E. (1995). Passive and active maternal smoking as measured by serum cotinine: The effect on birthweight. *American Journal of Public Health, 85,* 395–398.

Espin, O. M. (1993). Issues of identity in the psychology of Latina lesbians. In L. D. Garnets & D. C. Kimmel (Eds.), *Psychological perspectives on lesbian and gay male experiences* (pp. 348–363). New York: Columbia University Press.

Esposito, L. C. (1998). Regulating the Internet: The new battle against child pornography. *Case Western Reserve Journal of International Law, 30,* 541–566.

Estes, R. J., & Weiner, N. A. (2001). *The commercial sexual exploitation of children in the U.S., Canada, and Mexico.* Philadelphia: University of Pennsylvania.

Etherington, K. (1997). Maternal sexual abuse of males. *Child Abuse Review, 6,* 107–117.

Ethics Committee of the American Fertility Society. (1986, September). *Ethical considerations of the new reproductive technologies.* Birmingham, AL: The American Fertility Society.

Etonorgestrel implant (Implanon) for contraception. (2001). *Drug & Therapeutics Bulletin, 39*(8), 57–59.

Ettorre, E. M. (Ed.). (1980). *Lesbians, women, and society.* London: Routledge & Kegan Paul.

Everaerd, W., Laan, E. T. M., Roth, S., & van der Velde, J. (2000). Female sexuality. In L. T. Szuchman & F. Muscarella (Eds.), *Psychological perspectives on human sexuality* (pp. 101–146). New York: Wiley.

Fahrner, E. M. (1987). Sexual dysfunction in male alcohol addicts: Prevalence and treatment. *Archives of Sexual Behavior, 16,* 247–257.

Family Research Council. (1997). In focus: Talking points on partial birth abortion. Retrieved May 14, 1998, from www.frc.org/infocus/if97c31if.html

Farkas, G. M., Sine, L. F., & Evans, I. M. (1978). Personality, sexuality and demographic differences between volunteers and nonvolunteers for a laboratory study of male sexual behavior. *Archives of Sexual Behavior, 7,* 513–520.

Farmer, I. P., Meyer, P. S., Ramsey, D. J., Golf, D. C., Wear, M. L., Labarthe, D. R., & Nichaman, M. Z. (1996). Higher levels of social support predict greater survival following myocardial infarction: The Corpus Christi Heart Project. *Behavioral Medicine, 22,* 59–67.

Fassinger, R. E., & Morrow, S. L. (1995). Overcome: Repositioning lesbian sexualities. In L. Diamant & R. D. McAnulty (Eds.), *The psychology of sexual orientations, behavior, and identity: A handbook* (pp. 197–219). Westport, CT: Greenwood.

Fay, R. E., Turner, C. F., Klassen, A. D., & Gagnon, J. H. (1989). Prevalence and patterns of same-gender sexual contact among men. *Science, 243,* 338–348.

FDA approves NuvaRing contraceptive implant. (2002). *Journal of Gender Specific Medicine, 5*(2), 6.

Feeney, J. A. (1999). Adult romantic attachment and couple relationships. In J. Cassidy & P. R. Shaver (Eds.), *Handbook of attachment: Theory, research and clinical applications* (pp. 355–377). New York: Guilford.

Feeney, J. A. (2002). Attachment, marital interaction, and relationship satisfaction: A diary study. *Personal Relationships, 9,* 39–55.

Fehr, B. (1988). Prototype analysis of the concepts of love and commitment. *Journal of Personality and Social Psychology, 55,* 557–579.

Feingold, A. (1988). Matching for attractiveness in romantic partner and same-sex friends: A meta-analysis and theoretical critique. *Psychosocial Bulletin, 104,* 226–235.

Feldman, H. A., Goldstein, I., Hatzichristou, D. G., Krane, R. J., & McKinlay, J. B. (1994). Impotence and its medical and psychological correlates: Results of the Massachusetts Male Aging Study. *Journal of Urology, 151,* 54–61.

Feldman, M. P., & MacCulloch, M. J. (1971). *Homosexual behavior: Therapy and assessment.* Oxford: Pergamon Press.

Felmlee, D. H. (1994). Who's on top? Power in romantic relationships. *Sex Roles, 31,* 275–295.

Feng, D. (1999). Intergenerational transmission of marital quality and marital instability. *Journal of Marriage and the Family, 61,* 451–464.

Feray, J., & Herzer, M. (1990). Homosexual studies and politics in the 19th century: Karl Maria Kertbeny. *Journal of Homosexuality, 19*(1), 23–47.

Ferguson, S. L. (1998). Peer counseling in a culturally specific adolescent pregnancy prevention program. *Journal of Health Care for the Poor and Underserved, 9,* 322–341.

Ferin, M., Jewelewicz, R., & Warren, M. (1993). *The menstrual cycle: physiology, reproductive disorders, and infertility*. New York: Oxford University Press.

Ferris, D. G., Batish, S., Wright, T. C., Cushing, C., & Scott, E. H. (1996). A neglected lesbian health concern: Cervical neoplasia. *Journal of Family Practice, 43*, 581–584.

Festinger, L., Schachter, S., & Black, K. (1950). *Social pressures in informal groups: A study of human factors in housing*. New York: Harper.

Fields, J., & Casper, L. M. (2001a). America's families and living arrangements: March 2000. *Current Population Reports, P20-537*. Washington, DC: U.S. Census Bureau.

Fields, J., & Casper, L. M. (2001b). *America's families and living arrangements: Population characteristics*. Washington, DC: U.S. Census Bureau.

Fink, P. (1972). Dyspareunia: Current concepts. *Medical Aspects of Human Sexuality, 6*, 28–33.

Finkelhor, D. (1979). *Sexually victimized children*. New York: Free Press.

Finkelhor, D. (1980). Sex among siblings: A survey on prevalence, variety, and effects. *Archives of Sexual Behavior, 9*, 171–194.

Finkelhor, D. (1986). Sexual abuse: Beyond the family systems approach. *Journal of Psychotherapy and the Family, 2*, 53–65.

Finkelhor, D. (1987). The sexual abuse of children: Current research reviewed. *Psychiatric Annals, 17*, 233–241.

Finkelhor, D. (1990). Early and long-term effects of child sexual abuse: An update. *Professional Psychology: Research and Practice, 21*, 325–330.

Finkelhor, D. (1994). Current information on the scope and nature of child sexual abuse. *The Future of Children, 4*, 31, 46–48.

Finkelhor, D., & Baron, L. (1986). Risk factors for child sexual abuse. *Journal of Interpersonal Violence, 1*, 43–71.

Finkelhor, D., Mitchell, K. J., & Wolak, J. (2000). *Online victimization: A report on the nation's youth*. Alexandria, VA: National Center for Missing and Exploited Children.

Finkelhor, D., & Russell, D. E. H. (1984). Women as perpetrators: Review of the evidence. In D. Finkelhor (Ed.), *Child sexual abuse: New research and theory* (pp. 171–187). New York: Free Press.

First Breath Alliance. (1997). NRLC lauds AMA decision to endorse partial-birth abortion ban with only clarifying changes. Retrieved May 14, 1998, from www.firstbreath.org/970519a.htm. (Contains complete letter to Senator Rick Santorum from AMA.)

Fischer, J. L., & Sollie, D. L. (1993). The transition to marriage: Network suppport and coping. In T. H. Brubaker (Ed.), *Family relations: Challenges for the future: Vol. 1. Current issues in the family* (pp. 61–78). Newbury Park, CA: Sage.

Fisher, B. S., Cullen, F. T., & Turner, M. G. (2000). *The sexual victimization of college women*. Washington, DC: U.S. Department of Justice.

Fisher, H. (1992). *Anatomy of love: The natural history of monogamy, adultery, and divorce*. New York: Norton.

Fisher, J. M., & Heesacker, M. (1995). Men's and women's preferences regarding sex-related and nurturing traits in dating partners. *Journal of College Student Development, 36*, 260–269.

Fisher, R. D., Cook, I. J., & Shirley, E. C. (1994). Correlates of support for censorship of sexual, sexually violent, and violent media. *Journal of Sex Research, 31*, 229–240.

Fisher, S., & Greenberg, R. P. (1977). *The scientific credibility of Freud's theory and therapy*. New York: Basic Books.

Fisher, T. D., Pollack, R. H., & Malatesta, V. H. (1986). Orgasmic latency and subjective ratings of erotic stimuli in male and female subjects. *Journal of Sex Research, 22*, 85–93.

Fisher, W. A., & Grenier, G. (1994). Violent pornography, antiwoman thoughts, and antiwoman acts: In search for reliable effects. *Journal of Sex Research, 31*, 23–28.

Fitzgerald, L. F. (1993). *The last great open secret: The sexual harassment of women in the workplace and academia*. Washington, DC: Federation of Behavioral, Psychological, and Cognitive Sciences.

Fitzgerald, L. F., Drasgow, F., Hulin, C. L., Gelfand, M. J., & Magley, V. J. (1997). Antecedents and consequences of sexual harassment in organizations: A test of an integrated model. *Journal of Applied Psychology, 82*, 578–589.

Flannery, D. J., Rowe, D. C., & Gulley, B. L. (1993). Impact of pubertal status, timing, and age on adolescent sexual experience and delinquency. *Journal of Adolescent Research, 8*, 21–40.

Flaskerud, J. H., Uman, G., Lara, R., Romero, L., & Taka, K. (1996). Sexual practices, attitudes, and knowledge related to HIV transmission in low income Los Angeles Hispanic women. *Journal of Sex Research, 33*, 343–353.

Foa, E. B., Rothbaum, E. O., Riggs, D., & Murdock, T. (1991). Treatment of PTSD in rape victims: A comparison between cognitive-behavioral procedures and counseling. *Journal of Consulting and Clinical Psychology, 59*, 715–723.

Fogelman, K. R., & Manor, O. (1988). Smoking in pregnancy and development into early adulthood. *British Medical Journal, 297*, 1233–1236.

Foley, S., Kope, S. A., & Sugrue, D. P. (2002). *Sex matters for women: A complete guide to taking care of your sexual self*. New York: Guilford.

Food and drug administration: Birth control implant approved. (1991). *Journal of the American Osteopathic Association, 91*(1), 23.

Ford, R. P. K., Taylor, B. J., Mitchell, E. A., Enright, S. A., Stewart, A. W., Becroft, D. M. O., Scragg, R., Hassall, I. B., Barry, D. M. J., Allen, E. M., & Roberts, A. P. (1993). Breastfeeding and the risk of sudden infant death syndrome. *International Journal of Epidemiology, 22*, 885–890.

Fordney, D. (1978). Dyspareunia and vaginismus. *Clinical Obstetrics and Gynecology, 21*, 205–221.

Forrest, B. D. (1991). Women, HIV, and mucosal immunity. *Lancet, 337*, 835–837.

Fowers, B. J., & Olson, D. H. (1986). Predicting marital success with PREPARE: A predictive validity study. *Journal of Marital and Family Therapy, 12*, 403–413.

Fox, R. C. (1995). Bisexual identities. In A. R. D'Augelli & C. J. Patterson (Eds.), *Lesbian, gay and bisexual identities over the lifespan: Psychological perspectives* (pp. 48–86). New York: Oxford University Press.

Fox, R. C. (1996). Bisexuality in perspective: A review of theory and research. In B. A. Firestein (Ed.), *Bisexuality: The psychology and politics of an invisible minority* (pp. 3–52). Thousand Oaks, CA: Sage.

Foxman, B., & Chi, J. W. (1990). Health behavior and urinary tract infection in college-aged women. *Journal of Clinical Epidemiology, 43*(4), 329–337.

Foxman, B., Gillespie, B., Koopman, J., Zhang, L., Palin, K., Tallman, P., Marsh, J. V., Spear, S., Sobel, J. D., Marty, M. J., & Marrs, C. F. (2000). Risk factors for second urinary tract infection among college women. *American Journal of Epidemiology, 151*(12), 1194–1205.

Frackiewicz, E. J., & Shiovitz, T. M. (2001). Evaluation and management of premenstrual syndrome and premenstrual dysphoric disorder. *Journal of the American Pharmaceutical Association, 41*(3), 437–447.

Frank, E., Anderson, C., & Rubinstein, D. (1978). Frequency of sexual dysfunction in "normal" couples. *New England Journal of Medicine, 299,* 111–115.

Frankel, D. (1994). U.S. Surgeon General forced to resign. *Lancet, 344,* 1695.

Frantz, D. O. (1989). *Festum Voluptatis: A study of Renaissance erotica.* Columbus: Ohio State University Press.

Frayser, S. (1985). *Varieties of sexual experience: An anthropological perspective on human sexuality.* New Haven, CT: Human Relations Area File Press.

Frazier, A. L., & Colditz, G. A. (1995). Should we aim at prevention in youth? In B. A. Stoll (Ed.), *Reducing Breast Cancer Risk in Women* (pp. 209–206). Boston: Kluwer Academic Publishers.

Freeman, L. (1997). The state of women in the world: Legal status of abortion. Retrieved May 17, 1999, from www.snowcrest.net/freeman1/women/atlas/abortion.htm

Freetly, A. J. H., & Kane, E. W. (1995). Men's and women's perceptions of non-consensual sexual intercourse. *Sex Roles, 33,* 785–803.

Freud, S. (1953). Three essays on the theory of sexuality. In J. Strachey (Ed.), *The standard edition of the complete psychological works of Sigmund Freud* (Vol. 7) (pp. 123–246). London: Hogarth. (Original work published 1905)

Freud, S. (1955). The psychogenesis of a case of homosexuality in a woman. In J. Strachey (Ed.), *The standard edition of the complete psychological works of Sigmund Freud* (Vol. 18) (pp. 155–172). London: Hogarth. (Original work published 1920)

Freud, S. (1961). Some psychical consequences of the anatomical distinction between the sexes. *Collected works of Sigmund Freud* (Standard ed., Vol. 19) (pp. 248–260). London: Hogarth Press.

Freund, K. (1990). Courtship disorders. In W. L. Marshall, D. R. Laws, & H. E. Barbaree (Eds.), *Handbook of sexual assault: Issues, theories, and treatment of the offender* (pp. 195–208). New York: Plenum.

Freund, K., & Blanchard, R. (1986). The concept of courship disorder. *Journal of Sex and Marital Therapy, 12,* 79–92.

Freund, M., Lee, N., & Leonard, T. (1991). Sexual behavior of clients with street prostitutes in Camden, New Jersey. *Journal of Sex Research, 28,* 579–591.

Freund, M., Leonard, T. L., & Lee, N. (1989). Sexual behavior of resident street prostitutes with their clients in Camden, New Jersey. *Journal of Sex Research, 26,* 460–478.

Frey, K. S., & Ruble, D. N. (1992). Gender constancy and the "cost" of sex-typed behavior: A test of the conflict hypothesis. *Developmental Psychology, 28,* 714–721.

Fried, M. G., & Ross, L. (1995). Abortion rights should not be restricted. In C. Cozic & J. Petrikin (Eds.), *The abortion controversy* (pp. 90–94). San Diego: Greenhaven Press.

Friedman-Kien, A. (1995). Management of condylomata acuminata with Alferon N injection, interferon alfa-n3 (human leukocyte derived). *American Journal of Obstetrics and Gynecology, 172,* 1359–1368.

Friedrich, W. N., Fisher, J., Broughton, D., Houston, M., & Shafran, C. R. (1998). Normative sexual behavior in children: A contemporary sample. *Pediatrics, 101.*

Friman, P. C., Finney, J. W., Glasscock, S. G., Weigel, J. W., & Christophersen, E. R. (1986). Testicular self-examination: Validation of a training strategy for early cancer detection. *Journal of Applied Behavior Analysis, 19,* 87–92.

Fromuth, M. E. (1997). Hidden perpetrators: Sexual molestation in a nonclinical sample of college women. *Journal of Interpersonal Violence, 12,* 456–465.

Froster, U. G., & Jackson, L. (1996). Limb defects and chorionic villus sampling: Results from an international registry, 1992–1994. *The Lancet, 347,* 489–494.

Frye, M. (1992). *Willful virgin.* Freedom, CA: Crossing Press.

Fuendeling, J. M. (1998). Affect regulation as a stylistic process within adult attachment. *Journal of Social and Personal Relationships, 15,* 291–322.

Fullilove, M. T., Fullilove, R. E., Haynes, K., & Gross, S. (1990). Black women and AIDS prevention: A view toward understanding the gender rules. *Journal of Sex Research, 27,* 47–64.

Fullilove, M. T., Lown, E. A., & Fullilove, R. E. (1992). Crack'hos and skeezers: Traumatic experiences of women crack users. *Journal of Sex Research, 29,* 275–287.

Furstenberg, F. F., Jr., Brooks-Gunn, J., & Chase-Lansdale, L. (1989). Teenaged pregnancy and childbearing. *American Psychologist, 44,* 313–320.

Furstenberg, F. F., Jr., Geitz, L. M., Teitler, J. O., & Weiss, C. C. (1997). Does condom availability make a difference? An evaluation of Philadelphia's health resource centers. *Family Planning Perspectives, 29,* 123–127.

Gaddis, A., & Brooks-Gunn, J. (1985). The male experience of pubertal change. *Journal of Youth and Adolescence, 14,* 61–69.

Gage, A. J. (1998). Sexual activity and contraceptive use: The components of the decisionmaking process. *Studies in Family Planning, 29,* 154–167.

Gagnon, J., Giami, A., Michaels, S., & de Colomby, P. (2001). A comparison study of the couple in the social organization of sexuality in France and the United States. *Journal of Sex Research, 38,* 24–34.

Gagnon, J. H. (1985). Attitudes and responses of parents to preadolescent masturbation. *Archives of Sexual Behavior, 14,* 451–466.

Gagnon, J. H., Rosen, R. C., & Leiblum, S. R. (1982). Cognitive and social aspects of sexual dysfunction: Sexual scripts in sex therapy. *Journal of Sex and Marital Therapy, 8,* 44–56.

Gagnon, J. H., & Simon, W. (1973). *Sexual conduct: The social sources of human sexuality.* Chicago: Aldine.

Gagnon, J. H., & Simon, W. (1987). The sexual scripting of oral-genital contact. *Archives of Sexual Behavior, 16,* 1–25.

Galenson, E., & Roiphe, H. (1974). The emergence of genital awareness during the second year of life. In R. C. Friedman (Ed.), *Sex differences in behavior* (pp. 233–241). New York: Wiley.

Gall, S. A. (1995). Human papillomavirus infection and therapy with interferon. *American Journal of Obstetrics and Gynecology, 172,* 1354–1359.

Gallagher, J. (1996, July 11). Violent times. *The Advocate,* 33.

Galski, T., Thornton, K. E., & Shumsky, D. (1990). Brain dysfunction in sex offenders. *Journal of Offender Rehabilitation, 16,* 65–80.

Gamson, J. (1996, January/February). Do ask, do tell. *Utne Reader, 73,* 78–84.

Gannon, L. (1994). Sexuality and menopause. In P. Y. L. Choi & P. Nicholson (Eds.), *Female sexuality: Psychology, biology and social context* (pp. 100–124). New York: Harvester/Wheatsheaf.

Garcia, L. T. (1982). Sex-role orientation and stereotypes about male-female sexuality. *Sex Roles, 8*(8), 863–876.

Gardos, S. (1999). *Web MD Health: Sex during that time of month.* Retrieved June 27, 2002, from http://my.webmed.com/content/article/1687.50059

Garlick, Y., Marshall, W. L., & Thornton, D. (1996). Intimacy deficits and attribution of blame among sexual offenders. *Legal and Criminological Psychology, 1,* 251–288.

Garrow, D. (1998). First person: Common ground not likely for abortion adversaries. *Emory Report, 50*(18). Retrieved May 27, 1998, from www.emory.edu/EMORY_REPORT/erarchive//1998/January/erjanuary.26/1_26_98FirstPerson.html

Gay, J. (1986). "Mummies and babies" and friends and lovers in Lesotho. In E. Blackwood (Ed.), *The many faces of homosexuality.* New York: Harrington Park Press.

Gebhard, P. H., Gagnon, J. H., Pomeroy, W. B., & Christenson, C. V. (1965). *Sex offenders.* New York: Harper & Row.

Gebhard, P. H., & Johnson, A. B. (1979). *The Kinsey data: Marginal tabulations of the 1938–1963 interviews conducted by the Institute for Sex Research.* Philadelphia: W. B. Saunders.

Geer, J. H., & Broussard, D. B. (1990). Scaling heterosexual behavior and arousal: Consistency and sex differences. *Journal of Personality and Social Psychology, 58,* 664–671.

Genuis, S. J., & Genuis, S. K. (1995). Adolescent sexual involvement: Time for primary prevention. *The Lancet, 345,* 240–245.

Gidycz, C. A., & Koss, M. P. (1991). The effects of acquaintance rape on the female victim. In A. Parrot & L. Bechhofer (Eds.), *Acquaintance rape: The hidden crime* (pp. 270–283). New York: John Wiley & Sons.

Gigy, L., & Kelly, J. B. (1992). Reasons for divorce: Perspectives of divorcing men and women. *Journal of Divorce and Remarriage, 18,* 169–187.

Gijs, L., & Gooren, L. (1996). Hormonal and psychopharmacological interventions in the treatment of paraphilias: An update. *Journal of Sex Research, 33,* 273–290.

Gilbert, M. M. A. (2000). The transgendered philosopher. *The International Journal of Transgender, 4*(3), NP. Retrieved July 22, 2002, from www.symposion.com/ijt/gilbert/gilbert.htm

Gillespie, B. L., & Eisler, R. M. (1992). Development of the feminine gender role stress scale. *Behavior Modification, 16,* 426–438.

Gingiss, P. L., & Basen-Engquist, K. (1994). HIV education practices and training needs of middle school and high school teachers. *Journal of School Health, 64,* 290–295.

Giordano, J., & Beckman, K. (1985). The aged within a family context: Relationship, roles, and events. In L. L'Abate (Ed.), *Handbook of family psychology and therapy* (Vol. 1) (pp. 284–320). Homewood, IL: Dorsey.

Giovannucci, E., Rimm, E. B., Liu, Y., Stampfer, M. J., & Willett, W. C. (2002). A prospective study of tomato products, lycopene, and prostate cancer risk. *Journal of the National Cancer Institute, 94*(5), 391–398.

Gitlin, M. J. (1994). Psychotropic medications and their effects on sexual function: Diagnosis, biology, and treatment approaches. *Journal of Clinical Psychiatry, 55,* 406–413.

Glasier, A. F., Anakwe, R., Everington, D., Martin, D. W., van der Spuy, Z., Cheng, L., Ho, P. C., & Anderson, R. A. (2000). Would women trust their partners to use a male pill? *Human Reproduction, 15,* 646–649.

Glass, S. P., & Wright, T. L. (1992). Justifications for extramarital relationships: The association between attitudes, behaviors, and gender. *Journal of Sex Research, 29,* 361–387.

Glatt, A. E., Zinner, S. H., & McCormack, W. M. (1990). The prevalence of dyspareunia. *Obstetrics and Gynecology, 75,* 433–436.

Glenn, N. D., & Weaver, C. N. (1988). The changing relationship of marital status to reported happiness. *Journal of Marriage and the Family, 50,* 317–324.

Godding, P. R., McAnulty, R. D., Wittrock, D. A., Britt, D. M., & Khansur, T. (1995). Predictors of depression among male cancer patients. *Journal of Nervous and Mental Disease, 183,* 95–98.

Gold, S. N., Elhai, J. D., Lucenko, B. A., & Swingle, J. M. (1998). Abuse characteristics among childhood sexual abuse survivors in therapy: A gender comparison. *Child Abuse & Neglect, 22,* 1005–1012.

Gold, S. R., & Gold, R. G. (1993). Sexual aversions: A hidden disorder. In W. O'Donohue & J. H. Geer (Eds.), *Handbook of sexual dysfunctions: Assessment and treatment* (pp. 83–102). Boston: Allyn & Bacon.

Goldberg, B. (2002). Miscarriage. Retrieved November 26, 2002, from www.obgyn.net/displayarticle.asp?page=/women/articles/coffee_talk/ct009

Golding, J. (1995). Reproduction and caffeine consumption—a literature review. *Early Human Development, 43*(1), 1–14.

Goldman, R., & Goldman, J. (1988). *Show me yours: Understanding children's sexuality.* Ringwood, Australia: Penguin Books.

Goldstein, I., Lue, T. F., Padma-Nathan, H., Rosen, R. C., Steers, W. D., & Wicker, P. A. (1998). Oral sildenafil in the treatment of erectile dysfunction: Sildenafil Study Group. *New England Journal of Medicine, 338,* 1397–1404.

Goldstein, J. R. (1999). The leveling of divorce in the United States. *Demography, 36,* 409–414.

Goleman, D. (1991, October 22). Sexual harassment: It's about power, not lust. *The New York Times,* pp. C1, C12.

Gomez, C. A. (1999). Sex in the new world: An empowerment model for HIV prevention in Latina immigrant women. *Health Education and Behavior, 26,* 200–213.

Gomez, C. A., & Marín, B. V. (1996). Gender, culture, and power: Barriers to HIV-prevention strategies for women. *Journal of Sex Research, 33,* 355–362.

Gonzalo, I.-T., Swerdloff, R. S., Nelson, A. L., Clevenger, B., Garcia, R., Berman, N., & Wang, C. (2002). Levonorgestrel implants (Norplant II) for male contraception clinical trials: Combination with transdermal and injectable testosterone. *The Journal of Clinical Endrocrinology and Metabolism, 87*(8), 3562–3572.

Good, G. E., & Mintz, L. M. (1990). Gender role conflict and depression in college men: Evidence for compounded risk. *Journal of Counseling and Development, 69,* 17–21.

Goodchilds, J. D., & Zellman, G. L. (1984). Sexual signaling and sexual aggression in adolescent relationships. In N. M. Malamuth & E. Donnerstein (Eds.), *Pornography and sexual aggression* (pp. 233–243). Orlando, FL: Academic.

Goode, E. (1990). *Deviant behavior* (3rd ed.). Englewood Cliffs, NJ: Prentice-Hall.

Goodman, A. (1993). Diagnosis and treatment of sexual addiction. *Journal of Sex and Marital Therapy, 19,* 225–251.

Goodman, G. S., & Helgeson, V. S. (1988). Children as witnesses: What do they remember? In L. E. A. Walker (Ed.), *Handbook on sexual abuse of children: Assessment and treatment issues* (pp. 109–136). New York: Springer.

Goodson, P. (2000). Sex on the Internet: College students' emotional arousal when viewing sexually explicit materials on-line. *Journal of Sex Education and Therapy, 25,* 252–261.

Goodson, P., & Edmundson, E. (1994). The problematic promotion of abstinence: An overview of Sex Respect. *Journal of School Health, 64,* 205–210.

Goodson, P., McCormick, D., & Evans, A. (2001). Searching for sexually explicit materials on the Internet: An exploratory study of college students' behavior and attitudes. *Archives of Sexual Behavior, 30,* 101–118.

Gordon, M. (1978). *The American family: Past, present, and future.* New York: Random House.

Gordon, T. (1994). *Single women: On the margins?* New York: New York University Press.

Gorman, C. (1998, May 4). The downside of Viagra. Retrieved November 5, 1998, from http://www.time.com/time/magazine/1998/dom/908504/box1.html

Gorman, C. (2000, September 18). Who needs a period? More and more women are taking control of their monthly cycles. What are the risks and benefits? *Time, 156*(12). Retrieved July 3, 2002, from http://kenmzoka.com/20001202Julie.htm

Gosselin, C., & Wilson, G. (1984). Fetishism, sadomasochism and related behaviours. In K. Howells (Ed.), *The psychology of sexual diversity* (pp. 89–110). Oxford, England: Basil Blackwell.

Gosselin, C. C. (1987). The sadomasochistic contract. In G. D. Wilson, *Variant sexuality: Research and theory* (pp. 229–257). Baltimore: Johns Hopkins University.

Gosselin, C. C., & Eysenck, S. B. G. (1980). The transvestite "double image": A preliminary report. *Personality and Individual Differences, 1,* 172–173.

Gossett, J. L., & Byrne, S. (2002). Click here: A content analysis of Internet rape sites. *Gender and Society, 16,* 698–709.

Gottman, J. (1994). *Why marriages succeed or fail.* New York: Simon & Schuster.

Gottman, J., Coan, J., Carrere, S., & Swanson, C. (1998). Predicting marital happiness and stability from newlywed interaction. *Journal of Marriage and the Family, 60,* 5–23.

Gottman, J., & Levenson, R. W. (1992). Marital processes predictive of later dissolution: Behavior, physiology, and health. *Journal of Personality and Social Psychology, 63,* 221–233.

Gottman, J., Markman, H., & Notarius, C. (1977). The topography of marital conflict: A sequential analysis of verbal and nonverbal behavior. *Journal of Marriage and the Family, 39,* 461–477.

Gottman, J., Notarius, C., Gonso, J., & Markman, H. (1976). *A couple's guide to communication.* Champaign, IL: Research Press.

Gottman, J. M., & Silver, N. (1999). *The seven principles for making marriage work.* New York: Three Rivers.

Gowaty, P. A. (2001). Women, psychology, and evolution. In R. K. Unger (Ed.), *Handbook of the psychology of women and gender* (pp. 53–65). New York: Wiley.

Graber, B. (1993). Medical aspects of sexual arousal disorders. In W. O'Donohue & J. H. Geer (Eds.), *Handbook of sexual dysfunctions: Assessment and treatment* (pp. 103–156). Boston: Allyn & Bacon.

Graham, B. S. (1998). Infection with HIV-1. *British Journal of Medicine, 317,* 1297–1301.

Gray, J. (1997). *Mars and Venus in the bedroom: A guide to lasting romance and passion.* New York: HarperCollins.

Gray, J. A., Dore, G. J., Li, U. M., Supawitkul, S., Effler, P., & Kaldor, J. M. (1997). HIV-1 infection among female commercial sex workers in rural Thailand. *AIDS, 11,* 89–94.

Gray, V. (October, 2000). Newsstand seductress. *Brandweek, 41*(41), 80–82.

Greeff, A. P., & Malherbe, H. L. (2001). Intimacy and marital satisfaction in spouses. *Journal of Sex and Marital Therapy, 27,* 247–257.

Greeley, A. (1991). *Faithful attraction: Discovering intimacy, love, and fidelity in American marriage.* New York: Doherty.

Greeley, A. (1992). *Sex after sixty: A report.* Unpublished manuscript, University of Chicago, National Opinion Research Center.

Greeley, A. (1994). [Review of the Janus Report on sexual behavior]. *Contemporary Sociology, 23,* 221–223.

Green, A., Wray, C., & Baluch, B. (1993). On choosing a baby's sex: What the future generation thinks. A preliminary survey. *Psychological Reports, 73,* 169–170.

Green, B. L., & Kenrick, D. T. (1994). The attractiveness of gender-typed traits of different relationship levels: Androgynous characteristics may be desirable after all. *Personality and Social Psychology Bulletin, 20,* 244–253.

Green, E. C., Zokwee, B., & Dupree, J. D. (1995). The experience of an AIDS prevention program focused on South African traditional healers. *Social Science and Medicine, 40,* 503–515.

Green, R. (1978). Sexual identity of 37 children raised by homosexual or transsexual parents. *American Journal of Psychiatry, 135,* 692–687.

Green, R. (1985). Gender identity in childhood and later sexual orientation: Follow-up of seventy-eight males. *The American Journal of Psychiatry, 142,* 339–341.

Green, R. (1987). *The "sissy boy syndrome" and the development of homosexuality.* New Haven, CT: Yale University Press.

Green, R. (1992). *Sexual science and the law.* Cambridge, MA: Harvard University Press.

Green, R., & Fleming, D. (1990). Transsexual surgery follow-up: Status in the 1990s. *Annual Review of Sex Research, 1,* 163–174.

Greenberg, B. S. (1994). Content trends in media sex. In D. Zillmann, J. Bryant, & A. Huston (Eds.), *Media, children, and the family: Social, scientific, psychodynamic, and clinical perspectives* (pp. 165–182). Hillsdale, NJ: Erlbaum.

Greenberg, B. S., & Busselle, R. W. (1996). Soap operas and sexual activity: A decade later. *Journal of Communication, 46,* 153–160.

Greenberg, B. S., Sherry, J. L., Busselle, R. W., Hnilo, L. R., & Smith, S. W. (1997). Daytime television talk shows: Guests, content and interactions. *Journal of Broadcasting and Electronic Media, 41,* 426–441.

Greenberg, B. S., & Woods, M. G. (1999). The soaps: Their sex, gratifications, and outcomes. *Journal of Sex Research, 36,* 250–257.

Greenberg, M. (1985). *The birth of a father.* New York: Continuum.

Greenblat, C. (1983). The salience of sexuality in the early years of marriage. *Journal of Marriage and the Family, 45,* 277–289.

Greenfeld, L. A. (1997). *Sex offenses and offenders: An analysis of data on rape and sexual assault.* U.S. Department of Justice, Bureau of Justice Statistics. Retrieved 1999, from www.ojp.usdoj.gov/bjs/oyb/ascii/soo.txt

Greenhouse, S. (2001). *Infertility 101: Age's effect on fertility.* Retrieved September 24, 2002, from http://www.childofmydreams.com/infertility/basics/agerelated.html

Greenlees, J. (1997, January 17). Students tempted to enter sex trade. *Times Higher Education Supplement, 1263,* 12.

Greenspoon, J., & Lamal, P. A. (1987). A behavioristic approach. In L. Diamant (Ed.), *Male and female homosexuality: Psychological approaches* (pp. 109–128). New York: Hemisphere Publishing Corporation.

Greenwald, H. (1970). *The call girl.* New York: Ballantine Books.

Greer, G. (1992). *The change: Women, aging, and the menopause.* New York: Knopf.

Gregson, S., Nyamukapa, C. A., Garnett, G. P., Mason, P. R., Zhuwau, R., Caraël, M., Chandiwana, S. K., & Anderson, R. M. (2002). Sexual mixing patterns and sex differentials in teenage exposure to HIV infection in rural Zimbabwe. *Lancet, 9321,* 1896–2004.

Grenier, G., & Byers, E. S. (1997). The relationships among ejaculatory control, ejaculatory latency, and attempts to prolong heterosexual intercourse. *Archives of Sexual Behavior, 26,* 27–47.

Gribble, J. N., Miller, H. G., Rogers, S. M., & Turner, C. F. (1999). Interview mode and measurement of sexual behaviors: Methodological issues. *Journal of Sex Research, 36,* 16–24.

Grieco, A. (1987, March). Cutting the risks for STIs. *Medical Aspects of Human Sexuality,* 70–84.

Griffiths, M. (2000). Excessive Internet use: Implications for sexual behavior. *CyberPsychology and Behavior, 3,* 537–552.

Griffiths, M. (2001). Sex on the Internet: Observations and implications for Internet sex addiction. *Journal of Sex Research, 38,* 333–342.

Grimes, D. A., & Raymond, E. G. (2002). Emergency contraception. *Annals of Internal Medicine, 137*(3), 180–189.

Grimley, D. M., Prochaska, G. E., & Prochaska, J. O. (1993). Condom use assertiveness and the stages of change with main and other partners. *Journal of Applied Biobehavioral Research, 1,* 152–173.

Grimm, M. (2001). Reality bites. *American Demographics, 23.*

Grimmell, D., & Stern, G. S. (1992). The relationship between gender role ideals and psychological well-being. *Sex Roles, 27,* 487–497.

Grob, C. S. (1985). Female exhibitionism. *Journal of Nervous and Mental Disease, 173,* 253–256.

Gross, A. M., Bennett, T., Sloan, L., Marx, B. P., & Juergens, J. (2001). The impact of alcohol and alcohol expectancies on male perception of female sexual arousal in a date rape analog. *Experimental and Clinical Psychopharmacology, 9*(4), 380–388.

Grosser, B. I., Monti-Bloch, L., Jennings-White, C., & Berliner, D. L. (2000). Behavioral and electrophysiological effects of androstadienone, a human pheromone. *Psychoneuroendocrinology, 25*(3), 289–299.

Grosskurth, H., Mosha, F., Todd, J., Mwijarubi, E., Klokke, A., Senkoro, K., Mayaud, P., Changalucha, J., Nicoll, A., Kangina, G., Newell, J., Mugeye, K., Mabey, D., & Hayes, R. (1995). Impact of improved treatment of sexually transmitted diseases in rural Tanzania—randomised controlled trial. *Lancet, 346,* 530–536.

Groth, A. N., & Birnbaum, H. J. (1978). Adult sexual orientation and attraction to underage persons. *Archives of Sexual Behavior, 7,* 175–181.

Groth, A. N., & Birnbaum, H. J. (1979). *Men who rape: The psychology of the offender.* New York: Plenum Press.

Groth, A. N., & Burgess, A. W. (1980). Male rape: Offenders and victims. *American Journal of Psychiatry, 137,* 806–810.

Groves, R. M. (1987). Research on survey data quality. *Public Opinion Quarterly, 51,* s156-s172.

Gruber, J. E., & Bjorn, L. (1982). Blue-collar blues: The sexual harassment of women autoworkers. *Work and Occupations, 9,* 271–298.

Grunbaum, J. A., Kann, L., Kinchen, S. A., Lowry, R., Kolbe, L., Williams, B., & Ross, J. G. (2002). Youth Risk Behavior Surveillance—United States, 2001. *Journal of School Health, 72,* 313–339.

Grunbaum, J. A., Kann, L., Kinchen, S. A., Williams, B., Ross, J. G., Lowry, R., & Kolbe, L. (2002). Youth Risk Behavior Surveillance—United States, 2001. *Morbidity and Mortality Weekly Report, 51*(SS-04), 1–64.

Gutierrez, E. (2000, February 29). French connections. *Advocate,* 42–46.

Guttmacher, S., Lieberman, L., Ward, D., Radosh, A., Rafferty, Y., & Freudenberg, N. (1995). Parents' attitudes and beliefs about HIV/AIDS prevention with condom availability in New York City public high schools. *Journal of School Health, 65,* 101–106.

Guttman, C. (1999, September). The darker side of the Net. *UNESCO Courier,* 43–46.

Guy, D. J. (1991). *Sex and danger in Buenos Aires: Prostitution, family, and nation in Argentina.* Lincoln: University of Nebraska.

Gynecology Forum. (1997). Ectopic pregnancy: Overview of the problem. Retrieved November 26, 2002, from www.medforum.nl/gynfo/leading4.htm

Hacker, H. M. (1981). Blabbermouths and clams: Sex differences in self-disclosure in same-sex and cross-sex friendship dyads. *Psychology of Women Quarterly, 5,* 385–401.

Haffner, D. W. (1997). The really Good News: What the Bible says about sex. *SIECUS Report, 26,* 3–8.

Hair, W. M., & Wu, F. C. (2000). Male contraception: Prospects for the new millennium. *Asian Journal of Andrology, 2,* 3–12.

Hall, G. C. N. (1995). Sexual offender recidivism revisited: A meta-analysis of recent treatment studies. *Journal of Consulting and Clinical Psychology, 63,* 802–809.

Hällström, T., & Samuelsson, S. (1990). Changes in women's sexual desire in middle life: The longitudinal study of women in Gothenburg. *Archives of Sexual Behavior, 19,* 259–268.

Halperin, D. M. (1990). *One hundred years of homosexuality and other essays on Greek love.* New York: Routledge.

Halpern, C. T., Joyner, K., Udry, J. R., & Suchindran, C. (2000). Smart teens don't have sex (or kiss much either). *Journal of Adolescent Health, 26*(3), 213–225.

Halpern, C. T., Udry, J. R., & Suchindran, C. (1997). Testosterone predicts initiation of coitus in adolescent females. *Psychosomatic Medicine, 59*(2), 161–171.

Halpern, C. T., Udry, J. R., & Suchindran, C. (1998). Monthly measures of salivary testosterone predict sexual activity in adolescent males. *Archives of Sexual Behavior, 27*(5), 445–466.

Halpern, J., & Sherman, M. A. (1979). *Afterplay: A key to intimacy.* New York: Pocket Books.

Hamer, D. H., Hu, S., Magnuson, V. L., Hu, N., & Pattatucci, A. M. L. (1993, July 16). A linkage between DNA markers on the X chromosome and male sexual orientation. *Science, 261,* 321–327.

Hamilton, C. E., Falshaw, L., & Browne, K. D. (2002). The link between recurrent maltreatment and offending behavior. *International Journal of Offender Therapy & Comparative Criminology, 46*(1), 75–94.

Hamilton-Boyles, S., Ness, R. B., Grisso, J. A., Markovic, N., Bromberger, J., & CiFelli, D. (2000). Life event stress and the association with spontaneous abortion in gravid women at an urban emergency department. *Health Psychology, 19*(6), 510–514.

Hanafin, H. (1996). Overview of surrogacy parenting: An overview of the psychological evaluation and counseling in surrogacy parenting. American Surrogacy Center. Retrieved January 23, 1997, from www.surrogacy.com/psychres/article/eval.html

Hanenberg, R., & Rojanapithayakorn, W. (1998). Changes in prostitution and the AIDS epidemic in Thailand. *AIDS Care, 10,* 69–80.

Hansen, K. A., & Gidycz, C. A. (1993). Evaluation of a sexual assault prevention program. *Journal of Consulting and Clinical Psychology, 61,* 1046–1052.

Harding, R. (1995). Sustained alterations in postnatal respiratory function following suboptimal intrauterine conditions. *Reproduction, Fertility, & Development, 7*(3), 431–441.

Hareven, T. K. (Ed.). (1977). *Family and kin in American urban communities, 1700–1930.* New York: Franklin Watts.

Harkness, C. (1992). *The infertility book: A comprehensive medical and emotional guide.* Berkeley: Celestial Arts Publishing.

Harlap, S., Kost, K., & Forrest, J. D. (1991). *Preventing pregnancy, protecting health: A new look at birth control choices in the United States.* New York: Alan Guttmacher Institute.

Harnish, R. J., Abbey, A., & DeBono, K. G. (1990). Toward an understanding of "the sex game": The effects of gender and self-monitoring on perceptions of sexuality and likeability in initial interactions. *Journal of Applied Social Psychology, 20*(16), 1333–1334.

Harris, A. C. (1996). African-American and Anglo-American gender identities: An empirical study. *Journal of Black Psychology, 22,* 182–194.

Harris, C. R. (2002). Sexual and romantic jealousy in heterosexual and homosexual adults. *Psychological Science, 13,* 7–12.

Harris, N. S., Thompson, S. J., Ball, R., Hussey, J., & Sy, F. (2002). Zidovudine and perinatal human immunodeficiency virus type 1 transmission: A population-based approach. *Pediatrics, 109*(4). Retrieved May 31, 2002, from http://www.pediatrics.org/cgi/content/full/109/4/e60

Harris, R., Whittemore, A. S., Itnyre, J., Collaborative Ovarian Cancer Group. (1992). Characteristics relating to ovarian cancer risk: Collaborative analysis of 12 U.S. case-control studies. III. Epithelial tumors of low malignant potential in white women. *American Journal of Epidemiology, 136,* 1204–1211.

Hart, B. L., & Leedy, M. G. (1985). Neurological bases of male sexual behavior: A comparative analysis. In N. Adler, R. W. Goy, & D. W. Pfaff (Eds.), *Handbook of behavioral neurobiology* (pp. 373–422). New York: Plenum.

Hass, A. (1979). *Teenage sexuality.* New York: Macmillan.

Hatano, Y. (1991). Changes in the sexual activities of Japanese youth. *Journal of Sex Education and Therapy, 17,* 1–14.

Hatcher, R. A., Trussell, J., Stewart, F., Stewart, G. K., Kowal, D., Guest, F., Cates, W., & Policar, M. S. (1994). *Contraceptive technology* (16th rev. ed.). New York: Irvington Publishers.

Hatfield, E., & Rapson, R. (1993). *Love, sex, and intimacy: Their psychology, biology, and history.* New York: HarperCollins.

Hatfield, E., & Rapson, R. (1996). *Love and sex: Cross-cultural perspectives.* New York: Allyn & Bacon.

Hatfield, E., Sprecher, S., Pillemer, J. T., Greenberger, D., & Wexler, P. (1988). Gender differences in what is desired in the sexual relationship. *Journal of Psychology and Human Sexuality, 1,* 39–52.

Haugaard, J. J., & Reppucci, N. D. (1988). *The sexual abuse of children: A comprehensive guide to current knowledge and intervention strategies.* San Francisco: Jossey-Bass.

Hauri, D., Knonagel, H., & Konstantinidis, K. (1989). Radical prostatectomy in cases of prostatic carcinoma: The problem concerning erectile impotence. *Urologia Internationalis, 44,* 272–278.

Hawaleshka, D. (2001, February 19). Peeping Toms go electronic. *Maclean's, 114*(8), 24–26.

Hawton, K. (1982). The behavioral treatment of sexual dysfunction. *British Journal of Psychiatry, 140,* 94–101.

Hawton, K. (1992). Sex therapy research: Has it withered on the vine? *Annual Review of Sex Research, 3,* 49–72.

Hawton, K., Catalan, J., & Fagg, J. (1992). Sex therapy for erectile dysfunction: Characteristics of couples, treatment outcome, and prognostic factors. *Archives of Sexual Behavior, 21,* 161–176.

Hawton, K., Catalan, J., Martin, P., & Fagg, J. (1986). Long-term outcome of sex therapy. *Behaviour Research and Therapy, 24,* 665–675.

Hawton, K., Gath, D., & Day, A. (1994). Sexual function in a community sample of middle-aged women with partners: Effects of age, marital, socioeconomic, psychiatric, gynecological, and menopausal factors. *Archives of Sexual Behavior, 23,* 375–395.

Hazan, C., & Shaver, P. (1987). Romantic love conceptualized as an attachment process. *Journal of Personality and Social Psychology, 52,* 511–524.

Healy, D. L., Trounson, A. O., & Andersen, A. N. (1994). Female infertility: Causes and treatment. *The Lancet, 343,* 1539–1544.

Heath, R. G. (1972). Pleasure and brain activity in man: Deep and surface electroencephalograms during orgasm. *The Journal of Nervous and Mental Disease, 154,* 3–18.

Heaton, J. A., & Wilson, N. L. (1995). *Tuning in trouble: Talk TV's destructive impact on mental health.* San Francisco: Jossey-Bass.

Hebditch, D., & Anning, N. (1988). *Porn gold: Inside the pornography business.* London: Faber & Faber.

Hecht, M. A., & LaFrance, M. (1998). License or obligation to smile: The effect of power and sex on amount and type of smiling. *Personality and Social Psychology Bulletin, 24,* 1332–1342.

Heilbrun, K., Nezu, C. M., Keeney, M., Chung, S., & Wasserman, A. L. (1998). Sexual offending: Linking assessment, intervention, and decision making. *Psychology, Public Policy, and Law, 4,* 138–174.

Heiman, J. R. (1977). A psychophysiological exploration of sexual arousal patterns in females and males. *Psychophysiology, 14*(3), 266–274.

Heiman, J. R. (2002a). Psychologic treatments for female sexual dysfunction: Are they effective and do we need them? *Archives of Sexual Behavior, 31,* 451–455.

Heiman, J. R. (2002b). Sexual dysfunction: Overview of prevalence, etiological factors, and treatments. *Journal of Sex Research, 39,* 73–79.

Heiman, J. R., & Grafton-Becker, V. (1989). Orgasmic disorders in women. In S. R. Leiblum & R. C. Rosen (Eds.), *Principles and practice of sex therapy: Update for the 1990s* (2nd ed.) (pp. 51–88). New York: Guilford.

Heiman, J. R., & LoPiccolo, J. (1988). *Becoming orgasmic: A sexual and personal growth program for women* (Rev. ed.). New York: Prentice-Hall.

Hendrick, S. S., & Hendrick, C. (1993). Lovers as friends. *Journal of Social and Personal Relationships, 10,* 459–466.

Hendrick, S. S., & Hendrick, C. (1995). Gender differences and similarities in sex and love. *Personal Relationships, 2,* 55–65.

Hendrick, S. S., Hendrick, C., & Adler, N. L. (1988). Romantic relationships: Love, satisfaction, and staying together. *Journal of Personality and Social Psychology, 54,* 980–988.

Henshaw, S. K. (1998). Unintended pregnancy in the United States. *Family Planning Perspectives, 30,* 24–29, 46.

Henshaw, S. K. (2001, March 5). *U.S. teenage pregnancy statistics with comparative statistics for women aged 20–24.* New York: Alan Guttmacher Institute.

Henshaw, S. K., Singh, S., & Haas, T. (1999). The incidence of abortion worldwide. *International Family Planning Perspective, 25,* S30–S38.

Herdt, G. H. (1981). *Guardians of the flutes: Idioms of masculinity.* New York: McGraw-Hill.

Herdt, G. H. (1984). *Ritualized homosexuality in Melanesia.* Berkeley: University of California Press.

Herdt, G. H. (1987). *The Sambia: Ritual and gender in New Guinea.* Fort Worth, TX: Harcourt Brace Jovanovich.

Herdt, G. H. (1992). Coming out as a rite of passage: A Chicago study. In G. Herdt (Ed.), *Gay culture in America.* Boston: Beacon Press.

Herdt, G. H., & Nanda, S. (Eds.). (1994). *Third sex, third gender: Beyond sexual dimorphism in culture and history.* New York: Zone Books.

Herek, G. M. (1984). Beyond "homophobia": A social psychological perspective on attitudes toward lesbians and gay men. *Journal of Homosexuality, 10*(½), 1–21.

Herek, G. M. (2002). Are some heterosexuals more likely to be prejudiced than others? Retrieved September 12, 2002, from http://psychology.ucdavis.edu/rainbow/html/prej_corr.html

Herek, G. M., Jobe, J. B., & Carney, R. M. (Eds.). (1996). *Out in force: Sexual orientation and the military.* Chicago: University of Chicago Press.

Herek, G. M., Kimmel, D. C., Amaro, H., & Melton, G. B. (1991). Avoiding heterosexist bias in psychological research. *American Psychologist, 46,* 957–963.

Herndon, J., Strauss, L. T., Whitehead, S., Parker, W. Y., Bartlett, L., & Zane, S. (2002). Abortion Surveillance—United States, 1998. *Morbidity and Mortality Weekly Report, 51*(No. SS-3), 1–32.

Hesse-Biber, S. J. (1996). *Am I thin enough yet? The cult of thinness and the commercialization of identity.* New York: Oxford University Press.

Heyl, B. S. (1979). *The madam as entrepreneur: Career management in a house of prostitution.* New York: Transaction Publishers.

Hibbard, D. R., & Buhrmester, D. (1998). The role of peers in the socialization of gender-related social interaction styles. *Sex Roles: A Journal of Research, 39*(3–4), 185–202.

Hickman, S. E., & Muehlenhard, C. L. (1997). College women's fears and precautionary behaviors relating to acquaintance rape and stranger rape. *Psychology of Women Quarterly, 21,* 527–547.

Hickman, S. E., & Muehlenhard, C. L. (1999). "By the semi-mystical appearance of a condom": How young women and men communicate sexual consent in heterosexual situations. *Journal of Sex Research, 36,* 258–272.

Hidalgo, M., Bahamondes, L., Perrotti, M., Diaz, J., Dantas-Montiero, C., & Petta, C. (2002). Bleeding patterns and clinical performance of the levonorgestrel-releasing intrauterine system (Mirena) up to two years. *Contraception, 65*(2), 129–132.

Hildesheim, A. (1997). Human papillomavirus variants: Implications for natural history studies and vaccine development efforts. *Journal of the National Cancer Institute, 89,* 752–753.

Hill, C. T., Rubin, Z., & Peplau, L. A. (1976). Break-ups before marriage. The end of 103 affairs. *Journal of Social Issues, 32,* 147–168.

Hill, M. S., & Fischer, A. R. (2001). Does entitlement mediate the link between masculinity and rape-related variables? *Journal of Counseling Psychology, 48*(1), 39–50.

Hilliard, R. B., & Spitzer, R. L. (2002). Change in criterion for paraphilias in DSM-IV-TR. *American Journal of Psychiatry, 159,* 1249.

Hinck, S. S., & Thomas, R. W. (1999). Rape myth acceptance in college students: How far have we come? *Sex Roles: A Journal of Research, 40,* 815–832.

Hines, T. M. (2001). The G-spot: A modern gynecologic myth. *American Journal of Obstetrics and Gynecology, 185*(2), 359–362.

Hirschfeld, R. M. A. (1999). Management of sexual side effects of antidepressant therapy. *Journal of Clinical Psychiatry, 60*(Suppl. 14), 27–30.

Hirschfeld, S. J. (2002). 21% of women surveyed in the latest national poll report having been sexually harassed at work. Retrieved January 15, 2003, from http://fm.employmentlawalliance.com/ela/FMPro?-DB=ela+articles.fp5&-Format=article.html&-RecID=40&-Find

Hite, S. (1976). *The Hite Report.* New York: Macmillan.

Hite, S. (1979). *The Hite Report on female sexuality.* New York: Knopf.

Hite, S. (1981). *The Hite Report on male sexuality.* New York: Knopf.

Hite, S. (1987). *Women and love, a cultural revolution in progress.* New York: Knopf.

Ho, G. Y. F., Bierman, R., Beardsley, L., Chang, C. J., & Burk, R. D. (1998). Natural history of cervicovaginal papillomavirus infection in young women. *New England Journal of Medicine, 338,* 423–428.

Hobson, B. M. (1987). *Uneasy virtue: The politics of prostitution and the American reform tradition.* New York: Basic Books.

Hock, E., Schirtzinger, M. B., Lutz, W. J., & Widaman, K. (1995). Maternal depressive symptomatology over the transition to parenthood: Assessing the influence of marital satisfaction and marital sex role traditionalism. *Journal of Family Psychology, 9,* 79–88.

Hodges, F. M., Svoboda, J. S., & Van Howe, R. S. (2002). Prophylactic interventions on children: Balancing human rights with public health. *Journal of Medical Ethics, 28,* 10–16.

Hodson, D. S., & Skeen, P. (1994). Sexuality and aging: The hammerlock of myths. *Journal of Applied Gerontology, 13,* 219–236.

Hoff, T., Greene, L., McIntosh, M., Rawlings, N., & D'Amico, J. (2000). *Sex education in America: A view from inside the nation's classroom.* Meno Park, CA: The Henry J. Kaiser Family Foundation.

Hogben, M., & Byrne, D. (1998). Using social learning theory to explain individual differences in human sexuality. *Journal of Sex Research, 35,* 58–72.

Høigärd, C., & Finstad, L. (1992). *Backstreets: Prostitution, money, and love* (K. Hanson, N. Sipe, & B. Wilson, Trans.). University Park: Pennsylvania State University Press. (Original work published 1986).

Hollender, M. H., Brown, C. W., & Roback, H. B. (1977). Genital exhibitionism in women. *American Journal of Psychiatry, 134,* 436–438.

Holt, R. R. (1989). *Freud reappraised.* New York: Guilford.

Holtzman, D., & Rubinson, R. (1995). Parent and peer communication effects on AIDS-related behavior among U.S. high school students. *Family Planning Perspectives, 27,* 235–240.

Hook, E., Sondheimer, S., & Zenilman, J. (1995). Today's treatment for STDs. *Patient Care, 29,* 40–56.

Hook, E. W., & Handsfield, H. H. (1990). Gonococcal infections in the adult. In K. Holmes, P. Mardh, P. Sparling, P. Wiesner, W. Cates, S. Lemon, & W. Stamm (Eds.), *Sexually transmitted diseases* (2nd ed.) (pp. 149–165). New York: McGraw-Hill.

Hooker, E. (1956). The adjustment of the male overt homosexual. In H. M. Ruittenbeck (Ed.), *The problem of homosexuality in modern America* (pp. 141–161). New York: Dutton.

Hoon, P. W., Bruce, K., & Kinchloe, B. (1982). Does the menstrual cycle play a role in sexual arousal? *Psychophysiology, 19,* 21–26.

Hopkins, J. (2000). Reason and orgasm in Tibetan Buddhism. In J. Runzo & N. M. Martin (Eds.), *Love, sex, and gender in the world religions* (pp. 271–285). Oxford, England: Oneworld Press.

Hopman, E. H., Rozendaal, L., Voorhorst, F. J., Walboomers, J. M., Kenemans, P., & Helmerhorst, T. J. (2000). High risk human papillomavirus in women with normal cervical cytology prior to the development of abnormal cytology and colposcopy. *British Journal of Obstetrics and Gynecology, 107*(5), 600–604.

Hopwood, N.J., Kelch, R. P., Hale, P. M., Mendes, T. M., Foster, C. M., & Beitins, I. Z. (1990). The onset of human puberty: Biological and environmental factors. In J. Bancroft & J. M. Reinisch (Eds.), *Adolescence and puberty* (pp. 29–49). New York: Oxford University.

Horn-Ross, P. L., Whittemore, A. S., Harris, R., Itnyre, J., Collaborative Ovarian Cancer Group. (1992). Characteristics relating to ovarian cancer risk: Collaborative analysis of 12 U.S. case-control studies. Neo epithelial cancers among adults. *Epidemiology, 3,* 490–495.

Hotvedt, M. E. (1990). Emerging and submerging adolescent sexuality: Culture and sexual orientation. In J. Bancroft & J. M. Reinisch (Eds.), *Adolescence and puberty* (pp. 157–172). New York: Oxford University.

How predating works. (2002). Retrieved November 16, 2002, from www.pre-dating.com/works.html

How reliable are condoms? (1995, May). *Consumer Reports,* pp. 320–325.

Howes, R. J. (1998). Plethysmographic assessment of incarcerated nonsexual offenders: A comparison with rapists. *Sexual Abuse: Journal of Research & Treatment, 10,* 183–194.

Hoyenga, K. B., & Hoyenga, K. T. (1993). *Gender-related differences: Origins and outcomes.* Boston: Allyn and Bacon.

Hsu, B., Kling, A., Kessler, C., Knapke, K., Diefenbach, P., & Elias, J. E. (1994). Gender differences in sexual fantasy and behavior in a college population: A ten-year replication. *Journal of Sex and Marital Therapy, 20*(2), 103–118.

Hucker, S. J., & Bain, J. (1990). Androgenic hormones and sexual assault. In H. E. Barbaree, W. L. Marshall, & S. M. Hudson (Eds.), *The juvenile sex offender* (pp. 193–202). New York: Guilford.

Huebner, D. M., Davis, M. C., Nemeroff, C. J., & Aiken, L. S. (2002). The impact of internalized homophobia on HIV prevention interventions (1). *American Journal of Community Psychology, 30*(3), 327–348.

Hughes, J. O., & Sandler, B. R. (1987). *Friends raping friends: Could it happen to you?* Washington, DC: Association of American Colleges, Project on the Status and Education of Women.

Human Rights Campaign. (2002). Quick facts: Same-sex marriage and civil unions. Retrieved September 12, 2002, from http://www.hrc.org/issues/marriage/quickfacts.asp

Humphreys, L. (1970). *Tearoom trade: Impersonal sex in public places.* Chicago: Aldine de Gruyter.

Hunt, M. (1974). *Sexual behavior in the 1970s.* Chicago: Playboy Press.

Hunter, J. A., & Mathews, R. (1997). Sexual deviance in females. In D. R. Laws & W. O'Donohue (Eds.), *Sexual deviance: Theory, assessment, and treatment* (pp. 465–480). New York: Guilford.

Hurtig, A. L., & Rosenthal, I. M. (1987). Psychological functioning in early treated cases of female pseudohermaphroditism caused by virilizing congenital adrenal hyperplasia. *Archives of Sexual Behavior, 16,* 209–222.

Huston, A. C., & Alvarez, M. M. (1990). The socialization context of gender role development in early adolescence. In R. Montemayor, G. R. Adams, & T. P. Gullotta, (Eds.), *From childhood to adolescence: A transition period.* London: Sage.

Hyde, J. S. (1996). *Half the human experience: The psychology of women* (5th ed.). Lexington, MA: D.C. Heath and Co.

Hyde, J. S., DeLamater, J. D., Plant, E. A., & Byrd, J. M. (1996). Sexuality during pregnancy and the year post partum. *Journal of Sex Research, 33,* 143–151.

Hyde, J. S., Klein, M. H., Essex, M. J., & Clark, R. (1995). Maternity leave and women's mental health. *Psychology of Women Quarterly, 19,* 257–285.

Hynie, M., Lydon, J. E., Cote, S., & Weiner, S. (1998). Relational sexual scripts and women's condom use: The importance of internalized norms. *Journal of Sex Research, 35,* 370–380.

Icard, L. (1986). Black gay men and conflicting social identities: Sexual orientation versus racial identity. *Journal of Social Work & Human Sexuality: Social Work Practice in Sexual Problems, 4(1/2),* 83–93.

Infectious Diseases Society of America. (2002). IDSA news release: HIV/AIDS: Global rates of infection fact sheet. Retrieved January 9, 2003, from www.idsociety.org/newsroom/nr_hivfacts_11-17-00.htm

Innala, S. M., & Ernulf, K. E. (1989). Asphyxiophilia in Scandinavia. *Archives of Sexual Behavior, 18,* 181–189.

International Herpes Management Forum (2002a). Genital herpes: The facts. Retrieved May 15, 2002, from http://www.ihmf.org/general/resources03.asp

International Herpes Management Forum (2002b). Herpes simplex and pregnancy. Retrieved May 20, 2002, from http://www.ihmf.org/general/resources04.asp

International Perinatal HIV Group. (2001). Duration of ruptured membranes and vertical transmission of HIV-1: A meta-analysis from 15 prospective cohort studies. *AIDS, 15*(3), 357–368.

Intons-Peterson, M. J., & Roskos-Ewoldsen, B. (1989). Mitigating the effects of violent pornography. In S. Gubar & J. Hoff (Eds.), *For adults users only: The dilemma of violent pornography* (pp. 218–239). Bloomington: Indiana University Press.

Iversen, T., Tretli, S., Johansen, A., & Holte, T. (1997). Squamous cell carcinoma of the penis and of the cervix, vulva and vagina in spouses: Is there any relationship? An epidemiological study from Norway, 1960–1992. *British Journal of Cancer, 76,* 658–660.

Jack or Jill? (1993). *The Lancet, 341,* 727–728.

Jacklin, C. N., & Baker, L. A. (1993). Early gender development. In S. Oskcamp & M. Costanzo (Eds.) (pp. 41–57), *Gender issues in contemporary society* (pp. 41–57). Newbury Park, CA: Sage Publications.

Jackson, J. L., Calhoun, K. S., Amick, A. A., Maddever, H. M., & Habif, V. L. (1990). Young adult women who report childhood intrafamilial sexual abuse: Subsequent adjustment. *Archives of Sexual Behavior, 19,* 211–221.

Jacob, S., Hayreh, D. J., & McClintock, M. K. (2001). Context-dependent effects of steroid chemosignals on human physiology and mood. *Physiological Behavior, 74*(1–2), 15–27.

Jacob, S., Kinnunen, L. H., Metz, J., Cooper, M., & McClintock, M. K. (2001). Sustained human chemosignal unconsciously alters brain function. *Neuroreport, 12*(11), 2391–2394.

Jacob, S., & McClintock, M. K. (2000). Psychological state and mood effects of steroidal chemosignals in women and men. *Hormones & Behavior, 37*(1), 57–78.

Jacobs, C. D., & Wolf, E. M. (1995). School sexuality education and adolescent risk-taking behavior. *Journal of School Health, 65,* 91–95.

Jacobson, J., Jacobson, S., & Sokol, R. (1996). Increased vulnerability to alcohol-related birth defects in the offspring of mothers over 30. *Alcohol Clinical and Experimental Research, 20*(2), 359–363.

Jaget, C. (1980). *Prostitutes—Our life.* Bristol, England: Falling Wall Press.

Jakobovits, L. A. (1965). Evaluational reactions to erotic literature. *Psychological Reports, 16,* 985–994.

Jankowiak, W. R., & Fischer, E. F. (1992). A cross-cultural perspective on romantic love. *Ethology, 31,* 149–155.

Janssen, E., & Everaerd, E. (1993). Determinants of male sexual arousal. *Annual Review of Sex Research, 4,* 211–245.

Janus, S. S., & Janus, C. L. (1993). *The Janus Report on sexual behavior.* New York: Wiley.

Jehl, D. (1999, June 20). For shame: A special report. Arab honor's price: A woman's blood. *New York Times.*

Jelovsek, F. R. (2000). Lifestyle choices and female infertility. Retrieved September 24, 2002, from www.wdxcyber.com/ninfer06.htm

Jenks, R. J. (1998). Swinging: A review of the literature. *Archives of Sexual Behavior, 27,* 507–521.

Joffe, M., Chapple, J., Paterson, C., & Beard, R. W. (1994). What is the optimal caesarean section rate? An outcome-based study of existing variation. *Journal of Epidemiology and Community Health,* 48, 406–411.

Johnson, A. M., Mercer, C. H., Erens, B., Copas, A. J., McManus, S., Wellings, K., Fenton K. A., Korovessis, C., Macdowall, W., Nanchahal, K., Purdon, S., & Field, J. (2001). Sexual behaviour in Britain: Partnerships, practices, and HIV risk behaviours. *Lancet, 358,* 1835–1843.

Johnson, S. (1991). *Forbidden.* New York: Bantam Books.

Jones, J. T., & Cunningham, J. D. (1996). Attachment styles and other predictors of relationship satisfaction in dating couples. *Personal Relationships, 3,* 387–399.

Jones, R. E. (1991). *Human reproductive biology.* San Diego: Harcourt Brace Jovanovich.

Jordan, B., & Davis-Floyd, R. (1993). *Birth in four cultures* (4th ed.). Prospect Heights, IL: Waveland Press, Inc.

Jordan, T. R., Price, J. H., & Fitzgerald, S. (2000). Rural parents' communication with their teen-agers about sexual issues. *Journal of School Health, 70,* 338–345.

Josefson, D. (2000). FDA approves device for female sexual dysfunction. *BMJ: British Medical Journal, 320,* 1427.

Jung, P. B., Hunt, M. E., & Balakrishnan, R. (2001). *Good sex: Feminist perspectives from the world's religions.* New Brunswick, NJ: Rutgers University.

Juni, S., & Grimm, D. W. (1993). Sex-role similarities between adults and their parents. *Contemporary Family Therapy, 15*(3), 247–251.

Kahn, A., Mathie, V., & Torgler, C. (1994). Rape scripts and rape acknowledgement. *Psychology of Women Quarterly, 18,* 53–66.

Kaiser Family Foundation. (2000). *Sex education in America: A series of national surveys of students, parents, teachers, and principals.* Menlo Park: CA: Author.

Kaiser Family Foundation. (2002a). Kaisernetwork.org: Daily health policy report. Retrieved January 9, 2003, from www.kaisernetwork.org/daily_reports//rep_index.cfm?hint=3&DR_ID=10180

Kaiser Family Foundation. (2002b). *Sex education in America: A view from inside the nation's classrooms.* Menlo Park, CA: Author.

Kaiser Family Foundation/ABC Television. (1998, September). *Sex in the 90s: 1998 National survey of Americans on sex and sexual health.* Menlo Park, CA: Kaiser Family Foundation.

Kaiser Family Foundation & American Social Health Association. (1998). *STDs in America: How many cases and at what cost?* Menlo Park, CA: Kaiser Family Foundation.

Kaiser Family Foundation & *Glamour* Magazine. (1998). *Survey of men and women on sexually transmitted diseases.* Menlo Park, CA: Kaiser Family Foundation.

Kalichman, S. C. (1998). *Preventing AIDS: A sourcebook for behavioral interventions.* Mahwah, NJ: Erlbaum.

Kalichman, S. C., & Belcher, L. (1997). AIDS information needs: Conceptual and content analyses of questions asked of AIDS information hotlines. *Health Education Research, 12,* 279–288.

Kalichman, S. C., Hunter, T. L., & Kelly, J. A. (1992). Perceptions of AIDS susceptibility among minority and nonminority women at risk for HIV infection. *Journal of Consulting and Clinical Psychology, 60,* 725–732.

Kalichman, S. C., & Rompa, D. (1995). Sexually coerced and noncoerced gay and bisexual men: Factors relevant to risk for human immunodeficiency virus (HIV) infection. *Journal of Sex Research, 32,* 45–51.

Kaplan, A. G., & Sedney, M. A. (1980). *Psychology and sex roles: An androgynous perspective.* Boston: Little, Brown.

Kaplan, H. (1974). *The new sex therapy: Active treatment of sexual dysfunctions.* New York: Brunner/Mazel.

Kaplan, H. S. (1977). Hypoactive sexual desire. *Journal of Sex and Marital Therapy, 3,* 3–9.

Kaplan, H. S. (1979a). *Disorders of desire.* New York: Brunner/Mazel.

Kaplan, H. S. (1979b). *Making sense of sex.* New York: Simon & Schuster.

Kaplan, H. S. (1987). *Sexual aversion, sexual phobias, and panic disorder.* New York: Brunner/Mazel.

Kaplan, H. S. (1995). Sex aversion disorder: The case of the phobic virgin, or, an abused child grows up. In R. C. Rosen & S. R. Leiblum (Eds.), *Case studies in sex therapy* (pp. 65–80). New York: Guilford.

Kaplan, S. A., Reis, R. B., Kohn, I. J., Ikeguchi, E. F., Laor, E., Te, A. E., & Martins, A. C. (1999). Safety and efficacy of sildenafil in postmenopausal women with sexual dysfunction. *Urology, 53,* 481–486.

Karim, S. S. A., & Ramjee, G. (1998). Anal sex and HIV transmission in women. *American Journal of Public Health, 88,* 1265–1267.

Karofsky, P. S., Zeng, L., & Kosorok, M. R. (2001). Relationship between adolescent-parental communication and initiation of first intercourse by adolescents. *Journal of Adolescent Health, 28*(1), 41–45.

Kassam, Z. (2000). Politicizing gender and religion: Love for women, love for Islam. In J. Runzo & N. M. Martin (Eds.), *Love, sex, and gender in the world religions* (pp. 223–237). Oxford, England: Oneworld Press.

Kaufman, A., Divasto, P., Jackson, R., Voorhees, D., & Christy, J. (1980). Male rape victims: Noninstitutionalized assault. *American Journal of Psychiatry, 137,* 221–223.

Kauth, M. R., & Landis, D. (1994, July). The U.S. military's "don't ask, don't tell" personnel policy: Fear of the open homosexual. In D. Landis (Chair), *Prejudice and discrimination in large organizations.* Symposium conducted at the Second International Congress on Prejudice, Discrimination and Conflict, Jerusalem, Israel.

Keane, M. (1998). Television and moral development in China. *Asian Studies Review, 22,* 475–504.

Kelaher, M., Ross, M., Rohrsheim, R., Drury, M., & Clarkson, A. (1994). Dominant situational determinants of sexual risk behavior in gay men. *AIDS, 8,* 101–105.

Kelley, M. L., & Parsons, B. (2000). Sexual harassment in the 1990s. *Journal of Higher Education, 71,* 548–568.

Kellogg, J. H. (1888). *Plain facts for old and young: Natural history and hygiene of organic life.* Burlington, IA: I. F. Segner.

Kelly, J. A., Amirkhanian, Y. A., McAuliffe, T. L., Granskaya, J. V., Borodkina, O. I., Dyatlov, R. V., Kukharsky, A., & Kozlov, A. P. (2002). HIV risk characteristics and prevention needs in a community sample of bisexual men in St. Petersburg, Russia. *AIDS Care, 14,* 63–76.

Kelly, M., Strassberg, D., & Kircher, J. (1990). Attitudinal and experiential correlates of anorgasmia. *Archives of Sexual Behavior, 19,* 165–177.

Kempe, R. S., & Kempe, C. H. (1984). *The common secret: Sexual abuse of children and adolescents.* New York: W. H. Freeman and Co.

Kempner, M. E. (1998). Special report:1997–1998 sexuality education controversies in the United States. *SIECUS Report, 26,* 16–26.

Kendall-Tackett, K. A., Williams, L., & Finkelhor, D. (1993). Impact of sexual abuse on children: A review and synthesis of recent empirical studies. *Psychological Bulletin, 113,* 164–180.

Kendrick, K. M., & Dixson, A. G. (1986). Anteromedial hypothalamic lesions block proceptivity but not receptivity in the female common marmoset (Callithrix jacchus). *Brain Research, 375,* 221–229.

Kenney, J., Reinholtz, C., & Angelini, P. J. (1997). Ethnic differences in childhood and adolescent sexual abuse and teenage pregnancy. *Journal of Adolescent Health, 21,* 3–10.

Kenrick, D. T., & Trost, M. R. (1993). The evolutionary perspective. In A. E. Beall & R. J. Sternberg (Eds.), *The psychology of gender* (pp. 148–172). New York: The Guilford Press.

Kenyatta, J. (1953). *Facing Mount Kenya: The tribal life of the Gikuu.* London: Secher & Warburg.

Kenyon-Jump, R. (1992). *Detection of sexual cues: An assessment of nonaggressive and sexually coercive males.* Unpublished doctoral dissertation.

Kerlinger, F. N. (1973). *Foundations of behavioral research* (2nd ed.). New York: Holt, Rinehart, & Winston.

Kersten, K. (1996). Commentary: Girls in school. "All Things Considered," National Public Radio. Retrieved June 8, 1999, from www.amexp.org/publications/npr/npr121096.htm

Key, K., Denoon, D., & Boyles, S. (1996, December 16). Positive genital warts vaccine Phase IIA trial results reported. *AIDS Weekly Plus,* 15–16.

Kidd, S. A., & Kral, M. J. (2002). Suicide and prostitution among street youth: A qualitative analysis. *Adolescence, 37,* 411–431.

Kiecolt-Glaser, J. K., McGuire, L., Robles, T. F., & Glaser, R. (2002). Psychoneuroimmunology and psychosomatic medicine: Back to the future. *Psychosomatic Medicine, 64,* 15–28.

Kikiros, C. S., Beasley, S. W., & Woodward, A. A. (1993). The response of phimosis to local steroid application. *Pediatric Surgery International, 8,* 329.

Killing girls and aborting female fetuses. (1993, May 1). *New Scientist,* p. 13.

Kilpatrick, D. G. (2000). *Rape and sexual assault.* Retrieved October 21, 2002, from www.vawprevention.org/research/sa.shtml

Kilpatrick, D. G., Best, C. L., Saunders, B. E., & Veronen, L. J. (1988). Rape in marriage and in dating relationships: How bad is it for mental health? *Annals of the New York Academy of Sciences, 528,* 335–344.

Kim, J. H., Skates, S. J., Uede, T., Wong, K., Schorge, J. O., Feltmate, C. M., Berkowitz, R. S., Cramer, D. W., & Mok, S. C. (2002). Osteopontin as a potential diagnostic biomarker for ovarian cancer. *Journal of the American Medical Association, 287*(13), 1671–1679.

Kimmel, M. S. (2000). *The gendered society.* New York: Oxford University Press.

Kimmel, M. S., & Linders, A. (1996). Does censorship make a difference? An aggregate empirical analysis of pornography and rape. *Journal of Psychology & Human Sexuality, 8,* 1–20.

King, M., & Woollett, E. (1997). Sexually assaulted males: 115 men consulting a counseling service. *Archives of Sexual Behavior, 26,* 579–588.

Kingsberg, S. A. (2002). The impact of aging on sexual function in women and their partners. *Archives of Sexual Behavior, 31,* 431–437.

Kinsey, A. C., Pomeroy, W. B., & Martin, C. E. (1948). *Sexual behavior in the human male.* Philadelphia: W. B. Saunders Co.

Kinsey, A. C., Pomeroy, W. B., Martin, C. E., & Gebhard, P. H. (1953). *Sexual behavior in the human female.* Philadelphia: W. B. Saunders.

Kinsman, S. B., Romer, D., Furstenberg, F. F., & Schwarz, D. F. (1998). Early sexual initiation: The role of peer norms. *Pediatrics, 102,* 1185–1193.

Kirby, D. (1999). Reflections on two decades of research on teen sexual behavior and pregnancy. *Journal of School Health, 69,* 89–94.

Kirby, D. (2001). *Emerging answers: Research findings on programs to reduce teen pregnancy.* Washington, DC: National Campaign to Prevent Teen Pregnancy.

Kirby, D., Brener, N. D., Brown, N. L., Peterfreund, N., Hillard, P., & Harrist, R. (1999). The Seattle school condom availability program: Subsequent changes in sexual behavior and condom use. *American Journal of Public Health, 89,* 182–188.

Kirby, D., Coyle, K., & Gould, J. B. (2001). Manifestations of poverty and birthrates among young teenagers in California zip code areas. *Family Planning Perspectives, 33*(2), 63–69.

Kirkwood, M. K., & Cecil, D. K. (2001). Marital rape: A student assessment of rape laws and the marital exemption. *Violence Against Women, 7*(11), 1234–1253.

Klein, N. A., Goodson, P., Serrins, D. S., Edmundson, E., & Evans, A. (1994). Evaluation of sex education curricula: Measuring up to the SIECUS guidelines. *Journal of School Health, 64,* 328–333.

Kleinpeter, C. H., & Hohman, M. M. (2000). Surrogate motherhood: Personality traits and satisfaction with service providers. *Psychological Reports, 87*(3 Pt. 1), 957–970.

Klonoff-Cohen, H., Cross, J., & Pieper, C. (1996). Job stress and preeclampsia. *Epidemiology, 7,* 245–249.

Klüver, H., & Bucy, P. C. (1939). Preliminary analysis of functions of the temporal lobes in monkeys. *Archives of Neurology and Psychiatry, 42,* 979.

Knight, R. A., & Prentky, R. A. (1990). Classifying sexual offenders: The development and corroboration of taxonomic models. In W. L. Marshall, D. R. Laws, & H. E. Barbaree (Eds.), *Handbook of sexual assault: Issues, theories, and treatment of the offender* (pp. 23–52). New York: Plenum.

Kobayashi, J., Sales, B. D., Becker, J. V., Figueredo, A. J., & Kaplan, M. S. (1995). Perceived parental deviance, parent–child bonding, child abuse, and sexual aggression. *Sexual Abuse: A Journal of Research and Treatment, 7,* 25–44.

Kodera, K. (1996). Gender and space in Japanese society: An illusion of "motherhood." *International Review of Sociology, 6,* 465–478.

Koelle, D. M., & Wald, A. (2000). Herpes simplex virus: The importance of asymptomatic shedding. *Journal of Antimicrobial Chemotherapy, 45,* 1–8.

Kolodny, R. C. (1981). Evaluating sex therapy: Process and outcome of the Masters & Johnson Institute. *Journal of Sex Research, 17,* 301–318.

Kon, I. S. (1987). A sociocultural approach. In J. H. Geer & W. T. O'Donohue (Eds.), *Theories of human sexuality* (pp. 257–286). New York: Plenum.

Kon, I. S. (1999). Sexuality and politics in Russia, 1700–2000. In F. X. Eder, L. Hall, & G. Hekma (Eds.), *Sexual cultures in Europe: National histories* (pp. 197–218). New York: Manchester University Press.

Koss, M. P. (1988). Hidden rape: Incidence, prevalence, and descriptive characteristics of sexual aggression and victimization in a national sample of college students. In A. W. Burgess (Ed.), *Rape and sexual assault* (Vol. II) (pp. 1–25). New York: Garland.

Koss, M. P., & Dinero, T. E. (1989). Discriminant analysis of risk factors for sexual victimization among a national sample of college women. *Journal of Consulting and Clinical Psychology, 57,* 242–250.

Koss, M. P., & Gaines, J. A. (1993). The prediction of sexual aggression by alcohol use, athletic participation, and fraternity affiliation. *Journal of Interpersonal Violence, 8,* 94–108.

Koss, M. P., Heise, L., & Russo, N. F. (1994). The global health burden of rape. *Psychology of Women Quarterly, 18,* 509–537.

Koss, M. P., & Heslet, L. (1992). Somatic consequences of violence against women. *Archives of Family Medicine, 1,* 53–59.

Koss, M. P., Woodruff, W. J., & Koss, P. G. (1991). Criminal victimization among primary care medical patients: Prevalence, incidence, and physician usage. *Behavioral Sciences and the Law, 9,* 85–96.

Koster, A., & Garde, K. (1993). Sexual desire and menopausal development: A prospective study of Danish women born in 1936. *Maturitas, 16,* 49–60.

Kothari, P., & Patel, R. (1989). Sexual grounding: The missing link of the sexual response cycle. *Sexual and Marital Therapy, 4,* 65–74.

Kovacs, A., & Osvath, P. (1998). Koro (genital retraction syndrome): A symptom or a disease? *Psychiatria Danubina, 10,* 45–51.

Kraaykamp, G. (2001). Trends and countertrends in sexual permissiveness: Three decades of attitude change in the Netherlands. *Journal of Marriage and the Family, 64,* 225–240.

Kraemer, G. W., Ebert, M. H., Lake, C. R., & McKinney, W. T. (1984). Hypersensitivity to d-amphetamine several years after early social deprivation in rhesus monkeys. *Psychopharmacology, 82,* 266–271.

Krafft-Ebing, R. von. (1936). *Psychopathia sexualis.* (F. J. Rebman, Trans.). New York: Physicians & Surgeons Book Co. (Original work published 1886)

Krane, R. J., Goldstein, I., & de Tejada, I. S. (1989). Impotence. *New England Journal of Medicine, 321,* 1648–1659.

Kresin, D. (1993). Medical aspects of inhibited sexual desire disorder. In W. O'Donohue & J. H. Geer (Eds.), *Handbook of sexual dysfunctions: Assessment and treatment* (pp. 15–51). Boston: Allyn & Bacon.

Kreuter, M., Sullivan, M., & Siosteen, A. (1996). Sexual adjustment and quality of relationship in spinal paraplegia: A controlled study. *Archives of Physical and Medical Rehabilitation, 77,* 541–548.

Kristol, I. (1999). Liberal censorship and the common culture. *Society, 36,* 5–11.

Ku, L., Sonenstein, F. L., Lindberg, L. D., Bradner, C. H., Boggess, S., & Pleck, J. H. (1998). Understanding changes in sexual activity among young metropolitan men: 1979–1995. *Family Planning Perspectives, 30,* 256–263.

Ku, L. C., Sonenstein, F. L., & Pleck, J. H. (1992). The association of AIDS education and sex education with sexual behavior and condom use among teenage men. *Family Planning Perspectives, 24,* 100–106.

Ku, L. C., Sonenstein, F. L., & Pleck, J. H. (1994). The dynamics of young men's condom use during and across relationships. *Family Planning Perspectives, 26,* 246–251.

Kuhn, T. S. (1970). *The structure of scientific revolutions* (2nd ed.). Chicago: University of Chicago.

Kuhnle, U., & Krahl, W. (2002). The impact of culture on sex assignment and gender development in intersex patients. *Perspectives in Biological Medicine, 45*(1), 85–103.

Kuiper, B., & Cohen-Kettenis, P. (1988). Sex reassignment surgery: A study of 141 Dutch transsexuals. *Archives of Sexual Behavior, 17,* 439–457.

Kuliev, A., Jackson, L., Froster, U., Brambati, B., Simpson, J. L., & Verlinsky, Y. (1996). Chorionic villus sampling safety. Report of the World Health Organization/EURO meeting in association with the seventh international Conference on Early Prenatal Diagnosis of Genetic Diseases, Tel-Aviv, Israel, May 21, 1994. *American Journal of Obstetrics and Gynecology, 174,* 807–811.

Kumar, R. (1994). Postnatal mental illness: A transcultural perspective. *Social Psychiatry and Psychiatric Epidemiology, 29,* 250–264.

Kunkel, D., Cope, K. M., & Biely, E. (1999). Sexual messages on television: Comparing findings from three studies. *Journal of Sex Research, 36,* 230–236.

Kunkel, D., Cope-Farrar, K., Biely, E., Farinola, W. J. M., & Donnerstein, E. (2001). *Sex on TV (2): A biennial report to the Kaiser Family Foundation February 2001.* Menlo Park, CA: Henry J. Kaiser Family Foundation.

Kunz, J. (2002). Teen pregnancy and negative life outcomes: What is the relationship? *Social Work Today, 2*(15), 20.

Kurdek, L. A. (1991). The dissolution of gay and lesbian couples. *Journal of Social and Personal Relationships, 8,* 265–278.

Kurdek, L. A. (1995). Lesbian and gay couples. In A. R. D'Augelli & C. J. Patterson (Eds.), *Lesbian, gay, and bisexual identities over the lifespan: Psychological perspectives* (pp. 243–261). New York: Oxford.

Kurdek, L. A. (1995). Predicting change in marital satisfaction from husbands' and wives' conflict resolution styles. *Journal of Marriage and the Family, 57,* 153–164.

Kurdek, L. A., & Schmitt, J. P. (1987). Partner homogamy in married, heterosexual cohabiting, gay, and lesbian couples. *Journal of Sex Research, 23,* 212–232.

Kutchinski, B. (1991). Pornography and rape: Theory and practice? Evidence from crime data in four countries where pornography is easily available. *International Journal of Law and Psychiatry, 14,* 147–164.

Kyes, K. B. (1995). Using fear to encourage safer sex: An application of protection motivation theory. *Journal of Psychology and Human Sexuality, 7,* 21–37.

Laan, E., Everaerd, W., van Bellen, G., & Hanewald, G. (1994). Women's sexual and emotional responses to male- and female-produced erotica. *Archives of Sexual Behavior, 23,* 153–169.

Ladas, A. K., Whipple, B., & Perry, J. D. (1982). *The G spot and other recent discoveries about human sexuality.* New York: Holt, Rinehart and Winston.

Lafayette, L. (1995). *Why don't you have kids?* New York: Kensington Publishing.

Lam, T. H., Shi, H. J., Ho, L. M., Stewart, S. M., & Fan, S. (2002). Timing of pubertal maturation and heterosexual behavior among Hong Cong Chinese adolescents. *Archives of Sexual Behavior, 31*(4), 359–366.

Lambert, B. (1988, September 20). AIDS among prostitutes not as prevalent as believed, studies show. *The New York Times,* p. D9.

Landry, D. J., Kaeser, L., & Richards, C. L. (1999). Abstinence promotion and the provision of information about contraception in public school district sexuality education policies. *Family Planning Perspectives, 31*(6), 280–286.

Lang, R. A., Langevin, R., Checkley, K. L., & Pugh, G. (1987). Genital exhibitionism: Courtship disorder or narcissism. *Canadian Journal of Behavioral Science, 19,* 216–232.

Langevin, R. (1983). *Sexual strands: Understanding and treating sexual anomalies in men.* Hillsdale, NJ: Erlbaum.

Langevin, R. (1990). Sexual anomalies and the brain. In W. L. Marshall, D. R. Laws, & H. E. Barbaree (Eds.), *Handbook of sexual assault: Issues, theories, and treatment of the offender* (pp. 103–113). New York: Plenum.

Langevin, R., & Lang, R. A. (1987). The courtship disorders. In G. D. Wilson (Ed.), *Variant sexuality: Research and theory* (pp. 202–228). Baltimore: Johns Hopkins University.

Langevin, R., Paitich, D., Ramsay, G., Anderson, C., Kamrad, J., Pope, S., Geller, G., Pearl, L., & Newman, S. (1979). Experimental studies of the etiology of genital exhibitionism. *Archives of Sexual Behavior, 8,* 307–331.

Langevin, R., Paitich, D., & Russon, A. E. (1985). Voyeurism: Does it predict sexual aggression or violence in general? In R. Langevin (Ed.), *Erotic preference, gender identity, and aggression in men: New research studies* (pp. 77–98). Hillsdale, NJ: Erlbaum.

Langevin, R., Wortzman, G., Wright, P., & Handy, L. (1989). Studies of brain damage and dysfunction in sex offenders. *Annals of Sex Research, 2,* 163–179.

Langfeldt, T. (1990). Early childhood and juvenile sexuality, development and problems. In M. E. Perry (Ed.), *Handbook of sexuality VII: Childhood and adolescent sexology* (pp. 179–200). Amsterdam: Elsevier.

Lanier, C. A., Elliott, M. N., Martin, D. W., & Kapadia, A. (1998). Evaluation of an intervention to change attitudes toward date rape. *Journal of American College Health, 46,* 177–180.

Lanyon, R. I. (1986). Theory and treatment in child molestation. *Journal of Consulting and Clinical Psychology, 54,* 176–182.

Larimer, M. E., Lydum, A. R., Anderson, B. K., & Turner, A. P. (1999). Male and female recipients of unwanted sexual contact in a college student sample: Prevalence rates, alcohol use, and depression symptoms. *Sex Roles: A Journal of Research, 40,* 295–308.

Larson, D. E. (Ed.). (1996). *Mayo Clinic family health book: The ultimate illustrated home medical reference* (2nd ed.). New York: William Morrow.

Larsson, I., & Svedin, C. (2002a). Sexual experiences in childhood: Young adults' recollections. *Archives of Sexual Behavior, 31*(3), 263–273.

Larsson, I., & Svedin, C. (2002b). Teachers' and parents' reports on 3- to 6-year-old children's sexual behavior—a comparison. *Child Abuse & Neglect, 26*(3), 247–266.

Laumann, E. O., Gagnon, J. H., Michael, R. T., & Michaels, S. (1994). *The social organization of sexuality: Sexual practices in the United States.* Chicago: University of Chicago.

Laumann, E. O., Paik, A., & Rosen, R. C. (1999). Sexual dysfunction in the United States: Prevalence and predictors. *Journal of the American Medical Association, 281,* 537–544.

Laver, S. M. L., van der Borne, B., Kok, G., & Woelk, G. (1997). A preintervention survey to determine understanding of HIV and AIDS in farmworker communities in Zimbabwe. *AIDS Education and Prevention, 9,* 94–110.

Lawrence, P. B. (1994). Breast milk: Best source of nutrition for term and preterm infants. *Pediatric Clinics of North America, 41,* 925–941.

Lawson, A. L. (1999). Women and AIDS in Africa: Sociocultural dimensions in the HIV/AIDS epidemic. *International Social Science Journal, 51,* 391–401.

Learner, N. (1999). Fighting for equality in Japan. *Progressive, 63,* 15.

Leary, M. F., & Downs, D. L. (1995). Interpersonal functions of the self-esteem motive: Self-esteem as a sociometer. In M. Kernis (Ed.), *Efficacy, agency, and self-esteem* (pp. 123–144). New York: Plenum.

LebanonHealth. (2002). Miscarriage. Retrieved November 21, 2002, from www.lebanonhealth.com/condi/38944.htm

Leder, J. M. (1991). *Brothers and sisters: How they shape our lives.* New York: St. Martin's.

Ledray, L. E. (1986). *Recovering from rape.* New York: Henry Holt.

Lee, J. A. (1973). *The color of love.* Toronto: New Press.

Lee, J. A. (1988). Love-styles. In R. J. Sternberg & M. L. Barnes (Eds.), *The psychology of love* (pp. 38–67). New Haven, CT: Yale University Press.

Lee, J. K. P., Pattison, P., Jackson, H. J., & Ward, T. (2001). The general, common, and specific features of psychopathology for different types of paraphilias. *Criminal Justice and Behavior, 28,* 227–256.

Lee, W. R., Hall, M. C., McQuellon, R. P., Case, L. D., & McCullough, D. L. (2001). A prospective quality-of-life study in men with clinically localized prostate carcinoma treated with radical prostatectomy, external beam radiotherapy, or interstitial brachytherapy. *International Journal of Radiation Oncology, Biology, & Physics, 51*(3), 614–623.

Lehigh Valley Hospital and Health Network. (1998). How Viagra works. Retrieved April 20, 2000, from http://www.lvhhn.org/search

Leiblum, S. R. (1995). Relinquishing virginity: The treatment of a complex case of vaginismus. In R. C. Rosen & S. R. Leiblum (Eds.), *Case studies in sex therapy* (pp. 250–263). New York: Guilford.

Leiblum, S. R., & Rosen, R. C. (Eds.). (1988). *Sexual desire disorders.* New York: Guilford.

Leiblum, S. R., & Rosen, R. C. (Eds.). (2000). *Principles and practice of sex therapy* (3rd ed.). New York: Guilford Press.

Leitenberg, H., & Henning, K. (1995). Sexual fantasy. *Psychological Bulletin, 117,* 469–496.

Lemieux, R., & Hale, J. L. (2000). Intimacy, passion, and commitment among married individuals: Further testing of the Triangular Theory of Love. *Psychological Reports, 87,* 941–948.

Lenders, C. M., Hediger, M. L., Scholl, T. O., Khoo, C., Slap, G. B., & Stallings, V. A. (1994). Effect of high sugar intake by low-income pregnant adolescents on infant birth weight. *Journal of Adolescent Heath, 15,* 596–602.

Lenihan, G. O., Rawlins, M. E., Ebefiy, C. G., Buckley, B., & Masters, B. (1992). Gender differences in rape supportive attitudes before and after a date rape education intervention. *Journal of College Student Development, 33,* 331–338.

Lerman, S. E., & Liao, J. C. (2001). Neonatal circumcision. *Pediatric Clinics of North America, 48*(6), 1539–1557.

Lesser, E. K., & Comet, J. J. (1987). Help and hindrance: Parents of divorcing children. *Journal of Marital and Family Therapy, 13,* 197–202.

Letourneau, E., & O'Donohue, W. (1993). Sexual desire disorders. In W. O'Donohue & J. H. Geer (Eds.), *Handbook of sexual dysfunctions: Assessment and treatment* (pp. 53–81). Boston: Allyn & Bacon.

LeVay, S. (1991). A difference in hypothalamic structure between heterosexual and homosexual men. *Science, 253,* 1034–1037.

LeVay, S., & Nonas, E. (1995). *City of friends: A portrait of the gay and lesbian community in America.* Cambridge, MA: The MIT Press.

Lever, J. (1994, August 23). Sexual revelations. *The Advocate,* 17–24.

Lever, J. (1995). Bringing the fundamentals of gender studies into safer-sex education. *Family Planning Perspectives, 27,* 172–174.

Levin, R. J. (1992). The mechanisms of human female sexual arousal. *Annual Reviews in Sex Research, 3,* 1–48.

Levine, R., Sato, S., Hashmoto, T., & Verma, J. (1995). Love and marriage in 11 cultures. *Journal of Cross-Cultural Psychology, 26*(5), 554–571.

Levine, S. B. (1998). *Sexuality in mid-life.* New York: Plenum.

Levine, S. B., & Agle, D. (1978). The effectiveness of sex therapy for chronic secondary psychological impotence. *Journal of Sex and Marital Therapy, 4,* 235–258.

Levinger, G. (1976). A social psychological perspective on marital dissolution. *Journal of Social Issues, 32,* 21–47.

Levinger, G. (1980). Toward the analysis of close relationships. *Journal of Experimental Social Psychology, 16,* 510–544.

Levitan, M. (1988). *Textbook of human genetics.* New York: Oxford University.

Levitt, E. E., Moser, C., & Jamison, K. V. (1994). The prevalence and some attributes of females in the sadomasochistic subculture: A second report. *Archives of Sexual Behavior, 32,* 465–473.

Levy, G. D. (1989). Relations among aspects of children's social environments, gender schematization, gender role knowledge, and flexibility. *Sex Roles, 21*(11/12), 803–823.

Lewes, K. (1988). *The psychoanalytic theory of male homosexuality.* New York: Simon & Schuster.

Lewis, D. O., Shankok, S. S., & Pincus, J. H. (1979). Juvenile male sexual assaulters. *American Journal of Psychiatry, 136,* 1194–1196.

Lewis, L. A. (1984). The coming-out process for lesbians: Integrating a stable identity. *Social Work, 29*(5), 464–469.

Lewontin, R. C. (1995). Sex, lies, and social science. *The New York Review of Books, 42,* 24–29.

Libman, E., Fichten, C. S., & Brender, W. (1985). The role of therapeutic format in treatment of sexual dysfunction. *Clinical Psychology Review, 5,* 103–117.

Liebert, R. M., & Liebert, L. L. (1995). *Science and behavior: An introduction to the methods of psychological research.* Englewood Cliffs, NJ: Prentice-Hall.

Lindsey, K. (1977, November). Sexual harassment on the job. *Ms.,* 47.

Linehan, M. M. (1993). *Cognitive-behavioral treatment of borderline personality disorder.* New York: Guilford Press.

Linz, D. (1989). Exposure to sexually explicit materials and attitudes toward rape: A comparison of study results. *Journal of Sex Research, 26,* 50–84.

Linz, D., Donnerstein, E., & Penrod, S. (1987). The findings and recommendations of the Attorney General's Commission on Pornography: Do the psychological "facts" fit the political fury? *American Psychologist, 42,* 946–953.

Linz, D., & Malamuth, N. (1993). *Communication concepts 5: Pornography.* Newbury Park, CA: Sage Publications.

Lipner, J. J. (2000). The god of love and the love of god in Christian and Hindu traditions. In J. Runzo & N. M. Martin (Eds.), *Love, sex, and gender in the world religions* (pp. 51–87). Oxford, England: Oneworld Press.

Lippert, T., & Prager, K. J. (2001). Daily experiences of intimacy: A study of couples. *Personal Relationships, 8,* 283–298.

Little, B. C., Hayworth, J., Benson, P., Hall, F., Beard, R. W., Dewhurst, J., & Priest, R. G. (1984). Treatment of hypertension in pregnancy by relaxation and biofeedback. *The Lancet,* 865–867.

Litz, S. (1996). Screening surrogates. American Surrogacy Center. Retrieved January 23, 1997, from www.surrogacy. com/psychres/article/screen.html

Liu, D., Ng, M. L., Zhou, L. P., & Haeberle, E. J. (1997). *Sexual behavior in modern China.* New York: Continuum.

LNG IUS. Clinical information for providers. (2001). Association of Reproductive Health Professionals. Retrieved October 9, 2002, from http://www.arhp.org/healthcareproviders/onlinepublications/clinicalproceedings/ndiccp/clinicalinfo.cfm?ID=164

Lobel, M., DeVincent, C. J., Kaminer, A., & Meyer, B. A. (2000). The impact of prenatal maternal stress and optimistic disposition on birth outcomes in medically high-risk women. *Health Psychology, 19*(6), 544–553.

Lock, J., & Steiner, H. (1999). Gay, lesbian, and bisexual youth risks for emotional, physical, and social problems: Results from a community-based sample. *Journal of the American Academy of Child and Adolescent Psychiatry, 38,* 297–304.

Lohr, B. A., & Adams, H. E. (1995). Sexual sadism and masochism. In L. Diamant & R. D. McAnulty (Eds.), *The psychology of sexual orientation, behavior, and identity: A handbook* (pp. 256–269). Westport, CT: Greenwood.

London, K. A., & Wilson, B. F. (1988). Divorce. *American Demographics, 10,* 22–26.

Long, P. J., & Jackson, J. L. (1991). Children sexually abused by multiple perpetrators: Familial risk factors and abuse characteristics. *Journal of Interpersonal Violence, 6,* 147–159.

Long, P. J., & Jackson, J. L. (1993, November). Depression, sexual satisfaction, self-esteem, and physical symptoms among childhood sexual abuse survivors. Presented at the annual meeting of the Association for the Advancement of Behavior Therapy, Atlanta, GA.

LoPiccolo, J., & Friedman, J. (1988). Broad-spectrum treatment of low sexual desire: Integration of cognitive, behavioral, and systemic therapy. In S. R. Leiblum & R. C. Rosen (Eds.), *Sexual desire disorders* (pp. 107–144). New York: Guilford.

LoPiccolo, J., & Lobitz, W. E. (1972). The role of masturbation in the treatment of orgasmic dysfunction. *Archives of Sexual Behavior, 2,* 163–171.

LoPiccolo, J., & Stock, W. E. (1986). Treatment of sexual dysfunction. *Journal of Consulting and Clinical Psychology, 54,* 158–167.

Los Angeles County Department of Health Services. (1998, Spring). STD Chalk Talk. Retrieved July 26, 2000, from www:lapublichealth.org/std/news/chalk/chalk.htm

Losch, M., Dungy, C. I., Russell, D., & Dusdieker, L. B. (1995). Impact of attitudes on maternal decisions regarding infant feeding. *The Journal of Pediatrics, 126,* 507–514.

Loth, D. (1961). *The erotic in literature: A historical survey of pornography as delightful as it is indiscreet.* New York: Julian Meissner.

Lottes, I., & Weinberg, M. (1997). Sexual coercion among university students: A comparison of the U.S. and Sweden. *Journal of Sex Research, 34,* 67–76.

Loulan, J. (1984). *Lesbian sex.* San Francisco: Spinsters Ink.

Loulan, J. (1987). *Lesbian passion: Loving ourselves and each other.* San Francisco: Spinsters/Aunt Lute.

Lovdal, L. T. (1989). Sex role messages in television commercials: An update. *Sex Roles, 21,* 715–724.

Loy, P. H., & Stewart, L. P. (1984). The extent and effects of the sexual harassment of working women. *Sociological Focus, 17,* 31–43.

Lucas, A., Brooke, O. G., Morley, R., Cole, T. J., & Bamford, M. F. (1990). Early diet of preterm infants and development of allergic or atopic disease: Randomised prospective study. *British Medical Journal, 300,* 837–840.

Lugaila, T. A. (1998). Marital status and living arrangements: March 1998. *Current Population Reports, P20-514.* Washington, DC: U.S. Census Bureau.

Lugalla, J. L. P., & Emmelin, M. A. C. (1999). The social and cultural context of HIV/AIDS transmission in the Kagera region, Tanzania. *Journal of Asian and African Studies, 34,* 377–403.

Luke, B. (1994). Nutritional influences on fetal growth. *Clinical Obstetrics and Gynecology, 37*(3), 538–549.

Lukianowicz, N. (1972). Incest: I. Paternal incest. II. Other types of incest. *British Journal of Psychiatry, 120,* 301–313.

Lundberg, P. O. (2001). The peripheral innervation of the genital organs of women. *Scandinavian Journal of Sexology, 4,* 213–225.

Luster, T., & Small, S. A. (1997). Sexual abuse history and problems in adolescence: Exploring the effects of moderating variables. *Journal of Marriage & the Family, 59,* 131–142.

Lutgendorf, S. K., Starr, K., McCabe, P., Ironson, G., Klimas, N., Fletcher, M. A., Kumar, M., Schneiderman, N., & Cleven, K. (1997). Cognitive-behavioral stress management decreases dysphoric mood and herpes simplex virus type 2 antibody titers in symptomatic HIV-seropositive gay men. *Journal of Consulting and Clinical Psychology, 65,* 31–43.

Lytton, H., & Romney, D. M. (1991). Parents' differential socialization of boys and girls: A meta-analysis. *Psychological Bulletin, 109*(2), 267–296.

Maccoby, E. E. (1990). Gender and relationships: A developmental account. *American Psychologist, 45*(4), 513–520.

Maccoby, E. E. (1998). *The two sexes: Growing up apart, coming together.* Cambridge, MA: The Belknap Press.

Maccoby, E. E., & Mnookin, R. H. (1992). *Dividing the child: Social and legal dilemmas of custody.* Cambridge, MA: Harvard University Press.

MacDonald, J. (1973). *Indecent exposure.* Springfield, IL: Charles C. Thomas.

MacDonald, N. E., Wells, G. A., Fisher, W. A., Warren, W. K., King, M. A., Doherty, J. A., & Bowie, J. R. (1990). High-risk STD/HIV behavior among college students. *Journal of the American Medical Association, 263,* 3155–3159.

MacFarquhar, E. (1994, September 12). Population wars. *U.S. News and World Report,* pp. 54–57.

Macharia, K. (1997, November). Homosexuality: My perspective. Retrieved October 7, 1999, from www.qrd.org/qrd/www/culture/black/discussion/perspective.html

Mackay, J. (2001). Global sex: Sexuality and sexual practices around the world. *Sexual and Relationship Therapy, 16,* 71–82.

MacLean, P. D. (1962). New findings relevant to the evolution of psychosexual functions of the brain. *Journal of Nervous and Mental Disease, 135,* 289–301.

MacPhee, D. C., Johnson, S. M., & van der Veer, M. C. (1995). Low sexual desire in women: The effects of marital therapy. *Journal of Sex and Marital Therapy, 21,* 159–181.

Madalinska, J. B., Essink-Bot, M-L., de Koning, H. J., Kirkels, W. J., van der Maas, P. J., & Schröder, F. H. (2001). Health-related quality-of-life effects of radical prostatectomy and primary radiotherapy for screen-detected or clinically diagnosed localized prostate cancer. *Journal of Clinical Oncology, 19*(6), 1619–1628.

Magnusson, C. (2001). Adolescent girls' sexual attitudes and opposite-sex relations in 1970–1996. *Journal of Adolescent Health, 28*(3), 242–252.

Mahler, K. (1996). Delay in first sex is seen among British teenagers in sex education program. *Family Planning Perspectives, 28,* 83–84.

Major, B., Richards, C., Cooper, M. L., Cozzarelli, C., & Zubek, J. (1998). Personal resilience, cognitive appraisals, and coping: An integrative model of adjustment to abortion. *Journal of Personality and Social Psychology, 74,* 735–752.

Makler, A., Reiss, J., Stoller, J., Blumenfeld, Z., & Brandes, J. M. (1993). Use of a sealed minichamber for direct observation and evaluation of the in vitro effect of cigarette smoke on sperm motility. *Fertility and Sterility, 59,* 645–651.

Malamuth, N. M. (1986). Prediction of naturalistic sexual aggression. *Journal of Personality and Social Psychology, 50,* 953–962.

Malamuth, N. M. (1998). An evolutionary-based model integrating research on the characteristics of sexually coercive men. In J. G. Adair, D. Belanger, & K. L. Dion (Eds.), *Advances in psychological science, volume 1: Social, personal, and cultural aspects* (pp. 151–184). Hove, England: Psychology Press/Erlbaum.

Malamuth, N. M., Addison, T., & Koss, M. (2000). Pornography and sexual aggression: Are there reliable effects and can we understand them? *Annual Review of Sex Research, 11,* 26–91

Malatesta, V. J. (1989). On making love last in a marriage: Reflections of 60 widows. *Clinical Gerontologist, 9,* 64–67.

Malatesta, V. J., Pollack, R. H., Crotty, T. D., & Peacock, L. J. (1982). Acute alcohol intoxication and female orgasmic response. *Journal of Sex Research, 18,* 1–17.

Malatesta, V. J., Pollack, R. H., Wilbanks, W. A., & Adams, H. E. (1979). Alcohol effects on orgasmic-ejaculatory response in human males. *Journal of Sex Research, 15,* 101–107.

Malatesta, V. J., & Robinson, M. S. (1995). Hypersexuality and impulsive sexual behaviors. In L. Diamant & R. D. McAnulty (Eds.), *The psychology of sexual orientation, behavior, and identity: A handbook* (pp. 307–326). Westport, CT: Greenwood.

Malecontraceptives.org. (2002). Experimental methods. Retrieved October 10, 2002, from www.malecontraceptives.org/methods/index_frame.htm

Maletzky, B. M. (1997). Exhibitionism: Assessment and treatment. In D. R. Laws & W. O'Donohue (Eds.), *Sexual deviance: Theory, assessment, and treatment* (pp. 40–74). New York: Guilford.

Manderson, L. (1992). Public sex performances in Patpong and explorations of the edges of imagination. *Journal of Sex Research, 29,* 451–475.

Mansfield, P. K., Koch, P. B., & Voda, A. M. (1998). Qualities midlife women desire in their sexual relationships and their changing sexual response. *Psychology of Women Quarterly, 22,* 285–303.

Maranto, G. (1996, September). Should women in their 40s have mammograms? *Scientific American, 275*(3), 113.

March of Dimes Birth Defects Foundation. (1993). Eating for two: Nutrition during pregnancy. Retrieved April 8, 1998, from http://www.noah.cuny.edu/pregnancy/march_of_dimes/pre_ preg.plan/eating42.html

March of Dimes. (2002a). Folic acid FAQ. Retrieved September 23, 2002, from http://www.mofdimes.com/professionals/690_1403.asp

March of Dimes. (2002b). Pregnancy after 35. Retrieved September 25, 2002, from http://www.modimes.org/search/MsmGo.exe?grab_id=33703458&extra_arg=&page_id=550&host_id=1&query=Pregnancy+after+35&hiword=PREGNANCY+AFTER+35+PREGNANT+PREGNANCIES+

Marchbanks, P. A., McDonald, J. A., Wilson, H. G., Folger, S. G., Mandel, M. G., Daling, J. R., Bernstein, L., Malone, K. E., Ursin, G., Strom, B. L., Norman, S. A., Wingo, P. A., Burkman, R. T., Berlin, J. A., Simon, M. S., Spirtas, R., & Weiss, L. K. (2002). Oral contraceptives and the risk of breast cancer. *The New England Journal of Medicine, 346,* 2025–2032.

Marcuse, L. (1965). *Obscene: The history of an indignation* (K. Gershon, Trans.). London: MacGibbon and Kee. (Original work published 1963)

Margolin, G., & Wampold, B. E. (1981). Sequential analysis of conflict and discord in distressed and nondistressed marital partners. *Journal of Consulting and Clinical Psychology, 49,* 554–567.

Marín, B. V., Gómez, C. A., & Hearst, N. (1993). Multiple heterosexual partners and condom use among Hispanics and non-Hispanic whites. *Family Planning Perspectives, 25,* 170–174.

Marin, B. V., & Marin, G. (1992). Predictors of condom accessibility among Hispanics in San Francisco. *American Journal of Public Health, 82,* 592–595.

Markman, H. J. (1981). Prediction of marital distress: A 5-year follow-up. *Journal of Consulting and Clinical Psychology, 49,* 760–762.

Markman, H. J., & Floyd, F. (1980). Possibilities for the prevention of marital discord: A behavioral perspective. *American Journal of Family Therapy, 8,* 29–48.

Markowitz, L. M. (1993, March/April). Understanding the differences. *Networker,* 50–59.

Marks, N. F. (1996). Flying solo at midlife: Gender, marital status, and psychological well-being. *Journal of Marriage and the Family, 58,* 917–932.

Markstrom-Adams, C. (1989). Androgyny and its relationship to adolescent psychosocial well-being: A review of the literature. *Sex Roles, 21,* 325–340.

Marshall, W. D. (1989). Pornography and sex offenders. In D. Zillman & J. Bryant (Eds.), *Pornography: Research advances and policy considerations* (pp. 185–214). Hillsdale, NJ: Erlbaum Associates.

Marshall, W. L. (1988). The use of sexually explicit stimuli by rapists, child molesters and nonoffender males. *Journal of Sex Research, 25,* 267–288.

Marshall, W. L., & Barbaree, H. E. (1990). An integrated theory of the etiology of sexual offending. In W. L. Marshall, D. R. Laws, & H. E. Barbaree (Eds.), *Handbook of sexual assault* (pp. 257–275). New York: Plenum.

Marshall, W. L., Barbaree, H. E., & Butt, J. (1988). Sexual offenders against male children: Sexual preferences. *Behaviour Research and Therapy, 26,* 383–391.

Marshall, W. L., Barbaree, H. E., & Christophe, D. (1986). Sexual offenders against female children: Sexual preferences for age of victims and type of behaviour. *Canadian Journal of Behavioral Science, 18,* 424–439.

Marshall, W. L., & Eccles, A. (1993). Pavlovian conditioning processes in adolescent sex offenders. In H. E. Barbaree, W. L. Marshall, & S. M Hudson (Eds.), *The juvenile sex offender* (pp. 118–142). New York: Guilford.

Marshall, W. L., & Hambley, L. (1996). Intimacy and loneliness, and their relationship to rape myth acceptance and hostility toward women among rapists. *Journal of Interpersonal Violence, 11,* 586–593.

Marshall, W. L., & Marshall, L. E. (2000). The origins of sexual offending. *Trauma, Violence, and Abuse, 1,* 250–263.

Marshall, W. L., Payne, K., Barbaree, H. E., & Eccles, A. (1991). Exhibitionists: Sexual preferences for exposing. *Behaviour Research and Therapy, 29,* 37–40.

Marshall, W. L., & Serran, G. A. (2000). Improving the effectiveness of sexual offender treatment. *Trauma, Violence, and Abuse, 1,* 203–222.

Marteau, T. M. (1993). Sex selection: "The rights of man" or the thin edge of a eugenic wedge? *British Medical Journal, 306,* 1704–1705.

Martin, A. (1993). *The lesbian and gay parenting handbook.* New York: HarperCollins.

Martin, C. W., Anderson, R. A., Cheng, L., Ho, P. C., van der Spuy, Z., Smith, K. B., Glasier, A. F., Everington, D., & Baird, D. T. (2000). Potential impact of hormonal male contraception: Cross-cultural implications for development of novel preparations. *Human Reproduction, 15,* 637–645.

Martin, N. M. (2000). Loving the goddess in Hinduism. In J. Runzo & N. M. Martin (Eds.), *Love, sex, and gender in the world religions* (pp. 89–111). Oxford, England: Oneworld Press.

Martinson, F. M. (1994). *The sexual life of children.* Westport, CT: Bergin & Garvey.

Marván, M. L., & Cortés-Iniestra, S. (2001). Women's beliefs about the prevalence of premenstrual syndrome and biases in recall of premenstrual changes. *Health Psychology, 20*(4), 276–280.

Marván, M. L., Vacio, A., & Espinosa-Hernandez, G. (2001). A comparison of menstrual changes expected by pre-menarcheal adolescents and changes actually experienced by post-menarcheal adolescents in Mexico. *Journal of School Health, 71*(9), 458–461.

Marx, B. P., Van Wie, V., & Gross, A. M. (1996). Date rape risk factors: A review and methodological critique of the literature. *Aggression and Violent Behavior, 1,* 27–45.

Masheter, C. (1991). Postdivorce relationships between ex-spouses: The roles of attachment and interpersonal conflict. *Journal of Marriage and the Family, 53,* 103–110.

Massey, D. R., & Christensen, C. A. (1990). Student teacher attitudes to sex role stereotyping: Some Australian data. *Educational Studies, 16,* 95–107.

Mast, C. K. (1990). *Sex Respect: The option of true sexual freedom: Teacher manual* (rev.). Bradley, IL: Respect Inc.

Masters, W. H., & Johnson, V. E. (1966). *Human sexual response.* Boston: Little, Brown.

Masters, W. H., & Johnson, V. E. (1970). *Human sexual inadequacy.* Boston: Little, Brown.

Masters, W. H., & Johnson, V. E. (1979). *Homosexuality in perspective.* Boston: Little, Brown.

Masters, W. H., Johnson, V. E., & Kolodny, R. C. (1994). *Heterosexuality.* New York: HarperCollins.

Matek, O. (1988). Obscene phone callers. *Journal of Social Work and Human Sexuality, 7,* 113–130.

Mathewes-Green, F. (1997). Free love didn't come cheap. *Christianity Today, 41,* 68–69.

Mathews, R., Hunter, J. A., & Vuz, J. (1997). Juvenile female sexual offenders: Clinical characteristics and treatment issues. *Child Abuse: A Journal of Research and Treatment, 9,* 187–199.

Mathews, R., Matthews, J. K., & Speltz, K. (1989). *Female sexual offenders: An exploratory study.* Orwell, VT: Safer Society Press.

Maticka-Tyndale, E., Elkins, D., Haswell-Elkins, M., Rujkarakorn, D., Kuyyakanond, T., & Stam, K. (1997). Context and patterns of men's commercial sexual partnerships in northeastern Thailand: Implications for AIDS prevention. *Social Science and Medicine, 44,* 199–213.

Maticka-Tyndale, E., Herold, E. S., & Mewhinney, D. (1998). Casual sex on spring break. *The Journal of Sex Research, 35,* 502–516.

Maxwell, K. (1996). *A sexual odyssey: From forbidden fruit to cybersex.* New York: Plenum.

Mayer Labs. (2002). eZ·on bi-directional condoms. Retrieved October 8, 2002, from www.mayerlabs.com/consumer/products/ezon.asp

Maypole, D. E. (1986). Sexual harassment of social workers at work: Injustice within? *Social Work, 31,* 29–34.

Mbizvo, E. M., Msuya, S. E., Stray-Pederson, B., Chirenje, M. Z., Munjoma, M., & Hussain, A. (2002). Association of herpes simplex virus type 2 with the human immunodeficiency virus among urban women in Zimbabwe. *International Journal of STD and AIDS, 13*(5), 343–348.

McAdams, D. P., & de St. Aubin, E. (1992). A theory of generativity and its assessment through self-report, behavioral acts, and narrative themes in autobiography. *Journal of Personality and Social Psychology, 62,* 1003–1015.

McAnulty, R. D. (1995). The paraphilias: Classification and theory. In L. Diamant & R. D. McAnulty (Eds.), *The psychology of sexual orientation, behavior, and identity: A handbook* (pp. 239–255). Westport, CT: Greenwood.

McAnulty, R. D., & Adams, H. E. (1991). Voluntary control of penile tumescence: Effects of an incentive and a signal detection task. *Journal of Sex Research, 28,* 557–577.

McAnulty, R. D., & Adams, H. E. (1992). Validity and ethics of penile circumference measures of sexual arousal: A reply to McConaghy. *Archives of Sexual Behavior, 21,* 177–186.

McAnulty, R. D., Adams, H. E., & Dillon, J. A. (2001). Sexual deviation: The paraphilias. In H. E. Adams & P. Sutker (Eds.), *Comprehensive handbook of psychopathology* (3rd ed.). New York: Plenum.

McAnulty, R. D., Adams, H. E., & Wright, L. W. (1994). Relationship between MMPI and penile plethysmograph in accused child molesters. *Journal of Sex Research, 31,* 179–184.

McAnulty, R. D., & Loupis, J. (1999, November). *Religiosity and fundamentalism in child molesters.* Paper presented at the joint meeting of the Society for the Scientific Study of Sexuality and the American Association of Sex Educators, Counselors, and Therapists, St. Louis, MO.

McAnulty, R. D., Satterwhite, R., & Gullick, E. (1995, March). *Topless dancers: Personality and background.* Paper presented at the meeting of the Southeastern Psychological Association, Savannah, GA.

McArthur, M. J. (1990). Reality therapy with rape victims. *Archives of Psychiatric Nursing, 4,* 360–365.

McCabe, M. P. (1999). The interrelationship between intimacy, relationship functioning, and sexuality among men and women in committed relationships. *Canadian Journal of Human Sexuality, 8,* 31–39.

McCaghy, C. H., & Hou, C. (1994). Family affiliation and prostitution in a cultural context: Career onsets of Taiwanese prostitutes. *Archives of Sexual Behavior, 23,* 251–266.

McCandlish, B. M. (1985). Therapeutic issues with lesbian couples. In J. C. Gonsiorek (Ed.), *A guide to psychotherapy with gay and lesbian clients.* New York: Harrington Park Press.

McCann, L., Pearlman, L. A., Sakheim, D. K., & Abrahamson, D. J. (1988). Assessment and treatment of the adult survivor of childhood sexual abuse within a schema framework. In S. M. Sgroi (Ed.), *Vulnerable populations: Evaluation and treatment of sexually abused children and adult survivors* (Vol. 1) (pp. 77–101). New York: Lexington Books.

McCarn, S. R., & Fassinger, R. E. (1996). Revisioning sexual minority identity formation: A new model of lesbian identity and its implications for counseling and research. *Counseling Psychologist, 24,* 508–534.

McCarthy, B. W. (1989). Cognitive-behavioral strategies and techniques in the treatment of early ejaculation. In S. R. Leiblum & R. C. Rosen (Eds.), *Principles and practice of sex therapy: Update for the 1990s* (2nd ed.)(pp. 298–318). New York: Guilford.

McCarthy, B. W. (1995). Learning from unsuccessful sex therapy patients. *Journal of Sex and Marital Therapy, 21,* 31–38.

McCleskey, K. (2000). History of contraception. Retrieved June 6, 2000, from http://benji.colorado.edu/~mcck/

McConaghy, N. (1993). *Sexual behavior: Problems and management.* New York: Plenum.

McCoy, N. L., & Pitino, L. (2002). Pheromonal influences on sociosexual behavior in young women. *Physiological Behavior, 75*(3), 367–375.

McDermott, D. H., Zimmerman, P. A., Guignard, F., Kleeberger, C. A., Leitman, S. F., & Murphy, P. M. (1998). CCR5 promoter polymorphism affects HIV-1 disease progression. *Lancet, 352,* 866–871.

McFarland, C., Ross, M., & DeCourville, N. (1989). Women's theories of menstruation and biases in recall of menstrual symptoms. *Journal of Personality and Social Psychology, 57*(3), 522–531.

McGregor, J. A., & French, J. I. (2000). Bacterial vaginosis in pregnancy. *Obstetrical and Gynecological Survey, 55*(5 Supplement 1): S1–19.

McGuire, R. J., Carlisle, J. M., & Young, B. G. (1965). Sexual deviations as conditioned behavior: A hypothesis. *Behavior Research and Therapy, 2,* 185–190.

McKay, M., Fanning, P., & Paleg, K. (1994). *Couple skills: Making your relationship work.* Oakland, CA: New Harbinger.

McKenna, K. Y. A., Green, A. S., & Smith, P. K. (2001). Demarginalizing the sexual self. *Journal of Sex Research, 38,* 302–311.

McLaren, A. (1991). *A history of contraception: From antiquity to the present day.* Cambridge, MA: Basil Blackwell, Inc.

McMahon, K. (1990). The *Cosmopolitan* ideology and the management of desire. *Journal of Sex Research, 27,* 381–396.

McWhirter, D. P., & Mattison, A. M. (1984). *The male couple.* Englewood Cliffs, NJ: Prentice-Hall.

Mead, M. (1975, January). Bisexuality: What's it all about? *Redbook,* 6–7.

Meana, M., Binik, Y. M., Khalife, S., & Cohen, D. R. (1997). Dyspareunia: Sexual dysfunction or pain syndrome? *Journal of Nervous and Mental Diseases, 185,* 561–569.

Meckstroth, K. R., & Darney, P. D. (2001). Implant contraception. *Seminars in Reproductive Medicine, 19*(4), 339–354.

Meisler, A. W., Carey, M. P., Lantinga, L. J., & Krauss, D. J. (1989). Erectile dysfunction in diabetes mellitus: A biopsychosocial approach to etiology and assessment. *Annals of Behavioral Medicine, 11,* 18–27.

Men's Health Institute. (1999). Sex and relationships. Retrieved November 17, 1999, from http://www.sexandhealth.com/preview/index.html

Meredith, M. (2001). Human vomeronasal organ function: A critical review of best and worst cases. *Chemical Senses, 26*(4), 433–445.

Meriggiola, M. C., Costantino, A., & Cerpolini, S. (2002). Recent advances in hormonal male contraception. *Contraception, 65*(4), 269–272.

Meritor Savings Bank, FSB v. Vinson, 477 U.S. 57 (1986).

Meschke, L. L., Zweig, J. M., Barber, B. L., & Eccles, J. S. (2000). Demographic, biological, social, & psychological correlates of the timing of first intercourse. *Journal of Research on Adolescence, 10*(3), 315–338.

Messenger, J. (1971). Sex and repression in an Irish folk community. In D. C. Marshall & R. C. Suggs (Eds.), *Human sexual behavior: Variations in the human spectrum.* New York: Basic Books.

Messman, T. L., & Long, P. J. (1996). Child sexual abuse and its relationship to revictimization in adult women: A review. *Clinical Psychology Review, 16,* 397–420.

Metcalf, M. G., Braiden, V., Livesey, J. H., & Wells, J. E. (1992). The premenstrual syndrome: Amelioration of symptoms after hysterectomy. *Journal of Psychosomatic Research, 36*(6), 569–584.

Metts, S., Sprecher, S., & Regan, P. C. (2000). Communication and sexual desire. In P. A. Andersen & L. K. Guerrero (Eds.), *Communication and emotion.* Orlando, FL: Academic Press.

Metz, M. E., & Miner, M. H. (1998). Psychosexual and psychosocial aspects of male aging and sexual health. *Canadian Journal of Human Sexuality, 7,* 245–260.

Metz, M. E., & Prior, J. L. (2000). Premature ejaculation: A psychophysiological approach for assessment and management. *Journal of Sex and Marital Therapy, 26,* 293–320.

Meuwissen, I., & Over, R. (1992). Sexual arousal across phases of the human menstrual cycle. *Archives of Sexual Behavior, 21,* 101–119.

Meyer, S. L., Vivian, D., & O'Leary, K. D. (1998). Men's sexual aggression in marriage: Couple's reports. *Violence Against Women, 4,* 415–435.

Meyer-Bahlburg, H. F. (1984). Psychoendocrine research on sexual orientation: Current status and future options. *Progressive Brain Research, 61,* 375–398.

Meyers, M., Diamond, R., Kezur, D., Scharf, C., Weinshel, M., & Rait, D. S. (1995). An infertility primer for family therapists: 1. Medical, social, and psychological dimensions. *Family Process, 34,* 219–229.

Michaud, D. S., Augustsson, K., Rimm, E. B., Stampfer, M. J., Willet, W. C., & Giovannucci, E. (2001). A prospective study on intake of animal products and risk of prostate cancer. *Cancer Causes and Control, 12*(6), 557–567.

Mickelson, K. D., Kessler, R. C., & Shaver, P. R. (1997). Adult attachment in a nationally representative sample. *Journal of Personality and Social Psychology, 73,* 1092–1106.

Middleton, D. R. (2002). *Exotics and erotics: Human cultural and sexual diversity.* Prospects Heights, IL: Waveland Press.

Mihalik, G. J. (1988). More than two: Anthropological perspectives on gender. *Journal of Gay and Lesbian Psychotherapy, 1*(1), 105–118.

Milhausen, R. R., & Herold, E. S. (1999). Does the double standard still exist? Perceptions of university women. *Journal of Sex Research, 36,* 361–368.

Miller, A. H., & Adams, J. E. (1996). *Sexualities in Victorian Britain.* Bloomington: Indiana University.

Miller, B. (1998). *Families matter: A research synthesis of family influences on adolescent pregnancy.* Washington, DC: National Campaign to Prevent Teen Pregnancy.

Miller, B., & Marshall, J. C. (1987). Coercive sex on the university campus. *Journal of College Student Personnel, 28,* 38–47.

Miller, B. C., & Moore, K. A. (1990). Adolescent sexual behavior, pregnancy, and parenting: Research through the 1980s. *Journal of Marriage and the Family, 52,* 1025–1044.

Miller, K. S., Levin, M. L., Whitaker, D. J., & Xu, X. (1998). Patterns of condom use among adolescents: The impact of maternal-adolescent communication. *American Journal of Public Health, 88,* 1542–1544.

Miller, L., & Notter, K. M. (2001). Menstrual reduction with extended use of combination oral contraceptive pills: Randomized controlled trial. *Obstetrics & Gynecology, 98*(5 Pt. 1), 771–778.

Miller, N. (1995). *Out of the past: Gay and lesbian history from 1869 to the present.* New York: Vintage Books.

Miller, N. B., Smerglia, V. L., Gaudet, D. S., & Kitson, G. C. (1998). Stressful life events, social support, and the distress of widowed and divorced women. *Journal of Family Issues, 19,* 181–203.

Milner, J. S., & Dopke, C. A. (1997). Paraphilia not otherwise specified: Psychopathology and theory. In D. R. Laws, & W. O'Donohue (Eds.), *Sexual deviance: Theory, assessment, and treatment* (pp. 394–423). New York: Guilford.

Milsten, R., & Slowinski, J. (1999). *The sexual male: Problems and solutions.* New York: Norton.

Minichiello, V., Marino, R., Browne, J., Jamieson, M., Peterson, K., Reuter, B., & Robinson, K. (2000). Commercial sex between men: A prospective diary-based study. *Journal of Sex Research, 37,* 151–160.

Mischel, W. (1999). *Introduction to personality* (6th ed.). Fort Worth, TX: Harcourt Brace.

Mitchell, J. E., Baker, L. A., & Jacklin, C. N. (1989). Masculinity and femininity in twin children: Genetic and environmental factors. *Child Development, 60,* 1475–1485.

Mofenson, L. M., & the Committee on Pediatric AIDS. (2000). Technical report: Perinatal human immunodeficiency virus testing and prevention of transmission. *Pediatrics, 106*(6), p. e88. Retrieved May 31, 2002, from http://www.pediatrics.org/cgi/content/full/106/6/e88?

Mohr, J. W., Turner, R. E., & Jerry, M. B. (1964). *Pedophilia and exhibitionism.* Toronto: University of Toronto.

Mok, S. C., Chao, J., Skates, S., Wong, K., Yiu, G. K., Muto, M. G., Berkowitz, R. S., & Cramer, D. W. (2001). Prostasin, a potential serum marker for ovarian cancer: Identification through microarray technology. *Journal of the National Cancer Institute, 93*(19), 1458–1464.

Mol, B. W. J., Van der Veen, F., & Bossuyt, P. M. M. (2002). Symptom-free women at increased risk of ectopic pregnancy: Should we screen? *Acta Obstetrica et Gynecologia Scandinavica, 81*(7), 661–672.

Money, J. (1976). Childhood: The last frontier in sex research. *The Sciences, 16,* 12–27.

Money, J. (1980). *Love and love sickness: The science of sex, gender difference, and pair-bonding.* Baltimore: Johns Hopkins University.

Money, J. (1984). Paraphilias: Phenomenology and classification. *American Journal of Psychotherapy, 38,* 164–179.

Money, J. (1986). *Lovemaps: Clinical concepts of sexual/erotic health and pathology, paraphilia, and gender transposition in childhood, adolescence, and maturity.* New York: Irvington.

Money, J. (1991). *Biographies of gender and hermaphroditism in paired comparisons: Clinical supplement to the Handbook of Sexology.* New York: Elsevier.

Money, J., & Ehrhardt, A. (1972). *Man and woman, boy and girl.* Baltimore: Johns Hopkins University.

Money, J., & Lamacz, M. (1989). *Vandalized lovemaps.* Buffalo, NY: Prometheus.

Money, J., & Lehne, G. K. (1999). Gender identity disorders. In R. T. Ammerman & M. Hersen (Eds.), *Handbook of prescriptive treatments for children and adolescents* (2nd ed.) (pp. 214–228). Boston: Allyn & Bacon.

Money, J., Schwartz, M., & Lewis, V. G. (1984). Adult erotosexual status and fetal hormonal masculinization and demasculinization: 46,XX congenital virilizing adrenal hyperplasia and 46,XY androgen-insensitivity syndrome compared. *Psychoneuroendocrinology, 9,* 405–414.

Monk-Turner, E., & Purcell, H. C. (1999). Sexual violence in pornography: How prevalent is it? *Gender Issues, 17,* 58–68.

Monto, M. A. (2001). Prostitution and fellatio. *Journal of Sex Research, 38,* 140–146.

Moore, K. A., McCabe, M. P., & Brink, R. B. (2001). Are married couples happier in their relationships than cohabiting couples? Intimacy and relationship factors. *Sexual and Relationship Therapy, 16,* 35–46.

Moore, N. B. (1986). Cross-cultural perspective: Family life education as a force for strengthening families. *Marriage and Family Review, 10,* 91–115.

Moore, S., & Halford, A. P. (1999). Barriers to safer sex: Beliefs and attitudes among male and female heterosexuals across four relationship groups. *Journal of Health Psychology, 4,* 149–163.

Moore, S., & Rosenthal, D. (1993). *Sexuality in adolescence.* New York: Routledge.

Morais, R. C. (1999). Porn goes public. *Forbes, 163,* 214–221.

Morales, K., & Inlander, C. B. (1991). *Take this book to the obstetrician with you: A consumer's guide to pregnancy and childbirth.* Reading, MA: Addison-Wesley.

Moranis, R. J., & Tan, A. L. (1980). Male-female differences in conceptions of romantic love relationships. *Psychological Reports, 47,* 1221–1222.

Morell, V. (1995). Attacking the cause of "silent" infertility. *Science, 11,* 775–777.

Morokoff, P. J. (1978). Determinants of female orgasm. In J. LoPiccolo & L. LoPiccolo (Eds.), *Handbook of sex therapy.* New York: Plenum.

Morokoff, P. J. (1986). Volunteer bias in the psychophysiological study of female sexuality. *Journal of Sex Research, 22,* 35–51.

Morokoff, P. J. (1988). Sexuality in perimenopausal and postmenopausal women. *Psychology of Women Quarterly, 12,* 489–511.

Morrell, M. J., Dixen, J. M., Carter, C. S., & Davidson, J. M. (1984). The influence of age and cycling on sexual arousability in women. *American Journal of Obstetrics, 148,* 66–71.

Morris, K. (2000). Candidate receptor turns on human pheromone debate. *The Lancet, 356,* 835.

Morris, M., Podhista, C., Wawer, M. J., & Handcock, M. S. (1996). Bridge populations in the spread of HIV/AIDS in Thailand. *AIDS, 10,* 1265–1271.

Morrison, D. M., Leigh, B. C., & Gillmore, M. R. (1999). Daily data collection: A comparison of three methods. *Journal of Sex Research, 36,* 76–81.

Morrison, L. A. (2002). Vaccines against genital herpes: Progress and limitations. *Drugs, 62,* 1119–1129.

Morrow, G. D., Clark, E. M., & Brock, K. F. (1995). Individual and partner love styles: Implications for the quality of romantic involvements. *Journal of Social and Personal Relationships, 12,* 363–387.

Morry, M. M., & Winkler, E. (2001). Student acceptance and expectation of sexual assault. *Canadian Journal of Behavioural Sciences, 33,* 188–192.

Mosely, R. P., & Paget, S. (2002). Liquid-based cytology: Is this the way forward for cervical screening? *Cytopathology, 13*(2), 71–82.

Moser, C. (1988). Sadomasochism. *Journal of Social Work and Human Sexuality, 7,* 43–56.

Moser, C., & Levitt, E. E. (1987). An exploratory-descriptive study of a sadomasochistically oriented sample. *Archives of Sexual Behavior, 23,* 322–337.

Mosher, D. L. (1970). Psychological reactions to pornographic films. *Technical reports of the Presidential Commision on Obscenity and Pornography* (Vol. 7). Washington, DC: U.S. Government Printing Office.

Mosher, D. L. (1988). Pornography defined: Sexual involvement theory, narrative context, and goodness-of-fit. *Journal of Psychology and Human Sexuality, 1,* 67–85.

Mosher, D. L. (1991). Ideological presuppositions: Rhetoric in sexual science, sexual politics, and sexual morality. *Journal of Psychology and Human Sexuality, 4,* 7–29.

Mosher, D. L., & McIan, P. (1994). College men and women respond to X-rated videos intended for male or female audiences: Gender and sexual scripts. *Journal of Sex Research, 31,* 99–113.

Mosher, W. D., & Pratt, W. F. (1990). *Fecundity & infertility in the United States 1965–1988: Advance data-192.* Washington, DC: National Center for Health Statistics.

Mroczek, D. K., & Kolarz, C. M. (1998). The effects of age on positive and negative affect: A developmental perspective on happiness. *Journal of Personality and Social Psychology, 75,* 1333–1349.

Muehlenhard, C. L. (1988). "Nice women" don't say yes and "real men" don't say no: How miscommunication and the double standard can cause sexual problems. *Women and Therapy, 7,* 95–108.

Muehlenhard, C. L., & Cook, S. W. (1988). Men's self-reports of unwanted sexual activity. *Journal of Sex Research, 24,* 58–72.

Muehlenhard, C. L., & Linton, M. A. (1987). Date rape and sexual aggression in dating situations: Incidence and risk factors. *Journal of Counseling Psychology, 34,* 186–196.

Muehlenhard, C. L., & Long, P. (1988, May). Men's versus women's reports of pressure to engage in unwanted sexual intercourse. Paper presented at the Western Regional Meeting of the Society for the Scientific Study of Sex, Dallas, TX.

Muehlenhard, C. L., & McCoy, M. L. (1991). Double standard/double bind: The sexual double standard and women's communication about sex. *Psychology of Women Quarterly, 15,* 447–461.

Muehlenhard, C. L., & Rodgers, C. S. (1998). Token resistance to sex. *Psychology of Women Quarterly, 22,* 443–463.

Mulhall, J. P. (2000). Current concepts in erectile dysfunction. *American Journal of Managed Care, 6,* S625–S631.

Muller, D., Roeder, R., & Orthner, H. (1973). Further results of stereotaxis in the human hypothalamus in sexual deviation. First use of the operation in addiction to drugs. *Neurochirurgia, 16,* 113–126.

Munjack, D. J., & Kanno, P. H. (1979). Retarded ejaculation: A review. *Archives of Sexual Behavior, 8,* 139–150.

Murphy, J. J., & Boggess, S. (1998). Increased condom use among teenage males, 1985–1995: The role of attitudes. *Family Planning Perspectives, 30,* 276–281.

Murray, D., Cox, J. L., Chapman, G., & Jones, P. (1995). Childbirth: Life event or start of a long-term difficulty? Further data from the Stoke-on-Trent controlled study of postnatal depression. *British Journal of Psychiatry, 166,* 595–600.

Murray, F. S., & Beran, L. C. (1968). A survey of nuisance telephone calls received by males and females. *Psychological Record, 18,* 107–109.

Murrin, M. R., & Laws, D. R. (1990). The influence of pornography on sexual crimes. In W. L. Marshall, D. R. Laws, & H. E. Barbaree (Eds.), *Handbook of sexual assault* (pp. 73–91). New York: Plenum.

Mustanski, B. S. (2001). Getting wired: Exploiting the Internet for the collection of valid sexuality data. *Journal of Sex Research, 38,* 292–301.

Myers, L. (1995, December 3). U.S. leads industrialized world in rape. *The Charlotte Observer,* p. 8A.

Myers, L., & Morokoff, P. J. (1986). Physiological and subjective sexual arousal in pre- and post-menopausal women taking replacement therapy. *Psychophysiology, 23,* 283–292.

NARAL. (1998). Factsheet: "Justifiable homicide" and the anti-choice movement. Retrieved June 5, 2000, from www.naral.org/mediaresources/fact/homicide.html

Nathan, S. G. (1986). The epidemiology of the *DSM-III* psychosexual dysfunctions. *Journal of Sex and Marital Therapy, 12,* 267–281.

National Abortion Federation. (1996). *Incidents of violence and disruption against abortion providers, 1995.* Washington, DC: Author.

National Cancer Institute. (2001). Human papillomavirus and cancer. Retrieved May 21, 2002, from http://cis.nci.nih.gov/fact/3_20.htm

National Cancer Institute. (2002). Lifetime probability of breast cancer in American women. Retrieved June 24, 2002, from http://cis.nci.nih.gov/fact/5_6.htm

National Center for Health Statistics. (1995). Advance report of final divorce statistics, 1989 and 1990. *Monthly Vital Statistics Report, 43*(9), *Supplement.* (DHHS Publication No. 95–1120). Hyattsville, MD: Public Health Service.

National Gay & Lesbian Task Force Policy Institute. (1991). *Anti-gay/ lesbian violence, victimization and defamation in 1990.* Washington, DC: Author.

National Household Survey on Drug Abuse. (2001). *Tobacco and alcohol use among pregnant women.* Retrieved January 14, 2003, from www.samhsa.gov/oas/2k2/PregAlcTob/PregAlcTob.htm

National Institute of Allergy and Infectious Diseases, National Institutes of Health. (1998, July). *Fact sheet.* Bethesda, MD: Author.

National Institute of Allergy and Infectious Diseases, National Institutes of Health. (2001). Fact sheet: Human papillomavirus and genital warts. Retrieved March 12, 2002, from http://www.niaid.nih.gov/factsheets/stdhpv.htm

National Institute of Allergy and Infectious Diseases, National Institutes of Health. (2002). Fact sheet: Treatment of HIV infection. Retrieved June 1, 2002, from http://www.niaid.nih.gov/factsheets/treat-hiv.htm

National Institute of Environmental Health Sciences. (2001, March). NIEHS news features: Uterine fibroids. Retrieved July 2, 2002, from http://www.niehs.nih.gov/oc/crntnws/2001mar/fibroids.htm

National Institute on Drug Abuse. (2002). MDMA (Ecstasy). Retrieved July 12, 2002, from http://www.nida.nih.gov/Infofax/ecstasy.html

National Institute on Media and the Family. (2000a). Children and television. Retrieved July 17, 2002, from www.mediaandthefamily.org/research/fact/childrenandtv.shtml

National Institute on Media and the Family. (2000b). Media's effect on girls: Body image and gender identity. Retrieved July 17, 2002, from www.mediaandthefamily.org/research/fact/mediaeffect.shtml

National Institutes of Health. (1997). *Interventions to prevent HIV risk behaviors. NIH Consensus Statement, 1997 February, 11–13,* 15 (2). Bethesda, MD: Author.

National Institutes of Health. (1998). NIH news release: Landmark study shows behavioral interventions reduce HIV-related sexual risk behavior. Retrieved January 9, 2003, from www.nih.gov/news/pr/jun98/nimh-18.htm

National Institutes of Health. (2000). Press release: NIH announces new international network to study HIV prevention strategies. Retrieved June 2, 2002, from www1.od.nih.gov/ormh/press_rel/intl_aids_network.html

National Victim Center, Crime Victims Research and Treatment Center. (1992, April 23). *Rape in America: A report to the nation.* Arlington, VA: Author.

National Women's Health Information Center. (1998). Retrieved October 27, 1999, from www.4woman.org/faq/syphilis

Nayir, A. (2001). Circumcision for the prevention of significant bacteriuria in boys. *Pediatric Nephrology, 16*(12), 1129–1134.

Nelson, H. D. (2002). Assessing benefits and harms of hormone replacement therapy: Clinical applications. *Journal of the American Medical Association, 288*(7), 882–884.

Nelson, J. (1980). Gayness and homosexuality: Issues for the church. In E. Batchelor, Jr. (Ed.), *Homosexuality and ethics.* New York: Pilgrim Press.

Neugebauer, R., Kline, J., Stein, Z., Shrout, P., & Warburton, D. (1996). Association of stressful life events with spontaneous abortion. *American Journal of Epidemiology, 143,* 588–596.

Newcomer, S., & Udry, J. R. (1987). Parental marital status effects on adolescent sexual behavior. *Journal of Marriage and the Family, 49,* 235–240.

Newton, E. (1972). *Mother Camp: Female impersonators in America.* Englewood Cliffs, NJ: Prentice-Hall.

Nichols, M. (1990). Lesbian relationships: Implications for the study of sexuality and gender. In D. P. McWhirter, S. A., Sanders, & J. M. Reinisch (Eds.), *Homosexuality/heterosexuality: Concepts of sexual orientation* (pp. 350–364). Oxford: Oxford University Press.

Nichols, M. (1995). Sexual desire disorder in a lesbian-feminist couple: The intersection of therapy and politics. In R. C. Rosen & S. R. Leiblum (Eds.), *Case studies in sex therapy* (pp. 161–175). New York: Guilford.

Nieva, V. F., & Gutek, B. A. (1981). *Women and work: A psychological perspective.* New York: Praeger.

Nixon, E. (1965). *Royal spy: The strange case of the Chevalier D'Eon.* New York: Reynal & Co.

Nordland, R., Bartholet, J., Johnson, S., Hosenball, M., Nadeau, B., Dickey, C., & Stone, B. (2001, March 19). The Web's dark secret. *Newsweek, 12,* 44–52.

Norris, J., Nurius, P. S., & Dimeff, L. A. (1996). Through her eyes: Factors affecting women's perception of and resistance to acquaintance sexual aggression threat. *Psychology of Women Quarterly, 20,* 123–145.

Nottelmann, E. D., Inoff-Germain, G., Susman, E. J., & Chrousos, G. P. (1990). Hormones and behavior at puberty. In J. Bancroft & J. M. Reinisch (Eds.), *Adolescence and puberty* (pp. 88–123). New York: Oxford University.

Nurnberg, H. G., Gelenberg, A., Hargreave, T. B., Harrison, W. M., Siegel, R. L., & Smith, M. D. (2001). Efficacy of sildenafil citrate for the treatment of erectile dysfunction in men taking serotonin reuptake inhibitors. *American Journal of Psychiatry, 158*(11), 1926–1928.

Nurnberg, H. G., Hensley, P. L., Lauriello, J., Parker, L. M., & Keith, S. J. (1999). Sildenafil for women patients with antidepressant-induced sexual dysfunction. *Psychiatric Services, 50,* 1076–1078.

Nusbaum, M., & Schwarz, R. (2000). Men and infertility. Retrieved September 24, 2002, from www.acig.com.from_home/acog_districts/dist_notice.cfm?recno=1&bulletin=702

Nye, R. A. (1999). Sex and sexuality in France since 1800. In F. X. Eder, L. Hall, & G. Hekma (Eds.). *Sexual cultures in Europe: National histories* (pp. 91–113). New York: Manchester University Press.

O'Brien, M. J. (1991). Taking sibling incest seriously. In M. Q. Patton (Ed.), *Family sexual abuse: Frontline research and evaluation* (pp. 75–92). Newbury Park, CA: Sage.

O'Carroll, R., & Bancroft, J. (1984). Testosterone therapy for low sexual interest and erectile dysfunction in men: A controlled study. *British Journal of Psychiatry, 145,* 146–151.

Ochs, E. P., & Binik, Y. M. (1999). The use of couple data to determine the reliability of self-reported sexual behavior. *Journal of Sex Research, 36,* 374–384.

O'Donohue, W., & Geer, J. H. (1993). Research issues in the sexual dysfunctions. In W. O'Donohue & J. H. Geer (Eds.), *Handbook of sexual dysfunctions: Assessment and treatment* (pp. 1–14). Boston: Allyn & Bacon.

O'Donohue, W., Letourneau, E., & Geer, J. H. (1993). Premature ejaculation. In W. O'Donohue & J. H. Geer (Eds.), *Handbook of sexual dysfunctions: Assessment and treatment* (pp. 303–333). Boston: Allyn & Bacon.

Ogden, G. (1999). *Women who love sex: An inquiry into the expanding spirit of women's erotic experience.* Cambridge, MA: Womanspirit Press.

O'Grady, R. (2001). Eradicating pedophilia: Toward the humanization of society. *Journal of International Affairs, 55,* 123–141.

Ogundipe-Leslie, M. (1984). Nigeria: Not spinning on the axis of maleness. In R. Morgan (Ed.), *Sisterhood is global.* New York: Anchor.

O'Hanlan, K. (1995, June 27). In the family way: Insemination 101. *The Advocate,* 49–50.

O'Hanlon, K. A., & Crum, C. P. (1996). Human papillomarvirus-associated cervical intraepithelial neoplasia following lesbian sex. *Obstetrics and Gynecology, 88,* 702–703.

Okami, P. (1995). Childhood exposure to nudity, parent–child co-sleeping, and "primal scenes": A review of clinical opinion and empirical evidence. *Journal of Sex Research, 32,* 51–64.

Okami, P., & Goldberg, A. (1992). Personality correlates of pedophilia: Are they reliable indicators? *Journal of Sex Research, 29,* 297–328.

Oliver, C. (1995, April). Freak parade. *Reason, 26,* 52–55.

Oliver, M. B., & Hyde, J. S. (1993). Gender differences in sexuality: A meta-analysis. *Psychological Bulletin, 114,* 25–51.

Olsen, J. A., Weed, S. E., Ritz, G. M., & Jensen, L. C. (1991). The effect of three abstinence-based sex education programs on student attitudes toward sexual activity. *Adolescence, 26,* 631–641.

Olsen, O. (1997). Meta-analysis of the safety of home birth. *Birth, 24,* 4–13.

Olson, S. H., Mignone, L., Nakraseive, C., Caputo, T. A., Barakat, R. R., & Harlap, S. (2001). Symptoms of ovarian cancer. *Obstetrics & Gynecology, 98*(2), 212–217.

Oncale v. Sundowner Offshores Services, Inc., 523 U.S. 75 (1998).

O'Neil, J. M. (1990) Assessing men's gender role conflict. In D. Moore & F. Leafgren (Eds.), *Problem solving strategies and interventions for men in conflict* (pp. 23–38). Alexandria, VA: American Counseling Association.

O'Neil, J. M., Helms, B., Gable, R., David, L., & Wrightsman, L. (1986). Gender Role Conflict Scale: College men's fear of femininity. *Sex Roles, 14,* 335–350.

Oosterhuis, H. (1999). The Netherlands: Neither prudish nor hedonistic. In F. X. Eder, L. Hall, & G. Hekma (Eds.). *Sexual cultures in Europe: National histories* (pp. 71–90). New York: Manchester University Press.

Oppenheim, M. (1994). *The man's health book.* Englewood Cliffs, NJ: Prentice-Hall.

Orbuch, T. L., & Harvey, J. H. (1991). Methodological and conceptual issues in the study of sexuality in close relationships. In K. McKinney & S. Sprecher (Eds.), *Sexuality in close relationships* (pp. 9–24). Hillsdale, NJ: Erlbaum.

Ornoy, A., & Arnon, J. (1993). Clinical teratology. *Fetal Medicine, 159,* 382–390.

Osborn, C. A., & Pollack, R. H. (1977). The effects of two types of erotic literature on physiological and verbal measures of female sexual arousal. *Journal of Sex Research, 13*(4), 250–256.

Ossana, S. M., Helms, J. E., & Leonard, M. M. (1992). Do "womanist" identity attitudes influence college women's self-esteem and perceptions of environmental bias? *Journal of Counseling and Development, 70,* 402–408.

Oster, H. (1999). Rubella vaccination while pregnant. Retrieved December 15, 1999, from www.allhealth.com/womens/pregnancy/ga/0,4801,1885-128082,00.html

O'Sullivan, K. (1979). Observation of vaginismus in Irish women. *Archives of General Psychiatry, 36,* 824–826.

O'Sullivan, L. F. (1995). Less is more: The effects of sexual experience on judgments of men's and women's personality characteristics and relationship desirability. *Sex Roles: A Journal of Research, 33,* 159–181.

O'Sullivan, L. F., & Allgeier, E. R. (1998). Feigning sexual desire: Consenting to unwanted sexual activity in heterosexual dating relationships. *Journal of Sex Research, 35,* 234–244.

O'Sullivan, L. F., & Byers, E. S. (1992). College students' incorporation of initiator and restrictor roles in sexual dating interactions. *Journal of Sex Research, 29,* 435–447.

O'Sullivan, L. F., & Byers, E. S. (1993). Eroding stereotypes: College women's attempts to influence reluctant male sexual partners. *Journal of Sex Research, 30,* 270–283.

O'Sullivan, L. F., & Gaines, M. E. (1998). Decision-making in college students' heterosexual dating relationships: Ambivalence about engaging in sexual activity. *Journal of Social and Personal Relationships, 15,* 347–363.

O'Sullivan, L. F., Meyer-Bahlburg, H. F. L., & Watkins, B. X. (2001). Mother-daughter communication about sex among urban African American and Latino families. *Journal of Adolescent Research, 16,* 269–293.

Overholser, J. C., & Beck, S. (1986). Multimethod assessment of rapists, child molesters, and three control groups on behavioral and psychological measures. *Journal of Consulting and Clinical Psychology, 54,* 682–687.

Oxygen Media. (2002). The Oprah Winfrey show: Sylvia Ann Hewlett. Retrieved September 24, 2002, from www.oprah.com/tows/pastshows/tows_2002/tows_past_20020501_b.jhtml

Padero, M. C., Bhasin, S., & Friedman, T. C. (2002). Androgen supplementation in older women: Too much hype, not enough data. *Journal of the American Geriatric Society, 50*(6), 1131–1140.

Painter, K. (1996, April 24). Female sterilization not a sure bet. *USA Today,* pp. 1A, 6D.

Painter, K., & Farrington, D. P. (1998). Marital violence in Great Britain and its relationship to marital and non-marital rape. *International Journal of Victimology, 5,* 257–276.

Palace, E. M. (1995). A cognitive-physiological process model of sexual arousal and response. *Clinical Psychology: Science and Practice, 2,* 370–384.

Palella, Jr., F. J., Delaney, K. M., & Moorman, A. C. (1998). Declining morbidity and mortality among patients with advanced human immunodeficiency virus infection. *New England Journal of Medicine, 338,* 853–861.

Palermo, G. D., Cohen, J., Alikani, M., Adler, A., & Rosenwaks, Z. (1995). Intracytoplasmic sperm injection: A novel treatment for all forms of male factor infertility. *Fertility and Sterility, 63,* 1231–1240.

Palosaari, U. K., & Aroo, H. M. (1995). Parental divorce, self-esteem and depression: An intimate relationship as a protective factor in young adulthood. *Journal of Affective Disorders, 35,* 91–96.

Panchaud, C., Singh, S., Feivelson, D., & Darroch, J. E. (2000). Sexually transmitted diseases among adolescents in developed countries. *Family Planning Perspectives, 32*(1), 24–32, 45.

Parker, H. N. (1997). The teratogenic grid. In J. P. Hallett & M. B. Skinner (Eds.), *Roman sexualities* (pp. 47–65). Princeton, NJ: Princeton University.

Parker, R. G., Herdt, G., & Caballo, M. (1991). Sexual culture, HIV transmission, and AIDS research. *Journal of Sex Research, 28,* 77–99.

Parks, K. A., & Miller, B. A. (1997). Bar victimization of women. *Psychology of Women Quarterly, 21,* 509–525.

Parrinder, G. (1987). A theological approach. In J. H. Geer & W. T. O'Donohue (Eds.), *Theories of human sexuality* (pp. 21–48). New York: Plenum.

Parrot, A. (1991). Institutionalized response: How can acquaintance rape be prevented? In A. Parrot & L. Bechhofer (Eds.), *Acquaintance rape: The hidden crime* (pp. 355–367). New York: Wiley.

Parrot, A., & Bechhofer, L. (Eds.) (1991). *Acquaintance rape: The hidden crime.* New York: Wiley.

Parry, B. L. (2001). The role of central serotonergic dysfunction in the aetiology of premenstrual dysphoric disorder: Therapeutic implications. *CNS Drugs, 15*(4), 277–285.

Partsch, C. J., & Sippell, W. G. (2001). Pathogenesis and epidemiology of precocious puberty. Effects of exogenous oestrogens. *Human Reproduction Update, 7*(3), 292–302.

Pastore, L. M., & Savitz, D. A. (1995). Care-control study of caffeinated beverages and preterm delivery. *American Journal of Epidemiology, 141*(1), 61–69.

Pastore, M. (2001). Search engines, browsers still confusing many Web users. *CyberAtlas.* Retrieved January 17, 2003, from http://cyberatlas.internet.com/big_picture/applications/article/0,,1301_588851,00.html

Patterson, C. J. (1995). Lesbian mothers, gay fathers, and their children. In A. R. D'Augelli & C. J. Patterson (Eds.), *Lesbian, gay, and bisexual identities over the lifespan: Psychological perspectives* (pp. 262–290). New York: Oxford.

Patterson, G. R. (1974). A basis for identifying stimuli which control behavior in natural settings. *Child Development, 45,* 900–911.

Patton, W., & Mannison, M. (1995). Sexual coercion in high school dating. *Sex Roles: A Journal of Research, 33,* 447–466.

Paul, E. L., McManus, B., & Hayes, A. (2000). "Hookups": Characteristics and correlates of college students' spontaneous and anonymous sexual experiences. *Journal of Sex Research, 37,* 76–89.

Peck, D. L. (1993). The fifty percent divorce rate: Deconstructing a myth. *Journal of Sociology and Social Welfare, 20*(3), 135–144.

Peck, M. S. (1978). *The road less traveled.* New York: Simon & Schuster.

Peckham, M. (1969). *Art and pornography: An experiment in explanation.* New York: Basic Books.

Pedersen, B., Tiefer, L., Ruiz, M., & Melman, A. (1988). Evaluation of patients and partners 1 to 4 years after penile prosthesis surgery. *Journal of Urology, 139,* 956–958.

Peirol, P. (1997, May). Minority homosexuals invisible in their world: Gay men and women in Canada's ethnic communities feel surrounded by homophobia, marginalized by gay culture. Retrieved October 29, 1999, from www.fc.net/~zarathus/abroad/chinese_minority_homosexuals_feel_invisible_to_their _world.tx

Peplau, L. A. (1982). Research on homosexual couples: An overview. *Journal of Homosexuality, 8,* 3–8.

Peplau, L. A., & Amaro, H. (1982). Understanding lesbian relationships. In W. Paul & J. D. Weinrich (Eds.), *Homosexuality as a social issue.* Beverly Hills, CA: Sage.

Peplau, L. A., & Gordon, S. L. (1983). Women and men in love: Sex differences in close heterosexual relationships. In V. E. O'Leary, R. K. Unger, & B. S. Wallston (Eds.), *Women, gender and social psychology.* Hillsdale, NJ: Erlbaum.

Perachio, A. A., Marr, L. D., & Alexander, M. (1979). Sexual behavior in male rhesus monkeys elicited by electrical stimulation of preoptic and hypothalamic areas. *Brain Research, 177,* 127–144.

Perkins, C. A. (1997, July). Age patterns of victims of serious violent crime. *Bureau of Justice Statistics: Special Report.* Washington, DC: U.S. Department of Justice, Office of Justice Programs.

Perse, E. M., & Rubin, A. M. (1990). Chronic loneliness and television use. *Journal of Broadcasting and Electronic Media, 34,* 37–54.

Person, E. S. (1980). Sexuality as the mainstay of identity: Psychoanalytic perspectives. *Signs, 5,* 605–630.

Person, E. S. (1987). A psychoanalytical approach. In J. H. Geer & W. T. O'Donohue (Eds.), *Theories of human sexuality* (pp. 385–410). New York: Plenum.

Person, E. S., Terestman, N., Myers, W. A., Goldberg, E. L., & Salvadori, C. (1989). Gender differences in sexual behaviors and fantasies in a college population. *Journal of Sex and Marital Therapy, 15*(3), 187–198.

Petersen, A. (1985). Pubertal development as a cause of disturbance: Myths, realities, and unanswered questions. *Genetic, Social, and General Psychology Monographs, 111,* 205–232.

Peterson, J., & Marin, G. (1988). Issues in the prevention of AIDS among Black and Hispanic men. *American Psychologist, 43,* 871–877.

Petrick, W. (1995). The hall of contraception. Retrieved May 14, 1998, from http://desires.com/1.6/Sex/Museum/museum1.html

Phillips, K. A., Flatt, S. J., Morrison, K. R., & Coates, T. J. (1995). Potential use of home HIV testing. *New England Journal of Medicine, 332,* 1308–1310.

Piaget, J. (1952). *The origins of intelligence in children.* New York: International Universities.

Piccinino, L. J., & Mosher, W. D. (1998). Trends in contraceptive use in the United States: 1982–1995. *Family Planning Perspectives, 30,* 4–10, 46.

Pierce, R., & Pierce, L. (1985). Analysis of sexual abuse hotline reports. *Child Abuse and Neglect, 9,* 37–45.

Pillard, R. C., & Bailey, J. M. (1998). Human sexual orientation has a heritable component. *Human Biology, 70,* 347–365.

Pillard, R. C., & Weinrich, J. D. (1986). Evidence for a familial nature of male homosexuality. *Archives of General Psychiatry, 43,* 808–812.

Pimentel, E. E. (2000). Just how much do I love thee? Marital relations in urban China. *Journal of Marriage and the Family, 62,* 32–48.

Pithers, W. D., & Cumming, G. F. (1989). Can relapses be prevented? Initial outcome data from the Vermont Treatment Program for Sexual Aggressors. In D. R. Laws (Ed.), *Relapse prevention with sex offenders.* New York: Guilford.

Pithers, W. D., Kashima, K. M., Cumming, G. F., Beal, L. S., & Buell, M. M. (1988). Relapse prevention of sexual aggression. In R. A. Prentky & V. L. Quinsey (Eds.), *Human sexual aggression: Current perspectives* (pp. 244–260). New York: New York Academy of Sciences.

Planned Parenthood Association of Utah. (1996). Birth control methods. Retrieved May 14, 1998, from www.xmission.com/~ppau/method.html

Planned Parenthood Federation of America, Inc. (1997). Safe surgical abortion before six weeks' gestation available through new technologies. Retrieved May 14, 1998, from www.plannedparenthood.org/Library/abortion/SaveSurg.html

Planned Parenthood Federation of America, Inc. (1998). Legal questions and answers about so-called "partial-birth" abortion bans. Retrieved May 14, 1998, from www.plannedparenthood.org/Library/abortion/LegalQuest.html

Planned Parenthood of Southeastern Pennsylvania. (1996). Planned Parenthood® Interactive: Medical abortion facts. Retrieved June 6, 2000, from www.ppsp.org/methmiso.html

Plant, R. (1986). *The pink triangle: The Nazi war against homosexuality.* New York: H. Holt & Company.

Plouffe, L. (1985). Screening sexual problems through a simple questionnaire. *American Journal of Obstetrics and Gynecology, 151,* 166–169.

Pocs, O., & Godow, A. G. (1977). Can students view parents as sexual beings? *Family Coordinator, 26,* 31–36.

Podgers, J. (1996, April). Trends in the law: Passing marks for sex ed. *American Bar Association Journal,* 44–45.

Polaschek, D. L. L., Ward, T., & Hudson, S. M. (1997). Rape and rapists: Theory and treatment. *Clinical Psychology Review, 17,* 117–144.

Pomeroy, W. B. (1972). *Dr. Kinsey and the Institute for Sex Research.* New York: Harper & Row.

Pomeroy, W. B., Flax, C. C., & Wheeler, C. C. (1982). *Taking a sex history: Interviewing and recording.* New York: Free Press.

Poniewozik, J. (1999, August). Sex on TV is . . . not sexy! *Time,* 86–88.

Poole, M., & Isaacs, D. (1993). The gender agenda in teacher education. *British Journal of Sociology of Education, 14,* 275–284.

Popkin, B. M., Adair, L., Akin, J. S., Black, R., Briscoe, J., & Flieger, W. (1990). Breast-feeding and diarrheal morbidity. *Pediatrics, 86,* 874–882.

Potterat, J. J., Rothenberg, R. B., & Muth, S. Q. (1998). Pathways to prostitution: The chronology of sexual and drug abuse milestones. *Journal of Sex Research, 35, 333–341*

Powell, B. B. (1998). *Classical myth* (2nd. ed.). Upper Saddle River, NJ: Prentice Hall.

Powell, E. (1991). *Talking back to sexual pressure.* Minneapolis: CompCare Publishers.

Prince, V., & Bentler, P. M. (1972). Survey of 504 cases of transvestism. *Psychological Reports, 31,* 903–917.

Proto-Campise, L., Belknap, J., & Wooldredge, J. (1998). High school students' adherence to rape myths and the effectiveness of high school rape-awareness programs. *Violence Against Women, 4,* 308–328.

Pruthi, S. (2001). Amenorrhea: When menstruation goes away. Retrieved July 3, 2002, from http://www.mayoclinic.com/invoke.cfm?id=HQ00224

Purnine, D. M., & Carey, M. P. (1997). Interpersonal communication and sexual adjustment: The role of understanding and agreement. *Journal of Consulting and Clinical Psychology, 65,* 1017–1025.

Quadland, M. C. (1985). Compulsive sexual behavior: Definition of a problem and an approach to treatment. *Journal of Sex and Marital Therapy, 11,* 121–132.

Quinsey, V. L., Chaplin, T. C., & Carrigan, W. F. (1979). Sexual preferences among incestuous and nonincestuous child molesters. *Behavior Therapy, 10,* 562–565.

Quinsey, V. L., Chaplin, T. C., & Upfold, D. (1984). Sexual arousal to nonsexual violence and sadomasochistic themes among rapists and non-sex offenders. *Journal of Consulting and Clinical Psychology, 52,* 651–657.

Quintero, R. A., Puder, K. S., & Cotton, D. B. (1993). Embryoscopy and fetoscopy. *Obstetrics and Gynecology Clinics of North America, 20,* 563–581.

Rabkin, J. G., & Harrison, W. M. (1990). Effect of imipramine on depression and immune status in a sample of men with HIV infection. *American Journal of Psychiatry, 147,* 495–497.

Rado, S. (1940). A critical examination of the concept of bisexuality. *Psychosomatic Medicine, 2,* 459–467.

Rajamanoharan, S., Low, N., Jones, S. B., & Pozniak, A. L. (1999). Bacterial vaginosis, ethnicity, and the use of genital cleaning agents: A case control study. *Sexually Transmitted Diseases, 26,* 404–409.

Randall, R. S. (1989). *Freedom and taboo: Pornography and the politics of self divided.* Berkeley: The University of California Press.

Randolph, A. G., Hartshorn, R. M., & Washington, A. E. (1996). Acyclovir prophylaxis in late pregnancy to prevent neonatal herpes. A cost-effective analysis. *Obstetrics and Gynecology, 88,* 603–610.

Ranke-Heinemann, U. (2002). Female blood. Retrieved from http://www.womanpriest.org/body/ranke.htm

Rankow, E. J., & Tessaro, I. (1998). Cervical cancer risk and Papanicolaou screening in a sample of lesbian and bisexual women. *Journal of Family Practice, 47,* 139–143.

Rapaport, K., & Burkhart, B. R. (1984). Personality and attitudinal characteristics of sexually coercive college males. *Journal of Abnormal Psychology, 93,* 216–221.

Raspberry, W. (2001, July 27). What's love got to do with it? *The Washington Post,* p. A31.

Ravart, M., Trudel, G., Marchand, A., Turgeon, L., & Aubin, S. (1996). The efficacy of a cognitive behavioural treatment model for hypoactive sexual desire disorder: An outcome study. *Canadian Journal of Human Sexuality, 5,* 279–293.

Reamy, K. J., & White, S. E. (1987). Sexuality in the puerperium: A review. *Archives of Sexual Behavior, 16,* 165–186.

Rechy, R. (1963). *City of night.* New York: Grove Press.

Redbook. (1999). 5,000 married men confess what keeps sex [with you] hot. Retrieved November 17, 1999, from http://redbook.women.com/rb/marriage/features/89conf13.htm

Redmon, J. B., Carey, P., & Pryor, J. L. (2002). Varicocele—the most common cause of male factor infertility? *Human Reproduction Update, 8*(1), 53–58.

Redmond, G. P. (1999). Hormones and sexual function. *International Journal of Fertility and Women's Medicine, 44*(4), 193–197.

Reece, E. A. (1999). First trimester prenatal diagnosis: Embryoscopy and fetoscopy. *Seminars in Perinatology, 23*(5), 424–433.

Reece, R. (1987). Causes and treatments of sexual desire discrepancies in male couples. *Journal of Homosexuality, 14,* 157–172.

Reece, R. (1988). Special issues in the etiologies and treatments of sexual problems among gay men. *Journal of Homosexuality, 15,* 43–57.

Regan, P. C. (1996). Rhythms of desire: The association between menstrual cycle phases and female sexual desire. *Canadian Journal of Human Sexuality, 5*(3), 145–156.

Regan, P. C. (1997). The impact of male sexual request style on perceptions of sexual interactions: The mediational role of beliefs about female sexual desire. *Basic & Applied Social Psychology, 19,* 519–532.

Regan, P. C. (2000). Love relationships. In L. T. Szuchman & F. Muscarella (Eds.), *Psychological perspectives on human sexuality* (pp. 232–282). New York: John Wiley & Sons, Inc.

Regan, P. C., Kogan, E. R., & Whitlock, T. (1998). Ain't love grand! A prototype analysis of the concept of romantic love. *Journal of Social and Personal Relationships, 15,* 411–420.

Regenstein, Q. R., & Reich, P. (1978). Pedophilia occurring after onset of cognitive impairment. *Journal of Nervous and Mental Disease, 166,* 794–798.

Reibstein, J., & Richards, M. (1993). *Sexual arrangements.* New York: Scribner's.

Reichert, T., Lambiase, J., Morgan, S., Carstarphen, M., & Zavoina, S. (1999). Beefcake or cheesecake? No matter how you slice it, sexual explicitness in advertising continues to increase. *Journalism & Mass Communication Quarterly, 76,* 7–20.

Reid, R., & Lininger, T. (1993). Sexual pain disorders in the female. In W. O'Donohue & J. H. Geer (Eds.), *Handbook of sexual dysfunctions: Assessment and treatment* (pp. 335–366). Boston: Allyn & Bacon.

Reinisch, J. M. (1990). *The Kinsey Institute new report on sex: What you must know to be sexually literate.* New York: St. Martin's.

Reinisch, J. M., & Beasley, R. (1990). *The Kinsey Institute new report on sex: What you must know to be sexually literate.* New York: St. Martin's.

Reis, B., & Saewyc, E. (1999). Eighty-three thousand youth: Selected findings of eight population-based studies as they pertain to anti-gay harassment and the safety and well-being of sexual minority students. Retrieved November 11, 2002, from www.safeschools-wa.org

Reisman, J. A., & Eichel, E. W. (1990). *Kinsey, sex and fraud: The indoctrination of a people.* Lafayette, LA: Lochinvar-Huntington House.

Reiss, I. L. (1964). The scaling of premarital sexual permissiveness. *Journal of Marriage and the Family, 26,* 188–198.

Reiss, I. L. (1967). *The social context of premarital sexual permissiveness.* New York: Holt, Rinehart & Winston.

Reiss, I. L. (1986). *Journey into sexuality: An exploratory voyage.* Englewood Cliffs, NJ: Prentice Hall.

Reiss, I. L. (1989). Society and sexuality: A sociological explanation. In K. McKinney & S. Sprecher (Eds.), *Human sexuality: The societal and interpersonal context* (pp. 3–29). Norwood, NJ: Ablex.

Reiss, I. L. (1993). The future of sex research and the meaning of science. *Journal of Sex Research, 30,* 3–11.

Reiss, I. L. (1995). Is this the definitive sexual survey? [Review of *The social organization of sexuality: Sexual practices in the United States*]. *Journal of Sex Research, 32,* 77–85.

Reiss, I. L., & Lee, G. R. (1988). *Family systems in America* (4th ed.). New York: Holt, Rinehart, and Winston.

Reiss, I. L., & Leik, R. K. (1989). Evaluating strategies to avoid AIDS: Number of partners vs. use of condoms. *Journal of Sex Research, 26,* 411–433.

Remez, L. (2000). Oral sex among adolescents: Is it sex or is it abstinence? *Family Planning Perspectives, 32,* 298–305.

Renaud, C. A., & Byers, E. S. (1999). Exploring the frequency, diversity and content of university students' positive and negative sexual cognitions. *Canadian Journal of Human Sexuality, 8,* 17–30.

Rennison, C. M. (2002). *Rape and sexual assault: Reporting to police and medical attention, 1992–2000.* Washington, DC: U.S. Department of Justice.

Renshaw, D. C. (1988). Profile of 2,376 treated at Loyola Sex Clinic between 1972 and 1987. *Sexual and Marital Therapy, 3,* 111–117.

Resick, P. A., & Schnicke, M. K. (1992). Cognitive processing therapy for sexual assault victims. *Journal of Consulting and Clinical Psychology, 60,* 748–756.

Resnik, H. L. P. (1972). Eroticized repeated hanging: A form of self-destructive behavior. *American Journal of Psychotherapy, 26,* 4–21.

Reuters. (1999). Viagra works for women, too. Good results from small controlled study. Retrieved April 20, 2000, from http://archive.abcnews.go.com/sections/living/DailyNews/Viagrawomen_OSO499.html

Richards, K. (1997). What is a transgenderist? In B. Bullough, V. L. Bullough, & J. Elias (Eds.), *Gender blending* (pp. 503–504). Amherst, NY: Prometheus Books.

Richards, M. H., & Larson, R. (1993). Pubertal development in the daily subjective states of young adolescents. *Journal of Research on Adolescence, 3,* 145–169.

Rigby, W. (2002). New treatment reduces women's cycles to 4 a year. Retrieved July 3, 2002, from http://news.mysanantonio.com/story.cfm?xla=kens5&xlb=200&xlc=623898&xld=200

Riger, S. (1991). Gender dilemmas in sexual harassment policies and procedures. *American Psychologist, 46,* 497–505.

Riley, P. (1994). *The X-rated videotape star index 1994.* Buffalo, NY: Prometheus.

Rind, B., & Tromovitch, P. (1997). A meta-analytic review of findings from national samples on psychological correlates of child sexual abuse. *Journal of Sex Research, 34,* 337–355.

Rinehart, N.J., & McCabe, M. C. (1997). Hypersexuality: Psychopathology or normal variant of sexuality? *Sexual and Marital Therapy, 12,* 45–60.

Roan, S. (2002, August 13). Norplant contraceptive off the market. *Post-Gazette.com: Health & Science.* Retrieved October 9, 2002, from www.Pittsburghpost-gazette.com/healthscience/20020813hnorplant4.asp

Roberts, D. F., Foehr, U. G., Rideout, V. J., & Brodie, M. (1999). *Kids and media at the new millennium: A comprehensive national analysis of children's media use.* Menlo Park, CA: Henry J. Kaiser Family Foundation.

Roberts, T. A., Goldenberg, J. L., Power, C., & Pyszczynski, T. (2002). "Feminine protection": The effects of menstruation on attitudes toward women. *Psychology of Women Quarterly, 26*(2), 131–139.

Roberts, Y. (2000). Let's think of sex as the Dutch do. *New Statesman, 129,* 16.

Robinson, B., Walters, L., & Skeen, P. (1989). Response of parents to learning that their child is homosexual and concern over AIDS: A national study. In F. Bozett (Ed.), *Homosexuality and the family* (pp. 59–80). New York: Harrington Park Press.

Robinson, B. W., & Mishkin, M. (1966). Ejaculation evoked by stimulation of the preoptic area in monkeys. *Physiology and Behavior, 1,* 269–272.

Robinson, I., Zeiss, K., Ganja, B., Katz, S., & Robinson, E. (1991). Twenty years of the sexual revolution, 1965–1985: An update. *Journal of Marriage and the Family, 53,* 216–221.

Robson, W. L. M., & Leung, A. K. C. (1992). The circumcision question. *Postgraduate Medicine, 91,* 237–244.

Rochman, B., Tippit, S., & Peterzell, J. (1994, August 15). Apologists for murder: The FBI launches a probe of abortion-clinic violence, shining a spotlight on extremists who defend homicide. *Time,* p. 39.

Rodgers, K. B. (1999). Parenting processes related to sexual risk-taking behaviors of adolescent males and females. *Journal of Marriage and the Family, 61,* 99–109.

Rodriguez, I., Greer, C. A., Mok, M. Y., & Mombaerts, P. (2000). A putative pheromone receptor gene expressed in human olfactory mucosa. *Natural Genetics, 26*(1), 18–19.

Rogers, C. (1951). *Client-centered therapy: Its current practice, implications, and theory.* Boston: Houghton Mifflin.

Roheim, G. (1933). Women and their life in Central Australia. *Journal of the Royal Anthropological Institute of Great Britain and Ireland, 63,* 207–265.

Rokach, A. (1990). Content analysis of sexual fantasies of males and females. *The Journal of Psychology, 124*(4), 427–436.

Rolfs, R. T., Goldberg, M., & Sharrar, R. G. (1990). Risk factors for syphilis: Cocaine use and prostitution. *American Journal of Public Health, 80,* 853–857.

Romans, S. E., Martin, J. L., Anderson, J. C., O'Shea, M. L., & Mullen, P. E. (1996). The "anatomy" of female child sexual abuse: Who does what to young girls? *Australian & New Zealand Journal of Psychiatry, 30,* 319–325.

Rooney, B. L., Thompson, J. E., Schauberger, C. W., & Pearse, C. A. (1996). Is twelve-percent cesarean section rate at a perinatal center safe? *Journal of Perinatology, 16,* 215–219.

Roosa, M. W., Reyes, L., Reinholtz, C., & Angelini, P. J. (1998). Measurement of women's child sexual abuse experiences: An empirical demonstration of the impact of choice of measure on estimates of incidence rates and of relationships with pathology. *Journal of Sex Research, 35,* 225–233.

Rooth, G. (1972). Changes in the conviction rate for indecent exposure. *British Journal of Psychiatry, 121,* 89–94.

Rooth, G. (1973a). Exhibitionism outside Europe and America. *Archives of Sexual Behavior, 2,* 351–362.

Rooth, G. (1973b). Exhibitionism: Sexual violence and pedophilia. *British Journal of Psychiatry, 122,* 705–710.

Rosen, R. C. (1991). Alcohol and drug effects on sexual responses: Human experimental and clinical studies. *Annual Review of Sex Research, 2,* 119–179.

Rosen, R. C. (1995). A case of premature ejaculation: Too little, too late? In R. C. Rosen & S. R. Leiblum (Eds.), *Case studies in sex therapy* (pp. 279–294). New York: Guilford.

Rosen, R. C., & Ashton, A. K. (1993). Prosexual drugs: Empirical status of the "new aphrodisiacs." *Archives of Sexual Behavior, 22,* 521–543.

Rosen, R. C., & Beck, J. G. (1988). *Patterns of sexual arousal: Psychophysiological processes and clinical applications.* New York: Guilford.

Rosen, R. C., & Leiblum, S. R. (1988). *A sexual scripting approach to problems of desire.* New York: Guilford.

Rosen, R. C., & Leiblum, S. R. (Eds.). (1995a). *Case studies in sex therapy.* New York: Guilford.

Rosen, R. C., & Leiblum, S. R. (1995b). Treatment of sexual disorders in the 1990s: An integrated approach. *Journal of Consulting and Clinical Psychology, 63,* 877–890.

Rosen, R. C., Leiblum, S. R., & Spector, I. (1994). Psychologically based treatment for male erectile disorder: A cognitive-interpersonal model. *Journal of Sex and Marital Therapy, 20,* 67–85.

Rosenberg, P. S., & Biggar, R. J. (1998). Trends in HIV incidence among young adults in the United States. *Journal of the American Medical Association, 279,* 1894–1900.

Rosenthal, D. A., Smith, A. M. A., & de Visser, R. (1999). Personal and social factors influencing age at first sexual intercourse. *Archives of Sexual Behavior, 28*(4), 319–334.

Ross, L. R., & Spinner, B. (2001). General and specific attachment representations in adulthood: Is there a relationship? *Journal of Social and Personal Relationships, 18,* 747–766.

Ross, M. W. (1991). A taxonomy of global behavior. In R. A. P. Tielman, M. Carballo, & A. C. Hendricks (Eds.), *Bisexuality and HIV/AIDS: A global perspective* (pp. 21–26). Buffalo, NY: Prometheus Books.

Ross, M. W., & Need, J. A. (1989). Effects of adequacy of gender reassignment surgery on psychological adjustment: A follow-up of fourteen male-to-female patients. *Archives of Sexual Behavior, 18,* 145–153.

Rosser, B. R. S., Short, B. J., Thurmes, P. J., & Coleman, E. (1998). Anodyspareunia, the unacknowledged sexual dysfunction: A validation study of painful receptive anal intercourse and its psychosexual concomitants in homosexual men. *Journal of Sex and Marital Therapy, 24,* 281–292.

Rothberg, A. R. (1987). An introduction to the study of women, aging, and sexuality. *Physical and Occupational Therapy in Geriatrics, 5,* 3–12.

Rotheram-Borus, M. J., Meyer-Bahlburg, H. F. L., Koopman, C., Rosario, M., Exner, T. M., Henderson, R., Matthieu, M., & Gruen, R. S. (1992). Lifetime sexual behaviors among runaway males and females. *Journal of Sex Research, 29,* 15–29.

Rotheram-Borus, M. J., Rosario, M., Meyer-Bahlburg, H. F. L., Koopman, C., Dopkins, S. C., & Davies, M. (1994). Sexual and substance use acts of gay and bisexual male adolescents in New York City. *Journal of Sex Research, 31,* 47–58.

Rothschild, A. J. (2000). Sexual side effects of antidepressants. *Journal of Clinical Psychiatry, 61*(Supplement 11), 28–36.

Rousar, E. (1990). *Valuing's role in romantic love.* Unpublished doctoral dissertation, Pacific Graduate School of Psychology, Palo Alto, CA.

Rowland, D. L. (1995). The psychobiology of sexual arousal and behavior. In L. Diamant & R. D. McAnulty (Eds.), *The psychology of sexual orientation, behavior, and identity: A handbook* (pp. 19–42). Westport, CT: Greenwood.

Rowland, D. L. (1999). Issues in the laboratory study of human sexual response: A synthesis for the nontechnical sexologist. *Journal of Sex Research, 36,* 3–15.

Rowland, D. L., Greenleaf, W. J., Dorfman, L. J., & Davidson, J. M. (1993). Aging and sexual function in men. *Archives of Sexual Behavior, 22,* 545–557.

Rowland, D. L., & Slob, A. K. (1992). Vibrotactile stimulation enhances sexual response in sexually functional men: A study using concomitant measures of erection. *Archives of Sexual Behavior, 21,* 387–400.

Royal Society of Chemistry. (1997). Elixirs of love. Retrieved April 23, 2000, from http://www.chemsoc.org/chembytes/ezine/1997/lurv.htm

Rozee, P. D., & Koss, M. P. (2001). Rape: A century of resistance. *Psychology of Women Quarterly, 25,* 295–311.

Rubin, A. M., & Adams, J. R. (1986). Outcomes of sexually open marriages. *Journal of Sex Research, 22,* 311–319.

Runzo, J., & Martin, N. M. (Eds.). (2000). *Love, sex, and gender in the world religions.* Oxford, England: Oneworld Press.

Russell, D. E. H. (1982). *Rape in marriage.* New York: Macmillan.

Russell, D. E. H. (1983). The incidence and prevalence of intrafamilial and extrafamilial sexual abuse of female children. *Child Abuse and Neglect, 7,* 133–146.

Russell, D. W. (1996). UCLA Loneliness Scale (Version 3): Reliability, validity, and factor structure. *Journal of Personality Assessment, 66,* 20–40.

Russell, K. (2001). Netherlands becomes first nation to allow same-sex marriages. *Lesbian News, 26,* 16.

Saarinen, U. M., & Kajosaari, M. (1995). Breastfeeding as prophylaxis against atopic disease: Prospective follow-up study until 17 years old. *The Lancet, 346,* 1065–1069.

Sadker, M., & Sadker, D. (1994). *Failing at fairness: How America's schools cheat girls.* New York: Charles Scribner's Sons.

Safran, C. (1976, November). What men do to women on the job: A shocking look at sexual harassment. *Redbook,* pp. 148, 149, 217, 218, 220, 222, 224.

Saghir, M. T., & Robins, E. (1969). Homosexuality: Sexual behavior of the female homosexual. *Archives of General Psychiatry, 20,* 192–201.

Saghir, M. T., & Robins, E. (1973). *Male and female homosexuality.* Baltimore: Williams & Wilkins.

St. James, M. (1987). The reclamation of whores. In L. Bell (Ed.), *Good girls/bad girls: Sex trade workers and feminists face to face* (pp. 81–87). Toronto: The Women's Press

St. John, W. (2002, April 21). Young, single, and dating at hyperspeed. *The New York Times,* section 9, p. 1–2.

St. Lawrence, J. S., & Scott, C. P. (1996). Examination of the relationship between African American adolescents' condom use at sexual onset and later sexual behavior: Implications for condom distribution programs. *AIDS Education and Prevention, 8,* 258–266.

Sakheim, D. K., Barlow, D. H., Beck, J. G., & Abrahamson, D. J. (1984). The effect of an increased awareness of erectile cues on sexual arousal. *Behaviour Research and Therapy, 22,* 151–158.

Salmans, S. (1996). *Prostate: Questions you have. . . answers you need.* Allentown, PA: People's Medical Society.

Saluter, A. F., & Lugaila, T. A. (1996). Marital status and living arrangements: March 1996. *Current Population Report, 496, Series P-20.*

Sampson, R. (2002). *Acquaintance rape of college students. Problem-Oriented Guides for Police series, no. 17.* Washington, DC: U.S. Department of Justice.

Sanday, P. R. (1981). The socio-cultural context of rape: A cross-cultural study. *Journal of Social Issues, 37,* 5–27.

Sandelands, L. E. (2001). *Male and female in social life.* New Brunswick, NJ: Transaction.

Sanders, G. (1982). Social comparison as a basis for evaluating others. *Journal of Research in Personality, 16,* 21–31.

Sanders, R. C. (1993). Ultrasonic clues to the detection of chromosomal anomalies. *Obstetrics and Gynecology Clinics of North America, 20,* 455–483.

Sanders, S. A., & Reinisch, J. M. (1999). Would you say you "had sex" if. . . . *Journal of the American Medical Association, 281,* 275–277.

Sandfort, T. G. M., & de Keizer, M. (2001). Sexual problems in gay men: An overview of empirical research. *Annual Review of Sex Research, 12,* 93–120.

Sandman, C. A., Wadhwa, P. D., Chicz-Demet, A., Dunkel-Schetter, C., & Porto, M. (1997). Maternal stress, HPA activity, and fetal/infant outcome. *Annals of the New York Academy of Science, 814,* 266–275.

Sandnabba, N. K., & Ahlberg, C. (1999). Parents' attitudes and expectations about children's cross-gender behavior. *Sex Roles: A Journal of Research, 40*(3–4), 249–263.

Sands, K. M. (2000). *God forbid: Religion and sex in American public life.* Oxford, England: Oxford University.

Santelli, J. S., Lindberg, L. D., Abma, J., McNeely, C. S., & Resnick, M. (2000). Adolescent sexual behavior: Estimates and trends from four nationally representative surveys. *Family Planning Perspectives, 32,* 156–167.

Santelli, J. S., Robin, L., Brener, N. D., & Lowry, R. (2001). Timing of alcohol and other drug use and sexual risk behaviors among unmarried adolescents and young adults. *Family Planning Perspectives, 33*(5), 200–205.

Santtila, P., Sandnabba, N. K., Alison, L., & Nordling, N. (2002). Investigating the underlying structure in sadomasochistically oriented behavior. *Archives of Sexual Behavior, 31,* 185–196.

Sarkis, M. (2001). Female genital cutting: An introduction. FGM Education and Networking Project. Retrieved March 22, 2002, from www.fgmnetwork.org/intro/fgmintro.html

Sarrell, P., & Masters, W. (1982). Sexual molestation of men by women. *Archives of Sexual Behavior, 11,* 117–131.

Sarwer, D. B., & Durlak, J. A. (1997). A field trial of the effectiveness of behavioral treatment for sexual dysfunction. *Journal of Sex and Marital Therapy, 23,* 87–97.

Saunders, B. E., Villeponteaux, L. A., Lipovsky, J. A., Kilpatrick, D. G., & Veronen, L. J. (1992). Child sexual abuse as a risk factor for mental health disorders among women: A community sample. *Journal of Interpersonal Violence, 7,* 189–204.

Saunders, E., Awad, G. A., & White, G. (1986). Male adolescent sex offenders: The offenders and the offense. *Canadian Journal of Psychiatry, 31,* 542–549.

Savic, I., Berglund, H., Gulyas, B., & Roland, P. (2001). Smelling of odorous sex hormone-like compounds causes sex-differentiated hypothalamic activations in humans. *Neuron, 31*(4), 661–668.

Savin-Williams, R. C. (2001). Suicide attempts among sexual-minority youths: Population and measurement issues. *Journal of Consulting and Clinical Psychology, 69,* 983–991.

Scarce, M. (1997). *Male on male rape: The hidden toll of stigma and shame.* New York: Plenum.

Schachter, S. (1964). The interaction of cognitive and physiological determinants of emotional state. In L. Berkowitz (Ed.), *Advances in experimental social psychology (Vol. I).* New York: Academic.

Schacker, T. (2001). The role of HSV in the transmission and progression of HIV. *Herpes, 8*(2), 46–49.

Schaeffer, A., & Nelson, E. (1993). Rape-supportive attitudes: Effects of on-campus residence and education. *Journal of College Student Development, 34,* 175–179.

Scheig, R. (1991, March). The hepatitis viruses: Who's at risk? *Medical Aspects of Human Sexuality,* 23–26.

Schiavi, R. C. (1990a). Chronic alcoholism and male sexual dysfunction. *Journal of Sex and Marital Therapy, 16,* 23–33.

Schiavi, R. C. (1990b). Sexuality and aging in men. *Annual Review of Sex Research, 1,* 227–249.

Schiavi, R. C. (1999). *Aging and male sexuality.* Boston: Cambridge University Press.

Schiavi, R. C., Schreiner-Engel, P., White, D., & Mandeli, J. (1988). Pituitary-gonadal function during sleep in men with hypoactive sexual desire and in normal controls. *Psychosomatic Medicine, 50,* 304–318.

Schiavi, R. C., Schreiner-Engel, P., White, D., & Mandeli, J. (1991). The relationship between pituitary-gonadal function and sexual behavior in healthy aging men. *Psychosomatic Medicine, 53,* 363–374.

Schiavi, R. C., & Segraves, R. T. (1995). The biology of sexual function. *The Psychiatric Clinics of North America, 18,* 7–23.

Schiavi, R. C., White, D., Mandeli, J., & Levine, A. C. (1997). Effect of testosterone administration on sexual behavior and mood in men with erectile dysfunction. *Archives of Sexual Behavior, 26*(3), 231–242.

Schiffman, M. H., & Brinton, L. A. (1995). The epidemiology of cervical carcinogenesis. *Cancer, 76,* 1888–1901.

Schlegel, A. (1995). The cultural management of adolescent sexuality. In P. R. Abramson & S. D. Pinkerton (Eds.), *Sexual nature, sexual culture.* Chicago: University of Chicago.

Schlegel, A., & Barry, H. (1991). *Adolescence: An anthropological inquiry.* New York: Free Press.

Schlosser, E. (1997, February 10). The business of pornography. *U.S. News and World Report,* 42–40.

Schmidt, G., & Sigusch, V. (1970). Sex differences in responses to psychosexual stimulation by films and slides. *Journal of Sex Research, 6,* 268–283.

Schmidt, G., Sigusch, V., & Schafer, S. (1973). Responses to reading erotic stories: Male-female differences. *Archives of Sexual Behavior, 2,* 181–199.

Schmitt, D. P., Shackelford, T. K., & Buss, D. M. (2001). Are men really more "oriented" toward short-term mating than women? A critical review of theory and research. *Psychology, Evolution and Gender, 3,* 211–239.

Schneider, P. (1997). 5 off-limits drugs for pregnant women. *Parents,* p. 50.

Schoub, B. D. (1993). *AIDS and HIV in perspective.* New York: Cambridge University Press.

Schover, L. R., & Jensen, S. B. (1988). *Sexuality and chronic illness: A comprehensive approach.* New York: Guilford Press.

Schreiner-Engel, P., & Schiavi, R. C. (1986). Lifetime psychopathology in individuals with low sexual desire. *Journal of Nervous and Mental Disease, 174,* 646–651.

Schultz, S. (2001, April 2). The pill has company: The patch, the ring, the shot. *U.S. News & World Report Archive.* Retrieved October 7, 2002, from http://www.usnews.com/usnews/issue/archive.htm

Schvaneveldt, P. L. (2001). Academic goals, achievement and age at first intercourse: Longitudinal, bi-directional influences. *Adolescence, 36*(144), 767–787.

Schwartz, I. M. (1999). Sexual activity prior to coital initiation: A comparison between males and females. *Archives of Sexual Behavior, 28*(1), 63–70.

Schwartz, M., & Nogrady, C. (1996). Fraternity membership, rape myths, and sexual aggression on a college campus. *Violence Against Women, 2,* 148–162.

Scott, J. E., & Cuvelier, S. J. (1993). Violence and sexual violence in pornography: Is it really increasing? *Archives of Sexual Behavior, 22,* 357–371.

Scott, S. J., & Mercer, M. A. (1994). Understanding cultural obstacles to HIV/AIDS prevention in Africa. *AIDS Education and Prevention, 6,* 81–89.

Sears, W. (1995). *SIDS: A parent's guide to understanding and preventing sudden infant death syndrome.* Boston: Little, Brown.

Sedlak, A., & Broadhurst, D. (1996). *Executive Summary of the Third National Incidence Study of Child Abuse and Neglect.* Westat, Inc.

Segal, Z. V., & Marshall, W. L. (1985). Heterosocial skills in a population of rapists and child molesters. *Journal of Consulting and Clinical Psychology, 53,* 55–63.

Segal, Z. V., & Stermac, L. E. (1990). The role of cognition in sexual assault. In W. L. Marshall, D. R. Laws, & H. E. Barbaree (Eds.), *Handbook of sexual assault* (pp. 161–174). New York: Plenum.

Segraves, R., Saran, K., Segraves, K., & Maguire, E. (1993). Clomipramine versus placebo in the treatment of premature ejaculation: A pilot study. *Journal of Sex and Marital Therapy, 19,* 198–200.

Segraves, R. T. (2002). Female sexual disorders: Psychiatric aspects. *Journal of Psychiatry, 47,* 419–426.

Segraves, R. T., Croft, H., Kavoussi, R., Ashcer, J. A., Batey, S. R., Foster, V. J., Bolden-Waton, C., & Metz, A. (2001). Bupropion sustained release (SR) for the treatment of hypoactive sexual desire disorder (HSDD) in nondepressed women. *Journal of Sex and Marital Therapy, 27,* 303–316.

Seid, R. P. (1994). Too "close to the bone": The historical context for women's obsession with slenderness. In P. Fallon & M. A. Katzman (Eds.), *Feminist perspectives on eating disorders* (pp. 3–16). New York: The Guilford Press.

Seidman, S. A. (1999). Revisiting sex-role stereotyping in MTV videos. *International Journal of Instructional Media, 26,* 11–23.

Seidman, S. N., & Reider, R. O. (1994). A review of sexual behavior in the United States. *American Journal of Psychiatry, 151,* 330–341.

Semans, J. H. (1956). Premature ejaculation: A new approach. *Southern Medical Journal, 49,* 353–358.

Seoud, M. A., Nassar, A. H., Usta, I. M., Melhem, Z., Kazma, A., & Khalil, A. M. (2002). Impact of advanced maternal age on pregnancy outcome. *American Journal of Perinatology, 19*(1), 1–8.

Seto, M., Maric, A., & Barbaree, H. E. (2001). The role of pornography in the etiology of sexual aggression. *Aggression and Violent Behavior, 6,* 35–53.

Seto, M. C., & Kuban, M. (1996). Criterion-related validity of a phallometric test for paraphilic rape and sadism. *Behavior Research and Therapy, 34,* 175–183.

Sevcik, K. (2001, December). Sex secrets around the world. *Marie Claire, 8*(12), 106–111.

Sevely, J. L. (1987). *Eve's secrets: A new perspective on human sexuality.* London: Bloomsbury.

Sexual Health InfoCenter. (2001). Gonorrhea. Retrieved May 14, 2002, from http://www.sexhealth.org/std/gonorrhea.shtml

Sexuality Information and Education Council of the United States, National Guidelines Task Force. (1991). *Guidelines for comprehensive sexuality education: Kindergarten–12th grade.* New York: Author.

Sexuality Information and Education Council of the United States. (1998). SIECUS looks at states' sexuality laws and the sexual rights of their citizens. *SIECUS Report, 26,* 4–15.

Shaffer, D. (1999). *Developmental psychology: Childhood and adolescence* (5th ed.). Pacific Grove, CA: Brooks/Cole.

Shah, D., & Button, J. C. (1998). The relationship between psychosocial factors and recurrent genital herpes simplex virus. *British Journal of Health Psychology, 3,* 191–213.

Shapiro, B. L. (1997). Date rape. *Journal of Interpersonal Violence, 12.*

Shapiro, B. L., & Chwarz, J. C. (1997). Date rape: Its relationship to trauma symptoms and sexual self-esteem. *Journal of Interpersonal Violence, 12.*

Sharp, D. (2002). Telling the truth about sex. *Lancet, 359,* 1084.

Sharpe, M. J., & Heppner, P. P. (1991). Gender role, gender-role conflict, and psychological well-being in men. *Journal of Counseling Psychology, 38,* 323–330.

Sharpsteen, D. J. (1991). The organization of jealousy knowledge: Romantic jealousy as a blended emotion. In P. Salovey (Ed.), *The psychology of jealousy and envy* (pp. 31–51). New York: Guilford Press.

Sheeran, P., Abraham, C., & Orbell, S. (1999). Psychosocial correlates of heterosexual condom use: A meta-analysis. *Psychological Bulletin, 125,* 90–132.

Shen, W. W., & Hsu, J. H. (1995). Female sexual side effects associated with selective serotonin reuptake inhibitors: A descriptive clinical study of 33 patients. *International Journal of Psychiatry in Medicine, 25,* 239–248.

Shepela, S. T., & Levesque, L. L. (1998). Poisoned waters: Sexual harassment and the college climate. *Sex Roles: A Journal of Research, 38,* 589–611.

Shepherd, G. (1987). Rank, gender, and homosexuality: Mombasa as a key to understanding sexual options. In P. Caplan (Ed.), *The cultural construction of sexuality* (pp. 240–270). London: Tavistock Publishers.

Shepherd-Look, D. (1982). Sex differentiation and the development of sex roles. In B. B. Wolman (Ed.), *Handbook of developmental psychology* (pp. 403–433). Englewood Cliffs, NJ: Prentice-Hall.

Sherman, B. L., & Dominick, J. R. (1986). Violence and sex in music videos: TV and rock 'n' roll. *Journal of Communication, 36,* 79–93.

Sherman, S. L., DeFries, J. C., Cottesman, I. I., Loehlin, J. C., Meyer, J. M., Pelias, M. Z., Rice, J., & Waldman, I. (1997). Behavioral genetics '97: ASHG statement. Recent developments in human behavioral genetics: Past accomplishments and future directions. *American Journal of Human Genetics, 60,* 1265–1275.

Sherwin, B. B., Gelfand, M. M., & Brender, W. (1985). Androgen enhances sexual motivation in females: A prospective, crossover study of sex steroid administration in the surgical menopause. *Psychosomatic Medicine, 47,* 339–351.

Shi, L. (1999). Experience of primary care of racial and ethnic groups in the United States. *Medical Care, 37*(10), 1068–1077.

Shields, W. M., & Shields, L. M. (1983). Forcible rape: An evolutionary perspective. *Ethology and Sociobiology, 4,* 115–136.

Shingleton, H., & Heath, C. W. (1996, February 16). Letter to Dr. Peter Rappo, American Academy of Pediatrics from the American Cancer Society. Retrieved 1999, from www.nocirc.org/position/acs.html

Shires, A., & Miller, D. (1998). A preliminary study comparing psychological factors associated with erectile dysfunction in heterosexual and homosexual men. *Sexual and Marital Therapy, 31,* 37–49.

Shitata, A. A., & Gollub, E. (1992). Acceptability of a new intravaginal barrier contraceptive device (Femcap). *Contraception, 46*(6), 511–519.

Shostak, M. (1981). *Nisa, the life and words of a !Kung woman.* Cambridge, MA: Harvard University Press.

Shotland, R. L., & Craig, J. M. (1988). Can men and women differentiate between friendly and sexually-interested behavior? *Social Psychology Quarterly, 51,* 66–73.

Shotland, R. L., & Goodstein, L. (1992). Sexual precedence reduces the perceived legitimacy of sexual arousal: An examination of attributions concerning date rape and consensual sex. *Personality and Social Psychology Bulletin, 18,* 756–764.

Shotland, R. L., & Hunter, B. A. (1995). Women's "token resistance" and compliant sexual behaviors are related to uncertain sexual intentions and rape. *Personality and Social Psychology Bulletin, 21,* 226–236.

Shu, X-O., Hatch, M. C., Mills, J., Clemens, J., & Susser, M. (1995). Maternal smoking, alcohol drinking, caffeine consumption, and fetal growth: Results from a prospective study. *Epidemiology, 6,* 115–120.

Shulman, L. P. (2000). Expanding contraceptive choices: Lunelle monthly contraceptive injection. *International Journal of Fertility and Women's Medicine, 45*(2), 190–194.

Shulman, L. P., & Elias, S. (1993). Amniotic and chorionic villus sampling. *Western Journal of Medicine, 159,* 260–268.

Sibai, B. M., & Anderson, G. D. (1991). Hypertension. In S. G. Gabbe, J. R. Niebyl, & J. L. Simpson (Eds.), *Obstetrics: Normal and problem pregnancies.* New York: Churchill, Livingstone.

Sibai, B. M., Odlind, V., Meador, M. L., Shangold, G. A., Fisher, A. C., & Creasy, G. W. (2002). A comparative and pooled analysis of the safety and tolerability of the contraceptive patch (Ortho Evra/Evra). *Fertility & Sterility, 77*(2 Suppl. 2), S19–26.

Siegel, J. M., Golding, J. M., Stein, J. A., Burnham, M. A., & Sorenson, S. B. (1990). Reactions to sexual assault: A community study. *Journal of Interpersonal Violence, 5,* 229–246.

Siegel, K., Karus, D., Epstein, J., & Raveis, V. H. (1996). Psychological and psychosocial adjustment of HIV-infected gay/bisexual men: Disease stage comparisons. *Journal of Community Psychology, 24,* 229–243.

Siegel, K., Krauss, B. J., & Karus, D. (1994). Reporting recent sexual practices: Gay men's disclosure of HIV risk by questionnaire and interview. *Archives of Sexual Behavior, 23,* 217–230.

Signorielli, N. (1989). Television and conceptions about sex roles: Maintaining conventionality and the status quo. *Sex Roles, 21,* 341–360.

Signorielli, N., & Bacue, A. (1999). Recognition and respect: A content analysis of prime-time television characters across three decades. *Sex Roles: A Journal of Research, 40*(7–8), 527–544.

Signorielli, N., McLeod, D., & Healy, E. (1994). Gender stereotypes in MTV commercials: The beat goes on. *Journal of Broadcasting and Electronic Media, 38,* 91–101.

Sigusch, V., Schmidt, G., Reinfeld, A., & Wiedemann-Sutor, I. (1970). Psychosexual stimulation: Sex differences. *Journal of Sex Research, 6,* 10–24.

Sikkema, K. J., Koob, J., Cargill, V., Kelly, J., Desiderato, L., & Roffman, R. (1995). Levels and predictors of HIV risk behavior among women living in low-income housing developments. *Public Health Reports, 6,* 707–713.

Silbert, M. H., & Pines, A. M. (1981a). Occupational hazards of street prostitutes. *Criminal Justice and Behavior, 8,* 395–399.

Silbert, M. H., & Pines, A. M. (1981b). Sexual child abuse as an antecedent to prostitution. *Child Abuse and Neglect, 5,* 407–411.

Simmons, R., Blyth, D., & McKinney, K. (1983). The social and psychological effects of puberty on white females. In J. Brooks-Gunn & A. Petersen (Eds.), *Girls at puberty.* New York: Plenum.

Simon, P. M., Morse, E. V., Osofsky, H. J., Balson, P. M., & Gaumer, H. R. (1992). Psychological characteristics of a sample of male street prostitutes. *Archives of Sexual Behavior, 21,* 22–44.

Simon, W. (1992). [Review of *Kinsey, sex and fraud: The indoctrination of a people*]. *Archives of Sexual Behavior, 21,* 91–93.

Simon, W. (1994). Deviance in history: The future of perversion. *Archives of Sexual Behavior, 23,* 1–20.

Simon, W., & Gagnon, J. H. (1987). A sexual scripts approach. In J. H. Geer & W. T. O'Donohue (Eds.), *Theories of human sexuality* (pp. 363–383). New York: Plenum.

Simons, R., & Whitbeck, L. (1991). Sexual abuse as a precursor to prostitution and victimization among adolescent and adult homeless women. *Journal of Family Issues, 12,* 361–380.

Simpson, J. A., Rholes, W. S., & Nelligan, J. S. (1992). Support seeking and support giving within couples in an anxiety-provoking situation: The role of attachment styles. *Journal of Personality and Social Psychology, 62,* 434–446.

Singer, J. J. (1968). Control of male and female sexual behavior in the female rat. *Journal of Comparative and Physiological Psychology, 66,* 738–742.

Skipper, J. K., & McCaghy, C. H. (1970). Stripteasers: The anatomy and career contingencies of a deviant occupation. *Social Problems, 17,* 391–405.

Slade, H. B. (1998). Cytokine induction and modifying the immune response to human papilloma virus with imiquimod. *European Journal Dermatology, 8,* 13–16.

Slupik, R. I., & Allison, K. C. (1996). *The American Medical Association complete guide to women's health.* New York: Random House.

Smallbone, S. W., & Dadds, M. R. (1998). Childhood attachment and adult attachment in incarcerated adult male sex offenders. *Journal of Interpersonal Violence, 13,* 555–573.

Smith, A. M. A., Rosenthal, D. A., & Reichler, H. (1996). High schoolers' masturbatory practices: Their relationship to sexual intercourse and personal characteristics. *Psychological Reports, 79,* 499–509.

Smith, C. H. (1989). Acute pregnancy-associated hypertension treated with hypnosis: A case report. *American Journal of Clinical Hypnosis, 31,* 209–211.

Smith, T. D., Bhatnagar, K. P., Shimp, K. L., Kinzinger, J. H., Bonar, C. J., Burrows, A. M., Mooney, M. P., & Siegel, M. I. (2002). Histological definition of the vomeronasal organ in humans and chimpanzees, with a comparison to other primates. *The Anatomical Record, 267*(2), 166–176.

Smith, T. W. (1994). Attitudes toward sexual permissiveness: Trends, correlates, and behavioral connections. In A. S. Rossi (Ed.), *Sexuality across the life course* (pp. 63–97). Chicago: University of Chicago.

Smolak, L. (1993). *Adult development.* Englewood Cliffs, NJ: Prentice-Hall.

Smukler, A. J., & Schiebel, D. (1975). Personality characteristics of exhibitionists. *Diseases of the Nervous System, 36,* 600–603.

Snodgrass, M. C. (1989). An investigation of the relationships of differential loneliness, intimacy, and changing attributional style to duration of loneliness in adult women. *Dissertation Abstracts International, 49,* 3109.

Snyder, H. M. (1991, January 15). To circumcise or not. *Hospital Practice,* 201–207.

Sobo, E. J. (1993). Inner-city women and AIDS: The psycho-social benefits of unsafe sex. *Cultural Medicine and Psychiatry, 17,* 455–485.

Socarides, C. (1968). *The overt homosexual.* New York: Grune & Stratton.

Socarides, C., & Volkan, V. (1990). *The homosexualities: Reality, fantasy, and the arts.* Madison, CT: International University Press.

Solanki, S. L., Potter, W. D., Brown, R., & Ewan, P. (1996). Suitability of polyurethane condom by latex-sensitive individuals. Retrieved June 5, 2000, from www.aegis.com/pubs/aidsline/1997/jan/m9712295.html

Solomon, R., & Liefeld, C. P. (1998). Effectiveness of a family support center approach to adolescent mothers: Repeat pregnancy and school drop-out rates. *Family Relations, 47,* 139–145.

Somers, P. J., Gervirtz, R. N., Jasin, S. E., & Chin, H. G. (1989). The efficacy of biobehavioral compliance interventions in the adjunctive treatment of mild pregnancy-induced hypertension. *Biofeedback and Self-Regulation, 14*(4), 309–318.

Sommers, C. H. (1994). *Who stole feminism? How women have betrayed women.* New York: Touchstone.

Sonenschein, D. (1987). On having one's research seized. *Journal of Sex Research, 23,* 408–414.

Sonenstein, F. L., Ku, L., Lindberg, L. D., Turner, C. F., & Pleck, J. H. (1998). Changes in sexual behavior and condom use among teenaged males: 1988 to 1995. *American Journal of Public Health, 88,* 956–959.

Sonnenstuhl, P. (1996). Introduction to midwifery. Retrieved September 24, 2002, from www.efn.org/~djz/birth/midwifefaq/intro.html

Soper, D. (1991, February). Disseminated gonococcal infection. *Contemporary Obstetrics & Gynecology,* 97–99.

Soper, D. E., Brockwell, N.J., & Dalton, D. P. (1991). Evaluation of the effects of a female condom on the female lower genital tract. *Contraception, 44*(1), 21–29.

Sophie, J. (1985/1986). A critical examination of stage theories of lesbian identity development. *Journal of Homosexuality, 12,* 39–51.

Southerland, D. (1990, May 27). Limited "sexual revolution" seen in China: Nationwide survey shows more liberal attitudes developing in conservative society. *The Washington Post,* p. 32.

Spector, I. P., & Carey, M. P. (1990). Incidence and prevalence of sexual dysfunctions: A critical review of the empirical literature. *Archives of Sexual Behavior, 19,* 389–408.

Spencer, J. M., Zimet, G. D., Aalsma, M. C., & Orr, D. P. (2002). Self-esteem as a predictor of initiation of coitus in early adolescents. *Pediatrics, 109*(4), 581–584.

Spenger, P. (1999, September 30). The porn pioneers. *The Guardian (Online),* 2–3.

Spira, A., et al. (1993). *Les comportements sexuels en France.* Paris: La Documentation Francaise.

Spitz, A. M., Velebil, P., Koonin, L. M., Strauss, L. T., Goodman, K. A., Wingo, P., Wilson, J. B., Morris, L., & Marks, J. S. (1996). Pregnancy, abortion, and birth rates among U.S. adolescents—1980, 1985, and 1990. *Journal of the American Medical Association, 275,* 989–994.

Spitze, G., & Logan, J. (1989). Gender differences in family support: Is there a payoff? *Gerontologist, 29,* 108–113.

Sprecher, S. (1986). The relationship between inequity and emotions in close relationships. *Social Psychology Quarterly, 49,* 309–321.

Sprecher, S. (1988). Investment model, equity and social support determinants of relationship commitment. *Social Psychology Quarterly, 51,* 318–328.

Sprecher, S., Aron, A., Hatfield, E., Cortese, A., Potapova, E., & Levitskaya, A. (1994). Love: American style, Russian style, and Japanese style. *Personal Relationships, 1,* 349–369.

Sprecher, S., Barbee, A., & Schwartz, P. (1995). "Was it good for you, too?": Gender differences in first sexual intercourse experiences. *Journal of Sex Research, 32,* 3–15.

Sprecher, S., & Hatfield, E. (1996). Premarital sexual standards among U.S. college students: Comparison with Russian and Japanese students. *Archives of Sexual Behavior, 22,* 261–288.

Sprecher, S., McKinney, K., & Orbuch, T. L. (1987). Has the double standard disappeared? An experimental test. *Social Psychology Quarterly, 50,* 24–31.

Sprecher, S., McKinney, K., & Orbuch, T. L. (1991). The effects of current sexual behavior on friendship, dating, and marriage desirability. *Journal of Sex Research, 28,* 387–408.

Sprecher, S., Metts, S., Burleson, B., Hatfield, E., & Thompson, A. (1995). Domains of expressive interaction in intimate relationships: Associations with satisfaction and commitment. *Family Relations, 44,* 203–212.

Sprecher, S., & Regan, P. C. (1996). College virgins: How men and women perceive their sexual status. *Journal of Sex Research, 33,* 3–15.

Sprecher, S., & Regan, P. C. (1998). Passionate and companionate love in courting and young married couples. *Sociological Inquiry, 68,* 163–185.

Stack, S. (1998). Marriage, family, and loneliness: A cross-national study. *Sociological Perspectives, 41,* 415–432.

Stack, S., & Eshleman, J. R. (1998). Marital status and happiness: A 17-nation study. *Journal of Marriage and the Family, 60,* 527–537.

Stack, S., & Gundlach, J. H. (1992). Divorce and sex. *Archives of Sexual Behavior, 21,* 359–367.

Standberry, L. R., & Rosenthal, S. L. (1999). The epidemiology of herpes simplex virus infections in adolescents. *Herpes, 6*(1), 12–13.

Standford, C. B. (2000). Darwinians look at rape, sex, and war. *American Scientist.* Retrieved October 30, 2002, from www.americanscientist.org/bookshelf/Leads00/Stanford.html

Stanton, A. L., Lobel, M., Sears, S., & DeLuca, R. S. (2002). Psychosocial aspects of selected issues in women's reproductive health: Current status and future directions. *Journal of Consulting and Clinical Psychology, 70*(3), 751–770.

Stanton, C. K., & Gray, R. H. (1995). Effects of caffeine consumption on delayed conception. *American Journal of Epidemiology, 142*(12), 1322–1329.

Staples, R., & Johnson, L. B. (1993). *Black families at the crossroads: Challenges and prospects.* San Francisco: Jossey-Bass.

Steele, J. R. (1999). Teenage sexuality and media practice: Factoring in the influences of family, friends, and school. *Journal of Sex Research, 36,* 331–342.

Steele, V. (1996). *Fetish: Fashion, sex, and power.* New York: Oxford University.

Stein, J., Golding, J., Siegel, J., Burnham, M., & Sorenson, S. (1988). Long-term psychological sequelae of child sexual abuse: The Los Angeles Epidemiologic Catchment Area Study. In G. Wyatt & G. Powell (Eds.), *Lasting effects of child sexual abuse* (pp. 135–154). Newbury Park, CA: Sage.

Stein, P. J. (1975). Singlehood: An alternative to marriage. *The Family Coordinator, 24,* 489–503.

Stein, Z. A. (1990). HIV prevention: The need for methods women can use. *American Journal of Public Health, 80,* 460–462.

Steinman, D. L., Wincze, J. P., Sakheim, D. K., Barlow, D. H., & Mavissakalian, M. (1981). A comparison of male and female patterns of sexual arousal. *Archives of Sexual Behavior, 10*(6), 529–547.

Stenson, P., & Anderson, C. (1987). Treating juvenile sex offenders and preventing the cycle of abuse. *Journal of Child Care, 3,* 91–102.

Stephenson, J. (2000). Genital herpes vaccine shows limited promise. *JAMA: News and Perspectives, 284.* Retrieved May 14, 2002, from http://jama.ama-assn.org/issues/v284n/15/ffull/jmn1018-2.html

Stermac, L. E., Segal, Z. V., & Gillis, R. (1990). Social and cultural factors in sexual assault. In W. L. Marshall, D. R. Laws, & H. E. Barbaree (Eds.), *Handbook of sexual assault: Issues, theories, and treatment of the offender* (pp. 143–159). New York: Plenum.

Stern, K., & McClintock, M. K. (1998). Regulations of ovulation by human pheromones. *Nature, 392*(6672), 177–179.

Stern, S. E., & Handel, A. D. (2001). Sexuality and mass media: The historical context of psychology's reaction to sexuality on the Internet. *Journal of Sex Research, 38,* 283–291.

Sternberg, R. J. (1986). A triangular theory of love. *Psychological Review, 93,* 119–135.

Sternberg, R. J. (1988). *The triangle theory of love: Intimacy, passion, commitment.* New York: Basic Books.

Sternberg, R. J. (1993). What is the relation of gender to biology and environment? An evolutionary model of how what you answer depends on what you ask. In A. E. Beall & R. J. Sternberg (Eds.), *The psychology of gender.* New York: Guilford Press.

Sternberg, R. J. (1998). *Cupid's arrow: The course of love through time.* New York: Cambridge University.

Sternfeld, B., Quesenberry, C. P., Eskenazi, B., & Newman, L. A. (1995). Exercise during pregnancy and pregnancy outcome. *Medicine & Science in Sports and Exercise, 27,* 634–640.

Sternfeld, B., Swindle, R., Chawla, A., Long, S., & Kennedy, S. (2002). Severity of premenstrual symptoms in a health maintenance organization population. *Obstetrics and Gynecology, 99*(6), 1014–1024.

Stevenson, M. R. (1988). Promoting tolerance for homosexuality: An evaluation of intervention strategies. *Journal of Sex Research, 25*(4), 500–511.

Stevens-Simon, C., & White, M. M. (1991). Adolescent pregnancy. *Pediatric Annals, 20,* 322–331.

Stock, W. (1993). Inhibited female orgasm. In W. O'Donohue & J. H. Geer (Eds.), *Handbook of sexual dysfunctions: Assessment and treatment* (pp. 253–277). Boston: Allyn & Bacon.

Stolberg, S. (1994, May 19). Cesarean birth rate leveling off. *Los Angeles Times,* p. B-4.

Stoller, R. J. (1991). *Pain and passion: A psychoanalyst explores the world of S & M.* New York: Plenum.

Stone, K. M., Grimes, D. A., & Magder, L. S. (1986). Personal protection against sexually transmitted diseases. *American Journal of Obstetrics and Gynecology, 155,* 180–189.

Storms, M. D. (1981). A theory of erotic orientation development. *Psychological Review, 88,* 340–353.

Straneva, P. A., Maixner, W., Light, K. C., Pedersen, C. A., Costello, N. L., & Girdler, S. S. (2002). Menstrual cycle, beta-endorphins, and pain sensitivity in premenstrual dysphoric disorder. *Health Psychology, 21*(4), 358–367.

Strassberg, D. S., Kelly, M. P., Carroll, C., & Kircher, J. C. (1987). The psychophysiological nature of premature ejaculation. *Archives of Sexual Behavior, 16,* 327–336.

Strassberg, D. S., & Lowe, K. (1995). Volunteer bias in sexuality research. *Archives of Sexual Behavior, 24,* 369–382.

Strommen, E. F. (1989). "You're a what?" Family member reactions to the disclosure of homosexuality. *Journal of Homosexuality, 18*(1/2), 37–58.

Struckman-Johnson, C., & Struckman-Johnson, D. (1997). Men's reactions to hypothetical forceful sexual advances from women: The role of sexual standards, relationship availability, and the beauty bias. *Sex Roles, 37,* 319–333.

Stuart, F. M., Hammond, D. C., & Pett, M. A. (1987). Inhibited sexual desire in women. *Archives of Sexual Behavior, 16,* 91–107.

Stubbs, M., Rierdan, J., & Koff, E. (1989). Developmental differences in menstrual attitudes. *Journal of Adolescent Health Care, 25,* 117–130.

Studd, M. V. (1996). Sexual harassment. In D. M. Buss & N. M. Malamuth (Eds.), *Sex, power, conflict: Evolutionary and feminist perspectives* (pp. 54–89). New York: Oxford University Press.

Stuntz, R. C. (1986). Physical obstructions to coitus in women. *Medical Aspects of Human Sexuality, 20,* 125–133.

Stylianos, S. K., & Vachon, M. L. S. (1993). The role of social support in bereavement. In M. S. Stroebe & W. Stroebe (Eds.), *Handbook of bereavement: Theory, research, and intervention* (pp. 397–410). New York: Cambridge University Press.

Sullivan, K. M., & Adzick, N. S. (1994). Fetal surgery. *Clinical Obstetrics and Gynecology, 37,* 355–371.

Sundet, J. M., Kvalem, I. L., Magnus, P., & Bakketeig, L. S. (1988). Prevalence of risk-prone behaviour in the general population of Norway. In F. A. Fleming, M. Carballo, & D. F. Fitzsimmons (Eds.), *The global impact of AIDS.* London: Alan R. Liss.

Susser, I., & Stein, Z. (2000). Culture, sexuality, and women's agency in the prevention of HIV/AIDS in Southern Africa. *American Journal of Public Health, 90,* 1042–1049.

Syed, T. A., Cheema, K. M., Khayyami, M. Ahmad, S. A., Ahmad, S. M., Ahmad, S., & Ahmad, S. A. (1995). Human leukocyte interferon-alpha versus podophyllotoxin in cream for the treatment of genital warts in males. A placebo-controlled, double-blind, comparative study. *Dermatology, 191,* 129–132.

Symons, D. (1979). *The evolution of human sexuality.* New York: Oxford.

Symons, D. (1987). A evolutionary approach: Can Darwin's view of life shed light on human sexuality? In J. H. Geer & W. T. O'Donohue (Eds.), *Theories of human sexuality* (pp. 91–125). New York: Plenum.

Taffe, J. R., & Dennerstein, L. (2002). Menstrual patterns leading to the final menstrual period. *Menopause, 9,* 32–40.

Talbot, M. (2002, October 13). Men behaving badly. *New York Times Magazine,* 52–57.

Tanith. (2000). The history of abortion. Retrieved October 11, 2002, from www.she-net.com/she-zine/feb00/abortion.html

Tannen, D. (1990). *You just don't understand: Women and men in conversation.* New York: Plenum.

Tantleff-Dunn, S., & Thompson, J. K. (1995). Romantic partners and body image disturbance: Further evidence for the role of perceived—actual disparities. *Sex Roles, 33,* 589–605.

Tasker, F., & Golombok, S. (1995). Adults raised as children in lesbian families. *American Journal of Orthopsychiatry, 65*(2), 203–215.

Tavris, C., & Sadd, S. (1987). *The Redbook Report on female sexuality.* New York: Dell.

Taylor, B., & Wadsworth, J. (1984). Breastfeeding and child development at five years. *Developmental Medicine and Child Neurology, 26,* 73–80.

Taylor, C. C. (1990). Condoms and cosmology: The "fractal" person and sexual risk in Rwanda. *Social Science and Medicine, 31,* 1023–1028.

Taylor, G. R. (1970). *Sex in history.* New York: Harper & Row.

Taylor, J. (1995, September). The long, hard days of Dr. Dick. *Esquire,* 120–123.

Telford, A. (1997, September/October). Sex in advertising. *Communication Arts,* 84–88.

Templeman, T. L., & Stinnett, R. D. (1991). Patterns of sexual arousal and history in a "normal" sample of young men. *Archives of Sexual Behavior, 20,* 137–150.

Thelen, M. H., Sherman, M. D., & Borst, T. S. (1998). Fear of intimacy and attachment among rape survivors. *Behavior Modification, 22,* 108–116.

39 Viagra deaths confirmed. (1998, July 24). *Tulsa World* Online. Retrieved November 16, 1998, from http://library.northernlight.com/BM19980727010159226.html?cb=0&sc=0#doc

Thoits, P. A. (1995). Identity relevant events and psychological symptoms: A cautionary tale. *Journal of Health and Social Behavior, 36,* 72–82.

Thomas, C. (2000). Vermont court imposes homosexual agenda. *Human Events, 56,* 9.

Thomas, J., & Rogers, C. (1983). A treatment program for intrafamily juvenile sexual offenders. In J. Greer & I. Stuart (Eds.), *The sexual aggressor: Current perspectives on treatment* (pp. 127–143). New York: Van Nostrand Reinhold.

Thompson, R. S. (1990). Routine circumcision in the newborn: An opposing view. *The Journal of Family Practice, 31,* 189–196.

Thompson, T. L., & Zerbinos, E. (1995). Gender roles in animated cartoons: Has the picture changed in 20 years? *Sex Roles: A Journal of Research, 32,* 651–673.

Thornhill, R., & Palmer, C. T. (2000). *A natural history of rape: Biological bases of sexual coercion.* Cambridge, MA: The MIT Press.

Thornhill, R., & Thornhill, N. (1983). Human rape: An evolutionary analysis. *Ethology and Sociobiology, 4,* 137.

Thornton, A., & Camburn, D. (1989). Religious participation and adolescent sexual behavior and attitudes. *Journal of Marriage and the Family, 51,* 641–653.

Thornton, A., & Young-DeMarco, L. (2001). Four decades of trends in attitudes toward family issues in the United States: The 1960s through the 1990s. *Journal of Marriage and the Family, 63.*

Tiefer, L. (1986). In pursuit of the perfect penis: The medicalization of male sexuality. *American Behavioral Scientist, 29,* 579–599.

Tiefer, L. (1991). Historical, scientific, clinical and feminist criticisms of "The Human Sexual Response Cycle" model. *Annual Review of Sex Research, 2,* 1–23.

Tiefer, L., Pedersen, B., & Melman, A. (1988). Psychosocial follow-up of penile prosthesis implant patients and partners. *Journal of Sex and Marital Therapy, 14,* 184–201.

Tielmann, G., Juul, A., Skakkebaek, N. E., & Toppari, J. (2002). Putative effects of endocrine disrupters on pubertal development in the human. *Best Practices Research in Clinical Endocrinology and Metabolism, 16*(1), 105–121.

Tjaden, P., & Thoennes, N. (2000). *Full report of the prevalence, incidence, and consequences of violence against women: Findings from the National Violence Against Women survey.* Washington, DC: U.S. Department of Justice.

Today's new contraceptive options. (2001). Association of Reproductive Health Professionals. Retrieved October 9, 2002, from http://www.arhp.org/healthcareproviders/onlinepublications/healthandsexuality/ndic/today.cfm?ID=221

Tolman, D. L., & Diamond, L. M. (2001). Desegregating sexuality research: Cultural and biological perspectives on gender and desire. *Annual Review of Sex Research, 12,* 33–74.

Tong, R. (1984). *Women, sex, and the law.* Totowa, NJ: Rowman & Littlefield.

Trager, O. (1992). *Abortion: Choice and conflict.* New York: Facts on File, Inc.

Travin, S., Cullen, K., & Protter, B. (1990). Female sex offenders: Severe victims and victimizers. *Journal of Forensic Sciences, 35,* 140–150.

Troiden, R. R. (1989). The formation of homosexual identities. *Journal of Homosexuality, 17,* 43–73.

Troutman, B. R., & Cutrona, C. E. (1990). Non-psychotic postpartum depression among adolescent mothers. *Journal of Abnormal Psychology, 99,* 69–78.

Truman, D., Tokar, D., & Fischer, A. R. (1996). Dimensions of masculinity: Relations to date rape supportive attitudes and sexual aggression in dating situations. *Journal of Counseling and Development, 74,* 555–562.

Trumbach, F. (1977). London sodomites: Homosexual behavior and Western culture in the eighteenth century. *Journal of Social History, 2,* 1–33.

Tuller, D. (1994, January 10). The latest thinking on safe sex. *San Francisco Chronicle,* p. D-7.

Tuller, N. R. (1978). Couples: The hidden segment of the gay world. *Journal of Homosexuality, 3,* 331–343.

Turner, A. M., & Greenough, W. T. (1985). Differential rearing effects on rat visual cortex synapses. I: Synaptic and neuronal density and synapses per neuron. *Brain Research, 329,* 195–203.

Turner, A. N., & Ellertson, C. (2002). How safe is emergency contraception? *Drug Safety, 25*(10), 695–706.

Twelve major cancers. (1996, September). *Scientific American, 275,* 126–132.

Tyler, K. A., Hoyt, D. R., & Whitbeck, L. B. (1998). Coercive sexual strategies. *Violence and Victimization, 13,* 47–61.

U.S. Census Bureau. (1990, December). Household and family characteristics: March 1990 and 1989. *Current Population Reports, P-20, No. 447.* Washington, DC: U.S. Government Printing Office.

U.S. Census Bureau, Population Division, Fertility & Family Statistics Branch. (1999). Marital status and living arrangements: March, 1998 (update). *Current Population Series Survey Reports.* Retrieved June 15, 2000, from www.census.gov/population/www/socdemo/ms-la.html

U.S. Department of Education, National Center for Education Statistics. (2000). *Educational equity for girls and women* (NCES 2000-030). Washington, DC: U.S. Government Printing Office.

U.S. Department of Health and Human Services/Public Health Service. (1999, May 5). *Healthy people 2000 progress review: Maternal and infant health.* Retrieved December 10, 1999, from http://odphp.osophs.dhhs.gov/pubs/hp2000/PROGRVW/materinfant/maternalprog.htm

U.S. Department of Justice. (1986). *Attorney General's Commission on Pornography: Final Report.* Washington, DC: U.S. Government Printing Office.

U.S. Department of Justice. (1999). American Indians and crime. Retrieved October 16, 2002, from www.ojp.usdoj.gove/bjs/pub/press/aic.pr

U.S. Department of Justice, National Institute of Justice, & U.S. Department of Health and Human Services, Centers for Disease Control and Prevention. (1998). *Prevalence, incidence, and consequences of violence against women: Findings from the National Violence Against Women Survey.* Washington, DC: U.S. Government Printing Office.

U.S. Merit Systems Protection Board. (1995). *Sexual harassment in the federal workplace: Trends, progress, continuing challenges.* Washington, DC: U.S. Government Printing Office.

U.S. News Online. (1997). How the abortion pill works. Retrieved May 14, 1998, from www3.usnews.com/usnews/issue/970303/3ru48b.htm

Uauy, R., & DeAndraca, I. (1995). Human milk and breast feeding for optimal mental development. *American Institute of Nutrition,* 2278S–2280S.

Udry, J. R. (1993). The politics of sex research. *Journal of Sex Research, 30,* 103–110.

Ugwumadu, A. H. (2002). Bacterial vaginosis in pregnancy. *Current Opinions in Obstetrics and Gynecology, 14,* 115–118.

UNAIDS (Joint United Nations Programme on HIV/AIDS). (1998). *HIV/AIDS: The global epidemic.* New York: Author.

UNAIDS (Joint United Nations Programme on HIV/AIDS). (1999a). *Acting early to prevent AIDS: The case of Senegal.* New York: Author.

UNAIDS (Joint United Nations Programme on HIV/AIDS). (1999b). *AIDS epidemic update: December 1999.* New York: Author.

UNAIDS/WHO (Joint United Nations Programme on HIV/AIDS & World Health Organization). (2001). *AIDS epidemic update: December 2001.* New York: Author.

UNAIDS (Joint United Nations Programme on HIV/AIDS). (2002). *Report on the global HIV/AIDS epidemic 2002.* Geneva, Switzerland: Author.

UNAIDS/WHO (2002a). *AIDS epidemic update: December 2002.* Geneva: Author.

UNAIDS/WHO (2002b). *Zimbabwe: Epidemiological fact sheets on HIV/AIDS and sexually transmitted infections, 2002 update.* Geneva: Author.

Unger, J. B., Kipke, M. D., Simon, T. R., Johnson, C. J., Montgomery, S. B., & Iverson, E. (1998). Stress, coping, and social support among homeless youth. *Journal of Adolescent Research, 13,* 134–158.

Unger, R., & Crawford, M. (1992). *Women and gender: A feminist psychology.* New York: McGraw-Hill.

Utne, M. K., Hatfield, E., Traupmann, J., & Greenberger, D. (1984). Equity, marital satisfaction, and stability. *Journal of Social and Personal Relationships, 1,* 323–332.

Valliant, P. M., Gauthier, T., Pottier, D., & Kosmyna, R. (2000). Moral reasoning, interpersonal skills, and cognition of rapists, child molesters, and incest offenders. *Psychological Reports, 86*(1), 67–75.

van Berlo, W., & Ensink, B. (2000). Problems with sexuality after sexual assault. *Annual Review of Sex Research, 11,* 235–257.

Vande Berg, L. R., & Streckfuss, D. (1992, Spring). Prime-time television's portrayal of women and the world of work: A demographic profile. *Journal of Broadcasting and Electronic Media, 36,* 195–208.

Vander, A. J., Sherman, J. H., & Luciano, D. S. (1994). *Human physiology: The mechanisms of body function* (6th ed.). New York: McGraw-Hill.

Van Dyk, A. C. (2001). Traditional African beliefs and customs: Implications for AIDS education and prevention in Africa. *South African Journal of Psychology, 31,* 60–67.

VanLandingham, M., Grandjean, N., Suprasert, S., & Sittitrai, W. (1997). Dimensions of AIDS knowledge and risky sexual practices: A study of northern Thai males. *Archives of Sexual Behavior, 26,* 269–294.

Van Ness, S. R. (1984). Rape of instrumental violence: A study of youthful offenders. *Journal of Offender Counselling, Services, and Rehabilitation, 9,* 161–170.

Van Oost, P., Csincsak, M., & De Bourdeaudhuij, I. (1994). Principals' and teachers' views of sexuality education in Flanders. *Journal of School Health, 64,* 105–109.

Vanwesenbeeck, I. (2001). Another decade of social scientific work on sex work: A review of research 1990–2000. *Annual Review of Sex Research, 12,* 242–290.

Vanwesenbeeck, I. (2001). Psychosexual correlates of viewing sexually explicit sex on television among women in the Netherlands. *Journal of Sex Research, 38,* 361–368.

Vanwesenbeeck, I., Bekker, M., & van Lenning, A. (1998). Gender attitudes, sexual meanings, and interactional patterns in heterosexual encounters among college students in the Netherlands. *Journal of Sex Research, 35,* 317–327.

Van Wyk, P. (1984). Psychosocial development of heterosexual, bisexual, and homosexual behavior. *Archives of Sexual Behavior, 13,* 505–544.

Vas, C. J. (1969). Sexual impotence and some autonomic disturbances in men with multiple sclerosis. *Acta Neurologica Scandinavica, 45,* 166–182.

Ventura, S. J., Martin, J. A., Curtin, S. C., & Mathews, T. J. (1999). Births: Final data for 1997. *National Vital Statistics Report, 47*(18).

Ventura, S. J., Martin, J. A., Curtin, S. C., Mathews, T. J., & Park, M. M. (2000, March 28). Births: Final data for 1998. *National Vital Statistics Reports, 48,* 1–100.

Ventura, S., Mathews, T. J., & Hamilton, B. (2002). Teenage births in the United States: State trends 1991–2000. An update. *National Vital Statistics Reports, 50*(9). Hyattsville, MD: National Center for Health Statistics.

Viera, A. J., Clenney, T. L., Shenenberger, D. W., & Green, G. E. (1999). New pharmacologic alternatives for erectile dyfunction. *American Family Physician, 60,* 1159–1167.

Villalon, D. (2002, October 6). Rape drug detectors: California UWCA branch distributes devices to spot date-rape drugs. Retrieved October 17, 2002, from http://abcnews.go.com/sections/scitech/DailyNews/daterape_detection021006.html

Virtanen, S. M., Räsänen, L., Aro, A., Lindström, J., Sippola, H., Lounamaa, R., Toivanen, L., Tuomilehto, J., Åkerblom, H. K., & Childhood Diabetes in Finland Study Group. (1991). Infant feeding in Finnish children < 7 yr of age with newly diagnosed IDDM. *Diabetes Care, 14,* 415–417.

Vittorio, C. C., Schiffman, M. H., & Weinstock, M. A. (1995). Epidemiology of human papillomaviruses. *Dermatologic Clinics, 13,* 561–574.

Voeller, B. (1991). AIDS and heterosexual anal intercourse. *Archives of Sexual Behavior, 9,* 319–325.

Wabrek, C., & Wabrek, A. (1974). Sexual difficulties and the importance of the relationship. *Journal of Gynecological Nursing, 3,* 32–35.

Wadhwa, P. D., Herbel, K., Dunkel-Schetter, C., Chicz-Demet, A., & Sandman, C. A. (1998, March). *Prenatal stress and infant development: A preliminary study.* Paper presented at the meeting of the Society for Behavioral Medicine, New Orleans, LA.

Waigandt, A., Wallace, D. L., Phelps, L., & Miller, D. A. (1990). The impact of sexual assault on physical health status. *Journal of Traumatic Stress, 3,* 93–102.

Wakefield, H., & Underwager, R. (1994). *Return of the Furies: An investigation into recovered memory therapy.* Peru, IL: Open Court.

Wakefield, J. (1987). Sex bias in the diagnosis of primary orgasmic dysfunction. *American Psychologist, 42,* 464–471.

Walboomers, J. M., Jacobs, M. V., Manos, M. M., Bosch, F. X., Kummer, J. A., Shah, K. V., Snijders, P. J., Peto, J., Meijer, C. J., & Munoz, N. (1999). Human papillomavirus is a necessary cause of invasive cervical cancer worldwide. *Journal of Pathology, 189*(1), 12–19.

Waldner-Haugrud, L., & Magruder, B. (1996). Homosexual identity expression among lesbian and gay adolescents. *Youth & Society, 27,* 313–333.

Waldner-Haugrud, L. K., & Gratch, L. V. (1997). Sexual coercion in gay/lesbian relationships: Descriptives and gender differences. *Violence and Victims, 12,* 87–98.

Walker, B. (2002). Bob Walker's official New Orleans area wedding guide: Louisiana's Covenant Marriage law. Retrieved November 16, 2002, from www.walkerpub.com/covenant_marriage.html

Walsh, R. A. (1994). Effects of maternal smoking on adverse pregnancy outcomes: Examination of the criteria of causation. *Human Biology, 66*(6), 1059–1092.

Walster, E. (1971). Passionate love. In J. B. Murstein (Ed.), *Theories of attraction and love* (pp. 85–99). New York: Springer.

Walters, J. (1997). Invading the Roman body: Manliness and impenetrability in Roman thought. In J. P. Hallett & M. B. Skinner (Eds.), *Roman sexualities* (pp. 29–43). Princeton, NJ: Princeton University.

Wang, C., & Swerdloff, R. S. (2002). Male contraception. *Best Practice & Research: Clinical Obstetrics & Gynaecology, 16*(2), 193–203.

Wang, C-T., & Daro, D. (1997). *Current trends in child abuse: The results of the 1996 annual fifty state survey.* Chicago: The National Center on Child Abuse Prevention Research, The National Committee to Prevent Child Abuse.

Wang, P., Cong, S., Dong, X, Chen, Z., & Ma, C. (1991). A genetic study of human interferon-induced repair of DNA damage in hepatitis B patients. *Mutation Research, 262,* 125–128.

Ward, L. M., & Rivadeneyra, R. (1999). Contributions of entertainment television to adolescents' sexual attitudes and expectations: The role of viewing amount versus viewer involvement. *Journal of Sex Research, 36,* 237–249.

Warshaw, R., & Parrot, A. (1991). The contribution of sex-role socialization to acquaintance rape. In A. Parrot & L. Bechhofer (Eds.), *Acquaintance rape: The hidden crime* (pp. 73–82). New York: Wiley.

Wartik, N., & Felner, J. (1994). Is breast self-exam out of touch? *Ms., 5*(3), 65–69.

Washington State Department of Health. (2002). Fact sheet: Teen pregnancy. Retrieved November 13, 2002, from www.doh.wa.gov/Topics/teenpreg.htm

Waterman, A. S. (1982). Identity development from adolescence to adulthood: An extension of theory and a review of research. *Developmental Psychology, 18,* 341–358.

Waterman, A. S., & Archer, S. L. (1990). A life-span perspective on identity formation: Developments in form, function, and process. In P. B. Baltes, D. L. Featterman, & R. M. Lerner (Eds.), *Life-span development and behavior* (Vol. 10). Hillsdale, NJ: Erlbaum.

Webb, G. (2001). Sex and the Internet. *Yahoo! Internet Life, 7*(5), 88–98.

Webb, P. (1975). *The erotic arts.* Boston: New York Graphic Society.

Weeks, G. R., & Hof, L. (1987). *Integrating sex and marital therapy: A clinical guide.* New York: Brunner/Mazel.

Weeks, M. R., Schensul, J. J., Williams, S. S., Singer, M., & Grier, M. (1995). AIDS prevention for African-American and Latina women: Building culturally and gender-appropriate interventions. *AIDS Education and Prevention, 7,* 251–263.

Weeks, R., & Widom, C. S. (1998). Self-reports of early childhood victimization among incarcerated adult male felons. *Journal of Interpersonal Violence, 13,* 346–361.

Weinberg, M. S., Lottes, I. L., & Gordon, L. E. (1997). Social class background, sexual attitudes, and sexual behavior in a heterosexual undergraduate sample. *Archives of Sexual Behavior, 26,* 625–642.

Weinberg, M. S., Lottes, I. L., & Shaver, F. M. (1995). Swedish or American heterosexual college youth: Who is more permissive? *Archives of Sexual Behavior, 24,* 409–437.

Weinberg, M. S., Shaver, F. M., & Williams, C. J. (1999). Gendered sex work in the San Francisco Tenderloin. *Archives of Sexual Behavior, 28,* 503–521.

Weinberg, M. S., Williams, C. J., & Calhan, C. (1994). Homosexual foot fetishism. *Archives of Sexual Behavior, 23,* 611–626.

Weinberg, M. S., Williams, C. J., & Calhan, C. (1995). If the shoe fits . . . Exploring male homosexual foot fetishism. *Journal of Sex Research, 32,* 17–27.

Weinberg, M. S., Williams, C. J., & Pryor, D. W. (1994). *Dual attraction: Understanding bisexuality.* New York: Oxford University Press.

Weinberg, M. S., Williams, C. J., & Pryor, D. W. (2001). Bisexuals at midlife: Commitment, salience, and identity. *Journal of Contemporary Ethnography, 30*(2), 180–208.

Weinberg, T. S. (1994). Research on sadomasochism: A review of sociological and social psychological research. *Annual Review of Sex Research, 5,* 257–279.

Weiner, D. N., & Rosen, R. C. (1997). Medications and their impact. In M. L. Sipski & C. J. Alexander (Eds.), *Sexual function in people with disability and chronic illness: A health professional's guide* (pp. 85–114). Gaithersburg, MD: Aspen Publishers.

Weinhardt, L. S., & Carey, M. P. (1996). Prevalence of erectile disorder among men with diabetes mellitus: Comprehensive review, methodological critique, and suggestions for future research. *Journal of Sex Research, 33*(3), 205–214.

Weinhardt, L. S., Forsyth, A. D., Carey, M. P., Jaworski, B. C., & Durant, L. E. (1998). Reliability and validity of self-report measures of HIV-related sexual behavior: Progress since 1990 and recommendations for research and practice. *Archives of Sexual Behavior, 27,* 155–180.

Weir, S. S., Roddy, R. E., Zekeng, L., & Ryan, K. A. (1999). Association between condom use and HIV infection: A randomized study of self-reported condom use measures. *Journal of Epidemiology and Community Health, 53,* 417–422.

Weisner, T. S., Garnier, H., & Louky, J. (1994). Domestic tasks, gender egalitarian values and children's gender typing in conventional and nonconventional families. *Sex Roles, 30*(1/2), 23–54.

Weller, A., & Weller, L. (1992). Menstrual synchrony in female couples. *Psychoneuroendocrinology, 17,* 171–177.

Weller, L., Weller, A., & Roizman, S. (1999). Human menstrual synchrony in families and among close friends: Examining the importance of mutual exposure. *Journal of Comparative Psychology, 113*(3), 261–268.

Weller, R. A., & Halikas, J. A. (1984). Marijuana use and sexual behavior. *Journal of Sex Research, 20,* 186–193.

Wellings, K., Field, J., Johnson, A. M., & Wadsworth, J. (1994). *Sexual behaviour in Britain: The National Survey of Sexual Attitudes and Lifestyles.* London: Penguin Books.

Welshimer, K. J., & Harris, S. E. (1994). A survey of rural parents' attitudes toward sexuality education. *Journal of School Health, 64,* 347–352.

Werneke, U., & Crowe, M. (2002). Review of patients with erectile dysfunction attending the Maudsley psychosexual clinic in 1999: The impact of sildenafil. *Sexual and Relationship Therapy, 17,* 171–185.

Wertz, D. C., & Fletcher, J. C. (1993). Prenatal diagnosis and sex selection in 19 nations. *Social Science and Medicine, 37,* 1359–1366.

Wessells, H., Lue, T. F., & McAninch, J. W. (1996). Penile length in the flaccid and erect states: Guidelines for penile augmentation. *Journal of Urology, 156*(3), 995–997.

West, D. J., & de Villiers, B. (1993). *Male prostitution.* New York: Haworth Press.

Whipple, B. (1995). Research concerning sexual response in women. *The Health Psychologist, 17,* 16–18.

Whipple, B. (2000). Beyond the G spot. *Scandinavian Journal of Sexology, 3*(2), 35–42.

Whipple, B., Myers, B. R., & Komisaruk, B. R. (1998). Male multiple ejaculatory orgasms: A case study. *Journal of Sex, Education, and Therapy, 23,* 157–162.

Whitaker, D. J., & Miller, K. S. (2000). Parent–adolescent discussions about sex and condoms: Impact on peer influences of sexual risk behavior. *Journal of Adolescent Research, 15*(2), 251–273.

Whitaker, D. J., Miller, K. S., May, D. C., & Levin, M. L. (1999). Teenage partners' communication about sexual risk and condom use: The importance of parent-teenager discussions. *Family Planning Perspectives, 31,* 117–122.

Whitam, F. L. (1987). A cross-cultural perspective on homosexuality, transvestism, and trans-sexualism. In G. D. Wilson, *Variant sexuality: Research and theory* (pp. 176–201). Baltimore: Johns Hopkins University.

Whitbeck, L. B., Yoder, K. A., Hoyt, D. R., & Conger, R. D. (1999). Early adolescent sexual activity: A developmental study. *Journal of Marriage and the Family, 61*(4), 934–946.

White, G. L. (1981a). Jealousy and partner's perceived notion for attraction to a rival. *Social Psychology Quarterly, 49,* 24–30.

White, G. L. (1981b). A model of romantic jealousy. *Motivation and Emotion, 5,* 295–310.

White, G. L., & Mullen, P. E. (1989). *Jealousy: Theory, research, and clinical strategies.* New York: Guilford.

White, M. I. (1993). *The material child: Coming of age in Japan and America.* New York: Free Press.

Whitley, B. E. (1990). College student contraceptive use: A multivariate analysis. *Journal of Sex Research, 27,* 305–313.

Whittemore, A. S., Harris, R., Itnyre, J., Collaborative Ovarian Cancer Group. (1992). Characteristics relating to ovarian cancer risk: Collaborative analysis of 12 U.S. case-control studies. II. Invasive epithelial ovarian cancers in white women. *American Journal of Epidemiology, 136,* 1184–1203.

Widmer, E. D., Treas, J., & Newcomb, R. (1998). Attitudes toward nonmarital sex in 24 countries. *Journal of Sex Research, 35,* 349–358.

Wiedeman, G. H. (1974). Homosexuality: A survey. *Journal of the American Psychoanalytic Association, 22,* 651–696.

Wiederman, M. W. (1997). The truth must be in here somewhere: Examining the gender discrepancy in self-reported lifetime number of sex partners. *Journal of Sex Research, 34,* 375–386.

Wiederman, M. W. (1999). Volunteer bias in sexuality research using college student participants. *Journal of Sex Research, 36,* 59–66.

Wiederman, M. W. (2001). *Understanding sexuality research.* Toronto: Wadsworth.

Wiegers, T. A., Keirse, M. J. N. C., van der Zee, J., & Berghs, G. A. H. (1996). Outcome of planned home and planned hospital births in low risk pregnancies: Prospective study in midwifery practices in the Netherlands. *British Medical Journal, 313,* 1309–1313.

Wiehe, V. R. (1998). *Sibling abuse: The hidden physical, emotional and sexual trauma.* Newbury Park, CA: Sage.

Williams, D. B., Morley, K. H., Cholewa, C., Odem, R. R., Willand, J., & Gast, M. J. (1995). Does intrauterine insemination offer an advantage to cervical cap insemination in a donor insemination program? *Fertility and Sterility, 63*(2), 295–298.

Williams, D. R., & Rucker, T. D. (2000). Understanding and addressing racial disparities in health care. *Health Care Financial Review, 21*(4), 75–90.

Williams, J. E., LaRose, R., & Frost, F. (1981). *Children, television and sex role stereotyping.* New York: Praeger.

Williams, W. L. (1986). *The spirit and the flesh: Sexual diversity in American Indian culture.* Boston: Beacon Press.

Williard, J. (1991). *Juvenile prostitution.* Washington, DC: National Victim Resource Center.

Willis, B. M., & Levy, B. S. (2002). Child prostitution: Global health burden, research, needs, and interventions. *Lancet, 359,* 1417–1423.

Wilson, G. D., & Cox, D. N. (1983). Personality of paedophile club members. *Personality and Individual Differences, 4,* 323–329.

Wilson, G. D., & Gosselin, C. (1980). Personality characteristics of fetishists, transvestites, and sadomasochists. *Personality and Individual Differences, 1,* 289–295.

Wincze, J. P., & Carey, M. P. (2001). *Sexual dysfunction: A guide for assessment and treatment* (2nd ed.). New York: Guilford.

Wingood, G. M., & DiClemente, R. J. (1992). Cultural, gender, and psychosocial influences on HIV-related behavior of African-American female adolescents: Implications for the development of tailored prevention programs. *Ethnicity & Disease, 2,* 381–388.

Wingood, G. M., & DiClemente, R. J. (1998). Pattern influences and gender-related factors associated with noncondom use among young adult African American women. *American Journal of Community Psychology, 26,* 29–41.

Winick, C., & Evans, J. T. (1994). Is there a national standard with respect to attitudes toward sexually explicit media material? *Archives of Sexual Behavior, 23,* 405–419.

Winick, C., & Kinsie, P. M. (1971). *The lively commerce: Prostitution in the United States.* Chicago: Quadrangle Books.

Winikoff, B., & Wymelenberg, S. (1992). *The contraceptive handbook: A guide to safe and effective choices.* New York: Consumer Reports Books.

Wise, T. N., & Meyer, J. K. (1980). The border area between transvestism and gender dysphoria: Transvestic applicants for sex reassignment. *Archives of Sexual Behavior, 9,* 327–342.

Witt, S. D. (2000). The influence of peers on children's socialization to gender roles. *Early Child Development & Care, 162,* 1–7.

Wittchen, H. U., Becker, E., Lieb, R., & Krause, P. (2002). Prevalence, incidence and stability of premenstrual dysphoric disorder in the community. *Psychological Medicine, 32*(1), 119–132.

Wolchik, S. A., Braver, S. L., & Jensen, K. (1985). Volunteer bias in erotica research: Effects of intrusiveness of measure and sexual background. *Archives of Sexual Behavior, 14,* 93–107.

Wolchik, S. A., Spencer, S. L., & Lisi, I. S. (1983). Volunteer bias in research employing vaginal measures of sexual arousal: Demographic, sexual and personality characteristics. *Archives of Sexual Behavior, 12,* 399–408.

Wolff, C. (1971). *Love between women.* New York: Harper & Row.

Women under assault. (1990, July 16). *Newsweek,* p. 23.

Women's choices: Pluses and minuses. (2002, September 23). *U.S. News & World Report Archive.* Retrieved October 7, 2002, from http://www.usnews.com/usnews/issue/archive.htm

Women's Sports Foundation. (1998). *The Women's Sports Foundation report: Sport and teen pregnancy.* East Meadow, NY: Author.

Wong, C., & Tang, C. S. (2001). Understanding heterosexual Chinese college students' intention to adopt safer sex behaviors. *Journal of Sex Research, 38,* 118–126.

Wood, J. C. (2001). *When men are women: Manhood among the Gabra nomads of east Africa.* Madison: University of Wisconsin.

World Health Organization (1993, November). *World Health Organization urges sex education in schools to prevent AIDS.* WHO Press Release.

World Health Organization. (1997). Fact Sheet 153: Female genital mutilation. Retrieved April 18, 2000, from www.who.ch/inf-fs/en/fact153.html

World Health Organization. (1999). WHO/FHE/MSM/94.14. Indicators to monitor maternal health goals. Retrieved May 19, 2000, from http://www.who.int/rht/documents/MSM94–14/9414.htm

World Health Organization (WHO). (June, 2000). Fact sheet number 241: Female genital mutilation. Retrieved June 24, 2002, from http://www.who.int/inf-fs/en/fact241.html

World Health Organization. (2002). *Scaling up antiretroviral therapy in resource-limited settings: Guidelines for a public health approach: Executive summary.* Geneva: Author.

Wright, A. L., Holberg, C. J., Taussig, L. M., & Martinez, F. D. (1995). Relationship of infant feeding to recurrent wheezing at age 6 years. *Archives of Pediatric and Adolescent Medicine, 149,* 758–763.

Wulf, D., Frost, J., & Darroch, J. E. (1999). *Microbicides: A new defense against sexually transmitted diseases.* New York: Alan Guttmacher.

Wulfert, E., & Wan, C. K. (1995). Safer sex intentions and condom use viewed from a health belief, reasoned action, and social cognitive perspective. *Journal of Sex Research, 32,* 299–311.

Xantidis, L., & McCabe, M. P. (2000). Personality characteristics of male clients of female commercial sex workers in Australia. *Archives of Sexual Behavior, 29,* 165–176.

Yankelovich Partners, *Time/CNN Poll,* January 5, 1995.

Yates, A. (1978). *Sex without shame: Encouraging the child's healthy sexual development.* New York: William Morrow.

Yates, A., & Wolman, W. (1991). Aphrodisiacs: Myth and reality. *Medical Aspects of Human Sexuality, 25,* 58–64.

You, H. S., & Malley, M. K. (2000). Young adult attachment styles and intimate relationships with close friends: A cross-cultural study of Koreans and Caucasian Americans. *Journal of Cross-Cultural Psychology, 31,* 528–534.

Youn, G. (2001). Perceptions of peer sexual activities in Korean adolescents. *Journal of Sex Research, 38,* 352–360.

Young, K. S., Griffin-Shelley, E., Cooper, A., O'Mara, J., & Buchanan, J. (2000). Online infidelity: A new dimension in couple relationships with implications for evaluation and treatment. In A. Cooper (Ed.), *Cybersex: The dark side of the force* (pp. 59–74). Philadelphia: Brunner Routledge.

Zabin, L., Hirsch, M. B., Smith, E. A., Streett, R., & Hardy, J. B. (1986). Evaluation of a pregnancy prevention program for urban teenagers. *Family Planning Perspectives, 18,* 119–126.

Zaviacic, M. (2001). The human female prostate and its role in women's lives: Sexology implications. *Scandinavian Journal of Sexology, 4,* 199–211.

Zavos, P. M., Correa, J. R., Antypas, S., Zarmakoupis-Zavos, P. M., & Zarmakoupis, C. N. (1998). Effects of seminal plasma from cigarette smokers on sperm viability and longevity. *Fertility and Sterility, 69,* 425–429.

Zelnik, M., & Kantner, J. F. (1980). Sexual activity, contraceptive use and pregnancy among metropolitan area teenagers: 1971–1979. *Family Planning Perspectives, 12,* 30–36.

Zhuravleva, V. (2001). The health behavior of adolescents and sexually transmitted diseases. *Russian Education and Society, 43,* 72–91.

Ziadeh, S., & Yahaya, A. (2001). Pregnancy outcome at age 40 and older. *Archives of Gynecology and Obstetrics, 265*(1), 30–33.

Ziergler, S., & Krieger, N. (1997). Reframing women's risk: Social inequalities and HIV infection. *Annual Review of Public Health, 18,* 401–409.

Zilbergeld, B. (1999). *The new male sexuality (revised ed.).* New York: Bantam Doubleday Dell.

Zillman, D. (1978). Attribution and misattribution for excitatory reactions. In J. H. Harvey, W. Ickes, & R. F. Kidd (Eds.), *New directions in attribution research* (Vol. 2) (pp. 335–368). Hillsdale NJ: Erlbaum.

Zillman, D. (1984). *Connections between sex and aggression.* Hillsdale, NJ: Erlbaum.

Zillman, D. (1986). *Effects of prolonged consumption of pornography.* Paper presented for the Surgeon General's Workshop on Pornography and Public Health, Virginia.

Zillman, D., & Bryant, J. (1986). *Pornography's impact on sexual satisfaction.* Unpublished manuscript, Indiana University, Bloomington.

Zillman, D., & Bryant, J. (1988). Effects of prolonged consumption of pornography on family values. *Journal of Family Issues, 9,* 518–544.

Zucker, K. J. (1995). Gender identity disorders: A developmental perspective. In L. Diamant & R. D. McAnulty (Eds.), *The psychology of sexual orientation, behavior, and identity: A handbook* (pp. 327–354). Westport, CT: Greenwood.

Zucker, K. J., & Blanchard, R. (1997). Transvestic fetishism: Psychopathology and theory. In D. R. Laws & W. O'Donohue (Eds.), *Sexual deviance: Theory, assessment, and treatment* (pp. 253–279). New York: Guilford.

Zucker, K. J., & Bradley, S. J. (1995). *Gender identity disorder and psychosexual problems in children and adolescents.* New York: Guilford.

Zucker, K. J., Bradley, S. J., Kuksis, M., Pecore, K., Birkenfeld-Adams, A., Doering, R. W., Mitchell, J. N., & Wild, J. (1999). Gender constancy judgments in children with gender identity disorder: Evidence for a developmental lag. *Archives of Sexual Behavior, 28*(6), 475–502.

Zverina, J., Lachman, M., Pondelickova, J., & Vanek, J. (1987). The occurrence of atypical sexual experience among various female patient groups. *Archives of Sexual Behavior, 16,* 321–326.

name index

subject index